Acclaim for *James the Brother of Jesus*

'Robert Eisenman's *James the Brother of Jesus* is less a book than an irresistible force. Once opened . . . [it] bulldozes your prejudices, flattens your objections, elbows aside your counter-arguments, convinces you.'
—*Toronto Globe and Mail*

'Encyclopaedic . . . fascinating.'
—Karen Armstrong, *The Times*

Powerful . . . expert . . . A thrilling essay in historical detection this passionate quest for the historical James refigures Christian origins.'
—*The Guardian*

'Eisenman is too careful a historian and too passionate a believer to attempt merely to debunk two thousand years of history. His is not an effort to replace Jesus with James, but to rescue the younger brother from the oblivion to which the blatantly fictionalized Book of Acts consigned him . . . Eisenman's course through the evidence is so logical and his narrative so compelling that one emerges after one thousand pages wondering how this demythologized, internally consistent understanding of early Christianity could have been kept out of sight for so long.'
—*The Scotsman*

'Blown away! The breadth and detail of Eisenman's investigations are breathtaking, as are its implications . . . Eisenman shows us how to crack the codes of theological disinformation, to listen to the long-faded echoes, to find handholds up what seemed an insurmountable climb to a peak from which to view the hitherto unseen landscape of early Christianity . . . Mind-blowing . . . Breathtaking . . . A Masterpiece!'
—*The Journal of Higher Criticism*

'Fascinating reading'
—*The Kirkus Review*

'What a book! Impressive in elegance and painstaking scholarship . . . Magnificent . . . A tour de force.'
—Neil Asher Silberman, author of *The Hidden Scrolls*

'A tremendous work of historical scholarship . . . Expert . . . Fascinating . . . Unparalleled . . . Apocalyptic . . . A great book.'
—*The Jerusalem Post*

'Enthralling . . . immense . . . Compelling . . . Massive in its learning and relentless in its argument . . . *James the Brother of Jesus* offers a stunning reinterpretation of 'Jamesian Christianity' as the very opposite of the Christianity that has come down to us. Eisenman's book places us at the center of these controversies with often surprising results . . . It delivers us into an unfamiliar world of punning wordplay, trenchant allusion, and ruthless polemic, where nothing – including the person of Jesus – is quite what it seems . . . In helping us return to and deepening our understanding of Christianity's origins, Eisenman has done a service to believer and sceptic alike . . . A massive display of provocative scholarship.'
—*The Oregonian*

'Eisenman is like the Renaissance scientists, who had to hand-craft all the intricate parts of a planned invention. His book is an ocean of instructive insight and theory, a massive and profound achievement.'
—Robert M. Price, author of *Deconstructing Jesus*

'This book will live and live and live!'
—A. Auswaks, Reviewer, *The Jerusalem Post*

'I permanently admire (this) superb book.'
—Harold Bloom, author of *Jesus and Yahweh: The Names Divine*

THE NEW TESTAMENT CODE

THE CUP OF THE LORD, THE DAMASCUS COVENANT, AND THE BLOOD OF CHRIST

Robert Eisenman, is the co-author of *The Facsimile Edition of the Dead Sea Scrolls* and *The Dead Sea Scrolls Uncovered* and the author of the bestselling *James the Brother of Jesus*. He is Professor of Middle East Religions and Archaeology and Director of the Institute for the Study of Judeo-Christian Origins at California State University, Long Beach; and Visiting Senior Member of Linacre College, Oxford University. He was a Senior Fellow at the Oxford Centre for Postgraduate Hebrew Studies and a United States National Endowment for the Humanities Fellow-in-Residence at the Albright Institute of Archaeological Research in Jerusalem, where the Dead Sea Scrolls first came in.

He was the leader of the worldwide campaign of 1987-92 to break the academic and scholarly monopoly over the Dead Sea Scrolls, freeing them for research for all interested persons regardless of their affiliation or credentials. As a consequence of this, he was the consultant to the Huntington Library of San Marino, California on its decision to open its archives and allow free access to the Scrolls.

In 2002-2003 he was the first to publicly announce that 'the James Ossuary,' which so suddenly and miraculously appeared, was fraudulent, and he did so on the same day it appeared on the basis of the actual inscription itself, and what it said, not as a result of any external 'scientific' or 'pseudo-scientific' measurements.

By the same Author

The Dead Sea Scrolls Uncovered
The Dead Sea Scrolls and the First Christians
James the Just in the Habakkuk Pesher
Maccabees, Zadokites, Christians and Qumran: A New Hypothesis of Qumran Origins
James the Brother of Jesus
A Facsimile Edition of the Dead Sea Scrolls

THE NEW TESTAMENT CODE

THE CUP OF THE LORD,
THE DAMASCUS COVENANT,
AND THE BLOOD OF CHRIST

ROBERT EISENMAN

WATKINS PUBLISHING
LONDON

Distributed in the USA and Canada by Sterling Publishing Co., Inc.
387 Park Avenue South, New York, NY 10016

This edition first published in the UK and USA 2006 by
Watkins Publishing, Sixth Floor, Castle House,
75–76 Wells Street, London W1T 3QH

1 3 5 7 9 10 8 6 4 2

Designed and typeset by Dorchester Typesetting Group Ltd

The use of the cover image is based on an initial cover design
by Nadav Eisenman

Manufactured in the United States of America

Library of Congress Cataloging-in-Publication Data Available

ISBN-10: 1-84293-186-5
ISBN-13: 978-1-84293-186-8

For information about custom editions, special sales, premium and
corporate purchases, please contact Sterling Special Sales
Department at 800-805-5489 or specialsales@sterlingpub.com.

www.watkinspublishing.com

It is related that the children of Zadok the Priest, one a boy and the other a girl, were taken captive to Rome, each falling to the lot of a different officer. One officer resorted to a prostitute and gave her the boy. The other went into the store of a shopkeeper and gave him the girl in exchange for some wine (this to fulfill Joel 4:3: '*And they have given a boy for a harlot and sold a girl for wine*'). After awhile, the prostitute brought the boy to the shopkeeper and said to him, '*Since I have a boy, who is suitable for the girl you have, will you agree they should cohabit and whatever issues be divided between us?*' He accepted the offer.

They immediately took them and placed them in a room. The girl began to weep and the boy asked her why she was crying? She answered, '*Should I not weep, when the daughter of a High Priest is given in marriage to one (like you), a slave?*' He inquired of her whose daughter she was and she replied, '*I am the daughter of Zadok the High Priest.*' He then asked her, where she used to live and she answered, '*In the upper marketplace.*' He next inquired, '*What was the sign above the house?*' and she told him. He said, '*Have you a brother or a sister?*' She answered, '*I had a brother and there was a mole on his shoulder and whenever he came home from school, I used to uncover it and kiss it.*' He asked, '*If you were to see it now, would you know it?*' She answered, '*I would.*' He bared his shoulder and they recognized each other. They then embraced and kissed till they expired.

Then the Holy Spirit cried out, '*For these things I weep*'!
(Lamentations *Rabbah* 1:16.46 and *Gittin* 58a).

You will deliver the Enemies of all the Countries into the hand of the Poor (the *Ebionim*) to cast down the Mighty Ones of the Peoples, to pay (them) the Reward on Evil Ones...and to justify the Judgements of Your Truth... You will fight against them from Heaven...for You commanded the Hosts of Your Elect in their thousands and their Myriads, together with the Heavenly Host of all Your Holy Ones,...to strike the Rebellious of Earth with Your awe-inspiring Judgements...For the King of Glory is with us...and the Angelic Host is under His command...(They are) like clouds, moisture-laden clouds covering the Earth – a torrent of rain shedding Judgement on all that grows
(The War Scroll from Qumran, XI.17-XII.10 and XIX.1-2).

'*Of what use are graven images, whose makers formed a casting and images of Lying...?*' The interpretation of this passage concerns all the idols of the Nations, which they create in order to serve...These will not save them on the Day of Judgement ...'*But the Lord is in His Holy Temple. Be silent before Him all the World*'! Its interpretation concerns all the Nations who but serve stone and wood. But on the Day of Judgement, God will destroy all the Servants of Idols and Evil Ones off the Earth
(1QpHab, XII.10-XIII.4 on Habakkuk 2:18-19).

Contents

Illustrations and Maps

60 The entrance to Petra, Herod's mother's place-of-origin and the capital of the '*Arab*' King Aretas, her possible kinsman (and also, therefore, the possible '*kinsman*' of Paul). (Robert Eisenman)

61 Column XVI of 4QD271 describing how Abraham was threatened by '*the Angel Mastemah*' ('*Satan*') for not circumcising all members of his household, whereupon he promptly did so. (*FEDSS*)

62 The amphitheatre at Hellenistic Petra, a city Paul may have visited when he speaks in Galatians 1:17 of '*going into Arabia.*' (Robert Eisenman)

63 The ruins of Pella across the Jordan in Perea, to which the Community of James was reputed to have fled after his death. (Robert Eisenman)

64 The ruins of Palmyra, a key city on the trade route going North to Syria, Adiabene, and beyond. (Robert Eisenman)

65 The Cave 4 parallel to CDVI where the all-important '*going out to dwell in the Land of Damascus,*' '*digging of the Well,*' and '*the New Covenant*' to be erected there are mentioned (*FEDSS*)

66 The ruins of Hellenistic Jerash, like Pella, another city of '*the Decapolis*' but further inland. (Robert Eisenman)

67 A scene from old Damascus, down the walls of which Paul allegedly escaped '*in a basket*' from the '*Arab*' King Aretas and the venue of many important allusions at Qumran. (Robert Eisenman)

68 The City of Edessa ('*Antioch Orrhoe*') with the Pool of Abraham in the foreground and the Plain of Haran – Abraham's childhood home – in the background. (J.B. Segal, *Edessa: The Beloved City*, reprinted by permission of Oxford University Press)

69 The end of the Second Part ('*the Second Letter*') of *MMT* speaking of '*the works of the Torah which would be reckoned for your Good*' as *per* Abraham in Genesis 15:6, James, and Paul. (*FEDSS*)

70 The *MMT* passage banning '*things sacrificed to idols*' so important to James' directives to overseas communities and '*Sicarii Essene*' martyrdom/resistance practices. (*FEDSS*)

71 Baptism scene of the Mandaeans/'*the Subba^c of the Marshes*'/ '*Masbuthaeans*'/'*Elchasaites*' of Southern Iraq. (E. S. Drower, *The Mandaeans of Iraq and Iran*, reprinted by permission of Oxford University Press)

72 Mandaean Elders and Priests. (E.S. Drower, *The Mandaeans of Iraq and Iran*, reprinted by permission of Oxford University Press)

73 The First Column of CD mentioning '*the Root of Planting,*' '*the Teacher of Righteousness,*' and '*the Pourer out*'/'*Spouter of Lying.*' (S. Schechter, *Fragments of a Zadokite Work*, Cambridge, 1910)

74 4Q268, paralleling the First Column of the Cairo *Genizah*

version, showing the link with earlier material instructing '*the Sons of Light to keep away from the Paths*' / '*the Ways (of pollution).*' (FEDSS)

75 Voluptuous Hellenistic sculpture found around Italica in Spain, the birthplace of both Trajan (98-117 CE) and Hadrian (117-138 CE). (Robert Eisenman)

76 Bust of Hadrian who ruthlessly suppressed the Bar Kochba Revolt and rebuilt Jerusalem under his own name as '*Aelia Capitolina.*' (Robert Eisenman)

77 Amphitheatre at Italica, birthplace of Trajan and Hadrian and perhaps home of '*the Regiment*' mentioned in Acts 10:2. (Robert Eisenman)

78 Sumptuous reconstructed floor mosaic found in ruins in the area of Italica. (Robert Eisenman)

79 Silver Sestertius with portrait of Trajan, under whom Egyptian Jewish Community was wiped out in disturbances around the years 105-115 CE. (www.Forumancientcoins.com)

80 Silver dinar with portrait bust of Hadrian. (Robert Eisenman)

81 The Pinnacle of the Temple with the Kedron Valley tombs – in particular, the Monument of Absalom just visible below. (Robert Eisenman)

82 Rock-cut '*Tomb of Zadok*' in the Kedron Valley below the Pinnacle of the Temple next to James' – a hiding place mentioned in the Copper Scroll. (Robert Eisenman)

83 The Tomb attributed by pilgrims to James, but an inscription identified it as that of the '*Bnei-Hezir*' Priest Clan ('*the Boethusians*') and probably at the root of the burial legends about Jesus. (Robert Eisenman)

84 Burial chambers inside '*the Tomb of St. James.*' (Robert Eisenman)

85 The excavated entry to the family Tomb of Queen Helen of Adia-bene built for her and her son Izates by her second son Mono-bazus. (C. W. Wilson, *Ordinance Survey of Jerusalem*, London, 1865)

86 Absalom's Monument next to James' Tomb. It or pyramids like it probably stood above Queen Helen's Family Tomb on the other side of Jerusalem. (Robert Eisenman)

87 Column IV of the Psalm 37 *Pesher* describing how '*the Violent Ones of the Gentiles took Vengeance*' on the Wicked Priest for what he did to the Righteous Teacher and referring to '*the Church of the Poor seeing Judgement.*' (The Huntington Library)

88 Burial niche inside the Family Tomb of Queen Helen of Adiabene. (Robert Eisenman)

89 Ruins surrounding the steps of the Temple in Jerusalem with the Pinnacle and Mount of Olives Cemetery in the background. (Robert Eisenman)

90 Tomb directly alongside James,' attributed to Zechariah the Prophet, but the designation probably has more to do with '*Zachariah ben Bariscaeus*,' the '*Rich*' collaborator '*cast down*' by Revolutionaries from the Temple wall into the Kedron Valley below. (Robert Eisenman)

91 The Temple steps upon which James lectured the People when he was supposedly '*cast down*' by '*the Enemy*' Paul. (Robert Eisenman)

92 The Third Column of the Nahum *Pesher* referring to '*messengers*'/ '*Apostles*' to '*the Gentiles*' and '*deceiving*' converts with '*a Lying Tongue*.' (The Huntington Library courtesy of Bill Moffett)

93 '*The Golden Gate*,' towards which the Romans made their final adoration of their standards after storming and burning the Temple in 70 CE. (Wilson, *Ordinance Survey of Jerusalem*, 1865)

94 What is left of '*Herod's Palace*' in Jerusalem where Saulos and his Herodian colleagues took refuge at the beginning of the Uprising. (C. W. Wilson, *Ordinance Survey of Jerusalem*, London, 1865)

95 Greek/Hebrew warning block in the Temple forbidding non-Jews to enter its sacred precincts on pain of death. (Robert Eisler, *The Messiah Jesus and John the Baptist*, Dial Press, 1931)

96 Fragment from the Genesis *Pesher* (49:14) identifying '*the Sceptre*' as '*the Messiah of Righteousness*' (singular) and '*the Branch of David*.' (FEDSS)

97 4Q*Berachot*/'*The Chariots of Glory*' '*cursing*' Belial as '*the Angel of the Pit*.' (FEDSS)

98 The ruins of strategic Emmaus where Jesus appeared to '*Cleopas*' and Jewish defenders were sealed in their caves and starved to death by the Romans. (Robert Eisenman)

99 A passage verifying the presence of CDVII at Qumran evoking '*the Star who came to Damascus*,' '*the Doresh*,' '*the Sceptre*,' '*the Nasi*,' and '*destruction by the hand of Belial*.' (FEDSS)

100 Columns IV-V of the Nahum *Pesher* referring to '*the Nilvim*' rejoining '*the Glory of Judah*,' '*the Cup*,' '*perishing by the sword*,' and '*going into captivity*' (The Huntington Library)

101 The ruins of the seaport at Caesarea, where Paul visited '*Philip*' and was incarcerated for two years by Felix in the Palace of Agrippa II, his putative '*kinsman*.' (Robert Eisenman)

102 The Synagogue at Gamala just above the Sea of Galilee in the Gaulon, the birthplace of '*Judas the Galilean*' (the progenitor of '*the Zealot Movement*'). (Robert Eisenman)

103 The two '*Camel*'-like humps from which Gamala received its name and from which the first Jewish mass suicide occurred in 67 CE as the Romans made their bloody way down from Galilee. (Robert Eisenman)

104 Ruins near Mt. Gerizim in Samaria where the Samaritan Redeemer figure, '*The Taheb*,' crucified by Pontius Pilate, performed his '*Signs*.' (Robert Eisenman)

105 The Western or '*Wailing Wall*,' the only part of Temple left standing after its destruction in 70 CE. (Robert Eisenman)

106 Columns XI-XII of the Habakkuk *Pesher* referring to how the Wicked Priest both '*swallowed*' the Righteous Teacher and '*destroyed the Poor*' and how '*the Cup of the Right Hand of the Lord*' would then '*come around*' and '*swallow him*.' (John Trever)

107 The last Column XIII of the Habakkuk *Pesher* evoking '*the Day of Judgement*' on '*Idolaters*' and '*Evil Ones*' and announcing that '*God is in His Holy Temple, let all the world be still*.' (John Trever)

108 Coin from '*Year 2*' of the Uprising against Rome depicting a ceremonial amphora on the obverse and a grape leaf with the logo '*the Freedom of Zion*' on the reverse. (Robert Eisenman)

109 The Colosseum, built by Vespasian from the proceeds of the Temple Treasure and the numerous slaves he took, the survivors among whom (martyrs all) probably died in it. (Robert Eisenman)

110 The underground walkways of the Priests in the Jerusalem Temple which survived its destruction by Vespasian, Titus, Titus' mistress Bernice, and Philo's nephew Tiberius Alexander. (Robert Eisenman)

111 The Arch of Titus, celebrating his victory over the Jews, still standing in the Roman Forum today – his father Vespasian's Colosseum visible just behind it. (Robert Eisenman)

112 Vespasian's '*Judea Capta*' coin, displaying his image on its obverse and the Roman dominion over a weeping Judean woman on its reverse – the palm tree signifying the Jewish State. (Roel Oostra: Archiv MVG)

113 The image on the Arch of Titus showing his great Triumph, the Jewish captives carrying their sacred objects, particularly the seven-branched, gold candelabra given by Queen Helen to the Temple – presumably melted down to help to pay for the Colosseum. (Roel Oostra: Archiv MVG)

114 Jewish Revolutionary coin from the rare Year 4 depicting the real '*Cup of the Lord*' ('*the Cup*' of *Divine Vengeance*?) and bearing the logo '*the Redemption of Zion*.' (www.Forumancientcoins.com)

Preface

Many significant things are happening these days in the field of New Testament Studies and Christian Origins. Principal among these, of course, is the sudden and almost miraculous appearance of a '*Gospel*' attributed to '*Judas*' – meaning, '*Judas Iscariot*.' Not only is the very concept of such a surprising Gospel a shock (no doubt, part of its point), though it has been known at least since the Second Century when the early Church theologian Irenaeus condemned it (part of the reason, certainly, for its disappearance or being, as it were, '*put out of the way*'); but even now it will do much to help remove the taint of anti-Semitism (despite its being decidedly antinomian or anti-'*Mosaic*' or '*Sinaitic Covenant*'-oriented itself) from the whole tradition – abetted by the tendentious picture in the received Gospels, the Book of Acts, and not moderated in any way by Paul (on the contrary) – that to some extent coalesced around this '*Judas*.' This character (also called '*the Iscariot*' in John), it is now widely recognized, was to no small degree normally seen as representative of '*Jews*' and '*the Jewish Nation*' generally and contributed, thereby, to portraying them in the most negative light conceivable – to say nothing of the same effect a portrait of this kind had on the whole '*Sicarii*' or '*Zealot Essene Movement*' we shall elaborate in this book and from which, we contend, the pseudonym derived.

Just as importantly and perhaps even more to the point, such a '*Gospel*' goes a long way towards illustrating the way the literature we have before us, including the four orthodox Gospels, developed; and it *is 'a literature'* – that is, '*philosophical*' or, if one prefers, '*Mystical*' or '*Neoplatonic*' or, as the Gospels themselves, '*Mysteryizing*' or '*Magical*' – but '*a literature*' all the same and *not 'history*,' one layer varying, building upon, reiterating, or responding to another; and all the time putting metaphysical or theological ideas in the Greco-Roman-Egyptian manner or the literary format of personalized and Hellenized '*God tales*' or '*Man-God*'/'*God-Man tales*' – and/or for that matter, as here in Judas' Gospel, '*dialogues*.'

Should one prefer to put this proposition in a different manner: as the advocates of the Jewish Neoplatonic and aristocratic philosopher Philo of Alexandria in Egypt (where much of this literature probably got its start before it spread Westwards across the Mediterranean as well as to points further East) – an older contemporary of the Gospel literary character '*Jesus*' (called by Paul '*Christ Jesus*' or '*the Lord Jesus*'), Paul himself, and the

Jewish historian Josephus in the next generation – would probably put it, '*allegorical*' or '*allegorizing*' but, once again, not '*history*.'

Paul also puts it like this in Galatians 4:24, but there he is talking about what most of us (though not scholars) would call '*the Old Testament*' or, as he would put it, the '*Mosaic*' or '*Sinaitic Covenant which is Agar*' (he means by this '*Hagar*,' but how he achieves this fairly derogatory synthesis, the reader will have to see later). It is these materials that Paul, like Philo, is interpreting in an '*allegorical*' manner. But where the picture of 'Jesus' that has come down to us is concerned (about whom Paul appears to know very little except for the fact that *he was 'crucified'* and, as far as he was concerned, proclaimed the doctrine of '*Communion with*' his own '*Blood*'); these are '*New Testament*' or '*New Covenant*' materials being depicted or humanized allegorically directly at their inception, not retrospectively. This is an important difference between Philo and Paul.

Moreover, as just emphasized, this is being done in the manner of the old Hellenistic or Hellenizing Greco-Roman and Egyptian '*God*'/'*Man-God tales*' which these societies had for so long been so adept at creating or recreating – not *in relation to the Deity*, as in the Hebrew Bible, but by actually *picturing the Deity itself being incarnated and walking around on this Earth* and, then, going back, returning, or '*being assumed*' back up to '*Heaven*.'

There are even works-in-the-making that will assert that what many regard as the first Gospel, the one attributed to '*Mark*' (even though names of this kind seem to have been attached relatively late in the process of '*Gospel manufacture*' or the back-and-forth and reverberating process of *tradition proliferation* – not so different from '*Hadith manufacture*' in Islam – one tradition, as we shall see, bouncing off, responding to, and developing another, if any sense can be made out of the whole process at all), is even masking a personality and activities connected with one or another of the First-Century '*Herodians*' or Herodian Kings in '*Palestine*' or '*Judea*' – in this period, basically interchangeable designations – known in the histories of Josephus and his Egyptian and Roman contemporaries as '*Marcus Agrippa*'–Agrippa I (37–44 CE) or Agrippa II (49–93 CE) – individuals named after a favorite of Augustus who won him the Battle of Actium over Anthony and Cleopatra and to whom the first embodiment of Hadrian's world-famous later '*Pantheon*' was dedicated (there is not a little irony in this).

These, of course, were his and their Greco-Roman names. All these '*Herodians*' had several names (sometimes, like '*the Maccabeans*' preceding them, one based on a Hebrew original and the others, Latin or Greek) – in the case of '*Marcus Agrippa*,' there seem only to have been two Latin names. But this '*Agrippa*' – I or II, it makes no difference – also had important connections to Egypt and the large Jewish Community there (itself virtually wiped out in apparently '*Messianic*' and internecine strife that occurred there under Trajan, c. 98–117 CE).

Where Egypt was concerned, not only was it the venue of much of this early '*Gospel-theorizing*' or '*manufacture*' as one can see from the case of '*The Gospel of Judas*'(to say nothing of quite a few others, such as '*The Gospel of Mary Magdalene*' or '*The Gospel of Thomas*,' that is to say, '*Judas Thomas*'); it was also the locale where Vespasian – the father of the new Roman Imperial Line succeeding, in the midst of '*the Jewish War*,' Julius Caesar's and Augustus' '*Julio-Claudians*,' namely, '*the Flavians*' (from whom Josephus himself derived his Latin familial name, '*Flavius Josephus*,' i.e., much like his modern cinemagraphic counterpart '*Ben Hur*,' whose novelized biography to some extent mirrored Josephus' own, he was adopted into a noble Roman family, though this time it was *the new Imperial One*, this obviously for services rendered such as writing books extolling them and at one point even, like Yohanan ben Zacchai in Rabbinic literature, *actually proclaiming Vespasian* '*Messiah*' or *the one who was to come out of Palestine to rule the World*!) – first seems to have considered putting forth a claim to the Roman Imperial Throne. In this, Vespasian was encouraged by persons connected to this same Philo, including his nephew Tiberius Alexander and even Josephus himself, to say nothing of Agrippa II and his sister Bernice – the presumable prototype for many of the '*prostitutes*'/ '*harlots*' allusions, one encounters in Gospel imaging – the mistress of Vespasian's son and Emperor-to-be Titus.

Their father, Agrippa I (37-44 CE) – both Agrippa II and his sister Bernice had been accused of '*incest*' with each other as even Josephus reports – seems to have been one of the first to consider making these kinds of Imperial or, in '*Jewish*' terms, '*Messianic*' claims for himself in the East when he too passed through Egypt some thirty years before on his way back from having been freed by Caligula from imprisonment by the Emperor Tiberius (the end of whose reign, '*Prophet*'-like, Agrippa also seems to have predicted). To add to this, several '*Herodian*' family members (for example, Agrippa I's daughter and Bernice's sister Mariamme – her other sister Drusilla married the infamous Roman Governor Felix – had divorced a previous husband who had only been Treasurer of the Temple, to do so; obviously he wasn't quite '*Rich*' enough) married into Philo's own family, that of '*the Alabarch of Alexandria*,' probably the '*Richest*' in all Egypt, deriving its wealth from control of the Red Sea/India and East Asian trade and the Leader of the Jewish Community there. So there was a good deal of connection of this branch of the '*Maccabean Herodian*' Family with Egypt in this period.

Then, too, there is the whole question of the group in Egypt, Philo himself identifies as the '*Theraputae*' or '*Healers*,' a quasi-Gnosticizing and esotericizing, Asclepius-like '*overseas*' or foreign version of those, both he and Josephus designate in Palestine as '*Essenes*'; but probably in almost no way resembling '*the Essenes*' considered to have authored the Dead Sea Scrolls except perhaps in their organization, their '*monastic*' or, at least, *self-abnegating* life-style, and their '*Pythagorean*'-like clothing (though in Palestine '*white linen*' could also be seen, as we shall see, as the garb of '*Priests*' in general and, in particular, '*the High Priest*').

In this work, we shall make it clear – as we have in previously in *James the Brother of Jesus* (Penguin, 1998/Watkins, 2002) – that, not only were Paul's own '*Herodian*' connections real, overt, and more familial than most might think; but Paul's whole agenda, which he often announces of for Jews first, '*but Greeks as well*,' was neither alien or inimical to Herodian family interests and designs for an extended '*Imperium*' in the East, so a '*Gospel*' presentation that was somehow related to or embodying an initial impetus of this kind would not have been at all odd. One could also say the same – as we shall demonstrate in this book – about the way 'Jesus' is portrayed in the normative Gospels as they have been bequeathed to us, that is, as '*a Friend of tax-collectors*' (the '*Friend*' terminology being very important in all venues, such as the Letter of James, the Dead Sea Scrolls, the *Talmud*, and even the Koran), '*Sinners*,' '*prostitutes*' – all terms, as we shall show, with particular relevance where '*Herodians*' were concerned – but even, '*a glutton and a wine-bibber*'; that is, someone who was not keeping dietary regulations and, unlike James or even John the Baptist, not a '*Nazirite*' or '*Holy from his mother's womb*' and certainly not '*a vegetarian*'!

But from our perspective, unfortunately (or, perhaps, fortunately), none of these ascriptions, familiar, comfortable, and beguiling as are, have anything at all to do with '*the Historical Jesus*' if, ultimately, we are able to identify him in any real way – on the contrary. But none of this, as just alluded to, would be strange or new to the perspective we embrace in this book, though the manner in which the various and layered traditions, that were ultimately incorporated into the Gospels, occurred is probably a little more complex than just ascribing the first embodiment of them to a given Herodian Family member whoever he may have been (if he was) or however much he may have contributed to their original inception (if he did).

We also make a point in this book of the possible incorporation or '*blending*' of Samaritan traditions into the story of 'Jesus' as it has been presented to us in the Gospels as they have come down to us; and, indeed, not only could this explain something of the anti-'*Jewish*' or anti-'*Judean*' strain one encounters in these '*stories*' (in itself, a self-contradiction), but also the very fact of '*Jesus*'' name, as these '*Gospels*' seem finally to have settled upon it, '*Jesus son of Joseph*' – and, deriving from this, as we shall see, the alleged '*ossuary*' containing this name – even though '*Jesus*'' actual father was not supposed to be '*Joseph*' at all.

Rabbinic tradition, as we shall also see, is quite familiar with the idea of there being two '*Messiahs*' (though not the two '*Messiahs*' many allege to be part of the Qumran tradition), one a Northern One it calls '*the Messiah ben*' or '*son of Joseph*' – '*Joseph*' being the patronymical name of the Northern Kingdom even in the Prophets, the paradigmatic hero of which, '*Joshua*' (*i.e.*, in Greco-Roman transliteration, '*Jesus*') himself being a '*son of Joseph*' both prototypically and lineally – and a Southern One, '*the Messiah ben Judah*,' *i.e.*, the '*Judean*' or '*Davidic*' one, '*David*' being his prototypical forerunner as well. Of course, our '*Jesus*' in Scripture meets both of these specifications being considered in some recondite manner both a '*son of Joseph*' and a '*son of David*' at one and the same time!

This being said, the actual name attached to the '*Samaritan*' Redeemer figure in this period was '*the Taheb*' or '*Restorer*' and he, very definitely, was to be a kind of '*Joshua* ('*Jesus*') *Redivivus*' or '*Joshua incarnated*' or '*reincarnated*' as, of course, '*Jesus*' was to some degree in Scripture. But more to the point, this '*Taheb*' (who also has much in common with another '*Magician*'-like figure or '*Miracle-worker*,' '*Simon Magus*' and a colleague of his '*Dositheus*,' both of whom are described in the Pseudoclementine literature as '*Disciples of John the Baptist*' and both '*Samaritans*') was very definitely executed by Pontius Pilate – in fact, '*crucified*,' as the events of the story set forth in the Gospels would have it and a pivotal theme in Paul, as we shall delineate, in his allegorical and theological transformation of '*the Lord Jesus*'s death into a World-Saving event. That is, '*Jesus*' is not only named '*the Saviour*' – '*Joshua*' literally meaning '*Saviour*' in Hebrew – but *he actually was* '*the Saviour*,' a new theological concept at this point as far as Old Testament Scripture is concerned.

But these quasi-Messianic or Salvationary events did not transpire in Jerusalem, as Gospel narrative would place them; *they occurred in Joseph and Joshua's City*, '*Shechem*' *in Samaria* (today's '*Nablus*' as *per* Arabic transliteration, *i.e.*, in Greco-Arabic, '*the New City*' built upon the Hebrew '*Old City of Shechem*') or, at least, outside it on Mt. Gerizim where '*Joshua*' originally called all the Tribes together and '*made them swear to observe the Law and keep the Covenant*.' The *Talmud* adds '*Lod*' or '*Lydda*' as the locale where '*the Messiah ben Joseph*' was crucified. To some extent this is supported by Josephus who actually does record a number of Jewish and Samaritan '*Revolutionaries*' or Messianists '*crucified*' at this time at '*Lydda*' (today's '*Lod*'). Nor does Josephus record any other actually verifiable crucifixions under Pontius Pilate in Jerusalem in this period (unless it be the interpolated one inserted into his *Antiquities*, c. 93 CE, which he neglected to mention earlier in his *War*). But even more tellingly, we shall be able to show that the name of this Samaritan '*Taheb*' is actually known to Acts and does appear in Acts 9:32–42's curious description of events surrounding '*Peter*'s miraculous curings and raisings at '*Lydda*'/'*Lod*' – albeit rather cryptically, but we shall be able to '*decode*' it.

But all these things have to do with '*overseas Messianism*,' as it were, or '*Neoplatonic*,' '*Mystery-Religion*,' '*Salvationary*' or '*Enlightenment*' literature outside of Palestine's or Judea's borders. This is not really what we are interested in or what is going to be the subject of this book except peripherally. In this book, what we are interested in is '*Messianism*' *within the borders of* '*Palestine*,' as the Romans called it, or '*the Land of Judah*'/'*the Wilderness of Judea*,' as the Scrolls sometimes rather archaically refer it, and, to some extent, the area contiguous to it to the East as far north as Northern Syria and Northern Iraq – '*the Land of the Edessenes*' and '*Adiabene*' (modern Kurdistan) – what, to a certain degree, we shall encounter in the terminology '*the Land of Damascus*' in the Dead Sea Scrolls.

It is these documents that came to light or materialized and changed everything. The even more miraculous discovery – than the Gospel of Judas, miraculous as it was – of the Dead Sea Scrolls, nineteen centuries after they had seemingly been secreted away in caves, has come back to haunt us all like some unexpected '*time capsule*' out of the past. Obviously, the people who wrote them and then deposited or secreted them away did not, therefore, die in vain. It is these documents that have happened to change everything, finally giving us the tools to penetrate the darkness of how all these peculiar literary creations, we now know, came into being and how the history of '*the Messianic Movement in Palestine*,' as it would perhaps be best to call it, was transmuted into something entirely different, wholly alien and Greek – or perhaps, more accurately, Egypto-Greco-Roman (if one likes, as just suggested, even to some extent '*Herodian*') – but, in any event, the very opposite of what was happening in Palestine/Judea in these pivotally-foundational times where the history of man and womankind is concerned.

This is what – if someone with a more religious bent of mind were to describe it – is '*miraculous*' about their being found and this, almost exactly at the moment when the new Jewish State was in the process, it would appear, of being born. This is what gives us an entirely new perspective on these events, which those who came before us did not have and, therefore, could not use in, for example, something like their '*Quest for the Historical Jesus*.' They did not have the control the Scrolls provide and had little or nothing to compare things with, for they did not know (except for the often hostile bits sometimes afforded them in Rabbinic literature or Josephus) what a native Palestinian '*Messianic Movement*' might actually look like – a '*Movement*' most people now content themselves by calling '*Essene.*' But now we do and this makes all the difference.

This is why our scholarship today is so different and this is why we can now do research that our forebears and predecessors – even the most perceptive or incisive among whom – could not do, being often obliged to rely on what actually were '*mythologized*,' retrospective, or '*fantasizing*' presentations, bordering even sometimes on dissimulation or disinformation. Now, what we actually have before us here in these Scrolls is the literature of '*the Messianic Movement in Palestine*' – homogeneous, pointed, unadulterated, and uncompromising. Call it by whatever name one might wish. Actually, what it really is, is the literature of '*extreme Naziritism*' – therefore, probably the somewhat bowdlerized New Testament nomenclature '*Nazoraean*' – or even '*Revolutionary*' or '*Messianic Sadduceeism*' (*i.e.*, '*Zadokitism*' or '*Zaddikitism*').

This is what I have been trying to point out in my several works over the last twenty or more years. It was for these reasons, too, that I felt obliged to try to break the academic and scholarly monopoly and the literal stranglehold over the publication and interpretation of the Dead Sea Scrolls (the two were, in fact, interrelated) that previously obtained from approximately 1952-1991 (in fact, ever since '*the International Team*' took over responsibility for their publication) – or, as I expressed it elsewhere, to try '*let a thousand voices sing.*' The only way to do this was to allow any interested person to approach all the documents that existed in a totally free manner, independent of mind-numbing academic analyses – and I put this forth in the Introduction I did with Professor James Robinson of the University of Claremont (one of the key individuals in breaking the Nag Hammadi logjam, the partial reason I invited him to participate in the parallel campaign to help break the monopoly over the Dead Sea Scrolls, though we were of wholly different mindsets) to the *Facsimile Edition of the Dead Sea Scrolls.*

Having said this, it is the Dead Sea Scrolls that have, as if by some miracle, changed everything. They have given us the native Palestinian documents that did not go through and were left, as it were, untouched by the editorial processes of the Roman Empire (either the reason or the result, obviously, of their having been put in caves in the first place), again an ancient '*time capsule*' – '*Palestinian Messianism*' before it went overseas and became Hellenized – from the perspective of the present writer, an additional contradiction in terms. It is for this reason that these documents differ so much from the ones found, for example, at Nag Hammadi in

Upper Egypt or, for that matter, the Romanized Gospels as they have both been chosen for and come down to us. Here in the Scrolls was real '*Palestinian Messianism*' as raw as it may seem and, at the same time, *real Palestinian Revolutionary Apocalypticism*. It is these documents that give us the '*yardstick*,' as just alluded to, along with a perspicacious reading of Josephus and few other sources, to measure the others and, as the Pseudoclementine *Homilies* quote 'Jesus' as putting it, '*to determine false coin from true*.'

This I have tried to do in my work up until now and for this, too, I consider this generation to be a fortunate, even a '*blessed*' one. I did this in *James the Brother of Jesus* in 1997-98 and I have tried to do it in my other work – for example, in the collection of essays and translations, *The Dead Sea Scrolls and the First Christians*, 1996 and Barnes & Noble/Harper Collins/Sterling, 2004. In *James the Brother of Jesus*, I promised a sequel because five hundred pages had been cut from the end of it (basically the last ten chapters of this book). But in the meantime other newer matters had been clarified for me and other subjects explored in far more detail and depth than I did in *James the Brother of Jesus*, which accounts for the additional pages and the finally equal length of this *The New Testament Code*.

In *James the Brother of Jesus* I started the process of deciphering the *modus operandi* of the more '*literary-romantic*' portions of the Gospels and the Book of Acts (this is to put things as kindly and diplomatically as possible). One thing Paul was not was '*literary-romantic*' – a hater not a lover, a polemicizer not a conciliator or accommodator and, certainly not an artist – but he was a rhetorical dialectician (or, as some might prefer perhaps to term it, '*a gymnast*') and an allegorizer of the first order, though with hardly an ounce of human sympathy for those who might have opposed him or whom he thought stood in his way in some manner (therefore, I say, definitely not a '*literary-romantic*'); and, like the Gospels and the Book of Acts, hardly a historian at all.

However this may be, this is the sequel I promised at that time. Though it took years longer than I projected, I think I have gone about as far in the direction of such '*decipherment*' as one might. I do think that to some degree I have '*cracked the codes*' of some of the '*theological disinformation*' – as one of my more appreciative reviewers put it – involved in these documents and I do think (as he also expressed it) that we are looking out at '*a hitherto unseen landscape of almost unimaginable beauty and splendor.*' This position was echoed by another reviewer, whom I seem to have struck – to use his also not-unflattering words (though some may think otherwise) – as someone '*who has been shown a revelation of stunning splendor.*' I hope he is correct in this evaluation. Moreover, I hope my earlier and present readers will find this to be true and that some of this '*landscape*' is either imparted to or shared with them. This is the most any author can legitimately hope for or has a right to expect from his work. Moreover, if 'Jesus' were alive today – existent or non-existent in the form he has been presented to us – and, if there had been things that had been done and said in his name that were not his; it is my view that he would expect – nay require – his most sincere, ardent, and dedicated supporters and followers to find this out, there being nothing worse than having things done in or attributed to one's name in either life or legacy that were not one's own. This would be his charge to them and their obligation.

In my case, however, I have to admit to having an additional hope in mind – the reader will forgive it if there is any *hubris* here – to, at least, have done my small part in helping to open people's minds and, in so doing, contribute to making sure no future '*Holocausts*' of the type we all just witnessed in the last Century (and have been witnessing over these last nineteen and a half centuries) ever transpire again. I hope that for that alone we have put that '*Evil Demon*' – as the Gospels sometimes refer to it – to rest, have done with all the slogans of real disinformation, and finally come to grips with how amazing the times pictured in the Dead Sea Scrolls really were and how incomparably brave and precious all these *real* First-Century '*Martyrs*' were – and we are not speaking here of those perhaps retrospectively incorporated into the First Century.

'*Martyrs*' of a more Hellenized or spiritualized kind came later, but not perhaps in First-Century Palestine and not among those who were taken to Rome to help build Vespasian's Colosseum (on the whole constructed with the proceeds plundered from the Jerusalem Temple – Titus admits as much in 79 CE in the items he depicts on the Triumphal Arch that still stands in his name in the ruins of the Roman Forum today), many to subsequently die in it; and, like the Death Camp now memorialized like some vast Temple of either Doom or Demonic Destruction at Auschwitz, the most macabre of historical reversals and ironies – how pathetic and yet how tragic.

In my dedication page I have tried to impart some of these feelings to the reader. What '*the Holy Spirit*' really did in those terrible days was '*weep*,' as it would have done as well in our own too-tragic times – their counterpart. It '*wept*,' as the *Talmud* puts it in the story, I excerpted, about the two children of the High Priest Zadok taken as captive to Rome in the wake of the First Jewish Revolt (we will cite it again at the end of Chapter 11: '*The Dogs who Licked Poor Lazarus' Sores*'). Actually, it probably didn't even do that but, if there were one and if we were going to get into the realm of '*artistic*' expression, *it should have* – that is, '*wept*'!

But what it most certainly did not do was cry out the familiar Synoptic Gospel: '*This is my only-begotten Son. In him I am well pleased*' or even, as the Apocryphal Gospel of the Hebrews quoting Psalm 2:7 is reported by Jerome – and echoed in Hebrews 1:5 – to have rephrased it (before people of his mindset made sure it too, like the Gospel attributed to Judas, disappeared): '*At this moment I have begotten him*,' except in the mind of the latterday Greco-Roman artificers or their retrospective '*man-god*'/'*god-man*' overwrite/rewrite specialists (that is, their philosophical or theological aboriginal script/scripture-writers).

I hope all my readers will find as much to plumb in this work as I have in writing it. I wish to thank all those who helped me to prepare and execute it both editorially and substantively. Without their help, I could never have brought it to fruition or into the final form we now have. This includes all the students I have had over the years who patiently bore and simultaneously motivated my expositions, analyses, and syntheses.

In particular, I wish to express my appreciation and thanks to my wife Heather, who also patiently bore up and stuck with it, allowing me to explore areas of mutual interest to us both. It is she who never let a solecism or a misspelling pass – spellcheck notwithstanding. Nevertheless I am sure any that have (and there will not be a few) are all of my own doing. For the same reasons, I wish to thank all my children: Lavi, Nadav, Sarah, and Hanan and Sara, some of whom also actually worked on this manuscript, designed the cover, and helped me get over the rough spots, while at the same time even accompanying or representing me in the field.

For footnote availability, the reader should see the 'Note on Translations and Endnotes' at the end of the book. Thanks also go to all the students and associates who helped me in the preparation of this manuscript: Chris Chung, Cheryl Thompson, Ron Dubay, Christine Abrego, Peter Madrid, Doug Wallace, Michael Rahlwes, Tessa Dick, and Linda O'Dell. In particular, I wish to thank my research assistants Noelle Bautista, Nancy Meyer, Kevin Skull, and Alfred Perez, and my able hard-drive specialist Mark Cooper, who did patient servitude beyond the call of duty. I would also like to thank Zdzislaw Kapera, Robert Price, Florentino Garcia Martinez, David Patterson (*z"l*), Robert Morgan, Peter Flint, Neil Asher Silberman, Michael Baigent, John Collins, Howard Firth, Harold Bloom, and J.-F. L'Huilier who stuck with my work while others complained.

In the end, I wish to thank my two long-suffering editors, Michael Mann and Penny Stopa, without whose patient fortitude this work could never have been accomplished. Thanks, too, go to their very fine typesetter, Graham Baylis, and their Senior Associate, Duncan Baird who, together with these others, made this work possible.

Robert Eisenman   Fountain Valley, California. May, 2006

PART I

PRELIMINARIES

I

Names, Concepts, and Places:
The Anti-Semitic Peter and
Herodians at Antioch

Christianity and Essenism

In a book aimed at demonstrating the relationship of the Dead Sea
Scrolls to Early Christianity, one should perhaps begin with the proposition that there were not two Messianisms at the end of the First
Century/beginning of the Second Century in Palestine – only one. Nor
was there really any such thing at this time as '*Christianity*' *per se*, Christians having first been called '*Christians*,' according to Acts 11:26, in the
early to mid-Fifties of the Common Era in a place called '*Antioch*' in
Northern Syria (a denotation we shall have cause to question below).

So why use the term '*Christian*' at all? Because one must communicate and, in order to do so, one must use words however misleading or
inadequate these may be. At the outset it should be appreciated that the
use of questionable or imprecise terminologies of this kind – especially
when taken according to their superficial meaning – often produces all
the confusion surrounding these matters. The author takes the proposition that there was no such thing as '*Christianity*' in the First Century in
Palestine, along with the one about there being only one Messianism in
Palestine or the Land of Israel in the First Century (in his view, the one
found in the Dead Sea Scrolls[1]), as truisms or tautologies. The two – that
is, the points about there being only one '*Messianism*' and no such thing
as '*Christianity*' in Palestine in the First Century – are more or less equivalent anyhow. At the very least they are contrapositives, the one entailing
the other, though the first-time reader might not appreciate them as such
at this point.

One needs only one final proposition to complete the structure of
mutually interconnected terminologies we are talking about and that is,
'*Essenism*' was what '*Christianity*' was in First-Century Palestine, certainly
before the fall of Masada in 73 CE – whatever meaning one might wish
to give to the '*Christianity*' we are talking about at this point. This is not

3

to say precisely what one might mean by 'Essenism' either, only that if one is calling documents like the Dead Sea Scrolls 'Essene,' then one must define Essenism – whether inclusive of 'Jesus' or without him – by what the Scrolls themselves say it is and not by what the often tendentious or inaccurate descriptions of the various commentators such as Josephus, Philo, or early Christian writers might say it is.[2]

'Essenism' flourished sometime before the fall of the Temple in 70 CE – how long before, it is unnecessary for our purposes to determine – after which it seems to have become absorbed into one or more of the several Movements known to early Church writers (called 'heresiologists' in the jargon of the field) as 'Ebionites,' 'Elchasaites,' 'Masbuthaeans' (known in Southern Iraq and in the Koran as 'the Subbaᶜ' or 'Sabaeans' – that is, 'Immersers' or 'Daily Bathers'), 'Manichaeans,' and even 'Christians' themselves. All of these are not necessarily separate or mutually exclusive terminologies. In fact, they may be designating the same phenomenon from the standpoint or native tongue of a different observer whether writing in Greek, Aramaic, Syriac, or some other language. This brings us back to our original proposition, namely that there was no such thing as 'Christianity' in Palestine in the First Century, that is, no belief in 'Jesus' as 'the Christ' per se, only 'Essenism' (whatever meaning one might want to give to this) and this probably not until well into the Second Century sometime before the Bar Kochba Uprising.[3]

'Antioch,' 'Ananias,' and 'Jude the Brother of James'

Though the 'Antioch' in Acts is generally considered on the basis of retrospective historical consensus to be Antioch-on-the-Orontes in Syria (the 'Antioch' that is closest to the Mediterranean), there were at least *four* 'Antioch's in 'Asia' at this time – the founder of the Seleucid Dynasty in Syria after Alexander the Great's death having apparently harbored an inordinate affection for his father who actually was named 'Antiochus'.

These included 'Antioch-in-Pisidia,' now part of Turkey, described at length in Acts 13:14–50. Here Paul delivers his first exhortative in the Synagogue there on the Sabbath, an exhortative which has much the style of the last Columns of the Damascus Document from the Cairo Genizah (and from Qumran) directed at 'Israelites and God-Fearers' alike.[4] There was 'Antioch-by-Callirhoe' or 'Carrhae' on the Upper Euphrates in the region of Abraham's place-of-origin 'Haran' in Northern Syria – also now Southern Turkey – what Eusebius will denote as 'the Land of the Edessenes,' a city which eventually became known as 'Edessa.' This city –

4

famous ever after not only in the history of the Crusades, but also in 'Holy Shroud' historiography and hagiography[5] — is my choice, historically speaking, for the real 'Antioch' in Paul's Letters and in Acts.

Finally, there was 'Antiochia Charax,' 'Charax Spasini' or presentday Basrah at the mouth of the Tigris River on the Persian Gulf and in the birthplace of the Third-Century religious teacher, the founder of Manichaeism, Mani. In Josephus, Charax Spasini was the place where Izates, the favorite son of Queen Helen of Adiabene (characterized by Josephus, as we shall see, as her 'only begotten'[6]) first met the itinerant merchant cum missionary 'Ananias,' an individual also apparently appearing in both Eusebius and Acts. In the latter, he rather greets Paul in 'Damascus' at the time of the latter's conversion on 'the Damascus Road.'[7] Adiabene was the area around the source of the Tigris in Northern Iraq, roughly equivalent to modern-day Kurdistan and not very distinct from what Eusebius calls 'the Land of the Edessenes' or 'Osrhoeans' (Assyrians) 'beyond the Euphrates' above.[8]

Not only does this 'Ananias' play a role in Acts 9:9–19's picture of Paul's encounter in Damascus on 'a street called the Straight' at the house of one 'Judas'[9]; but a similar 'Ananias' plays a prominent role in Eusebius' narrative of yet another conversion — that of 'King Agbarus' or 'King Abgarus' of the Osrhoeans (and characterized by him as 'the Great King of the Peoples beyond the Euphrates'), a narrative Eusebius claimed to have found in 'the Royal Archives of Edessa' – 'Antioch-by-Callirhoe' – and to have personally translated into the Greek from Syriac or Aramaic into Greek.

To complete the circle of similar personages in these parallel conversion narratives, a namesake of the 'Judas,' at whose house Paul is supposed to have stayed in 'Damascus,' also appears in the story Eusebius conserves. In this version, 'Ananias' is the courier between 'Jesus' and 'King Agbarus' or 'Abgarus.' In Josephus' picture of Izates' conversion (also a 'King'-to-be at another such 'Antioch'), he is associated with another unnamed teacher (Paul?). Together they get in among the women in Izates' father 'Bazeus'' ('Agbarus'?) harem and teach that circumcision is unnecessary for conversion.[10]

The 'Judas' in the account Eusebius claims to have found in the Royal Archives at Edessa is 'Judas Thomas,' that is, 'Judas the Twin' – in John, the patently redundant 'Didymus Thomas' or 'Twin Twin,' both 'Didymus' in Greek and 'Thoma' in Aramaic meaning 'Twin'; in the Gospel of Thomas, 'Didymus Judas Thomas,' most probably Jesus' third brother 'Judas' or 'Jude the brother of James' in the Letter by that name in the New Testament; and in the Koran, even 'Hudhud' a bird![11] In Eusebius' discussion of these events (derived partially from other sources too) this 'Judas' has something to do with a 'Disciple' named 'Thaddaeus' – in orthodox Apostle lists in the Gospels, an '*Apostle*' as well.[12]

To bring this particular cluster of appellatives full circle, the latter is rather referred to in Matthew 10:3 as '*Lebbaeus* (the '*Oblias*' in the account of James' death in Eusebius *via* Hegesippus?[13]) *who was surnamed Thaddaeus*.' In Mark 3:18 this is simply '*Thaddaeus*,' but in Luke 6:16 and Acts 1:13 he is replaced by someone called '*Judas (the brother) of James*' – again probably *the third brother of Jesus named* '*Judas*' or '*Jude*.'[14] One admits the difficulty in following all these convolutions, but the new reader might consult my earlier work *James the Brother of Jesus* (Penguin, 1998/ Watkins, 2002) where most of these complexities are worked out in detail.

Stephen and '*the Hellenistai*'

Notwithstanding this plethora of confusing overlaps, the Community Acts 11:26 appears to be describing as '*Christian*' in its picture of early events at '*Antioch*' is certainly a '*Hellenistic*' or '*Greco-Judaic*' one – if it can really be said to be '*Judaic*' (a proposition we will ultimately call into question). Six lines earlier, Acts 11:20 refers to it or the Community preceding it as '*Hellenist*' (*Hellenistas*). As just remarked, one must be careful of such denotations as they may represent a circumlocution or euphemism for something entirely different – sometimes, in fact, something just the opposite. This would be true, for example, in the '*dispute*' between '*Hellenists*' (*Hellenistai*) and '*Hebrews*' in Acts 6:1–5 over '*the daily ministration for widows*' (*diakonia*) and '*waiting on tables*' (*diakonein*) which serves to introduce the highly-polemicized and largely fictional story about some one Acts ultimately ends up calling '*Stephen*.'[15]

In this story, as we shall see further below, '*the Hellenistai*' (6:1) are probably not '*Hellenes*' or '*Hellenists*' at all nor are '*Hebrews*' probably Hebrews. In it '*Hebrews*' most likely refers to principal Apostles as *per* Paul's use of the term in 2 Corinthians 11:22 to depict those he is contemptuously dismissing as '*Super Apostles*' or '*Apostles of the Highest Degree*.' Nor is the '*dispute*' between so-called '*Hellenists*' and '*Hebrews*,' pictured in Acts 6:1–6's run-up to its introduction of this '*Stephen*,' probably about '*serving tables*' or '*ministering to widows*,' however picturesque or charming the circumstances of this episode appear to be.

Nor can it be said that '*Stephen*' – as just remarked, probably not even an historical personage in Palestine at this time (at least not in the context and circumstances presented by Acts[16]) – is one of '*the Hebrews*' as the episode impenetrable, implies. Neither in this presentation is he one of '*the Hellenist on*,' though in the final analysis he probably is and, archetypically speaking at least, typifies what a '*Hellenist*' might have been if one existed at this time – basically one of Paul's newly-converted Gentile followers.

So do the other six members of '*the Seven*' enumerated here in Acts 6:5, all with patently Grecian names – two seemingly right out of Plato ('*Timon*' and '*Parmenas*'[17]). A third, the never-heard-of-before-or-since '*Nicolaus, a proselyte from Antioch*' (thus!), probably reflects one of Josephus' sources, the wily Herodian diplomat *cum* historian '*Nicolaus of Damascus*.'[18] Notwithstanding, it should be observed that in the Damascus Document there are certainly a species of Gentile proselytes or converts delineated who are far more exacting, scrupulous, and demanding, Judaically-speaking, than any of these '*deaconizing Seven*' in Acts.[19] In actuality, Stephen like '*Ananias*' and '*Judas Thomas*' above represents another of these '*doppelganger*' characters as well.

In the parallel source represented by 1 Corinthians 16:15, another '*Stephen*,' that is, he or a namesake of his, is referred to by Paul as '*the first-fruit in Achaia*' – meaning presumably Paul's first convert on the Greek mainland, probably in Corinth – '*the members of whose house appointed themselves to the service (diakonia) of the Saints*.' Of course to the perspicacious reader, the telltale employment of the usages '*diakonia*'/'*diakonein*,' upon which the modern English word '*deacon*' is based, seals the philological overlap. Not only does Paul allude to the excellence of this '*service*' including, one would assume, '*table service*' (*diakonian* – 16:17–18); but I think it can safely be said that this passage is the basis for Acts 6's multiple references to '*ministering*' (*diakonia* – 6:1), '*service*' (*diakonein* – 6:2), or '*Ministry*' (*diakonia* – 6:4) above which form the backbone of its introduction to '*Stephen*' – '*diakonia*' or its variants being repeated three times in four lines in case we missed the point!

Of course, all this sometimes playful and always purposeful obfuscation typifies Acts' bizarre and often malevolent sense of humor or word-play. In Josephus – if one acknowledges the parallel of identical names cropping up in chronologically-parallel narratives however dissimilar or unfamiliar the context or circumstances may superficially appear – '*Stephen*' is '*the Emperor's servant*' with dispatches and monetary tender from abroad (presumably from Corinth too), who is beaten and robbed by rampaging Jewish Revolutionaries almost within eyeshot of the walls of Jerusalem in the aftermath of the Passover stampede in the Temple of 49 CE.[20]

This stampede, in which Josephus estimates – depending on which source one is following, the *War* or the *Antiquities* – some 300 or 3000 people were trampled to death (extra zeroes not being terribly germane in ancient numeration – 300 being the more likely figure, much like similar stampedes with which one is familiar in our own time during modern Muslim pilgrimages to Mecca), was occasioned by a Roman Centurion on guard on the roof of the Temple arcade who lifted up his tunic and derisively exposed himself to the crowd, presumably to show at one and the same time both his uncircumcision and his contempt. He then turned around and, bending over, expelled a rude noise at the pilgrims assembled below. One should perhaps note that this is an example of what the writer would consider to be the *real* stuff of history and not romance, historical retrospective, or make-believe.

From this perspective, the '*Stephen*' in Josephus and the '*Stephen*,' Paul refers to in what was later to be Nero's summer capital Corinth as his '*firstfruit of Achaia*,' are not two separate individuals (in a modern context, one can imagine Bin Laden using similar terminology to describe new '*Disciples*' in one of his preferred geographical locales). Nor is the character whose demise Acts refurbishes into a vicious attack by horrid Jewish agitators – including a High Priest and rump Sanhedrin which, whatever the circumstance, would not have convened a special session to consider the case of an ethnic Greek such as '*Stephen*' (whatever his beliefs – the case of James being another matter entirely[21]) – *to replace the attack by Paul on the fabled Leader of 'the Jerusalem Church'* James the Just '*the brother of the Lord*.' All the elements are there as conserved in that important counterweight to the presentation in the Book of Acts, the Pseudoclementine *Recognitions*.[22]

There is one last '*Stephen*' of note in this circle of relevant '*Stephen*'s at this time and that is the '*Stephen*' responsible for the assassination of Domitian. (81–96 CE) Domitian had wreaked singular destruction on the circle of influential early Christians in Rome, beginning with Epaphroditus (seemingly Paul's colleague in Philippians 2:25 and 4:18 and, in a previous embodiment, Nero's secretary for Greek letters – not to mention the influential person Josephus pays homage to in his *Vita* as encouraging all his works[23]) and ending with Flavius Clemens, probably the very '*Clement*' featured in Pseudoclementine narrative just mentioned above.[24] Nor, seemingly, was Josephus exempt from Domitian's wrath, not surprisingly in view of Josephus' own connection probably with this same '*Epaphroditus*,' towards whom Domitian seems to have had a more than ordinate animus since he ultimately had him executed as well – probably along with Flavius Clemens and possibly even Josephus in the events leading up to Domitian's own assassination in 96 CE.[25]

This '*Stephen*' is the servant or slave of Flavia Domitilla, for whom one of the earliest and largest Christian catacombs in Rome – '*the Domitilla*

Catacomb' – is named. She was a relative of the Emperor and either the wife or niece of this very dame Flavius Clemens.[26] In regard to this name '*Flavia*,' one should remember Josephus' own adopted patronym, '*Flavius Josephus*.'There can be little doubt that Stephen's assassination of Domitian was in the nature of revenge for the execution of Flavius Clemens and probably encouraged by Flavia Domitilla herself.

If the character Josephus presents us with in the late Forties was identical to Acts' and Paul's '*Deaconizing*' and '*table-waiting*' Stephen above, how much fun it would have been for the author of Acts to transform an attack on James in the Temple at Passover in the hated Pseudoclementine *Recognitions* by Acts' own narrative hero Paul (clearly dubbed in the *Recognitions* as '*the Man who is our Enemy*'[27]) into an episode delineating an attack '*by the Jews*' – and invested with *the substance and circumstances of the two attacks on James* as reported in all early Church sources and Josephus – on the archetypical Gentile believer '*Stephen*.' The Czar's minions in *The Protocols of the Elders of Zion* (based on a recently discovered text attacking the Emperor Louis Napoleon of France[28]) could not have imagined a better scenario. Unfortunately it just did not happen.

Paul's attack on James, '*Hellenists*' at Antioch, and '*Elymas Magus*' on '*Cyprus*'

Not only does Acts randomly mix into its account materials from James' '*fall*' from the Pinnacle of the Temple as set forth by Hegesippus – material delightfully parodied in the Synoptics' picture of the '*temptation of Christ by the Devil*' on the Pinnacle of the Temple[29] or James' '*headlong*' fall from the Temple steps in the Pseudoclementine *Recognitions* (itself parodied in the '*headlong*' one '*Judas Iscariot*' takes in '*the Field of Blood*' in Acts 1:18–19[30]) – not to mention the actual stoning of James that follows in Hegesippus, Clement, and the two Apocalypses of James from Nag Hammadi[31]; but in all these accounts, the several descriptions of how '*Stephen*'/'*James*' '*cries out with a loud voice*' (Acts 7:60) or the Jewish crowd '*cried out*' (Acts 7:57) are exactly the same.[32] So basically are the final words attributed to Stephen who, '*seeing the Heavens open*' (in replication of the vision James is portrayed as having of *the Son of Man* '*sitting on the right hand of the Great Power*' *before he too was* '*cast down*' *from the Pinnacle of the Temple* in Eusebius via Hegesippus – '*Stephen*' having, it will be recalled, *been* '*cast out of the City*'[33]), '*falls to his knees*' (so does James in Hegesippus' report but, rather earlier, *in the Holy of Holies*) and, Christlike, both utter the words, '*Lord, do not lay this Sin to them*' (Acts 7:60).[34]

This is to say nothing of the chapter-long speech Stephen is portrayed as making *to the High Priest and Sanhedrin* prior to his stoning, telling them their whole history up to the building of the Temple by Solomon (Acts 7:2–53) – as if a *'Jewish'* Sanhedrin would need such a review! – but which rather ends with the *'killing all the Prophets'*-accusation (or rather *'libel'*) first made by Paul in Thessalonians 2:15 and contains elements from the Letter of James about *'keeping the Law'* and an actual phrase based on Ezekiel 44:7 used in the Habakkuk *Pesher* from the Dead Sea Scrolls, the *'uncircumcised heart.'*[35]

Not only is this speech clearly lifted from Joshua's *'Farewell Address'* to the assembled Tribes on Mounts Ebal and Gerizim in Joshua 24:2–15, but Joshua 24:32 actually points the way to the source of the glaring error *'Stephen'* makes in Acts 7:16, where he identifies Abraham's burial site as *'the tomb which Abraham bought for a certain sum of money from the Sons of Hamor in Schechem'* and not the one *a hundred miles or so further South which Abraham bought from Ephron the Hittite at Mamre in Hebron.* This mistake, as anyone familiar with such august gatherings would easily understand, would have caused eruptions of laughter. Moreover, the mistake is easily comprehensible as a too-hasty reading of Joshua 24:32, immediately following it, where the burial place of Joshua's ancestor Joseph, *'the plot of ground Jacob bought for a hundred pieces of silver from the sons of Hamor the father of Shechem'* is specifically evoked.[36]

To further point up the artificiality of this episode, Acts has Stephen (*in whose face one could 'see the face of an Angel'*) now predicting – like Jesus in the Gospels – that *'Jesus the Nazoraean would destroy this Place'* (meaning,*'the Temple'*) and *'change the customs delivered by Moses'* (6:14–15). This is certainly written after the fall of the Temple in 70 CE, only here it is not God or the Romans who will be coming to *'destroy this place'* but now *'Jesus the Nazoraean'* and the metamorphosis is complete. Of course, not only does *'Stephen'* (in place, one must suppose, of the allegedly *'Judaizing'* Leader of *'the Party of the Circumcision,'* James) almost become a 'Jesus' himself; his suffering and torment at the hands (importantly, *of 'the Jews'*) almost replicates that of his Biblical prototype 'Jesus' as well.

Figuratively, the name *'Stephen'* means *'Crown'* in Greek, an image, for instance, which Eusebius makes much of two centuries later in characterizing him as *'the first after our Lord…to receive the Crown answering to his Name of the Victorious Martyrs of Christ.'*[37] But, as both H.-J. Schoeps and myself have shown, the execution by stoning carried out by Eusebius' *'murderers of the Lord'* and Stephen's reaction to it (to say nothing of the crowd's) have as much or more to do with James' fate and martyrdom than any archetypical Gentile convert by the name of *'Stephen'* at this moment in early Church history in Palestine. In fact, the very '*Crown*,' we are speaking about here, was also often used to describe the hair of unshorn '*Nazirites*' like James.[38]

'*Hellenists*' may be '*Gentiles*' or '*Hellenizers*' but, in the writer's view, sometimes they may even represent '*Zealots*.' If the parallels with contemporary episodes in Josephus delineating the attack on '*the Emperor's Servant Stephen*' not very far from the walls of Jerusalem itself by crazed Revolutionaries, as well as those with the disputes running through Books XIX–XX of the *Antiquities* between '*Greeks*' and '*Jews*' in Caesarea ('*Hellenists*' and '*Hebrews*' in Acts) or '*Zealots*' and toadying Jewish turncoats, are recognized as the real historical templates underlying these chapters in Acts – transmogrified here *via* the magic of art in the interests of retrospective theology – then this is certainly the case.[39] There is a precedent for this, namely the use of '*Canaanites*' or '*Cananaeans*' in Mark and Matthew based on the Hebrew word '*Kanna'im*' or '*Zealots*'.[40] This is easily recognized in the shift from '*Simon the Cananaean*' or '*Canaanite*' in Apostle lists in Matthew 10:4 and Mark 3:18 to '*Simon Zelotes*' in Luke 6:15 and Acts 1:13. This, in turn, parallels the shift already called attention to above from '*Thaddaeus*' to '*Lebbaeus surnamed Thaddaeus*' in Mark and Matthew to '*Judas (the brother) of James*' in Luke (no doubt, too, '*Jude the brother of James*' in the Letter ascribed to his name[41]).

There are also problems with designations such as '*Cypriots*' or '*Cyrenians*' which do not always represent what they seem. Take for example the case of Simon *Magus*' double in Paphos on '*Cyprus*' in Acts 13:4–12, the supposedly '*Jewish*' magician and '*false prophet whose name was Bar-Jesus*.' This name is further alluded to as '*Elymas Magus*' in the Greek of Acts 13:8, basically another redundancy of the kind of '*Twin Twin*' regarding '*Didymus Thomas*' above, since '*Elymas*' in Greek is a synonym of '*Magus*.' Nor is this to mention the virtual repeat of this episode in '*the Seven Sons of Sceva*' episode in Acts 19:10–20 – supposedly the sons of a '*Jewish High Priest*,' who were also going around '*Asia*' casting out '*Evil spirits*' or '*practising magical arts*' – the very name of whom '*Sceva*' in Hebrew itself meaning '*Seven*.' It is in this episode on '*Cyprus*,' too, right at the beginning of Paul's first missionary journey, as Acts depicts it, that Paul meets his namesake one '*Sergius Paulus*,' the former never seemingly called '*Saulos*' ever again. Nor is the latter ever heard from again. Neither is this to mention that Simon *Magus*' place of origin and principal theater of operations, according to both early Church accounts and the Pseudoclementines (but not Acts), seems originally to have been '*Samaria*,' the town of '*Gitta*' there being his birthplace.[42]

What am I saying? Actually, sometimes '*Cyprus*' may mean '*Samaria*' because the earlier confrontation between Simon *Magus* and Peter in the aftermath of the '*Stephen*' episode in Acts 8:14–24 – being parodied here in Acts 13:6–12's '*Elymas Magus*' episode – almost certainly took place either in '*Samaria*' or '*Caesarea*,' the closest major coastal city to Samaria, as it does, for instance, also in the Pseudoclementines. '*Caesarea*' is also the locale in which Josephus places the character he calls in the *Antiquities* 'a *Magician called Simon*.'[43] In some manuscripts this is '*Atomus*,' an almost-certainly garbled allusion to the characteristic doctrine assigned to '*Simon Magus*' according to the Pseudoclementines and early Church reports, *the incarnated* or '*Primal Adam*'-ideology of which, for Paul in 1 Corinthians 15:22 and 45–48, Jesus is '*the Second*' or '*Last*' – '*the Lord out of Heaven*.'[44]

The reason for this particular geographical confusion – above and beyond the purposeful obfuscation involved – is probably because Jews in this period (including Josephus) *often referred to 'Samaritans' as* '*Cuthaeans*.'[45] This seems, in some convoluted manner to have become confused in translation with '*Kittim*,' an important usage also in the Dead Sea Scrolls which, despite the fact that its earliest signification must surely have been '*Crete*,' even in the Bible represents Cyprus, the closest island of any size in the direction of Crete off the Judean coast.[46] This is to say nothing of the additional possible confusion between '*Cuth*,' '*Kitte*,' and '*Gitta*' in the above-mentioned allusion to Simon *Magus*' birthplace.

Herodians at Antioch

Notwithstanding all these points, among these founding members or '*Hellenists*' in the Christian Community of Antioch (where '*the Disciples were first called Christians*' – 11:26), as Acts presents them, were even individuals of *the Herodian genus*. Though not himself expressly listed as a founding member of the Community in Acts, a good example of this kind of individual would be '*Titus*' (in other presentations, also possibly '*Timothy*' – not always distinguishable from one another[47]), '*the son of a certain Jewish believing woman whose father was a Greek*' (Acts 16:3). The situation described by this last would be typical of descendants of either of Herod's two '*Jewish*' wives both named '*Mariamme*' ('*Mary*').[48]

Another individual of this genus – who along with '*Judas Barsabas*' (to say nothing of Barnabas and Paul) is described as bringing the '*letter*' containing James' directives to overseas communities '*down to Antioch*' in Acts 15:27 – is Silas (in other vocabularies also possibly '*Silvanus*,' its equivalent in Latin, and, like '*Titus*' and '*Timothy*,' not always distinguishable one from the other). In coeval materials in Josephus from the Forties to the Sixties CE, an individual called 'Silas' is the Commander of King Agrippa's bodyguard in Caesarea.[49] This, like many of the parallels noted above, may simply be coincidental, but if these other equivalences hold – and their number does begin to mount up – there is no reason to think it is. Both 'Silas' and 'Judas,' interestingly enough, are referred to in Acts 15:32 as 'Prophets,' 'strengthening and exhorting the brothers by much discourse.' Not only is this 'Prophet' designation – or usually rather 'pseudo-prophets' – being widely used in Josephus in this period; but in this imagery of 'Strengthening' we again have language paralleling what we shall encounter in both the Damascus Document from Qumran and early Church accounts of James.[50]

Another of these match-ups, officially listed among these five founding 'certain ones' or 'some' – almost always an expression, whether in Acts or Paul's Letters, involving either disparagement or an unwillingness to be straightforward or forthcoming[51] – and 'the prophets and teachers of the Assembly at Antioch' (Ecclesian[52]) in Acts 13:1, is 'Niger.' A parallel 'Niger' in Josephus – possibly another coincidence but also possibly not – is a pro-Revolutionary turncoat Herodian 'Man-of-War' who participated in the first battles of the War. Later he is military chieftain of the unruly 'Idu-maeans' on the other side of the Jordan in Perea (whoever these might be considered as being – as we shall see as we progress, possibly 'the Violent Ones of the Gentiles' mentioned in the Habakkuk and Psalm 37 Peshers as responsible for the destruction of the Wicked Priest, 'paying him the Reward with which he rewarded' the Teacher of Righteousness and his followers among 'the Poor,' that is, 'destroying them,' and in the second-named as 'taking vengeance upon him for what he had done to the Righteous Teacher'[53]).

It should be appreciated, too. that the national affiliation 'Idumaeans' (Biblically-speaking, 'the Edomites,' a euphemism as well in the Talmud for both Romans and Herodians) further solidifies an 'Herodian' connection for these 'Violent Ones of the Gentiles' (as they are called in the Dead Sea Scrolls) or 'Men-of-War,' despite their pro-Revolutionary orientation – Herod's mother having been of either 'Idumaean' or 'Arab' extraction and Herodians generally, therefore, being popularly known as 'Idumaeans.'[54] In Josephus, this 'Niger' suffers a terrible fate at the hands of his erstwhile comrades, who do not seem to have considered him either loyal or revolutionary enough; and the agonizing portrait of his death carrying his own cross out of the city is, in the author's view, seemingly the template for the picture of Jesus' last moments in the Gospels – itself possibly even penned by one of this 'Niger''s disillusioned followers.[55]

Another of these 'certain ones' at Antioch is a sometime traveling companion of Paul, called in Paul's Letters and here in Acts, 'Barnabas.'

However, in Acts 4:36 he was called a '*Cypriot Levite named Joses.*' Not only is there once again the issue here of what actually is intended by the designation '*Cypriot*,' but also the interesting coincidence that '*Joses*' is the name in the Synoptic Gospels of Jesus' fourth '*brother.*' Nor is this to say anything about the basic overlap or resemblance of names like '*Barnabas*'/'*Barsabas*'/and '*Barabbas*,' their signification, or the connection of, at least, some, such as '*Joseph Barsabas*' and '*Jesus Barabbas*,' with similar-sounding names among the members of Jesus' family generally.[56] Further penetration of these tantalizing connections, however, is perhaps not possible.

Be these things as they may, a third of these so-called '*prophets and teachers*' of '*the Church at Antioch*' in Acts 13:1 (equivalent to '*the Hellenists*' above in Acts 11:20'?) is '*Saulos*' or '*Paul*' himself.[57] It should be appreciated that '*Ecclesia*' in Greek ('*Church*' in English and related European '*Tongues*') is '*ʿEdah*' in Hebrew, itself an extremely important usage across the board in Qumran documents usually translated in English as '*Congregation.*' We use the word '*Qumran*,' the Arabic denotation for the location where the Scrolls were found, interchangeably with the Scrolls themselves and their content, a practice in wide use in the field. '*Assembly*' – called '*the Jerusalem Assembly*' by some; '*the Jerusalem Church*' by others – is also an important usage for all descriptions of James and the Council of Elders ('*Presbyters*' in Acts 15:2–4, 22, 21:18, *etc.*), he headed, not only in Acts but in the Pseudoclementines as well.[58]

The fourth of these five '*prophets and teachers*' in Acts 13:1 is '*Loukios the Cyrenian*,' most probably an approximation for the alleged author of Acts and the Gospel under his name, and, like Barnabas, a seeming traveling companion of Paul. Here '*Cyrenian*' probably does represent the area of Cyrenaica (presentday Libya) next to Hellenistic Egypt, from where '*Lukas*' presumably came, and a wide area of revolutionary '*Sicarii*' activity even after the Temple fell in 70 CE,[59] though this is probably not the case for someone like '*Simon the Cyrenean*' in the Gospels, portrayed as carrying the cross for Jesus in Mark 15:21 and Luke 23:26 and who apparently resides in Jerusalem.

Together with appellatives like '*Barnabas*,' '*Lebbaeus*,' and '*Barsabas*,' it is a cognomen of some kind, but so in reality too is '*Niger*,' the reference to whom actually reads, '*Simeon who was called Niger.*' In Greek '*Niger*' means '*Black*,' in which case it could have overtones with another interesting character in the contemporary '*Antioch- by-Callirhoe*': '*Abgar the Black*' or '*Agbar Uchama*' in Eusebius' fabulous correspondence.[60] In Semitic languages generally it can, it would appear, also carry the connotation, '*shoemaker*', whatever one wishes to make of that in the context we are discussing above – if anything.

The 'Simeon' aspect of the appellation is curious as well since it is a name most often associated with 'Simeon bar Cleophas,' the successor to James and second successor to Jesus in the Leadership of 'the Jerusalem Church,' considered by most to be the cousin germane of both.[61] But if 'Cleophas,' who is normally represented in early Church tradition as the 'brother' of Jesus' father 'Joseph' and the husband of 'Mary the mother of James, Joses, Simon, and Judas,'[62] is the same as 'Clopas' in John 19:25, 'Cleopas' in Luke 24:18, and most likely 'Alphaeus' in Synoptic Apostle lists; then 'Simeon bar Cleophas' is probably hardly distinguishable from Jesus' second brother 'Simon' and not his 'cousin germane' as early Church sources would have it, in which case, he is also probably to be identified with 'Simon the Cananaean'/'Simon the Zealot' in Gospel Apostle lists above and possibly even another 'Simon,' 'Simon (the father)' or '(brother) of Judas Iscariot' in John 6:71 – but this would take a little more exposition beyond the present scope of these present 'Preliminaries.'[63]

It should be noted, too, that 'Peter' or 'Cephas' (n.b., the homophonic relation of 'Cephas' to 'Cleophas' and, for that matter, 'Caiaphas'[64]) – another of these 'Twin Twin' repetitions, 'Peter' in Greek and 'Cephas' in Aramaic both meaning 'Rock' – normally considered to be 'Simon Peter' the successor to Jesus in orthodox Christian tradition, is at one point anyhow referred to as 'Simeon.' This comes, yet again, during the crucial succession of speeches in Acts 15's portrayal of the fabulous 'Jerusalem Council' (15:14), speeches which have much in common with earlier ones at the beginning of Acts (2:14–3:26) and a parallel set of speeches in the Pseudoclementine *Recognitions* just prior to the portrayal there of *Paul's physical assault on James.*

We say 'fabulous' and 'portrayal' because Acts' narrative is just this, an artistic and retrospective recreation. The points it makes have almost nothing in common with the picture Paul provides in Galatians 1–2 and, as well, very little in common with what we know of what Leaders like James or Simeon bar Cleophas actually would have said from other sources. On the other hand, they will have important terminological connections with well-known allusions in, for instance, the Damascus Document.[65] This would make the 'Simeon' in question in Acts 15's portrait of the 'Jerusalem Council' (not to mention the 'Simon' who suddenly appears in Luke 24:34's presentation of the aftermath of 'Jesus'' first post-resurrection appearance on 'the road to Emmaus' to 'Cleopas' and an unnamed other[66]) to have more in common with *James' successor in* 'Ebionite' or 'Jewish Christian' tradition, 'Simeon bar Cleophas,' than with Jesus' successor in more Western orthodox sources and tradition, 'Simon

Cephas' or *'Peter.'*

Mix-ups of this kind surround the pivotal character known variously as *'Simon'/'Peter'/'Cephas'*/and/or *'Simeon'* whom, we have much cause in Palestine anyhow at this time to identify with *'Simeon bar Cleophas,'* James' successor in the Leadership of *'the Jerusalem Church'* and the so-called *'cousin germane of our Lord'* – Jerome's ploy of identifying the brothers of Jesus as *'cousins'* already having taken hold in the literature by this point.[67] This is to say nothing about the fact that, according to the historiography of Acts, at the time of the date of the supposed *'Jerusalem Council,'* the character it is calling *'Peter'* had already fled the country with a death sentence on his head for having escaped from prison after having been arrested and, indirectly therefore, caused the death of the prison guards (12:4–19).[68] This anyhow is Acts' testimony if it can be trusted.

In our view, sometimes it can but only rarely, and this more in its later stages – after the introduction of the *'We Document'* in 16:10 directly following *'the Jerusalem Council,'* the delivery of James' *'Letter'* to the *'Apostles, Elders, and brothers at Antioch,'* the split between Barnabas and John Mark and Paul and Silas, and Paul's circumcision of *'Timothy'* – than in its earlier stages and/or narrative. So it is difficult to imagine that the orthodox *'Peter'* could, somehow, suddenly have returned to peacefully participate in this *'Council'* in Acts 15:6–30 whatever its proceedings.

'Manaen the Foster Brother of Herod the Tetrarch'

This brings us to the fourth person mentioned in Acts 13:1 – preceding *'Saulos'* and just before *'Saulos'* is renamed *'Paulos'* in Acts 13:9 – the fifth among these *'Prophets and teachers'* of *'the Antioch Assembly,'* *'Manaen the foster brother of Herod the Tetrarch.'* This is one of the most revealing testimonies in New Testament Scripture because it unequivocally – and, one might say, even unashamedly – reveals that *there were 'Herodians' involved in the foundation of the Church at 'Antioch' where 'Disciples were first called Christians'* around 55 CE. This is no insignificant datum.

In *James the Brother of Jesus,* I expressed the opinion that what one has in such instances is a species of shell-game.[69] We identified this sort of *'shell-game'* with regard to the *'Central Triad'* of *'the Jerusalem Church'* depending on which source and which and whose *'brother'* one is talking about – *Peter, James, and 'John his brother'* in the Gospels and *'James, Cephas, and John'* in Galatians. In the manner in which these *'Central Three'* are presented in the Gospels, the most famous *'James'* appears to be *'the brother of John'* and, therefore, one ends up with the well-known *'John and James the two sons of Zebedee'* or *'the two Sons of Thunder'/'the Thunder Twins'* however one wishes to express it, none of which formulations appears historically very realistic.

It only takes a little reconstruction to arrive at the '*Cephas, John, and James his brother*' – meaning '*James the brother of the Lord*' – as '*the Central Three*' according to Paul's testimony in Galatians 1:19 and 2:9. The epithet '*his brother*' would then no longer apply to '*James the brother of John*,' a character nowhere mentioned by Paul; but rather – and this probably more accurately – '*James the brother of Jesus*.' This was obviously how Paul saw it and, because of this, made no mention of any '*James*' other than '*the brother of the Lord*' and seems to know no other. This would appear to be the thrust of most traditional extra-Biblical literature too, where more is known about '*James the Just*' or '*James the brother of Jesus*' (to be fair, in Galatians 1:19 he is only referred to as '*James the brother of the Lord*') than someone called '*James the brother of John*' as in Mark 3:17 and 5:37, unless '*John*' and '*the Lord*' can be considered to mean the same thing – a dubious proposition.

In any event, this other '*James the brother of John*,' historical or otherwise, conveniently disappears from Scripture in Acts 12:2 just prior to Acts' introduction of this other '*James*' in 12:17. This disappearance of '*James the brother of John*' consonant with the sudden appearance of the really significant James just a few lines later, off-hand or otherwise is, from the standpoint of early Church history in Palestine, the really significant information as well. This '*James*' appears, as it were, unheralded and unintroduced though the text appears to think we already know or should know who he is.[70]

The same is true of the reference to one '*Manaen the foster brother of Herod the Tetrarch*' as one of the principal members of the founding Community at Antioch in Acts 13:1. We shall have more to say about which '*Antioch*' is intended here in due course, but '*Manaen*' is probably defective as there is no other known personality with such a name in any source one can point to, unless it be '*Mani*' a century or two later.[71] Rather the appellation, as it stands in Acts, probably represents a corruption of the '*Ananias*,' we have already met above, who forms a setpiece of the presentation of Paul's conversion in Damascus in Acts 9:12–17. In this sense '*Damascus*' in Acts can simply be seen as a parallel to or write-in for '*Edessa*' and what is going on there at about this time or, even possibly, '*Adiabene*' in Josephus – all fairly contiguous areas.[72]

The same can probably be said for a '*certain Mnason*,' mentioned further along in Acts 21:16 at the time of Paul's climactic final encounter with James. Not only do we have the telltale '*certain*' or '*someone*' in this designation (we shall have occasion to further point up as we proceed), but, once again, the picturesque description of him as '*an old Disciple, a Cypriot*' who, for some unexplained reason, *has a house in Jerusalem where Paul and his companions stay*. He may constitute a variation on '*Ananias*' above as well or, for that matter, some other unidentified personage as, once again, there is no one by this name in any other historical context from this Period one can specify.

Properly speaking, the character being referred to in multiple contexts as '*Ananias*' probably should have been mentioned among '*the Prophets and teachers of the Antioch Assembly*' anyhow – whichever the '*Antioch*' one might have in mind at this time.[73] Though Acts places him in '*Damascus*,' he or a namesake of his is clearly functioning, according to Eusebius' source, in Edessa where he is associated with the conversion of the King there, Abgarus or Agbarus, '*the Great King of the Peoples beyond the Euphrates*.'

Also in Josephus' account of the conversion of Queen Helen (possibly one of '*Agbarus*'' wives as we shall see below – and, perhaps even, his principal one) and her favorite son Izates at the beginning of the all-important Book Twenty of *The Antiquities* ending with the death of James, yet another character called '*Ananias*' is to be met in two locales, once in the South at the mouth of the Tigris at Charax Spasini (modern-day '*Basrah*' – also '*Antiochia Charax*') and, following this, on the Upper Euphrates closer to Edessa or '*the Land of the Edessenes*' – possibly including '*Adiabene*' adjoining it. Nor do we consider all of these to be separate renderings or episodes.

The women, such as '*Helen of Adiabene*' in this '*Great King*''s harem – also possibly his sister or half-sister (as, for instance, Sarah was supposed to have been Abraham's) – whom '*Ananias*' and another companion Josephus mysteriously declines to mention (Paul?) get in among and convert, '*have a horror of circumcision*.' This last, in turn, is perhaps the principal issue behind Paul's polemics in Galatians, a Letter being addressed seemingly to those in either a Northern Syrian or an '*Asian*' context. This is perhaps why Abraham plays such an important role in its polemics, not those only directed against erstwhile companions but also those in the Letter of James, in some respects its ostensible answer – Abraham himself being celebrated as having originated in this area. This is also true of the derivative later polemics in the Koran.[74]

To go back to the '*Herod the Tetrarch*,' to whom this '*Manaen*' is supposed to have stood in a quasi-fraternal relationship: not only is this '*Herod*' well known as the eventual husband of the sister of King Agrippa I, Herodias, but he or she would seem to bear much of the responsibility for the death of John the Baptist, whichever presentation of these events one chooses to follow − either that of the Gospels or of Josephus.[75] It is hardly credible that an individual with such a background and called, therefore, '*the foster brother of Herod the Tetrarch*' could have been reckoned among the founding '*Prophets and teachers of the Church at Antioch*,' as Acts would have it, unless the apposition were accidentally or purposefully displaced − which is what we meant by alluding to a '*shell-game*' in the first place − and it rather applied, not to an insignificant unknown such as '*Manaen*,' but rather to Paul himself.

I have expressed the position, which we shall develop in much greater detail in due course below, that Paul was an '*Herodian*,' one of the proofs of which were his greetings to his '*kinsman Herodion*' ('*the Littlest Herod*') at the end of Romans 16:11 − presumably Herod the Sixth, the son of Aristobulus and Salome, to whose household he appears already to have sent greetings in the previous line (16:10).[76] The '*Salome*' in question is, of course, the very person whose dance is pictured in the Synoptic Gospels as being the immediate cause of John's demise, a dance never mentioned in Josephus though her marriage to another of her mother's uncles, '*Philip*,' is. In the Synoptics, this '*Philip*' evolves into her mother's first husband, an individual Josephus rather identifies as actually having been named '*Herod*' not '*Philip*.' In Josephus, it is rather Salome's husband, as we just said, who is named '*Philip*,' '*who died childless*'.[77]

As it turns out, just such a relative of '*Herod the Tetrarch*' (elsewhere, '*Herod Antipas*') named '*Saulos*' does exist in the Herodian family at this time. Furthermore, as described by Josephus, he is involved in activities not unsimilar, as we shall see, to Paul's as well − namely, leading a riot in Jerusalem after the death of James perilously similar to the riot led by Paul described in Acts 8:1−3 directly following '*the stoning of Stephen*' or the riot which Paul, described as '*the Enemy*,' is pictured as leading in the Pseudoclementine *Recognitions* that ends up in James being thrown, not from '*the Pinnacle of the Temple*' but '*head-long down the Temple steps*.'[78] He is also involved, like his namesake '*Paul*,' in an appeal to Caesar − in both, '*Nero Caesar*' − but more about all these things in due course.[79]

If Paul and not '*Manaen*' was '*the foster brother of Herod the Tetrarch*,' identical with the individual called '*Saulos*' in Josephus; it would not be at all surprising if he were also involved earlier in his career in the death of John the Baptist and his flight from Damascus at this time (as *per* the picture in 2 Corinthians 11:32−33 − not the sanitized and refurbished one in Acts 9:23) in order to escape the soldiers of King Aretas related to these circumstances. The circumstances were that this '*Paul*' or '*Saulos*' was in Damascus − the *real* '*Damascus*' and not the more complex one in the Scrolls or the one revised in Acts 9:2−25 − on a mission of some sort in support of his *'kinsman'* or *'foster brother'* Herod the Tetrarch, the recently-acquired husband of the despised Herodias, the marriage of whom triggered the death of John. Actually Aretas, the *'Arab'* King of Petra further South, had just taken military control of Damascus at this time.[80]

To put this more succinctly: if we sometimes consider constructs like *'the foster brother of Herod the Tetrarch'* to be laterally displaced, we can arrive with far more sense at the insight that, in the early Christian Community at Antioch (whichever 'Antioch' one might ultimately think this to be) *'where Christians were first called Christians,'* the individual brought up with Herod the Tetrarch was Paul not *'Manaen'* (the likely original of which was *'Ananias'*) – precisely that *'Saulos'* who eight lines further along in Acts 13:7 receives his Greco-Latin name after a far too felicitous exchange with *'Sergius Paulos'* (pictured as the Roman proconsul of *'Cyprus'* at this time).

Elsewhere *'Paul'* is pictured as having made the assertion of having persecuted *the followers of the Way unto death'* (Acts 22:4 and Galatians 1:13 and 23). This is just the conclusion we would arrive at in our interpretation of the curious double version of Paul's *descent down the walls of Damascus 'in a basket'* to *escape the representatives of King Aretas trying to arrest him* in 2 Corinthians 11:32–33. Via the miracle of art, Acts 9:23 refurbishes this – while at the same time injecting another fairly virulent dose of Hellenistic anti-Semitism – into *a descent by Paul down the walls of Damascus in a basket 'to escape the Jews.'* It is now *'the Jews'* who are presented as the ones who *'want to kill him'* and not *'the Ethnarch of Aretas'* as in 2 Corinthians 11:32 above.

In fact, a Monarch by the name of *'Aretas'* did play a role in the circumstances surrounding John the Baptist's death, but he was on the same side as John because Herod the Tetrarch (*'Herod'* in the Gospels) had divorced his original wife (this *'Aretas'* daughter) to prepare the way for his marriage to Agrippa I's sister and Salome's mother, Herodias. As Josephus puts it in the *Antiquities*, the people were glad at Herod's discomfiture in the subsequent mini-war he fought with Aretas over this affair and took it as a sign of God's vengeance or displeasure *'at what he (Herod) had done to John.'*[81] In addition, it is apparent that *'the Jews'* in Josephus' diverging account *were on the same side as John and not against him* as the Gospels often portray – John being a popular religio-political reformer for the mass of Jews who, according to Josephus, seemed willing to do *'anything he should suggest'* including Revolution; while, on the other hand, the Herodians were a Greco-Arab alien Dynasty imposed on them by the Romans from outside, *most of whom not even considered as Jews!*[82]

This is backed up as well by later Syriac/Armenian sources which claim – reliably or not – that their ruler '*Abgar*' ('*Abgar the Black*'?) helped Aretas in his campaign against Herod Antipas or Herod the Tetrarch,[83] the individual we are supposed to think had a '*foster-brother*' among the earliest '*Prophets and teachers*' of the '*Christian*' Assembly at Antioch named '*Manaen*.' Once again, our suggestion is that the actual '*foster brother*' of Herod the Tetrarch was not '*Manaen*' but Paul himself, which makes perfectly good sense in the context. This is particularly true when one considers Paul's Roman Citizenship (which all Herodians possessed[84]), his consistently pro-Roman orientation both as pictured in Acts and in his letters, his easy entrée as a young man into Jerusalem upper-class circles, including the letters he gets from the High Priest *to arrest those* '*of the Way*' *in* '*Damascus*' (Acts 9:2) – to say nothing of the ease with which his nephew later (whoever *he* may have been) is able to communicate with the Chief Captain of the Roman Guard in the Temple who is holding Paul in protective custody (Acts 23:19) and, finally, his incarceration in '*Herod* (Agrippa II)'*s Palace in Caesarea*' in what appears rather a loose form of house arrest than an actual incarceration in Acts 23:35.

Therefore we have alluded to him as '*the Herodian Paul*' and, therefore too, it is possible to assert that Paul not '*Manaen*' (whoever he might have been) would have more likely been *the one brought up with Herod the Tetrarch*, a fact Acts' Lukan artificer would have been at pains to obscure. With only a slight lateral displacement – just as with '*James his brother*' meaning '*James the brother of John*' (not '*James the brother of Jesus*') above – this is exactly what one ends up with and this embarrassing fact is easily over-written and erased. These things as they may be, these are the kinds of analyses and insights one is able to achieve and will achieve further below if one pursues this kind of information without preconceptions or prior commitment and with a modicum of common sense and intelligence.

The Anti-Semitic Peter

Another rewarding avenue of analysis are the speeches attributed to Peter in Acts and the contrast of these with the portrait of Peter in the Pseudoclementines. In Acts, Peter is presented as a mouthpiece for anti-Semitic invective, but this kind of Peter is hardly, if ever, in evidence in the Pseudoclementines, whichever version one consults, the *Homilies* or the *Recognitions*. In our view, the Pseudoclementines do not simply parallel Acts; rather, *they are based on the same source as Acts, to which they are the more faithful*. This is certainly the case with the *Recognitions*, the

First Book of which links up with Acts in an almost point-for-point manner – albeit approaching most issues from a completely opposite ideological orientation. In addition there is the common vocabulary not only with Acts, but also documents at Qumran like the Damascus Document.

There are some five or six speeches attributed to Peter in Acts. In almost every one, rather like the '*Stephen*' just noted above, he is presented as making the same telltale '*Blood libel*'-accusation which is never even alluded to in the Pseudoclementine narratives. Rather, in the latter, Peter emerges as a gentle soul, never quick to anger – the archetypical '*Essene*' as it were – who, like those described in Josephus, '*wears threadbare clothes*' *and arises at dawn to greet the sun in prayer, following which he always immerses himself* – that is, in the Pseudoclementines *Peter is a Daily Bather*.[85] Finally in the Pseudoclementines, he is the inveterate '*Jamesian*,' preaching absolute adherence to a more faithful rendition of James' directives to overseas communities even than those depicted in Acts.[86]

It is obviously this sort of portrait that is being deliberately gainsaid in Acts. Not only does Peter receive a '*Paulinizing*' vision in Jaffa where he learns not to make distinctions between '*Holy and profane*,' nor '*to call any man profane*' (Acts 10:14–15 and 28) just in time to greet the representative of the Roman Centurion Cornelius (10:19–22); this vision, of course, makes it possible for him to come and visit Cornelius' house and keep '*table fellowship*' with him – the prototype for the whole '*Gentile Mission*' of Paul and the opposite of the outcome of the confrontations in Antioch in Galatians 2:11–14 after the representatives from James '*come down*' from Jerusalem. In this last Peter parts company with Paul and together with Barnabas *chooses no longer to keep company with him in either* '*work or purse*' (the language of Qumran – *cf.* Acts 15:39 above[87]), in return for which Paul accuses both of them of '*hypocrisy*' (Galatians 2:13).

But, of course, the position of *the real* '*Peter*' comes across even here in his exclamation in response to the Heavenly Voice (in Hebrew, '*Bat Chol*') accompanying this storybook vision of a tablecloth descending from Heaven, commanding him '*three times*' to '*eat*' *unclean foods* and '*not separate Holy from profane*': '*no Lord no, I have never eaten any profane or unclean thing*' (Acts 10:14). Indeed, Peter becomes the swing figure exploited in Acts at every opportunity to make the point of its anti-Semitic invective. How completely unhistorical, if we are to judge by the Pseudoclementines, and how sad.

The first of these speeches occurs in Acts 2:14–36 when Peter speaks on Pentecost to the '*Jews and Pious persons from every Nation of those under Heaven who were dwelling in Jerusalem*' (Acts 2:5 – *thus*), addressing them:

'*You took him with your lawless hands and, having crucified him, put him to death,*' meaning '*Jesus the Nazoraean, the man set up by God with mighty works and wonders, and signs which God worked through him*' and '*given up*' with '*the foreknowledge of God*' (Acts 2:22–23). Now quoting Scripture, Peter continues making *the second of these 'Blood libel' accusations*:

> *He was a Prophet and knowing that God had sworn to him with an oath...to sit upon His Throne* (and quoting '*David,*' as Acts puts it in 2:29–35 from Psalm 110, also popular material in the Scrolls and the same material we have already seen '*Stephen*' quote in 7:49 above[88]), *the Lord said to my Lord, 'Sit at My right hand until I place your Enemies as a footstool beneath your feet.' So therefore, let all the House of Israel know that God made him both Lord and Christ – this same Jesus whom you crucified* (Acts 2:30–36 – here the second accusation).

This in its totality is his first speech, '*standing with the Eleven*' *to the Assembled Multitudes on Pentecost* and the doctrinal invective it contains is patent. The '*Peter*' pictured here was surely not going to win many friends or influence many people in Jerusalem with this kind of language, but the speech obviously was not intended for the ears of those living in Jerusalem despite its context and the ostensible greeting of the opening line to '*all you who inhabit Jerusalem*'; but rather to the wider cosmopolitan audience to which it has always been found more meaningful.

The next speech follows almost immediately in the next Chapter when '*Peter and John go up to the Temple at the ninth hour*' (3:1). Acts is always interested in this type of detail ('*James*' for some reason is now absent and it should be obvious to the reader by now why). *After straightening out a cripple's crooked bones* (thus), Peter again launches into a like-minded speech, clearly paralleling ones in the debates on the Temple steps recorded in the First Book of the Pseudoclementine *Recognitions*. In that version of quasi-parallel proceedings which pictures one Apostle speaking after another, Peter finally precedes James in a speech to the Assembled Multitudes, but the message is completely different from the one here in Acts.[89]

The issue under discussion in the *Recognitions* is the nature of the Messiah and the '*Primal Adam*' ideology; but in Acts at this juncture, Peter rather *berates the crowd over the fact of his miracle-working*:

> *Men, Israelites, why do you wonder at this...as if we made him walk by our own Power* (this, an allusion to '*the Great Power*' ideology we shall presently also encounter in the Pseudoclementine *Recognitions*)...*The God of Abraham*

and Isaac and Jacob, the God of our Fathers, glorified His Servant Jesus, whom you delivered up (here the third instance of the '*Blood libel*' accusation being attributed to Peter), *denying him in the presence of Pilate after he had decided to release him. But you denied the Holy and Righteous One* (this furthers the accusation) *and demanded that a man who was a murderer be given to you instead* (3:12–14).

This is totally the approach of the Gospels, but neither here nor in them is it explained why Pilate as Roman Governor should have offered the Jewish crowd this kind of choice between '*Barabbas*,' as the Gospels flesh this out, and 'Jesus.'

Still, to drive the point home and, as in the preceding chapter, making the '*Blood libel*' accusation two times in the same speech, '*Peter*' is made to add:

And you killed the author of life whom God raised up from the dead (this is the fourth such accusation – not a very good proselytizing technique), *of which we are the witnesses* (3:15).

Here Acts gives the number of those who heard and, therefore, believed as '*five thousand*' (4:4), but this is the number Josephus originally gives for the number of '*the Essenes*,' as we shall see, as well as the number of the original followers of the Maccabees.[90] It is also, to be sure – continuing the parallel – the number of James' followers in the Pseudoclementine *Recognitions* who flee down to the Jericho area after James has been thrown down and left for dead in the riot allegedly instigated by Paul in the Temple and, of course, the number of people before whom Jesus performs his '*signs*' or miracles '*in the wilderness*' in the Gospels (though sometimes this alternates with '*four thousand*').[91]

The next occurrence of this sort of accusation again follows almost immediately. It takes place before the High Priest, the Prefect Alexander (Philo's nephew Tiberius Alexander – Titus Caesar's military Commander during the siege of Jerusalem and, with him, responsible for the destruction of the Temple – which would put the timeframe, given the scenario of the Gospels, in the mid-Forties, not a very likely chronology[92]), the Rulers, Elders, other High Priests, and Scribes representing, as stated further along, '*the Sanhedrin*.' Here Peter is presented as saying:

Rulers of the People (this parallels a phrase in the all-important Qumran Damascus Document, '*Kings of the Peoples*' – a euphemism there, as we shall see, seemingly for '*Herodians*'[93]) *and Elders of Israel, if we are tried today for a good work to a lame man who has been cured* (at Qumran and in Judaism generally '*good works*' were normally thought of as '*works of the Law*' not Hellenistic-style miracles or Asclepius-like curings), *let it be known to you all and all the People of Israel that it is in the name of Jesus Christ the Nazoraean, whom you crucified* (the standard theological formula and *the fifth such accusation put into Peter's mouth in three chapters*), *whom God raised from the dead. It is by him that he standing before you has been made whole* (4:8–10).

The fourth speech of this genre Peter makes again occurs in the very next chapter, this time directly paralleling the picture in the Pseudoclementine *Recognitions* because he and all the Apostles have been '*standing*' (the '*Standing*' notation is of extreme importance in the Pseudoclementines as well and it relates to that of '*the Great Power*' – we have already encountered a hint of it in 2:11 and now in 4:10 above[94]) and preaching in the Temple (5:12). The standard arrest then takes place, though the prisons must have been exceptionally large since now one has to do with '*all the Apostles*' not just Peter and John; and after a miraculous escape, once again, they (*Peter and all the Apostles* not just Peter and John) are '*standing in the Temple and teaching the People*.' In addition, like the Essenes and the picture of Peter's '*daily-bathing*' in the Pseudoclementine *Homilies*, the time now is '*at dawn*' (5:21).

Yet again they ('*Peter and the Apostles*') are arrested and placed before what is now called '*the Sanhedrin*,' a body that must have found it unusual, if not more than a little inconvenient, to have so many meetings in so short a span of time. Responding to the High Priest's admonishment '*not to teach in this Name*' ('*Name*' also being an extremely important usage both here and throughout the literature at Qumran[95]), '*filling Jerusalem with*' and '*bringing upon us the Blood of this Man*' (this last, '*filling Jerusalem with Blood*,' etc., too being specifically alluded to in the Habakkuk *Pesher* at Qumran as we shall see [96]); Peter insists, '*It is right to obey God rather than men*' (5:29 – usages such as these comparing '*God*' to '*men*' will also be reminiscent of polemical repartee between James in the Letter ascribed to his name and Paul in his letters[97]).

Peter then completes his defence (5:30–31) with the sixth allusion to the '*Blood libel*' accusation in just four chapters (not a very politic defence in the circumstances but then, as just pointed out, the formula is *not meant for these circumstances*):

The God of our Fathers raised up Jesus, whom you killed by crucifixion (literally '*hanging on a tree*' – a punishment forbidden in Judaism and expressly condemned, as we shall show, in the Dead Sea Scrolls[98]), *a Prince and a*

Saviour whom God has exalted by His right hand (based, as '*the Priest after the order of Melchizedek*' elsewhere, on the phraseology, of Psalm 110).

These words, '*by His right hand*', are the ones Jesus uses in last appearances in the Gospels and the proclamation attributed to James in the speech he makes on the Pinnacle of the Temple before being stoned in early Church texts and the Second Apocalypse of James from Nag Hammadi.[99] It will also be part of the climactic *Pesher* on Habakkuk 2:16's '*Cup of the right hand of the Lord*' which will be exploited to describe how '*the Cup of the Wrath of God would swallow him*' ('*the Wicked Priest*') as a '*Reward*' for what he did to '*the Righteous Teacher*' and his followers among '*the Poor*' (*i.e.*, '*the Ebionites*').[100]

This is the last in this series of speeches attributed to Peter making this accusation but, should the reader have missed the previous ones, the message is pretty obvious. It is followed by yet another in the next chapter , not really distinct or separate from it – but this time, as we have seen, attributed to '*Stephen*' (Acts 7:48–56), the historicity of whom we have already called into question above. As Stephen reformulates this libel he again refers, as Peter, to '*Heaven is My Throne and Earth a footstool for My feet*' from Isaiah 66:1–2 and Psalm 110:1. He also adds a reference to '*circumcision*' – in this case, the '*uncircumcised heart*' from Jeremiah 9:26, Ezekiel 44:7–9 and Romans 2:29, a usage specifically applied in the Habakkuk *Pesher*, as just noted, to the destroyer of the Righteous Teacher at Qumran, known now rather famously as '*the Wicked Priest*.'

'*Stephen*''s presentation, which is no more accurate than '*Peter*''s, is as follows:

O you stiff-necked and uncircumcised in heart and ears (these too!), *always resisting the Holy Spirit* (now directed at the Jews as a whole and not just '*the Wicked Priest*' as in the Habakkuk *Pesher* or '*the Turners-aside from the Way*' or '*Removers of the Bound*' in the Qumran Damascus Document[101]), *as your Fathers were* ('*Fathers*' also being a common allusion in the Damascus Document[102]), *so are you. Which one of the Prophets did your Fathers not persecute* (as we have already suggested and will see further below, most of this is based on Paul in 1 Thessalonians 2:15 – in fact, most of the Old Testament Prophets seem not to have been badly treated, certainly not by '*the People*', but these terrible formulae have remained)? *And they killed the ones who prophesied the coming of the Just One* (vocabulary more in keeping, it would appear, with James' cognomen than 'Jesus''), *of whom you now have become the Betrayers and murderers* (7:51–52 – the seventh and, as just remarked, a recapitulation of the previous six attributed to '*Peter*').

Here the characterization of '*Judas Iscariot*' in the Gospels has now been turned against the Jewish People as a whole – not only illustrating the true intent of such characterizations but, sadly, as he has always subconsciously been taken to represent these last nineteen hundred years. It is probably also useful to remark that allusion to such '*Betrayers*' or '*Traitors*' is again known in the literature at Qumran, in particular and as usual, in both the Habakkuk *Pesher* and Damascus Document.[103]

Sadly, as well, this accusation has been picked up and repeated *ad nauseam* in the Koran even to this day as almost a setpiece of anti-Semitic vilification, notwithstanding the fact that, as just observed, there is hardly a single prophet in the Old Testament '*the Jews*' can actually be accused of having killed – not Moses, not Nathan, not Elijah, not Elisha, not Amos, Micah, or Hosea, not Isaiah, not Jeremiah, not Ezekiel, *etc.* (unless it be perhaps Zechariah though the circumstances surrounding his death are far from certain[104]).

The charge is actually anticipated in Paul, who makes the same accusation in a probably uninterpolated section of 1 Thessalonians 2:14–16 as we just saw:

> *For brothers, you become the imitators of the Assemblies of God in Judea...because you also suffered the same thing from your own Countrymen as they* (presumably '*the Assemblies*') *did from the Jews, who both killed Jesus and their own Prophets and expelled you* (as '*the Essenes*' and the Community responsible for the Dead Sea Scrolls did Backsliders[105]), *displeasing God and being the Enemies of the whole Human Race* (here is the final diabolical piece in this terrifying polemic).

It should be clear to even new readers that what one has here is an extremely telling reversal of '*the Enemy*' accusations in both the Pseudo-clementine *Recognitions* and James 4:4, to say nothing of Matthew 13:13–44's '*Parable of the Tares*' and not to mention Paul's awareness of these accusations in Galatians 1:20, 4:16, and elsewhere.[106] Historically, despite its patent untruth, this accusation has proved to be of the utmost durability and probably formed, as just suggested, the basis of most of the invective so far excerpted – not to mention the intractability of the '*Devil People*' accusation worldwide.

Of course, Stephen then goes on to have the vision reported of James when he is stoned in all early Church sources, punctuated as in these by the actual vocabulary of '*crying out*,' '*crying out with a loud voice*,' *etc.* – expressions, just noted, forming the backbone of Hegesippus' tradition. There is also the allusion to '*falling asleep*' so conspicuous in the parallel scenario in the *Recognitions* and in Paul.[107] This vision actually uses the language of '*seeing Heaven open and the Son of Man standing at the right hand of God*' (Acts 7:56) of Peter's last speech and the final last-breath words of both James in Early Church accounts and Jesus in the Synoptics.[108]

One last speech is recorded of Peter before his arrest, escape abroad, and final unlikely return and appearance before the so-called '*Jerusalem Council*.' It follows his vision of the Heavenly tablecloth (again here, *n.b.*, the language of '*Heaven opening up*'), in which he learns '*not to call any man profane or unclean*' (Acts 10:11, 15, and 28 above). We have already stressed the '*Paulinization*' going on here. Contrary to the clear portrait of '*Peter*' and/or '*Cephas*' by Paul in Galatians, not to mention Peter as the thoroughgoing '*Jamesian*' in the Pseudoclementine *Homilies* and *Recognitions*[109]; this apocryphal episode turns Peter into a rank-and-file '*Paulinist*.' Yet, even here, *the real Peter* shines through. For instance, in his first response to the Heavenly Voice ('*Bat Chol*' in Hebrew) instructing him to '*kill and eat*,' to which Peter answers, as already signaled, '*No Lord, for I have never eaten anything profane or unclean*' (10:14). This is so unequivocal that it contradicts even the portrait later on in Galatians where Peter is presented as following a more middle-of-the-road approach and Paul has the temerity to accuse both him and Barnabas of '*hypocrisy*' (2:13).

But this passage in Acts is clearly written by a Gentile as well – probably in either Alexandria or Rome – one of the numerous '*Hellenists*' or Gentilizing '*Greeks*' (should we add '*anti-Semitic*' or should we just say anti-'*Jewish Christian*'/anti-'*Jamesian*'?) noted above. This is because it has Peter stating in his first conversation with the Roman Centurion Cornelius – raising him up after the latter '*fell at his feet*' – having already just learned on a rooftop in Jaffa that '*table fellowship*' with and *visiting Gentile homes* was permitted:

> You know that it is not lawful for a Jewish man to join himself with (in the language of the Damascus Document at Qumran, become '*Joiners*' or '*Nilvim*'[110]) or come near one of another Race (Acts 10:28).

Not only is this patently inaccurate, but no Jew could have ever written or said it – even a Backslider or turncoat like Josephus – as the issue was far more complex than this. It had to do with purity regulations and/or contracting impurity or defilement and would even have applied to contact with – to use the vocabulary of the Qumran Habakkuk *Pesher* – non-'*Torah-Doers in the House of Judah*,' meaning '*Jews*'[111]). Rather, this is how Jews would have been perceived by uncomprehending outsiders – since it is not that Jews could not go near foreigners; it is only that one would find it difficult to keep '*table fellowship*' (as the issue is referred to in contemporary scholarship) with them or be in touch with people *not keeping the Law*, whether '*Renegade*' or Backsliding Jews or Gentiles.

To repeat, this could not have been written by someone who was Jewish. Rather it is how Jewish behaviour might or would have appeared to non-Jewish and certainly jaundiced and even hostile eyes. In particular, this is how an anti-Semitic individual (possibly even one of the ubiquitous '*Hellenists*' mentioned above) would have framed such an observation – not patently the historical Peter, at least not as he is depicted (in our view, more faithfully) in documents like the Pseudo-clementines unless, of course, one views Peter as a man hobbled by anti-Semitic stereotypes, which the present writer does not.

The character delineated as '*Cornelius*' is also an impossibility, for it would not have been possible to find at this time a '*Righteous and God-fearing Centurion*' of the Caesarean contingent of Roman Soldiers, '*highly spoken of by the whole Nation of the Jews*' (Acts 10:22 – '*Pious*' and '*doing many good works on behalf of the People and praying to God continually*' as Acts 10:2 puts it preceding this). Not only is it hard to refrain from outright guffawing here, this is an obvious inversion and clear overwrite because, as even Josephus has attested, the Caesarean regiment of Roman Soldiery was among the most brutal in Palestine. It was they more than any other Roman troops that goaded the Jews into revolt, so much so that when Titus – not someone particularly known for his liberality or largesse and certainly not his concern for the Jews – had finally pacified the country in 70 CE, the Caesarean regiment was the first to be banished from it because of its previous record of unmitigated cruelty.[112]

In fact, like so many of these epithets, the descriptions '*the Righteous One*,' '*Pious*,' '*highly spoken of by the whole Nation of the Jews*,' and '*supplicating God continually*,' apply more appropriately to someone like James than anyone else one can specify in this Period. Notwithstanding, even here I have already expressed the opinion that what one really has to do with is a refurbishment of the visit of '*a certain Simon the Head of an Assembly* ('*Ecclesia*,' i.e., '*Church*'/'*Congregation*') *of his own in Jerusalem*,' as described by Josephus, to the household of Agrippa I (37–44 CE) in Caesarea '*to see what was done there contrary to Law*' – the reason of course being, that Agrippa I was perhaps the only '*Herodian*' highly spoken of by a goodly portion of the Jews not only because of the Maccabean blood on his father's side (*via* Herod's original Maccabean wife Mariamme), but also, contrary to the behaviour of other Herodians, his self-evident attempts at conciliating his fellow Countrymen.[113] Even the *Talmud* portrays this Agrippa's concern to ingratiate himself over such matters.[114]

In other words, the 'Simon' at this time in Josephus was a 'Zealot' who wanted to bar mixed-blood persons or foreigners from the Temple, not admit them, as Acts portrays its 'Simon,' his contemporary. But, as we shall see in the end, even the name 'Cornelius' will have particular relevance towards some of the issues circulating in this Period and beyond – especially 'the Lex Cornelia de Sicarius et Veneficis,' attributed to the legendary Roman General, Publius Cornelia Scipio, but probably not put into real effect until after the First Jewish Revolt by Nerva (96–98 CE) and repressively applied by Hadrian (117–38 CE) to discourage both Revolution and 'circumcision' across the board.[115]

Again Peter repeats in the speech he now makes to this 'Cornelius' on going into his house – for perhaps the seventh or eighth time (depending on whether one includes the one attributed to Stephen) – the usual 'Blood libel.' If we had not got the point by now, we would perhaps have gotten it after this. After describing how 'God anointed Jesus, who was from Nazareth, with the Holy Spirit and with Power' (the 'Great Power' ideology again) and how Jesus then went around 'doing good (as in 10:2 earlier, note the 'Jamesian' language of 'doing' here, now attached to Hellenistic curings and other miracles) and 'healing all who were being oppressed' – significantly not by Rome, but 'by the Devil' (Diabolou)! – Peter now adds, 'which he did both in the Country of the Jews and in Jerusalem' (this clearly an exposition aimed and directed at non-Jews), but 'whom they (the Jews) put to death by hanging on a tree' (Acts 10:39 – the typical description of crucifixion Acts has already had Peter use in 5:30 and used by Paul in Galatians 3:13).

By way of introduction to these matters, Peter alludes to two points, important in many descriptions of James: 1) 'God is not a respecter of persons' (10:34), which is a fundamental setpiece of all early Church descriptions of James – already highlighted above and parodied by Paul at the beginning of Galatians, 'do I persuade men or God or do I seek to please men' (1:10).[116] 2) 'In every Nation, he who fears Him (God) and works Righteousness is acceptable to Him' (10:35), which is basically the approach of the Damascus Document with its emphasis on 'works Righteousness' and, in particular, at the end of the exhortative section of the Cairo recension, where 'fearing God' and 'God-Fearers' are several times evoked – to whom its 'New Covenant in the Land of Damascus' is also clearly addressed – but 'God-Fearers' who obey the Law not those who disobey it.[117]

Like Stephen's speech above, the very introduction to these points – supposedly spoken by 'an Angel of God' ('a man in bright clothing at the ninth hour of the day') to another of these ubiquitous 'certain ones' Acts is always referring to (this time the Roman Centurion Cornelius – 10:1–4 and 30–33) – is reminiscent of the opening appeals of the Damascus Document, which we shall further elucidate as we proceed. As Acts puts this, *'Now therefore...hear all the things which God has commanded you, and... opening his mouth, etc.'* – here again, the telltale plays on *'uncircumcising'* one's ears, eyes, and ultimately one's heart, we have already encountered in the speech attributed to Stephen above.

In the Damascus Document the parallel position runs as follows:

> *Hear now all you who know Righteousness and consider the works of God...hear now, all you who enter the Covenant and I will unstop your ears...etc., etc.*[118]

And later:

> *And God shall heed their words and will hear and a Book of Remembrance* (the phrase is echoed almost actually verbatim in Acts 10:31, this time in the 'Angel''s words addressing Cornelius above: *'Your prayer was heard and your good works'* or *'alms were remembered before God'*) *shall be written out before Him for God-Fearers and those considering His Name* (here the 'Name' and 'naming' imagery, we have already referred to, in Acts 4:10 and 5:28 above[119]), *until God shall reveal Salvation (Yesha*^{c}*) and Righteousness to those fearing His Name* (and of course, the imagery of 'Righteousness' and 'God-fearing,' to say nothing of the Hebrew equivalent to the actual name 'Jesus'/'Yesha^c' itself).[120]

In the last line, as we shall have cause to repeatedly point out as we progress too, the reference will actually be to *'seeing Jesus'* (Yeshu^{c}a) or *'seeing His Salvation'*:

> *And their hearts will be strengthened and they shall be victorious...and they shall see His Salvation (Yeshu^{c}ato), because they took refuge in His Holy Name* ('Name' imagery again).[121]

2

The Attack by Paul on James, the Memorial Mausoleum at Qumran, and the James Ossuary

The Attack by Paul on James on the Temple Steps

Perhaps the most astonishing notice in all extra–Biblical literature is the one found in the Pseudoclementine *Recognitions* describing *an actual physical assault by Paul on James on the Temple steps in Jerusalem*. Nor should one fail to remark the absence of this attack from the parallel account known as the Pseudoclementine *Homilies*, which appears to refashion its narrative of early Christian history to expressly avoid mentioning it.[1] The same is true, of course, of Acts where, as we already observed, the assault on the archetypical Gentile Christian believer '*Stephen*,' which introduces Paul and which Paul '*entirely approved of*' (8:1), replaces it.

As Acts 8:3 describes these things, '*Saul*' (or '*Paul*') then proceeds to '*ravage the Assembly in Jerusalem, entering their houses one by one, dragging out men and women to be delivered up into prison.*' This mayhem continues into the next chapter with the picture of Paul '*breathing threats and murder* (in other words, even in the portrait in Acts, Paul is extremely violent) *against the Disciples of the Lord*' (this last phraseology, too, not very differ-ent from allusions found in the Scrolls[2]), obtaining letters from the High Priest '*to Damascus, to the synagogues*' (itself a very peculiar if not a defec-tive usage – if we take '*synagogue*' according to its Greek meaning, '*council and pedagogical center*' then, keeping in mind the plural in both, it is pos-sible to see a parallel here to the '*Camps*' in '*the Land of Damascus*' in the Dead Sea Scrolls as well[3]), advising that, '*if he found any who were of the Way* (again, a known terminology at Qumran based on Isaiah 40:3[4]), *whether man or woman, he should bring them bound to Jerusalem*' (Acts 9:1–2).

For its part the *Recognitions*, as already remarked, starts off with the parallel picture of *debates on the Temple steps*, the most important speakers in which are Peter and James. In Acts' picture, of course, as already under-scored, James is totally missing or deleted from such activities while in the *Recognitions* it is John who plays almost no role. In the midst of these debates, a man identified only as the '*Enemy*' (in margin notes, he is often identified as Paul) bursts upon the scene and leads a riot of killing and mayhem on the Temple Mount, paralleling that in Acts above, in the course of which he actually takes a club from the pile of faggots next to the altar and assaults James, '*casting him headlong*' *down the Temple steps* where he leaves him for dead.[5] No wonder this assault is nowhere to be found in more orthodox accounts; nor, for that matter, in the *Homilies*.

The '*headlong*' phraseology in *Recognitions* is important as it links up with testimony in Jerome about James' death and what seems to be yet another variant – Acts 1:18's obscure picture of the '*headlong*' fall Judas Iscariot takes '*as a Reward for Unrighteousness*' *in a Field* '*of Blood*' (this '*Reward*' language too will be important at Qumran[6]). Since the '*Enemy*' then obtains letters from the High Priest and pursues the early Christian Community down to Jericho on his way to Damascus, the relationship of said events with the activities of Paul in Acts 9:1–25 is for all intents and purposes confirmed. In the author's view, this is *real* '*Essene*' history not that of what we call '*Christianity*'.

'*Christianity*' is to be found in the refurbished portraits one finds in the Gospels and Acts. We have to see the Pseudoclementines – romantic history or literary romance perhaps, but so is Acts – as *history from the inside*, from the perspective of persons or personages in '*the Essene Movement*' as it were. Identities which are only hinted at through circumlocutions and tantalizing *nom-de-guerres* in the Dead Sea Scrolls, in the Pseudoclementines are spoken of overtly and by name. Through them we get, perhaps, a clearer picture of the divisions of '*Early Christianity*' in Palestine in the First Century and a handle on persons only vaguely hinted at in the Scrolls or totally obliterated in Acts.

As in Hegesippus, Jerome, the *Recognitions*, and Acts, we must carefully consider all these episodes involving the usages '*throwing down*'/'*casting down*'/'*headlong*'/or '*causing to stumble*.'[7] In the Habakkuk *Pesher*, for example, this last is exactly what is said to happen to the followers of '*the Righteous Teacher*' – there called, as already alluded to, '*the Poor*' or '*the Perfect of the Way*' (compare this with '*those of the*' or '*this Way*' in Acts 9:22 above, denoting individuals in the '*synagogues*' or '*the Jews who dwelt in Damascus*' whom Paul '*confounds*') – when the Wicked Priest '*appeared to them at the completion of the Festival of their Rest*' (thus – Yom Kippur).[8] Not only is '*the Wicked Priest*' in this episode described as '*not circumcising the foreskin of his heart*' and '*swallowing them*,' but also '*causing them to stumble*' or, quite literally, '*casting them down*.' According to the Habakkuk *Pesher*, he does this in the process of '*conspiring to destroy the Poor*,' the last being coeval with those '*Torah-Doers*' referred to as '*the Simple of Judah doing Torah*' in both Habakkuk and Psalm 37 *Peshers* and to whom, Habakkuk

2:4's *'the Righteous shall live by his Faith'* is rightfully considered to apply.[9]

Unlike Peter in Acts 10:15, these *'Simple' Torah-Doers* have not yet learned *'not to call any thing'* or *'any man profane or unclean'*; but rather, in the manner of Josephus' *'Zealots'* and/or *'Essenes'* (in some instances, as we shall eventually see, probably interchangeable denotations), they refuse *'to call any man Lord'* or *'eat forbidden things'* (quite different from New Testament portraiture). In the version of this testimony preserved in the Third-Century heresiology attributed in Rome to one 'Hippolytus,' this last becomes more specifically – and probably more accurately – *'things sacrificed to idols,'* a prohibition intrinsic, as we shall see as well, not only to James' directives to overseas communities in Acts but the document Qumran scholars refer euphemistically to as *'MMT'*.[10]

For Hippolytus, said *'Essenes'* (actually he calls them, as we shall see, *'Zealot Essenes'* or *'Sicarii Essenes'*) are prepared to undergo any sort of bodily torture, even death, rather than *'eat things sacrificed to idols'* or *'blaspheme the Law-giver'* (meaning Moses).[11] They are also, as the Scrolls make plain, *'the Ebionites'* or *'the Ebionim'* (*the Poor*),[12] in all early Church heresiologies the direct successors of *'the Essenes'* and virtually indistinguishable from what these same heresiologists are calling *'Elchasaites'*/*'Masbuthaeans'*/*'Sampsaeans'*/or *'Sabaeans'* – the last-mentioned, in later Islamic lore, doubtlessly indicating *'Daily Bathers.'* We shall have more to say about all these terminologies presently when discussing the *'Nazoraean'* or *life-long 'Nazirite'* language of *'abstention'* or *'keeping away from (lehinnazer) things sacrificed to idols'* or *'the pollutions of the idols'* one finds both in the Scrolls and in Acts.[13] These *'Ebionites'* are also the followers of James *par excellence*, himself considered (even in early Christian accounts) to be the Leader of *'the Poor'* or these selfsame *'Ebionites.'*[14]

To go back to the attack by Paul on James: as already signaled, James did not die in this attack. He was only left for dead, *'breaking,'* as the Pseudoclementines and later Jerome make clear, *one or both his legs*.[15] James does not die for another twenty years, the two episodes being neatly telescoped or conflated into one in both the description of *'Stephen'*'s stoning in Acts and early Church accounts of James' death. James, rather, is carried out of the Temple to a house – not the *'house'* of *'the Disciple Jesus loved'* as in the Gospel of John (19:26) but, rather, a house James possesses in Jerusalem. This is also the gist of Acts 12:12 when Peter, after his escape from prison, goes to the house of *'Mary the mother of John Mark'* – another character never heard of before or since (more Gentile Christian dissimulation?). No, *Mary the mother of James!* There he, quite properly, leaves a message for *'James and the brothers'* that *he is going abroad*. As already remarked, this constitutes the introduction of the real James in Acts, the other James having conveniently been removed just ten lines earlier in Acts 12:2.

The next morning, the Disciples numbering some '*five thousand*' – the actual number according to Josephus of '*the Essenes*,' as we have seen, not to mention those in Acts 4:4 just converting to Christianity following Peter's third enunciation of the '*Blood libel*' charge above – carry James' inert body down to Jericho. In the meantime the '*Enemy*'/Paul gets letters from the High Priest – in passing, it should be remarked that these '*letters*' are the only ones Paul ever receives. They are not from James, the proper appointment procedure as set forth in the Pseudoclementine *Homilies* and endlessly and sarcastically belittled, as we shall delineate, in 2 Corinthians 3:1–16, 5:12, 9:1–3, 10:8–18, *etc.*[16]

Paul pursues the members of the Early Christian Community (should we rather at this point be saying '*Essenes*'?) through Jericho on the way to Damascus where he misses them because, in the meantime, James together with all his followers have gone outside of Jericho (Qumran?) to visit the tomb of two of the brothers '*who had fallen asleep*' (*n.b.*, the parallel language in Acts 7:60 above). The detail and geographical precision here, as in the matter of the assault in the Temple preceding it, is impressively convincing. The tombs of these brothers *miraculously* '*whitened of themselves every year*,'

> because of which miracle the fury of the Many against us was restrained, because they perceived that our brothers were held in Remembrance before God (again the '*Remembrance*' language from the end of the Damascus Document and that of the '*Angel*' approving Cornelius' Righteous behaviour and charitable works in Acts 10:31–35, but now in the Pseudoclementines. This is to say nothing about what is to be encountered in 1 Corinthians 11:24 and 'Last Supper' scenarios in the Gospels such as in Luke 22:19).[17]

This is the kind of startling originality one encounters in this first section of the *Recognitions*. Not only do we have the notice of an attack on James by the '*Enemy*' Paul, from which James will still be limping a month later when it came to sending out Peter on his first missionary journey – *from somewhere outside of Jericho* – to Caesarea (and not to Samaria) where he does however, encounter Simon *Magus*; but who would have thought to place *the entire 'Early Christian' Community to the number of some five thousand* in these environs, that is, before the discovery of the Dead Sea Scrolls some nineteen hundred years later just a few miles south of Jericho at Qumran?

Yet here we have just such a testimony in these incomparable notices in the Pseudoclementines which do not simply, in the writer's view, parallel but are rather based on the same source as Acts – to which they are the more faithful. This is certainly the case concerning the *Recognitions*, the First Book of which, as already observed, links up with Acts in a point-for-point manner, albeit from a completely-opposite ideological orientation. Then, of course, there is the common vocabulary, not only with Acts but also the Damascus Document from Qumran – as, for instance as just noted, the phraseology, '*remembered before God*,' in the *Recognitions* at the end of the last part of the historical exposition of the Damascus Document where, as with the '*Angel*'s words to Cornelius in Acts, *the thrust is primarily directed at 'those who fear God' or 'who are God-Fearers.'*

Recently a team of students under my direction and the field leadership of archaeologists Hanan Eshel and Magen Broshi in Israel discovered a burial monument of just this kind at the head of the Qumran cemetery, *upon which the some thousand or so graves located there appear to have been keyed.*[18] Depending on the orientation of its entrance, the sun could easily have come through in a special fashion once a year, possibly at the time of the equinox or some other key calendrical moment – in the account we have in the Pseudoclementines *Recognitions*, it is the time of Passover – and the sepulchres inside could *have 'miraculously whitened of themselves every year'* just as the above notice describes – but, of course, this is only speculation. In further digging at the site by Richard Freund of Hartford University the next year (2002), it turned out that there was at least one male body in the tomb whereas the previous year, it had been thought that *there were only two female bodies in a state of secondary burial in the tomb.*[19] Plus, the monument or enclosure is in such a spectacular orientation that it not only overlooks the Dead Sea and the hills of Moab or Perea across the way, but it would have been visible from a long way off by all those coming down either south from Jericho or north up from Ein Gedi, Wadi Murabbaᶜat, and Masada.

Most of the graves in this graveyard are oriented North and South, though the burial or burials within the enclosure appear to be oriented east and west so as, it would appear, '*at the Resurrection' to 'stand up' facing the Temple.* Nor would the North-South orientation of most other graves at Qumran be very surprising since, if the Community was a group of '*Hemero-Baptists*' or '*Daily Bathers*' ('*Masbuthaeans*'/'*Essenes*'/'*Sabaeans*'/'*Elchasaites*' in the language of the various heresiologists we have mentioned above), then at least some of these, as the Muslim Encyclopaedist al-Biruni avers, were intent on '*facing*' or '*praying towards the Dome of Heaven.*'[20] That is to say their bodies were probably oriented facing North (not South and Mecca, as would have been the case for Muslims).

Though this was the direction of the prayer of all such '*Daily Baptists,*' one assumes burials would have been oriented in the same manner.

As noted, most of the graves in the Qumran and other cemeteries in the surrounding area, aside from those in the enclosure or mausoleum and a handful of others, seem oriented in a North-South direction.[21] Though confusion has crept in because of what seem to be later beduin over-burials oriented East and West in the Qumran cemeteries, this does seem to have largely been the case.[22] However one interprets this, this passage in the Pseudoclementine *Recognitions* does *unequivocally place James and all his Community in the Jericho area* and, what is more, it does testify to the existence of just such a highly-revered burial monument or mausoleum. Again, the detail of all this is startling. It is from here, as just remarked, that *James sends out Peter on his first missionary journey to confront Simon Magus in Caesarea, not in Samaria* as Acts would appear to mistakenly confuse it with other notices in early Church literature having to do with Simon's place of origin and his having very likely made claims to being the Samaritan '*Taheb*' or '*Messiah.*'[23]

To make this all the more remarkable, when Peter does arrive in Caesarea on this journey, he meets '*Zacchaeus*' – the same '*Zacchaeus,*' presumably, whom the Gospels in their usual obscurantism call '*a little man*' and '*a tax-collector,*' who scrambles up a tree in order to see Jesus *as he passed through Jericho on the way to Jerusalem* not, as for instance in the case of '*the Hostile Man*' or Paul, *as he passed through Jericho on his way to Damascus* (Luke 19:2–8 – it would have to be Luke the author too of Acts). '*Zacchaeus*' then invites '*Jesus*' – not Peter as in the Pseudoclementines above or, for that matter, King Agrippa to his '*Temple-barring*' critic '*Simon*' in Josephus above) – into his house *in Jericho now and not Caesarea!* How peculiar all this overlap of sources is but, once again, it is the more down-to-earth *Recognitions which seems the more historical.*

In the more realistic and less fanciful *Recognitions*, it is when '*Zacchaeus*' inquires after James' well-being that Peter responds and tells him that *James is recuperating and still limping on one leg* – n.b., the detail here – thereby testifying to the fact that *James broke one* or *both his legs in the fall he took down the Temple steps after the attack on him by Paul.*[24] The same point is then picked up in a slightly different manner in Jerome's account of James' demise based largely on the Second-Century source Hegesippus, but also going back probably to other '*Jewish Christian*' sources.

In his account, not only does Jerome insist that *James wore the breastplate of the High Priest* and *actually went into the Inner Sanctum of the Temple at least once* – presumably on *Yom Kippur* in the manner of High Priests generally (possibly, even, the same '*Yom Kippur*' which will be referred to in the Habakkuk *Pesher* in connection with the demise of its hero '*the Righteous Teacher*' and, as we shall argue, the putative cause of the San-hedrin trial for blasphemy '*pursued*' against him by his nemesis '*the Wicked Priest*' – Ananus[25]); but also that *James' legs 'were broken' in the fall he took when he was 'cast down,'* now not necessarily '*headlong' down the steps of the Temple* but, as in normative Church accounts stemming from Hegesip-pus, *from the Pinnacle of the Temple.* These same '*broken legs,*' however, once again reappear via the magic of art in Gospel accounts of 'Jesus'' death, a feature drawn in them – or so it would seem – from Josephus.[26]

The Memorial Mausoleum at the Head of the Qumran Graveyard

Several events have made an impression in the worlds of Dead Sea Scrolls research and Early Christian studies in recent years – for some, anyhow, perhaps not completely unrelated to one another. The first, as just sig-naled above, was the discovery of the burial enclosure or mausoleum at the head of the cemetery at Qumran. A second and most sensational was the ossuary allegedly connected to James' name. The third was the pub-lication of the Gospel of Judas which we shall treat more fully in our conclusion. However, like the Nag Hammadi '*Apocalypse of James*' with which it was found, what it illustrates is how creative and layered the lit-erature surrounding these subjects – and *it was a literature not history* – became in the 2nd–3rd Centuries CE. Moreover, unlike the orthodox '*New Testament,*' it was not '*anti-Semitic*' though it was antinomian. On the contrary, some of it could be positively philo-Semitic as long as it served a Neoplatonic end. Finally, it demonstrated what an important character '*Judas Iscariot*' ('*the Iscariot*') actually was both literarily and theologically.

To examine the first '*event*' more formally – in July of 2001 in the course of investigations mapping the lay-out and burials of the cemetery at Qumran, a burial enclosure or ceremonial mausoleum was found at the head of the graveyard on a finger of land closest to and with the most prominent prospect of the Dead Sea.[27] Since it was upon this promontory and the funerary monument built upon it that the rest of the one thousand or so graves in the cemetery appear to have been ori-ented, one could state with some assurance that *the structure was at the head of the graveyard at Qumran.* Though earlier it had been inexplicably missed by Qumran archaeologists, it was clearly an object, therefore, of some veneration – a Holy Site or Saints' Tomb probably visited on a regular basis by the entire Community responsible for the Dead Sea Scrolls – just as described in the Pseudoclementine *Recognitions* above.

The enclosure was discovered owing to the initiative of two members of the contingent on this expedition who were under my direction, Dennis Walker and Ron Dubay.[28] However controversy immediately broke out concerning whether the monument or burial shrine harbored ancient or modern graves or whether the two sets of remains that were found in a state of secondary burial – meaning that they had initially been buried elsewhere, but were expressly reburied here because of the importance of the place – were beduin women, ancient or modern?[29]

That the site was of some consequence was immediately clear to me from the moment it was reported to me by telephone from the shores of the Dead Sea the night they discovered it, because it reminded me of this all-important notice in the Pseudoclementine *Recognitions*. Here we had a notice about just such a memorial mausoleum from this period however fantastic. It was my view then that this *was* the actual burial monument described so reverently in the Pseudoclementine *Recognitions* or something very much like it and that this impressive monument at the head of the Qumran graveyard, found so fortuitously by my representatives, was just the kind of highly-venerated Saints' tomb or '*tomb of the two brothers that miraculously whitened of itself every year*' reported in the *Recognitions* and of such significance to the members of James' Community that it was the focus of an annual pilgrimage for them. But in the aftermath of the discovery, so confused did its particulars become, because of the subsequent disagreements that erupted, it was impossible to see this with any clarity and little of certainty emerged concerning it at the time.[30] In the process, the extremely interesting connection between it and this notice in the Pseudoclementine *Recognitions* was lost.

However in the follow-up expedition in Summer 2002, upon further groundscanning and digging underneath the find of the previous summer, as just signaled, an additional complete and *indisputably male skeleton was discovered*. This time *it was not in a state of secondary burial*; rather it was nicely laid out and surrounded in the same stratigraphic layer by pottery that definitively placed it in the First Century CE, a date Professor Eshel and my students had already arrived at the previous year from the indications found *in situ* of the pottery surrounding the secondary burials.[31] The additional find was duly reported again in *Time* Magazine and in newspapers around the world – this time in August, 2002.[32]

Now there was no doubt that the skeleton was a completely preserved male, probably middle-aged and buried in a straightforward manner within the structure or funerary enclosure, the orientation of which burial *was East to West facing the Temple, not North to South*. Subsequent radar observations have now shown an additional signature or signatures underneath this indicating something else, perhaps another body, perhaps only an object of some kind. Should this turn out to be a second body, then, of course, we would have an absolutely perfect match with this startling notice in the *Recognitions* – though the reader should not become too optimistic as archaeological work at suspected grave sites in Israel is a difficult proposition at any time. Nevertheless, at the very least, we have proof that in both Communities – the early Christian in Palestine and the one at Qumran – a mausoleum or burial enclosure of some kind, somewhere south of Jericho along the Dead Sea, was held in high esteem, perhaps even venerated, and visited as a Saints' tomb by the respective members of both Communities. It will be left to the arguments in this book to see if we can bring the connections between this early '*Christian*' Community of James as delineated in the Pseudoclementine *Recognitions* and the Community represented by the Dead Sea Scrolls closer together than this – closer than most are willing to admit – but the resemblances are doubtlessly there and they are striking.

The Call for AMS Carbon Testing of the Scrolls

But what then has principally held researchers back from making these kinds of connections in the past? Primarily it is the chronology of Qumran based on external data such as archaeology and palaeography and, more recently, the newly-employed technique of AMS radiocarbon dating. I have covered the first pair of these matters thoroughly in two previous books subjecting the archaeology and palaeography of Qumran to intense and thoroughgoing criticism.[33] However, I share some of the responsibility for the issue of radiocarbon dating having arisen in the first place and the procedure itself being employed regarding the Scrolls.

This occurred in the following manner: in March–June of 1989, Professor Philip Davies of Sheffield University in England and I suggested in a letter to the Israel Antiquities Authority that in *lieu* of granting proper open access to the rest of the unpublished corpus of the Dead Sea Scrolls to the entire scholarly community and all others so inclined – then the reigning issue in Scrolls Studies and a thing the Antiquities Authority at that time seemed unwilling to do – it conduct such tests (tests which, in any event, we considered to be well within its powers).

At the time, however, we included two caveats: 1) that opposition scholars be included in the process to ensure objectivity and that the concerns of such scholars – those that had prior to this felt the most need for such tests – be fairly and properly addressed; and 2) that '*relative dating*' as opposed to '*absolute dating*' (meaning, '*earlier vs. later in the same test run*') should be the goal in order to test the palaeographic sequences – at the time, considered almost sacrosanct and more or less inviolable – and, consequently, the claims for palaeographic accuracy in Qumran Studies. It was my firm opinion then and still is now that the margins-of-error in C-14 testing are of such magnitude as to render attempts at *absolute dating* impossible, *relative dating* (that is, *earlier vs. later in the same test run,* being sufficient to overturn the over-inflated claims for accuracy in palaeographic dating[34]), therefore, being the best that could be reasonably expected from a given cluster of tests because the inherent methodological errors in such a situation would presumably cancel themselves out.

These suggestions and concerns were laid out in two letters sent to Amir Drori, then Head of the Israel Antiquities Authority which oversaw such matters. The first was on May 6, 1989 and to it we also attached the relevant literature on the new *'AMS'* methods of carbon testing which consumed far less materials than previously was the case, in the event he was not familiar with them (we presumed, probably correctly, that he was not). The second was sent on June 15th, 1989 after no response was received from the first (except from then Head of the International Team, John Strugnell – to whom we had originally written in March – who spurned our requests[35]). In the event, neither was answered, nor were either of the two caveats we raised observed when the Antiquities Authority then proceeded *to announce its intention to run precisely such tests in September,* 1989 (in response obviously to our requests).

I was also indirectly responsible for the second run of carbon tests in 1995. This transpired in the following manner: at the request of the NOVA Program on *The Secrets of the Dead Sea Scrolls* being prepared for broadcast in 1991–92, I had been asked at the last moment (I had already done some 3–4 hours of filming for them previously, but all of this had ended up on the *'cutting room'* floor) to participate in some additional filming they wished to conduct at the Huntington Library in San Marino, California. This was because the pivotal role played by that Institution in opening its archives earlier that September – for which I was the consultant – had suddenly been appreciated by NOVA's Producers and they wanted to *'shoehorn'* something in concerning this at the last moment.[36]

Furthermore, in order to heighten viewer interest in the shots they were planning to do at the Library, they asked me to bring along a student, to whom I could be shown giving tuition from the photographs the Library had theoretically newly just made available to scholars like myself (actually, it really had not[37]). After several local students I had more directly and personally trained proved unavailable on such short notice, I asked Greg Doudna who was then doing graduate studies at Cornell University – a program I had helped him in his decision to enter and whom I suspected would welcome the opportunity (he did) – if he would like to participate because at conferences he had shown a certain amount of solicitude towards my work.

Of all the disappointments I have experienced in Qumran Studies – and there have been many – and mistakes I made in the struggle to free the Scrolls, this turned out perhaps to be one of the most painful and ill-considered. E. J. Brill's sudden cancellation of the *Facsimile Edition,* which James Robinson and I had prepared for them, in April, 1991 (after dissension broke out at the '*Official Team*'s Madrid Conference the preceding month), ten days before the planned date of publication and then turning to this same '*Official Team*' to do what amounted basically to the same publication the next year, was another. This had the effect of depriving Professor Robinson and myself of a chance to break the monopoly a full six months before the Huntington Library stepped in.

Hershel Shanks' own addition of a highly unusual and cartoon-like '*Publisher's Foreword*' to the *Facsimile Edition,* Professor Robinson and myself had previously prepared for the E. J. Brill publication, thereby undercutting it and bringing upon ourselves a series of interminable lawsuits which took years to settle, rank a very close second and third. Finally, my co-editor Michael Wise's sharing the photographs of the previously unpublished Scrolls, which I had supplied him in confidence, with students and other university associates and mentors and proceeding after that to do a completely new translation of all the Dead Sea Scrolls with two new colleagues, while at the same time allowing them to redo the translations we had previously published together without a word of personal explanation or apology to me, were a fourth and fifth.[38]

However these things may be, I invited Mr. Doudna, then an unknown graduate student, to stay at my house the night before filming in order to save him lodging expenses as he had been obliged to pay his own round-trip airfare from Ithaca. In conversation that evening, I shared with him my concerns over the accuracy of carbon-dating tests generally and the way '*the results*,' which had recently been announced, were being presented in magazines like the *Biblical Archaeology Review*[39] and over '*the Pandora's Box*' I had opened. At the same time, I acquainted him with the entire new process of AMS carbon dating and its pitfalls – a subject which he himself admitted to knowing little or nothing at the time – but which he has since made his life's work. In this work he has also, more recently, been taken up by '*Network*' or '*Consensus*' scholars as a world-class expert[40] – though rarely if ever with any admission or a word of acknowledgement of how he came to be involved in this aspect of his career in the first place.[41]

That night I explained to him my dissatisfaction with the way the results were being presented, primarily as an attack upon myself even though Professor Davies and I had been the ones who had originally first officially called for such tests. I also delineated for him what I considered the over-inflated claims for accuracy that were being made and the under-emphasis on the margin-of-errors involved by those seizing on the '*results*' of these tests, such as they were.[42] Since I thought any letter from myself to the *Biblical Archaeology Review* – which had just summarized these '*results*' – expressing such dissatisfaction and my unease with the way they were being applied by '*Consensus Scholars,*' who had run the tests, would just appear self-serving; I suggested that as a relative unknown and an outsider, as it were, he might write just such a letter. At the same time I outlined for him the points I thought should be made about the unreliability and shortcomings of the '*tests*' that were done.

Apparently I did this too well because, from all reports, upon returning to Ithaca he became completely absorbed by the subject, leading ultimately even to giving up his graduate studies there (from my perspective, I imagined he envisioned the inherent possibilities in the whole subject and decided to move in that direction. In the event, after a financial settlement from Cornell and a detour to the University of Chicago – also partially arranged by myself through my erstwhile colleagues teaching there – he did later finish at the University of Copenhagen in Denmark[43]); and, instead of the letter to the *Biblical Archaeology Review* I had roughed out for him, *he wrote one proposing he should personally pay for a new round of carbon testing.*[44] Given the outcome of the earlier run and the questionable way in which its results were being taken advantage of, this was not something I was very enthusiastic about seeing repeated.

On the other hand, it was a proposal I knew would be eagerly taken up by Hershel Shanks, the Editor of the *Biblical Archaeology Review*, who would immediately see the public-relations possibilities inherent it – just as he had two years before when he had taken up the *Facsimile Edition* of the previously-unpublished Qumran photographs Professor Robinson and I had prepared for Brill, though not before delaying three to four months (in order to give a previous project of his, Wacholder and Abegg's computerized restoration of Qumran texts from the official Concordance of the Scrolls, a chance to take hold[45]), so that, once again, we missed the chance to be the first to break the monopoly, and involving us in a lawsuit that took almost ten years to sort out – and, as he had two years before that, when he restarted his campaign to help free the Scrolls after I sent him a copy of the computer printout of all the unpublished Scrolls held by the Israel Antiquities Authority at the Rockefeller Museum.[46]

Be this as it may, Doudna's revision of my suggestions resulted in another round of AMS carbon testing, now conducted by the Center of the University of Arizona previously involved in the testing of the Turin Shroud (tests which had themselves been fraught with controversy[47]). The new tests proved to be even more skewed than the first but – probably partially because of the oral excursus I had given Mr. Doudna to begin with – focused on more pivotally decisive Qumran documents in terms of chronology and importance.[48] Aside from the general attempt to press '*absolute dating*' from an insufficiently-precise-process-to-begin-with, given the time period involved, this had been my principal objection to the first set of tests – as, earlier, those initiating the tests showed no particular awareness of which documents were pivotal to the debate.

Not only this – but because, to be sure, of my chagrin at being totally frozen out of the process only to have the tests then exploited by persons who had previously never even thought of doing AMS C-14 tests and who – from my perspective – had no real sense of their limitations and, in my view, the tendentious way in which the tests were conducted and, thereafter, being reported (a concern which turned out to be as true, in my opinion as well, for the second run as much as for the first)[49]; I had preferred to let things stay where they were, realizing little or nothing would come out of the second round of tests, given the personalities and prior assumptions of those who would be conducting them.

The Weakness of the '*Results*'

To criticize these '*results*' would take a very lengthy excursus. I started this process in the first part of *James the Brother of Jesus* (Penguin, 1998) by pointing up the multiple inaccuracies involved in such testing, including the inherent imprecision of using dendrochronology as a control (tree-ring analysis on which most attempts at absolute chronology were based); the lack of any really firmly-attested palaeographic '*pegs*' between approximately 225 BC and 115 CE, the possible timeframe of the Scrolls; the impurities introduced by various cleansings and other procedures – including the actual inks used by the scribes – particularly where oft-consulted documents like the Habakkuk *Pesher* were concerned; and the inability to tell when a given skin or plant, from which the parchment or papyrus was produced, was actually utilized even if it could be determined with any precision when it had stopped growing or was killed; and *the tendency of radiocarbon tests generally, therefore, to archaize.*[50]

But, more important perhaps even than any of these, whatever the pretensions of a given lab and the various investigators involved, *the analysis of the tests did involve interpretation* – interpretation based on the abilities of the investigators involved and, as the recent revelations concerning the FBI Crime Lab in Washington D.C. have so vividly demonstrated, a certain number of preconceptions. In the parallel case of a laboratory even as prestigious as that, it was found that *researchers came out with 'results' generally in keeping with the preconceptions of those initiating the tests*[51]; and, in the case of laboratories probably not even as prestigious or well-regulated as that in Qumran Studies, as we shall see, '*the results*' that were achieved were often just that – tendentious interpretations of raw data that itself may not have been particularly accurate in the first place.

This is particularly the case with the tests that were run, almost all of which either began or included in their reports an uncalled-for and fairly harsh attack on my own and like-minded research positions. Not only this, but aside from my own efforts, recent investigators have pressed these points even further and it has since turned out that, just as I initially thought, researchers in all the three labs involved in the two runs of testing that were done regarding the Dead Sea Scrolls in 1989–91 and 1994–95 were using an imprecise and outdated dating curve (even though the newer dating curves were readily available at least by the time of the second reports in 1995, if not the first[52]) which made their '*results*,' such as they were, appear older than they actually were.[53] This is something of what is involved in the '*archaizing*' effect alluded to above.

In fact, it has also since been shown that where radiocarbon dating is concerned, multiple sample variations in a single source – that is, different pieces from varying parts of the same parchment or papyrus – can often be even greater than some of the margins-of-error reported in the tests that were done, which for the most part, reportedly, were based on single sample testing[54]; and, despite the pretensions at arriving at some finality in terms of '*absolute dating*,' the results that were achieved turned out generally to be '*skewed*.' In other words, *nothing of any absolute certainty was obtained at all* – but the opposite. In fact, as a recent paper I helped prepare in *Qumran Studies* (revised from an earlier one in the *Qumran Chronicle*) has shown, the results to some extent actually more favor some of the hypotheses set forth in this book not *vice versa* but, because of a certain degree of wishful thinking and self-serving analysis, the public was left with the completely opposite impression.[55]

This was true even of a document like the Habakkuk *Pesher* which, as a result of these tests, was being used to try to undercut positions like the ones embraced in this book. It was, palaeographically-speaking, exactly comparable to the case of the Psalm 37 *Pesher*, a document to which it was also completely related both ideologically and historiographically.[56] Yet in trying to press that document back into the First

Century BC to attack positions like those in this book, analysts ignored the fact that the carbon dating of the Psalm 37 *Pesher* – which because it had been handled and cleaned less, relatively speaking, was altogether more reliable and secure – came out to be dated well into the second half of First Century CE, exactly the position of this book.[57]

The reason I was so sure about my positions right from the beginning was because I knew that 1) given the results of both palaeographical studies and those alleged of archaeology and AMS carbon dating, no sense whatever could be made of the Scrolls themselves – that is, '*the external data*' *defeated the clear thrust of* '*the internal data.*' Put another way, these so-called external attempts to measure chronology rendered the internal data – or what the Scrolls themselves had to say – moot or completely contradictory.[58] 2) Most of the principal Qumran sectarian Scrolls, meaning those new Scrolls that had never been seen before, had to have been written at about the same time or, at least, in probably close chronological proximity – say within fifty years of one another, whatever the palaeographers, archaeologists, or analysts of carbon testing might say – *and this because they contained the same dramatis personae and repeated the same points in the same form with the same vocabulary over and over again.*

Nor could this have been otherwise for, if they had been written at varying times (and one is not including here Biblical texts represented in the Qumran library or even known apocryphal or pseudepigraphic texts, such as Enoch, Jubilees, Daniel, or the Giants Literature which by the time of the composition in their wake of the more sectarian Qumran documents probably had had time to become standardized), they would have included historical markers pointing to varying times of compositions. In American history, for instance, it would probably make a difference if a document were written during the time of Abraham Lincoln or John Kennedy, two leaders assassinated in similarly brutal circumstances. But the sectarian Qumran documents do not do so. To think that they were all written at varying times would be like thinking people alive today would be reading with intense interest – and considering them applicable to their own time and place – documents referring to George Washington's time or President Polk's War against Mexico.

This is what the results of carbon testing seem to imply because of the multiple variables and imprecisions involved. A good beginning in the criticism of these results has been made in two recent articles and a whole host of lesser ones. The first of these was by G. A. Rodley and B. E. Thiering, the latter known for some of her perhaps over-imaginative theories of Qumran origins but, in this instance, producing the most solid and straightforward of scientific presentations. In it, they demonstrated that the parties at the University of Arizona who conducted the second run of carbon-dating tests (for which even more extravagant claims were made for accuracy than the first) *used the wrong dating curve.*[59]

A second paper by two statisticians, Steve Braunheim and Joseph Atwill, has now been published in *Qumran Studies*.[60] Since I helped in its preparation (though the technical research was completely their own), I can attest that it carries these arguments further than Rodley and Thiering and demonstrates that there is absolutely no certainty arising from the two runs of carbon testing. Furthermore, the multiple uncertainties involved effectively defeat the claims, such as they are, for any final *'precision'* or *'accuracy'* – as Braunheim and Atwill refer to it – in these tests.[61]

Not only had researchers before 1998 been using the wrong dating curve – this includes both sets of tests, those done in 1991–2 and those in 1994–5 – which made documents appear older than they actually were (sometimes by as much as 50, 100, or even 200 years[62]); but it should be appreciated that, when these results are interpreted, there are in fact, even according to *'Establishment'* theorizing, *two sigmas*: one encompassing the time span that radiocarbon theory posits they would contain the actual date 68% of the time; the second, a far wider time span, that would theoretically include the date 95% of the time. This is not to mention the issue of impurities, cleansing, biological age of the animal whose skin was being used at death, and such like already remarked above.

But when announcing the *'results'* of these tests in a public manner, those responsible almost uniformly confined themselves to the *'one-sigma'* not the *'two-sigma'* results. One English specialist, well known for his conventionally *'Establishment'* views, announced that even a single counter-indicative such result, even if not wholly accurate, would *'damage almost beyond repair the hypothesis proposing a Christian connection.'*[63] But this statement was not only factually inaccurate, it is in fact wrong in principle as well – at least from the standpoint of the discipline of statistics.

It is of little import, but worth pointing out as well, that this same English scholar constantly assumes that I consider the Qumran characters known as *'the Wicked Priest'* and *'the Man of Lying'*/*'Scoffer'* or *'Spouter of Lying'* to be identical, thereby all-too-easily dismissing my association of the latter with Paul or, at least, a Paul-like Teacher. This is like setting up a *'straw man'* and then proceeding to demolish what was inaccurate to begin with – and he has had this characterization of my position in the Introductions to both his Fourth Edition of *The Dead Sea Scrolls in English* and *The Complete Dead Sea Scrolls* with a footnote to my *'Dead Sea Scrolls Uncovered'* until now (but omitting any page reference – presumably, because it isn't there) concluding, thereby that *'theories'* like mine *'fail the basic credibility test*' and '*are foisted on the texts*.'[64] Nor has he ever retracted what on the face of it is patently an unfair mischaracterization.

In making such an assertion what he does demonstrate, however, is that he cannot have ever carefully read the theories of mine he is dismissing but, rather, is accepting what appear to be inaccurate characterizations of them on the basis, perhaps, of secondhand opinion or hearsay. His criticism, therefore, is doubly offensive for, had he actually read my work with care, *he would at least know that above all* – and this contrary to the rank and file of the majority of Qumran commentators – *what I have done is carefully and absolutely distinguish between these two characters, a position I have taken from the earliest stages of my work and still insist on today!*[65]

To consider, therefore, that I '*assign the part*' of '*the Wicked Priest*' at Qumran to '*Paul*' is not only a misleading characterization of my position that subjects me to ridicule, but an all-too-easy victory. Would all such arguments could so easily be won. Rather, what he seems to have done is confused my opinion with both his own and that of the general run of Qumran specialists but, in particular, the earliest advocate of the '*Jewish Christian*' hypothesis, Joel Teicher of Cambridge University, *who did made the unconvincing error of presenting Paul as the Wicked Priest and Jesus the Righteous Teacher in the early days of Qumran research in the Fifties!*[66]

But the reason Professor Vermes is also totally mistaken in the first contention where my work is concerned (about the impossibility of a '*Christian connection*' even if there were *only a single counter-indicative result*) is because, *when dealing with an array of items expressed in units of probability, the results of the entire sample must be considered.* One statistical outlier, that is, a single result outside a pattern determined by multiple other results, even if it were accurate, is always within the realm of the possible and no single data point can ever produce information that has greater meaning than that provided by the array in which it is contained. This is a statistical postulate obviously well beyond the comprehension or expertise of many either reading these articles or doing Qumran research – myself perhaps included – but it is well made and fully explained in the Braunheim-Atwill articles mentioned above.[67]

When it comes to analyzing the results of carbon testing where Qumran documents are concerned, it should be observed that these '*sigma*'s or time spans are not narrow, whatever the test run involved. Where the first '*sigma*' is concerned, the time span can range to over a hundred years. When the second is taken into consideration, it can then be extended in some cases to over even two hundred years. Right from the start, therefore, this is considerably beyond the margin-of-era required to date individual scrolls with the accuracy necessary to affect the present chronological debate or arrive at '*absolute dates*.'[68]

Where evaluating these '*results*' is concerned, aside from individual tastes or interests, a good deal of attention was focused on the date of the Habakkuk *Pesher*, a document which doubtlessly received innumerable cleansings and much individual handling and actually describing historical events and naming *dramatis personae* – albeit with the infuriating circumlocutions so familiar to persons doing Dead Sea Scroll research. Initial reports gave it a date of 104–43 BC, which sent researchers scurrying to date all the *dramatis personae* and the *sitz-im-leben* of the Qumran documents back before approximately 50 BC.[69] This was particularly true where G. Doudna above was concerned who, in his ideas about a '*Single-Generation Hypothesis*' (unfortunately, in my view, he was probably dealing with '*the wrong Generation*') not only gave away, to some extent, his own agenda but cheerfully considered he had solved the problem of Qumran origins, when patently he had not.[70] But then according to the new 1998 calibration, this first *sigma* calibration had to be corrected to 88–2 BC, though the retractions never made the same impression as the initial assertions and few ever knew and still remain unaware that the initial reports – such as they are – were inaccurate and flawed.[71]

Moreover several other matters also impinged on '*the results*' that all those untutored in the vagaries of carbon testing took to be '*certain*' and as '*confirming the results of palaeography*.' The true skeptic might properly reply to such over-enthusiastic claims or pretensions, '*it is so if you think so*.'[72] In the first place, in doing their testing, as signaled above as well, it turns out that, owing to conservation concerns, for the most part only one sample was taken from each item tested. In a recent paper, N. Caldararo pointed out that, in general, such a measurement technique ignores the greater precision multiple samples from the same host would provide and contributes to the inaccuracy of the technique.[73] Following this up R. E. M. Hedges also demonstrated that there can be great differences between multiple samples taken from the same host and these must be included when calculating the *sigma*-range, meaning that a one-sample variance is much less accurate than one obtained from multiple samples taken from the same host.

When considerations such as these, therefore, are taken into account, the first-*sigma* corrections for the Habakkuk *Pesher* would undoubtedly move well into the First Century and it is impossible to tell what would happen to the two-*sigma* range which in the tests that were done – and this not incuriously and uniquely – for some reason virtually agreed with the one-*sigma* range. Put in another way, when sample-to-sample variations and other variables, such as calibration errors, acquiescent and tendentious interpretation, and uncertainly regarding the length of time between the death of an animal or plant and the ultimate use of its skin as parchment or its fibre as papyrus for writing, are taken into account, *then the corrected standard deviations boost the margins-of-error in question by approximately another century either upwards or downwards.*

Another point, already alluded to above and of key significance, is that it has long been appreciated that, palaeographically-speaking, the Habakkuk *Pesher* and the Psalm 37 *Pesher* – including many events and *dramatis personae* which are the same in both – are basically equivalent. Both were in, as already underscored, what is referred to in the field as '*Herodian semiformal script*' dated by the palaeographers to approximately 30–0 BC. But when the Psalm 37 *Pesher* was dated by radiocarbon, even the first-*sigma* range came out to be between 29–81 CE and its second-*sigma* extended the range to 5–111 CE. In our view, if one had to choose, this would be the far more likely dating of the document in question – '*Pesharim*' generally at Qumran being found in single exemplars only.

Rather, dominated by their preconceptions, our radiocarbon analysts and their ideological confrères, dating Scrolls solely on the basis of palaeography – that is, on the basis of the inexact palaeographic sequences they have posited[74] – who cast themselves as the ones asking for and conducting the tests (sound similar to the FBI Crime Lab in Washington D.C. which usually rendered the conclusions those sponsoring the tests desired and the reason why we called for '*Opposition Scholars*' to be included in the process in the first place?), chose to highlight the radiocarbon dating of the former because it suited their preconceptions.

Recently, however, a document was found among the fragments from Cave 4, which appears to mention the name of a known High Priest whose tenure dated from 46–47 CE, thus providing vivid '*internal evidence*' negating any idea that the documents were deposited in this Cave prior to this time.[75] *Pace* modern attempts, based on this imperfect interpretation of radiocarbon-testing analysis, to make it seem as if all documents were deposited in the caves before about 40–50 BC – *a perfectly absurd* and, from my perspective, *an absolutely untenable conclusion that ignores 100–150 years of perhaps the most vital Palestinian history.*

The new calibration also produced a significant change for the range of 4Q267, considered the earliest fragment – palaeographically speaking – of the Damascus Document, bringing its two-*sigma* range well into the First Century; but we have already stated the opinion that all such documents like the Habakkuk, Psalm 37, the Isaiah *Peshers*, the Messianic compendiums like the *Florilegium* and Testimonia, we shall examined in more detail below,[76] and the Damascus Document have been written at approximately the same time because of their mention of and focus upon the same *dramatis personae* and associated contemporary events. *If one dated to one certain moment in time then, probably, all dated to approximately that moment* – and this should not always be the earliest chronological measurement but rather, probably, the chronological mean.

Finally, it should be concluded that there is nothing in the results of the two runs of radiocarbon dating that precludes any of the ideas or analyses set forth in this book. There is absolutely no finality on these matters and not even a presumption of one. Nor did the two runs that were done, which produced an extremely uneven or skewed set of results, demonstrate the reliability of palaeography as most '*Consensus Scholars*' took them or imagined them to do. In the best case scenario, perhaps – in the worst case, absolutely not.[77] Rather, when taken as a whole, C-14 testing results showed that neither palaeography nor C-14 dating *was a sufficiently precise enough tool to conclusively contribute to the debate over the accurate dating of the Dead Sea Scrolls*. In fact, C-14 testing generally supported and did not preclude the premise that some of the Scrolls were produced well into the First Century CE if not later.

Let us repeat this proposition because it is important: the results of carbon testing – such as they are – contain nothing in them which would nullify any of the ideas or positions argued in this book. All things being equal, they probably do just the opposite. Though some may provide useful information, they may just as likely be wildly inaccurate. It is for this reason one must turn to what we call '*the internal data*' as a control. If the results of these tests and other external measurements such as archaeology and palaeography – some (including in the case of '*the James Ossuary*,' as we shall see below, '*patina analysis*') really not exact sciences in the true sense of the term at all – conflict with '*the internal data*'; then, regardless of one's confidence in them, they must be jettisoned.

Nor for my part would there be any point in writing a book such as this were one to hold as sacrosanct the interpretations of data produced only by '*external measurements*' of this kind. This is the situation in Dead Sea Scrolls research today, the conclusions concerning which have been rendered inchoate and vacuous by the uncritical and superficial reliance on external data or parameters such as these. As opposed to this, this book will focus more on the internal ones and see what sense can be made of these.

Internal vs. External Data

It has been my position from the beginning that there are two kinds of data at Qumran, 'external' and 'internal.' 'External' are things like archaeology, palaeography, and carbon dating, but these rather turn out to often be either imprecise or unreliable. In a situation of the kind represented by the materials and discoveries at Qumran, when there is a contradiction between the results of such disciplines and 'the internal data' – meaning, *what the documents themselves say*, to which the rest of this book will be dedicated – then 'the internal data' must take precedence, given the quality and kind of 'the external data' that exists for Qumran.

What, for instance, might be considered 'internal data'? Primarily the most important allusions at Qumran. These include references such as 'making a Straight Way in the wilderness,' alluded to twice in the Community Rule and, as is well known, associated with the teaching and coming of John the Baptist 'in the wilderness' in the Synoptic Gospels.[78] A related terminology is 'the New Covenant,' a phrase originally based on Jeremiah 31:31 and a central theme of the Damascus Document, known of course as the basis of the word, 'New Testament' (i.e., the 'New Covenant').[79] Equally important is the allusion to and exposition of Habakkuk 2:4, perhaps the climax of the Habakkuk *Pesher* and perhaps the central Scriptural building block of early Christian theology as set forth by Paul in Romans, Galatians, and Hebrews and, of course, in James.[80]

Related to these and, in particular, this last are the repeated reference to the two 'Love Commandments' of 'Piety' and 'Righteousness' (I will capitalize important concepts throughout this book, just as I will italicize important phrases and ideas whether in quotations or part of my own exposition) – in Josephus defined as, 'loving God' and 'loving your neighbor as yourself' – and 'Justification' theology generally. Not only are these the essence, allegedly, of Jesus' teaching in the Gospels and James' in the Letter ascribed to his name in the New Testament and in early Church literature generally,[81] but they are also the basis in the picture provided by Josephus of John the Baptist's teaching and a central category of 'Essene' doctrine as well.[82]

Then there is the wide use of 'Zealot' and 'Nazirite' terminology (in the sense of 'Nazoraean' or 'Nazrene'), designations known to the First Century but not clearly attested to in any consistent manner earlier.[83] Related to these is 'the Poor' (in early Church literature, 'the Ebionites'), the only really clearly identifiable term of self-designation in the Dead Sea Scrolls, a nomenclature also designating the followers of James *par excellence* and the group succeeding or basically coeval with 'the Essenes.'[84] In a controversial reference in the Habakkuk *Pesher* – a document which, together with the Psalm 37 *Pesher* above, definitively denotes the followers of 'the Righteous Teacher' as 'the Poor,' that is, we are definitely in the realm both of 'the Ebionites' and of 'Ebionite' literature. Not only would both of these be '*destroyed*' or '*swallowed*' by '*the Wicked Priest*' but, in turn, he would be made to '*drink the Cup of the Wrath of God*' and '*paid the Reward which he paid the Poor*' (*i.e.*, '*the Ebionim*')![85]

Here '*the Cup of the Lord*' relates to Divine Vengeance which is, once again, also the sense of parallel allusions in the New Testament Book of Revelation. Again there is an allusion to the same theme in the Psalm 37 *Pesher* and, as opposed to the superficial analyses early on in Qumran Studies, the allusion – as we shall see more fully – has nothing whatever to do with the '*drunkenness*' of the Wicked Priest or consonantly *any* '*banquet*' or '*dinner party*' *he might have been attending*,[86] except metaphorically in that, as in Revelation 14:8–10 and 16:19, '*drinking his fill*' of such a '*Cup*' has to do with '*drinking his fill of the Cup of the Wrath of God*' or *the Divine Vengeance which would be visited upon* or '*paid*' *the murderer of the Righteous Teacher for what he* ('*the Wicked Priest*') *did to him* ('*the Righteous Teacher*') *and his followers among* '*the Poor.*'[87] The attestation of this usage in Revelation, not to mention the allusion to '*the Poor*' connected in some man- ner with James in Galatians 2:10, again, should be seen as chronologically definitive '*internal data*' no matter what the '*external.*'

To name a few other such First-Century dating parameters: there is the insistence on '*fornication*' as descriptive of the behaviour of the Ruling Establishment in the '*Three Nets of Belial*' section of the Damascus Document. In it, regardless of its meaning in any other context, '*fornication*' is specifically defined in terms of '*polygamy*,' '*divorce*,' '*marrying nieces*' and, curiously enough, '*sleeping with women during their periods*,' all things that, taken as a whole, can be said to be descriptive of '*Herodians*' and not '*Maccabeans.*'[88] Among Herodians, in particular '*niece marriage*' was rampant and an aspect of purposeful family policy.[89]

Another of these '*Nets*' had to do with '*pollution of the Temple.*' Not only was this a matter not unrelated to '*things sacrificed to idols*,' mentioned above and – as we shall see further below – in relation to Hippolytus' '*Sicarii Essenes*' and in the Qumran document known as '*MMT*'; it is likewise a matter connected, as we shall stress, to James' directives to overseas communities, where it is also expressed in Acts 15:20 in terms of the variation '*pollutions of the idols.*' Interestingly enough, too, this condemnation of '*eating things sacrificed to idols*' is even found and grouped together with both '*fornication*' and the language of '*being led astray*' in Revelation 2:20.[90] These are additional First-Century dating parameters.

Much debate, too, has crystallized about the term '*the Kittim*,' so important to the literature and outlook of Qumran especially in the Commentaries ('*the Pesharim*'), the War Scroll, and those documents related to it.[91] Several references are absolutely critical for the correct elucidation of this seemingly purposefully obscure allusion and archaism. The first is in the Nahum *Pesher* where '*the Kittim*' are specifically identified as '*coming after the Greeks.*'[92] Several others come in the Habakkuk and Psalm 37 *Peshers* where, in the former anyhow, they are specifically described as '*pillaging the Temple.*'[93] Josephus is very specific about this point and makes it quite plain that there was *no 'pillaging of the Temple' by the Romans* either in 63 BC under Pompey because they wished to ingratiate themselves with the People; nor by Herod in 37 BC who, Josephus tells us, actually had the soldiers paid out of his own pocket expressly to avoid such a happentance.[94]

That leaves only Vespasian and his son Titus who did, in fact, *plunder the Temple in 70 CE, and used the proceeds afterwards to pay for the abomination now famously referred to worldwide as 'the Colosseum.*'[95] There can be a no-more definitive chronological placement of the Habakkuk *Pesher* than this extremely telling allusion and this is what is meant by a proper appreciation of '*the internal data*' being frustrated or rendered meaningless by inept and over-inflated interpretation of and reliance upon '*the external.*' Of course, in this context, too, there is the decisive reference to *the Kittim 'sacrificing to their standards and worshipping their weapons of war,*' which we shall further discuss in due course as well.[96] It has been pointed out by numerous commentators, but seemingly to little avail, that this is *Roman military practice not Hellenistic* or *Greek* – and, specifically, *Imperial Roman from Augustus' time forward*, since the Emperor whose bust was on the standards had, commencing in that period, been deified and worshipped as a God.[97]

Just as telling is the reference, immediately following this in the same document, to how these same violent and brutal '*Kittim,*' *who conquered* '*Nation after Nation,*' *had* '*no pity even on the fruit of the womb*' – Josephus describes just such carnage by the Sea of Galilee in 67 CE in the run-up to the siege of Jerusalem two years later, where the Romans did actually kill just such infants – and '*whose eating was plenteous,*' '*parcelled out*' their *taxes like fishermen catching fish in their nets.*'[98] Here, to be sure, one has a combination of motifs familiar in the '*fishermen*' and '*nets*' themes in the Gospels – of course, as always, with reverse or more effectively trivializing signification. Matthew 17:25–27 even goes so far in response to matters concerning *the paying of 'tribute'* (in this case, delineated in terms of *paying the Temple tax*) to actually portray Jesus as sending his favorite Apostle '*Peter*' (also a Galilean '*fisherman*') to the Sea of Galilee to retrieve the required coinage *out of the mouth of a fish!*

In addition, however, it is clear that what is being described in this pivotal section of the Habakkuk *Pesher*, as we shall see further too, is the well-known Roman administrative practice of '*tax-farming*,' particularly among the petty Kings in the East (like the '*Herodians*' who functioned as Roman juridical and '*tax-gathering*' officials – in the Gospels, that is, '*Publicans*'!), and which the Romans practised so assiduously in the Eastern part of the Empire (therefore, the alleged '*Census*' referred to in Luke).[99] Once again, these petty or Eastern Kings were specifically referred to in Roman juridical language, as we shall also see further, as '*Kings of the Peoples*' – of which such '*Herodians*' were prototypical.[100] Here, too, the exact phraseology actually appears in the Damascus Document in describing just such kinds of '*pollution*,' which included even '*polluting the Temple Treasury*,' '*robbing of Riches*,' and '*approaching near kin for fornication*' – meaning, '*marriage with nieces*' and '*close family cousins*.'

Of course, once one has accepted such evidence, it must be accepted, as we have been trying to point out, that all '*sectarian*'-style texts – or those referred to also as '*extra-Biblical*' at Qumran – have to have been written at more or less the same time since they all *use the same vocabulary, refer to the same dramatis personae*, and *express basically the same concerns and orientation*. As hard as this may be to appreciate for those making superficial analyses on the basis of pseudo- or quasi-scientific '*external data*,' this is true and defeats both palaeographic theorizing and archaeological reconstructions, such as they are, not to mention the 'wishful thinking' embedded in the unrealistic expectation or inflation of '*the results*' of radiocarbon test-data analysis. To be sure, there may be copies made of copies, but all of the key '*extra-Biblical*' or '*sectarian*' texts – except some very early apocryphal and pseudepigraphic texts – particularly those including real historical indications or dating parameters, *had to have been written in more or less the same period of time*.

One could go on perhaps endlessly to give examples of allusions or expressions from the Scrolls demonstrating a First-Century CE provenance but not a particularly earlier one. Two of the most telling of these are '*the House of his Exile*' or '*his Exiled House*,' used in the Habakkuk *Pesher* to describe a final confrontation of some kind between '*the Wicked Priest*' – clearly *the Establishment High Priest* – and '*the Righteous Teacher*,' which seems to have ended up in the destruction of the latter along with a number of his followers referred to, as just noted, as '*the Poor*' (*Ebionim*).[101] No sense whatever has ever been made of this '*House of Exile*' by any commentator (including, as far as I can see, the above-mentioned Professor Vermes of Oxford); but, as we shall demonstrate, it clearly relates to *the 'Exile' of the Sanhedrin around the Thirties to the Sixties of the Common Era*, frequently attested to in the *Talmud*[102] (therefore, the '*House*' in question is '*his House*,' meaning *the High Priest's 'House*' and not the 'house' of the Righteous Teacher as per the usual exposition – Hebrew typically being imprecise in genitives of this kind), *from its place of sitting in the Great Stone Chamber on the Temple Mount to a 'House' outside its precincts* (not unlike the trial at 'the House of the High Priest' in the Luke 22:54/Matthew 26:57) – the implication being that, because of this, all capital sentences imposed in this Period under such jurisdiction *were to be considered unlawful* or *invalid*.

Finally there is the reference in the Damascus Document to '*raising*' or '*re-erecting the fallen Tabernacle of David' in a Land seemingly North of 'Damascus*.'[103] But this usage is also one expressly attributed to and expounded by James in his speech at the famous '*Jerusalem Council*' in Acts 15:16, which we shall elaborate in considerable more detail in the second part of this book. Another such allusion, expressly attributed to James in early Church accounts of the circumstances leading up to his death (to say nothing of 'Jesus'"[104]), is the proclamation of '*the coming of the Heavenly Host upon the clouds of Heaven*' which will, as we shall also see, form the backbone of two extensive apocalyptic sections of the War Scroll.[105]

There, of course, it is '*the Star Prophecy*' of Numbers 24:17 which is being both evoked and expounded and, once again, we have come full circle, because according to Josephus this was the '*ambiguous Prophecy*' – '*ambiguous*' because it was capable of multiple interpretations – that '*most moved*' *the Jews to revolt against Rome*.[106] To put this in another way: this '*Prophecy*,' referred to upwards of three times in the extant corpus at Qumran, together with Isaiah 10:34–11:5, also extant in *Pesher*-form in at least two contexts at Qumran, was *the driving force behind the Revolt against Rome* – again, yet another *unambiguous dating parameter*. One need not mention, of course, the fact of the emergence of the whole '*Christian*' tradition, itself another response to this '*ambiguous*' Prophecy. Then, of course, there is the very term '*Damascus*' itself, the esoteric meaning of which we shall attempt to delineate at the end of this book. Though one could go on, this is the kind of powerful '*internal evidence*' that exists for a First-Century provenance of many crucial and interrelated '*sectarian*' texts at Qumran.

The James Ossuary

Recently – possibly as a direct result of all the attention I and several others have focused on James over the last several years – an ossuary '*was discovered*' or, should we rather say, suddenly surfaced, containing a trace of remains and allegedly bearing the inscription in Aramaic '*James the son of Joseph the brother of Jesus*.' Much discussion concerning this ossuary ensued including *coffee table*-style books, television documentaries, and endless polemics (exploitation?) about both its palaeography and the very authenticity of the artifact itself. Most of this occurred in the same magazine, *The Biblical Archaeology Review*, already mentioned in connection with the *Facsimile Edition* and other disputes concerning carbon dating and the breaking of the monopoly on the Dead Sea Scrolls.[107]

Not only did the present writer question its authenticity from the first day of its appearance when its '*discovery*' was presented to the press in a release by Hershel Shanks, *BAR*'s above-mentioned Publisher, but my article '*A Discovery That's Just too Perfect*' (October 29th, 2002) was perhaps the first to do so in a systematic manner and appeared ten days later on the *Los Angeles Times* Op-Ed Page. The reason I was invited by its editors to write this piece was probably because of my role as consultant to the Huntington Library on its decision to open its archives and, as it were, '*free the Scrolls*'; but also because mine had been the most widely-circulated comments in the press then questioning the authenticity of the ossuary – and this, once again, *on the basis of 'the internal' not 'the external' evidence*. But even now the preponderance of '*external*' evidence, concerning the ossuary, has more and more turned to support its being – to some degree anyhow – a forgery, at least that is the conclusion of an Israeli panel of experts that investigated the matter and police action has even been undertaken against its proprietor.[108]

That the ossuary was old and from the period in question never really was the point of contention. Such ossuaries are plentiful in the Jerusalem area, some inscribed – some even uninscribed. They could be bought in a fairly good state of preservation by any collector from the antiquities dealers in the Old City of Jerusalem and elsewhere for perhaps a few hundred dollars – '*in the old days*,' when the owner of this particular '*ossuary*' claims it came into his family's possession, much less. The question rather was, as the present writer saw it, whether people would have thought to use words such as those inscribed – in a fairly abnormal manner – *on the reverse of this ossuary* to refer to someone like James at this time at all, not whether the inscription was really that of '*James the brother of Jesus*' (the subject, to some extent, of this and my earlier book), the seeming general preoccupation of those originally supporting the ossuary's authenticity. So interested were these last in proving the existence of '*Jesus*' that at the beginning anyhow they were not really addressing the question of its possible fraudulence in any serious manner – a fraudulence that would have raised the value of the ossuary from about $200 to say $2,000,000 or more![109]

This was the present writer's point. It was obvious that the unusual character of the inscription made it clear that those who had executed it aimed it at those who held the family of *'Jesus'* in high regard and meant it to be taken for *the real burial repository of the bones of his illustrious 'brother,' also known as 'James the Just.'* Though I had everything to gain personally by its being taken as authentic having, as it were, *'written the book'* on the subject and a tremendous amount of additional attention would, therefore, have been focused on James, increasing my sales proportionately[110]; furthermore, despite the fact that many urged me out of self-interest to keep silent, I found it impossible to do so and felt it all the more incumbent upon myself to speak out on the issue since it was obvious to me, from an historical and ideological point-of-view, that the inscription could not in any way be considered to be authentic – and this, once again, from the perspective of the *'internal'* not the *'external evidence.'* As just observed, my point rather was that the inscription reflected what a latterday observer – probably modern or, at the very least, some early Pietist from the Third or Fourth Century CE after the doctrinal view of 'Jesus,' as we know it from *'Scripture,'* had had time to develop – would have thought should be written about James or what we, the heirs to the tradition, would have wished or expected to see written.[111] That's why I termed it *'A Discovery that was just too Perfect.'*

But this was not what the palaeographers were saying, the most well-known of whom were, on the contrary, literally *'falling all over one another'* to extol the excellence of *'the bookhand'* (the term used to describe formal or semi-formal scripts) as a perfect representative of First-Century Judean script – but this, not surprisingly, would be a simulation any artificer would have been most anxious to achieve.[112] And here, I think, we have come to the limits of palaeography as a *'scientific'* discipline. They were saying that *both* scripts involved were authentic – and there were ostensibly *two* hands on the ossuary, *one formal* or *semi-formal* and the other more *cursive*. This distinction was obvious to even the amateur or most-unpracticed observer but had never been mentioned in the first reports about the ossuary.[113] Moreover, I think, by making such over-hasty and emotionally excited judgements reflecting what they *wished* to be true, not what actually *was true*, they basically discredited palaeography as a serious and objective study to be applied to the wider issue of the chronological dating of the Dead Sea Scrolls.

One of the ossuary's principal palaeographic advocates, a Sorbonne-trained French *'epigrapher'* – as he was referred to – who had made the original determination of its authenticity, had even gone so far as to date it to 63 CE! What precision and such a miniscule margin-of-error – typical one might add of pseudo-scientific practices and the arrogance of those relying solely on the measurement of *'external data'* in this field.

Nor, doubtlessly, had it escaped him that, according to Josephus, James had died in 62 CE and, therefore, such an inscription (if authentic) could not have been executed before 62 CE – say, for instance, 61 CE![114]

'*Epigraphy*,' as some might call it, or palaeography aside – the inscription on the back of the ossuary did perhaps, as already suggested, come into being because of some of the attention I myself had called to James in *James the Brother of Jesus* (Viking, 1997/Penguin, 1998), which was known in Israel and had been reviewed in *The Jerusalem Post* on April 22nd, 1997 using such superlatives as: '*a tremendous work of historical scholarship*,' '*apocalyptic*,' '*expert*,' '*great*,' and '*this book will live and live and live*.'[115] In its Introduction, I had even said – concerning the paucity of historical information about 'Jesus' himself, to say nothing of his having '*several brothers, one of whom was called James*' –

In fact, taking the brother relationship seriously may turn out to be one of the only confirmations that there ever was a historical Jesus[116];

and I assume that the artificers of the ossuary had at least read this far in my book.

A pity they did not read further because, had they done so they would have known that, according to three observers anyhow – Hegesippus, Eusebius, and Jerome – James' burial site was known and its marker still extant seemingly in their own times (all had lived in Palestine at one time or another), namely, the Second, Fourth, and Fifth Centuries.[117] This means that at least till then – a century or two, that is, before the Muslim conquest – *James was buried in the ground in the normal manner and there would have been no ossuary*! Again, this is the insight or determination that paying close attention to the '*internal data*' would have brought them. However, so excited were so many to get a First-Century witness to 'Jesus' that they obviously did not do so.

This being said, as I saw it, James was so famous in his own right – which would have been even more pronounced if he were '*the Righteous Teacher*' from Qumran as well – that few, if any, would have thought he needed to be identified by the additional appellative '*the brother of Jesus*.' A cognomen such as this was rare in any event in ossuary inscriptions from the First Century in Palestine and only one or two have ever been discovered.[118] As already suggested, too, this sounded more like what a modern believer, not an ancient one, already schooled in the fact that 'Jesus' was so much more important and famous than his '*brother*' James, would have expected to see and thought should been required to identify him. Nor is this to say anything about the whole problem of '*the*

Historical Jesus,' the existence of whom is only undoubted by modern observers, well-schooled, as just remarked, in the Gospels and attendant literature as ancient writers, for the most part, hardly mention him at all.[119] Certainly he is not identified in any way in the Dead Sea Scrolls.[120]

Then there is the whole question of who the father of James – to say nothing of 'Jesus' – actually was in early Church tradition and, once again, whether a '*Joseph*' ever really existed as such except in the modern believer's imagination, again schooled in the genealogies and historical pretensions of the Gospels, since 'Jesus' was not even supposed to have been '*the son of Joseph*' but rather '*the Son of God*.'

We have quite a few other names of persons associated with and related to James, some clearly in a patrilineal manner – for instance '*Cleophas*,' called in early Church tradition '*the brother of Joseph*' and the '*uncle*' germane of Jesus;[121] '*Alphaeus*' (Matthew 10:3 and *pars.*), certainly a corruption of '*Cleophas*'; '*Clopas the husband of Mary*' ('*the sister of the mother of the Lord*' – thus! – John 19:25); and '*Cleopas*' *the first to see Jesus on the road to Emmaus* (Luke 24:18). So one might have expected to see something like '*James the son of Cleophas*,'*James the son of Alphaeus*,' or even '*James the Just*' ('*ha-Zaddik*' in Hebrew), but not necessarily '*Joseph*' as such, as the modern adept or believer might expect. There is also the mysterious '*Lebbaeus*' in Matthew 10:3, possibly corresponding to James' cognomen '*Oblias*' in Hegesippus' report in the Second Century, meaning – or so it would seem – '*the Protection of the People*.'[122]

These are the kinds of problems associated with James' parentage if not Jesus' and still one hasn't even approached the problem of how and in what manner '*Joseph*' could have been considered Jesus' father even if he did exist. Nor is this to say anything about the question, which we shall treat further below, of whether when one speaks of '*Joseph*,' one is not simply speaking of the '*Messiah Ben Joseph*' designating in Talmudic lore a tribal affiliation in the Northern Kingdom (as he would have been referred to as well in Samaritan tradition) as opposed, for instance, to the '*Messiah ben Judah*' designating a Messianic individual in the Southern Kingdom.[123] Finally, as already alluded to as well, the writer raised the point about whether it can safely be said that James was even buried in a manner such as this and his bones collected in an ossuary with a First-Century CE inscription on it.

Actually, I covered many of these points in *James the Brother of Jesus* and the reader who wishes to be acquainted with this kind of data would be well-advised to consult it. In that prequel to this volume, I collected many of the notices from early Church literature which generally describe *how James was stoned under the Pinnacle of the Temple* and *buried in the normal manner where he fell* after '*a laundryman*' had given him a *coup de grace* with his club (*thus!*).[124] Whether these traditions can be relied upon and were not exaggerated is a question an individual reader will have to judge for him or herself. If, however, one goes according to the gist of these testimonies, *then James was not laid out in a rock-cut tomb at all –* unless, that is, burial traditions purporting to be descriptive of how Jesus was interred were, as we shall also argue to some degree as we proceed, actually descriptive of how James was interred – but simply buried in the ground in the normal manner, in which case his remains would not have been collected in an ossuary at all, at least not in the First Century and not as far as any of the above sources were aware.

This may well have happened at a later time, when Pious pilgrims could have come, dug up his body, and reburied it in an ossuary of the kind, say, that one finds in Santiago de Compostela in Spain, said to have been brought there by Pious pilgrims in the Eighth or Ninth Century CE and belonging, allegedly, to the other '*James*' – '*James the brother of John.*'[125] There are some traditions, too, associated with the Armenian Church of St James that also claim to have an ossuary belonging to James buried beneath the altar of that Church but these,too, too seem to be later traditions certainly unknown or, at least, not remarked in any literary manner before Jerome's testimony in the early Fifth Century to actually having seen James' burial marker in the Kedron Valley where he fell.[126] But, once again, then why is the inscription on the ossuary – which according to first reports was homogeneous throughout – and the epigraphy of First-Century origin? Of course, despite these initial reports, the inscription is certainly *not homogeneous throughout*, but why would later epigraphers then use a purportedly First-Century script to reformulate it?[127]

The reader should appreciate that ossuaries were used when persons were laid out in rock-cut tombs and, in Palestine, this primarily in the First Century. After the mortal flesh rotted away, the bones were sometimes collected by loving relatives or admiring followers and preserved in the ceremonial limestone boxes now referred to as '*ossuaries.*' This might have been the case for James – one cannot say, but one has no indication of it in the traditions preserved about James. Rather, as we saw, they tell us a totally different story.

Nevertheless, James may have been buried in a rock-cut tomb in the manner reported of 'Jesus,'[128] as there are oral traditions in the form of pilgrims' tales associating James with a tomb now identified as '*the Tomb of the Bene Hezir*' in the Kedron Valley beneath '*the Pinnacle of the Temple.*' Next to this are those known to tradition as '*the Tomb of Absalom,*' '*the*

Tomb of Zechariah' and, as it would seem from the latterday document found at Qumran known as the Copper Scroll (documenting, as well, it would appear, *the hiding places of the Temple Treasure*), '*the Tomb of Zadok*' or perhaps even '*the Zaddik*' ('*the Just One*,' as James was called as we saw in all traditions associated with his name).[129] This last-named is difficult to pinpoint with any precision, but it is probably one of these, that is, either '*the Tomb of Saint James*' or '*the Tomb of Zechariah*' just referred to above.[130]

There can be little doubt that the rock-cut tombs in the Kedron Valley beneath the Pinnacle of the Temple that we are speaking about here are upper-class tombs from the Maccabean, Hellenistic, or even Herodian Periods, all most likely '*Priestly*.' This is certainly the case for '*the Tomb of the Bene Hezir*,' '*the Bene Hezir*' being one of the twenty-four Priestly courses in the Temple referred to in Ezra and Nehemiah and clearly denoting an important '*Herodian High-Priestly*' Line.[131] This funerary monument contains an inscription plaque with this reference – therefore the name – enumerating the names of the Priests in this line. The inscription makes it fairly clear that this was the family mausoleum of High Priests known to both Josephus and in the *Talmud* as '*the Boethusians*,' an incredibly wealthy High-Priestly clan that Herod imported from Egypt after marrying a daughter of a scion of this line named Mariamme in place of his Maccabean wife (also named Mariamme), whom he had executed for alleged adultery with his brother-in-law, another '*Joseph*' (the original '*Joseph*' and '*Mary*'?).[132]

Therefore, it is certainly not without the realm of possibility that the burial of James did take place in just such a rock-cut tomb as that of '*the Bene Hezir*' ('*the Tomb of St. James*' of Christian pilgrimage tradition) just as Jesus' burial is portrayed in the Gospels in '*a Rich Man's tomb*' – once again, another '*Joseph*' – now called, most incredibly, '*Joseph of Arimathaea*.'[133] Still, as things have since transpired, the authenticity of this ossuary ascribed to James which so suddenly materialized as if out of nowhere – its inscriptions and the smattering of remains therein – has now been seriously invalidated, not only because of the lack of secure provenance and a known transmission tradition, but also because of the behaviour and reputation of those who claim, not only to have owned it, but to have been its custodians and conservers, the credibility of whom is now in serious question and the subject of an ongoing police inquiry in Israel itself.[134] We do not say this with any great sense of celebration, but simply as a statement of fact to counteract some of the exaggerated and wildly implausible claims that have been and are still being made regarding it on the part of those having virtually no knowledge at all and who appear to be either capitalizing, exploiting, or profiteering off its notoriety.

One says here '*inscriptions*' because, as already remarked, it is obvious – and this even to the amateur – despite the initial expert testimony
to the contrary, that *there are two different hands in evidence in the inscription*
even as we presently have it: one, as just noted, formal and ceremonial,
finely chiseled by an extremely precise hand – the first part, '*James the son
of Joseph*,' by which name there could have been numerous persons in the
Jerusalem of the day – and the other, rough, done in cursive script, not
finely incised but indistinct and obviously executed with a different tool.
This is the second part, '*the brother of Jesus*,' a rare though not unheard of
ascription in Second Temple times, as already indicated.[135]

Not only is this an unlikely combination, but even the content of the
second inscription – which was obviously added – raises serious issues.
In the first place there is the disagreement about who the father of James
in early tradition really was, the phraseology '*Jesus the son of Joseph*' or
'*Jesus ben Joseph*' being just too pat from a theological point-of-view. In
the second place, at the time of James' death, as also already underscored
above, few if any would have felt the need to further identify him as '*the
brother of Jesus*' in this manner, because James was so famous in the
Jerusalem of his day as '*the Righteous*' or '*Just One*' as to need no further
identification. This would, as just explained too, rather reflect the attitude
of a more recently-believing Christian, say from the early or mid-200's
onwards – even up to the present – not anyone in the time of James,
which those who authenticated the epigraphy of this inscription insisted
and are, to some degree, still insisting today!

But new questions, too, have arisen concerning the strongest argument for authenticity those asserting this claim could muster and that
had to do with the '*patina*.' At the time in my *Los Angeles Times* Op-Ed
piece, I wrote:

> *The only really strong point the arguers for the authenticity have is the so-called
> patina, which was measured at an Israeli laboratory and appears homogeneous.
> As this is a new science, it is hard for me to gauge its value. Still, the letters do
> seem unusually clear and incised and do not, at least in the photographs, show a
> significant amount of damage caused by the vicissitudes of time.*[136]

But, as has since become apparent in subsequent investigations and
analyses, just as I originally thought, '*patinas*' are now being routinely fabricated in archaeological antiquities forgeries, the faking of which have
now assumed the dimensions of a firestorm.[137]

In fact, that it would seem the individual claiming ownership of this
ossuary (to say nothing of its authenticity) was not long before involved

in another much-publicized and highly questionable antiquities discovery, 'the Joash Inscription,' having to do with a ceremonial object found allegedly from the First Temple, the patina of which has since come under severe questioning and scrutiny by Israeli researchers as well.[138] It now turns out that, according to the Committee established by the Israel Antiquities Authority to investigate such claims (which has now gone so far as to *actually declare the James ossuary a fraud*), not only is the '*patina*' on '*the Joash Inscription*' fraudulent, but the one on '*the James Ossuary*' now turns out not to be homogeneous as originally announced and, according to it, there are observably severe discontinuations in it.[139]

So the question remains, is the inscription on '*the James Ossuary*' an ancient addition done by some faithful pilgrim at some later date or is the whole a modern reproduction? For the present writer, the sudden appearance of this ossuary *at the height of all these debates surrounding the figure of James and his importance* (in my view, as already stressed, partially engendered by my *James the Brother of Jesus*) is just a little too fortuitous to be credited, though it would be nice if it were true. Still, as is the case with many such forgeries, it is often impossible either to know or say with any finality and perhaps only one's Faith will answer questions such as these.

But it does not matter. Whatever one's answer is, the finding of this ossuary, real or imitation, as well as the discovery of the burial enclosure or mausoleum at the head of the graveyard at Qumran, have focused people's attention on matters relating to James and, as a consequence, the Dead Sea Scrolls and burial monuments such as these as never before. To add to these, now we have the new discovery of '*The Gospel according to Judas*' which will concentrate people's attention on the '*literary*,' ahistorical character of many such narratives, while at the same time also help to blunt the negative connotations associated with the title '*the Iscariot*.'[140]

In the end these are wholesome developments and there can be no objection to them. They are good things and broaden peoples' perspectives in a manner, the effect of which is impossible to finally calculate. Nor is it possible to say where the interest engendered by such things will lead, but for the general public it can only be considered a positive and not a negative. It is safe to say that in and of itself such interest is healthy not harmful and leads to a closer and fuller regard for *real* historical truth and an abandonment of historical '*shibboleths*.' It is as a response to interests and needs such as these that the present book is intended. It is hoped, therefore, that the reader will find much in it that will be helpful in providing deeper insight and illumining questions and interests of this kind.

PART II

THE NEW COVENANT IN THE LAND
OF DAMASCUS

3

Essene Bathers in the East and
Abraham's Homeland

Life-long Naziritism and the '*Perfect Holiness*' Lifestyle

The traditions about James' '*Holiness from his mother's womb*' or life-long
Naziritism, vegetarianism, and abstention from sexual relations are to be
found, as we have already alluded to, in the early Church fathers Hegesippus, Origen, Eusebius, Jerome, and Epiphanius.[1] Though many of
these notices go beyond what is normally associated with a '*Nazirite*' or
'*Perfect Holiness*' life-style,[2] they persist in all sources relating to James and
among all groups seemingly descended or claiming descent from him.
They also appear, not surprisingly, to relate to what numerous persons in
different contexts are calling '*Essenes*.'

Where James' sexual continency – his '*life-long virginity*' as Epiphanius
graphically describes it[3] – is concerned, this may, in any event, have been
a concomitant of his '*life-long Naziritism*,' as it was of people contemporary with and not too different from him, such as the individual
Josephus' calls '*Banus*' and those he denotes as '*Essenes*.'[4]

Obliquely too, it provides a clue as to how this claim came to be
reflected – or retrospectively absorbed as the case may be – into the more
familiar one of *Mary's life-long 'virginity*' or, as this was first seemingly
enunciated in the early Second Century, her '*perpetual virginity*.'[5] The '*perpetual*' aspect of this claim can certainly with more justification anyhow,
be applied to James since, even according to orthodox theology, '*Mary*'
(if she can be pinpointed in any real way and was not just a reflection of
the earlier '*Joseph and Mary*' story in the Herodian family machinations
mentioned above[6]) had at least one son and perhaps even more, not to
mention at least one daughter.[7]

The claim of Mary's '*perpetual virginity*,' in any event, had an anti-
James undercurrent to it meant to deny the credibility of there actually
being any '*brothers*' as such or, as the polemic shook out, '*half-brothers*,'
'*cousins*' (this is how Jerome and, following his lead, Catholicism to this
day ultimately approached the issue), or '*milk brothers*.'[8] Incredibly
enough, the claim for Mary's '*perpetual virginity*' is first made in a text: *The*

Protevangelium of James, which is attributed to James and actually put into his mouth, the implication being, of course, that he, the closest living 'relative,' heir, and even successor, would have known about these kinds of things better than anyone else – and no doubt he did.[9]

The motifs of sexual continency and abstention from meat or vegetarianism, whether part of a '*Nazirite*' oath procedure of some kind – '*temporary*' or '*life-long*' – are also to be seen in the notices from Rabbinic literature and Acts about exactly such kinds of '*Nazirite*' oaths on the part of extreme irredentists or revanchists – again '*temporary*' or '*life-long*'.[10] In Acts 23:12–21, as we saw, such persons vow '*not to eat or drink' until they have killed Paul*, the implication being that they *will not eat meat or drink wine*. In contemporary Rabbinic sources, the implication shifts to *waiting until the Temple should be reborn* or *rebuilt*; and the interconnectedness of these imageries to Paul's and the Gospels' presentations of *Jesus' body as Temple* should be clear.[11]

From 1 Corinthians chapters 8–12, where he is actually discussing James' directives to overseas communities (in particular, '*keeping away from food sacrificed to idols*' – the Hebrew equivalent of '*keep away*' or '*abstain from*' in the vocabulary of the Damascus Document being the phraseology of '*lehinnazer*,' which is based on the same Hebrew root *N-Z-R* underlying the English words '*Nazirite*' or '*Naziritism*'); Paul himself speaks about '*eating and drinking*,' to wit, '*have we not every right to eat and drink?*' (9:4) Such challenges not only lead up to his ultimate allowing of '*eating*' or '*partaking of things sacrificed to idols*' – in fact, '*all things sold in the market place*' (10:25) – and his '*for me all things are lawful*' allusions (10:23 repeating 6:12), but also his climactic final formulation of '*Communion with*' the body and blood of *Christ Jesus* (10:16).

The Gospels also emphasize this kind of Naziritism when they describe John the Baptist as '*coming neither eating nor drinking*' – this, as opposed to the more Paulinized description of '*the Son of Man*' or '*Jesus coming eating and drinking*' in Matthew 11:18–19 and Luke 7:33–34. Such ideologies are immediately reinforced by the portraits of 'Jesus' as '*a glutton*,' '*wine-bibber*,' and '*a friend of tax-collectors and Sinners*' that follow – this '*friend of tax-collectors and Sinners*' phraseology parodying ones like '*the Friend of the Emperor*' so common in Roman court usages and the portrait of Jesus '*eating and drinking with publicans and Sinners*' generally throughout the Gospels.[12]

As Paul develops this ideology and these esotericisms in his final enunciation of the true meaning of '*the Cup of the Lord*' and '*drinking*' it as '*the New Covenant in (the) Blood*' of Christ, he totally reverses the life-long or temporary Nazirite notion of '*not eating or drinking*' and rather aims at those *who would 'eat this bread and drink' this Cup 'unworthily'* (1 Corinthians 11:27). In a final crowning, and what might be construed as a cynical reversal of this ideology, such persons now become *'guilty of the body and blood of the Lord,'* a frightening accusation in any context, as the history of the Western World has demonstrated. Using this imagery, which we already have found present in the Habakkuk *Pesher*, such persons will now actually *'drink vengeance to themselves, not seeing through to the Blood of Christ'* (11:29), an equally terrifying imprecation.[13] As we shall see towards the end of this book, one understanding of this phraseology will be that such persons do not understand the word *'Damascus'* according to its proper or esoteric sense – such things, as he would have it in Galatians 4:24 (when speaking about *'casting out the slave woman'* and *'Agar which is Mount Sinai in Arabia'*) *'being allegory.'*[14]

By contrast, as we just remarked, in Rabbinic sources such 'temporary' or life-long Nazirite oaths shift and take on a wholly different, more nationalistic – even *'Zionistic'* – sense of *'not eating or drinking' until one should see the Temple rebuilt.*[15] For these sources and Karaism to follow, including later witnesses like the Eleventh-Century, Spanish-Jewish traveler Benjamin of Tudela, such oaths are a consequence of *mourning for the destruction of the Temple* and *waiting for it to be rebuilt* which, in turn, blossom into a full-blown Movement, *'the Mourners for Zion,'* the origins of which, though clouded in obscurity, have to be understood in terms of the events of this period.[16]

Such a period of *'waiting'* relating to the rebuilding of the Temple resembles nothing so much as the well-known one associated with *'the Disciple Jesus loved'* at the end of the Gospel of John or that *'delay'* in the Habakkuk *Pesher*, which goes in Christianity later by the name of *'the Delay of the Parousia,'* based in the *Pesher* on Habakkuk 2:3:

> *If it tarries, wait for it, for it will surely come and not delay* (introducing the even more famous *'the Righteous shall live by his Faith'* from Habakkuk 2:4 that follows).

The notion of such *'Mourners for Zion'* is highly underestimated in the history of this period and deserves a good deal more attention than it usually gets. There can be little doubt that one can still discern its influence, however metamorphosized, in the black garments worn by Jewish *'Hassidic'* groups to this day – to say nothing of *'Christian'* ones. It also paves the way for the development of Karaism in Judaism which, with the appearance of Dead Sea Scrolls material in Jerusalem at the beginning of the Ninth Century, reached what some might consider a final fruition.[17]

'Karaism' itself certainly grew out of movements such as these 'Mourners for Zion' forming part of its own ideology.[18] 'The Mourners for Zion' themselves had already been functioning in Palestine and places further East prior to the emergence of Karaism in the Seven Hundreds CE. In fact, such 'Mourners' were already influencing a series of 'Messianic' Uprisings in the East in areas being treated in this book, namely Kurdistan, Northern Iraq, and Persia, a happenstance that may not be coincidental.[19]

Nor is it too much of a stretch to put the Crusaders in a similar category as these 'Mourners' and undoubtedly a case can be made that these 'Mourners for Zion' had a tenuous, even if underground, influence on groups like 'the Templars' and, if real, possibly the now infamous inner coterie known to some as 'the Prioré de Sion,'[20] both of which preserving some semblance of their name. This may even extend to 'the Cathars' / 'the Pure' whose Priests, carrying on this theme of 'mourning,' however bizarre, actually wore black rather than the more typical white. In Jerusalem, unfortunately, all such Jewish groups were probably liquidated in the general blood-letting that occurred in 1099 after it fell at the end of the First Crusade – a possible consequence of their own success – though perhaps not before many of their ideas were communicated to groups such as the Templars (and 'the Prioré,' if it ever really existed – a doubtful proposition).

Notices such as 'life-long Naziritism' and 'Perfect Holiness' – 'Holiness from his mother's womb,' as all our descriptions of James put it – are also to be found in Gospel descriptions of John the Baptist and in the way Paul describes himself in Galatians 1:15–16 – seemingly in competition with James – as 'separated' or 'chosen' by God from his 'mother's womb' to 'reveal His Son in' him. They are also found in the Dead Sea Scrolls, particularly in the Hymns.[21]

We have just seen how the Gospels of Matthew and Luke insist that John 'came neither eating nor drinking,' seemingly implying that like James thereafter John too was a vegetarian.[22] As Luke also puts this earlier in the form of a prophecy, once again, by 'an Angel of the Lord':

> He shall be great before the Lord and never drink wine or strong drink and he shall be filled with the Holy Spirit even from his mother's womb. (1:15)

This clearly implies that, for Luke anyhow, John like James was 'a lifelong Nazirite,' a condition that apparently entailed for Matthew and Luke – as in early Church descriptions of the details of James' life – in addition to abstaining from wine and strong drink, abstention from meat.[22]

Extreme Nazirites may have insisted, in the manner of James, on going as far as vegetarianism as Judas Maccabee in a previous epoch seems to have done when, according to 2 Maccabees 5:27, he '*withdrew into the wilderness along with about nine other companions*' – '*the Ten Just Men*' of Jewish mystical lore, upon whose existence the continued existence of the universe was predicated[23] – '*Rechabite*'-style, '*eating nothing but wild plants to avoid contracting defilement.*' The situation 2 Maccabees is describing here at the beginning of Judas' Revolt against the Hellenizing Seleucids in Syria would appear to have been particularly applicable when 1) the Temple had been defiled; 2) was no longer functioning; or 3) the charge of '*pollution of the Temple*' or the corruption of its sacrifice practices was in the air or perceived as valid.

This charge in particular, as alluded to above, is fundamental to almost all Qumran documents, as it is in so-called '*Jewish Christian*' or '*Ebionite*' ones.[24] The rationale here would be that, *with the corruption* or '*pollution of the Temple*,' the permission to eat meat – which in biblical terms was dependent upon Noah's atoning sacrifice after the flood in Genesis 8:20–9:17 – was no longer viable or had been withdrawn. At Qumran too, as among '*Essene*' groups generally (not to mention those following John the Baptist, if they can be differentiated in any real way from the previous two), the practice of '*bathing*' was fundamental – in large part '*daily bathing.*'[25]

Extreme purity regulations, however, to the extent of abstaining from meat or wine, are not clearly articulated either at Qumran or in the various descriptions of '*Essenes*' that have come down to us.[26] In the Scrolls, the latter may have rested on the distinction between '*new wine*' and older more alcoholic kinds, since '*wine*' is generally referred to quite freely in them but not what kind of wine, a distinction that does not go unnoticed in Gospel commentary.[26] On the other hand, '*pure food*' – whatever might have been meant by this either in Qumran documents or among '*Essenes*' – was insisted upon for all full-fledged participants in such groups, meaning those in the higher stages of Community membership,[27] and this may have involved a certain amount of vegetarianism not very different from that reflected in these descriptions of James and implied in the ones about John.[28] Certainly Paul's remonstrations against precisely such kinds of persons, whom in Romans 14:1–15:2 and 1 Corinthians 8:7–15 he refers to in the most intemperate manner conceivable, basically calling vegetarians like James '*weak*' (certainly '*weak in Faith*' or '*having weak consciences*' – '*conscience*,' as we shall repeatedly see, being one of his favorite euphemisms for '*keeping the Law*'[32]), make one suspect that special dietary observance of this kind did include what others perceived of as vegetarianism.

'Nazirite' Bathing Groups in the East

'Nazirite' or *'bathing'* groups such as at Qumran or in Northern Syria are variously referred to by early Church fathers and others as *'Nazoraeans,'* *'Ebionites,'* *'Elchasaites,'* *'Sampsaeans,'* *'Masbuthaeans,'* *'Sabaeans,'* *'Naassenes,'* *'Jessaeans,'* and *'Essenes.'*[30]. In fact, whatever the term *'Essene'* might have meant, there is every likelihood that it was generically applied, at least by Palestinian and Egyptian commentators of the First Century (namely Josephus and Philo) and the Second-Century, Early Christian heresiologist Hippolytus, to all bathing groups of this kind. In other words, however one chooses to define the term – and there is even now no agreement on this definition[31] – *'bathing'* is an integral aspect of it – in particular *'daily bathing'* (*'Hemerobaptists'* in early Church sources; *'Masbuthaeans,'* *'Sobiai'* or *'Sabaeans'* in Syriac, Aramaic, and Arabic ones).

Writers from these times – *'heresiologists'* in some vocabularies, that is cataloguers of *'heresies'* (the designation is significant in illustrating their outlook) – were fond of multiplying these groups into an endless panoply of schisms and sects depending on whose writings they had seen, whether they understood the terminologies they were seeing or not, or were themselves able to pronounce or transliterate the terms in an accurate manner.[32] Though the term *'Essene'* may have been popular in Palestine or Egypt, in a different tradition, the very same group may have been known by a different appellative based on a somewhat different linguistic root or phraseology.

'Sabaeans,' for instance, a term that has come down to us through the Koran and Islamic usage, is probably the same as what goes in Aramaic and Syriac sources as either *'Masbuthaeans'* or *'Sobiai,'* that is, *'Bathers'* or *'Immersers.'* It is also probably interchangeable with what the Fifth-Century heresiologist Epiphanius, somewhat mysteriously, calls *'Sampsaeans,'* which he thinks, because of a homophonic root in Hebrew meaning *'sun,'* has something to do with their worship of the sun.[33] Perhaps he is right, as many of these groups do seem to have *prayed at dawn to greet the rising sun*, but the term probably has more to do with consonantal confusions as expressions were transliterated from one language to another.

Though many of these writers think they are eponymous designations referring to a person – as *'Christianity'* does *'the Christ'* – usually the founder; often they are conceptual describing some aspect of the tradition that seemed particularly significant to the commentator – as, for instance, *'the Elchasaites'* and their eponymous founder *'Elchasai.'*[34] Notwithstanding, almost all really are but an adumbration probably of the same basic ideological orientation regardless of chronology or place. Therefore in these catalogues, the same group may at times be called '*Essene*' or at other times, '*Ebionite*,' '*Elchasaite*,' '*Sampsaean*' (basically the same as '*Elchasaite*' anyhow), '*Jewish Christian*,' '*Sabaean*,' or some other such appellation. What all the foregoing, anyhow, would have in common is an emphasis on '*bathing*.'

According to most of these early Church heresiologists, these groups mostly inhabited the area around the Dead Sea, particularly the Eastern side of the Jordan in what was called '*Perea*' or the area around Damascus and north from it – referred to in the Damascus Document as '*the Land of Damascus*' and, even possibly, in Matthew 4:15 as '*Galilee of the Gentiles*' – on up to Northern Syria and beyond across the Euphrates to the Tigris (what more latterly is often referred to as '*the Fertile Crescent*'). '*Perea*,' it should be observed, was the area on the other side of the Jordan where John the Baptist, particularly important in most of these traditions, is pictured as originally operating. Not only is this an area in which there are extremely attractive warm water springs, in fact it is well known that John was even executed there at the Maccabean/Herodian Fortress of Machaeros.[33]

Recently, as already signaled, with renewed exploration of the Trans-Jordanian area, graves have been found with the same puzzling North-South orientation evidenced by the graves at Qumran as well as at other habitations further south along the Dead Sea.[34] One has yet to make sense of this orientation, but in the realm of '*bathing groups*' such as '*Essenes*,' '*Ebionites*,' '*Elchasaites*,' '*Masbuthaeans*,' and their successors further East. That, according to Muslim heresiologists, many of these *turned towards* '*the vault of Heaven*' or *the North* in their daily ministrations, is one way of making sense of this puzzling orientation.[35] In fact, it can be seen as comprising one proof that the Qumran '*Essenes*' basically followed the same pattern as these other Transjordanian or Northern Mesopotamian '*bathing*' groups even as early as the First and Second Centuries CE.

Matthew 4:15's '*Galilee of the Gentiles*' makes it clear it is based on Isaiah 8:23 – 9:1, where the '*Galil*' or '*Circle*' being referred to as '*seeing a great light*' ('*Galil*' meaning '*Circle*' in Hebrew) is quite explicitly designated as *being* '*beyond Jordan*.' In this sense, the term really means '*the Region*' or '*Circle of the Gentiles*' beyond the Jordan River – normally, as just remarked, referred to as '*the Fertile Crescent*' – not the '*Galilee*' in Northern Israel as the Gospels take it to be. These are the same areas in which one encounters a bewildering plethora of petty kings – '*the Kings of the Peoples*,' as already signaled, as Roman sources designate them ('*Ethnē*'/'*Peoples*' in Greek; '*Gentium*'/'*Gentiles*' in Latin – as evidenced for example by Paul's 'Gentile Mission' allusions).[38]

We have already seen that this expression, 'the Kings of the Peoples,' is also used in a key portion of the Damascus Document where 'the Kings' of the Ruling Establishment referred to are also alluded to as 'the Princes of Judah' and their offences, such as 'fornication,' 'incest,' 'pollution of the Temple,' and illegally amassing 'Riches,' are vividly delineated.[39] This also provides, as we saw too, a good dating tool if such were needed and a further indication that the Sitz-im-Leben (life setting) of documents making references such as this was Roman – in particular Imperial Roman – and not Seleucid or Hellenistic.[40] In fact, all such petty, Greek-speaking, tax-farming 'Kings' in the Eastern areas of the Empire should probably be included in this category as this was how they were referred to in Roman jurisprudence – 'the Peoples' (Ethnon/Gentium – "Am' or "Amim' in Hebrew) being the subject 'Peoples' in Asia Minor, Northern Syria and Mesopotamia, and even Palestine.

In this regard, the allusion to 'tax-farming' is particularly appropriate since this is an issue having singular resonance with Gospel portrayals of people involved in such activities, especially in the picture of those called 'publicans' or 'tax-collectors' interacting with or 'keeping table fellowship' with 'Jesus' or 'the Messiah.' It should be appreciated that a picture such as this also had political or theological implications as, of course, did the charged reference to 'prostitutes' usually accompanying it – the point being that one should not object to or disapprove of such persons, but rather conciliate them or accommodate them.

This issue of 'tax-farming' is also reflected, as already remarked, in a key portion of the Habakkuk Pesher expounding Habakkuk 1:14–15, 'taking up fish with a fish-hook and catching them in a net,' and has a significant relationship to Gospel portraiture. Here of course one has actual allusion to 'fish' and 'fish-hook's not to mention 'net's. It is in this context, too, that the tantalizing pseudonym 'the Kittim,' in exposition of Habakkuk 1:17's 'his eating is plenteous,' was delineated as:

> parceling out their yoke and their taxes (here the 'tax-farming' allusion) consuming all the Peoples year by year, giving many over to the sword ... and having no pity even on the babes in the womb –

a terrifying indictment resonating with (as we saw as well, but it bears repeating) Josephus's portrayal of what actually occurred in these times around the Sea of Galilee in 67 CE by contrast to more heart-warming and folksy Gospel portraiture.[41]

The Descendants of Queen Helen of Adiabene

The same Rulers can also sometimes be found referred to in Roman sources as '*Arabs*.'[42] Not only must the Herodian family in Palestine, which also gained footholds as model Roman bureaucrats in Lebanon, Syria, and Asia Minor in this period, be reckoned among such '*Arabs*'; but so should '*Kings*' like the First-Century Northern Syrian Monarch, Eusebius calls '*Agbarus*' or '*Abgarus*' – in variant manuscripts even '*Albarus*' or '*Augurus*' – '*the Great King of the Peoples beyond the Euphrates*.'[43] It is to Constantine's Bishop Eusebius, formerly Bishop of Caesarea in Palestine and responsible for some of the most far-reaching innovations concerning the '*Christianity*' ultimately adopted into the Roman Empire, that we owe this latter title – the use of the term '*Peoples*' in it being both revealing and giving it an aura of credibility.[44]

Terminologies such as '*Kings of the Peoples*' and '*Arab*' should also probably extend to families like the one Josephus, the *Talmud*, and Eusebius himself refer to as '*the Royal House of Adiabene*' on the borders of this '*Abgar*' or '*Agbar*'s Kingdom '*beyond the Euphrates*' – basically today's Kurdistan. Neighboring the Parthian or Persian Empire further East, it is an area which would include the now familiar cities of Mosul, Arbil, and Kirkuk.[45] Nor is it really clear whether these two dynasties, the Edessene and that of Adiabene, contiguous as they were – *n.b.*, the common use of the term '*'Ad*' or '*'Adi*'[46] – can be distinguished in any real way from one another. Some Armenian and Syriac sources suggest they cannot.[47] Whether they can or not, all had strong political and marital connections with each other.

Eusebius claims to have personally found and translated the account of Agbarus' conversion to what he considers to be '*Christianity*' from a document in the Royal Archive at Edessa. As we have described, for Strabo and Pliny this is originally '*Antioch Orrhoe*' (meaning '*Assyrian Antioch*') or '*Antioch-by-Callirhoe*' (a tributary of the Euphrates) as opposed to '*Antioch-on-the-Orontes*' further West (the former capital of the Seleucid Kingdom and the '*Antioch*' everyone thinks they are talking about when speaking of '*Antioch*') or '*Antioch in Pisidia*' in Asia Minor (Acts 13:14). Eusebius dates Agbarus' conversion to 29 CE, extremely early by any reckoning and about the same time, not incuriously, that Josephus provides the parallel story of the conversion of Queen Helen of Adiabene and her family (presumably including her husband).[48] The story is to be found at the beginning of the all-important Book Twenty of the *Antiquities*, climaxing with the account of the death of James in 62 CE and ending with an enumeration of all the High Priests in the Temple up to the time of its destruction.

The '*Ad*'/'*Ed*' in '*Adiabene*' and '*Edessa*,' as we just saw, links up with the eponymous teacher in these areas, variously referred to in Apocryphal, Syriac, and Arabic sources as ''*Ad*,' ''*Adi*,' '*Addai*,' and even '*Thaddaeus*,' not to mention another name having a certain phonetic equivalence to this last, '*Judas Thomas*.'[49] Some Armenian sources, based probably on earlier Syriac ones, actually consider Queen Helen both King Agbar's wife and half-sister.[50] All these monarchs had multiple wives and large numbers of concubines and sister and half-sister marriage was, seemingly, one of the characteristic practices of the area, just as it appears to have been in the biblical story of Abraham and Sarah – also pictured as originating in Northern Syria/Iraq.

In fact, if one takes the chapter headings in Eusebius' narrative seriously, whether late additions or otherwise, the implication is that '*Agbarus*' or '*Abgarus, the King of the Osrhoeans*' ('*the Assyrians*') and '*the Great King of the Peoples beyond the Euphrates*' ('*Adiabene*' being precisely one of those areas '*beyond the Euphrates*') and Helen, designated in such headings as '*the Queen of the Osrhoeans*,' are linked by marriage as well. In addition, Eusebius identifies Agbar as '*Abgar Uchama*' or '*Abgar the Black*' – in Syriac sources seemingly Abgar III who died around 45–50 CE.[51]

Even this designation, however recondite, has real bearing on the parallels – even, in fact, the parodies – of these 29–30 CE timeframe conversions in the peculiar stories Acts provides: the first of these, as already signaled, being Paul's conversion in Acts 9:9–20 *at Damascus* '*on a Street called the Straight*' – tellingly, '*neither eating or drinking*' – at '*the house of one Judas*' (the parallel in other sources would probably be either '*Judas Barsabas*,' '*Judas Thomas*,' or '*Judas the brother of James*'[52]). It is here Paul is pictured as meeting '*a certain Disciple by the name of Ananias*,' as we already saw as well, also prominent in Eusebius' story of the conversion of King Abgar as well as Josephus' description of the conversion of Queen Helen and her sons.[53]

The second of these stories is the one Acts 8:26–40 provides of the conversion of the '*Ethiopian Queen's eunuch*' *on the road to Gaza*. As I have already argued in my Preliminary remarks and in *James the Brother of Jesus*, there was no '*Ethiopian Queen*' at this time except in the annals of Strabo's *Geography* some seventy-five years before. There she is designated rather as the Nubian '*Queen of Meroe*' up the Nile in today's Sudan or Nubia. This is a notice, not only picked up by Pliny in his *Natural History* in the 70s of the Common Era, but undoubtedly also the source of Acts' somewhat misleading co-option of the appellative '*Kandakes*' to describe her.[54] Nor would or did such a '*Queen*' send her '*Treasury Agents*' some thousand miles north up to Jerusalem laden with coin, as Acts 8:27 would have it, and certainly not in approximately 25 BC.

Not only would such a trip have been impossible for anyone from Nubia carrying such '*treasure*' – to say nothing of '*Ethiopia*' – but there is no record that the principal court officials of such '*Queens*' (or for that matter '*Kings*') were '*eunuchs*,' there being no harems there to protect. This was rather a custom of states dominated culturally by and on the border of Persia, such as Helen's or her husband's where there actually were '*eunuchs*.' In fact, it was Queen Helen, probably part of a huge harem of her putative brother and greater '*King*' (the one, as we have seen, called in Eusebius, '*the Great King of the Peoples beyond the Euphrates*') who did, in fact, in this period send her 'treasury agents' to Jerusalem.

This is the picture, of course, one gets in Josephus, the *Talmud*, and Eusebius dependent upon them, all of whom make it clear that from thence (either Palestine or Jerusalem), she and her sons Izates and Monobazus – *both of whom circumcised themselves!*[55] – sent these agents down to Egypt and out to Cyprus to buy grain to relieve '*the Great Famine*' that, as Acts paraphrasing Josephus puts it, '*was then over the whole world*' (11:28 – the '*Great*' here seemingly being appropriated from Eusebius' Edessene Chancellery Office records above designating Abgarus as '*the Great King of the Peoples*'). It is because of these 'famine relief' efforts that in all these sources (including later Armenian ones) Helen and/or her sons win undying fame. It is also possible to conclude that it is for this reason Acts 8:26–27 refers to this '*Queen*'s agent as being '*on the road to Gaza*,' the traditional gateway to Egypt.[56]

Acts 11:27–30, of course, puts Paul among those who brought '*famine relief*' up from '*Antioch*' to Jerusalem. '*Philip*,' too, in 8:26 received his command to '*go down from Jerusalem to Gaza*' from a mysterious '*Angel*' of some kind – upon which way he then encounters this curious '*eunuch*' of '*the Ethiopian Queen*' – in response to a mysterious oracle by an unknown '*prophet*' pointedly named '*Agabus*' – an obvious garbling, as we shall argue below, of '*Agbarus*'/'*Abgarus*,' clearly indicating the source from which Acts lifted the narrative. For his part, as we shall see below as well, Paul never mentions such a visit in his version of these events in Galatians 1:17–20 and denies, on pain of an oath that he was '*not lying*,' that he had ever been to Jerusalem in the '*fourteen years*' since the visit when he saw '*none save Peter*' and '*James the brother of the Lord*' and his return – again '*as a result of a revelation*' (*apocalypsin*) – taking Barnabas and Titus with him, to lay before '*those considered something*' the gospel *as he proclaimed it* '*among the Peoples*' (2:1–2 – as usual, the pivotal reference to '*Peoples*' – Ethnesin).[57]

Acts 12:1–24 not only conspicuously fails to delineate this *'famine-relief'* mission *'to the brothers dwelling in Judea'* (*cf.*, CD, Columns 4–6 on *'going out from the Land of Judah to dwell in the Land of Damascus'*) except, curiously, to announce its conclusion in 12:25 and somewhat backhandedly allude, as well it might (though without any prior introduction), to James in 12:17; but it is doubled by another trip Paul and Barnabas make *'up to Jerusalem'* which Acts describes in some detail, starting in 15:1–2 when introducing the storied *'Jerusalem Council.'* Of course, if Paul and Barnabas did actually make such a trip, as Acts seems to think they did, with *'famine-relief funds'* from *'the Disciples'* in Antioch (where Christians *'were first called Christians'* – 11:26) up to the *'the Presbyterous'* (*'Elders'*) in Jerusalem; this would probably, in effect, put both him and Barnabas among the representatives of either Queen Helen, her husband, and/or her sons Izates and Monobazus, at the conversion of whom Josephus has already placed (*along, curiously, with an unnamed other*) a namesake of Paul's companion *'in Damascus,'* *'Ananias.'*[58]

It should also be appreciated that, first of all, the trip by Paul and Barnabas up *'to the Elders in Jerusalem'* described in Acts 15:2 is begun, not as in Acts 11:27 by *'Agabus'* *'coming down from Jerusalem to Antioch'* but by *'some coming down from Judea'* and *'teaching the brothers that unless you were circumcised according to the tradition of Moses, you could not be saved'* (15:1). Second of all, it is in fact rather the conversion of Helen's favorite son Izates – according to later Syriac sources, *'King Ezad'*[59] – and his brother Monobazus who, after reading the passage about *Abraham circumcising all his household* in Genesis 17:9–14, insist on being circumcised as opposed to Ananias and his unnamed companion's teaching.

This would also appear to be the butt, as we just saw, of Acts' somewhat disingenuous and even rather malicious description of its Queen's *'treasury agent'* as a *'eunuch,'* there being no indication of the practice, nor for that matter the harems connected with it, in *'Ethiopia'* at the time – such usages being generally a fixture of Persian cultural ambiances such as *'Adiabene'* and *'Edessa.'* Nor is this to mention the perceived relative *'blackness'* of these Northern Syrian, Mesopotamian *'Kings'* or *'Queens'* – possibly reflected in Agbarus' cognomen in Eusebius as *'Uchama'* – meaning *'Black'* – and the perception, in Roman texts, already noted above, of all of them anyhow as *'Arabs'*!

Elchasaite Bathing Groups across Jordan, and *'the Subbaᶜ'* of the Marshes

One of the groups which seems to have flourished in both Palestine, and across Jordan, and further East in these times were *'the Elchasaites.'*

Though the sources regarding them are unclear, they first come to the fore about 100 CE, and are considered to have taken their name from their leader, one '*Elchasai*.' Nevertheless, the precise meaning of this term, probably a title in any event, is debated. Some, preferring to consider its Aramaic root, define it as '*Hidden Power*'; others, '*the Righteous*' or '*Perfect One*.'[60] If the latter, then the connection in this period with James-type leaders or other '*Zaddikim*' ('*Righteous Ones*,' such as those leading the Community at Qumran) is patent.

One interesting etymology, noted by an early commentator, is a corruption of the Greek word '*Ecclesia*,' '*Assembly*' or '*Church*,' though this is probably far-fetched.[61] If it is not far-fetched then, according to this view, no such person '*Elchasai*' really ever existed as such in Palestine and we are simply back among the descendants or successors of the original '*Jerusalem Assembly*' or '*Church*' of James the Just or further terminological derivatives (or confusions) – '*Ecclesia*' literally meaning '*Assembly*' in Greek or what the Dead Sea Scrolls would refer to as '*the ͨEdah*.'[62]

If '*Elchasai*' is a title, then depending on the language one is using, it is not very different from the usage '*Righteous Teacher*' at Qumran or one of his ideological descendants. This is the problem with many such denotations. It is never really clear whether they come from Greek, Hebrew, Aramaic, Syriac, old Persian or Pahlevi, or later Arabic. Therefore names like either '*Bazeus*' or '*Monobazus*' – the most prominent name among Helen's relatives and descendants, the second no doubt of Persian derivation – could well have been equivalent to what goes in more Semitic renderings as '*Agbarus*' or '*Abgarus*.' This is also true, as we saw, for the confusions one encounters between Greek and Aramaic names such as '*Peter*' or '*Cephas*,' not to mention Greek and Latin ones like '*Silvanus*' or '*Silas*' and '*Timothy*' or '*Titus*.'

However this may be, the leader of these '*Elchasaites*' in Palestine – if they existed in any separate way and were not simply local variations of groups like '*the Essenes*' or '*Ebionites*' – would certainly have been a contemporary of James' '*cousin*' – as already suggested, possibly his putative '*brother*' – Simeon Bar Cleophas, who reigned over what was left of James' '*Jerusalem Assembly*' and, according to reports in early Church literature (themselves difficult to credit where chronology is concerned), survived into and was crucified under Trajan's reign![63]

Nor is this to say anything about another putative contemporary of this '*Elchasai*' and '*Simeon*,' '*Simeon bar Yohai*,' the eponymous founder of *Zohar* tradition.[64] Epiphanius together with Hippolytus, our main sources for this bewildering plethora of sectarian and bathing groups, relates '*the Elchasaites*' to both '*Nasaraeans*' (or '*Nazoraeans*') and '*Ebionites*'.[65] Nor does

Epiphanius distinguish to any extent between these last, that is, 'Nazo-raeans' and 'Ebionites' – whatever he intends by such designations. For him 'Elchasai' was originally an 'Ossaean' (clearly he means 'Essene' here) with followers on both sides of the Dead Sea and further north in Syria and Northern Iraq. These latter areas, in turn, are where the conversions of King Abgar/Agbar and Queen Helen's family occurred – whether to Christianity or Judaism, or something in between.[66]

These Elchasaites also seem to have spread down into Southern Iraq. In the Koran and later Arab sources they are referred to as 'Sabaeans,' a term itself – despite innumerable confusions even in Islamic sources – going back, as already suggested, to Greco-Aramaic and Syriac usages like 'Sobiai' and 'Masbuthaeans,' that is, 'Immersers' or 'Daily Bathers.' Again, this was the same area where Queen Helen's favorite son Izates was living at Charax Spasini (today's Basrah). Curiously this town, which was a trading center at the mouth of the Tigris, was another of those cities known as 'Antioch' – this time, 'Antiochia Charax,' the fourth we have so noted.

It is here this highly favored son of Queen Helen (strikingly, Josephus uses the term 'only begotten' that the Synoptic Gospels use to describe Jesus[67]) was living when he was converted in the Twenties of the Common Era to something Josephus presents as approximating 'Judaism.' In his version of this episode – introducing, as we saw, the all-important Book Twenty of his Antiquities – Izates was converted by the Jewish teacher, we mentioned above, named Ananias.[68] We say 'approxi-mating' here, because what Ananias and his unnamed companion taught (whom, given the circumstances and teaching involved, we take to be Paul) did not require circumcision – a strange sort of Judaism!

'Ananias,' whom Josephus refers to as 'a merchant,' also appears in par-allel texts like the one Eusebius claims he found in the Royal Archive of the Edessa describing 'Agbarus'' conversion to what Eusebius thinks is 'Christianity,' though the date is only 29–30 BC or thereabouts. It is not incurious, as already remarked (but one cannot remark curiosities such as this too often), that he also appears in Acts' presentation of the aftermath of Paul's conversion at a house of one 'Judas' on 'a street called the Straight' in Damascus.[69]

Just as in Scroll delineations of its 'New Covenant in the Land of Dam-ascus,' Acts also considers the conversion of the character it most cares about to have taken place 'on the road to (or 'in the Land of') Damascus,' which might have wider implications, as we shall eventually see, than the first-time reader might initially imagine.[70] One consequence of this cor-respondence is that the 'Covenant' in the first might simply be reversing *the other*, that is, unlike the more '*Paulinizing*' one in Acts, Qumran's '*New Covenant in the Land of Damascus*' – in which '*the Penitents of Israel who went out from the Land of Judah to dwell in the Land of Damascus*' (also called '*the Princes*' who go out with '*the Nobles of the People(s)*'[71]) '*to dig the well of living waters*' with their '*staves*' (in Hebrew, a homonym for '*laws*'/ '*hukkim*') – rather insisted on '*separating Holy from profane*' as well as '*setting up the Holy Things according to their precise specifications*.'[72]

Not only did Mani (216–277 CE), the founder of Manichaeism, reportedly come from an '*Elchasaite*' family living in the same general locale in Southern Iraq as Izates when he was converted – a place the sources refer to as '*Mesene*'[73]; '*the Mandaeans*,' who represent themselves as the followers of John the Baptist and are in all things absolutely indistinguishable from these same '*Elchasaites*,' inhabit Southern Iraq down to this very day.[74] They have been referred to in Arab texts for over a thousand years as '*Sabaeans*' – again, Arabic for '*Baptizers*' or '*Daily Immersers*' (not persons from Southern Arabia as normative Islam usually considers the term to mean) and, in popular parlance, used by Arabs then and still today, '*the Subbaᶜ of the Marshes*.' These Mandaeans also refer to their priest class as '*Nasuraiya*,' that is, '*Nazoraeans*' (compare this with the town of Naziriyya recently fought over by US forces in the war in Iraq), though it seems to have taken a Saddam Hussein to all but eradicate them by draining the marshes – attempts to reverse which are now seemingly underway.[75]

This is the area that in later times ultimately becomes a hotbed of Shiᶜite Islam as it clearly still is today. The key seems to have been '*the Primal Adam*' ideology associated, according to all commentators, with groups like '*the Ebionites*' and '*Elchasaites*.' It, in turn, was transformed into what became '*the Imam*' or '*Hidden Imam*' idea so integral to 'Shiᶜite' though not Sunni Islam.[76] The '*Hidden Imam*' idea is basically a variation of this '*Primal Adam*' or '*Standing One*' notation fundamental, according to the Pseudoclementines, Hippolytus, and Epiphanius, to groups like the Ebionites, Elchasaites, Jewish Christians, and, even before these, Simon *Magus*.[77]

The idea would also appear to be present in one form or another in Qumran documents and echoes of it are identifiable across the breadth of New Testament literature – though not perhaps to the uninitiated reader – in the never-ending allusions to '*standing*' one encounters in it.[78] Like '*the Elchasaites*' preceding them, the Manichaeans were precursors of Islam and, for the most part – in this part of the world anyhow, probably absorbed into it. Indeed, Muhammad has many doctrines in common with the traditions represented by both groups, in particular, the idea of '*the True Prophet*' or '*the Seal of the Prophets*' and the importance of Abraham in the salvationary scheme he is delineating.[79]

The Land of Noah and Abraham's Religion

The connection to Abraham of traditions relating to religious ideas arising in these areas should not be underestimated. It is important to realize that Edessa, the capital of Eusebius' '*Great King of the Peoples beyond the Euphrates*,' is basically the sister city of Haran some thirty miles south. Haran is well known in the Bible as Abraham's place of origin before he received the call to depart for the Land of Israel (Genesis 11:28–32), a fact its inhabitants are not slow to advertise to this day. Nor were they in ancient times as Abraham's fame grew more and more legendary. As already underscored, it was at Edessa that Eusebius claimed to have originally come upon the King Agbar conversion narrative he translated.

Not only do shrines and legends connecting Abraham with sites in this area persist to this day, Paul and Muhammad – whose respective salvationary schemes, while not always distinguishable from one another, pivot on the spiritual status of Abraham – both emphasize their common connection to '*the Faith*' or '*Religion of Abraham*.'[77] So does the ideologically opposite and, in this sense, parallel salvationary scheme set forth in the Letter of James and, if one looks carefully, one can detect the same ideological focus on Abraham across the breadth of the Qumran corpus, in particular in the Damascus Document, where one would expect to find it, but also in the '*Letter*' or '*Letters*' known as '*MMT,*' the source latterly of so much controversy in Dead Sea Scrolls Studies.[78]

Paul makes his allusion to Christianity being 'Abraham's Religion' in Galatians 3:6–4:31 and Romans 4:1–22 and 9:7–9, even going so far as to claim that Christians were *the true* '*Heirs to*' or '*Children of the Promise*' and '*were justified*' in the way '*Abraham was justified*' – his famous '*Justification by Faith*' polemic.[82] James, authentic or otherwise, against whom many of these positions appear to be directed, likewise evokes the salvationary state of Abraham (2:21–24, paraphrasing Genesis 15:6).

In James however, as is well known, Abraham '*is justified by works*,' his '*Faith*' rather '*Perfected*' or '*made Perfect*' – according to some translations '*completed*' – *by works*.' This then fulfills the biblical passage about Abraham's '*Belief*,' that he '*believed God and it was counted*' or '*reckoned to him as Righteousness*.' It is as a result of this that, according to James 2:22–23, '*he was called Friend of God*,' all terminologies well-known to the Dead Sea Scrolls.[83] This position, of course, is the opposite of that of the stated opponent of James – '*the Empty*' or '*Foolish Man*' (2:20) – that Abraham *was saved* '*by Faith only*' and thought by most to reflect the position that can be identified with Paul in Galatians 2:16–3:7 above.[84]

For his part, Muhammad varies this only slightly and includes even the emphasis on Abraham's willingness to sacrifice his son, fundamental both to James 2:21 and the Letter to the Hebrews 11:17 but at odds with them (according to orthodox Islamic doctrine) as to whether it was Isaac or Ishmael who was to be sacrificed as an example of Abraham's '*Faithfulness.*'[85] Nor is Muhammad very clear in the Koran about whether this was a demonstration of either Abraham's '*Faith,*' '*works,*' or both.

However this may be, claims such as these generally come in Koranic passages connected to '*ʿAd and Thamud,*' '*Hud and Salih,*' and '*the Land of Noah.*'[86] In such ideological contexts, these geographical allusions also seem to be evocative of Northern Syria/Iraq, Abraham having never really visited '*Arabia*' in the classical meaning of that term – Islamic claims to the contrary about his building the Kaʿabah in Mecca notwithstanding. Also, just as the Koran associates '*the Land of Noah*' with '*ʿAd and Thamud,*' '*Hud and Salih;*' according to both Josephus and Hippolytus, '*Adiabene*' was the land where Noah's ark landed.[87]

For Muhammad, just as in Paul's new 'Christianity,' Islam is '*Abraham's Religion*' (for Paul, strictly speaking, the term is '*Abraham's Faith*'). But as in the Dead Sea Scrolls and the Letter of James, Muhammad goes even further designating Abraham as '*the Friend of God*' – the epithet for him ever after in Islam to this day to the extent that '*al-Khalil*' ('*the Friend*') is used in place of Abraham's very name itself.[88] The only difference between Muhammad's arguments, as they develop in the Koran, and Paul's, however, is that for Paul, Abraham's '*Faith*' (using the language of Genesis 15:6) '*was reckoned to him as Righteousness*' *before the revelation of the Torah* or *the Law to Moses* and, therefore, *Abraham* – as he puts it so inimitably – *could not have been* '*justified by the Law.*' For Muhammad, following Paul's ploy, it was rather '*Abraham's Religion*' that *came before both Judaism and Christianity* or, as he so inimitably puts it in the Koran, as well, before either Judaism or Christianity *could corrupt* '*the Religion of Abraham*' *with their* '*lies*' (2:145–56). One should note that, in using this language of '*Lying,*' he demonstrates, once again, a certain linguistic commonality with all three: the Letter of James, the Dead Sea Scrolls, and with Paul.[89]

If these arguments were directed to the inhabitants of Northern Syria (as to some extent, in the writer's view, they are in the Dead Sea Scrolls as well), then the evocation of Abraham's salvationary status is perhaps neither accidental nor very surprising, particularly where those seeing themselves as inhabiting '*Abraham's homeland*' were concerned. As just pointed out, too, important documents in the Dead Sea Scrolls such as the Damascus Document and the one I named '*Two Letters on Works Righteousness*' ('*MMT*') follow the same basic approach.[90]

'*MMT*' actually uses the language of '*works reckoned as Righteousness*' (only really to be found elsewhere in the Letter of James) in *addressing the* '*King*' it compares to David, who would appear to be its respondent; and '*his People*,' that is, as we shall see, seemingly *a foreign* '*People*.'[91] By implication, this compares the salvationary state of this '*King*' with Abraham's salvationary state, providing further evidence that this '*King*' is probably a foreigner and linking him to the individual Eusebius is calling '*the Great King of the Peoples beyond the Euphrates*' and, even perhaps, Queen Helen's son '*Izates*' (as we saw, seemingly '*Ezad*' in Armenian/Syriac sources) – if the two, in fact, can be differentiated in any real way.[92]

In the same vein, Muhammad's subsequent ideological reliance on Abraham – prefigured, as it were, by Paul – is not so surprising either. Certainly Paul visited this area. But, in our view, so did Muhammad. Plainly he was heir to the traditions, however garbled, stemming from these lands as suggested by the striking references he provides to them in the Koran.[93] If Muhammad participated in the caravan trade, as the *Biographies of the Prophet* insist, then surely he visited the trading center Charax Spasini (modern Basrah) at the Southern end of the Tigris. It is here, in our view, he would have become familiar with the kinds of ideologies and new salvationary schemes we have been delineating above.

But he may also have gone even further North into Northern Iraq and Syria, which the stories he conserves about '*cAd and Thamud*' seem to suggest, since this is where '*cAdi*' ('*Addai*'/'*Thaddaeus*') and '*Thomas*' (probably '*Thamud*' in the Koran – in some versions of the traditions '*Judas Thomas*' or, even '*Judas Barsabas*'/'*Thaddaeus*'/or '*Jude the brother of James*') were so important.[94] To put this in another way, many of his stories about '*Arabian Prophets*' – in the Koran, '*Hud*,' '*Salih*,' and '*their Lands*' (which were seen as including '*cAd*' and '*Thamud*,' not to mention '*the Land of Noah*' often connected to these) – are all names linked in earlier sources, to legendary heroes of the Northern Mesopotamian region. These include, '*cAdi*' or '*Addai*,' '*Judas Thomas*,' '*Judas Barsabas*,' and '*Judas (the brother) of James*,' all corresponding to '*Hud*' in the Koran itself derived from the Hebrew '*Yehudah*'/'*Judah*.'[95] Not only was '*cAdi*'/ '*Addai*' the indigenous prophetical archetype for this region and, in some pagan pockets, as for instance '*the Yazidis*,' is still so today[96]; but '*Salih*,' who also figures prominently in these stories and translates out in Arabic as '*Righteous One*,' would in our view represent James, the name of whom also carries the same cognomen in all traditions.[97]

The identification in the Koran of some of these stories with both Noah and the land in which his ark came down only further strengthens these connections, because stories such as those about Helen's Kingdom of Adiabene or 'the Kingdom' her son Izates was said to have received from his father,[98] as just signaled, also evoke the association of Noah and his ark with these areas. Nor is the ark, whatever its mythology, generally thought to have come to rest in Arabia *per se*, so these Koranic stories, whatever their pretensions, really could not relate to 'Arabian Prophets' in the sense of 'the Arabian Peninsula'; though contrary to modern, more Fundamentalist belief, many of the traditions do connect the place where the Ark came to rest with Northern Iraq, that is, what we now familiarly call Kurdistan.[99]

Not only does Muhammad allude to Abraham's being 'the Friend of God,' this position is in fact fully developed – even perhaps for the first time – in the beginning exhortation in the Qumran Damascus Document where both Paul's 'Justification' theology and James' 'Royal Law according to the Scripture' are also evoked.[100] Just as in the *Surah* of the Cow, *Surah Two*, the principal *surah* of the Koran where the term 'Muslim' is ultimately defined as 'he who surrenders to God' and Abraham is designated as *the first 'Muslim'*; these early columns of the Damascus Document, as well as the letter attributed to James, are using the term 'Friend' exactly parallel to the way the Koran is using the expression 'Muslim.'[101]

Nor are such foci surprising in a text like the Damascus Document which, as its name implies, focuses on 'the New Covenant in the Land of Damascus,' in particular, the region 'north of Damascus' where for it, at some point, 'the fallen tent of David' was going to be re-erected.[102] As we shall see, Acts 15:16 puts the same words about 're-erecting the fallen tent of David' into James' mouth in its portrait of his speech at the Jerusalem Council above, another incontrovertible parallel between Acts' portrait of events it considers central to the development of the early Church and Qumran's picture of its own history.[103] The position of this book will be that, not only are all these allusions parallel, but they argue for a parallel chronological provenance for documents in which they are to be found. In addition, they are directed towards *conversion activities in areas where Abraham's name and his salvationary state were looked upon with more than a passing reverence.*

Not surprisingly, too, when James does send his messengers Silas and Judas Barsabas 'down from Jerusalem' to this region in Acts 15:22–35, it is to 'Antioch' they direct their steps – the only question being, as we have suggested, which 'Antioch' was intended. Was it the one assumed in normative Christian tradition and by all commentators (though never proven) '*Antioch-on-the-Orontes*,' where nothing of consequence appears to have been happening in this period, or the more historically signifi- cant Syriac '*Antioch-by-Callirhoe*' or '*Antiochia Orrhoe*,' also known as Edessa and all but indistinguishable from Abraham's city Haran, where all these incredible conversions were going on and Abraham's name was held in such regard? As far as I can see, the answer should be obvious – the second.

Izates' Conversion and Circumcision

The connection of so many of these traditions and ideologies with Abraham is not simply fanciful as the theme, whether in the Koran, earlier Christian writings, Josephus, the *Talmud*, and even in the Dead Sea Scrolls, is too persistent to be ignored. Not only do the people of Urfa connect the spring at Callirhoe (from which '*Antiochia-by-Callirhoe*' or '*Edessa Orrhoe*' derives its name) to Abraham to this day, but he was said to have been born in one of the caves in its environs as well.[104] Like the legends connected to both the births of John the Baptist and Jesus in Luke's '*Infancy Narrative*' and the Protevangelium of James, Abraham too, according to these 'apocryphal' traditions, was said to have *been 'hidden' by his mother* there.[105]

For Josephus, this is the Kingdom near Haran which was originally given to Helen's favorite son Izates by his father (whom Josephus calls '*Bazeus*' – whatever or whomever is intended by this).[106] Josephus calls this area, which '*Bazeus*' (evidently defective) gave Izates, '*Carrae*,' thus tightening even further the connection between Eusebius' '*Great King of the Peoples beyond the Euphrates*' and the Royal House of Adiabene. If this was '*Carrhae*' just south of Edessa – namely, the place of Abraham's origin '*Haran*' – then, of course, we are once again in the framework of Abraham's homeland and heritage – *all the more reason why Izates should take Abraham for his role model.*

The etymological development from Haran to present day Urfa, the name by which Edessa goes in Turkey to this day, is also not completely irrelevant, going from Haran to Hirru to Orhai to Orrhoe to Osrhoe – the Kingdom over which '*Agbarus*' reigned according to Eusebius – and finally to '*Ruha*' in Arabic, from which the present day Turkish '*Urfa*' is derived.[107] Of course, one could arrive at '*Ruha*' from a simple inversion of the original 'Haran' as well.

In the story of Izates' conversion, the portrayal of Abraham as the role model for Izates' ultimate decision to have himself circumcised, as opposed to Paul's position on this issue and the position of Izates' original teacher 'Ananias,' is pivotal as well. As we saw, *'Ananias'* is also a principal player in Acts' picture of parallel events – *'Damascus'* there, corresponding to the picture in the Scrolls, taking the place of wherever it was in Northern Syria or Iraq that Helen's family was living at the time of her conversion. The story, as already remarked, is also to be found in the *Talmud's* presentation of these events and, in my view, by refraction in the New Testament's picture, as we saw, of *the conversion of 'the Ethiopian Queen's eunuch' as well.*[108]

In the *Talmud* and Josephus, which both focus on the same event, Izates is reading the passage about *Abraham circumcising his whole household* – in Genesis 17:12 supposed to include even the *'stranger dwelling among them'* (conversely and significant, ideologically speaking, in Acts 8:32–33 *'the Ethiopian Queen's eunuch'* is reading *'the Suffering Servant'* passage from Isaiah 53:7–8) when the more *'Zealot'* teacher *from Galilee,* whom Josephus is referring to as *'Eleazar'* (*'Lazarus'?* – in the parallel represented by Acts 8:30 this character becomes *'Philip'*), convinces Izates and Monobazus his brother that they should circumcise themselves too. Whereupon, they immediately do so.[109]

Basically, the issue parallels the thrust of the Letter of James (2:10 – echoed as well both by the Gospel 'Jesus' and the Dead Sea Scrolls[110]), that *he who 'keeps the whole of the Law yet stumbles on one small point is guilty of (breaking) it all.'*[111] It is at this point that James 2:21–22 goes on to evoke Abraham's willingness to *sacrifice his son Isaac* to stress the point that *Abraham was 'saved by works and Faith working together'* as opposed, presumably, to his unidentified interlocutor's insistence that *Abraham 'was saved by Faith' alone.*

For his part, *'the Ethiopian Queen's eunuch'* – *'on his chariot'* – who is reading *'the Suffering Servant'* passage from Isaiah in Acts when a teacher named *'Philip'* calls him to be baptized, immediately orders his chariot to stop, whereupon both Philip and the eunuch went down into the water, and Philip baptized him. In our view, what we essentially have here is a 'Gentile Christian' parody of Izates' conversion replete with a sarcastic characterization of circumcision as castration which would have had particular meaning for Roman audiences especially after Nerva's time (96–98 CE), and all the more so, after Hadrian's (117–138 CE).[112]

Par contra, using Abraham as their prototype, both Josephus and the *Talmud* emphasize the *'circumcision'* aspect of the conversion process despite the fact that at least Josephus portrays Queen Helen, the mother of Izates and Monobazus, as *'having horror of circumcision'* because it would put her in ill repute with her people. Despite her conversion, allegedly to Judaism, '*circumcision*' as such was evidently not part of the religion she was taught by Ananias and his unnamed companion above.[113] Consequently, not only is this the pivotal point in the controversy between '*Ananias*' and '*Eleazar*' over Izates' conversion above, but it is also the background against which Paul develops his whole polemic in Galatians, in particular, the dispute at 'Antioch' in Galatians 2:7–12 where Paul calls the '*some from James*,' of whom Peter '*was afraid*' and, after whose coming, '*separated himself and withdrew*' from '*eating with the Gentiles*' (Ethnon), '*of the Circumcision*' or '*the Party of the Circumcision*.'[114]

Therefore, just as the '*Philip*'/'*Ethiopian Queen's eunuch*' conversion episode is a Gentile Christian parody of the Izates/Monobazus one – replete, as we just explained, with *derisive caricature of circumcision as castration*; this whole tangle of data is echoed in Acts 15:1–3's seemingly parallel portrayal of basically the same situation in its run-up to the so-called 'Jerusalem Council,' when these ubiquitous '*some*' – already referred to several times earlier in Acts (these same '*some*' even appear in the Gospels[113]) – '*come down from Judea*' to Antioch and '*teach the brothers that unless you were circumcised, you could not be saved*.'

Nor is it inconsequential that Abraham's paradigmatic support for circumcision is also cited by the Damascus Document at Qumran.[115] This occurs in the Damascus Document after evoking Deuteronomy 23:24 and 27:26, emphasizing the necessity of '*keeping the Commandments of the Torah*' and '*not to depart from the Law*' even at '*the price of death*'[116] and is put as follows:

> *And on the day upon which the man swears upon his soul* (or '*on pain of death*') *to return to the Torah of Moses, the Angel of Mastema* (meaning here '*Divine Vengeance*' – in other vocabularies '*Satan*')[115] *will turn aside from pursuing him provided that he fulfills his word. It is for this reason Abraham circumcised himself on the very day of his being informed* (of these things).[118]

Just as in the case with Izates' and Monobazus' conversion, the reference is to Genesis 17:9–27 and Abraham's obligation therein set forth, to '*circumcise the flesh of his foreskin*' and that of all those in his household – this last being an important addendum – which, the biblical passage adds, *he accomplished* '*on that very day*' although he was ninety-nine years old.

But, of course, not only is this exactly what Column Sixteen of the Damascus Document above specifies; it is exactly what Izates and Monobazus do when the more 'zealous' teacher '*Eleazar from Galilee*' points this out in the text they are reading. Just as in Acts 8:38's depiction of the '*Ethiopian Queen's eunuch*' immediately jumping down from '*his chariot*,' the emphasis is on the instantaneousness of the response. In passing, it should also be appreciated that in Islam – a religious tradition requiring, just like the '*some from James*,' circumcision – thirteen is the age, as in Ishmael's circumcision by Abraham in Genesis 17:27 above, by which time boys are circumcised to this day.

Not only does the Damascus Document – like the Letter of James and the Koran following it – designate Abraham as '*a Friend of God*,' it does so in the same breath that it describes Abraham as '*a Keeper of the Commandments of God*.' This last is also, as we shall see, basically the esoteric definition of '*the Sons of Zadok*' (possibly too '*the Sons of Righteousness*' or '*of the Righteous One*') in the Community Rule at Qumran.[119] In fact, in the Koran, as we saw, just as in James 2:21–23, the parallel is to the new terminology in Arabic '*Muslim*' or '*one who has surrendered*' to God's will. Of course, *being 'a Keeper not a Breaker'* is repeatedly emphasized throughout the Dead Sea Scrolls and is a fundamental ideology of James 2:8–12 as well, particularly in the background to its statement of both '*the Royal Law according to the Scripture*' to '*love your neighbor as yourself*' and '*keeping the whole Law, but stumbling on one small point*' bringing upon one the '*guilt of (breaking) it all*.'

To bring us full circle: one could conclude, therefore, that *being 'a Keeper*,' '*a Friend of God*,' and even '*a Muslim*' are basically all parallel denotations and that, in all contexts, Abraham is so designated because he *responds positively to God's 'testing' and is prepared to carry out God's Commandments.* In James 2:21 and in Hebrews 11:17, in particular, this '*surrendering to God's will*,' as it is put in the Koran, is deemed a kind of '*test*.' It is also worth remarking and certainly not insignificant that in Hebrews the term '*only begotten*' is applied to Isaac just as in Josephus it is to '*Izates*' and in the Synoptic Gospels to 'Jesus.'[120]

4

Peter as a '*Daily Bather*' and '*the Secret Adam*' Tradition

Sabaeans, Masbuthaeans, and '*the Subba^c of the Marshes*'

To go back to '*Elchasai*,' Hippolytus tells us that he was supposed to have '*preached unto men a new remission of sins in the second year of Hadrian's reign*' (119 CE). In addition he calls him '*a certain Just Man*,' meaning '*Elchasai*' too was '*a Righteous One*' – again, the manner of how all early Church sources refer to James and the Dead Sea Scrolls refer to '*the Teacher of Righteousness*'/'*Righteous Teacher*.'[1] Hippolytus reports as well that Elchasai insisted (like the '*some from James*' above) that '*believers ought to be circumcised and live according to the Law*.'[2]

Of course, '*circumcision*' is a practice insisted on in Islam to this day but, even more importantly, in Arabic '*Elchasai*' can also mean '*Hidden*.' We have already touched upon how the '*Hidden*' terminology can relate to stories about the birth of John the Baptist and Jesus in the Infancy Narrative of Luke and the Protevangelium of James, to say nothing about Edessan stories about Abraham. Nor is this to mention the whole tradition of '*the Hidden Imam*' in Shi^cite Islam, which we shall discuss further below. In Jewish mystical traditions as incorporated in the *Zohar*, a parallel allusion occurs in the description of how Noah '*was hidden in the ark*' to escape '*the Enemy*' who wanted to kill him.[3] Though an odd story, to say the least, to be found in an allegedly 'medieval' document like the *Zohar*, it does bring us back, however circuitously, to how the ark was related by Hippolytus and Josephus to Queen Helen's and Izates' homeland and, not surprisingly, in the Koran to the story of the destruction of the Tribe of '^cAd' and the messenger sent to it, Hud (that is '*Judas*' – in Hebrew, '*Yehudah*'; in Arabic, '*Yehud*').[4]

In Arabic too, the root of '*Subba^c*,' a term related to those Hippolytus calls '*Sobiai*' whom he identifies with '*the Elchasaites*,'[5] is '*to plunge*' or '*immerse*,' which is the same for Aramaic and Syriac. In fact, John the Baptist is actually known in Arabic as – and this not just by Mandaeans who take him as their paradigmatic teacher – '*as-Sabi^c*,' meaning '*the Baptizer*' or '*Immerser*.'[6] This leads directly into the issue of what can be

90

understood by those called 'Sabaeans' in the Koran,[7] who must be seen as basically the same group as 'the Subbaᶜ' or Hippolytus' 'Sobiai' (and, as we shall see, Epiphanius' 'Masbuthaeans') despite slight variations in spelling and later Islamic ideological attempts to obscure it.

The reason for this was not really malice, but rather simply historical misunderstanding or shortsightedness, Muslims having forgotten what the term originally meant and deciding, therefore – despite the disparity in roots – that it related to an earlier cultural group in Southern Arabia with a phonetically similar (though not identical) name.[8] In time, the term was used (perhaps with more accuracy) to designate a more Gnosticizing group in Northern Iraq, allegedly composed of 'Star-Gazers.'[9] The reason all this is so important is that in the final analysis, the whole ideology relating to it became the basis of the Islamic notion of 'the People of the Book' or 'Protected Persons.'[10]

Nevertheless, as Muhammad uses the term in the Koran – often within the context of discussions about Abraham[11] – he does so to designate a group intermediate between Jews and Christians, about whom he appears to have personal knowledge. All three he describes as 'believing in Allah and the Last Day and doing good works' (2:62). The perspicacious reader will immediately recognize these as the exact parameters of the debate between Paul and James, particularly as set forth in the Letter of James with its insistence on 'Faith (in Koranic terms that is, 'Belief') and works working together,' while at the same time citing Abraham's willingness to sacrifice Isaac.[12] One should also remark the accent on 'doing' and 'works' in all such contexts, emphases strong throughout the Dead Sea Scrolls and all ideologies associated with James though not Paul.[13]

Muhammad uses almost the precise words, in another extremely telling passage to describe one particular community among those he labels 'Peoples of the Book,' with whom he seems particularly familiar and of whom, unusually fond. The people of this community, as he puts it, 'recite the revelations of Allah in the night season' – which is certainly paralleled by those Josephus is calling 'Essenes' and in the literature found at Qumran[14] – and:

> believe in Allah and the Last Day and enjoin Right conduct and forbid indecency ('fornication' at Qumran, a category prohibited both in the 'Three Nets of Belial' section of the Damascus Document and James' directives to overseas communities as reported by Acts), and vie with each other in good works, for they are of the Righteous ('Salihin').[15]

'Salihin' in Arabic is the same root as and the plural of that 'Salih,' who

with '*Hud*' (a contraction of Yehudah – Judas as we have seen), is a messenger to '*ᶜAd*' (Addai/Adiabene) and a '*brother*' to the Tribe Muhammad
calls '*Thamud*' – a corruption, in our view, of '*Thomas*' or, if one prefers,
'*Judas Thomas*,' the same '*Judas Thomas who taught the truth to the Edessenes*'
in early Christian literature previously.[16]

Essenes, Ebionites, and Peter as '*a Daily Bather*'

Epiphanius refers to '*Essenes*' not only as '*Ossaeans*,' but also '*Esseneans*' or
'*Jessaeans*' – the last, he claims, after David's father and Jesus' forbear '*Jesse*'
or, for that matter, '*Jesus*" very name itself.[17] However, he also seems to
appreciate that '*Essene*' can derive from the Hebrew root, '*to do*,' that is,
'*Doers*' (Hebrew, '*ᶜOsim*') or '*the Doers*'/'*Doers of the Torah*' we shall meet
in due course in the Dead Sea Scrolls and the thrust of the language of
'*doing*' or '*works*' in all doctrines associated with James or ascribed to him.
The Letter of James also actually uses '*Doers*,' meaning '*to do the Law*,'
three different times.[18] In another important overlap, the same usage
appears in the all-important Habakkuk *Pesher*, which we shall analyze in
more detail, crucially surrounding the exposition of '*the Righteous shall
live by his Faith*' so dear to Pauline exposition.[19]

Whatever one might think of the validity of Epiphanius' derivations
and though his '*Essenes*' are hardly distinguishable from those he is also
calling '*Ebionites*'; as he sees it, before Christians were called '*Christians*'
in Antioch in Acts – that is, around the time of Paul's and Helen's Famine
relief efforts in the mid-Forties – in Palestine they were known as
'*Essenes*' and, after that, '*Nazoraeans*.'[20] From our perspective, this is about
right with the reservation that Epiphanius and other early Christian
writers have little or no idea what these denotations actually
signified.

In fact, for the group called '*Galileans*' among '*the Seven Sects of the Circumcision*' comprising Judaism of this period according to Hegesippus (c.
150 CE) as conserved in Eusebius (c. 320 CE) – including '*Pharisees*,' '*Sadducees*,' '*Essenes*,' '*Samaritans*,' '*Baptists*,' etc. – Epiphanius substitutes the
term '*Nazoraeans*.'[21] In doing so, he provides testimony, however indirect, that the group, most instinctively refer to as '*Zealots*' – otherwise
missing from both Epiphanius' and Hegesippus' enumerations and often
called '*Sicarii*' both by their opponents or detractors and hardly distinguishable from Eusebius' '*Galileans*'[22] – were from their perspective all
but indistinguishable from '*Nazoraeans*,' the same group most consider
coextensive with '*Christians*.' Once again, this brings home the point that
the literature concerning these matters in this period is, depending on

the perspective of the writer, filled with and confused by many names for the same basic movement.

Though these '*sects*,' as Eusebius and Epiphanius like to call them, also include another group both refer to as '*Hemerobaptists*' or '*Daily Bathers*,' Eusebius – again dependent on Hegesippus – in effect, repeats himself by including in the same list yet another group he calls '*Masbuthaeans*.' Once again, this terminology represents a Greek attempt to transliterate groups like Hippolytus' '*Sobiai*' and the Aramaic/Syriac term for '*wash*'/'*immersed*,' that is, '*Baptizers*.' This not only moves into the Arabic '*Subba^c*' as we saw, and is basically the same root of Hippolytus' '*Sobiai*' above, but also the same Arabic/Islamic '*Sabaeans*,' some incarnations of whom seem certainly to have been based in the neighborhood of Abraham's Haran in Northern Syria.

Epiphanius for his part multiplies these basically parallel or synonymous groups by introducing others in the course of his narrative like '*the Sampsaeans*,' yet another attempt to approximate the Arabic/Syriac '*Sabaeans*' in Greek. In this context, one should appreciate the epigraphical mix-ups between '*P*' and '*B*' in Arabic (there being no '*P*' as such in Arabic) and juxtapositions of letters that occur when names move from one language to another, as for example '*Abgarus*' to '*Agbarus*' from Semitic to Western languages. Once more we have come full circle, because Epiphanius not only locates these '*Sampsaeans*' around the Dead Sea and further east across the Jordan and in Northern Iraq, but proceeds to observe that they are not to be distinguished from '*the Elchasaites*,' which should have been obvious in the first place.[23]

What Epiphanius, who actually was someone of Jewish Christian or '*Ebionite*' background from Palestine – though he later removed to mainland Greece – has apparently done is confuse the terms '*Sabaeans*,' '*Sobiai*,' or '*Masbuthaeans*' reflecting more Semitic usage, with the linguistic approximation in Greek '*Sampsaean*.' Nor does he, yet again, distinguish their doctrines to any extent from the '*Nasarenes*' or '*Nazoraeans*,' whom he definitely identifies as doctrinally following James, and chronologically, following '*the Ebionites*' whom we know followed James.[24]

Since all such '*Essene*' or '*Sabaean*'-type groups were '*Daily Bathers*' of one kind or another, despite confusing early Church testimony that might gainsay this, it would appear that James was one as well.[25] This is also the way Peter is portrayed both in the Pseudoclementines and by Epiphanius, the one probably dependent on the other.[26] So was James' contemporary, the teacher Josephus cryptically denotes as '*Banus*,' the transliteration of whose name has not yet been solved (though via the

Latin, it probably points to his 'bathing' activities), and with whom Josephus seems to have spent a quasi-'Essene' style novitiate 'in the wilder-ness' – the reason probably he knows so much about 'Essenes.'[27] Nor is it without relevance, when considering these things, that in the Pseudo-clementines as well, *Peter is also portrayed as a definitive 'Jamesian.'*[28]

For the '*Subba^c*' of Southern Iraq, obviously so designated because of their bathing practices, just as with so-called '*Essenes*,' these rituals included daily ablution and purification in addition to a more all-encompassing immersion. This immersion was known to them even then as '*Masbuta*' – from which clearly Eusebius via Hegesippus gets his '*Masbuthaeans*' – and it included both the notion of washing away of sins and even a '*laying on of hands*,' the Priest interestingly enough laying one hand on his own head,[29] all notions except the last known to Christianity.[30]

Actually, Epiphanius includes the note about Peter being a '*Daily Bather*' in the context of his discussion of those he is calling '*Ebionites*' – an honoured term of self-designation in widespread use at Qumran.[31] Not only does he think that the terminology '*Ebionites*,' like that of the '*Elchasaites*' above, relates to a teacher called '*Ebion*' – meaning that, as he sees it, '*Ebion*' is a person not a concept; he also seems to think that, as the '*Elchasaite*' teacher in Hippolytus above, this '*Ebion*' went to Rome.[32] It is at this point he observes:

> *They say that Peter was a Daily Bather even before he partook of the bread.*[33]

That is, Peter is a complete '*Essene*.'

Epiphanius combats this description in the most vituperative manner imaginable, insisting that it was *because* '*the Ebionites*' were so '*lewd and filthy that they bathed so often*'![34] His approach is reminiscent of how Eusebius characterizes '*the Ebionites*.' Coming from Caesarea in Palestine, Eusebius like Epiphanius also knew Hebrew. In an ideological reversal that should by this time be all too familiar, he characterizes these same '*Ebionites*' in a manner as vituperative and dissimulating as Epiphanius following him and other 'Church Fathers' such as *Irenaeus* and Origen preceding him.[35] This he does by insisting in a derisive play on the Hebrew meaning of their name that they were called '*the Poor*' because of '*their mean and poverty-stricken notions about the Christ*,' meaning that what today we would call *their 'Christology*' was '*poverty-stricken*'! – an exposition even the beginning reader will recognize as both dissimulating and malevolent.[36]

However, by contemptuously and sarcastically depicting Ebionites as *seeing 'Christ' as merely a man, generated by natural not supernatural means, advanced above other men in the practice of Righteousness or virtue, and only 'a prophet,'* Eusebius inadvertently gives us insight into their actual doctrines. Where the matter of '*a Prophet*' is concerned, one will be able to immediately discern the outlines of the '*True Prophet*' ideology of the Ebionites, which is such a set-piece of the Pseudoclementine literature and reflections of which are also discernible in the Dead Sea Scrolls, in particular, the Community Rule, proceeding down through Elchasaism, Manichaeism, and ultimately into Islam.[37]

This is the same spirit of malicious invective with which Epiphanius a century later ridicules the '*daily bathing*' of these same Ebionites (not to mention, by implication, *similar activity on the part of Peter*). However, unlike Eusebius, rather than the extreme '*poverty*' of their Christological notions, he focuses on their practice of '*daily bathing*' *of this type, while following an extreme purity regime and avoiding fornication.*[38] Nevertheless the reader should note how both writers intemperately appeal to popular prejudice to undermine and obscure the true sense of these appellations and the practices underlying them.

For the writer, the aspects of their conduct Epiphanius records, for the most part probably drawing on the Pseudoclementines, are rather *the true parameters of Peter's existence* – these, as opposed to childish episodes incorporating ideological reversal as, for instance, the descent of '*the table cloth*' from Heaven '*by its four corners*' in Acts 10:11, in which Peter learns *not to make distinctions between Holy and profane and to call no food unclean* (10:12–16 repeated in 11:8), the very opposite of communities such as at Qumran and groups like those following James like '*the Ebionites.*'

Not only is this kind of approach in Acts similar in genre to Eusebius and Epiphanius, in some cases in Acts these reversals are even more blatant. For instance, as we saw in Chapter Two, in some five–six different episodes in almost a drumbeat fashion, Peter is presented as a mouthpiece for anti-Semitic invective, in particular, the '*Blood libel*' *accusation of having killed Christ.*[39] In truth, this seems to be about the only real ideological point the author of Acts seems even to know about '*Peter*,' so often is it repeated in his speeches and notwithstanding its marked contrast with the kinder, less strident and more noble picture of Peter one finds in the Pseudoclementines.[40]

Aside perhaps from the material in Galatians, which relates Peter to these same areas of Northern Syria where groups such as the Ebionites, Elchasaites, and Masbuthaeans appear to have been prevalent at this time (as to some extent they still are today), materials delineating Peter's pious '*Essene*'-like behaviour – for instance, that he wore 'threadbare clothes' and, as among 'Essenes' and at Qumran, he prayed every morning at dawn and bathed every day (this '*before partaking of bread*' as Epiphanius conserves it above) – are perhaps the only properly historical materials about Peter we have.[41] As an aside, it should perhaps also not go unremarked that, like Epiphanius' mysterious teacher '*Ebion*' and Hippolytus' '*Elchasaite*' teacher he thinks is called '*Sobiai*,' Peter too reportedly ended up going to Rome. Whether accurate in Peter's case – for which Acts provides no verification – it would certainly appear to be accurate in the case of Hippolytus' '*Elchasaite*' teacher named '*Sobiai*' above.

One of the reasons for the kind of daily '*purification*' activity Epiphanius so derogatorily dismisses, known not only to the Pseudo-clementines but also so characteristic of the '*sectaries*' at Qumran – at least among those extreme '*Essenes*' Hippolytus insists on also calling either '*Zealot*' or '*Sicarii*'[42] – is that even casual contact with Gentiles was thought to be polluting in some manner. This, of course, immediately gives rise to issues like the '*table fellowship*' one above between the '*some from James*' who '*came down to Antioch*' and Paul in Galatians 2:11–14. In the 'Heavenly tablecloth' episode, just cited above too, even Peter is pictured as citing this excuse in Acts 10:14 when he is at the point of learning he '*should not call any man unclean nor any thing profane*' and *could eat forbidden foods.*

Notwithstanding, it is just the opposition to allowing persons, who either *were not circumcised and did not keep the Law*, to discuss matters relating to it that were the key issues for those extreme '*Essenes*' whom Hippolytus insists were called either '*Zealots*' or '*Sicarii*,' a picture in some ways more accurate and more incisive than the received Josephus.[43] In fact, Hippolytus' picture of '*Essenes*,' which agrees with Josephus on all important points, seems to be based on an alternate version of Josephus' works, perhaps the earlier one he claims to have written in Aramaic for his co-religionists in a more Persian cultural framework.[44]

Not only did normative '*Essenes*,' according to the received portrait in Josephus, refuse to eat on pain of death and whatever the torture they were subjected to, '*forbidden things*'; as Hippolytus refines this picture, what those he refers to as '*Zealot*' or '*Sicarii*' Essenes refused to eat were the Jamesian category of '*things sacrificed to idols*' (Acts 15:29 and 21:25). No wonder Epiphanius is so enraged at the picture of Peter he finds in allegedly '*Ebionite*' literature – but more about these things later. To repeat – his materials bring us back to the location of these groups in Northern Syria and Southern Iraq, the two areas Josephus focuses upon in his story of the conversion of Queen Helen, her two sons Monobazus and Izates, and possibly also her husband '*Bazeus*' – if his identity could be precisified in any final way.

Sabaeans and Manichaeans and the Ban on '*Things Sacrificed to Idols*' and '*Carrion*'

Arabic sources pick the story up from here. Now using the terminology '*Sabaean*,' the Arab chronologer and historian al-Biruni (c. 850) contends that the remnants of '*the Sabaeans*' in the area around Haran in Northern Syria – obviously still there in his own time – were:

> the remnant of Jewish tribes remaining in Babylon when the other tribes left it for Jerusalem in the days of Cyrus and Artaxerxes.[45]

It should be remarked that even the Eleventh-Century Jewish traveler Benjamin of Tudela encounters an '*Elchasaite*' Synagogue in Mosul (the former area of '*Adiabene*') that he still reckons as one of *the three groups of 'Jews*' he observes living there.[46] On the other hand, for Epiphanius, these '*Daily Bathers*' he is calling either '*Elchasaite*' or '*Sampsaeans*' are neither '*Jews, Christians, or Greeks*' but something else.[47]

For al-Biruni they, like the Manichaeans descending from them, *prayed towards the North*, which they considered as already remarked, as '*the middle of the dome of Heaven and its highest place.*'[48] This notice, as we saw, is extremely interesting in view of the fact that at Qumran (which a majority of scholars has always referred to as '*Essene*' – whatever might be meant by this), the 1200 or so graves found there are almost all aligned on a North-South axis, as are those in settlements further south along the Dead Sea and now others across Jordan – clearly, therefore, related to Qumran.[49] Since the normal orientation of Jewish graves was towards Jerusalem and Muslim graves towards Mecca, this presented something of a puzzle to a majority of observers.[50] If these graves are rather those of '*Sabaean*'-like bathing groups, among whom we should group those known as '*Essenes*' and their '*Elchasaite*'/'*Ebionite*' successors, perhaps, as already suggested, they need remain puzzled no longer.

According to al-Biruni, again exhibiting the emphasis on the importance to sectarians in these areas of these various biblical patriarchs before and after the flood, the Sabaeans held that Noah's grandfather Methusaleh had another son besides Noah's father Lamech (Genesis 5:25–29) called '*Sabiᶜ*' from whom they derived their name (*cf.* John the Baptist and the derivation of his name, '*as-Sabiᶜ ibn Yusufus*,' according to the '*Sabaeans*' or '*Subbaᶜ of the Marshes*' in Southern Iraq above).[51] He also says they were led by '*Holy Men*,' called by them '*Siddiks*,' which once again, however circuitously, brings us to the Community led by James and the one portrayed in the documents at Qumran – not to mention the one founded by '*Elchasai*' as described by Epiphanius – '*Siddik*' like '*Salih*' in Arabic being equivalent to the term *Zaddik/'Righteous One'* in Hebrew.

According to another Arab writer two hundred years later in the Eleventh Century, the Encyclopaedist Ibn al-Nadim – also called 'The *Fihrist*' – the Sabaeans had an offshoot in Southern Iraq also called '*Sabaeans*.' These are clearly identical to, as just signaled above, 'the *Subba*ᶜ' of the Marshes.' As in al-Biruni, praying towards the North formed a distinct part of their rituals. Additionally, according to Ibn al-Nadim, they also *abstained from marrying close relatives*, which would obviously also include the ban on nieces and close family cousins at Qumran.[52] As we saw, these things came under the general category of '*fornication*' at Qumran, another of the bans associated with James' directives to overseas communities.

Nor do such '*Subba*ᶜ' countenance divorce, except under strict conditions – once again, part of these same Qumran and early Christian prohibitions to similar effect. Perhaps more importantly, the *Fihrist* fully delineates the '*Sabaean*' ban on '*carrion*,' a ban also reflected in some of the strictures in *MMT* which we shall analyze further below.[53] Bans such as these, perhaps more than anything else, firmly link such '*Sabaeans*' to James and his directives to overseas communities as recorded in Acts 15:19–29 and 21:25 above, directives so assiduously avoided by Paul in 1 Corinthians 6:12–11:16 but firmly restated in the Koran by Muhammad in succession to such '*Sabaeans*.'[51] In these directives, as should be familiar by now, James banned '*blood, fornication, strangled things, and things sacrificed to idols*.'

These are also the same bans laid out by Peter in the Pseudoclementines, which are now being implicitly ascribed to 'Jesus' in his role as '*the True Prophet*.' In them, James' ban on '*strangled things*,' as imperfectly set forth in Acts, is now, quite properly, being clarified and enlarged into '*carrion*.' As the Pseudoclementine *Homilies* expresses these directives, Peter speaking in the name of '*the True Prophet*':

> *abstain from the table of demons* (Paul, of course, uses the same phraseology in the context of delineating his doctrine of '*Communion with the blood of Christ*' in 1 Corinthians 10:19–22, but to opposite effect, *arguing against Jewish dietary regulations and Jewish sacrifices in the Temple*), that is, *from food sacrificed to idols, animals which have been suffocated* (here Acts' '*strangled*

things') or caught by wild beasts (this now, quite clearly, *'carrion') and from blood* (here too James' ban on *'blood,'* now integrally connected to the one on *'carrion').*[54]

This is repeated later in the same section and the context is now, not only the ban on *'blood,'* but also on *'shedding blood'* or *'manslaughter'* of the description of Noah's sacrifice in Genesis 9:4–6, to which even *the ban on 'tasting dead flesh or filling themselves with that which is torn of beasts'* – in other words, once again, *'carrion'* – is definitively added.

Compare this with how this same ban on *'carrion'* would appear to be ascribed by the 'Sabaeans' of Southern Iraq above seemingly to Noah's father Lamech's brother 'Sabi^c.' Here the ascription is rather to *'a certain Angel'* speaking to Noah and his descendants after the Flood and it reads:

(...they should not) *shed blood or taste dead flesh, or fill themselves with that which is torn of beasts or that which is cut or that which is strangled* (once again, the ban attributed to James in Acts on *'strangled things,'* but more clearly developed) *or anything else which is unclean* (this, in contrast to Acts' picture of Peter's *'tablecloth'* vision presuming to terminate distinctions between *'clean and unclean').* But those who do not follow My Law, you not only shall *not touch* (this totally gainsaying what Peter claims to have learned from his *'tablecloth'* vision in Acts *'to call no thing'* or *'any man profane or unclean,'* but also the exact picture of those Hippolytus is called *'Sicarii* Essenes' – also a ban reproduced in the Damascus Document but clearly alien to Paulinism[55]) *but also do no honour to, but rather flee from their presence.*[56]

Not only does this sound very much like what Peter is pictured as explaining to Cornelius in Acts 10:28 *'that it is not lawful for a Jewish man to attach himself or come near one of another race'*; but also like Paul in 2 Corinthians 6:16–7:1, the only really Qumran-sounding passage in all his letters where, in speaking about *'the Temple of God with idols'* and making defective reference to *'Belial'* from Qumran, he avers, *'touch no unclean thing'* and *'one should purify oneself of every pollution of flesh and spirit, Perfecting Holiness in fear of God.'*[57]

These bans normally attributed to James (another *'Righteous One'* in the *'Noahic'* tradition) are, to repeat, almost precisely set forth in some five different places in the Koran, once again, as in the Pseudoclementine *Homilies* with *the ban on 'strangled things'* quite clearly reproduced as *'carrion'* and followed as part of Islamic dietary law to this day.[58] This cannot be accidental.[59]

On the one hand, these *'Sabaeans,'* delineated so straightforwardly by ibn al-Nadim, move directly into Manichaeism. As such, they too are direct descendants of the 'school' of James and carry on the extreme Rechabite/Nazirite/Nazoraean practices of *abstaining from wine, meat, and sexual intercourse*.[60] In fact the only difference between so-called '*Manichaeans*,' following their Third-Century founder/'*True Prophet*'/ teacher Mani and other '*Sabaean*' groups such as the Ebionites, Elchasaites, Essenes, and the like, was that the Manichaeans abjured the '*daily bathing*' part of the extreme purity regimen considering it unnecessary. This abjuration followed into Islam as well – sand in Islam taking the place of water purification at least where prayer was concerned – just as the '*True Prophet*' part of their ideology did through its '*Prophet*'/'*Seal of the Prophets*,' Muhammad, who doubtlessly saw himself as a successor of sorts to Mani.

On the other hand, the '*daily bathing*' aspect of this purity-oriented regimen was carried on by the equally Gnosticizing group, mentioned by ibn al-Nadim above, whom we now call '*Mandaeans*.' These '*Mandaeans*' as we saw, also originally styled themselves '*Nasuraia*' or '*Nazoraeans*' or, at least, this is the name they give their '*Priests*' or inner core of adepts.[61] In fact, the name '*Nasuraia*' conserves the original Hebrew meaning of the '*Nazoraean*' terminology, that is, '*Keepers*' – in the Hebrew of the Prophets, '*Notzrei ha-Brit*'/'*Keepers of the Covenant*' which, in turn, is a synonym of the Qumran '*Shomrei ha-Brit*,' the definition in the Community Rule of the all important '*Sons of Zadok*.'[62] Though, where the Mandaeans were concerned, this probably moved into *the more Gnosticizing* '*Keepers of the Secrets*'; in Palestine earlier, the meaning would more likely have been, '*Keepers of the Law*' or '*Torah*.'[63] '*The Keepers of the Secrets*' connotation, however, most likely leads us to the real meaning of the '*Elchasai*' terminology, as it does the '*Hidden Imam*'-terminology in Shi'ite Islam succeeding to it in these same areas.

For the Mandaeans, the '*Secret Adam*'-ideology – *the vast cosmic Adam that preceded the creation of the world* – was known as '*the Adam Kasia*' (the same as '*the Adam Kadmon*' in *Kabbalah*, itself equivalent to '*the First*' or '*Primal Adam*' of Paul in 1 Corinthians 15:22–58, and Peter's '*Teaching*' in the Pseudoclementines) or '*the Hidden*' or '*Secret Adam*' – again, '*the Primal Adam*' of Ebionite terminology.[64] As this moves on later into Islamic Sufism, this becomes '*the Insan al-Kamil*'/'*Perfect Man*' of poets like Ibn al-ʿArabi.[65] In Hippolytus, it will be remembered, a book was brought to Rome in the SecondYear of Hadrian's reign (119 CE) '*alleging that a certain Just Man Elchasai had received*' it in a town in Persia (Adiabene?) and '*gave it to one called Sobiai*.' As we saw above, this last is clearly no more a man's name than '*Elchasai*' or '*Ebion*.' Rather it is a title relating to the central ideology of these groups, '*bathing*.'

These Mandaeans also possessed a book called *The Haran Gawaita* – notice even the name here '*Haran*' from the claim that they originally descended from emigrants from Palestine that first went into the areas of Haran and Medea (our '*Thaddaeus*'/'*Judas Thomas*' stories now framed from a different perspective) and, thereafter, into Southern Iraq. As we shall see, these stories about an '*emigration*' or '*flight*' across Jordan to Northern Syria parallel claims in the Dead Sea Scrolls – in particular, the Damascus Document again – of an '*emigration*' across Jordan, out '*from the Land of Judah to dwell in the Land of Damascus*,' where '*the New Covenant in the Land of Damascus*' – to '*set up the Holy Things according to their precise specifications*' – was to be erected.[66]

But they are also to some extent echoed in the '*Pella Flight*' tradition of the Jerusalem Church, we shall also analyze more extensively below, not to mention traditions about Judas *Thomas* sending Thaddaeus to work in these areas, following on after himself – traditions we have already remarked above. Not only are these integral to Eusebius' Edessan Chancellery Office narrative, they are also part and parcel of apocryphal literature generally.[67] Of course, if we take the allusion to '*Damascus*' in whatever context, as an esotericism that can include going even further afield than to just a city – an esotericism not unlike the use of the word '*Arab*' in Roman sources – the correspondence grows even more precise.

Mandaean Tradition and '*the Taheb*,' '*Tabitha*,' and '*Tirathaba*'

For these Mandaeans of Southern Iraq, John the Baptist was their teacher and one of their titles for him was, as we saw, '*as-Sabi^c ibn Yusufus*,' '*the Baptizer the Son of Joseph*.' Not only does the second part of this title echo similar ascriptions related to '*Jesus*'' parentage in Christian tradition, where in John 1:45 and 6:42 he is denoted a '*son of Joseph*'; but a second '*Messiah*,' called '*the Messiah ben Joseph*' or '*the Messiah the Son of Joseph*' – this as opposed to the Davidic Messiah/'*the Messiah ben Judah*' – was also considered to have been executed in Rabbinic tradition in the region of Lydda possibly even by crucifixion.[68]

Not only does this title – which the Gospels take as definitively genealogical even though 'Jesus' *was not supposed to have been* '*Joseph*''s *son* – possibly imply an overlap with Samaritan Messianic pretensions; but the title, '*Son of Joseph*,' dovetails perfectly with '*Samaritan*' tradition, since the Samaritans generally considered themselves '*Sons of Joseph*,' that is, *descendants of the Biblical* '*Joseph*.' In the Dead Sea Scrolls, too, the curious additional parallel represented by the terminology '*Ephraim*'/'*the Simple of Ephraim*' (in the Nahum *Pesher* grouped alongside '*the Simple of Judah doing Torah*') should not be overlooked – '*Ephraim*' being another biblical euphemism for '*Samaria*.'[69]

The issue of what to make of this '*Son of Joseph*' in Messianic tradition is fraught with difficulties and we have already referred in our preliminary remarks to similar issues regarding the appearance of this cognomen in the fraudulent inscription on the ossuary purporting to be the burial box of James that recently 'surfaced' containing the same allusion to '*the Son of Joseph*.' Of course we take the ossuary along with its inscription to be spurious, but the very fact that those who created it felt obliged to include it is significant.[70] In the *Talmud*, as tenuous as its traditions sometimes are, there certainly is indication of a Messianic individual, as just observed, *crucified in the Lydda region* – an area *contiguous to and on the periphery of Samaria*.[71] Here too there would appear to be some substance to the story as there certainly was a Messianic '*Restorer*' or '*Redeemer*' tradition in the adjacent area of Samaria at this time, alluded to in Josephus and denoted in Samaritan tradition, '*the Taheb*.'[72]

This individual may or may not have been equivalent to or reflected in stories about the famous '*Simon Magus*,' known in the Pseudoclementine *Recognitions* and other early Church writings to have come from the Samaritan village of Gitta, whom we know was often supposed to be *imitating* '*Jesus*.'[73] In fact, according to these same *Recognitions* and/or *Homilies*, he and a colleague of his, Dositheus – both '*Disciples*' of John the Baptist – were principal originators of '*the Secret Adam*'/'*Primal Adam*' ideology. Therefore, too, in some versions of Josephus, his *alter ego and double in Caesarea* – another Rasputin-like '*magician called Simon*' in the employ of the Roman Governor Felix and the Herodian family[68] – *is even referred to as* '*Atomus*,' probably a Greco-Latin corruption of '*Adam*' reflecting the principal doctrine associated with his person, '*the Primal Adam*.'[75]

It should be remarked that Caesarea, the Roman administrative center in Palestine and the closest large seaport to Samaria, was also the locale of the initial confrontation between Peter and the '*Simon Magus*' in the Pseudoclementine literature as well. Nor can there be any doubt that something of these matters is being reflected in Acts 8:4–25's portrayal of the confrontations between both '*Philip*' and Peter with Simon Magus over Simon's Messianic ('*Primal Adam*'?) posturing '*in many villages of the Samaritans*.' But in Acts, these confrontations occur *in Samaria, not Caesarea – seemingly reflecting Simon Magus' place of origin* – and '*Philip*' only goes to Caesarea later, after his encounter with '*the Ethiopian Queen's eunuch.*' Furthermore, Acts 8:17–24 portrays the Simon *Magus* affair somewhat disingenuously, as having basically to do with *buying the 'Power' imparted by 'laying on hands' for 'money.'* While the vocabulary is probably accurate, the import is misleading – probably purposefully. In addition, it is employing both the '*Great Power*' vocabulary attributed to Simon *Magus* in the Pseudoclementines and of the Elchasaites *cum* Mandaeans and the '*laying on of hands*,' which becomes such an integral fixture of the practices of these same Mandaeans.[76]

In any event, the episode ends inconclusively enough with: '*and they* (seemingly inclusive of Simon *Magus* not without him) *preached the Gospel in many villages of the Samaritans*' (8:25). However this may be, '*Philip*' then turns into the protagonist of the conversion, '*on the way which goes down from Jerusalem to Gaza*' (8:26) of '*the Ethiopian Queen's eunuch*' before suddenly dematerializing – '*the Spirit of the Lord took Philip away so that the eunuch never saw him again*' (8:39 – thus). '*Having been found at Azotus*' – a little north of Gaza but south of Jaffa – modern-day Tel Aviv – once again, he '*preached the Gospel in all the cities* (inclusive probably of '*Lydda*') *until he came to Caesarea*' (8:40), where he seems to have been going in the first place since he had there '*four virgin daughters who were prophetesses*' (21:9)!

For his part Peter, after this somewhat inconclusive confrontation with Simon *Magus* – pictured in Acts, as we saw, as taking place in Samaria not Caesarea – follows '*Philip*' and he, too '*passes through all*' (9:32 – whatever this means). Nevertheless he actually does '*go down to the Saints that lived at Lydda.*' While there, however, what he is doing – in place presumably of the crucifixions occurring there in both Josephus and the *Talmud* – is rather *curing* '*a certain*' *paralytic* by the name of Virgil's hero in *The Aeneid*, '*Aeneas*,' '*who had been lying in bed for eight years*' (9:33 – thus; sometimes it really is hard to refrain from laughing). Because '*Lydda was nearby Jaffa*,' the Disciples, having heard Peter was there – preparatory to his coming '*tablecloth*' vision – invite him to come to Jaffa to raise, as we shall see, '*a certain Disciple* (like the Roman Centurion Cornelius, about to appear in the next Chapter, '*full of good works and charity*') *named Tabitha*' – female because the form in Aramaic is feminine – '*which being interpreted means Dorcas*' (now '*gazelle*' in Greek!), who had '*become ill and died*' (9:36–38). This is all supposed to be taken seriously.

But to go back to Simon's Samaritan origins, which Acts seems unaware of or, at least, never makes clear – we must rather wait for the Pseudoclementines and Churchmen like Clement of Alexandria, Irenaeus, and Eusebius to clarify these.[77] In the Pseudoclementines, as already explained, Peter becomes the hero of a whole string of similar confrontations with Simon *Magus* north to Lebanon and Syria, but *beginning with this one in Caesarea which probably really was historical.*[78] For its part, as we already saw as well, Acts 8:10 in the midst of what for it is a first confrontation in Samaria even describes Simon – like '*Elcha-sai*'/'*the Hidden Power*' – as '*the Power of God which is Great.*' However this may be, its emphasis throughout this whole fantastic *and certainly unhis-torical episode* (if it is historical, it has been tampered with) on '*Power*' and '*laying on of hands*' – both cornerstones of '*Mandaean*' tradition – is *nothing less than startling.*[79]

Nor can there be any doubt as well that the New Testament is inor-dinately sympathetic to individuals of a '*Samaritan*' background as opposed to a '*Judean*' or '*Jewish*' one.[80] Over and over again in the works of early Church heresiologists we hear about individuals from a Samar-itan cultural milieu being the recipients of John the Baptist's teaching and its offshoots – the implication, as we have been suggesting, of this curious Mandaean notation for John the Baptist of '*as-Sabiᶜ ibn Yusufus*' in the first place.[81] In the Pseudoclementine *Recognitions*, for instance, both Simon *Magus* and an individual named '*Dositheus*' – both also later portrayed as heads of '*sects*' of their own just as '*Ebion*,' the Ebionites, and '*Elchasai*,' the Elchasaites – are portrayed, as we saw, as *Samaritan* '*Disci-ples*' *of John the Baptist.*[82]

'*Dositheus*,' also seemingly referred to in Josephus as '*Doetus*' or '*Dortus*' (and the head supposedly – according to the heresiologists – of his own sect '*the Dositheans*'[83]) is evidently one of those crucified in the disturbances between Samaritans and Jews at Lydda.[84] He also seems to reappear in the '*Dortus*'/'*Dorcas*' story in Acts 9:36–43 above where, as we just saw, Peter resurrects someone in Jaffa he calls by the supposed Aramaic equivalent of the Greek name '*Dorcas*' – '*Tabitha*' a '*Doe*'! As Acts 9:43 expresses this in its own inimitable way – again using the language of '*a certain*': '*and he (Peter) stayed many days in Jaffa with a certain Simon*,' but now the '*Simon*' the text is talking about is not '*Simon Magus*' but allegedly '*Simon a tanner*'! This occurs in Acts, right before the orthodox '*Simon*''s '*tablecloth*' vision where, it will be recalled, Peter gets '*Paulinized*,' *learning to call* '*no man profane*,' and just following Peter's brief sojourn in the same '*Lydda*' – a town we just heard about in the *Talmud in connection with the crucifixion of* '*the Messiah ben Joseph*' and in Acts, the scene of Peter's *curing of another* '*certain*' *paralytic, so curiously named* '*Aeneas*,' *by invoking the name of the Messiah* '*Jesus.*'[85]

The magical words, Peter is depicted as uttering here, are illustrative: '*Aeneas, rise up, Jesus the Christ* – which can just as well be translated as '*the Saviour the Christ*' – *has healed you*' (9:34), as they may point the way to a solution of many of the historical problems raised in this book. What we are trying to say here is that '*the Saviour the Christ*' may originally have been part of a magical formula, invoked in such healing attempts in a Hellenistic milieu and around which many of these miracle tales then came to be fashioned. It also, of course, takes the place of the crucifixion of '*the Messiah ben Joseph*' – whose counterpart this '*Joshua*' most certainly was – here at Lydda according to the *Talmud*.

Certainly the '*Taheb*' traditions among the Samaritans have something to do with all these relationships but, in the writer's view, they also have something to do with the Gospel presentations of stories about Pontius Pilate and Jesus. The name '*Jesus*' itself has to be seen as related to the '*Taheb*' who was, in fact, just such a '*Joshua*' or '*Jesus redivivus*' ('Joshua' being the scion of the principal Northern Tribe of Ephraim). So does the title '*Son of Joseph*,' from which the Talmudic '*the Messiah ben Joseph*' is derived – '*Joseph*' being the patronymic hero of the North. In particular, this is true of Joshua's tribe, Ephraim (the preferred son of Joseph according to the blessing of his father Jacob in Genesis 48:13–20), all of whom were seen as '*Sons of Joseph par excellence*.'

Though surviving Samaritan tradition is difficult in the extreme to penetrate, what does emerge is that there is a '*Redeemer*' figure, referred to there as 'the *Taheb*' – from this, possibly, the curious '*Disciple named Tabitha*' ('*which being interpreted is Dorcas*' – thus!), whom Peter is pictured as resurrecting after she had already '*been washed*' in Acts 9:37–41 above. Certainly the two names are homophonic and it is not a very long stretch to see them as anagrams of the kind, as we shall see, of '*Sicarios*' and '*Iscariot*'). If true, this is an incredible transformation, once again, pointing up the *modus operandi* and mischievous dissimulation embodied in New Testament narrative of this kind.

We have already seen that the term '*the Taheb*' actually would appear to mean '*the Restorer*' and what this '*Joshua redivivus*' or '*Restorer*' was supposed to restore was the Mosaic legacy as represented by the figure of '*Joshua*' – '*Jesus*.'[86] In fact, this is something of what Josephus portrays when he presents '*the tumult*' in Samaria that was so serious that it really did end up in *Pontius Pilate's recall from Palestine*.[87] This is highly underestimated and a rare occurrence even in view of the brutality shown by other Roman governors. In this episode, an individual, obviously supposed to be '*the Taheb*' (though Josephus never actually calls him this), is clearly trying to present himself as a '*Joshua*' or '*Jesus redivivus*,' since he wishes to lead a massed multitude up to Samaria's '*Holy Mountain, Mt. Gerizim*' where Joshua had originally read the Mosaic Law to the assembled tribes (Joshua 8:33–35).

The way John the Baptist is presented in Josephus, whose effect on the crowd (which *'seemed prepared to do anything he would suggest'*; for the Samaritan agitator, it is: *'Lying he considered of little consequence and he contrived everything to please the crowd'*) at almost precisely the same time (a synchronicity that needs to be explored) is comparable in almost every way.[88] What the Samaritan *'Impostor'* prevails on the crowd to do is to restore *'the sacred vessels,'* presumably of the Temple, that had allegedly been *'deposited in that place by Moses.'*[89] But, as Josephus portrays it, these crowds, which had congregated *'at a certain village called Tirathaba'* (here, of course, once again our *'certain'* language as in Acts' portrait of *'Tabitha'* above – but, what is even more striking and more definitive, now there really are *the unmistakable traces of the name Acts has played upon or garbled in transcription to produce 'Tabitha,' and here we really do have an anagram*) were now set upon and slaughtered by *'a great troop of horse and men'* commanded by Pontius Pilate.

Others were taken alive, *'the principal and most powerful of whom'* Pilate ordered to be crucified just as Christian tradition considers its *'Jesus'* to have been.[90] These must have included the individual claiming to be *'the Taheb'* unless – like Simon *Magus* seemingly in the episode involving *'the Egyptian' on the Mount of Olives* later in Acts (clearly comprising further *'Joshua redivivus'* activity[91]) – he managed to escape. There is no comparable story in the received Josephus – unless it be that of the *'pseudo-prophet Jesus ben Ananias,'* whom we shall consider in a more definitive manner presently, but this transpires under a later Prefect or Procurator, Festus[92] – about Pilate's interaction with Jewish or Samaritan crowds and a Messianic *'Restorer'* or *'Redeemer'* figure, whom he cruelly and brutally crucified and for which he was ultimately actually recalled, unless it be this.[93]

Nor can there be much doubt that we have in these activities the kernel of events being transformed in Acts' picture of Peter's encounter with *'a certain Tabitha which interpreted is Dorcas'* and, in Josephus, probably *'Dortus'* or *'Doetus.'* Pace as well, recent popular presentations of Pontius Pilate, under whom this *'tumult'* allegedly occurred – particularly in the cinema – as a harmlessly benign governor. Such overlaps of *'the Taheb'* story – including the common denotation *'Son of Joseph'* – with that of the *'Jesus'* or the *'Christ'* make it seem pretty certain that there was some original or underlying version of materials about this *'Son of Joseph'/ 'Taheb'* personality, owing its origins to and based upon Samaritan originals, that went into the Gospels. But further than this it is impossible to go.

This amazing transformation of *'the Taheb'* and/or *'Tirathaba'* into

'*Tabitha*' – most likely we have a progression here and all three are related – is perhaps, as we saw, a more vivid indication of the New Testament's working method than even the transformation of the circumcised convert Izates, reading Genesis 17 on God's instructions to Abraham, into '*the Ethiopian Queen's eunuch*' reading Isaiah 53:7 – interpreted for him by Philip as '*the Gospel of Jesus*'[94] – immediately going down into the water and being baptized.

But unfortunately one must go further – just as Josephus characterizes the Samaritan Messiah as '*considering Lying of little import*,' there are historical lies here, lies – however benignly-intentioned – meant to undermine, belittle, and deceive, which unhappily have done their work all too well over the last two thousand years and are still, sad to have to say, so doing.

'*The Nasuraia*,' '*the Keepers*,' and Mandaean Tradition Continued

To go back to Mandaean tradition, according to which Jesus – also acknowledged to be one of these '*Keepers*' or '*Nasuraia*' ('*Nazoraeans*') – corrupted John the Baptist's message, '*perverting the words of the Light and changing them into Darkness*.'[95] Once again, a lot of this would appear to have to do with how Simon *Magus* is portrayed both in the Pseudo-clementines and in Acts. But the words could also have come right out of the literature at Qumran where, as in the Gospel of John, such '*Light*' and '*Dark*' imagery is widespread.[96]

In the Scrolls, too, paralleling this issue of '*corrupting the words of Righteousness*' (*cf.* Acts 8:23's description of Simon as '*consumed by bitter gall and chained in Unrighteousness*' and of the '*Restorer*' in Josephus as '*one who thought Lying of little consequence and contrived everything to please the multitude*'), there is also '*the Spouter of Lies*,' who *embodies* '*the Lying Spirit*' and *follows the* '*Way of Darkness*' *as opposed to that of* '*Light*.'[97] Needless to say, this kind of '*Light*' and '*Dark*' imagery is widespread in Mandaean literature and is also a foundation piece of Manichaeism – though, it should be appreciated, it may just as well reflect Persian '*Zoroastrian*' influences too.

For the *Haran Gawaita*, with '*his brother*' – here now our James or even possibly the '*Judas Thomas*'/'*Judas the Twin*'/'*Judas Barsabas*' traditions already signaled above (note again in this last just the slightest hint of the '*Saba*ᶜ'/'*Sabaean*' notations we have been exploring[98]) – *Jesus converted* '*all Nations, bringing the People unto themselves*.'[99] Again this, too, is reflective of the widespread '*People*' or '*Peoples*' terminology we shall be encountering throughout the literature at Qumran and, of course, historical portions of the New Testament.[100] These, Mandaean tradition now asserts, *'were called Christians and named after Nazareth'*![101]

What has occurred in this account is that the orientation of Paul (or even possibly Simon *Magus*, not inconsequentially confused with Paul in Pseudoclementine tradition[102]) – who is never mentioned either in Mandaean Scripture or the Koran – in particular, his *'Gentile Mission,'* is now *being confused with that of 'Jesus' and even attributed to him.* This should not be surprising as the same thing has happened for the last nineteen centuries in Western culture because of some extremely successful re-write activities in both the Gospels and the Book of Acts. Otherwise, very real echoes of historical fact, however garbled and misunderstood, are being conserved – in particular, the coupling of *'Jesus'* and *'his brother'* in leadership positions. As we just saw, this coupling could also possibly be James and Judas *Thomas*, the latter doubled in Northern Syrian tradition as *'Thaddaeus'/'Addai'* and, at Nag Hammadi, even as *'Theudas'* – itself possibly a corruption of either *'Judas Thomas'* or *'Thaddaeus,'* or perhaps even both.[103]

In this regard, it should be recalled, that the latter, called *'Lebbaeus surnamed Thaddaeus'* in Matthew 10:3 (probably based on either *'Belial'* in the Scrolls or Hegesippus' cognomen for James, as conserved in Eusebius, *'Oblias'*[104]) is even replaced in Luke 6:16 by *'Judas of James,'* which becomes *'Judas the brother of James'* in Jude 1:1. It is even possibly further transmogrified in John 6:71 into *'Judas (the brother) of Simon Iscariot,'* himself appearing as *'Simon the Zealot'* in Luke and *'Simon the Cananaean'* in Mark and Matthew.[105] The reason all these shifts and transmutations are so important is probably because – as we have been at pains to point out – of the single notice in the document Eusebius claims to have translated from the Edessan Chancellery records that *'Thomas'* (later *'Judas Thomas'*) *sent 'Thaddaeus' on his mission to King Agbarus to evangelize the Edessenes,* thereupon following him not only there but, according to apocryphal tradition, on journeys that take him *all the way to India.*[106]

As far as we can discern, however, the two *'Apostles'* or *'Disciples'* – the sources are unclear regarding distinctions such as this[107] – are the same person, the key being the *'brother'* or *'twinning'* relationship subsumed in the designations *'Thomas'* (*'Thamud'* in Arab sources, as we have already seen) and *'Judas of James'* (*'Hud'* in these same Arabic sources), to say nothing of *'Addai'* (*'Ad'* in Arab sources – but note also *'Adiabene'*) for *'Thaddaeus.'*[108] Nevertheless, in our view *something historical is being conveyed in Eusebius' document* and that is, in the final analysis, *someone sent his 'brother' to evangelize 'the Peoples beyond the Euphrates.'* Since the source is quite clear that *this was not Jesus* but, at the same time, somehow included both 'Judas Thomas' and 'Thaddaeus'; then, in our view, this is nothing but an echo of James, the Successor, Archbishop, or Bishop (at Qumran, 'the Mebakker' as we shall see[109]) *sending his brother 'Judas of James'* – as he does after Acts' *'Jerusalem Council,' 'Judas Barsabas' to evangelize the Edessenes.* Whatever one might wish to conclude, in the Mandaean tradition echoing these things these *'two brothers'* (whoever they are thought of as being) *not insignificantly, operate from 'Mount Sinai.'* [101]

Joseph Barsabas Justus and the Sabaeans

Continuing the application of 'Sabaean' terminology to John in Mandaean tradition, John's father is called '*Abba Saba Zachariah*,' echoing the Aramaic '*Abba*' ('*Father*') denotations in Christian Scripture, to say nothing of the '*Saba*' in '*Barsabas*' again. The Mandaean tradition too, dating the exodus of John the Baptist's followers from across Jordan to the year 37–38 CE (around the time, as well, of Pontius Pilate's destruction of the Samaritan '*Restorer*' and his followers above), more or less agrees with the date Josephus gives for John the Baptist's execution across Jordan in Perea. Josephus puts this, as we have seen, at the end of both Pontius Pilate's Governorship and Herod Antipas' Tetrarchy, well past the normal date for Jesus' execution given in the Gospels of between 30–33 CE.[111]

It is interesting that for Josephus, John the Baptist like '*the Essenes*' taught '*Piety towards God and Righteousness towards one's fellow man*' – the '*Righteousness*'/'*Piety*' dichotomy we have already called attention to above – clearly recognizable throughout the Dead Sea Scrolls, the Letter of James, and considered the essence of 'Jesus'' teaching in both the Gospels and by the early Church polemicist Justin Martyr.[112] For Josephus, John the Baptist was executed by Herod the Tetrarch because he feared that John was so popular that the people would do anything he might suggest. In other words, the execution of John was a preventative one, because Herod feared John might lead an Uprising.[113]

In fact, Josephus portrays John as being so popular – unlike the somewhat more tendentious depiction of him in the Gospels[114] – that he says the people considered Herod's defeat by King Aretas (in the war they fought because Herod had divorced Aretas' daughter in order to marry Herodias) as punishment for what he had done to John. This is to say that John the Baptist *was a popular leader* and his death resulted from this, and not from some '*seductive dance*' performed by Herodias' daughter (unnamed in the Gospels, but Josephus tells us she was '*Salome*'), the subject of popular imagination every since.[115]

But this mini-war between King Aretas and Herod, which probably had something to do with the picture of Paul's escape down the walls of Damascus in a basket in 2 Corinthians 11:32–33, in order to evade '*the Ethnarch of Aretas*' *who wanted to arrest him* (not as per Acts 9:22–24's somewhat more malevolent portrayal, '*the Jews*' *who wanted* '*to kill him*' – Aretas, the '*Arab*' King of Petra having just conquered the city only a short time before), does not seem to have occurred until approximately 37 CE.[116] Therefore, John could not have been executed much before that time since the divorce by Herod of Aretas' daughter was ostensibly driving the hostilities.[117]

Christian sources are extremely insistent (particularly Hippolytus, but also Epiphanius two centuries later) that '*Elchasai*' had '*a book*,' that is, the one Hippolytus says was given to '*Sobiai*' above ('*Sobiai*' of course, apparently relating to '*Masbuthaeans*' or '*Sabaeans*'). Hippolytus actually gives the name of the '*Syrian*' follower who brought this book to Rome as '*Alcibiades*' – another of these seeming corruptions as expressions moved from Aramaic or other Semitic languages into Greek, this time, patently, of the name '*Elchasai*' as it was transliterated from Aramaic or Syriac. Hippolytus' younger contemporary, Origen, also claims to have seen this '*book*' while residing in Caesarea on the Palestine coast.[118]

Modern scholars have been attempting to reconstruct this '*book*' attributed to *Elchasai*. All acknowledge it to have been '*Jewish Christian*' or '*Ebionite*' and related to a book that also has only recently come to light, *The Mani Codex*.[119] Among the previously inaccessible manuscripts from the Dead Sea Scrolls, another book, *The Book of Giants*, which has recently come to light, was also known to Manichaean sources.[120] That Muhammad seems to know about this '*book*' or '*books*' seems clear from his insistent designation of the group he is calling '*Sabaeans*,' together with Jews and Christians as one of the three '*Peoples of the Book*' or '*Protected Persons*'/'*Dhimmis*.'[121] Curiously enough, he is not perceived as having included Mani's followers in this category and, therefore, they were later persecuted by Muslims. Nevertheless, in so far as they were not distinguishable from '*Elchasaites*,' they too were probably also originally subsumed under this notation '*Peoples of the Book*.'

Nor does Muhammad mention Mani any more than he does Paul. Neither do any of these other groups, presumably because Paul and Mani were, ideologically speaking, so close, and because all, including '*the Ebionites*' or so-called '*Jewish Christians*' – the Mandaeans do not mention Paul either except to speak mysteriously about an '*Enemy*'[122] – *were so violently opposed to Paul.* It is, however, not without interest as we have seen that, even in the Book of Acts, Paul has a companion with the Mani-like name, 'a certain Mnason' (21:16 – if this is not just another garbling of someone like 'Ananias' again), called there 'an early Disciple' and 'a Cypriot' – this last, as already underscored, *often a stand-in for Samaritan*.[123]

As we saw, Josephus calls the stand-in he knows for Simon *Magus* in Caesarea – the 'Magician' also designated in some manuscripts as 'Atomus' – as *coming from 'Cyprus'.* On the hand, Acts 13:6 calls the 'certain magician and Jewish false Prophet' – again the inversion of the 'True Prophet' ideology – it pictures Paul as encountering on 'Cyprus,' 'Bar Jesus,' a name it admits is equivalent to the redundant 'Elymas Magus' (that is, 'Magician Magician'!) Not only does Acts depict this 'magician' standing side-by-side with Paul's namesake, 'the Proconsul Sergius Paulus,' just as Josephus does the 'Magician' he knows as 'Simon' with the Roman Prefect Felix; but it also pictures Paul as addressing him as follows:

> O Son of the Devil ('Diabolou' that is, 'Belial'), *full of guile and all cunning, the Enemy of all Righteousness* (*i.e.*, the reversal of the Pseudoclementine 'Enemy' terminology as applied either to Paul or, as the case may be, Simon *Magus*), *will you stop perverting the Straight Ways of the Lord* (13:10 – again the allusions to 'the Upright' or 'Straightening,' favorite allusions at Qumran based on the proverbial Isaiah 40:3 '*make a straight Way in the wilderness*')?[124]

In any event, this 'Mnason' – also referred to with the qualifier 'a certain' again and 'an old Disciple' from 'Cyprus' – like the 'Judas on a street called the Straight' in Acts earlier (to say nothing of, the 'certain Simon a tanner' with whom Peter stays in Jaffa and the other 'a certain Disciple' named 'Tabitha' at Lydda) has a house in Jerusalem at which Paul stays.[125]

Then, too, in the Book of Acts, as it has come down to us, Paul has another, even earlier, colleague called 'Manaen' described, as we saw, as one of the original founders of the 'Church at Antioch' (whichever 'Antioch' may be intended by this, the one 'on-the-Orontes' or 'by-Callirhoe') and 'a foster brother of Herod the Tetrarch' (13:1). This is the same 'Herod,' we have already highlighted as well, involved with matters relating to John the Baptist's death, in connection with which Paul's curious escape 'down the walls of Damascus in a basket' from the representative of 'King Aretas' in 2 Corinthians 11:32–33 may have occurred. This is the same 'King Aretas' who fought the mini-war with Herod because he had divorced his (Aretas') daughter to marry Agrippa I's sister and his (Herod's) 'niece,' Herodias.[126]

But, as we have already suggested as well, this denotation 'Manaen' for a founding member of 'the Church at Antioch' probably points to a garbling of the name of Paul's other, more well-known, companion, 'Ananias,' missing from this enumeration and whom we have likewise already delineated in some detail above. As for the *'foster brother'* part of the designation or *'the man brought up with'* this same *'Herod'* responsible for the death of John the Baptist, as argued in our Preliminaries, this most probably (via a deft bit of editorial displacement) *represents Paul himself not Ananias.*[127]

Except for a few historians like al-Biruni and *The Fihrist* above, Muslims, as already indicated, generally think that the *'Sabaeans,'* about whom the Prophet speaks so familiarly and approvingly in the Koran,[128] were from Southern Arabia and an area called 'Saba'' (today's Yemen) from which they probably disappeared as an identifiable group almost a thousand years previously – that is, in the era not long after Solomon's time. Like the Christians before them, they 'forget' or, simply, just do not know that there were *'Sabaeans'* of the kind we have delineated above (namely *'Elchasaites'* or *'Masbuthaean* Baptizers'), making the same anachronistic genre of mistake Acts makes in its evocation of *'the eunuch of the Ethiopian* Queen' it calls *'Kandakes'* (this also playing on the Roman view of *'circumcision'* as self-mutilation or a kind of castration).[129]

In fact, as we saw, according to Strabo of Cappadocia (Pliny's source and the one probably behind Acts' disparaging bit of caricature), the last Queen by this name ruled Meroe in Sudanese Nubia on the Upper Nile up until about 20 BC.[130] Likewise, the confusion in spellings and vocabularies – that is, *'Sabaean'* spelled with the Semitic *'ayin,'* meaning *'Daily Bather,'* and *'Sabaean'* spelled with the Semitic *'alif,'* as in *'Sheba'* of *'the Queen of Sheba,'* that is, *'Shebaeans'* or *'Sabaeans,'* may have been the source behind Acts 8:27's original error or dissimulation in this regard.

Of course, in Acts (if not the Koran) these kinds of confusions or mis-translations (really mis-transliterations) may be disingenuous derision, tinged with a touch of unconscious (or perhaps not so unconscious) racism – in Greco-Roman eyes all *'Arab'* Queens from this part of the world being simply dark or black, that is, *'Ethiopian.'* This would certainly include the all-important Queen of Adiabene, whose *'Treasury Agents'* actually *did take the road to Gaza and El-Arish,* the traditional gateways to Egypt (and, for that matter, the oft-heard about *'Cyprus'*), as we have seen, to buy grain to relieve the famine – *'the Great Famine'* that Acts 11:28 has the *'Prophet'* it calls *'Agabus'* (parodying *'the Great King of the Peoples beyond the Euphrates'* Eusebius calls *'Agbarus'* or *'Abgarus'* – these kinds of transliteration mix-ups already proliferating), *'signify by the Spirit, was about to come a severe famine over the whole inhabitable world.'*

For their part, Muslims persist in this confusion even though the root of the word '*Sabaean*,' as we saw, as it pertains to '*the Peoples of the Book*' in the Koran and Islamic ideology thereafter, is completely different from the one used to designate the name of the Kingdom in Southern Arabia, '*Saba*'' – from which '*the Queen of Sheba*' presumably came. Actually this really is Southern Arabia not Ethiopia.[131] In fact, in telling her story Muhammad, once again, specifically evokes the telltale names of '*Hud*' (now '*Hudhud*' and *supposed to be a bird!*), '*Thamud*,' and '*Salih*,' so much a part of the nomenclature of these Northern Syrian, though not Southern Arabian, conversion stories.[132]

On the other hand, if Acts is genuinely simply confused in styling the monarch, the Greeks and Romans at this time knew as '*Queen Helen of Adiabene*,' as '*Queen of the Ethiopians*' – mistaking '*Sabaean*' for '*Shebaean*' – then it is also providing just the slightest hint that this Helen may have espoused the kind of Judaism represented by such '*Sobiai*' or '*Masbuthaeans*' in Northern Syria or Mesopotamia, Talmudic claims of her adoption of mainstream Judaism notwithstanding.[133] The reader should remember that the Medieval Jewish traveler, Benjamin of Tudela, was still listing the '*Elchasaite Synagogue*' he encountered in this area as '*Jewish*,' as we saw, *as late as the Eleventh Century*. If Acts likewise is mistaking '*Shebaean*' for '*Sabaean*,' then it would provide proof that the appellation '*Sabaean*' was already in use among '*bathing*' groups in Northern Mesopotamia and Syria at the time Acts was being put into its final form.

This is possibly the implication behind names like '*Judas Barsabas*' and '*Joseph Barsabas Justus*,' also to be found in Acts but nowhere else and themselves both confusing and hard to distinguish from each other.[134] '*Judas Barsabas*' (whom, as should be clear by now, we do not distinguish from '*Judas the brother of James*,' '*Judas Thomas*,' '*Judas Zelotes*,' '*Lebbaeus who was surnamed Thaddaeus*,' and even, perhaps – as will become more and more obvious – '*Judas Iscariot*'), like '*Agabus*' before him in Acts 11:27, '*goes down from Jerusalem to Antioch*' with Barnabas, Paul, and Silas, not to predict '*the Famine*' but to deliver James' letter. With Silas and also like '*Agabus*,' he is also called '*a Prophet*' in Acts 15:32 – so too, according to Josephus, was '*Theudas!*'[135]

'*Joseph Barsabas Justus*,' it will be recalled, is the defeated candidate in the election to fill the '*Office*' (*Episkopon* – the actual word Acts 1:20 applies) of another '*Judas*' – '*Judas Iscariot*,' even though this '*Iscariot*' was *never presented as holding such an 'Office'/Bishopric' or title in the first place*.[136] Not only are these '*Barsabas*' names (to say nothing of quasi-related '*Barabbas*' ones) tied to the known names associated with Jesus' family members; but we would say that this '*Joseph Barsabas Justus*' (the '*Justus*' part of which in Acts 1:23 is actually retained in the Latin and not in its

Greek equivalent – the '*Joseph*' part of which once again being, in our view, the alleged patrimony) relates to the missing introduction and election of James in Acts ('*Justus*,' not just in all Latin versions of his name, but also sometimes even in Greek[137]) to succeed 'Jesus' in the '*Office*' of '*Bishop of the Jerusalem Assembly.*'[138]

So one can conclude that we have clear evidence that this group of '*Sabaean*' Daily Bathers, closely associated with what early Christian heresiologists like Hippolytus or Epiphanius are calling either '*Nasarenes*'/ '*Nazoraeans*' (referred to as '*Nasranis*' in Arabic to this day), '*Essenes*'/ '*Ossaeans*,' '*Ebionites*,' or '*Elchasaites*,' existed at least as early as Acts' transmutation of materials about Queen Helen of Adiabene into the '*Queen of Sheba*,' '*Meroe*,' '*Ethiopia*,' or what have you. In addition, they are also to be connected – at least where Northern Mesopotamia and Syria were concerned – with the missionary activities of someone called '*Judas*' ('*Hudhud*,' *a bird, in the story about the Queen of Sheba in the* Koran!) or '*Addai*' (that is, '*Thaddaeus*' – in some manuscripts called '*Judas the Zealot*'; in other contexts,' as we have seen, '*Judas of James*'/'*Judas the brother of James*' and in the Second Apocalypse of James from Nag Hammadi, even '*Theudas the brother of the Just One*'[139]).

It should, also, be emphasized that, aside from the still extant Mandaean '*Nasoraia*' in Southern Iraq, these '*Nasrani*' – '*Christians*' in Islam; '*Notzrim*'/'*Keepers*' as we have seen in Judaism – give way in Northern Syria to a secretive group even today known by insiders as '*Nusayri*' (an obvious allusion to their Judeo-Christian/'*Nasrani*' origins) and by outsiders, as ''*Alawwis*' (the plural of ''*Ali*') – this last though also secret alluding to the series of '*Hidden Imams*' or '*Secret Adams*' succeeding ''*Ali*' (and possibly another, even earlier, teacher ''*Adi*').[140]

Nor should it go unremarked that these '*Nusayri*,' to which the present-day President of Syria belongs, as did his father, were also said to follow another native Northern Syrian prophet, as just signaled, that even today they call by the telltale name of ''*Adi*'![141] Although primarily a Shi'ite group, as the name '*Alawwi*' suggests, there are in this ''*Alid*' notation the traces of the Islamic '*Imam*' doctrine – ''*Ali*' being '*the Hidden Imam*' *par excellence* for Shi'ite Muslim groups of no matter what derivation. The secretive nature of these groups, including related ones such as '*the Druze*' in Southern Lebanon, Syria, and Israel/Palestine (named after a Twelfth-Century Isma'ili Shi'ite agitator al-Darazzi), is not unrelated also to '*the Secret Adam*' idea so prized by Gnostic-style groups preceding them in these same areas.

Though a little more straightforward than these later, perhaps more Gnosticizing doctrines of '*Sabaean*' or '*Daily Bathing*' groups, first reported in Irenaeus' description of '*the Ebionites*' or Hippolytus' description of '*the Elchasaites*';[142] the hint of the same or a similar conceptuality is already present across a wide range of key documents pertaining to groups such as those at Qumran, including the Damascus Document, the Community Rule, the War Scroll, Hymns, etc.[143] The same conceptuality is to be found in Paul in 1 Corinthians 15:20–58 above which includes, as we have alluded to, not only the language of '*the First Adam*,' but the '*Heavenly Secret*' as well.

Though originally based on an Arabic root meaning '*being*' or '*standing before*' – in normative *Sunni* Islam meaning only in prayer (*i.e.*, '*the Prayer Leader*') – in Shi^cite Islam, '*the Imam*' becomes something far more exalted, even bordering on the supernatural, as '*the Christ*' in Christianity. What the '*Imam*'-doctrine became in Shi^cite Islam was an incarnationist notion of the Divine specifically coming to rest in or on ^cAli and the members of his family and/or their descendants.

Nevertheless, this Shi^cite Islamic doctrine of '*the Imam*' is nothing other than the Ebionite/*Elchasaite* '*Hidden*' or '*Secret Adam*' ideology, '*the Adam Kasia*' of the Mandaeans or '*the Christ*' (whatever this was supposed to mean) as theologians such as Paul proceed to translate it into Greek. This last – now referred to as '*the Holy Spirit*' – is pictured in the Gospels as coming to rest on Jesus' head in the form of a dove when he emerges from the baptismal waters (the probable origin of Muhammad's '*Hudhud*'/'*a bird*').

The transfer of this doctrine of multiple Christs, *Imam*s, or ^cAlis that could be seen as incarnated in any given individual or at any given time and place became extremely useful for Shi^cite Islam, ^cAli being Muhammad's closest living 'relative' and, according to some – like James and Jesus' other relatives in Christianity – his rightful and only authentic heir. Of course in this kind of derivative or later thinking, ^cAli or '*the Imam*' is the heir of 'the Prophet' not of a supernatural being as 'Christianity' would have us believe 'Jesus' is. But even in Ebionite tradition – reflected seemingly in John 6:14 and 7:40 – it should be appreciated that 'Jesus' was considered to be '*the True Prophet*' referred to in Deuteronomy 18:15–19, a fundamental conceptuality of the Pseudoclementines and a biblical proof-text also extant and subjected to exegesis at Qumran.[144] So was Mani and, following this of course, Muhammad in Islam.

Not only is the framework for all these ideas already present in the Qumran documents earlier; but this idea of '*standing*' (at the root of both the *Elchasaite*/Ebionite ideology of '*the Standing One*' and '*the Imam*' doctrine in Islam – to say nothing of '*the Christ*' in Christianity[145]) is widespread as well at Qumran – in particular, in the Damascus

Document, where it can even mean, depending on the context, 'resurrection' and/or the coming or return of the Messiah *'at the End of
Days.'*[146]

In addition to relating to the Ebionite/*Elchasaite* doctrine of *'the
Standing One'* – itself indistinguishable from the notions of *'the Primal'*
or *'Secret Adam'* above, and probably reflected in the *Book of Giants* as
well – traces of it run through all the Gospels and Jesus and/or his
Apostles are repeatedly placed in a varying set of circumstances and
descriptions in which they are alluded to – *often for no apparent contextual
reason* – as *'standing.'*[147] Along with the ideology of *'the True Prophet,'* it is a
basic conceptuality of the Pseudoclementines, which give detailed
descriptions of it in several places and where it is also depicted, surprising as this may seem, as the basic component of the ideology of the
Samaritan *'pseudo-Messiah'* or *'Magician'* Simon *Magus* – as already underscored, along with *'Dositheus,'* both *'Disciples'* of John the Baptist.[148]

The Relationship of Theudas, Barsabas, and Paul

Finally, early Christian tradition – namely in the hands of the Second-
Century theologian Clement of Alexandria (actually named *'Titus
Flavius Clemens'* and, therefore, probably a descendant of the first
'Clement' and a *'Flavian'*) – is aware that Paul and the individual most call
'Theudas' (certainly a variation of the Hebrew *'Judas'* – and possibly as we
have seen even a contraction of *'Judas Thomas'* – specifically, *'Thoma'/
'Yehudah'/'Theudas'* – and a variation obviously of the name *'Thaddaeus'*)
knew each other and the one was a disciple of the other or *vice versa*. This
is the implication of some of the things we have been saying above as
well.

In fact in some Syriac sources, the replacement for *'Thaddaeus'* in
Lukan Apostle lists, *'Judas of James,'* is again replaced, by another variation,
'Judas the Zealot.'[149] This inevitably brings us back to that other *'Judas,'*
surnamed *'the Iscariot,'* so demonized in Gospel history. In turn, this last
in the Gospel of John – itself having no Apostle lists – is rather
characterized as either *'Judas (the son)'* or *'(brother) of Simon Iscariot.'*[150] For
his part *'Simon Iscariot'* starts this circle all over again and, just as *'Judas
Iscariot'* is to *'Judas Zelotes,'* is itself patently not unconnected to the name
found in the Apostle lists of Luke/Acts, *'Simon Zelotes'/'Simon the
Zealot.'*[151]

Not only is it possible to look upon this *'Theudas'* as a double for
*'Thaddaeus'/'Judas Thomas'/'Judas (the brother) of James'/*and now *'Judas
the Zealot,'* but in the Second Apocalypse of James from Nag Hammadi,

as we saw as well, he is described, as either the '*father*' or '*brother of the Just One*' – the latter being James' cognomen. It is, as the reader will immediately recognize, the sobriquet with which we started this whole discussion and which Acts 1:23 attaches to that '*Joseph Barsabas Justus*' it portrayed as the defeated candidate in the election *to fill* '*the Office*' of '*Judas Iscariot*' – a sobriquet which for some reason Acts finally felt unwilling to discard!

The Second Apocalypse of James from Nag Hammadi also makes it clear that this '*Theudas*' was the one to whom James transmitted his teachings.[152] Just as interesting, where both Apocalypses of James are concerned, the role of '*Theudas*' in the Second Apocalypse is doubled by that of '*Addai*' in the First – both clearly being variations of '*Thaddaeus*.' In addition, both are placed in some relationship to James, whether familial or doctrinal.[153] These are very curious notices and add to the sense that something very mysterious is being concealed behind the name '*Theudas*.'

For Josephus, as we saw, '*Theudas*' is a Messianic contender and another of these '*Jesus*'/'*Joshua redivivus*'-types of the late Thirties – the early Forties CE. Though Josephus labels him a '*Deceiver*' or an '*Impostor*,' nevertheless, he cannot hide the fact that '*the multitudes*' thought of him '*as a Prophet.*'[154] According to him, what Theudas attempted to do – in the manner of '*Jesus*' in the Gospels[155] – was to lead a reverse exodus back out into the wilderness and, '*Joshua*' or '*Jesus*'-like, part the River Jordan to let the multitudes go out 'with all their belongings' rather than come in. Presumably the reason behind this was because the land was so corrupted and polluted by a combination of both Herodian and Roman servitors – why else?

This is exactly the kind of reverse exodus '*out from the Land of Judah to dwell in the Land of Damascus*' that forms the central setpiece of the Damascus Document, providing it with its name. Not only was the aim of this '*to dig the Well of Living Waters*,' there '*to re-erect the Tent of David which is fallen*';[156] but this is the context of the evocation of '*the New Covenant in the Land of Damascus*,' the principal legal requirements of which were, as we shall see, '*to love, each man, his neighbor as himself*' ('*the Royal Law according to the Scripture*' of the Letter of James) and '*to set the Holy Things up according to their precise specifications*' – that is, '*to separate Holy from profane*' and not to mingle them or abolish such distinctions.[157]

It is also, of course, exactly the kind of activity that Josephus rails against in both – so strong was his antipathy to its practitioners – the *War* and the *Antiquities*, in particular as he puts it, '*leading the People out into the wilderness, there to show them the signs of their impending freedom*' or 'redemption' – the word changes from the *War* to the *Antiquities*.[158] Josephus calls such leaders '*Impostors*,' '*Magicians*,' '*Deceivers*,' '*religious frauds*,' or '*pseudo-Prophets*' – '*in intent more dangerous even than the bandits*' or '*Innovators*' (meaning, '*Revolutionaries*,' but with the secondary meaning too, of course, of religious '*innovation*'), with whom they made common cause.[159]

This is exactly the kind of activity '*in the wilderness*' on the other side of the Jordan or Lake Gennesaret that the Gospels portray 'Jesus' as engaging in when they picture him as '*multiplying the loaves*,' '*the fishes*,' and '*the baskets*' of grain to feed '*the multitudes*' (at Qumran, '*the Rabim*'), who *went out* with him to these locations, and there *performing other such magical* '*signs and wonders*.'[160] It is also the kind of activity Josephus depicts the unknown Deceiver as engaging in at '*Tirathaba*' and on '*Mount Gerizim*' – in his case, to show '*the multitudes*' the sacred vessels that Moses had supposedly caused to be buried there – and, in addition, explains why the Gospels are so insistent on repeatedly delineating all these so much more *Hellenized* '*mighty works and wonders*,' like raisings, curings, and exorcisms, on the part of their '*Messianic*' leader '*Jesus*.'

First of all, '*Theudas*' is another of those characters like James, John the Baptist, '*James and Simon the two sons of Judas the Galilean*,' '*Sadduk a Pharisee*,' '*Onias the Righteous*' ('*Honi the Circle-Drawer*'), the Samaritan '*Restorer*,' and others whom, for one reason or another, Josephus left out of the *Jewish War* but included in the *Antiquities* twenty years later – at that point, evidently feeling secure enough to mention them.[161] Secondly and perhaps more important, the note about '*Theudas*,' he does provide, comes right after his long excursus on the Queen Helen story at the beginning of Book Twenty, the book basically *reaching a climax with the death of James*. Strikingly too, it both introduces his description of '*the Great Famine that was then over Judea*' and Queen Helen's famine-relief activities relating to it and is itself immediately followed by his notice about the crucifixion of '*the two sons of Judas the Galilean*' in 48 CE, which will produce the well-known anachronism in Acts 5:36–37 concerning both Theudas and this '*Judas*' we shall discuss further below.[162]

Nor is Acts unaware of Theudas' importance and it is certainly not incurious that the beheading of '*Theudas*' in the mid-Forties CE parallels the execution '*with a sword*' in Acts 12:1–29 by '*Herod the King*' of '*James the brother of John*' (thus) – as already suggested, one should keep one's eye on these '*brother*' denotations.[163] This chapter, which is sandwiched between both the notice about '*a Prophet called Agabus*' (paralleling, of course, how Josephus denotes '*Theudas*' as '*a Prophet*' and how Acts will later refer to '*Judas Barsabas*') predicting '*the Famine*' and Paul and Barn-abas' '*famine relief*' mission to '*Judea*' on behalf of the '*Antioch*' Community and their '*return*' (Acts 11:29–30 and 12:25), while studiously avoiding providing any details concerning this mission; actually goes on to intro-duce James and another character called 'Mary *the mother of John Mark*' – whoever she might have been – to whom Peter goes to leave a message for '*James and the brothers*' (12:12–17).[164]

Since Josephus loves detailing the executions of troublesome agitators of any kind, that the beheading of '*James the brother of John*' – a character never alluded to in any of Paul's works either – is missing from the *Antiquities* is astonishing. In our view, however, *it is not missing*. Rather the concomitant beheading of '*Theudas*' at this juncture in the *Antiquities* has simply been replaced in Acts by the execution of this James, '*with the sword*' and it is the '*brother*' aspect of the whole tangle of notices that *pro-vides the clue to the overwrite*.[165]

Notwithstanding these things, Acts 5:36–37's anachronism regarding '*Theudas*,' '*Judas the Galilean*,' and '*the Census of Cyrenius*' comes in a speech attributed to another of these ubiquitous '*certain*' ones – this time, '*a certain Pharisee named Gamaliel*' we shall also have cause to discuss further below. This anachronism has to do with a too hasty reading of the above notice about '*Theudas*' in the *Antiquities* as well. The problem is that Acts via the Pharisee Patriarch Gamaliel – another character men-tioned parallel-wise but to very different effect in the Pseudo-clementine *Recognitions*[166] – pictures '*Judas the Galilean*' as both '*arising in the days of the Census*' (that is, 7 CE), but coming after '*Theudas*,' whom it depicts as '*rising up*' before him and '*claiming to be somebody*' (in Josephus, of course, what he claimed to be was '*a Prophet*' – the '*True Prophet*'?).

In fact, it is the unraveling of this anachronism that definitively dates Acts as having been written *sometime after the publication of the Antiquities in 93* CE. The reason is quite simple: the notice about Theudas' beheading in the *Antiquities* is immediately followed by both the panegyric to Queen Helen's own famine relief activities around 46 CE and the notice about the crucifixion of Judas the Galilean's '*two sons*' in 48 CE not, as in Acts 5:37, the destruction of Judas and his followers. It is at this point that Josephus adds the statement describing 'Judas' which Acts then carelessly reproduces, oblivious of the anachronism. In the *Antiquities*, this reads: '*that same Judas who caused the people to revolt from the Romans at the time Cyre-nius came to take a Census of their belongings*.' This represents the source both of the presentation of the birth of 'Jesus' in Luke and the anachronism represented by the faulty chronological sequencing in Acts at this point.[167]

Early Christian tradition too – as also reproduced by Clement, whose complete family name, as we saw, '*Titus Flavius Clemens*' probably implies he was a descendant of Vespasian's cousin, Flavius Clemens (executed by Domitian as a seeming secret Christian) – in some manner associates Theudas' teaching with another individual descended from '*Essene*'/ '*Ebionite*' tradition. This is Valentinus, also an Alexandrian flourishing in the early to mid-100s, one of the first definitively-identifiable '*Gnostics*.'[168] Not only is this forebear of Clement – possibly even his grandfather – all but indistinguishable, in our view, from the first '*Clement*,' who was the second or third '*Bishop*' or '*Pope*' in Rome (in succession to Peter) depending on who is doing the reckoning; he is also, in our view, the eponymous hero of the Pseudoclementines, a proposition that in view of his importance makes a good deal of sense.[169]

The Domitian (81–96 CE), who executed Flavius Clemens, was also responsible for the execution of Josephus' patron Epaphroditus – possibly Paul's '*brother, co-worker, and comrade-in-arms*' in Philippians 2:25 and 4:18 – and also possibly *Josephus' own mysterious disappearance from the scene at around this time* as well.[170] Domitian's execution of Flavius Clemens was apparently accompanied by the execution or exile of his niece (or wife), Flavia Domitilla, after whom one of the biggest Christian catacombs in Rome, the '*Domitilla Catacomb*' is named.[171] Both, as their prénoms probably imply, were members of Vespasian's family circle originally intended at some point to succeed him. It is also worth noting that this execution(s) triggered Domitian's own assassination – this time by Domitilla's own '*servant*,' another of these curious '*Stephen's*.'[172]

Origen (185–254 CE), who succeeded Clement in Alexandria, also shows some awareness of '*Theudas*' as a 'Messianic' individual of sorts or part of the Messianic tradition.[173] These are peculiar notices, indeed, and hint at something very important, as already remarked, lying behind the name '*Theudas*.' This is particularly the case when they are ranged alongside Paul's own testimony both about '*traveling*' around with women and knowing '*the brothers of the Lord*.' His self-justifying protestations these details comprise come in response to accusations in 1 Corinthians 9:1–4, obviously complaining about his '*eating and drinking*' – a theme we have already explicated to some extent above.

The whole theme is particularly instructive when ranged beside those quasi-'*Nazirites*' in Acts 23:12–14, already cited above, who take precisely the opposite kind of oath, namely, '*not to eat or drink*' and this, in particular, '*not until they have killed Paul*.' As we saw as well, the theme also provides insight when ranged against those '*Mourners for Zion*' who, in Talmudic literature, take an oath '*not to eat or drink until they see the Temple restored*.'[174]

Of equal importance, in the lines leading up to this testimony to his acquaintance with '*the brothers of the Lord*,' are the questions Paul himself confirms were being raised both as to the legitimacy of his '*Apostleship in the Lord*' and his claim of '*having seen Jesus Christ our Lord*' (1 Corinthians 9:1–3), not to mention what he refers to in Galatians 2:4 as '*the freedom*' he enjoys – by which he clearly means '*freedom from the Law*' and '*freedom from circumcision*' – '*in Christ Jesus.*'[175] It is because of his pique over being asked such questions that he then asserts his 'authority,' as he puts it, not only '*to eat and drink*' (by which he again means, *inter alia*, not to have to keep in any scrupulous manner Mosaic purity and/or dietary laws), but also *to travel with women*, another accusation which by induction one can tell was clearly being lodged against him.

His response to this last is – itself followed by a whole litany of additional famous self-serving retorts, such as '*is it only Barnabas and I who do not have the authority to quit work*,' '*who ever serves as a soldier at his own expense*' (again, the same military metaphor we have already encountered above relative to his '*fellow soldier and fellow worker*' Epaphroditus in Philippians 2:25), or the equally famous evocation of Deuteronomy 25:4, '*You shall not muzzle an ox treading out corn*,' while at the same time making it crystal clear that what was on his mind was '*the Law of Moses*' (1 Corinthians 9:8–9):

> Do we not have the authority to take around a sister, a wife, as the other Apostles do and (as do) the brothers of the Lord and Cephas (1 Corinthians 9:5 – here the reference is specifically '*Cephas*,' as in Galatians 2:9, *and not* '*Peter*,' whatever one might wish to make of this)?

Not only is the allusion to '*the brothers of the Lord and Cephas*' separate and distinct from '*the other Apostles*'; but, for our purposes, this last clearly demonstrates that Paul knew '*the brothers of the Lord*' or, if one prefers, '*of Jesus*,' in particular, the third brother known in the various sources, as we have been developing them, as '*Judas (the brother) of James*'/'*Judas the Zealot*' or '*Thaddaeus*'/'*Theudas*'/'*Judas Thomas*' ('*Judas the Twin*') and that they – or at least '*Judas*' – did have families.

This, in turn, concurs with materials from Hegesippus, as conserved by Eusebius, claiming that the descendants of Jesus' third brother, '*Judas*' (or '*Jude*' if one prefers – the two are the same in Greek and it is only in English translation that a difference emerges), *were questioned in either Vespasian's or Domitian's time – or both – and executed in Trajan's.*[176] In fact, the variant source, we have already referred to above which designates '*Lebbaeus who was surnamed Thaddaeus*' or '*Judas of James*' as '*Judas the Zealot*,' confirms this too and even knows where this '*Judas the Zealot*' was buried – '*Berytus*' or '*Beirut*.'[177] Therefore, unlike James and the individual '*Simeon bar Cleophas*,' who succeeded James – normally seen as James' first '*cousin*,' but whom we consider to be the putative second brother of Jesus (his parallel in Apostle lists being, as we have just underscored, '*Simon the Zealot*' or possibly even, in our view, '*Simon Iscariot*'),[178] *these notices imply that Judas at least was married and had children – even grandchildren.*

5

James as 'Rain-Maker' and 'Friend of God'

James in the Temple as 'Opposition High Priest'

It is primarily to Eusebius, Epiphanius, and Jerome (mostly via Hegesippus in the Second Century) that one must also turn to get a picture of James' person – in particular, what he was doing on the Temple Mount and the nature of the clothing he wore there.[1] All present James, whether a product of their imagination or otherwise, as functioning as an 'Opposition' High Priest of some kind and doing the sort of things in the early Sixties CE, if not before, that a High Priest normally did – what kind of High Priest, we shall attempt to delineate as we proceed.[2]

Not only does Epiphanius present these things even more forcefully than Eusebius – in this he is supported by Jerome – actually citing Clement of Alexandria and Eusebius as his sources, insisting that *James actually wore the diadem* or *head-plate of the High Priest with the inscription 'Holy to God' on it*; but also that *he went into the Holy of Holies* or *Inner Sanctum of the Temple, if not regularly, at least once* – there to render a '*Yom Kippur*'-style atonement, on behalf of the whole People.[3]

In the received Eusebius, again obviously relying on Hegesippus (Eusebius relies on Clement for other things – namely the election of James to succeed his brother as '*Bishop*' or '*Archbishop*' of the Jerusalem Community or, to use more precise vocabularies, '*Assembly*'), this is reduced somewhat or, as the case may be, garbled. There Eusebius claims, rather obscurely, that James '*used to go into the Temple ('Sanctuary') regularly alone.*' Moreover he provides the description of '*his supplication on behalf of the People on his knees before God*' until they '*turned as hard as camel's hide*' – the more general '*Sanctuary*' or '*Temple*' being substituted for Epiphanius' and Jerome's more specific '*Holy Place*' or '*Holy of Holies*'/'*Inner Sanctum.*'[4]

Furthermore Eusebius reports that James was called '*the Righteous*' or '*Just One*' and '*Oblias*' (which Hegesippus appears to define as '*Protection of the People*' – the root of the mysterious '*Lebbaeus*' above?) *on account of 'his exceeding great Piety,*' and that these titles, which were applied to him, were to be found by searching Scripture – or, as he so inimitably puts it, '*as the Scripture declares concerning him*' – him and, one might add, Jesus.[5] Nevertheless, his presentation of James '*kneeling before God*' in '*the Temple alone*' is patently impossible unless he means by this, as Epiphanius and Jerome do, '*the Holy of Holies*' or '*Inner Sanctum of the Temple,*' since '*the Temple*' as a total entity was a public building and no one ever went into it '*alone*' as he puts it – there '*to intercede on his knees for the forgiveness of the People*' – at least not in its public parts or outer precincts.

So, if we are to credit Eusebius' redaction or transcription of Hegesippus, a solitary atonement of this nature – just as Epiphanius and Jerome declare – would have had to have taken place in the '*Inner Precincts*' (the Inner Sanctum or the Holy of Holies itself), and this by the High Priest only once a year, on *Yom Kippur*. So if James ever really did go into the Temple '*by himself*' in the manner all three describe, then the version conserved by Epiphanius and Jerome – if not more detailed – is certainly the more comprehensible.

All three also make much of the '*linen clothes*' James was supposed to have worn – just as Josephus predicates of those he designates as '*Essenes*' and that '*Banus*' with whom he (Josephus) spent a two-year novitiate in the Fifties CE.[6] *Banus*, he tells us, *took only cold baths and wore only* '*clothes that grew on trees*' – a charming way in the Greek, clearly, to translate the idea of *wearing only linen*.[7] Once again, Epiphanius also adds the additional detail (perhaps real – perhaps imagined) that *he wore no footwear*.[8] This last, of course, was true of all Priests and persons generally when entering the Temple, just as it is in all mosques to this day.[9]

While this is found in no other source other than in Epiphanius, for his part he is missing another tradition about James mentioned in all the other sources – namely the practice definitive also of Josephus' '*Essenes*' of *not anointing himself with oil*.[10] Eusebius adds to this last, again doubtlessly relying on Hegesippus, *he did not* '*go to the baths,*' but this too is probably garbled. For his part, Epiphanius reproduces this as '*he did not wash in a bath.*'[11] Both are probably wrong or perhaps it would be more appropriate to say their true intent or meaning has been lost in transmission or translation.

The reason for this is once again simple: if James did go on the Temple Mount in the manner they describe, then he would have had to have taken a cold-water, ritual immersion-style bath, as all persons entering its hallowed precincts did. There would have been no exceptions to this – none, and this is probably the root of the conundrum. In fact, the mistake is similar to the one made in reading Josephus' descriptions of those he calls '*Essenes,*' namely, that '*they preferred being unwashed*' or, more accurately probably, '*they preferred having dry skin*' – once again meaning, that when they did take '*baths*' or, more properly, '*immerse themselves*' they did not '*anoint themselves*' or use oil in the Greco-Roman manner. It patently did not mean they did not bathe.[12]

This, at once, both illumines the problem and provides the solution. What these '*Daily Bathing*' Essenes did was not go to *Roman baths*, for certainly Josephus' '*Essenes*' were '*Daily Bathers*.' So was the individual Josephus calls '*Banus*' (a name presumably based in some manner on – probably via the Latin – and implying '*bathing*'), as certainly was James despite these testimonies to the contrary.[13] What such testimonies must be understood as saying is that they *did not take* '*hot*' *baths, but rather* '*cold*' *ones*, just as Josephus relates '*Banus*' did.[14] Nor did they, as was common in such bathing establishments, '*anoint the skin with oil*' – both being, as it were, two sides of the same coin.

In fact, many of these practices are to be found in Ezekiel 44:17–31's presentation of the reconstructed Temple, in particular his description in 44:15 of '*the Priests, the Levites who were the Sons of Zadok*,' so dear to sectarian exegetes at Qumran and the basis of their understanding of *who these* '*Sons of Zadok*' *actually were*.[15] First of all, the exegesis of this passage takes off from an allusion to, '*they shall stand before Me*,' in the same line to develop an eschatological definition of '*the Sons of Zadok*' that involves '*the Last Days*.'[16] As this is put in the Damascus Document, they '*shall stand in the Last Days*,' which can also mean '*go on functioning*' or, as Paul might express it in 1 Corinthians 15:51 above, explaining the '*Mystery*' or '*Heavenly Secret*' he is about to tell, '*we shall not all fall asleep*' or '*die*.'[17]

As the present writer interprets this, it is reserved for two classes of '*the Righteous*,' those who have already died and those still alive. In this sense, the allusion can have two meanings, one for the Righteous living '*going into the Kingdom alive*'; and the other, for the Righteous dead '*being resurrected*.' Of course in the other vocabularies we have set forth in previous chapters and playing off the underlying allusion to '*standing*' in Ezekiel 44:15 as well; the allusion to '*the Sons of Zadok*' would be equivalent to '*the Standing Ones*.'[18] As the exegesis also progresses and illustrating the basic truth of this eschatological sense, they are also said to '*justify the Righteous and condemn the Wicked*' (in Hebrew literally, '*make the Righteous righteous*' and '*the Wicked wicked*'), which can only mean a participation in what popularly goes by the name of '*the Last Judgement*,' an image familiar to normative Christianity as well.[19]

As the exegesis in the Damascus Document makes clear, this is the proper order of '*Justification*' theology as opposed to its reversal two columns earlier in the same document in the universe as co-opted by Belial.[20] There the opposite order is expressed of *'justifying the Wicked* (one can even read here, should one wish, *'justifying the Sinners'*) *and condemning the Righteous.'* As painful as this may be for many readers to appreciate, from the perspective of Qumran, this would probably be how the stance expressed in the New Testament might have appeared, especially that of many well-known passages to this effect in the Gospels as they have come down to us.[21] It would also be the way many of Paul's opponents would have thought to characterize the approach he was taking – to say nothing of what he was, in fact, doing.[22]

Be these things as they may, the passage in question in Ezekiel 44:15–16 reads as follows:

> *But the Priests, the Levites (who are) descendants of Zadok* (in Hebrew literally *'Bnei-Zadok'/'Sons of Zadok'*), *who kept* (*shamru*) *the charge* (also possibly *'watch'/'mishmarah,'* from the same Hebrew root *Sh-M-R* as *'keep'*) *of My Temple when the Sons of Israel strayed from Me. They shall approach Me to serve Me and they shall stand before Me* (here the allusion to *'standing'* so important to the various traditions emphasizing it above) *...They shall come into My Temple and they shall draw near My table to minister unto Me* (or *'serve Me'* – perhaps the same kind of *'serve'/'table service'* already alluded to in our discussion of the appointment of *'Stephen'* and the others *'to serve the tables'* of *'the Twelve'* in Acts 6:1–5 and 1 Corinthians 16:15 – a *'table'* Paul, too, in 1 Corinthians 10:21 in the course of his polemics curiously compares to *'the Table of Demons'* though, admittedly, the sense here is obscure[23]) *and keep My charge* (*'shamru et mishmarti'* again).

One should perhaps also note here language that could be construed as particularly important as well to *'Samaritans.'* This is especially true when it is understood that even to this day the few remaining *'Samaritans'* consider their name to be based on the same Hebrew root just highlighted above, *Sh-M-R/'Shomer.'* That is to say that *'Shomronim'* (the underlying Hebrew for *'Samaritans'*) did not only mean *coming from the city called 'Samaria'* in the Eighth to the Seventh Century BC; but for some, just as here in Ezekiel and at Qumran, it may also have been seen as alluding to *'keeping charge of My Sanctuary'* in the right way – meaning, *'keeping the Law'/'keeping the Covenant,'* the actual definition of *'the Sons of Zadok'* in the Community Rule at Qumran.[24]

It is difficult to understand what all this might mean, only that the echoes of Samaritan Messianism – already emphasized above in the matter of Pontius Pilate's brutal execution of *'the Taheb'*-like Samaritan *'Deceiver'* and his followers and in connection with the several *'Disciples'* of John the Baptist from this same area – may be enjoying a reflection in these usages at Qumran as well.

The special characteristics of James' person and behaviour, described in the reports about him, preserved by Eusebius and supported by Epiphanius and a little more cursorily in Jerome, are for the most part associated with those Josephus and others are calling *'Essenes'* as well. In addition to common characteristics such as these, however, the reports about James go even further and, to a certain degree, reflect what is also to be found in Ezekiel's description of these *'Sons of Zadok'* now *'serving'* in the newly reconstructed Temple, including *'wearing only linen and no wool,' 'no razor coming near his head'* (a variation of what Ezekiel 44:20 is describing as *'not shaving'* or *'cutting their hair'* but rather *'polling it'*), and the Nazirite-like requirement of *'drinking no wine.'*

As Ezekiel 44:17 puts the first of these:

> *And it will be, when they ('the Priests, the Levites who are Sons of Zadok') enter into the gates of the Inner Court, they shall wear only linen garments and no wool shall touch their flesh.*

It is at this point, too, that they are enjoined, *not to 'shave their heads'* (44:20 – as Hegesippus puts it with regard to James, *'no razor came upon his head'*), but rather *'only to poll their hair'* and, while they are *'in the Inner Court'* of the Temple, *'to drink no wine'* (44:21).

The twin requirements about *'wearing only linen'* and *'no wool touching their flesh'* are particularly interesting, especially when trying to link James up with other notices at Qumran.[25] Even the ban on *'carrion,'* associated with James' directives to overseas communities in Acts 15:20–29 and 21:25 (not incuriously, preceded in 21:24 by James' *'temporary Nazirite'* oath-procedure injunction to *'shave their heads'*) and, even more specifically, in the Pseudoclementines, is also to be found in Ezekiel 44:31's description of these *'Sons of Zadok'* in the New Temple who

> *were to eat no flesh of anything dying naturally or that has been savaged, either a bird or any other living creature.*

A more perfect description of the ban on *'carrion'* in James' instructions to overseas communities is not to be found.[26]

James as 'Rain-Maker,' Noah the First 'Zaddik,' and the Eschatological 'Rain' and 'Flood' Tradition.

Strikingly, Epiphanius provides yet another curious detail about James, missing from the descriptions provided by these various other sources: that *once during a famine he brought rain*, that is, *James was a 'Rain-maker.'*[27] In this regard, it is useful to recall that whatever else Epiphanius might have been, he was a Palestinian and, originally probably, 'an Ebionite' or 'Jewish Christian.' Whether this activity attributed to James took place during 'the Famine,' introducing Josephus' 'Theudas' episode and so important to Paul's and Queen Helen's 'famine-relief' activities, is impossible to say. However, if it did occur 'at the time of the Famine,' then it would make this notice in Epiphanius *all the more meaningful.*[28]

Alluding to this event in between his description of James *wearing the diadem of the High Priest and entering the Holy of Holies* and the general drift of the information he provides about James being called 'the Righteous' or 'Just One,' Epiphanius describes the rain-making on his part as follows:

> *Once during a famine, he lifted his hands to Heaven and prayed, and at once Heaven sent rain.*[29]

This 'rain-making' ascribed to James is no ordinary matter. Though it is impossible to judge the truth or falseness of the tradition – it is no more fantastic than many similar reports about 'Jesus' in the New Testament – still, if authentic, the notice has to be considered connected to James' 'Noahic' status as 'the Just One,' like Noah, 'Perfect and Righteous in his generation' (Genesis 6:9).[30]

Here we come to some uniquely Palestinian concepts, common to early Church traditions about James and ideologies permeating the Dead Sea Scrolls as opposed to more Greco-Hellenistic ones found in the letters of Paul and scriptural representations of 'Jesus' as the Gospels portray him. Not only does James' status of 'Zaddik' – to say nothing of his 'rain-making' – remount to his relationship to the first biblical 'Zaddik,' Noah, and his salvationary activity at the time of the first apocalyptic Flood (the second such episode, centering on Lot and relating to the function and fundamental status of 'the Zaddik' in the world in Genesis 18:17–32, comes just prior to the next apocalyptic biblical catastrophe);[31] it bears on James' participation, like 'the Sons of Zadok' and 'the Elect of Israel' at Qumran generally, in the final apocalyptic Judgement on mankind or, at least, his calling down this Judgement in the Temple in terms of images first evoked by the apocalyptic visionary Daniel –

images also attributed to 'Jesus' in the Gospels and later to be found in climactic passages in the Dead Sea Scrolls.[32]

This idea of participation in final apocalyptic Judgement is outlined in the Habakkuk *Pesher* from Qumran with regard to '*the Elect of Israel*' and dominates climactic portions of the presentation in the War Scroll.[33] In fact, in this document as already remarked, one can actually find a description of *the coming of the Messiah with the Heavenly Host in final apocalyptic Judgement.* But this is also the case in the Damascus Document's crucial exegesis of Ezekiel 44:15, just highlighted above, where the all-important '*Sons of Zadok*' are identified as '*the Elect of Israel called by name who will stand in the Last Days*' ('*stand up,*' if the sense is that of resurrection), and '*justify the Righteous and condemn the Wicked*' – all allusions which, as we saw, must be considered eschatological.[34]

In Hegesippus' Second-Century portrait conserved by Eusebius in the Fourth, James is pictured as calling down this Judgement in the Temple in terms of the imagery of the Messiah coming on the clouds of Heaven (described in terms of the coming of '*the Myriads of Angels and Spirits*' or '*the Heavenly Host*' in the War Scroll from Qumran[35]), first evoked, as just noted, in apocalyptic visions of Daniel 7:13–14. The same proclamation is attributed to 'Jesus,' albeit perhaps retrospectively, in several key places in the Gospels.[36] There Jesus is described in two separate contexts – first in '*the Little Apocalypses*' – as proclaiming that '*they shall see the Son of Man coming on the clouds of Heaven with Great Power and Glory*' (Luke 21:27). Both Mark 13:27 and Matthew 24:31 add the '*sending of His Angels*' and '*Elect from the four winds*' to this array. Not only should one note the overlap in general with the '*Elect*' language in various contexts in the Scrolls in which '*the Holy Angels*' also appear, but the '*Elchasaite*'/Simon *Magus*/Pseudoclementine-like language of the '*Power*'/'*Great Power.*'[37]

The same proclamation is repeated at '*the High Priest's house*' in response to the patently absurd question, '*are you the Christ, the Son of God*' (we say '*patently absurd*' because neither the language of '*the Christ,*' or that of '*the Son of God*' relative to the Jewish Messiah had even begun to circulate in Palestine at that time, so no one at '*the High Priest's house*' would even have thought to phrase the question in those terms):

> *and you shall see the Son of* Man *sitting at the right hand of Power and coming on the clouds of Heaven* (Matthew 26:63–64/Mark 14:61–62).

Not only is this the exact proclamation attributed to James in the Temple in 62 CE, three and a half years before the outbreak of the War against Rome, in response to basically the same question (here attributed to '*the Scribes and the Pharisees*,' James standing on '*the Pinnacle of the Temple*' – *cf.* too its reflection, not surprisingly, in the speech attributed to James' stand-in '*Stephen*' in Acts 7:55–56[38]); but it will also be the kind of visionary proclamation that will be set forth in climactic portions of the War Scroll from Qumran, as we shall see, both in terms of '*cloud*' imagery and *the coming of rain*. This is the same '*coming*' and '*sending of rain*' which as '*the Sermon on the Mount*' in Matthew 5:45 too will aver – in describing how to be '*Sons of Your Father who is in the Heavens*' (plural '*Divine Sonship*' as at Qumran[39]) and '*Perfect as Your Father who is in the Heavens is Perfect*' (plural, too, as in the Hebrew '*Shamaim*' – '*Heavens*' is plural) will '*fall on the Just and Unjust alike*.'[40]

The Rabbinical catalogue of traditions called *The Abbot de Rabbi Nathan* (*The Fathers according to Rabbi Nathan*) associates '*rain-making*' or rains coming in their proper season with *proper Temple service*.[41] This theme of '*proper Temple service*,' performed by unpolluted Priests and expressed in terms of '*choosing a High Priest of higher purity*,' is a favorite one in this period.[42] In these important passages in the *Abbot de Rabbi Nathan*, there is just the slightest hint of a link to the kinds of sacrifice and offering of thanks Noah made to God after the Flood in Genesis 8:15–9:17 above. At the very least, Noah's salvationary activities in this episode are connected to the coming of rain; and, in the '*rainbow sign*' material at its close, its cessation. In some sense, therefore, where these very obscure concepts of '*eschatological rain*' or '*flood*' are concerned, Noah can be viewed as the first atoning Rain-maker; and his salvationary activities, associated with the coming of rain and its cessation.

The repetition of both of these themes, that is, the coming of rain and its cessation, will also be ascribed to the prototypical prophet Elijah, as they will to the odd person we shall discuss more fully below, '*Nakdimon ben Gurion*' – James' contemporary, who at a time of drought is also pictured as '*making rain*' like James.[43] Both themes, that is, the bringing of rain and its cessation, will be evoked too in apocalyptic portions of the Letter attributed to James where, to come full circle, the whole ideology of bringing and halting rain is connected to '*the efficacious prayer of the Just One*' (5:17–18).[44]

Not only was Noah the first '*Righteous One*' or '*Zaddik*' ('*Righteous and Perfect in his generation*'), a fact that our literature is not slow to remark; but, for the Rabbinic sages, so '*Perfect*' was he that *he was born circumcised*![45] However bizarre this claim might seem to us today – the Rabbis still contend such persons, while rare, do exist and, medically speaking, the condition is not theoretically impossible – it connects the '*circumcision*' ideal to the '*Perfection*' one and, by implication, that of the *atoning, rain-making 'Zaddik'* – all themes in one way or another related to the extant picture of James. In another sense, the Primordial Flood that wiped all life from the earth except '*Noah the Righteous*'[46] and his family can be seen as an eschatological one and there is certainly a note of this in Genesis 9:8–9:17's account of the promise God makes to Noah after his '*Righteous*' sacrifice when He displayed for him '*the Rainbow Sign.*'

Canny as ever, the Gospels pick this eschatological sense up as well, in apocalyptic statements attributed to 'Jesus' in the '*Little Apocalypses*' again though the '*sign*' for Matthew 24:17/Mark 13:14 is Daniel's '*Abomination of the Desolation standing where it ought not to stand*'; while for Luke 21:20, prescient as ever too, it is '*Jerusalem surrounded by armies*' – fairly convincing evidence that all three were written after the fall of the Temple.[47] This is how Kabbalistic Jewish documents like the Medieval *Zohar* – that itself may go back to Second Temple sources – see the '*Flood*' as well, asserting that Noah '*who sought Righteousness,*' '*withdrew*' or '*hid himself in the ark.*'

In other notices in the *Zohar*, this is expressed as:

Noah was hidden in the ark on the Day of the Lord's Anger and was placed beyond the reach of the Adversary.

In this passage, not only do we have hints of the '*Hidden*' terminology that will so permeate the New Testament and apocryphal texts associated with John the Baptist – portrayed in the Synoptics, though not in John, as an 'Elijah *redivivus*'[48] – to say nothing of derivative Islamic ideologies; but also 'the *Enemy*' sobriquet so strikingly applied to the assailant who attacked James on the Temple Mount in the Pseudoclementine *Recognitions*. Not only is this '*Enemy*' fundamental to '*Jewish Christian*' or '*Ebionite*' theology about Paul, but it is also to be found in Matthew's '*Parable of the Tares*' – probably the single instance of a pro-'*Jewish Christian*' or '*Ebionite*' parable in the Gospels (13:25–40). It is applied, too, to the opponent of the author of the Letter of James 4:4[49] ('*by making yourself a friend of man, you turn yourself into an Enemy of God*') and known to Paul in Galatians 4:16 ('*your Enemy have I then become by speaking Truth to you*'), most likely in debate with or response to James where, by implication, it is reversed.[50]

All lead into a new, albeit ephemeral, ideology from this period – also reflected in the War Scroll from Qumran as just signaled – '*eschatological rain.*' Not surprisingly – aside from James' related proclamation in the Temple in early Church witnesses to the circumstances surrounding his death – '*rain-making*' and the theme of '*coming eschatological Judgement*' are also intrinsic to James' Letter, not to mention the one ascribed to '*Jude the brother of James*' – his putative brother.[51] As we shall see in more detail as we proceed, in some of the most splendid eschatological imagery of any biblical document, James 5:8–11, – following its condemning '*the Rich*' for '*killing the Righteous One*' (5:6) and just before evoking Elijah's saving activity of both *bringing and stopping the rain* – evokes the theme of the imminent '*coming of the Lord*' or '*the Lord of Hosts,*' that is, of coming eschatological Judgement.

Here not only does one find an extremely aggressive apocalypticism, asserting that '*the cries of the reapers have reached the ears of the Lord of Hosts,*' but also a double entendre playing off the parallel theme of '*the Last Judgement,*' '*the Rich have amassed for themselves treasure in the Last Days*' (5:3). It ends amid the splendid imagery of '*spring*' and '*late rain*' (5:7) – imagery known, as we shall see, in similar contexts to the *Talmud*[52] – by evoking *final eschatological Judgement on all mankind* and, along with it, the just-mentioned *efficacious Power of the* '*prayer of the Just One*' (James 5:9–16). This last theme is connected in James to the '*Zealot*' priestly fore-runner Elijah – '*Zealot*' because of the repeated description of him in Kings and derivative notices as having '*a burning zeal for God*' (1 Kings 19:10).[53] As James 5:17–18 puts this – he both '*prays for it not to rain*' and then, after '*three years and six months,*' to rain again[54]

In other words, James' activity is being compared to that of Elijah, who, in 1 Kings 18:1–45, brings on a whirlwind – imagery duplicated, as we shall see, in introductory portions of the Nahum *Pesher* from Qumran not originally available in earlier translations of Qumran documents, not to mention in Ezekiel (aside from Isaiah, perhaps Qumran's favorite prophet).[55] In such a context, therefore, James too can be viewed as a '*Zealot*' and, indeed, he is indisputably presented as such – or at least the majority of those who follow him are – in the last notice about him in Acts 21:21. There James is presented as explaining to Paul that the majority of his followers in the so-called '*Jerusalem Assembly*' or '*Church*' are '*Zealots for the Law.*'

This is also the implication behind Paul's defensiveness over the '*Enemy*' epithet in Galatians 4:15–19 above, an allusion which flows directly into just such an evocation and three times in the next two lines plays off and clearly displays Paul's obsession with the idea that *those opposing him are consumed by* '*zeal,*' that is, *they were* '*zealous to exclude,*' (as of course those called '*Zealot*' or '*Sicarii Essenes*' in Hippolytus would have been[56]), not – as he then puts it so disingenuously[57] – '*zealous for the right thing.*' Not only were they, therefore, '*Zealots for the Law*'; they were certainly '*zealous for circumcision.*'[58]

Also in the allusion to Elijah in the Letter of James above, there is just the slightest hint of the kind of prefiguration, in the '*zeal*' being referred to in '*the efficacious prayer of the Just One,*' of James' own '*efficacious prayer*' and '*zeal.*' In the same way that Synoptic tradition represents Elijah as prefiguring John the Baptist – both, as it were, fulfilling the same kind of incarnationist function – the implication of this evocation of Elijah's powerfully '*zealous*' rain-making in this Letter is that James, too, is one of these pre-existent '*Priestly*' rain-makers, '*consumed by a burning zeal*' and an '*Elijah redivivus.*' Nor should it be forgotten that the evocation in it of both '*early and late rain*' (5:7), once again, *has to do with coming eschatological Judgement.*

Numerology, '*Eating and Drinking*', and the Pre-Existent *Zaddik*

In the subject matter of the Letter of James, therefore, there are hints of both the kind of atonement James ('*the Just One*') is depicted as making in all early Church sources in the Holy of Holies of the Temple on at least one particular Day of Atonement – if not many – and the proclamation '*on the Pinnacle of the Temple*' he is pictured in these same sources, as having made just before he was finally killed.[59] This last, as we just saw, is that of '*the Son of Man sitting on the right hand of the Great Power*' – one of the actual definitions in Aramaic, it will be recalled, that Epiphanius gives of the term '*Elchasai,*' namely '*Great Power*' – and '*about to come* (in the manner of Daniel 7:13) *on the clouds of Heaven.*' It is also repeatedly attributed, as we just saw as well, to Jesus in several Gospel contexts, particularly in '*the Little Apocalypses.*'

While the timeframe spoken of in James 5:17 of '*three years and six months*' is not precisely the more general one 1 Kings associates with Elijah's rain-making when it speaks of how '*after three years*' Elijah commanded that the drought be ended (18:1), still the two are basically the same and this is clearly the point the writer of James is intent on conveying. For its part, Luke 4:24–25, which now has Jesus *compare his own miracles to Elijah's*, also evokes '*three and a half years*' to describe the period when '*Heaven was shut up and there was a great famine throughout the land.*'

Even more significantly, whether coincidentally or otherwise, this timeframe is also that of Daniel 12:7's chronology of '*a time, two times, and a half*' or, as this is more or less repeated in Daniel 8:14 earlier, '*two thousand three hundred evenings and mornings.*' In Daniel, this timeframe is

usually thought of as relating to the interruption of the perpetual sacrifice at the time of the Maccabean Uprising, when Antiochus Epiphanes
erected *'the Abomination of the Desolation' in the Temple* – thought to have
been a statue of the Olympian Zeus[60] – alluded to as well in Daniel 8:13
and 12:11 together with allusions to *'the End Time'* (1 Maccabees 1:55).

But an alternative scheme of reckoning could just as easily have seen
this chronology as applying to the time between the death of James in
62 CE and the stopping of sacrifice in the Temple on behalf of Romans
and other foreigners and the rejection of their gifts by the *'zealous'* lower
priesthood *approximately three and a half years* later, an event which started
the Uprising against Rome and the cataclysmic events unleashed
thereby.[61]

If one accepts the relationship of this with Daniel, then this whole
cluster of notices can, in fact, throw light on how the timeframe in Daniel
was seen in the Second Temple Period. The presence of this reference to
'three and a half years' at this juncture in the Letter of James – not present
per se, as we just saw, in 1 Kings 18's account of Elijah's miracle, evoked in
this Letter, but rather an important yardstick in Daniel's eschatology –
might be an indication both of *how James' death was seen by his followers* and
*how the coming of this final apocalyptic Holy War, represented by the Uprising
against Rome, must have been seen by its participants.*[62]

Even early Church sources like, those collected by Eusebius, take a
similar view of the relationship of James' death to the cataclysmic events
that, as far as they were concerned, immediately followed his death and
were not unrelated to it.[63] It should be appreciated that even earlier than
Eusebius, Origen claims to have seen – in the copy of Josephus's works
he too evidently found in the library of Caesarea – a statement connecting James' death and not Jesus' directly to the fall of Jerusalem that
followed it, to which he, like Eusebius thereafter, took great umbrage –
the reason perhaps why the notice has disappeared from all normative
copies of Josephus ever since.[64]

However these things may be, the *Talmud* devotes a whole section of
one of its oldest and most accurate books, *Tractate Taᶜanith*, to the subject
of *'rain-making.'* In doing so, it evokes Isaiah 45:8 about

> *the Heavens pouring down Righteousness (Zedek) and the Earth opening and
> bringing forth Salvation (Yeshaᶜ), and Justification (Zedakah) growing up
> together (with them).*

This is clearly one of the most triumphant 'Messianic' passages in Scripture, culminating in the assertion in Isaiah 45:17 of Israel's redemption

or, as the text expresses it, 'Israel will be saved in the Lord with an everlasting Salvation' (Yeshuᶜa). Recently a number of Qumran texts emphasizing precisely this kind of 'saved'/'saving'/'Salvation' (Yeshaᶜ/Yeshuᶜa/yizzil) have come to light, – these in addition to the several known notices of this kind in the Damascus Document, the Community Rule, and the Habakkuk Pesher.[65] The rich vocabulary of the passage quoted above – in fact, the whole section of Isaiah in which it is found – is important regarding the subject of such 'Messianism' as well.

Talmud Taᶜanith specifically interprets this passage from Isaiah to mean that 'rain will not fall unless Israel's sins are forgiven' which, by implication, associates these matters somewhat with Yom Kippur or, at least, the central activity of that commemoration, atonement. Here we are beginning to encounter not one but several of the themes connected to James' activities in our sources, including one that we have already highlighted above, his praying for the forgiveness of the People in the Temple, and the other, of course, his rain-making.

In the same passages, Taᶜanith compares 'the day on which rain falls to the day on which Heaven and Earth were created,' evoking the same imagery of 'spring rain' which we just encountered in the Letter of James above regarding the imminent 'coming of the Lord.'[66] This not only ends by alluding to Elijah's efficacious 'rain-making,' but also evokes another allusion related to Isaiah 45:8, that of 'the farmer waiting for the precious fruit of the Earth' (James 5:7).

It should also be observed that the same imagery regarding James' person will be encountered below in the crucial appointment passage of James as successor to his brother in the Gospel of Thomas, namely:

> In the place where you are to go (presumably Jerusalem), go to James the Just, for whose sake Heaven and Earth came into existence (Logion 12).[67]

This last might just as well be 'were created,' as Talmud Taᶜanith expresses it above; and, just as the allusion in Taᶜanith relates to 'rain-making' or the fall of rain, in the Gospel of Thomas, it relates to James' Zaddik-status.

The word, Taᶜanith uses in connection with the coming of such 'spring rain,' is the Hebrew 'yoreh,' the primary meaning of which is 'pouring down.' 'Yoreh' is, of course, homophonic for the designation 'moreh' or 'teacher' in Hebrew; and exactly the same usage appears on at least one occasion in the Qumran Damascus Document as a variation on the 'Teacher of Righteousness,' that is, instead of his being a 'Moreh ha-Zedek,' he is a 'Yoreh ha-Zedek' – meaning, 'he pours down Righteousness' just as, presumably, these 'spring rains' do.[68]

These are admittedly complex imageries but the reader will, at least, appreciate the fertility of the ancient artificer's mind and that they are certainly present in the documents before us where they are being formulated with great precision. Jerome, in his work, also interprets this passage in Isaiah in terms of, or as implying, *coming eschatological Judgement*. In his translation, however, it does not simply involve '*letting the clouds pour down Righteousness*,' but '*let the clouds pour down the Just One*,' an important variation where James is concerned – to say nothing of '*the Teacher of Righteousness*' from Qumran![69] In the War Scroll from Qumran too, as we saw and shall delineate further below, these clouds '*pour down Judgement*' (*Mishpat*).[70]

In connection with these themes of '*Heaven and Earth*' and James' '*rain-making*,' just highlighted in connection with the Gospel of Thomas above; not only do these words have to do with James' pre-existent '*Zaddik*'-status but the '*Pillar*' imagery Paul employs to designate the Leadership of '*the Jerusalem Assembly*' in Galatians 2:9, itself probably based on '*the Zaddik the Pillar*' or '*the Zaddik the Foundation of the world*' phraseology found in Proverbs 10:25 – again, as Paul uses the term, therefore alluding to James' '*Zaddik*'-status.

The same kinds of references to '*Heaven and Earth*' also appear in the Synoptic Gospels. In Matthew 5:18 and Luke 16:17, for instance, Jesus is presented as saying things like:

Heaven and Earth shall pass away but not one jot or tittle shall pass from the Law;

and in a variation in '*the Little Apocalypses*' above, all three Gospels – in the context, it should be emphasized, of alluding to '*seeing the Son of Man coming on the clouds of Heaven with Power*' – speak of '*Heaven and Earth passing away*' but not *Jesus' words*.[71] The version in Matthew 24:30–34 goes, however, even further because it actually compares – not insignificantly – '*the coming of the Son of Man*' to '*the days of Noah*,' then evoking obscure imagery about how '*they were eating and drinking, marrying and giving in marriage, until the day when Noah entered into the ark*' (24:37–38).

Not only do assertions such as these further reinforce the connection of these kinds of eschatological allusions to '*the first Zaddik*' Noah's paradigmatic '*rain-making*' and soteriological activity; but these seemingly tendentious references to '*eating and drinking*' (to say nothing of '*marrying and giving in marriage*') also connect to the '*eating and drinking*' theme we have called attention to above – particularly as reflected in Paul's polemical discussions in 1 Corinthians 8:1–11:34 – as the bone of contention between Paul and James and, by extension, the several prohibitions relating to these in James' directives to overseas communities. Not only do these relate – where one of these, '*fornication*,' was concerned – to the '*marrying and giving in marriage*' theme above, but also of the kind of temporary '*Nazirite*' oath procedures so inimically opposed to Paul's positions.[72]

In turn, this last complex of issues has a direct link to what the Rabbis (and perhaps others) were subsuming under the phraseology '*the Noahic Covenant*' – itself classically associated with similar prohibitions (in particular, '*manslaughter*,' '*idolatry*,' and '*fornication*') – and to Noah's paradigmatic salvationary personality.[73] This 'Covenant' has relevance not only to James functioning as the '*Bulwark*' or '*Protector of the People*' and his '*Oblias*' status as reported in early Church testimony (itself possibly even relating to the puzzling '*Lebbaeus*' denotation)[74]; but also the actual terms of his directives to overseas communities, as recorded in Acts and refracted in Paul's polemics in 1 Corinthians and in the Pseudoclementine Homilies. Most noteworthy among these, of course, is the fundamental requirement to '*abstain from blood*,' a prohibition Noah also received in the context of the atoning sacrifice he is pictured as making in Genesis 9:5 at the end of the Flood episode.[75]

These Noahic prohibitions, because of the theory behind them that they were imposed upon Noah in the aftermath of the Flood, were seen at least by the Rabbis (and probably by others as well) *as being applicable to all mankind* and *not specifically to Israel alone.* They also included the categories of '*pollutions of the idols*,' as Acts 15:20 at one point puts it (elsewhere, this category is expressed as '*things sacrificed to idols*,' the same formulation, we have seen, employed by Muhammad in the Koran in regard to Islamic dietary restrictions and by Hippolytus in his description of '*Sicarii Essenes*'' willingness – *on account of which* – *even to martyr themselves*[76]), and '*fornication*' – two of the other categories of James' prohibitions reflected in 1 Corinthians by Paul, the Pseudoclementines, and now in the curious '*Letter*' or '*Letters*' Qumran scholars refer to as '*MMT*.'[77]

One can well imagine that Noah was seen as a vegetarian too (as James was, John the Baptist appears to have been, and Peter is portrayed as being in the Pseudoclementines[78]), at least during the actual period of '*the Flood*' itself – this before his sacrifice at its end when the permission to eat meat was restored and connected, importantly, to '*blood*' vengeance (Genesis 9:5). This last, too, of course, inevitably entailed both the prohibition on '*blood*' as well as the one of '*manslaughter*.' As Genesis 9:4 puts this in its own inimitable way: because '*the life (of the living being) was in the blood,'* Noah learns not to consume flesh with blood in it.

Not only is this prohibition on *'blood'* also a cornerstone of James' directives, if one looks closely at it, one can see how Paul has allegorically turned it around in his *'communion with the Blood of Christ'* polemic arising out of his discussions of James' directive on *'things sacrificed to idols,'* his own insistence on *'all things are lawful to'* him, and *'drinking the Cup of the Lord'* but not *'the Cup of Demons'* in 1 Corinthians 8:4–13 and 10:17–32.[79]

Though *'strangled things'* (*'carrion'* as the Pseudoclementines, the Koran, and now Ezekiel, no doubt, correctly conserve it[80]), the last category in James' prohibitions to overseas communities as portrayed in Acts 15:19–29 and 21:25 above, are not specifically evoked in the picture of Noah's sacrifice in Genesis; *'killing'* – which may be seen as related – in the sense that *'carrion'* has been *killed by other beasts* – is, since the *'blood vengeance'* that then follows is connected to *both 'man and beast.'*

The *Zohar's* *'Zaddik-the-Pillar-of-the-World'* and the *'Zealot'* Priesthood

We have already delineated the applicability of the *'Zaddik'*-notion to the persons of both James and Noah by calling attention to the Medieval *Zohar's* references to Noah. One of these passages also explains the *'Pillar'*-notation as applied by Paul to James, Cephas and John and connected to his understanding of *'the Central Three'* in Galatians 2:9.[81] It reads in part:

> *Noah was a Righteous One...after the Heavenly ideal* (here, clearly a variation of the *'Primal Adam'*/incarnated *'Imam'*-concept in Pseudoclementine, Ebionite, and Islamic contexts – in Christianity, even *'the Christ'*). *Scripture says, 'the Righteous One is the Pillar of the world'* (Proverbs 10:25)...*So Noah was called 'Righteous'* (Zaddik) *below...a true copy of the Heavenly ideal, and...an incarnation of the world's Covenant of Peace* (i.59b on *'Noah'*).[82]

It is interesting that this foundational, allegedly Medieval, work of *'Kabbalah'* tradition also seems to understand the *'Oblias'* or *'Protection-of-the-People'* notation as it was applied to James in early Church literature.

One encounters an excellent approximation of this, most notably in the section entitled *'Phineas,'* the paradigmatic *'Zealot'* High Priest and progenitor of the line of *'Zadok.'* One should add that, as such, he was also the ancestor of Elijah, Jesus ben Yehozedek, the High Priest of the return from Exile, and Joiarib, the first and principal Priestly course in the Temple from which the Maccabees claimed descent.[83] It reads as follows:

*When God desires to give healing to the Earth, He smites one Righteous One
...with suffering...to make atonement...and sometimes all his days are passed in
suffering to Protect the People (iv.218a–b on 'Phineas').*

The connection of this with Christian materials relating to the presentation of the scriptural 'Jesus' should be obvious and one could not have a better picture of '*the Suffering Righteous One*' than this. But it is also hard to believe that its relevance to materials related to James and, by extension, his '*Zaddik*'-status among persons of the '*Zealot*'/'*Sicarii*' mindset – for whom 'Phineas' was such an important paradigmatic archetype – could be simply accidental or fanciful.[84]

'*The Covenant of Peace*,' referred to as being '*sealed with Noah*' in this '*Zaddik-the-Pillar-of-the-world*' passage, can be seen as just another adumbration of '*the Zadokite Covenant*' detailed in Ezekiel's vision of the reconstructed Temple – in turn forming the basis, as we just saw, of the exposition of '*the Sons of Zadok*' in the Damascus Document from Qumran.[85] But it should also be observed that, aside from being evoked by Ezekiel (34:25 and 37:26 – a prophet of perhaps quintessential importance at Qumran) regarding *the eternal promises of the Davidic Kingship*, this '*Covenant*' is evoked, too, at the end – not insignificantly – of Ecclesiasticus (called by academics after its putative author '*Ben Sira*') in relation to Phineas – *again the prototypical archetype of the* '*Zealot*' *orientation.*[86]

In another, not incurious parallel, this same '*Covenant of Peace*' is evoked in the climax of the Qumran War Scroll's exposition of '*the Star Prophecy*' – a prophecy found, as it will emerge, in at least two other locations in the Qumran corpus – in the context of which, as just underscored, *the coming of the Heavenly Host upon the clouds* '*to shed Judgement like rain* upon all that grows' is evoked.[87] *Ben Sira* or Ecclesiasticus calls '*Phineas son of Eleazar, third in Glory*' after Moses and Aaron. It then affirms, that '*because of his zeal*' and '*because he stood firm*,'

*(he) atoned for Israel. Hence a Covenant of Peace was sealed with him, making
him Ruler of both Temple and People and securing to him and his descendants
the High Priestly dignity for ever (45:23ff.).*

The whole stems from the original use of these terms to picture Phineas in Numbers 25:6–15. There, because of his '*zeal*' ('*like that of the Lord's*') in turning away pollution from the wilderness camp of Israel and the Divine '*Wrath*' that would have ensued over the twin issues of *mixing with foreigners* and *intermarriage;* he was vouchsafed this eternal '*Covenant of Peace*' and '*the right to perform the atonement over the Sons of Israel*' in *perpetuity.* This puts things about as succinctly as one can put them and explains the basis of all these allusions. Phineas is therefore like Noah is therefore like Elijah is therefore like James – or, in orthodox Scripture, if one prefers, James' reflection 'Jesus.' Perhaps even more germane, in Rabbinic tradition, Phineas is also a *'Rainmaker,'* meaning that, like Elijah, he is one of these Heavenly incarnated forerunners.[88]

For 1 Maccabees 2:23–27, this is the same Covenant that is extended to the progenitor of the Maccabean family and, by implication, his sons after him in perpetuity because he *killed backsliders who were cooperating with foreign power* or *foreign edicts abolishing both Covenant and Law.* In doing so, to use the words 1 Maccabees uses, *'he acted as Phineas did against Zimri son of Salu,'* crying out, *'Let everyone who has zeal for the Law and takes his stand on the Covenant, come out and follow me.'* The *'Zealot'* nature of this Covenant, therefore – in spite of the fact of its being characterized *'a Covenant of Peace'* – should be clear.

This is the ethos, too, which is reflected in the burningly apocalyptic section of the War Scroll. The language of *'come out'* is also not unimportant here, being reflected both in the words Paul evokes in 2 Corinthians 6:17 above (to wit, *'therefore come out from among them and be separated, saith the Lord, and the unclean touch not'*) and, of course, the general ethos of the Dead Sea Scrolls, in particular, *the exodus from 'the Land of Judah to the Land of Damascus.'*[89]

Ben Sira, echoing 1 Kings 19:10–14 above, also sees Elijah as having this same *'burning zeal for the Law,'* for which reason *'he was taken up to Heaven itself.'* Aside from the allusion to Enoch in Genesis 5:21–24 (which produced an inordinate interest in this character in the Second Temple Period[90]) and the one, it alludes to, about Elijah in 2 Kings 2:1, this is one of the earliest *'Heavenly ascent'* motifs. Again the subject is also reflected by Paul in this same 2 Corinthians – this time in the important description in 12:2–5: *'I knew a man fourteen years ago'* (the same time span he specifies in Galatians 2:1 between his first and second returns to Jerusalem, both of which times he met James[91]) *'who was caught up to the Third Heaven'* (in the next line, *'Paradise'* – *'Pardes'* in the *Zohar*[92]), *'where he heard unspeakable sayings that it is not permitted a man to speak'* (was this *'man'* James?[93]). It is also perhaps reflected in the document associated by tradition with James, the *Ascents of James.*[94]

The Hebrew version of *Ben Sira* was found for the first time in 1897 in the repository of Medieval Hebrew manuscripts known as the Cairo *Genizah,* where the most complete exemplar of the Damascus Document, which we still use today, was also originally found.[95] In 1964 it was discovered again in, of all places, the ruins of the *'Sicarii'* stronghold of

Masada, where the '*Zealot*' hold-outs from the Jewish War committed suicide in 73 CE.[96] Previously it had only been known through Greek and other languages. Not only does it give the original of the notation in English, '*Famous*' or '*Illustrious Men,*' as '*Anshei-Hesed*'/'*Men of Piety*' ('*Hesed*' being in Hebrew a word which in some contexts is also trans- lated as '*Grace*'); it associates this '*perpetual Covenant*' – '*the Covenant of Peace*' which was sealed with Phineas and his descendants in Numbers and with those for whom God's '*Servant David*' was to be '*a Prince forever*' in Ezekiel – with those it refers to, as well, as '*the Sons of Zadok.*'

As already explained above, this term was first coined by Ezekiel in his vision of the new or reconstructed Temple.[97] In his vision, such '*Sons of Zadok,*' as we have seen, were described as '*keeping charge of My Sanctuary*' and *preserving it from pollution*, material fundamental to the Qumran 'Dam- ascus' or 'Zadokite' Document – therefore its name.[98] Not only were they to *clothe themselves* like James (who, it should be recalled, was pictured in early Church tradition as wearing both the mitre and breastplate of the High Priest) and '*the Essenes,*' only '*in linen garments*'; but like James too, as we also saw, '*no wool was to come upon their flesh*' and '*no razor was to come upon their heads*' (Ezekiel 44:17). Rather, as already underscored, '*they were to poll their hair*– missing from descriptions of James, but probably to be inferred.

In emulation of Phineas' '*zeal*' presumably too, they were instructed in 44:7 to *bar uncircumcised persons and foreigners generally from the Temple*,[99] motifs with a particular resonance to the events we have been describ- ing above and, no doubt, the epitome of what was meant by *proper Temple service*. No doubt, too, this was the way James was seen by his supporters, the majority of whom even Acts acknowledges, as already signaled, were '*Zealots for the Law.*' Here, then, all our key terminologies converge: '*the Zealot,*' '*the Zadokite*' (or, if one prefers, '*the Zaddikite*'), and what one might call '*the Jewish Christian.*'

In the light of these materials in Ezekiel and, no doubt, those in the Scrolls, it is a not incurious bit of disingenuousness that Josephus in the *Jewish War* rather characterizes the '*Zealot*' decision in 66 CE, on the part of the probably 'Jamesian' Lower Priesthood, to stop sacrifice on behalf of Romans and other foreigners and reject their gifts in the Temple that triggered the Uprising against Rome, as '*an Innovation with which our Fore- fathers* ('*Rishonim*'/'*the First*' at Qumran) *were unacquainted.*'[100]

6

Other Rain-Making 'Zaddik's in the 'Primal Adam' Tradition

Honi the Circle-Drawer or Onias the Just, 'the Friend' or 'Beloved of God'

For the *Talmud*, several other individuals are associated with 'rain-making.' The first, Honi the Circle-Drawer – 'Onias the Just' in Josephus[1] – is a 'Rain-maker' in both Jerusalem and Babylonian *Talmud*s (that is, the traditions as they were transmitted in both Palestine and Mesopotamia). 'Circle-drawing' itself perhaps relates to the 'Essene' Sabbath observance practice – also reflected at Qumran – of drawing a perimeter, outside of which a given individual would not move even to defecate.[2] In Honi's case, the circles are the ones to which he confines himself – also, most likely, not exiting from them even to relieve himself – in order to cause rain to fall.

He is a 'Rain-maker' in Josephus as well, where he also bears the tell-tale cognomen, as we just saw, 'the Just' or 'Righteous One.'[3] This manifestly prefigures the epithet early Church texts always ascribe to James, who – if John the Baptist's family and Jesus' family were indeed related as the Gospel of Luke depicts – may also have been *Honi's putative descendant as well.*

As Josephus describes it – with a good deal more precision, as usual, than Talmudic texts – *Onias put an 'end to a certain famine...praying to God,'* thereby echoing the Letter of James and prefiguring 'the Famine' all sources refer to in the 46–48 CE period.[4] As in James' final triumphant evocation of Elijah praying for it *both to rain and not to rain* and the efficacious 'prayer of the Just' or 'Righteous One much prevailing,' Honi also prays for it *both to rain and not to rain.*[5] This is the focus of Talmudic accounts as well. The Jerusalem *Talmud* will actually compare his situation to Elijah's in the manner in which *he importuned God like 'a Son to a Father.'* Therefore, Honi too, again like one of his putative descendants John the Baptist (possibly 'Hanin' or 'Hanan the Hidden,' as we shall see, in Talmudic sources below), is an 'Elijah redivivus.'[6] But for the *Talmud*, this 'sonship' relation of Honi to God will also present something of a problem.

In his description of what has to be seen as a parallel situation, Josephus will describe this Honi — that is, the character he calls '*Onias the Righteous*' — as the '*Beloved*' or '*Friend of God whose prayers God heard*.' In this context it is important to remark that '*Friend of God*' and '*Son of God*' are, for all intents and purposes, synonyms. As explained above, since '*Friend of God*' — applied in James 2:21–24 to Abraham in the context of describing how he was '*made Righteous*' or '*justified by works*,' not just '*by Faith*' because of the willingness he displayed to sacrifice his son Isaac — is equivalent to how Muhammad designates Abraham attaching the new term '*Muslim*' to him; '*Muslim*,' too, can be considered yet another synonym of these other two — just as '*the Christ*,' '*the Primal Adam*,' or even '*the Sons of Zadok*' in other ideological environments spinning off from these can — that is, '*Muslim*' = '*Friend of God*' = '*Son of God*.'

Just as James applies the '*Friend of God*' terminology to Abraham because, when he was '*tested*' he '*put his Faith in God*' and '*offered his son Isaac on the altar*' (a similar proposition, but from the Pauline viewpoint, is expressed, as already remarked above, in Hebrews 11:17); James also reflects the kind of prayer Honi is pictured as making in Rabbinic literature above — namely, '*of talking to God like a Son*' (here, the '*sonship*' motif really is being brought into the equation). It does so three chapters later in 5:13–18, as we saw, when it climactically evokes '*the fervent working prayer of the Just One much prevails*,' citing Elijah as its paradigm (who in its language, both '*prayed for it not to rain*' and '*three years and six months*' later for it to rain). But the '*Friend*' — or '*Son*' — notation would obviously apply to other like-minded and fervently praying suppliants as well.

To close another of these fundamental language circles, the Damascus Document — in setting forth its sacred history at the end of Column Two and the beginning of Column Three, now specifically developed in terms of those '*who kept the Commandments*' or were '*Keepers*' (in the Community Rule, the definition of '*the Sons of Zadok*' and a focus, as we have seen, of the Letter of James as well) — uses the same kind of terminology to describe the first person it denotes as '*a Friend of God*' — Abraham. '*He (Abraham) was made a Friend of God because he kept the Commandments and did not choose the will of his own spirit*' (like Paul?).[7]

To be precise, in place of '*Friend*' the Damascus Document (CD) is using another basic synonym to refer to Abraham and his descendants, Isaac and Jacob, '*Beloved of*' or '*by God*.' CD also applies yet another fundamental terminology to them: '*Heirs of the Covenant forever*.' These are all persons Muhammad in the Second *Surah* of the Koran (*The Cow*) groups along with Ishmael as the first '*Muslims*' as well.[8] This usage,' '*Heirs to the Covenant*,' is another pivotal usage Paul appears to know as well, only he changes it into 'Heirs according to' or 'of the Promise' (Galatians 3:29, Hebrews 6:17, etc. – in James 2:5, in the context of the 'Piety' Commandment of 'loving God,' 'Heirs to the Kingdom').[9]

This language of the 'Beloved of God' is also possibly reflected in that of 'the Disciple Jesus loved' or 'the Beloved Apostle' in the Gospel of John.[10] It is this language of 'making oneself a friend of men and thereby turning oneself into an Enemy of God' of James 4:4 too, which Paul is so anxious to counter, as we saw – particularly in the introduction to Galatians regarding the accusation that was obviously circulating at the time concerning him of 'seeking to please men' (1:10). It is also in 4:16 above: 'so by speaking Truth to you, your Enemy have I become,' itself obviously both responding to and incorporating the parallel 'Jamesian' aspersion just cited above as well.

Paul also uses these kinds of allusions as a springboard to parody another description applied to James in early Church literature, again dependent upon Hegesippus, of 'not deferring to persons.'[11] Oblivious of its original meaning here and in the Letter of James and, showing his usual mastery of repartee and rhetorical inversion, Paul reverses this in Galatians 2:6, attacking the very 'importance' of the Jerusalem 'Pillars' whose 'repute nothing conferred' nor 'made any difference' to him – for 'God does not accept the person of men.' So in this sort of nimble verbal exchange, Paul actually uses the phraseologies of his interlocutors to attack the very Leadership of 'those of repute' or 'reckoned to be something' of 'the Jerusalem Church' or 'Assembly' itself, presumably including James.

Elsewhere he varies this phraseology with 'God has no favorites,' but by implication he is using these allusions to attack those he refers to in 2 Corinthians 11:5 and 12:11 as the 'Highest' or 'Super Apostles,' who certainly comprise this Leadership and whom he also contemptuously dismisses as 'Hebrews' (11:22). Another thing these 'Super Apostles' or those he calls 'dishonest workmen' in 2 Corinthians 11:13 do, adding additional thrust to his scorn and playing off their attachment as 'Hebrews' to 'written letters' and/or 'letters written in stone' (his double entendres are always cruelly dismissive as well), is 'recommend themselves' or 'write their own letters of recommendations' (3:1–7 and 10:12–18).[12]

Not only are these 'Apostles' (Paul calls them 'Pseudo-Apostles' in 2 Corinthians 11:13 above, doubling this, as we just saw, with 'dishonest workmen disguising themselves...as Servants of Righteousness, whose End shall be according to their works' – another parody, both of expressions at Qumran and 'the Last Days'/'works Righteousness' doctrines found both there and in James) manifestly indistinguishable from the Leadership of the Jerusalem Assembly who, throughout Galatians as already remarked, *appear to be insisting on circumcision*; the attack would also be on Jewish claims to *'chosenness'* generally, as it is on the *'written words'* incorporating it (*cf.* Paul's attack on *'written words'* in 2 Corinthians 3:1–11 and throughout the letter, just noted above). Correlatively the attack supports *'the Gospel as (he – Paul) taught it among the Peoples'* (*Ethnesin* – Galatians 2:2) opposed, or so it would appear, to James' *'circumcision'* one. Such are his rhetorical and polemical skills.

For James 2:5, of course, it is *'the Poor of this world ('the Ebionim'* or *'Ebionites') whom God chose as Heirs to the Kingdom He promised to those that love Him.'* This last, it will be recalled, is the second part of the *'Righteousness'/'Piety'* dichotomy or the first of the two *'love'* Commandments. For Muhammad in the Koran 2:130–36, the Damascus Document's *'Beloved of God'* – Abraham, Isaac, and Jacob (Muhammad adds *'Ishmael'* to these) – *are now rather 'Muslims,'* that is, *those who have 'surrendered to God,'* an alternative, as just explained, to the use of *'Friend'* in James – *'Beloved'* at Qumran.

For Muhammad, therefore, *'Abraham's Religion'* is simply *'Islam,'* just as for Paul, prefiguring him, it was *'Christianity.'* Muhammad even refers to Abraham and, for instance, those *'Sabaean'*-like *'People of the Book,'* who follow him, as being *'of the Salihin'* – or *'of the Righteous'* (Koran 3:113). These last, it was explained, *'believe in Allah and the* Last Day, *enjoin Righteousness, forbid fornication* (one of the categories of James' directives to overseas communities and, as we saw, one of the most important of *'the Three Nets of Belial'* in the Dead Sea Scrolls),[13] and *'vie with each other in good works.'* For James, too, and Josephus (who actually calls Onias *'a Righteous Man'* (*Zaddik*) and *'Beloved of God'*), *'the Zaddik,'* the true *'Friend'* or *'Beloved of God,'* can actually intercede with God through *'his prayer'* to bring rain in times of extreme drought or famine. Therefore these ascriptions, such as *'the Beloved of God'* and *'Righteous One'* attached to Honi's name and echoed in Talmudic accounts as well, have more than routine significance.

The Stoning of Honi the Circle-Drawer as Prefiguring James

Josephus' description of the death of Honi is, not surprisingly, missing from Talmudic accounts which – while continuing the theme of his *praying for rain* – also have *Honi waking from a long sleep in his grandson's time* and *praying rather for his own death!* One will have to acknowledge, as we proceed, the odd sense of humor of some of these Talmudic hagiographers though, unlike that of Acts, at least it is not overtly malevolent.[14]

In Josephus' account, not only did Honi *once pray for rain in the midst* of a famine, but God also 'took vengeance upon them' (the Pharisees who stone him) by sending the most violent hurricane or cyclone. This is the same 'whirlwind' symbolism from the story of Elijah, 'a whirlwind' also signaled in Ezekiel's prophecies and evoked in detail in the First Column of the Nahum *Pesher* from Qumran. In Ezekiel 13:12–14, as we shall see, this will be directed against 'the wall upon which the daubers slapped plaster,' a crucial image in the Damascus Document too, for those it calls 'the Seekers after Smooth Things' or 'the Pharisees' as well[15] – in Ezekiel 13:10 'those who lead (the) People astray, crying "Peace" when there is not peace!'[16] It should be appreciated that Honi's death is clearly the work of the Pharisees (those who backed Salome Alexandra's older, more Pharisee-minded son, Hyrcanus II – c. 76–40 BC) – therefore doubtlessly too, the *Talmud's* reticence as heir to Pharisaic tradition in speaking of it. Both *Talmuds* hint at the reasons for Honi's stoning, but do not in fact mention that he was stoned. It is left to Josephus to apprise us of this.[17]

The circumstances behind this stoning in Josephus are important both in that *they exactly prefigure the death of James* (Honi's putative descendant and heir in the 'rain-making' tradition he represented) and in the insight they provide into the political configurations of the time.[18] According to Josephus, Honi is stoned by these Pharisaic supporters of both Salome Alexandra and her son Hyrcanus II. The disapproval of Honi by Pharisaic leaders, in particular Salome Alexandra's 'kinsman' Simeon ben Shetach, will also emerge in these same Rabbinic sources and, by implication too, the reason for his stoning.[19] Ostensibly, this was his refusal to condemn Hyrcanus' younger and more nationalist brother Aristobulus II (c. 67–49 BC), the Priestly supporters of whom had taken refuge in the Temple after Aristobulus' untimely capture by deceit by the Romans and were refusing to surrender.[20] This is the background to Honi's stoning.

The time is Passover, 65 BC, two years before the Romans under Julius Caesar's associate-to-be Pompey stormed the Temple with the help of these more collaborationist Pharisees, thereby putting an end to an independent Jewish State.[21] The attitude of *Aristobulus' Priestly supporters in the Temple* must be seen as 'proto-Zealot' or, what should perhaps be called, 'Purist Sadducee,' and even later – as, for instance, like those at Qumran – 'Messianic Sadducees'[22] ('Sadducee' being a transliteration into Greek of the Hebrew, 'Zadduki' or 'Zaddoki,' the 'Z-D-K' root of which also carrying the secondary meaning of 'Righteousness' or 'being Righteous'). This is, also, the sense clearly of 'the Sons of Zadok'/'of the Zaddik' at Qumran.[23]

Ranged against these 'Purist Sadducees' is a newer more accommodating or compromising group, familiar from portraits in the New

Testament and Josephus purporting to depict the First Century CE, that should be called '*Herodian Sadducees*' or even '*Boethusian Sadducees*' after the High Priest of that name ('*Boethus*') whom Herod brought in from Egypt after doing away with most, if not all, of the Maccabees. Those he did not murder he married![24]

Aristobulus' supporters patently have an attachment to national independence and oppose any accommodation to foreign rule in Palestine while the proto-Pharisees who oppose him – even at this time – just as patently do not. The same can be said of Aristobulus' father, Alexander Jannaeus (c. 104–76 BC), who was opposed as well by the same kind of '*Pharisees*' and must be seen as one of these *original* '*Purist*' or *more nationalistic* '*Sadducees.*'[25] Nor was Alexander a collaborationist or accommodating '*Sadducee*' of the stripe of the later ones in the Herodian Period we have just highlighted above. Nor, certainly, was his father John Hyrcanus (c. 134–104 BC).[26]

On the other hand, Alexander Jannaeus' wife, Salome Alexandra (d. 67 BC), the kinswoman of the '*Simeon ben Shetach*' just mentioned above who was one of the original foundational '*Pairs*' and transmitters of Pharisee tradition according to the '*Abbot*' literature (*The Pirke Abbot* and *The Abbot de Rabbi Nathan* we shall have cause to refer to further below), is manifestly pro-Pharisaic. Josephus makes it very plain that even her husband Alexander Jannaeus knows this.[27] Moreover he is very straightforward in identifying as '*Pharisees*,' the people who were responsible for the stoning of Honi the Circle-Drawer and the collaborators who co-operated with the Romans the first time they stormed the Temple in 63 BC. So is Salome's oldest son Hyrcanus II, executed by Herod in 29 BC, meaning '*a Pharisee.*' He allies himself with Herodian family interests and together with such '*Herodians*' must be seen as primarily responsible for bringing the Romans into the country and paving the way for the Roman/Herodian takeover and an end of Jewish independence.[28]

For his part Aristobulus – later poisoned by Pompey's supporters on his way back to Palestine with two legions after Caesar had freed him in 49 BC – had earlier been unable to debase himself before Pompey in the 65–63 events. As Josephus – no friend of resistance-minded Maccabeans, though proud of his own well-advertised Maccabean blood[29] – describes the episode at that time (in fact, a fateful one and perhaps a turning point in Jewish history[30]): Aristobulus '*turned sick of servility,*' *returned to Jerusalem to take refuge with his* '*purist Priestly*' *supporters in the Temple before his duplicitous capture by the Romans*. Aristobulus, therefore, is patently not a '*Pharisee*,' nor an accommodating or collaborationist '*Sadducean*' of '*the Herodian Period*' thereafter – the one most are familiar with through the rather distorted historical lens of the Gospels and the Book of Acts. This later breed of 'Sadducees,' as Josephus makes clear, were 'dominated by the Pharisees in all things' and supported and were supported by the Herodian Dynasty, even paying bribes to Roman Governors for the privilege of serving as High Priests.[31] This is clearly not the behaviour of any truly credible 'Maccabean' High Priest.

These matters are very complex. Plus they have been highly polemicized over the last two millennia. Nevertheless in this context Honi the Circle-Drawer or Onias the Just emerges as supporting, not opposing Aristobulus' 'Purist Sadducean' Priestly followers who had taken refuge in the Temple. One should keep this in mind when it comes to considering the deaths of James and other like-minded Messianists in the next century. Just as Honi's James-like cognomen 'the Just' implies – so admired was Honi by the general population because of his 'Righteousness' and 'Piety' that, when the Pharisees outside the Temple attempted to force him to condemn the supporters of Aristobulus within, he refuses to do so. Whereupon they (the Pharisees) immediately stone him.[32] As already suggested, this refusal is the ostensible reason for his stoning, but the legal justifications at this point for this are hazy. The real reasons however, which are similar to those behind the stoning of James (his putative descendant and heir) one hundred and twenty-seven years later, will emerge in the Talmudic sources we shall note below.[33]

In the picture provided by Josephus (certainly based on a source like Nicolaus of Damascus – as already mentioned, an Herodian diplomat in Rome – and not his own view), Aristobulus' 'Purist Sadducean' supporters are the lower priests in the Temple responsible for the daily sacrifices. As Josephus describes it, they have paid the Pharisees outside the city besieging them in the Temple (with help from the 'Arab' King of Petra in support of Hyrcanus II, itself arranged by Herod's father Antipater[34]) in good faith for animals to make the necessary sacrifices prescribed for Passover.[35] As usual, in these pivotal situations, the time is Passover and, once again – if such were needed – we have a good example of the scrupulousness of such 'nationalist' or 'Purist Sadducees' even under extreme duress, their unwillingness to resort to bribery, and their 'Piety,' putting proper 'Temple service' even above their own safety.

Even in the picture provided by Josephus – not someone who would normally be very sympathetic to their cause (as already noted, certainly based on a source and probably not his own perspective) – the Pharisees cheat them and refuse to hand over the animals, Aristobulus II's supporters besieged inside the Temple, had already paid for.[36] These are key moments and turning-points in the history of the period and, even perhaps as already suggested, Jewish history as a whole. Not only does Josephus (or his source) literally describe the behaviour of these presumable '*Pharisees*' who betray their trust – even if to their political and religious opponents – as '*Impiety towards God*' (the opposite, of course, of the '*Piety towards God*' so highly sought after by such opposition groups as '*Sicarii Essenes*' or '*Proto-Christians*');[37] these points are, not surprisingly, missing from Talmudic accounts. On the contrary, this must be seen as the '*Zealot*' presentation of the affair – the '*Rabbinic*' we shall encounter presently.

It should also be borne in mind that these Priestly supporters of Aristobulus *in the Temple* are the same hold-outs who, one or two years later, are ultimately cut down while faithfully *proceeding with the sacrifices in the midst of the Roman assault on the Temple* – another example of their extreme '*Piety*' and what, once again, has to be considered '*proper Temple service*' *according to a Righteousness-oriented* '*Purist Sadducean*' *or* '*Zealot*' *mentality in this period*. In fact, so '*zealous*' were they in this regard, *even at the expense of their very lives*, that, as Josephus himself avers, the Romans were themselves amazed.[38] This is what has to be considered as the attitude or orientation of '*Purist*' or, what becomes in the Herodian Period, '*Opposition Sadducees*,' namely, those in our view who ultimately come to be called '*Zealots*' or '*Essenes*' *such as those at Qumran*.

For his part, Josephus also notes, rather laconically and almost as an afterthought, that most of the killing in the assault as it was finally conducted by Pompey on the Temple Mount was carried out by the opponents of these '*Torah*-doing,' '*Covenant-keeping*,' Priestly partisans of Aristobulus (and, by extension, Honi), who *have to be seen as Pharisees*. It is they who *actually cooperated with the Romans in storming the Temple* (with Herod's father, Antigonus' help).[39] These '*Pharisees*,' Talmudic attempts at heroicization or idealization notwithstanding, have to be seen as characterized over the next hundred and thirty years – even in the picture Josephus, a self-professed Pharisee, himself provides – *by unstinting support for Herod, his heirs, and Roman rule in Palestine generally*.[40]

Because of said '*Impiety*,' Aristobulus' '*Zealot*'-minded Priestly supporters pray to be avenged on their own countrymen of the opposite persuasion, in response to which God now '*sends*,' as Josephus describes it, '*a violent windstorm*' – or '*whirlwind*' – which '*destroyed the fruits of the whole country*.'[41] This is an obvious case of '*pietistic*' intercession or, as Tractate *Taʿanith* would have it in describing Honi, '*importuning God like a Son to the Father*.' At the same time, it is the inverse of the situation, pictured in Isaiah 45:8 above and evoked in the same Tractate, of '*the Heavens raining down Righteousness*' and *the Earth* '*causing Salvation to spring up and*

Justification to grow.'[42] Rather the event Josephus describes in his *Antiquities* (as usual it is missing from the *War*) is more like that delineated in the Qumran War Scroll and the passage from Ezekiel 13, remarked above, on *'the Daubers on the Wall'* in the Damascus Document – who *'cry "Peace" when there was no peace'* – as it is that in Matthew's *'Little Apocalypse'* of the Heavens *'raining down' Judgement 'on the Just and Unjust alike.'*[43]

Not only should this be viewed as punishment for the *'Impiety'* of the Pharisee besiegers of Aristobulus' supporters' in cheating them (*n.b.*, how this theme of *'cheating'* is clearly also present in James 4:3–4:9 on *'the Rich' cheating the mowers in the field* and a similar *'Judgement'* is being patiently awaited), and an answer to the prayers of *Pious 'Zadokite'* or *'Righteous'* Priests attempting to do proper *'Temple service'* in the midst of all the carnage; but it is also Vengeance for the stoning of Honi, *'the Righteous'* and *'Beloved of God,'* by these same persons that preceded it. Though, strictly speaking, Josephus does not specify that this Vengeance is for Honi's death; nevertheless, at the same time, he does not distinguish between the two succeeding events to any extent, nor for that matter the punishment for them. But the cause of the punishment – *the 'Impiety' of the besiegers* on both counts – should be clear and it is re-echoed, as we have suggested, one hundred and twenty-five years later *in the events surrounding the stoning of James* and *the punishment inflicted*, according to the view of his supporters – conserved, it would seem, in at least one version of Josephus and in Hegesippus – *for this.*[44]

Both *Talmud*s recount the complex of views surrounding Honi's behaviour, but particularly the Palestinian one has Honi debating Simeon ben Shetach, already mentioned above as the most famous Pharisee Leader of the time and the kinsman of Alexander Jannaeus' wife, Salome Alexandra.[45] In this account, the issue is whether, in originally *'importuning God as a Son to a Father' to bring the rain and fill the cisterns* and, thereafter, *praying for the rain to cease* (both obvious cases of *'Zaddik'*-style intercession of the kind signaled in the Letter of James in its evocation of *'the efficacious prayer of the Just One'* – an evocation, it should be appreciated, that came after its appeal for *'the coming of the Lord'* and *Divine Judgement* in the allusion in 5:9 of *'the Judge stands at the Door'*), Honi was not guilty of *'blasphemy'* or, as the Jerusalem *Talmud* puts this, *'profanation of the Name'*; and here, significantly enough, *the comparison with Elijah is cited!*[46] Though not expressed in so many words, this is obviously Simeon ben Shetach's position, in *pronouncing the ban on Honi* – *'profanation of the Name'* being a way of expressing the infraction of *'blasphemy,'* in turn, *a pivotal motif in all early Church accounts of James' stoning too.*[47]

Honi's response, as conserved in the *Talmud*, alludes to *his exalted status 'among the People'* – a status also not unsimilar to that reported of James as *'Protection of the People'* in early Church accounts[48] – and their recognition of him as the *'Friend of God'* and *'Zaddik.'*[49] Though arcane, the gist of this response is that, *for the sake of 'the contrary decision' or 'adjudication by a Zaddik' or 'Just One,' God would annul a punitive decree or banning*, even one as extreme as this one on *'profanation of the Name'* or *'blasphemy'* clearly being pronounced upon him, according to this account in Tractate *Ta'anith*, by the Pharisee Establishment in the person of its most prominent representative, Salome Alexandra's kinsman, Simeon ben Shetach.[50]

If this Talmudic account is to be credited, not only do we have in it the confirmation of Honi's status – reported as well in Josephus and anticipating that of James – as *'the Just,' 'Righteous One,'* or *'Zaddik' of his generation*, but a reflection of the background issue that eventually led to his stoning. As in the stoning of James the Just one hundred and twenty-five years later, against a similar backdrop and for similar reasons; this can be seen as having been occasioned by accusations on the part of the Pharisaic Establishment of *'Profanation of the Name,'* or, to put this in another way, *pronouncing the forbidden Name of God* as James must have done at least once, probably in the year 62 CE, if the account of his *Yom Kippur*-style atonement in the Inner Sanctum of the Temple as an 'Opposition' High Priest of some kind, as reported in all sources, is to be credited.[51]

Other Rain-Making 'Zaddik's in the 'Hidden' or 'Secret Adam' Tradition

Not only does Josephus designate Honi, who *'prayed to God to end the drought'* and *'whose prayers God heard and sent them rain,' 'Zaddik'* and *'Beloved of God'*; he also describes how in the midst of all these troubles Honi *'hid himself,'* obviously for protection but also yet again suggesting the *'Hidden'*-ideology we have been highlighting above.[52] This *'Hidden'* notation is picked up in the *Talmud* in terms of a *'Rip van Winkle'*-style extended-sleep narrative, connected to Honi's person, and is also applied in it to another of Honi's putative descendants, presented as another in this series of archetypical *'Rain-makers,' 'Hanan'* or *'Hanin ha-Nehba,'* that is, *'Hanan the Hidden.'*[53] This *'Hanin'* or *'Hanan'* (in English *'John'*) is portrayed as the son of one of Honi's daughters, making him a grandson of Honi on the female side. Moreover, not only is the individual called *'John the Baptist'* in the Gospels and in Josephus often identified with *'Hanan the Hidden,'* but some texts have Elizabeth, John the Baptist's mother, as *the daughter of one 'Anon,'* that is, *'Onias'* or *'Honi.'*[54]

It should be recalled that according to the Infancy Narrative of Luke, John's mother and Jesus' mother were kinswomen (1:36) both, therefore, presumably carrying priestly blood at least on their mothers' side.[55] We have already seen how in the Second-Century '*Infancy Gospel*' ascribed to James and called therefore, *The Protevangelium of James*, John's mother Elizabeth *tried to 'hide' her son in a cave* (22:3). But in the same narrative, Mary too is described as '*hiding*' *the infant Jesus in a cave* (18:1) whereas in the semi-parallel materials in Luke, Elizabeth is alternatively described as, rather, '*hiding herself for five months*' (1:24).

Muhammad, in *Surahs* 3 and 19 of the Koran, also knows something of this '*Hidden*' ideology as applied to both John and Jesus and there, too, events surrounding their respective mothers are likewise conflated.[56] He also shows some familiarity with the '*Primal Adam*' doctrine we have been discussing above, pronouncing, for instance, in *Surah* 3:19 that '*the likeness of Jesus with Allah is as the likeness of Adam*' – a perfect statement of the doctrine; or in 19:17, in describing how God's '*Spirit*' was sent to Mary, that '*it assumed for her the likeness of a Perfect Man,*' again betraying more than a little contact with groups conserving this kind of doctrine in Syria and Iraq.[57] Once again, just like those '*People of the Book*' in 3:113–14 above, '*who recite the revelations of Allah in the night season*' and '*believe in Allah, the Last Day, enjoin Righteousness, and forbid fornication*' – a perfect 'Jamesian' combination, including the idea of '*belief and works working together*' – he also knows that John, Jesus, and Elijah (the grouping of these three together is in itself telling) '*are of the Righteous*' (6:85 – also see 3:39 on John as '*chaste*' or '*virgin and a Prophet of the Righteous*').

Since we have already encountered this same '*Hidden*' and '*Zaddik*' language in the Medieval *Zohar* above (again represented as a conduit for underground traditions, '*Kabbalah*' being based on the Hebrew/Arabic/Aramaic word, '*lekabbel*'/'*to receive*') – there used to describe the prototypical, rain-making *Zaddik* Noah '*the Righteous,*' who '*hid himself in the ark…on the Day of the Lord's Anger to escape from the Enemy*' – it is difficult to escape the impression that these allusions are not simply accidental and that the ideology behind them is connected in some way with the rain-making '*Zaddik*' or '*Friend of God.*'

It has also gone into Shi'ite Islam, attaching itself to the '*Imam*'-concept and producing in all functioning Shi'ite ideologies of whatever kind ('*Fiver,*' '*Sevener,*' or '*Twelver*'[58]) the notion of '*the Hidden Imam.*' This in turn is, as we have seen, but a variation of the Ebionite/Naassene/Elchasaite '*Secret Adam*' or '*Hidden Power*' doctrine or '*the Christ*' that descends – in Christian scripture, *in the form of a dove* – to be incarnated in any time or place in a variety of recipients usually connected in a familial manner to one another (in more Far Eastern contexts this looks suspiciously like the '*Buddha*' doctrine but it also can be considered Neoplatonic).[59]

As this is expressed in the Pseudoclementine *Recognitions* – considered, as should by now be clear, an '*Ebionite*' or '*Jewish Christian*' work – in the context of allusion to '*the rule of Righteousness*':

> *Know then that Christ* (now it is the '*Christ*' who is the '*Secret Adam*' or '*Hidden Power*'), *who was from the beginning and always, was ever present with the Pious, though secretly, through all their generations – especially with those who waited for him, to whom he frequently appeared* (1.52 – this '*waiting*' doctrine also appears in the Gospel of John in regard to '*the Beloved Disciple*' and will do so again in the Habakkuk *Pesher* from Qumran in regard to '*the Last Days*' or final eschatological Judgement. We have already seen a variation of it as well in James 4:7–10 above in *those who wait patiently* '*for the coming of the Lord*.')[60]

In earlier, more Palestinian, terms this same doctrine might be described as the '*pre-existent Zaddik*.' John the Baptist – himself possibly identical with Honi the Circle-Drawer or Onias the Just's grandson '*Hanan*' or '*Hanin ha-Nehba*' – is referred to in Mark 6:20 as '*a Just Man and Holy*' and considered, in the Synoptics anyhow, an *Elijah redivivus* (Matthew 11:14 and pars.), meaning, an Elijah *come-back-to-life* or an incarnation of Elijah. This is not true for the Gospel of John which, as we saw, is specifically intent on denying this point (1:21–25).

For his part, Josephus calls John '*a good Man*,' and both he and Mark apply the same word in Greek to him, '*Man*'/'*Andros*,' a term that fairly permeates the sections of the Koran and other like-minded documents where John and Jesus are being referred to.[61] John is also referred to as '*Enosh*' – '*Enosh*' meaning '*Man*' in Aramaic – in Mandaean Scripture, which is probably the origin of Muhammad's several references to him using a similar vocabulary. '*Man*,' of course, in Hebrew translates out as '*Adam*,' so once again, whether coincidentally or not, we are in the framework of the '*Primal*' or '*Secret Adam*' tradition so familiar to the Pseudoclementines and known to Paul in 1 Corinthians 15:22–49.[62] Of course Jesus is portrayed in Gospel tradition, figuratively or literally, as '*the Son of Man*.' This characterization may be at the root of the confusion between '*the Son of Man*' as it has come down to us in Christian Scripture and Daniel 7:13's original allusion to: seeing '*one like a son of man coming on the clouds of Heaven*,' on which it is supposed to be based, meaning literally, someone who *looked like a* '*man*' but who – since he *was riding on the clouds of Heaven* – was *not really a man but something more.*[63]

This ideology of '*the Last*' or '*Secret Adam*,' in turn, bears an eschato-logical dimension of '*the Lord out of Heaven' shedding Judgement* that brings us back both to James' ever-recurring proclamation in the Temple of '*the coming of the Son of Man with the Heavenly Host in Glory*' and the scenario of final apocalyptic War led by the Messiah – also expressed in terms of '*the clouds shedding Judgement like rain*' as we saw – in the War Scroll from Qumran.

Peculiar as it may seem, this kind of phraseology is also reflected in the Qumran Hymns, a document that repeatedly refers to its author's '*spirit of zeal*,' '*the soul of the Poor One*' (*Ebion*), and '*standing with the Army of Holy Ones and coming together with the Community of the Sons of Heaven*' in a War which shall '*scourge the Earth and not cease till the appointed destruction*.'[64] Hymns also asserts that God appeared to its author *in His 'Power as Perfect Light*.'[65] It is in this context that it refers to *both 'Man'* (*Enosh*) *and 'the Son of Man'* (*Ben-Adam*), while at the same time alluding to '*Perfection of the Way*' and '*Justification*,' concluding:

> *The Way of Enosh (Man) is not established, except by the Spirit God created for him to make Perfect a Way for the Sons of Man (Adam) in order that they will know all His works with His Mighty Power* (here, the Elchasaite '*Hidden*' or '*Great Power*' language yet again) *and the abundance of His Mercies on all the Sons of His Choice.*[66]

Aside from yet another telltale reference to '*standing*' above and the idea of '*Chosenness*' or '*election*,' this allusion to '*Sons of His Choice*' is a par-allel, should one choose to regard it, to Paul's '*Children of the Promise*,' already remarked in Romans 9:8 and Galatians 3:29–4:29 above, to say nothing of '*Sons*' or '*Children of God*' in both the Gospels and the Scrolls.[67]

In Mark, it is rather Herod the Tetrarch who calls John '*a Just Man and Holy*' (that is, in Hebrew, '*Zaddik and Kedosh*') – however incredible this may seem – and it is he who, '*hearing him gladly*,' supposedly wished to '*keep him safe*' ('*hide*' him?)! It would be hard to refrain from guffawing were it not for concern over what some might call their '*Faith*.' It should be appreciated that the words, 'a *Just Man and Holy*,' are almost precisely those used in Early Christian tradition to describe James who was not only referred to as a '*Just One*,' but also as *wearing the High-Priestly diadem with the words 'Holy to God' inscribed upon it*. Moreover the texts go even further than this, as already remarked, in the contention that he was '*considered Holy from his mother's womb*.' But so too, probably, was John the Baptist, particularly in Mark 6:20 above, but even more so in Luke.

Though Luke 1:15 does not use precisely this terminology, as it expresses this in the words of '*an Angel of the Lord standing at the right of the altar*' (our '*standing*' language again – this time used to characterize, '*an Angel*'), it is almost the same:

> For he shall be great before the Lord and shall never drink wine or strong drink and he shall be filled with the Holy Spirit even from his mother's womb,

that is, not only did John like James '*not drink wine or strong drink*' but, like James too, *he was* '*a Nazirite*' or '*Holy from his mother's womb.*' One also finds this kind of language in Paul who in Galatians 1:14, it should be recalled, claimed to be '*chosen from* (*his*) *mother's womb*' as well – that is, '*chosen*' to have '*His* (*God's*) *Son revealed in*' him!

This allusion to '*being Holy from* (*one's*) *mother's womb*' is actually replicated, as already remarked, with even more pertinence in sections of the Qumran Hymns, a document which also uses the phraseology of '*a Wall of Strength that will not shake or move from its Foundations*' – prominent imagery in various descriptions of James in early Church texts. These not only include the sobriquet '*Oblias*' or '*Protection of the People,*' but an allusion also to providing Jerusalem with '*a Bulwark*' – both undoubtedly connected to characterizations such as the one above.[68] In fact, the language of this '*extreme Holiness*' regime permeates the Damascus Document which even goes so far as to employ the nuance and metaphor of Naziritism or, what we shall call as we proceed, the language of '*N-Z-R*' – the root, that is, of '*the Nazir.*'[69]

These, then, are the categories of the '*Opposition,*' rain-making *Zaddik* or '*redivivus*' tradition. So '*Righteous,*' for instance, is Elijah and so '*consumingly zealous,*' as 1 Kings 19:10–14 would put it, that he does not die but is *taken up to Heaven alive* (2 Kings 2:1–11) – '*in a whirlwind*' no less. It is perhaps for this reason that, prefiguring Jesus, he was seen as being able to come back to earth and alive again or, as it were, become incarnated. We have already seen how the Jerusalem *Talmud* actually compares Honi to Elijah, even to the extent – incomprehensibly in our view – of applying the same '*ban*' or '*blasphemy*' charge, Simeon ben Shetach leveled against Honi, *to Elijah*! Notwithstanding, in the style of Noah, Elijah is perhaps the paradigmatic primordial '*Rain-maker*' and '*Zaddik.*' It is perhaps for this reason that James 5:16–18 in conclusion refers to him, as previously underscored, as a '*Man, who in a prayer, prayed for it*' both to rain and '*not to rain*' and, perhaps even more to the point, as an example of *the saving Power* '*of the prayer of the Just One.*'

The fact of Elijah's '*consuming zeal for the Lord of Hosts,*' as already underscored as well, is twice referred to in the all-important chapter – 1 Kings 19. Here the reference is specifically to *the Lord God of Hosts.* Again, this is almost exactly the language of the proclamation of James 5:1–8, following its allusion to how the workers, being cheated in the fields by '*the Rich,*' were advised *to wait 'patiently until the coming of the Lord'* (the '*of Hosts*' part already specifically evoked in 5:4). This is varied slightly, but significantly in the light of new concerns over martyrdom in time of Holy War, in Mattathias' final testament to his sons in 1 Maccabees 2:49–94, which rather asserts:

> This is the time to have a consuming zeal for the Law and to give your lives
> for the Covenant of our Forefathers (in the language of the Damascus Document's prefatory exhortation, 'the Covenant of the First'[70]).

To this, 2:58 added the pivotal, that '*for his consuming zeal for the Law, Elijah was caught up into Heaven itself.*'

Curiously, it was in 1 Kings 19:4–15 that Elijah was not only described as *taking refuge in a cave* – '*hiding himself*' once again? – to escape from Jezebel and King Ahab after having just made rain and slaughtering all their prophets of '*Baal*' (another variation of the '*B-L-ᶜ-language*' so important to Qumran and early Church symbolism?[71]); but also as '*going into the wilderness.*' There, he '*sat under a carob tree*' and '*wished to die*' (a feature of the tradition complex that will also reappear in '*Honi*' stories in Rabbinic literature)[72] before significantly, as this is put in 1 Kings 19:15, *making his way to 'the wilderness of Damascus.*' This motif of '*sitting under a tree*' will also resurface in these *redivivus*-type stories about Honi, as it will in their mutation in the one about '*Nathanael*' – a *stand-in*, in our view, *for 'James*' in the New Testament in the Gospel of John 1:49–51. Notices such as these show Honi, just like John, to be another of these *Elijah redivivuses*, not only in the matters *of being placed under ban* and *being a Rain-maker, but also as to his basic persona.*[73]

In an additional tradition stemming from this period Elijah, in turn, is considered to have been the incarnation of another of these High-Priestly primordial Rain-makers, the archetypical '*Zealot*' *High Priest Phineas.*[74] It is possible, therefore, to conclude that this '*redivivus*' or incarnationist '*rain-making*' tradition is, in some manner, connected to the parallel one about High-Priestly '*zeal*' and/or '*Perfect Holiness*' and '*Righteousness*' as determining one's qualifications to serve at the altar of God in the Temple.

In Numbers, it was this Phineas who killed backsliders and persons intermarrying with foreigners *to prevent 'pollution' in the archetypical desert camp*.[75] But just as Elijah's '*consuming zeal for the Law*' is referred to in the speech attributed to Mattathias in 1 Maccabees 1:58 above, Mattathias himself – whose own *Phineas-like 'zeal' in killing collaborating backsliders* was already depicted earlier in 1 Maccabees 1:24 – likewise, invokes Phineas' paradigmatic '*zeal for the Law*' in this farewell Testament to his sons (1:54). This he puts as follows – in the process tacitly declaring his own legitimate '*Zadokite*' ancestry and, consequently, that of his family descending from Phineas:

> *Phineas our father, in return for his burning zeal, received a Covenant of Everlasting Priesthood* (the incongruously-designated '*Covenant of Peace*' again).[76]

Abba Hilkiah Makes Rain

The Babylonian *Talmud* also refers to another mysterious, *rain-making* grandson of *Honi the Circle-Drawer/Onias the Righteous* contemporary with James, '*Abba Hilkiah*.'[77] These '*Abba*'-names, which like the similar '*Abu*' family names in Arabic signify '*Father*,' are very curious. They are not unlike the parallel '*Barsabas*' or '*Barabbas*' names normally connected in some manner, as we saw, with either James, Jesus, or other members of the 'Messianic' family such as '*Joseph*,' '*Judas*,' '*Justus*,' etc. – '*the Desposynii*' as these are called in early Church texts.[78] It has even been suggested that '*Abba*'-names, such as these, may in some manner denote '*Essenes*' which, in the more general way the term seems to be used, probably has an element of truth to it.

To give an additional example from the *Talmud*, Rabbinic literature ascribes the catalogue of what are usually referred to as '*the Zealot woes*,' to one '*Abba Joseph bar Hanin*' – identity otherwise unknown – that is, '*the Son of Hanin the Father of Joseph*,' a very curious designation indeed. This catalogue of '*woes*' attacks the various High-Priestly families in the Herodian Period in the most extreme manner conceivable and is expressed as follows:

> *Woe unto me for the Boethusians. Woe unto me for their curses. Woe unto me from the Sons of Ananus* (the family pictured in both Scripture and Josephus as being involved in the execution of Jesus and the judicial murder of James). *Woe unto me for their slanders...For they are the High Priests, their sons are Treasurers, their sons-in-law are Captains of the Temple, and their servants smite the People with clubs.*[79]

Not only is this a completely surprising passage utterly atypical of the *Talmud* – therefore the reference to it as '*the Zealot woes*' – but one should note the references to both '*Boethusians*' and '*Sons of Ananus*,' the condemnatory attitude towards both, and the references to '*Treasurers*,' '*Captains of the Temple*,' and how '*their servants beat the People with sticks*,' all subjects conspicuous in Josephus' picture of the progression of events leading up to the War against Rome in the Sixties CE.[80]

The note in these '*Zealot woes*' about the High Priests *sending* '*their servants to beat the People with sticks*' actually echoes two notices in Josephus' *Antiquities*, one just preceding the stoning of James and the other right after it. In both notices, the High Priests are described as '*sending their servants to the threshing floors*,' beating the People '*with sticks*,' and *stealing the tithes of the* '*Priests of the Poorer sort*.'[81]

Not only does the repetition of this notice indicate some confusion on Josephus' part about events surrounding the death of James (or at the very least some overlap), but in the Pseudoclementine *Recognitions* and in events surrounding '*the stoning of Stephen*' – the reflection of the stoning of James in Acts – Paul is implicated in similar kinds of attacks. Once again, there is the problem here, which we shall discuss further, of a chronological disconnect.[82] Of course, whatever else might be meant by the allusion to '*Priests of the Poorer sort*,' it certainly reflects the manner in which all accounts refer to the followers of James.

This language of '*woe*' in these notices, also reflects the language Josephus attributes to another interesting character, we have already called attention to above, named '*Jesus ben Ananias*.' He is unknown to the *Talmud*, but we shall presently associate him with the direct aftermath of James' death, as well as the well-known '*Pella Flight*'-tradition of the early Church – the legendary flight of James' followers across the Jordan after his death before the fall of Jerusalem.[83] This '*Jesus*,' as we shall see, seems to have appeared during *Succot*/Tabernacles, 62 CE, just following the death of James and, according to the picture in Josephus, *for the next seven and a half years he prophesied the downfall of Jerusalem* before he too was killed by an errant Roman projectile just prior to the fall of the city.[84] Though only Josephus seems to know of him, we shall argue that Acts 21:10–14's garbled account of the second appearance of the '*prophet called Agabus*' warning Paul *not* '*to go up to Jerusalem*,' *rather than to leave it*, is but a thinly disguised reflection of the warning of this mournful '*prophet*' Josephus calls '*Jesus*.'

For his part, though '*Abba Hilkiah*' is never heard from again in any Talmudic legend, the substantive second part of his name, '*Hilkiah*,' is certainly Priestly and surfaces at various critical junctures in pre- and post-Exilic history. He plainly appears to have been a member of the original High Priest line, *meaning he was a 'Zadokite'* and, as such, *a direct lineal descendant of the 'Zadok' who functioned as High Priest in David's time* (1 Chronicles 6:13 and 6:45). Not only was one of his forebears seemingly involved with the Prophet Isaiah (Isaiah 36:3–22), but Ezra himself is pictured – in what is probably an artificial genealogy anyhow, borrowed from Jesus Ben Yehozedek, the son of the last High Priest of the First Temple and, therefore, a 'Zadokite' as well[85] – as one of his descendants (Ezra 7:1–5). The latter takes Ezra back through 'Hilkiah' to 'Zadok' and, from thence, to Phineas – that is, Ezra *himself*, according to the overt implications of this genealogy, *is at the same time both a 'Zadokite' and a 'Zealot High Priest.'* The only problem is that the genealogy is, as just underscored, *basically the same one accorded Jesus ben Yehozedek* – the first High Priest of the Return.[86]

In Nehemiah, the name 'Hilkiah' is that of a 'Priestly' clan rather than of a single individual and appears twice, probably redundantly: once among the Priestly returnees with Zerubbabel in the Sixth Century BC and, a second time, among those listed as hearing Ezra read the Law in the Fifth.[87] The Prophet Jeremiah, who has close connections to another curious clan with 'Priestly' characteristics known as 'the Rechabites' (the clan into which, according to Talmudic tradition, Honi's putative descendants appear to intermarry, *the description of whom in Jeremiah 35 is very important for understanding the missing introduction to James at the beginning of Acts*,[88]) is designated as a 'son of Hilkiah' in Jeremiah 1:1. Though this might simply be a coincidence, the chronology is right, especially if we are talking about the original Hilkiah – the one involved in the Reform of Josiah (640–609 BC)[89] – who seems to have found the missing Book of Deuteronomy in the Temple in the Seventh Century BC (2 Kings 22:3–12)!

Another descendant – perhaps confused with an individual by the same name – said to have been the son of the Temple Scribe, Shaphan (himself associated with the first Hilkiah involved in the Reform of Josiah above), seems to have delivered a letter in Jeremiah 29:3 from Jeremiah to the exiles in Babylonia.[90] Most importantly of all, the most well-known and probably original 'Hilkiah,' as just signaled, precipitated the Reform of Josiah by mysteriously finding an additional Book of the Law in the Temple that most commentators take to be the biblical Deuteronomy. In other words, *the Biblical book we now all know as Deuteronomy would in some manner appear to be associated with his person.*[91]

It is interesting that just as Jonadab son of Rechab, connected to the founding of the 'Rechabites' and highlighted in Jeremiah 35:3–19, seems to have literally *stood behind Jehu in his chariot* (841–814 BC) – *a previous reformer* and *the King Elijah anointed on his 'way' to 'the wilderness of Damascus' after witnessing Jehu's 'zeal for the Lord' in destroying the devotees of Baal and Ahab's descendants* in 2 Kings 10:16[92] – so too did this original 'Hilkiah' appear to *stand behind Josiah's Reform and the Covenant he made 'beside the Pillar' to keep the Commandments and destroy all idols of Baal*, not to mention '*all the idolatrous Priests whom the Kings of Judah had previously ordained*' (2 Kings 23:1–5).[93] It is perhaps useful to remark that this '*standing beside the Pillar*' is another important bit of imagery found in the description of James' death in the document from Nag Hammadi, mentioned above and known as the Second Apocalypse of James.[94]

Even more germane on the popular level, *Jonadab son of Rechab's standing behind Jehu on his chariot* in 2 Kings 10:15–17 – another prototypically '*Zealot*' episode evoking, at once, both *Jehu's 'zeal for the Lord'* and Elijah's directive from God in 1 Kings 19:15–16 to return '*to the Way to the wilderness of Damascus*' and anoint Jehu '*King of Israel*' – is, of course, the paradigm used by Acts 8:26–30 to produce its patently disingenuous palimpsest of Philip being instructed by '*an Angel of the Lord*' to *jump up on the 'chariot' of 'the Ethiopian Queen's eunuch*' and *stand behind him* to decipher the true meaning of Isaiah 53's '*Suffering Servant*.'

It should also be appreciated that these '*Zealot*' intimations of the original instructions of the '*Rechabite*'/'*Nazirite*' Jonadab ('*Nazirites*' and '*Rechabites*' being, in fact, in this period basically interchangeable characterizations)[95] to Jehu *to rid Israel of all 'the devotees of Baal*' – itself a usage charged with significance – probably bears in some sense on the program as it was being set forth to Queen Helen's more '*Zealot*'-inclined son Izates (in due course, himself apparently to become King of both Adiabene and the Edessenes), here being refurbished via the magic of literary recreation in Acts.

These '*Zealot*' and '*Zadokite*' connections to the original Hilkiah in 2 Kings, coincidental or otherwise, are not inconsequential, nor are the ones to Jeremiah's family and the implications these may have concerning the '*Rechabite Priestly*' tradition connected to James and his '*cousin*' (also, possibly, *his putative brother*) called, as we have seen in early Church tradition, '*Simeon bar Cleophas*.'[96] In the version of the death of James conserved in Hegesippus via Eusebius, the witness to the stoning of James – depicted there as '*crying out*,' '*Stop, the Just One is praying for you*,' and identified by Epiphanius in the next century *as Simeon bar Cleophas* – is described as '*a Priest of the Sons of Rechab*,' an appellation that may be – as we have been intimating – just another circumlocution for '*Essenes*' or '*Ebionites*.'[97] In Acts this same stoning would appear to be transformed, as we have also already suggested – again via the magic of artistic recreation – into *the stoning of 'Stephen'* and the *'witness'* becomes the means by which James' and Simeon's arch-enemy Paul is first introduced to the reader.[98]

Further than this it is impossible to go. Nevertheless the circumstances surrounding *'Abba Hilkiah'*'s *'rain-making,'* described in Rabbinic tradition as *'a time of drought,'* certainly are striking and parallel the traditions about James in Hegesippus, the Pseudoclementines, and the notice in Epiphanius about James' *rain-making.*[99] In the Babylonian *Talmud*, for example, so frightened are the Rabbis of *Abba* Hilkiah that they will not approach him. Rather, they send little children to him, while he is *'working in the fields,'* to ask *him to make rain.*[100] The same motifs reappear in a tradition preserved by Jerome relative to James' pre-eminent *'Holiness,'* that James was held in such reverence among the people of Jerusalem and considered *'so Holy'* that *the little children used to try 'to touch the fringes of his garments as he passed by.'*[101] Not only are both James and *'Abba Hilkiah,'* therefore, more or less contemporary, making rain in a time of drought; both individuals are treated by all who approach them – friend and enemy alike – with a kind of *reverential awe bordering on fear.*[102]

A similar, albeit less convincing, portrait of 'Jesus' in the Synoptic Gospels has come down to us as orthodox tradition – another probable instance of real traditions relating to James' person being retrospectively absorbed into the portraits of Jesus. The individuals involved in the *'touching'* activity relative to Jesus' person or garment run the gamut from women with an unstoppable discharge of menstrual blood (*sic!*) to these same *'little children,'* as well as the blind, paralytics and, as a prelude to one curing or raising incident, *even a Roman centurion!*[103] The comedy of these episodes, sacred or profane, should not be ignored and *all must be strenuously doubted or taken to a certain extent as a parody* – often malevolent parody – of cherished Jewish beliefs, customs, and taboos.

The note, in the Babylonian *Talmud's* version of the Rabbis sending *'little children'* to ask *Abba* Hilkiah to make rain, of his being *'in the fields'* not only dominates the story, but to some extent parallels the allusion in the Letter of James to *the workers 'in the fields' being cheated of their wages,* already underscored above. It will be recalled that, in James 5, this acts as a prelude to apocalyptic evocation *of the imminent 'coming of the Lord of Hosts' and final eschatological Judgement* ultimately expressed in terms of *'waiting patiently'* for *'the coming of spring rain.'* Again, we have come full circle and have the note of *'the coming of rain'* – to say nothing of that of *'waiting patiently'* which links up, as already remarked, with similar expressions in both the Habakkuk *Pesher* and the Gospel of John.[104]

Jacob of Kfar Sechania's Curious Tradition about *'Jesus the Nazoraean'*
and Judas *Iscariot's 'Bloody'* Suicide

We have already touched upon how, in regard to a previous *'Zaddik'*
Honi; the Pharisee opponents, who ultimately stone him, cheat the
resistance-minded Priests in the Temple, who are intent on carrying out
the Passover sacrifices according to their precise specifications. Moreover
these hold-outs are the same individuals whom Honi refuses to
condemn. To further extend the reverse parallel with the Letter of James,
in the Rabbinic legend, *Abba Hilkiah doesn't wish to cheat his employees.* As
in the case of another character in the *Talmud* paralleling James, *'Jacob of
Kfar Sechaniah'* or *'Jacob of Sihnin,'* the locale is probably Galilee.[105]

In the quasi-parallel pictures of both Hegesippus via Eusebius and the
Pseudoclementine *Recognitions*, the requests become those made to
James (either by *'the High Priests'* or *'the Scribes and the Pharisees'*) to come
to the Temple either to debate or to quiet the crowds *'hungering after the
Messiah'* at Passover and, in both, the motif of hesitant reverence is
strong.[106] In Hegesippus and early Church accounts dependent on him,
James then rather proclaims, as already remarked, the imminent coming
of *the Messiah 'on the clouds of Heaven'* (meaning, just as in the Letter of
James, *with the Heavenly Host*). In all sets of traditions however, Hegesippus, the Pseudoclementine *Recognitions*, and the Talmudic Tractate
Ta'anith; James or *Abba* Hilkiah, or both, are almost always presented as
hostile to the Herodian Pharisaic/Sadducean Establishment and treat its
emissaries with contempt.

'Jacob of Kfar Sechaniah' or *'Sihnin'* is another individual with the same
name as James in Rabbinic tradition. In the *Talmud*, he is the bearer of a
curious tradition about *'Jesus the Nazoraean,'* the only one Talmudic *literature conserves* or was allowed to conserve in this name![107] The tradition is
attributed to the allegedly *'heretical'* and obstreperous *'Rabbi Eliezer ben
Hyrcanus'* – *'obstreperous'* because of run-ins (interestingly enough, along
with another colleague, *'Rabbi Joshua'*)[108] with Rabban Gamaliel, the
grandson of Paul's professed teacher by that name.[109] In this tradition, as
he reports it, Eliezer meets this *'Jacob'* or *'James'* in Kfar Sechaniah or
Sihnin, presumably in Galilee. In response to a question Eliezer poses
him about *'a prostitute's hire'* or *'wages'* given or dedicated to the Temple – an odd question to begin with – Jacob replies with one of his own
about what *'Jesus the Nazoraean'* said on the subject.

Not only do we have the *'wages'* motif here that we just saw in the
material from James about *'the Rich'* cheating the workers in the field of *'their
wages'* and its inverse parallel in *Talmud Ta'anith's* portrait of *'Abba Hilkiah'*

not cheating the workers in his fields above (to say nothing of the ill-gotten *'hire'* or *'wages'* we shall see *'Judas Iscariot''cast into the Temple'* below – *a patently parallel issue*); but this is clearly a special case of *'gifts to the Temple'* in general, whether on the part of foreigners or other types of persons deemed impure for one reason or another (as, for example, the well-known *'harlots'* or *'prostitutes' who share 'Jesus'' table* according to Gospel portraiture – again, surely relevant here[110]) – the rejection of which *was so important for this period particularly in the run-up to the War against Rome* as Josephus presents it.[111]

Crucially, as just signaled, this Talmudic tradition, attributed to *'Eliezer ben Hyrcanus'* about *'Jacob of Kfar Sechania'* or *'Sihnin'* (phonically not completely, perhaps, unrelated to the usage *'Sicarii'*) in the name of *'Jesus the Nazoraean,'* parallels and, in the writer's view, is the actual basis for Matthew 27:3–10's depiction of Judas *Iscariot's 'thirty pieces of silver'* as *'the price' of 'innocent Blood'* – a portrait which embodies the three motifs of *'wages,' 'gifts to the Temple,'* and *'Blood,'* and, by implication, a fourth, the Damascus Document's *'pollution of the Temple.'*

Though not paralleled in any of the other Gospels, the version in Matthew is extensively revised in Acts 1:18–20. In Acts, Judas doesn't *'hang himself,'* but rather dies somewhat mysteriously and, something like James in early Church accounts, after *'a headlong fall'* – from where is unclear, but *into a 'Bloody Field' they called 'the Akeldama,'*[112] – *'his guts* (like James' head, previously) *all bursting open and blood gushing out'* (thus – Acts 1:18). Matthew 27:6's *'wages'* or *'price of Blood'* now metamorphose into Acts 1:19's *'the Field of Blood'* (*'called in their language* – as we just saw – *Akeldama'*) and, instead of a proof-text *allegedly from 'the Prophet Jeremiah,'* which Matthew 27:9 quotes as: *'I took the thirty pieces of silver, the price of him on whom they priced, on whom they of the Sons of Israel priced'* (*sic*); Acts 1:20 rather applies passages from Psalms 69:25 and 109:8, already remarked above – the second, in any event, in our view, leading into the *palimpsest of the missing election of James as 'Bishop' of the early Church.*[113]

However this may be, the problem is that *Matthew 27:9–10 is not quoting from 'the Prophet Jeremiah,'* as it mistakenly thinks or claims, but rather *from 'the Prophet Zechariah'* – and this not a little *disingenuously* – a matter which will, however tangentially, also have to do with the not-unconnected issue of *the missing introduction of James* in Acts.[114] The extant passage in Matthew – which, as it stands, is a loose quotation of Zechariah 11:12–13 – was, in its original context, actually an extremely angry one. Invoking the language of *'breaking My Covenant'* in Zechariah 11:10, this had to do with God instructing the Prophet to contemptuously 'cast' the paltry 'wages,' owed him for services rendered in shepherding His flock, 'into the Temple Treasury.'

Not only is this the proof-text which somehow Matthew 27:3–6 manages to apply to Judas Iscariot's 'betrayal of innocent Blood' and suicide (always an appropriate theme, however distorted, where 'Sicarii' are concerned, as already remarked, and quite a feat by any literary measure); but it is from this, too, that Matthew 27:3 (along with 26:15 and 27:9) gets its proverbial 'thirty pieces of silver,' which becomes such a useful quantitative element in its narrative but, once again, not paralleled in any of the other Gospels – though it will be pivotal for materials connected with Judas' criticism of Jesus in the 'Mary'/'Martha' affair and interlocked with Rabbinic tradition we shall delineate further below.[115] Furthermore, it is as a result of the evocation of this citation in Matthew that the High Priests respond and are able to explain that:

> It is not lawful to place them ('the pieces of silver') into the Treasury for it is the price of Blood (27:8).

For their part, the two passages Acts 1:20 quotes from Psalms will immediately give way in 1:21–26 to the election to replace 'Judas,' in which the individual with the curious name of 'Joseph Barsabas Justus' was the defeated candidate. Psalm 69, the source of the first citation, is also a source of many familiar proof-texts including: 'zeal for Your House consumes me' (69:9 – 'My Father's House' in John 2:16) and 'when I was thirsty, they gave me vinegar to drink' (69:21 – Matthew 27:34, 48 and pars.) – this, despite the fact that the Psalm is a completely 'Zionistic' one, which ends with the assertion that 'God will save Zion and rebuild the towns of Judah,' which will be 'handed down to His Servants' descendants and lived in by those who love His Name' (69:35–36). This last, of course, is exploited in James 2:5 above in 'the Kingdom prepared for those who love him' and throughout the Qumran Damascus Document as will become clear as we proceed.[116]

The original passage, as it appears in Psalms, calls out for the Lord's even more terrible 'vengeful fury' and 'hot anger' on the narrator's persecutors in the plural, so that 'their camp would be reduced to ruin and none would inhabit their tents.' This passage which, in its original context as just underscored, is at all times plural is pointedly changed to singular in the citation in Acts 1:18–20 above, where it is applied, as we saw, to the 'headlong fall' Judas Iscariot takes, 'all his bowels bursting open and gushing out,' in the 'Field of Blood called Akeldama.'

The second, from Psalm 109:8, reads: 'Let another take his Office'

(*Episcopate*) which, as we have already seen as well, has more to do with the position occupied by James in the progression of these events than any position ever held by the ephemeral individual the Gospels denote as '*Judas*' – whomever he may have been. What is, however, equally interesting is that the Psalm in question not only refers to '*Lying*'/'*a Lying Tongue*' (109:2), a favorite usage both at Qumran and in the Letter of James,[117] but it is completely '*Ebionite*' – meaning, like the Qumran Hymns, it repeatedly refers to '*the Poor*' (*Ebion*) as well as '*the Meek*' (*ʿAni*) – but even more to the point, to '*the soul of the Poor One*' (once again, '*Ebion*' – 109:16, and 22).[118]

In fact, the last two lines are classic in this regard and therefore, worth citing in full:

> *I shall praise Him* (the Lord) *among the Many* (*Rabim* – the designation given the rank and file at Qumran),[119] *for He shall stand* (once more, the by now familiar evocation of '*standing*') *at the right hand of the Poor* (*Ebion* – we have heard this before), *to save him* (*lehoshiʿa* – the verbal root of '*Yeshaʿ*' and '*Yeshuʿa*' – '*Salvation*,' and even '*Jesus*' above) *from the Judgements of his soul* (109:30–31).

One can imagine what the exegetes at Qumran would have made of this Psalm which, in substance, so much parallels Psalm 37 expounded there.[120] In the writer's view, Psalm 109 probably was too, that is, expounded at Qumran. Therefore it was on the basis of such vocabulary – namely '*Zaddik*'/'*Righteous*,' '*Rashaʿ*'/'*Evil*,' '*Ebion*'/'*Poor One*,' '*Belial*'/'*Ba-La-ʿa*,' '*Shamar*'/'*Keep*,' '*Sheker*'/'*Chazav*'/'*Lying*,' '*Rabim*'/'*Many*,' etc. – that they appear to have selected the texts they chose to expound, the commentary on it either not having been written down, not preserved, or not so far been found.[121]

Nor is it insignificant that a Psalm – the Greek rendering in which, of the Hebrew '*Pekudato*'/'*His Command*'[122] or '*Office*,' is '*Episcopate*' (109:8) – which makes so many references to both '*Lying*' and the '*Salvation of the Poor*' (this last, *the name of James' Community in whatever the source*), is evoked in Acts just at the point where, we have suggested, the introduction and/or election of James as successor to his 'brother' *should or would have occurred in a more 'Ebionite' text*. One should note that in 109:6–7 introducing this, the '*Judgement*' upon those '*returning Evil for Good, hatred for Love*' is to be executed – just as in the Damascus Document which invokes '*the Angel of Mastema*' *upon those neglecting circumcision* – by '*Satan standing at his* (the Evil Person's) *right hand*' to assure he will '*be condemned*.'

Matthew 27:10 also adds the curious phrase, '*as the Lord commanded me*' – nowhere to be found in the original of the received Zechariah 11:12 either in the Masoretic or the Septuagint – deformed, as this passage from Zechariah may be to suit the exegesis the Mattathean artificer desired.[123] Not only does Matthew 27:9 render this, '*the price of him who was priced, on whom they of the Sons of Israel set a price,*' again nowhere to be found in the original in Zechariah (in particular, '*the Sons of Israel*' has been purposefully introduced – curiously in place of '*the Meek*' or '*the Poor*' in Zechariah 11:11 – to serve the ignoble aims of the artificer. In fact, '*the Sons of Israel*' is nowhere to be found in the received version of Zechariah at all); but Matthew 27:10 does add – obviously attempting some conformation with Acts picture of '*the Akeldama*' – '*and gave them* ('*the thirty pieces of silver*') *for a Potter's Field.*' Once again, however, '*Potter's Field*' as well nowhere appears in the original of Zechariah 11:13, upon which it is ostensibly claiming to be based, which only conserves: '*and cast them to the Potter in the House of the Lord*' – in the context, as is generally agreed, carrying the meaning of '*Temple Treasurer*' or '*Treasury*'). *Nor can this be in any way reconciled with what appears in Matthew 27:10 however one chooses to rework it!*

Nevertheless, at this point Matthew 27:10 does conclude laconically with the addition of the single phrase, '*as the Lord commanded me,*' again as just noted, nowhere appearing in the original Zechariah but, in our view, pointing the way towards resolving the complex of issues surrounding these proof-texts. In order to understand this, one must appreciate that what was originally being described in the document underlying Acts *was the election to succeed 'Jesus'* (in Islam, if one likes, the '*Caliph*' or '*Khalifa*'[124]) *not the one 'to succeed Judas*' – if the two, that is, '*Judas*' and '*Jesus,*' can really be differentiated in any way. It is '*Jesus*' who is really '*missing*' at this point and in need of succession, not the ephemeral '*Judas.*' The latter's 'disappearance' or 'demise' is rather made up on the basis of the absurd use of this Biblical passage, bowdlerized and mistaken-attributed as it may be. Nor is the use of this emblematic name '*Judas*' – the name of a series of revered Jewish leaders including '*Judas Maccabee,*' '*Judas the Galilean,*' and evocative of the very nation itself – to say nothing of the secondary title '*Sicarios*'[125] either accidental or incidental, but rather insightfully calculated to incite intense anti-Jewish feeling, which it has not failed to do over the millennia, its originators having doubtlessly succeeded beyond even their wildest dreams! It is this, perhaps, that the '*new*' Gospel of Judas may help alleviate – since, while nevertheless still antinomian, it tries to portray '*Judas*' as 'Jesus'' favorite '*Disciple*' – but, of course, probably never to the extent necessary.[126]

'A Prostitute's Hire,' the *'Rechabite'* Introduction of James, and the
'Construction of a Latrine for the High Priests'

The description that would have been used at this point to introduce the
person of James in a proper historical narrative and explain how he came
to occupy the *'Office'* he did, namely that of *'Bishop'* or *'Mebakker'*[126] of
'the Jerusalem Church,' could easily have incorporated the proof-text
about *'the Poor'* from Psalm 109, which Acts applies to the *'election'* of the
almost unknown and never-heard-from-again *'Apostle'* by the name of
'Matthias' – a name already present for all intents and purposes in Apostle
lists (such as they are).[127]

To provide a more intimate description of who and what James, in
fact, actually was and how *'life-long Nazirites'* like him might have been
perceived at the time, it would have been even more striking to include
'the Prophet Jeremiah''s *unique delineation of the clan of 'Rechabites'* – the *'Jeremiah the Prophet'* so oddly intimated, but the quotation from whom is so
curiously missing in Matthew 27's picture of equally-tendentious parallel events – to whom James, as a life-long Nazirite and possibly even an
'Essene,' would have been thought either to resemble or relate. Not only
were such *'Rechabites'* important as actual prototypes of what *'Zealots'*
(*'Jonadab son of Rechab'* actually being so characterized in 2 Kings 10:16
above and, as such, another of these paradigmatic *'Zealot'* forerunners)
and, to some extent, *'Essenes'* – to say nothing of *'Nazoraeans'* – were
actually seen to be; but Jeremiah 35:3–19 really does provide a good
description of James as he has come down to us.

Principal among *'the commandments which Jonadab son of Rechab' gave to
his descendants* was the one *'to drink no wine'* (35:14), which such *'Rechabites'* held in common with *'Nazirites'* and which we would claim
basically to be at the core of this missing proof-text regarding James.
Regarding this *ban on 'drinking wine,'* it is certainly not incurious that in
the Synoptics, the picture of *'Judas Iscariot'*'s *'treachery'* actually occurs in
the context of *'the Last Supper'* where Jesus is pictured as announcing, following Paul in 1 Corinthians 11:25, *'This Cup is the New Covenant in my
Blood'* (Luke 22:20 and pars.). But in the Synoptics, this is accompanied
by the additional peculiar phraseology bearing on our subject and
reflecting these singular *'Rechabite'*/*'Nazirite'*/*'Jamesian'* restraints, *'I will
not drink henceforth of the fruit of the vine until the Kingdom of God shall come'*
(Luke 22:18 and pars.).[128] So here, of course, is the very ban on wine
right in the context of *'the Last Supper'* and Judas' imminent *'betrayal.'*

Furthermore, as Jeremiah reports, such *'Sons of Rechab'* were
instructed, again not unlike *'Essenes'* and Josephus' mysterious teacher

'*Banus,*' '*to build no houses,*' '*but to dwell in tents so that you may live many days upon the land which you inhabit*' (35:7). The '*tent*' theme is particularly important where '*Essenes*' were concerned and it is already to be encountered in the original of Psalm 69:25 underlying Acts 1:20 above and, like '*Essenes*' too (and it would appear, James, Peter, Simeon bar Cleophas, and Pseudoclementine '*Ebionites*' generally), they were '*long-lived.*'[129] Interestingly enough, 35:8 adds that, like '*the Sons of Zadok*' at Qumran as well and, in our view, '*the Nazoraean,*' Jacob of Kfar Sechania will now refer to in the tradition he will report about '*Jesus*' below, '*they kept them*' or, as Matthew 27:10 above would have it, *they did what they were '*commanded*' to do.*[130] One could say the same about groups like '*the Mandaeans*' in Southern Iraq, who still conform to teachings of this kind to this day. Nor should it go unremarked that '*drinking no wine*' is a fixture of Islamic practice even today.[131]

Where the '*command to drink no wine*' – which the Rechabites hold in common with the Nazirites and, of course, James as depicted in all early Church sources via Hegesippus – is concerned; it appears over and over in Jeremiah 35, setting down Jonadab's '*commandments*' to his sons on this subject and the wilderness lifestyle generally.[132] This command is repeatedly reiterated along with the words about '*being commanded*' together with the idea *of doing what one is directed to do*: e.g., '*we will drink no wine*' as '*our father commanded us*' (35:6), '*we have dwelt in tents* (again note here the overlap with the original allusion to '*tents*' in the original Psalm 69:25 so deftly transmuted in Acts 1:20 above) *and obeyed and done according that Jonadab our father commanded us*' (35:8–10), '*the words that Jonadab son of Rechab commanded his sons*' and '*they observed their father's commandment*' (35:14) and, finally the active as opposed to the passive: '*the sons of Jonadab the son of Rechab have set up the commandment of their father which he commanded them*' (35:16).

In fact, this allusion to '*setting up*' (*hekimu*) here is actually the pivotal usage employed in the Damascus Document to describe how '*those entering the New Covenant in the Land of Damascus were commanded* (here the '*commanded*' of both Jeremiah 35:6–16 and Matthew 27:10 again) *to set up the Holy Things according to their precise specifications.*'[133] It is also the basis in that document for both the '*re-erecting*' (or '*setting up*') *the fallen tent of David*' and '*raising the Covenant*' *and the Compact* (that is, '*the New Covenant*') *in the Land of Damascus*' itself [134] – the counterpart to '*the New Covenant in the Blood of Christ*' in Paul and the Gospels (note the parallel of '*Akeldama*' and '*Blood*' with '*Damascus*' and '*Blood,*' which we shall elucidate further in our conclusion).[135] Nor can it be overlooked, again, that this '*Covenant*' is the very opposite, of course, of '*the New Covenant*' that Peter *is taught* and, through him, that which was taught to *the 'household of the Roman Centurion in Caesarea' with the telltale name of 'Cornelius'* (the name of the Roman law in this period aimed at *'Sicarii'* and forbidding *'circumcision'* as a kind of bodily mutilation on pain of death – 'the *Lex Cornelia de Sicarius et veneficis*'[136]).

Jeremiah 35:18–19 concludes as follows:

> Therefore, thus saith *the Lord God of Hosts, the God of Israel* (the language James 5:4–8 uses in speaking about the imminence of Divine Judgement), *because you have obeyed the commandment of your father and kept all of his commandments* (again note, the pivotal allusion to *'keeping'/tishmiru*, so intrinsic to the definition of *'the Sons of Zadok'* at Qumran above) and *done all that He commanded you* (once again, too, the fundamental emphasis on *'doing'* which is such a striking element of the content of both the Letter of James and across the breadth of the documents at Qumran – in Hebrew, the root as we have seen, of the key usage, *'works'*),[137] *thus says the Lord of Hosts, the God of Israel, Jonadab son of Rechab shall not lack a man to stand before Me forever* (again too, the crucial emphasis on *'standing'* we have been stressing – here clearly with irrevocable effect).

This is the proof-text we consider to have actually been present in the original – probably *'Ebionite'* – source being drawn upon and so egregiously and disingenuously overwritten at this point in Acts 1:20. Its traces, as incredible as it may seem, are probably actually to be detected as well in the curious and patently implausible, related description of Judas Iscariot's *'Sicarii'*-like suicide in Matthew 27:3–10, itself incorporating a proof-text seemingly having, despite its parallel refurbishment, nothing whatever really to do with the events in question either.

The point – convoluted and preposterous as it may be – is that this episode (as the Talmudic one about *'Jesus the Nazoraean'* above) is ostensibly being presented as having to do with *the rejection by 'the Chief Priests and the Elders'* (the same *'Presbyteroi,'* who in Acts 15:2 and 22:18 trigger the so-called *'Jerusalem Council'* and are involved in the last confrontation of Paul with James?) of *'the price of Blood'* (*'innocent Blood'* a few lines earlier) *as 'unlawful' for inclusion 'in the Temple Treasury'* (27:6). Then, through the tendentious citation of Zechariah 11:11–12 and the mischievous inclusion of *'the Sons of Israel'* there (note, as well, the actual employment again, intentional or accidental, of the verb *'setting'* – that is, *'the Sons of Israel set a price on him who was priced'* not, for instance, *'setting up the Holy Things according to their precise specifications'* as in *'the New Covenant in the Land of Damascus'* above – note too here, how the word *'Blood'/'Dam'* is being moved around in these various allusions), one so-called '*traitor*'s defection is *being blamed upon a whole People* (a charge now decidedly reversed in '*the Gospel of Judas*'), but hardly to be considered as a serious accusation, despite the fact that it has been taken up historically as such by the mindless multitude obsessed, somehow, with '*Blood*' lust ever since!

Granted, this is a rather tortuous and round-about task for the novice reader to follow where this particular bit of dissimulation is concerned but, unfortunately, these are the kinds of twists and turns the serious scholar of New Testament history will have to follow if he or she really wishes to unravel the almost serpentine deformations incorporated in many of these '*traditions.*'

Aside from the '*Bloody-mindedness*' of all these kinds of New Testament passages – itself not without consequences where the new directive of '*drinking the Blood of Christ*' is concerned – the issue of '*sleeping*' or '*not sleeping with women during their menstrual flow,*' germane as well to these '*prostitutes*'' episodes and itself a matter patently not unrelated to '*Blood,*' is parodied, too, in the '*touching Jesus*' episode, already alluded to above regarding the woman with an over-abundant menstrual flow.[138] The issue of '*sleeping with women during their periods*' will, of course, also be pivotal in the '*Three Nets of Belial*' accusations in the Damascus Document where it is *the key point bridging the 'fornication*' and '*pollution of the Temple*' *charges* there. Not only is it related to that of '*a prostitute's hire,*' but the whole issue of *barring Herodians* and *gifts from* or *on their behalf in the Temple*, since Herodian Princesses, in particular, were seen by their '*Zealot*'-style opponents as no better than '*prostitutes.*' Therefore, too, the more cosmopolitan scenes of '*Jesus*' *eating with* '*prostitutes,*' '*tax-collectors,*' *and other* '*Sinners*' in the Gospels are included, in our view, to expressly counteract this.[139]

As this is explained in Columns Four to Five of the Damascus Document relating to those '*sleeping with women during their periods*' – itself a clear indication of how Herodians were perceived, to say nothing of their easy intercourse with their Roman overlords who were obviously also perceived in the same way – the identifying, laconic modifier is added (almost as an afterthought), '*and every one of them marry their nieces*' or '*close family cousins,*' thereby further strengthening the identification of the group involved in such activity with '*Herodians*' and not '*Maccabeans.*' Not only could this characterization not have applied to any Jewish Priesthood, regardless of its orientation; it certainly could not have applied to Maccabeans, about whom there is, in any case, no evidence of such policy.[140] Furthermore, as the Damascus Document makes plain, the charge, pointed and unique as it is, is but a special case of the ban on '*fornication*' in general and, because of the historical circumstance just alluded to, the one of '*pollution of the Temple*' connected to it in the '*Three Nets of Belial*' accusations, already signaled above.[141]

The explanation for this is simple. Those coming in contact with persons behaving in such a manner, that is, '*sleeping with women in their periods*' (namely, Herodians and their Roman overlords) – meaning in this period clearly the High Priests whom the Herodians and their Roman overlords appointed – thereby incur their '*pollution,*' a point also specifically made in the Damascus Document following these same accusations, namely, '*no one who approaches them can be cleansed* (these last are the persons who in the same passage are also described as those whose '*offspring are of vipers' eggs*'). *Like someone cursed, his house is guilty – unless he was forced.*'[142] Nor are they observing proper '*separation*' in the Temple, '*clean from unclean,*' '*Holy from profane,*' the concomitant part of the description of such persons in the Damascus Document.[143] This last, finally, also carries over to accepting gifts from and sacrifices on behalf of such persons (even the Emperor of Rome) in the Temple – the issue, as already explained, which was the immediate cause or and that triggered the War against Rome.[144]

It is, now, finally possible to return to Rabbi Eliezer ben Hyrcanus' encounter in Galilee with '*Jacob of Kfar Sechaniah*' in the *Talmud* and the opinion Jacob heard '*Jesus the Nazoraean*' express concerning what to do with '*the wages of a prostitute*' or '*a prostitute's hire*' (in this case, not the field laborer's '*hire*' or Judas *Iscariot*'s '*hire*' according to Matthew's tendentious portrayal) *given as a gift to the Temple*. It should now be clear how much this issue relates to the points we have just been making – the idea of its being '*the price of Blood*' (as transmuted and reformulated above in Matthew 27:6) having a direct bearing on precisely the perception of this kind of activity, namely gifts from persons '*sleeping with women in their periods*' or those incurring '*pollution*' from such persons doing service in the Temple and the manner in which the Herodian family was conducting itself in familial relations.

Not only is '*Jesus*'' response, as pictured in the *Talmud*, a good example of his sense of humor – refreshing for a change, to say the least – not normally considered present in most Gospel narratives (except by the writer); but, more germane, it completely gainsays New Testament traditions of a similar genre depicting '*Jesus*' as '*keeping table fellowship*' with '*prostitutes,*' '*tax-collectors,*' '*gluttons*' (a euphemism for persons not keeping dietary regulations), and other such individuals.[145] Moreover, the sardonic sense-of-humor displayed by this '*Jesus the Nazoraean*' in his response makes the whole Talmudic tradition, in the present writer's view, *even more credible*.

As Jacob transmits this – playing on this theme of '*the High Priests*' in the examples just cited, particularly that of '*Judas Iscariot*'s relation to them and his rather peculiar demise – *Jesus the Nazoraean's* answer is that it was appropriate to use gifts given to the Temple of this kind – that is, *from 'a prostitute's hire' to construct a latrine for the High Priests!* This is really very funny and a subject of some interest both in the *Talmud* and at Qumran, where the placement of the latrines, as it were, '*northwest of the camps*' is specifically indicated in the Temple Scroll and hinted at in the War Scroll.[146] Anyone who cannot see how this tradition, as it appears in the *Talmud*, has been transformed in the highly tendentious '*Judas Iscariot*' materials, also involving gifts to '*the Temple Treasury*' and so steeped in allusions – as they have come down to us – to '*Blood*,' is just unaware of and exhibiting no appreciation of the process of tradition manufacture and/or elaboration in this period.

We shall see how this elaboration continues, reverberating back and forth between *Talmud*, Gospels, and Acts, particularly as concerns the '*thirty pieces of silver*' which have become so proverbial and comparable allusions to *fabulous 'Riches' and precious ointments*, at times also involving '*Judas Iscariot*,' but also others, when it comes to considering the last and final '*Rain-maker*' in Talmudic tradition '*Nakdimon ben Gurion*' (or, as Josephus appears to call him, '*Gurion ben Nakdimon*'). Of course, just as some of the other characters we have been considering – such as '*Ananias*,' '*Agbarus*,' '*Theudas*,' and the Adiabenean '*Queen*' – the double or *alter ego* of this '*Nakdimon*' in the *Talmud* reappears in the Gospel of John as '*Nicodemus*' described, as we shall see in due course in John 3:1 below, as '*a man of the Pharisees*' and '*a Ruler of the Jews*' (thus!) and pictured in John 19:39 (along with '*Joseph of Arimathaea*') as '*bearing a hundred weight*' *of expensive 'ointments'* or '*perfumes*' with which he *helped prepare the body of 'Jesus' for burial*.

7

Revolutionary Messianism and the Elijah *Redivivus* Tradition

Elijah's Cave-Dwelling, Honi's Extended Sleep, and Revolutionary Messianism

Both the Palestinian and the Babylonian *Talmud*s now go on to relate a story about how Honi went to sleep for '*seventy years*' under '*a carob tree*' – not unlike Buddha '*under the Bodhi tree*' or, in the case of the Nathanael-type stand-in for James in the Gospel of John above, '*under a fig tree*.'[1] When Honi awakes in his grandson's generation nobody knew or recognized him, whereupon he immediately *prayed for death and died* – another example of the *Talmud*'s sense of humor.[2] This is a very curious even sardonic story. Not only are the number '*seventy*' and the element of '*carob tree*' significant for our period, but so too are Honi's *going to sleep* and *praying for death*.

The Palestinian *Talmud* even preserves a puzzling further variation of this story, which has Honi the grandfather of yet another individual, once again called '*Honi the Circle-Drawer*.'[3] Whether this individual is supposed to be the same as the one the Babylonian *Talmud* is calling '*Abba Hilkiah*,' with whom he would be contemporary – he probably is – or just another individual in the *redivivus* tradition, confused in the Palestinian *Talmud* with Honi, is impossible to say. Not only this, the Palestinian *Talmud* puts these events at the time of *the destruction of the First Temple* when they clearly must be seen in relation to or in the context of the destruction of *the Second*. What appears to be confusing these traditions is the '*redivivus*'-ideology they all seem to be wrestling with or trying to present, however imperfectly.

As with the descendants of the '*Hilkiah*' involved in Josiah's Reform and Jeremiah's forebear previously, we seem to be involved with a line or even a clan of such individuals much like '*the Rechabites*' – or should we rather call them '*proto-Essenes*' or '*Ebionites*'? – highlighted above as having to do with either James or his '*cousin*' (even his putative '*brother*'), Simeon Bar Cleophas. At least this is the information one can garner by superimposing Epiphanius' version of events on Eusebius'. Certainly we

have confusions of traditions, overlapping individuals and probably –
since they all seem to involve '*rain-making*' and '*falling asleep and waking
up later*' – a variation on the *redivivus* '*Zealot*' (and, as it will turn out,
'*Zadokite*') Priestly line coming down from Phineas through Zadok to
Elijah to Honi to either James or John the Baptist, or both.

This is exactly the theme we now encounter in the Palestinian
Talmud with regard to this second '*Honi the Circle-Drawer*,' for he too *goes
to sleep and wakes up again seventy years later – this time, supposedly in the time
of Zerubbabel after the Temple has already been destroyed and rebuilt again.*[4] The
'*seventy years*' involved here is certainly based upon Jeremiah 29:10's
numerology for the length of the Exile, a characterization which also
includes the notions of a '*Visitation*' and the vocabulary of '*the Wrath*,' all
of the utmost importance for the eschatological scheme of both the War
Scroll and Damascus Document at Qumran as well.[5] In Daniel 9:2–27,
this number '*seventy*' is actually referred to with reference to Jeremiah
and reinterpreted, not only in terms of '*the Period of Wrath*,' but also successive devastations of Jerusalem concluding importantly with *the setting
up of 'the Abomination of the Desolation' in the Temple.* Of course, according
to the chronology of the story of the '*second*' Honi in the Palestinian
Talmud, which puts him at the time of the destruction of the First
Temple, none of this makes any sense whatsoever.

Such is often the case with the *Talmud* based, as its traditions sometimes are, on garbled oral tradition and/or possible copyists' error. Still,
it is interesting that this '*second*' Honi goes to sleep '*in a mountain cave*'
rather than – as the first Honi – '*under a carob tree*.' This brings us to a possible solution to our problem – if there is one. As we have already
underscored above, Honi like John the Baptist is an Elijah *redivivus* or an
Elijah *come-back-to-life*. In fact, it is very probable that he, not John (since
John is most likely his descendant and one of these '*Hanin*''s or '*Honi*''s)
is the original behind the '*Elijah redivivus*' ideology as reported in the
New Testament.

What we are witnessing in later Gospel rewrites of this conceptuality – the Gospel of John, as we have seen, specifically denying the
ideology where John was concerned – are, once again, themes from
other narrative sources being absorbed into their '*Jesus*' story. We have
already remarked this happening with regards to elements from James'
biography.[6] It also happens regarding themes surrounding the series of
other charismatic agitators, '*Innovators*,' '*Impostors*,' or '*Pseudo-prophets*'
described in Josephus – the derogations are his not the author's – for
instance, '*Theudas*' leading the People across Jordan in a reverse exodus,
the Samaritan Messiah apparently brutally crucified along with a

number of his followers by Pontius Pilate, or '*the Egyptian*' on the Mount of Olives, for whom Paul is supposedly mistaken in Acts 21:38 (here, for instance, the terminology '*Sicarii*,' as we saw, was actually used to describe his followers), and others.[7] In Acts this kind of absorption of materials from other sources is raised to the level of art.

That this is the implication of the '*second*' Honi story (to say nothing of the first) is strengthened by its relation to the 1 Kings 19:10 story citing Elijah's '*burning zeal for the Lord of Hosts*,' as we saw – language also present in the Letter of James to some extent, to say nothing of the Gospel of John 2:17's '*zeal of Your House consuming me.*' Not only is Elijah '*filled with*' or '*consumed*' by such '*zeal*' but, in this episode, before going into the cave and, from thence, '*into the wilderness*' of Sinai '*to stand upon the mountain before the Lord*' and witness the miracles or '*earthquake*,' '*fire*,' and '*whirlwind*' (19:9–12), he also '*sits down under a carob tree*' and this, too, actually '*in the wilderness*' (1 Kings 19:4). Here *Elijah prays* – as in the Honi stories – that '*he might die*' and *he too then falls asleep!*

In the '*Honi*' stories the order is just reversed. In John 1:45–51's variation involving '*Nathanael*' above – where '*Jesus*' is now pictured as uttering (significantly just before '*Nathanael*' recognizes him as '*the Son of God*') the typically Greco-Roman anti-Semitic gibe, '*Behold an Israelite in whom there is no guile*' (*sic*), and in line with John's distinct denial that John the Baptist was '*the Elijah-come-back-to-life*' – it is now '*Nathanael*' not John who is '*the Honi*' or '*Elijah redivivus.*' The vision Jesus predicts '*Nathanael*' will see in return for having recognized him as '*the Son of God*' is, yet again, just another variation on the one accorded James in the Temple in early Church literature and Stephen in Acts 7:53–58 (before he, too, was '*cast out of the city*' – *ekbalontes* – and stoned[8]). Even '*the mountain cave*' element of the Palestinian *Talmud*'s '*second*' Honi story is prefigured in 1 Kings 19:8 above as '*the Mountain of the Lord in Horeb*' where Elijah – and '*Jesus*,' thereafter, according to additional Synoptic Gospel portraiture – is also now to spend '*forty days and forty nights.*'

But Elijah does not sleep for '*seventy years*,' as the Honi stories revamp this aspect of the story in the light of the new eschatology of *the coming* '*Wrath*' and the '*redivivus*'-tradition attaching itself to Honi's family line and that of '*rain-making*' *Zaddiks* generally. Rather in 1 Kings, Elijah is twice awoken by '*the Angel of the Lord*' and told to '*eat and drink*' – another important motif of the arguments between Paul and James, as we have been remarking, retrospectively incorporated into Gospel portraiture. This is because, during '*the forty days and nights*' he is about to spend – *like Moses on the Mountain in Sinai* – there presumably will be no food.

So now we have the twin themes of a Moses-like '*wilderness*' experience tied to '*a burning zeal for the Lord of Hosts*.' This ideological combination can, in turn, be read into the temporary '*Nazirite*' procedure of '*not eating and drinking*,' revised into the kind of vegetarianism and abstinence followed by even '*life-long Nazirites*' and later '*Mourners for Zion*' – positions which Paul consistently reverses to the extent even, as already signaled above, of '*drinking the blood*' of the Messiah (to say nothing of '*eating*' his flesh), as do the Gospels along with him even to the extent of portraying '*the Son of Man*' as '*coming eating and drinking*.'[9]

A good example of the opposite sort of behaviour, as we saw, are the temporary '*Nazirite*'-type oaths which the '*Sicarii*'-style assassins vow in Acts 23:21 '*not to eat or drink until they have killed Paul*' (for '*the Mourners for Zion*,' it will be recalled, it was '*not to eat or drink until they had seen the Temple rebuilt*' – in I Corinthians 3:9–17, Ephesians 2:21, and the Synoptics, of course, identical with '*Jesus*'[10]). Typically, Acts laconically describes such persons simply as '*Jews*'.

These '*Honi the Circle-Drawer*' stories in the two *Talmuds*, despite their confusion over which Honi is actually being referred to and when he lived, together with their expansion of Elijah's paradigmatic activity – whether '*falling asleep*' *under a carob tree* or '*in a mountain cave*' – must be seen as part and parcel of an incarnationist '*Zaddik*' or '*Primal Adam*' tradition which includes the elements of '*consuming zeal for the Lord*,' '*rain-making*' (probably to be taken more in its eschatological sense than a natural one), and '*the Friend of God*' ideology. Similar stories will be told in later Talmudic tradition about Simeon Bar Yohai, the progenitor of *Zohar* tradition, who together with his son *hides* '*in a cave*' *for years in the Trajan/Bar Kochba Period*.[11]

The only difference between the Hebrew version of this conception, as we encounter it in Palestine from the person of Honi onwards, and others – including that of '*the Christ*' and the later Shi'ite Islamic '*Imam*' further afield – is that in Palestine, the '*Zaddik*'-ideal becomes associated with the ongoing Revolutionary strife against all vestiges of foreign rule and concomitant '*consuming zeal for the Lord of Hosts*' directed against Jewish Law-breakers and backsliders too.[12] This, in turn, becomes entwined in the First Century CE in Palestine with the struggle against the Herodian Royal Family (if we can call it this, since groups embracing such ideas did not recognize it as '*Royal*' at all) and their hangers-on or collaborators. This would include the High Priesthood appointed by this family and the Roman Procurators in succession (or allied) to it – which, therefore, should be called, as we have already pointed out, the '*Herodian*' High Priesthood, by this time already being called '*Sadducees*' as well – and teachers like Paul.

This *'Zealot,' 'rain-making' Zaddik*-tradition attaches itself to putative second or third-generation descendants of Honi, such as John the Baptist and James, and, through them, the *'Messianic'*-ideal, no matter what definition of it one finally chooses to use. By contrast, the *'redivivus Elijah'*-tradition in its initial manifestation only attached itself to Honi. Where Paul is concerned, so practised was he in polemical dialectic and rhetorical debate that in Romans 13:2–3 he is even able to invert the issue of *'Law-breaking'* to encompass rather, *those who break Roman Law* (as he puts it so cannily, *'the Authorities God appoints' and their 'Ordinances'*) not Jewish Law and it is now patently Roman Law that is being referred to as *'the Ordinances of God'* not Mosaic.

Furthermore, in Romans 13:4–10, he even goes so far as to use *the 'all-Righteousness' Commandment,* *'love your neighbor as yourself* (in James 2:8 *'the Royal Law according to the Scripture'*), *to support paying taxes* (clearly to Rome), which every Government official – who in Paul's agile dialectic have now *suddenly been turned into 'the Servants of God'* (not, as one would elsewhere suspect – as at Qumran for instance – *'the Sons of Zadok'*) *has a right to expect.* In 2 Corinthians 11:13–15, as already remarked, he even turns this designation as it relates to the actual Leadership of the Movement around as well. Now this Leadership, whom he claims – like *'the Sons of Zadok'* at Qumran[13] – are being designated by some as *'Servants of Righteousness'* (which would clearly have to include James, Peter – *'Cephas'* in Galatians 2:9 – and John *'whose End shall be according to their works,'* vocabulary very close to what one also finds at Qumran[14]), are rather merely *'disguising themselves as Apostles of Christ'* and are, as we have seen as well, in reality only *'deceitful workmen'* and Satan-like *'Pseudo-Apostles'* (2 Corinthians 13:13)!

In 1 Corinthians 8:1–13, where he actually uses the *'Piety'* language of *'loving God'* and builds towards rejecting James' ban on *'things sacrificed to idols'* (viz., *'an idol is nothing in this world'* – *'nor if we eat are we better off, nor if we do not eat are we worse'*); Paul dismisses such *'scruples'* as the *'weak consciences'* of the ubiquitous *'some.'* In doing so, he actually uses the *'puffed up'* language we shall encounter, as we proceed, in the Habakkuk *Pesher,* based on Habakkuk 2:4 where it introduces the all-important biblical proof-text, *'the Righteous shall live by his Faith.'* But as Paul uses the expression, he applies it to what is clearly the Leadership of the Jerusalem Church, *'puffed up'* by its own *'Knowledge'* when it should be *'built up'* by *'love;'* or, as he so cannily puts it in 8:1 – using what we shall see to be the pivotal language of *'building'* – *'love builds up.'* For its part, the Habakkuk *Pesher,* introducing its key exegesis of this same *'the Righteous shall live by his Faith,'* actually interprets it in terms of the punishment the

Guilty '*will multiply upon themselves when they are judged*' – presumably at *the Last Judgement*, the *Pesher* always being very consistent on allusions of this kind to '*the Last Judgement*.'[15]

'*The Days of Noah*' and the Coming Eschatological Flood

Of course the biblical story about Elijah, in imitation of Moses, to say nothing of Noah, spending '*forty days and nights on the Mountain of God in Horeb*' prefigures Jesus' '*Temptation*' *for forty days and forty nights* '*in the wilderness*' as retold in Gospel narratives – with, to be sure as is usually the case, precisely the opposite effect since, as the Gospels retell it, the whole episode is viewed *as the result of* '*Devilish*' or '*Satanic*' *manipulation*.[16] The Pseudoclementine *Homilies* also alludes to this confrontation '*in the wilderness*' with the Devil but, according to it, the victors are those following James – '*Satan's servants*' being, in fact, '*Apostles*' such as Paul, who have no written credentials from James and do not teach his position on '*abstaining from blood, fornication, things sacrificed to idols, and carrion*,' but are rather sent to '*deceive*' – that is, it is they who are '*Satan's Servants*' or '*Deceivers*' not *vice versa*![17]

For their part, as the Synoptics (if not John) present this episode, the focus is shifted and it is rather aimed at just those kinds of charismatic Revolutionaries, to whom 'Jesus' (if he existed as such) must have belonged and who, together with extreme purity-minded '*Zaddik*' or '*Zadokite*' Leaders (who in other contexts go by the name of '*Nazirites*' or '*Nazoraeans*'), were indulging in the same sort of '*redivivus*' posturing that commentators like Josephus considered so fraudulent.[18] Josephus also basically evokes the same two themes of a '*wilderness*' sojourn and Satanic manipulation and, in his accounts, what these '*Impostors*' and '*Religious Frauds*' – '*who were in intent more dangerous even than the Bandit Leaders or Revolutionaries*' – were doing, as we have already explained, was '*leading the People out into the wilderness there to show them the signs of their impending Freedom*' or '*Redemption*' – '*signs*,' the Gospel narratives seem to imply, that were no better than '*Temptation by the Devil*.'[19]

Actually, scriptural stories about Elijah generally prefigure those about 'Jesus', including raising the dead, curing, etc., the only difference being that the more xenophobic portrayal of Elijah's attitude of apocalyptic '*zeal*' is, in almost every instance, jettisoned. On the contrary, guided by the anti-nationalist antinomianism of teachers like Paul, it has been totally reversed into the mirror opposite comprising an amorphous form of cosmopolitanism reflecting the ideals of the Roman '*Pax Romana*' wholly at odds with the normative ethos of Palestinian

'*Messianism*' as reflected in the Dead Sea Scrolls and the general '*Elijah redivivus*' tradition resting on '*a consuming zeal*' for either God or the *Torah* of Moses, or both.

In fact, if one looks closely at the above episode, where Elijah encounters '*the Angel of the Lord*' in a cave, one will even be able to detect the prefiguration of the earliest *surah*s of the Koran depicting, as they do, Muhammad's opening visionary experiences '*in a cave.*'[20] These include the theme of all-night vigils in caves such as this, coming out and wrapping himself in his '*cloak*' or '*raiment*,' and being told by the Angel – in this case, purportedly Gabriel – '*Arise and warn*' (*Surah* 84:1–2 – '*The Cloaked One*').[21] In Elijah's case, it will be recalled, it was, rather, '*Arise and eat*' – presumably to prepare himself for the journey to the Mountain of the Lord in Sinai![22]

For its part, the Palestinian *Talmud* also compares Honi's '*rain-making*' to Isaiah 54:9's '*this is like the days of Noah*,' which itself echoes or is echoed in the Synoptics' '*Little Apocalypses*' and, according to Gospel portraiture, words attributed to 'Jesus.' This reads in Matthew 24:37, '*But as the days of Noah, so shall be also the coming of the Son of Man.*' In it, such '*days*' are compared to final eschatological Judgement, just as they are in the *Talmud*. As Matthew 24:30, after speaking about '*the sun darkening*,' '*the stars falling*,' and '*the powers of Heaven being shaken*' – language, of course, picked up in early visionary *surah*s of the Koran as well[23] – puts this as we have seen:

> Then shall appear the sign of the Son of Man in the sky...and they shall see the Son of Man coming on the clouds of Heaven with Power and Great Glory (the *Elchasaite/Sabaean* '*Great Power*' – language we have been following).

As the Damascus Document from Qumran puts a similar idea in the summation at the end of its historical and exhortative section, as we saw as well: '*And they shall see Yeshuᶜato*' ('*His Yeshuᶜa*' or '*His Salvation*').[24] One should also note, by implication, that the Noahic '*Flood*' is being equated with '*the coming of the Son of Man on the clouds*' – once again, self-evident apocalyptic '*rain*' and '*storm cloud*'-imagery. This in turn is of course, as already underscored too, the key eschatological proclamation attributed to James in early Church accounts of the prelude to his death in the Temple on Passover – perhaps, even more likely, *Yom Kippur* since, as already signaled as well, James is depicted in these accounts as being in the *Inner Sanctum* of the Temple doing an atonement on behalf of the whole People, an activity normally associated with *Yom Kippur*.

Not only does the Jerusalem *Talmud* consider that rain is withheld for the sins of *idolatry, fornication, and murder* – or, as it puts it, '*polluting the ground with Blood because Blood pollutes the Land*'[25] – again the basic categories of James' directives to overseas communities and '*the Noahic Covenant*' generally; it also connects the story of Honi '*filling up cisterns, pits, and caverns*,' the implications of which we shall explore more fully below, with repeated reference to a '*Stone*' *in the Temple* (in this instance, '*the Stone of Lost Property*'). But this, too, contains just the slightest echo of the '*Hilkiah*' material, delineated in 2 Kings 23:4 above, in which Josiah is depicted as '*standing by the Pillar*' when he swears '*to keep the Covenant*.' This kind of '*Pillar*' or '*Stone*,' also, mysteriously reappears in the story of James' death in the Second Apocalypse of James from Nag Hammadi. Nor is this to mention '*Stone*' and '*Cornerstone*' symbolism generally at Qumran, particularly in the Community Rule, where the '*Wall that will not shake on its Foundations*' and '*Fortress*' imagery abounds – to say nothing of in the New Testament.[26] In this Second Apocalypse, James is pictured as '*standing beside the Pillar of the Temple beside the Mighty Cornerstone*' when his opponents decide '*to cast him down*' – the language of almost all these early Church accounts of his death.[27]

Curiously in this account – which is obviously drawn from the same material as the one Eusebius conserves from Hegesippus – after forcing him to '*stand in a pit*,' James' executioners place '*a stone on his abdomen*' oddly echoing the '*stoning*' aspect of the affair in more familiar contexts. But even here there is, also, either an echo or prefiguration of execution scenarios for '*blasphemy*' in the *Talmud's Mishnah Sanhedrin* where, in one description anyhow, *a heavy stone is placed on the malefactor's abdomen* and considered to be the equivalent of stoning![28]

We shall also presently see below how the last of these legendary Talmudic '*Rain-makers*' Nakdimon ben Gurion, already mentioned above, will be pictured as basically repeating Honi's miracle-working of '*filling up the cisterns, pits, and caverns*,' only in Nakdimon's case *he will* '*refill twelve Temple cisterns*' *to what is characterized as* '*overflowing*.'[29] This language of '*filling*' will then reverberate back and forth through a multitude of Talmudic and New Testament episodes, we shall examine in detail presently; until one's head will fairly spin from all the interconnections, rhetorical flourish, and word-play – word-play not so different from that we have already seen Paul use to such devastating effect in his method of allegorical and rhetorical repartee.[30]

Curiously too, the *Talmud* seems to think that in some manner the prophet Habakkuk prefigured Honi's '*circle-drawing*' and '*praying for rain*.'[31] One can, again, take this in an eschatological sense since Habakkuk will be seen as a key eschatological prophet for the sectaries at Qumran and, to be sure, early Christianity as well.[32] This parallel, however, is not simply fanciful for, in these sections on the prototypical Rain-makers in the *Talmud*, the prophecy in Habakkuk 2:1–2 of '*standing upon his Watchtower and fortifying himself firmly on his Bulwark*' – language strongly reminiscent, as well, of the imagery of early Church descriptions of James – is applied to the actual process of Honi *drawing his circle* and '*taking his stand' within it.*[33]

This prophecy also reappears in the Habakkuk *Pesher*, where it is expounded in terms of '*the Righteous Teacher*'s ability *to understand scriptural prophecy and foresee 'the appointed End.'*[34] The crucial exegeses of Habakkuk 2:3 and 2:4 on '*waiting for' the final vision* and '*the Righteous living by his Faith,*' that then directly follow, are interpreted in terms of what in Early Christian theology becomes known as '*the Delay of the Parousia*' and how those Jews '*who do the Torah*' (the '*doing*' here again being important in terms of '*Jamesian*' usage) *will* '*be saved' at the time of* '*the Last Judgement*' at the '*End of Time,*' while those following the more backsliding approach of a teacher very much resembling Paul – playing off the usage '*puffed up*' in the first part of Habakkuk 2:4 as we just saw – will have '*their guilt multiplied upon them when they are judged.*'[35]

In fact, the text of the Habakkuk *Pesher*, while somewhat damaged at this point, actually can be used, as we shall see, to clarify a questionable recension in the Cairo *Genizah* version of the Damascus Document – itself leading up to the all-important definition of '*the Sons of Zadok*' of Ezekiel 44:15. The text which presently reads *taking one's 'stand upon one's net'* (*metzudo*), a somewhat opaque allusion, probably should read – in view of the keen interest shown in this metaphor just detailed in the Habakkuk *Pesher* above – '*upon one's Watchtower*' (*mishmarti*).[36] In the Habakkuk *Pesher*, as we just saw, the exposition of this term '*Watchtower*' is eschatological and it is interpreted in terms of '*the Last Days,*' their '*delay*' or '*extension,*' and how '*God made known the Mysteries of the words of the Prophets*' – uniquely as it were – to '*the Righteous Teacher.*'[37]

Nor can there be any doubt that the interpretation of the all-important Habakkuk 2:4 that follows in the Habakkuk *Pesher*, '*the Righteous shall live by his Faith,*' expounded here at Qumran and in Galatians, Romans, and James, is, as we shall also see more fully as we proceed, '*eschatological*' as well, that is, its exposition *will relate to 'the Last Days*' or '*the Day of Judgement*' too.[38] As in the War Scroll, once again demonstrating the basic circularity of all these materials and their inter-relationships, the enemies in the Habakkuk *Pesher* at this juncture are '*the Kittim*' too – meaning, according to our interpretation, the Romans.

Simeon Bar Yohai, the Karaites, *Elchasai*, and Paul

A similar '*Hidden*' or '*disappearing*'/'*re-appearing*' tradition is associated in the *Talmud*, with the eponymous transmitter of *Zohar*-tradition in early Second-Century Palestine and a contemporary of '*Elchasai*,' Simeon bar Yohai. Simeon, was another Rabbi with distinctly '*Zealot*' attitudes, harboring an extreme antagonism towards Rome and all vestiges of Roman rule in Palestine. A '*Disciple*' of the equally '*Zealot*' Rabbi Akiba (who, as we shall see, seemed to have very real connections with the family of Queen Helen of Adiabene and perished in connection with the suppression of the Bar Kochba Uprising); Simeon was supposed to have '*hidden himself in a cave*' together with his son after the death of his mentor Rabbi Akiba, *eating nothing but carobs for some twelve years* (this number '*twelve*' will grow in importance when it comes to telling of the story of Nakdimon's '*twelve cisterns*' below) to escape Roman retribution (and even perhaps '*the Sicaricon*'![39]).

This note about his '*cave-dwelling*' is interesting relative to the Dead Sea Scrolls and other activity we have been observing including Koranic revelations in Islam thereafter. But it also tallies with traditions preserved by the Jewish Karaites, the sect opposed to Rabbinic Judaism in the Middle Ages. They asserted, not only that '*Jesus*" teaching was '*the same as*' someone they called '*Zadok*,' but that *the ban on* '*niece marriage*,' we know from writings, such as the Damascus Document and the Temple Scroll at Qumran, *was one of his (Jesus') fundamental teachings*.[40] Needless to say, this information is not conserved by any other source – thereby, meeting the criterion, when judging reliability, of uniqueness or originality.

Not only are the Karaites familiar with this '*ban on niece marriage*' and do they follow it themselves – whereas Rabbinic Judaism followed by Christianity and Islam do not – they also *attribute it, not surprisingly, to* '*Zadok*.' Even more to the point, in their heresiology, where '*cave-dwelling*' is concerned, a group they refer to simply as '*the Maghrarians*' or '*Cave-Dwellers*' is placed chronologically between the group led by the Teacher they refer to as '*Zadok*' and '*Jesus*.'[41] Of course, this would make it similar to a group Hippolytus in the Third Century is calling '*Sebuaeans*' (that is, '*Sabaeans*') or '*Naassenes*,' by which he appears to mean, as we saw, either '*Essenes*,' '*Nazirites*,' '*Nazoraeans*,' or '*Elchasaites*' – or some combination of these. That is, according to Karaite heresiology, first came '*Zadok*,' then '*the Cave-Dwellers*,' and then came '*Jesus*,' all linked in an unbroken progression of some kind.[42]

These matters will probably never be sorted out completely but that they relate in some manner to a '*Hidden*'-tradition, associated with a line of *Zaddiks* connected to Honi's family and taking Elijah as their proto-type, should be clear. That this line is also connected with '*rain-making*' – whether actual or eschatological – should also be clear. Regardless of the truth of Epiphanius' notice about James' '*rain-making*,' that such a proce-dure or ideology is connected to his person, even if only symbolically through his '*Zaddik*'-nature, is not insignificant. In this connection, the reappearance of all these Honi look-alikes just prior to the fall of the Temple in 70 CE should not go unremarked, nor should James' death in almost precisely the manner of Honi and for probably very similar reasons – in James' case (if not Honi's), *at the hands of a more accommodat-ing Priestly Establishment.*

That this line is also linked to the '*redivivus*'-ones, whether the '*Zealot*'-Priestly one stemming from Phineas and Elijah or the one the Synoptics suppose they are dealing with in portraying Elijah as reborn in John the Baptist, should also be clear. In turn, these lines are paralleled by the '*Jewish Christian*'/*Ebionite/Elchasaite* '*Primal Adam*' or '*Man*' – one in Pseudoclementine and *Sabaean* tradition described above. As Muhammad, another heir to this tradition – probably via '*the Sabaeans*' (that is, '*the Elchasaites*') either in Northern Syria or Southern Iraq or the Manichaeans descended from them – puts this in the Koran as we saw:

> *Behold, the likeness of Jesus with Allah is the likeness of Adam. He created him of the dust. Then He said unto him:* '*Be!*' *And he was* (3:59).

Paul himself shows great familiarity with this doctrine – again in key passages of 1 Corinthians that follow his version of Jesus' post-resur-rection sequences connected to a first appearance to James[43] – referring to it, as we also saw, as '*the Primal*' or '*First Man Adam*' or '*the Second Man*'/'*the Last Adam*' (15:21 and 45–48) and his whole discussion of these matters precedes his delineation of the state man will enjoy after the Resurrection.

This he describes in terms of the same '*secrecy*' and triumphalism we have already encountered regarding the '*Hidden Power*' ideology of the *Elchasaite* '*Sabaeans*,' namely their '*keeping the secrets*,' and their vari-ations on Isaiah 45:8's God triumphantly '*raining down Salvation*' (1 Corinthians 15:51–54). In these Isaiah materials above (45:14), one should also note the reference to '*Sabaeans*' with an '*alif*,' meaning South-ern Arabians from '*Sheba*' south of Cush, not '*Sabaean*' with an '*ayin*' as the usage occurs in Islamic documents meaning, as already sufficiently underscored, via the Syriac, '*Bather*.'

As Paul describes this earlier in the same letter when explaining, it will be remembered, that he *does not 'speak in the words taught of human Wisdom but in the words taught by the Holy Spirit, communicating spiritual things spiritually,'*

> *But we speak the Wisdom of God in a Mystery, that which* God *has hidden and predetermined before the ages for our Glory* (1 Corinthians 2:7–15).

It is his use of the word '*Glory*' in passages such as these that will be paralleled in the Habakkuk *Pesher* when describing its principal Adversary to precisely the opposite effect – more of the verbal repartee going on in this period. In the latter, this '*Glorying*' or '*Self-Glorification*' is connected to an individual, as already remarked, it calls '*the Liar*' or '*the Spouter of Lying*' (also '*the Scoffer*' or '*Comedian*') and whom it describes as '*leading Many astray*' (note the usage '*Many*' here) *with* '*Lying for the sake of his own Glory*' – sound familiar?[44]

For his part, Epiphanius sets forth one of the best descriptions of this '*Secret*' or '*Second Adam*' doctrine imaginable in a passage in which he describes how '*the False Prophet Elchasai joined...those called Sampsaeans* (Sabaeans), *Osseneans* (Essenes), *and Elchasaites*' (here the basic coextensiveness of these three groups again). This, he puts, as follows:

> *Some of them say that Christ is Adam and the first to be made and given life by the Spirit of God* (compare this with Muhammad in the Koran above). *Others of them say that he is from above, having been created before everything, being Spirit and above the Angels and Lord of all* (this is almost word-for-word reflected in the Koran),[45] *and is called 'Christ'...but He comes here when he wants, as when he came in Adam* (our basic incarnationism again)...*He came also in the Last Days* (language we have already seen as fundamental in the Dead Sea Scrolls) *and clothed himself in Adam's body...*[46]

Two hundred years, before, Irenaeus in Western Europe, in discussing '*the Ebionites*' whom he already knew were hostile to and had rejected Paul, puts the same proposition in similar terms:

> *Therefore, do these men reject the commixture of the Heavenly wine and wish it to be the water of the world only, not receiving God so as to have union with Him* (or '*be in Communion with Him*'), *but they remain in that Adam who...was expelled from Paradise* (here his contempt is evident) *not considering that, as at the beginning of our formation in Adam, that breath of life proceeded from God...so also in the Last Days* (notice the commonality with Epiphanius'

vocabulary above and that of the Dead Sea Scrolls) *the Word of the Father and the Spirit of God, having become united with the ancient substance of Adam's formation, rendered Man living and Perfect, receptive of the Perfect Father* (here, too, of course, the '*Perfection*' doctrine found in the Dead Sea Scrolls and enjoying a faint echo in New Testament Scripture as well – but even more strikingly as Muhammad's view of God's '*Spirit*' sent to Mary in *Surah* in 19:17 above, '*assuming for her the likeness*' *of the* '*Perfect Man*').[47]

Though Irenaeaus, living in Lyons in Transalpine Gaul, never mentions groups like Epiphanius' '*Elchasaites*' or '*Sabaeans*' – denotations which were mainly only known in the East and probably had not traveled that far West (for instance, Western authors like him, Hippolytus, and Tertullian, do not seem to even know Hegesippus); still it should be clear that this kind of theorizing about '*Adam*' was alive and well even in the Western Empire.

For the Koran (2:34 and variously) and Islam thereafter, as with Epiphanius' '*Ebionites*' and '*Elchasaites*,' *Adam is above the Angels who prostrate themselves to him, 'all save Iblis*' – the '*Belial*' we shall encounter throughout the Dead Sea Scrolls and the Arabic equivalent of what Paul refers to defectively in 2 Corinthians 6:15 as '*Beliar*' (in linguistic theory, two letters being sufficient to establish a loan).[48] In other words, this '*Primal*' or '*Supernatural Adam*' is '*the Son of Man*' ('*Man*' and '*Adam*,' as we have seen, being for all intents and purposes indistinguishable in Hebrew) or, as the newer Greek usage now developing in the West would put it, '*the Christ*' who '*in the Last Days*' *was going to* '*come upon the clouds of Heaven*' *leading the Heavenly Host.* It is extraordinary that we should have to go as far afield as Irenaeus in France to explain this tantalizing allusion to '*Christ*' as '*Perfect Man*' in the Koran!

As Paul puts it in line with his teaching '*spiritual things spiritually*' in 1 Corinthians 2:13–15 above and his Philo-like poetic allegorizing (in Galatians 4:24, even admitting, 'such things are allegory'):

> *So also it has been written* (it is unclear where): '*The First Man Adam* (meaning, '*the Primal Adam*') *became a living soul; the Last* (or '*Second*') *Adam became a life-giving Spirit*' (this is, to be sure, the doctrine Irenaeus is describing above),

concluding, as we saw above:

> *The First Man is out of the earth, made of dust. The Second Man* (meaning 'Jesus'), *the Lord out of Heaven* (1 Corinthians 15:45–47).

Again, this is a perfect rendition of the '*Man*' or '*Adam*'-ideology we have been encountering, *the First Adam 'made of dust'* (which Paul repeats twice more in 1 Corinthians 15:48) prefiguring Muhammad, as just underscored above, on '*the likeness of Jesus with God being the likeness of Adam.*' This gave rise to the idea of '*Jesus*' as '*Second Adam*,' the Heavenly Judgement-bringer and Paul's '*Lord out of Heaven.*'

One immediately sees that, as we have been attempting to illustrate, this is a '*redivivus*'-tradition paralleling the one involving '*rain-making*' and Priestly '*zeal*' attaching itself to Phineas, Elijah, and Honi or, if one prefers, Elijah's incarnation in John. Likewise, '*the Son of Man*' (that is, '*the Son of Adam*'), based on the notice in Daniel 7:13 about '*one like a Son of Man coming with the clouds of Heaven*' ('*Man*' here expressed as '*Enosh*' in Daniel's Aramaic) is but a variation of '*the Lord out of Heaven*' or '*Second Adam*' notation. However this time, in addition to the supernatural dimension as in 'Christianity'-to-come, it also carries an eschatological one, that is, '*the Son of Man*' is now combined in the new Hebrew '*Messianic*'-ideology with the additional imagery of '*the Messiah coming on the clouds of Heaven*' to render final apocalyptic Judgement on all mankind.

This in turn, as we shall demonstrate in the War Scroll from Qumran at length below, is expressed in terms of '*rain*' – now *eschatological rain* – in turn, carrying with it the connotation of a '*Last Judgement*' that in the words of the War Scroll and Matthew 5:45 above, *will fall on* '*the Just and Unjust alike*' or '*upon everything that grows.*'[49] The same ideology is also to some extent announced in the Letter of Jude, in which Jude uses a passage freely quoted from Enoch 1:9:

> *The Lord will come with myriads of his Holy Ones to execute Judgement against all and condemn all the ones who were ungodly among them regarding all their works of ungodliness which they did in an ungodly way* (n.b., here the double emphasis on both Jamesian – but not Pauline – '*works*' and '*doing*' which we shall, as stressed, also find so prevalent at Qumran).[50]

Enoch is an extra-biblical text using apocalyptic imagery, inspired seemingly by the same visionary impetus as Daniel, which, though widely copied and expanded in post-biblical times, never penetrated either Jewish or Christian canons despite being highly prized in sectarian environments such as at Qumran.[51] Not only is this passage from Enoch, which is quoted in Jude 1:14, extant in fragments found at Qumran – and, because of this testimony to its antiquity, therefore, very likely from Enoch's original autograph[52] – Jude 1:11 preceding it and allusion to '*Adam*' in 1:14 as well (Jude 1:6–7 also refers to *a 'Great Day of Judgement' of 'everlasting fire'* and *'fornication'*), instead of using the language of Paul's defective *'Beliar'* or the Damascus Document's *'Belial,'* employs like Revelation 2:14 the linguistically-related usage *'Balaam'* – two letters, as already signaled to, being sufficient in linguistic theory to establish a loan.[53]

In fact Revelation 2:14 conflates James' directives to overseas communities with the Damascus Document's *'Three Nets of Belial.'* This is expressed in the latter in terms of the *'nets'* with which *'Belial'* attempted *'to ensnare Israel,'* presenting them *'as three kinds of Righteousness'* – nothing of course could better express Herodian family policy than this. On the other hand, Revelation rather expresses this as:

> *Balaam taught Balak* (again the variations on *'Belial'*) *to cast* (*balein* – and this too, including in Greek the pivotal *'casting'* usage) *a snare before the Sons of Israel* (is this the language, which Matthew 27:9 borrowed, of *'the Sons of Israel setting a price'* when it loosely quoted Zechariah, attributing it to Jeremiah?) *to eat things sacrificed to idols and commit fornication.*[50]

All the key usages for both the Scrolls and the Paul/James polemic are here.

Replete with other language such as *'grumbling,' 'boasting,'* and *'Light and Dark'* imagery so familiar both in a 'Jamesian' context and in the Dead Sea Scrolls,[55] Jude (which is actually ascribed to *'the brother of James'* – the reference here, as we have seen, is not the indefinite *'of James,'* but the actual Greek *'brother'* designation, *'adelphos'*) uses the Messianic-style imagery of *'Salvation,' 'stars,'* and even *'clouds'* (*'clouds without water'* in 1:12). It puts this scenario for *apocalyptic Messianic 'Judgement upon the clouds'* – intending doubtlessly by *'Lord'* here, *'the Messiah,'* or, as it appears at this point and elsewhere in Paul, *'the Lord Jesus Christ'* (1:12–17, 21, and 25).[56] This could not be more parallel to the exegesis of *'the Star Prophecy'* in the War Scroll from Qumran as we shall see in due course below.

For Paul, in discussing his ideas about *'the First Man Adam'* and *'Jesus'* as *'Second Adam'* being *'the Lord out of Heaven,'* this *'coming of the Son of Man on the clouds of Heaven'* is transformed into a discussion simply about the difference between earthly and Heavenly existence. But in his masterful use of rhetorical allegory, Paul also appears to be playing on language familiar as well from the 'Messianic' portions of the War Scroll and the exposition of *'the Star Prophecy'* from Numbers 24:17, it contains in Columns Eleven to Twelve.[57] In referring to Adam as being *'formed out of the dust'* (1 Corinthians 15:48), the War Scroll's triumph of *'those bent in the dust over the Mighty of the Peoples'* now appears to be transformed in Paul into *'the First Man'* (*'the Primal Adam'*) or *the earthly man 'formed out of the dust.'*[58]

Likewise, the War Scroll's idea of *the 'Victory'* by *'the Star'* Messiah *together with 'the Poor'* (*'the Ebionim'* again), *'the Downcast of Spirit'* (compare this to *'the Poor in Spirit'* in Matthew 5:3's *Sermon on the Mount*) or *'those bent in the dust,'* and the *Heavenly Host upon the 'clouds;'* Paul now likens to *'a Mystery,'* meaning, *'Mystery,'* in the sense of a Hellenistic *'Mystery.'* This *'Mystery'* in 1 Corinthians 15:51 – in other words, this *'Victory'* – is now the one that God *'gives us by our Lord Jesus Christ'* and, in the typical Hellenizing allegorizing style – which he characterizes as *'teaching spiritual things spiritually'* in 1 Corinthians 2:13 above – it is now *'Victory'* over *death, not 'Victory'* over Rome or, as the War Scroll so exuberantly expresses this concept, *Victory 'over the Mighty of the Peoples'* or *'the Kittim.'* As Paul so deftly transposes this *'Victory'* in 1 Corinthians 15:55, it becomes,

> *Death where is your sting? O Hades* (note now, the complete Hellenization of the vocabulary here), *where is your Victory?*

Muhammad and Paul

For Islam too (probably following Ebionite, Sabaean and/or Manichaean tradition), Jesus is a *'Second Adam'* in the sense that he was *the only other man after Adam who did not have a human father.* As Muhammad puts this proposition in the Koran and all of Islamic doctrine dependent on this thereafter – as in the case of the *'Mary'/'Perfect Man'* material in Irenaeus above, but this time actually incorporating the approach to Jesus' procreation pioneered two centuries before Islam by St Augustine, *himself originally a Manichaean – Jesus was the son of Mary only,* meaning *he did not have a father, only a mother.*[59] Nor did Adam who, for all intents and purposes, *did not even have a mother*! In this sense, as already suggested, *'Jesus'* really is, at least ideologically-speaking, a *'Second Adam.'*

This ideology of *'the Last'* or *'Secret Adam,'* as we saw, bears an eschatological dimension which, in turn, brings us back both to James' proclamation in the Temple at Passover time (in our view, more likely around the time either of *Yom Kippur* or *Succot*) of *'the coming of the Son of Man'* together with the *Heavenly Host 'on the clouds of Heaven'* (compare this with *'the Lord coming with myriads of his Holy Ones to execute Judgement'* in Jude 1:14 claiming to be based on Enoch 1:9 above) and the scenario of the final apocalyptic War led by the Messiah expressed in terms of 'clouds shedding Judgement like rain' in the War Scroll from Qumran ('spring rain' in James).

This is not the only ideology descending either directly from James and/or 'Ebionite Christianity' that Muhammad preserves in the Koran. He also preserves James' directives to overseas communities as recorded in Acts 15 and 21 and refracted in 1 Corinthians 6–11. These become the basis of subsequent Islamic dietary Law as we saw, that is, 'abstain from (in the 'Nazirite' language of the Hebrew Damascus Document 'lehinnazer') blood, swine flesh, things sacrificed to an idol, and carrion' (Koran 2:173, 6:146, 16.115, etc.). Even the word 'carrion,' being used here in the Koran, recapitulates the delineation of these things, as we have seen as well, in the Pseudoclementine Homilies, with which Muhammad and Muslim tradition generally clearly seem to have been in touch and a delineation which takes the place of and is more precise, as already underscored, than anything Acts is trying to describe by the phraseology employed in it – 'strangled things.'

In fact, showing his prescience in these things, at one point Muhammad even preserves Acts' 'strangled' allusion in conjunction with other aspects of the 'carrion' notation, definitively defining it – along with 'beating,' 'goring,' 'falling,' and 'things torn by carnivorous animals' – as things not given the prescribed death cut (Koran 5:3), meaning, the cut at the throat with a knife as in Jewish religious observance too. This is strict Muslim and Jewish orthodox usage still (known in the latter as 'kashrut'; in the former as 'halal,' – meaning 'legal,' 'lawful,' or 'permissible'), no doubt conserving, as we have said, the real meaning of what Acts was attempting to convey so imprecisely in the Greek, the partial or defective translation of which has come down to us in the manner in which these all-important 'Jamesian' directives to overseas communities were expressed in the New Testament in Acts.

For Muhammad, as we saw, Zachariah, John, Jesus, and Elijah are all also 'of the Righteous' (Koran 6:86–Arabic: 'min as-Salihin' and the same word root one encounters in the important 'Hud and Salih' stories in the tradition to which he is the heir above). The emphasis on Zachariah – 'Abba Saba Zachariah' in Mandaean tradition as we saw – however exaggerated, almost certainly shows Mandaean tradition to be the true route or the source of the transmission of information of this kind.

Muhammad also utilizes Paul's understanding of Abraham coming before the Law and therefore the impossibility, logically speaking, of his having been 'saved' or 'Justified' – in more precise Hebrew usage, 'made Righteous' – by it. However, like the Mandaeans, Ebionites, and other more 'Eastern' descendants of anti-Pauline traditions of this kind, he never once mentions Paul – this, despite the fact that he is using the latter's basic spiritual and theological approach as already suggested, to create the third 'Western Religion' that his new '*Islam*' represents. Not only is this the second major world religion created on the basis of 'Abrahamic' polemical arguments which invoke Abraham's genealogical and/or spiritual status as paradigmatic, but in so doing Muhammad provides further vivid testimony, if such were needed, of the '*Ebionite*' anti-Pauline strain of the tradition to which he is the heir, to say nothing of where he might have encountered these ideas.

Having said this, like Paul he masterfully shifts the thrust of his dialectic ever-so-slightly laterally so as to characterize the new '*Faith*' he is preaching (not Christianity) as *the 'Religion of Abraham'* – not Paul's '*Faith of Abraham*' – '*Islam*' as he now characterizes it, coming not only *before Mosaic Law* (as Paul, in perhaps the foundational Western theological position, so cunningly represents it), but *before both Judaism and Christianity as well*.[60] In the process, by implication, Muhammad brushes aside Paul's position, stemming from a somewhat tendentious exposition of Genesis 15:6, that '*Christianity*' not Judaism was the true '*Faith of Abraham*.'[61] What Muhammad, and Muslims thereafter, think they are doing is returning to the purity of the original monotheism of '*Abraham's Religion*' or, as they would put it, *before it was corrupted by Jewish* and *Christian 'Lies*' or '*Lying*.'

Where allusion to this kind of '*Lying*' is concerned, at Qumran – succeeded by Ebionite/*Elchasaite*/Mandaean/and Manichaean polemic – it is a teacher resembling Paul, or even Paul himself, who is designated as '*the Man of Lies*' or '*the Spouter of Lying*.' What this adversary does is, as we shall see – through '*Lying*,' '*lead the People astray into a trackless waste without a Way*,' '*without the signposts which the Ancestors* ('*the First*') *laid down*,' meaning, of course, the *Mosaic Law* or *Torah*.[62] In like manner, Muhammad varies Paul's presentation of Christians as the true, if allegorized, '*Children of Abraham*' (Galatians 3:9, 4:31, etc.) – this in the section where Paul triumphantly concludes in an astonishing display of inverse polemical invective, '*therefore cast out (ekbale) the slave woman and her son*' (4:30 – more of the '*casting out*' language so dear to Essenes where the treatment of backsliders is concerned, and Acts 7:58's picture of the way its hero '*Stephen*' is treated by *the Jews* and their Sanhedrin above).[63]

Paul arrives at this triumphant recommendation after drawing the fairly cynical contrast between '*the children of the slave woman Hagar*' (for him and his rather mean-spirited use of allegory, *this is* '*Israel*', not *Muhammad's later 'Arabs*') and '*the children of the free woman Sarah*,' meaning his new overseas '*Children of the Promise*' or '*Christian*' Communities such as those in Galatia, '*free of the Law*' (4:28–31)![64] The key point for him here of course, is the contrast between 'slavery' and 'freedom' and, in a straightforward presentation of his rhetorical method, in Galatians 4:24, it will be recalled, he even admits 'such things are allegory.'

To add to these complexities of mutually inverted polemics, Muhammad proudly signals his own physical descent and that of all Arabs with him *from this very same 'Hagar' via Ishmael*, a foundational cornerstone of Islamic doctrine, and the same 'bond-servant', Paul has just so contemptuously dismissed, insisting in a free rendering of Genesis 21:10 that – as a representative, obviously, of *all 'Law-keeping'* and *Torah-doing Jews*[65] – *she should have been 'cast out'*!

Even the words 'cast out,' Paul uses here, are pivotal for the kind of allegorical and rhetorical invective he is involved in, of which he has already shown himself to be the consummate master, since the words 'casting out' (here, *ekbale*), 'casting down' (*kataballo*), and their derivatives (in the Gospels used to express *what 'fishermen' do with their 'nets'* or how *'pearls are cast before swine'* or, in one divergent tradition, *how 'the tares'* or *'rotten fish' are 'cast into a furnace of fire'*[66]) are reflections of the language all early Church texts employ when describing the death of James (that is, he was 'cast down' from either *'the Pinnacle of the Temple'* or *'its steps'*) and how groups like 'the Essenes,' as already signaled, would have treated backsliders of a Pauline genre – that is, 'cast them out' (*ekballo*).[67]

Not only is this the kind of language the Gospels use to treat the cluster of allusions to what are perhaps Jesus' favorite miracles, *'casting out demons'* or *'Evil spirits,'* and/or *the way 'the Disciples'* or *'Apostles' 'cast down' their 'fishermen's nets'*; they also are a reflection of the way texts such as the Damascus Document, as we saw, characterize *the 'nets' which the diabolical adversary Belial 'casts down' in order to 'deceive Israel.'*[68] In Revelation 2:14, as we just saw too, these are *'the nets Balaam taught Balak to cast before Israel (balein) to eat things sacrificed to idols and commit fornication'* – two key categories of James' directives to overseas communities, the first anyhow gainsaid by Paul in 1 Corinthians 8:8–12 above.

Even *the* term 'Belial' in Hebrew, like 'Balaam' and 'Balak' in Revelation above – not to mention 'Babylon' in Revelation as well and 'Beelzebub' in the Gospels – represents a variation of this language circle.[69] Not incuriously, in the Hebrew the homophonic analogue of this language carries the connotation of 'swallowing,' which the Habakkuk *Pesher* will actually apply, as we shall see, to the fate of 'the Righteousness Teacher,' as it will – following a confrontation of some kind on *Yom Kippur* where the Hebrew equivalent of this 'casting down' language in Greek will also be employed – to his followers denoted as 'the Ebionim' or 'the Poor' (the early Christian nomenclature, as we have seen, for 'the Ebionites').[70]

Just like Paul – and no doubt Mani too, probably his direct source – Muhammad presents himself as an '*Apostle to the Gentiles*,' in this case, one specific group of '*Gentiles*' or '*Peoples*,' the Arabs who, in truth, via Ishmael, according to the biblical genealogist, *actually were descended from Abraham* (though, of course, all such claims are to some extent mythical). Clearly Muhammad means by this, having accepted the biblical genealogy, not just in the '*spiritual*' and/or '*allegorical*' sense favored by Paul in both 1 Corinthians and Galatians above ('*such things*,' as we just saw, in Galatians 4:24 being characterized, as '*allegories*'), but by direct descent as well,

Not only does Paul claim in a concomitant use of '*allegorization*' of this kind – a method to some extent, as we have remarked, dependent upon his older Jewish intellectual contemporary, the famous Philo of Alexandria[71] – that the Jews, whether physically or spiritually, or both, *are the descendants of Abraham's 'bondservant Hagar'* (Galatians 4:21–24); in the pointed nature of his allegorical polemics (but allegory with a calumniatory, sometimes even scurrilous, bite) he identifies this '*Agar*' in Galatians 4:25 *as 'Mount Sinai in Arabia.*' By so doing, he patently signals that what he really means by this inverted metaphor is *their attachment to the Law of Moses*, so strikingly portrayed in the *Torah* – with which he was certainly familiar – *as having been revealed there.* This '*allegorical*' and free-wheeling use of Scripture, anyhow, is hardly very subtle but, in fact, actually fairly blunt.

In continuing these inverted metaphors, just as with his equating of '*God's Law*' with '*Roman Law*' and citing the second part of the '*Righteousness*'/'*Piety*' dichotomy, '*loving your neighbor as yourself*,' as *a reason to pay Roman taxes* in Romans 13 above; he goes even further by playing on, and at the same time reversing, the two fundamental concepts '*freedom*' and '*slavery*' so crucial *to this period.* For Paul here and throughout the corpus attributed to him, '*freedom*' always means *freedom from Jewish Law*; and 'obedience,' *obedience to the Roman Authorities never the Jewish.* As he puts it in Galatians 4:31 concluding this virtuoso rhetorical performance: '*So brothers, we* – who '*are like Isaac, Children of the Promise*' (meaning, *the Children of Sarah not Hagar*) – *are not children of the slave woman but of the free (woman).*' In other words, in a breathtaking rhetorical display of inverse polemics, as just underscored, *it is the Jews who are now 'the Children of Hagar*'; and Paul's new '*Christian*' believers, '*the Children of Sarah*'!

He fleshes this out further in Romans 4:1–5:10 and 8:28–9:11 in pursuit of his arguments, just delineated, presenting Christianity as '*the Religion*' or '*Faith of Abraham.*' Not only is this letter addressed like the

Letter of James above '*to those who love God*' – namely, those like '*the Essenes*' who practise the first of the two '*all Righteousness*' or '*Love*' Commandments – '*Piety towards God*' – but just as in Galatians, this is constantly punctuated by protestations that he '*does not lie*' or '*I lie not*' (Romans 9:1 but note, as well, the canny: '*If in my Lie, the Truth of God overflows to His Glory, why am I still judged?*' in 3:7), protestations which in both Galatians 4:16 above and now Romans 5:10 even include allusion to the '*Enemy*' epithet applied to him in '*Jewish Christian*' or '*Ebionite*' invective as already fully described.[72]

In fleshing out this '*freedom vs. slavery*' polarity here in Galatians 4:22–31 as well, he adds geographical insight to rhetorical skills, in relation to which his use of '*Arabia*' as a synonym for '*Mount Sinai*' in 4:25 is pivotal. As he develops this particular inverse metaphorical allusion, *the Covenant* '*which is Hagar,*' as we saw, *is the one of* '*slavery.*' This is clearly to be associated with Moses' '*Covenant,*' as already also explained, and Paul says as much himself by *overtly identifying this* '*Covenant*' *with* '*Mount Sinai in Arabia.*' Once again, in his view '*slavery*' is slavery to *Jewish* or *Mosaic Law* and '*freedom,*' *freedom from this Law, not freedom from Rome.* Contrariwise, for the 'Zealot,' '*Sicarii,*' and probably '*Essene*' practitioners of Holy War in defence of the same '*Sinaitic*' or '*Mosaic Covenant*' which he is so clearly parodying, '*slavery*' would be *slavery to the rule of Rome*; and '*freedom,*' *freedom from it* (namely, *Rome*), *not freedom from the Law*, as Paul so disparagingly transforms it.

PART III

THE NEW TESTAMENT CODE:
NAKDIMON AND NICODEMUS

8

'Do Not Throw Holy Things to Dogs'

Nakdimon Ben Gurion's Rain-Making and his Twenty-one Years of Grain Storage

Finally the Babylonian *Talmud* tells us about another individual who was a contemporary of James and prayed for rain just before the fall of the Temple in 70 CE.[1] It calls this individual, as already remarked, '*Nakdimon ben Gurion*.' Josephus, reversing the name of the same or similar character into '*Gurion the son of Nakdimon*,' actually calls him in the original Greek, '*Nicodemus*,' corresponding to the '*Nicodemus*' pictured in the Gospel of John, as we saw, bringing an expensive mixture of perfume ointment consisting of myrrh and aloes to prepare Jesus's body for burial (19:40). We shall see how these motifs of expensive '*ointments*' and '*perfumes*' play out in the various traditions incorporating elements of this kind below.

In fact, the *Midrash Rabbah* on *Genesis* (a Rabbinic compendium of historical and folkloric materials presented in a kind of Qumran-style, full-length '*pesher*' or commentary on Genesis) actually also calls this '*Nakdimon*' even in the Hebrew, '*Nicodemon*' (i. e., '*Nicodemus*').[2] Not only does it – along with Rabbinic sources generally portray him – as being like James *able to go into the Temple and make rain at the time of another of these ubiquitous 'famines'* – this one apparently during the siege of the Temple by the Romans in 68–70 CE[3] – but, as in the '*Elijah*' and '*Honi*' traditions prefiguring him, *he is able to bring the sunshine as well.*[4]

Two sources, Tractate *Taᶜanith* explicitly and the *Abbot de Rabbi Nathan* – henceforth *ARN* – implicitly, connect the Hebrew root of his name, '*Na-Ka-Da*' – meaning, '*to pierce*' or '*break through*,' as the sun '*pierces*' or '*breaks through the clouds*' – as reflective of this miracle based on their portrayal of him as, supposedly, *being able to bring the sun back after it had already set* – a dubious proposition to say the least illustrating, albeit unwittingly on their parts, the somewhat childish or credulous manner in which Talmudic tradition is manufactured as well.

ARN puts this proposition in the following manner, '*the sun broke through again*' and '*continued shining for his sake*.'[5] For its part, *Taᶜanith* draws the logical conclusion comparing him even more flamboyantly to Joshua and Moses – though why Moses should have been included at this point is not immediately clear – declaring that '*for the sake of three, the sun broke through.*' At this point *ARN* even quotes Joshua 10:13–14's '*the sun stood still and delayed its setting,*' meaning that – like the renowned '*Joshua*' – so astonishing were '*Nakdimon*''s abilities and so favored by God was he that he too could even *make* '*the sun stand still*' – another '*Joshua*'/'*Jesus redivivus*' or '*Jesus*'-like '*sign*' or '*miracle*' tradition.

All of these traditions about '*Nakdimon*' (if this was really his name and not a pseudonym of some kind), however bizarre, are very curious and give the impression that there was more underlying the events being described than might initially have been supposed – especially when the other designated '*Rain-makers*' and quasi-contemporaries preceding him, such as James, '*Abba Hilkiah*,' and '*Hanin ha-Nechba*,' are taken into account.

Just as in the case of the latter two, it is obvious that we have a combination of themes based on the portraits of Elijah and/or Honi the Circle-Drawer (Josephus' '*Onias the Righteous*') in biblical and Rabbinic narrative and in Josephus. In the *ARN* – perhaps related to Moses' inclusion as being able '*to make the such shine through*' above – the circles Honi drew and in which he stood to pray to bring the rain are ascribed to Moses as well – in Moses' case, the prayer to God (presumably as another of these '*Friend*'s), he supposedly made, *to cure Miriam's leprosy*.[6] Josephus, as we saw, also pictures '*the Essenes*' as employing a similar procedure of perimeter-drawing in the matter of their Sabbath toilet observances.[7]

These points aside, it is hardly credible that, according to the details of the picture of '*Nakdimon*'s incredible abilities – clearly evoking his '*Piety*,' '*Zaddik*'-status, and '*Friendship with God*' – someone as '*Rich*' as Nakdimon ('*Gurion ben Nicodemus*' in Josephus above) was legended to have been in Rabbinic tradition, could be thought of as having accomplished anything remotely resembling the '*rain-making*' and other miraculous feats attributed to him in these sources. The conclusion will probably have to be that the same kind of subversion of native Palestinian materials is going on in Jewish or Rabbinic tradition (after the fall of the Temple, there was no real distinction between the two) that we have already encountered in Early Christian tradition embodied in the Gospels and in the Book of Acts.

*Ben Kalba Sabu*ᶜ*a* and Nakdimon ben Gurion Supply Jerusalem with Enough Grain to Last for '*Twenty-one Years*'

In Rabbinic notices generally, Nakdimon is one of a class of individuals the Dead Sea Scrolls, for instance, and the Gospels would refer to as 'Rich' – in some cases even ostentatiously so.[8] One of these fabulously wealthy types with whom Nakdimon is often associated is another person with a seemingly tantalizing pseudonym, referred to as 'Ben Kalba Sabuᶜa' ('the Son of the Dog' in Aramaic – female 'Dog' in homophonic Hebrew). In the notices about Ben Kalba Sabuᶜa, just as with Nakdimon above, his name is expounded in terms of things he has done or the actual meaning of his name – therefore the description (such as it is) reads: 'no Poor were ever turned away from his door;' and, when 'they came to his house hungry as a dog, they went away filled' ('Sabuᶜa' in Aramaic also carrying the sense of 'being filled').[9]

Not only are some of these allusions important for usages relating to the subjects we have been discussing above, but the 'dog'/'female dog' aspect (kalba) of the exposition echoes, ever so slightly, the episode in the Gospels about Jesus' encounter with the 'Canaanite'/'Cananaean' (in Hebrew, as we shall see, also possibly 'Zealot'/'Kanna'im') or 'Greek Syrophoenician woman,' where 'Jesus' complains about 'taking the children's bread and casting it to the dogs' (Matthew 15:26 and Mark 7:28 – 'balein' once again and actually 'kunariois'/'little dogs') which we shall treat in more detail below.[10] No less important, the second part of 'Ben Kalba Sabuᶜa''s name – the 'Sabuᶜa' or 'filled' cognomen – can also, as we shall see more fully (no pun intended) below and as I have already been at some pains to point out, carries with it the sense in both Syriac and/or Aramaic of being 'immersed' or 'to bathe.'[11]

As we shall also discuss in more detail below, both 'Nakdimon' and 'Ben Kalba Sabuᶜa' will intimately be tied with the important number 'twenty one' – 'Nakdimon' in the number of wells he will be able 'to fill' in his miraculous 'cistern-filling' activities at a time of drought, and 'Ben Kalba Sabuᶜa' (one possible reading of whose name, with a little extra imaginative insight will also be, as just implied, 'the Son of the Sabaean Dog' or 'of the Sabaean Bitch'), the number of years that either he or Nakdimon (this will depend on the source which, in data of this kind, infuriatingly, often overlap[12]) could have fed the total population of Jerusalem had not the Zealots in their monstrousness burned his or Nakdimon's immense granary reserves and mixed mud with them![13]

Here it is worth remarking that the Talmud, though purporting to represent a tradition of meticulous observation of Law, is just about always – like its alter ego and mirror reversal the New Testament – anti-Zealot. It is worth remarking, too, that this number 'twenty-one,' associated both with Nakdimon's 'drought relief' activities and either his or Ben Kalba Sabuᶜa's 'grain-supplying' ones (the 'eating and drinking' theme again), is also, according to Talmudic tradition the amount of time of Queen Helen of Adiabene's *three successive Nazirite oath periods*. These had been laid upon her by the Rabbis, oddly enough, for perceived infractions of the biblical law of adultery, the rules pertaining to which, in particular, *those concerning 'the suspected adulteress'* – a plaque concerning which she had erected in gold in the Temple courtyard![14] – are to be found in Numbers 5:11–31. Interestingly enough and, not incuriously too, where these thematic combinations are concerned, these rules are found in Numbers *just proceeding the rules appertaining to vows of the Nazirites and their oaths* (Numbers 6:1–21).

Where Nakdimon's perhaps even more interesting colleague, *Ben Kalba Sabuʿa*, is concerned, he is also associated in some manner with the fabulous tomb, remarked in all sources – as we have already alluded to above – which Queen Helen and her son called '*Monobazus*' built in Jerusalem.[15] Originally, Monobazus had evidently built it for his apparent brother, Izates, but ultimately it came to be identified as a mausoleum for the whole family. So durable was it that it still exists today and can be easily visited.[16] Another point that will bear on this data complex – not only did the famous '*Zealot*' Rabbi Akiba, at the time of the Second Jewish Revolt, marry *Rachel, 'Ben Kalba Sabuʿa's daughter*, but one of Akiba's more well-known students will turn out to be an individual also called in all sources '*Monobaz*' – a descendant obviously in the next generation of this same Helen or *Ben Kalba Sabuʿa*, or both, and probably this Rachel's brother – but more about these matters below.[17]

Finally, both Nakdimon and *Ben Kalba Sabuʿa* are associated in these traditions with a third individual, again depicted as fabulously wealthy and cryptically denoted by another curious *nom à clef*, '*Ben Zizzit Ha-Keset*'[18] – whatever one might finally choose to make of this.[19] Another individual will be grouped with these other three fabulously-wealthy potentates in these traditions – more, actually, because of *his daughter 'Martha's Riches' and extravagant behavior* (in one tradition she is referred to, apparently mistakenly, as '*Miriam*'/'*Mary*' – as we shall see, more of the confusion one often encounters in these traditions)[20] than his own. He is called '*Boethus*,' a name obviously meant to evoke the reigning representative of that family Herod brought in from Egypt to take over the High Priesthood after he had disposed of his Maccabean wife by the same name as this, '*Mariamme*' – that is, two more instances of these confusing '*Miriam*'s or '*Mary*'s.[21]

To go back to Nakdimon's *cistern-filling, water-supply*, and *famine-relief efforts* (ascribed in this period now to six separate persons we can specify: Queen Helen, her son Izates, Paul and Barnabas, *Ben Kalba Sabuʿa*, and

Nakdimon, to whom we could certainly add a seventh; in some of his miraculous '*works*,' 'Jesus' himself) – not only does Nakdimon promise in Talmudic *Tractate Gittin* (the implication being during the final Roman siege) *to supply Jerusalem with enough grain for* '*twenty-one years*' (in *ARN*, as we just saw, it is Nakdimon's colleague '*Ben Kalba Sabuᶜa*' who promises this, but in the slightly different time-frame of '*twenty-two years*')²²; Nakdimon is also pictured as giving '*twelve talents of silver*' as surety to an unidentified '*Rich*' foreign '*lord*' or '*grandee*' of some kind to advance him '*twelve cisterns of water*' so that he could fulfill his promise *to fill the Temple cisterns* by that amount.²³ One should not only keep an eye on the numbers '*twelve*' and '*twenty-four*' in these traditions but, as we shall see further below, all allusions to '*full,*' '*fill,*' '*filling,*' '*sated,*' or '*satiated.*'

The story, which appears in both *Taᶜanith* and *ARN* and is pictured as taking place *inside the Temple*, is recondite in the extreme. Nevertheless, it is within the context of fulfilling these promises that Nakdimon – like James – is pictured as '*making rain*' and, therefore, one of these prototypical '*Rain-maker*'s – in fact, *so much rain does he make for the benefit of pilgrims coming to Jerusalem to celebrate the Passover that he* '*fills*' *the Temple water cisterns* '*to overflowing.*'²⁴ The characterization of this process as '*overflowing*' will be another key motif to watch in these intertwining stories as we proceed.

Not only is *the* '*Rich*' *foreigner* or '*lord,*' with whom Nakdimon is involved in these Rabbinic traditions, said either *to have had something to do with* '*bathing*' or *gone to* '*bathhouses*' *himself*; but where '*rain-making*' and '*sunshine-bringing*' are concerned, Nakdimon is pictured – like Elijah, Honi, and even Muhammad in the Koran – several times as '*wrapping himself in his cloak*' – in his case anyhow, if not Muhammad's or these others, undoubtedly implying *his prayer shawl*.

In the story Nakdimon's relations with *the* '*Rich*' *lord* or '*master*' will resemble some of the situations involving '*Rich*' *masters* and *their servants* to be encountered in 'the Parables' told by Jesus below. In the story too, there is just the slightest hint again of *the theme of* '*Rich*' *gifts to the Temple on behalf of foreigners* repeatedly signaled, as we have seen, in the run-up to the War against Rome and so important where issues regarding *gifts of this kind* and '*pollution of the Temple*' generally in the Dead Sea Scrolls are concerned. In addition, the efforts of Nakdimon and his colleague *Ben Kalba Sabuᶜa* to relieve the famine and supply Jerusalem with grain '*for twenty-one years*' ('*twenty-two*' for '*Ben Kalba Sabuᶜa*' above, as we just saw) also mirror to some extent, as already suggested, the '*famine relief*' efforts in the Forties of Queen Helen of Adiabene and her son Izates, detailed in both Josephus and Rabbinic sources – not to mention those of Paul and his nascent '*Antioch*' Community in Acts.

The time span of '*twenty-one years*' will also bear a relationship to aspects of the Queen Helen story – in this instance, as already just remarked as well, *reflective of the time span of the three successive, seven-year Nazirite-oath penances laid upon her for obscure reasons by the Rabbis.*[25] Furthermore, where gifts to the Temple on the part of '*Rich*' foreigners are concerned; it should be appreciated that Helen, her husband, and/or her sons *were also involved in giving the golden candelabra to the Temple which stood in front of its entrance*, before Titus took it as booty to Rome using it in his victory celebrations. It is now famously pictured on the Arch dedicated there to his name.[26] Of course, this same Titus and Vespasian his father also used the other monies they accumulated from '*plundering the Temple*' *to build the Colosseum*, the most brutal of all Roman entertainment venues and another excellent example of ironic historical reversal.

Helen and/or her husband ('*Bazeus*' in Josephus – '*King Monobaz*' in the *Talmud*) are also credited with having given the golden handles for vessels used on *Yom Kippur* in the Temple and, as just underscored as well above, the gold plaque containing – strikingly in terms of her personal story (the *three successive, seven-year Nazirite oath penances* certainly seeming to have something to do with possible '*fornication*' and/or '*adultery*' charges that were leveled against her)[27] – *the 'suspected adulteress' passage from Numbers* 5:11–31 – a passage, not incuriously and as just remarked, preceding the one delineating all the Nazirite oath procedures in Numbers 6:1–21 – *all points never adequately explained in our sources.*[28]

Perhaps even more germane, this woman, whom we have elsewhere referred to as the '*Sabaean Queen*' and whom Acts, as we saw, would appear to refer to in somewhat less flattering terms, actually *did send her Treasury agents up to Jerusalem to supply it with grain during the 44–46 CE famine* and we have already explained in some detail the relationship of this whole series of circumstances to Acts 8:26–40's story of *the conversion of 'the Ethiopian Queen's eunuch.*'[29] But, in addition, *the 'twenty-one years' of her three successive Nazirite oaths* can be seen, should one choose to remark it, *as the amount of time between this first famine and the stopping of sacrifice on behalf of foreigners and the rejection of their gifts in the Temple* that began the Uprising against Rome in 66 CE.[30] Nor should it be overlooked that this '*Famine*' in approximately 45 CE seems to have been the occasion for '*Theudas*'' Messianic-style reverse exodus above – mentioned, so anachronistically in Acts, and in Josephus and Eusebius, alongside *Queen Helen's own 'famine-relief' efforts* – which included, it will be recalled, a '*Joshua*'/'*Jesus redivivus*' parting of the Jordan River in reverse and *an attempted Damascus Document-style exodus across the Jordan.*

Regarding the additional penalty of '*twelve talents of silver*' Nakdimon
had promised to pay if he was late in fulfilling the surety he had
pledged, his Rich creditor finally asks him either to *refill the cisterns
by the stipulated date or pay the additional 'twelve talents'* (one needs to
watch these various multiples or repetitions of '*twelve*' – now, apparently, mounting to '*twenty-four*').[31] It is at this point in this oddly-labored
story – which has many overtones, as we shall see below, of the '*feeding
the multitudes*' and '*giving to drink*' miracles 'Jesus' performs in the Gospels,
on several occasions pictured as '*multiplying loaves*' and, in one celebrated
instance, *even turning water into wine!* – that Nakdimon's/Nicodemus'
'*rain-making*' occurs and he actually *goes into the Temple and* (like James)
prays for rain.

As this is described in Talmudic tradition:

He *wrapped himself in his cloak and stood up to pray*' (notice, another
instance, perhaps coincidentally – perhaps not, of the '*standing*' allusion
which we have been calling attention to in so many contexts in the
Gospels, Acts, and the Dead Sea Scrolls above. Not only does this relate
to '*the Primal Adam*' ideology reflected in the supernatural activities of
these '*rain-making*' '*Zaddiks*' and referred to in Ebionite/Elchasaite tradition as 'the *Standing One*,' as we have seen; it may also be the reason why
the '*feet*' *of this gigantic figure* – perhaps the only thing visible to ordinary
mortals, since *he was supposed to have stood some* '*ninety-six miles*' *high*[32]
and an element which will become evermore prominent in these traditions as we proceed – might have taken on such extraordinary
significance).

The Jerusalem *Talmud* even knows the words of Nakdimon's prayer. Nor
is this to say anything, as just indicated, about the traditional Jewish activity of '*wrapping oneself in a prayer shawl*,' also a part of these traditions. Of
course, we have already encountered this theme of '*wrapping himself in a
cloak*' (again, '*prayer shawl*' evidently being intended) when Elijah's '*consuming zeal for the Lord of Hosts*' in a cave on Mount Sinai was evoked in 1
Kings 19:9–14 above, not to mention its reflection in the circumstances
of Muhammad's earliest revelations in the Koran, when in his first visions
(*in a cave as well*) he pictures himself or, supposedly, '*the Angel Gabriel*' pictures him, as '*wrapping himself in a cloak*' or '*being wrapped in a cloak*'![33]

It is not unremarkable that in this prayer, in which Nakdimon is pictured as claiming that it was not for his '*own Glory*' nor that of his own
'*house*' but rather *for God's* '*Glory*' that he would perform the '*sign*' or
'*miracle*' – namely, *filling the cisterns in order that there should be enough water*

in the Temple to accommodate even those on pilgrimage.[34] In the process, as we shall see in more detail below too, Nakdimon is pictured as speaking, intentionally or otherwise, in terms of allusion to his *'father's house,'* the cry, of course, that John 2:17 above – evoking Psalm 69:9 – puts into 'Jesus' mouth when depicting his *'consuming zeal'* and *'purification of the Temple.'*

It should be recalled that in *Ta'anith's* picture of Honi's paradigmatic *'rain-making,'* it was because of Honi's use of almost the same language that the famous Pharisee leader, Simeon ben Shetach, considered pressing *'blasphemy'* charges against him (and by extension, it should be appreciated, Elijah – since Honi like his seeming descendant *'Hanin'* or *'John the Baptist' was being compared to Elijah) because he was 'speaking to God like a son.'*[35] According to *Ta'anith,* this was because in his prayer – much like Nakdimon's prayer in *Ta'anith* here as well – Honi had added the words about being *'looked upon as one of (God's) household.'* In this connection, Simeon was only prevented from doing so by the conclusion which he is pictured as stating himself: *'If he were not Honi, I would have excommunicated him'!*[36]

All this is rife with meaning for future events and, from the reader's perspective, it is important to see that this issue of *'blasphemy,'* presaged in these *'Friendship'/'Sonship'* claims by these *'rain-making''Zaddik's/'Adam redivivus'es,* is the prototype for the portrait in the Gospels of similar charges, pictured as being leveled against 'Jesus' either by the High Priest or the Jewish Sanhedrin. As these present things, the reason behind the *'blasphemy'* charge is always the perceived claim of Divine *'Sonship,'* which either Jesus is pictured as making or which was retrospectively being made on his behalf by his Hellenizing enthusiasts or partisans.[37] Put in another way, when evaluating the New Testament's focus on *'the Son of God'* motif in the context of accusations of *'blasphemy,'* it is well to keep one's eye on the controversy being generated by language of this kind in the case of *'rain-making'* Zaddiks and Elijah *redivivus*es like Honi as a template or fore-runner for the picture in the New Testament of the same accusations against the person pictured in the Gospels as being called *'Jesus'* or *'Saviour.'*

Nakdimon Fills the Cisterns and Hanan *the Hidden* Locks Himself in the Toilet

However all these things may be – in *'Nakdimon''s* case, as Rabbinic story-telling would have it, *'Immediately the sky was covered by clouds until the twelve wells were filled with water'* in a torrent so strong that they *'filled beyond overflowing*' (again, it is important to pay attention both to the '*filling*' notices here as well as to the '*overflowing*'). There now ensues much wrangling about '*the wages which were held back*' from Nakdimon by the foreign lord or those Nakdimon held back from him; whereupon Nakdimon, once more, *enters the Temple, wraps himself in his cloak a second time, and prays* (*like Elijah before him* and '*the efficacious prayer*' *of James*' '*Just One*') *for it not to rain.* This time he is even pictured as evoking '*the Beloved*' or '*Friend of God*' language (so similar to that of '*the Son of God*' in other contexts), we have been describing above with regard to James, Honi, and Abraham in writings like the Damascus Document, Tractate *Ta'anith* and the New Testament.

This wrangling over payment due and not performed, to some degree, *reflects Josephus' account of the stoning of Honi as well*, when the Pharisees besieging the Temple refuse to provide the Priests inside with the animals they have already paid for. It was, it will be recalled, at this point that the Maccabean Aristobulus' and Honi's supporters *inside the Temple pray to God*, who then sends '*a whirlwind*' or an intense rainstorm to '*repay them for both their Impiety*' and, presumably, *their prior* '*Impiety*' *in having stoned Honi.*[38]

In fact, *Ta'anith* makes the connection between the two characters Nakdimon and Honi in almost the very next line, when it adds the curious statement that '*his name was not Nakdimon but Boni.*' As if this were not surprising enough, in the very same breath it revises its position on the original significance of '*Nakdimon*''s name by *explaining that he had only been called* '*Nakdimon*' '*because the sun broke through (nikdera) on his behalf*!'[39] But this is what we have been trying to point out from the beginning. The *Talmud*, in the often garbled nature of transmission of this kind, is clearly implying that when it is talking about '*Nakdimon*,' it really is talking about '*Honi*' or, more comprehensibly, a Honi *redivivus*, as very little, if anything else, can make sense out of this ludicrous alias. As puzzling as this may be, *aside from the absurdity of this tomfoolery*, there is no doubt that in this story we are dealing in some manner, once again, with the '*redivivus*' traditions associated with Honi – a complex that *really would have confused the abilities of even the most-informed of later redactors.*

Nor is this to say anything about the real reason for Honi's stoning – and, consequently, that of the related tradition surrounding the rain-making and stoning of James – namely, *refusing to cooperate with the dictates of foreign power.* Whether, because of the chronology of the episode, Nakdimon is to be identified with another of these '*redivivus*' grandsons of Honi, such as '*Abba Hilkiah*,' '*Hanan Ha-Nehba*,' or even James, is impossible to say with any certainty given the nature of Talmudic story-telling. It should be pointed out, however, that where the description of Nakdimon's colleague '*Ben Kalba Sabuᶜa*' as '*never turning the Poor away from his door*' above is concerned and further characterizations of a similar genre we shall encounter regarding these same several pseudonymous '*Rich*' celebrities below'; '*Abba Hilkiah*,' too, has a wife who '*stays at home and gives bread to the Poor*.'[40]

In another startling variation on these traditions regarding '*Hanan*'/'*Hanin*''s cognomen, '*Ha-Nehba*'/'*the Hidden*'; the Talmudic tradition, playing off the usage '*to hide*,' sarcastically observes that he was given this cognomen '*because he used to hide himself in the toilet*.'[41] Again, this story is typical of Talmudic narrative which, like the Gospels, is often so absurd and malicious that it fairly jolts one and makes one laugh outright. But this is the way writings of this kind often treat their ideological opponents and this one carries clear overtones of the Jacob of Kfar Sechania story told to Eliezer ben Hyrcanus above, the Rabbi excommunicated by the Patriarch Gamaliel II (the grandson of Paul's alleged teacher in Acts 22:3 by the same name – Gamaliel I), about '*Jesus the Nazoraean*''s position on gifts from prostitutes' earnings given to the Temple, whose answer to which was, it will be recalled – again not without a touch of scurrilous humor typical of Talmudic story-telling – *that they should be used to build an outhouse for the High Priests*.

Surely this question (to say nothing about its parody involving Jesus' putative cousin '*Hanin*' providing, even if only indirectly, perhaps additional confirmation of the veracity of the original) and 'Jesus'' purported response to it are important, as we saw, not only vis-a-vis persons perceived as being themselves no better than '*prostitutes*' (among whom should perhaps be included the last Herodian Princess, Titus' mistress, Bernice; her sister Drusilla, who divorced her first husband to marry the brutal Roman Governor Felix – himself pictured in Acts as standing with her and genially conversing with Paul; and even possibly Queen Helen herself[42]), but also the picture of 'Jesus' in the Gospels keeping '*table fellowship*' *with* '*prostitutes*,' '*publicans*,' *and* '*tax-collectors*.'

Moreover the '*Nakdimon*' pictured in these Talmudic '*miracle tales*' with their oddly tortuous plot-lines does not leave things there. Now '*Nakdimon*' asks the foreign lord *to pay him* for the excess wells of water produced out of the '*overflow*' his efforts had produced. In so doing, according to the convoluted logic of these stories, he gives his creditor *a chance to object that the day was already done and the sun already gone, so he (the creditor) owed Nakdimon nothing* – thus setting the stage for Nakdimon's even more celebrated, next miracle! In the turgidity of the material, as it has come down to us, it is in order to both meet this objection and collect for the overflow that Nakdimon performs the miracle, from which he supposedly derived his name, namely, *making the sun 'shine through,' 'pierce through the clouds'* or, in the manner of the Lord's special dispensation to Joshua, *'make the sun stand still.'*

Though it would be hard to get more convoluted than this still, to use the episode's own language, something does seem *'to shine through.'* Not only are the two times *'twelve'* or *'twenty-four wells'* or *'cisterns,'* one is dealing with in the matter of what is finally *'being filled,'* also reflected in the several exchanges between Nakdimon and his creditor over *'the twelve talents of silver'*; it can be seen as reflecting the number of the priestly courses in the Temple, *'twenty-four,'* we have already alluded to above – for whatever this might be seen to be worth. Be this as it may, one can, in fact, draw an even more impressive connection to Epiphanius' description of the Ebionite/*Elchasaite 'Standing One'* above or *'the High Power which is above God the Creator'* and thought of, as well, in terms of being *'the Christ and the Great Power of the High God which is superior to the Creator of the world,'*[43] the dimensions of which he reckons as:

> *Twenty-four schoeni or ninety-six miles in height* (as we saw) *and six schoeni or twenty-four miles in width.*[44]

Rabbi Akiba's *'Disciples'*

But there is even a more germane parallel than either of these, specifically relating to the Royal House of Adiabene we have been following. This one involves the *'Zealot'* Rabbi Akiba, referred to above, who supported the Bar Kochba Uprising in 132–36 CE, one of the important students of whom was also called *'Monobaz.'* It is the allusion to two times either *'twelve talents of silver'* or *'twelve cisterns of water'* involved in the Nakdimon stories above which, more likely, *echoes the double period of twelve years 'the Poor shepherd,'* Rabbi Akiba, reportedly worked to earn the right to marry Nakdimon's *'Rich'* colleague, *'Ben Kalba Sabuᶜa's daughter.'*[45]

Called Rachel in the *ARN* above, as we saw, in her model faithfulness *'Ben Kalba Sabuᶜa'*'s daughter is not only pictured as encouraging this *'Poor'* country boy in his studies and, rather than marry him immediately, paying for the two consecutive *'twelve-year'* (*'twenty-four year'* in all) study periods, Rabbi Akiba seems to have spent with the famous, quasi-heretical Rabbi Eliezer ben Hyrcanus just referred to above.[46] Of course, in Talmudic tradition, Rabbi Akiba was not only one of the most nationalist rabbis, he was also the rabbi who proclaimed Bar Kochba *'the*

Messiah' at the time of this Uprising from 132–36 – much to the reported derision of his peers and confrères (applying the famous '*Star Prophecy*' from Numbers 24:17 to him, a prophecy we have already seen reflected in the New Testament and at Qumran and reflected in Josephus as well[47]) – and a time in which he too was ultimately martyred in the cruelest of ways.[48]

Called '*Ben Kalba Sabuᶜa's shepherd*,' Rabbi Akiba was also pictured as twice returning to his wife Rachel with '*twelve thousand Disciples*' – again, note the striking numerology – that is, '*twenty-four thousand*' in all, no doubt evocative of *the number of adepts ready to participate with Bar Kochba in the Second Jewish Revolt against Rome*.[49] Though the geographical provenance of Rabbi Akiba's several departures and returns is unclear, his teacher R. Eliezer ben Hyrcanus, as we saw, was considered a '*Christian*' sympathizer of sorts and, certainly, was perceived of as actually knowing a tradition from '*Jesus the Nazoraean*' via '*Jacob of Kfar Sechania*' ('*Kfar Sihnin*' – James?) about '*the prostitutes' wages*' and the High Priest's '*outhouse*' above.

Not only does the gist of this tradition incorporate quite an acute sense of humor, often missing from New Testament accounts, as already observed; '*Jesus the Nazoraean*''s purported response via Jacob of Sihnin (elsewhere called '*Kfar Sama*' or '*Kfar Sechania*' – a '*Sicarii*' spin-off?) about using said '*hire*' to '*build the High Priest an outhouse*' (a response Eliezer ben Hyrcanus obviously also felt to be quite humorous, since he conserved it) is also perhaps not unrelated to the '*toilet drain*' parable we shall see ascribed in the Gospels to 'Jesus' as well. Nor is this to say anything about its further ribald adumbration in Talmudic satire of Hanin '*locking himself in the outhouse*' just mentioned above.[50]

Eliezer's testimony to '*Jesus the Nazoraean*' in the *Talmud* is one of the most convincing concerning this personage on record, though its wry humor and intense anti-Establishmentism is quite different from Gospel portrayal. Ultimately excommunicated by the Rabbis for being a little too self-assertive and opposing Rabban Gamaliel II, Lamentations *Rabbah* also calls '*Eliezer*,' '*Liezer*,' a name we shall see to have no little significance below.[51] Chronological difficulties aside, he or a prototype of his, is still one of the best candidates for the mysterious '*Galilean*' Rabbi, named '*Eliezer*' in Josephus, who countermands Ananias' and his companion (Paul?)'s teaching on the matter of the unnecessariness of circumcision as a prerequisite for the conversion of the male members of Queen Helen's household.[52]

Even more to the point, the *Talmud* specifically denotes one of Rabbi Akiba's students as '*Monobaz*,' as we have seen, who certainly must be seen as a descendant of this Rich and famous family. Not only is *'Monobazus'* the name of Queen Helen's second son, as we just saw, in Josephus' episode about his and Izates' *'circumcision'* above and probably the name of her husband *'Bazeus'* as well (itself probably defective, but possibly also a generic variation in a Persian linguistic framework of the more Semitic name or title *'Abgarus'* or *'Agbarus'*[53]); it is the name as well of one of the two descendants of this same Queen Helen who *both distinguish and martyr themselves in the opening engagement of the Jewish War against Rome in 66* CE *at the Pass at Beit Horon.*[54]

In conclusion therefore, for the *Talmud*, Rabbi Akiba, one of the most nationalist Rabbis and himself martyred in the Second Jewish War against Rome, was for all intents and purposes *involved with the family of Queen Helen of Adiabene* in two ways. In the first, one of its descendants was clearly his *'Disciple'*; in the second, he more than likely married one of its daughters who, in turn, not only encouraged, but *paid for the twenty-four years of study he pursued* that seem to have matured into extreme revolutionary sympathies as well as *the materialization eventually of twenty-four thousand 'Disciples.'*

This, of course, would necessitate the additional conclusion that *Ben Kalba Sabuᶜa* is a *nom à clef* for the scion of that family, two descendants of which – one also called *'Monabazus'* and the other, *'Kenedaeus'* (the root *inter alia* of Acts 8:27's mysterious own bowdlerization of Queen Helen's name, *'Kandakes'*)[55] – lost their lives in the opening engagement of the First Jewish War against Rome, blocking the advance of Roman reinforcements on Jerusalem at the Pass at Beit Horon, an heroic death reminiscent of Leonidas at the Pass of Thermopolae – a not unimpressive revolutionary heritage.[56]

Ben Kalba Sabuᶜa's Doorstep and *'Casting Holy Things to Dogs'*

To turn to further traditions about *'Nakdimon'*'s colleague – Talmudic literature calls by the curious pseudonym *'Ben Kalba Sabuᶜa'* – involved with him according to the *ARN* in *promising to replenish Jerusalem's grain supplies for not 'twenty-one' but 'twenty-two years'*: one possible reading of his name, as already suggested, could be taken as a derogatory reference to one or another of the descendants of the legendary convert to Judaism (or nascent *'Christianity'* – there being no real difference between the two at this point, except the requirement of *'circumcision'* or lack thereof) in Northern Syria or Mesopotamia, Queen Helen of Adiabene. Taken according to this sense, *'Kalba'* in both Aramaic and Hebrew signifying *'dog'* (as it does in Arabic – in both it and Hebrew, if read phonetically, '*female dog*' or '*bitch*'), the only question really is whether to impute to it in English translation only the masculine sense of the Aramaic or the feminine of both the Hebrew and Arabic as well.

Even if this doubly derogatory feminine sense of '*the Son of the Sabaean Bitch*' (which we are imputing to it on ideological grounds) turns out not to be present – the writer considers it is, linking up with various allusions to '*dogs*' in the New Testament episodes we shall delineate below and elsewhere (in particular in '*MMT*') – all such Talmudic circumlocutions, pseudonyms, or euphemisms must be taken seriously. Nor can there be any doubt of the more than simply ordinary significance of a veiled reference to someone ('*Nakdimon*') having a connection to someone else ('*Ben Kalba Sabuᶜa*'), whose name in the Syriac or Aramaic actually, also, carries with it the sense of '*bathing*' or '*bathers*' – these last in Arabic, as we saw, referred to as '*Sabaeans*' and, in all three, the use of the letter ᶜ*ayin* as opposed to *alef* is determinant.

In the Talmudic descriptions of Ben Kalba Sabuᶜa, another theme – aside from the repetitious evocations of '*dog*' or '*dogs*' to expound his name – and one, as we shall see, despite some slight variations, always prominent in New Testament narrative as well, is the one of being '*sated*,' '*satiated*,' '*full*,' or '*filled*.' We have already encountered this theme in the matter of '*filling*' Nakdimon's or his '*Rich*' patron's cisterns above, but it will be of equal prominence in Gospel narratives as it will be, to some extent, in the Dead Sea Scrolls.[57] Catchwords or the use of phrases such as this will lead to a goodly number of other key words or usages in a variety of contexts. Unfortunately this was how many of these ancient manuscripts usually resonated with each other, that is, however maddeningly it may sometimes seem, *via the use of common keywords*.

Tractate *Gittin*, supported by *ARN*, tries to make sense of Ben Kalba Sabuᶜa's name, in the process developing quite a humorous play upon it. It expounds it, as already underscored above, as follows – saying he was called this because,

One came to his door hungry as a dog and went away filled.[58]

Not only is this last usage, '*sabuᶜa*' or '*filled*,' related in both Syriac and Aramaic to '*immersion*,' it carries with it in Hebrew the additional sense of '*sated*' or '*satiation*,' which is the whole point of the Talmudic attempt at exposition. Here one should also pay especial attention to the verb '*come*' or '*came*,' which will reappear in a dizzying number of New Testament contexts as well – more than would normally be expected. The same will be true to a somewhat lesser degree of the expression 'his door,' 'doorway,' 'stoop,' or 'porch,' instances of the use of which we have already started to encounter in the case of 'Abba Hilkiah''s wife above.

This is particularly true of Luke 16:22's further variant on the motif of these 'dogs' having to do with 'a certain Poor man named Lazarus' (here, too, our 'a certain' language again) with a 'body full of sores who was laid at the doorstep' (this 'laid at'/'laid down' motif will reappear in the additional Nakdimon story, we shall highlight below, in 'the woollen clothes laid down for him by the Poor, so his feet would not touch the ground' – here, too, 'the Poor' allusion we just saw with regard to 'Ben Kalba Sabuᶜa's doorstep,' Abba Hilkiah's house, and Luke's characterization of 'Lazarus') of 'a certain Rich man clothed in purple and fine linen' – this 'Poor man Lazarus' himself being characterized, in turn, as 'wanting to be satisfied from the crumbs that fell from the Rich man's table,' while 'the dogs came and licked his sores'!

Of course, anyone with a modicum of insight will easily be able to see that here we already have many of the motifs, we have been calling attention to above, including 'the Poor' and 'the Rich man,' 'the doorstep,' the pivotal allusion to 'being satisfied,' to say nothing of his body being 'full of sores,' and of course 'the dogs,' which we shall be analyzing more thoroughly as we proceed. Furthermore, this whole thematic complex, as we shall see as well, will move into other material in John about this 'Lazarus' ('Liezer' above?) – the body of whom was resurrected after it 'had already begun to stink' (11:39–44) – who will have 'two sisters,' 'Mary' and 'Martha' – names we shall also encounter in those of the daughters in these Talmudic 'Rich Men' stories – who will themselves be involved in what we shall in turn see to be tell-tale 'perfume' and 'expensive spikenard ointment' ministrations (John 11:1–3 and 12:1–6).

In Matthew 15:21–28 and Mark 7:24–30, the references to 'dogs' will also occur, but here they will relate, to what Jesus did with 'a Canaanite' ('Cananaean')/'Greek Syrophoenician woman' out of whose 'daughter' he 'casts a demon' or 'an unclean spirit' (as he will in Luke 8:2, which has no 'Canaanite'/'Cananaean woman' episode, and later in Mark 16:9, 'from Mary Magdalene'). In this context, Mark 7:26 will actually use the term 'ekballe' so important in other milieux, as we have already seen and shall see further (for instance, in Mark 16:9 a propos of Mary Magdalene, a variation of the same term 'ekbeblekai' will be used; whereas Matthew 15:17 – which does not conserve any description of this kind concerning 'Mary Magdalene' – rather reserves this usage for the food Jesus says 'goes into the belly and is cast – 'ekballetai' – into the toilet bowl' preceding his 'withdrawal into the parts of Tyre and Sidon'), to express how 'the children should first be satiated' or 'filled' (our 'satiated'/'filling' language). Of course, both Matthew 15:26/Mark 7:27 conclude with the famous saying of 'Jesus': '*it is not good to take the children's bread and cast it (balein) to the dogs.*'

An earlier version of this same '*casting Holy Things to dogs*' phrase (here '*balete*') but to opposite effect, that is, *don't give anything to* '*dogs*' – intending no doubt, as will become clear, '*Gentiles*' and/or '*backsliding Jews*' (the '*casting down*' will reappear in the second part of the injunction, to '*cast no pearls before swine*') – is to be found in Matthew's Sermon on the Mount. It combines this same language of '*casting down*' with '*dogs,*' but this time Jesus is speaking to '*his Disciples*' who '*came to him,*' not to '*the Canaanite*'/'*Greek Syrophoenician woman*' and reads in the more native Palestinian or normative Hebrew manner,

> *Do not give Holy Things to dogs, nor cast down your pearls before the swine, lest they should trample upon them with their feet* and, *turning around, rend you* (Matthew 7:6 not paralleled in the other Gospels – curiously, here too begin those odd '*feet*' allusions we shall encounter so omnipresently in both Talmudic and New Testament tradition below).

Once again one should note here the expression we have been calling attention to as endlessly repetitive, the '*casting out*'/'*casting down*' language (*balein/ballo/ekballo*), not only relating to what happens to Stephen in Acts 7:58 (they '*cast him out of the city*' – *ekbalonte*) and early Church literature to James ('*cast down*' either from the steps of the Temple by '*the Enemy*' Paul in the Pseudoclementine *Recognitions* or, in early Church literature, *from* '*the Pinnacle of the Temple*' by the allegedly angry Jewish mob before, like Stephen, he too is stoned), but in Josephus to what his prototypical '*Essenes*' do to backsliders – namely, '*cast them out*' (*ekballo*).[59]

It is also related as we saw – at least homophonically – to the '*Ba-La-ʿa*' or '*swallowing*' language (the root is a homophone) one encounters in Hebrew in the Dead Sea Scrolls relative to what '*the Wicked Priest*' does to '*the Righteous Teacher*' and his followers – called there '*the Poor*'/*the Ebionim*' – that is, '*swallows them.*'[60] This, in turn, points to the characteristic activity of the Romans and/or their Herodian agents (the '*ʿAmim*' and the '*Yeter ha-ʿAmim*' of the Habakkuk *Pesher*[61]), '*swallowing,*' itself related to another seeming variation, '*Balaam*' – whose name in the *Talmud*, anyhow, is phonetically interpreted to mean '*swallowing the People,*' which the Herodians did *so conspicuously.*[62]

To complete this circle, a term like '*Balaam*' cannot really be distinguished in any way from '*Belial*' in the Scrolls, a name based on the same root. In the New Testament, this not only moves into allusions like '*Beliar*' and '*Diabolos,*' also based on parallel roots; but, not insignificantly, in a book like Revelation, as we saw as well, it goes back to the original 'Balaam' (and 'Balak,' too, a further variation – to say nothing of 'Beelzebub' or, for that matter even, 'Babylon') and his 'net' or 'nets,' terminology that will be so pivotal to the Damascus Document's delineation of the conduct of the then reigning Establishment – *the Herodians.*[63]

In Matthew 7:6 too of course, as we just signalled, is one of the first adumbrations of the language of '*feet*,' a motif which will be so prominent in many of the traditions below. Here, also, the '*dogs*' are '*dogs*' (*kunes*), as they are in Luke's alternate version of how they rather '*came and licked the Poor man Lazarus' sores*' ('*the crumbs*,' to be sure, still '*falling from the table*') – not '*kunaria*'/'*little dogs*,' as in Mark/Matthew's '*Greek Syrophoenician*'/'*Canaanite woman*''s retort (whom, of course, *is also portrayed* in Mark 7:25 as '*falling at Jesus' feet*'), but the effect is the same. In fact, if one takes these several motifs – in particular, that of '*casting down Holy Things to dogs*' or '*swine*' or '*casting down crumbs to dogs under the table*' – as a single cluster, Jesus' caution here in Matthew 7:6 can actually be seen as a reply in advance to the later complaint by this Canaanite/Greek Syrophoenician woman – which, in due course, finally does give way to *his curing* '*her daughter*.'

That these kinds of Gospel portraits involving allusions to '*dogs*' do, in fact, have to do with '*Gentiles*' is made clear in the version of this encounter conserved in, of all places, the Pseudoclementine *Recognitions*. In the repartee, as it is presented there, the '*dogs*' are overtly identified as *a Hebrew way of referring to Gentiles* and the woman in question actually gets a name, '*Justes*' – the feminine equivalent of '*Justus*.'[64] Whether this is an earlier or derivative version of the encounter in Mark and Matthew above has to be decided, but in the writer's view – just as in the instance of the Pseudoclementine *Homilies'* more complete delineation of what '*the strangled things*' in James' directives to overseas communities actually were or the *Recognitions'* portrayal of *who the real* '*Zacchaeus*' *was in* '*Caesarea*' *not* '*Jericho*'[65] – the version in the Pseudoclementine *Recognitions*, which definitively ties down these correspondences, is more complete and also probably earlier.

To show the link between all three sets of material as the Gospels preserve them, that is, Matthew and Mark's '*Canaanite*'/'*Greek Syrophoenician woman*''s '*the crumbs falling from the master's table*' (thus)/'*the little dogs under the table eating the children's crumbs*' and the earlier '*not throwing Holy Things to dogs*'; it would be well to set out more fully out the description of the man, Luke alluded to, as '*a certain Poor One* (in the language of the early Church, '*an Ebionite*'):

Now there was a certain Rich Man and he was clothed (as we shall see, like Nakdimon) *in purple and fine linen, enjoying himself in luxury daily* (this usage too will repeatedly reappear in the Rabbinic traditions we shall cite below – in particular, the one about the amount of money *'daily,'* *'Nakdimon's daughter Miriam'* will need just *to fill* 'her perfume basket'!). *And there was a certain Poor Man named Lazarus* (we shall see from the matter of *'the smell'* his body was later said to emit in John 11:39 below that this probably corresponds to *'Eliezer ben Hyrcanus'* above, the *'smell of whose bad breath'* becomes so celebrated in Rabbinic legend), *who was laid out on his doorstep, whose body* was *full of sores and he was desiring to be filled* (in the Greek, this really is the *'satisfied'* or *'filled'* of Nakdimon's *'rain-making'* above or of *'the Poor,'* who came to Ben Kalba Sabuᶜa's *'house hungry as a dog and went away filled'* above, not the more familiar English translation *'fed'*) *from the crumbs* (the same *'crumbs,'* presumably, that *'fell'* – in the *'Greek Syrophoenician'/'Canaanite woman'*'s retort to Jesus in Matthew and Mark above – to *'the little dogs under the table'*) *which fell from the Rich Man's table, so that even the dogs came to lick his sores* (16:19–21).

One could not get much closer to the Talmudic notice purporting to decipher *'Ben Kalba Sabuᶜa'*'s name just cited above, i.e., *'no Poor were ever turned away from his door,'* than this – always making allowances, of course, for the contemptuous disparagement inherent in the parody. Nor can such linguistic coincidences even in translation be considered acciden-tal, the *'desiring to be filled'* or *'satiated'* – not to mention even the *'came,'* or *'coming,'* to say nothing of *'being laid at,'* *'the Rich Man's doorstep,'* the allu-sion to *'daily,'* which we shall repeatedly now encounter below, and, of course, the *'Poor'* – going a long way towards establishing the linguistic connection to the Talmudic depiction of its *'Ben Kalba Sabuᶜa.'* The per-son or persons who created this description certainly knew what he or they were doing.

In a climactic section of the Qumran Habakkuk *Pesher,* already called attention to above, we shall see a similar allusion to *'being filled,'* this time applied to *'the Wicked Priest'* who *destroys the Leader of the Scroll Commu-nity,* *'the Righteous Teacher'* and *his followers* among *'the Poor'* – as just noted, specifically designated as *'the Ebionim.'*[66] This *'Priest'* (the meaning being, of course, *'the High Priest'*), as a result of his *'walking in the ways of satiety'* – often misconstrued by consensus Qumran scholars as implying *'drunkenness,'* but which is rather evocative of his *'bloodthirstiness'* – would *'drink his fill'* of *'the Cup of the Wrath of God,'* meaning, as we shall see and as in directly parallel passages in Revelation in the New Testament already remarked above, *the Divine Vengeance which would be taken on him for what he did to 'the Righteous Teacher.'*[67] In the Habakkuk *Pesher*, this is reinforced in the very next lines by the words: '*and he (the Wicked Priest) will be paid the reward he paid the Poor*' – namely destruction.[68]

Nakdimon's Daughter '*Miriam*,' Boethus' Daughter '*Martha*,' and '*Lazarus*'' Two Sisters

The notices about these fabulously wealthy individuals in the *Talmud* – just as in the case of the '*Greek Syrophoenician*'/'*Canaanite woman*' above – also usually involve their daughters or, sometimes even, their daughters-in-law. For instance, in the case of '*Nakdimon's daughter Miriam*' ('*Mary*,' according to New Testament transliteration), *ARN* also describes '*her couch*' as '*overlaid with a spread worth twelve thousand dinars.*' Here of course, not only do we have allusion to the '*twelve thousand*' again, which we have already encountered above in the number of '*Rabbi Akiba's Disciples*,' to say nothing of the various figures descriptive of *the amount of Nakdimon's surety* or *the number of 'cisterns' he filled* and the variation of the language of '*laying out*' which the allusion to '*overlaid*' contains; but the allusion here to '*couch*' also forms part of the Talmudic exposition of the name of Nakdimon's other '*Rich*' colleague, variously called '*Ben Zizzit Hakeseth*' or '*Siset Hakkeset*,' a name which the *ARN* also expounds in terms of, as we shall see, the '*silver couch upon which he reclined before the Great Ones of Israel.*'[69]

A similar allusion to '*couch*' will, as these usages move into ever-widening circles, comprise part of the tradition *ARN* conserves about the great wealth of as well Rabbi Akiba, the hero of its narrative who started in poverty so extreme as to be virtually inexpressible. Rabbinic hyperbole aside, in later life after he had obviously inherited his father-in-law *Ben Kalba Sabuᶜa*'s wealth (the latter having at first disinherited both him and his daughter for marrying without his permission but, when later witnessing his son-in-law's great fame, became reconciled to them both); Rabbi Akiba supposedly '*mounted his couch with a ladder of gold,*' while '*his wife (Rachel) wore golden sandals*' (allusions to '*footwear*' of various kinds or the lack thereof will also be a setpiece of our traditions) and '*a golden tiara*' reportedly shaped like *the City of Jerusalem*. Not only does this tradition, once again doubtlessly, remount to his father-in-law Ben Kalba Sabuᶜa's '*Riches*,' to say nothing of Queen Helen's family's – Ben Kalba Sabuᶜa's putative forebears – *own expensive gifts to the Temple* (which included both the seven-branched candelabra at its entrance, taken to Rome for his '*Triumph*' by Titus, and the plaque with the passage from Numbers dealing with '*the suspected adulteress*' above, *both also of gold*); but also a youthful promise he (Rabbi Akiba) had made to his wife in the winter after their marriage when *they had nothing but straw upon which to sleep* (a prototype of the '*Jesus in the manger*' story?).[70]

For her part, Nakdimon's daughter is characterized in the Talmudic Tractate *Kethuboth* as already underscored – Rabbinic hyperbole again notwithstanding – as needing:

> *an allowance of four hundred dinars daily just for her perfume basket.*

Even this she is pictured as being contemptuous of, saying to the Rabbis who administered it (presumably because by this time *she was apparently a widow*), '*May you grant such a pittance to your own daughters!*'[71] The speech we have here, as we shall see below, seemingly mixes with one attributed elsewhere (in Lamentations *Rabbah*) to '*Boethus' daughter Miriam*' (again, actually meaning '*Martha*' but, as we said, these mix-ups are common and they will continue and become quite blatant in the Gospel of John), unless we have *two widows here both awaiting the levirate decision to remarry* (another important theme in the Synoptics[72]) – a doubtful proposition.

Motifs such as these, in particular the costliness of the '*perfumes*' or '*ointments*,' to say nothing of the allusion to '*daily*,' as noted in Luke's description of his '*a certain Rich Man*' – the one with the '*certain Poor man named Lazarus lying on his doorstep*,' will be mainstays in Gospel accounts of *events leading up to Jesus' death and burial*. For example, one of these '*expensive perfume*' or '*ointment*' episodes rather occurs *at Lazarus' own house* '*in Bethany*' in the Gospel of John 11:1–3 (repeated in 12:1–11) and relates notably to Lazarus' '*two sisters*,' *Mary* ('*Miriam*' in Hebrew) and the other, *Martha* ('*Boethus*'' daughter's name, as we just saw).

A small piece of this tradition will also appear as a separate episode earlier in Luke 10:38–42, this time '*in a certain village*' at the house of '*a certain woman named Martha*,' not at Lazarus' house – '*Lazarus*' (who will appear later in Luke 16:20 as just remarked) having been excised. Nevertheless, even in this episode, Mary will be '*sitting at (Jesus') feet*' and the argument, pregnant with significance – as we shall elucidate further below, breaks out over '*serving*' ('*diakonian*' – the same '*serving*' we have already seen relative to the complaints of '*the Seven*' against '*the Twelve*' over '*serving tables*' in Acts and Paul's allusion to the good '*service the Saints received*' at '*the house of Stephen, the first-fruit of Achaia*' – thus! – in 1 Corinthians 16:15).

In the two remaining Synoptics, Matthew and Mark, a different piece of this tradition – but still incorporating the '*expensive spikenard ointment*' and '*Bethany*' elements from John, as well as the '*alabaster flask*' detail from yet another such encounter, three chapters earlier in Luke 7:37–50, in which Jesus eats at '*the house of the Pharisee*' – will take place '*at Simon the Leper's house*' but now *the woman who 'comes' is unnamed* (Matthew 26:6–13/Mark 14:3–10). She is also unnamed in Luke 7:37 where she is called, conspicuously, '*a woman of the city who was a Sinner.*'

Not only does this episode include a good deal of emphasis, as in John, on '*kissing (Jesus') feet,*' '*wiping them with the hairs of her head,*' and '*anointing his feet with ointment*' but now, rather, a parable Jesus tells to *an unidentified* '*Simon*' (not the '*Simon the Leper*' in the argument over the '*three hundred pieces of silver*' value of '*the alabaster flask of very precious spikenard ointment*' in Matthew 26:7 and Mark 14:5, nor the '*Judas of Simon Iscariot*' – obviously now one of those called '*his Disciples*' in Matthew 26:9 above – in the argument, we shall discuss below, over the same issue in John 12:4), comparing this '*woman who was a Sinner*' and '*the Pharisee*' (it is now '*the Pharisee*' whom, we ultimately will find out, is called '*Simon*' who is *doing the complaining,* just as '*Martha*' in Luke and '*Judas*' in John) to '*two debtors who owed a certain creditor,*' one '*five hundred pieces of silver and the other fifty*' – clearly another anti-'*Jerusalem Church*' parable because it is about '*great Sinning*' rather than '*great Righteousness.*'[73] Furthermore, compare this, too, with Acts 15:5 above about '*certain of those of the sect of the Pharisees*' whose insistence on '*circumcision*' triggers '*the Jerusalem Conference,*' to say nothing of the certain parallel with *the debt of 'twelve talents of silver' Nakdimon 'owes' his creditor.*

In John 11–12, the more complete and imposing presentation of '*Lazarus*' ('*Eliezer*'?) and his two '*sisters,*' Mary and Martha are pictured in two successive episodes as '*anointing (Jesus') feet*' (just as in Luke 7:37–50's presentation of *the unidentified female* '*Sinner*') – at least '*Mary*' does (12:2–3, prefigured not a little anachronistically in 11:2). Martha, it seems, *is only doing the 'serving'* (12:2), *a matter about which we have just seen Luke* 10:40 *picture her as complaining bitterly above.* Also note the allusion to '*feet*' which Mary will anoint with '*a hundred-weight of ointment of pure spikenard of great price*' in John 12:3 and which *the unidentified* '*Sinning Woman*' just did as well in Luke 7:38. Prior to this, of course, in John 11:32, when Jesus is about *to resurrect her* '*brother*' *Lazarus* – like *Ben Kalba Sabuᶜa's* daughter greeting one of the heroes of Talmudic narrative, Rabbi Akiba, below – '*seeing Jesus, Mary fell at his feet.*'

Of course, this element of Jesus' *feet* – which we have already tied to '*the Primal Adam*'-ideology above – whether '*Mary*' or her stand-in *is* '*sitting*' at them, '*wiping them with her hair,*' '*kissing them,*' or '*anointing them with expensive ointment of pure spikenard,*' will repeatedly reappear in tradition after tradition. Also the locale, specifically noted in John 11:18 and

12:1 as being 'in Bethany,' will be the connecting link between the several traditions, since Mark 14:3 and Matthew 26:7 will picture the same basic incident as taking place at 'Simon the Leper's house in Bethany,' when the 'woman comes' with 'the alabaster flask of pure spikenard ointment of great worth' to anoint him (Matthew actually reads, dropping the 'spikenard,' 'with an alabaster cask of very precious ointment' as already underscored).

The Woman at 'Simon the Leper's House,' Jesus' Feet, and Rabbi Eliezer's Bad Breath

To drive home the motif of 'feet' and, as it will turn out, several others in John, 'Mary' (Hebrew, 'Miriam'/Arabic, 'Maryam') is not only pictured, not once but twice, as wiping 'his feet with her hair' (first alluded to anachronistically in 11:2 then repeated in 12:3 – twice as well in Luke 7:38 and 7:44 above), but also as 'falling down at' Jesus' 'feet' (11:32). As already underscored, we shall see this motif of 'falling down at his feet' continually repeated – most interestingly, as it will turn out, twice too in Rabbinic tradition in Kethuboth's story about how Ben Kalba Sabuʿa's daughter Rachel 'falls down at' Rabbi Akiba's feet after his several returns from study with his several times 'twelve thousand Disciples.' In this tradition, Rachel is also pictured, not as 'wiping (his feet) with her hair' as here in John, but as simply rather 'falling at his feet and kissing them.'[74]

But we have just seen this motif, too, in Luke 7:38's picture of the portrait of 'a woman of the city who was a Sinner.' In fact, this 'kiss' – somewhat like the mystical 'kiss' of Knowledge which Jesus gives James in the Two Apocalypses of James at Nag Hammadi (in the orthodox Gospels, the 'kiss' of betrayal 'Judas Iscariot' gives 'Jesus' – itself actually counter-indicated in the picture in this First Apocalypse[75]) – portrayed as very 'ardent' or 'loving,' becomes the source of 'Jesus'' complaint against 'Simon' above, whom he seems to feel did not 'love him' enough and did not show him enough adoration or obeisance – the typical ideological approach of these 'Gentilizing' Greek Gospels.

Not only do we have this 'serving' theme in John 12:3's picture of Martha doing the 'serving' (diakonei) while Mary goes about her 'anointing his feet' and 'hair wiping' ministrations – an activity that in Luke 10:40's version of this affair causes all the trouble; this allusion, as already indicated, cannot be disconnected from the issue of 'daily serving' (diakonia) in Acts 6:1–4's 'deacon'-appointment introduction of its 'Stephen' episode above, in which the 'Seven Men' are described as 'full of the Holy Spirit' in 6:3 and Stephen, as well, in 6:5, 6:8, and 7:55 (note too, the curious parallel with Luke 16:20's 'Poor Man' Lazarus above, whose body was rather described as '*full of sores*' – '*full of sores*' replacing '*full of the Holy Spirit*' in Acts 7:55 above).

Going back to John 12:3, however, after '*Martha does the serving*' in 12:2, then, it is rather '*the house*' which is described, pointedly and strikingly, as '*filled with the smell of the ointment*' or '*the perfume*' – here, not only our '*filled*'/'*full*' allusion but also that of '*the ointment*' or '*perfume*,' now combined with the new one of '*the smell*' or '*the odour*.' This theme of Martha's '*serving*' rather than Mary's *expensive anointment* and *hair-wiping ministrations* will form the basis of Luke 10:38-42's more compressed and obviously derivative version of these events, already examined in some detail above, specifically now *at 'Martha's house'* (10:38). This episode is the second of these basically interchangeable encounters in the same Gospel – the first, as we saw, at '*the house of the Pharisee*' (a write-in clearly for what is being represented as the '*James Party*' in both Acts and Galatians) who, in the guise of '*Simon*,' will bear the brunt of the '*creditor*'/ '*wages*'-parable rebuke.

This being said, it is still of the utmost importance to note, once again, the allusion to '*fill*'/'*full*'/'*being filled*' we have been focusing on in all these different episodes: the first being in '*the house was filled with the smell* (in the sense of '*perfume*') *of the ointment*' in John 12:3; a second being '*the Poor*' coming to '*Ben Kalba Sabuᶜa*''s house '*hungry as a dog and going away filled*'; a third, in Luke 16:20 (the analogue of the second) about '*Poor Lazarus*' under '*the Rich man's table*,' his body '*full of sores*,' '*desiring to be filled*'; and a fourth, of course, the one with which we began, *Nakdimon* '*filling*' his '*twelve*' to '*twenty-four cisterns*' even to '*overflowing*.' This is to say nothing about what will be seen to be additional motifs and spin-offs, using the same language, as we proceed.

For instance, as already intimated, this '*smell*' or '*odor*' motif will reappear with surprising ramifications in Talmudic tradition having to do with '*dung*' – as always the Talmudic counterparts to this matter are nothing, if not more colorful, earthy, and amusing – in particular, *the '*dung*' Rabbi Eliezer ('*Lazarus*'' namesake) puts into his mouth because he was hungry on the Sabbath but which gave him bad breath*. Nor is this to mention the '*dung*' which we shall encounter in other scenarios and traditions relative to these spoiled daughters or daughters-in-law of these proverbial '*Rich*' parvenus and relative to Rabbi Yohanan ben Zacchai himself in the matter, we will elaborate in more detail as we proceed, of his two '*Disciples*' putting '*dung*' into his coffin to convince both '*the Zealots*' and the Romans not to stab (or '*pierce*') him with their swords because he was already, indeed, dead.[76]

Where Eliezer ben Hyrcanus himself is concerned, the '*dung*' in question allows this same Rabbi Yohanan b. Zacchai, his mentor and the proverbial founder of Rabbinic Judaism – through his founding the Academy at Yavneh in the wake of this fortuitous escape from Jerusalem – and a supposed '*Friend of the Emperor*' (one wonders if this, too, does not have an analogue in the '*Friend of God*' denotations already highlighted above),[77] to observe and turn what was essentially the negative impression the young Rabbi Eliezer, as we saw, was making into a positive:

> *Just as an offensive smell came forth from your mouth, so shall a great name go forth from you in (teaching) Torah.*[78]

The relation of this to Jesus' retort to '*the Pharisees*,' called by him in this episode (which introduces his encounter, importantly enough, with and exorcism of the '*Canaanite*'/'*Syrophoenician woman's daughter*' in Matthew 15:21–28/Mark 7:24–30) '*Blind Guides*' – the '*Jamesian Party*' again and evoking, as we shall see in due course, the individual called '*the Maschil*' at Qumran[79] – about '*that which enters the mouth going down into the belly and being cast out (ekballetai) the toilet bowl*' in Matthew 15:17 above (echoed in Mark 7:19 but without the '*ekballetai*'), should be patent. As this reads in several different versions in Matthew 15:11 (and in more prolix fashion in Mark 7:15 and 7:20), purporting to respond to disputes concerning '*the Pharisees*'' (Mark 7:3 adds, as we shall presently see as well, '*and all the Jews*'') insistence on '*eating with clean hands*' and *purity regulations generally* – together with pointed allusion to the Qumran Damascus Document's language of '*hear and understand*' in Matthew 15:10 (and, again, in a more prolix fashion in Mark 7:18–20)[80]:

> *Not that which enters into the mouth defiles the man but that which goes forth from the mouth, this defiles the man.*

In fact, Matthew 15:18 adds (bowdlerized somewhat in Mark 7:19 above):

> *but the things going forth out of the mouth come forth out of the heart* (here the actual '*coming*' allusion of the Yohanan ben Zacchai speech above and so common in all these episodes) *and they defile the man.*[81]

To repeat the original point: once more the negative parallel with *the 'great odour' of the Torah 'going forth out of the mouth of Rabbi Eliezer* should be clear.

Furthermore, this allusion to both the '*stench*' of Rabbi Eliezer's breath in the *ARN* and the lovely '*smell of the ointment*' of pure spikenard '*filling*' *Lazarus' house* in John 12:3 is presaged even earlier in the *doppel-ganger* in John 11:39 in the context of *Lazarus'* (not '*Jesus*") startling resurrection. There the '*stink*' of Lazarus' body – not *unlike Rabbi Yohanan's body above with the 'dung' in his coffin* – dead '*for four days*,' as we saw, becomes a key component of more of '*Martha*''s complaining in 11:21–22,[82] duplicated in 11:32 above about '*Mary*''s complaint that, if '*Jesus*' had been there, her '*brother would not have died*' – complaints presumably that come before Luke 10:40's version of the episode where they rather metamorphose back into the issue of '*table service*' (*diakonian*) again, '*Martha*' as in John 12:2 *doing all the 'serving*' (*diakonein*), while her sister '*Mary*,' now '*sitting at Jesus' feet*' no less, *enjoys all the attention!*

Jesus' response is classic and suitably arcane: '*Mary has chosen the good part*,' which directly echoes a phrase at the end of the First Column of the Cairo Damascus Document referring to '*those who sought Smooth Things and chose illusions*' – normally considered Pharisees but, in the writer's view, also intended to include Pauline Christians – '*they chose the fair neck*,' a passage generally based on Isaiah 30:10–13, meaning, seemingly, '*they chose the easiest way*.'

Another variation of the '*anointment*' aspect of this cluster of traditions is to be found in the picture in Matthew and Mark of Jesus' encounter with *the unnamed woman carrying the alabaster flask* at '*Simon the Leper's house*.' While still '*at Bethany*' as in John, this is not, as we saw, '*Martha's house*' or even '*Lazarus*'' (though, in reality, it is), but this unknown '*woman with the alabaster cask*' at '*Simon the Leper's house*' (Matthew 26:7/Mark 14:3), the reference to whom is clearly a blind as elsewhere in Luke 7:40 this is '*Simon the Pharisee*' and in John 12:4 even '*Simon Iscariot*' as we saw. Paralleling Lazarus' '*sister Mary*' in John, it is now rather this unnamed woman who '*comes*' in with '*an alabaster cask of very precious ointment*' (this is Matthew 26:7, Mark 14:3 still preserving the '*alabaster flask of pure spikenard ointment of great value*,' as in John as well)[83] *to anoint Jesus*' '*head*' and not '*his feet*,' as '*Mary*' is pictured as doing in John 12:3. Literally in Mark 14:3/Matthew 26:7, she '*poured it on his head while he reclined*,' meaning – as in the case of the anointment by the unknown woman Sinner at '*the House of the Pharisee*' in Luke 7:36 above, which also *pictures* '*Jesus*' as '*reclining*'[84] though in this case it is back to '*anointing his feet*' again *and much else* – he was '*eating at the table*' or '*dining*.'

It should be reiterated that the connecting piece between Matthew and Mark, on the one hand, and John, on the other, is the specific bit of information that *both* were taking place '*at Bethany*.' Of course, it would also be well to note in passing the motif of Jesus dining with some of these forbidden classes of people, such as '*the woman from the city who was a Sinner,*' for instance, in Luke 7:37 above and, now, the new woman identified only as *coming* 'with an alabaster cask' or 'flask' in Matthew and Mark (in Luke 7:37, she 'brought an alabaster flask').

Both Mark and Matthew repeat John 12:3's allusion to 'pure spikenard ointment of great price' – Mark verbatim, though Matthew discards the 'pure spikenard' and 'great price' in favor of 'precious ointment,' as we have seen – again demonstrating the two sets of material to be integrally related (just like the several in Luke, if we did not already know it). Luke even discards Matthew's 'precious' keeping only the 'alabaster flask of ointment.' John rather discards the 'alabaster flask' part of the phrase – though conserving all the rest – substituting an entirely new expression, 'a hundred weight' or 'litra' to be encountered again in his later picture of 'Nicodemus having come,' 'bearing about a hundred weight of mixture of myrrh and aloes' (19:39 – n.b., here, too, the combination with 'coming' again). While we shall have a good deal more to say about this latter notice later, this in itself – even if only indirectly – again demonstrates the basic interconnectedness of the 'Nicodemus' and the 'Mary'/'Miriam' scenarios at least as far as the Gospel of John is concerned.

Once more, the 'precious ointment,' 'perfume,' and/or 'spikenard' is the point of the various presentations – as it will be in the Talmudic ones involving 'Nakdimon's daughter Miriam,' 'Boethus' daughter Martha,' and others – in particular, its value, whether it be the 'four hundred dinars' of the 'Nakdimon's daughter Miriam' episode and its variations or the 'hundred weight of ointment of pure spikenard of great value' and its variations, to which Matthew, Mark, and ultimately Luke add the additional note of the 'alabaster flask.'

Though the locale 'at Bethany' in Matthew and Mark is the same as in John and the unnamed woman – who becomes 'Mary' ('Miriam') in John – is pictured as 'anointing his head' rather than 'his feet,' nevertheless the note of 'precious ointments' or 'pure spikenard' is absolutely the same. In Lamentations *Rabbah*, it will be recalled, typical of the mix-ups in this kind of information based, as it is, on imperfect oral transmission or even possibly copyist error, 'Miriam' is misidentified as 'Boethus' daughter' not 'Nakdimon''s or 'Nicodemus'' and the amount is augmented to 'five hundred dinars.' Elsewhere in Talmudic tradition, as we shall see, 'Boethus' daughter' – returning to her correct identification as 'Martha' – to show her arrogant extravagance, is pictured as requiring 'a Tyrian gold dinar every Sabbath eve just for her sweetmeats' ('spice puddings' according to some translations).[85] Here, the 'weekly' motif takes the place of the 'daily' one in the traditions already underscored above, but the effect is the same.

Of course, there is the usual ever-recurring allusion in all these episodes – in the Gospels as well as in the notice about *the Poor 'coming'* *to 'Ben Kalba Sabuᶜa"'s door 'hungry as a dog and going away filled'* – of *'coming'/'came.'* One might remark, too, the somewhat less common one of *'pouring out'* – as in the case of the woman with the *'alabaster flask'* in Matthew and Mark, who *'pours out'* *the precious ointment on Jesus' head*. The use of this expression will become ever more pivotal as we proceed, especially when one considers both *'the Man of Lying'* at Qumran (in some descriptions, *'the Pourer out of'* or *'Spouter of Lying,'*[86] characterized in the Damascus Document – in the very same passage as the one containing *'choosing the fair neck,'* just highlighted above – as *'pouring out over Israel the waters of Lying'*[87]) and Jesus' *'blood'* in 'New Testament'/'New Covenant' *Communion* scenarios in the Synoptics (Matthew 26:28 and *pars*.) – generally characterized as *'poured out for (the) Many'* too.[88]

In Luke 10:38–42, to bring us back full circle, the same encounter takes place, as already underscored several times, *at 'Martha's house'* – no relation to 'Lazarus' indicated and no suggestion of *'in Bethany'* whatsoever but, rather, the far vaguer *'a certain village'* (earlier in Luke 7:37, as will be recalled, it was *'in the city'*). Still Martha is pictured as *'complaining'* (*cf.* both the complaints of Nakdimon's daughter above and Boethus' daughter below about the paltriness of the allowance the Rabbis were willing to provide them). About what? Not about the parsimony of the Rabbis, as *'Miriam'* Nakdimon's daughter or *'Martha'* Boethus' daughter complain but rather, as we just saw, *her sister Mary anointing Jesus' 'feet' while she had to do all the 'service'*!

9

Mary '*Anoints*,' Martha '*Serves*,' Judas *Iscariot* '*Complains*'

'*Judas Iscariot*' not '*Martha*' Complains about not '*Giving to the Poor*'

As John will now present this scenario, these '*complaints*,' as already remarked, will rather migrate into the mouth of '*Judas Iscariot*' over Mary's waste of such '*expensive ointment*' or '*perfume*' (the Rabbis, it will be recalled, were trying to stop this sort of wastefulness in the matter of Nakdimon's daughter '*Miriam*''s profligate use of her '*widow*''s allowance) and, in a further charged addition, *her lack of concern for* '*the Poor*' (12:4–8). Not only is the playfulness of these Gospel craftsmen really quite humorous but, as already underscored, is is not completely unconnected with the Talmudic theme of the Rabbis' stinginess, on the one hand and *Ben Kalba's Sabuᶜa's* contrasting concern for '*the Poor*' on the other.

Of course, the same '*diakonian*' used here in Luke 10:40 to express Martha's concern at having to do '*so much serving*' will go on to occur three times in four lines, as we have seen, in the picture Luke draws as well in Acts 6:1–4 and there it is not only coupled with the word '*daily*' but also the theme of '*widows*.' In this presentation, the '*complaints*' ('*murmuring*,' it is called[1]) were those of supposed '*Hellenists*' against '*the Hebrews*' in the matter of '*their widows being overlooked in the daily serving*' (whatever was meant by this and however far-fetched it may seem) and formed the backdrop to its introduction of '*Stephen*.'[2]

But even here, the various notes about the '*widows*,' '*the daily service*,' and the issue of '*waiting on tables*' reverberate with our other sources in the manufacture of these traditions, the one about Nakdimon's and/or Boethus' daughters being '*widows*' and either their '*daily*' or '*weekly*' allotment of '*perfumes*,' '*sweetmeats*,' or '*pension*' (to say nothing of Luke 16:18's '*Rich Man clothed in purple and fine linen luxuriously enjoying himself daily*') and the other, *Martha's problem with Mary* as Luke 10:40 portrays it.

Whereas in Acts 6:2 the complaints these '*Hellenists*' make are detailed in terms of having to '*wait on tables*' (diakonein), not just while '*the widows were overlooked*' (meaning obscure), but while '*the Twelve were drawn away from service (diakonia) of the word*' (6:4 – in 6:2 '*the word of God*'); '*at Martha's house*' here in Luke, it is rather *Martha having to do 'so much service*' – much like the alleged '*Hebrews*' in Acts 6:2 (clearly meant as a euphemism for '*the Jerusalem Apostles*'[3]) – while her sister Mary does nothing but '*sit at Jesus' feet and listen to his words*' (note the play off the allusion to '*the word*'/'*word of God*' in Acts 6:2-4 just signaled above).

In Mark 14:10–11 and Matthew 26:14–16, the corresponding encounter at '*Simon the Leper's house*' at '*Bethany*' is immediately followed by evocation of *Judas Iscariot's departure to betray Jesus 'to the Chief Priests*' for '*thirty pieces of silver*,' though now the '*complaints*' will be by '*His (Jesus')*' *Disciples*' in Matthew 26:8 (compare this with Rabbi Akiba or Rabbi Yohanan ben Zacchai's '*Disciples*' in quasi-parallel Talmudic narrative just alluded to above[4]) or the ever-ubiquitous '*some*' in Mark 14:4. With regard to the '*silver*' motif in these last, it will be important to have regard to the same motif in the exposition of '*Ben Zizzit Ha-Kesset*'*s* name, already encountered above, to say nothing of the '*twelve talents of silver*' in the surety required in the story of Nakdimon's miraculous '*rain-making*' – but more about both of these things later.

The parallel episode '*at Bethany*' to that in Mark and Matthew in John's account rather takes place, as has now become clear, at '*Lazarus*'' *house* – the same '*Lazarus*' who is described in Luke 16:19–22 *as 'a certain Poor Man laid at the doorway of a certain Rich Man*,' '*whose sores the dogs came and licked*' (again note the allusion, '*come*'/'*came*'). In the parallel Rabbinic material about Nakdimon it was '*the Poor*' *who came to Nakdimon's '*door*,' though both are manifestly the same. Nor should one forget the parallel to the predicate '*laid at*' in the description of *Nakdimon's daughter Miriam's bed* as '*being overlaid with a spread worth twelve thousand silver dinars*.' There will be more. Notwithstanding in Luke 10:38, as already mentioned, this is not *the house of 'a certain Poor one named Lazarus*' but, rather, of '*a certain woman named Martha*' – location unspecified and expressed *only as 'a certain village*,' but never mind.

To go back to the dispute between Judas *Iscariot* and Jesus in John 12:5-8 and the '*three hundred dinars*' – reflecting the '*four hundred dinars*' in Rabbinic legend about the value of '*Miriam's (Mary's) perfume box*' – that '*Judas*' felt '*should have been given to the Poor*' (we shall presently see how even this number is parodied in Matthew 27:3-5's picture, already encountered above, of '*the thirty pieces of silver*' '*Judas*' allegedly '*cast into the Temple*'): as with the motif of '*serving tables*' in Acts 6:2-4 above, the allusion to '*the Poor*' is also repeated *three times in four lines*, just in case we missed the point. Hopefully, we didn't – we got it. Still, if the reader's head begins to reel by this time, it would not be surprising since the multiplicity of these repeating references does become dizzying.

Nevertheless one would be well-advised to keep going, preferably with a Greek-English Interlinear translation of the Gospels at one's side in order to catch these linguistic nuances and overlaps.

Instead of being used to characterize the '*Lazarus*' in Luke, '*whose body was full of sores*' (the '*filled*' allusion) and '*licked by dogs;*' John 12:5 now puts this same allusion to '*the Poor*,' as we just saw, into the mouth of the arch-villain in Christian tradition, '*Judas the son*' or '*brother of Simon Iscariot*' – this last, as also already underscored, replaced in Mark and Matthew by the encounter with '*Simon the Leper*,' another bit of not-so-subtle disinformation perhaps *even more malevolent than the original 'Judas Iscariot' libels*. It should be recalled that following the anointment of Jesus' head '*with precious ointment of pure spikenard*' by the unnamed woman at '*Simon the Leper's house at Bethany*,' we had already encountered '*Judas*' – tantalizingly referred to in Mark 14:10 as '*Judas the Iscariot*' as opposed to the more normative '*Judas Iscariot*' in Matthew 26:14 (in John 12:4 and 13:26 at this juncture, '*the son*' or '*brother of Simon Iscariot*') – '*going out to betray him to the Chief Priests.*'

In Matthew and Mark, the whole sequence then leads directly into Jesus announcing – to use the 1 Corinthians 11:25 phraseology of Paul – '*This is the Cup of the New Covenant in my blood*' and, as Matthew 26:28 and Mark 14:24 now add, '*which is poured out for the Many.*' Here Paul's 1 Corinthians' 11:24–25, '*drink it in remembrance of me*,' has been transformed in Mark 14:9 and Matthew 26:13 into Jesus' rebuke to '*his Disciples*' (in Mark 14:4 above, the '*some*') over their parallel '*complaints*' about the unnamed woman *at 'Simon the Leper's house's* wastefulness and the Gospel being preached throughout the world '*in remembrance of*' or '*as a memorial to her*,' namely, the unnamed woman (with her obvious '*Gentile Christian*' overtones), who had just '*anointed him*,' '*pouring out*' (again the pivotal '*pouring out*' allusion) *the expensive ointment of pure spikenard upon his head.*

Of course, the whole phraseology is reprised in the last section of the exhortation of the Damascus Document where it is stated *(to repeat):*

> *A Book of Remembrance will be written before Him for God-Fearers* (that is, '*Gentiles*') *and for those reckoning His Name until God shall reveal Salvation* ('*Yesha'* – in Greek, '*Jesus*' as we saw) *and Justification (Zedakah) to those fearing His Name* (again, the repetition of the '*God-Fearers*' allusion, which has to be seen as *inclusive of Gentiles*).[5]

It should be appreciated that in Matthew 26:8–16/Mark 14:3–9's version of this cluster of complaints about the costliness of the perfume that the unnamed woman (*Martha's sister 'Mary'* in John) had wasted, the above allusion to *'the Poor'* is put into the mouth of *'his Disciples' taken as a whole* (26:8 – in Mark 14:4, the *'some'* as we saw), not Judas alone as in John 12:4. The addition, however, in John 12:7 – following Mary's *anointing Jesus' feet,* then *'washing them with her hair' – 'she has kept it for the day of my burial,'* is common to all three!

In Matthew 26:12 this reads: *'in pouring this ointment upon my body this woman did it for my burial'* while, in Mark 14:8, it changes slightly to: *'she came beforehand to anoint my body for burial'* (again, note here the addition – pertinent or otherwise – of the verb *'come'/'came'*). Of course, not only does Mark 14:3 add *'of pure spikenard'* from John 12:3 to Matthew's less precise *'alabaster flask of very precious ointment'*; even more to the point in Mark 14:4, the very next line, those making the complaints now become, as just signaled, the even more general, yet ever ubiquitous, *'some.'*

It should perhaps be reiterated at this point that the use of the basically interchangeable *'some'/'a certain'* and/or *'certain ones'* generally in Gospel and Acts portraiture (all really the same word in Greek) is particularly important where individuals having a connection of one kind or another with James' 'Jerusalem Church' are concerned – called, not irrelevantly, in early Church accounts, *'the Ebionim'* or *'the Poor'*: as, for instance, Paul's Galatians 2:12's *'some came from James'* following, to be sure, James' important admonition *'not to forget to remember the Poor'* in 2:10; or, provoking the so-called *'Jerusalem Council'* above, Acts 15:1's *'some came down from Judea, teaching the brothers, according to the Law of Moses, that unless you were circumcised you cannot be saved.'* Also note the perhaps not completely unconnected usage in both cases again of the verb *'to come'* and the *'Salvation'* motif of the Damascus Document above connected, of course, with the theme of *'circumcision'* once more.

In Rabbinic tradition, it is important to observe, as well, that the description of Nakdimon's wealth comes amid debate over *the sincerity or lack thereof of his charity* and notices questioning *the reality of his concern for 'the Poor'* which, in the writers' view, are laterally transferred and only slightly refurbished in these striking polemics of John's *'Judas the son'* or *'brother of Simon Iscariot'* or Mark's telltale *'some'* and Matthew's *'his Disciples'* with *'Jesus'* over the wastefulness of these various women either anointing *'his head'* or *'his feet'* with *'precious ointment'* or *'pure spikenard,'* to say nothing of *'wiping them with (their) hair'*!

The notice in Tractate (Marriage Contracts), which triggers this debate, Rabbinic hyperbole aside (already alluded to above), literally reads:

When he (as bizarre as this may seem, Nakdimon) *walked from his house to the house of study, woollen clothes were laid out beneath his feet and the Poor followed behind him gathering them up.*[6]

Of course, here we have the typical motifs of '*being laid out,*' '*the Poor,*' and '*his feet,*' with which we began our discussion. In addition, there is also the one of '*woollen clothes,*' an allusion which will recur in other sources. Not only does it echo Ezekiel 44:17's requirement for '*Zadokite*' Levites or '*Priests*' serving at the altar of the Temple above; but, in particular, also Epiphanius' description of James in the context of his depiction of the atonement he made in the *Inner Sanctum* of the Temple on behalf of the whole People, that is, that *he* '*wore no woollen clothes.*'[7] In this description, Epiphanius also includes the note about James' footwear or lack thereof, again probably echoing the strictures of Ezekiel's '*Zadokite Covenant*' as we saw. Furthermore, we also shall encounter some of the same motifs in descriptions of '*Ben Zizzit Ha-keset*' below.

In addition to these, however, Jerome for example preserves a tradition (that we saw as well above) about how James was held in such awe among the People and considered '*so Holy*' that the little children used to try '*to touch the fringes of his garments*' *as he passed by* – here, a variation of the '*clothing*' motif we shall encounter so insistently as we proceed.[8] A similar portrait – albeit perhaps somewhat less convincing – of the crowd's response to Jesus has come down to us as orthodox tradition in the Synoptic Gospels, another probable instance of a real tradition relating to James being retrospectively absorbed and attached to '*Jesus*' instead.[9] The individuals involved in this '*touching*' activity of Jesus' person or '*garments*' in these accounts, as already remarked, run the gamut from women with *an overflow of menstrual blood* to these same '*little children,*' '*the blind,*' paralytics, and, in the prelude to one curing or raising, even a Roman Centurion![10] The humor of these sketches should not be overlooked and, no matter how amusing many of them may be, as we have stressed, all should be rejected and looked upon as parody – in some cases, *malevolent parody* – of *cherished Jewish beliefs* or *taboos*.

However, what should be appreciated is that not only do we have in these legendary portraits of '*Nakdimon*' the theme of '*the Poor*' – the name, as just emphasized, of the Community, James is said to have headed in Jerusalem – but also the inversion of the '*touching his clothes*' theme, just underscored above, in that now it was '*Nakdimon*' who was held in such reverence by '*the Poor*' that they even followed after him making it possible for his '*feet*' *not to have to touch the dirt of the ground*; or, vice versa perhaps, his wealth was so great that he could afford to abandon such *'clothes'* in a *display of false charity on behalf of these same 'Poor.'* In either case, the point is the same and, as we shall see further below, integrally connected to *'Judas Iscariot'*'s complaints.

In a further adumbration of this Nakdimon's *'feet'* and *'clothes'* story, we shall also see that it will be *'Miriam the daughter of Boethus'* (actually, as we have seen, this is reversed – the tradition, as will become ever clearer as we proceed, should have read *'Martha the daughter of Boethus'*), for whom on *'Yom Kippur'* (another important motif in both the James story above and, as we have been indicating, in notices referring in the Habakkuk *Pesher* to the destruction or death of *the Righteous Teacher from Qumran* and *his followers from among 'the Poor'*[11]) not *'woollen clothes'* or *'garments'* but rather *'cushions'* or *'carpets' were laid from the door of her house to the Temple* (the *'laid out'* and *'doorstep'*-motifs from both the *'Nakdimon'* and Luke's *'Poor man Lazarus licked by dogs'* stories), so that *'her feet might not be exposed.'*[12] Here, once again too, the telltale motif of *'feet'* – now *'her feet'*! We shall encounter such details again, as already implied, not only in the details about *Boethus' daughter's 'feet'* but the *'feet'* of many of these other legendary characters so intrinsic to our discussion and how they, too, were *'exposed.'*[13]

'The Poor You have with You Always but You do not Always have Me'

But to go back to Nakdimon – in relation to the *'woollen garments'* which were *'laid out for his feet'* which *'the Poor'* then *'gathered up,'* the Rabbis debate the point, whether *he really cared about the Poor* and *practiced real charity,* rather concluding, *he did this 'for his own glorification.'*[14] This leads them into discussions of an aphorism, seemingly well known at the time, *'in accordance with the camel is the burden,'* which they interpret as meaning, *the Richer the man the more he should bear.* It will not escape the reader that the elements of this saying are very familiar and will lead, in turn, to interesting ramifications relative to comparable (or derivative) sayings attributed to 'Jesus' in Scripture, also *comparing 'camels' to 'Rich' men,* to say nothing of other formulations we shall encounter, not only in the Gospels, but also in the Scrolls, about *'Glory'* or *'glorying.'*[15]

In fact, from a certain perspective, one might perhaps say the same thing, the Rabbis are saying about Nakdimon, about Jesus' words in the three traditions conserved above, to wit, *'the Poor you have with you always, but you do not always have me'* (John 12:8 and pars.) – a kind of *'glorying'* or, if one prefers, *'vainglory.'* We have seen other examples of this somewhat unseemly portrait of 'Jesus' – which the writer does not consider at all historical but which, rather, resembles what Greco-Hellenistic *'gods'* required in the service due them[16]: for example, in Jesus' rebuke of Simon in Luke 7:44–46 above – directed too at 'the Pharisee' at whose 'house' he was dining – in the matter of not welcoming him sufficiently, by which he means their 'not bathing (his) feet with her tears,' nor 'wiping them with the hair of her head,' nor 'anointing (them) with ointment,' nor lovingly 'kissing (them)'; and of course, the response here is precisely the impact of the Talmudic aphorism cited with regard to Nakdimon above – to quote freely: 'whoso loved much, much is forgiven' (meaning the woman who had 'many Sins'). Par contra: 'whoso loved little, little is forgiven' – one couldn't get much more 'Pauline' than this.

But in John, Judas ('of Simon Iscariot')'s statement about 'selling (the perfume) for three hundred dinars' and giving the proceeds 'to the Poor' (12:5) is followed by the narrational aside (itself preceding 'Jesus'' rebuke, 'the Poor you have with you always but you do not always have me' in 12:8):

> He ('Judas of Simon Iscariot') did not say this because he cared about the Poor, but because he was a thief and held the purse (12:6)!

Not only is 'being a thief and holding the purse' being substituted for the phrase, 'his own self-glorification,' in Talmudic literature, which would not exactly have fit the context; but for the first time, we hear that Judas was 'the Purser' of 'the Twelve,' a position familiar in 'Essene' practice.[17] It is also the first time we have heard about this wretched knavery! In Matthew 26:9–15 and Mark 14:3–10, it will be recalled, it also comes directly after Jesus is pictured as saying: 'The Poor you have with you always, but you do not always have me,' that 'Judas Iscariot' is rather depicted as 'going out to the High Priests' in order 'to betray him' (literally, 'deliver him up').

This being said, in Acts 5:1–13 we are confronted with an odd little episode as well about 'a certain Ananias' (familiar phraseology) and 'his wife Sapphira.'[18] In the manner of 'Essenes' too, they are pictured as required to give the proceeds of the sale of 'a possession' of theirs and 'lay it at the feet of the Apostles' (n.b., again both the language of 'the feet' and 'laying' something 'down' in an entirely new context) and, when they 'kept back part of the price,' both die in a horrendous manner (at Peter's direction!). This is followed by the laconic comment, 'And many signs and wonders (the motif of 'signs' again) among the People came to pass by the hands of the Apostles,' and Acts' narrational 'glue': 'more believers were added to the Lord, multitudes both of men and women' (5:12–14).

But, even more importantly, it is preceded by the words:

> A great fear came upon the whole Assembly (Ecclesian) and on all who heard

these things (5:11).

These resemble nothing so much as the words with which the first prefatory letter to the Pseudoclementine *Homilies* – called 'The Epistle of Peter to James' – ends, where *the assembled 'Elders,'* after hearing James speak, are described as *'being in an agony of terror.'*[19] The whole scene transpires in the wake of James reading the attack in the letter – he has just received from Peter overseas – on the *'lawless and trifling preaching of the man who is my Enemy'* (considered almost unanimously by all commentators as an attack upon Paul), because of which *'some from among the Gentiles* (the ubiquitous *'some'* allusion, now rather turned around and aimed, seemingly, at Pauline communities) *have rejected my preaching about the Law.'*

This is followed both by Peter's and then James' injunction endorsing it, *'not to communicate the books of my preaching'* to anyone who has not *'been tested and found worthy according to the initiation of Moses'* which, James immediately makes clear, meant *'a probation of six years'* before being *'brought to a river or a fountain which is living water, where the regeneration of the Righteous takes place'* (the language here, of course, is completely that of the Community Rule of the Dead Sea Scrolls[20]). Moreover, James adds at this point, *'which we ourselves, when we were regenerated, were made to do for the sake of not sinning'* – featuring the same concentration on *'forgiveness for sin'* which was the original issue in the parable Jesus tells in Luke 7:47 about the alien woman, who having *'loved much,'* *'had her many sins forgiven'* with which we began this whole circle of notices.

It would also, at this point, be well to observe that Acts 8:34–38's portrait of Philip, three chapters later, *now baptizing 'the eunuch of the Ethiopian Queen'* – the parody embodied in which we have already expounded at some length above – would in no wise have been countenanced according to the position both Peter and James are pictured as enunciating here which would, as we just saw, rather have *required 'a probationary period of no less than six years.'*[21] In fact, Acts' picture of this *'baptism'* after this chance or casual meeting *'on the road,'* as it were – following which even Acts 8:39 avers, *'the eunuch never saw (Philip) again'* – can be thought of as specifically intended to counter-indicate the position of both James and Peter as reflected in this curious letter from Peter to James prefacing the Pseudoclementine *Homilies* and the powerful effect it had upon those who heard James read it.

However this may be, it is at this point that *'the Elders,'* who have been listening to both James read Peter's letter and James' own admonitions thereafter, now *take the oaths to 'keep this Covenant,'* thereby having *'a part with the Holy Ones'* – language, once again, that is almost a facsimile of that found in Qumran documents[22] – in particular, emphasizing that they *'will not lie'* (cf. Paul's protestations to this effect in the letters attributed to him[23]).

This is, of course, the basic gist of the episode in Acts with which we began, which described how *'Satan filled'* the hearts of *'Ananias'* and *'Sapphira,'* causing them, in *'keeping back part of the value of the land,'* *'to lie to the Holy Spirit'* and *'lie'* not just to men but *'to God'* (5:3–4). It is at this point that *the 'great fear (that) came upon all who heard these things'* is depicted in Acts 5:5 that so much parallels and reverberates with *the 'agony of terror'* in this prelude to the Pseudoclementine *Homilies*, characterizing the frightened reaction of all those present when they heard James allude to how they *would be accursed, both living and dying, and be punished with everlasting punishment'* if they should *'lie.'*[24] In the author's view, the implied parallel between the two accounts could not be more exact.

That having been said – to go back to Jesus' comment to *'Simon the Pharisee'* concerning the woman *'who washed his feet with her tears,'* *'ardently kissing them,'* and *'dried them with the hair of her head'* in Luke 7:44–47 above, to the effect that to *'who so loves much, much is forgiven'* – one could not get much closer to the Rabbis' reaction to Nakdimon's treatment of *'the Poor'* – *'in accordance with the camel is the burden'* – than this either! Whereas in Nakdimon's case, the use of the expression *'the Poor'* served to introduce the fact that they were contemptuously allowed to *'gather up the woollen clothes that had been laid,'* so his feet would not have to touch the ground; in John 12:5–6 (rephrased in Matthew 26:8 and Mark 14:3 and attributed to either *'the Disciples'* as a whole or the *'Some'*), it forms the crux of the ideological exchange between *'Jesus'* and *'Judas the son* (or *'brother')* of Simon Iscariot'* (in Matthew and Mark, anyhow, *'about to deliver him up'* or *'betray him'*[25]) concerning these same *'Poor'* – the latter character, as already suggested, capable of being seen or actually having been seen as representative of all Jews or at the very least, anyhow, those of the *'Ebionite'/'Zealot'* strain of thinking – namely Epiphanius' *'Sicarii Essenes'* already called attention to above.

Martha's Complaints, Mary's Wastefulness, and Nakdimon's Daughter's Arrogance

Let us go over all these points again, repetitive or dizzying as this may be. John does so on several occasions, so why shouldn't we? As already remarked, in John 11:2 earlier, Mary *'the sister of the sick man Lazarus'* had been described as *'anointing the Lord with ointment and wiping his feet with her hair.'* In Luke 7:38 and 44 above, where 'Jesus' is pictured as telling '*a parable*' to another '*Simon,*' 'at '*the house of the Pharisee,*' it is yet another unnamed '*woman of the city who was a Sinner,*' who was '*kissing his feet,*' '*anointing them with ointment,*' and '*wiping his feet with the hairs of her head*'! By contrast, in John 12:2-3, *while 'Martha served,*' it was '*Mary*' who was rather described – just as in Mark's variation *at* '*Simon the Leper's house*'– as '*bringing in a hundred weight of expensive ointment of pure spikenard*' and, more specifically at least in John, *anointing Jesus' feet with it* '*and wiping them with her hair.'* Nor should the aside about '*the house being full of the smell of the perfume*' be ignored. At this point the complaining is not being done by Martha over the issue of '*table service,*' as in Luke's version of the events at '*Martha's house*'; but rather by '*Judas*' Simon Iscariot's '*son*' or '*brother,*' who (though also alluded to earlier in John 6:71 as '*about to deliver him up being one of the Twelve*' – '*delivering up*' being another usage of extreme interest in the eschatology of the Dead Sea Scrolls[26]) is now presented in a really substantive manner.

In Matthew and Mark's '*Simon the Leper*' scenarios, of course, as we have several times now remarked, it was '*the Disciples*' or the mysterious '*some*' who did the '*complaining*' over the value of *the precious ointment the unnamed woman had poured over Jesus' head* – in Mark 14:5, again reckoned as '*three hundred dinars*' as in John 12:5; in Matthew 26:9, only as the more indeterminate, *it was worth* '*much.*' It is at this point that '*Judas the Iscariot*' is introduced into the narrative, not '*complaining*' as in John, but as *immediately going out* '*to deliver him up*' (Mark 14:10). Here Matthew 26:15 too, now finally gives its quantification to the amount, '*thirty pieces of silver,*' to be picked up in 27:3 and 27:9 that follow in Matthew's (but not the other Gospels') '*casting the pieces of silver into the Temple*' scenario in the next chapter – a figure not to be considered independent, clearly, of the '*three hundred dinars*' in Mark 14:5 and John 12:5, the one simply being a decimal multiple of the other.

Actually in John 11:21 earlier, Martha had, as we saw, already been complaining to some extent to Jesus that, if he had come sooner her '*brother would not have died,*' and following this, in 11:39, about *the* '*stink*' or '*smell*' *of Lazarus' rotting corpse already dead* '*for four days.*' It is then directly after this in more or less a repeat of all these things in the next chapter too, that John 12:5 has '*Judas the son*' or '*brother of Simon Iscariot, one of his Disciples*' and '*the man who was going to deliver him up,*' say:

Why wasn't this ointment sold for three hundred dinars and the money given to the Poor?

Not only has the 'Simon' of the 'Simon the Leper' encounter in Matthew/Mark above now plainly floated into the material about 'Judas' here in John (or vice versa); but the valuation of 'three hundred dinars' of 'the precious ointment of pure spikenard' in John and Mark, as just underscored, is nothing but a reformulation of the 'thirty pieces of silver' Judas Iscariot then receives for the price of his 'betrayal' or 'delivering him up' in Matthew 26:15 (unparalleled in either John, Mark, or Luke). It should also be observed that in the curious material that follows in Matthew 27:3–10 about 'the price of blood,' in which Matthew thinks it is citing 'Jeremiah,' but which is actually rather a free translation of Zechariah 11:12–13 about throwing 'the wages of thirty pieces of silver into the Temple Treasury' (this really does appear in Zechariah 11:13); Matthew quotes 'the Chief Priests' as saying 'it is not lawful to put them (the alleged 'thirty pieces of silver') into the Treasury, for it is the price of blood.'

Aside, however, from attributing this proof-text to the wrong prophet – a comparatively minor error – this again echoes the response Eliezer ben Hyrcanus reported hearing from Jacob of Kfar Sechania about what 'Jesus the Nazoraean' taught concerning whether it was lawful or not to give 'the wages' earned from 'a prostitute's hire' to the Temple. As already to some extent suggested, this is an extremely charged statement in view of the perceived behavior of Herodian princesses such as Herodias, Bernice, and Drusilla – and possibly even that of Helen of Adiabene herself. 'Jesus'' response, that it was permissible to 'use them to build an outhouse for the High Priest,' is also probably, as we said, the only real historical notice about him remaining in the whole of the Talmud, the rest having long ago fallen victim to years of censorship.[27]

Nevertheless, even the reference to 'High Priest' here plays back into the notices in the Gospels about 'Judas Iscariot going to the High Priests in order to betray him' – further amplified in the picture of these same 'High Priests' refusing to put Judas' 'pieces of silver' into 'the Treasury because it was the price of blood' here in Matthew 27:6. Moreover, the connection of this Talmudic tradition – possibly even going back to James – to this material uniquely developed in Matthew out of the price for 'the precious ointment of pure spikenard' which 'should have been given to the Poor,' quoted in John 12:5 in a speech attributed to 'Judas Iscariot' as well, should be patent.

Not only do we have here the matter of the poorly-explained issue of why 'Judas'' 'wages' or 'hire' would not be acceptable in the Temple; but also the issue of the 'price of blood,' in this instance carrying the additional meaning of 'menstrual blood' which was so abhorrent to the priest class – to say nothing of the people generally – and, once again, a key concern of the Damascus Document from Qumran.[28] Just as important is the additional play in the amount of '*three hundred dinars*' for '*the measure of ointment of pure spikenard of great value*' of John 12:5 (in Mark 14:3, '*alabaster flask of ointment of pure spikenard of great value*') on the Talmudic tradition citing '*four hundred dinars*' as the allowance provided by the Rabbis for Nakdimon's daughter Miriam's/Mary's '*daily perfume basket*.' In Lamentations *Rabbah*, even this is augmented by another hundred dinars, as we saw, to '*five hundred dinars*' which, in turn, suggests the '*four*' to '*five thousand*' augmentations in the number of followers Jesus is pictured as feeding – in Matthew 15–16/Mark 6–8 as well – in the several '*multiplication of loaves*' / '*wilderness exodus*' episodes which we shall presently examine in more detail below.[29]

This '*dinar*' theme will reappear over and over again in these Talmudic narratives about these various '*Rich*' daughters. So will the one related to it about '*levirate marriage*,' implied in the Rabbis having to provide '*maintenance*' or an '*allowance*' to support these '*widows*.' As we shall see further below, this will have to do, not only with Nakdimon's daughter '*Miriam*,' but Boethus' daughter '*Martha*' – the issue of '*the levir*' being of particular importance where the remarriages of both were concerned.[30]

Nor do a '*hundred dinars*' matter very much as the valuations of these precious '*perfumes*,' '*spikenards*,' or '*ointments*' move from one tradition to the other. In these overlaps and interdependencies it is always useful to remark, as we have already done, the *Talmud*'s this-worldly earthiness – or what some would call its vulgarity or crassness; others, reality (particularly noticeable in the above story about Jesus' opinion of '*the High Priest's privy*,' which is actually quite funny) – as opposed to the New Testament's more idealized and Hellenized other-worldliness which, no doubt, accounts for its enduring appeal despite the obviously secondary nature of many of its traditions.

The points concerning this cluster of usages stemming from Nakdimon's '*rain-making*,' his and his colleague Ben Kalba Sabuᶜa's extravagant '*Riches*,' and their daughters' or daughters-in-law's *expensive perfumes* are so important that it would also be well to look at them, too, again with more precision. It is important to do so, not only because they are so complex, but because they bear to some extent both on how the Gospel narratives themselves were put together, but also, as it will turn out, the details of the preparation of Jesus' body, his tomb and, as we shall finally suggest, even perhaps the legendary '*Tomb of St James*.'

In these Rabbinic traditions paralleling Luke's '*a certain Rich Man clothed in purple and fine linen who used to feast every day in splendor*,' the third of this trio or quartet of fabulously '*Rich*' individuals in Jerusalem's last days, '*Ben Zizzit*,' was supposedly so characterized, it will be remembered, because he used *to lie at the head of the Great Ones of Israel on a silver couch*.[31] Not only does this incorporate a pun on his cognomen '*Hakkeset*' which, depending on how it is transcribed, can either mean '*cushions*'/'*couch*' (*keset*) or '*seat*' (*kise*); it can also be seen as involving a play on the '*silver*' (*kesef*) or '*silversmith*' motifs, we have been encountering above as well. Elsewhere, it was rather Nakdimon's daughter, who supposedly '*needed an allowance of four*' or '*five hundred dinars daily just for her perfume basket*,' whose '*couch was overlaid with a spread worth twelve thousand dinars*.'[32] Moreover, we have already remarked the reverberations of all these figures with the various '*expensive ointment*' or '*precious spikenard*' allusions in Gospel parallels.

In the *ARN* '*Ben Zizzit*' is rather called '*Sisit Hakkeset*,' but the play is still clearly on the word '*keset*' which can mean either '*cushions*' or '*couch*' as we just saw. In *Gittin* (the Talmudic Tractate on '*Divorce*') however, where he is called '*Ben Zizzit Hakeseth*,' the interpretation is provided, as previously signaled, that this was because '*his fringes (zizzit) used to trail on cushions*,' so the play is on both: the fact of '*his fringes*' and their '*trailing on cushions*.' But there the important addition appended:

> Others say he derived the name from the fact that his seat (*kise*) was among the Nobility (or '*Great Ones*') of Rome,[33]

which varies the one on '*lying at the head of the Great Ones of Israel on a silver couch*' just noted with regard to him above. Whoever he was, however, he was clearly *an Establishment person of some kind*.

Nevertheless in this cluster of traditions, whether evoking Nakdimon, his colleagues '*Ben Zizzit*' and '*Ben Kalba Sabuᶜa*,' or the Rich Herodian High Priest '*Boethus*,' it cannot be emphasized too often that their daughters or daughters-in-law are almost always named '*Miriam*' (Mary) or '*Marta*' (Martha). '*Boethus*,' whose daughter '*Martha*' is actually described in these traditions as '*one of the Richest women in Jerusalem*,' seems to have had his grandiose family tomb in the Kedron Valley beneath the Pinnacle of the Temple from which James, according to early Church tradition, '*was cast down*.'[34] It is perhaps not unrelated that this same tomb, as already remarked, has always been referred to, for some reason, in early Christian pilgrimage tradition as well as '*the Tomb of St James*.'[35] This clan (called '*the Boethusians*') which Herod, as we have seen, imported from Egypt in the previous century after executing his Maccabean wife, the first '*Mariamme*'/'*Miriam*'/or '*Mary*,' and marrying the second, the next '*Mariamme*' or '*Mary*' of that generation, was therefore always absolutely beholden to the Herodian family and the Establishment Herod had created.

Mary's Perfume Allowance and Martha's Spice Puddings

In further traditions about this Nakdimon's daughter or his daughter-in-law (we will see an additional parallel to these '*daughter*'s in the case of the *Syrophoenician/Canaanite woman's* '*daughter*' out of whom '*Jesus casts*' an '*evil spirit*' or '*demon*' below), *ARN* specifies the actual reason the Rabbis were supervising her allowance, namely, as already indicated, '*she was awaiting a decision by the levir*' – meaning *the decision by her deceased husband's brother to allow her as a widow to remarry* (the concomitant being, of course, that she was obviously without children at this point otherwise the procedure would have been unnecessary).

This is patently another theme that will reappear in New Testament tradition, most famously, as already signaled, in John the Baptist's protests over Herodias' marriage to Herod Antipas, to which picture we would most strenuously object. It was also probably the reason for all these '*widow*'/'*in-law*' confusions in the first place. In the case of Herodias' remarriage, for starters, this is presented as having taken place *after a divorce* – which was probably true, because her various '*uncle*'s, as it were, were vying with each other for this connection since Herodias' brother, Agrippa I, was on his way towards becoming the first '*Herodian*' King since their grandfather's demise forty years before; and theirs was the preferred line within the family carrying Maccabean blood through their grandmother '*Mariamme*' (the first of these '*Mary*'s just mentioned above[36]) – so it is not clear if the issue of '*levirate marriage*' ever applied.

In the second place, already explained too, Herodias had not *previously been married to anyone called* '*Philip*' at all. In fact, she seems to have been married to another son of Herod, *also called* '*Herod*' (the son of Herod's second or '*Boethusian*' wife, also named '*Mariamme*') *and another of her uncles*. The '*Philip*' involved in the story actually did – according to Josephus who makes a special point of it, the only point he does make concerning him – *die childless* and in any event, as already remarked as well, *actually was rather married to Herodias' daughter Salome*![37] In Salome's case, her remarriage to another close '*cousin*,' the son of Agrippa I's brother – also called '*Herod*' as we have seen, this one '*Herod of Chalcis*' – and possibly that '*Aristobulus*' Paul refers to so congenially in Romans 16:10 before mentioning '*Herodion*' ('*the Youngest Herod*' – probably Herod VI, their son) – *probably did involve the issue of levirate marriage!*

But the parameters surrounding John's objections to Herodias' divorce and remarriage to another of her uncles, Herod Antipas – the '*Herod the Tetrarch*' mentioned as the '*foster brother of Manaen*' in Paul's incipient '*Antioch Community*' in Acts 13:1 above[38] – probably should have been the proscriptions detailed in principal Dead Sea Scrolls over the more inte-grally-connected issues of '*marriage with nieces,' polygamy, and* – particu-larly where such '*Princes*' or '*Princesses*' were concerned – '*divorce,' marriage with non-Jews, close family 'cousins,' and the like*.[39]

In the *Talmud*, the traditions about this much-derided daughter of Nakdimon become even more absurd. Instead of the '*four hundred*' or '*five hundred dinars*' she needs '*for her perfume basket daily*,' in *Kethuboth* ('*Mar-riage Contracts*') – in the same context of '*waiting for the levir*' – she or Boethus' daughter Martha are now said to need '*a Tyrian gold dinar every Sabbath evening* (here our '*dinar*' theme again as well as the '*weekly*'/'*daily*' one, together with a new one – that of '*Tyre*') *just for sweetmeats*' or '*spice puddings*' as we saw.[40] Even the reference to '*Tyrian*' or '*Tyre*' here will have its ramifications for allusions in Matthew and Mark to the same locale in their account of 'Jesus'' encounter with the '*Canaanite*'/'*Greek Syrophoeni-cian woman*' and '*her daughter*,' to say nothing of '*Sidon and Tyre*' elsewhere in Synoptic allusion.[40] It can also possibly be connected in Christian tra-dition to the story about Simon *Magus* and *the consort with the curious name of 'Helen,' he was reported to have found 'in a brothel of Tyre*,' itself, in turn, possibly bearing elements of the story of '*Queen Helen of Adiabene*,' not to mention the issue of her '*suspected*' *alleged adultery*, already called attention to above.[42]

This notice in the *ARN* that she was awaiting a levirate marriage (that is, as we just saw, *the permission of her brother-in-law for her to remarry*) fleshes out many of the allusions we have already been encountering above. Such bizarre and fanciful detail as '*her sweetmeats*' or '*spice puddings*' aside, so many coincidences in detail with the '*Judas Iscariot,*' '*Mary,*' '*Martha,*' '*precious Spikenard,*' '*dinars*' complex of materials can hardly be considered purely accidental. The '*dinars*' theme – both as actual '*dinars*' and as '*pieces of silver*'[43] – will reappear in another famous variation, whether related or not, the portrayal of '*Judas Iscariot*'/'*the Iscariot*''s '*betrayal*'/'*delivering up*' of Jesus or his objection to '*Mary*'/'*Miriam*''s extravagant waste of '*precious perfume*' (her '*perfume box*'?). Of course Judas' cognomen in this regard, in the light of the many '*Sicarii*' connections to these episodes above, is, as we have been highlighting, not insignificant; while the '*every single Sabbath eve*' and '*spice puddings*' motifs patently rep-resent more Rabbinic hyperbole.

In fact, as *Kethuboth* – in the context also of '*awaiting the decision of the levir*' – had already put the matter earlier, it is rather '*the daughter-in-law of Nakdimon ben Gurion*' to whom the Rabbis grant such an allowance and now this is expressed in terms of '*two se'ahs of wine for her sweetmeats*' or '*spice puddings every week*.'[44] Again we have the repetition of the motif of chronological regularity expressed in '*weekly*' terms not '*daily*' ones.

This being said, in Lamentations *Rabbah* – typical of this kind of tradition confusion or migration – the Rabbis go back to the '*daily*' not the '*weekly*' framework for these activities and, as we just saw and will see further below, grant this allowance of '*two se῾ahs of wine*' with respect only to the widowhood and not the remarriage of '*Miriam the daughter of Boethus*' (*sic*) after the death of her husband Jesus ben Gamala. This '*Jesus*' was murdered, it will be recalled, along with Ananus ben Ananus and other collaborating High Priests '*appointed by Herodians*' by those Josephus calls '*Idumaeans*' and their confederates, whom he is at this point finally willing to identify as '*Zealots*' – in our view, probably *taking vengeance, if not for* '*the Righteous Teacher*' *at Qumran, then certainly for the death of James*.[45]

Never mind that it is '*Martha the daughter of Boethus*' that is really meant here – this is the third interlocking tradition about such '*daily*' or '*weekly*' allowances granted by the Rabbis to these improvident '*daughter*'s. Showing that we are not dealing with separate traditions – for her part in *Kethuboth*, Nakdimon's '*daughter-in-law*' (name, of course, not provided) is, once again, pictured as being contemptuous even of this, standing up and declaring once more, '*make such a grant for your own daughters*'! To be sure, this is precisely what '*Nakdimon's daughter Miriam*' (the *real* '*Mary*' or '*Miriam*' in these traditions) was pictured as saying in respect of *her daily allowance of* '*four*' to '*five hundred dinars*' thereafter in both *Kethuboth* above and Lamentations *Rabbah* below.[46] That we have here, too, but a slight variation of the tradition about Nakdimon's '*daughter*' is made clear when one Rabbi, probably sarcastically, defers even to this – noting by way of explanation in his response that '*she was a woman awaiting the decision of the levir.*'

Here of course, as just suggested, we have what appears to be a further confusion, this time between '*Nakdimon's daughter-in-law*' and '*Martha the daughter of Boethus*' – herself *awaiting a second marriage to Josephus' friend, the highly-regarded, though unfortunate, High Priest Jesus ben Gamala*. In fact, this is made clear in Lamentations *Rabbah* as well, which, in talking about this '*Miriam the daughter of Boethus*' (what is meant here is, of course, '*Martha the daughter of Boethus*,' but in the New Testament too, confusions such as these – particularly where '*Mary*' and '*Martha*' are concerned, as we have been suggesting – are common), provides the description below of how, in order for her to see her husband Joshua ('*Jesus*') ben Gamala

read in the Temple on Yom Kippur, carpets (or 'cushions') were laid from the doorway of her house to the entrance of the Temple so that her feet would not be exposed. Nevertheless they were exposed.

It is at this point Lamentations *Rabbah* makes the addition that when her husband Joshua (ben Gamala) died, the Rabbis allowed her *two se'ahs of wine daily.*[47]

Once again we have the '*daily,*' '*allowance,*' and telltale '*feet*'/'*foot exposure*' themes, we have already encountered regarding '*Nakdimon's daughter Miriam*' above. Moreover, this is obviously just a variation of another tradition about '*Nakdimon,*' the one about '*when he walked from the door of his house to the house of study, the Poor gathered up the woollen clothes laid down under his feet.*' Of course, aside from the additional laconic remark, '*nevertheless they were exposed,*' which really is very striking, there is also the repetition of the '*doorway,*' '*cushions*'/'*carpets,*' something '*being laid down*' (in Luke's episode about '*the dogs*' at the '*Rich Man's door,*' '*someone*' or '*a certain Poor One named Lazarus*') and, as ever, '*her* (if not '*his*') *feet*' themes.

The '*Rabbi Eleazar ben Zadok*' Traditions and '*In Accordance with Camel is the Burden*'

Another Rabbi – interestingly enough one '*Eleazar ben Zadok*' with whom many of these traditions are connected ('*Zadok,*' possibly his father, was another Rabbi widely associated in Talmudic tradition with '*mourning for the Temple,*' praying and fasting '*for forty years*' before the fall of Jerusalem and, as we have signaled, a name paradigmatic in the Dead Sea Scrolls as well[48]) – on the subject of '*Nakdimon's daughter Miriam*'*'s overweening pride* quotes a verse from Song of Songs 1:8, '*go your way forth by the footsteps of the flock and feed your offspring,*' adding seemingly by way of exposition,

> May I not live to behold the consolation (of Zion) if I do not see her gathering barley corns from beneath the feet of horses in Acco.

Here, of course, we have the '*feet*'/'*footsteps*' theme again, to say nothing of a new one, '*barley corns*' or '*grain.*'[49]

This same '*Rabbi Eleazar ben Zadok*' quotes the aphorism in the same Lamentations *Rabbah* and elsewhere, '*May I not live to behold the consolation*' – meaning, '*of Zion*' – concerning similar suffering and the '*feet*' of another '*Mary,*' not '*Nakdimon's daughter Miriam*' but, once again, '*Miriam the daughter of Boethus.*'[50] Again he obviously means '*Martha,*' but this is the same genre of confusion between '*Mary*' and '*Martha,*' as we have been repeatedly remarking, that found its way into the Gospels – particularly John. Even in this last, '*Martha,*' as we saw, is quoted as saying to Jesus, '*If you had been here, my brother (Lazarus) would not have died*' (11:21). Eleven lines later in John 11:32, 'Mary' – now also portrayed as 'falling down at his feet' – is depicted as saying precisely the same thing: 'If you had been here, my brother would not have died.' This is the sort of tradition overlap we have been speaking about. It is eerie and probably not accidental.

The same basic tradition about Nakdimon's daughter will again be told in Kethuboth, this time in the name not of 'Rabbi Eleazar ben Zadok' but of 'Rabbi Yohanan ben Zacchai,' pictured – to some extent like 'Jesus' is in the Gospels (Matthew 21:7 and pars.) – as 'outside Jerusalem riding a donkey while his Disciples followed after him.'[51] But what Rabbi Yohanan now sees, unlike 'Eleazar ben Zadok' above, is this 'girl picking barley corns' or 'grain from among the dung of Arab cattle' – here again the 'barley corns' or 'grain' theme, but now connected with the one about 'dung' we have already remarked previously and shall have cause to remark further. One should also not ignore how in the Gospel version of this tradition, in Luke 19:36 'his Disciples,' after 'having thrown their garments on the ass of a colt' (in Mark 11:7, 'epebalon'/'cast their clothing'), 'laid out their garments in the way.' Though in Matthew 21:8/Mark 11:8/John 12:18, this second part is specifically attributed rather to 'the Many' or 'the multitudes' (sic) but, whatever the sense here 'the garments' are being pictured as 'laid out' or 'spread' much as in the 'Nakdimon ben Gurion' or 'Mary the daughter of Boethus' tradition.

It is interesting that in the context of this same cycle of traditions which started with those about the Talmudic 'Rich Men' – in particular, the ones about 'the Poor' who 'came to Ben Kalba Sabuᶜa's door hungry as a dog and went away filled' (as always, n.b., the 'coming' allusions) and the promise both he and Nakdimon ben Gurion made to supply everyone in Jerusalem with 'grain' for twenty-one or twenty-two years (in connection with 'the Zealots' having burned all the grain, or used 'the loaves' – another important motif, as we shall presently see, in Gospel portraiture – as bricks to reinforce the walls 'and plastered them over with clay'[52]) – ARN provides the following tradition that:

When Vespasian came to destroy Jerusalem...(and) looked at their excrement ('dung') and saw there was no sign of corn (that is, 'barleycorns') in it (meaning 'only straw'), he said to his troops, 'If these who eat nothing but straw, kill so many of you in this fashion, how many of you they would kill if they ate every-thing you eat and drink (here another incidence of the 'eating and drinking' motif we have already encountered in Paul's evocation of 'drinking the Cup of the New Covenant' of the Lord in 1 Corinthians 11:23–29 above, 'the Mourners for Zion' who vow not 'to eat or drink' until they have seen the Temple restored – or, alternatively in Acts 23:12–21, 'until they had killed Paul' – and the Synoptic Gospels of Matthew 11:19 and Luke 7:34 in how '*the Son of Man came eating and drinking*').[53]

Clearly, not only are these several episodes about *Nakdimon's* and *Boethus'* '*daughter's* not two separate traditions – '*the feet of horses in Acco*' in the *ARN* having now been interchanged with '*the dung of Arab cattle*' in *Kethuboth*; but they also incorporate the resultant '*famine*,' '*grain*,' and '*dung*' motifs. This is to say nothing about the various '*grain*' and '*loaves*' traditions both in these sources and, in particular, those related to '*Jesus*'' miracles we shall presently encounter in all four Gospels below.

However these things may be, the tradition about '*Nakdimon's daughter*' Miriam, in the name of Rabbi Yohanan ben Zacchai, now contrasts *the condition he finds her in after the fall of the Temple* with the prodigiousness of her dowry, '*a million dinars besides what was added from her father-in-law's house*' (again the confusions over '*in-law's* – once again, in our view, intending '*Nakdimon*'). This is followed up in *Kethuboth*, as well, by another description of Nakdimon's incredible wealth, the one depicting '*the Poor*' above, '*gathering up the woollen clothes that had been laid for his feet*' (once again, pay particular attention to '*the Poor*,' '*laying down*,' '*woollen clothes*,' and '*his feet*'), in turn, followed by the Rabbinic discussion of the issue of the sincerity of his proverbial charity, the apparent meaning of which, it will be recalled, was that this was *not real charity to treat* '*the Poor*' *in this way, even though they probably* '*gathered up*' *and kept* '*the woollen clothes*.'[54]

It is at this point in *Kethuboth* that the important aphorism is added evoking the pivotal motif, as already underscored above, of '*the camel*' relating to '*his Riches*' and *his* '*charity*,' that is, '*in accordance with the camel is the burden*' – meaning that *extraordinary charity was only to be expected on the part of one so* '*Rich*.' However, the same aphorism is quoted later in this same Tractate with perhaps even more justice in relation to *recovering the dowry of* '*Martha the daughter of Boethus*,' already characterized above as awaiting permission of '*the levir*' to marry Josephus' friend, Jesus ben Gamala.[55] He was High Priest from 63 CE directly following James' death until 65 CE, when he was brutally dispatched along with the individual actually responsible for James' judicial murder, Ananus ben Ananus, by '*the Zealots*' and their '*Idumaean*' allies – as we have already described – as the Uprising against Rome moved into what can best perhaps be termed its '*Jacobite*' phase in 68 CE.[56]

The reason one says '*with more justice*' here is because the allusion to '*gamal*' or '*camel*' would more appropriately play on the name of this '*Boethusian*' High Priest, of which it actually constitutes a part, meaning, it would seem, the town of Gamala from where he – and, interesting enough, '*Judas the Galilean*' like him – seems to have come (curiously enough, the same place for which Josephus was supposed to have prepared defences).[57] This '*Gamala*' was so named because of its situation on an inland mesa overlooking the Sea of Galilee that had the shape of the hump of a camel. Nor is this to say anything about the curious '*eye of the camel*' aphorisms connected these '*Poor Man*'/'*Rich Man*' allusions in famous discourses attributed to 'Jesus' we shall discuss further below.

Notwithstanding, the 'Boethus' then, to whom this '*Jesus b. Gamala*' became connected through his '*Rich*' daughter '*Martha*,' was – as previously explained – one of the more accommodating High-Priestly clans, willing to live both with Roman power in Palestine and its Herodian representatives – a fact that may have explained this '*Jesus*'' rather violent death, as it did that of his even perhaps more accommodating colleague, Ananus ben Ananus, *responsible for the death of James*.

Judas' Concern for '*the Poor*' Revisited and James' Charge to Paul '*not to Forget to Remember the Poor*'

To go back to John and to make the connection with these stories about Nakdimon's or Boethus' '*daughter*' even more plain, the narrator in John 12:6 in an aside reflecting the Talmudic debates on Nakdimon's real or alleged charity, adds as we saw, '*he said this not because he cared about the Poor, but because he was a thief*' – but now, of course, the reference is not to Nakdimon's false '*charity*' but this time rather Judas *Iscariot*'s. Clearly this statement, made by the narrator, makes no sense without presupposing knowledge of the previous Rabbinical debates about the legitimacy of Nakdimon's charity – one can probably assume, therefore, that the author of John had already either read or heard this tradition.

Since this issue of '*being a thief*' is a new theme we haven't heard before – at least not in the Gospels – the narrator, fairly running away with himself, proceeds then to impart the interesting new fact that – as already underscored – *since Judas had charge of the common purse*, '*he used to help himself to what was put therein*' (12:6). Given the symbolic nature of the character represented by '*Judas*,' as we have been delineating it, this is perhaps more of the covert anti-Semitism one finds, for instance, in Acts' portrayal of its basically non-existent '*Stephen*' (to say nothing of '*Peter*').

In the parallel Synoptic material in Matthew and Mark '*at Simon the Leper's house*' where, it will be recalled, it is '*the Disciples*' or the ubiquitous '*some*,' not '*Judas of Simon Iscariot*' alone, who are indignant and are the ones who do the complaining about *the wastefulness of the woman with* '*the alabaster flask*' who poured the '*precious ointment of pure spikenard*' on Jesus' head rather than '*his feet*.' Nevertheless it is, as always, '*the Poor*' who form the crux of the complaints, as they do in the '*Nakdimon*,' '*Lazarus*,' and now these '*Judas Iscariot*' materials. We shall see below how these allusions also play off Rabbi Akiba's response to those who would contend *they* '*were too Poor to study Torah*,' namely, '*Was not Rabbi Akiba very Poor and in straitened circumstances?*'[58]

In both sets of tradition, John and the Synoptics, Jesus is pictured as saying something clever about his own coming death, specifically (as we saw): '*The Poor you have with you always, but you will not always have me*.' Of course, none of this can be taken as the least bit historical but rather as we have been showing, simply more rhetorical repartee playing off the matter of '*the precious ointments*' and/or '*perfumes*' and 'Jesus'' coming burial scenario, either meant for the anointment of his body or simply the antidote to noxious odours – to say nothing of the picture of the '*perfume box*' of Nakdimon's pampered daughter '*Miriam*' in the *Talmud*.

As John 12:7 sees these things, the exchange sets the stage for Jesus' death, not only because of the comment he is portrayed as making (echoed as well in Matthew 26:12/Mark 14:8): '*to leave her alone because she has kept it for the day of my burial*'; but also in John 12:10 because '*the Chief Priests*' then '*plot together so they might also put Lazarus to death*' (here, of course, not only the '*Chief Priests*' motif of the Eliezer ben Hyrcanus tradition about '*the toilet*' for the '*High Priest*' above, but also the mixing of the stories of both '*Lazarus*' and '*Jesus*') because *many of the common Jews* – when '*seeing Lazarus*,' '*raised from the dead*' – would '*believe on Jesus on account of him*' (thus –12:9–11).

Not only do we have here the usual Pauline theological note, but this side comment appears so totally confused that, at first, it is impossible to decipher it. Not only does it draw on the '*Judas Iscariot*' materials in the Synoptics (note, for instance too, how in Matthew 26:4, introducing these materials – like John 12:10 above on its '*Lazarus*' – it is '*the Chief Priests*' and '*Elders of the People*,' who '*plot together in order that they might seize Jesus*' and '*kill him*'![59]); but in normative theology it is because of Jesus' resurrection not Lazarus' that one is supposed to believe.

For Matthew 26:10–13 and Mark 14:7–10, anyhow, the whole presentation is framed – unlike in John, where the framework is rather that of Judas Iscariot's complaints about '*the Poor*' – *within the context of the worldwide Gentile Mission* or, as both express this through the picture of their 'Jesus'' rejoinder to '*his Disciples*' on the act ('*a good work*') of the woman who *anointed his head* with '*the very precious ointment*' while '*he reclined*':

Wherever this Gospel is preached throughout the whole world that which this woman did will also be spoken of as a memorial for her.

One should note here the 'Jamesian'/Dead Sea Scroll emphasis on what *'this woman did'* or *'doing'* – even the expressed allusion in Matthew 26:10/Mark 14:6 that *'she has done a good work towards me'*[60] – in three lines out of four in both these passages. This is to say nothing of the allusion to *'memorial'* or *'remembrance'* in Matthew 26:13/Mark 14:9, which we have already called attention to in the Damascus Document above Nor is this to say anything about James' words as reported by Paul in Galatians 2:10 about not forgetting to *'remember the Poor,'* which he says he *'was indeed most anxious to do'* (note here, again the emphasis on *'doing'*) and which we shall have cause to elaborate more fully below – but now with quite another signification.[61] Moreover the *'good work,'* referred to now in both Matthew and Mark, is *'breaking the alabaster flask'* and *'pouring'* the *'very precious pure spikenard ointment,'* it contained, *'on his* ('Jesus") *head'* – not a *'work'* of either *Torah* or *of the Law.*

John's account, of course, like Acts' entire *'Stephen'* episode – not to mention the Synoptic *'Lazarus'/'Canaanite woman'* episodes – is replete with anti-Semitism; and this episode, in particular, where *'the Chief Priests'* are represented as not only *wishing to kill Jesus* (cf. Matthew 26:4 above) *but Lazarus as well – on account of (the)* *'many of the Jews [,' 'seeing what Jesus had done,,' ']* *were believing on Jesus because of him'* (John [11:45 and]12:10-11) – is a particularly noteworthy example, the reference to *'the Jews'* portraying them as a completely *'alien'* People. Notwithstanding, the retrospective and mythological nature of the whole scenario in both sets of materials should be patent.

Of course, whereas Matthew and Mark have no *'dogs licking Lazarus under the table'* episode, Luke has no *'Canaanite'/'Syrophoenician woman'* encounter. Nevertheless, just as the thrust of Matthew and Mark's *'Canaanite'/'Greek Syrophoenician woman"s* (meaning that she is presumably a Gentile in the region of Sidon or Tyre) retort to Jesus implies that she, in particular, has something to teach even Jesus; or, put this in another way, *the Jewish Messiah 'Jesus'* has something to learn even from a lowly Gentile believer. In particular, the *'Tyre'* allusion in Matthew 15:21 and Mark 7:24 – interestingly, in Luke 6:17 the *'parts'/'coasts of Tyre and Sidon'* allusion is tied rather to one about the People *'trying to touch'* Jesus, *when* *'the power went* out of him' – will have, as already suggested, real importance in traditions about some of these women, such as, for instance, Simon *Magus'* companion *'Helen,'* whom Christian tradition says he found *'in the brothels of Tyre,'* to say nothing of the *'Tyrian gold dinar'*

Boethus' daughter '*Martha*' or Nakdimon's daughter '*Miriam*' is said '*to need every Sabbath evening just for her sweetmeats*' or '*spice puddings*'!

'*The Crumbs that Fall from the Rich Man's Table*'

The polemic in the Lukan counterpart of these two presentations – where, as we saw, '*the dogs*' rather *lick Lazarus' sores* and do not just '*eat the crumbs under the table*' and where Lazarus is presented as '*a certain Poor Man desiring to be filled from the crumbs*' under '*a certain Rich Man's table*,' himself described as '*clothed in purple and fine linen*' (how believable is this?) – ends in a fulsome attack on Judaism, the Law, and Jewish '*blindness*' generally in the face of such seemingly overwhelmingly convincing miracles as *Jesus*' (*not Lazarus*') *coming resurrection from the dead*.

In Luke 16:22–31, this is expressed in the manifestly mythological picture of the afterlife that follows – this in place of the picture of '*Jesus*'' resurrection of Lazarus '*from among the dead*' in John. As Luke 16:22 laconically depicts this, '*the Poor Man* (meaning '*Lazarus*') *died and he was carried away by the Angels into the bosom of Abraham*' (the counterpart, as just indicated, unmistakably of Lazarus' resurrection in John – now abstracted into a parable or an allegory). At this point, then, '*the Rich Man also died*' and, '*being in the torment of Hades*' (one could hardly get a more Hellenized version of the afterlife than this), '*cried out for mercy*' to '*Abraham afar off*' – presumably meaning '*in Heaven*,' '*Lazarus on his bosom*' (16:23).

Though there is no hint here of Lazarus' resurrection into the present world but rather this '*far-off*' one or '*Heaven*'; still Abraham's rebuke in the doctrinal discussion that follows of '*the Rich Man*' as one of the followers of '*Moses and the Prophets*' (here the Pauline theological implications are completely in evidence since the '*Poor Man*,' '*carried away by the Angels into the bosom of Abraham*,' is being pointedly differentiated from '*the Rich Man*' only following '*Moses and the Prophets*') does turn on the theme that, even if '*one came to them* (emphatically meaning the present-day '*Jews*') *from the dead, they would not be repent*' (16:30).

Not only do these passages from Luke anticipate the next step in John 11:17–45, that is, Jesus' resurrection of Lazarus, '*four days in the tomb*' and already '*stinking*' (to whom in 11:34 even the predicate, '*having been laid*,' is applied); but the very next line in Luke 16:31 reiterates, with even clearer bearing on John's narrative, again with the signification of *a final conclusion by Abraham presented as answering Lazarus' query:* '*even if someone were to rise from the dead, they* (again meaning, '*the Jews*'), *would not be persuaded*.' Moreover, as if to add insult to injury, the words Luke puts into Abraham's mouth here seem to carry an echo of the language used in the opening exhortative of the Damascus Document, to wit, *'hear, all you who know Righteousness'* and *'hear me, all who enter the Covenant,'*[62] but as always with reverse dialectical effect, that is, how could *'they be persuaded'* (meaning *'the Jews'* again), since *they don't even 'hear Moses and the Prophets' (thus)*!

The themes here in Luke parallel, of course, the *'Lazarus'* episode in John, including even the precise antithesis of this,

> Then many of the Jews, who came to Mary and saw what Jesus did, believed on him (11:45 – here too, of course, the omnipresent *'coming,' 'doing,'* and *'believing on'* usages).

While others, it seems (the ubiquitous *'some'* again), *'went to the Pharisees and told them what Jesus had done'* (11:46 – again, the repetition of the *'doing'* theme; in 11:47, now *'doing many signs'!*). This then provokes the next step in John's plot-line (no pun intended), namely, the picture of *'the Chief Priests* (as in Matthew 26:4 above) *plotting together how they might kill' Jesus* as well as Lazarus (11:47-53 – n.b., in this scene how *even Caiaphas is pictured as 'prophesying'!*) just as in 12:10–11, immediately following, they will then do regarding *'Lazarus.'*

To leave *'Lazarus'* for the moment – in Mark 7:25–27, Jesus is pictured as *'casting out (ekbale) unclean spirits'* or *'demons' from 'the Greek Syrophoenician woman's daughter'* (note that here too, she is depicted as *'falling at his feet'* and *'the children'* are characterized as about *'to be filled'* or *'satisfied'*) and in 7:24, the implication seems simply to be of his *'hiding'* (the *'hidden'* language once again) *in a non-Jewish household* – the allusion to *'unclean spirits'* carrying with it its own additional polemic in terms of Jewish *'cleanliness'* requirements we shall highlight further as we proceed.

On the other hand, in Matthew 15:21–28 – where the *'casting'* allusion is not used in relation to *'casting unclean spirits'* out of the *'Canaanite woman's daughter'* as in Mark 7:26, but rather in relation to *'the crumbs falling from the tables of their masters,'* now expressed in terms of *'taking the childrens' bread and casting it (balein) to the little dogs'* – the anti-Jewish and pro-Gentile Mission slant, as in *'Lazarus being carried away by the Angels into Abraham's bosom'* in Luke 16:22 above, is plain. This is achieved in Matthew 15:24 by having the episode clearly prefaced by Jesus' assertion, *'I was not sent except to the lost sheep of the House of Israel,'* just as the counterpart in Luke 16:21's *'Poor Lazarus wanting to be filled from the crumbs which fell from the Rich Man's table'* – note the parallel with Mark 7:27's *'let the children first be filled'* – is prefaced by its compressed version of Matthew 5:18's Sermon on the Mount, starting with *'not serving two masters'* in 16:13 and ending with the *'not a jot or tittle shall pass from the Law'* assertion in 16:17.

This is also true of Luke 6:17's earlier evocation of Matthew/Mark's *'coasts of Tyre and Sidon'* (in Matthew 15:21 and Mark 7:31, this is *'parts'* or *'borders of Tyre and Sidon'*), which is immediately followed in 6:18–19 by *'those troubled by unclean spirits also coming,' 'the whole crowd seeking to touch him (Jesus),' 'the Power going out of him and healing them'*![63], and reprising another part of Matthew's *'Sermon on the Mount,'* starting with *'Blessed are the Poor'* in 6:20 and ending with the *'house built without a foundation'* in 6:49.[64] One should also not fail to observe that the *'coming'* and *'falling'* in Mark 7:25 above is rather that of the *'Greek Syrophoenician woman falling at Jesus' feet,'* whereas in Matthew 15:27 and Luke 16:21, the *'falling'* remains that of *'the crumbs from the table.'* But now, unlike in Luke, in Matthew *'the crumbs fall to the little dogs'* while *'their masters'* take the place of the *'Rich Man'* in Luke!

In all these traditions we are, once more, face to face with the kinds of inversions or polemical reversals we shall see in Paul's reversal of James' position on *'things sacrificed to idols'* and eating *'unclean foods'* in 1 Corinthians 6-12 both, as we have alluded to it above and will treat further below. In the first place, there is the play on the allusion to *'dog'* or *'dogs'* (singular or plural, masculine or feminine is beside the point) – already signalled in relation to the *Talmud's* rather droll exposition of *'Ben Kalba Sabuᶜa'*'s pseudonym; but now, in addition to the allusion to them in Luke's *'Poor Lazarus'* episode, there is the evocation of them in Matthew/Mark's depiction of Jesus' *'exorcism'/'curing'* of the *'Greek Syrophoenician'/'Canaanite woman's daughter'* in the explanation that *'even the dogs under the table eat the children's crumbs'/'eat the crumbs that fell from their masters' table.'*[65]

As these expand in other directions to encompass Luke's the *'Poor man Lazarus longing to be filled from the crumbs that fell from the Rich Man's table,'* the issue turns, as we saw – as it did in John – into *one involving 'Resurrection.'* In fact, Luke 16:19–31's version of the scenario of the *'certain Poor Man Lazarus'* under *'a certain Rich Man'*'s *'table,' 'his sores licked by dogs,'* does not quite end up in a discussion of whether this was *'true charity,'* as in the case of *'Nakdimon'* in Talmudic tradition above; but rather it does go on to picture the Rich Man's torment in Hell (*'Hades'*), *'suffering in this flame,'* moving on, as already underscored, into the anti-Semitic attack on the stiff-neckedness of *'the Jews'* and the presentiment of Jesus' coming resurrection and *'return from the dead,'* to which the pointed comment is attached: *'even then they would not be persuaded'* (16:31).

For its part, in John's picture of these all-important goings-on at

Lazarus' house – paralleled, however abbreviated, by what takes place in Luke *at 'Martha's house'* (in Matthew/Mark, as we saw, *at 'Simon the Leper's house'*), the Synoptic presentation of '*Judas Iscariot going to the Chief Priests*' to '*deliver him up*' or '*betray him*' (Matthew 26:14–15 and pars.) *is included*; but now rather in the characterization of Judas as '*the son*' or '*brother of Simon Iscariot*' (John 12:4 and 13:29–31 – the second, pivotally, at '*the Last Supper*') – in other words, the '*Simon*' characterized as '*the Leper*' in both Matthew and Mark (or even '*Simon the Pharisee*' earlier in Luke), only now with completely different signification. Put in another way, in place of '*Simon the Leper*' or '*Simon the Pharisee*' in these Gospels, as already remarked, we should now have to probably read '*Simon the Cananaean*,' '*Simon Zelotes*,' or even '*Simon Iscariot*.'

Though the complaints about '*the Poor*,' that '*Judas*' is pictured as making against 'Jesus' in John 12:4–8, are folded into those '*the Disciples*' and the '*some*' make against *the woman who* '*anoints*' *Jesus*' *head at* '*Simon the Leper's house*' in Matthew and Mark – only in John they are far more theoretical or theological – as already suggested, they also mirror *Nakdimon's daughter 'Miriam''s* (or *his unnamed daughter-in-law's*) *complaints*, albeit reversed. *Now the amounts are not too little* as in Talmudic tradition, *but too costly* as in the Gospels. It is worth observing, yet again, that this is often the way this kind of data moves from one tradition to the other – much in the way the whole ethos of the Dead Sea Scrolls is largely reversed in New Testament reformulation.

Of course, in Luke's abbreviated and clearly secondary version of these encounters, Martha is pictured as *complaining about Mary 'sitting at Jesus' feet' while she has to do all the 'serving'*; whereas her Talmudic counterpart rather *complains either about the paltriness of her 'daily perfume allowance'* or *the stinginess of the weekly 'widow' allocation the Rabbis are prepared to allot her.* On the other hand in John, to repeat and just to get these things straight – as with '*the Disciples*' in Matthew/the '*some*' in Mark and inverting the sense of Nakdimon's daughter Miriam's complaints in the *Talmud* – '*Judas of Simon Iscariot*' is rather *complaining about Mary's profligacy in wasting such 'expensive perfume'* or '*pure spikenard ointment*' *and not 'giving it to the Poor.'* In John as well, it should be recalled that the famous '*thirty pieces of silver*' of Matthew 26:15/27:3's '*Judas Iscariot*'s '*price of blood*'/'*suicide*' scenario (itself significant) – in Mark 14:11, it will also be recalled, this was only the more indeterminate '*silver*' or '*money*' and no numerical amount was attached, all the rest being the same – *is now augmented some tenfold.* Thereupon Judas is depicted as crying out, as we saw, '*Why was this ointment not sold for three hundred dinars and given to the Poor?*' – a noble sentiment, but the amount in the one is basically reconfiguring the amount of the other.

Notwithstanding, in Mark 14:5's '*Simon the Leper's house*' scenario, we now rather get *John 12:5's more precise formulation* for the value of the '*precious spikenard ointment*' of '*three hundred dinars*' (the '*some*' now '*complaining*' or '*murmuring*' – not either '*the Disciples*' in Matthew or '*Judas*' in John) as opposed to the vaguer '*much*' in Matthew 26:9 or the '*money*,' Mark 14:11 *then goes on to designate as Judas Iscariot's betrayal 'price.'* This is not surprising as only Matthew had the precise amount of this last (supposedly taken, it will be recalled, from '*the Prophet Jeremiah*' when it was, in fact, '*Zechariah*'!). Accordingly and unlike in John and Mark, therefore, in Matthew 26:9 the price of '*the precious ointment*' now becomes the somewhat less precise – '*the Disciples*' now doing the objecting:

> *For what, this waste? This ointment could have been sold for much and given to the Poor.*

Were one to ask which of these multiple variations and spin-offs came first, it would be perhaps impossible to say. Still, it should be observed, that the relationships are far more complex than is generally thought, since Mark here is clearly dependent on John and not Matthew. But in the writer's view, it doesn't really matter, since almost all are secondary anyhow – most probably actually going back to these hyperbolic amounts conserved in Talmudic tradition about these ostentatiously '*Rich Men*''s '*daughters*' or '*daughters-in-law*.'

'*Don't Forget to Remember the Poor*' and '*the Camel and the Eye of the Needle*'

Nevertheless, if we were to take this ideological exchange on the subject of '*the Poor*' here in John (revamped in Matthew and Mark, but deleted altogether in Luke in favor of the '*Poor Lazarus under the table*' episode – also dependent to some extent on John) as symbolic of the whole period and the Judas '*the Iscariot*,' John 14:22 alludes to, simply as representative of the more historical '*Judas the Galilean*,' the founder of both '*Zealot*' and '*Sicarii*' Movements as far as Josephus is concerned[66] – and, in our view, *the entire 'Messianic' Movement contemporary with them*[67]; then one can see by John's clear concern to counter-indicate Judas' rebuke of '*Jesus*' over '*Mary*''s '*wastefulness*' (again, moved ever so laterally in Matthew and Mark in line with their plot-line) that *taking wealth of '*the Rich*' and giving it to '*the Poor*'* was a cornerstone of the ideology of these '*Movements*' – therefore the designation '*the Poor*.' Furthermore, this same ideology was, in 'Jesus'' retort to this same 'Judas' (in John later, 'the Iscariot' – in Matthew, 'his Disciples;' in Mark, the ubiquitous 'some'), at the same time now being aggressively undermined, Hellenized – the kind of obeisance being demanded by 'Jesus' here being typical of that paid to any number of Hellenistic Deities[68] – and, in the interests of 'the Pax Romana,' pacified.

Though this historical point just barely shines through the patent attempt at dissimulation on the part of these New Testament narratives, so layered and artfully constructed, as we have seen, are they; still, it is exactly what one would expect since even Josephus makes it clear that 'the Innovators' ('Revolutionaries') responsible for the War against Rome – aside from burning the palaces of the 'Rich' Herodians and High Priests (including, ultimately, butchering Josephus' friend Jesus ben Gamala and the individual responsible for James' judicial murder, Ananus ben Ananus) and burning all the debt records – 'wished to turn the Poor against the Rich,'[69] meaning, one has in his account one of the first clearly-documented class struggles in written history.

One should also appreciate in these ideological exchanges between 'Judas' and 'Jesus' on the subject of 'the Poor,' the echo – no matter how laterally-displaced the context may sometimes seem – of James' admonition relative to the continuance of Paul's 'Gentile Mission' in Galatians 2:10 that he (Paul) should 'only' not forget 'to remember the Poor,' which (as we saw) he says he 'was most anxious to do' (n.b., again the stress on 'doing').

Not surprisingly, this occurs right after the allusion in Galatians 2:6–9 to 'James, Cephas, and John' – 'these reputed Pillars' (whoever 'Cephas' was supposed to have been, 'Peter' or another), not that 'their importance' or 'repute meant anything to' him. Echoing 'Jesus'' declaration to the 'Canaanite'/'Cananaean woman' in Matthew 15:24 above: 'I was not sent except to the lost sheep of the House of Israel' (in Mark 7:27, this is: 'It is not good to take the children's bread and cast it to the dogs')[70]; these 'Pillars,' according to him, were to be 'the Apostleship of' and supposed only to go 'to the circumcision,' while he and Barnabas were 'to go to the uncircumcision' or 'the Gentiles.'

Also, not surprisingly, it is followed two lines later by the note about the 'some from James' who came down from Jerusalem (2:12 – again picked up, however obscured, in the objections by the 'some' in Mark 14:4 above) and how Peter, whose habit before had been to 'eat with the Gentiles' ('Ethnon'), then immediately 'separated himself (that is, from Paul and from 'table fellowship with Gentiles' generally) for fear of those (or the 'some') of the circumcision' (again, one should pay careful attention to the all-important 'some' allusions here).

In this context too, then, one sees both 'Judas Iscariot' and 'Simon Zelotes'

('*Simon Iscariot*'?) as representing the more '*Zealot*'/'*Sicarii*' orientation of the '*Essenes*'/'*Judeo-Christians*' (an appellative that should be used advisedly)/'*Qumran sectarians*' (it should also be used advisedly), particularly if '*Sicarii*' also carries with it the sense of '*forcible circumcisers*,' as we shall argue at the end of this book only – in the sense of the Roman ban on such '*bodily mutilations*' generally, '*the Lex Cornelia de Sicarius et Veneficis*'[72]; while Jesus embraces the more overseas Hellenizing and Paulinizing line – including displaying (in the manner, for instance, of the Dionysus-like God in Euripides' *The Bacchae*[73]) not a little derisive contempt – '*the Poor*' being *unimportant as compared to him,* that is, to put it in the manner of the three above-mentioned Gospels, '*the Poor you have with you always, but you do not always have me.*'

Regarding Nakdimon's '*charity*,' Rabbinic tradition, as we saw, picks up this theme as well, concluding that – like the '*Riches*' of '*the Unrighteous*' we shall encounter in Luke 16:1-12's '*Parable of the Unfaithful Servant*' about *another* '*certain Rich Man*'/'*lord*'/or '*master*' and the collection of his '*debts*' below (again, leading into his version of the '*Sermon on the Mount*' in 16:13-18 – itself leading into the '*Poor Man Lazarus under the Rich Man's table*' material in 16:18-31) – his *allowing* '*the Poor*' *to gather up* '*the woollen clothes that had been laid*,' so that '*his feet*' would not have to touch the dirt of the ground, was not real charity. Their conclusion was rather, that it was for '*self-glorification*' only. It was at that point, it will be recalled, that they went on to cite the aphorism, '*in accordance with the camel is the burden*' which, in the context, obviously meant, *the richer he was the more he owed.*[74]

Though we showed this to have an equally obvious corollary in the matter of the wealth acquired by Josephus' friend '*Joshua ben Gamala*' – *whose patronym meant* '*camel*' – when he married Boethus' daughter '*Martha*'; this too, with just the barest amount of reshuffling, had an easily-recognizable parallel in the favorite Synoptic aphorism about '*a Rich Man*,' '*a camel*,' and '*the eye of a needle*' – whatever one might ultimately take this to mean – *actually comparing the* '*Rich Man*' *to the* '*camel*':

> *Easier would it be for a camel to go through the eye of a needle than for a Rich Man to enter the Kingdom of God* (Matthew 19:24 and pars.).[75]

The relationship of this curious saying – the meaning of which is, admittedly, obscure and has been debated – to these '*Rich Man*' and '*camel*' aphorisms in the *Talmud* should be patent.

That in the Synoptics the dictum comparing these two is delivered following another allusion to '*allowing the little children to come unto*' him (Matthew 19:13-15 and pars. – again, note the allusion to '*coming*') – this time uttered in the context of Jesus '*touching*' *the little children*, not their '*touching*' *him* (as in earlier Gospel scenarios and Jerome's testimony about the way the Jerusalem populace reacted to James) – is certainly also interesting. So is the ban on '*divorce*' and '*fornication*' preceding this rather saccharine portrait (once again, one can just picture a '*God*' such as Dionysus, Apollo, or even Osiris, being portrayed in this manner) in Matthew 19:3-12 and Mark 10:2-12, which much echo similar strictures in the Damascus Document and Temple Scroll from Qumran.[76] In all three Synoptics, this series of commandments preceding this '*camel*'/'*eye of a needle*' pronouncement, which even include a number of the Ten Commandments, finally ends with the emphatic directive – Matthew 19:21 even evoking the earlier admonition attributed to Jesus in 5:48's '*Sermon on the Mount*' to '*be Perfect even as your Father who is in the Heavens is Perfect*'[77] – to '*sell all that you have and give to the Poor*,' not the more cynical inversion of this in the '*Judas Iscariot*'/'*Simon the Leper*' scenarios already adequately delineated above.

Not only is the demand, attributed to 'Jesus,' delivered this time *with positive, not negative effect* – meaning, now '*the Poor*' are of primary importance and not of secondary significance behind the '*God-Man Jesus*' – but in Matthew 19:19 anyhow; in the context of yet another enunciation of the '*all-Righteousness*' Commandment '*you shall love your neighbor as yourself*' – the first part of the '*Righteous*'/'*Piety*' dichotomy, so cynically manipulated by Paul in Romans 13:8-9, and a fixture of the salvationary scheme set forth in the Damascus Document at Qumran of '*the New Covenant in the Land of Damascus*.'[78]

It will be recalled that in Paul's dialectic in Romans 13, '*loving your neighbor as yourself*,' was to some degree being used to countenance *the payment of* '*taxes*' *to* '*the Servants of God*' – implying that it was the '*Roman Authorities*,' not the '*Jerusalem Church*' or Qumran Leadership, who were '*the Servants of God*' and to whom such '*love*' in the form of '*tribute was due*,' the very opposite of what the Revolutionary Movement begun by '*Judas the Galilean*' had demanded.[79] The reason for this, according to Paul's initial, somewhat self-serving polemic in 13:1, was that *since* '*there was no Authority except from God, those presently considered* '*the Authorities*' *had been appointed by God*'!

It was this commandment too – '*the Royal Law according to the Scripture*' in James 2:8, which Josephus pictures as the fundamental principle, by which '*Essenes*' conducted themselves towards their fellow man, as opposed to *their duties towards God* – '*loving God*,' which was the first.[80] It was this that *dictated the* '*poverty*' *regime* of groups such as these '*Essenes*' and their counterparts, '*the Ebionites*' or '*the Poor*.' The implied rationale was that you could not demonstrate 'love for your neighbor' or 'Righteousness towards your fellow man' if you made economic distinctions between such a one and yourself[81] – therefore, Jesus' directive here in the Synoptics: 'If you would be perfect, sell what you have and give to the Poor.'

Both Matthew and Mark add in the same line the note about *storing up 'Riches'* or *'Treasure in Heaven'* which, in turn, so much echoes the language in James 5:3 but in an approbatory not condemnatory way, that is, *not attacking 'the Rich'* ('*the Riches of whom were rotting away and whose clothes were all moth-eaten*') *but praising 'the Poor'* or, at least, *those giving all their possessions 'to the Poor'* (Matthew 19:21/Mark 10:21). A few lines earlier, in Matthew 19:17, anyhow, there is to be found the reiteration of two other, important Qumranisms, namely, '*keep the Commandments*' (the definition of '*the Sons of Zadok*' at Qumran – in Mark 10:19 and Luke 18:20 expressed only as the less emphatic '*knowing the Commandments*') and, more importantly still, the recommendation to '*be Perfect*,' already enunciated, as we just saw, in the Sermon on the Mount earlier.[82]

Preceding these commandments in Matthew 19:12, leading up to this pronouncement about the '*Rich Man*' and the '*camel*' and at the conclusion of banning both '*fornication*' and '*divorce*' in 19:2–11 (based, as at Qumran, on '*male and female He created them*' in Genesis 1:27 and '*two by two they went into the ark*' in 7:9); there occur the odd passages in support, seemingly, of celibacy (rather than worrying over '*fornication*'/'*adultery*') about those who were '*eunuchs from the mother's womb*,' those '*made eunuchs by men*,' and '*those making themselves eunuchs for the sake of the Kingdom of Heaven*.'

Here too, not only do we have an echo of the *ARN's* view of how Noah's '*Perfection*' involved his having '*been born circumcised*' (nor is this to say anything about the others *ARN* lists so physically '*perfected*' – namely, *Adam, Shem, Jacob, Joseph, Moses, David, Jeremiah, Job, Zerubabel,* even *Balaam*![83]), but also the note about James *being,* according to early Church tradition, *born 'a Nazirite from his mother's womb*' – to which Paul sets up his own competitive claim in Galatians 1:15 of having, likewise, '*been selected*' or '*chosen from his mother's womb*' and the reflection of which claim we have already identified as being made by the author of the Qumran Hymns.[84] Compare all this, too, with Paul similarly in 1 Corinthians 7:2-40 on both '*fornication*' and '*circumcision*,' which even includes the reference to his own celibacy in 7:7-8 and allusion to '*keeping God's Commandments*' in 7:19, the Qumran language both of '*for your own good*' and '*casting a snare before you*' ('*epibalo*') in 7:8 and 7:35, and Paul (like '*the Mebakker*' in the Damascus Document and James in Acts 15:19) *making Judgements* as well.[85]

There is also the odd occurrence of Origen in the Third Century castrating himself, apparently not unconnected to this recommendation attributed to 'Jesus' in Matthew 19:12, as just indicated, to '*make themselves eunuchs.*' It was, seemingly, because of this act that the term '*Sicarius*' was applied to him[86] – an act, however, that Jerome in the Fifth Century, in his Letter 84 to Pammachius and Oceanus, ridicules by applying Paul's attack on '*the Zealots*' in Romans 10:2–6 to it, declaring that Origen did this out of '*zeal for God, but not according to Knowledge*' (*Gnosis*).[87]

In these curious allusions we have further confirmation that both '*Zealots*' and '*Sicarii*' were practising what in our view should be termed, '*forcible circumcision,*' just as Hippolytus avers in the testimony – evidently drawn from a variant version of Josephus he was familiar with – *of just such* '*Sicarii*' or '*Zealot Essenes.*'[88] The same is also true of Acts' story of *the conversion of 'the Ethiopian Queen's eunuch,*' which we have already analyzed as involving a play on the practice of '*circumcision*' and other such '*bodily mutilations,*' according to the view of the Roman *Lex Cornelia de Sicarius et Veneficis* then coming into wider effect,[89] in particular, the circumcision of Queen Helen of Adiabene's two sons, Izates and Monobazus, as recorded as well in Josephus.

We have already seen that in the Lukan material leading up to evocation of '*a certain Rich Man clothed in purple and fine linen*' in 16:19 – which in 16:17 incorporates its version of Matthew 5:17's '*not one jot or tittle*' aphorism, to say nothing of these allusions in Mark and Matthew to '*adultery*' and '*fornication*' – the allusion to '*Heaven and Earth*' has the following variation:

> *Easier would it be for Heaven and Earth to disappear than for even a tittle of the Law to fail* (16:17).

The motif of '*Heaven and Earth*' here is, of course, important and, as already previously remarked, one finds it echoed in the designation of James as Successor in *Logion* 12 of the Gospel of Thomas – which, not surprisingly, also explains the true nature of '*the Zaddik*' and, by implication, the meaning of Paul's '*Pillar*' imagery with regard to James and his two colleagues, '*Cephas and John,*' in Galatians 2:9 just mentioned above:

> *In the place where you are to go* (meaning, apparently, Jerusalem), *go to James the Just for whose sake Heaven and Earth came into existence.*S

IO

'Every Plant which My Heavenly Father has not Planted Shall be Uprooted'

'Even the Dogs Eat the Crumbs under the Table'

Let us try to summarize a few of these things. As we have seen, Luke's variation on these 'Rich,' 'dogs,' 'crumbs,' and 'filling' motifs combine Talmudic 'sated as a dog,' 'Rich,' 'coming,' and 'Poor' allusions with Mark and Matthew's 'Canaanite'/'Greek Syrophoenician woman''s retort to Jesus: 'even the dogs eat of the crumbs which fall from the table of their masters.' This is Matthew 15:27. Mark 7:28 has: 'even the dogs under the table eat of the children's crumbs.' Not only are all these textual variations noteworthy, one should not forget Jesus' apparent prior rejoinder to the − again in Matthew 7:6's Sermon on the Mount:

> Do not give what is holy to dogs, nor cast (balete) your pearls before swine (here, it is important to note, the 'casting' or 'balete' is associated with the 'swine' not the 'dogs').

Notwithstanding, it is difficult to miss the connection of this with Jesus' pronouncement in Matthew 15:25 later seemingly obviating it:

> It is not good to take the children's bread and cast it (here 'balein') to the dogs, lest they should trample them with their feet.

Here the 'feet' motif in what has to be considered an odd milieu indeed, but it will have overtones with Talmudic materials, below about the fate of these same 'Rich Men's daughters' and various references to their own 'feet' and those of animals.

This curious depiction of what transpired at this 'Rich Man's house' − all 'clothed in purple and fine linen' (the counterpart of the 'woollen clothing' allusion in the episode about 'Nakdimon's house,' 'his feet,' and 'the Poor'?') − in Luke is also a bridge to John's picture of what went on at 'Lazarus' house,' and the issues debated there, as we just saw, again against the background of multiple evocation, once more, of Jesus' 'feet,' 'the Poor,' and

Lazarus' two sisters' *'precious spikenard ointment'* or *'perfume'* ministrations.

Just as Matthew and Mark's encounter on the *'parts'/'borders'* – in Luke, as we saw, *'the shores' of Tyre and Sidon'* with the *'Greek Syrophoenician'/'Canaanite woman'* is absent from Luke and John; the *'Lazarus'* episodes in John and Luke, incongruous as they may be, are missing from Matthew and Mark. There is however a caveat here – the particulars of John's *'Lazarus'* encounter partly turn up in Matthew and Mark's *'Simon the Leper'* episode and partly in Luke's picture of the goings-on at *'Martha's house'* – the connecting links being the *'Bethany'* locale, the repetitive use of the verb *'to come,'* the ever-present evocation of *'the Poor,'* the recurrent use of the telltale *'some'/'certain ones,'* and the whole activity of *'anointing'* Jesus' *'head'* or *'feet.'* Nor does John have any *'dogs under the table'* episode. Rather it evolves into something entirely different – an albeit recognizable scenario.

Still like Luke's *'a certain Poor man named Lazarus'* and the complaints of *'the Disciples'* or *'the some'* in Matthew and Mark about *'giving to the Poor,'* the adumbration of these themes in John both alludes to *'the Poor'* and moves into a number of other usages of the utmost importance for this tradition-cluster centering around this set of *'Rich' Men and women* in Palestine. In particular, it moves from the way John transforms Luke's resurrection scenario (*'carried away by the Angels'* after his death *'to the bosom of Abraham'*) to allusions to Jesus' coming burial scenario (in our view, ultimately having to do with members of the Royal Family of Adiabene) to these constant evocations of *'costly perfumes,' 'precious ointments,'* and *'his'* or someone's/something else's *'feet.'* In turn, these bring us full circle back to the original Talmudic allusions regarding these fabulously *'Rich' Men, their daughters,* and, of course, as we have been seeing over and over again, *'the Poor'* coupled with evocations of these *Rich Men* or women's *'feet.'* Admittedly, all these overlaps and variations are hard to follow without following the actual texts directly, but the reader should do his or her best.

Not only does this idea of being ostentatiously *'Rich'* find expression in Luke's version of the *'Lazarus'* material – to wit, *'a certain Poor man Lazarus ('laid at his doorstep') longing to be filled from the crumbs falling from the Rich Man's table'*; it also constitutes a part of the picture in the Synoptics of *'Joseph of Arimathaea's coming'* to claim and prepare Jesus' body for burial in *'his'* (Joseph's) tomb in Matthew 27:57 and *pars*. Despite the widespread familiarity with the name *'Nicodemus,'* this picture in the Synoptics involves no *'Nicodemus'* and it is, rather, only in John that *'Joseph of Arimathaea'* is associated with this other character called *'Nicodemus'* (*'Nakdimon'*) who also *'came'* – *'the one who first "came" to Jesus by night* (there are two more '*coming*'s here) *bearing a mixture of myrrh and aloes about a hundred weight*' (19:39 – '*litras*,' the same '*litra*' we encountered in John 12:3's picture earlier of the amount of '*ointment of pure spikenard of great worth*' with which Mary anointed Jesus' '*feet*' – in the Synoptics, it will be recalled, the measure was only expressed in terms of '*an alabaster flask*'/'*cask*' and not '*litras*').

As we also saw above, in his original introduction of this '*Nicodemus*' or '*Nakdimon*,' John called him '*a man of the Pharisees, a Ruler of the Jews*' – a bit of an exaggeration obviously – '*Pharisees*' often being substituted in New Testament parlance (as, for instance, in Acts 15:5 provoking *the* '*Jerusalem Council*') for '*the Party*' or the '*some insisting on circumcision*' of James.

Not only do all the various tomb and burial scenarios include motifs of '*linen*,' '*cloth*,' or '*clothes*,' there is often the mention, as just underscored, of the verb '*to come*' as, for example, in John 12:1's Jesus '*coming to Bethany where was Lazarus who had died and whom he raised from the dead*.' In Luke's further variation on these themes, *the dogs* '*come*' as well – as they do in Matthew 15:27's '*Canaanite woman*''s rejoinder to Jesus, that '*even the dogs eat of the crumbs that fall from their master's table*' (in Mark 7:28, it will be recalled, this was rather '*the Rich Man's table*') – though only '*to lick*' *Poor Lazarus*' '*sores*,' an allusion, one supposes, that would also have included '*his feet*' (that is, if it wouldn't have tickled so much!). Here, however, it is rather '*Poor Lazarus*' who is going to *eat* '*the crumbs*.' No doubt, Luke should have included the '*dogs under the table*' portion of the '*Canaanite*'/'*Greek Syrophoenician woman*''s retort to 'Jesus' which, of course, is implied, since that is where '*the crumbs*' (in Mark 7:28, '*the children's crumbs*') would have '*fallen*' if there had been any!

John's '*Cana in Galilee*' and God's '*Glory*'

Aside from these '*Rich*,' '*Poor*,' '*fall*,' '*filled*,' '*doorstep*,' '*dog*,' and '*came*' motifs; one should also not ignore, in Matthew 15:22's version of '*a woman, a Cananaean came out*' to him, the possible play on the '*Cananaean*'/'*Zealots*'-theme generally. This must of necessity be seen as, early on, including the phrase '*Cana of Galilee*' in John 2:1–11 as well (later too, in John 4:46 and 21:2). One must also see in the second part of this expression, '*Galilee*,' another possible play on Eusebius' version (seemingly based on Hegesippus), in delineating the number of Jewish '*sects*' at the time of Jesus, of '*Galileans*' as an alternate nomenclature for '*Zealots*.'[1] In this passage, it was '*in Cana of Galilee*' that Jesus '*fills*' – in the manner of *Nakdimon's* '*twelve cisterns*' above (for *Ben Kalba Sabu'a*, Luke, and further along in

John, it will be recalled, it was '*Poor Lazarus*' and '*the room*' that were '*filled*') – '*six stone water vessels to the brim*,' then *turning them into* '*wine*' (John 2:9). It is this '*filling to the brim*' aspect of the tradition which sharpens the relationship with *Nakdimon's* '*filling*' *the Rich Lord's water cisterns* '*to overflowing*' above. In 2:6 it was '*the master of the feast's* '*six stone water vessels standing* (note the '*standing*' usage again) *according to the* '*purification*'/'*cleansing (practices) of the Jews*' (this last phrase in itself confirms this as having been written *by Gentiles for Gentiles*).

This is one of the notorious '*signs*' or '*miracles*' Josephus refers to so scathingly in his several descriptions about how these '*wonder-workers*' or '*Impostors*' led the people out into the wilderness, there '*to show them the signs of their impending freedom*' or '*Redemption*.' It was such '*Impostors*' and '*religious frauds*,' it will be recalled, that he (Josephus) considered more dangerous even than '*the Revolutionaries*' or '*Innovators*' (the actual term he uses for these last[2]). For John 2:11, the theme recurs with the words: '*These were the beginning of the signs Jesus did in Cana of Galilee*.'

Not only does the description of the performance of this first miracle in John include a possible esoteric play (like the '*hundred baths of oil*' we shall encounter in due course in Luke below) on James' '*drinking no wine*' and *cold water* '*bathing*' habits[3]; but it is in this context and following that John 2:1 and 2:12, too, actually evokes '*his (Jesus') mother and his brothers*.' It is also as a consequence of these '*signs*' or '*miracles*' that John, unlike the Synoptics, portrays '*his Disciples as believing on him*' because '*he revealed his Glory*' (2:11).[4]

Furthermore, it is directly after this episode that John 2:13–17 – perhaps not insignificantly – positions its version of the expulsion of the money-changers from the Temple. To this, it is – once again – '*his Disciples*' (as '*the Disciples*' in the Rabbi Yohanan or Rabbi Akiba traditions) who apply the famous line from Psalm 69:9, '*zeal of Your House consumes me*.' We have already seen a variation of this line applied in Tractate *Ta'anith* and *ARN* above in the prayer Nakdimon makes to God regarding his own '*miracle*' of '*filling*' the water cisterns of the Temple. Probably not coincidentally, it is at this point that John 3:1 first introduces the character it calls '*Nicodemus, a Ruler of the Jews*,' a character missing from the other Gospels, with whom, John 3:3–22 pictures '*Jesus*' as then carrying on quite a sophisticated discussion about '*Christology*,' '*Light and Darkness*,' and '*born-again*' theology.

Again this discussion begins with Nicodemus, who '*comes to Jesus by night*,' saying to him (in quasi-parallel to the words the *Talmud* uses to describe Nakdimon, '*for whose sake the sun delayed its setting*'): '*no one is able to do the miracles that you are doing unless God is with him*' (John 3:2 – n.b., the correspondence to the '*doing*' ideology here, now connected to '*signs*' or '*miracles*'s). It also contains an allusion like the one Paul uses in 2 Corinthians 12:2–4 in speaking about '*knowing a Man in Christ fourteen years ago*' (the same timeframe as in Galatians 1:19 and 2:1 between the two meetings he has with James), who '*was caught away to the Third Heaven*' or '*Paradise*,' where '*he heard unutterable things.*' In John 3:12–13 this is: '*Will you believe if I say to you Heavenly things? No one has gone up into Heaven*' except '*the Son of Man who is in Heaven.*'

But more arresting than any of these and, in our view, further indicative – perhaps even definitively so – of dependence on Rabbinic tradition – if one actually examines the prayer Nakdimon is pictured as making in both *Ta°anith* and *ARN* (and, one might add, the one Honi is pictured as making prior to this too in *Ta°anith*, part of which we have partially recorded above); the words Nakdimon is portrayed as using *to fill the Temple water cisterns and bring the rain* are as follows:

> *Master of the Universe, it is revealed and known to You that not for my own glory did I do this, nor for the Glory of my Father's House did I do this* (n.b., the same emphasis on '*doing*' of Nicodemus' words above), *but only for Your Glory I did it, so that there might be water for the pilgrims.*'6

In the Honi episode in *Ta°anith* that precedes this, it will be recalled, it was because Honi added the words '*because I am looked upon as one of Your Household*,' meaning God's '*Household*' (it is this which is almost exactly the gist of Nicodemus' introductory declaration to Jesus above: '*no one is able to do these miracles unless God is with him*'), that the Pharisee '*Father*,' Simeon ben Shetah, is said to have declared: '*If he were not Honi, I would have excommunicated him.*'

But here in *ARN/Ta°anith*, the matter of '*Glory*,' whether God's or Nakdimon's, as we can see, forms the backbone and basis of the prayer. It cannot be accidental that in the sequence in John 2:2–2:11 above, after '*filling six stone water-vessels with water*' in 2:6–7 (here, of course, the '*filling*' is not of Nakdimon's '*twelve water cisterns*' but only '*six water-vessels*') at the marriage '*in Cana of Galilee*,' which Jesus then promptly *turns into wine*, the following words are added by the narrator:

> *This was the beginning of the miracles Jesus did at Cana in Galilee, revealing his Glory, and his Disciples believed on him* (2:11 – note, again the Talmudic emphasis on '*doing*' coupled with the additional emphasis on '*his Disciples*').

What should be immediately clear is that the '*Glory*' Jesus '*reveals*' here, goes right back to the '*Glory*,' just noted, that was '*revealed*' and '*known to*' God in the matter of Nakdimon's rain-making – in his case, so that '*the pilgrims would have enough water for the Festival*,' if not '*wine*' for the '*Cananaean*' marriage celebration.

The resemblance is uncanny; the sequencing precise; and, in the writer's view, this unexpected result of comparing the '*Glory*' evoked in both episodes is proof on the order of that achieved concerning the dependence of Luke's presentation in Acts of the conversion of '*the Ethiopian Queen's eunuch*' (who was reading Isaiah 53:11 when '*Philip*' – like '*Jonadab the son of Rechab*' in 2 Kings 10:15 – jumped up on the back of his chariot and asked him whether he knew the significance of what he was reading) on the Talmudic presentation of the conversion of Queen Helen's two sons, who were reading Genesis 17:10–14 on *how Abraham circumcised his whole household 'including the foreigner not born within it*' which formed the climax of *James the Brother of Jesus* (Penguin, 1998).[7]

It is also important to note that Jesus' '*mother*,' who requests him to replenish '*the wine supply*' for the '*marriage in Cana of Galilee*,' as we saw, goes unnamed here (John 2:1–4). Nor is she designated as '*Mary*' anywhere else in John, but always only as '*his mother*' or '*Jesus' mother.*' The reason for this is quite simple. In John 19:25, '*Mary (the wife) of Clopas*,' one of the witnesses to the crucifixion, is expressly designated as '*his mother's sister*'! It would be as hard for us, as it evidently was for John, to imagine there could be *two* sisters in the same family named '*Mary*.'

We have already treated this subject to some extent in our '*Preliminaries*.' John knows only *three* '*Mary*'s. The first of these is this '*Mary (the wife) of Clopas*,' just referred to above. '*Clopas*,' as we have already seen, was Jesus' '*uncle*' in traditional literature, the father therefore of *his cousin*, '*Simeon bar Cleophas*,' and according to this reckoning – since this '*Mary*' is clearly the '*mother*' of all the '*brothers*' – his putative '*brother*' as well.[8] In Matthew 27:56 and 61, this same '*Mary*' is also called '*Mary the mother of James and Joses*'[9] and '*the other Mary*' (in Mark 15:40, '*Mary the mother of James the Less and of Joses and Salome*' – in 15:47 however, *only* '*of Joses*'[10]).

The second '*Mary*,' John knows, is the '*Mary*' of the '*Mary*'/'*Martha*' duality, whose brother John considers to be '*Lazarus*' and whom we have already fully discussed above. The third is '*Mary Magdalene*,' about whom we shall have more to say in connection with the '*Canaanite woman*' out of whose daughter Jesus '*casts an unclean spirit*' ('*demon*' in Matthew, where the '*casting*' has more to do with '*the children's bread*' and '*the little dogs*') and who has presently become such an intense subject of international interest.[11] The narrational voice in John was, as just remarked, presumably aware of the improbability of there being *two 'sisters' by the same name* – entailing, therefore, a *'Mary the sister of her own sister Mary'* – it being only our subconscious that fills in the name *'Mary'* for the more-guarded references only to *'his mother'* in John.

The Unfaithful Servant and *'the Twelve Water Cisterns'*

In Luke, *'the dogs under the table who lick Poor Lazarus' sores '* (*'Lazarus'* rather *'eating the crumbs'*) in 16:19–31 – the Synoptic counterpart to *'casting the children's crumbs to the dogs under the table'* in Matthew and Mark – follows directly upon, as we have already remarked, the abbreviated version in 16:15–18 of Matthew 5:17–18's *'not one jot or tittle'* allusion (itself preceded in Matthew 5:14–16's *'Sermon on the Mount'* by a series of *'Light'* notices, including an allusion to *'Glorifying'* not unfamiliar to John 1–3 above – the discussion, John's *'Jesus'* had with this *'Nicodemus'* above, being to some extent simply a continuation of this Gospel's *'Light Prologue'*).

The idea in Luke 16:16–17 of *'one tittle of the Law not failing'* is not only preceded by its version of Matthew 6:24's *'a servant not serving two lords'* (Luke 16:13), but the whole sequence, leading up to this *'Poor Lazarus on the Rich Man's doorstep,...his sores licked by dogs'* episode, follows another very tortuous parable in 16:1–15, traditionally referred to as *'the Parable of the Unfaithful Servant.'* While we have referred to this *'Parable'* to a certain extent above, it is worth looking at it in more detail, since it actually begins with the introduction of the whole theme of the rest of the Chapter 16 to follow – namely, *'a certain Rich Man.'* Not only is this *'Rich Man,'* as in the *'Nakdimon'* episodes, once again alluded to as *'lord'* or *'master'* in 16:5; but the Parable includes for our purposes, the key motifs, of haggling over the numbers of his *'bath'*-storage facilities, just alluded to in the *'Nakdimon'* parallels, but also of *'grain'* or *'wheat'*-provision amounts (16:6–8, which are, of course, part and parcel of all these *'Rich Men'* supplying Jerusalem with enough *'grain'* or *'barley corns'* for *'twenty-one or twenty-two years'* in the *Talmud* and Josephus above[12]).

Just as with the *'six stone water-vessels'* Jesus *'fills to the brim'* in John 2:7 or the *'two hundred dinars of loaves'* (here we really are getting close to Talmudic evaluations, for instance, of the value of *'Nakdimon's daughter Miriam's perfume basket'*) and *'twelve handbaskets of wheat and barley'* (the same *'wheat and barley'*- motifs, *Gittin* will specifically connect to Nakdimon's or *Ben Kalba Sabuᶜa's* famine-relief efforts) that follow in 6:7–13 in these *'signs'/'miracle'* episodes – climaxed it would seem by John 6:10's version of the famous 'feeding the five thousand' (at the conclusion of which in 6:14, it should be appreciated, Jesus is specifically identified as the Ebionite 'True Prophet': viz., 'this is truly – note the play on 'True' in the word 'truly' here! – the Prophet that is coming into the world'); once again this convoluted 'Unfaithful Servant Parable,' which then leads in Luke into 'the dogs licking Lazarus' sores' while he 'longed to be filled from the Rich Man's crumbs,' must ultimately be seen as another variant or spin-off of these basic 'Nakdimon'-miracle tales from Rabbinic tradition, themselves turning on the theme of haggling with the 'Rich' lord over 'twelve talents of silver' and 'filling the twelve water cisterns' – the same amounts, of course, as the 'twelve handbaskets of wheat and barley' just encountered in John above.

Not only does this seemingly purposefully obscure parable – in Luke's run-up to its 'crumbs falling from the Rich Man's table'-counterpart to the same thematic variations in Mark and Matthew (none of which can be considered in the least historical) – include, in approaching the issue of the untrue nature of the 'Riches' of 'the Unrighteous,' the same genre of personage again referred to by the 'master' or 'lord' denotation (in 16:5 and 8, 'kurios' / 'kurion'); from the outset in 16:1; it raises the same telltale concern over their 'wastefulness' – here that the manager or representative was 'wasting his (the 'master''s) goods.' In these abstruse exchanges we already saw that another important Qumranism, 'the Sons of Light' (16:8), was incorporated – but there are also additional allusions to 'digging' in 16:3 and 'scoffing' in 16:14 which, as we shall see below, are so pivotal to concerns in crucial Qumran documents as well.[13]

No less telling, the whole discussion from 16:8–14, supposedly between 'the master' and his 'unjust servant' and dealing with 'false Riches,' 'the Unrighteous,' 'the Pharisees' (another motif we shall encounter below, too, in the run-up to Matthew/Mark's picture of 'Jesus'' encounter with the 'Canaanite' / 'Greek Syrophoenician woman'[14]), 'making yourselves friends of this world' (compare with James 4:4 above), and 'servants,' reflects not a little Paul's own barely concealed attack on the Jerusalem 'Apostles' in 2 Corinthians, called by him in 11:22 'Hebrews' and 'Super Apostles' or 'Apostles of the Highest Degree' in 12:11.

In making this attack Paul uses – as per the 'Christ' and 'Beliar,' 'Righteousness' and 'Lawlessness,' 'Light' and 'Darkness,' and 'Temple of God' with 'Temple of idols' comparisons earlier in 2 Corinthians 6:5-7:1– the quasi-Qumranism, 'Satan transforming himself into an Angel of Light,' and compares this to how 'pseudo-Apostles (clearly meaning the 'Hebrew,' 'Super Apostles' just mentioned above) turn themselves into Servants of Righteousness.' We have already seen that this last, too, was almost a total Qumranism.[15] It is co-extensive as well with what Paul is also referring to in 2 Corinthians 11:13 as '*Apostles of Christ.*' Furthermore, this in turn is preceded in 11:12, one should note, by the additional important Qumranism, '*cutting off,*' which we shall see to be of such consequence in the Damascus Document's historiography – to say nothing of its parody as well by Paul in Galatians 5:12 above, who uses it somewhat crudely to attack those who '*are troubling*' his communities with '*circumcision*'![16]

It is, therefore, during the course of this rather tortured '*Parable*' in Luke 16:1–16, ending with '*not serving two masters*' and '*forcing the Kingdom of Heaven,*' that the twin motifs of '*baths*' and '*grain*'/'*wheat*' are raised and over which '*the unjust servant*' bargains with '*his master's debtors.*' It is these motifs which so parallel those in the Nakdimon '*rain-making*' tradition of *bargaining over* '*the lord's*' *water cisterns* (in our view, Luke 16:6 transforms this into '*a hundred baths of oil*') or his '*supplying Jerusalem with enough grain for twenty-one years*' – e.g., the '*hundred cores of wheat*' that Luke 16:7 here considers *owing* '*the master's servant.*' Both amounts actually incorporate the '*hundred*' numeration, multiples of which form so much a part of the '*perfume*'/'*precious ointment*' traditions and their further adumbration in the various Gospel '*dinar*' descriptions already detailed above.

The quantification of '*a hundred baths of oil*' is, of course, probably basically meaningless – '*oil*' not usually being either *provided* or *measured in* '*baths.*' Once again, it probably plays on '*the bathing habits*' of James and those '*Essenes,*' he and Peter so much resemble, all of whom, too, probably *took only cold* '*baths*' as well as refusing '*to anoint themselves with oil.*'[17] That both kinds of allusions form the backbone of Nakdimon's '*miraculous water-supply*' and '*famine-relief*' activities – the latter also attributed to Nakdimon's two '*Rich*' colleagues, *Ben Kalba Sabuᶜa* and *Ben Zizzit* – is of considerable importance.

But the interchanges between '*the lord's servant*' and '*his master's debtors*' in Luke 16:5–6 also include the *pro forma* element of *haggling over numbers* – now '*fifty,*' '*eighty,*' and '*a hundred.*' In the Nakdimon stories, it is the haggling over the number of wells and who owes whom and what amount. It is this '*haggling*' that Luke uses as a springboard to produce his version of the famous aphorism, '*no one can serve two lords*' ('*God and Mammon*'), already quoted above and better known in Matthew's '*Sermon on the Mount.*' In Luke 16:13, in keeping with the business nature of the parable and playing on the '*lord*' theme, this reads:

> No servant can serve two lords, for either he will hate the one and love the other or he will hold to the one and despise the other. You cannot serve God and Mammon.

It is at this point, too, that these Chapter 16 preliminaries give way in Luke to its version of Matthew 5:18 – taking off from the allusion to '*not coming to abolish the Law and the Prophets but to fulfill them*' in 5:17 (in Luke 16:16, this is, conflating various passages from Matthew 5:17–18 and 11:12-13, '*The Law and and the Prophets were until John*'): '*Verily I say unto you, that until Heaven and Earth pass away, not one jot or tittle shall pass away from the Law until all these things are accomplished.*'

Luke 16:17 puts this statement, as we have seen, in line with its version of the '*greedy*,' '*scoffing*' *Pharisees* (often a stand-in, as we have already underscored as well, for '*the Jerusalem Church*' of James the Just) *seeking to* '*justify themselves before men*,' *but whose '*hearts God knows*' (this, of course, connected to '*heart*'-imagery at Qumran – in particular, the Damascus Document in which, for instance, '*God knew the works of those who sought Him with a whole heart before ever they were created*,'[18] not to mention the whole issue between Paul and James of '*trying to please men*' and '*Justification*,' we shall further elaborate as we proceed):

> *Easier would it be for Heaven and Earth to pass away than for one tittle of the Law to fail* (again, the conflation inherent in these kinds of passages should be obvious).

In 16:18 this is immediately followed by the ban on '*divorce*' which, as in the Damascus Document too and in Matthew 5:32 and 19:9, is linked as we saw, to the whole issue of '*fornication*.'[19] Here too Jesus' attack on '*the Pharisees*' must be seen as equivalent to similar ones on the ever-present '*some*,' already signalled above. It is also reflected in Jesus' like-minded attack on the Pharisees as '*Blind Guides*' in Matthew 15:1–20 and Mark 7:1–23, in the context of declaring '*eating with unwashed hands does not defile the man*' and '*all foods clean*,' leading up in both to the '*not taking the children's bread and casting it to the dogs*' episodes in 15:21–28 and 7:24–30, which we shall analyze further below.

We have already seen too how this '*Poor*' motif is echoed in the complaints at '*Simon the Leper's house*' in Matthew and Mark and those of '*Judas of Simon Iscariot*' at '*Lazarus' house*' in John and Jesus' rather vainglorious response in all three, '*the Poor you have with you always, but you do not always have me.*' However, as we have also already suggested, this exchange cannot be completely differentiated from the one in Rabbinic literature concerning the extreme '*poverty*' of the key Rabbinic hero, Rabbi Akiba, when he was young. In fact at one point, to illustrate Rabbi Akiba's '*poverty*,' at the time he married '*Ben Kalba Sabuᶜa's daughter*' before her father became reconciled to their marriage, his wife Rachel is portrayed as *having to 'sleep on straw'* and *picking it 'from his (Rabbi Akiba's) hair.'*

One should pay particular attention here to the *'hair'* motif once more, but this time it is now *Rabbi Akiba's 'hair'* and not either *'Lazarus''* sister *'Mary''s 'hair'* nor that of *the unidentified female 'Sinner'* in Luke, *'anointing' Jesus' feet* and *'wiping them with her hair'*![20] One should also note here the theme of *'straw,'* so important in the picture in both Josephus and the *Talmud* – should one again choose to regard it – of *'the Zealots'* (*'the Barjonim'/'Biryonim'* in the *Talmud*) burning Ben Kalba *Sabuʿa's*/ Nakdimon's and/or *Ben Zizzit's 'grain'* stores or mixing, in their desperation, such *'grain'* or *'straw'* with the bricks they used to shore up Jerusalem's defences.[21] Nor is this to say anything about the portraits of the *'feet'* of these various *'Rich' Men's daughters*, we have been highlighting and will highlight further below, both during and after the War against Rome, amid *'the straw'* and *'mud'* of various Palestinian cities as, for instance, Jerusalem, Lydda, or Acre.[22]

It is at this point that Tractate *Nedarim* (on the bride's dowry) depicts Rabbi Akiba as promising his wife *'a golden Jerusalem'* – apparently the tiara, noted above, in vogue among the ladies of the day depicting the city of Jerusalem and manifestly an *'irredentist'* statement of some kind. But it also depicts the Prophet Elijah as coming to Akiba *in the guise of a mortal* (the *'Elijah redivivus'* theme, we have been underscoring, and an essential element too of Gospel portraiture at least in the Synoptics) and *crying out at the door, 'Give me some straw for my wife is in confinement and I have nothing for her to lie on'* (the root perhaps, as already suggested, of the *'no room at the inn'* scenario in Luke 2:5–17). Not only is this, *'crying at the door,'* a theme both present in the Letter of James 5:9 and the proclamation in the Temple at Passover attributed to James in all early Church literature[23]; the tradition as a whole is, in some manner and in the characteristically *'earthy'* Talmudic style, obviously both comparing and connecting Rabbi Akiba with the Prophet Elijah. At this point, in typical Rabbinic style, Rabbi Akiba is pictured as wryly observing to his wife, *'You see there is a man who lacks even straw'*!

These things as they may be, following allusion to Rabbi Akiba's teacher, *'Rabbi Eliezer b. Hyrcanus'* (*'Lazarus'*?), and pivotal usages such as *'uprooting,' 'casting,'* and *'hidden'* – all of which we shall encounter again, as we proceed, in the run-up in Matthew 15 and Mark 7 to the exorcism of the *'Canaanite'/'Greek Syrophoenician woman's daughter'*[24] – *ARN* notes how Rabbi Akiba's example *will condemn all the Poor for, when they will be accused* (Judas Iscariot's or *'the Disciples''* accusation against either Lazarus' sister *'Mary'* or *'the woman with the alabaster flask'* about *'anointing' Jesus'* head or 'his feet'?), 'Why did you not study Torah?' (the content of these stories or traditions are, as should by now be fully appreciated, almost always one hundred and eighty degrees inverted) and they plead, 'Because we were too Poor' ('the Poor you have with you always' paradigm in the above episodes?); the response will be, 'Was not Rabbi Akiba very Poor and in straitened circumstances?'[25]

However dramatic this may be, the allusion to 'uprooting' connected to this notice in the *ARN*, which – at least in Matthew – precedes Jesus' exchange over 'not taking the children's bread and casting it to the little dogs' as well, will be a particularly important one. Here in Matthew it will be found in another rebuke Jesus makes in a polemical exchange about 'the Pharisees' as 'Blind Guides' – in this instance, not to the 'Canaanite woman,' but to his own 'Disciples' again (more and more 'Jesus' begins to sound like a disgruntled Ruler of some kind – say, Agrippa II in retirement in Rome when, after the Revolt, things did not turn out exactly as he might have preferred[26]):

> Every plant which my Heavenly Father has not planted shall be rooted up (Matthew 15:13).

The inverted parallel to this – which, as at Qumran and as we shall show further below, will also involve a 'Guide' or 'Maschil'[27] – will be present in the Damascus Document's dramatic opening imprecation about how 'God' caused:

> a Root of Planting to grow (the parallel is here!) from Israel and from Aaron to inherit His land and to prosper on the good things of His Earth.[28]

The linguistic interdependence of this and much else in the depiction of 'Jesus'' arguments in Matthew 15:1–20 and Mark 7:1–23 (leading up to his exchange with the 'Canaanite'/'Greek Syrophoenician woman' in (Matthew 15:21–28 and Mark 7:24–30) with the 'scribes and Pharisees from Jerusalem' should be clear to all but the most stubbornly obdurate reader. This is Matthew 15:1, but in Mark 7:1 this changes into the even more pregnant 'the Pharisees' and – the telltale – some of the scribes who had come from Jerusalem' – thus, (again note both the 'coming' and the 'some') and a euphemism it would appear, once again, evocative of Paul's interlocutors from James' 'Church'/'Assembly' in Jerusalem.'

'Suffer the Little Children to Come unto me and Do not Hinder them'

In *ARN*, this exchange concerning Rabbi Akiba's *incredible application to* '*studying Torah*,' as opposed to *those claiming to be 'too Poor' to do so*, is directly followed by yet another, equally striking allusion – this time to '*little children*' and/or Rabbi Akiba's *own 'little children.'* It reads, as we saw:

> *If they plead, 'we could not study Torah' because of our little children* (that is, instead of '*because we were too Poor*'), *the response should be,* '*Did not Rabbi Akiba have little children too?*'

Not only should it be clear that this bears on Jesus' admonition to '*Let the children first be filled*' and '*it is not good to take the children's bread and cast it to the little dogs*' in both Matthew and Mark – upon which we shall elaborate still further below (all allusions for the moment to 'being *filled*' aside) – but also to the several references to '*little children*' throughout the Gospels.[30] As we have already remarked, perhaps the most striking and well-known example of these is the one that comes just following the imaginative presentation concerning '*fornication*' and '*adultery*' in Matthew 19:12 (itself clearly playing off Column Four of the Damascus Document on the same subject[31]) about '*eunuchs from the mother's womb*' and '*those making themselves eunuchs for the sake of the Kingdom of Heaven,*' just preceding allusions, too, to '*keeping the Commandments*' in 19:17 and '*a Rich Man not entering into the Kingdom of Heaven*' in 19:24 – all just reviewed above as well.

Just as the rebuke to the woman *who came to him with an alabaster cask of very precious ointment* at '*Simon the Leper's house*' in Matthew 26:7 later and that to '*his Disciples*' about '*planting,*' '*uprooting,*' and '*Blind Guides*' in Matthew 15:12 earlier; this is, once again, *aimed at 'the Disciples,'* now pictured as *objecting to 'Jesus'* having '*laid hands*' on '*little children*' (Matthew 19:13-15 and *pars.*). In response, in what is now becoming something of a pattern, Jesus immediately rebukes these same '*Disciples,*' making the now celebrated remark: '*Suffer the little children to come unto me.*' Similarly, preceding this there is yet another, equally proverbial rebuke – *again directed against 'the Disciples'* – insisting that,

> *unless you become as the little children, you shall in no wise enter the Kingdom of the Heavens* (Matthew 18:1-4 and *pars.*)

Not only should the interconnectedness of all these '*Kingdom of Heaven*' allusions be obvious, but that all have to do with castigating those – as, for example, the unnamed *circumcisers 'confusing'* or '*troubling*' *Paul's new* '*Gentile Christian*' communities in Galatians 5:12 above – throwing up inconsequential legal barriers (such as '*circumcision*') should be obvious as well. We mean by '*inconsequential*,' '*inconsequential*' *as deemed by Paul* since, as he also puts this in the same Galatians 5:14 – again clearly both alluding to and pre-empting the sentiment expressed in James 2:8–2:10:

> For the whole of the Law is fulfilled in one sentence, you shall love your neighbor as yourself.

Here too, strikingly, he evokes his '*freedom*' ideology, by which he always means '*freedom from the Law*' and not '*freedom from Rome*,' and pointedly characterizes his opponents as '*biting and devouring one another*.'[33]

It should be equally obvious, too, that, once again, these are all anti-'*Jerusalem Church*' aspersions, since they are usually followed up by and tied to equally proverbial statements like '*the First shall be Last and the Last shall be First*' (Matthew 19:30, 20:16 and pars.) – again patently having to do with Paul's new '*Gentile Christian*' communities and those, like him, making no such insistences on seemingly *picayune legal requirements for* '*Salvation*.' Why '*patently*,' because Paul first made the allusion to being '*last*' in his 1 Corinthians 15:8 'Jesus' sighting-order determinations – also, importantly enough, citing James even if albeit defectively[33] –

> And last of all he appeared, as if to one born out of term (or '*to an abortion*'), also to me.

But '*the First*' is an extremely important expression at Qumran, carrying with it the signification of '*the Forefathers*' or '*the Ancestors*' and the sense is always *those who observed* or *gave the Torah*, while '*the Last*' – aside from Paul's evocation of it regarding his own post-resurrection appearance role – usually has to do with '*the Last Times*' or '*the Last Days*,' denoting the '*present*' or '*Last Generation*' as opposed to '*the First*.'[34] On the other hand, in the Gospels, once again absolutely turning Qumran ideology on its head, '*the Last*' are these '*simple*' or '*little children*' – completely representative of Paul's new '*Gentile Christians*,' knowing or required to know little or nothing about such onerous legal requirements, yet still in a state of '*Salvation*,' or, as it were, '*in Jesus*.' The '*simile*,' '*symbolism*,' '*parable*,' or '*allegory*'[35] – as the case may be – in all these allusions is not hard to figure out, despite endless scholarly attempts at evasion or posturing to the contrary.

Mark 10:13–14, followed by Luke 18:16–17,[36] is even more severe, rather expressing Matthew's '*little children*' incident as follows:

> And they brought little children to him that he might touch them, but the

Disciples rebuked those who brought them (here, of course, we have both '*the little children*' and '*Disciples*' usages, but now the issue is not expressed in terms of '*laying on hands*' but of '*touching*,' as it was earlier in both Mark 5:22–43 and Luke 8:40–56 in the case of the woman who '*came*' to him with *an endless 'fountain' of blood* in the midst of the '*Jairus' little daughter*' episode we shall examine further in due course below). *But when Jesus observed this, he was very displeased and he said unto them, 'Suffer the little children to come to me and do not hinder them.'*

Not only is this a good deal stronger than Matthew and one would have to be completely simplistic not to realize it was directed both *against Jews and the the Jerusalem Apostles* and *for the new 'Gentile Mission' of Paul*; but we have the '*touching*' motif too that we have already encountered in several *miraculous 'curing'* episodes above (when '*the Power*' often '*goes out of him*'[37] – and, even more importantly and most particularly, in Jerome's testimony regarding James concerning how '*the little children*' or '*the People used to run after him and try to touch the fringes of his garment as he passed by.*'[38]

Nor is this to say anything about the statement, following the rebuke comparing Rabbi Akiba's dedication to '*Torah study*' to that of those *claiming to be 'too Poor*' or *making the excuse of having 'little children*' above, '*that Rabbi Akiba started studying Torah and by the end of thirteen years he taught Torah in public.*' For whatever it's worth, like the picture of Rabbi Akiba's wife about to give birth to a child in a quasi-manger and being visited by '*the Prophet Elijah*' above having points in common with Luke 2:7; this is not completely unrelated to the picture in Luke 2:46 of 'Jesus' *teaching in the Temple* – though the age cited in the Lukan tradition *is* '*twelve years old*' and that in the Rabbi Akiba one, '*thirteen*,' close enough. Of course in Luke, the number is always '*twelve*,' as it is for the 'age' of Jairus' '*little daughter*,' the number of years the '*certain woman*' *had been sick* '*with a flow of blood*' and, as it will be, for '*the twelve baskets full of broken pieces*' below.

We have also already encountered several usages in John not dissimilar to ones found in the Rabbi Akiba tradition, particularly concerning his wife. This is most in evidence in the picture both of how she and ultimately her father – Rabbi Akiba's father-in-law *Ben Kalba Sabuᶜa* – '*falls on his (or 'her') face and kisses his (Rabbi Akiba's) feet.*'[39] The parallel this represents, however far-fetched, with John's portrayal of Lazarus' sister Mary '*falling down at his feet*' in John 11:32 and similar portrayals of the unknown female '*Sinner*' with the '*alabaster flask of ointment*' at '*the Pharisee's house*' in Luke 7:37, '*falling at his feet*,' '*wiping them with the hairs of her head*,' and '*kissing them lovingly*' should not be overlooked.

In John too, as should by now be indelibly fixed, it is *'Judas ('the son'* or *'brother') of Simon Iscariot'* who makes the complaint about not *giving the price of the precious ointment 'to the Poor'*; whereas the *'plotting'* normally associated with his name and evoked in 12:10 (it will also be evoked in the Dead Sea Scrolls[40]), interestingly enough is as we saw, not between Judas and the High Priests, as in the Synoptics (Matthew 26:15 and pars.).[41] Rather, the *'plotting'* 'takes place only between *'the High Priests'* themselves since, in John, the Synoptic *'thirty pieces of silver'* or *'dinars'* motif is entirely missing in favor of the *'three hundred dinars'* for the value of the *'precious spikenard ointment.'*

In John 11:50, too, the motive of the High Priests – since *'many of the Jews were coming to Mary and seeing what Jesus did (to Lazarus)'* – is rather that,

> *it was better that one man should die for the People than that the whole Nation should perish.*

Nor is the *'plotting'* or *'betrayal'* at this point in John 12:10–11, as we have seen, about *identifying* or *betraying Jesus per se* as in the Synoptics; but rather the *'plotting'* is about *putting Lazarus back to death*, since it was on his account that *'many of the Jews were leaving and believing on Jesus'*! It should be emphasized again that this *'plotting'* theme will also be conspicuous in the Scrolls, most notably in the Habakkuk *Pesher* and the *'plotting'* evoked there on the part of *'the Wicked Priest'* is rather to *'consume,' 'eat,'* or *'destroy* (compare with Paul in Galatians 5:14 above) *the Righteous Teacher.'*[42] Once again, it should be clear that what we are witnessing here are numerous rewrites of the same or similar material as one tradition reworks, absorbs, or transforms another.

Feeding *'Five Thousand'* with *'Five Loaves and Two Fishes,' 'Filling Twelve Baskets,'* and *'the Children First being Filled'*

To go back to the presentation of *'Jesus''* encounter with the *'Cananaean'/'Greek Syrophoenician woman'* in Mark and Matthew (so frequently pointed up above – the familiar notice, once more, in Mark 7:25 of now the Greek Syrophoenician woman *'falling down at his feet'* aside): the exchange between the two of them has to do with another of these *'daughter's* who, like her mother – though she comes from *'the border areas'/'parts of Sidon and Tyre'* (in other words, *she is supposed to be a Gentile*, which Mark 7:26 makes clear by mentioning her *'race'/'genei'*) – goes unnamed. Notwithstanding, what she wants Jesus to do in Mark

7:25 (as in the case of 'Mary Magdalene' in Luke 8:2 above, yet another 'Mary,' 'from whom seven demons had gone out' – n.b., 'here' is grouped with two other unknown women, one with 'Herodian' connections) 'to cast' (ekballe) 'an unclean spirit' – 'a demon' in both Mark 7:26 and Matthew 15:22 – 'out of her daughter.'

Jesus' response – seemingly playing on the non-Jewish origins of this mother and her daughter – turns, as we saw, on the following statement:

> First to be filled (or 'sated'/'satisfied' – language related to 'the Poor' at 'Ben Kalba Sabuᶜa's doorstep' and the 'certain Poor One Lazarus longing to be filled' with which we began the whole discussion) should be the children (again, compare with the exchanges, just signaled above, relating to either 'the Poor' or 'Rabbi Akiba's little children'). It is not good to take the children's bread and cast it (balein) to the little dogs (paralleling, too, 'the little children' above, once again increasing the 'Gentile Christian' overtones of this episode).

This is from Mark 7:27, the fuller exposition. Matthew 15:26, for its part, omits the allusion to 'filled' and, therefore, the first reference to 'children,' but it does pick up the second, that is, 'it is not good to take the children's bread and cast it to the little dogs,' as well as the reference to 'balein.' Moreover, in Mark 7:25 too, as already indicated, the 'daughter' is actually even her 'little daughter' and 7:24–25 also includes the usual telltale introductory usage 'a certain woman,' the fact that Jesus 'could not be hidden,' and the mother, once again, both 'coming' and 'falling at his feet.'

Not only does the omnipresent 'casting' language introduce and permeate the episode but, as also just remarked, Mark's use of the 'satiated' or 'filled' vocabulary mirrors or, at least, evokes that in Luke's account of the 'Poor Man Lazarus longing to be filled' – to say nothing of his 'dogs' – again showing the basic interconnectedness of these three encounters, not to mention the Talmud's 'Ben Kalba Sabuᶜa,' the cognomen of whom in Aramaic, as we saw, actually means 'filled' and to whose 'door one came hungry as a dog and went away filled'!

As already sufficiently underscored, we shall ultimately also actually encounter this same language of 'being filled,' 'sated,' or 'satiated,' in the Habakkuk Pesher's description of the final destruction of 'the Wicked Priest,' in which the latter is depicted – as in Revelation – as 'drinking the Cup of the Wrath of God to filling' or 'to satiation.'[43] This last means 'to the dregs' or – paralleling similar significations in Revelation 14:10 and 16:19 above[44] – that 'he would drink his fill' of the Divine Vengeance which 'would come around to him' for what he had done to 'the Righteous Teacher' and those of his followers (called 'the Poor' or 'Ebionim' – in our view, James and his Community, pointedly referred to in early Church literature, as will by now have become crystal clear, as '*the Ebionites*' or '*the Poor*').[45]

To continue along this line and the whole circle of allusions centering around the usage '*to fill*' – as already signaled too, there is a slight hint here, should one choose to remark it, of Nakdimon '*filling*' his own '*baths*' or '*water cisterns*' or those of the '*master*' or '*lord*' with whom he is negotiating. Nor is this to mention '*the six stone water-vessels*' at the wedding '*in Cana of Galilee,*' which Jesus '*filled, revealing his Glory*' in John 2:6 or '*the twelve handbaskets of fragments from the five barley loaves*' which '*the Disciples*' will '*fill*' from the '*overflow*' or '*remains*' in the '*feeding the five thousand*' (*on the other side '*of the Sea of Galilee*'*) in John 6:13 and other various spin-offs, we shall treat more fully below (no pun intended).

In fact, this decisive encounter with the '*daughter*' of the '*Canaanite*'/ '*Greek Syrophoenician woman*' in Mark and Matthew is sandwiched between two others, the first in both Matthew 14:13-23 and Mark 6:30-46: the feeding of the '*five thousand in a place in the desert*' (we shall see the second presently) involving this same overflow in John 6:9–13 of '*twelve baskets full of fragments,*' meaning, of course, as in John, of '*barley loaves*' or '*grain.*' So important was this episode evidently thought to be that now one even finds it in Luke (9:10–17). In fact in Matthew 14:20 and Luke 9:17, it is the '*multitudes*' or the telltale '*Many,*' who are again characterized as being '*satisfied*' or '*sated,*' while in John 6:12 this comes across as '*when*' or '*after they were filled.*'

All four now also include the additional motif of '*five loaves and two fishes,*' adding up to the number '*seven,*' a numeration that will grow in importance as we proceed,[46] and, of course, all four also have the characteristic allusion to '*and they did all eat and they were satiated*' or '*filled*' (Matthew 14:20 and *pars.* – in John 6:12, as just alluded to, '*when they were filled*'). To these Mark 6:37 and John 6:7, in line with their respectively more extensive storylines, add the additional *pro forma* important allusion to '*two hundred dinars of bread*' – again, the '*bread*' of '*the children*' above – or '*loaves*' (in John 6:13, '*loaves*' – more intelligibly, no doubt, of '*barley*' or '*wheat*'). Once again then here, not only do we have another indication of intertextuality between John and Mark as against the other Synoptics, but also, an additional variation on both the '*hundreds*' and the '*dinars.*'

Interestingly enough, in John 6:1-5's account of these '*twelve handbaskets*' and '*two hundred dinars*' – where, as in all four (at this point), it is the same '*five thousand*' who are being fed – the time is specifically denoted as being '*near Passover, the Feast of the Jews*' (6:4). Once again, as above, this is clearly being aimed at non-Jews, and for the same reasons, the whole episode in John 6:3 being equated with Moses' *Exodus* sojourn in the desert – Jesus being portrayed as *'going up into the mountain'* *'with his Disciples'* (repeated in Matthew 14:23 and Mark 6:46, but with different sequencing). This time in John, however, it is *'Philip'* rather than *'the Disciples'* (as in the Synoptics) who – in response to 'Jesus'' question, on *'seeing a great crowd,'* *'whence shall we buy loaves that these may eat?'* – replies in terms of the *'two hundred dinars'* (6:5-7). In the Synoptics this is turned around and it is *'the Disciples'* who raise this question not 'Jesus' (Mark 6:36 and *pars.*) Notwithstanding, in Luke 9:12 it is *'the Twelve'* who recommend sending *'the Many'* away.

Be these things as they may, it is here Philip responds that even *'two hundred dinars (worth) of loaves are insufficient for them.* In Mark 6:37 it is *'his Disciples'* who again make this response, but note, in particular, the *'dinars'* / *'pieces of silver'* motif – this time, as just indicated, in a factor of *'two hundred's* not *'three,'* *'four,'* or *'five.'* Here, too, *'Andrew the brother of Simon Peter,'* *'one of his Disciples'* (thus), suddenly also appears. One wonders what would be the effect of switching one or another of the other *'Simon's* in here, *e.g.,* *'Simon the Cananaean,'* *'Simon the Leper,'* or even *'Simon Iscariot'* – *'Andrew'* basically being a derivative of the Greek *'Andros'* / *'Man'* (*'Enosh'* / *'Bar-Adam'* in Aramaic and *'Ben-Adam'* in Hebrew)?[47] He brings forward *'a little boy,'* not the *'little daughter'* of Mark 7:25 above (here too, the variation on the *'little children'* theme, we just saw above, in Jesus' request to *'his Disciples,'* *'to let the little children to come unto'* him *in order that he should 'lay hands on'* or *'touch them'* in the run-up to the *'Rich man,'* *'camel,'* and *'eye of the needle'* scenario in all three Synoptics, now reduced to just *'one small boy'* and accompanied, this time, by the *'wheat'* or *'barley'* motif). It is he, the *'little boy'* as opposed to *'the Disciples'* or *'the Twelve'* in the Synoptics, who now has the *'five barley loaves and two small fishes,'* out of which 'Jesus' *will perform another of his great 'signs'* (John 6:9–14 – once more note the important emphasis on *'doing'* but now, yet again, in a more Hellenistic framework of *'magic'*).

It is interesting, too, that these portraits of Jesus *'feeding the five thousand'* in Mark 6:30–46 and Matthew 14:13–23 come directly after the description of John the Baptist's execution by *'Herod'* (Mark 6:14–29/ Matthew 14:1–12), in particular, their depiction of John's *'head' being brought to Herodias'* *'daughter'* (unnamed) *'upon a platter.'* Not only is this a completely inaccurate portrait, as we have seen, but it is probably based on the picture in Josephus of how Nero's Jewish-leaning wife Poppea – who, according to him, in the period just prior to the Revolt against Rome, *'was interested in religious causes'* – prevailed upon Nero to *behead his former wife,* whom he had previously only exiled, and, thereafter, have *her head* brought to *her* *'on a platter'*![48] If this is so, then we have in this

Gospel rewrite, yet another marvelous example of pro-Roman and Hellenizing, anti-Jewish disinformation.

In any event, Jesus then takes '*the loaves*' and '*the little fishes*' (*sic*) and gives them to his Disciples and, as we just saw, '*when they were full*' (once again, this '*filled*'/'*satiated*' usage really *is* here), '*they gathered up the fragments*' or '*broken pieces*' ('*the broken pieces*'/'*fragments*'-motif from the Synoptics above), '*filling up twelve handbaskets with broken pieces*' *from* '*the overflow*' (John 6:11–13 – here of course the '*overflow*' theme, together with yet another allusion to '*filling*,' as in the Nakdimon story and his '*filling up*' the lord's '*twelve cisterns to overflowing*,' which is to say nothing of '*the twelve handbaskets*,' that is, Nakdimon's '*twelve water cisterns*,' etc., etc.).

It is at this point, showing just how important the implications of all these various numbers were to the authors of these traditions, that John 6:14 actually has '*the men*' – seemingly meaning '*his Disciples*,' though perhaps '*the Many*' and probably picking up from the '*five thousand men*' that '*were filled*' in all four accounts previously – overtly identify Jesus, once again (as in 2:11 earlier and '*the miracles he did in Cana of Galilee*' *where he turned water into wine,* '*revealing his Glory, and his Disciples believed on him*'!), '*seeing the sign that he had done*' (again note, the more Gentilizing, overseas '*Christian*' nature of the '*doing*' or the '*works*' – certainly not meant as '*works of the Torah*,' but rather more magical, Greco-Roman, god-like '*miracles*'), as *the Ebionite* '*True Prophet who is coming into the world*.' Here, in the enigmatic wording of this obscure prophecy, perhaps the real sense and basis of all these ideological allusions to '*coming*,' we have been repeatedly encountering throughout these traditions.

Now only '*Seven Loaves and a Few Small Fishes*' to Feed '*Four Thousand*' and Queen Helen's '*Famine-Relief*' Activities

More interesting even than this, the whole episode from Mark 6:32–44 and Matthew 14:15–21 is repeated a chapter or two later in Mark 8:4–9 and Matthew 15:33–38, where the number '*seven*' will begin to take on its definitive signification (in fact, a third version, as we shall see, will occur in Mark 8:16–21 and Matthew 16:7–12 that will try to explain the discrepancies between the first and the second), in a direct follow-up to the curing of the Canaanite/Greek Syrophoenician woman's daughter.

Not surprisingly, this repetition is not to be found, in either John or Luke. In other words, the healing of this '*daughter*' in Mark and Matthew – also not to be found in John or Luke, at least not in the form of Mark and Matthew – is couched between two episodes basically saying or repeating the same thing only, as we shall now see, the figures are different. It is here that the curious mix-ups or overlaps between '*five*' and '*four thousand*' occur (*the number of* '*the Essenes*' in Josephus, *the followers who flee with James after Paul's attack* in the Pseudoclementines, and '*the number of the men who believed*' *after* '*Peter and John*' *were first arrested* in Acts 4:4 – in Acts 2:41, after '*Peter*''s earlier speech referring to '*the True Prophet*,' it was '*three thousand*'), which we have already identified as of the same genre as those in Rabbinic accounts of the '*daily*' *amounts of four–five hundred dinars required* '*to fill*' *Nakdimon's daughter Miriam's* (or *his* '*daughter-in-law*''s) '*perfume basket*.' Again, the figures are different, but only by a factor of ten, and the point is more or less the same.

It is immediately made clear in this second version of this picture of those '*fainting away*' from hunger and '*needing to be fed in the wilderness*' in Mark 8:2 and Matthew 15:33 – yet a third in Mark 8:16–21 and Matthew 16:7–12, as just remarked, will by way of explanation directly follow this second – that we are dealing with the same *Messianic* '*signs in the wilderness*,' also just underscored in John 2:18, 4:48, and 6:30 above and which Jesus discusses in detail in the intervening material in Mark 8:11–15 and Matthew 15:12-14 and 16:1–12. In the same manner as Jesus' attack on '*the Pharisees*' as '*Blind Guides*' and dietary regulations in Matthew 15:12-20 (both of which we shall directly analyze below) in the prelude to his encounter in Matthew 15:21–28 and Mark 7:24–37 with the '*Greek Syrophoenician*'/'*Canaanite woman's daughter*'; these second and third '*signs from Heaven*'/'*feeding*'/'*filling*' episodes occur in the context of an attack in Matthew 16:6 (reprised in Matthew 16:11–12) on what Jesus now refers to as, playing on the '*loaves of bread*' motif, '*the leaven of the Pharisees and Sadducees*' – in Mark 8:15, '*the leaven of the Pharisees and the leaven of Herod*'!

It is these same '*signs and wonders*,' about which Josephus becomes so agitated in his condemnations of those he calls '*Impostors*' and '*miracle-workers*' above who, as we saw, were '*showing the People the signs of their impending freedom*' or – depending on which of his two works one is quoting – '*the signs of their Redemption*' and whom, he considered, '*more dangerous even than the Revolutionaries*' (or '*Innovators*' – an alternate, perhaps more accurate, translation). As we have seen as well – even this '*freedom*,' Paul much abuses and allegorizes into something anti-Mosaic, turning it against those he euphemistically refers to in 1 Corinthians 8:7–13 as '*having scruples*' or '*with conscience*' – his code, it will be recalled, for '*observing the Law*.'

It should also be appreciated that all these '*feeding*' episodes and any other ones evoking '*barley*,' '*wheat*,' or '*grain*' usually reflect to some degree the celebrated '*famine relief*' efforts of Queen Helen of Adiabene (in Josephus, for instance, grouped together – as we have seen above – with the performance of just such a miraculous 'sign' or 'wonder,' that is, 'parting the Jordan River in reverse' – by the curious character he denotes only as 'Theudas'[49]), who sent her 'treasury agents' to buy grain for Jerusalem to places as far away as 'Egypt and Cyprus.'[50] Activities such as these are, in turn, reflected in Paul and Barnabas' 'Antioch' activities in Acts 11:28–30 and 12:25, where 'Christians' were 'first called Christians' (11:26).[51]

Of course, Acts promises to tell us this story of Paul and Barnabas' 'famine relief' mission but, in the space between these two notices, does nothing of the kind. However this may be, the interesting thing is that Acts follows up its original notice about 'all the Disciples deciding to send relief to the brothers dwelling in Judea' (also referred to as 'the Elders'/'Pres-byterous' – note the parallel, too, here with those 'dwelling' in 'the Land of Judah' in the Damascus Document above[52]) 'by the hand of Barnabas and Saul' in 11:29–30 with the note about 'Herod the King' beheading 'James the brother of John' in 12:1–2 (i.e., executed him 'with the sword').

Of course too, as already to some extent remarked, if we follow Jose-phus' sequencing, what the author of Acts probably originally overwrote here was 'Judas the brother of James,' not 'James the brother of John' – or rather even, 'Theudas' (elsewhere, as we have already also suggested, 'Thad-daeus'), the delineation of whose 'signs' in leading the People out in the wilderness comes in Josephus in between his two notices about 'the Famine' and the undying fame of Queen Helen of Adiabene's 'famine relief' activities.[54]

In Mark 8:5–6 and Matthew 15:34–35, however, the picture of 'five loaves and two fishes' of the first 'feeding' episode (of course, childishly mythologized so as to appeal to the reader's grossest credulity) disappear in favor of their sum, that is, 'seven loaves and a few little fishes' (in Mark 8:5–6, only 'seven loaves,' Matthew 15:34–36's 'and a few little fishes' – note the incidence of the adjective 'little' – having already dropped away!). Of course, in Matthew 15:37/Mark 8:8, after 'the Multitude' or 'the Many' had eaten 'and were filled' (once more, the 'satiation'/'sated' imagery of all the earlier episodes!); there is the matter again of 'the overflow' or 'remainder' of all the 'fragments' or 'broken pieces' which – instead of the 'twelve handbas-kets full' of the earlier delineation (Matthew 14:20/Mark 6:43) – are now reckoned as 'seven handbaskets full' (Matthew 15:37/Mark 8:8 – again note the allusion to 'full'), evidently absorbing by a kind of refraction the number 'seven' from the quantification 'seven loaves' just preceding it.

This last, as we have already explained, patently corresponds to the 'overflow' in the Nakdimon story of his 'twelve cisterns filled to overflowing,' even more which, in a twist that only a Talmudic mind would appreciate, Nakdimon *then tries to resell back to the 'lord'* or *'master.'* To be sure, in all four Gospels previously, this was *'twelve baskets filled with broken pieces'* (Matthew 14:20/Mark 6:43/Luke 9:17/and John 6:13, the latter adding *'from the five barley loaves'*) and it will be *'twelve'* again when the third version in Mark 8:19 makes the final reconciliation and recapitulation of all these materials!

In the Nakdimon story, it will be recalled, it was, when the *'lord' hesitated to repay the surety of 'twelve talents of silver,'* that Nakdimon (like *'Joshua'* – in other contexts, *'Jesus'*) *made the sun reappear after it had already set*, because of which he allegedly received his *nom à clef 'Nakdimon,'* meaning *'Shining Through.'* But more significant even than this – just like *'those who went to Ben Kalba Sabuʿa's door hungry as a dog and went away filled,'* the *'Poor man Lazarus wanting to be filled from the scraps that fell from the Rich man's table'* and, still more germane at this point perhaps, *'the children who should first be filled'* before *'the dogs under the table'* in the *'Greek 'Syrophoenician woman's daughter'* episode – Jesus is asked in the matter now of the *'seven handbaskets full'* (as opposed to *'twelve handbaskets full'* previously), *could all these 'be filled'* or *'satisfied'* (Mark 8:4/Matthew 15:33)? In both Gospels, as we saw, the right answer is given – this time by the narrator – *'and they did eat and were satiated'* or *'filled'* (Mark 8:8/Matthew 15:37).

For good measure both episodes are then, as just remarked, *recapitulated yet a third time* – though here the ostensible venue of the action is *'on a boat'* going across the Sea of Galilee from *'Dalmanutha'* to *'Bethsaida'* in Mark; in Matthew, only somewhere called *'the borders of Magdala'*[54] – because *'they had forgotten to take the bread'*! (Matthew 16:5–11/Mark 8:17–21). But the whole point is obviously to reconcile the two earlier versions in some way (that is, the ones in Matthew 14:13–23/Mark 6:30–46 and Matthew 15:32–38/Mark 8:1–9, leading up to the harmonization of the third); so one has the clear indication in both Gospels that the narrator is not only well aware of the contradictions, but views all three episodes as part of a single whole.

Now both quantities for the number of those fed are cited, *'five thousand'* and *'four thousand'* (Matthew 16:9–10 and Mark 8:19–20), but after some complicated number crunching – calisthenics might be more accurate – Mark, in particular, finally comes up with *'the twelve handbaskets full of broken pieces'* for the number *'taken up'* or *'filled,'* which was the original of all four Gospels in the first place – corresponding, of course, to *Nakdimon's 'twelve cisterns'* or *'water pools,'* with which we began the whole excursus. Nor is the whole complex unrelated, as we shall see, to both Helen of Adiabene's and Paul and Barnabas' *'famine-relief'* efforts.

For its part, Matthew 16:11–12 satisfies itself – since its main interest is the continuation of the attack on '*the leaven of the Pharisees and Sadducees*' – to speak portentously only about the more general '*bread*' and its '*leaven*.' Here 'Jesus' speaks to his followers like some divine '*Dionysus*,' '*Asclepius*,' or '*Apollo*' come down to sort out their problems. After warning about '*the leaven of the Pharisees and the leaven of the Herodians*' above (Mark 8:15 – in Matthew, just alluded to, this changes to '*the leaven of the Pharisees and Sadducees*'), both have 'Jesus' questioning '*his Disciples*,' '*Do you yet not perceive*' or '*understand*' (Matthew 16:9/Mark 8:17 and 21 – I hope we do) – Matthew 16:10 then having its 'Jesus' manfully trying to summarize the whole convoluted issue of the numbers as follows:

> *Do you not yet perceive, nor remember* (in Mark 8:17 as in Matthew 16:5 addressed to '*the Disciples*,' but – more in the manner of the language of the Qumran Damascus Document – this is: '*nor understand? Have you hardened your hearts*'[55]) *the five loaves and the five thousand and how many handbaskets you took and the seven loaves and the four thousand and how many handbaskets you took?*

In the end, as just remarked, it is left to Mark 8:19 to come up with the right answer: '*They said to him, "Twelve"*'!

If we now add to this the '*two hundred dinars*' given by Mark 6:37 – reprised, as we saw, in John 6:7 where it was put, not surprisingly, into the mouth of the always useful '*Philip*' (the hero of Acts 8:26–39's '*Ethiopian Queen's eunuch*' conversion episode) – we basically have all the numbers and their multiples or variations from the Talmudic Nakdimon/Boethus/and their daughters/daughters-in-law traditions – the '*seven*'s, for instance, having to do with the three '*seven*'- year, temporary Nazirite-style penances put upon Queen Helen of Adiabene by the Rabbis. It is, also, always useful to again remark that the variation of the '*loaves*' (whatever the final number), as opposed to '*the twelve baskets full of fragments*' simply corresponds to the addition of the element of the '*twelve talents of silver*' over and above the '*twelve water cisterns*' in the Nakdimon miracle-stories.

Nor is any of this, finally, to say anything of Nakdimon and his colleagues' '*twenty-one*' or '*twenty-two years*' of grain-storage activity *to relieve the famine in Jerusalem* – though actually it does. We have already explained that this '*twenty-one years*' in Rabbinic tradition reflects, in turn, the three successive seven-year Nazirite oath-style penances – just remarked above – supposedly (and curiously) placed upon Queen Helen of Adiabene by the Rabbis for reasons which were unclear, but very likely having to do with adultery or some such similar issue (therefore her interest in having the passage on the *'adulterous woman'* from Numbers 5:13–31 – itself followed by the one on *'Nazirite oaths'* in Numbers 6:1-21 – placed in an expensive plaque of gold leaf on a wall of the Temple courtyard[56]).

But we have just seen in these various *'fainting of hunger in the wilderness'* and *'longing to be filled'*/*'needing to be fed'* descriptions in the Gospels (poeticized allusions, obviously, to a situation requiring *'famine relief'*); the constant reiteration of the number *'seven'* in the *'seven baskets full of fragments'* and *'the seven loaves'* valuations, to say nothing of the *'five loaves and two fishes,'* from which *'they all ate and were satisfied'* in Mark 8:4-8 and pars. Compare this with the Rabbinic *'Ben Kalba Sabuᶜa'* tradition, a name in itself having either to do with *'dogs,'* *'immersion,'* or *'being satiated'* or *'filled,'* and how they *'came to his door hungry as a dog and went away filled.'*

Can anyone really doubt that those initially responsible for these traditions in the Gospels, such as they are – and I use the expression *'tradition'* charitably – knew the truth about what was going on in Palestine in this period and the real issues actually being debated there, but rather substituted these often nonsensical and sometimes even ridiculous miracle tales that so much appeal to the naive and credulous, not only at that time but, it would seem, at all times and in all places since? *'The Truth,'* as one might refer to it, really *'will* – to use the words of John 8:32 – *set you free'* and, in a very real sense, it has to do with these *more Revolutionary, Messianic heroes* and *Movements,* themselves probably connected in some manner to the activities of Queen Helen of Adiabene and her descendants – *new converts to Judaism far more 'zealous'* (as we have been seeing) *than any 'Herodian' ones.*

'Eating with Unwashed Hands Do not Defile the Man' and *'Making all Foods Clean'*

One last point that should at this juncture perhaps be made. The encounter with the unnamed *'Cananaean'*/*'Syrophoenician woman,'* out of whose *'daughter'* Jesus *'casts an unclean spirit'* or *'demon'* (in Acts 8:27, the code will no longer be *'Cananaean'* but now *'the Ethiopian Queen Kandakes,'* *'the treasury agent'* of whom, naturally enough – playing on the whole *'zealotry'*/*'Sicarii'* theme – was a *'eunuch'*[57]), is also preceded in Mark 7:1-23 (very prolix for Mark, usually the most compressed of the Gospels) and somewhat less so in Matthew 15:1–20 by the pro-Pauline polemics – in Mark 7:6–7 and Matthew 15:9 quoting Isaiah 29:13, having to do with *'teaching as doctrines the commandments of men.'*

This is a very important allusion and plays off the critique of *'the Enemy'* Paul, mirrored in Galatians 1:10–11's *'seeking to please men'* – and even before this in 1:1, where Paul makes the claim of being *'an Apostle not through men or of man.'* This is also true of Galatians 4:16, just alluded to above, where – attacking *'the Zealots'* in 4:17–18 (*'zeloute'/'zelouson'*) – Paul asks unctuously whether it was *'by speaking the Truth to you, your Enemy have I become?'* As already described, too, this reverses James 4:4 to just the opposite effect and also, by playing off the *Abraham as 'Friend of God'* motif in James 2:23 before that, signaling the true origin of *'the Enemy of God'* designation. James reads: *'by making yourself a friend of man you turn yourself* (or *'transform yourself*) *into an Enemy of God.'*

Furthermore and even perhaps more germane, these polemics in Mark 7:1–23 and Matthew 15:1–20 actually evoke the famous Talmudic Tractate, *Pirke Abbot* (*The Traditions of the Fathers* which, as we have already seen, has as its variation the *ARN* or *The Fathers According to Rabbi Nathan*) – here in Mark 7:3–5 and Matthew 15:2, *'The Traditions of the Elders.'* This designation *'Elders'* or *'Presbyteron'* is used, as we have seen, at various junctures in the Gospels and the Book of Acts and is the actual designation for James' *'Jerusalem Community'* in both Acts 21:18 and the Pseudoclementine *Homilies* above.[58] In perhaps the most convoluted reasoning we have yet encountered in our discussion, these polemics also invoke the Mosaic Commandment, *'Honor your father and your mother'* (Mark 7:10/Matthew 15:4) and, in doing so, leave no doubt that we are, in fact, dealing – as we shall see – with *'the Fathers.'* Just as importantly, in Mark 7:1–5 (to some degree paralleled in Matthew 15:1–4 and 12), *'the Pharisees'* are invoked as well – three times in five lines! As we have several times had cause to remark, this is an expression that often acts as a *'blind'* for those of the *'Jamesian'* persuasion within the early Church – as, for example, in Acts 15:5 at the renowned *'Jerusalem Council,'* the elusive *'some who believed'* of *'the sect of the Pharisees,'* who provoked the *'Council'* by their insistence *on 'circumcision'* and *'keeping the law of Moses'* (thus)!

Not only have we just encountered these same *'Pharisees'* in the two *'filling those fainting from hunger'*-signs episodes in both Mark 8:11–14 and Matthew 16:1–12 above, but in this run-up to the *'dogs eating of the crumbs falling from their master's table'* episode (in the variation in Luke 16:21, *'the Rich Man's table'*), the evocation of these same *'Pharisees'* is being used to attack those of the James school over the issue of *'table fellowship with Gentiles'* (an issue clearly being raised by Paul in Galatians 2:11–14 above). Moreover, there is the additional derivative attack, which now seems to us, if not bizarre, at least primitive, on the Jewish People as a whole – in this case, plainly, meant to include *'the Jerusalem Community'* of James, and others of this mindset – that '*eating with unwashed hands does not defile the man*' (Matthew 15:20/Mark 7:2–3).

Not only is this attack framed in terms of the charged words, '*keeping*,' '*breaking*,' and '*holding fast to*,' familiar in Dead Sea Scrolls' texts like the Damascus Document above,[59] but it derogates '*washing one's hands before eating*' only to the level of a '*tradition of men breaking the* (obviously '*Higher*') *Commandment of God*.' In the odd logic being displayed in this clearly pro-Pauline exposition, the meaning of this last would appear to be the Mosaic Commandment and that of humanity generally, to '*honor your father and your mother*' (Mark 7:8–9/Matthew 15:3 and 15:19).

The argument, which is childish and self-serving in the extreme, seems to turn on the point that, since one's parents might have '*eaten with unwashed hands*,' the Commandment not to do so – which the Gospel 'Jesus' is pictured as dismissing here merely as '*a Tradition of the Elders*' (meaning '*a tradition of men*' above) – would be contradicting the Higher Commandment (the one he is terming a '*Commandment of God*') *not to dishonour them*! This appears to be the gist of what seems a very tortured and largely unintelligible argument but, to judge by the time spent on it in Mark as well as Matthew, *clearly a pivotal one* as well. Still, should the reader feel it represents the true words of the 'Jesus,' he or she holds sacred or admires, then that person is welcome to do so. But the conclusion is ridiculous, namely '*don't wash your hands before eating*,' a scientifically-proven imprudence. As stated, the writer sees it as a striking example of retrospective pro-Pauline polemics (that is, '*Paulinization*') and, consequently, feels it to be a service historically-speaking to rescue 'Jesus' from this particular bit of prejudiced sophistry.

Furthermore, these polemics clearly also evoke Paul's attack on Peter in Galatians 2:13 above, in which Paul accuses him of '*hypocrisy*' ('*hypokrisei*'). In this regard, it is actually the nominative of this word in Greek ('*Hypokriton*') that Mark 7:6 portrays 'Jesus' as using in commencing his attack on '*the Pharisees and some of the Scribes*' (note the telltale allusion to '*some*' here and, equally pointedly as we shall see further below, in Matthew 15:1's '*Scribes and Pharisees from Jerusalem*'), '*Well did Isaiah prophesy concerning you Hypocrites as it is written* (in Isaiah 29:13), *this People honor Me with the lips but the heart is far away from Me*.'

Moreover, vocabulary such as '*lips*,' '*heart*,' and '*vain*'/'*vanity*' is absolutely fundamental to the Qumran lexicon, as it is some extent the Letter attributed to James.[60] In fact, as we have been trying to illustrate, to unravel these things takes quite a good deal of sophistication – which is why history before the discovery of the Dead Sea Scrolls has been so slow to do so (the key or '*Rosetta Stone*,' as it were, just not being available) – because the people who put them together were extremely clever and, if the truth were told, artful. Nor did we have the rudimentary data to deconstruct them. Now we do. Here, once again, the last word belongs to Plato who wished to bar just such persons from his ideal 'Republic,' that is, the people who spun these kinds of 'mystery'-oriented miracle tales about the 'gods,' by which the average people lived, and in so doing , misled them.[61]

Both Mark 7:6–7 and Matthew 15:7–9 picture 'Jesus' as using this passage to attack the 'vanity' of those who 'teach as their doctrines the commandments of men,' meaning, 'the Traditions of the Elders' just mentioned in Mark 7:5 and Matthew 15:2 above. Not only is this clearly an attack on what in Rabbinic parlance would be called 'oral tradition,' but it turns around the parameters of Paul's debates with those of the 'Jamesian' school or, if one prefers, inverts their arguments turning them back against themselves.[62] Again, the meaning both the Gospels of Mark and Matthew are clearly ascribing to their 'Jesus' from the start here is that 'Hypocrites' of this kind, following 'the Tradition of the Elders,' are 'forcing people to wash their hands before eating,' something which most people nowadays, as just remarked, would consider as not only normal, but hygienic; however in Paul's inverted invective something Paul (to say nothing about 'Jesus') would obviously consider quite reprehensible.

In Galatians 2:13, as we just pointed out, Paul uses the abstract noun, 'hypocrisy' ('hypokrisei'), of this nominative 'Hypocrite,' to attack 'Peter' or 'Cephas,' as the case may be, in the context of referring to the proverbial 'some from James' who 'came down' from Jerusalem to Antioch, so often alluded to above. He even accuses Peter 'and the rest of the Jews' with him (sic) – including his erstwhile traveling companion 'Barnabas' (whoever he may have been) – in 2:13 of, not just propagating 'their hypokrisei' but 'not walking Upright' (another usage basic to the Community Rule at Qumran paralleled, too, in Acts 21:24 above in Paul's final confrontation with James[63]) and 'jointly dissembling' as well. The reason for this last, it will be recalled, is that prior to the 'coming' of these 'some from James' down to 'Antioch,'

He ('Cephas' or 'Peter')was eating with the Peoples (Ethnon – in the Scrolls, in addition to 'foreigners,' often a code or nom a clef for 'Herodians'[64]); but when they came, he drew back and separated himself (a 'Nazirite'-style usage evoked in somewhat parallel manner by Paul in the pivotal series of allusions in 2 Corinthians 6:17–7:1 above and, once again, a basic ideological concept of the Dead Sea Scrolls – in particular, in the Community Rule's exposition of the famous 'make a straight way in the wilderness' pericope from Isaiah 40:3) *for fear of those of the circumcision* (Galatians 2:12).[65]

This allusion to *'those of the circumcision'* is also intrinsic to Acts 11:2–3's description of how these same *'those of the circumcision'* complained that Peter *'ate with uncircumcised men'* (the *'table fellowship'* theme again coupled with the *'circumcision'* one). This came after Peter's *'heavenly tablecloth'* vision, in which he learned to call *'no man'* or *'no thing'* either *'profane or unclean'* (10:15 and 28), after which he promptly went to visit the house of the Roman Centurion Cornelius – described in Acts' own inimitable way, as we saw, as a *'Pious One and Righteous,' 'fearing'* and *'supplicating God continually'* (that is, in more familiar terminology, *'a God-Fearer'*), and *'esteemed by the whole Nation of the Jews' (sic)*, whose *'works were remembered before God'* (11:2 and 11:30 – this last, as we have seen as well, a set-piece along with several allusions to *'God-Fearers'* or *'Fearing God'* of the final exhortation in the Qumran Damascus Document too[66])!

This whole episode in Mark 7:1 and Matthew 15:1, as already alluded to, also begins with this same idea of *'the Pharisees and some of the Scribes coming down from Jerusalem'* (in Mark 8:15 and Matthew 16:6, it will be recalled, this allusion morphs into the polemical derogation of *'the leaven of the Pharisees and the leaven of Herod'* or *'the leaven of the Pharisees and Sadducees'*). Here the *'some of the scribes'* clearly corresponds to the *'some from James'* and *'those of the circumcision'* in Galatians 2:12 and Acts 11:2 above. Their complaint is now portrayed as being about *'seeing some* (the always telltale *'some'* again) *of his Disciples'* (again *'the Disciples'*) *eating with unwashed'* or *'polluted hands'* (Mark 7:2; in Matthew 15:1, this becomes *'not washing their hands when they eat bread'*).

But of course we have already seen that these same allusions to *'coming down from Jerusalem'* and *'circumcision'* recur in Acts 15:1's picture of events triggering the celebrated 'Jerusalem Council' above. Not only do they basically recapitulate the scenarios just highlighted in Acts 11:2 and Galatians 2:12 about the objections of the *'some'* or *'those of the circumcision'* to the Gospel, Paul was *'proclaiming among the Gentiles'* (compare with Paul's own words to this effect in Galatians 2:2); once again they are followed up, as we have seen, by allusion in Acts 15:2 – as in Mark 7:1 and Matthew 15:1 – to *'the Elders in Jerusalem' (Presbyterous)* and in 15:5, *'the Heresy of the Pharisees'* (*'Airesious'* – the use of which terminology already denotes a certain sectarianism), to say nothing of Peter's being, as usual, the first to speak, though here somewhat more conciliatorily than in previous speeches attributed to him and even though he had according to Acts 12:17–19 already fled the country with a presumable death sentence on his head.

Acts 15:1 reads – it will be recalled though it bears repeating –

And some, having come from Judea, were teaching (edidaskon – we have already seen the same usage in Mark/Matthew's Septuagint-based translation of Isaiah 29:13 above, which is a little more elaborate than the Masoretic[67]) the brothers that, unless you are circumcised, you cannot be saved.

Here the usage '*Judea*' is substituted for '*Jerusalem*' in Mark and Matthew above (in Acts 11:2 this is rather turned around and '*Peter*' goes '*up to Jerusalem*'), but this is made good by the mention of '*the Elders in Jerusalem*' in the very next line 15:2 and then again in 15:4. Even more importantly, the same allusion to '*teaching*' (*didaskontes/diduskalias*), being employed here, is repeated twice each in Mark 7:7 and Matthew 15:9 – presumably, just so we would not miss the point (we don't; we get it) and forms the basis of the whole polemic there. Therefore and in this manner, the whole circle of all these interconnected allusions is complete.

'*Spitting on the Tongue*,' '*Unstopping Ears*,' and '*Declaring all Things Clean*'

As in all of the previous episodes above, the denouement of this '*abolishing purity requirements*'/'*table fellowship*' episode in Mark 7 and Matthew 15, which sets the stage for the '*Canaanite*'/'*Greek Syrophoenician woman*'/'*dogs under the table*' encounter that follows in the same chapters and further legitimizes the Pauline Gentile Mission; once more has 'Jesus' in 7:17 *entering a* '*house*' (as he does yet again in Mark 7:24). In Mark 7:17, this is typically '*away from the multitude*' to rebuke '*the Disciples.*' In Matthew 15:15 there is no house[68] and the rebuke is – because of Galatians 2:11-14 – as per usual, *only to Peter*. Still, '*the multitude*' from Mark 7:17 (which probably should be read '*the Many*' or '*the Rabim*,' the term, as we have seen – unlike '*the Sons of Zadok*' – applied *to the rank and file at Qumran*) are the ones already portrayed earlier in Mark 7:14 and Matthew 15:10 as the ones being addressed by Jesus on the subject of '*pure foods*,' '*unwashed hands*,' '*Blind Guides*,' and '*Uprooted Plants*.'

In both Gospels, Jesus' discourse begins with the words, '*hear and understand*,' again seemingly playing off the opening exhortations of the Damascus Document at Qumran which read, significantly as we saw, '*hear, all you who know Righteousness, and understand*' (1.1) –

and now listen to me all who enter the Covenant ('the New Covenant in the Land of Damascus' demanding both 'purity' and 'separating the Holy from the profane') and I will unstop your ears (2.2).[69]

But in Mark 7:16 in the midst of Jesus' attack on *'the Tradition of the Elders'* and *'purifying all food'* preceding this, the same *'ears'* metaphor from Column Two of the Damascus Document, just reproduced above, actually appears, to wit, *'If anyone has ears, let him hear.'*

This is not the only place it appears in this episode. Mark's 'Jesus' repeats this in 8:18, in the midst of the third and harmonized version of *'the feeding of the four thousand'* episode: *'Having eyes, do you not see? Having ears, do you not hear'*? But Mark even goes further than this. It also appears in the nonsense material that intervenes in 7:32–37, following his version of *'the dogs under the table'* episode in 7:24–30, in the miracle that 'Jesus' is then pictured in 7:33–35 as doing in *'laying hands'* on a *deaf and dumb person, curing him*. For its part, Matthew 15:29–31 omits this and, at this point in 15:31, only depicts *'the Rabim'* as, once again, *'glorifying the God of Israel'* after, once again, having *'thrown down at his feet' the 'dumb,' 'maimed,' 'blind,'* and *'lame,'* they *'had with them,'* for him to cure.

These things also involve the process of *'unstopping someone's ears,'* but Mark now rather proceeds to dramatize it in the form of a deaf and dumb person *whose 'ears' will literally now be 'unstopped'* (7:32). This miracle – not specifically depicted in Matthew except by the more general allusion to their *'seeing the dumb speaking'* in 15:31 – takes place after Jesus *left* 'the borders of Tyre and Sidon' and, the unnamed Greek Syrophoenician woman's daughter, *'lying on the bed,' 'the demon having departed'* (7:30–31). Jesus then somehow *'came to the sea of Galilee'* from *'the borders of Tyre and Sidon'* (in the manner in which Philip, somewhat disembodiedly, in Acts 8:26-40 *gets to Caesarea after having taken the road from Jerusalem to Gaza*) – this, after going *'through the midst of the borders of the Decapolis,'* that is, on the other side of the Sea of Galilee and known to Gospel writers, as well as to the readers of Josephus, as another predominantly Gentile area![70]

In Mark, 'Jesus'' activity comes here, as we just saw, right before 8:1–9 and 14–21's second and third versions of Jesus' *'multiplication of the loaves'* miracle. So, not only is the performance of miracles on behalf of *'Gentiles'* – as for instance, the earlier *'Greek Syrophoenician woman's daughter'* – continued, but so obsessed is Mark with this metaphor from the Qumran Damascus Document, of *'unstopped ears'* and, in the process, trivializing it and reducing it to the level of banality; that he is now prepared to depict 'Jesus' as performing yet another miracle in a predominantly Gentile area – and this, despite the fact that in both 8:10–13 and Matthew 16:1–4 to follow, in response yet again to more *'Pharisee'* prodding (in Matthew, both *'Pharisee' and 'Sadducee'* prodding), he impatiently asserts:

Why does this generation seek a sign (the '*sign*' language again, but this time together with the language of '*seeking*' we shall see, in due course, to be so important to the eschatological scheme of the Damascus Document below[71] – in Matthew 16:4, '*this adulterous generation*')? *Verily I say unto you, there shall be no sign given unto this generation.*

What is this miracle? Why Mark 7:33–34 now depicts Jesus as '*unstopping the ears*' of '*a deaf man*' in the following manner:

Putting his fingers into his ears and having spit, (he) touched his tongue (thus) *and, looking up to Heaven* (in the manner of Stephen in Acts 7:26 and early Church depictions of the death of James), *he groaned and said* '*Ephphatha,*' *that is,* '*be opened*' (this is real Hellenistic magic, the language being Aramaic, but even explained and translated for the benefit of *the Greek audience*, certainly not the Hebrew), *and immediately his ears were unstopped*!

Need one say more?

However the reader might respond to the imbecility of the picture of this '*miracle*' – based, as we contend it is, on reducing serious allusions in the Damascus Document to the level of idiocy – to go back to Matthew 15:16: there the rebuke about '*being yet without understanding,*' as already remarked, *is directed at Peter alone not at* '*the Disciples.*' Notwithstanding, prior to this, after '*calling the Multitude*' or '*the Many to him*' (15:10, reprised in Mark 7:14), Jesus does actually address '*the Disciples*' in Matthew in 15:12 as well. There the reproof he gives '*the Disciples*' concerning staying away from '*the Pharisees*' and '*leaving them alone*' (in 16:6–12 later, as we saw, '*the leaven of the Pharisees*' repeated multiple times) – which includes the '*Blind Guides,*' '*planting,*' and '*uprooting*' allusions we have already called attention to above and shall do so further below – comes in the wake of his enunciation of the following famous doctrine:

Not that which enters the mouth defiles the man, but that which proceeds out of the mouth, this defiles the man (15:11 – in Mark 7:15, this changes into the more prolix and obviously derivative, '*There is nothing from without the man that going into him can defile him. Rather the things that proceed out of the man are those that defile him*').

This allusion to '*the Pharisees,*' the evocation of whom initiated the whole series of encounters right from the beginning of Mark 7:1 and Matthew 15:1, comes – as Matthew 15:12 now phrases it – because '*the Disciples*' reported to Jesus that '*the Pharisees were offended by what they heard him saying'* (the reader should appreciate, it would be so easy to read here, *'what they heard Paul saying'* – as, for example, *'John Mark'* evidently was in Acts 13:13 and 15:38 above when he *'withdrew from them in Pamphylia'*[72]). It must be reiterated that expressions like *'the Pharisees,'* regardless of their overt meaning in any other context, have a covert meaning as well and this is the key to understanding *'The New Testament Code'* such as it is. They – like *'the Scribes'/'some of the Scribes who came down from Jerusalem'* coupled with them in Matthew 15:1 and Mark 7:1 above – are, in this context in the Gospels, a stand-in for *'the James Community'* in Jerusalem. Not only did this *'Community'* insist on *'circumcision'*, but also its legal consequences, such as purity regulations that included measures of bodily hygiene like *'washing their hands'* that seem, in the picture Mark and Matthew are presenting, to so upset their 'Jesus' here.[73]

It is also perhaps not without relevance that an expression like *'Pharisees'* – *'Perushim'* in Hebrew – carries with it, too, the meaning of *'splitting away'* or *'separating themselves from,'* the implication being that, in some contexts, it can even be understood as *'heretics'* which, in fact, is one of the appositions Acts, applies to it in 15:5 above. Nor should the reader overlook the fact that Matthew's picture of 'Jesus' reproving the Pharisees follows his exhortation to *'the Many'/'the Rabim'* in 15:10 to *'hear and understand'* (in Mark 7:14, *'hear me all of you and understand'*) – a phrase, as we just saw, that has to be seen as comparable to CDi.1's: *'Now hear, all you who know Righteousness and understand the works of God.'* Matthew 15:14 also pictures 'Jesus' as calling these *'Pharisees,' 'Blind Guides'* (an allusion we shall presently show to be charged with significance) because of their complaints against his teaching that *'eating with unclean hands does not defile the man'* (15:20), as well as related matters concerning purity and dietary regulations, themselves having a bearing on the key issue in Galatians 2:11–14 above of *'table fellowship with Gentiles.'*[74]

It is at this point that 'Jesus' in Matthew 15:14 as well, then cautions *'his Disciples'* (none of this paralleled now in Mark) to *'leave them alone'* – the sense of which allusion will be of particular importance when it comes to discussing the exegesis of *'the Way in the wilderness'* of Isaiah 40:3 in the Community Rule below. Before doing so, however, it would be well to point out that even the line in Matthew 15:19, preceding 15:20 on *'eating with unclean hands not defiling the man'* just cited and echoed in Mark 7:21–23, enumerates *'the things which proceed out of the mouth'* (thereby, according to the discourse being attributed here to 'Jesus,' *'coming forth out of the heart'* and, most famously, therefore *'defiling the man'*) as: *'Evil thoughts, murders, adulteries, fornications, thefts, lies, blasphemies – these are the things that defile the man'* (Mark 7:22 adds *'greedy desires,*

Wickednesses, deceit, lustful desires, an Evil eye, pride, and foolishness').

But this catalogue of *'Evil'* inclinations almost precisely reprises one of the most famous passages in the Community Rule from Qumran as well – *'the Two Ways'*: *'the Ways of Darkness'* and *'the Ways of 'Light.'* In this document, *'the Spirit of Evil' / 'Ungodliness'* or *'of Darkness'* is depicted even more lengthily as:

> *greediness of soul, stumbling hands in the Service of Righteousness* (the comparison of this with Paul's attack in 2 Corinthians 11:15 above on the 'False Apostles' who *'transform themselves into Servants of Righteousness'* should not be hard to appreciate), *Wickedness and Lying, pride and proudness of heart, duplicitousness and deceitfulness, cruelty, Evil temper* (there is a lot of Paul in this – to say nothing of Mark 7:21–23 above), *impatience, foolishness, and zeal for lustfulness* (the opposite, of course, of proper *'zeal'* – *'zeal for the Law'* or *'zeal for the Judgements of Righteousness,'* as it is expressed in the Hymns from Qumran[75]), *works of Abomination in a spirit of fornication, and ways of uncleanness in the Service of pollution* (now we are getting into it – as opposed to the proper *'Service of Righteousness'* of *'true'* Apostles above, all issues of *'table service,'* for instance, aside), *a Tongue full of blasphemies* (the *'Tongue'* imagery of the Letter of James[76]), *blindness of eye and dullness of ear* (this, too, momentarily reappearing in the Gospel episode we shall now describe), *stiffness of neck and hardness of heart* (as will this) *in order to walk in all the Ways of Darkness and Evil inclination.*[77]

'Blind Guides,' the Qumran 'Maschil,' and 'Walking in the Way of Perfection'

This is quite a catalogue, but the parallels with Matthew and Mark do not stop here. Even the allusion to *'Blind Guides,'* to say nothing of *'leave them alone,'* which Matthew depicts Jesus as applying to *'the Pharisees,'* actually seems to parody the pivotal character evoked at Qumran (in particular, in the Community Rule again, but also in the Hymns), *'the Maschil'* or *'the Guide.'* He is defined, just like *'the Teacher of Righteousness'*), as instructing *'the Many'* in the Ways of Righteousness.[78]

In the Community Rule this *'Maschil'* or *'Guide'* is pictured, *inter alia*, as *'doing the will of God'* (that is, *'being a Doer'* not *'a Breaker'* in the manner of the recommendations in James 1:22–25 – nor should one forget, in this regard as well, all the *'signs'* or *'miracles,'* 'Jesus' is depicted as *'doing,'* in John 2:11, 2:23, 6:2, 6:14, etc.) and

> *studying all the Wisdom that has been discovered from age to age,' to separate* (the

language of 'separation' again, just evoked above in the 'leave them alone' allusion) and evaluate the Sons of the Righteous One (here, the usage really is 'the Sons of the Righteous One' or 'the Zaddik,' not the more usual Qumran and New Testament 'Sons of Righteousness' – in Hebrew, 'Zedek,' without the definite article) according to their spirit (this harks back to the 'Two Spirits' passage just elaborated above as well, but it is also a usage that will reappear in Paul's 1 Corinthians 2:10–15 on 'communicating spiritual things spiritually') and fortify (another crucial usage at Qumran, paralleled in known imageries connected to the person of James[79]) the Elect of the Age according to His will as He commanded and, thereby, to do His Judgement (once more the 'Jamesian' emphasis on 'doing,' we have been emphasizing so constantly above) on every man according to His spirit.[80]

This does begin to become New Testament-like. Not only does it hark back to the 'Two Spirits,' with which we began this discussion, and Paul's 'knowing the things of man according to the spirit of man which is in him' of 1 Corinthians 2:11–15 just remarked above; but this description of 'the Guide' in the Community Rule then goes on to actually evoke two allusions, 'clean hands' and 'not arguing with the Sons of the Pit' – in other words, the 'leave them alone,' in fact, just encountered in passages from Matthew 15:14 and to a certain extent in Mark 7:8 above (the latter to be sure not quite in the same context); and, perhaps even more strikingly, yet another – the third (as just remarked as well), 'the Pit,' an allusion known throughout the Dead Sea Scrolls and which we shall presently encounter in Jesus' further disparagement of these 'Blind Guides' as we proceed:

(The Maschil shall allow) each man to draw near according to the cleanness of his hands (here, the 'hands' allusion) and his wisdom and, thus, shall be his love together with his hate. Nor should he admonish or argue with the Sons of the Pit (here again Jesus' directive to 'the Disciples' in Matthew 15:12–14, just highlighted above a propos of 'the Pharisees,' to 'leave them be').

Furthermore, 'the Guide' or 'Maschil' is commanded in this telling concluding exhortation of the Community Rule to rather:

conceal the counsel of the Torah (that is, 'the Law') from the Men of Evil ('the Men of the Pit' or 'Ungodly' above), confirming the Knowledge of the Truth and Righteous Judgement to the Elect of the Way ('the Elect' is, of course, a very widespread and important terminology at Qumran, as is 'the Way'[81])... comforting them with Knowledge, thereby guiding them in the Mysteries of the Marvelous Truth...,that is, to walk in Perfection each with his neighbor.[82]

We shall hear more about all these concepts presently.

The *'walking in Perfection'* part of this last allusion is also clearly part of Paul's Qumran-style instructions in 2 Corinthians 6:15–7:1 which, it will be recalled, not only refer to *'Beliar,'* compare *'Light with Darkness,'* *'the Temple of God with idols'* and *'Righteousness to law-breaking,'* but also include that command: *'Therefore, come out from among them and be separated,'* *'touching no unclean thing,'*

> *making ourselves clean from every defilement of the flesh and spirit, Perfecting Holiness in the fear of God'* (paralleling allusions such as the words of Matthew 5:48's 'Jesus' in *'the Sermon on the Mount,'* *'be Perfect as your Father in Heaven is Perfect'* and *'fearing God'* and *'God-Fearers,'* as we saw, being fundamental conceptualities at the end of the final exhortation of the Qumran Damascus Document[83]).

The Community Rule's *'walking in Perfection, each with his neighbor'* is easily recognizable as the *'loving your neighbor as yourself'* – called in James 2:8: *'the Royal Law according to the Scripture'* – the second of the two *'All Righteousness'* Commandments (*'Piety'/'Hesed,'* that is, *'Righteousness'/'Zedek'*), the first being *'loving God,'* which we shall momentarily also encounter below and present too – as already indicated as well – in James 2:5 on *'the Kingdom (God) promised to those who love Him.'*[84]

Of perhaps even more significance, this leads directly into the second citation of Isaiah 40:3's *'preparing a Straight Way in the wilderness'* passage:

> *For this is the time of the preparation of the Way in the wilderness. Therefore he* (*'the Maschil'* – in Matthew above, Jesus' *'Blind Guide'*) *should guide them in all that has been revealed that they should do in this Time* (n.b., again, the pivotal emphasis on *'doing'*) *to separate* (here again too, the Nazirite-like directive to *'come out from among them and be separate,'* just enunciated by Paul in 2 Corinthians 6:17 as well) *from any man who has not turned aside his Way from all Evil* (including, of course, *from these 'Sons of the Pit,'* just alluded to above as well).

To further demonstrate the interconnectedness of these kinds of these kind of usages, the denotation *'the Sons of the Pit'* is immediately reprised in these climactic passages from the Community Rule:

> *These are the rules of the Way for the Guide in these Times* (presumably *'the Last Times'* of other Qumran documents and the Gospels): *Everlasting hatred for the Sons of the Pit in a spirit of secrecy, to leave them to their Riches*

(here the language of '*the Pit*' coupled with express allusions both to '*Riches*' and '*leaving them alone*' – nor is there any hint of the idea of '*loving your enemy*' in these passages – the opposite[85]) and *the suffering (ʿamal) of their hands, like the slave to his Ruler and the Meek before his Lord.*

Not only do we have the '*master*' and '*lord*' vocabulary here, but also again that of '*hands*' – this time in the sense of '*that which their own hands have wrought*' – the same '*hands*' presumably that were to remain '*unwashed*' when eating in 'Jesus'' crucial '*toilet bowl*' homily in both Matthew and Mark above. Furthermore, the implication of the whole simile embodied in this passage, would appear to involve '*the Judgement Day*,' since the Hebrew '*ʿamal*' – as in the all-important Isaiah 53:11 proof-text and the Qumran Habakkuk *Pesher*, seemingly like the Gospels dependent upon it – is eschatological and also part of the vocabulary here.[86] The conclusion of all this is quite extraordinary:

> *And he* (both '*the Maschil*' and the rank and file) *shall be as a man zealous for the Law* (now our '*Zealot*' vocabulary joined in an integral manner to the exposition of the '*making a straight way in the wilderness*' proof-text – the term here is actually '*Hok*'/'*Law*,' not '*Decree*' and certainly not, as in some translations, '*precept*'[87]), *whose Time will be the Day of Vengeance* (meaning, in this context, '*the Last Judgement*' but, once again, *without a touch of non-violence*[88]), *to do* (yet again, the vocabulary of '*doing*' we have underscored above as so intrinsic to the Letter of James and which we shall further encounter in the Habakkuk *Pesher* below) *all His will in all the work of his hands* ('*hands*' again [89])...*delighting in all the words of His mouth* (the '*mouth*' vocabulary of Jesus' '*what comes into the mouth*' or '*goes forth from the mouth*' above) *and in all His Kingdom as He commanded* (the '*Rechabite*' vocabulary of '*commanding*' – a noble thought).[90]

The reader should pay particular attention to all these usages, but especially: '*doing the will of God*'; '*separating the Sons of the Righteous One*' and '*not disputing with the Sons of the Pit*,' but '*leaving them to their Riches*' and '*the works of their hands*'; and finally '*doing all His will in all the work of his* ('*the Maschil*'s or the adept's) *hands*' and '*delighting in all the words of His mouth*.'

'*Every Plant shall be Uprooted*' and the Messianic '*Root of Planting*' Imagery

In conclusion, one should also remark that leading into this allusion to the Pharisees as 'Blind Guides' in Matthew 15:14, Jesus is pictured as evoking the 'plant' or 'planting' vocabulary that Paul also uses with regard to 'God's plantation' or 'growing place' and 'God's building' in 1 Corinthians 3:6's: 'I planted, Apollos watered, but God caused to grow.' In the writer's view this, too, plays off the Messianic 'plant' and 'planting' imagery at Qumran in general,[91] in particular, 'the Root of Planting' with which the Damascus Document follows up its opening imprecation to 'hear and understand.' This reads, as we have already partially seen, as follows:

> And in the Age of Wrath...He (God) *visited them and caused a Root of Planting to grow* (these are some of the same words Paul uses in 1 Corinthians 3:6–8 above) *from Israel and Aaron to inherit His Land* (Paul's 'field' or 'growing place' imagery, just cited in 1 Corinthians 3:9 above) *and to prosper on the good things of His Earth.*[92]

In Matthew 15:13–14 the preliminary characterization introducing Jesus' 'Leave them alone, they are 'Blind Guides'' reproof about 'the Pharisees' reads:

> But he answered, saying, 'Every plant which My Heavenly Father has not planted shall be uprooted'!

Of course the 'uprooting' or 'rooting up' language here is exactly the same as 'the Root of Planting' just encountered in these opening exhortation of the Damascus Document – the 'uprooting' playing off the 'Root of Planting' that God 'caused to grow'; and the 'Planting,' the 'Planting' part of the 'Root' imagery. Likewise, Paul's parallel 'Apollos planted, I watered, and God caused to grow' from 1 Corinthians 3:6 above, not only plays off, but is an actual *verbatim quotation* of the remainder of this all-important preliminary metaphor in the Damascus Document.

But in addition in these pivotal allusions in 1 Corinthians 3:6–11 to 'God's Plantation' and 'God's Building' – of which Paul himself is 'the architect' or 'builder' just as he was 'the gardener' or 'husbandman' in the previous few lines; Paul also uses the further imagery of 'laying the foundations,' widespread at Qumran – in particular, in both the Damascus Document and the Community Rule, but also in Hymns.[93]

In fact, these imageries are preceded in 1 Corinthians 2:4–6 by material in which Paul attacks 'the wisdom of men' and 'the wisdom of the age.' One should compare allusions such as these to the Community Rule (1QS 9.12–13)'s instructions to 'the Maschil' to:

Do the will of God (again, the *'doing'* vocabulary) *in accord with everything that has been revealed from age to age* and *study all the wisdom that has been discovered according to the law of that age.*

One can't get a much closer fit than this or, for that matter, the Damascus Document's *'the Root of Planting'* to Matthew's *'every plant which my Heavenly Father has not planted shall be uprooted.'*

Here too Paul evokes *'the perfect'* and *'their wisdom'* and speaks of *'the Rulers of this Age,'* another usage not so different from the allusion in the Community Rule to *'the Wisdom of God'* above (as opposed to *'human wisdom'*) *revealed as if 'in a Mystery'*[94] – *'Mysteries'* in the Community Rule having to do with *'walking Perfectly,'* *'the Rulers of the Age,'* and *'making a straight Way in the wilderness'* already fully cited above.[95]

Later, speaking of *'the reward each shall receive according to his own labor'* and attacking *'the words which human wisdom teaches,'* Paul rather evokes, in 1 Corinthians 2:13–14 above, as we just saw as well, concerning *'the words the Holy Spirit teaches'* and *'communicating spiritual things spiritually.'* The perspicacious reader will be able to discern counterparts to all these usages in just the material we have already quoted from column Nine of the Community Rule, defining the character and the function of *'the Guide'* above. This could partially, but not exhaustively, include *'doing Judgement on each man according to his spirit'* (the *'doing'* vocabulary yet again), *'leaving the Men of the Pit to their Riches and the work of their hands'* (meant eschatologically), *'being as a man zealous for the Law whose Time is the Day of Vengeance to do (God's) will in all work of his hands,'* and *'delighting in all that has been said by his mouth.'*

Even more telling, all these imageries that Paul uses in 1 Corinthians 3:9–14 evoking *'building,'* in particular, himself as *the 'wise architect,'* his Community as *'God's Building,'* and the *'laying the foundations'* and *'building up'* language, we have already encountered above, would appear to be very familiar to the author of the Habakkuk *Pesher* who uses the very same imagery of *'the architect'* and/or *'building up'* to attack its omnipresent adversary, *'the Man of Lies'* or *'Spouter of Lying'* as

building a worthless city upon blood and erecting an Assembly upon Lying (the *'Ecclesia'/'Church'* language of the New Testament) *for the sake of his Glory*[96] –

Here, once again, we have the language of *'Glory'* or *'glorying,'* we have been underscoring above and, in our view, and allusion to a Community like Paul's, *'built upon'* the idea of *'Communion with the blood of Christ.'*[97]

In addition to this, one should appreciate that in 1 Corinthians 2:7, preceding the above, Paul has just used the same language of '*the wisdom of God*,' '*Mystery*,' and of '*Glory*' when he asserts:

> But we speak the Wisdom of God in a Mystery which God has hidden and pre-ordained for our Glory before the Ages.

Here not only the same '*Glory*,' just alluded to in Column Ten of the Habakkuk *Pesher* above, but also '*the Ages*,' just encountered in 1QS 9.13 above, which is to say nothing, of course, of the language of '*Hidden*' and '*Mystery*' already several times underscored above as well.

Furthermore, the idea of '*God's Building*,' '*God's House*,' or '*God's Temple*' – all more or less synonymous in Hebrew – which Paul goes on to apply in 1 Corinthians 3:9–17 to his new '*Gentile Christian*' Community, is nothing less than the imagery of '*House of the Torah*,' used throughout the Damascus Document to describe '*the Community*' it is addressing in its final exhortative above – not to mention '*the House of Faith God built*' earlier '*for them*' in Column Three of the Damascus Document (leading up to the decisive exposition of '*the Sons of Zadok*' proof-text from Ezekiel 44:15), '*the likes of which never stood from ancient times until now*.'[98]

Neither is this to say anything about the allusions to '*the Men of Perfect Holiness*' or '*the Perfection of Holiness*,' leading into the two evocations of '*the House of the Torah*' in the last Column of this exhortative (Column Twenty of the Cairo *Genizah* version) or '*those fearing God*' ('*the God-Fearers*') or the '*Hesed*' ('*Grace*' or '*Piety*') God would show '*to the thousands of them that love Him*,' following it.[99] Not only is this last easily recognizable as the first part of the '*Hesed*'/'*Zedek*' dichotomy, the two '*Love*' Commandments we have frequently alluded to above; it is once more, of course, exactly equivalent to what Paul has just enunciated in 1 Corinthians 2:9 – phrasing this as '*the things which God has prepared for those that love Him*' – and the variation of both one finds in James 2:5, also spoken about earlier above, concerning how '*God chose the Poor*' ('*His Elect*' and '*Rich in Faith*' – *cf.* the allusion to '*House of Faith*' in CD/the Damascus Document 3.19 earlier as well) to be '*Heirs to the Kingdom which He promised to those who love Him*.'

The very next line in Matthew 15:14 continues the borrowing:

> They are Blind Guides leading the Blind and, if the Blind lead the Blind, both will fall into the Pit.

Here one has in both subject and predicate, the image of '*the Maschil*' just as in several of the passages quoted from the Qumran Community Rule above. Nor is this to say anything, once more, of yet another adumbration of the language of *'falling,'* we have already encountered throughout the numerous Gospel passages we have analyzed above.

But more importantly and combined with this is the language and imagery of '*the Pit,*' just underscored as well – in particular, that of '*the Sons of the Pit*' used to attack all the enemies of the Community including, presumably, *persons of the mindset of Paul.*[100] Even more to the point, we are again in the process of *one reversing the other*, that is, *someone using the very language of another person* and *turning it back on that other person to undermine him.* Here, note too, that in Matthew 15:14 it is both '*the Blind Guides*' and '*the Blind*' they lead who, metaphorically, *will fall into* '*the Pit*'!

Can anything be more cynical and derisive than this and can any of it be accidental? The author seriously doubts it. This is the reason for the extensive detail employed in trying to elucidate all these usages above. Indeed, this whole allusion at this point in Matthew, which seems innocuous enough, actually plays on yet another seemingly completely-unrelated passage. This concerns regulations governing the Sabbath in the Damascus Document as well, most of which are generally counter-indicated in the Gospels. In the process, Matthew 15:12-14 makes fun of and shows its 'Jesus'' contempt for it too, namely, *if a man's* '*beast falls into a pit on the Sabbath, he shall not lift it out.*'[101]

But even here, the borrowing does not stop. In the very next lines from this First Column of the Damascus Document, one comes upon, as we have already to some extent seen, the final linchpin of all this borrowing. This comes in the very introduction of the renowned '*Righteous Teacher*' himself – '*the Guide of all Guides,*' as it were. It reads in its entirety, following right after the allusion to '*God having visited them and caused a Root of Planting to grow*' and the words '*to inherit His Land and to prosper on the good things of His Earth,*' parts of which we have already quoted above:

And they were *like blind men groping for the Way* ('*the Way in the wilderness*' and, as we have seen, the name for early Christianity in Palestine as recorded in Acts on at least three different occasions – more impressive '*internal*' as opposed to '*external*' evidence for the ambience of material such as this[102]) *for twenty years* (the time elapsed, perhaps, between the death of whomever '*the Messiah Jesus*' is supposed to represent and the elevation of James[103]). *And God considered their works, because they sought him with a whole heart* (again both the '*works*' and '*heart*' language, together now with a new imagery, we have already called attention to above, the '*seeking*' language of '*the Doresh ha-Torah*' or '*Seeker after the Torah*' we shall encounter further below) *and He raised up for them* (we shall encounter this '*raising up*' language, again below too, in our discussion of '*the raising up the Tabernacle of David which is fallen*' and *in a Land 'North' of 'Damascus*' later Columns of the Damascus Document and the like-minded exposition of Numbers 24:17's '*Star Prophecy*' in a compendium of pro-David proof-texts from Qumran known as '*the Florilegium*' – both to some extent interpreting these things in terms of '*raising up in Zion*' this '*Doresh ha-Torah*' *who would 'stand up' together with the Messiah 'to save Israel' in 'the Last Days'* [104]) *a Teacher of Righteousness to guide them in the Way of His heart* (though based on a slightly different root, the '*guiding*' language here is a variation of that of '*the Way*,' again combined with that of the '*heart*'). [105]

Of course, nothing could show the interconnectedness of all these imageries better than the appearance of this allusion to '*being like blind men*' and how they were to be '*guided by the Teacher of Righteousness*' in '*the Way*' of God's '*heart*,' following directly upon the one to '*planting*' the all-important Messianic '*Root*,' which God then '*caused to grow*' (the '*caused to grow*' here using the exact same language as the Messianic '*Branch of David*' we shall presently encounter in these other documents and contexts [106]) and preceding the equally pivotal introduction of the proverbial '*Teacher of Righteousness*' here in the Damascus Document as well.

The reason for all this borrowing, parody, and derogation has to have been that so original and impressive were these new ideas and usages, we now know from the discovery of the Dead Sea Scrolls, and so well versed were some of the original creators of much of the above-material from the Gospels, to say nothing of the material in Paul, that they were unable to resist repeatedly playing off them and, as I have been at pains to point out, reversing or inverting the actual original sense or meaning. This was, not only intentional and, in my view, political – but it also resulted from a kind of playful malevolence; that is, it gave the people who were originally responsible for creating the traditions upon which many of these documents are based – people, mostly probably in Rome, who had lost everything because of many of the ideas excerpted from the Scrolls above – a good deal of pleasure and they had a lot of fun doing so. That is to say, they really derived a lot of pleasure from shoving this version of '*the Messiah*' or '*the Saviour*' down the throats of the People who had originally created him.

11

The Dogs who Licked Poor
Lazarus' Sores

'Casting Unclean Spirits out' of Daughters and *'Toilet Bowl'* Issues again:
the Themes Migrate

At this point, it would be well to review the sequencing of these all-important passages from Matthew 14–16 and Mark 6–8 dealing with *'making all foods clean,'* the permissibility of activities in predominantly non-Jewish or Gentile areas, and the several *'signs'*-miracle performances, in particular ones bearing on *'famine relief,'* evidently a major historical event in the period from the 40s to the 60s CE which left, judging by reports about it in Josephus, Acts, and Talmudic literature – and their reflection as well in early Church accounts – a deep impression upon all considering it.

There are also, in the portrayal of these things, the reverberations of the *'casting out'/'casting down'* vocabulary sometimes used with regard to *'casting out unclean spirits'* (*ekballe*) or *'evil demons'* (*balein*), and sometimes in the polemics surrounding Paul's contention in 1 Corinthians 6:13 of *'food being for the belly and the belly for food'*; or, as Matthew 15:17 will ultimately portray 'Jesus' as so graphically expressing this:

> *Everything that enters the mouth, goes into the belly, and is cast out (ekballetai) down the toilet bowl.*

As these episodes progress, starting in Matthew 14:13–23 and Mark 6:30–46 with Jesus' first *'multiplication of the loaves'/'feeding the five thousand'* (in the manner of *'the religious frauds'* and *'pseudo-prophets'* in *'the wilderness'* in Josephus – in Luke 9:10, *'in a desert place of a city called Bethsaida;'* in John 6:1, *'on the other side of the Sea of Galilee, which is the Sea of Tiberius!'*), they move from *'the Pharisees and some of the scribes from Jerusalem'* (sic), holding to *'the Tradition of the Elders'* and objecting to *'his Disciples eating with unwashed hands'* (a euphemism, as should by now be clear, for complaints against persons *of the orientation of Paul's 'Gentile Mission'*) into the arguments over *'teaching the doctrines of men'* as opposed to '*the Commandments of God*' (Matthew 15:1–9 and Mark 7:1–14).

In Matthew 15:10, as we saw, these give way to the attacks on '*the Pharisees*' as '*Blind Guides*' (a euphemism at this point, if not elsewhere, for the Leadership of '*the Jerusalem Church*' of James the Just and/or the Leadership of the Community at Qumran, should one choose to regard it) and the contention that '*the Plant*,' which they made claims – in the Damascus Document at Qumran – *to have* '*planted*,' would '*be rooted up*.' The characterization of this '*Plant*' included the immediate further assertion that '*both*' the followers whom they '*led*' ('*the Blind*') and themselves, '*the Blind Guides*' or '*the Leaders*,' would then '*fall into*' the same '*Pit*' to which they so graphically consigned others (again in the Qumran Damascus Document).[1] This is about as near to a definitive proof that the authors of these passages in the Gospel of Matthew knew the Qumran Damascus Document as one could provide.

These attacks culminate in both Matthew and Mark in attacks on '*Peter*' or '*the Disciples*,' or both – attacks continuing the '*toilet bowl*' analogy but adding a new one, as per Paul's '*all things to me are lawful*' and '*I personally am free*' protestations in 1 Corinthians 6:12 and 9:1 and the point ultimately of the whole exercise – *these things Jesus said* '*making all foods clean*' (Mark 7:19, of course, gets the point. Matthew, atypically here, is a little more reticent) which all '*the Disciples*' and '*Peter*' are unable '*to perceive*' being '*yet*' or '*also without understanding*' (7:17/15:16).

To reinforce the matter of '*making all foods clean*' and the permissibility of activities in predominantly non-Jewish or Gentile areas, these episodes then move on to the curing of the '*Canaanite*'/'*Syrophoenician woman's daughter*' in the '*border areas of Tyre and Phoenicia*' and ultimately the one-two additional versions of Jesus' '*multiplication of the loaves*'/'*famine relief*' miracles, all basically utilizing the parameters of Nakdimon's '*famine relief*' efforts and his own great miracle of '*filling*' the lord's '*twelve cisterns to overflowing*.' In Matthew and Mark, this already worried-over curing of the '*Syrophoenician woman's daughter*' in the '*Tyre and Sidon borderlands*' is itself sandwiched between their respective versions of either the '*feeding the four*' to '*five thousand*' scenario (according to Mark 7:37, '*in the border areas of the Decapolis*') and their presentation of Jesus' polemics on '*unwashed hands*,' '*bodily purity*,' and the ritually neutral character of '*food going down the toilet bowl*.'[2]

At the risk of some repetition, it would be well to go over this episode one final time, just to get it absolutely clear, since only then can one complete the picture of the strange dislocations and vocabulary transferences taking place from Gospel to Gospel and from Rabbinic tradition to New Testament. Once again, Mark 7:24 begins his version of '*casting out'* of *'the unclean spirit'* (*'ekballe,'* the same *'casting out'* that Matthew 15:17, leading into this, used in its version of the *'the toilet bowl'* scenario – it should be kept in mind that, not only does Matthew 15:22's *'demon'* turn into Mark 7:25's *'unclean spirit,'* but in Mark 7:19 earlier, the food had only *'gone down the toilet drain'* and not *'been cast forth'* (*ekballetai*) as in Matthew 15:17 above) with the *pro forma* notice about how Jesus *entered 'a house'* – owner's name unspecified . A few lines earlier in Mark 7:17 it was Jesus entering *'into the house'* of another unnamed person, this time, *'away from the multitude'/'the Many,'* both of which *'entrance's* are missing from Matthew 15:15 and 15:22's version of the same events. Nor does Matthew 15:26 use Mark's *'ekballe'* (*'cast out'* or *'cast forth'*) in its picture of the exorcism but rather the slightly less virulent usage *'balein'* (*'cast'* or *'throw'* – no *'out,' 'forth,'* or *'down'* included).

In this *'house,' 'the Disciples'* prod him (Jesus) – paralleling *'Peter'*'s similar prodding in Matthew 15:15 – to expound *'the Parable,'* but which *'parable'* is intended is difficult to comprehend, since what follows is more in the nature of *'a simile'* or *'homily'* and not *'a parable.'* Be this as it may, 'Jesus' now provides the afore-referenced *'Parable,'* to wit, *'whatever goes into the man goes out into the toilet drain,'* the point of which according to Mark 7:19 was, as just underscored, *'making all foods clean.'* In 7:24, however, taking advantage of the issue of whose house 'Jesus' was staying in when the *'Greek woman, a Syrophoenician by Race came and fell down at this feet,'* Mark once again alludes to the *'Hidden'* ideology already called attention to above. He does so with the words – *'whose house, Jesus wanted no one to know, but it'* or *'he could not be hidden.'*

Before proceeding, it is worth noting the evocation of another such *'parable'* in *ARN* tradition, already alluded to above as well, which couples an allusion to being *'hidden'* with *'a parable'* centering on Rabbi Akiba's *'Poverty'* being a reproach to those *'claiming to be too Poor to study Torah.'* This *'Parable'* too, as we saw, was surrounded by allusions to *'casting down,' 'uprooting,'* the *'hidden being brought to light,'* and the additional motif of those pleading they *'could not study Torah on account of (their) little children,'* allusions not unsimilar to many we shall continue to encounter in this picture of Jesus *'casting the unclean spirit out of'* the Syrophoenician woman's daughter.[3]

Mark 7:25's description of this *'certain woman,'* as he terms her, *'whose little daughter had an unclean spirit'* (at this point, as we just saw, Matthew 15:22 prefers the language of her *'daughter being miserably possessed by a demon'*) is, once again, instructive too in view of the subject of *'cleanliness'* or *'uncleanliness'* – in *'the Parable'* that just preceded it – of what was or was not just *'cast'* or *'gone down into the toilet bowl.'* So is the language of 'casting out' with which Mark 7:26 begins its version of how the woman approached Jesus, i. e., 'she besought him to cast (ekballe) the demon out of her daughter.' (n.b., at this point, too, Mark, having already used the 'unclean spirit' allusion in 7:25 to describe her, now picks up Matthew's earlier 'demon' language as well).

Though we have already gone over most of this before, it is not without profit to repeat these transferals to show how such slight differences in vocabulary move from and are re-absorbed in one redaction or occurrence to another. In fact, the reason repetition of these motifs is helpful is that they show, curiously, that it is not so much the event itself that is so important to the various narrators, redactors, or artificers, but rather the use of a given expression, wording, or phraseology and finding a convenient context in which to employ it. To the modern mind this is – as it was, most probably, earlier as well – a rather incomprehensible way to proceed, which is why so few over the years have either grasped or bothered making an issue of it.

Of course, to make the circle of all these usages complete, Mark's 'let the children first be filled' and the Talmud's 'going away full' are likewise now making their appearances in Luke's 'a certain Rich man clothed in purple and fine linen' variation, but the connecting link between all of them should always be seen as the allusion to 'dog' or 'dogs.' We have already pointed out the reason why Mark 7:26's 'casting out'/'ekballe' allusion is missing from Matthew 15:22's initial version of the 'Cananaean woman''s request to Jesus – despite the fact that its variation does finally come into play in both versions of Jesus' proverbial response ultimately to both unnamed women's requests: 'It is not good to take the children's bread and cast (balein) it to the dogs' (n.b., again, always 'the dogs' motif – Mark 7:27/Matthew 15:26) – and this should by now be clear. The reason is that Matthew 15:17 used the word 'ekballetai' to characterize what Jesus had said a few lines earlier concerning what was 'cast out down the toilet bowl' – and, therefore, of no legally-efficacious import – whereas Mark 7:19 had not, only noting a little more prosaically, as we have seen, that it had 'gone out into the toilet drain'!

Of course Mark 7:27's otherwise fuller version of this all-important exchange with the Syrophoenician woman uses the more ideologically-charged expression 'sated' or 'filled' (again also missing, as already emphasized too, from Matthew 15:26 at this point) to introduce its version of 'not casting the children's bread to the dogs' – namely, 'Let the children first be filled.' On the other hand, both Gospels use the omnipresent 'came' or 'come' (Matthew three times – the second, in describing how 'the Disciples,' typically, 'came' to him and tried to get him to send the woman away *'because she was crying out after' them*; and the third, how the woman, *'having come, bowed down to him'* – 15:23 and 15:25), that is, in Matthew 15:22, for instance, the unnamed woman, *'having come out of the border areas of Tyre and Sidon, cried out to him'*; whereas in Mark 7:25, paralleling Matthew 15:25 just cited above, she simply *'came and fell at his feet'* which, even more importantly, evokes once again yet another favorite allusion, *'his feet'*! Of course in Luke 16:21's version of these materials, this meta-morphoses into *'even the dogs came and licked his feet'* – meaning *'Lazarus,'* not *'Jesus'*! – and the circle of these allusions spreads ever wider.

The rest of this encounter we have already largely analyzed. In Matthew 15:27 the woman, in uttering the celebrated *'even the little dogs eat of the crumbs which fall from their masters' table,'* incorporates the *'falling'* usage just employed in Mark 7:25's *'she fell at his feet'* – which is to say nothing of its evocation of the omnipresent *'lord'* or *'master'* motif from Column Nine of the Community Rule, Gospel parables probably not unrelated to it, and the Talmudic story about Nakdimon's *'master's water cisterns'* – perhaps coincidental, perhaps not. For its part, Mark 7:28's version of the unnamed woman's proverbial retort to Jesus is then framed – somewhat differently than Matthew 15:27's above, no doubt because, in the odd mindset of its authors or redactors, the *'falling'/'fell'* usage had already been employed two lines previously in her *'falling at his feet'* – in terms of the equally celebrated,

> and she answered, saying to him, *'Yea Lord, but even the little dogs under the table eat of the children's crumbs.'*

Not only is there no *'falling'* allusion here at all, because Mark had just used it in the previous sentence to describe how the Greek Syrophoeni-cian woman *'fell at his (Jesus') feet'* (though there is an allusion to *'Lord'* should one choose to regard it); *'the crumbs'* now migrate, therefore, from the *'masters' table'* to *'the little dogs eating under the table'* and now they are *'the children's.'* Again there is *'the dogs'* allusion here, but the *'little'* from the *'little children'* of Gospel narrative generally and those in the Rabbinic *'Parable'* about Rabbi Akiba's *'Torah study'* (to say nothing of the Syro-phoenician woman's *'little daughter'* earlier), has migrated to the *'little dogs'*![4]

Of course, the *'under the table'* theme too, just as the *'coming'* one, will now migrate to Luke's version of the *'dogs'* (now normal size and not *'little'*) *'coming,'* not to *'eat the crumbs,'* but to lick the *'Poor Man Lazarus' sores'* – *'under the table.'* Again, it is worth keeping in mind that, just as Luke has no Canaanite/Greek Syrophoenician woman *'dogs'* episode, Mark and Matthew have no *'dogs licking Lazarus' sores'* episode – and John has no '*dogs*' episode at all!

'*Casting out Mary Magdalene's Seven Demons*' and '*Casting Down the Toilet Bowl*' Again

Moreover, these circuitous machinations do not end here. In other accounts, the woman out of whose daughter Jesus casts '*an unclean spirit*' or '*demon,*' as we have already suggested to some degree above, will transmogrify into '*Mary Magdalene out of whom he ('Jesus') cast seven demons*' (Luke 8:2 and Mark 16:9 – here it is not '*ekballe*' but '*ekbeblekai,*' together now with not one but '*seven demons*'!). Regarding this last and taking into account the persistent '*Tyre*' allusions in Mark and Matthew above, it is not completely unwarranted to identify yet another mutation in this circle of materials in the parallel represented by the portrait of Simon Magus' '*Queen,*' called – like '*the Queen of Adiabene*' – '*Helen*' in all early Church sources who is perhaps not totally unrelated to this '*Northern Syrian*' or '*Arabian Queen,*' whom we have had occasion to mention so frequently above and who is depicted in clearly hostile early Church sources as having, significantly, been picked up by Simon *in a brothel in Tyre*. Perhaps we can dismiss a certain amount of hyperbole here too.

The perspicacious reader will quickly recognize as well that the '*crumbs that fall from their masters' table*' of Matthew 15:27 now also migrate over to Luke 16:20. It is instructive too to recall that, in Luke 16:20–21's version of these events, '*the crumbs*' are rather those that now '*fall from the Rich man's table*' to '*a certain Poor Man named Lazarus*' – '*the Rich Man*' replacing Matthew 15:27's '*their masters,*' as we saw, though the '*falling*' in Matthew has nothing to do with anyone '*kissing*' or '*licking*' Jesus' '*feet.*'[5] However, now it is '*Lazarus,*' as repeatedly noted, who '*wants to be satisfied*' or '*filled from the crumbs which fell from the Rich Man's table*' and whose sores '*even the dogs came and licked,*' not the '*children should first be filled*' of Mark 7:27's further variation of it – again, it should be appreciated, none of this being the least bit historical, just a good deal of further word-play.

To go back to Matthew and Mark, so convinced is Jesus by the unnamed '*Canaanite woman*''s clever riposte – as if disagreements over '*purity*' issues of this kind could simply be solved by lighthearted and casual rhetorical give-and-take or one-upmanship – that he proceeds '*to cast unclean spirits*' *out of Gentiles* too in areas *outside of Palestine* proper (that is, in '*Tyre and Sidon*' and later even '*the Decapolis*'). The Pauline '*Gentile Mission,*' implicit in this depiction, is well served as is ideologically-speaking, where legal requirements are concerned, *the child-like simplicity of these 'little' people*, since that is really what is at stake in these episodes and this debate. Nor is this to say anything about the debate and resolution of the *'unclean'* foods issue that precedes and introduces it in both Gospels, now transformed into the patently trivializing and dissimulating one of *'possession by unclean spirits'* or *'demons.'* This is continually true of the *modus operandi* of the Gospels and probably just about every reference to *'unclean spirits'* or *'demons'* should be seen in this context

In this connection, too, one should pay particular attention to Paul's reference to *'the table'* in the Temple in the same breath as *'the table of demons'* in 1 Corinthians 10:21 above, implying an interconnection of sorts if one could actually understand, through all the dissimulation here, what was actually being said.[6] Not only does this come in continuation of his wrestling in 10:18–20 with the question of *'things sacrificed to idols'* (*'what then do I say, that an idol is anything or that which is sacrificed to an idol is anything?'*), it precedes his second evocation of his *'all things lawful being lawful for me'* pronouncement in 10:23, concluding in 10:25 with:

> Eat everything that is sold in the marketplace, in no way making inquiry on account of conscience (his euphemism, as we have seen, for having regard to or questions pertaining to *'the Torah'* or *'the Law'*).[7]

For its part Luke 8:2, lacking the Syrophoenician woman's daughter episode, attaches these *'unclean'* or *'Evil spirits,'* as we just mentioned, to its introduction of Mary Magdalene, *'out of whom seven demons had gone,'* and here we have the same conundrum – as in the case of the *'toilet bowl'* situation – only in Mark, anyhow, now reversed. As should be readily apparent, this last in Luke now combines Mark 7:19's *'going out,'* as in his *'going out down the toilet bowl,'* with Matthew 15:22's *'my daughter is miserably possessed by a demon.'*[8]

There is also just a suggestion in both of these descriptions – for whatever it's worth – of the language of Luke's *'Seven sons of Sceva'* episode in Acts 19:13–18, portrayed as *going around* (the *Diaspora* presumably) *exorcizing 'Evil spirits.'* Not only are they themselves, once again, referred to by the ubiquitous *'some,'* but so is the sub-class in Acts 19:13, to which they seem to have appertained, namely, *'some of the Jews wandering around exorcizing Evil spirits'*! It too, though, is clearly another nonsense episode paralleling Paul's encounter with *'Elymas Magus'* (*'Magician Magician'* – Simon *Magus*?) in Acts 13:8 in *'Cyprus'* earlier.

In the encounter with the clearly pseudonymous *'Seven sons of Sceva'* (himself characterized in 19:14 as *'a Jew'* and *'a High Priest'*!), though the locale is uncertain, it would appear to be *'Asia'* once again – the ubiquitous *'Jews from Asia'* who make trouble for Paul *'in the Temple,' 'stirring up the multitude'* who *'laid hands on'* Paul in Acts 21:27 thereafter? Nevertheless, it does appear to have just an element of truth underlying it, that is (aside from the telltale *'some'* attached to yet another use of *'doing'* in the phraseology, *'who were doing this,'* viz., *'Jews wandering around exorcizing Evil spirits in the Name of the Lord Jesus,'* i.e., *'the Lord Saviour'*), if one could substitute the words *'going around teaching the James position on table fellowship,' 'bodily purity,'* or *'dietary regulations'* for the words, *'exorcizing Evil spirits.'* Furthermore, it does draw on the overlap to the unsophisticated mind between the number *'Seven'* – *'Sheva^c'* (also meaning *'oath'* in Hebrew) – and *'Sceva'* in Greek transliteration, as certainly no *'High Priest'* was ever named *'Sceva'* in Hebrew!

Where the evocation of the number *'Seven'* is concerned, there is in it just a touch of the *'Seven Brothers'* story in 2 Maccabees (to say nothing of the *'Philip the Evangelist who was of the Seven'* and had *'four virgin daughters who were prophetesses'* in Acts 21:8–9 – sic!), parodied by a further nonsense episode in the Synoptics featuring an exchange – this time between *'Jesus'* and *'the Sadducees'* – over the frivolous issue of which brother, a woman who had married all *'Seven'* would *be considered married to after the Resurrection* (one says *'nonsense'* and *'frivolous'* here because *'the Sadducees'* purportedly did not believe in *'the Resurrection of the dead'* anyhow and this is an extremely childish view of what *'the Resurrection'* was supposed to have been all about – Matthew 22:25–33 and pars.).[9]

Be these things as they may, earlier in Luke 8:2–3 Mary Magdalene is part of a group also referred to, as we just saw, by the ubiquitous *'some'* usage again (in this case, *'some women'*), all portrayed as having *'been cured'* by Jesus *'of Evil spirits'* – this last the equivalent to the *'unclean spirit'* besetting the *'Syrophoenician woman's daughter'* in Mark 7:25 above. These included, as already observed, *'Susanna'* and *'Joanna the wife of Chuza, a steward of Herod.'* This last is reinforced by the episode in Acts 13:1, where Luke portrays, in an enumeration which also includes the expression *'some in Antioch,'* at least one *'Herodian'* among *'the prophets and teachers of the Church at Antioch.'* That being said, the implication of the first notice, anyhow, is that Luke, therefore, is picturing 'Jesus' as *being willing to 'cure' even Herodians.*[10] Furthermore, though Mary Magdalene and Joanna will reappear later in Luke's depiction of events at *'the empty tomb,' 'Susanna'* is never heard from again either in Luke or anywhere else for that matter (unless it be in the picture of her original biblical prototype).

Later Luke 24:10 groups Mary Magdalene and Joanna with another 'Mary' – this time, *'Mary (the mother) of James,'* all pointedly denoted in 24:10 once again as *'some.'* For Mark 16:1, the parallel trio is *'Mary Magdalene and Mary the mother of James and Salome'* – *'Salome'* here (whether in the genitive or nominative) clearly taking the place of '*Joanna*' – and it is now these, as in a number of other instances already sufficiently 'worried over' above, '*who bring perfumes*' or '*aromatics that they might come and anoint him.*' Once again we have the '*coming*' allusion coupled with the '*anointing*' one, but now we have two more '*Mary's coming to Jesus* to '*anoint him*' (living or dead, as in this case – it hardly matters).

While in Luke 24:10 it is this trio who report '*these things*' – meaning, *the empty tomb, the two Angels* '*in shiny white clothes,*' and *what they said* – '*to the Apostles*'; in Mark 16:5, as in Matthew 28:2, only one Angel '*clothed in a white robe*' is seen in the empty tomb. Of course Mark's version of such post-resurrection appearances is considered defective by most scholars. Still for Mark 16:9, Mary Magdalene alone, as we just saw, is – as in John 20:14–17, for whom there are (as in Luke 24:4) '*two Angels sitting in the tomb in white clothing*' (20:12, the complexity of these inter-relationships becoming legion) – the recipient of Jesus' first post-resurrection appearance. This she duly reports, as in John 20:18, '*to the Disciples*'; whereas in Matthew it is the two '*Mary's* who report the '*Angel of the Lord,*' '*with a gaze like lightning and his clothing white as snow,*' and the fact of *the empty tomb* to '*the Disciples*' (28:2–3). In Luke 24:4 and 10, it is '*two men*' – later identified as '*Angels*' – and now it is *the three women*, including '*Joanna and Mary (the mother) of James,*' making the report, this time, '*to the Apostles.*'

Of course for John, too, it is '*the Disciple whom Jesus loved*' who '*outruns Peter*' for the honor and is the '*first*' *to enter the empty tomb*, where he sees the linen cloths and the napkin for his head rolled up to one side – Mary still '*standing*' outside weeping – but no Angels (20:2–11). It was only, after this and '*the Disciples had gone home* (thus!), that Mary '*stooped down into the tomb*' and gets her vision of the '*two Angels in white*' and following this, as usual, *Jesus* '*standing*' *behind her* (n.b., '*the Standing One*' - ideology again). So in the end in John we have '*three*' people entering the tomb, but not the '*three*' reported in the Synoptics. For Matthew 28:7–8, it is only '*Mary Magdalene and the other Mary*' (whoever she may be – probably James' and, dare we say, Jesus' mother) who experience this and they are instructed to report this at one point, as just signaled, '*to the Disciples*' – and, at another (28:10), '*to my brothers*' – as Mary Magdalene is in John 20:17 – not, as in Luke 24:10, '*to the Apostles.*'

It is perhaps because of the nature of such a post-mortem encounter with Jesus that Mark 16:9 includes at this point Luke 8:2's earlier characterization of '*Mary Magdalene*' as having *been possessed by* '*seven demons.*' Instead, however, of '*going out of* her – as Luke and Mark 7:19's own picture of Jesus' words concerning what '*went out into the toilet bowl*' – now the '*seven demons*' are characterized, as we have already seen, as being '*cast out of her*' (*ekbeblekai*) by Jesus. The usage is, as already underscored as well, yet another variation of his own '*ekballe*' earlier in his version of the Greek Syrophoenician woman's request to Jesus '*to cast the demon out of her daughter*' (Mark 7:26) and the '*ekballetai*' in Matthew 15:17's version of the food '*cast out down the toilet drain*' excursus preceding this.

Mary Magdalene, Jairus' Daughter, the Woman with '*the Fountain of Blood*' and Jesus' '*Feet*' Again

Interestingly enough, the parallel at this point in Matthew 28:9 which, while ignoring the allusion in Mark to '*casting out*' vis-a-vis Jesus' treatment of Mary Magdalene's '*seven demons*,' once more picks up another important notation from this circle of related usages – that of *Jesus' 'feet.'* We shall continue our consideration of these sometimes repetitious allusions, because the mutual reverberations resound back and forth in so many different combinations and permutations that something edifying usually emerges from their analysis, even if only because of the slightly differing contexts with or perspectives from which they start.

As Matthew 28:9 puts this – now, as just underscored, with only two women: '*Mary Magdalene and the other Mary*' (presumably '*James' mother*' in Luke 24:10 since, in this manner, the narrative safely *avoids mentioning her relation to 'Jesus*'[11]) and like Mark 16:5, which probably derived from it, only one Angel '*whose face was as lightning and his clothing white as snow*':

> *Lo and behold Jesus met them…and they came to him, took hold of his feet* (note, still another allusion to '*coming to him*' combined again with '*his feet*'), *and worshipped him!*

So now we have two '*Mary*'s '*coming to*' Jesus and *falling at* '*his feet*' – not one as in John and Luke's '*Mary*,' '*Martha*,' and '*Lazarus*' scenarios – one called '*Mary Magdalene*' and the other '*Mary the mother of James and Salome*' (Mark 16:1 – or, should one consider it warranted, '*of Jesus*'). Elsewhere – as in Mark 15:47 – this '*Mary*' is called '*Mary the mother of Joses*' and, in Mark 15:40 earlier, '*Mary the mother of James the less and Joses*.' We have already treated to some extent in *James the Brother of Jesus* these multiple confusions and overlaps between '*mothers*,' '*brothers*,' and '*cousins*' of Jesus (including even the one presumably between '*Joses*' and '*Jesus*' himself) as the doctrine of the supernatural Christ gained momentum in the early Second Century and beyond.[12]

This allusion to '*falling at his feet*' is also reprised in Mark 7:25's picture of the '*Greek Syrophoenician*' woman (whom we have already connected to some extent to the picture of Mary Magdalene – to say nothing of Queen Helen of Adiabene) *'falling at his feet'* above. It is also reprised, as we have several times had cause to remark, in John 11:32's picture of Lazarus' sister *'Mary'* – after Jesus *'came'* to Bethany the second time – and how after *'coming'* to him, *she 'fell at his feet'* (*'come'* repeated about seven times in eight lines – not to mention a number of other times throughout the episode).[13]

But this same *'Mary'* had earlier in John 11:2 (repeated more dramatically in 12:3) had already *taken 'the litra of precious spikenard ointment and anointed Jesus' feet'* with it, *'the house being filled with the odor of the perfume.'* The same allusion to *'feet,'* it will be recalled, was replicated in Luke 10:38–42 above, but this time it was *'Mary sitting at Jesus' feet' while Martha complained about having to do 'so much serving.'* Again in this last, it should not be forgotten, there is the possible play in *Jesus' response to Martha's complaint over Mary's having 'left her alone to serve'* in Luke 10:42 (note here, too, the other variations on this in the *'leaving them'* and *'the Sons of the Pit alone'* allusions we have already considered in Matthew 15:14 above) on this *'(she) has chosen the good part,'* in the critique of *'the Lying Spouter'* and *'the Seekers after Smooth Things'* – *'the Pharisees'* and *'the Pauline Christians,'* as we have defined them – at the end of the First Column of the Cairo Damascus Document.[14]

These last were described in CD1.19, as should be recalled, in terms of *'choosing the fair neck'* (evidently meaning *'the good part'* or *'the easiest way'*) and connected to *'seeking Smooth Things'* and *'watching for breaks'* in the passage from Isaiah 30:10–13 being drawn on there. The reason the Damascus Document gives for applying this allusion (*'choosing the fair neck'*) to such persons is because *'they chose illusions,' 'condemning the Righteous and justifying the Wicked'* – the opposite, it should be appreciated, plainly of the proper *'Justification'* activity by *'the Sons of Zadok'* later in the same Document of *'justifying the Righteous and condemning the Wicked,'* *'transgressing the Covenant and breaking the Law.'*[15]

Nor is this to mention that the issue of these *'feet'* is so much a part of these Talmudic traditions, not only regarding the various daughters of these proverbial *'Rich Men,'* but also *'the Poor'* (concerning whom, in Gospel representations of conflicts between *'Jesus'* and *'Judas Iscariot'* or *'the Disciples,'* as we saw, *'Jesus'* allegedly asserts, *'you have with you always'*), who *'gather up the woollen garments that were laid down'* so the *'Rich'* Nakdimon's *'feet'* would not have to touch the ground. Again there is the motif of *'touching'* here, already variously underscored above in episodes involving the *'touching'* of both Jesus' and James' person, fringes, or clothes. Moreover this same *'touching'* theme, along with a number of other motifs, will again intrude into the incidents surrounding another character – this time, in the Synoptics – named '*Jairus*' and designated as '*a Ruler*' (compare with how John 3:1 designates '*Nicodemus*' above) or '*Ruler of the Synagogue,*' and yet another individual whose daughter will need to be cured (Matthew 9:18–26/Mark 5:21–43/Luke 8:40–56).

Here, too, in both Mark 5:22 and Luke 8:41, '*Jairus*' is described as '*falling at his (Jesus') feet.*'[16] This is interrupted by the '*coming*' of another in this endless series of unnamed women – this one now described as '*with a flow of blood for twelve years*' (Mark 5:25/Luke 8:43/Matthew 9:20). Here, again, there is another use of the miraculous number '*twelve,*' which will then be the age of Jairus' daughter in Mark 5:42 and Luke 8:42 and, of course, Jesus' age in Luke 2:42 when '*sitting among the teachers in the Temple,*' and the number of '*talents*' and '*water cisterns*' in the Nakdimon story, to say nothing of the '*twelve handbaskets full of broken pieces,*' '*gathered up*' (like '*the Poor*' do Nakdimon's '*woollen clothes*' above) in the aftermath of Jesus' miraculous '*famine relief*'/'*signs*' demonstrations in all Gospels.

The curing of this '*woman with a flow of blood*' who, like '*the Cananaean woman's daughter*' in Matthew 15:28 above, will also ultimately be described as '*saved by her Faith*' (interestingly this affirmation is missing from Mark 7:29 which only has Jesus saying – as in the stories, we shall momentarily encounter below, attributed to '*Rabbi Yohanan ben Zacchai*' and/or '*Rabbi Eleazar ben Zadok*' about both Nakdimon's daughter '*Miriam*' and Boethus' daughter '*Martha*' in the aftermath of the fall of the Temple – '*Go your way*'[17]), is sandwiched in between the two halves of the '*raising*'/ '*healing of Jairus' daughter*' (Mark 5:25–34 and *pars.*). Not only does it, like these other '*touching*' incidents above, once again have to do with '*touching his clothing,*' '*border of his garment,*' and '*the Multitude*' or '*Rabim*' of Qumran allusion; but it is also possible to see it, as previously suggested, as *making fun of Jewish scrupulousness over* '*blood*' and *issues related to* '*blood*' *generally* – concerns particularly strong, not only at Qumran, but also in James' directives to overseas Communities as reiterated in Acts.[18]

In fact, Mark 5:29 actually uses the language of '*drying up the fountain of her blood,*' instead of '*the flow of her blood,*' to describe her state regarding this matter. One possible way of looking at this modification in Mark is as an amusing caricature of the Damascus Document's pointed concern over '*blood*' generally ('*the Forefathers*' having been '*cut off because they ate blood in the wilderness*' – and *the Temple Establishment* as well, because they were in contact with '*those sleeping with women during the blood of their periods*'[19]). Perhaps even more to the point, it is possible to see it as a disparaging play on the language in this same Damascus Document of '*the Fountain of Living Waters,*' which was the essence of what it conceived of as '*the New Covenant in the Land of Damascus*' – this '*New Covenant*' itself clearly an affront to those being characterized in it, as well, as '*having turned back from it and betrayed it*'![20]

Once again, too, Mark is uncharacteristically more expansive and, not only does *the woman with* '*the fountain of blood*' *for twelve years* '*come and fall down before*' *Jesus* (5:33), but Mark would also appear to be having a lot of fun generally – if we can consider its author(s) as this well-informed and having this degree of sophistication – over the whole connection, pivotal to the Damascus Document's historiography, between '*the New Covenant in the Land of Damascus*' and '*the Well*' or '*Fountain of living waters*' that was literally or figuratively '*to be dug*' there – now here in Mark 5:29 (if, as we said, we can give him credit for this amount of sophistication) being caricatured in terms of '*the fountain of her blood.*'

We will see this '*blood*' usage, which so horrified those at Qumran and was so abhorred by them, in the context of the imagery of '*the New Covenant in the Land of Damascus,*' in particular the '*Blood*' (*Dam*) and the '*Cup*' (*Chos*) which make up the syllables of this denotation in Greek and Paul's '*the Cup of the New Covenant in (his) blood*' (1 Corinthians 11:25) as we proceed.[21] Be these things as they may, Jesus is now pictured as '*coming to the Ruler of the Synagogue's house*' and, as with '*Lazarus*' and the '*Greek Syrophoenician woman*' in Tyre and Sidon, now raising or curing *his* '*daughter*' (Mark 5:35–43 and *pars.*).

As these motifs reverberate back and forth from one Gospel to the other, and to the *Talmud* and then back, the same '*Mary*' who in Luke '*sat at*' and, in John, '*fell at*' or '*anointed his feet*' (while Judas *Iscariot* and/or Martha '*complained*'), as we have on several occasions pointed out, '*washed his feet with her hair.*' In fact, this notice clearly so appealed to John that, as just highlighted, he repeated it twice in 11:2 and 12:3.

'*Jairus*' Kisses '*Jesus*' Feet,' Ben Kalba Sabu'a Kisses '*Rabbi Akiba's Feet,*' and Eliezer ben Jair

To go back to '*Jairus,*' whose story – which had been interrupted for some reason – is now resumed in all three Gospels. He too, as we saw, is characterized in Mark 5:22 as '*falling at (Jesus') feet,*' the '*Multitude gathered around him.*' We shall see the connection of these two successive characterizations of persons '*falling at Jesus feet*' in the same episode – one a '*Ruler of the Synagogue,*' whatever '*Synagogue*' this may have been in such circumstances; and the other, another unnamed '*certain woman*' who '*comes*' to him with a *twelve-year* '*issue,*' '*flow,*' or '*fountain of blood*' – to the story in Rabbinic tradition about how both Rabbi Akiba's wife and his important father-in-law '*fall at his feet*' below.

In the tradition about '*Jairus' daughter*,' not only does the picture of '*the flute players and the crowd*' in Matthew 9:23 identify this as a typical scene one would encounter across the Mediterranean in this period (though not perhaps in Palestine), but allusion to the all-important catchwords, '*master*' or '*lord*,' we have encountered above (in the sense of those coming out of '*the Ruler's house*' saying to Jesus, '*Why trouble you the master any further?*' – Mark 5:35/Luke 8:49), also appears. But even more to the point, just as the '*certain woman, whose daughter had an unclean spirit*' '*came and fell at Jesus' feet*' later in Mark 7:25 and Matthew 15:25 above, not only does Jesus speak with regard to the '*woman with the twelve-year issue of blood*' in the patently '*Paulinizing*' manner, '*your Faith has cured you*' (presumably, once again meaning, she was a '*Gentile*' – Mark 4:34/Luke 8:48[22]); but, as in the '*little daughter*' of the woman who was a '*Greek Syrophoenician by race*' also in 7:25, Mark 5:23 applies the diminutive '*little*' to '*the Ruler of the Synagogue by the name of Jairus*'' '*little daughter*.'

Finally, even more important than any of these, Mark 5:41 – being the most prolix of any of these accounts as we have seen – actually also uses a variation of the phrase Acts 9:40 applies to '*Tabitha*' (in 9:39 leading up to this – also portentously called '*Dorcas*' as we saw[23]) at Jaffa, after Peter traveled there from Lydda to resurrect her, *i.e.*, '*Tabitha arise*' – '*get up!*' Here in Mark, this becomes – not '*Tabitha*' (which we have already previously proposed as a quasi-anagram or phoneme for the Samaritan '*Taheb*'[24]) – but '*Talitha cumi, which interpreted means* (that is, translated from Aramaic into Greek), *little girl, I say unto you, arise.*' Of course, however the diminutive '*little*' (now applied to the '*maid*' or '*girl*') may be, it is hardly conceivable that the use of the Aramaic '*talitha*' for '*little*'/'*young girl*'[25] at this point in Mark is not in some way connected to the related use of the Aramaic '*Tabitha*' for the name of '*a certain Disciple (female) at Jaffa*,' cured or resurrected by Peter in Acts 9:40 in an almost precisely parallel way, is accidental or merely coincidence.

But to take the case, as well, of Rabbi Akiba in the *ARN* above. We have already seen how when he and his new wife Rachel, *Ben Kalba Sabuᶜa*'s daughter, married despite the fact '*he was so Poor*' and despite her father's vow to disinherit her; they not only had to sleep on straw, but how the even more vivid and tender Talmudic tradition dramatized this by picturing him as '*picking the straw out of her hair.*'[26] We also suggested that this episode could be seen as a variation on Luke's picture of Jesus' birth in a manger, for it also pictures '*Elijah the Prophet*' in the guise of a man '*coming*' to them in a clearly *redivivus* manner and *begging some straw, since his wife was in labor and* '*there was nothing for her to lie on.*' It was at this point that the tradition pictures Rabbi Akiba as remarking, as we saw as well, '*there is a man*' *who was so Poor, that* '*he lacks even straw*'![27]

In fact, so many of these New Testament traditions seem to go back to stories about Rabbi Akiba and his well-known colleagues of the previous generation, such as Rabbi Yohanan ben Zacchai and Eliezer ben Hyrcanus that any casual connections such as these should immediately be remarked. In the first place, not only was Rabbi Akiba a '*ben Joseph*,' meaning, his name *literally was* '*Akiba ben Joseph*,' a point the present writer – because of the numerous contradictions surrounding Jesus' parentage and the kind of problems already highlighted concerning the recently-surfaced ossuary in the name of '*Jacob (James) the son of Joseph (the) brother of Jesus*' – finds more credible with regard to Akiba than, for instance, '*Jesus*.'[28] Notwithstanding, as already signaled, in the stories we have about Rabbi Akiba's relations with his wife (*Ben Kalba Sabuᶜa*'s daughter) and her father, we are also *twice* confronted with the references to '*falling down before him and kissing his feet*.'[29]

The first occurs when, after having been secretly married to Ben *Kalba Sabuᶜa*'s daughter, R. Akiba returns a second time after his two stays of '*twelve years*' at the academy – location unspecified, but probably in '*Lydda*,' though it may have been further afield (here all our number '*twelve*'s again of the Nakdimon story and its spin-offs) – with '*twenty-four thousand Disciples*' and, like Martha's sister Mary and therefore Lazarus' as well (as already suggested, possibly even a play on R. Akiba's own teacher, the famous 'heretical' teacher Rabbi Eliezer b. Hyrcanus, or Eliezer ben Jair below, or both) and the unnamed '*woman in the city who was a Sinner*' with the alabaster flask who accosts Jesus at '*the Pharisee's house*' in Luke 7:38 above, she '*falls down before him and kisses his feet*.'[30] The second comes right after this, when *Ben Kalba Sabuᶜa*, Rachel's father, hears that '*the Great Man had come to town*' and, prevailing upon Rabbi Akiba to help him annul his vow to disinherit his Rachel – just like the Great '*Jairus*,' styled a '*Ruler of the Synagogue*' in the story about the resurrection of his daughter above (Mark 5:22) – '*he (Ben Kalba Sabuᶜa) falls down before him (R. Akiba) and kisses his feet*.'[31]

But '*Jairus*' too, as we just suggested, is a name celebrated in Jewish tradition, since '*Eliezer ben Jair*' is the famed commander of the final stand at Masada and a second-generation descendant of the equally-famous founder of the '*Zealot*' or – if one prefers – '*Sicarii Movement*,' '*Judas the Galilean*.' Is there more here than meets the eye? From our perspective, there is. Just like the co-option of Rabbi Yohanan's father's name '*Zacchaeus*' (in Hebrew, '*Zacchai*') in Luke 19:2–8 – itself probably based on Peter's visit to confront Simon *Magus* in Caesarea where, in the

Pseudoclementine *Recognitions*, he stays at '*Zacchaeus' house*' (possibly the real father of Rabbi Yohanan ben Zacchai[32]); '*Theudas*' in '*Thaddaeus*'; now this '*Ben Jair*' in '*Jairus*'; and even '*Judas the Galilean*' himself in '*Judas Iscariot*' and/or '*Judas Zelotes*'; it would not be unfruitful to speculate about the connection of the theme of the resurrection of '*Jairus' daughter*' with that of the '*Zealot*' or '*Sicarii*' mass suicide on Masada since, from modern archaeological research, we now know that the sectaries were adepts of the idea of '*the Resurrection of the dead*' – the '*bones*' passage from Ezekiel 37 having been found as if purposefully buried underneath the synagogue floor there.[33] In addition, more recent revelations concerning the Dead Sea Scrolls – exemplars of which were also found at Masada – make it crystal clear that the Qumran sectaries also believed in the doctrine of '*the Resurrection of the dead*.'[34] We will leave it to the reader to decide what the connection of all these things may be – if any.

Where R. Akiba is concerned, the '*Zealot*' Rabbi of his generation and considered by most to be the spiritual force behind the Bar Kochba Uprising;[35] in addition to the several notices above, he was also said to have – like Jesus, '*the Essenes*,' John the Baptist, and James – taught the twin Commandments of the '*All Righteousness*'-ideology: the first, in his advocacy as a fundamental precept of *Torah*, '*You shall love your neighbor as yourself*' – '*Righteousness towards one's fellow man*' as Josephus labels it in his *Antiquities* Book Eighteen description of John the Baptist, to say nothing of that of '*the Essenes*'' advocacy of it preceding this and, of course, '*the Royal Law according to the Scripture*' as it is put in the Letter of James.[36]

The second is even more dramatic and parallels to some extent Hippolytus' picture of those he calls '*Sicarii*' or '*Zealot Essenes*' who, during the First Uprising, are portrayed as willing to undergo any sort of torture rather than '*blaspheme the Law-Giver or eat things sacrificed to idols*.'[37] Tractate *Berachot*/'*Blessings*' in the *Talmud* (now at the time of *the Second Jewish Uprising*), takes up the picture from there. In the midst of graphically detailing how Rabbi Akiba was tortured to death by the Romans – presumably for his support of the 'Messianic' pretender, Shimon Bar Kochba, to whom he applied '*the Star Prophecy*' of Numbers 24:17 above:

> *A Star shall come out of Jacob and a Sceptre shall rise out of Israel, and he shall smite the corners of Moab and destroy all the sons of Seth* (compare this with the quotation of the same passage in Column Eleven of the Qumran War Scroll from below, just preceding the first evocation there of '*the coming of the Heavenly Host on the clouds of Glory*'[38]).

It provides the following gruesome picture: though his flesh is '*flailed from his body with iron combs'* and *'his body is then drawn and quartered,'* nevertheless Rabbi Akiba welcomed his martyrdom as a chance to fulfill the first of the two *'All Righteousness'* Commandments, that of *'Piety towards'* or *'loving God,'* we have at several points had cause to refer to above:

> You shall love the Lord your God with all your heart and with all your soul... even if you must pay for it with your life.[39]

One will, of course, find this Commandment too, not only attributed to 'Jesus' and John the Baptist in Scripture but also, as already observed, in the Letter of James in *'the Kingdom prepared for those who love Him'* – *'loving God'* being equivalent to *'Piety towards God'* – and, no less pivotally, in the Damascus Document from Qumran.[40]

To go back to this theme of the *'hair'* of these celebrated *'daughter's,* Rabbi Akiba's wife Rachel, *Ben Kalba Sabuʿa's* daughter – whom some called *'a Galilean'* because, like others spending their early years in this locale and called by this designation, she was said to have *been buried in Galilee* – to show her virtue and constancy was also said *to have 'sold her hair' to pay for her husband's studies because they were so Poor.*[41] The resemblance of this to some of the *'hair-wiping'* traditions above is uncanny and it really does, of course, bear on these traditions about Mary in John and others, *'wiping Jesus' feet with her hair,'* while *'the Disciples'* or *'Judas Iscariot'* protest that *'the value'* of such *'ointment of pure spikenard oil'* should have been *'sold and given to the Poor.'*

For the *Talmud* too, the issue of *'hair'* will now be linked to *'Boethus' daughter'* for whom, it will be recalled, the same *'cushions'* or *'carpets'* – pictured in the above traditions as having been *'laid on the ground'* (*before they were gathered up by 'the Poor'*), so Nakdimon's *'feet'* would not have to *'touch the ground'* (note again how, in Luke 16:19–20, the *'certain Poor Man named Lazarus, who was full of sores'* is *'laid at the doorstep'* of *'a certain Rich Man clothed in purple and fine linen and feasting in splendor daily'* – n.b., in particular, the *'laid at the gate'* and *'daily'* themes and now how it is not *'the cisterns'* or *'granaries'* that are *'full,'* but rather *'Lazarus'* whose body is *'full of sores'*) – are *'laid so that, when she walked from her house to the entrance to the Temple to see her husband* (Josephus' friend, the Boethusian High Priest, Jesus ben Gamala) *read the Torah on the Day of Atonement'* (as we have seen too, always an interesting motif whether connected to the death of James or that of *'the Righteous Teacher'* from Qumran[42]), her *'feet'* too *'would not get dirty.'*[43]

It was also she, it should be remembered, not just *'Nakdimon's 'daughter-in-law,'* to whom the Rabbis grant *'two se'ahs of wine daily'* after the death of her husband '*as a precaution against dissoluteness*' (here the '*daily*' and '*dissoluteness*' themes of the Lukan pericope above). Furthermore, to show how far she had fallen after the destruction of the Temple, it is also she, this same '*Martha the daughter of Boethus*' (called here '*Miriam*'), the '*hair*' of whom – Rabbinic exaggeration aside – '*Rabbi Eleazar ben Zadok*' now *sees* (not, as in the case of '*Nakdimon's daughter Miriam*' – also cited in this passage, '*picking grain among the horses' hoofs in Acco*') the Romans '*bind to the tails of Arab horses and make run from Jerusalem to Lydda*'!⁴⁴

Here of course, our '*hair*' motif starts to replicate. Neither should one overlook the point about '*from Jerusalem to Lydda*' (Peter's route in Acts above), nor the '*Zadok*' denotation in Rabbi Eleazar's patronym.⁴⁵ Where Boethus' daughter's '*cushions*' are concerned, we have already observed that aside from deriving the name of another of these '*Rich*' colleagues of Nakdimon, '*Siset Hakkeset*'/'*Ben Zizzit Hakeseth*,' from the '*silver couch upon which he used to recline before all the Great Ones of Israel*,'⁴⁶ Tractate *Gittin* also derived it from '*his fringes*' (*zizzit*), which '*used to trail on cushions*' (*keset*). To be sure, like the material about many of these same sorts of things in the New Testament, much of this is hyperbole or what is perhaps even worse, pure nonsense; – but, for the purposes of tracing the migration of these motifs and this vocabulary from one story to another and across the boundaries of cultural tradition, it doesn't really matter – that is, which is more nonsense and which less so.

'*The Centurion's Servant*,' More '*Poor Widow*'s and Temple Destruction Oracles

Finally, to go back yet again to Luke and the much-overlooked encounter with another woman '*carrying an alabaster flask of ointment*' at someone called '*Simon the Pharisee's house*' at the end of Chapter Seven, who '*washed*' Jesus '*feet with (her) tears*' and '*wiped them with (her) hair*' – which comes, as it does, before most of the materials, we have been considering at such length above, even come into play and so innocuous that most hardly even notice it – in it, Luke, as we saw, combines all these themes. It would be worthwhile, therefore, to go over it once again, but this time in more detail.

In a series of curings that begin with Luke 7:1–10's evocation – as in his Acts 10's '*Heavenly tablecloth*' vision/'*Pious*' Roman Centurion Cornelius' *conversion*-affair – of '*a certain Centurion*' who is also described like this '*Cornelius*' as '*loving our Nation and building a synagogue for us*.' Were it not for concern over wounding the tender sensibilities of those claiming to '*believe*,' it would be hard once again to refrain from an outright guffaw here. In Acts 10:2 and 10:22, it will be recalled, it was *'Pious,' 'Righteous,'* *'a God-Fearer,' 'doing many charitable works for the People, praying to God continually,'* and *'borne witness to by the whole Nation of the Jews'* – equally laughable – though these particular allusions in Acts were more than likely aimed at either Domitian or the Emperor Trajan whose father, as we saw, *really had been a Centurion in Palestine* conspicuously singled out by Josephus for his bravery; still, where the idea of *'building a synagogue for us'* is concerned, this notice in Luke 7:5 seems more to be consistent with what Vespasian or Titus did for R. Yohahan ben Zacchai when he appeared before him after his escape from Jerusalem applying *'the Messianic Prophecy'* to him.[47] Though extremely confusing and replicating much of Acts 10:1–18's more detailed story of *'Peter'*'s visit to Cornelius – instead of sending *'two servants'* and another *'Pious Soldier'* to invite Peter *'to his house'* as in Acts 10:7 and 22, *'the Centurion'* here in Luke 7:3 is somehow able to send the *'Presbyterous'* or *'Elders of the Jews'* to Jesus *'to ask him to come in order to cure his servant'* (sic).

Moreover, as Jesus *'was already not too distant from the house'* (Luke 7:6 – in Acts 10:9, it was *'as the two servants drew near' the house'*), the Centurion has a change of heart and now sends his *'Friends'* (note, the *'Friend'* / *'Friendship of God'* vocabulary here) to tell Jesus not to bother to come – presumably because of the embarrassment this might cause a *'Jewish Messiah'* in the eyes of persons, such as the *'some from James'* in Galatians 2:12 opposing *'table fellowship with Gentiles'* – because he *'was unworthy for (Jesus) to come under (his) roof'* (here, of course, the kind of *'roof'* language – though the parallel is not exact – of *'Peter going up on the roof to pray, about the sixth hour'* in Acts 10:9 above; plus, the modesty on the part of the Roman Centurion here really is quite remarkable).

While in Luke 7:6–10 Jesus stops just before actually entering the Centurion's house and, at this point, is made to announce *'to the Multitude'* again the *pro forma, 'not even in Israel have I found such great Faith'* thereby, seemingly, curing *'the Centurion's servant'* by remote control from outside the house; in Acts – where *'Peter'* actually enters the Centurion's house, who then *'falls down at his feet worshipping'* him (thus)! – the issues are rather that of the *'pouring out'* (the *'pouring out'* language again of both the Dead Sea Scrolls and Jesus at *'the Last Supper'*) of the *Holy Spirit upon Gentiles as well'* (10:45) and *'God also giving the repentance of life to Gentiles'* (11:18), not just *'curing the Centurion's servant.'*

The version of this encounter one finds in Matthew 8:5–13 is somewhat different. In the first place, it directly follows *'the Sermon on the Mount,'* including the passage: *'Do not give what is Holy to dogs, nor Cast (balete) your Pearls before swine, lest they should trample them with their feet in*

Matthew 7:6 (here '*casting*,' '*dogs*,' and '*feet*' allusions again). Secondly, it also directly follows another '*touching*' and '*cleansing*' episode in Matthew 8:3 – in this case, the '*cleansing*' of '*a leper*' (the '*Simon the Leper*' of Mark and Matthew later?), who '*came and worshipped him*' (the '*worshipping him*' of Acts 10:25's Cornelius' greeting '*Peter*' above). In Luke 7:18–22 following these curings and raisings, it should be appreciated that these motifs drift into the allusion to '*the lepers being cleansed*' and the multiple references to '*coming*' we shall discuss further below. In this exchange between 'Jesus' and John (not paralleled in Matthew until 11:2–19, *when John is supposed already to be 'in prison'*) – just as the '*Centurion*' sends his '*two servants*' to Peter in Acts 10:7 above, John is now pictured as sending '*two certain (ones) of his Disciples*' to query Jesus with the apocalyptically-charged, '*Are you the one who is to come?*' – language we shall eventually see reflected in '*the Doresh ha-Torah*' ('*the Seeker after the Law*') who came to *Damascus*' in Ms. A of the Damascus Document and '*the coming of the Messiah of Aaron and Israel*' in Ms. B and in '*the Star who would come out of Israel*' from Numbers 24:17 in Ms. A and the Qumran *Testimonia* below.[48]

But in Matthew 8:5, it is neither the '*Presbyterous of the Jews*' or the '*Friends of the Centurion*' who come to Jesus on '*the Centurion*''s behalf, but now '*the Centurion*' himself; and here, not only does he again refer to his servant '*being laid out in the house*' (8:6) – as in the multiple references to the '*Rich Men*' or their daughters' '*garments*'/'*cushions*' being '*laid out*' in Talmudic scenarios or Luke's '*Poor Man Lazarus at the Rich Man's door*' above, to say nothing of the approximately *seven* references to '*come*' or '*coming*' in as many lines from 8:5–11 below and, of course, in 8:8 the '*roof*' of both Luke and Acts above – but now even, after commenting as in Luke on the Centurion's '*great Faith*,' the '*Go your way*' (8:13) of the several Talmudic stories attributed to either '*Yohanan ben Zacchai*' or '*Eleazar ben Zadok*' about the '*hair*' or '*feet*' of these same '*Rich Men's daughters*.' Moreover, the perspicacious reader will also immediately discern that, as we shall see further below, this same '*Go your way*' has now migrated down in Luke 7:22 into the outcome of Jesus' exchanges with '*the Disciples of John*' over the question of '*the One who is to come*.'

Finally, in this healing, Matthew is even more anti-Semitic and pro-Pauline than Luke – if this is possible. To his version of Jesus' compliment to the Centurion of '*not even in Israel have I found such great Faith*' (8:10) – also more or less repeated in Matthew 15:28 later in his version of the '*cleansing*' of the '*Cananaean woman's daughter*,' *viz.*, '*O woman, great is your Faith*' – is now attached the additional ideologically-charged and pointed comment, including this '*Centurion*' among '*the Many*' who '*shall come from East and West*' and '*recline (at the table* – Luke 7:36–37's '*table fellowship*' theme that will now take place at '*the house of the Pharisee*' below and elsewhere) *with Abraham and Isaac and Jacob in the Kingdom of the Heavens*' (*sic*). In the portrait of '*Heaven and Hell*' that concludes the '*certain Poor Man*' laid at the gate of the '*Rich Man clothed in purple and fine linen*' in Luke 16:22–31, this will be '*Lazarus on the bosom of Abraham.*' In the same breath, Matthew reverses the '*casting out*' language, Josephus used to illustrate '*Essene*' treatment of backsliders, to say nothing of his own later '*casting out down the toilet bowl*' parable and the way Luke will portray the Jewish crowd as '*casting*' Stephen '*out of the city*' in Acts 7:58:

> But the Sons of the Kingdom (clearly meaning, the original '*Heirs to the Promise*'/the Jews, though it can be seen, even here, as a synonym for what Qumran is denoting as '*the Sons of Zadok*' above) *shall be cast out into the outer darkness* (8:12 – *pace* ideas of Matthew as the most '*Jewish*' of all the Gospels. This is pure '*Gentile Mission*' material[49]).

To add insult to injury, Matthew adds here, '*and there shall be much weeping and gnashing of teeth*' (yes, and it would be hard to imagine anything otherwise in the context here).

To go back to the further resurrection episode in Luke 7:11–17 that intercedes between this '*healing*' of '*the Centurion's servant*' and the exchange between '*the Disciples*' of John and Jesus – using the language of '*coming*,' '*touching*,' '*Many*,' '*glorifying God*' and basically paralleling the raising of '*Jairus*'' daughter' that follows at the end of the Chapter Eight, the pregnant expression '*arise*' (found, for instance, throughout the Damascus Document, where it also appears to mean '*be resurrected*'[49]); Luke portrays Jesus as resurrecting the '*only son*' (here actually the '*only begotten son*,' paralleling John 1:14, 3:16, Hebrews 11:17, the Synoptics on Jesus, and the same expression Josephus uses to characterize the '*sonship*' of Helen of Adiabene's favorite son Izates[50]) '*in a city called Nain*' of a bereaved '*widow*' – another of the *Talmud*-like '*widow*' scenarios which Luke, in particular (but also Mark), appears to have found so attractive.

Not only should one note in this regard, for example, '*the widows overlooked in the daily serving*' in Luke's introduction of '*Stephen*' in Acts 6:1 above (here again, both the '*serving*' and '*daily*' evocations); but in both Luke 21:1–5 and Mark 12:41–44, there is the proverbial and particularly charged episode of, again, the '*certain Poor widow casting her two mites into the Treasury*' (here '*ballousan*'/'*ebelen*') – '*charged*' because, while missing at this point in the parallel attacks in Matthew 23 on '*the Pharisees*' as '*Hypocrites*' (Galatians 2:13's attacks, on Peter and Barnabas as '*Hypocrites*' for '*separating themselves*' like the '*some from James*'), '*Blind Guides*,'

'*Offspring of Vipers*,'[51] and '*slaying all the Prophets*' (Paul in Thessalonians 2:15) as well as on '*Jerusalem*,' the '*House*' of which '*will be left desolate*' (*i.e.*, this was written after the fall of the Temple!); it is so similar to the later scenario in Matthew 27:3–10 of 'Judas *Iscariot*,' casting his '*thirty pieces of silver*' ('*the price of blood*' – here in Matthew 23:30, this is '*communion*'/'*partaking in the blood of the Prophets*' – more '*blood libel*' accusations) into '*the Temple Treasury*' prior to his alleged '*suicide*,' that it too probably has simply been transferred and revamped.

In any event, like Judas' '*casting*' his '*thirty pieces of silver*' into '*the Temple Treasury*,' it deals with what emerges as one of the pivotal issues for this period, that of '*sacred gifts given to the Temple*' – in this instance, on the part of '*the Rich casting (ballontas) their gifts into the Treasury*' (but also on the part of '*Gentiles*' generally) as opposed to those '*cast*,' as Luke 21:4/Mark 12:43 would have it, by '*this certain Poor widow*' ('*cast*'/'*casting*' repeated five times in four lines!) '*out of her poverty*.' Of course, as in the resurrection of the '*only-begotten son*' of '*the widow of Nain*' (Adiabene), the overtones of this episode with the gifts to the Temple from another probable '*widow*,' Queen Helen *of Adiabene* (whose gifts included the famous seven-branched gold candelabra which was taken to Rome in Titus' victory celebration and there, presumably melted down to help build – of all places – the Colosseum!) should be obvious.

Furthermore, Jesus' attitude towards '*the Poor*' and '*poverty*' in the matter of the '*certain Poor widow*''s '*two mites*'– again missing, not only from Matthew, but John as well – is a far cry from what it is in John 12:5's picture of his response to '*Judas Iscariot*''s complaints about '*the Poor*' over the wastefulness of '*Lazarus*'' sister Mary '*anointing his feet with expensive ointment of spikenard*.' On the other hand, this time it does once again bear a resemblance to the *Talmud*'s picture both of Rabbi Akiba's '*poverty*' as opposed to his '*Rich*' father-in-law, Ben Kalba Sabuᶜa's '*superfluity*' and Rabbi Eliezer's '*poverty*,' whose '*fame*' would in due course, like '*this Poor widow*''s '*be worth more than all the rest*' (Luke 21:3/Mark 12:43).[52]

The encounter with this second '*widow*' here in Luke 21:1-5,whose '*two mites*' were '*worth more than all the rest*,' is pivotal too; because, in both it and Mark, it introduces Jesus' telltale oracle, delivered to '*his Disciples*,' starting in the very next line (21:6 and 13:2 – in Mark 13:1 '*going forth out of the Temple*' and now paralleled in Matthew 24:1– 26:1 picking up from the allusion to '*your House being left unto you desolate*' in 23:38 above) and so patently based on Josephus' description in *The War* of Titus' destruction of the Temple, which dates all three Synoptics (as almost nothing else can), giving them a *terminus a quo* of 70 CE: '*There shall not be left a stone on top of a stone that shall not be thrown down*.'[54] Here, too, Jesus is not only called '*Teacher*' (as opposed, for instance, to those Matthew 23:7–8, somewhat pejoratively refers to as calling their '*Leader*,' '*Rabbi*'[55] – '*Teacher*' carrying with it, in the writer's view, something of the sense of '*the Righteous Teacher*' at Qumran); but the whole discourse he now delivers on '*going out from the Temple*' (in Luke 21:1, this comes after '*he sees the Rich/ballontas casting their gifts into the Treasury*'!) is replete with multiple allusions to the telltale language of '*leading astray*' (in Matthew 24:5 and 11, '*leading Many astray*'[56]) as well as that of '*the Elect*,' '*delivering up*,' '*false Christs and false prophets*,' '*misleading*' or '*deceiving with (great) signs and wonders*.'

In addition, 'Jesus' is depicted, in this material leading up in all three Gospels to both '*the Little Apocalypses*' and '*the Poor widow casting her two mites into the Treasury*,' as pointedly characterizing the '*Rich*' and those he pictures as *occupying* '*the Chief Seats in the Synagogues*'[57] as '*going to receive a greater*' or '*more abundant Judgement*' – that is, in proportion to their '*Riches*' (Luke 20:47/Mark 12:40). Furthermore, this phraseology is replicated almost precisely in the Qumran Habakkuk *Pesher*'s picture – *in exposition of, it should be noted, Habakkuk 2:4* – of how the punishment '*of the Wicked* (in particular, '*the Wicked Priest as a consequence for what he did to the Righteous Teacher*' and those of his followers among '*the Poor*'[58]) would be *multiplied upon themselves*' when they '*were judged*'.' Moreover, this means, of course, on '*the Last*' or '*Day of Judgement*' (*n.b.*, in particular, that even here the verb '*eating*' or '*devouring*' is used to express this in both Luke 20:47 and Mark 12:40 just as it is in the Habakkuk *Pesher*[59]).

For its part Matthew 24:2, while retaining Mark's '*going forth from the Temple*' but discarding the '*widow's two mites*' material – since it has held back the use of the '*casting coins into the Temple Treasury*' presentation for its '*Judas Iscariot*' betrayal/death scenario (only the amounts will the two episodes differ) – embeds 'Jesus'' oracle of the destruction of the Temple at the end of its general '*woes*' – '*woes*' not unlike or really separable from those of the curious '*prophet*' in Josephus, '*Jesus ben Ananias*,' after the death of James leading up to the destruction of the Jerusalem, which we shall consider in more detail below[60]; '*woes*,' too, which throughout the whole of Matthew 23 are used to attack the '*Rabbis*,' '*Pharisees*,' '*Hypocrites*,' '*Blind Ones*,' '*fools*,' '*Blind Guides*,' and just about every person or concept of any consequence in this period (in particular, concepts fundamental to Qumran ideology[61]), finally giving way, as in the other two Synoptics, to '*the Little Apocalypse*' in Chapter Twenty-Four and, of course, to the typical proclamation ascribed to James in all early Church literature of '*seeing the Son of Man coming (together with the '*Elect*') on the clouds of Heaven with Power and great Glory*' (Matthew 24:30/Mark 13:26/

Luke 21:27).

But these *'woes'* are also reminiscent of the *'woes'* R. Yohanan pronounces to *'his Disciples'* when he goes forth from Jerusalem in the *ARN* above. Of course, these *'woes'* too, like those continually pronounced by *'Jesus ben Ananias'* above − however preposterous, as we have seen, they may be − are far more credible than any of these *'woes'* being pronounced in the Gospels, since at least they are not happening forty years before the events in question, but actually consonant with the occurrences. Furthermore, they are not a vicious and even incendiary attack on such *'Blind Guides'* and all of its associated innuendo in which our Gospel artificers − which, though supposedly talking about *'Love'* (Matthew 22:36−40 and *pars.*), actually seem full of hatred − put all their favorite anti-Semitic invective, including the one about *'Serpents, Offspring of Vipers'* (23:33 and *pars.*) and that about *'Jerusalem, Jerusalem, who kills the Prophets and stones those who have been sent to her'* (note, even *'Jesus ben Ananias'* here was neither stoned or killed − at least not by Jersualemites!). In fact, the *ARN* at this point even recounts a tradition that echoes the one about either James or Jesus being tempted to jump or actually *'being cast down from the Pinnacle of the Temple.'* This is Vespasian's General who was forced to *'cast himself down from the roof of the Temple'* because he disobeyed and refused to carry out an order from Vespasian to destroy the Temple, but rather left the Western (or *'Wailing'*) Wall as a sign of the Emperor's great strength![62]

However this may be, at the end of this *'Little Apocalypse'* in Matthew, preceding both *'the Son of Man coming in his Glory'* in 25:31 and in *'two days'* being *'delivered up to be crucified'* in 26:1, there occurs (uniquely in Matthew 25:14−30) another one of these *'talents,' 'servants,' 'lord'* and, this time even, *'digging in the earth'* parables/scenarios − this one involving delivering *'five talents'* to the one *'good and Faithful servant'* and to another *'two'* (our *'seven cisterns'* of the Nakdimon bartering with his *'lord'* earlier?) and a third one who will get only *'one'* (numbers which seem completely arbitrary − any seemingly will do). After much bantering and business psychology (obviously representing the Mediterranean bourgeois of the day) and even mentioning *'money-lenders'* and *'interest'* (25:27); again, as in Nakdimon's doubling the amounts of his *'lord's cisterns,'* the amounts are also somehow doubled to ten and four (25:20−28) while the *'wicked and slothful servant,'* who only *'dug in the ground* (in our view, a parody of *'the Diggers'* in Column Six of the Damascus Document, who *'dug the Well of Living Waters in the Land of Damascus'* which we shall treat further below and around which *'the New Covenant'* there is proclaimed[65]) *and buried his lord's money,'* would have his *'taken from him and given to him with ten talents*' (the other '*Faithful servant*,' who with smart business sense doubled his to '*four*,' now seemingly having gone by the boards!).

Of course, parabolic or otherwise, this is monetary venture capitalism with a vengeance, well-suited to the ethos of the *Imperium Romanum*, however manifestly at odds with '*the Poor of this world*' and '*Heirs to the Kingdom promised to those that love him*' of James 2:5 above. In any event, once again, there was to be much '*weeping and gnashing of teeth*' and this '*worthless bondservant*' was '*to be cast out (ekballate) into the Darkness*' (25:30 – my, my, most violent and a little sad that '*the servant*' who did not go to '*the money-lenders*' and double '*his lord*''s investment should be treated so harshly and callously even if only symbolically). It is hard to imagine, even if uttered completely symbolically or interpreted allegorically in the most Philo-like manner, that this had anything to do with Palestinian '*Messianism*' whatsoever, nor '*the Blessed of (the) Father inheriting the Kingdom prepared for them from the Foundation of the World*' of Matthew 25:34 that follows, but once again, as just noted, Roman and Herodian venture capitalism with a vengeance.

The '*Only-begotten Son*,' '*God Visiting His People*,' and '*the Sign*' of '*the Coming of the Son of Man*'

On the other hand – since Jesus is not '*going forth from the Temple*' at this point in Luke, but simply continuing on from his '*widow's two mites*' homily – Luke 21:5–6, unlike Matthew and Mark, uses the ever-recurring '*some*' to provoke him into uttering the dire prognostication above about the destruction of the Temple – '*there not being left one stone upon stone that shall not be thrown down*' – as simply part of the discourse which continues relatively seamlessly, then too, from 21:8–36 into its version of '*the Little Apocalypse*.' But the '*some*' who provoke this and, in the manner of '*the Righteous Teacher*' in the Scrolls, call Jesus '*Teacher*' as well (21:7), do so because they were speaking, seemingly admiringly, about the pivotal question of '*sacred gifts to the Temple*' – which, as just remarked, we shall discuss further, particularly as it acted in the run-up to and as the immediate cause of, the War against Rome – and expensive decorations obviously being given to the Temple by '*the Rich*' (as opposed to those of '*the Poor widow*'), doubtlessly meant to include and specifically aimed at, in particular, those given by persons such as the celebrated Queen Helen of Adiabene above.[66]

Even more importantly finally, in describing the implications of this '*raising*' of the '*only begotten son*' of the '*widow of Nain*' (probably '*Adiabene*,' as no one has or probably ever will point out a geographical locale in

Palestine consonant with this 'Nain' and we have already underscored how Josephus calls Queen Helen's son her 'only begotten' as well); Luke 7:12–14 actually pictures 'the bier' of the 'only-begotten son' of this 'widow' outside 'the Gate of the City.' In this regard, one should pay particular attention to the well-known tomb – built by Queen Helen's second son, Monobazus, for her and Izates, *who did in fact pre-decease her*, near the Gate of the City of Jerusalem where it is still extant today – then decorated, as is meticulously described by Josephus, with three large pyramids![67]

Moreover, Luke 7:16 then uses exactly the same allusion we have already encountered in the opening lines of the Damascus Document, picturing the crowd as crying out – on seeing 'Jesus'' miracle and taking him for 'a Prophet' – 'God has visited His People.'[68] In the Damascus Document, in the context of 'the Root of Planting' passage already highlighted above, this is God 'visited them and caused a Root of Planting to grow from Israel.' But the allusion 'visited them,' is often used (very often in conjunction with 'delivered them up' as we shall see) throughout the Damascus Document, usually implying retribution or the execution of Divine Judgement.[69] Nothing probably could represent a greater distortion or reversal of Qumran ideology, as far as the import of this expression 'God visited' is concerned, than what one finds here in Luke 7:16. Of course, in reality, there probably never was any 'Poor widow of Nain' either but, as just remarked, this is a direct attack (however veiled – those 'who had ears' would 'understand') on the illustrious Queen of Adiabene herself, probably perceived by 'some' (no pun intended) as a 'Rich widow,' her husband – whoever he might have been – having already died by the time of her emergence as an importance presence on the Palestinian scene.

For its part, Luke 7:16 employs this allusion to 'God visiting His People' in the context of having the crowd 'glorifying God'[70] and then crying out 'a Great Prophet has arisen among us.' Once again, we have the verb 'arising' here, as already indicated, used throughout the Damascus Document where the 'arising of the Messiah of Aaron and Israel at the End of Days' is concerned but also, as we shall presently see, in the 'Messianic' *Florilegium* regarding 'the Branch of David who will arise' / 'stand up *in Zion together with the Doresh ha-Torah in the Last Days*' – 'the Tent of David which is fallen' of Amos 9:11 ('the Sceptre' of Numbers 24:17 in the War Scroll, *Testimonia*, and Genesis *Pesher*, where 'the Staff' or 'Mehokkek' is 'between his feet' and 'the Messiah of Righteousness' is identified with both 'the Sceptre' and 'the Branch of David who will come') who 'will arise to save Israel' too.[71] Furthermore, and also perhaps even more importantly, in speaking about such a 'Great Prophet,' the crowd's exclamation once again echoes 'the True Prophet' ideology of the Ebionites, Elchasaites and, in succession to these, the Manichaeans and Islam[72] – an ideology definitively evoked as well, not only in the build-up to this evocation of '*the fallen Tent of David*' here in the 'Messianic' *Florilegium*, but also in the climactic Column Nine of the Community Rule above.[73]

In fact, playing on this ideology of '*the True Prophet coming into the world*' (as, for example, in John 6:14 quoted above, '*This is truly the Prophet that is coming into the world*' – which is probably the reason for all these '*coming*' allusions so proliferating the notices we have been highlighting, to say nothing of the '*Standing*' ones, and part and parcel of '*the Star*' who '*will come out of Jacob*' of '*the Star Prophecy*' in Ms. A of the Damascus Document and the *Testimonia* above and the '*coming of the Messiah of Aaron and Israel*' in Ms. B, we shall analyze further below[74]); this '*coming*' allusion, like the '*casting*' ones just alluded to in Luke 21:1–4 as well, is played on three times in just three lines in the prelude to Jesus' discussion in Luke 7:24–30 of the '*Greatness*,' '*baptism*,' and '*Prophethood*' of John the Baptist who, for some reason, erupts into the text at this point both in it and the Gospel of Matthew. This occurs, as we saw, in the question Luke 7:18–20 has now John allegedly send to Jesus – '*Are you the One who is coming?*' – again (as in the case of the '*two servants*' of Acts 10:7's '*Pious Centurion*') via '*two certain ones*' – now two '*of his (John the Baptist's) Disciples*.'

Not only will John (like James later) be portrayed in 7:31–34 – amid phrases like '*the Son of Man came drinking and eating*,' '*a friend of tax-collectors and Sinners*' (not, it should be noted, '*a Friend of God*' – *cf.* James 4:4 on '*making yourself a friend of the world*' and '*transforming yourself into an Enemy of God*' above), '*the tax-collectors justifying God*' (this one is really absurd), the '*little children*' again, and John even being perceived by some as '*having a demon*'! – as '*neither eating meat nor drinking wine*' (Luke 7:33–34/Matthew 11:18–19); but it is at this point in the narrative, as we just saw, that John's '*Disciples*,' '*coming to*' Jesus, ask him, '*Are you the One who is coming*' and here Jesus is made to answer as well – in the manner of comments, we have already considered above and shall review further below, based on Song of Songs 1:8: '*O you fairest among women, go your way forth by the footsteps of the flock and feed your offspring*,' attributed to Rabbis like Yohanan ben Zacchai and Eleazar ben Zadok concerning the miserable state of our same '*Rich men's daughters*' after the fall of the Temple – '*Go your way*' (Luke 7:22/Matthew 11:4 – though none of these materials are paralleled at this point in Mark; *cf.* the same kind of remark in Mark 7:29, already remarked above, to the '*Syrophoenician woman*' in the matter of '*the demon having left*' her daughter!).

To return to Luke 7:22's picture of how 'Jesus' responds to John's '*two Disciples*' (in Matthew 11:2, only '*his Disciples*') by preaching about '*the*

1 ABOVE: View of the Qumran marl, mainly consisting of Cave 4 but also 5-6, with the settlement across the wadi and Dead Sea in the background.

2 ABOVE: The Mausoleum or Burial Monument at the Head of the Qumran Cemetery (discovered by two CSULB students) with the Dead Sea in the background.

3 ABOVE: Another view of the Mausoleum, discovered by two CSULB students, containing the so-called '*Burial Monument of the Righteous Teacher*' and dominating the graveyard.

4 LEFT: The graves in front of the Mausoleum showing the north/south orientation of '*Essene*'/'*Sabaean*' bathing groups.

5 BELOW LEFT: Another view of the north/south orientation of the some nine hundred graves in the main cemetery.

6 BELOW: The fragment from 4QD266 preceding Column I of the Cairo Damascus Document mentioning '*the Sons of Light keeping away from*' (*linzor*/ Naziritism).

7 Above: The excavated Mausoleum showing its splendid location over-looking the Dead Sea and the east/west orientation of its burials.

8 Below: Column III of the Psalm 37 *Pesher* mentioning both '*the Penitents of the Wilderness*' and '*the Assembly*' or '*Church of the Poor*' (*Ebionim*).

9 Below Right: A view of the excavated grave, in which one adult male buried in an east/west orientation facing Jerusalem and two secondary females burials were found so far.

10 ABOVE: The lookout overlooking the Kedron's effluence to the Dead Sea, discovered by the author's son Hanan Eisenman by following the Second Temple Period pottery-trail leading to it.

11 BELOW LEFT: Another view of the lookout around which rare coins from Year 4 of the Revolt against Rome were found.

12 ABOVE RIGHT: The impressive doorway of the structure connected to the lookout.

13 BELOW: Columns VII-VIII of the Habakkuk *Pesher* containing '*the Delay of the Parousia*' and the anti-Pauline exposition of Habakkuk 2:4: '*The Righteous shall by his Faith.*'

14 ABOVE: The terrace of the lookout, showing its strategic location over-looking both the mouth of the Kedron and the wharf.

15 ABOVE: The wharf at Khirbat Mazin at the effluence of the Wadi Kedron on the Dead Sea.

16 RIGHT: Columns VIII–IX of the Community Rule, twice quoting Isaiah 40:3's *'Preparing a Way in the Wilderness'* and referring to *'zeal for the Day of Vengeance.'*

17 ABOVE: Cave 4 overlooking the Wadi, from which the lion's share of the Qumran manuscripts came.

18 ABOVE RIGHT: Periodic water pouring down into the Wadi Qumran from the Bethlehem Plain, the storage of which made habitation at Qumran possible.

19 LEFT Columns I-II of the Community Rule, like 4QD266, 'cursing' all those *departing from the right or left of the Torah.'*

20 ABOVE: The author standing in the mouth of Cave 4 during the 1991–2 CSULB radar groundscan.

21 ABOVE: The artificially hollowed-out water channel at the top of the Wadi Qumran, the *raison d'etre* of the Community.

22 ABOVE RIGHT: The also artificially hollowed-out interior of Cave 4 where most of the manuscripts appear to have been stored.

23 ABOVE: Cave I where the first and most complete manuscripts were found in 1947 in neat storage jars.

24 LEFT: Cave II, the last manuscript-bearing cave found in the mid-Fifties, from which the Temple Scroll apparently came.

25 BELOW LEFT: A piece of the *Pesher* on Isaiah 10:33-11:5, containing the Messianic Prophecy on '*Lebanon being felled by a Mighty One*' and '*the Branch*' from '*the Root of Jesse.*'

26 BELOW: Column II of the Nahum *Pesher* describing how '*the Kittim*' came after the Greeks and in which, contrary to Paul, crucifixion or '*hanging a man alive upon a tree*' is condemned.

27 RIGHT: The first radar groundscan of the Qumran cliffs, carried out by the author together with the CSULB Team in the winter of 1991-2.

28 BELOW: The first groundscan of the ruins on Qumran plateau in which it became clear that no real earthquake damage had occurred to the installations at Qumran.

29 BELOW RIGHT: Members of the CSULB Team and author's son groundscanning inside Cave 4.

30 LEFT: The CSULB Walking Survey of 1990–92 charting all caves from Qumran in the North to Ein Gedi in the South.

31 ABOVE: Member of the CSULB Survey Team inspecting lintel doorway of a cave 20 kilometers south of Qumran.

32 ABOVE: The 1990 Walking Survey visiting the ruins of the Judean Desert Fortress of Hyrcania (also Khirbat Mird) not far from Mar Saba where Herod kept all his treasure.

33 LEFT: The Herodian three-tier step Palace at the northern end of Masada, the Dead Sea in the distance at dusk.

34 BELOW: A view from Masada of the Roman siege camp, the Dead Sea in the distance.

35 ABOVE: The ramp the Romans built using Jewish prisoners as slave-labor to finally take Masada in 73 CE, but not before all its inhabitants committed suicide.

36 ABOVE LEFT: The storage bins at Masada, the contents of which were not burned when the inhabitants committed mass suicide, to show they '*chose death over slavery*' not hunger.

37 ABOVE: The entrance to the large water cistern that made life tenable at Masada.

38 LEFT: The text mentioning '*the Son of God*' from Cave 4.

39 ABOVE: The pilings of the Roman-style hot steam bath at Masada.

40 RIGHT: One of the frescoed murals and pillars in the three-tier luxurious palace built by Herod on Masada.

41 RIGHT: Herod's Palace at Herodion, the Fortress dedicated to his name and in which he is reputed to be buried – author sitting in the distance.

42 BELOW: 4Q285 identifying '*the Root of Jesse*' from Isaiah 11:1-5 with '*the Branch of David*' and, in turn, '*the Nasi of the Assembly*' ('*the Nasi Israel*' found on Bar Kochba coins).

43 ABOVE: Herod's winter Palace in Jericho where he had Jonathan, the last Maccabean High Priest, drowned when he came of age.

44 RIGHT: The Greek Orthodox Monastery in Wadi Kelt, also possibly the site of Kochabe, from where Bar Kochba might have come.

45 LEFT: The mouth of the Wadi Murabba^cat south of Qumran on the Dead Sea leading up to the Bar Kochba Caves further inland.

46 ABOVE: Further along the Wadi Murabba^cat in the Judean Desert leading inland to the Bar Kochba Cave.

47 ABOVE: The Cave further into the Wadi Murabba^cat where letters actually signed by Bar Kochba and his lieutenants were found.

48 ABOVE: The walls of the Judean Desert Monastery of Mar Saba (note its name), one of the oldest – the Wadi Kedron flowing down to the Dead Sea from Jerusalem in the background.

49 LEFT: The Qumran proof-text called '*The Testimonia*,' including '*The True Prophet*' of Deuteronomy 18:18-19, '*the Star Prophecy*' (from which '*Bar Kochba*' took his name), and the anti-Herodian Joshua 6:26.

50 ABOVE: The Qumran *Florilegium*, containing the promises to '*David's seed*' and referring to '*the fallen Tabernacle of David*,' '*the Sceptre to save Israel*,' and '*the Branch*.'

51 LEFT: Palm tree coin from Bar Kochba mentioning '*Shimᶜon*' (*Nasi Israel*) on the obverse and '*the Freedom of Jerusalem*' on the reverse.

52 ABOVE: The Herodian Fortress of Machaeros where John the Baptist was executed in Perea across the Dead Sea from the Wadi Kedron, the wharf, and Qumran.

53 LEFT: Hot volcanic river flowing down on the East side of the Dead Sea beneath Machaeros where Herod probably bathed during his final fatal illness.

54 BELOW LEFT: The Last Column of the Damascus Document from 4QD266, mentioning a reunion of the Desert '*Camps*' every year at Pentecost '*to curse*' (as in 1QS but unlike in Paul) '*those who depart to the right or left of Torah.*'

55 BELOW: Column xx of Ms. B of CD, which actually refers to '*the Standing up of the Messiah of Aaron and Israel,*' '*seeing Yeshu𝖼a*' ('*Jesus*' or '*Salvation*'), and '*a Book of Remembrance for God-Fearers.*'

blind seeing,' 'the dumb hearing,' again *'the lepers being cleansed,' 'the dead being raised,'* and *'the Poor* (here again, of course, *'the Poor'* terminology) *having the Gospel preached to them'*; both Luke and Matthew use patently Paulin-izing language to present him as blessing those who find *'no occasion of stumbling'* or *'being scandalized in'* him (clear counterparts of Paul's *'stum-bling block'* and *'scandal of the cross'* aspersions in 1 Corinthians 1:23, 8:9, Galatians 5:11, and Romans 9:32–3, 11:9, 14:13, etc.).

In addition, after these either *'depart'* or *'go their way,'* both Gospels pic-ture Jesus as yet again evoking *'the True Prophet'* ideology and applying it to John (7:26/11:9-10) while at the same time querying *'the Many'* about, *'going out into the wilderness'* – in the manner of Josephus' *'false prophets,' 'Impostors,'* and *'Deceivers'* – to say nothing of having him depict John as *'a reed shaken by the wind'* (7:24/11:7 – the *'Windbag'* allusion we shall presently encounter below in the Damascus Document?[75]). Moreover, they conclude by having 'Jesus,' in the manner of a scriptural exegete, himself also apply *'the preparation of the Way'* passage from Isaiah 40:3 and the Qumran Community Rule[76] to John, portraying *'the tax-collectors'* as *'having been baptized with the baptism of John'* (Luke 7:26–34/Matthew 11:10–19 – what could be more misguided and laughable than this?). This is the context in which John is portrayed, accurately for a change, as either a *'Rechabite'* or a *'Nazirite,'* that is, *'John came neither eating or drinking* (though nonetheless, as we just saw, thought by some as *'having a demon'*!) whereas Jesus, on the contrary, *'came eating and drinking'* (the omnipresent *'come'* again). It is here, too, that the famous and pointed *'glutton,' 'wine-bibber,'* and *'friend of publicans and Sinners'* barbs are evoked, which end in the plainly nonsensical: *'and Wisdom is justified by Her works'* (in Luke 7:35: *'by all Her Children'* – thus)!

It is at this point, too, that Jesus is portrayed as visiting yet another *'house'* in Luke 7:36–37 (again not paralleled in either Matthew or Mark), now that of *'the Pharisee,'* already discussed in some detail above, and keep-ing *'table fellowship'* with him (the *'table fellowship'* theme again) or, as this is also put in the passage, *'reclining'* or *'eating with him'* (7:36–37 – this is the same *'recline'* that we just encountered above in the matter of Jesus' proposed visit in Matthew 8:5–13 to the house of another *'Pious'* Roman Centurion (that is, in addition to the one in Acts 10:1) *'to cure his servant'* (the *'servant'* theme again) and *'the Many that shall come from the East and West and recline with Abraham, Isaac, and Jacob in the Kingdom of Heaven'* – also preceded in Matthew 8:2–3 by another of these ubiquitous *'leper(s) coming and worshipping him'* and Jesus *'touching him,' 'making him clean'* (the incessant *'touching'* and *'making clean'* themes again)

There are also additional possible allusions of this genre to *'go your way*,' depending on how one wishes to translate the usage in the Gospels, in particular in Matthew 5:23–4's '*Sermon on the Mount*' in the key context of '*gifts to the Temple*' again – '*leave your gift before the altar and go your way*'; in Matthew 8:1–13, following the miracle of Jesus '*making the leper clean*' and before curing the paralytic '*servant*' of the humble and over-modest Roman Centurion (here, we have something in the order of a Roman military-recruiting manual), where it is now the '*some of the Kingdom*,' as we saw, who '*shall be cast (ekblethesontai) into outer Darkness*' and the Centurion's '*Faith*' is '*Greater than all in Israel*' (8:10); in John 4:50, after curing the '*little child*' of another supplicating '*nobleman*,' this one in '*Galilee*' and '*the second of the signs Jesus did on coming out of Judea to Galilee*' (the only one that comes to mind in these locales would be one or another of the '*Herod*'s – n.b., again the '*coming*'); in Mark 10:21, after '*allowing the little children to come unto*' him and '*laying hands upon them*,' once again, '*touching them*' and '*blessing them*' – this followed by yet another suppliant (this one unnamed), '*running up*,' '*kneeling down to him*,' and again calling him '*Teacher*' (10:13–20 – one should once more note the parallel with Qumran both here and in the '*coming out of Judea to Galilee*' materials, just indicated in John 4:54 above); and finally in Mark 10:52 and 11:2, following '*the camel*' and '*the eye of the needle*' allusions in 10:25, leading into Jesus in '*Bethany*' again riding on '*the colt*,' and culminating – contrary to the complaints of the '*some*' again – in the '*Many spreading their garments before him on the way*' (11:5–8), exactly in the manner of '*the Poor*' in the '*Nakdimon*'/'*Jesus ben Gamala*' stories above.[77]

In this picture in Mark 11:7 too, so enthusiastic are the People that they even '*cast (epebalon) their garments on the colt*' as well. The same episode occurs in Luke 19:29–36 but before this, even more interestingly, in 17:11–19 the one '*falling on his knees*' of Mark 10:17 becomes one of '*ten lepers*' ('*standing at a distance*'), who now rather '*falls on his face*' and happens to be '*a Samaritan*' (i.e., now we have '*a Samaritan leper*'! – but it basically shows the interchangeability of all these expressions) and the '*ten lepers*' of Luke 17:12 turn into, in Mark 10:41, '*the Ten*' Disciples who '*complain about*' or '*are jealous of James and John*' (*sic*)!

To go back to Luke 7:37: it was at this point, as will be recalled, that yet another woman appeared, called '*a woman in the city*' and '*a Sinner*,' bringing the *pro forma* '*alabaster flask of ointment*' (the clear meaning here, of course, is that of '*Gentile*' as per Paul's Galatians 2:15 allusion to '*Gentile Sinners*,' the '*tax collector*' in Luke 18:13 and 19:7 – obviously supposed to represent '*Herodians*,' or the '*Greek Syrophoenician woman*' from Sidon or Tyre in Matthew 15 and Mark 7; but there is also the idea of an '*Am ha-Aretz*' or an unclean '*Person of the Country*' from the *Talmud* – possibly also intending '*Herodians*'[78]). Once again, one should compare this with the woman with the '*alabaster flask of ointment*' at '*Simon the Leper's house*' in Mark 14:3 and Matthew 26:7, an episode missing from Luke where, as we saw, it has already been replaced in 10:38–42 both by the visit to '*Martha's house*' ('*in a certain village*') and in 16:19–31 the '*Lazarus under the table whose sores were licked by dogs*' episode (this one also mentioning, just as Matthew 8:11 above, '*Abraham's bosom*'; but now instead of '*Isaac and Jacob*,' '*Moses and the Prophets*') – '*the lepers being cleansed*' already having been mentioned along with '*the blind*,' '*the lame*,' '*the deaf*,' and '*the Poor*' in Jesus' earlier response to John's '*certain two*' (as usual, unnamed) '*Disciples*' in Luke 7:22 and this same '*Simon*,' albeit now identified as '*the Pharisee*' not '*the Leper*,' about to be mentioned in Luke 7:40 (again showing the basic transmutability of all these terminologies!).

At the risk of some redundancy, the reader will bear with us if we repeat some of the points of this episode, since they are so remarkable and the issues at stake are so momentous. Now '*standing behind* (again, the further adumbration of the '*Standing*' notation encountered throughout all the Gospels – even '*the ten lepers standing at a distance*' in Luke 17:12 above – reflecting, just as the '*coming of the True Prophet*' in 7:18–20 preceding it, 'the *Standing One*' or '*Primal Adam*'-ideology[79]), *weeping at his feet*' (in Luke 8:41 to follow, it will be '*Jairus, a Ruler of the Synagogue*,' who '*falls at his feet*,' while in Luke 17:16 above, '*the leper*' who '*was a Samaritan*' only '*fell on his face at his feet*'!) while '*the Pharisee*' – like Judas Iscariot, Martha, and '*the Disciples*' in other such episodes – whom we have discovered and shall discover again was called '*Simon*,' *complained*,

> *she began to wash his feet with her tears and she was wiping them with the hairs of her head*' (as we saw, one should compare this, in particular, with John 12:3's '*Mary anointing the feet of Jesus and wiping his feet with her hair*' previously, but also some of the Talmudic episodes relating to Rabbi Eliezer ben Hyrcanus and Rabbi Akiba above).

It is not hard to see that we have all our imageries in just this one sentence, but so carried away by this time is Luke that he doesn't stop here but rather goes on (to repeat), '*And she was lovingly kissing his feet and anointing them with ointment*' (7:38).

Now we really do have all our themes, and motifs, but '*the Pharisee*' – like '*the Pharisees*' as '*Blind Guides*' and in the '*Unwashed Hands*' Parable, leading up to exorcizing the '*Greek Syrophoenician*'/'*Cananaean woman*''s daughter episode in Mark 7:23–30 and Matthew 15:21–28 but, significantly, not in Luke (here in Luke 8:1–3, this leads directly into the introduction of the '*certain women who had been cured of Evil spirits*,' including '*Mary Magdalene, out of whom*,' as we have also seen, '*seven demons had gone, and Joanna the wife of Chuza, a steward* – more of the '*steward*' allusions we shall immediately encounter below – *of Herod, and Susanna and many others*,' all portrayed as '*being with him*' like '*the Twelve*' and '*ministering to him* – '*diakonoun*' again – *out of their substance*') – yet again raises both the issue of such a woman '*touching him*' and '*the True Prophet*' characterization (this time as applied to 'Jesus'), namely, '*if he were (such) a Prophet*,' how could he allow such a woman ('*a Sinner*') to '*touch him*' (presumably meaning because she was either a Gentile or alluding to the defective state of her '*purity*' – 7:39)?

It is at this point that Jesus starts to talk to someone he now, as just noted, suddenly addresses as '*Simon*' who responds by calling him '*Teacher*' again (7:40). Just as in the '*Simon the Leper*' episode in Matthew 26:6–13 and Mark 14:3–9, this obviously should have been '*Simon Peter*' but, except for the rebuke which is about to follow in Matthew 26:34 and Mark 14:30 – like the rebuke to either '*the Disciples*' or '*Peter*' over misunderstanding the point about food '*not defiling the man*' in Matthew 15:10–20 and Mark 7:14–23 above – '*Simon Peter*' was never part of the episode. Not only does Jesus now clearly mean, as just signaled, that '*the Pharisee*,' with whom he is now '*reclining*' Socratic-style and discoursing in a dialectical manner, is called '*Simon*'; but what is really being picked up here is the '*Simon*' from the '*Simon the Leper's house*' encounter '*in Bethany*' in Matthew 26:6 and Mark 14:3 (to say nothing of the allusion to '*Simon Iscariot*' in John 12:4) – and the dizzying circle of these variations and elaborations continues. Of course, we are also in the area of the '*table fellowship*' issue too, since Jesus has been invited '*to eat*' and '*reclined (at the table) at the house of the Pharisee*' (7:36) – how symbolic!

Again, though Simon has done nothing but offer him '*table fellowship*' (by now, it should be obvious that this '*Pharisee*,' as just underscored, is supposed to be a caricature of '*Simon Peter*,' since this was the issue that so divided him from Paul in Galatians 2:11–2:17 above); Jesus launches into a lengthy diatribe, ending with the usual refrain from the '*Jairus*' (who also, as we just saw, '*falls at his feet*')/'*woman with the twelve-year flow of blood*' and '*Cananaean woman's daughter*' episodes and now, as just underscored too, the '*Centurion*' whose '*Faith was greater than all in Israel*' as well, that is to say, '*Your Faith has saved you*' (Luke 7:50). It also incorporates the same '*creditor*'/'*debtor*' haggling over numbers, we have already encountered in Luke 16:1–15's parable about '*the Unfaithful Servant*,' to say nothing of Matthew 25:14–30's equally-mercantile capitalist parable above about how those who, having seemingly invested their money with '*money-lenders*,' doubled the number of their '*talents*' and the '*interest*' earned from '*two*' to '*four*' and '*five*' to '*ten*' (*n.b.*, this one ostensibly advanced in response to a question in 25:11 from '*ten virgins*' – the counterpart to Luke 17:12's '*ten lepers standing at a distance*' who were '*Samaritans*'? – the '*ten virgins*' themselves being the subject of an equally-mercantile parable from 25:1–10 (preceding this one about the '*worthy*' and '*unworthy servants*') involving '*five wise (virgins)*' and '*five foolish*' which even seems to end in 25:10 with the allusion to '*shutting the door*,' we have already called attention to and will call attention to further in Column Six of the Damascus Document below[80]); and in Matthew 18:21–35 where, again in response to Peter (which also involved, not one, but two additional '*falling at his feet*'s), the numbers were '*seven*,' '*seventy*,' '*ten thousand talents*,' and '*one hundred dinars*.'

Though in Luke 16:1–18 which, it will be recalled, was again about '*a certain Rich Man's steward*' and his '*baths of oil*' – and alluded to '*the Sons of Light*,' '*digging*,' speaks of '*the Unrighteous steward*,' evokes like James 4:4 above '*making yourselves friends of the Unrighteous Mammon*', and is directed yet again against '*the Pharisees*' – the haggling is over the numbers '*eighty cors*' or '*measures of wheat*' and '*a hundred*,' either '*cors of wheat*' or '*baths of oil*.' Here in Luke 7:41, it is '*five hundred dinars*' as opposed to '*fifty*' but, in any event, all have a good deal in common with '*Nakdimon*''s '*cistern*' negotiations with which we started in Chapter Eight. It also reflects the '*three hundred dinars*'-numerical variations of both the '*Simon the Leper*' and John 12:5's '*Judas of Simon Iscariot*'/'*Lazarus*'/'*house in Bethany*' encounters and Matthew 26:15's tenfold reduction of this in the amount then '*appointed to*' Judas by '*the Chief Priests*' to '*betray*' or '*deliver him up*.' Nor is this to say anything about the '*one hundred dinars*'-amount owed by '*the fellow debtor*' in Matthew 18:29 above or the '*hundred baths of oil*' or the '*hundred measures of wheat*' in Luke 16:1–18's equally mercantile parable. But even more germane than this, aside from the parallel represented by the haggling between '*Nakdimon*' and '*his lord*' over the number of '*cisterns of water*' that were owed or '*needed filling*,' it even more precisely corresponds to the '*four*' to '*five hundred dinar*' amounts Rabbinic tradition reckons as the value of Nakdimon's daughter's '*perfume basket*'!

These parallels being as they may, now complimenting '*Simon*' in Luke 7:43 – in the typical style of Platonic dialogue – as '*having judged rightly*' (this in response to his own '*creditor*'/'*debtor*' analogy, again regarding '*a certain debtor*' and the debt he owed a '*money-lender*'); Jesus nevertheless then turns and, in 7:44, addresses – in the self-centered style we have now come to expect (the style of Hellenistic gods visiting mere mortals on Earth) – '*Simon the Pharisee*' with a complaint we were not expecting at all. This, too, we have partially reproduced above but, once again, it is worth reproducing it in full:

> *Do you see this woman? I entered your house, but you gave me no water for my feet. Yet she washed my feet with tears and wiped them with the hairs of her head* (here, not only do we have the perpetual reiteration of the '*feet*' and '*hairs*' themes, but also the doubled repetition of Lazarus' sister Mary '*wiping Jesus' feet with her hair*' in John 11:2 and 12:3). *You gave me no kiss* (this is the same kind of '*kissing*' of the Rabbi Akiba episode above, when he returns to meet his wife after years of study or that of her father, '*Ben Kalba Sabuᶜa*,' when he has heard how famous Akiba had become), *but since I came in she has not ceased lovingly kissing my feet. You did not anoint my head with oil* (as already several times remarked, it is Jesus who – paralleling his '*Poor you have with you always, but you do not always have me*' retort in Matthew 26:11, Mark 14:7, and John 12:8 – appears the real egoist here. Though, again. this might do in Hellenistic circles but never Hebraic), *but she anointed my feet with ointment*' (meaning the expensive '*aromatic ointment of pure spikenard*' above – Luke 7:44–46).

As we noted, this is about the fifth, sixth, or seventh such episode to use these themes but, I think, we can safely say, this one just about says it all.

Miriam's Hair, Casting Martha's Silver into the Street, and the Stink of R. Eliezer's Bad Breath

To go back to Lamentations *Rabbah*, after the material about R. Eleazar ben Zadok swearing on '*the Consolation of Zion*' if he did not see the Romans binding Boethus' daughter's hair '*to the tails of Arab horses and making her run from Jerusalem to Lydda*'; the narrative switches back in the very next passage to Nakdimon ben Gurion's daughter '*Miriam*' ('*Mary*'). It is here that it noted how '*the Rabbis allowed her five hundred dinars daily to be spent on her store of perfumes*' – the '*five hundred dinars*' we just saw in Luke 7:41 above in Jesus' rebuke to '*Simon the Pharisee*' (however similar to those of '*Simon Peter*' elsewhere, clearly meant to be a likeness of Matthew/Mark's '*Simon the Leper*' – himself a variation of the '*Simon Iscariot*' in John 12:4?) – over another unnamed '*woman in the city*' with '*an alabaster flask of ointment*' (now only identified as '*a Sinner*') washing Jesus' '*feet*' again '*with her tears*' and '*wiping them with her hair*' (the '*feet*' of both the '*Shiloh*' Prophecy and '*the Standing One*' above?). Nor is this to say anything about the '*daily*' (the '*daily*' of the Nakdimon's daughter '*perfume*'/'*dinar*' quote?) self-indulgent luxury engaged in by Luke 16:19's '*Rich Man clothed in purple and fine linen*' while *the 'sores'* – which *'Poor'* Lazarus' body *'were full of '* – were *'licked by dogs.'*

It is here Lamentations *Rabbah* quotes the passage from the Song of Songs 1:8, just remarked above as well and again attributed to Rabbi Eleazar, '*O thou fairest among women, go your way forth among the footsteps of the flock and feed your offspring*' (in the original, this is literally '*gediyot* / '*kids,*' which for some reason is reinterpreted here in the text as '*geviyot* / '*bodies*' – the sense of which translates out in English as '*offspring*' – typical of the wordplay of this period which will be of no small significance in the Habakkuk *Pesher's* description of the desecration of the Wicked Priest's '*corpse*' and other usages, such as '*uncovering their festivals*' for '*uncovering their privy parts,*' we shall consider in more detail below[81]). The same oath about '*seeing the Consolation of Zion*' is uttered again by R. Eleazar ben Zadok, this time in connection with his having seen Nakdimon's daughter '*gathering barley grains from beneath the feet of horses in Acco*' – here, of course, '*the feet*' are now '*the feet of horses*'; but, as ever, it is important to have regard for the '*feet,*' '*footsteps,*' '*barley grains,*' and '*hair*' motifs, we have so consistently been following above. Nor is this to forget the possible echo of this '*go your way*' phraseology in the several Gospel passages just remarked above as well.

In this material in Lamentations *Rabbah*, which follows the note about '*the Rabbis granting*' Boethus' daughter, '*Miriam*' (*sic*), the widow's allowance of '*two se'ahs of wine daily*' (again, of course, there is the '*daily*' usage here) after the death of her husband, Josephus' friend '*Jesus ben Gamala*' (here the evocation about '*the camel*' and '*his burden*' that will, as we shall see, be applied to this situation in *Gittin* below will be of more than ordinary import – nor do the Rabbinic sources evince very much concern over the circumstances of this '*Jesus'*' death); now the '*feet*' will be '*her feet,*' not '*the feet of horses in Acco,*' and here, of course, occurs the note about '*carpets being laid for her from the door of her house to the entrance of the Temple* occurs (a sort of awe not completely unsimilar to the 'Jesus' entry-into-Jerusalem scenario also just remarked above), *so her feet would not be exposed*' – the Talmudic narrator then sardonically adding, as we have pointed up as well, '*nevertheless they were exposed.*'[82]

In case the reader is unfamiliar with or confused by these various sources, it is important to realize that the same tradition is related in Tractate *Kethuboth*, but there it is rather attributed to R. Yohanan ben Zacchai, '*leaving Jerusalem riding upon an ass, while his Disciples followed him*' (R. Yohanan too, it seems – just like '*Jesus*' and Rabbi Akiba above – had '*his Disciples*' and he, too, '*rides upon an ass*' or '*donkey,*' though unlike '*Jesus*' entering Jerusalem on Good Friday, as just remarked above, *he is leaving*

Jerusalem). Again it should be noted – for whatever it's worth – how even here in this version of Jesus *'riding on an ass'/'the colt of an ass'* material in Mark 11:2 and Luke 19:30 – though not, once again, in the third Synoptic Matthew 21:7 – Jesus appears to be using the equivalent in Greek of the expression *'go your way'* above in Hebrew.

Here in *Kethuboth* the exchange between Rabbi Yohanan and Nakdimon's daughter, *'picking barley grains out of the dung of Arab cattle,'* is more detailed and focuses even further on the utter reversal of her fortune and the complete obliteration of the *'Riches'* of both her father and her father-in-law's house (whoever he may have been – thus seemingly continuing the mix-up in Rabbinic sources between *'Boethus'' daughter Martha'* and *'Nakdimon's daughter Miriam'*[83]). Moreover, here, too the ever-present motif of *'her hair'* is added. Now *'standing up'* to answer the *'Master''s* questions (*n.b.*, Rabbi Yohanan like Jesus is also being called *'Master'* here),

> She *wrapped* (not *'wiped'* as in John and Luke above) *herself with her hair and stood before him* (another of those *'stood'* allusions though here, probably without the same import).

It is in this context that the Talmudic narrators asked the question concerning whether Nakdimon practised *'true charity'* itself related, as we saw, to complaints by 'Judas *Iscariot,'* *'the Disciples,'* the *'some,'* and characters like *'the Pharisee'* named *'Simon'* above, about why Jesus' *'feet'* were being either *'washed,'* *'wiped with hair,'* *'anointed,'* or *'kissed'* and the *'dinar'* equivalent of the *'precious spikenard ointment'* which should have *'been sold and given to the Poor.'*

It is at this point in *Kethuboth*, too, that the above, now familiar, description, *'when he walked from his house to the house of study, woollen clothes were spread beneath his feet and the Poor followed behind him gathering them up'* (and which, as we also just saw, perhaps not completely unrelated to the matter of Jesus' entry into Jerusalem) is added which not only includes the *'feet'* and *'the Poor'* themes, but after which the narrators comment that this was not *'true charity'* but, rather, *'he did it for his own Glorification'* (one might, as already remarked, say the same about Gospel portraits of some of Jesus' more self-centered responses above). It is at this point too, just as in Lamentations *Rabbah* as we have seen, that the proverb is cited, *'in accordance with the camel is the burden'* – this last linking up with the familiar New Testament aphorism, *'easier would it be for a camel to go through the eye of the needle than a Rich Man to enter the Kingdom of God'* (Matthew 19:24 and *pars.* – it is also not unimportant to collate all these '*camel*' allusions[84]).

In the '*Mary daughter of Boethus*' material from Lamentations *Rabbah* above, for whom '*the carpets are laid*' so '*her feet*' would not touch the ground and about whom R. Eleazar ben Zadok is pictured as remarking concerning '*not living to see the Consolation (of Zion) if (he) did not see the Romans bind her hair to the tails of Arab horses and make her run from Jerusalem to Lydda*'; it was rather, as already underscored, one of the Mosaic woes, Deuteronomy 28:56, evoking,

> *The tender and delicate woman among you who would not adventure to put the sole of her feet upon the ground for tenderness and delicateness*

that is being cited to point out Boethus' daughter's precipitous reversal of fortune and how she died a beggar – not Song of Songs 1:8, as in the version that immediately follows in Lamentations *Rabbah* relative to this same R. Eleazar ben Zadok's comments about the downfall of '*Miriam the daughter of Nakdimon*' whom he now rather sees, as just pointed out, '*gathering barley corns from beneath the feet of horses in Acco.*'

The confusion over the names of these two '*daughters*,' whoever's daughters they are, also appears to drift – as we have been showing – into both John's '*Lazarus*' story and the segments of it that reappear in the Gospel of Luke where, instead of being two '*daughters*,' they now appear as two '*sisters*' who are either '*anointing*' Jesus' head with '*precious spikenard ointment*' or '*wiping his feet with their hair and bathing them with their tears*'; and even, according to what is basically the final presentation, *preparing his body for burial.* As we proceed, we will see how this brings us back to the '*Nakdimon*'/'*Nicodemus*' duality, who will *himself be involved in the preparation of Jesus' body for burial* according to the Gospel of John.

The shift here from '*anointing*' Jesus, presumably either for '*King*' or '*Messiahship*,' to preparing his body for burial takes place, as already observed, in the response Jesus is pictured as making to '*Judas Iscariot*'s complaint to him over the '*dinar*' value of the precious spikenard ointment which '*Judas*' – and, in the encounter at '*Simon the Leper*'s (not '*Simon Iscariot*'s) house,' the '*some*' or '*the Disciples*' – thinks '*should have been given to the Poor*' (John 12:5 and *pars.*). It is in this context that Jesus evokes the burial theme replying, as we saw, '*Let her alone. She has kept it for the day of my burial*' (the '*leave them alone*' of Matthew 15:14, now being applied in John 12:7 to Lazarus' and Martha's sister Mary and not '*the Pharisees*' or '*Blind Guides*' of the '*Uprooted Planting*'/'*Toilet Bowl*' Parable in Matthew 15:10–20; and, furthermore, not the reply to the '*some*' or '*the Disciples*' over '*the woman who came to anoint him with the alabaster flask of precious spikenard ointment at the house of Simon the Leper'* in Mark 14:3–9 and Matthew 26:6–13 above).

To understand all of these thematic twists and turns, overwrites and reversals, the reader should group together – as we have done – all these episodes both about Talmudic *'Rich'* persons (whether Ben Kalba *Sabuᶜa, Ben Zizzit*, Nakdimon ben Gurion, his daughter, or Boethus' daughter) and New Testament variations or enhancements. To show that the same overlaps and/or revisions are taking place in the *Talmud* as in the New Testament, later in *Kethuboth* this same aphorism, *'in accordance with the camel is the burden,'* is evoked once more, but this time it is applied – as already indicated – rather to *recovering the surety in the matter of a marriage contract (kethubah)*.[85] Now, since this is *Kethuboth* and not Lamentations *Rabbah*, it really is *'Martha'* who is involved and she is correctly identified as *'the daughter of Boethus'* and, as in the case of Nakdimon's treatment of *'the Poor'* previously, she is now being compared, somewhat anomalously, to *'the Poorest woman in Israel.'* Moreover, this is the context in which the aphorism, *'in accordance with the camel is the burden,'* is quoted – this time, to show that the twenty-five year limitation for recovery of a dowry was still applicable even though she was now *'Poor'* – *'Rich'* and *'Poor'* being equal before the law.[86] Of course this is to say nothing about her husband's patronym *'Gamala,'* which means *'camel'* in Hebrew, or the brutal circumstance of his death (along with that of James' judicial murderer, Jesus ben Ananias) at the hands of the so-called *'Idumaeans'* and *'Zealots.'*[87]

As *Gittin* picks up this material about *'Martha the daughter of Boethus,'* it too now calls her *'one of the Richest women in Jerusalem'* – this, once again, in the context of reference to these three *'Rich Men,'* Nakdimon ben Gurion, *Ben Kalba Sabuᶜa*, and *Ben Zizzit Hakeseth*.[88] Not only does *Gittin* reiterate here why *Ben Zizzit* was so designated, namely, either *'because his fringes (zizzith) used to trail on cushions'* (again, the *'cushions'/ 'clothes'/'garments'* theme) or because *'his seat (kiseh) was among the Great Ones of Rome'*; but also that these three were *'in a position to keep* (Jerusalem) *in supplies* (specifically denoted here as *'wheat and barley, wine, oil, salt, and wood') for twenty-one years'* at a time when *'the Biryonim'* were *'in control of the city.'* Though the chronology is important here, both in terms of Helen's three successive *'Nazirite'*-oath periods of seven years imposed upon her by the Rabbis and the successive numbers of cisterns in the Nakdimon *'rain-making'* scenario; as we have seen, this too would seem to be an exaggeration as, whoever these *'Rich Men'* are in the end determined to be, they cannot be thought of as being in control of Jerusalem for twenty-one years.[89]

This being said, the term '*Biryonim*' has been widely recognized as a Talmudic term to indicate '*Revolutionaries*' or '*Zealots*' – in fact, actually most probably '*Sicarii*.'[90] It has even been associated, as already indicated, with the term '*Simon Bar Jonah*,' which Jesus applies to Peter in Matthew 16:17. This is the scene in which Peter designates Jesus in 16:16 as '*the Christ, the Son of the Living God*' (in Mark 8:29 and Luke 9:20, only '*the Christ*' or '*the Christ of God*') and, seemingly, in return Jesus designates Peter as his Successor, '*the Rock upon which I will build my Church*,' giving him '*the keys of the Kingdom of Heaven*' (*sic* – 16:18). Though it has moved very deeply into the popular consciousness, the second part is notably missing from all the other Gospels, though it is – minus '*the keys*' and '*build my Church*' part – to some extent reflected in John 1:42 where Jesus, not only calls Peter '*Son of Jonah*' ('*Bar Jonah*'), but applies the term '*Cephas*' to him which, playing upon the meaning of '*Peter*' in Greek, he or the narrator actually interprets as meaning '*Stone*' ('*Petros*').

Nevertheless, in the scene as it develops in John 1:45–51, it is rather left to the individual we have elsewhere identified as a stand-in for James (in John – where otherwise James is nowhere mentioned), '*Nathanael*' ('*Given-by-God*') – because 1) Jesus first sees him like a Honi *redivivus* sitting '*under a fig-tree*' (1:48) and 2) he sees '*the Angels of God going up and coming down upon the Son of Man*' (1:51) – to identify Jesus as '*the Son of God*' and '*the King of Israel*' (1:49), the second of which we take to mean '*Messiah*.' Finally, as this scene draws to a close in Matthew 16:20, there is some indication that the designation is not widely known, at least not in Palestine, as Jesus tells Peter that '*he should tell no man he was the Christ*.'[91]

When the Rabbis, true to the political orientation of the Pharisees – those it would appear the Scrolls designate, *inter alia*, as '*the Seekers after Smooth Things*' (in this regard too, one should take note of Josephus' characterization of '*the Peace Party*' in Jerusalem, who send to the Romans outside Jerusalem at the beginning of the Uprising – via one '*Saulos*' whom we shall discuss further below – to come into the city and suppress it, as '*the principal Pharisees, the Chief Priests, and the Men of Power*,' the last clearly intending '*Herodians*'[92]) – wish '*to go out and make peace with*' the Romans, these '*Biryonim*,' according to the presentation of Tractate *Gittin* here (and this does seem to be accurate) '*prevent them*.' These same '*Biryonim*' are also described as '*burning all the stores of wheat and barley so that a famine ensued*' (here, of course, the real origin probably of many of the '*wheat and barley*' evocations above). Not only is this fact also borne out in Josephus' narrative,[93] it is reflected, it would appear, in '*the Famine*' with which we originally began this series of traditions circulating around the persons of Nakdimon ben Gurion and his colleagues.

It is in this context, too, that one of the final stories, chronologically speaking, is told about '*Martha the daughter of Boethus*' and, once again, this time *Gittin* has her *prenom* right.[94] As this is presented – and by now a certain tragic sadness has begun to envelop her story – after sending her servant out four different times: first to buy fine flour, next white flour, after that dark flour, then barley flour (clearly, four declining grades of quality, indicating how far the famine had progressed within the city) and finding there was none, suddenly she is described as '*taking off her shoes*'! Why she should do so at this point is unclear (unless she didn't want to get them '*dirty*') but, as is the way with these Talmudic traditions, it doesn't really matter – the allusion having made it possible for her to be barefoot again and for the final bit of information to emerge, that is, she then went out, but '*some dung stuck to her feet and she died*' (here again, both the '*feet*' and '*dung*' themes). Again, too, all of this is typical both of Rabbinic hyperbole and laconic understatement.

Once again, it is Rabbi Yohanan ben Zacchai who applies the passage from Deuteronomy 28:56 ('*The most tender and delicate of your women would not venture to set the sole of her feet upon the ground*' – previously applied above in Lamentations *Rabbah* by Rabbi Eleazar ben Zadok) – and this certainly with more justice – to the patheticness of Martha's fate and how he saw her reduced from her Rabbinic allowance of '*five hundred dinars daily just for her perfume box*' to '*gathering barley corns from beneath the feet of horses in Acco*' – though '*Rabbi Zadok*' (not '*Eleazar ben Zadok*,' seemingly perhaps, his father) is evoked in almost the very next sentence about the fast he supposedly observed '*for forty years so that Jerusalem might not be destroyed.*'[95]

In fact, so thin was he – R. Zadok, that is – that '*when he ate anything the food could be seen*,' meaning as it passed down his throat – more Talmudic hyperbole and fascination with earthly physicality as opposed to New Testament spiritual ethereality. It is in this context that the observation is made too that,

> *When Rabbi Zadok wished to restore himself, they used to bring him a fig and he used to suck the juice and throw the rest away* (here, yet another variation of the '*casting*' allusion, which then leads directly into those about Martha, '*when she was about to die*,' '*casting*' all her gold and silver '*into the street*,' we had already seen in this section of *Gittin*).

Nor is this description of Rabbi Zadok completely unrelated to some of the usages found in Matthew and Mark's picture of the '*Toilet Bowl*' Parable Jesus tells which, not only mentions *food going into his mouth* and seemingly '*down his throat*,' but '*casting the rest away*.' Even more to the point, this description of R. Zadok clearly correlates with and has many of the elements of depictions of James, including his perennial fasting and vegetarianism. Be this as it may, in another display of typical Talmudic earthiness or corporeality, it is now reported that some say,

> she ate the fig left by Rabbi Zadok (meaning the pulp he had discarded when he sucked out the juice), *became sick, and died!*[96]

Here, too, one should perhaps quote another Talmudic story, which in its pathetic sadness and tragicality has to be seen as defining this period – at least from the Judean point-of-view – and really does tug at the heartstrings. Clearly it did nothing of the sort to those who created the stories from the same period that found their way into the New Testament which show neither any such empathy or pity (or, for that matter, even '*charity*') and, however one might admire their artfulness or the cosmopolitanism of their spiritual message, in the circumstances, *are hard-hearted in the extreme.*

The story which is conserved, as usual, in two versions – one in Lamentations *Rabbah* and one here in Tractate *Gittin* – once more, seemingly, relates to this same Rabbi Zadok, now taken for a '*High Priest*' (though, since it is extant in two versions, it might be another).[97] In *Gittin*, it is told in relation to the children of a Rabbi named Ishmael ben Elisha, who probably is to be identified with another '*Boethusian*'-style '*High Priest*' in this period, Ishmael ben Phiabi.[98] But since most of our more reliable traditions from this time, particularly this kind of heart-rending material, seem to be emanating out of Lamentations *Rabbah* and the *ARN*, we will assume that the Lamentations one is more reliable although, where the sense and piteous impact of the story is concerned, it is immaterial. The story, which actually introduces this whole series of tales about '*Miriam the daughter of Boethus*' (thus) and the aphorism attributed to R. Eleazer ben Zadok in Lamentations *Rabbah,* reads as follows:

> It is related that the children of Zadok the Priest, one a boy and the other a girl, were taken captive to Rome (by Vespasian and Titus after the fall of the Temple in 70 CE), each falling to the lot of a different officer. One officer *resorted to a prostitute* (our '*harlotry*' allusion but now presented in a more normatively deprecating fashion) and gave her the boy (as a slave). The other went into the store of a shopkeeper and *gave him the girl in exchange for some wine* (this, in order to fulfill the text from Joel 4:3 in which is written: '*And they have given a boy for a harlot and sold a girl for*

wine' – here the use of biblical proof-texts to refer to present-day events of both the Dead Sea Scrolls and the Gospels). After a while the prostitute brought the boy to the shopkeeper and said to him, '*Since I have a boy, who is suitable for the girl you have, will you agree they should marry and whatever issues (from the union) be divided between us?*' He accepted the offer. They immediately took them and placed them in a room. The girl began to weep and the boy *asked her why she was crying?* She answered, '*Should I not weep, when the daughter of a High Priest is given in marriage to one (such as you), a slave?*' (here the imperiousness of the '*daughter of Boethus*'/'*Nakdimon's daughter*' traditions '*shines through*' – again, no pun intended).

He inquired of her *whose daughter she was* and she replied, '*I am the daughter of Zadok the High Priest.*' He then asked her, *where she used to live* and she answered, '*In the upper market place*' (the '*upper room*' of Luke 22:12 and Mark 14:15 '*Last Supper*' scenarios – scenarios going on to include '*henceforth not drinking of the fruit of the vine until the Kingdom of God shall come*'?). He next inquired, '*What was the sign above the house?*' and she told him. He said, '*Have you a brother or a sister?*' She answered, '*I had a brother and there was a mole on his shoulder and whenever he came home from school, I used to uncover it and kiss it*' (the several women '*kissing*' Jesus' feet in the various encounters above, soon to be followed by the odd discussion in John 13:1–11 – again mostly centered about Simon Peter and Judas of Simon *Iscariot's* imminent intention 'to betray him' – concerning Jesus' curious request to now rather '*wash*' the Disciples' '*feet*'?). He asked, '*If you were to see it, would you know it now?*' She answered, '*I would.*' He bared his shoulder and they recognized one another. *They then embraced and kissed till they expired. Then the Holy Spirit cried out* (this in both Lamentations *Rabbah* and *Gittin*), '*For these things I weep!*'[99]

One might opine, this is probably what any '*Holy Spirit*' (if there was one) would cry out in circumstances such as these – not some of the more romantic paradigms based on Greco-Roman tragi-comedies with which we are more familiar.[100]

Lamentations *Rabbah* then follows this up with more stories about '*Miriam the daughter of Boethus*,' though here she is called '*Miriam the daughter of Boethus Nahtum*' (*thus* – that is, '*Nakdimon*'), once again, clearly indicating the mix-up between the patronyms, '*Nakdimon*' and '*Boethus.*' Most likely we are probably dealing with Nakdimon's daughter and not Boethus' but, however this may be, the tradition which is conserved here – and which is followed by another one about '*Miriam the daughter of Nahtum*' (this one repeated in *Gittin,* but without any attribution and a 2 Maccabees 7:1–34 'Seven Brothers'-style martyrdom epic[101]) – claims that whichever 'Miriam' or 'Mary daughter of Nahtum' this was 'was taken captive and ransomed at Acco.'[102]

Because she was by this time so poor, the people had bought her a shift which, when she went to wash it in the sea, was carried away by a sudden wave, whereupon they bought her another one and the same thing happened. At that point she refused any further help and the story which, like the several Jesus 'Parables' in Luke 7:40–43, 16:1–13, and Matthew 18:12–35, already underscored above, also uses 'debt,' 'debtor,' and 'debt collection' language to have her conclude parabolically, 'Let the Debt Collector (meaning, God at 'the Last Judgement' and for her sins) collect His debt,' whereupon her garments were miraculously restored to her – a clearly symbolic resurrection story.

In the Maccabean-style 'Seven Brothers' martyrdom story that immediately follows – after the death of six of her other sons and quoting a whole series of biblical proof-texts a propos of these; this 'Miriam'/'Mary' actually alludes to her remaining child – much like the several Gospel recitals above evoking 'being with' or 'sitting down with Abraham in the Heavens' – 'going to talk to the Patriach Abraham.' To review these: in Matthew 8:6–13 'the Centurion' who wants his servant to be cured, but stops Jesus in the nick of time from entering his house, is complimented for having such 'Great Faith' – this really is unkind in the light of the pathetic and heart-rending materials we are analyzing here – as to enable him to 'sit down with Abraham while the Children of the Kingdom shall be thrown into outer Darkness'; Luke 13:24–35 puts this parabolically, alluding to 'seeing Abraham' while at the same time uses 'casting out' language, refers to 'shutting the door' and 'standing outside,' makes the 'killing the Prophets' accusation to predict the destruction of Jerusalem, ends – in a total parody of Qumran ideology – with the proverbial 'the First shall be Last and the Last shall be First'; and finally in 16:22–31 'Poor Lazarus,' after having 'his sores licked by dogs,' is 'carried away by Angels into Abraham's bosom.'

For its part, the woman Lamentations Rabbah is calling 'Miriam' or 'Mary' encourages her only remaining son to,

> Go to the Patriarch Abraham and tell him… that your mother actually built seven altars and offered up seven sons in one day. Whereas yours was only a test (cf. Hebrews 11:17 on Abraham's 'only-begotten' test), mine was in earnest,

at which point, 'while she was embracing and kissing him' (the language of 'embracing and kissing' now, not of Jesus' 'feet' but in the martyrdom-oriented ambiance of the death of a beloved child), 'he was slain in her arms.'

Tractate *Yoma* gives the name of this child as '*Do'eg ben Joseph*' (*i.e.*, parodying '*Jesus ben Joseph*' again?[103]) and '*the Sages calculated*' his age at '*two years, six months, six and a half hours*' (the '*six-six-six*' of Revelation 3:18?).

Not only have we already shown in this period the relationship of all such allusions to Abraham's intended sacrifice of Isaac to the ethos of the '*Sicarii*' suicide on Masada – itself clearly being reinforced by this episode, as we contend it is by the same example, evoked in James 2:21-4, of Abraham offering up Isaac, '*being justified by works*' thereby and '*called a Friend of God*' – but the story concludes, both realistically and pathetically, '*a few days later*' when '*the woman became demented and fell from a roof*' (again, the '*rooftop*' allusions). Furthermore, at this point a '*Bat Chol*' ('*Heavenly Voice*') issues forth, quoting Psalm 113:7–8 about '*raising the Poor from the dust and setting him up among Princes*' (another '*Ebionite*' text also quoted, as we shall see below, in the War Scroll from Qumran in its exegesis of the Messianic '*Star Prophecy*'[104]); and, once again, '*the Holy Spirit cries out* (as, indeed, it perhaps should), '*For these things I weep*'!

Of course, the tender pathos of the story of Zadok's two children as slaves in Rome, finding each other and dying in each other's arms, is surpassed in its affectiveness only by the Old Testament Joseph story, the '*Recognition*' theme of which is analogous (as it is in the Pseudoclementine *Recognitions*), though the outcome less tragic – obviously the times were less brutal. Whatever one's religious orientation, historically speaking it, has to be admitted that this Talmudic story is more convincing, at least as a representative picture of its times and the suffering endured, than any comparable story in the Gospels or Acts about '*Heavenly Voices*' crying out about human affairs, *e.g.*, those depicting '*the Holy Spirit*' (also a setpiece of this story) descending on Jesus '*as a dove*' while '*a voice out of Heaven*' cried out, '*This is my beloved son. In him I am well-pleased*' (Matthew 3:16–17 and *pars.*), to say nothing of the other '*Voice*' out of Heaven ('*the Bat-Chol*') in Acts 10:11–16, announcing concerning forbidden foods, dietary regulations, and '*table fellowship*,' '*Arise Peter, kill and eat*'!

But this, of course, is a matter of artistic taste and we are, once more, back in the contrasting worlds of Talmudic physicality and this-worldly quasi-realism and the New Testament one of other-worldly idealization and incorruptibility or, what in some vocabularies would be called, '*spiritualization*' or '*Hellenization*.' For the present writer, this episode, so tragically recorded in the *Talmud*, is real in the sense it represents what could have and, doubtlessly, did happen; the other being more in the nature of romanticization or mythologization in the manner of the foregoing Greco-Roman man-god traditions or retrospective theological polemics, completely unaffected by and casting a cold eye on these too-tragic times.

12

Rabbi Eliezer's Bad Breath and Lazarus' Stinking Body

Martha's Demise, the Fall of Jerusalem, and Levirate Marriage

So famous, obviously, was the demise of this '*Martha the daughter of Boethus*' that there is yet one more story about her precipitous fall now, as already signaled, with even more tragic overtones. Picking up from the '*casting out*' by Rabbi Zadok of the already-chewed fig-shred fibers, *Gittin* now quotes this final tradition as follows:

> *When Martha was about to die, she brought out all her gold and silver (cf.* James 5:3 *on the '*gold and silver*' of the '*Rich*') and cast it into the street, saying '*What good is this to me*,' thus giving effect to the verse, '*They shall cast their silver into the streets*' (Ezekiel 7:19 – also a favorite prophet at Qumran[1]).

Here we have the *pro forma* reinforcement by a scriptural proof-text as well as another variation of Matthew 27:3–5's version of Judas *Iscariot's* demise, which we have already characterized as both derivative and malicious.

Not only does the *Talmud* identify this '*Martha*' as '*one of the Richest women in Jerusalem*' (Josephus uses the same language in identifying her contemporary, the Herodian Princess Bernice, who was supposedly the incestuously-illicit partner of her brother Agrippa II and the future consort of Titus, the destroyer of Jerusalem[2]); in Tractate *Yebamoth* she is, therefore, pictured as *paying a bribe* (another favorite theme in New Testament recounting), seemingly to Agrippa II – called in the tradition '*King Yannai*,' the last Herodian King before the destruction of the Temple and the assumption of complete Roman control. It would appear that this was not simply to have her husband – again, Josephus' friend Jesus ben Gamala – appointed High Priest (c. 64 CE), but also to circumvent the normal levirate-marriage waiting period – she apparently having already been '*a Rich widow*' once before – so that he could, in line with her family's traditional High-Priestly status, then be appointed High Priest. Here, too, just as in New Testament reporting, the Rabbis speak in terms of there being 'a *conspiracy*' to secure his appointment and circumvent Mishnaic Law forbidding the consummation of such a marriage on the part of a High Priest – to say nothing of the implication of *there actually having been a 'bribe.'*[3]

In the description of this bribe to Agrippa II, the nephew of Herodias and brother to and alleged consort of the infamous Bernice above (*cf.* the probably accurate picture of both in Acts 25:13–26:32, *one of the longest continual episodes in the New Testament*), the amount is put at '*a tarkab*' or '*a measure of dinars*' – approximately two bushels. Not only do we have here the '*dinar*' theme again, but it is not unlike the '*hundred measures (cors) of wheat*' in the Lukan Parable of '*the Unrighteous Steward*' and the '*litra*' or '*measure of precious ointment of pure spikenard*' in John 12:3's '*Mary sister of Martha*'/'*Judas Iscariot*' remonstrations. Nor is this to mention '*Nicodemus*' bearing' the '*hundred litra measure of myrrh and aloes*' in John 19:39's later portrayal of the ministrations surrounding Jesus' burial.

In Tractate *Yoma*, all this is further reinforced (and with it, the parallel with Gospel portraiture) by the statement, recorded in the name of Rabbi Yohanan ben Torta,

And why all that, because they bought the (High) Priestly Office for money,[4]

though in *Kethuboth*, as we saw, at a seemingly later time she is also trying to recover her marital-contract security, which was a very high one.[5] Therefore, to close this subject, not only do we again have the language of the Judas *Iscariot* affair, both in the matter of the '*bribe*' of '*thirty pieces of silver*' (in Matthew 27:6, designated as '*the price of blood*') and the related sum of the '*three hundred dinars*' of his and others' complaints over '*the Poor*,' but also in the fact of the direct designation of the money involved as a '*bribe*.' In this convergence of motifs from these parallel, contemporary traditions, despite the disparity of their two sets of contexts; there is also just the faintest indication of '*the High Priests*' and either their involvement or that of their '*Office*' in the situation in some way.

Of course in the Talmudic traditions, the motives are quite different and, more in line with the Rabbinic generally, quite mundane or material, having to do, for instance, with bypassing Levirate marriage-rule maneuvering or recovering marital-contract surety in the face of one's own or one's family's economic situation having suffered a disastrous collapse; while in Gospel portraits in the New Testament the point is always the same (and often, in fact, just as or even more mean-spirited): to portray those making or accepting such bribes as conniving at or bringing the blundering or incompetent Roman Authorities around to schemes for the execution of Jesus as '*the Messiah*' or '*the Christ.*'

This is to say nothing of how Martha's '*silver*' in *Gittin* is at the time of her death '*being cast into the streets*' and not '*into the Temple*' or its '*Treasury,*' as in Judas *Iscariot*'s supposed action and the reaction to it of these same '*High Priests,*' as pictured in Matthew 27:5–7. To add to this, there is the matter of Matthew 27:9 supposedly quoting '*the Prophet Jeremiah*' – when in reality he is paraphrasing *Zechariah* – to characterize these events as a '*fulfillment*' of prophecy; while here *Gittin* is *accurately* quoting Ezekiel 7:19 and applying it to the analogous matter of Martha's '*gold and silver*' being '*cast into the street.*' Such a citation contributes the noteworthy additional implication of connecting the first fall of the Temple to the second, which is exactly the way the Damascus Document will handle similar passages in Ezekiel we shall consider in due course below.[6]

To extend these New Testament parallels just a little further into the, likewise, inaccurate or ahistorical presentation of the story of John the Baptist: in the *Mishnah*, the implications are that the '*bribe*' allowed Martha to bypass normal '*levirate*' marriage restrictions in order to marry Jesus ben Gamala since, as we just suggested, she seems to have been '*a widow*' – that is, her first husband *had apparently already died*. In such a situation, the theme of '*levirate marriage*' and/or the bypassing of the regulations concerning it makes sense, whereas in the Gospel variation of it – in the matter of John the Baptist's objections to Herodias' remarriage – it does not. The reason was, as we saw, that Josephus explicitly noted that Philip '*died childless*' which specifically means, of course, that *Herod Antipas could very well have been seen as raising up seed unto his 'brother'* had he married '*Philip*''s wife. Moreover, since he did not and since this '*Philip*''s wife was not Herodias but, in fact, *Herodias' daughter Salome*; none of it makes any sense whatsoever and, in the writer's view – as we see these cross-currents in thematic materials developing – most of it was drawn and rewritten from either improperly-digested or 'refurbished' Rabbinic materials of the kind we have just set forth above anyhow.[7]

However this may be, it is doubtful if '*levirate marriage*' even entered into the affair, where pseudo or questionable Jews such as the Herodians were concerned, but then the Gospel writers, operating from the sources we are trying to delineate and in an, as it were, overseas context, were presumably unaware of the opposition to '*niece marriage,*' '*divorce,*' '*polygamy,*' and '*marriage with close family cousins*' in the Qumran documents. All of these, as we have been emphasizing, figured prominently in '*Herodian*' marital practices and were apparently the issues between such '*Herodians*' and teachers like John the Baptist and the 'other' Simon – Josephus calls, '*Simon the Head of an Assembly of his own in Jerusalem*' – who wanted *to bar*

Herodians from the Temple as foreigners, which is to say nothing of their *'uncleanness'* as a result of all these behavioural patterns and concerning which, of course, *'Peter'* learns just the opposite in Jesus' admonishment of him in Matthew 15:15–20 (to say nothing of what he learns from the *'Voice out of Heaven'* in Acts 10:13–15) above. In any event, as we just saw and as Josephus tells us, *'Philip' never was married to Herodias, but rather to Salome her daughter.*[8]

Again, a footnote to all this is that Jesus ben Gamala whom Boethus' daughter Martha appears so desperately to have wished to marry and Josephus seems to have so loved, is killed alongside and in the same manner as the individual responsible for James' death, Ananus ben Ananus, whom we shall discuss in greater detail below. The persons responsible for these deaths are those Josephus is now formally willing to designate *'Zealots'* (he had not, as already underscored, used the terminology as such previously – only *'Sicarii'*[9]) and their *'Idumaean'* supporters.[10] In other words, in such a context both groups (the so-called *'Zealots'* and *'the Idumaeans'*) would appear to be *taking vengeance for the death of James*. Later in this book and elsewhere, I have and shall claim that this fact can be observed in at least two documents at Qumran.[11]

In fact, this killing, also, causes Josephus to forget his previous apparent rancor towards Ananus and rail against *'the Zealots,'* in particular, in the most intemperate manner conceivable. In excoriating the *'Impiety'* of those who flung the naked *'corpses'* of these two High Priests outside the city, without burial as food for jackals, he also makes the point that seems to have wound up – like so many of these other notices – as part of the narrative in the Gospel of John, that is, that *so scrupulous were the Jews in burial of the dead that they never even left the corpses of those who were crucified 'hanging up' on the crosses past nightfall* – though as John 19:32 frames this, it was rather on account of *'the Sabbath'* (*'a High Holy Day'*) that they did this.[12]

Martha *'Casts her Gold and Silver into the Streets'* and R. Yohanan is *'not Pierced'*

Before proceeding along these lines further, it would be well to go back to *Gittin's* descriptions of *'Ben Zizzit'* where it was claimed that he derived his name from, not only the *'seat'* or *'cushions'* he sat upon or *'his fringes'* which *'trailed on cushions'* (*keset*), but also because *'his seat* (*'kiseh'* playing off *'keset'*) *was among the Great Ones of Rome.'* Though here in *Gittin 'he sits among the Great Ones'* or *'Nobility of Rome,'* in the *ARN*, as will be recalled, *'he used to recline on a silver couch before the Great Ones of*

Israel' (once again, one should pay attention to the constant allusion to *'silver'*), both make it seem that *'Ben Zizzit'* was perhaps a derogatory expression for one or another of the Herodians – possibly Agrippa II, since his father Agrippa I was probably too respected in Rabbinic tradition to be characterized in such a manner.[13] However ludicrous traditions such as these may appear on the surface, all do display a certain peculiar, native Palestinian playfulness, as we have been underscoring, punning on the Hebrew for terms like *'seat,' 'cushions,'* or *'couch.'*

Directly following these expositions of *'Ben Zizzit'*'s name, *Gittin* goes on to tell its stories about *'Martha the daughter of Boethus'* (unlike Lamentations *Rabbah* it gets the patronym right), a name that time and time again inevitably seems to bring us back, as we have been suggesting, to the Gospel of John's stories about *'Lazarus''* two sisters, *'Mary'* and *'Martha'* and, in particular, the preciousness of the *'measure'* or *'weight of ointment of pure spikenard'* they used to minister either to Jesus' *'head'* or *'his feet.'* It is in illustrating how far *'Martha'* had sunk from her previous high station that *Gittin* gives us its version of the episode – also remarked, as we have seen, by Josephus – of how *'the Zealots'* had burned *all the stores of wheat and barley.*[14] This is the background it uses to illustrate how out of utter desperation, *because there was no grain left in the market, 'she took off her shoes,'* apparently because she didn't want to get them (the *'shoes'*) dirty in the mud, whereupon the *'dung stuck to her foot'* (a good inversion of both the *'foot'* and *'dung'* themes, to say nothing of Rabbinic whimsicality) *and she died.'*[15]

Aside from the earthy materiality of these stories and their self-evident tomfoolery – not to mention their utter confusion – once again here are the *'dung,' 'foot'/'feet,'* and *'sudden death'* themes, all of which have already been encountered in Luke and John about *'a Rich Man,'* the *'Cananaean woman'* and *'the dogs,' 'Poor Lazarus,'* his sisters, *'the Pharisee named Simon'* in Luke and, at least where the *'oil of pure spikenard'* was concerned, *'Simon the Leper'* and the *'woman with the alabaster flask'* in Matthew and Mark. Above and beyond the constant hyperbole or even *non sequiturs* of all these episodes and encounters, one should always keep one's eye firmly on these *'shoe,' 'foot,' 'barefoot,' 'precious ointment'/'perfume,'* and *'dinar'* themes as we have been doing.

In *ARN*, interestingly, the same story is told about how *'the Zealots'* burned all the grain in Jerusalem or *'mixed it with mud'* – this time directly connected to the name of *'Ben Kalba Sabuᶜa'* and the one about how, if *'one came to his door hungry as a dog, one went away filled.'*[16] Furthermore, not only is it explicitly connected to his *'twenty-one'* or *'twenty-two years'* of grain storage for Jerusalem, but also that of the themes of *'the loaves'* and 'dung'/'excrement' as well. This is achieved by having 'the Zealots' use 'the loaves,' which Ben Kalba Sabu'a had baked for all the citizens of Jerusalem, and 'brick up the walls with them.' Then, directly following this, another story connected with the city's fall about how, 'when Vespasian examined the dung of the besieged men,' who were by this time (because of 'the famine' and because 'the Zealots' had burned all Ben Kalba Sabu'a's stores) eating nothing but straw, 'and saw that it was without a trace of barley or corn, he said to his soldiers':

> If these men who eat nothing but straw can kill so many of you, how many more of you would they kill if they were to eat and drink like you?' (here too, yet another interesting variation of the 'eating and drinking' theme, already commented upon above).

It is at this point, too, that *Gittin* then launches into its climactic story about 'Martha,' the one we have been following about how, when she 'was about to die, she brought out all her gold and silver and cast it into the street,' thereby fulfilling the prophecy from Ezekiel 7:19 about *the destruction of Jerusalem and the fall of the Temple* (in this instance, as already indicated, *the First Temple* – in the Scrolls too, particularly in the Damascus Document and evoking the same Prophet, we shall encounter the same process at work[17]) and how the people would then have to 'cast their silver into the streets.' Of course, not only do we have the tragedy being so graphically illustrated by all events connected with these times (except in the Gospels, where it takes second place to other considerations), but the fact that the fall of the First Temple is being echoed in these traditions connected to the fall of the Second.

Of course, too, this story is certainly echoed, as we have been at pains to point out, by the one found in the Gospels about Judas *Iscariot 'casting down (his) pieces of silver into the Temple,'* itself supposed to be a variation – as previously underscored – of Zechariah 11:12–13's 'casting (his) silver to the silversmiths.' Not only does the 'silver'/'silversmith' motif, in turn, find an echo in the *ARN*'s Sisit Hakkeset 'sitting on silver cushions,' as already highlighted too, but also in the 'twelve thousand silver dinar' value of the bedspread 'Nakdimon's daughter Miriam' used or the 'twelve talents of silver' he promised to pay the foreign lord as surety for his 'twelve water cisterns.'[17]

In *Gittin*, these notices are immediately followed again, not surprisingly, by another about 'the Sicarii' referred to, as already explained above, as 'the Biryonim' and, picking up this theme of *the destruction of Jerusalem*, then moving into another series of stories about R. Eliezer ben Hyrcanus, R. Yohanan ben Zacchai, the Romans, the destruction of the

Temple, and ultimately, once more, even R. Akiba.[18] But the sequentiality is, yet again – not surprisingly – parallel and worth remarking since, just as the Gospels connect their *'Judas Iscariot' 'casting his silver into the Temple'* to the destruction of 'Jesus' (in Paul in 1 Corinthians 3:9–17 and 12:14–27, Matthew 26:61, and Mark 14:58 equivalent to *'the Temple'*[19]); so too *Gittin* connects Martha's *'casting her silver into the streets'* of Jerusalem with its stories about 'the *Biryonim*' (its *'Sicarii'*) and their direct role in bringing on *the destruction of Jerusalem*.

The story *Gittin* is telling, also recorded in Lamentations *Rabbah* in even more detail, is about *'Abba Sikkra'* (in the Lamentations and Ecclesiastes *Rabbah* tradition, *'Ben Battiah'*[20]), the head of *'the Sicarii'* or *'Biryonim in Jerusalem'* and *'the son of the sister of Rabbi Yohanan ben Zacchai'* – that is, Rabbi Yohanan's nephew. Even *Abba Sikkra*'s name here implies a connection to such *'Sicarii'* and the *'Abba'* part is extremely suggestive as well in terms of our earlier comments about *'Abba'* names – including *'Barabbas,' 'Abba Saba^c Zachariah,'* and *'Abba Joseph ben Hanin'* – playing an important role in many of these traditions.[21] This is also basically made explicit in Ecclesiastes *Rabbah* where the corruption *'Kisrin'* – not unlike similar corruptions such as *'Iscariot'* – has manifestly been substituted for *'Sikrin'* (*cf.* the village, called in some traditions *'Sihnin,'* seemingly 'in Galilee,' where James' stand-in *'Jacob'* – who tells Rabbi Eliezer the story about *'the High Priests' latrine'* – comes from).[22]

When Rabbi Yohanan sends for his nephew and berates him for *'killing all the People with starvation'* (because of having earlier burned all the stores), R. Yohanan requests a plan from him to enable him to escape from Jerusalem. His nephew then recommends he escape by means of a casket, presumably the only way out of the city at the time – *i.e.*, to be or pretend to be dead. This *'Abba Sikkra,'* a pseudonym if ever there was one, then tells him to even *'bring something that smells putrid'* and put it in the coffin so people would think he is dead.[23] Not only is this, once again, typical of Talmudic droll earthiness, the reader will immediately recognize the *'putrid smelling'* or *'stink'* motif of John 11:39's depiction of Lazarus' corpse (*'four days in the grave'* according to *'Martha'*), to say nothing of *'the dung,'* Rabbi Eliezer puts in his mouth so that his breath will smell *'putrid,'* we have already mentioned previously, but will have cause to discuss more definitively below. Nor is this to say anything about all the aromatic-ointment scenarios circulating about the issue of Jesus' body or feet in the other various parallels already sufficiently called attention to above as well.

In another such story about *'privies,'* illustrating the extreme physicality of Rabbinic tradition as opposed to the ofttimes extreme *'spirituality'* of the Greek, it is related that the heroic Rabbi Akiba, Rabbi Eliezer's student in the next generation, once followed Rabbi Joshua ('Jesus'?) '*into the privy to see how he conducted himself*' and observed that, '*entering sideways, he exposed himself only after he sat down and wiped himself (too) only after he had sat down and this solely with the left hand*' (a practice still followed throughout the Middle East to this day).[24]

However this may be, going back to R.Yohanan – the teacher of both R. Eliezer and R. Joshua in *Gittin* – when the guards at the gate want to '*pierce his casket with a lance*' (to make sure who or what was inside was dead), '*his Disciples*' in consternation (once again, we have here, now connected to R.Yohanan, the motif of '*his Disciples*') prevent them, saying,

> *Shall (the Romans) say, they have pierced our Master?*[55]

The guards then open the gates and allow the entourage to pass unimpeded and R.Yohanan goes on – not unlike Jesus both in Gospel '*Little Apocalypse*' and Matthew 24:2's '*not one stone upon another that shall not be cast down*' passages above – to evoke a passage from Isaiah 10:34, '*Lebanon shall fall by a Mighty One*' (actually extant among Qumran *Pesharim* and considered by most to be a part of what goes by the name of '*the Messianic Prophecy*'[26]), to predict Jerusalem's imminent downfall. In doing so, since passages such as this, employing exactly the same '*Lebanon*' imagery in multiple contexts, are extant and expounded at Qumran, he thereby solidifies the First-Century CE *sitz-im-leben* of all these types of '*Lebanon shall fall by a Mighty One*' allusions as *relating to the Temple and the First Century CE ambiance of this fall* and another hotly-vexed problem in the field of Qumran Studies is basically solved.[27]

This story itself also has a clear counterpart and possible parody in John 19:34's famous picture of a Roman soldier '*piercing (Jesus') side with a lance.*' Once again John, to say nothing of Luke and the others, certainly seems to be showing knowledge of or contact with – even perhaps dependency upon – the kind of allusions one finds in curious Talmudic traditions of this kind. Certainly Luke does in his portrait of the '*Rich Man dressed in purple*' and '*Poor Lazarus*' with '*his sores licked by dogs*' at '*his doorstep*' – but so, in our view, do the other Gospels in their various '*raising,*' '*curing,*' '*feeding,*' '*basket-filling,*' '*grain*' and '*loaves*'-multiplication, '*feet-kissing,*' '*hair-wiping,*' '*spikenard ointment,*' and '*Disciples*' stories we have so often been highlighting above.

But the Scriptural warrant John quotes for this is, once again (as in Matthew 27:3–10 above in Judas *Iscariot* '*casting the thirty pieces of silver into the Temple*') a passage again from *Zechariah* (though in 27:9, as previously underscored, it was supposed to be from '*the Prophet Jeremiah*') – this time Zechariah 12:10, '*they shall look upon him whom they pierced*.'[26] Curiously the proof-text quoted with it in John 19:36 is from Exodus 12:46, '*not a bone of it* (that is, *the lamb) shall be broken*,' which has to do with eating the paschal meal and again referencing the matter of *taking Jesus' body down from the cross before nightfall without 'breaking his legs.'* But here the resemblance ends. In the context in Exodus, it is preceded in 12:43–45 and followed in 12:48 by an absolute insistence on '*circumcision*' and '*no foreigner who is not circumcised*' taking part in such a ceremonial meal. To be sure, this is the very opposite of the way John, the other Gospels, and, of course, Paul insist on putting such passages to use but, as we have already seen, anything goes where the use of Philo's method of '*allegorical interpretation of Scripture*' as applied to the purported '*Passion of the Christ*' is concerned.[27]

'*Lebanon shall Fall by a Mighty One,*' '*the Branch of David,*' and '*the Messiah of Righteousness*'

Notwithstanding, the passage R. Yohanan is pictured as using here, '*And Lebanon shall fall by a Mighty One*' from Isaiah 10:34, has since, as just remarked, turned up among Qumran proof-texts known as '*Pesharim*'/ '*Commentaries*.' There, while baffling to so many Qumran scholars, the exegesis is similar to what we have in Tractate *Gittin* above, in which Rabbi Yohanan specifically asserts that '*Lebanon* – no doubt implying not only the white linen worn by the Priests in the Temple (to say nothing of that worn by '*Essene*' membership generally), but also its woodwork made of cedarwood from Lebanon – *refers to the Temple*'![30]

Interesting, too, the same proof-text turns up in the parallel version of these events, the *ARN* – as, in fact, it does in Lamentations *Rabbah*.[31] There, in *ARN*, a whole series of such '*Lebanon*' and '*cedarwood*' proof-texts, for the most part from Zechariah 11:1–3 (a prophet we have just seen referred to in Matthew and John above, but also in tandem here in these Isaiah *Peshers* from Qumran[32]), are specifically denoted as referring to the Temple and, in particular, its fall in 70 CE.

Passages such as '*wail O cypress tree, for the cedar tree is fallen*' and '*the strong forest has come down*' from Zechariah 11:2 in this list are expressly characterized as '*referring to the Temple*.' Likewise, Zechariah 11:1, '*Open your doors, O Lebanon, that the fire may consume your cedars*' (this is the very same verb '*eat*' or '*consume*' we have encountered and shall encounter again in the Habakkuk *Pesher* below[33]), is graphically interpreted as '*the High Priests in the Temple taking their keys*' (Peter's '*keys to the Kingdom*' in

349

Matthew 16:19 above?) as '*unworthy custodians*' and '*throwing them into the sky to the Holy One, the Master of the Universe.*'

Here the '*white*' implicit in the Hebrew of the designation '*Lebanon*' clearly refers to the '*white garments*' of the Temple '*Priests*' – just as, for instance, it does in the Habakkuk *Pesher* of '*Lebanon*' as '*the Community Council*,' presumably because of *their* '*white linen garments.*'[34] Not only is this identity made explicit in the latter, but it should also not be forgotten that in the Community Rule – as to some extent in Paul in 1 Corinthians 12:12–27 above – '*the Community Council*' functions as or is esoterically identical with '*the Temple.*' Furthermore, it is seen as '*atoning for sin*' that '*they may obtain Lovingkindness for the Land without the flesh of holocausts and the fat of sacrifices*' (thus).[35]

Not only shall we encounter this same phraseology '*Lovingkindness*' or '*Hesed*' below in the material about R. Joshua's '*woes*' that precedes the citation of these '*Lebanon*' passages in the *ARN* where R. Joshua, following R. Yohanan out of the city and on '*seeing it in ruins*,' cries out '*woe*' (here, of course, Jesus' '*woes*' in Matthew 23:12–24:19, both in the Temple and upon leaving it, when looking back at Jerusalem and predicting its destruction – as well those in '*the Little Apocalypse*' above) and R. Yohanan consoles '*his Disciple*' by quoting Hosea 6:6 on '*desiring Lovingkindness and not sacrifice*,' upon which the above passage from the Community Rule is based; but elsewhere it is rather stated that the reason '*Lebanon*' stands for the Temple was that '*there Israel's sins were made white.*'[36]

While this last explanation is perhaps typical of Rabbinic passivity, it does throw light on the curious allusion to being '*made white*,' we have already encountered, in the matter of '*the tombs of the two brothers*' above in the Pseudoclementine *Recognitions* that '*miraculously whitened of themselves every year*,' presumably meaning on Yom Kippur or perhaps in some more recondite manner. That this passage from Zechariah 11:1, '*Open your doors, O Lebanon, that the fire may devour you*,' refers to the coming destruction of the Temple is also made clear in *Yoma* (another Tractate of the *Talmud*, again, about Yom Kippur) which also cites three other '*Lebanon*' passages as referring in some manner to '*the Temple*' as well, *viz.*, Psalm 72:16, Nahum 1:4 (also extant and expounded at Qumran where '*Lebanon*' again gives every indication of being either '*the Temple*' or '*the Community Council*'), and Isaiah 35:2.[37]

While the presentation in the *ARN*, like the one in *Gittin* and Lamentations *Rabbah* ('*the three Gospels*'?), knows the names of Rabbi Yohanan's *two* '*Disciples*' – R. Eliezer and R. Joshua – but unlike either of those accounts, it makes no mention of his nephew, '*Abba Sikkra*' or '*Ben Battiah*,' nor of '*the Biryonim*' he leads, nor even the matter of Rabbi

Yohanan's body '*not being pierced.*' For Lamentations *Rabbah*, which basically reproduces the same story (though it divides '*Nakdimon ben Gurion*'
into two separate '*Councillors,*' '*Ben Nakdimon*' and '*Ben Gurion*' – thus! –
and for it, the '*woe*' will rather be the one R. Yohanan exclaims, not his
acolyte R. Joshua[38]), these events all occur '*three days*' after '*Ben Battiah*
('*Abba Sikkra*' in *Gittin*) *burned all the stores.*' For it too, it is R. Yohanan,
not Vespasian, who sees the people virtually reduced to starvation when
he witnesses them '*seething straw,*' presumably to distill its substance into
juice and, at this point, it is he that pronounces the '*woe*' (which, however,
because of his nephew's objections, he claims was rather '*wah*' – again
more Rabbinic tragic comedy or, should we say, even slapstick?). In its
version of events, it is Ben Battiah then, who leads R. Yohanan's coffin
out of the city while R. Eliezer and R. Joshua, carrying the head and the
feet, bring up the rear. Furthermore, it is *he who prevents the Jewish Guards*,
not *the Romans*, from '*piercing the body of (their) Master*' in order to determine if he was really dead[39]!

All three, however, then go on to picture R. Yohanan as evoking and
applying, '*He shall cut down the thickets of the forest with iron and Lebanon
shall fall by a Mighty One*' of Isaiah 10:34 to Vespasian, either hailing him
obsequiously as a kind of reverse '*Messiah*' and foreseeing his imminent
appointment as '*King*' or '*Emperor.*'[40] At Qumran, as already remarked,
while the extant *Pesher* on Isaiah 10:34 is unfortunately fragmentary at
this point, it does seem, typically, to be just the reverse of these Rabbinic
texts and Josephus; and the '*Mighty One*' appears to refer to a '*Jewish
Messiah*' – '*the cutting down of the thickets of the forest*' and '*the tallest of the
lofty ones*' to '*the Army of the Kittim.*' Nevertheless, in the writer's view,
what cannot be denied is that all are referring in this period to *the fall of
the Temple* in 70 CE – Josephus and the Rabbinic from a more pessimistic
point-of-view; the one at Qumran, just the opposite.

Josephus, in fact, does testify to precisely this state of affairs at the end
of the *Jewish War* when he provides what he considers to be the authentic exegesis of '*the World Ruler Prophecy*' (seemingly this prophecy from
Isaiah 10:34, as we just saw, combined with Numbers 24:17), applying it
– as already underscored as well and like the Rabbinic – to Vespasian as
opposed to those more misguided persons of his own race who considered it applied to '*one of their own*' (*sic*!).[41] For its part, Lamentations
Rabbah even portrays R. Yohanan as crying out – as Josephus himself
earlier seems to have done – presumptuously and obsequiously, '*Vive
Domine Imperator*'/'*Long live Lord Emperor*'! Note here, in particular, how
this flies in the face of Josephus' own picture or either '*the Zealots*' or '*the
Essenes*' as '*refusing to call any man, Lord.*' [42] Of course, this is wildly

inaccurate or, at least anachronistic, since by this time in 70 CE, Vespasian had already departed for Rome.[43] He did so the year before – '*the Year of the Three Emperors*' – in 68–69 CE – leaving the siege of Jerusalem in the hands of his son Titus, ably assisted by his second-in-command, Philo's nephew, the ever-present ideal Roman bureaucrat, Tiberius Alexander (also referred to in Acts 4:6 some twenty-five years earlier) and other nefarious types, such as Josephus himself, Agrippa II, and his sister (Titus' mistress and aspiring empress-to-be) Bernice, who make their appearance at the climax of Acts 25:13–26:32 – as we have seen, one of the longest (if not the longest) continuous episodes in Acts. Of course, Josephus, probably more accurately, *actually did by his own testimony apply* '*the World Ruler Prophecy*' *to Vespasian in Galilee* in 67 CE after his own ignominious surrender there and it is upon this that these Rabbinic stories are probably based.[44]

The same prophecy is extant, as we just saw as well, along with others involving '*Lebanon*' from Isaiah 14:8 and 29:17 but, because of the poor state of its (their) preservation, the interpretation is obscure. Nevertheless, the one from Isaiah 10:34 (the ones from Isaiah 14:8 and 29:17 are too damaged to tell – but, as in the Rabbinical to say nothing of the Gospels above, they are combined with material from Zechariah, evidently 3:9 and 11:1) clearly refers to '*the Kittim*' as '*Conquerors*' and its interpretation either parallels or, with more justice, anticipates the Talmudic though, seemingly, from the opposite point-of-view as just described.

Notwithstanding, just as in *ARN*, it is immediately followed by the celebrated passage from Isaiah 11:1–5 about '*a Shoot coming forth from the Stem of Jesse and a Branch growing out of his Roots*' which makes the whole *Pesher* even more '*Messianic.*'[45] Furthermore, the exegesis is also aggressively '*Messianic*,' that is, it is interpreted in terms of the '*standing up*' or '*arising in the Last Days*' or '*at the End of Days*' of '*the Branch of David*' / '*the Zemach-David* already alluded to above and all very clearly singular – meaning, in the traditional sense, *a singular David Messiah* – to whom God was going to grant '*a Throne of Glory and a Crown of Holiness.*'[46] As *per* Isaiah 11:4 – and, as it were, Numbers 24:17 ('*the Star Prophecy*' above) – he was going to '*smite his enemies*' with '*the Sceptre*' or '*Rod of his mouth*' / '*the Spirit of his lips*' and '*rule over all the Nations,*' '*judging all the Peoples*' ('*Amim*) *with* '*his sword.*'

Not only should one compare this with Matthew 10:34's '*I have come not to bring Peace but a sword*' and is it clearly singular (again, a singular normative Davidic '*Messiah*' as *per* '*early Christian*' denotation drawn from the same proof-texts); but it is fiercely and apocalyptically '*Messianic*' linking up with the text Michael Wise and myself originally found in 1990 about '*the Branch of David*' (also '*the Zemach-David*'), which we called '*The Messianic Leader*' or '*Nasi ha-ʿEdah*').⁴⁷ This text, which was only a fragment, also evoked Isaiah 10:34, alluding *inter alia* to both '*woundings*'/'*piercings*' and '*the Kittim*,' and , in the spirit of Isaiah 11:4 to follow, probably referring to '*judging the Peoples with the sword of his mouth*.'

Moreover, this was how I always saw the militancy of this text, newspaper reports or the views of my colleagues – who actually found and originally translated the text in a more '*Christian*'-like manner – notwithstanding.⁴⁸ As we shall see in due course, this '*Nasi ha-ʿEdah*' will appear in Ms. A of the Damascus Document where he will again be identified as '*the Sceptre who will stand up*' or '*arise out of Israel*' of Numbers 24:17 (in Ms. B, as we shall also see, this will be transformed into '*the Messiah of Aaron and Israel*' – in our view, again an idiomatic singular⁴⁹), who '*will smite all the sons of Seth*' (a synonym clearly for '*the Evil Ones*'/'*the Kittim*'/or '*the Enemies of God*' of the Isaiah *Peshers, et. al.* above).

In turn, in the document known in Scroll Studies, as we have seen, as '*The Genesis Pesher*' (in our publication of it we called it, with a nod to John Allegro, '*The Genesis Florilegium*'), in exposition of '*the Shiloh Prophecy*' of Genesis 49:10–11 (so-called because of references in it to the '*coming*' of the figure known – perhaps defectively – as '*Shiloh*'), both '*the Sceptre*' and '*the Branch of David*' are once again evoked and now, for the first time, the all-important Messianic '*feet*.' Moreover, because of the curious allusion in it to '*tethering his donkey*' or '*the colt of its she-donkey*,' it is probably also being evoked in all four Gospels in Jesus''*Messianic*' entry into Jerusalem (Matthew 21:1–11 and *pars.* above), to say nothing of its imagery at this point which fairly saturates Revelation.⁵⁰

In it, too, '*the Staff*' (*Mehokkek*), which will re-appear in numerous contexts below – in particular, in the Damascus Document's exposition of both Numbers 21:18 and Isaiah 54:16 – is pictured as being '*between the Shiloh's feet*' and interpreted as '*the Covenant of the Kingdom*.' In Ms. A of the Damascus Document, as we shall see below, it will be '*the Interpreter*' or '*Doresh ha-Torah*' who '*went out from the Land of Judah*' to '*dig the Well of Living Waters in the Land of Damascus*' of Numbers 21:18 – '*the Instrument for His works*' of Isaiah 54:16 and '*the Star*' evoked along with '*the Sceptre*' in Numbers 24:17 above and, as we shall see, the Messianic *Florilegium* as well. It is worth remarking as well that '*Shiloh*' is also designated as '*the name of the Messiah*' in the various Messianic allusions that follow the evocation of the '*Lebanon*' quote from Isaiah 10:34 in Lamentations *Rabbah* above.⁵¹

But here in the Genesis *Pesher*, both *'the Sceptre'* and *'the Branch of David'* are distinctly identified with *'the Messiah of Righteousness,'* who in turn is identified with *'the coming of the Shiloh,'* to whom and to whose *'seed,' 'the Covenant of the Kingdom of His People'* was given *'unto Eternal generations because he kept the Torah'* – *'keeping'* being the basis of the definition, as we have seen, of *'the Sons of Zadok'* at Qumran. However these things may be and whatever the reader may make of the final meaning of these things, the reader should appreciate that *'the Branch of David'* being referred to in these Isaiah and Genesis *Peshers*, is certainly also the same as *'the Nasi ha-ʿEdah'* being evoked in both the famous fragment above, most now consider an addition to the War Scroll, and in the Damascus Document's exposition of *'the Sceptre'* from *'the Star Prophecy,'* not to mention the language used on the coinage from the period of the Bar Kochba War (132–36 CE) in the denotation there of *'Bar Kochba' / 'the Star'* as *'the Nasi-Israel.'*[52] To complete the circle, *'the Sceptre'* and its analogue, *'the Branch of David,'* now turn up in these Messianic allusions from Isaiah 10:21–11:5 in the various versions of the Isaiah *Pesher*, so we clearly really do have here a circle of Messianic allusions.

Rabbi Yohanan and Rabbi Joshua's *'Woes'* and Rabbi Eliezer's *'Putrid Breath'* Again

Therefore when R. Yohanan applies *'the Mighty One'* terminology of Isaiah 10:34 to, however improbably, Vespasian in the various Rabbinic milieux above as well, the implication is that he also – perhaps cynically, perhaps otherwise – is somewhat disingenuously applying *'the Star'* or *'Shiloh' Prophecies* to him as well – as we have just seen Josephus doing. This story as the *ARN* presents it, while not paralleled in *Gittin*, is however with slight modifications to be found in Lamentations *Rabbah* and, to some extent, in Ecclesiastes *Rabbah*, though in these, as already remarked, it is R. Yohanan who is exclaiming *'woe'* because of his nephew (Ben Battiah), who has burned the storehouses, condemning the people to starvation.

This parallels the much longer series of *'woes,'* we saw Jesus pictured as making in the Temple in the Gospel of Matthew 23:13–38 (though not in the other three), ending in the clearly retrospective reproof, *'Jerusalem, Jerusalem, which kills the Prophets'* and the additional – equally retrospective – prognostication, *'your house (will) be left desolate unto you.'* In Luke, these *'woes'* come earlier in 11:46–52, after Jesus visits Martha's house, when another *'certain Pharisee'* had invited him to dine with him and noticed *'he had not first washed before eating'* (11:38). The parallel to this was clearly the '*unwashed hands*'/'*Traditions of the Elders*' material in Matthew 15:1–20 and Mark 7:1-23 above, also in response to '*the Pharisees and some of the Scribes from Jerusalem*' (*i.e.*, in '*the New Testament Code*,' '*the James Party*'), when Jesus, it will be recalled – in attacking '*the Pharisees*' as '*Blind Guides*' – expounded for '*Peter*''s benefit, after pronouncing the pivotal '*every plant which my Heavenly Father has not planted shall be uprooted*,' the '*Toilet Bowl*' Parable.

It is following this extensive list of '*woes*' in Matthew 23 that 'Jesus,' upon leaving Jerusalem and the Temple and turning back – just as R. Yohanan and his '*Disciple*,' R. Joshua, above – to look at it, pronounced the devastating prediction, '*There shall not be left here one stone upon stone that shall not be thrown down*' (Matthew 24:1–2 and *pars.*), before proceeding to the Mount of Olives to set forth '*the Little Apocalpyse*' in all three Synoptics. Of course for the *ARN*, as opposed to both Lamentations and Ecclesiastes *Rabbah*, it is R. Joshua (just as in the Synoptics – '*Jesus*' and '*Joshua*' being analogues) who, when looking back at the Temple and seeing it in ruins, as already underscored, utters his own mournful '*woe*'; and it is at this point that R. Yohanan (not Ben Battiah who rebukes him) is rather comforting '*his Disciple*' at the sight they are now both witnessing by evoking Hosea 6:6 above, that is, it is '*Mercy*' or '*Lovingkindness*' (literally, '*Hesed*'/'*Piety*') which the Lord '*desires, not sacrifice*' – then going on to counsel him that he should now pray three times a day as Daniel had done in Babylon (Daniel 6:1)![53]

Following this and the picture of his application of the Isaiah 10:34 citation, '*Lebanon shall fall by a Mighty One*,' to Vespasian and his rise to power; *ARN* even depicts the Romans as '*catapulting a pig's head*' into the Temple upon its altar, not unlike the report of some modern military tactics today. In fact in *Gittin,* R. Yohanan is portrayed as obsequiously characterizing this rise to power by Vespasian as '*the Good News*'/'*the Gospel*' and quoting Scripture, Proverbs 15:30: '*Good News fattens the bone*,' as applying to it![54] Moreover, before his application of the other '*Lebanon*' and '*cedar tree*' passages – including that of Zechariah 11:1–3 on '*Lebanon opening (its) doors so fire might consume ('eat') its cedars*' – both to it and the fall of the Temple; *ARN* also pictures R. Yohanan as sitting and waiting, trembling by the side of the road, as Eli had done '*for the ark of the Lord*' in 1 Samuel 4:13, when he and '*his Disciples*' (another Gospel parallel?) hear that '*Jerusalem was destroyed and the Temple in flames*,' whereupon '*they tore their clothes, wept, and cried aloud in mourning*' (*i.e.*, the first note of '*Mourning for Zion*' or, as we have elsewhere expressed it, '*the Mourners for Zion*').[55]

Not only do these speeches by R. Yohanan parallel what we have just seen 'Jesus' is supposed to have said about '*there shall not be left here one stone upon stone (of the Temple) that shall not be thrown down*' (Matthew 24:1–2 and *pars.*) when he and '*his Disciples*' are leaving the Temple as well; but also another speech 'Jesus' is pictured as making in Matthew 26:61 and Mark 14:58 before '*the Chief Priests, the Elders, and the whole Sanhedrin*' about '*being able to destroy the Temple of God and in three days build it up.*' The application of Isaiah 10:34 and Zechariah 11:1–3 in these Rabbinic traditions to these pivotal events and their picture of R. Yohanan's appearance before the Emperor-to-be – either Vespasian or his son Titus (Talmudic tradition is really unable to distinguish between historical points as fine as these) – must also have included '*the Star Prophecy*' extant, as we have seen, in at least three separate contexts in known documents at Qumran.[56]

This picture of R. Yohanan (after his humiliating escape from Jerusalem) obsequiously applying these kinds of '*prophecy*' to Vespasian's rise to power is, perhaps – as previously indicated – more accurately linked to Josephus, who in the *Jewish War* had already explained how he used this precious '*oracle*' to predict Vespasian's coming elevation to Emperor and save, as it were, his own skin.[57] That this '*oracle*' had to include, among other things, the prophecy that '*a world Ruler would come out of Palestine*' seems to the author to be a given.

In the parallel and more detailed version of this encounter in Lamentations *Rabbah*, it is after R. Yohanan applies the passage from Proverbs 15:30 about '*the Good News fattening the bones*' in it as well to Vespasian's elevation to Emperor that Vespasian asks him whether he has any other '*friend or relative*' in Jerusalem he wished to save. Yohanan is then pictured as sending his '*two Disciples,*' R. Eliezer b. Hyrcanus and R. Joshua, back to Jerusalem to bring out Rabbi Zadok. Not only is this a parallel, should one choose to regard it, to John the Baptist sending his '*two Disciples*' to Jesus in Luke 7:20/Matthew 11:2 above to ask the Messianically-charged question, '*Are you the one who is to come or must we look for another?*'; but also the episode in all three Synoptics, just underscored above as well, of 'Jesus' sending his '*two Disciples*' to find the '*ass tied and a colt along with her*' in Matthew 21:1–11 and *pars.* Though paralleled in John 12:14, the note about the '*two Disciples*' is missing and Jesus rather finds '*an ass's colt*' himself. Nevertheless both it and Matthew 21:4 specify this episode as '*fulfilling that which was spoken by the Prophet.*' Again, the language of '*the Prophet*' should be familiar here, though this time – unlike the mistake about '*Jeremiah the Prophet*' in Matthew 27:9 above as well – he goes unnamed. However, the meaning clearly is Zechariah 9:9, actually quoted in Matthew 21:5, but also, as we have just seen, obviously the

'*Shiloh*' Prophecy of Genesis 49:11 as well.

Of course with regard to these ideas, *viz.*, '*a colt being tethered to the vine*' of both Genesis 49:11 and the Gospels, the '*coming of the Messiah*' alluded to in the query attributed to John and the ever-recurrent motif of '*the Messiah's 'feet*,' one should note the tradition in both Lamentations *Rabbah* and Song of Songs *Rabbah*, ascribed to Simeon bar Yohai – the legendary progenitor of *Zohar* tradition as we have seen – interpreting the passage, '*He has spread a net for my feet*,' from Lamentations 1:13 in terms of '*seeing a colt tethered to a tree*' and '*looking for the feet of the Messiah*' again.[58] Curiously, though these allusions have no apparent connection except an esoteric one, still in all these traditions – that is, Jesus' '*Messianic*' entry into Jerusalem in Synoptic (Matthew 21:7–8 and *pars.*), both the '*Nakdimon*' and '*Martha the daughter of Boethus*' ones about '*woollen garments*' or '*cushions*' being spread beneath their '*feet*' in Rabbinic, and now this one relating to '*looking for the Messiah's feet*' from Lamentations and Song of Songs *Rabbah* in the *Midrash* – the motif of having '*garments spread beneath the feet*' is conspicuous.

To go back to Rabbi Zadok: when Vespasian saw him, he was supposed to have wondered why Rabbi Yohanan would bother to bring out such an '*emaciated old man*.' Whereupon Yohanan is pictured as responding, a little less obsequiously this time and in a variation of Vespasian's words in *ARN* above on *examining the* '*dung*' *of those besieged in Jerusalem* and *finding only straw in it*, '*Two like him and you would have never taken Jerusalem even with double your Army*.' It should be appreciated that here in Lamentations *Rabbah*, too, R. Yohanan himself sees the people in the market in Jerusalem '*seething straw and drinking its product*'; and it is this he takes as a sign to leave, asking '*can such men withstand the Armies of Vespasian*' (*cf.* the expression, '*the Armies of the Kittim*,' in the Habakkuk *Pesher* below and note the persistent motif of someone – like the followers of James – receiving a '*sign*' either '*to leave Jerusalem*' or '*go up to*' it).[59]

In parallel materials about Rabbi Yohanan in *Kethuboth*, he is once again pictured as we saw, like Jesus in reverse, '*leaving Jerusalem riding upon a donkey while his Disciples follow him*.'[60] It is at this point that he was supposed to have encountered Nakdimon ben Gurion's daughter Miriam and now she is the one, as we saw as well, '*picking barley grains out of the dung of Arab cattle*,' not as in the tradition Lamentations *Rabbah* quotes in the name of R. Eleazar ben Zadok about Boethus' daughter Miriam '*picking barley grains among the horses hoofs at Acco*' (concerning which R. Eleazar was supposed to have cited the verse from Song of Songs 1:8, '*O fairest among women, go your way forth among the footsteps of the flock and feed your bodies*' – '*geviotayik*' / '*your bodies*,' not '*gediyotayik*' / '*your kids*' as in the biblical text).

In Miriam's conversation now with R. Yohanan in *Kethuboth* (and not Rabbi Eleazar ben Zadok as later in *Kethuboth* and in Lamentations *Rabbah*) – whom she also addresses, as we saw, as '*Master*' – the only thing she really requests of him (R. Yohanan), after '*standing up*' and '*wrapping herself in her hair*' (this, of course, the parallel to Lazarus' sister '*Mary*' wiping Jesus' *feet with her hair* in John 11:2 and 12:3 above, to say nothing of Luke 7:38's '*woman of the city, a Sinner, with the alabaster flask*' wiping Jesus' *feet with her hairs*'), is '*feed me*' (our '*dog*'/'*dogs*' or '*Ben Kalba Sabuᶜa*'s '*Poor*'/'*Lazarus under the table*' language and that of other '*feeding*' episodes we have already outlined so extensively above again?); however we are clearly dealing with the same episode.[61] It is here, too, that Rabbi Yohanan enters into his discourse on '*the Riches*' of both Miriam's father's and father-in-law's houses, noting in an aside to '*his Disciples*' how the marriage contract he signed reckoned her surety at '*one million dinars*' and comparing it, by implication, to the abject poverty of her present fallen status.

In fact, *Kethuboth* ('*Marriage Contracts*') again does not specifically name '*the daughter of Nakdimon ben Gurion*' in this episode, '*Miriam*' or '*Mary*,' though we know this was her name; and, interestingly enough, it does not immediately follow this up with the variant tradition about Rabbi Eleazar ben Zadok, that we just noted was found in Lamentations *Rabbah* as well, in which he too applied the verse from Song of Songs 1:8 to her pathetic condition after he sees her '*picking barley grains among the horses' feet at Acco*'; but now we definitely are apprised that this is supposed to be '*Nakdimon's daughter*' – again no prenom added. Nor, in either of these traditions in *Kethuboth* or Lamentations *Rabbah*, is she explicitly going out '*barefoot*,' as *Gittin* relates rather of '*Boethus' daughter Martha*' above who died when '*some dung stuck to her foot*' (pay attention here to the '*dung*' motif again). There, it will be recalled, Rabbi Yohanan rather applied the verse from Deuteronomy 28:56 above about '*the tender and delicate woman who would not set the sole of her foot upon the ground*' to Boethus' daughter Martha's equally pathetic demise, a passage we have already seen, as just noted, '*R. Eleazar ben Zadok*' apply in Lamentations *Rabbah* to '*Boethus' daughter Miriam*'!) – she whom, after '*binding her hair to the tails of Arab horses*,' the Romans made '*run from Jerusalem to Lydda*' (here, once again, one should pay particular attention to the '*hair*' motif).[62]

In a final passage relating to all these themes from Genesis *Rabbah*, already highlighted above and paralleled with only slight modifications in *ARN*, it will be recalled that the '*dung*' is now rather what R. Eliezer ben Hyrcanus (called in the text '*Liezer*' – '*Lazarus*' in New Testament parlance – and alleged, as we have seen, to have either 'Jewish Christian' sympathies or contacts) puts into his mouth when still a ploughman with his brothers in his father's field, thus either purposefully or because her was hungry giving himself bad breath (more hyperbole).[63] He goes to study with R.Yohanan ben Zacchai, again probably in Lydda, and when this '*stench*' is brought to the attention of '*the Master*,' as in New Testament '*parables*,' R.Yohanan allegorizes it, characterizing his '*breath*' as '*a sweet fragrance*.' Not only are these the words applied to the '*Righteousness*' of the Community Council in the Qumran Community Rule or by Paul to his colleague, Epaphroditus, in Philippians 4:18,[64] but R.Yohanan also provides the following exposition (already paraphrased above in the *ARN* version) of them:

> As the smell of (Rabbi Eliezer's) *mouth became putrid for the sake of the Torah, so will the sweet fragrance of (his) learning become diffused from one end of the World to the other (ARN adds: 'because of his mastery of Torah').*

First and foremost, it should be immediately plain that this is but a variation (or *vice versa*) of the famous '*Parable*' we have been analyzing in such detail above, attributed to '*Jesus*,' in which he rebukes either '*Peter*' or '*the Disciples*' as being '*so*' or '*even yet without understanding*' (Mark 7:17-18/Matthew 15:15-16). To paraphrase this rebuke:

> A man is not known by what goes into the mouth. That cannot defile the man. But the things which go forth out of the mouth, they defile the man.

The language of both these expositions is, of course, almost completely parallel only, as usual, the Gospel version is, as it were, '*cleaned up*' and, in line with the Greek or Hellenistic cultural expression generally, made more elegant and less mundane.

Having said this, however, both Matthew and Mark still retain the rather course '*toilet bowl*' metaphor, itself patently related to the motif of the '*dung*' in *ARN* and Lamentations *Rabbah*. On the other hand, whereas in Mark 7:19, it will be recalled, the aim of '*the Parable*' was to '*declare all foods clean*'; in Matthew, it was to assert that '*eating with unwashed hands does not defile the man*' (15:20). Nevertheless, it should be clear that both versions are totally antithetical to what the authors of the R.Yohanan anecdote had in mind, the thrust of which was to see the learning of *Torah* '*diffused from one end of the World to the other*,' which was just the reverse and would have horrified both Matthew and Mark – and all the other Gospels too for that matter.

First of all, not only is this another excellent example of ideological inversion or reversal, but it should be quite clear that there is borrowing going on here. The only problem is to determine in which direction the '*borrowing*' is taking place or, to use the language of Matthew's allusion here, '*proceeding*.' The fair-minded reader will undoubtedly query, how do you know which way the '*borrowing*' is going? The answer should be plain – '*borrowing*,' for the most part, goes from the more primitive to the more sophisticated or, if one wishes, from the more vulgar to the more polished or more elegant and rarely, if ever, the other way round – from the more sophisticated to the more primitive.

In this instance the Rabbinic (despite protestations one might hear also on this score to the contrary) is clearly the more primitive or more vulgar – the Gospel, as it were, the more '*elegant*' or, if one prefers, the more '*Hellenized*.' In this case, anyhow, the Talmud's physicality rescues it from the charge of '*borrowing*' and unfortunately, sad as it may be to have to say, one can clearly envision the core of the ideological thrust of assertions of this kind emanating out of sophisticated circles on the highest '*cosmopolitan*' cultural level in either Alexandria or Rome – more likely the latter – but working off what 'they' would have seen as the more '*base*' (that is, the more '*realistic*' or '*crude*') Judaic – meaning '*not idealized*' – material.

Lazarus, Liezer, Amraphel, and Ephraim

But to go back to our other historical parallels – not only have we seen the same sort of '*stench*' referred to in the story of the advice R. Yohanan's nephew '*Abba Sikkra*' or '*Ben Battiah*,' '*the Head of the Sicarii of Jerusalem*,' gives R. Yohanan '*to put a clod of something smelling very putrid*' into his coffin (in the picture of his somewhat dishonorable or even cowardly escape from Jerusalem – the reader will see *there is honesty here however droll*), so people would think he was dead; but it also finds a reflection, however shadowy, in both of John 11–12's '*Lazarus*'/'*Eliezer*' stories.

Though what we shall now summarize is, again, to a certain extent repetitious of previous material or what we have just pointed out in a secondary or more cursory manner in other contexts, it would be useful to review all this material about '*smells*' or '*odours*' one last and hopefully conclusive time. In so doing, however redundant this may seem, at least these things will indelibly imprint themselves on the reader's consciousness (as they have the author's) and, as is often the case, some new insight might and, in this case, does emerge. In this type of study, such summations are necessary where the material is as complex as that before us.

Let us take the second passage from John 12:3–5 first: when '*Mary*' Lazarus' sister '*takes the pound* ('*litran,*' as opposed to 'the *tarkab of dinars*' above, the parallel Talmudic measure relative to the '*bribe*' Boethus' daughter gives to Agrippa II) *of ointment of pure spikenard of great price*' to anoint Jesus' '*feet and wipe them with her hair*'; the house was said to have '*been filled* (the '*full of*' language again) *with (its) odour*' or '*smell,*' that is, *the sweet* '*smell*' of the pure '*perfume.*' It is this '*litran*' about which '*Judas the son*' or '*brother of Simon Iscariot*' (here, of course, the '*Abba Sikkra*' parallels) complains, reckoning it at '*three hundred dinars.*'

To press the point home and, with it, the further parallels with Nakdimon's '*feet*' never touching the ground because of '*the cushions laid for him by the Poor*' and the questionable pretense he made of charity (or, for that matter, '*Boethus*' daughter Martha' who *made no such pretense when she walked from her house to the Temple* and whose '*feet,*' likewise, *appeared to floated on air*), exemplified also in other stories about '*dog*'s and/or '*the Poor coming to his door* ('*the Rich Man*''s or '*Ben Kalba Sabuʿa*''s) *and going away filled*'; the text, as we have already underscored, has Judas add to the above complaint about the '*dinar*' value of the ointment: '*it should have been sold and given to the Poor,*' then opining, as we have seen as well,

> He did not say this because he cared about the Poor, but because he was a thief and held the (common) purse, carrying away whatever was put in it (12:6 – now the text really is revealing its agenda and growing extreme).

To make the connection with Jesus' coming '*death and burial*' even more plain, John 12:7 then has Jesus add before that bit of egocentrism which has become proverbial, '*the Poor you have with you always but you do not always have me,*' we have already emphasized sufficiently above too:

> Let her alone (echoing '*the Blind Guides*' rebuke in Matthew 15:14 and the admonition relative to '*the Sons of the Pit*' in the Scrolls[65]). She has kept it (*the expensive spikenard perfume*) for the day of my burial.

Interestingly enough, even this tradition about Jesus' attitude towards the respect he was owed by '*his Disciples*' has a parallel from the life of Eliezer ben Hyrcanus. R. Eliezer, even at the point he was about to die too and after he has been excommunicated by Rabban Gamaliel (the grandson of Paul's alleged teacher by the same name), when his '*Disciples,*' '*Rabbi Akiba and his colleagues,*' come to see him on his deathbed (in spite of the ban R. Gamaliel had placed upon him) and they discourse Socrates-style about the '*cleanness*' or '*uncleanness*' of things contained in '*unclean vessels*' (a subject that will also be discussed at length, as we shall see below, in *MMT*[23]); he is pictured as suddenly blurting out:

> *I fear for the Disciples of this generation, for they will be punished by death from Heaven.*[67]

When they ask him, '*Master, what for?*,' he replies in the manner of Jesus' various rebukes to '*his Disciples*' or '*the Apostles*' over all the women '*anointing him*' and '*kissing his feet, wiping them with their hair*':

> *Because, they ('you') did not come and attend upon me.*

In particular, he singles out his principal '*Disciple*,' Akiba *ben Joseph* (the '*ben Joseph*' part of this phraseology is most noteworthy), whom we know died a horrifying and terrible martyr's death (he was drawn and quartered and pulled apart by horses) in the next generation for his support of the Bar Kochba Revolt. Not only did Akiba, according to Rabbinic lore, designate Bar Kochba '*the Star*' of Numbers 24:17, thereby bestowing upon him his cognomen[29;] but when he was asked by R. Eliezer, '*why you did not attend upon me?*' and he answered, *because he* '*did not have time,*' R. Eliezer is reported to have replied (much in the manner of Jesus to the two '*Sons of Thunder*,' pictured in Matthew 20:20-28/Mark 10:35-45 as having '*to drink the Cup*' that he would have to drink or *having to* '*take up the cross and follow*' him – in the context of all these '*follow me*' allusions, one should also note the evocation of '*spilling the blood of Zechariah between Temple and altar*,' a peculiar concern of the Gospels such as Matthew 23:35 and Luke 11:51), '*the manner of your death will be the hardest of them all.*'[68]

It is at this point too that John 12:9-11, right after picturing Jesus as referring to his '*burial*' and right before his finding '*a young ass colt*' to sit on, then incorporates the curious tradition that '*a great crowd of Jews*' gathered, '*not because of Jesus only, but that they might see Lazarus whom he raised from the dead*' (12:9); whereupon '*the Chief Priests*,' it will be recalled, '*plotted together that they might also put Lazarus to death*' (*sic!* – 12:10).

In a seeming further, like-minded reflection from the life of Rabbi Eliezer ben Hyrcanus (who seemed to sympathize, as we have seen, with sectarian '*Nazoraeans*' like 'Jesus',[69] argued with R. Yohanan's other '*Disciple*,' R. Joshua,[70] others from Rabbi Yohanan's school,[71] and Rabban Gamaliel, whose sister he had married and by whom he was arbitrarily excommunicated,[72] and was considered so *'Great'* that, *when he sat before 'the Great Ones of Israel'* – including *'Ben Sisit Hakkeset, Nakdimon ben Gurion, and Ben Kalba Sabuᶜa'* – his face was *'as luminous as the light of the sun and the beams emanated from it like the rays from Moses' face*[73]*)*; John 12:9–11, as already remarked, seems to think that *'the High Priests'* were acting in this way *'because many of the Jews were leaving and believing in Jesus because of him'* (*Lazarus*)! We have already commented on the bizarreness of this accusation. Nevertheless, it would be well to note that this passage about the light of Rabbi Eliezer's face being *'as luminous as the beams emanating from Moses' face'* would also appear to have another inverse parallel in the attack by Paul in 2 Corinthians 3:7-18 on just this claim, asserting that Moses, when coming out of the Tent of Meeting, by putting a veil over his face (Exodus 34:33-35) was concealing the fact that the light of *'the Old Covenant'* (or *'the Torah'*) *had been extinguished'* or *'annulled.'*[74]

Directly after this, of course, John 12:12-15 has the material about Jesus *'coming'* with *'his Disciples,' 'riding on a young ass colt,'* supposedly fulfilling the passage from Zechariah 9:9 already remarked above, *'your King is coming,' 'riding on a young donkey – a colt the foal of a donkey.'* Nonetheless, once again, here too the context of this whole passage in the Hebrew Zechariah, including both the chapters preceding and following it, could not be more aggressively nationalistic, irredentist, and Zionist, *wishing destruction on all of Zion's enemies and rejoicing on the whole 'House of Judah'*![75]

Even more telling with regard to this motif of *'smells'* above is the previous story John 11:17–44 tells about *'Martha meeting' Jesus, while 'Mary was still sitting in the house.'* In this incident, it transpires that, since Martha has *'secretly'* told her that *'the Master'* had come, it is now Mary who *'arises'* (11:21–11:28) and *'goes to the tomb that she might weep there'* (11:31– yet another adumbration of the *'weeping'* theme we encountered in the story of R. Yohanan and *'his Disciple,'* R. Joshua, *'mourning for the fall of the Temple'* and the *'weeping'* they mutually indulge in when contemplating its *'ruins.'* Nor is this to say anything about R. Akiba's own *'weeping'* when he encounters R. Eliezer's body being carried on the highway from Lydda and the *'woes'* he then exclaims,[76] nor R. Yohanan's *'weeping'* when he contemplates his own death,[77] nor that of *'the Holy Spirit'* or what the two children of Zadok the High Priest exchange in the Talmudic story, just recounted above, when they find each other in Rome and expire in each other's arms).

Nor is this 'Jesus'' tomb that *'Mary'* goes to – as in the case of one or both of the two *'Mary'*'s, *'Mary Magdalene'* and *'the other Mary'* – in John 11:31 above, but here the tomb of *'Lazarus,'* who had been in the cave blocked by the stone *'for four days'* (thus – 11:38-39). The point is that, '*when she came*' in the *pro forma* manner – just like R. Akiba's wife over and over again in the Rabbinic stories about him – she, once again, '*falls at his (Jesus') feet.*' Now, specifically tying this '*putrid stench*' both to Lazarus ('*Eliezer*' – the '*Liezer*' of the Genesis *Rabbah* version of the story about Eliezer's bad breath above[78]) and the '*smell*' of his dead body (also paralleling '*the smell*' of R. Yohanan's body above where, depending on the tradition, R. Eliezer and R. Joshua were '*the two Disciples*' conducting it past either the Roman or Jewish sentries outside Jerusalem); John has Jesus now direct '*Martha the sister of him that died*' to '*take away the stone*' (11:39). Whereupon, as usual, she once again complains but this time, as we saw, *about the putrid stench,*

> Lord, he (or '*it*') *already stinks for it has been four days* (since, that is, he was put into the tomb).

So instead of the '*smell*' of Mary's '*litra of ointment of pure spikenard of great price,*' '*filling the house with the smell of the perfume*' in John 12:3, it is now Mary's '*sister Martha*' evoking *the putrid stench of Lazarus' dead body.* So that perhaps would be sufficient for the parallels involved in the '*smells*' of all these various contexts involving either '*Lazarus,*' '*Eliezer,*' '*Mary,*' '*Martha,*' or eventually even, as we shall presently discuss, '*Nicodemus*'/'*Nicodemon.*'

To go back to the story of R. Eliezer ben Hyrcanus in *ARN* who, when only a young man (some say twenty-two – others say twenty-eight), was also pressed by R. Yohanan to discourse about *Torah* before '*all the Great Ones of Israel*', obviously meaning before a Synod or Sanhedrin of some kind. For Genesis *Rabbah*, the discourse R. Eliezer is pressed to present is before '*the Great Ones of the Land*' whom, it names, as including '*Ben Zizzit Hakeseth, Nikodemon ben Gurion* – i.e., '*Nakdimon*' or '*Nicodemus*' – and *Ben Kalba Sabuᶜa.*' By the same token, it is this incident – plus the story of '*the cattle dung*' which he put into his mouth the night before he was to give this, '*causing a putrid smell to rise from his mouth*' – which the *ARN* also uses to introduce its stories about the three grandees there '*Sisit Hakkeset,*' '*Nakdimon ben Gurion,*' and '*Ben Kalba Sabuᶜa*'.[79] For Ecclesiastes *Rabbah* in its discussion of R. Yohanan's nephew '*Ben Battiah,*' the Head of '*the Sicarii*' of Jerusalem, it was four such '*Councilors*' in Jerusalem at this time, '*each capable of supplying the city with grain for ten years*': '*Ben Zizzit, Ben Gurion, Ben Nakdimon, and Ben Kalba Sabuᶜa.*'[80] In fact, *ARN* then goes on to say something similar about '*Ben Sisit Hakkeset*''s name to what it did in its story, just preceding this, • about both R. Eliezer ben Hyrcanus and R. Yohanan, that is, that they called him this '*because he used to recline on a silver couch before the Great*

Ones of Israel' (for *Gittin*, it will be recalled, it was rather '*because his seat was among the Great Ones of Rome*').[81] Such are the inconsistencies of Rabbinic literature as well.

For Genesis *Rabbah*, which like *ARN* starts off with the note about '*the clods of dung Rabbi Eliezer used to put into his mouth until it emitted a putrid smell*,' now these three – as just indicated – are called '*the Great Ones of the Land*' (in *Gittin*, which has no '*dung*' incident, they were – something like Luke notes about its various '*Rich Men*' – '*three Men of Great Riches*'[82]) and R. Eliezer's lecture is delivered just as his father, who has come to disinherit him for studying *Torah*, sees him so elegantly holding forth in such exalted company and then rather bequeaths his whole fortune to him. The perceptive reader will immediately see that there are overtones here of the initial estrangement between R. Akiba and *his* father-in-law, '*Ben Kalba Sabu*ᶜ*a*' – whom we have already identified as a scion of some kind of the Royal House of Adiabene – before an eventual reconciliation occurs for not unsimilar reasons. This too results in R. Akiba's eventual great wealth. Of course in the latter's case, there is always the additional curious story of his second marriage – Rachel, the putative descendant of Queen Helen's family, having already disappeared somehow from his biography by this point – to the wife, clearly in the time of either Trajan or Hadrian, of a wealthy Roman aristocrat *who had converted for his sake!*[82]

However this may be, the description of this scriptural exegesis session – before what almost resembled '*a Sanhedrin*' of important personages (when R. Eliezer b. Hyrcanus – '*whose face*,' as we saw, '*shone like the beams of light emanating from Moses' face*' – was reconciled with his father) – in Genesis *Rabbah* reads almost like a *Pesher* on Psalm 37, a *Pesher* extant at Qumran. Moreover, Genesis *Rabbah* makes it very clear that the actual verse he is expounding (before '*the Great Ones of the Land*') is a verse *actually subjected to exegesis at Qumran*. Be this as it may, now Eliezer ben Hyrcanus (not '*Ben Zizzit*') is '*sitting before them*' – '*the Great Ones of the Land*' – expounding a verse from Psalm 37:14–15:

> The Wicked have drawn the sword and bent the bow to cast down the Meek and the Poor (Ebion) and to slay the Upright of the Way (Yesharei-Derek)

But, of course, this is a classic Qumran-style '*wilderness*' passage including not only allusions to '*Ebion*' ('*the Poor*'), '*the Meek*' (ᶜ*Ani*), and '*the Way*'/'*the Upright of the Way*,' but also another important variation on the '*casting down*' language, imagery which – as we shall presently also see – is to be found in the Habakkuk *Pesher* as well.[83] And what is so marvelous about all this is that, as just observed, *a 'Pesher' on the same verse is actually extant at Qumran* – palaeographically speaking, as already indicated, contemporary with the Habakkuk *Pesher*.[84]

As far as Eliezer is concerned, the verse, '*the Wicked have drawn the sword and have bent the bow,*' refers to '*Amraphel and his companions*' (Genesis 14:1–15), which is the reason for the placement of this incident at this point in Genesis *Rabbah*. However in the Psalm 37 *Pesher* at Qumran, more to the point, the exegesis of this passage has to do with '*the Wicked of Ephraim and Manasseh*' – in any event, the first of these is both a homophone and an anagram of the '*Amraphel*' above.[85] This is immediately followed up in the *Pesher* by references to both '*the Doers of the Torah*' and '*the Penitents of the Desert*' ('*the Congregation*' or '*Church of God's Elect*' – later '*the Church of the Poor*' or '*the Ebionites*'), '*who shall possess the High Mountain of Israel forever*' – also defined in Psalm 37:20, that follows, as '*those who love the Lord*' and '*the pride of His pastures.*'[86]

There is no telling what R. Eliezer might have made of these further allusions and why his surprising exposition, '*this refers to Amraphel and his companions,*' should have so impressed the assembled grandees (including his father, who immediately bequeathed him his whole estate whereas earlier he was on the point of disinheriting him); but if it has anything to do with Qumran, then its exposition would concern:

> *The Evil Ones of Ephraim and Manasseh, who sought to lay hands on the Priest (i.e., 'the High Priest' – a synonym at Qumran for 'the Righteous Teacher') and the Men of his Council ('the Community Council' at Qumran) at the time of the testing (or 'trial' – literally, 'refining' as in metal work) that came upon them. But God will redeem them from their hand and later they will be given over to the hand of the Violent Ones of the Gentiles for Judgement*[89] –

by anyone's standard, a crucial exposition we shall evaluate further below when it comes to analyzing the Habakkuk *Pesher*, because of the numerous overlaps and commonalities in vocabulary between the two *Pesharim*.

Not only is this yet another testimony – if such were needed – of the chronological provenance of these Qumran allusions as relating to the First Century and not before, in particular, the period of the War against Rome; but almost all commentators see these references as covert allusions to the Establishment, possibly Herodians or Romans – possibly Pharisees and Sadducees. Nor can it be emphasized too much that the finding of this pseudonym '*Amraphel*' here in the Genesis *Rabbah*, placed in the mouth of Eliezer ben Hyrcanus, the one rabbi whose sympathies with sectarian movements in Palestine has always been suspected, is a striking reminder of the uniqueness of these scriptural expositions; and that the knowledge of them and the events they represented continued after the generally-assumed deposit-date for the Scrolls in the Qumran caves – in the period around 70 CE and the fall of either the Temple or Masada or both (of course, there is no reason they could not have been deposited later, as I have argued, any time up to the Bar Kochba Revolt of 132–36 CE and its suppression[88]).

Furthermore, when talking about 'the Simple of Ephraim fleeing their Assembly' and 'those who mislead them' and, once more, 'joining (themselves to) Israel ('nilvu'/'ger-nilveh'/'Nilvim'[89]) when the Glory of Judah shall arise' (presumably meaning 'the Messiah' – cf. John 12:16 and 12:28 above referring to Jesus' 'Glorification' in the context of reference to 'his Disciples' not understanding the meaning of his coming to Jerusalem 'riding on a donkey') in another Pesher, that on Nahum; this 'joining' allusion can mean 'Gentiles' generally in the sense of 'God-Fearing' Nilvim (or 'Joiners' – an expression actually used in the interpretation of the all-important passage from Ezekiel 44:15 on 'the Sons of Zadok' in the Damascus Document, we have already discussed to some extent above and will discuss further[90]), pro-Revolutionary Herodians, or even 'Samaritans' per se as, for instance, in the way this latter term is used in the Gospels.[91]

Where this 'Glory' too is concerned, it should be appreciated that not only is Zechariah 9:9, 'your King is coming' – 'Righteous,' 'humble,' and 'bearing Salvation' – above[92] (it would be nice to find a Pesher on this passage at Qumran – just the kind of passage usually subjected to exegesis there); but the evocation of it in John 12:15 also refers back in 12:17 to how 'the Many bore witness...when he called Lazarus out of the tomb' previously and the passage anticipating this in John 11:4. In turn, this passage speaks, not only of 'the Glory of God' and how he 'was to be Glorified' when he would 'do this sign' (11:4 and 12:18) but also, most portentously, to Lazarus as being 'the one you love' (John 11:3). Of course, this is the same kind of language that 'the Many' are also pictured as using in Matthew 15:31, when they too were said to have 'Glorified the God of Israel,' following their having seen 'signs' like that of the resurrection of the 'Cananaean woman's daughter.'

But also at the conclusion of all these 'Mary'/'Martha'/'Lazarus'-activities in John 12:23 and 12:28, when Andrew and Philip – again 'two Disciples' – tell him that 'certain Greeks' are also coming 'to worship at the Feast' (presumably 'the Feast of Passover' in Jerusalem); Jesus is pictured as responding in 12:23 using similar language, 'the time has come for the Son of Man to be Glorified' (cf. this same theme repeated in Acts 11:18 after

Peter explains to 'those of the circumcision' why he 'went in and ate with uncircumcised men' – who upon 'hearing these things were silent and Glorified God, saying, truly God gave repentance unto life to the Gentiles too'), and again in 12:28, when he is pictured as crying out, 'Father, Glorify Your Name,' yet one more 'Voice out of Heaven' materializes and calls down, 'I both have Glorified it and will Glorify it again'! So obviously, this 'arising of the Glory of Judah' was very much on the mind of Gospel craftsmen.

However this may be, what these 'Evil Ones of Ephraim and Manasseh' (for R. Eliezer, it will be recalled, 'Amraphel and his companions' – and n.b., too, how for some reason John 11:54 mysteriously refers at this point to 'a city called Ephraim' in 'the country near the desert' where 'he stayed with his Disciples'!) do in the Psalm 37 Pesher, in 'casting down the Meek and the Poor,' is lay hands on the Righteous Teacher (called in the Pesher, as just remarked and as in the Habakkuk Pesher as well, 'the Priest' – which in the context obviously means 'the Opposition High Priest' of the Community) and the Men of his Council (that is, 'the Assembly' or 'Church of the Poor' – once again, just as this 'Council' is described in the Habakkuk Pesher and, should we say, by Paul as well?[93]), 'for which they will be delivered into the hands of the Violent Ones of the Peoples ('Arizei-Go'im,' that is, probably pro-Revolutionary Herodian Men-of-War as, for instance, those in Josephus called 'Idumaeans,' responsible for the death of the High Priest Ananus and his colleague, Martha's most recent husband, the Boethusian High Priest 'Jesus ben Gamala' – cf. here, too, the note of 'delivering up,' as in all portrayals of 'Judas Iscariot' in the Gospels. Of course, also here it is 'the Sicarii' or 'the Zealots' who are working with 'the Idumaeans' in exacting this vengeance) for Judgement.'[94] In the Habakkuk Pesher, 'the Wicked Priest' not only will have 'to drink the Cup' he forced 'the Righteous Teacher' to 'drink' ('the Cup' which, when it 'comes round to him,' will be called 'the Cup of the right hand of the Wrath of God'), but he would also be 'paid the reward he paid the Poor.'[95]

In the meantime 'the Penitents of the Desert' ('Priests' according to the Damascus Document's exegesis of Ezekiel 44:15 above, which we shall analyze further below [96]) here in the Psalm 37 Pesher – as we just saw, also 'the Assembly' or 'Church of His Elect' and 'the Assembly of the Poor'[97] – shall be 'saved and live for a thousand generations' (this, too, has its parallel in the Damascus Document where 'those that hold fast to the New Covenant in the Land of Damascus' and 'walk in these things in Perfect Holiness' are also promised 'to live for a thousand generations'[98]) and 'all the Glory of Adam shall be theirs' (and this too is paralleled in the Damascus Document[99] – a variation on 'the Primal Adam' ideology we have been highlighting, not to mention 'the Glory of Judah' as well, just alluded to, in John's language of

'*Glorifying*' and '*Glorification*' above) and '*they shall possess the whole Earth as an inheritance*' (also this is paralleled in '*the Root of Planting*' material at the outset of the Damascus Document).[100]

In the exposition by Eliezer ben Hyrcanus, just referred to in Genesis *Rabbah* above, '*the Poor and the Meek*' are rather designated as '*Lot*,' saved in this archaic episode in Genesis 14:14–15 by Abraham and his servants who '*fell upon them* ('*Amraphel and his companions*') *at night*' and '*pursued them as far as Hobab north of Damascus*.' '*The Upright of the Way*' are, of course, Abraham and his household; the '*sword*' of whose enemies described as '*entering their own heart*'[101]; and this is the important correspondence between the two *Peshers*, that is, '*the sword*' of their Enemies '*will come around to*' them. Having said this, it is not difficult to work out the correspondences – but the whole is, of course, basically Talmudic disinformation with nothing like the clarity and precision, we just pointed out and will point out further in documents like the Psalm 37 *Pesher*, the Habakkuk *Pesher*, and the Damascus Document below. Moreover, there is the significant additional point of correspondence in the '*north of Damascus*' allusion which will enjoy, as we shall also see, a significant parallel in the Damascus Document from Qumran.[102]

In this same Psalm 37 *Pesher*, the allusion to '*those who love the Lord*' (37:20 – '*the Piety Commandment*,' we have so often referred to above), who are also called '*the Pride of the Pastures*' (the '*Plantation*' or '*Husbandry*' imagery, we have also been highlighting, in the several contexts of the Damascus Document, Paul in 1 Corinthians 3:6–9, and even in the parody of the '*Pasturage*' of this kind '*being uprooted*' in Matthew 15:13[103]), has another parallel, as we have underscored too, in the Letter of James (to say nothing of the Damascus Document just noted above[104]), in '*the Kingdom promised to those who love Him*' – in James 2:4, expressly denoted as '*the Poor*' whom '*God chose*' (that is, '*His Elect*,' '*Rich in Faith and Heirs to the Kingdom*') preceding its exposition of '*the Royal Law according to the Scripture*' – the '*all-Righteousness Commandment*' – in 2:5–8.

Here in the Psalm 37 *Pesher*, they are '*the Assembly*' or '*Church of His Elect*' as well (also referred to *inter alia*, as just remarked, as '*the Assembly*' or '*Church of the Poor*'). These '*shall be Leaders and Princes* – like '*Shepherds*' – *of the flock among their herds*.'[105] This too enjoys a parallel in the Damascus Document's exegesis of Numbers 21:18 about '*the Well which the Princes dug, which the Nobles of the People dug with the Staff* ('*Mehokkek*') – '*the Well being the Torah*,' '*the Diggers*' being '*the Penitents of Israel who went out from the Land of Judah to dwell in the Land of Damascus*,' and '*the Staff*' being '*the Interpreter of the Torah who* (just like Elijah and later Paul) *came to Damascus*' and probably elsewhere.[106]

13

Barring the Dogs from the
Wilderness Camps

'MMT'

Perhaps the key to many of these puzzles and interrelationships comes
in the curious document, remarked above, scholars refer to as '*MMT*' but
which I called, following allusions in its opening and closing lines, '*Two
Letters on Works Righteousness.*'[1] As it turns out, in a passage in it about
'*dogs*' (in this case, '*being barred from the Holy Camp*' – identified in the
'*Letter(s)*' with '*the Temple*') most of what we are speaking about here is
paralleled and, perhaps, even more clearly explained.[2]

In the succession of events leading up to the ultimate publication of
the document, in which I participated, I took it to be *two* '*Letters*' – the
only '*Letters*,' it would appear, in the entire corpus at Qumran and something in the nature of 1 and 2 Corinthians or Thessalonians in the New
Testament – therefore the name I accorded it which I saw as, not only
an altogether more accurate way of referring to it, but also as pointing
towards critical subject matter in the proverbial debate between Paul and
James.

Gratifyingly, much of this way of looking at it has since been recognized – in particular, the use of the charged expression, '*works*,' as a
translation of the term '*ma°asim*' (based on the Hebrew root '°-S-H'),
which carries with it the sense of '*doing*' as in '*doing the Torah*' (and not
'*acts*' or '*deeds*' as some well-known translators of Qumran documents –
who shall remain nameless – would have it). By extension and deriva-
tively, this would extend to the whole way the usage, '*justify*' or
'*Justification*' – based on the celebrated phrase or '*proof-text*' from Isaiah
53:11, '*My Servant, the Righteous One (Zaddik) will justify (yazdik) Many*'
or, more literally, '*make Many Righteous*, is employed at Qumran, not only
in *MMT* but also the centrally-important Damascus Document and the
parallel '*New Testament*' (this latter, clearly, not '*in the Land of Damascus*'
but in the milieu of manifestly '*Paulinized*' Communities in Asia Minor
and further west).[3]

This allusion, occurring in the first line, speaks about '*some works of the*

Torah' (complimenting an allusion in the last one to '*doing*'), from which the scholarly designation '*MMT*'/'*Some Works of the Torah*' above – originally for some reason (before my emendations), mystifyingly translated as '*Some Words of the Torah*,' though expression '*Words*' never appeared in this line – was derived. Presumably the '*Letter*' or '*Letters*' then intended to go on to air certain subjects that would be of interest to its recipient. These included, in the first instance, '*purity*' issues and '*sacrifices*' that could end up in '*pollution of the Temple*,' in particular, the affect '*Gentile gifts*' or '*sacrifices*' and matters relating to aspects of relations with '*Gentiles*' generally could have on the '*Holiness*' of the Temple (subjects of intense interest too in the New Testament, as we have been encountering them and, as it were, at Qumran).

The usual view of this document, because of certain allusions in the second part ('*the Second Letter*') evoking and seemingly comparing its recipient to '*David*,'[4] was that this was directed towards a '*Jewish*' or '*Herodian King*,' though which '*King*' this might be in this period – other than Agrippa I (37-44CE), already mentioned above, who presumably would not have needed such tuition – is hard to imagine. It is for these reasons, too, that I have considered this document to be addressed to a newer and, therefore, even perhaps *more* '*zealous*' *convert to Judaism* who, while nevertheless a '*King*,' would not only need and be interested in such instruction but would, in fact, be desirous of having it.[2]

Accordingly, this allusion to '*works of the Torah*' is also picked up towards the end of the second part of this document – called in scholarly parlance '*the composite document*,' because it is made up of a reconstruction from some six or seven different document fragments and, consequently, what probably should be seen as the end of the Second '*Letter*' – showing it to be interested in both '*the Law*' and/or '*the Torah*' as, for instance, in the Letter of James, but not the other way round, as in Paul.[3]

This reads:

Now as to what we have written you concerning some works of the Torah (that is, there was an earlier letter – a situation, as just remarked, somewhat equivalent to Letters in the corpus attributed to Paul like 1 and 2 Corinthians or 1 and 2 Thessalonians), *which we reckoned* (the same '*reckoned*' in the Hebrew as in Genesis 15:6 above, but now concerning those '*works*' and not just the '*Faith*' that was going to be '*be reckoned to Abraham as Righteousness*') *for your own well-being* (seemingly the '*well-being*' or '*welfare*' of the '*King*,' to whom '*the Second Letter*,' anyhow, appears to be addressed and, of course, someone who would be interested in *Abraham's*

'*Salvationary*' *state* and/or *how he 'was justified'*) *and that* (i.e., again, the same '*well-being*') *of your People* (this allusion certainly makes it look as if we are dealing with the '*welfare of a People*' outside the borders of Palestine proper – perhaps Adiabene or '*the Land of* someone like '*Abgarus*' or '*Agbarus, the Great King of the Peoples beyond the Euphrates*,' again either '*the Osrhoeans*' or those inhabiting the contiguous Lands a little bit further East in areas such as '*Adiabene*' or modern-day Kurdistan, who, coming from the region of '*Abraham's Homeland*' certainly would have had an interest in his '*Salvationary state*').

Because we see that you possess discernment and knowledge of the Torah (acknowledgement of the King's sincerity, even perhaps his conversion but, in any event, hardly descriptive of any Herodian '*King*' one might be able to imagine – except perhaps, as just observed, Agrippa I, though even he with difficulty)...*that you may distance yourself from* ('*keep away from*') *Evil thoughts and the counsel of Belial* (the '*keeping away from*' language of James' directives to overseas communities in Acts 15:20, 15:29, and 21:25 above and that permeating the Damascus Document above, where it is expressed in terms of the same Hebrew root as that underlying the language of '*Naziritism*'[5]), *so that at the End Time* (again, the same '*End Time*' that we have already encountered above in the Damascus Document as well and shall encounter further in the Habakkuk *Pesher* below[6]), *you will rejoice* (meaning clearly '*at the Resurrection*') *when you find this collection of our words* ('*Mikzat*' again) *to have been True and it* (your '*doing*' these '*works of the Torah* – with an emphasis, as in the Damascus Document and the Letter of James again, on '*doing*' based on the same Hebrew root, as just explained, as '*works*' – and '*what is Upright and Good before Him*'/'*God*') *will be reckoned to you as Righteousness*.'[7]

But, of course, this is '*Justification*' theology with a vengeance.[8] It is using the same phraseology of '*being reckoned to you as Righteousness*,' based on the Genesis 15:6 passage, we have also just highlighted above, describing Abraham's '*Faith*.' This is the same passage which Paul employs in both Romans 4:2–5:1 (here Paul actually uses the phrase, '*justified by works*,' found here in *MMT*, but to gainsay it where Abraham was concerned) and Galatians 3:6, to develop his understanding of '*Christian*' *Salvation*, that is, '*Salvation by Faith*' – this last, in turn, polemically refracted (in the spirit of the '*works Righteousness*' stance of *MMT* just outlined above) in James 2:23–24 which rather delineates the '*testing*' of Abraham *through the offering of Isaac* and, therefore, why '*he was called a Friend of God*.'

The allusion we are interested in, concerning the subject we have been setting out in this section, dovetails very nicely with the words Matthew 7:6 attributes to 'Jesus' in its formulation of the *'dog'/'dogs'* theme in its version of *'the Sermon on the Mount'*: *'Do not give that which is Holy to the dogs'* (*'nor cast your pearls before the swine lest they trample on them with their feet'* – n.b., the *'feet'* motif again). The way this is expressed, to be polemically gainsaid in the encounter with the *'Greek Syrophoenician'/'Canaanite woman,'* as we have seen, also reflects the ethos of Qumran literature in general – again, most notably, that of the Damascus Document – of *'setting up the Holy Things according to their precise specifications'* (directly amplified in the pivotal *'Jamesian'* demand that immediately follows, *'to love each man his brother'*) and *'separating Holy from profane,'*[9] we already called attention to, an ethos, of course, which is the opposite of what *'Peter'* is pictured as *'learning'* in Acts 10:13–14, 10:28, and 11:9 and elsewhere in the Gospels. As such, for all intents and purposes this last position embodies the original *'Palestinian'* Jewish approach to such matters before it went overseas to be transmogrified into the thematic variants and reversals in the New Testament – some quite amusing – which we have been setting out above.

Like the *'Letter'* Judas Barsabas and his colleagues Paul, Barnabas, and Silas are pictured as *'taking down to Antioch from Jerusalem'* in Acts 15:29–32, containing James' directives to overseas communities, *MMT* is, as just signaled, also a letter (or letters) of some kind.[9] Before proceeding, it should also be remarked that the actual words with which *MMT* closes above (*'Then you shall rejoice at the End of Time when you find this collection of our words to have been True and it will be reckoned as justifying you –* literally, as we just saw, *'reckoned to you as Righteousness'* or *'Justification'/'Zedakah'*– *your having done what is Upright and Good before Him for the sake of your own Good –'consolation'* or *'well-being'*; the Hebrew here is *'Tov'*) – *and for the sake of Israel'*), are essentially reproduced in Acts 15:30–31's version of the outcome or aftermath of this *'Council:'*

> They went to Antioch and, gathering the Multitude (*'the Many'*), they delivered the letter and, having read it, they rejoiced at the consolation' (*'good,' 'comfort,'* or *'well-being,'* meaning, which it – the *'letter'*– provided).

Again, the correspondences are nothing short of remarkable. Nor is this to say anything of the intended destination of this *'letter,' 'Antioch'* – in our view, *'Antioch-by-Callirhoe'* or *'Antioch Orrhoe,'* the capital city of King Agbarus above (*'Agbar the Uchama'* – *'the Black'*?) and possibly *'King Ezad'* ('Izates'?) in succession to him.[10]

In *MMT* above, the ban on gifts and sacrifices from and on behalf of foreigners in the Temple, which we have identified as the immediate issue triggering the War against Rome in 66 CE, is basically the subject of the whole first section from approximately 1.3–1.12. The way this is being formulated, this includes the implication of '*pollution of the Temple*' (1.4–1.11), but even more importantly, the actual words that '*we consider the sacrifices which they sacrifice*' to be '*sacrifices to an idol*' (1.10–12). There cannot be too much debate about the presence of this all-important allusion in the '*First Letter*' (or '*Part*') of '*MMT*' at this point. In fact, if it is present, then the connections between it and the '*Jamesian*' position on this issue, to say nothing of those '*Zealot*' or '*Sicarii Essenes*' Hippolytus claims, as we shall see, are willing to undergo any sort of torture rather than consume such fare (in normative Josephus, this is only expressed in terms of the much less specific '*forbidden things*'), approach convergence.[11]

Paul clearly appreciates that this was the understanding of the vocabulary involved when he strenuously, if somewhat disingenuously, wrestles with the subject in 1 Corinthians 8:1–13 and 10:18–24 above. Again, one should note that he ends in 10:24 with a question that plays off the very words with which we have just seen '*MMT*' close, '*Let no one pursue his own well-being*' ('*welfare*,' or '*good*'), but rather '*each one that of the other*.' Even these last are the very words, we have also just highlighted, in the Damascus Document following its characterization of '*the New Covenant in the Land of Damascus*' as '*setting up the Holy Things according to their precise specifications*' and of the way '*each man should treat his neighbor*,' as well as at several other junctures.[12] In Paul's polemical repartee, these rather lead right into the repudiation of the essence of this '*New Covenant*' – as originally probably set forth in the Damascus Document from Qumran – in 1 Corinthians 10:25–26:

> *Eat everything that is sold in the market* (we have already outlined this above). *There is no need to inquire because of conscience* (Paul's euphemism for issues involving the Law[12]), *for the Earth is the Lord's and the fullness thereof.*

This last paraphrase, once again, even reflects the above proclamation with which the Cairo Damascus Document begins about '*God visiting them and causing a Root of Planting to grow...to inherit His land and to prosper on the good things of His Earth*.' This being said, it is difficult to get much more disingenuous than Paul in the above refinement of his 1 Corinthians 6:12 and 10:23 '*all things are for me lawful*' insistences. Obviously such instructions, whether in Paul or at Qumran, relate to James' rulings in '*the Letter*' ascribed to him in Acts 15 and 21 above, banning in the most unequivocal manner conceivable, '*things sacrificed to idols*,' to say nothing of the ban on '*blood*' immediately following this in all contexts.

Banning the Dogs from the Holy Camps

In fact, the first formulation of the prohibition on '*things sacrificed to idols*' in Acts 15:20 follows the characterization of James (in the manner of '*the Mebakker*' or '*Overseer*' in the Damascus Document, where the ban on '*blood*' is also a major obsession[14]) as '*judging*' and his charge '*to write them*' – meaning the '*Antioch*' Community above. In this first version of James' '*rulings*' – as already remarked – in Acts, the twin conceptualities of '*pollution of the Temple*' and '*things sacrificed to idols*' are combined in the following manner: '*abstain from* (at Qumran this is the Hebrew '*lehinnazer*'[15]) *the pollution of the idols.*' However it is formulated, the issue is labored over by Paul, as just indicated, in 1 Corinthians 8:1–13 and 10:14–33, but here rather leading into his own – and perhaps the original – presentation of '*the New Covenant*' of '*Communion with the body*' and '*the blood of Christ*' in 11:20–34, a formulation by implication, of course, just banned as a consequence of James' prohibition of '*blood*' above.

In the intervening material in 1 Corinthians 11:1–19, Paul also raised some issues having to do with marriage and woman's relationship to man, curiously mostly having to do with '*hair*' – in fact, peculiarly, her '*long hair*' which Paul considers to be '*to her Glory*' (11:15 – n.b., in another obvious attack on '*Nazirites*' such as James preceding this in 11:14, Paul insists that '*Nature itself does teach*' that if '*a man has long hair, it is a dishonor to him*' – sic; note the '*Teacher*' here is '*Nature*' not the Hebraic '*God*').

Marital issues are to some degree taken up as well in *MMT* in 1.39–49 and 78–92 – there however, once again, integrally connected to the third of James' all-important proscriptions '*to the Gentiles*' (*Ethnon*), '*fornication.*' In fact, '*fornication*' had already been evoked for comparative purposes in *MMT* 1.12 in the context of the '*things sacrificed to idols*' characterization earlier, that is, that sacrifices of this kind were either a '*seduction*' or a species of '*fornication.*' But the issue of '*fornication*' had already been dealt with at great length by Paul in 1 Corinthians 6:11–7:40 where he began his discussion of these pivotal directives by James to overseas communities while, at the same time, giving voice for the first time to his '*all things are lawful for me*' and '*food is for the belly and the belly for food*' admonitions, the first just cited above and the last the basis seemingly of Mark and Matthew's picture of Jesus' long excursus about food '*being thrown out through the toilet drain*' above.

The linkage of '*things sacrificed to idols*' to '*fornication*' was also fundamental, as already indicated as well, to the Damascus Document's '*Three*

Nets of Belial' accusations against the ruling Establishment (clearly, as will become ever more apparent as we proceed, *'the Herodians'* and their hangers-on).[16] Two of these charges were, in fact, *'fornication'* and *'pollution of the Temple,'* the ban on *'fornication'* being, as already to some extent observed, specifically defined in terms of *'niece marriage,' 'polygamy,'* and *'divorce.'*[17] At the same time, these were tied to a third, *'blood,'* just underscored above but this time expressed in terms of *'lying with a woman during the blood of her period'* – the linkage between all three, once more, growing out of not *'separating holy from profane,'* this time expressed, as just remarked as well, in terms of the charge of *not observing proper 'separation' procedures in the Temple.* The sense of this was that *'fornicating'* persons of this type (most specifically, including *'Herodians'*) were not being *properly banned from the Temple* and *their gifts and/or sacrifices not rejected* in the manner that they should have been.[18]

The ban on *'fornication'* of James' directives to overseas communities in whatever rendition – not to mention the one on *'blood'* – is widespread at Qumran in multiple documents.[19] In the strictures concerning it and marital relations generally here in *MMT,* 1.78–79, the purity-minded if somewhat ethnocentric reason why public *'fornication'* of any kind was to be abjured – this time, *by the whole People* – was that they were considered *'a Holy People'* and the biblical injunction, *'Israel is Holy,'* applied.[20]

The same reason is applied in *'the Composite Document'* to forbidding *'intermarriage,'* which is systematically considered part of the strictures concerning *'mixing'* in a wider sense – including, for instance, *'mixing different cloths'* or *'threads'* in the same garment or, even earlier, *mixing pure and impure liquids in the same vessel or conduit,* a parallel allusion to which we just saw in one of the *'Parables'* attributed to 'Jesus' above.[21] Not surprisingly, the issue of *'being a Holy People'* is considered particularly relevant to the status of *'the Sons of Aaron'* who, in their role as *'Priests'/'High Priests,'* wore the mitre upon which the words *'Holy to God,'* were engraved.[22] In this section of *MMT,* these *'Priests'* are termed – just as the *'three Priests'* part of (or added to) the twelve-member Community Council in the Community Rule[23] or, in an allegorization similar to Paul's *'members of the Community'* as *'the body of Christ'* or *'Jesus as Temple'* metaphor in 1 Corinthians 12:14–27 and Ephesians 2:20–22 above – *'the Holy of Holies'* or *'the Holiest of the Holy'* (1.82). The conclusion was, bearing again on James' ban on *'fornication'* – though there is some question about the reconstruction here – that they were not even *'to intermarry with the People'* nor *'defile their Holy seed with fornication.'*[24]

In conclusion, there is also the slightest echo of the fourth component of James' absolutely fundamental directives to overseas communities even as conserved in Acts, that of the ban on 'carrion,' so obviously garbled, as we shall explain further below, in Acts' Hellenizing paraphrase of the subject, 'abstain from strangled things,' but correctly delineated in full in the Pseudoclementine *Homilies* and, thereafter, in the *Koran* descending from both.[25] In '*MMT*' the ban on 'carrion,' already clearly enunciated in Ezekiel 44:31 where '*Bnei-Zadok*' Priests who were to '*serve at the altar*' and were '*not to eat anything dying of itself or torn*,' comes in the context of *the curious barring of the same omnipresent 'dogs'* we have been following above, only now '*from the Holy Camps*' (1.69–73).

In *MMT* this ban directly follows the one on '*mixing*' of various kinds, including multiple streams of poured liquids into a single vessel or down a single spout, just highlighted above, as well even as the general ban on '*the blind*' and '*the deaf*' (as always, counter-indicated across the Gospels) because – just as the banning of them from the Temple in the Temple Scroll – they would '*not be able to see to stay away from (such) unclean mixing and, to whom, such polluted mixing would be invisible.*' Moreover, where the latter were concerned, they would not even '*be able to hear the regulations*'! Since neither would, therefore, be able '*to perform them*' (literally '*to do them*' – the vocabulary of '*doing*' again), that is, '*do these regulations*,' they were not to be allowed '*to approach the purity of the Temple*' (1.52–57 – again concerns over '*cleanness*' vs. '*uncleanness,*' '*purity*' vs. '*impurity*' and, as usual, parabolically counter-indicated in the Gospels[26]).

The same would have to be said of '*dogs*,' but for a slightly different if related reason. As *MMT* 1.61–67 puts this:

> *Regarding dogs, one is not to bring dogs into the Holy Camps ('the Camps of Holiness') because they might eat some of the bones in the Temple while the flesh is still on them*

which, however primitive and seemingly intemperate this might appear to the modern ear, is perhaps the clearest statement yet of the reason for the whole concern over '*dogs*' we have been witnessing in these various contexts, that is to say, we are totally in the realm, once again, of '*carrion.*' Not only does this injunction incorporate the reason for the '*uncleanness*' of these '*dogs*' – which is now, simply, '*they eat the bones with the flesh still on them*' – but it specifically connects this '*uncleanness*' to the ban on '*carrion*' itself, *the fourth component of James' directives to overseas communities.*

This is now further explained and specifically connected to Jerusalem with the supplementary rationalization:

> *because Jerusalem is the Holy Camp, the place that He chose from all the Tribes*

of Israel, because Jerusalem is the Head of the Camps of Israel.[27]

Once again one has here the motif of the wilderness '*camps*,' we shall further delineate in Part Four below and, in particular, *Jerusalem* as '*the Head*' or '*Chief of the Camps of Israel.*'

We had already been prepared for something of this kind earlier because, prior to this in the context of extensive exposition of '*purity*' *issues relating to sacrifice* and *where to conduct it*, the principal status of Jerusalem had already been confirmed using this same archaizing '*Camp*' vocabulary. There, again alluding to the biblical wilderness '*Camp*' and '*Tent of Meeting*,' particularly concerning where impure waste from the Temple was to be disposed, Jerusalem had already been designated as '*the Camp*,' and, for these purposes, '*outside the Camp*,' defined as '*outside Jerusalem*'; and the same reason given, though a little more eloquently:'*for Jerusalem was the place He chose from all the Tribes of Israel as a dwelling place for His Name* (1.32–35 – again the reason for such reiteration, where the tuition of a foreign '*King*' might be concerned, should be self evident. A native one would not probably have required it).

One might actually be able to conceive of a '*Galut*' of these '*Holy Camps*' or '*Camps of Holiness*,' as this curiously idiosyncratic letter would put it – or, in the way, it will be put in the first line of the War Scroll, as we shall see as we proceed below, '*the Diaspora of the Desert*' which it, in turn, will be identifies as '*Benjamin*'![28] As this will be put in the Damascus Document's somewhat parallel exposition of '*the Star Prophecy*,' which will also reference '*the Tabernacle of David which is fallen*' from Amos 5:26–27 and 9:11–12 above – this will be '*re-erected*,' as we shall presently see as well, *in a Land 'north of Damascus*' which could also be reckoned as including these '*Camps of Holiness*' or wilderness '*Holy Camps*' being alluded to here in both the War Scroll and *MMT*.[29]

In the new situation defined by contemporary political realities, the flight across the Jordan, signaled so often in these various texts, and the movement, expressed archaically as '*going out from the Land of Judah ('Judea') to dwell in the Land of Damascus*' and specifically delineated in the Damascus Document as a prelude to '*erecting the New Covenant in the Land of Damascus*' (here, the use of '*erecting*' is the same vocabulary as '*erecting the fallen Tenet of David*' in Amos, CD, and the *Florilegium*); these '*Camps of Holiness*' or '*Holy Camps*' could actually even be conceived of as including, not just '*Transjordan*' or the New Testament's '*Perea*' or '*the Decapolis*, but also – as in the various '*heresiologies*' with which we began this analysis – far beyond, all the way up to Northern Syria including Carrhae or Edessa and even '*beyond the Euphrates*,' perhaps as far as

Adiabene in present-day Northern Iraq as well.[30]

'*Do not give Holy Things to Dogs*,' Gentile Gifts in the Temple, and '*Zealot*'/'*Sicarii Essenes*'

Instead of Mark and Matthew's '*Greek Syrophoenician woman*' comparing herself and her daughter to the '*dogs under the table*' or Luke's 'a certain *Poor man (Lazarus) wanting to be filled from the crumbs which fell from the Rich Man's table*' while '*the dogs licked his sores*' – not to mention the *Talmud's* equally silly exposition of '*Ben Kalba Sabuᶜa*'s name in terms of *the Poor* '*coming to his door hungry as a dog and going away filled*'; now the reason '*MMT*' gives for *banning the* '*dogs from the Camps of Holiness*' – carrying with it in particular, as already explained, the meaning of '*Jerusalem*' and '*the Temple*' as the '*Chief*' of these '*Holy Camps*' – is because '*the Dogs*' in such environments might '*eat the bones* (not '*the crumbs*') *with the flesh still on them.*' Here too, it is interesting that it is '*the flesh*' that interests our legal purists not just '*the bones*' – that is, '*the dogs*' are carnivores pure and simple and, thus, even their presence either '*in the camps*' or, more particularly, '*in the Temple*' would *violate the ban on the consumption of* '*carrion.*'

What we have here, as just signaled, is probably the original behind the whole circle of allusions regarding these telltale '*Dogs*' or '*Dog*.' Moreover it most certainly is also reflected in James' rulings to overseas communities in the ban he enunciates on what in Greek, as we have seen, is compressed into the single category of '*strangled things*' but which in other contexts – the Pseudoclementine *Homilies*, for example, or the Koran – is more fully and precisely defined as '*carrion.*'[31]

There also may be a secondary, more symbolic meaning behind all this and that is of the kind we are seeing in the Gospels, namely, *the use of this* '*Dogs*' *metaphor to relate to Gentiles*. In the light of the mutual polemics we have been following and the verbal repartee of the kind found in Paul's Letters, this arcane and curious allusion to '*Dogs*' from this native Palestinian Jewish document found in multiple copies at Qumran (the only '*letter*' or '*letters*' as such found there) therefore, might also be looked on as a veiled allusion to the same kind of thing Matthew 15:27 is intending in his allusion to '*even the little dogs eat of the crumbs falling from their master's table*' (Mark 7:28, as already explained, uses slightly different language: '*even the little dogs under the table eat of the children's crumbs*').

It would also be well to point out at this point that just as Matthew's presentation of the '*dogs under the master's table*' exchange is followed in 15:30–31 by the allusion to '*the dumb speaking, the maimed restored, the lame walking, and the blind seeing*' while the People, '*Glorified the God of Israel*' (in Mark 7:31–37 this is rather depicted by the picture of 'Jesus,' after '*departing from the borders of Tyre and Sidon*' and '*coming to the Sea of Galilee through the midst of the borders of the Decapolis,*' curing a deaf and dumb man by '*putting his fingers into his ears and spitting on his tongue*' – thus!); the barring the dogs from the Temple is preceded in '*MMT,*' as just remarked, by the material *barring the blind and the deaf from approaching* '*the purity of the Temple*' for reasons not unlike those signaled in Mark's vivid depiction of Jesus' restoration of the deaf-mute's speaking and hearing.

But there is also a lengthy passage almost directly following '*the barring of the dogs from the Temple*' in '*MMT*' dealing with the '*uncleanness*' and '*cleansing*' of lepers (1.67–76), a subject – as already underscored – treated throughout the Gospels in the context often of just another simple '*touch*' by Jesus – as, for instance, in Matthew 8:2–3 and *pars*, but also those just encountered in Luke 7:22 and 17:12 above.

In the writer's view this kind of corresponding subject matter – not to mention an often somewhat analogous sequentiality and what appears to be an almost systematic ideological inversion or reversal – occurs with such frequency that it can hardly be thought to be accidental or coincidental. Again, it should be appreciated that just these categories of persons being either *barred from the Temple* (in this context, the symbolic treatment of '*Jesus as Temple*' should always be kept in mind) or *kept at a distance* in documents at Qumran (this includes, '*wine-bibbers,*' '*Sinners,*' '*prostitutes,*' '*over-flowing*' *menstrual bleeders,* '*lepers,*' '*the deaf,*' '*the dumb,*' '*the blind,*' and '*the lame,*' '*gluttons,*' '*tax-collectors,*' and Roman '*Centurions*' to name but a few) are welcomed by 'Jesus,' not only in '*table fellowship,*' but also with a miraculous and healing '*touch*'![32] It is always hard to escape the impression that the people creating these traditions are laughing at what they knew to be native Palestinian '*scruples*' (as Paul would belittlingly characterize them) or what they saw as anachronistic superstitions – in the process, creating their own supernatural Greco-Roman and Hellenistic semi-divine '*Mystery*'-figure, such as an '*Asclepius,*' '*Dionysus,*' '*Apollo,*' '*Orpheus,*' '*Mithra,*' or '*Osiris*' or of the kind an Ovid, Virgil, Seneca, Petronius, or Apuleius might create, replacing these irksome, troublesome and, for the most part, even loathsome bans or taboos with this new, less offensive and more agreeable, less strident and more cosmopolitan man-god; and this, *in the very same environment of those insisting on such proscriptions* and, to add insult to injury, *picturing him as walking around in it* – but how successful, two thousand years-worth of success.

In Matthew the allusion to '*Dogs,*' as we have already seen, occurs in two separate contexts, once with regard to this '*Canaanite woman*' and, once at the end of '*the Sermon of the Mount*' – the one apparently in response to the other (if not 'Jesus' simply responding to himself). In Luke, as we saw – indirectly echoed in the '*Lazarus*' material in John – the '*Dogs*' allusion occurs in an entirely different context, in some ways even more closely linked to Talmudic '*Ben Kalba Sabuᶜa*' scenarios. However these things may be and however one interprets them, the references to '*Dogs*' in Mark and Mat-thew, anyhow, certainly *have something to do with Gentiles* or, at least, how these two Gospel writers *felt Jews looked upon Gentiles*, namely, *as being no better than '*Dogs*'*! The related materials in Luke and John (Luke acting as a kind of bridge to John) also have the not-unrelated reverse of these, that is, a not so thinly-disguised strain of anti-Semitism that runs through both of them.

If we take these allusions to '*Dogs*' in all contexts as involving something of the meaning implied in both Matthew and Mark of '*Gentiles*,' then even the reference to these same '*dogs*,' as we presently have it, in *MMT* can be seen, as well, as a kind of double entendre which, in addition to reflecting the ban on '*carrion*' of James' directives to overseas communities, is also in some manner evoking '*Gentiles*' or, at least, the way '*Gentiles*' were being seen or alluded to by Jews. This would include, in particular, where *MMT* is concerned, *the banning of Gentiles* and *the rejection of their gifts and/or sacrifices* – including those Josephus tells us were being offered '*daily*' on behalf of the Emperor – *from the Temple*, itself perhaps the over-riding theme of this period, at least where '*Zealots*,' '*Sicarii*,' or '*Innovators*'/'*Revolutionaries*' were concerned, again especially in the context of Josephus' description of events leading up to the War against Rome.[33]

If this is true – and the author feels that Matthew and Mark are at least playing on this theme (not to mention Matthew's earlier formulation of the reverse invective, '*Do not give Holy Things to dogs*' – here, the '*Holy Things*' links up with '*Holy Camps*' in *MMT*. It is this one is talking about when one speaks of 'code's in this period) – then, by extension, this pregnant allusion to '*even the dogs eating the crumbs under the table*' can also be seen as having to do with James' ban in both Acts and the Pseudo-clementine *Homilies* on '*things sacrificed to idols*,' itself reflected, as we have seen, in Paul's tendentious and rather self-serving discussions in 1 Corinthians 8–11 above. However general the formulation of this '*things sacrificed to idols*' may be in these three sources (four, if one includes *MMT*), the relationship is always to the Temple – as, for example, it is in Paul's discussion of the ban in 1 Corinthians 10:18–31.

This is also the way the allusion to *the barring of such '*Dogs*' on the basis of their not having '*kept away from carrion*' is presented in *MMT*. Nor is this to mention the strictures in the Temple Scroll *barring '*skins sacrificed* *to idols' and other unclean persons generally from the Temple related to it* – a ban, curiously enough, in this passage alluding in some manner to the person or word '*Bela*ᶜ.'³⁴ Both of these matters, namely the ban on '*things sacrificed to idols*' and that on '*Gentile gifts in the Temple*,' make up the bulk of *MMT*'s concerns up to the point of its consideration of Jerusalem as '*the Holy Camp*' which it also describes, as we saw, as '*the Place which He chose from among all the Tribes of Israel as a resting place for His Name*' and '*the Chief of the Camps of Israel*.'³⁵ Furthermore the ban on '*Dogs*,' '*because they might eat the bones with the flesh still on them*,' also *directly relates in its own way to the Temple*. 36

On the other hand and seen in the light of problems with Gentile conversion in this period generally, it doesn't take much imagination to see Matthew and Mark's version of the retort of the '*Cananaean*'/'*Greek Syrophoenician woman*' as encompassing the kind of response a person like Queen Helen of Adiabene or one of her descendants might have made to someone criticizing their expensive gifts in the Temple or, as the case may be, referring to them as '*Dogs*' – in this sense, Queen Helen would take the place of the '*Canaanite*'/'*Greek Syrophoenician woman*' in Matthew and Mark just as, in our view, '*Ben Kalba Sabuᶜa*' is a euphemism for one or another of her descendants or those of her sons.

In our view, too, just as the '*Queen Helen of Adiabene*' material re-emerges, however tendentiously, into Acts 8:27's story of '*the Queen of the Ethiopians*' and her '*eunuch*' treasury agent, so too Helen's legendary presence hovers, however obscurely, in the background of these Gospel materials as well, not only because of her and her family's wealth, legendary largesse, and '*famine relief*' efforts, but also because of there being in her story just the slightest suggestion of the '*prostitute*' or '*adultery*' motif – a motif present as well, as we have seen, in the matter of 'Jesus' having '*cast seven demons*' out of *Mary Magdalene* (the '*harlot*' character of whom is always lurking somewhere in the background of most traditions surrounding her) as it is with regard to Simon *Magus*' legendary traveling companion – the '*Queen*' named '*Helen*' he, too, supposedly *retrieved out of the bordellos of* '*Tyre!*'³⁷

To go back to the original point behind these two issues – *the ban on Gentiles in the Temple and the rejection of their gifts and sacrifices from it (including those on behalf of the Emperor)* – these according to Josephus were the essential last straws triggering the Uprising against Rome in 66 CE.³⁸ Josephus, as we have seen, disingenuously terms the banning of both of these by the more '*Zealot*'-minded lower priest class as '*an Innovation which our Forefathers were before unacquainted with.*' We say '*disingenuously*' here because he knows full well that these same persons – along presumably with their sacrifices – had been explicitly banned long before in Ezekiel 44:5–15's pointed '*Zadokite Covenant*,' the very same passage of central importance as well to the Damascus Document at Qumran which both delineated who and what these true '*Sons of Zadok*' were.[39]

Nor is it coincidental or accidental that when Paul comes to speak about such '*sacrifices on the part of Gentiles in the Temple*' in his likewise pivotal arguments in 1 Corinthians 10:14–22, leading up to announcing his position on '*Communion with the body*' and '*blood of Jesus Christ*' in 11:17–29 (again note how it is in the course of this in 11:14 he claims that '*Nature itself teaches that it is a dishonor to a man if he has long hair*,' clearly an outright attack, as already underscored, on Jewish '*Nazirites*' – again, too, it would be difficult to imagine a *more disingenuous statement than this since he knows the parameters of both Essenism and Messianism in Palestine*); he cautions his opponents in 10:22 in the same breath as he evokes '*drinking the Lord's Cup and the cup of demons*' and '*eating of the Lord's table and the table of demons*' (the '*demon*'/'*demons*' language of the Gospels above) with the threat of the very same '*zeal*' with which they probably had threatened him. Yet again, in invoking this '*zeal of the Lord*,' he is reversing in his usual rhetorical manner the language of his presumed interlocutors against themselves (in this case, seemingly, James' '*Zealots for the Law*' as *per* Acts 21:20 below). It is in such passages that one can be sure that Paul's opponents really were '*Zealots*' or '*Sicarii*' who had, of course, a diametrically opposed view of such '*idolatry*' to his own.

One should recall how in Hippolytus' description of those denoted as '*Zealot*' or '*Sicarii Essenes*' – Hippolytus conserving in the author's view an earlier and perhaps even more incisive version of Josephus' testimony on these matters – Hippolytus/Josephus emphasizes this very point, namely, the unwillingness of such '*Sicarii Essenes*' to eat '*things sacrificed to idols*' *even under the threat of the direst Roman torture or death*.[40] In the received version of Josephus – in which the latter acknowledges that these very same '*Essenes*' had participated and had distinguished themselves by their bravery in '*our recent war against the Romans*' – the unwillingness on their part to eat such fare even in the face of the direst torture or death is characterized, as already emphasized, only under the classification of the more general '*not eating forbidden things*.'[41]

It is in passages such as these that the account attributed to Hippolytus distinguishes itself by its greater precision and, for that matter, insight. In other words, putting Hippolytus and Josephus together, it is in connection with this ban – found both in '*MMT*' and James' directives to overseas communities in Acts, alluded to as well in the ban on '*skins sacrificed to idols*' in the Temple Scroll and worried over by Paul – that such '*Zealots*' or '*Essenes*' (good '*Jamesian*'s that they were) were prepared to martyr themselves. The testimony to their unwillingness to eat such fare is even backed up in Asia Minor in the correspondence between Pliny the Younger and Trajan about Revolutionary unrest in that area at a somewhat later period – the period in which Simeon bar Cleophas and the grandsons of Jesus' third brother Judas reportedly met their ends – and seemingly for precisely the same reasons.[42]

To close the circle again: aside from the fact that Acts 21:20 knows the majority of James' '*Jerusalem Church*' supporters were '*Zealots for the Law*' (*Zelotai tou Nomou*), the issue of '*Zealots*' is already present in the episode about 'Jesus'' encounter with the '*Greek Syrophoenician woman*' in Mark and Matthew as it stands. While Mark 7:25, which places the whole episode in '*the neighborhood of Tyre*' (again *n.b.*, '*the brothels of Tyre*' allusion in the slur about Simon *Magus*' consort above), identifies her in this latter manner, as we have seen; Matthew 15:22, on the other hand, identifies her as '*a Canaanite*' or '*Cananaean woman*' and for him, the region is now '*Tyre and Sidon.*' Elsewhere, the same appellation, as also already explained, is given in Mark 3:18 and Matthew 10:4 to Jesus' supposed Apostle '*Simon the Cananaean,*' another euphemism Luke 6:15 definitively unravels in its designation of '*Simon the Zealot*' ('*Zelotes*').[43]

It should also be appreciated that in Acts' patently incomprehensible arguments in the early Church between '*Hebrews*' and alleged '*Hellenists*' over who is '*to wait on*' or '*serve tables*' and *the distribution of the common fund*, which we have already variously deconstructed above; this term '*Hellenists*' (*Helleniston* – 6:1, reappearing too in 9:29 and 11:20; in Mark the reference is to '*Hellenis*') clearly conceals something more fundamental, that is, as in the matter of the '*Canaanite woman*' above, '*zealotry*' or '*Zealots*' (although in her regard in Matthew, the issue is inverted). In the context of such '*zealotry*' or '*Zealots,*' one should also recall the additional reverse play in the Greek on the same usage in Mark and Matthew's '*kunaria*'/'*little dogs*' (with the additional inclusion of the '*little*' from the '*little children*' usages tied to it; in Luke's related version about Lazarus' '*sores*' – not his '*bones*' – '*kunes*' or simply '*dogs*') on '*Kanna'im,*' the Hebrew for '*Cananaeans*'/'*Zealots.*'

Queen Helen's '*Eunuch,*' Circumcision, and '*the Lex Cornelia de Sicarius*'

One can go further than this. We have already seen that even though the whole episode regarding the '*Greek Syrophoenician*'/'*Canaanite woman*' seems to be missing from the third Synoptic account, in reality it is not.

Rather it reappears in the last of Jesus' parables about the '*Rich*' Men in Luke 16:19 about the '*certain*' one, '*who used to dress in purple and fine linen and feast in luxury every day.*' Nor is this parable paralleled, as already observed as well, in any of the other Gospels except for the name of the '*Poor Man who wished to be filled from the Rich Man's table crumbs*' – '*Lazarus,*' about whose '*sisters*' and the '*stink*' of whose body John for his part goes on, in turn, to give additional, not insignificant particulars.

As also analyzed previously, these details bring us right back to Talmudic stories about its '*Rich Men,*' Nakdimon, *Ben Kalba Sabu^ca*, Boethus, and their '*daughters.*' For its part, the '*daughter*' theme then takes us back even further, closing the circle of all these usages and returning us, yet again, to Mark and Matthew's '*Canaanite*'/'*Greek Syrophoenecian woman's daughter.*' As already suggested too, the last-named woman has much in common with Josephus' and Talmudic stories about Queen Helen and her legendary largesse or '*Riches*' (Luke's '*luxurious Rich Man with his daily feasting*'?)who, in turn, has interesting connections with Simon *Magus*' alleged consort or '*Queen*' also called '*Helen.*' The circle of these overlaps then even widens to include in Luke's Acts 8:27 another such '*Rich*' foreign woman with an interest in Jerusalem and apparent charitable giving, but now identified as '*Kandakes the Queen of the Ethiopians.*'[44]

This story about '*Kandakes*' too, aside from alluding to her fabulous wealth, as already pointed up, describes the Pauline-style conversion through baptism of her '*Treasury agent*'/'*eunuch*' (8:36–37). The latest '*Queen*' by the name of '*Kandakes,*' mentioned by Strabo in approximately 21 BC and echoed later by Pliny in his *Natural History* (the probable source of this particular transmogrification) was the Queen of Meroe in Nubia or modern-day Northern Sudan. Not only were there no Jewish-inclining '*Ethiopian Queen*'s to send (purpose unknown) their '*eunuch*'/'*Treasury agents*' up to Jerusalem in the late 30's or early 40's CE – a happenstance seemingly reflecting '*the Queen of Sheba*''s activities in Solomon's time a thousand years before; but there is no suggestion whatever of '*Christianity*' ever taking root there then (and hardly even today), the contacts of '*Ethiopia*' or, for that matter, '*Meroe*' with '*Christianity*' not having occurred until centuries later. Nor was she or any of her predecessors or successors ever remarked as having been particularly wealthy.[45]

This is not to mention the note of '*Zealotry*' seemingly present in the first syllable of her name, '*Kan*'/'*Ken,*' and echoed, as well, in the name of that descendant of Queen Helen, '*Kenedaeus*' (another of these seeming '^c*Arizei-Go'im*' in the Habakkuk *Pesher* we shall hear more about as we proceed[46]) who played a part in the 66 CE Uprising against Rome and apparently lost his life in its first serious engagement – the battle at the Pass at Beit Horon.[47] Linguistic connections and plays of this kind, however unlikely they may seem at first glance, should not be ignored, just as a similar correspondence in the name of 'the Canaanite woman' should not be ignored, nor blinds like so-called or alleged 'Hellenists.'

Nor is the the Treasury agent's 'eunuch' status a practice having anything to do with any African Kingdom at this time, but only Iraq and Persia and a hold-over from earlier Persian dynastic practices. As already alluded to, it is more than likely simply a poetic euphemism for 'circumcision' – in particular the 'circumcision' of Queen Helen's two sons, Izates and Monobazus (already sufficiently remarked above) – 'circumcision' in Roman eyes being looked upon (in exactly the manner of Paul's characterization of 'long hair' being 'against the teachings of Nature') as a kind of 'bodily mutilation' or 'castration.'

In this regard, as already noted, one should pay particular attention to the traditional body of Roman law, collectively known in this period as the 'Lex Cornelia de Sicarius et Veneficis' (c. 50 BC–150 CE) which even uses the term 'Sicarius' in connection with the ban on 'bodily mutilations' of this kind, the penalty for which was death.[48] The actual name 'Cornelius' associated with this legislation, as we saw as well, goes back to the famous Roman Commander, Publius Cornelius Scipio (c. 234–183 BC), but it really only came into serious effect under Nerva (96–98 CE) following the assassination of Domitian (81–96) and – it is important to add – in the wake of the ongoing unrest in Palestine/Judea[49]; and all the more so during and after the reign of Hadrian (117–136 CE – the last of these 'Italica Emperors') when another body of legislation also came into effect. This was known in the Talmud (perhaps defectively) as 'the Sicaricon' and involved the confiscation of enemy property, in particular, of those participating in the Bar Kochba Revolt against Hadrian and presumably earlier ones, and has to be associated in some way with this 'Lex Cornelia' and anti-circumcision legislation generally.[50]

We have also already emphasized the possible echo of this name in that of the 'Pious' Roman 'Centurion' in Acts (who was 'supplicating God continually,' 'doing so much charity to the People' – the 'doing' language again now reversed – and 'borne witness to by the whole Nation of the Jews,' because of which 'his works were remembered before God' – this last, of course, not only part of Paul's 'Last Supper' Communion language, but also that of the Pseudoclementine Recognitions above and the Damascus Document below[51]) of the 'Italica Regiment' in Caesarea, to whose house 'Peter' finally receives the command 'from Heaven' to visit, abolishing Mosaic Law for all time (meaning, of course too, that 'Jesus' never taught any such thing or why would 'Peter,' his closest associate, have been unaware of it of, for that matter, require a Paul-type '*vision*' to learn of it?).

Even Origen in the Third Century was referring to himself, in precisely the same manner, as a '*Sicarius*' because of the castration or bodily mutilation he was said to have performed upon himself![52] But in his case, he was probably following an equally tendentious statement Matthew 19:12 portrays 'Jesus' as making after '*withdrawing from Galilee and coming into the borders of Judea beyond Jordan*' (*thus*) and leading into the above material about allowing '*the little children to come unto him to touch him*' – in response to some very tough questioning from '*the Pharisees*' once again and similar to the Dead Sea Scrolls about different grades of '*marriage*,' '*divorce*,' '*fornication*,' and '*adultery*'[53] – about '*eunuchs making themselves eunuchs for the sake of the Kingdom of Heaven.*'

Nor in regard to this, too, should one forget those above, whom Hippolytus calls '*Sicarii Essenes*,' who offered the choice of forcible circumcision or death to anyone they heard discussing the Law who was not circumcised. Not only is this a forerunner of similar later Islamic alternatives, *i.e.*, '*Islam or the sword*'; it must also be seen as the other side of the coin to Josephus' derivation of the '*Sicarii*' terminology – the curved knife upon which he claimed the designation was based not, therefore, being just the assassin's knife as *per* the sense of his exposition of it, but also that of the circumciser. Moreover, among the practitioners of this '*Way*' the two, no doubt, functioned as one.[54]

This has to be seen as throwing a good deal of light on Galatians 2:12's reference to '*the some from James*' as '*the Party of the Circumcision*' and the '*some*' whom Acts 15:1–4 insists '*came down from Judea*' to Antioch – whichever the '*Antioch*' intended' – '*and were teaching the brothers that unless you were circumcised according to the law of Moses you could not be saved*' triggering, according to its historiography, '*the Jerusalem Council*' (*cf.* as well, the clearly tendentious portrait in Acts 10:45 and 11:2, too, concerning '*those of the Circumcision*' who '*were amazed that the gift of the Holy Spirit had been poured out on the Gentiles too*' – compare this with the portrait in the Scrolls of '*the Pourer out*'/'*Spouter*'/or '*Man of Lying who poured out on Israel the waters of Lying*'[55] – and argued with Peter, complaining that he '*went in unto uncircumcised men and ate with them*').

Of course, the whole issue of whether to circumcise or not to circumcise brings us right back to Josephus' and the Talmudic story about the conversion of Queen Helen, as well as that of her two sons Izates and Monobazus, their circumcision, and Helen's own apparently deep-seated, overtly expressed opposition to the practice.[56] This last, in turn – as just highlighted – bears on Luke's caricaturizing portrait of the conversion of '*the Ethiopian Queen's eunuch*,' who chooses to be baptized after

'*Philip*' encounters him reading a passage from Isaiah 53:7's '*Suffering Servant*' (which had, it should be appreciated, nothing whatever to do with baptism). But where the circumcision of Queen Helen's two sons in Talmudic tradition and Josephus are concerned, they are reading, as already explained, a passage about Abraham both '*circumcising himself*' and '*all the members of his household*,' including '*the foreigner dwelling among them*' – '*the Ger-Nilveh*' or '*Resident Alien*' of the Nahum *Pesher* above and a passage from Genesis 17:23–27 actually alluded to in the Damascus Document where Abraham was concerned as well[57] – which would have had more than a passing significance for persons in an '*Abrahamic*' locale, even perhaps those in the neighborhood of Haran such as '*Edessa*' in Northern Syria (Paul's '*Antioch*' above?), as it did the Koran as well.[58]

This brings us back to the Gospels of Luke and John on the issue of '*Dogs*,' '*Lazarus*,' his Resurrection, and '*the Poor*,' clearly combining in new ways and reflecting all the various Talmudic materials delineated above. The same can be said for Acts' picture of its '*Ethiopian Queen's eunuch*' reflecting, as already delineated, both materials in Josephus and the *Talmud* about the conversion via '*circumcision*' of Queen Helen's two sons, Izates and Monobazus. The '*Poor Man Lazarus*' – a designation reappearing in almost all Talmudic variations and the basis, of course, of the telltale Ebionite notation '*the Poor Ones*' – at the '*Rich Man's door*' in Luke moves on directly into the discussion of both his and '*the Rich Man*''s state after the Resurrection in Luke 16:22–31 as we have seen; whereas in John 12:9–11, the events circulating around Lazarus' '*Resurrection*' end up in the picture of '*Many of the Jews going astray* (note the use, once again, of this telltale Scrolls' vocabulary of '*going astray*'[59]) *and believing in Jesus because of (Lazarus') Resurrection*' and the High Priests, therefore, '*plotting together how they might also put Lazarus to death*' (*sic*).

For its part, it will be recalled, this rather anti-Semitic follow-up picture in Luke 16:22 depicts '*Lazarus*' – as seemingly the representative of all '*Jews believing in Jesus*' – now rather in some '*Angelic*' abode '*on the bosom of Abraham*,' not the real world as in John; whereas '*the Rich Man in Hades*' (seemingly meant to depict the state of most other Jews not '*believing in Jesus*') is now – like Lazarus earlier – longing to be '*comforted*' (16:24 – in the case of Lazarus earlier, it was '*longing to be filled*'). The conclusion is then reached in 16:30, clearly reflecting the picture in John 11–12 above, that '*even if one should go to them ('the Jews') from the dead, they would not repent*.' This is repeated in the next line as '*even if one should rise from the dead they would not believe*' (16:31 – now clearly implying the Resurrection *both* of Lazarus *and* Jesus), varying the report worrying the High Priests in John 12:9–11 above about '*the Jews believing on Jesus*' because of '*Lazarus whom he had raised from the dead*' and, again, plainly demonstrating the one Gospel to be but a variation of the other.

One should also note that in the Gospel of John's presentation of the whole story, Lazarus, the two Apostles, '*Thomas called the Twin*' (11:16 – in early Church literature and at Nag Hammadi, '*Didymus Judas Thomas*'[60]) and '*Judas Iscariot,*' figure prominently (both are important additions having to do with the '*Judas Barsabas*'/'*Thaddaeus*'/'*Theudas*'/'*Judas of Simon Iscariot*'/*Judas of James*' tangle we have highlighted previously[61]); as do the stories about Martha's '*serving*' and Mary's costly '*anointing ointment,*' not only for the purposes of '*anointing him*' (11:2) or '*washing his feet,*' but also for his burial (12:3–7) – the first account in Chapter Eleven clearly distinct from the second in Chapter Twelve, the second only reproducing the '*Simon the Leper*' and '*Simon the Pharisee*' stories elsewhere in the Synoptics.[62]

But nothing could better demonstrate that we are in the Talmudic context of determining the meaning of '*Ben Kalba Sabuᶜa*''s name (to say nothing of the '*Cananaean woman*''s '*crumbs under the master's table*'/'*dogs under the table eating of the children's crumbs*' response) than the way Luke describes its '*Poor man Lazarus*' as '*covered with sores*' and '*longing to be filled by the crumbs that fell from the Rich Man's table*' (here the '*longing to be filled,*' '*the crumbs falling from the table,*' and the '*Rich Man*' motifs now combined in different ways than in Talmudic tradition, Matthew, and Mark). To nail home the circularity of all these allusions, of course '*the Dogs,*' too, now appear in the whole configuration '*and come to lick his sores.*' Once again, one must reaffirm that the presence of this odd – and, of course, not only utterly fantastic, but mean-spirited and completely absurd – allegorical episode in Luke proves, as almost nothing else can, the accuracy of our understanding of the polemics involved in all these materials.

In fact, the whole episode regarding this Greek Syrophoenician/ Canaanite woman's rejoinder to Jesus, as we saw, is directly counter-indicated in Matthew 7:6's own version of '*the Sermon on the Mount*' earlier. As we have been arguing, it not only provides *the real meaning of* all these matters – both that in '*MMT*' and what '*the Greek Syrophoenician*'/'*Cananaean woman,*' with evident Gospel applause, is anxious to rebut – but, in rather putting things in terms of the '*casting down*' language again, namely, '*cast down pearls before swine,*' includes a possible anagram or homophone for '*Martha,*' that is, in Greek '*margaritas*' –'*pearls*'! It reads as already partially reproduced earlier:

> *Do not give Holy Things to dogs, nor cast down* (*balete* again) *your pearls before swine, lest they trample them under their feet*' (here the '*pearls*'/

'*margaritas*,' homonymous in Greek with '*Martha*,' and the '*trampling*' and '*foot*'/'*feet*' allusions should be carefully noted – we have been in this world before!).

Of course this whole statement, again attributed to Jesus, is completely in line with the essence of the Qumran approach, particularly that of the Damascus Document's '*separating the Holy Things from the profane*' above (though obviously not the mirror reversal of this: Peter's '*tablecloth*' vision and subsequent visit to the household of the Roman Centurion in Acts), as it is the ethos of the prohibition in '*MMT*' above about banning '*the dogs*' from the Temple and Jerusalem, defined in terms of '*the Holy Camp*' and '*the Chief of the Camps of Israel*.'

It also proves – in the author's view incontestably – that our analysis of the arcane twists and turns of some of these New Testament materials was absolutely right and that one has to be prepared to employ a peculiar form of logic in order to follow the incredibly complex and recondite mutual polemics of these documents.

Nakdimon, Ben Kalba Sabuᶜa's Tomb, Honi, and Boni

Nor is this to finally put to rest the whole issue of Acts' parody of '*the Ethiopian Queen*' above and her various look-alikes such as Queen Helen of Adiabene who seems to have supported the '*Zealot*' cause in Palestine in this period – or at least her sons and/or descendants did, as opposed to more collaboration-minded '*fellow-travelers*' of the Romans, such as '*the Herodians*.' In fact, it is our position, if '*MMT*' really was addressed to one or another of her sons, such as Izates or Monobazus, that, because of their self-evident '*wealth*,' they very likely helped in the support and upkeep of an installation like the one at Qumran.[62]

Nor does it put to rest the whole issue of the relationship to her of Simon *Magus*' '*Queen*' by the same name whom, as we have on several occasions now remarked, hostile sources assert he found among the fleshpots of Tyre in Phoenicia – the locale of Mark's version, anyhow, of this material about Jesus '*casting an unclean spirit*' from the daughter of the this '*Greek Syrophoenician woman*' who – like so many others in these traditions – was also depicted as '*falling at his feet*.' Nor, for that matter, Helen's own well-documented interest in '*the suspected adulteress*' passage from Numbers 5:12–29 – itself, either coincidentally or otherwise, leading into that on '*Nazirite oath*' procedures from 6:2–21 – a passage she is said to have hung in gold leaf on a commemorative plaque in the Temple Court.

This had to be saying something, presumably about her own biography, and it seems pretty obvious what that is, *don't make false accusations concerning someone in this regard*.[63] Like *Ben Kalba Sabuᶜa* and his '*twenty-one years*' of '*grain buying*' largesse according to Rabbinic sources, '*twenty-one years*,' as already underscored, also turned out to be the amount of time according to this same Talmudic tradition of Queen Helen's legendary three successive '*Nazirite oath*' penances – an inordinate amount of time, laid upon her somewhat disingenuously it would seem (presumably to get further contributions from her) by the Rabbis for real or imagined infractions, impurities, or sins of some kind, doubtlessly, having something to do with here marital behavior or perceived '*fornication*.'[64]

But these key numbers, '*twenty-one*' or '*twenty-two*,' are always associated with the years Nakdimon or *Ben Kalba Sabuᶜa*, as we saw – the legends here overlap – could have fed the total population of Jerusalem had not '*the Zealots*' ('*the Biryonim*' – '*the Sicarii*'?) either burned Nakdimon's immense grain storage reserves or mixed mud with them, or both.[65] This brings us back, not only to Helen and '*the Famine*,' but also to Paul, to say nothing of Acts' '*Ethiopian Queen*' since, according to Josephus and early Church tradition as already explained, it was Helen and/or her son Izates who sent their grain-buying agents to Egypt and Cyprus, dispensing their fabulous wealth to feed the inhabitants of Jerusalem in this period.[66]

As already noted, but worth recalling too, the *Talmud* though advertising itself as representative of a tradition supporting meticulous observation of Law is always – like its mirror opposite the New Testament – anti-Zealot. Where Nakdimon's associate '*Ben Kalba Sabuᶜa*' – '*the Son of the Sabaean Bitch*' – is concerned, two other traditions stand out. The first associates him in some manner with the fabulous tomb Queen Helen and Izates' brother '*Monobazus*' (probably Helen's son as well[67]), built in Jerusalem, her first son Izates having predeceased them (the reason given in the *Talmud* for her successive periods of Nazirite oaths[68]). But Helen's husband also seems to have been called by a variation of this name '*Bazeus*' and, as already suggested, it probably operated in a Persian cultural nexus something like '*Agbarus*' or '*Abgarus*' did in more Semitic circles or, for that matter, '*Herod*' and '*Caesar*' in Palestinian Greco-Roman ones.[69] This '*tomb*' material is reflected, too, in John's report of the '*precious ointment*' Mary was using to wash Jesus' '*feet*,' about which '*Judas Iscariot*' was said to have complained and which, Jesus then says – according to John 12:7 – '*should be kept for the day of (his) burial*.'

The Tomb of the Royal Family of Adiabene was so impressive (then and now – then apparently it had three large, pyramid-shaped monuments above it as we saw) that it is remarked in all sources, Talmudic, early Church, Syriac/Armenian, and Josephus.[70] Not only is '*Ben Kalba Sabuᶜa*' – himself often confused in these traditions with '*Nakdimon*' – associated in some manner with it (the reader should realize by now that the writer considers him to be identifiable with one or another of Helen's descendants), but '*Nicodemus*' in the Gospel of John (a Gospel along with Luke very much involved as well, as we have been demonstrating, in the transmission of these kinds of questionable and overlapping materials) is also to be associated with another such fabulous tomb.

In this instance he is the '*Rich*' merchant who John 19:39 portrays as '*also coming*' to prepare Jesus' body with precious ointments (a costly '*mixture of myrrh and aloes about a hundred weight*' – earlier he was described as '*a Ruler of the Jews*'!) before its placement in another legendary tomb, this time belonging to another such '*Rich*' individual identified only by the mysterious cognitive, '*Joseph of Arimathaea*' ('*a Disciple of Jesus, though secretly, for fear of the Jews*' – thus!). Not only had John 12:7 above already implied that '*Mary*' was supposed to have '*kept*' the '*litra of pure spikenard ointment of great value*' '*for the day of (his) burial*,' but in his introduction of '*Nicodemus*' earlier (3:1), he portrays the two of them as having a long discussion about how '*a man who is old can enter his mother's womb and be born a second time*' (3:4 – again something of '*the Primal Adam*' ideology of many of these early '*Judeo-Christian*' groups).[71]

Not only can one recognize as well – should one choose to regard them – several of the elements of early Church accounts of James' being,[72] but the discussion twice actually evokes in 3:16–18 (just as in John 1:14–18 earlier) the expression '*only begotten*' which Josephus applies to Helen's favorite (and perhaps '*only*') son Izates, for whom the burial monument we are discussing was originally constructed. In fact, the whole discourse could very well appertain to these Northern Syrian Sabaean '*bathing*' groups, we have been discussing as well, and would be very recognizable to the Southern Iraqi '*Mandaeans*' ('*the Subbaᶜ of the Marshes*') even today.[73] It actually rises to a crescendo, amid repeated evocation of '*Light*' and '*Dark*,' just as in John 1:18 as well, with 'Jesus' querying '*Nicodemus*' (one wonders why he would care – like Paul's account in 2 Corinthians 12:2–4, we have previously already connected to James,[74] of a man he '*knew in Christ fourteen years ago*' who '*was caught away*' to Heaven, where '*he heard unspeakable things it is not permitted a man to say*'), '*If I say to you Heavenly things will you believe*' (John 3:12 – again the typical '*Pauline*' phraseology of '*belief*')? John 3:13 then pictures Jesus as answering his own question with the seeming (though admittedly '*mystifying*') denial,

No one has gone up into Heaven except he who came down out of Heaven, the
Son of Man who is in Heaven (n.b., again even here the *'coming'* allusion).

Though following the Greek (and, in fact, Pauline) rhetorical and poetic
device of strophe, antistrophe, and epode, we have already called attention to above, this one really is a tongue-twister but, obviously, it was
meant to be *'mystifying.'*

These things as they may be, the second point about *'Ben Kalba
Sabuᶜa'* is that, as already underscored as well, the *'Zealot'* Rabbi of the
next generation, R. Akiba, married his daughter Rachel, again after some
three successive rejection periods totalling some 'twenty-one' years (here the correspondence with her putative forebear Queen Helen's three successive
'Nazirite' oaths, to say nothing of the number of years these two Talmudic *'Rich Men'* were supposed to have been able to supply Jerusalem with
grain before *'the Zealots'* spoiled it) – this purportedly because he was
only a *'Poor'* shepherd and *Ben Kalba Sabuᶜa* was so *'Rich.'*[75] Then finally
R. Akiba came to her with some *'twenty-four thousand'* students (two runs
of the important number *'twelve'* again but note, as well, the echo of the
'twenty-four schoeni in height' and *'twenty-four miles in width'* even of the
dimensions for the Pseudoclementine/*'Ebionite'* portrayal of the reincarnated *'Primal Adam'* or *'Standing One'/'Redeemer'/'Saviour'* figure above[76])
and, so impressed was she, that she finally married him. The stories vary
here as to whether they were already married when he was just a *'Poor'*
shepherd *'sleeping on straw'* above or whether this happened later, after her
father, hearing of his *'Great Name,'* finally became reconciled to him.[77]

Elsewhere in the *Talmud*, it is made plain that one of Akiba's students
was another of these *'Monobaz's*, obviously descended either from Helen
and her sons, Izates or Monobazus, or this supposed *'Ben Kalba Sabuᶜa,'*
or all three.[78] Our conclusion from all this is that these members of
Helen's family were not only instrumental in fomenting and financing
the First Uprising against Rome (for which commonweal they and not
the discredited and certainly despised Herodians – therefore the portrayal of their absolute *'Righteousness'* and extreme *'Piety'* and the
necessity, for example, of addressing a *'letter'* or *'letters'* such as *'MMT'* to
them – would be the heirs apparent or presumptive monarchs), and two
of her *'kinsmen'* or descendants, another *'Monobazus'* (whichever one this
was) and *'Kenedaeus,'* already referred to above, had already proved their
valor, dying in its first engagement; but also the Second – the significance
of R. Akiba's *'twenty-four thousand Disciples'* with whom he won *'Ben
Kalba Sabuᶜa'*'s daughter Rachel's hand. Moreover, they were also instrumental in the financing and support of the *'Movement'* represented by the

installation and correspondence at Qumran.

In any event, this associate of '*Ben Kalba Sabu'a*,' '*Nakdimon*' or '*Nicodemus*' – possibly one of the representatives of this family as well – was alleged by the *Talmud*, in the episode with which we started this whole discussion, to have gone into the Temple at a time of drought and, like James (in our view the '*Nazirite*'-style spiritual Leader both at Qumran and a designee of this family, around whom as '*the Zaddik*' of his generation most of these disparate '*Opposition*' groups revolved), *prayed for rain*.[79] So knowledgeable does the *Talmud* present itself as being regarding this episode that, as we saw, it even records the words of his prayer!

To go over the details of this event and refresh them in the reader's mind one last time: as the *Talmud* puts it, '*he* (Nakdimon/Nicodemus) *wrapped himself in his cloak* (this '*cloak*' motif repeated twice) and *stood up to pray*.' Again, one should remark the allusion to the '*standing*' motif here, perhaps coincidental, perhaps otherwise – allusions to '*standing*' being such an important element in all our sources about James, Jesus' post-resurrection manifestations and various other situations in the Gospels, and the Ebionite/Simon Magus/Elchasaite '*Standing One*' ideology forming the basis of it.[80]

In this prayer entreating God for sufficient water in the Temple to accommodate even those on pilgrimage, Nakdimon, the reader will recall, is made to speak of *his 'Father's House'* – the very cry, based on Psalm 69:9 above (a Psalm, however '*Zionistic*' its outlook, absolutely intrinsic to Gospel presentations of the events of Jesus' life[80]), John 2:17 puts into the mouth of its 'Jesus,' as already underscored, when speaking of his '*zeal*' for and desire *to purify the Temple*. Again too, we have the theme of '*supplicating*' or '*speaking to God like a son*,' for which the *Talmud* claims Simeon ben Shetah thought '*blasphemy*' charges should have been leveled against Honi, '*were he not Honi*,' to say nothing of Elijah![82]

But, as Josephus reports this affair, Honi was actually stoned by his opponents – an assortment clearly of anti-nationalist Pharisees basically collaborating with the Roman forces, whose entrance into the country had been connived at by Herod's father – when he refused to condemn the proto-'*Zealot*' partisans (who had taken refuge in the Temple) of the Maccabean pretender Aristobulus II, who had for his part refused to humble himself before Pompey.[83] It is for these reasons that Honi ('*Onias the Just*') – prefiguring his putative descendant James – was stoned, the ostensible justification for which, '*addressing God like a son*,' having, it would appear, already been provided (however disingenuously) in the *Talmud* above. Finally, as we saw and as Josephus reports too, it is rather his supporters besieged inside the Temple and not actually Honi who, like Elijah, *pray for rain and bring on a whirlwind!*[84]

Whatever one wishes to make of all these apparent correspondences and overlaps, where '*Nakdimon*' at least was concerned, the climax of the affair was that '*immediately the sky was covered by clouds until the twelve wells were filled with water*' even, as it is put, '*beyond overflowing*'! Again, it must be reiterated, this picture of Nakdimon cannot be any historical character like the fabulously '*Rich*' merchant Nakdimon and more likely conceals a story relating to someone of the religious significance of a James. Even this the *Talmud*, in its own inimical way, seems to suggest in virtually the very next statement, wherein it now states '*his name was not Nakdimon but Boni*,' opining, as already remarked above, that he was only called Nakdimon '*because the sun broke through on his behalf* (*nikdera*).[85]

Aside from the primeval stupidity herein evinced and the absurdity of this explanation for such denominative sleight-of-hand, there is no doubt that, in the tradition now before us, we are dealing with Honi's prefiguration of subsequent '*Zaddik*'s and the *redivivus* tradition associated with his name and that of his family. Nor is this to mention the underlying motif of the reason for his stoning and, of course, the related traditions surrounding the '*rain-making*' of James and his stoning – the '*blasphemy*' charge having to do with '*addressing God as a son*' and '*imploring Him*' like this, to say nothing perhaps of the more overarching one, *pronouncing the forbidden name of God* in the atonement James was pictured as performing in almost all sources in the *Inner Sanctum* of the Temple.

For the *Talmud*, this '*Boni*' together with one '*Thoda*,' *i.e.*, obviously '*Thaddaeus*' or '*Theudas*' above, becomes one of '*Jesus the Nazoraean*'s five '*Disciples*'; so it becomes clear that '*Boni*' must be thought of as a double for someone. In our view, this is either James – not only because of the allusion to his '*rain-making*' in Epiphanius, but because of the emphasis on such '*rain-making*,' so intensely evoked regarding Elijah, along with the '*fervent saving Power of the prayer of* other '*Just Ones*' in the apocalyptic conclusion of the New Testament '*Letter of James*' (5:16–18) – or '*Nicodemus*' in John, a Gospel which also includes yet another stand-in for James, '*Nathanael*' (John 1:45), missing from the Synoptics.

Interestingly enough in John 1:48–50, this last is portrayed as sitting '*under a fig tree*' (in Buddhism, '*the Bhodi Tree*'), which would seem to include just a hint of the manner in which the *Talmud* portrays Honi or his descendant '*Hanan the Hidden*,' as already underscored, as '*sitting under a carob tree for seventy years*' in another somewhat pungent *redivivus*-type story.[86] For its part John 1:51 also portrays 'Jesus,' as already remarked, as predicting that '*Nathanael*' will see a future vision of the kind ascribed to James in early Church accounts of the events leading up to his stoning (also finding a reflection, as we saw as well, in Acts 7:56's account of events surround the stoning of 'Stephen'), of

> the Heavens opened and the Angels of God ascending and descending on the Son
> of Man (in the War Scroll, it will be 'the Heavenly Host' that will so descend
> but one should note, in particular, this motif of 'the Heavens opening' par-
> alleled, of course, in both the pictures in Acts above and of James' death).

The third one of these 'Disciples' is called 'Nezer,' with obvious affinities to the imageries associated with Jesus and James, either having to do
with their respective, life-long 'Naziritism' or the prophetical 'Branch' or
'Nazoraean' vocabulary.[87] This passage in the Talmud actually applies the
all-important Messianic 'Root' or 'Branch' prophecies from Isaiah 11:1 and
14:19 to him – also to be found among the exegetical texts applied to the
Messiah at Qumran as it is, by implication, in the New Testament – 'a
Branch shall go forth out of its Roots' (see the 'Root'/'uprooting' imagery we
have already called attention to both in the Damascus Document and the
Gospel of Matthew) – but the second with inverted effect (probably to
counter the importance placed upon it in both these other two): 'casting
forth from your grave like an (abhorred) Nezer.'[88]

The last two 'Disciples' are called 'Matthai,' obviously 'Matthew,' and
'Nakai,' seemingly 'Nakdimon' again; but now this name is related to the
Hebrew root for 'naki' – 'clean' or 'innocent' – and not to 'shining through.'
Furthermore, Psalm 10:8 is cited about 'killing the Innocent,' another Zion-
istic psalm of the kind of Psalm 69 above, in this instance also repeatedly
referring to 'the Poor' or 'the Ebionim.'[89][90]

Again, this whole circle of materials is typical of information-pro-
cessing in the Talmud, itself sometimes even more haphazard and
humorous than that of the New Testament. That a fabulously wealthy
individual like Nakdimon should be seen as a 'Zaddik' or 'Friend of God'
or both, even 'speaking to God as a son' and going into the Temple and
praying for rain is about as preposterous as some of the inversions one
encounters in Paul and elsewhere in the Gospels and the Book of Acts.
In fact, we have something of the same disingenuousness going on in the
one as we do in the other and for the same reasons, though these Talmudic traditions are not nearly as well informed as New Testament ones
sometimes are. The conclusion, however, must be the same: there can be
little doubt that Nakdimon, who is performing some of the same miracles as Elijah and Honi and who is presented in this redivivus line, is a blind
for certain more Revolutionary persons and subversive events associated
with other individuals attached to this line.

Ananias, Nicodemus, Joseph of Arimathaea, and James

That this 'Nakdimon' is associated with another individual, also legended to have been fabulously wealthy and seemingly connected with the tomb of Queen Helen of Adiabene, as well as replicating some of the same activities – such as 'famine relief' (in Gospel portraiture, 'multiplication of the loaves' as we have seen) – she and her sons were supposed to have been involved in, further reinforces this suspicion. Here, too, the individual Josephus calls 'Gurion ben Nakdimon' – perhaps the same as this Nakdimon, perhaps his son (in one Talmudic source above, considered as we saw, a fourth 'Councilor' separate from Nakdimon), paralleling in this sense the Jerusalem Talmud's second 'Honi the Circle-Drawer' who is alleged to have appeared just prior to the fall of the Temple – is associated with another individual called 'Ananias the son of Sadduk' in last-ditch efforts in 66 CE to save the besieged Roman garrison in Jerusalem at the beginning of the Uprising.[90]

As always, there would appear to be two types of materials in these notices: one apocalyptic, uncompromising, and subversive; the other, more accommodating – even collaborating. We have already seen a man with the same name as this 'Ananias' involved, not only in Paul's conversion at 'Damascus' in the late Thirties in Acts, but also in the conversion of those in Queen Helen's household around the same period of time. He was even portrayed as being the tutor of Helen's son's Izates. In the contemporaneous conversion of 'the Great King of the Peoples beyond the Euphrates,' also in Northern Syria, in which both 'Thaddaeus' (a.k.a. 'Judas of James' in Luke) and 'Thomas' ('Judas Thomas' / 'Thoda' above – 'Thamud' in the Koran[91]) play important roles, there is also an intermediary named 'Ananias' involved as we have seen.

Not only are all these stories somewhat contemporaneous, but there is the common thread in them, too, that all are 'conversion' stories of some kind – either to Judaism or nascent 'Christianity.' In Josephus' version of the Helen material, the 'Ananias' involved is even portrayed, as just underscored, as Izates' tutor; in Eusebius' version of the 'Agbarus' / 'Abgarus' conversion, 'Ananias' is supposed to have brought the letter from King Agbarus in Edessa ('Antiochia Orrhoe') to Jerusalem and then back again. Nor can the latter be separated from the 'letter' again being sent to 'Antioch,' according to Acts 15:22–30's account, with James' directives to overseas communities with someone called 'Judas Barsabas' (supposedly a different 'Antioch' – there being four of them as we saw), in our view, a refraction of the 'letter' known in the Qumran corpus as 'MMT' above – itself addressed to a 'King' of some kind to whom Abraham's salvationary state has more than a passing importance. This would not be surprising, as we have been showing, in a Northern Syrian milieu.[92]

The '*Ananias*' here in Josephus – now connected to this '*Rich*' Nakdimon or his descendant or, in the Gospel of John's view of things, the '*Nicodemus*' who is a '*Rich Councilor*' and connected to another '*Rich*' individual who has an impressive tomb in Jerusalem (in Gospel lore, 'Joseph of Arimathaea') – seems to be personally acquainted with the Roman Commander of the Citadel named '*Mitelius*.'[94] This in itself again probably confirms his wealth, not to mention his influential status, and he does seem to be able to move around quite freely in the highest circles. Together with Gurion ben Nakdimon and a third personage, 'Antipas' – we shall encounter further below – he is able to convince Mitelius to surrender in exchange for a surety of safe passage – in other words, once again, he is acting as the intermediary.

This guarantee is broken by an individual Josephus calls '*Eleazar*,' who – like those in Hippolytus' picture of the Jewish sects above called '*Sicarii*' or '*Zealot Essenes*' – seems to want the Romans, or at least their commander, to circumcise themselves (or die), for at the last moment all are slaughtered except Mitelius, who *agrees not only to convert but also to be circumcised*.[94] One should note the quasi-parallel here with the '*Eleazar the Galilean*' who, in Josephus' picture of the conversion of Queen Helen's son Izates, insists on circumcision while the more moderate Pauline-type teacher '*Ananias*' (the above-mentioned merchant or courier) and his unnamed companion (Paul?) feel it unnecessary for Izates and Monobazus, his brother, to circumcise themselves – much to their mother Queen Helen's relief. Even if the chronology is a bit skewed, we certainly seem to be getting a convergence of themes in all these stories.

It should be remarked that the brothers '*Saulos and Costobarus*,' Josephus calls '*kinsmen of Agrippa*' (he means either Agrippa I or Agrippa II, probably Agrippa I[95]) and another '*kinsman of Agrippa*' Josephus calls '*Antipas*' (he will turn out to be the Herodian '*Temple Treasurer*'), as well as Philip the son of Jacimus, the Commander of Agrippa II's Army, are also involved in, not only seemingly Mitelius' surrender, but a parallel event contemporaneous with it, the surrender of Agrippa II's palace in which they had all taken refuge and which then seems to have been burned by these same '*Zealot*' Revolutionaries.[96]

Not only does Josephus identify this '*Antipas*' – like his putative kinsmen '*Helcias*' (an Herodian and a companion of Agrippa I in an earlier generation) and Helcias' son, '*Julius Archelaus*' (possibly this Antipas' brother or nephew) – as Temple Treasurer; but, as the Revolt moved into its more extremist or '*Jacobin*' phase (68–69 CE), this '*Antipas*' was eventually arrested and put to death by those whom Josephus, by this time, had actually begun calling '*Zealots*.'[97] As in the case of the butchering of James' executioner, the High Priest Ananus, and Jesus ben Gamala above, directly following this Antipas' execution, and the assassination of Ananus' brother Jonathan by those he had started to designate as '*Sicarii*' a decade or so earlier,[98] Josephus rails against the '*breach of the conditions of surrender*' constituted by the slaughtering of the Roman garrison and '*the pollutions of such Abominations*' this involved (familiar terminology in the Dead Sea Scrolls below[99]), partially because it seems to have occurred *on the Sabbath*. He calls it:

> the prelude to the Jews' own destruction...for it could not but arouse some vengeance whether by Rome or some Divine Visitation.[100]

Here, once again, we seem to be involved in another of these seeming reversals, so plentiful in this period in these materials. In the first place, the word '*Visitation*' permeates, as already underscored, the language of the Damascus Document where, in addition to the notion of '*Divine Vengeance*' and the '*Judgement*' associated with it, it would also appear to relate, at least in one formulation, to the '*coming of the Messiah of Aaron and Israel*' and a possible return, as well as to the Messianic '*Root of Planting*,' with which the document begins and which we have already called attention to above and will do further below.[101] Where the language of '*the pollutions of the Abominations*' is concerned, this too is present in the Damascus Document – in fact, as part of '*the Zadokite Statement*' there – but even more telling, it is exactly the kind of language one encounters in the Habakkuk *Pesher* in its attack on what would appear to be the more compromising '*Herodian*' Priestly Establishment for '*polluting the Temple of God*' and other '*Abominations*' committed there including, as we shall see, the apparent destruction of '*the Teacher of Righteousness*' and his followers among '*the Poor*.'[102] Here in Josephus, it is being used – as in the New Testament – with seemingly purposefully-inverted effect, to attack those of a '*Zealot*' mindset and not support them. Again, this latter orientation would appear to be the exact opposite of that at Qumran.

As Josephus presents these events, '*Philip*' anyhow (the '*Philip*' in the New Testament baptizing '*the Ethiopian Queen's eunuch*' on the road to Gaza or in Caesarea with '*the seven virgin daughters who were prophetesses*' – *sic*?) seems to have then fallen under a cloud regarding these events (that is, the Romans suspected him of treason) and he and '*Costobarus*' seemingly,[103] but not this '*Antipas*,' were sent to Nero – either at their own request (as Paul in Acts 26:32) or otherwise – for a hearing or to appeal their case. At this point, Nero seems to have been at Corinth in Greece (another important provenance of Paul's missionary and epistolary activities) and none of these are ever heard from again, at least not in Josephus.

It should be appreciated that the 'Saulos' in Josephus undergoes a similar fate and, following these events and his escape like 'Philip' from Agrippa II's palace, he re-emerges, as we have seen, as the intermediary between what should be seen as 'the Peace Party' in Jerusalem (identified in Josephus as 'the Sadducees, principal Pharisees, and the Men of Power' – this last obviously meant as a euphemism for 'Herodians') and the Roman Army outside it, an assignment that ends in almost total disaster.[104] After this ill-fated attempt on the part of the previously reigning Roman/Herodian Establishment in Jerusalem to invite the Roman Army into the city to attempt to suppress the Revolt, 'Saulos' too seems to have been sent to Nero in Corinth – again, either at his own request or otherwise – to report about the circumstances of this and the situation in Palestine generally, in particular in Jerusalem, a report that seems to have led directly to the dispatch of the General Vespasian from Britain with a large army to Palestine.[105]

The 'Ananias' who accompanied 'Gurion the son of Nicodemus' in the initial attempt to avoid war and save the Roman garrison hopelessly surrounded in the Citadel, in turn, seems to have had a connection with this same 'Ananus' above (the High Priest responsible, as already remarked, for the Sanhedrin trial and death of James). Even though Josephus hesitates to criticize this 'Ananus' – the opposite[106] – he does contemptuously describe the stratagems, both he and 'Ananias the son of Sadduk' used (which he claims to have ingeniously thwarted) to relieve him (Josephus) of his command in Galilee where he had been sent together with them as a representative of the Jerusalem Priestly Establishment.[107] Josephus describes this 'Ananias' as a Pharisee 'of the lower rank,' probably meaning the lower priesthood, and that he is a descendant of someone called 'Sadduk' is interesting (is this the R. Zadok or the 'Zadok the High Priest' of Rabbinic tradition ?), a point which cannot be further pursued on the basis of the available data.

The only other actual 'Sadduk,' Josephus alludes to, is the one in the Antiquities some sixty years before whom, curiously, he also calls 'a Pharisee' even though he associates him with 'Judas the Galilean' as the founder of 'the Fourth Philosophy' or what in other terminology usually goes by the name of 'the Zealot' or 'Sicarii Movement,' but which – as we have been attempting to point out – may also be a nom a clef for the 'Messianic' one.[108] Of course there is R. Yohanan's 'friend,' the Rabbi just discussed – in the Talmud he was also called 'Zadok' – who was said to have fasted for forty years to prevent Jerusalem from falling and whose emaciated physique even Vespasian is portrayed as having remarked when he allowed R. Yohanan to send his two favorite students, R. Eliezer and R. Joshua, back, after they had already escaped from Jerusalem, to rescue him. This was, it will be recalled, just prior to its fall when R. Yohanan too (like Josephus) allegedly applied either the '*Fall of Lebanon*' or '*the Star Prophecy*' (or both) to Vespasian.[109]

Once again, here in Josephus, the association of this '*Ananias ben Sadduk*,' in these crucial days having to do with the fate of Jerusalem, with a '*Nakdimon*' of some kind ('*Nicodemus*' in John as well as here in Josephus) who, in turn, in Rabbinic literature is portrayed as having a relationship with '*Ben Kalba Sabuᶜa*,' raises interesting questions about *Ananias*' and *Nakdimon's relationship to the conversion of the Royal House of Adiabene*. '*Nicodemus*' – '*Nakdimon*''s *alter* ego – is also portrayed as an influential '*Pharisee*' in John 3:1–9 and 7:50 (where he too is asked the question, '*are you also from Galilee*,' i.e., '*a Galilean*'?), though nevertheless a secret supporter of 'Jesus.' Curiously enough, this is also the role accorded the famous Pharisee Patriarch Gamaliel – Paul's purported teacher and the descendant of the Rabbinic hero Hillel – in the Pseudo-clementine *Recognitions* and to some extent too in Acts.[110] In the Gospel of John, too, Nicodemus joins the legendary '*Joseph of Arimathaea*,' as we have seen above, in preparing the body of Jesus for burial, '*binding it in linen cloth with the aromatics as is the custom among the Jews*' (19:40 – is this a Jew writing this narrative? It would seem doubtful).

In the Synoptics it is now '*Joseph of Arimathaea*' who is the '*Rich Councilor*' and owner of an impressive tomb in Jerusalem and it is he who is now the secret '*Christian*,' not '*Nicodemus*' – more dissimulation? Some have considered this name '*Arimathaea*' – certainly supposed to be a place name but not otherwise identifiable in Palestine – to be a pun on Josephus' name itself, that is, '*Joseph Bar Matthew*'/'*Joseph the son of Matthew*.'[112] In Luke 23:50, like so many other curious characters in early Christianity (the Roman Centurion, for example, in Acts 10:2 and 10:22 above), he, too, is called '*Good and a Just Man*,' that is, basically he is a '*Zaddik*' – the same words Herod applies to John the Baptist in Mark 6:20, namely, '*a Man Just and Holy*' (notice the telltale repetition of the word '*Man*' here – in other contexts often identified, as we have seen, with '*the Primal Adam*' and even John himself[113]) or which Pilate's wife applies to Jesus in Matthew 27:19. In addition to this, we have the re-emergence of the '*Zaddik*' theme again, so strong in all traditions about James – to say nothing of those relating to '*the Righteous Teacher*' at Qumran.[114]

It is hardly to be credited that either this '*Nicodemus*'/'*Nakdimon*' or the person the Gospels are calling '*Joseph of Arimathaea*' – if the two can really be separated – is a '*Zaddik*' or '*Friend of God*' and, in the former instance anyhow, a popular '*Rain-maker*' in the Temple. But in the *Talmud*, as we have been suggesting, aside from this '*rain-making*' and '*praying*' in *the Temple* – clear *leit-motifs* and/or residual vestiges of the James story – there is just the slightest suggestion of a connection between '*Nakdimon*' or his colleagues, '*Ben Kalba Sabuᶜa*' and '*Ben Zizzit*,' with the family of Queen Helen of Adiabene, whose fabulous tomb on the outskirts of Jerusalem is so familiar to all our sources. In fact, in the *Talmud*, the contracts this curious '*Nicodemus*'/'*Nakdimon*' undertakes with a foreign '*Lord*' or '*Ruler*' play a paramount role in his '*rain-making*,' as does the fabulous nature of the stores he supposedly purchases or amasses with these same colleagues to save Jerusalem during its '*Famine*' – enough, as we have repeatedly reiterated, to last for '*twenty-one years*,' the precise time of Queen Helen's three successive Nazirite-oath periods allegedly imposed on her for utterly obscure reasons by the Rabbis.

Can there be any doubt that the true provenance of much of this material – whether in the *Talmud* or New Testament – really appertains to the spectacular tomb these '*Kings*' and/or '*Queen*' from Northern Syria had originally erected for their '*favorite son*' Izates, whom Josephus also calls '*only-begotten*,'[115] and who had initiated the family's conversion to Judaism in the first place (now transformed into pro-Establishment and anti-'*Zealot*' story-telling, much as elsewhere in the Gospels and in Acts)? Moreover, that the notes about '*rain-making*,' '*Famine*,' and '*Naziritism*,' usually connected in some way with stories about these Royal personages from Adiabene, probably imply some relationship, however vague, between James and their conversions?

Likewise and *vice versa*, that these last may have been involved with someone the *Talmud* thinks '*made rain*,' who was an incarnation of '*Elijah*' in the '*Hidden Zaddik*'- tradition, but confuses with one or another of the descendants of Honi – to say nothing about the interest of all of these in '*extreme Naziritism*,' probably relates to the form of '*Judeo-Christianism*' – and I use the term loosely – these various Royal figures were being taught. That some of these figures, too, were later ultimately even willing to martyr themselves in this cause and that of Jewish independence in Palestine probably ties them, not only to the most extreme wing of '*the Zealot Party*' or '*Sicarii*' – '*Christian*' (to say nothing of '*Iscariot*'), as we shall see towards the end of this book, being a quasi-acronym of '*Sicarii*' – but to James as well.

PART FOUR

THE PELLA FLIGHT
AND THE
WILDERNESS CAMPS

14

The Wilderness Camps and Benjamin the *Golah* of the Desert

Rain-making, '*Theudas*,' and other Revolutionaries

Having attempted to decipher this curious relationship between '*Nakdimon*' in Rabbinic literature and '*Nicodemus*' in the Gospels, it should now be possible to return to the eschatological nature of '*rain-making*' and its relation to the proclamation that James is pictured as making in the Temple at Passover in all early Church accounts of '*the Son of Man sitting at the Right Hand of the Great Power and about to come on the clouds of Heaven*' – the same proclamation ascribed in Gospel portraiture to both Jesus and John the Baptist[1] but, where James is concerned, with perhaps more authenticity. It is impossible to know whether James was ever really called upon to make rain around this time or whether this was just an esoteric reckoning or a euphemism of some kind for the proclamation of the final initiation of the eschatological '*End Time*' since, as already alluded to, the War Scroll from Qumran speaks of just such an eschatological Judgement '*from*' or '*on the clouds with the Heavenly Host*' as James is pictured as making in all these early Church accounts.[2]

Perhaps the character Josephus denotes as '*Theudas*' performed '*signs and wonders*' of this kind too, since Josephus specifically applies the '*Impostor*'/'*pseudo-prophet*'/'*magician*' vocabulary to him meant to discredit just such individuals.[3] Not only does Theudas' name carry with it the distinct overtones of the character known as '*Thaddaeus*'/'*Judas Thomas*'/'*Judas the Zealot*'/'*Judas the Iscariot*' or even '*Judas the brother of James*' in Gospel portraiture or early Church literature; but, as already observed, he is clearly portrayed in Josephus as a '*Jesus*' or '*Joshua redivivus*'-type with '*Messianic*' pretensions as well.[4]

Certainly there was a '*Great Famine*' in the period 45–48 CE and various enterprises, like Paul's and/or Helen of Adiabene's '*famine-relief*' missions and '*Theudas*'' attempt to lead large numbers of followers out into the wilderness and repart the Jordan River in a reverse kind of exodus (as portrayed in Josephus, Eusebius, and, not a little anachronistically, in Acts) are not separable from it.[5] The number of followers

'*Theudas*' led out into the wilderness to display these '*signs*' is unclear; but right before discussing '*the Great Famine*' and how '*Queen Helen bought grain from Egypt for large sums of money and distributed it among the Poor*' (again, the '*Poor*' notation), Josephus calls it a '*majority of the masses*';[6] whereas Acts 5:36, a little more depracatingly – and *completely anachronistically* – terms the number of followers who '*joined*' the '*somebody*,' it calls '*Theudas*,' as only '*about four hundred*.'

Still, all these allusions to '*four hundred*,' '*four thousand*,' '*five thousand*,' and even '*six thousand*' followers, we have been following above, are important. Josephus, for instance, in his reckoning of the number of '*Essenes*' in the *Antiquities* puts their number at approximately '*four thousand*.'[7] This is the same number that Philo gives for '*those people called Essenes*' who '*derive their name from their Piety*' (thus!).[8] On the other hand, in Josephus, as well, there are initially '*six thousand*' close supporters of Alexander Jannaeus, who follow him out into the wilderness or into the mountains when he originally resists the incursion of '*Demetrius the King*.'[9]

For his part '*Theudas*,' as just noted, wished to leave Palestine and, Joshua-style, *part the waters of the River Jordan* but, now, rather in order *to depart* and *not to come in*. This, anyhow, was seen by the Romans as a subversive act, deserving of beheading. For Acts 4:4, to some extent anticipating '*Gamaliel*'s anachronistic reference to this same Theudas in Acts 5:36 above, '*five thousand*' is the number of '*believers*' who are added at this point to the early Church. Paralleling this and chronologically contemporaneous with these other events, for the Pseudoclementine *Recognitions* the number of James' followers, who flee with him down to the Jericho area after the riot in the Temple and physical assault on him led by '*the Enemy*' (Paul) is, not surprisingly, again '*five thousand*.' As in Acts 5:34 above, this too is followed by another parallel reference to '*Gamaliel*.'[10]

But the most important parallel to both '*Theudas*'' activities and those of Queen Helen of Adiabene and her surrogates, and inseparable as well from them, is 'Jesus' in the Gospels feeding the '*five thousand*' (Matthew 14:13–22 and *pars.* – in Matthew 15:38 and Mark 8:9 the number swings back, as already remarked, to '*four thousand*' and then '*five*' again). Regardless of discrepancies or repetitions of this kind and overlaps with other '*feeding*' episodes, all the Synoptics describe the locale of this one to '*the five thousand*' as being '*in the wilderness*' – meant to be either, as in '*Theudas*'' case, '*across Jordan*' or on '*the other side*' of the Sea of Galilee.

For its part John 6:4–71 reports another of these '*wondrous signs*'/'*wonder-working*' magical '*feeding*' episodes of the kind in 2:1–11 previously when 'Jesus' was pictured as *turning 'water into wine'* at '*Cana of Galilee'* — significant, as we saw, where '*Cananaean'*/'*Galilean'*/'*Zealot'* terminologies are concerned (the reader should always pay particular attention to double entendres in designations of this nature). This one, which again has to do with '*five barley loaves and two small fish'* and '*a little boy'* and occurs '*near the Passover, the Feast of the Jews* (thus — again, obviously a non-Jew writing this), is compared, therefore (paralleling '*Last Supper'* scenarios in the Synoptics and Paul, to '*eating the Living Bread'* and '*drinking his blood.'* Moreover, it even likens the '*feeding of the five thousand,'* that ensues, to the '*Forefathers* (another favorite Qumranism) *eating the manna* — called '*the bread of Heaven'* — *in the wilderness'* (John 6:31–58).

At the same time, using the Dead Sea Scrolls language of the '*works of God'* as well and plainly designating 'Jesus,' as in Pseudoclementine/ '*Ebionite'* ideology, '*the Prophet who is coming into the world'* (6:14 — for the Pseudoclementines, it will be recalled, this was '*the True Prophet'* while in the Qumran Community Rule it was, as here, simply '*the Prophet'*[11]); it goes on to develop in the purest of Philonic allegorical terms its version of Jesus' promulgation of the Eucharist (6:50–58[12]). It does so by comparing Jesus' '*flesh'* to '*the manna in the desert'* or, as it terms it, '*the Living Bread which came down out of Heaven'* (6:49–51), his '*flesh truly being food'* and his '*blood truly being drink.'* Moreover, he who '*eats'* and '*drinks'* it will '*have everlasting life'* and be '*raised on the Last Day'* (6:54–55 — again, more Qumran eschatological vocabulary[13]). The allegorical-like conclusion from all this, which has remained effective up to the present day — despite its basically being pure Hellenized Mystery Religion — is finally, therefore, '*he who eats my flesh* and *drinks my blood is living in me and I in him'* (6:56) — and this supposedly in Palestine and on the Passover no less![14]

These are precisely the kinds of '*signs and wonders'* that Josephus, of course, so rails against and is so anxious to condemn — to say nothing of James' outright ban on '*blood'* (one assumes this includes symbolically) in the picture of his directives to overseas communities in Acts 15:20, 29, and 21:25 above. In the case of Josephus, as we saw, such '*Impostors and religious frauds, who teamed up with the bandit chiefs, were more dangerous even than the Revolutionaries'* and he clearly views the kind of '*leading people out into the wilderness, there to show them the signs of their impending freedom'* that is being depicted here, both in John and the Synoptics, as the worst sort of Revolutionary subversiveness or imposture (here the contrast between the '*freedom from Rome'* as opposed to Paul's more allegorized '*freedom from the Law'* polemics again)..[15]

If James ever really had made rain, Josephus would have had to see it, too, in the same terms though, to be sure, this is not how he presents him in the *Antiquities*. There Josephus seems, otherwise, quite sympathetic to James and, as we have shown in other work, may even have spent time with him under the alias of the '*Banus*,' he refers to in the *Vita*, with whom he passed a two-year initiate in his late teens (as he seems to have done, to judge by his long description of them in the *War*, '*the Essenes*').[16]

Early Church sources picture James' proclamation in the Temple of the imminent coming of the Son of Man in response to the question put to him by the Temple Authorities about '*the Gate of Jesus*.'[17] This same designation, '*Son of Man*,' would also appear to be equivalent to the individual Paul refers to in 1 Corinthians 15:45–47 as '*the Second Man*'/'*the Last Adam*'/or '*the Lord out of Heaven*' – in the War Scroll, as we shall see below, quoting Isaiah 31:8: '*no mere Man*' or '*Adam*.'[18] Of course, according to other reckonings, such as those found in the Pseudoclementines and parallel incarnationist presentations, this same concept would be embodied in the doctrine known as '*the Primal Adam*.'

James' Proclamation and the Coming of the Angelic Host in the War Scroll

In these early Church sources there are also the constant notices about James praying in the Temple '*till his knees became as hard as a camel's*' and about '*all the importuning he did before God* – presumably *in the Holy of Holies – on behalf of the People*.' But this proclamation (in response to the question put to James in Hegesippus' original version of these accounts about '*What is the Gate of Jesus?*'), of '*the Son of Man coming on the clouds of Heaven*' (again, note the allusion to '*coming*') – the individual we have just seen Paul refer to in 1 Corinthians 15–16 as '*the Second Man*' or '*Last Adam, the Lord out of Heaven*' – and the '*Ebionite*'/'*Elchasaite*' note contained in it about '*sitting on the Right Hand of the Great Power*,' is precisely the exposition of '*the Star Prophecy*' from Numbers 24:17 in climactic passages from the War Scroll at Qumran ('*The War of the Sons of Light against the Sons of Darkness*'), another of those '*eschatological*' documents describing, among other things, the final apocalyptic war against all Evil on the Earth.[19]

The Star Prophecy ('*the Messianic Prophecy*' above and which we have already referred to with regard to Rabbi Akiba and Bar Kochba and other '*Messianic Prophecies*,' so important according to Josephus' testimony as a spur to Revolutionary activity in Palestine throughout the First Century, ending in the War against Rome and, by reflection, the birth of '*Christianity*'),[20] as we have seen, is also cited in at least two other pivotal contexts in known Qumran documents: the Damascus Document and the Messianic *Florilegium*, which we shall consider in more detail below.[21] In the War Scroll, it is definitively tied to the '*Messiah*' and combined with the note from Daniel 7:13 above about '*one like a Son of Man amid the clouds of Heaven*' and the imagery of final apocalyptic '*Judgement falling like rain on all that grows on Earth*.'[22]

Not only is the Prophecy important in helping us appreciate the '*Messianic*' thrust of these several notations, it also helps demonstrate just what was implied by the evocation of James' '*rain-making*' in the context of all the *importuning of God he did in the Temple* – presumably *in the Inner Sanctum* or *Holy of Holies* – until '*his knees became as hard as a camel's nodules*' (vivid testimony of this kind one should be chary of dismissing) in Epiphanius' version of Hegesippus' testimony about James. Whereas Epiphanius is only a Fourth–Fifth Century CE source; where James is concerned, he largely bases himself on Hegesippus, a Second-Century CE source about sixty years removed from the events in question.

Epiphanius, therefore, specifically ties this notice of James having made rain during a drought of some kind both to his

> *going into the Holy of Holies once a year, because he was a Nazirite and con-nected to the Priesthood* (Epiphanius' *actual words!*),

and his wearing the High Priestly '*diadem*' or '*Nezer*' ('*Crown*').[23] The first part is certainly something of what the *ARN* meant above by '*proper Temple service bringing rain in its season*'; while the second is not completely unconnected, with the play on James' death in the '*Stephen*' episode in Acts, whose name means, of course, '*Crown*' in Greek, specifically signaling in Eusebius' exposition of these events, '*the Martyr's Crown*.'[24]

The coupling of two of the most important '*Messianic*' prophecies from Numbers 24:17 and Daniel 7:13 in this climactic section of the War Scroll, as well as the citation of the first of these in both Damascus Document and Messianic *Florilegium* at Qumran and combining them there with the materials from Isaiah, we have already cited above, is about as important as Josephus' claim in a little-remarked testimony in the section about '*the signs and portents' for the destruction of the Temple* at the end of the *Jewish War* that '*the World Ruler Prophecy*' was the moving force behind the Uprising against Rome in 66–70 CE.[25] A better internal dating parame-ter for documents such as these Dead Sea Scrolls is hardly to be found.

To these the War Scroll, as just remarked, adds a third passage from Isaiah 31:8: '*Assyria shall fall by the sword of no mere Man and the sword of no mere Adam*,' not normally considered '*Messianic*' at all, but coupled with these other indications at this point in the War Scroll, it must be so construed. Not only do we have, yet again, just the slightest echo here of the '*Man*'/'*Adam*'/'*Primal Adam*'-ideology, we have been following; but all are applied to an apocalyptic *final Holy War* against '*the Kittim*' – who, in the such a context of citation of '*the Star Prophecy*' and this kind of imagery from Daniel at this point in the War Scroll, are certainly to be seen as the Romans.²⁶ These sections of Columns 10–11 of the War Scroll, reprised in Column 19, express the kind of apocalyptic '*Judgement*,' that is being alluded to, in terms of reference to '*the Heavenly Host*' and '*the hand of Your Messiah*.' These, in turn, are coupled with allusion to '*the hand of the Poor*' (our omnipresent '*Ebionim*' or '*Ebionites*' again) and '*the hand of those bent in the dust to humble the Mighty of the Peoples paying (them) the reward on Evil Ones*,'²⁶ '*justifying Your True Judgement on all the Sons of Earth*' – including '*the Enemies of all the Lands*' – all terms pregnant with meaning for the history of this period.²⁸

This notion of '*paying them the reward on Evil Ones*' is a widespread one at Qumran, particularly apparent in the Habakkuk *Pesher*, where it is applied to *the punishment visited upon the Wicked Priest for what he had done to the Righteous Teacher* (that is, *he had 'destroyed him*').²⁹ There, too, it unquestionably alludes to *the apocalyptic process of Final Judgement*, a point missed by most commentators.³⁰ It is also alluded to in the Psalm 37 *Pesher*, where it is applied to the fate of '*the Wicked Priest*' as well – '*at the hand of the Violent Ones of the Gentiles*' ('*Arizei-Go'im*) – but the whole context is one of final eschatological '*Judgement*' and the '*Salvation of the Righteous*' (*Zaddikim*) and '*the Congregation*' or '*Church of the Poor Ones*' (*i.e.*, once more, '*the Ebionites*'!).³¹ The Scroll concludes this eschatological exegesis of Number's 24:17's '*Star Prophecy*' and evocation of Daniel's '*Son of Man coming on the clouds of Heaven*' by speaking, as we have just seen, in terms of '*justifying (God's) True Judgement on all the Sons of Earth*' (as opposed presumably to '*the Sons of Heaven*' carrying it out), including '*the Enemies of all the Lands*' which, of course, can mean nothing other than all the foreign nations round about – again demonstrating the quasi-xenophobia of these Scrolls (here too, one should note, the telltale plural of '*the Enemy*'-terminology).

This whole climactic exposition of '*the Star Prophecy*' in the War Scroll follows its outlining the battle order of the formations, the slogans to be inscribed on the standards and weapons in this '*War*,' and the historical note, with which it commences, of *the* '*return of the Sons of Light, who are in Exile* ('*Golah*'), *from the Desert of the Peoples* (a term not without its parallel, of course, in Matthew 4:15's '*Galilee of the Gentiles*' or '*Peoples beyond the Jordan*') *to the camp in the wilderness of Jerusalem*.'³² Here too, in this opening evocation, '*Benjamin*' is defined in terms of this pregnant apposition 'the Golah' or 'Diaspora of the Desert,' which possibly includes 'the Sons of Levi and the Sons of Judah' and possibly does not; and the English term, 'Gentiles'/'Peoples' appears in the above phrase, 'the Desert of the Peoples,' just as it does in Matthew 4:15 where the Greek is 'Ethnon'/ 'Peoples.'³³

These passages in the first columns of the War Scroll read like the battle order of an army right out of the age of Cromwell and also parallel, in reverse, movement outlined in the Damascus Document, which twice refers to 'going out from the Land of Judah to dwell in the Land of Damascus' and which is to say nothing of the several reverse exoduses represented by 'Theudas' and those the Gospels picture 'Jesus' as making above.³⁴ In view of all that we have been describing about the location of groups like 'the Ebionites' or 'Nazoraeans,' the movement of what the Qumran documents (even those not so familiar, such as the pivotal 'MMT' above) are referring to as these 'camps' across the Jordan into the area of Damascus and beyond – possibly the Syrian Desert further north and east even as far 'North' as 'Assyria' (the classical 'Land of the Osrhoeans') and Adiabene – is significant.

Biblically-speaking, as we saw, this is also the direction Elijah is pictured as taking 'in the Way of the wilderness of Damascus' in 1 Kings 19:15 after his prototypical 'cave-dwelling' and 'rain-making' in 1 Kings 18. This is not to mention the various pictures of Paul in Acts, Galatians, and the Pseudoclementine *Recognitions* following a fleeing community into just these areas as well.³⁵ This emigration also bears on the legends of 'a flight' to the 'Pella' region – also across Jordan on 'the way to Damascus' – by James' 'Jerusalem Church' followers in response to some mysterious oracle after his death which we shall further elucidate below.

'Pella' was the nearest settled city across the Jordan leading up to Damascus and beyond in the great expanse of desert north and east along the so-called 'Fertile Crescent' as far as 'the Kingdom of the Edessenes' in Northern Syria and 'the Land of Adiabene' further east. By the same token, it is also possible to take the allusion to this 'Pella Flight' more generically as it might be the allusion to an emigration to 'the Land of Damascus' in the Qumran documents and the whole tangle of conflicting data relating to the same area in Acts, Paul's letters, the Pseudoclementine *Recognitions*, and Josephus – to say nothing of the similar flight tradition, where Northern Syria or Mesopotamia is concerned, after the death of John the Baptist in Mandaean literature.

Epiphanius expresses something of this, when speaking about 'the Ebionites' and 'Nazoraeans,' in the section in which he also refers to 'the Primal Adam'-ideology of 'Sampsaeans, Osseneans, and Elchaseans' (that is, *'the Sabaeans, Essenes, and Elchasaites'*). He says:

> *For the most part these settled in Perea, Pella a city in the Decapolis, Batanea*
> (the Roman province of the so-called *'Nabataean Arabs'* north of the
> Decapolis and east of Gaulonitus/*'the Golan'*), *and the Land of Bashan* (the
> classical name for these areas, overlapping most of these other locations
> as far north as Damascus).[36]

His meaning here, of course, is clear and he *was a* Palestinian – as we have
seen, allegedly a convert from Judaism or, more precisely perhaps,
'Ebionitism' – so whatever else might be intended, he is certainly speaking about *the other side of the Jordan River and further north in Syria* – *'on the
Way to Damascus'* as 1 Kings 19:15 above about Elijah might have put it.

In other delineations of such groups, Epiphanius also includes *'Moab'*
(directly east from the Fortress at Masada on the other side of the Dead
Sea, south of Perea and north of Arabian Petra) and *'Coele-Syria,'* north
of Damascus on the way up to Aleppo, Edessa (*'Antioch Orrhoe'*), and
points further East.[37] This is the area of primary interest to the War Scroll
from Qumran too, which speaks in its own archaizing manner of a *'War'*
against *'Edom,' 'Moab,' 'the Sons of Ishmael,' 'the Kittim of Assyria'* (probably
referring to the Romans but possibly, as some see it, the Seleucids preceding them – this cannot be determined with precision on the basis of
the reference as it stands), *'Aram-Naharaim'* (on the other hand, this *can be
determined on the basis of the information provided*, namely, *Northern Syria and
Iraq*), and *'the East as far as the Great Desert,'* also a straightforward geographical allusion.[38]

Where *'the Kittim'* are concerned, their armies are also specifically
denoted as being in Egypt as well. They too *'shall be crushed'* and *'their Rule
shall be ended.'*[39] As per the indication in Daniel 11:30 (though not 1 Maccabees 1:1), *'the Kittim'* in such references probably are the Romans,
which is also the implication of both the Habakkuk and Nahum *Peshers*,
where it is impossible to apply the allusion *to any group other than the
Romans*.[40] Though these may be *'Greeks'* or at least *'Macedonians,'* as per 1
Maccabees 1:1, it is difficult to imagine that such a term might refer to
any Grecian Period other than that of Alexander the Great *when there
may have been separate contingents of Macedonian troops in these areas.* One
certainly cannot refer to the Seleucids in this incredibly-inflated manner,
power-wise, by any stretch of the imagination.

Be this as it may, all these groups together with their allies are referred
to here in the War Scroll as *'the Sons of Darkness in the Army of Belial.'*[41] On
the other hand, those living *'in the camps,'* who must carry out this

struggle, *abetted by the Army of Heavenly Holy Ones* (in James' or Jesus' proclamations above, '*the Heavenly Host*'), are referred to by expressions like '*the Sons of Light*' or '*the People of God*.[42] '*The time is that* '*of Salvation* (Hebrew: '*ofYeshuʿa*') *for the People of God.*'[43] These last are also referred to as '*the Sons of Levi and the Sons of Judah and the Sons of Benjamin.*' Taken together, as we just saw, they or '*the Sons of Benjamin*' alone (probably the latter) are referred to as '*the Golat ha-Midbar*' / '*the Exile of the Desert*' or '*the Diaspora of the Desert*' or '*the Wilderness.*'[44] One should also note the parallel in this last reference to the addressee of the Letter of James 1:1, referred to as '*the Twelve Tribes which (are) in the Diaspora.*' It would be hard to imagine a closer fit.

Benjamin, the *Golah* of the Desert

The first two of these categories, '*the Sons of Levi and the Sons of Judah,*' are clearly the Priest Class and the People of Judah, the so-called '*Judeans*' or, as in contexts such as at Qumran, in the Gospels, and Josephus, *simply* '*Jews.*' But the third, '*Benjamin the Golah of the Desert*' – the only reference of this type in the whole Qumran corpus, is more puzzling and may provide a clue to what Paul was trying to say when referring to himself in Romans 11:1 and Philippians 3:5 as being of '*the Tribe of Benjamin.*'

It is sometimes suggested that '*Benjamin*' in this period is a reference to *all Diaspora Jews*. It may be, but this is not proved. As Paul uses the term, echoed in Acts 13:21 as well, aside from playing on the name of his namesake '*Saul,*' who actually was '*a Benjaminite*' – doubtlessly an important aspect of his use of it; there may also be a play on the '*Belaʿ*' / '*Belial*' / '*Edomite*' origins of Herodians, not to mention the way '*Sons of Belial*' and its parallel '*Balaam*' are sometimes used at Qumran and in the New Testament generally.[45] This rests on the proposition that Paul is an '*Herodian*' himself which, based on his reference in Romans 16:10–11 to his '*kinsman the Littlest Herod*' and '*the House of Aristobulus*' in Rome – as we shall explore further below, presumably Aristobulus V, Herod of Chalcis' son and the second husband of that '*Salome*' allegedly involved in the death of John the Baptist[46] – and other indicators, the present writer considers to be accurate.[47]

Not only does it turn out, through either confusion or acculturation, that '*Belaʿ*' is reckoned (like its other curious, genealogical overlap '*Balaam,*' just noted above as a variation of '*Belial*') as the '*Son of Beʿor*' and *the first of the Edomite Kings,* but '*Belaʿ*' also turns out to be, according to delineations such as those in Genesis and Chronicles, *the name of the principal 'Benjaminite' clan.*[48] Herodians, who were certainly seen as

'*Edomites*' ('*Idumaeans*' in this period being a Greco-Latin formulation for '*Edomite*'), may have been using this curious genealogical overlap to make – as Paul does – just such a '*Benjaminite*' claim.

Such a claim of descent from '*Benjamin*' – and, therefore, *descent from Jacob, though not Judah* – could easily translate itself into that of being '*of the Race of Israel*' (though not '*Jews*') and, '*a Hebrew of the Hebrews*,' as Paul puts it so tantalizingly in Philippians 3:5.[49] The term '*Benjamin*' therefore, in time, may also have come to apply to all such '*converts*,' such as these '*Herodians*' – if '*converts*' is the appropriate word. It may also have been expanded to include '*Gentiles*' generally, which could then possibly be seen as another aspect of this puzzling allusion. The allusion, '*the Sons of Benjamin*,' '*the Golah of the Desert*,' as it occurs in this opening passage in the War Scroll, as we just saw, does appear to carry something of this meaning while, at the same time, applying to a specific '*Golah*'/'*Galut*'/ or '*Diaspora in the Desert*,' that of, the '*Wilderness*' or '*Desert Camps*.'

Muhammad, while never mentioning Paul in the Koran, as we saw, as a latterday '*Apostle to the Gentiles*,' can be viewed (like Mani before him) as a Seventh- Century successor to Paul, particularly in the importance he attached to '*Abraham*.' This is especially true where Northern Syrian locales – Abraham's original *homeland* – were at issue. He and all Arabs after him pick up this '*Abrahamic*' – if not the 'Israelite' – aspect of the Hebrew genealogy by raising the claim of descent from '*Ishmael*.' In doing so, they are also making a quasi-'*Hebrew*' claim but, even more importantly, they are also like Paul – and here the transmission is direct – claiming to be '*Heirs*' to '*the Religion of Abraham*' (for Paul, '*the Children of*' or '*the Belief of Abraham*'[50]). In the case of Muslims, or at least Arabs, the sense is both genealogical *and* spiritual too. Paul may have been implying the same.

Another aspect of the puzzling allusion to '*Benjamin*,' as it is circulating in the First Century, may be its application to '*Gentiles*' generally, in particular, '*Gentile*' associates ('*God-Fearers*' in both the New Testament and, in the writer's view, even to some degree at Qumran[51]) or even '*Converts*.' The author considers this last the more-likely meaning of the term given the way it is used in the War Scroll. This is certainly some of the sense being reflected in the Damascus Document's crucial exegesis of '*the Zadokite Covenant*' from Ezekiel 44:15 too, which, as already explained, in addition to breaking open Ezekiel's original '*the Priests who are Sons-of-Zadok Levites*' by the deliberate insertion of *waw*-constructs (it then becomes '*the Priests, the Levites, and the Sons of Zadok*'); now interprets '*the Levites*' – playing on the original root-meaning of the word – as '*the Nilvim*' or '*Joiners with them*,' meaning, those '*joining*' the Priests (defined as '*Penitents in the wilderness*' – an abnormal and certainly unge-nealogical description of '*Priests*,' if there ever was one) *and* '*the Sons of Zadok*,' just noted above. All of these, it now implies – bringing us back to the various '*Damascus*' or '*Pella Flight*' traditions we shall analyze further below – '*went out from the Land of Judah to dwell in the Land of Damascus.*'[52]

This is also the way the Nahum *Pesher* would appear to be using the root, *L-V-Y/I*, the root of both '*Levites*' and '*Nilvim*'/'*Joiners*.' It ties it to the phrase '*ger-nilveh*,' that is, '*resident alien*' or '*the foreigner resident among them*' (to whom, as we saw, '*circumcision*' was seen to apply in the passage Izates was reading from Genesis 17 when he was queried by the Galilean '*Teacher*' Eleazar as to whether he understood '*the true meaning of what he was reading*'). The Nahum *Pesher* also ties it to another of its odd esoteri-cisms, '*the Simple of Ephraim*' which, as already suggested as well, may simply stand for '*Samaritans* – '*Ephraim*' being in this period the Land in which the Samaritans now dwelled.[53] This is to say nothing of the whole '*Amraphel*'/'*Ephraim*' circle of problems we have pointed out relative to the Psalm 37 *Pesher* too. That there was an originally non-Jewish cadre of '*Joiners*,' meaning '*Resident Aliens*' or '*God-Fearers*,' associated with the Community of Qumran, the author considers a self-evident truism.[54] That this is something of what is implied at this point by the '*Ephraim*' usage (if not that of '*Amraphel*'), the author also considers to be self-evident. To bring us full circle, the War Scroll is now applying these conceptualities to a specific '*Golah*' or '*Diaspora*' – '*the Golah of the Wilder-ness*' or '*Desert Camps*.'

The whole '*Benjamin*' or '*Golah of the Desert*' usage may also carry with it something of the way non-Jewish converts – those like the '*Nil-vim*'/'*Joiners*' in the Damascus Document's exegesis of Ezekiel 44:15 above, *who 'join' the 'Penitents in the wilderness'* (that is, '*the Priests and the Sons of Zadok*' – in the War Scroll, '*the Sons of Levi and the Sons of Judah*,' but all subsumed under the general heading of '*the Exiled Sons of Light*') *in 'going' out from the Land of Judah to dwell in the Land of Damascus*' – were looked upon in this period. This would include warriors such as Queen Helen's descendants, '*Monobazus*' and '*Kenedaeus*' from Adiabene ('*Aram Naharaim*' in the War Scroll), who lost their lives in the first engagement of the War against Rome at the Pass at Beit Horon, or even those '*Edomite Herodians*,' Josephus seems to be referring to as '*Idumaeans*' (in the Scrolls, also equivalent to '*the ᶜAmim*' or '*the Peoples*' or '*the Violent Ones of the Gen-tiles*,' we have already referred to above[55]), who come to the aid of those Josephus is ultimately willing to identify as '*Zealots*' and who butcher many of '*the High Priests*.' As we have seen, these include, in particular,

James' destroyer Ananus ben Ananus and Josephus' colleague, Jesus ben Gamala, Martha the daughter of Boethus' husband (could he be one of the models for the original 'Jesus'? He would be if Josephus had anything to do with the authorship of some of the materials we have been following).

It is possible even to draw a parallel to those Josephus is mysteriously picturing as 'Idumaeans' – identity unknown though at times they seem to be led by someone he calls 'Niger of Perea.'[56] Not only are they clearly 'Violent,' but they are just as clearly in league with those he is designating at this point as 'Zealots' (as just suggested, in the Qumran documents being referred to either as 'the Violent Ones' or 'the Violent Ones of the Gentiles' – at one point even, 'the Men-of-War') who take vengeance on 'the Wicked Priest' for what he did to 'the Righteous Teacher' in both the Psalm 37 Pesher and the Habakkuk Pesher[57] and who, in the latter, actually appear to attend 'the Righteous Teacher''s or 'the Priest''s ('in whose heart God put the insight to interpret the words of His Servants the Prophets') scriptural exegesis sessions.[58]

However these things may be, something like the terminology 'Benjaminite' is clearly circulating in the 'Diaspora' or 'Camps' beyond the Jordan and in the Damascus region. Since Paul – when he speaks in Galatians 1:17–18 of 'going away into Arabia' – has just as clearly spent time in these areas or, in the author's view, in this 'Diaspora' or in these 'Camps'; this may provide insight into the way Paul and Acts are using the term 'Benjamin,'[59] that is, the same way the War Scroll is using it. How much time Paul actually spent in these areas or 'Camps' would depend on how one chooses to interpret his reference to the 'three years' he says elapsed between his going 'into Arabia' and returning to Damascus and Jerusalem, not to mention the 'fourteen' additional years, he alludes to, as the time that elapsed before next he went up to Jerusalem in Galatians 2:1. In the writer's view, much of this time was spent 'in Arabia,' which in Roman parlance included the areas as far north even as Northern Syria and Northern Iraq or Adiabene (as already explained, today's Kurdistan centering around Mosul, Irbil, and Kirkuk – always a center of unrest).

It is also important to note that in the 'Letter' or 'Letters' to the King, just discussed above and paralleling both 'the Letter' to 'Abgarus'/'Agbarus'/ 'Augurus'/or 'Albarus,' mentioned in Eusebius and Syriac sources,[60] and the one in the New Testament, 'taken down to Antioch' by Judas Barsabas, et. al., from James; some regulations concerning these 'Camps' are discussed and Jerusalem, as we saw, is specifically denoted as 'the Holy Camp' and 'Chief of the Camps of Israel.' In our view, as should be by now clear, the 'Letter' in question, widely known as 'MMT,' is in fact the very one containing James' *directives to overseas communities,* carried down by Judas *Barsabas* and Silas – another individual with much in common with these *'war'*-like Herodians and, in Josephus, the name of the Head of Agrippa I's bodyguard[61]– to the *'Antioch'* refracted in the somewhat tendentious portrait in Acts 15:22–30.

It should also be noted that in the final triumphant evocation of what the Gospels call *'the Son of Man coming on the clouds of Heaven with Power'* at the end of the War Scroll, which repeats the whole description of eschatological *'rain'* and final apocalyptic *'Judgement'* at the hands of the Heavenly Holy Ones *'on the clouds,'* presented earlier in the same document in elucidation of *'the Star Prophecy'*; God is referred to – much like *'the Messiah'* in the Genesis *Pesher* above – as *'the God of Righteousness.'*[61] At the same time, it is stated that *'His is the Power, the battle is in His hands'* (the Ebionite/Elchasaite *'Great Power'*-usage again, this time with slightly more aggressive signification). Then, too, the wish is expressed, as we saw, that *'He'* or *'His Messiah'* (probably the latter) should *'smite the Nations'* or *'the Peoples, His Enemies, and devour'* or *'consume flesh with His sword.'*[62]

We have not only encountered this *'eating'* or *'devouring'* language at the end of Galatians 5:15, when Paul is criticizing those who are misleading his communities with *'circumcision'*; but this idea of *'eating'* or *'consuming'* will be a fixture of the Habakkuk *Pesher,* particularly in the manner in which the Wicked Priest *'consumes'* or *'destroys'* the Righteous Teacher and the way in which *'the Kittim* (in this case, clearly the Romans) *'consume all Peoples...with the sword'* as well.[63] On the other hand, here in the War Scroll the *'sword'* is rather referred to as *'the sword of God'* – pretty blood-curdling, but probably an accurate depiction of the desire of this group for Divine Retribution or, as it is often called, *'Vengeance.'*[64]

In this context, that of blessing God's *'Name'* and reference to His *'keeping the Covenant with us as of old'* (*'keeping the Covenant'* being, it will be recalled, the definition of *'the Sons of Zadok'* in the Community Rule and phraseology fraught with significance for this period[65]), the text now refers to *'the Gates of Salvation'* (*'Yeshuʿa'* – that is, in more Hellenized parlance, *'Jesus'*). These last, it claims, have been opened many times in the past.[66] The same usage is basically referred to in the question asked of James, *'What is the Gate to Jesus,'* in all accounts of his proclamation in the Temple on Passover of this *'coming of the Son of Man sitting on the right hand of the Great Power...about to come in Glory on the clouds of Heaven.'*[67] So here, then, we have the eschatological link between James' *'rain-making,'* his proclamation of *'Glory,'* and that of the final apocalyptic War against all Evil on the Earth and the delineation of these things in the War Scroll.

'*Galilee*' in the Gospels and the Massacre Conducted by Vespasian there

It is this picture in the War Scroll, too, of the movement '*from the camp in the Wilderness*' or '*Desert of the Peoples to the camp in the wilderness of Judea*' which, in its own way, can be thought of as being transformed in the Gospels to that of Jesus' movement, from his baptism by John and his '*Temptation in the wilderness*' (also seemingly '*of Judah*' or '*of Judea*'), northwards – after John, anticipating Jesus, '*was delivered up*' (always an important phraseology, as we have seen, across the whole spectrum of these documents[68]) to '*the Galilee of the Nations*' in Matthew 4:15. This, once again, basically also parallels the flight in Mandaean tradition of John's followers across the Jordan to Haran ('*Edessa*' or '*Urfa*') in Northern Syria and after that to Messene in Southern Mesopotamia. As the Gospels portray this, '*Galilee*' now becomes the domain of 'Jesus'' activities; and his Apostles, peaceful '*fishermen*' ('*casters of nets and fishers of men*') around the Sea of Galilee (Matthew 4:18–19 and *pars*.).

In turn, this latter picture plays to a certain extent on that of another character in Josephus' narrative, '*Jesus son of Sapphias*,' the Leader of the Galilean sailors and fishermen on the Sea of Galilee at the time of the outbreak of the War with Rome.[69] Accusing him of '*fomenting sedition and Revolution*' ('*Innovation*') in Tiberius[70] – typical of the accusations Josephus makes – Josephus tells how he burned the palace of Herod the Tetrarch (John the Baptist's murderer and, in our view, the putative '*kinsman*' of Paul in Acts 13:1), because it '*contained pictures of animals which was contrary to Law*.' Josephus, furthermore, claims '*Jesus*' also '*massacred all the Greek inhabitants there*.'[71] Curiously Tiberius, which was one of the cities founded by Herod Antipas, Tetrarch of Galilee and Perea, and the major city on the Sea of Galilee at this time, is conspicuously missing from Gospel portraits of events there.

Josephus portrays this '*Jesus*' and his (Josephus') own mortal enemy, '*a copy of the Laws of Moses in his hands*' (surely there is a certain amount of sarcastic parody and animosity going on in this picture at this point), *as trying to have him (Josephus) executed as a collaborator*. To add to that, he specifically identifies Jesus' followers as both '*Galileans*' and '*the Poor*' (or '*Poor wretches*').[72] Calling him '*the Leader of the Brigands*' (as in Gospel portraits of the two crucified with Jesus and other similar denotations in his own work, '*Lestai*' again[73]), Josephus can scarcely conceal his delight in describing how Vespasian and Titus came and, in the end, slaughtered many of this '*Jesus*'' followers while they were attempting to '*board their boats*' or '*swim out to sea*' – these last, of course, familiar motifs in Gospel iconography.[74]

Jesus and some of his other fishermen or boatmen, it seems, at the approach of the Roman army had already put out on the Lake (more Gospel portraiture?) in their little boats just out of bowshot. For his part, Josephus portrays the scene as follows:

> *Casting down their anchors (ekballon* – the '*casting down*' language, once again so prevalent in like-minded pictures in the Gospels[75]), *they closed up their boats one against the other like an army in battle formation and fought their enemy on the shore from the sea.*

At this point, Titus turned his attention instead to massacring the citizens of Tiberius, guilty and innocent alike. In these engagements, Josephus also accords generous mention to the gallantry of Trajan, the father and namesake of the future Emperor, consistently remarked throughout this picture of warfare in Palestine.[76]

Finally the Romans, moving east along the shore of the Lake to another city, Tarichaeae, at its confluence with the Jordan, themselves take to the Lake using bigger rafts. Here they overtake Jesus and his supporters, overturning their boats and spearing and decapitating so many in the water that

> *the whole lake was red with blood and covered with corpses, for not a man escaped ...and the beaches were strewn with wrecks and swollen corpses.*[76]

This is the end of Josephus' picture of the '*Galilean*' fishermen or boatmen and what happened on the '*Sea of Galilee*' or '*Lake Gennesareth*' – and this, in contrast to some others, *is clearly an 'eye-witness' one!*

Following this total collapse, Vespasian, who felt '*that nothing against the Jews could be considered an Impiety*' (this is verbatim – there are some others who have since felt the same way), *immediately executed some twelve hundred of the old and infirm*, who had not even participated in the fighting. *Six thousand of the more able-bodied he sent to Nero at Corinth to work on the canal* which Nero was having dug there. *Thirty thousand more he sold himself* and *he gave the remainder to King Agrippa (Agrippa II)*, who had originally invited Titus in to deal with the situation around the Sea of Galilee, since this was part of his domains. Whereupon Agrippa promptly sold them. *This is the man, together with his reputed consort Bernice* – later the mistress of Titus, the destroyer of both the Temple and Jerusalem – *who is presented so sympathetically in Acts and with whom Paul talks so congenially* in Acts 25:13–26:32 (as we have remarked, perhaps its longest continual episode).[78]

Agrippa II had received this Tetrarchy, which even Josephus allows was so rich that '*anything planted there grew immediately*' – true even to this day – in succession to his father Agrippa I (himself, seemingly portrayed in Acts 12:21–23), who had been given it and his other domains after Herod the Tetrarch (Herodias' husband '*Herod Antipas*') had been banished to Southen France by Caligula.[79] Actually Matthew 4:15, in describing the activities of the man it is calling 'Jesus,' quotes Isaiah 8:23–9:1 on '*the Galil of the Gentiles*' (literally, '*Circle*' or '*Wheel of the Gentiles*,' rephrased slightly here in Matthew to '*Galilee of the Peoples, the Way of the Sea beyond Jordan*'), pictures him as '*withdrawing*' to Nazareth and from thence, '*departing Nazareth and coming to dwell*' along the Sea of Galilee (language, once again for whatever it's worth, reminiscent of that in the Damascus Document's picture of the Community it is describing as '*departing the Land of Judah*' and coming '*to dwell in the Land of Damascus*').

The original of this in Isaiah, which does seem to refer to '*the far side of the Jordan*' (we have seen similar language to this in Mark 7:31's epilogue to the curing of the Syrophoenician woman's daughter), would be better approximated by terms like '*the Decapolis*,' '*Perea*,' Syria, and what presently goes by the name of '*the Fertile Crescent*' and the Peoples, mostly '*Arab*,' living along its sweep. Nor is there any '*wilderness*' or '*desert*' around the Sea of Galilee or near it, the extreme fertility of which was just indicated, where Jesus on several occasions, already underscored above, is portrayed either as '*multiplying the loaves and the fishes*' for his followers or sermonizing to them. On the contrary.

In following up this picture of Jesus' appearance by the Sea of Galilee and calling his principal Apostles – who, *being fishermen*, '*were casting a net into the sea*' (*ballontas* – once more, the vocabulary of '*casting*,' this time combined with '*net*' imagery of the kind encountered in the Damascus Document and Revelation relative to '*Balak*,' '*Balaam*,' or '*Belial*') or '*mending their nets*.' Matthew 4:25, in fact, speaks of Galilee in the same breath as '*the Decapolis, Jerusalem, Judea, and beyond the Jordan*,' which confuses things even more and shows an almost complete lack of geographical knowledge of this area. Mark 3:8 adds to this, '*from Idumaea and beyond the Jordan*' as well as '*those around Tyre and Sidon*.' Luke 6:17, for his part trying to make sense of all this, now drops the '*Decapolis, Idumaea, and across the Jordan*' and transforms it into '*the Sea Coast of Tyre and Sidon*,' whatever this was supposed to mean!

Regardless of these several non sequiturs, for Mark 3:9–10 the '*Many*' that he had cured were so great

that they pressed upon him so they might touch him (as Jerome above pictures the People in Jerusalem doing to James '*as he passed*' and as the woman with '*the fountain of blood*' and a number of others, already remarked above, do as well) *and the unclean spirits* (here the language of '*clean*' and '*uncleanness*' again), *when they beheld, fell down before him* (as well as the '*falling down*' language of many of the above episodes too), *crying out*, (however incredibly and demonstrating the basically imaginary character of the whole narrative) '*Truly you are the Son of God.*'

The marvelousness of this portrait notwithstanding, adding some more effusiveness about '*being cured of unclean spirits*' (Mark's vocabulary as opposed to Matthew's '*demons*'), Luke now, once again – as already signaled above – employs the '*Elchasaite*' language of '*Hidden Power*,' averring that '*Power came forth from him and healed them all*' (6:18). Then, like Matthew, it immediately moves on to its version of '*the Beatitudes*' of the Sermon on the Mount (6:20–6:49). For its part, Mark rather closes this episode with Jesus now angrily charging the masses – like James in the preface to the Pseudoclementine *Homilies*[80] or the Sabaean '*Keepers of the Secret*,' or even '*the Way in the wilderness*' portion of the Community Rule above[81] – '*not to make this known*,' that is, *what the unclean spirits cried out when they were cured* (more phantasmagoria – 3:12)!

One should contrast the historical reality or, rather, unreality of episodes such as these with the one from Josephus above about *the brutal, bloody, and uncompromising warfare that basically devastated settled life around the Sea of Galilee.* If there ever was an '*Historical Jesus*' around '*Gennesareth*' at this time (Luke 5:1 – the name Josephus also accords this Lake, the overlap of which with the term '*Nazareth*,' as it appears in Scripture, should not be overlooked) – on the face of it, a rather dubious proposition – this '*Jesus son of Sapphias*,' the *Leader of the* '*Galilean*' *boatmen* and '*the Poor*' *on the Sea of Galilee*, who together with his followers *poured his blood out into it*, was almost surely he.[82]

One should also remark that the picture of Jesus '*walking on the waters*' of the Sea of Galilee, incredible as it may be as well, has a much more likely counterpart and echo in the legends surrounding the Dead Sea further south in Judea and Perea, again the areas around which many of these quasi-'*Essene*' or '*bathing*' groups congregated. Here people *really do float on the surface of the waters and cannot sink* (because of the salt content of the water associated with its being below sea level) – a point Josephus does not neglect to make when he recounts, for the benefit of his Greco-Roman readers, how *Vespasian had Jewish captives, whose hands he had tied, thrown into these waters to see for himself that they did not sink* (this is the same Vespasian who – along with his son Titus – later had the Colosseum built over the remains of a lake, fashioned by Nero for his own private amusement on a site left by the fire in Rome; but this, rather to foster his own popularity for the public amusement of the Roman crowd *and* with monies, mainly consisting of the Temple Treasure, and additional captives he had come into possession of during his Judean campaigning!).[83] Again, the perspicacious reader should not fail to remark the counterpart to the point about '*not sinking*' in the various Gospel portraits of what happened relating to both '*Jesus*' and '*Peter*' on the Sea of Galilee.[84]

In fact, the whole picture in the Gospels of evangelical and religious activity around the Sea of Galilee at this time more likely reflects the situation circulating around the shores of the Dead Sea, which does seem to have been much busier than most would have thought,[85] '*Gennesareth*' and/or '*Galilee*'-type allusions perhaps acting as geographical stand-ins for designations like '*Nazirite*,' '*Nazoraeans*,' or '*Galileans*.' Nor is this to say anything about the phrase '*Cana in Galilee*' in John 2:11 and 4:46, almost certainly representing such a circumlocution – '*Cana*' (kana'/'zeal'), it will be recalled, in other contexts standing for '*Cananaean*' or '*Zealot*' and being where Jesus first '*turned water into wine*,' cured another '*little child*,' and, paralleling Josephus' descriptions of '*magicians*,' '*Impostors*,' or '*pseudo-prophets*,' '*did the first of his signs and revealed his Glory*' (John 2:11), '*having come out of Judea into Galilee*' (John 4:54)

Elsewhere, after the incident about the Greek Syrophoenician woman and '*casting down crumbs*' to dogs – almost certainly playing on and inverting the '*Letter*' or '*Letters*' known as '*MMT*' above, *barring 'dogs from the Holy Camp because they might eat bones with the flesh still on them*' – Mark, as we saw, again showing an almost total lack of geographical precision, has '*Jesus*' going from Tyre and Sidon to the Sea of Galilee '*through the midst of the coasts of the Decapolis*' (7:31). For his part, Matthew 19:1 has Jesus '*withdrawing from Galilee and coming to the coasts of Judea beyond Jordan*,' geographically speaking, again almost an impossibility. John 3:26 and 10:40, on the other hand, echoing Luke 3:3 on John the Baptist going '*into all the country around the Jordan*,' often has both John and Jesus as habitués of *these same regions beyond Jordan*.

Basically, however, the areas referred to in all of these notices are the ones we have been encountering in Hippolytus' and Epiphanius' testimonies to these '*Essene*' or '*Ebionite*'-like Judeo-Christian '*sects*,' including the various '*Arab*' Kingdoms, referred to by contemporary Latin and Greek authors – '*Arab*' Kingdoms in '*the Land of the Osrhoeans*' around Haran in Syria and Northern Mesopotamia as well as finally in Southern Mesopotamia, where Ananias first encounters Izates in the story of his and his mother Queen Helen's conversion and where, a century or two later, Mani was born.

The Regime of Extreme Purity in the Camps

The Qumran War Scroll also pictures what it considers to be the regime in these camps, this at the time it designates as '*the time of Yeshuᶜa*' –

> the time of Salvation for the People of God and Eternal destruction for all of the lot of Belial.

This time would appear to be consonant with the return of '*the Dispersion of the Sons of Light from the Desert of the Peoples* to *the camps in the wilderness around Jerusalem*'[87] – '*the Desert of the Peoples*' now clearly being synonymous, as we saw, with what Matthew 4:15 is calling '*Galilee of the Nations*' or '*Peoples*' above (*Ethnon*). For the War Scroll, '*no boy or woman is ever to enter the camps*' (compare this with the '*Jesus*' and '*the little children*' allusions in the various episodes and parables we have been considering above) during the whole period of their going out to what can only be described as, what Muslims would call even today, '*Holy War*.' Rather '*they shall all be Volunteers for War, Perfect in Spirit and body, preparing for the Day of Vengeance*'![88]

The expression '*Volunteers for War*' is similar to that found in 1 Maccabees 2:42's description of Judas Maccabee's army (Daniel's '*Kedoshim*' / '*Holy Ones*' or '*Saints*'), described at this point as '*Hassidaeans*' (Hebrew, '*Pious Ones*') '*each one a stout Volunteer on the side of the Law*.' Despite the conflicting testimony in 1 Maccabees 7:13, which portrays these same '*Hassidaeans*' – who appear to make up the bulk of Judas' most committed military contingent – as pacifistic, more compromising, and *willing to accept a High Priest appointed by foreign power* (in this case, by the Seleucids); in the view of the author, however, this must rather be balanced against 2 Maccabees 14:6 which implies just the opposite. I have treated this seeming contradiction at length in my short monograph *Maccabees, Zadokites, Christians and Qumran* in *The Dead Sea Scrolls and the First Christians* (Barnes and Noble, 2004), concluding that what we have here are rather terminological confusions and, actually, *the birth moment of 'the Pharisee Party*' – the latter, more-compromising '*Hassidaeans*,' being rather nascent '*Pharisees*' who split away from more aboriginal '*Zealot*' or '*Zadokite Sadducees*' over the issue of *foreign appointment of High Priests*.[89]

Another parallel is to be found in the recently-discovered '*Paean to King Jonathan*,' the pro-Maccabean attitude of which is patent.[90] Greeting its addressee – who can either be thought of as Alexander Jannaeus

(d. 76 BC); his great uncle, the first Maccabean Priest-King, Jonathan (*d.* 142 BC); or Alexander Jannaeus' own son Aristobulus II (*d.* 48 BC) – in adulatory, almost even '*Messianic*' terms, this text found by perspicacious Israeli text scholars and misidentified or overlooked for years, is really *a Hebrew Poem of Praise* or panegyric.[91] Not only this: it mysteriously alludes, in what can only be construed as the most approving terms, to '*the Joiners*' once again – the '*Nilvim*' of the Damascus Document's exegesis of Ezekiel 44:15 above – this time, '*the Joiners*' or '*Volunteers in the War of...*'[92] There the text breaks off.

Not only does it clearly disprove the notion, held by most 'Consensus Scholars,' that one or another of the Maccabees could in any way be viewed as '*the Wicked Priest*' (mentioned in two almost-certainly First-Century CE Qumran texts, the Habakkuk and Psalm 37 *Peshers*, as we have seen) and confirm my own position that the Scrolls must be seen as *pro-* not *anti-*Maccabean since they exhibit the same ethos as the Macca- beans – most notably, '*zeal for the Law*' and/or '*Covenant*'[93]; it also belies the widely-held parallel misconception that '*the Essenes*' *were* '*peaceful.*'

Maybe so-called '*Essenes*' were '*peaceful*' or *other-worldly* in Philo's Egypt, but in Josephus' Palestine they clearly participated, as he has testified and this definitively, in the final apocalyptic War against the Romans.[94] Nor can this War, as referred to in numerous Qumran documents, be considered simply a spiritual or symbolic war, as was likewise portrayed by numerous early Qumran scholars (and is still portrayed)[95] – at least as pictured by the Qumran documents themselves, a portrait for some reason they often incongruously ignore. This too is confirmed by a host of other extremely aggressive and war-like texts in the corpus at Qumran, some more recently released – some of long-standing.[96] Also the expression '*Day of Vengeance*' found at this juncture in the War Scroll is encountered – again probably definitively – in a climactic section, already underscored above, in the Community Rule. Not only does this quintessential conclusion contain, as we saw, the all-important John the Baptist-style '*this is the time of the preparation of the Way in the wilderness;*' but this expression '*the Day of Vengeance,*' itself a synonym for '*the Last Judgement*' and hardly very pacifistic, is linked in that section both to '*zeal for the Law*' and spiritualized '*atonement*' imagery.[97]

The implication of finding all these telltale usages linked together not only bears on the aggressiveness of the corpus, but also that the documents in which they occur must all be viewed as more or less contemporary or written at roughly the same time – regardless either of palaeographic or AMS carbon-testing indicators to the contrary[98] – since they are all using the same esotericisms, vocabulary, and allude on the whole to the same *dramatis personae*. There cannot be decades or even generations between their respective dates-of-origin as is the implication of most reigning 'Establishment' theorizing.

In the Community Rule, the use of this expression, '*the Day of Vengeance*,' rises out of the elucidation of a twice-repeated citation of the biblical proof-text (Isaiah 40:3), applied in the Synoptic Gospels to John the Baptist's '*mission*' in the wilderness.[99] After alluding to '*atoning for the land*' and '*suffering affliction*' and '*being confirmed in Perfection of the Way*' and '*separated as Holy*' – meaning, in a much underestimated ideology, that this is a '*Community of Consecrated Holy Ones*' or '*Nazirites*' – the text itself puts this in the following manner:

> *according to these Rules, they shall separate from the midst of the habitation of the Men of Ungodliness* (the '*separation*' ideology Paul himself evokes in 2 Corinthians 6:17, only elsewhere to counterindicate it[100]) *and go out into the wilderness to prepare the Way of the Lord, as it is written, 'Prepare in the wilderness the Way of the Lord. Make straight in the desert a Pathway for our God'* (Isaiah 40:3).[100]

The only difference between this ideology and other similar, more familiar ones is that '*the Way in the wilderness*' here is clearly defined as '*the study of the Torah*' which these '*Perfect*' / '*Separated*' / '*Consecrated*' / or '*Holy Ones*' are '*commanded to do*' exactly as it has '*been revealed from Age to Age*' and '*as the Prophets have revealed through His Holy Spirit*' (here the language of '*doing*' connected to that of '*the Holy Spirit*' which will not only reappear in the New Testament, but permeate the entire corpus at Qumran).[102]

This '*Jamesian*' emphasis on '*doing*,' which will be stressed even more forcefully, as we have seen and will see, in documents like the Damascus Document and the Habakkuk *Pesher* below,[103] is emphasized even further when this '*Way in the wilderness*' ideology is then reiterated in the Community Rule, but it is so important that, even though we have already reproduced parts of this, it is worth repeating the whole:

> *He shall do* (here the first use of the key allusion to '*doing*,' the basis as already stressed of the Hebrew usage '*ma'asim*' or '*works*') *the will of God in accord with everything that has been revealed from Age to Age...to separate* (see Paul in 2 Corinthians 6:17)...*to walk Perfectly* (also in 2 Corinthians 7:1) *each with his neighbor* (a variation on the James' '*Royal Law according to the Scripture*,' the first part of the '*Righteousness*' / '*Piety*' dichotomy, '*love your*

neighbor,' so important to all these *'wilderness'* groups[104])...*for this is the time of 'making a Way in the wilderness'* (the second quotation of this foundational Scriptural passage) *and they shall be instructed* (by *'the Maschil'* or *'Guide'* whom we have already discussed to some extent above) *in all that has been revealed that they should do* (again a reference to the all-important verb *'doing'*) *in this time, to separate* (here the *'separation'* ideology of the typical *'Nazirite'* or *'Rechabite'*) *from any man who has not turned his Way from Ungodliness...*

Everlasting hatred (the Qumran original of the New Testament reversal, *'love your enemy,'* totally in accord with the picture of James' admonitions to the Elders and the whole Assembly introducing the Pseudoclementine *Homilies* above[105]) *for the Men of the Pit* (the *'Pit'* vocabulary we have already called attention to in connection with that of *'the Maschil'* and, of course, Jesus' famous soliloquy on *'the Pharisees'* as *'Bind Guides'* above) *in a spirit of secrecy* (here, too, the *'Secret'/'Secrecy'* vocabulary we have also already called attention to *above*)...*Rather he shall be like a man zealous for the Law* (that is, *'a Zealot'* as, for instance, in Acts 21:20's characterization of the majority of the James' *'Jerusalem Church'* supporters as *'Zelotai'/ 'Zealots for the Law'*), *whose time is for the Day of Vengeance* (here again 'the Day of Vengeance' vocabulary), *to do* (the third occurrence of this pivotal usage in this particular passage) *His will in all the work* (the fourth) *of his hands and in all His Kingdom as He Commanded* (that is, here again one is instructed *'to do the Commandments'* and not ignore them and, to some extent, as Jonadab son of Rechab *'commanded'* to his descendants in the missing introduction to James of Jeremiah 35:1-19).[106]

That anyone could even conceive that allusions such as these relate to any century other than the First, even in the face of *'external* (albeit fallible) *data'* to the contrary – such as radiocarbon dating or palaeographic-sequencing typologies, which we have already subjected to extensive criticism in the Preliminary Section of this book and which are all subject to human error – shows a distinct lack of historical prescience or insight.

As already noted, such *'sectarian'* documents, themselves showing every indication of being from the last stages of Qumran ideology and not the first, must, because of internal consistencies of *sitz im leben* (life setting), vocabulary, *dramatis personae*, and fundamental conceptualities, all have been written at around the same time – other, more external, indications notwithstanding. This is what is meant by going according to the 'internal' evidence as opposed to the 'external' and the fallible 'results' of archaeology, carbon testing, and palaeography.[107] There are, in fact, internal indicators in documents other than the War Scroll and Community Rule, as we have been suggesting, which also show a distinct First-Century provenance – as, for instance, in the Habakkuk, Isaiah, Nahum, and Psalm 37 *Peshers*, the Messianic *Florilegium*, the Testimonia, and the like, as opposed to the 'external' and fallible 'results' of the data previously mentioned.[108]

The correspondence here between the War Scroll and the Community Rule on the subject of '*the Day of Vengeance*' is the kind of thing one is talking about that implies chronological contemporaneity. It is precise. The same is true of the Qumran Hymns, where similar allusions abound and '*the Day of Vengeance*' is, rather, referred to as '*the Day of Massacre*,'[109] but the effect is the same.

As the War Scroll ends up putting these things:

> *No one who is impure in the manner of sexual emissions (is to join their camps), for the Holy Angels are with their Hosts.*[110]

This allusion to '*the Heavenly Host*' actually being with '*the Walkers in the Way of Perfect Holiness*' and in their '*Desert*' or '*Wilderness Camps*' is again a pervasive one at Qumran, running through many of the documents, including more-recently revealed portions of the Damascus Document as it was found in Cave 4 at Qumran and not necessarily at Cairo.[111]

Not only does it have everything to do with the vision of *the Heavenly Host* '*coming on the clouds of Heaven*' dominating the proclamation James is pictured as making in all early Church literature, it absolutely explains *the regime of extreme 'purity'* followed in these '*camps*' where, unlike Paul's world-view as expressed in his Letters of '*all things being lawful to me*' (once more, he clearly means by this, '*lawful*' relative to '*Roman law*' not '*Jewish*'), '*Holy*' was absolutely to be '*separated from profane*' and '*the Holy Things*' were absolutely to be

> set up according to their precise specifications (that is, '*according to the Commandment of those who entered the New Covenant in the Land of Damascus*'), to love each man his brother as himself ('*the Royal Law according to the Scripture*' of the Letter of James 2:8 above), to strengthen the hand of the Meek (the early Church '*strengthening*'/'*Protection-of-the-People*'/'*Bulwark*' language as applied to James' role in the Community he directed in Jerusalem), *the Poor* ('*Ebion*' again), *and the Convert* (our cadre of Gentile '*Nilvim*' or '*Joiners*' yet again,'*attached to the Community*')...*and not to uncover the nakedness of near kin* (meaning, of course, *marriage with nieces and close*

cousins once more – *Herodian family policy*, as we have pointed out though, demonstrably, *not Maccabean*), *to keep away from fornication* (the exact language of James' directives to overseas communities as conserved in Acts, including even the phraseology, '*keep away from*,' based on the same Hebrew '*N-Z-R*' root as '*Nazirite*')...*to separate from all pollutions* (again the '*separation*' ideology)...(*and*) *walk in these things in Perfect Holiness* (that is, the '*Perfect Holiness*' regime; *cf.* Paul in 2 Corinthians 6:16–7:1 above, which includes even the '*walking*,' '*separation*,' and '*Perfection of Holiness*' usages) *on the basis of the Covenant of God, in which they were instructed, faithfully promising them, they would live for a thousand generations.*[112]

We shall see more about this '*thousand generations*' later but, once again, not only is this the exact opposite of the vision allegedly vouchsafed to Peter in Acts' '*descent of the Heavenly tablecloth*' episode (more amusing divertissement?); in fact, the whole regime of '*extreme purity*' in these '*Camps*' is the very opposite of that delineated in the Gospels as being followed and recommended by their 'Jesus,' portrayed as accepting of and finally even '*keeping table fellowship with*' a wide assortment of persons who would otherwise be considered absolutely '*unclean*' at Qumran.[113]

Interestingly enough, this description in the War Scroll now ends with a directive about the placement of the camp latrines out of sight, so '*no indecent nakedness will be seen surrounding any camp*,' markedly contrasting with the Gospel point of '*nothing from without defiling the man*.'[114] Not only do these '*latrines*' form a subject of some interest in the Temple Scroll which, where '*the Temple*' is concerned, places them to the northwest of the city, far enough away so that those sacrificing might not see or be seen by anyone so occupied;[114] it is a subject upon which Josephus also focuses in his extensive description of *the toilet-habits of the Essenes*.[116]

This is not to forget – New Testament amusing and fertile caricature aside – the *Talmud*'s own disparaging exposition and like-minded parody of Honi's grandson '*Hanan the Hidden*''s cognomen as having been applied to him '*because he used to hide himself in the latrine*.'[117] Nor should one forget the whole subject of such '*latrine*'s raised in the tradition associated with '*Jesus the Nazoraean*' in the *Talmud*, already reviewed above and relative to all these subjects, about what to do with '*a prostitute's hire*' given to '*the Temple*'; and Jesus' alleged response, as communicated to '*Jacob of Kfar Sechania*' via R. Eliezer ben Hyrcanus, recommending that it be used to construct '*a latrine for the High Priest*,' followed by the comment – not unlike Matthew 15:18's '*casting down the toilet drain*' allusion too – '*it was raised from filth and to filth it should return*.'[118]

15

James' Proclamation in the Temple and Joining the Heavenly Holy Ones

'Joining the Heavenly Holy Ones' in Hymns, the Community Rule, and the War Scroll at Qumran

This idea of striving for bodily and spiritual *'Perfect Holiness'* so as *not to pollute the purity of the Host of Heavenly Holy Ones* is a fixture of Qumran documents like the War Scroll and Hymns. It is also present in the Community Rule and Damascus Document – again demonstrating the basic homogeneity of all these documents and their simultaneity, chronologically speaking – that is, if we have demonstrated chronological ambiance (in our view, the First Century) for one such document employing usages of this kind, then we have basically demonstrated it for most or all such documents employing usages of this kind.

As this *'Communion' with the Sons of Heaven* is described in Hymns (how much closer to Paul's more Hellenized conceptuality of *'Communion with the body'* and *'blood of the Christ'* can one get without actually enunciating it?), which abounds with the imagery of *'the soul of the Righteous'* or *'Poor One,'* pre-existent and Divine sonship, and the idea, finally, of *'standing'* before God in a state of *'Perfect Light for all Eternity'*:

> *You have shaped him from the dust for an Eternal Foundation* (in Hebrew, *'Sod,'* which can also mean *'Secret'*) *and cleansed a straying Spirit of great sin* (here, possibly, the ideological underpinning for all the interest in the Gospels in portraying of 'Jesus' as *exorcizing 'unclean spirit'*s) *that it may stand on a plain with the Host of the Holy Ones* and *join with the Community of the Sons of Heaven* (and of course, as usual, the 'standing' notation).[1]

Here, too, the imagery of *'joining'* is now being used in a new fashion suggesting *'joining with Heavenly Beings.'* This is not unsimilar to Paul in 1 Corinthians 6:16–17 as well, where this imagery is rather applied to *'joining with harlots'* under the general rubric of the favorite Qumran subject *'fornication'* or, later in 12:12–28, where the *'joining'* is now with *'the body of Christ'* – echoed, for example, in Ephesians 2:19–22. In fact, the latter basically becomes '*the Household*' or '*Building of God*,' '*a Holy Temple in the Lord*,' and '*a Dwelling-place of God in the Spirit*,' all, of course, very allegorized or spiritualized and very much like what we see developing here in these allusions at Qumran from Hymns.[2]

'*Standing*' imagery is of course always important, as we have emphasized, particularly as it implies '*Resurrection*' and where the Ebionite/Pseudoclementine ideology of the '*incarnated Messiah*' or '*Primal Adam*' as '*the Standing One*' is concerned.[3] Therefore, too, as we have already suggested as well, throughout much of the imagery one gets in documents such as the Gospels, the subject of '*his feet*' or '*footwear*' becomes of such interest – presumably the only part of '*the Standing One's* body visible to a mere mortal – as, for instance, John 1:26–27, also evoking '*standing*' imagery, on even John the Baptist being '*unworthy to untie His* (Jesus') *shoe lace*' (itself probably having something to do with '*the Shiloh*' imagery).[4]

In the next column of Hymns, following evocation of this '*War*' *of the Heavenly Holy Ones that will scourge the earth until the appointed Destruction*, its author again describes God as *manifesting Himself in his Power* (the Ebionite/Elchasaite '*Great Power*' imagery again) '*as Perfect Light*.'[5] This comes right before yet another passage about '*the Way of Man* ('*Enosh*' – the name applied to John the Baptist in Mandaean literature) *and the Perfection of the Way of the Son of Man*' ('*Adam*' – Jesus' designation in Scripture) and reference, once again, to '*standing*' before God and being '*established victoriously*' forever.[6]

This idea of '*Victory*' is encountered throughout the Qumran Hymns and we have already called attention to how Paul uses it in 1 Corinthians 15:54–57 above in discussing '*the First Man*' and '*the Last Adam*' – a discussion in which he, once again, reverses the '*swallowing*' imagery so widespread and intrinsic to the Qumran mindset.[7] Aside from a clear play by Paul on the sort of language being used in the Habakkuk *Pesher* to describe '*the Righteous Teacher*' and his followers among '*the Poor*' being '*swallowed*' by '*the Wicked Priest*' (the sense there, as with the '*eaten*' that follows, clearly being '*destroyed*') and '*the Wicked Priest*,' in turn, *being* '*swallowed*' *by* '*the Cup of the Right Hand of God*,' a synonym for '*the Cup of the Wrath of God*'[8] – for Paul now, it is '*death being swallowed up in Victory*.' Paul means of course by this, '*the Victory*' which the Lord Jesus Christ *gives to his followers over death* and *not the victory of the Heavenly Host over God's enemies* as in the War Scroll and other like-minded such proclamations. Here Paul, as we have already remarked, is at his polemical, allegorical, and triumphant best.

In 1 Corinthians 15:51, using the '*secrecy*' imagery of his opponents – just alluded to in Hymns above and in the Community Rule earlier –

'*the Heavenly Secret*' or '*Mystery*' being referred to is, again, the '*Victory*' over death and the transformation of the body into the more supernatural substance of Heavenly Being. Paul uses the same language, yet again, in 2 Corinthians 2:14–15 to express the '*Triumph*' or '*Victory in the Christ*' (*thus!*) exemplified by those who '*are a sweet perfume of Christ to God,*' '*making the odour of the Knowledge* ('*Gnosis*') *of him manifest in every place*' (more rhetorical Hellenizing strophe/antistrophe/epode word-play?).

Again, this language of being '*a sweet perfume*' or '*odour*' is the same as the Community Rule applies to the '*building,*' '*Bulwark,*' and '*atonement*' activities of its Community Council (composed of '*Twelve Israelites*' and '*Three Priests*' – the '*Three Priests*' here, in another play, being a spiritualized '*Holy of Holies*' or '*Inner Sanctum for Aaron*'), namely, their being '*a sweet smell of Righteousness and Perfection of the Way.*'[9]

Again, the analogue with Paul should be patent. In exploiting the imagery – as Paul exploits it in 1 Corinthians and Ephesians above – of this '*Council*' as both '*House of Holiness*'/'*Temple for Israel*' and '*Holy of Holies for Aaron,*' the Community Rule then describes this '*Council*' – like '*the Righteous Teacher*' in the Habakkuk *Pesher* and '*the Sons of Zadok*' in the Damascus Document – as '*paying the Wicked their reward*'[10] – that is, just like these last, they participate in what now commonly goes by the denotation of '*the Last Judgement.*'

The Community Rule also applies a whole series of descriptions to this '*Council*' which precede and, as it were, serve to introduce its twofold quotation of '*the Way in the wilderness*' citation from Isaiah 40:3 and its exposition – ending, not insignificantly, as we saw, in evocation of '*being Zealots for the Law and the Day of Vengeance.*' These include: '*an Eternal Plantation*' (a metaphor, as we have underscored, also used at the beginning of the Damascus Document to describe the '*Visitation*' *by God that caused the Messianic* '*Root of Planting to grow out of Israel and Aaron*'[11]), '*a House of Perfection and Truth for Israel*' (again the '*House*' or '*building*' imagery found as well in Paul[12]), '*a tried Bulwark*' (again, the metaphor applied to James, both along with and paralleling the '*Oblias*' designation in early Church descriptions of his role in the Jerusalem of his day), '*a Precious Cornerstone which would not shake or sway on its Foundations*' (familiar imagery from Isaiah 28:16 that was also applied to Jesus in both the Gospels and also allegedly, for example, by Paul in Ephesians 2:20[13]), and '*an acceptable free will offering*' – totally spiritualized '*sacrifice*' and '*atonement*' and the same imagery we have already seen Paul apply to Epaphroditus in Philippians 4:18 above, but exactly parallel to what he and all others seem to have been applying to '*Jesus*' in early Christianity and ever after as well.

In these climactic metaphors in the Community Rule, the member of this '*Council*' would

> keep Faith in the Land with steadfastness and a humble spirit and atone for sin
> by doing Judgement (as always one should again note the 'Jamesian' empha-
> sis on '*doing*,' this time, '*doing Judgement*' – at Qumran, as we have seen, the
> basis of '*works' Righteousness*'/'*maᶜasim*') and *suffering affliction* (of course,
> the essence of the presentation of '*Jesus*' in Pauline theology and in
> Gentile Christianity generally, based on '*the Suffering Servant justifying
> Many*' from Isaiah 53:11).[14]

This Council was also to '*make atonement for the Land and render Judgement
on Evil*' (this is the same '*Judgement on Evil*' we shall encounter in the
Habakkuk and Psalm 37 *Peshers* below[15]) – the imagery once again of
both '*atonement*' and participation in '*the Last Judgement*.' It was also, in
further '*sacrifice*' and '*spiritualized atonement*' imagery, to

> offer up a sweet perfume with Everlasting Knowledge of the Covenant and Judge-
> ment (this is replaced by the offering up of the '*sweet perfume of Christ*'
> in 2 Corinthians 2:14-15 above).

Where the first part of this last metaphor is concerned, one should – as
just signaled – also have regard to Paul's description of Epaphroditus (his
'*brother, fellow-worker, and soldier*' in Philippians 2:25) as

> a sweet smell, an odour of an acceptable free will offering, well-pleasing to God
> (4:18).[16]

The parallel of course is precise.

Where the second part is concerned, evoking '*Everlasting Knowledge*'
or '*Gnosis*' once again – only this time, of course, with the not insignificant addition of '*of the Covenant*,' this reference to '*Judgement*' can likewise
be seen as transformed and enlarged upon by Paul in 1 Corinthians
11:24–29 above – following his version of '*Communion with the body*' and
'*the blood of Christ*,' a series of formulations he also claims to have '*received
from the Lord*' (one wonders in just what manner he '*received*' this) and
which he claims, also in a quasi-play on '*the night in which he was delivered
up*' in the very same line, he '*also delivered unto you*' (11:23 – *sic*!) – with
his own version of such an imprecation (we have already partially reproduced previously as well):

> So therefore whoever should eat this bread or drink the Cup of the Lord in an

unworthy way shall be guilty of the body and blood of the Lord (a terrifying accusation – but he even goes further, playing on the *'eating and drinking'* theme again)*...for he who eats and drinks unworthily, eats and drinks Judgement to himself* (the *'eating and drinking'* motif again, but this time, quite literally, *'with a vengeance'*)*, not seeing through to the body of the Lord.*[17]

The implications of all these things for subsequent history – especially in the light of his rather deprecating allusion with which he began in 1 Corinthians 1:18–19 to *'schisms'* and *'heresies among you'* and, even more recently, in what ultimately transpired in our times – is simply frightening.

For its part, in summation, for the Community Rule all these things are being done to *'prepare in the wilderness the Way for the Lord'* and *'establish an Everlasting Covenant of Laws'* – this last, anyhow, a one-hundred-and-eighty-degree inversion of Paul's understanding of what such a *'Covenant'* must finally turn out to mean or even what might have been *'prepared in the wilderness.'*

'The Sons of the Everlasting Foundation'

Hymns also takes up the idea of the *'First Man'* or *'Primal Adam being made of'* or *'rising out of the dust,'* encountered in these closing passages from Paul in 1 Corinthians 15:48, in a later, particularly exultant passage:

For the sake of Your Glory, You have purified Man (Enosh) of sin, that he may be made Holy (or *'consecrated'*) *to You* (that is, *'made'* either a *'Nazirite'* or a Priest) *from all the Abominations of uncleanness and guilty rebellion* (here the allusion to *'uncleanness'* again and the opposite, for instance, of the portrait of *'Jesus"* position on *'uncleanness'* in Matthew and Mark's presentation of his *'Toilet Bowl'* Parable, to say nothing about what Peter learns concerning *'calling things unclean'* in Acts' subsequent picture of his vision of *'the Heavenly tablecloth'*) *to be Sons of Your Truth with the Lot of Your Holy Ones* (here both the Divine *'Sonship'* motif and the *'Joining'* with the *'Heavenly Host'* or *'the Sons of Heaven,'* a different kind of *'Heavenly'* conjunction than what Paul is seemingly delineating and the opposite of what is to happen to those *'of the Lot of Belial'* in the War Scroll above[18])*, to rise from the dust of the worm-eaten dead as a Foundation* (the *'Foundation'* imagery just encountered in the Community Rule above or, as noted in this regard as well, possibly *'a Secret'*)*...to stand before You* (again, the *'standing'* imagery) *equal with the Eternal Host and the Spirits to be made Holy with all Eternal Being'*[19]

One could hardly get much closer to Paul and his strictures at the end of 1 Corinthians 15:51–57 above about the *'Heavenly Secret'* and *'being raised up incorruptibly,'* though *'changed,'* than this. These are the kinds of things one means by *'internal'* dating parameters being decisive or going according to the *'internal,'* not the *'external data.'*

'The Spirits,' referred to here, are also the same sort of *'Spirits'* we shall see below in the War Scroll's vision of *the Heavenly Host 'coming on the clouds' in final eschatological Judgement* and what, in Islam, is expressed by the usage *'Ginn'* (*'Genie'* in English).[20] One begins to understand to what all this emphasis by these *'Essene'/'Sabaean'/'Zealot'* and/or *'Messianic'* groups on *'purity,' 'Naziritism,' 'daily bathing,'* and the like related.

The Community Rule expresses similar ideas in its earlier columns, amid repeated allusion to *'Light and Darkness,' 'purifying oneself,'* and *'bathing,'* in outlining the stages in *'joining the Community of'* – and, therefore, *'Communion with'* – *the Heavenly Holy Ones'* – before ultimately building up to its two-fold evocation in its later Columns 8–9 of these important chronological indicators, *'making a straight Way in the wilderness'* and *'zeal for the Law and the Day of Vengeance:'*

> *No man from the House* (in the preceding line expressed as *'the House of the Community of God'*) *will move down from his allotted level or move up from his allotted standing* (yet another of these important allusions to *'standing,'* though perhaps this time with a somewhat different implication), *because all are in a Community of Truth, virtuous Humility, the love of Piety* (or *'Grace'*), *and thoughtful Righteousness, each towards his neighbor* (another variation on *'the Royal Law according to the Scripture'* in the Letter of James, *'love your neighbor as yourself'*) *in a Holy Community, the Sons of the Everlasting Foundation* (*'Sod'* – again also possibly *'Secret'*).[21]

Not only do we have here the two *'Love'* Commandments, portrayed as the essence of both Jesus' teaching in the New Testament and James' in all early Church sources, including the Letter ascribed to his name[22]; but the same language of *'each towards his neighbor'* is paralleled later in this *'Rule'* document and in pivotal sections of the Damascus Document having to do with *'separating Holy from profane'* and where *'the New Covenant in the Land of Damascus'* – *'to love each man his brother as himself'* – is also being defined.[23] Josephus alludes to this same combination, as we have emphasized and which I have already called the *'Righteousness'/ 'Piety'* dichotomy, as *'Piety towards God and Righteousness towards one's fellow man'* in his famous description of both John the Baptist and those he designates as *'Essenes.'*[24]

The rigidity of this communal hierarchy – characteristic of all the documents at Qumran – is paralleled in the Preface to the Pseudo-clementine *Homilies* in passages, already remarked above and represented as being James' speech to '*the assembled Elders,*' to which they react with '*fear and trembling.*'[25] As always, it is gainsaid and reversed in Paul's writings where, in his usual manner exploiting his masterful control of allegory, rhetoric, and polemics, while at the same time displaying seemingly prior knowledge of both the Qumran and '*Jewish Christian*' positions on these issues; he, at one and the same time, attacks both the favored position of James-like figures in the Leadership of '*the Jerusalem Church*' *and* the Hebrew/Jewish emphasis on '*chosenness*' with the customary assault on James and the '*Pillar*' Apostles. This he accomplishes, in particular as we have seen, with his opening salvos in the Letter to the Galatians relating to not being '*an Apostle from men or through men*' (1:1) and not '*seeking to please men*' or '*announcing a Gospel according to men*' (1:10–11); and later in Galatians 2:6 with his claim, '*God does not accept the person of man*' or, put in other words, '*God has no favorites.*'

Paul expresses a similar point in his famous depiction in 1 Corinthians 15:1–10 (starting off, not surprisingly, with yet another variation on the '*standing*' vocabulary, to wit, '*the Gospel...in which you also stand, by which you are also being saved*') of the order of Jesus' post-resurrection appearances. Though not without its interpolations[26], in some manner this seems to have been thought of as establishing one's position within the early '*Church*' or '*Assembly.*' It ends with the well-known:

> *And Last of all (he appeared) to me. I was born when no one expected it, as if to one born out of term* (or, to put it perhaps more accurately, '*as if to an abortion*' – 1 Corinthians 15:8).

This '*Last*' terminology and its counterpart, '*the First,*' as he expresses it here, is normally applied, as we just saw, to the '*standing*' of '*the First*' within the '*Jerusalem Church*' Hierarchy; but, in the Hebrew of the Damascus Document, '*the First*' also refers to '*the Ancestors*' or '*the Forefathers*' to whom, by implication, '*the First Covenant*' was vouchsafed.[27] The combination is also picked up in beloved though '*Paulinized*' sayings – spinning off, in the view of the present writer, from Paul's assertion here – attributed to 'Jesus' in Scripture, such as '*the Last shall be First and the First shall be Last*' (Matthew 19:30 and *pars.*).[28] The '*First*'/'*Last*' contraposition also permeates Qumran usage, where it has another important elaboration which contrasts '*the Covenant of the First*' with '*the Last Times*' or '*Last Days.*'[29]

The '*House*' or '*Household*' imagery, one encounters in the Community Rule's description of '*the Sons of the Everlasting Foundation*,' also occurs throughout the relevant literature. In other variations at Qumran, it becomes '*the House of the Torah*,' which the Damascus Document uses to describe '*the Community of God*' in its final summing-up passages having to do with *the Promises of 'the New Covenant in the Land of Damascus*' and those who have not '*turned aside*' and '*betrayed the Well of Living Waters*' that was being '*dug*' there.[30] In crucial passages again later in the Community Rule, which introduce '*the making a straight Way in the wilderness*' citations, this '*House*' imagery is – as in Paul – once again used allegorically, as we just saw, to characterize '*the Twelve Israelite*' *members of the Community Council* (the counterpart of '*the Twelve Apostles*' in the Gospels) as '*a House of Holiness for Israel*' – spiritualized '*Temple*' imagery again – and *the inner 'Three Priests*' as '*a House of the Holy of Holies for Israel*' (the counterpart of '*the Central Three*' in both Galatians 2:9 and the Synoptics[31]) – now spiritualized '*Inner Sanctum*' imagery.[32]

In 1 Corinthians 3:9-17 earlier, Paul had already used a variation of this '*House*'/'*Household*' imagery, preceded in 1 Corinthians 2:4–13 by '*the Secret*'/'*Mystery*'/'*being Hidden*' language in his discussion about '*teaching spiritual things spiritually*' and '*speaking Wisdom among the Perfect*' (any allusion to '*the Perfect*' or '*Perfection*' is always significant[33]). It is interesting that in reiterating this latter he actually is using the language of '*being Hidden*' which we have so focused upon earlier:

> We speak the Wisdom of God in a Mystery, Hidden and predetermined before the Ages for our Glory...which God has prepared for those who love Him (1Corinthians 2:7).

This last, of course, is the second part of the '*Righteousness*'/'*Piety*' dichotomy defined by Josephus, where '*Essenes*' were concerned, as we just saw – to say nothing of John the Baptist – as '*Piety towards God*.' As usual, one should compare this language with that of James 2:5, leading up to its citation of '*the Royal Law according to the Scripture*' in 2:9, on '*the Kingdom* – in his case, now specifically applied to the all-important '*Poor*' whom '*God chose*' – *promised to those who love Him*.'

This is the language, then, that Paul uses to introduce his '*building*' imagery in 1 Corinthians 3:9–17 above – imagery, once again, seemingly parodying or being parodied by Qumran documents such as the Habakkuk *Pesher* in its description of the nemesis of its Righteous Teacher, '*the Spouter of Lies*'/'*Man of Lying*,' as '*building a Community on blood*' and '*Lying*' (we shall decipher this '*building a Community on blood*' allusion in more detail towards the end of this book).[34]

Paul uses this language, not only by repeatedly playing on the *'laying the Foundation(s)'* symbolism, one encounters in Qumran documents like the Community Rule and Hymns above;[35] but by picturing himself as the *'architect,'* the Community he *'planted'* – which *'Apollos watered, but which God caused to grow'* – as *'God's building'* (compare this with *'God visiting them and causing a Root of Planting to grow out of Israel and Aaron to inherit His land and prosper on the good things of His earth'* in the famous introduction to the Damascus Document we have already covered above, regarding Jesus' alleged insistence in Matthew 15:13 on *'uprooting'* the things His *'Heavenly Father has not planted'*[36]) and, over and over again (once again seemingly parodying the Community Rule on *'the Twelve'* above being *'a Holy House'* or *'Temple for Israel'*) by speaking of *'the Holiness of the Temple of God'* (1 Corinthians 3:9–17).

Paul continues this imagery in 2 Corinthians 5:1, again tying it to some extent to discussion at the end of 1 Corinthians (12:12–27) of *'Jesus' as Temple* and *'the members'* of the Community as *'the parts of Christ's body'* (that is, the imagery of *'the Community as Temple'* again). Here, once again – echoing this same simile in the Scrolls – he picks up the *'building'* imagery by referring either to the Community or one's own body or both as *'a building from God, a House not made with human hands but Eternal in Heaven,'* which brings us right back to the Community Rule's language of *'the House'* as *'a Holy Community – the Sons of the Everlasting Foundation.'*

'Loving God' and *'Inheriting the Lot of the Holy Ones'*

The *'loving Piety'* – on which this *'Community of Truth,'* *'thoughtful Righteousness,'* and Divine *'Sonship'* is supposed to be based – is important as the first of the two *'Love'* Commandments Scripture also attributes to Jesus[37] – namely, as we just saw, *'loving God.'* As we just saw as well, both 1 Corinthians 2:9 and James 2:5 pick up the same formulation in *'the Hidden Wisdom of God in a Mystery'* (clearly a variation of the *'Logos'* doctrine of the Gospel of John and the equivalent in Greek of *'the Primal Adam'* in languages and cultures further East) or *'the Kingdom He prepared for those who Love Him,'* the latter in James preceding its enunciation in 2:8 of the second of these two *'Love'* Commandments (attributed to 'Jesus' in the Synoptics): *'Love your neighbor as yourself'* or, as Josephus would have it in his description of John the Baptist, *'Righteousness towards one's fellow man.'*

Paul alludes to such *'love of God'* – albeit very subtly – once again later in 1 Corinthians 8:3, this time in a crucial yet fulsome attack on the Jamesian Leadership of '*the Jerusalem Church*,' denoted by him somewhat facetiously as '*those who have Knowledge*' ('*Gnosis*' once again). This is yet another of those three-line rhetorical flourishes, more or less consisting of strophe, antistrophe, and epode, this time centering around this same celebrated Greek word '*Gnosis*,' meaning, '*knowing*' or '*known by*,' in the sense that '*if anyone loves God, then he is known by him*.'

This bravura rhetorical performance employs the same language of '*being puffed up*' that the Habakkuk *Pesher*, as already alluded to, applies to one of its two nemeses (in the sense of asserting that *his* – in this case, '*the Wicked Priest*''s – '*punishment will be multiplied upon him*' because he '*destroyed*' the *Righteous Teacher*[38]), and the '*building*' imagery, the *Pesher* also applies to the other ('*the Liar*' – in 1 Corinthians 8:1, it should be re-marked, Paul now caustically ties this same '*building*' language to the '*love*' metaphor, that is, '*but love builds up*'), to once again attack this same '*Jerusalem Church*' Leadership[39] – then leads into Paul's own tortured rejection in 8:3–13 of James' prohibition of '*things sacrificed to idols*' and his self-serving explanation of why such '*idols*' are '*nothing in this world*.'

Aside from portraying this '*Righteousness*'/'*Piety*' dichotomy as the essence of the teaching of both James and Jesus in early Church litera-ture, a variation based on a more Romanizing interpretation and allegiance is also to be found in Paul. For instance, in Romans 13:5–10, already cited earlier – in a characterization which, no doubt, would have sent his more '*Zealot*' critics or opponents into paroxysms of indignation, Paul uses the command to '*love one another*' (John 13:34–35 and 15:12) and the '*Royal Law according to the Scripture*' in James, '*love your neighbor as your-self*,' as already underscored, to recommend paying taxes to Rome!

Not only do both commandments permeate the Scrolls, as we have been underscoring as well, but Josephus picks them up in his references to the group he designates as '*Essenes*' to divide up his description of its practices on their basis.[40] Under '*Piety towards*' or '*loving God*,' he groups all the peculiarly '*Essene*' duties towards God, including daily bathing practices, extreme ritual cleanliness, and other ceremonial activities. Under '*Righteousness towards your fellow man*,' he groups all the others.[41] Moreover, even more importantly for our purposes and for documents like the Community Rule, which we have just been examining, and also for Gospel portraiture – in this area manifestly selective and ten-dentious – he unequivocally denotes in his *Antiquities* (about twenty years after his *Jewish War*) these two commandments as *the essence of John the Baptist's teaching* '*in the wilderness*,' that is to say, '*John taught Piety towards God and Righteousness towards one's fellow man*.'

In addition, to this he appends a description of John's baptism as '*a water cleansing*' or '*immersion*' for the body only, '*provided that the soul had already been previously purified by the practice of Righteousness*.'[42] A more precise description of John's baptism is probably not to be found. Furthermore, it could not agree more with the description found in Columns 4–6 of the Community Rule – but not with the more Paulinized portrait of these things we encounter in the New Testament, which includes '*Grace*' and '*baptism via the Holy Spirit*.' Though ideas such as these are alluded to to some extent in the Community Rule as well, nowhere in the New Testament do we find anything about '*daily baptism*' for bodily cleanliness or ritual purification as we find it in Josephus, Rabbinical literature, and/or in the Scrolls.[43]

As the Community Rule progresses, it also speaks both of a '*Visitation*' and the notion of '*concealing the Truth of the Mysteries of Knowledge*' (*Gnosis*),[44] which we have just encountered almost word-for-word in Paul above. Not only does it use the language he uses of '*Mystery*' and '*Victory*,' but it adds that of '*a Crown of Glory*' (imagery applied to '*Stephen*' in early Church literature, whose name in Greek, it will be recalled, literally translates out as '*Crown*'[45]) and '*Eternal Light*':

> *These are the Secrets of the Spirit* ('*Sod*' again, now plural – a variation also of Paul's '*not in words taught by Man's Wisdom but in words taught by the Holy Spirit imparting spiritual things spiritually*' approach in 1 Corinthians 2:13 above) *for the earthly Sons of Truth* and *the Visitation of all the Walkers in (the Holy Spirit) will be for healing and healthiness for long days...and Eternal joy in a Victorious life and a Crown of Glory with the imperishable clothing in Eternal Light.*

Here too is the theme of '*long-lived Essenes*,' which so permeates Josephus,' Philo's, and Hippolytus' descriptions of the members of this group, a theme also characteristic of the '*Jamesian*' Jerusalem Church and '*Ebionite*' literature generally, where James was supposed to *have lived for* '*ninety-six years*' and Simeon bar Cleophas, his '*brother*'/'*cousin*'/or successor in the Leadership of '*the Jerusalem Community*,' '*a hundred and twenty*.'[46]

One should also compare the language of '*a Crown of Glory*' and '*the imperishable clothing in Eternal Light*' in these concluding passages of the Community Rule with Paul's view of '*being raised up incorruptibly*' above in 1 Corinthians 15:52 and '*Ebionite*'/'*Elchasaite*' literature, generally, of being '*clothed with Adam*' or '*the Secret*' or '*Primal Adam*' putting on the clothing of men's bodies in multitudinous incarnations and, then, *taking it off again*.[47] In earlier descriptions of '*Holy Spirit*' baptism, the Community Rule finally reaches a climactic highpoint and wrestles with these '*Eternal*' matters with the words:

> *Then Truth, which wallowed in the Ways of Evil in the Government of Unright-*
> *eousness* (the Romans, the Herodians? – *cf.* too, Paul's '*so by speaking Truth*
> *to you, your Enemy have I become?*' in Galatians 4:16) *until the time of the*
> *appointed Judgement, will emerge Victorious in the world, and God with His*
> *Truth will refine all the works of man and purify for Himself the sons of men,*
> *perfecting all the Spirit of Unrighteousness within his flesh* (the overwhelming
> amount of Pauline vocabulary in these lines is clearly breathtaking) *and*
> *purifying it by means of the Holy Spirit from all Evil actions. He will pour upon*
> *him the Spirit of Truth like cleansing waters (washing him) of all the Abomina-*
> *tions of Lying.*[48]

Not only is this last indistinguishable from what goes by the name of '*the descent of the Holy Spirit*' or '*Holy Spirit Baptism*' in orthodox New Testament parlance, but, as can be seen, it is aimed squarely at the individual with '*the Lying Spirit*' or, in other words, a genus of individual character-ized by '*the Abominations of Lying.*' Once again, too, we have copious allu-sion to the language of '*Judgement*' ('*the Last Judgement*'), '*works,*' '*Truth,*' '*Victoriousness,*' '*purification,*' '*baptism,*' and '*Perfection.*' The text continues as follows:

> *And he shall be plunged into the Spirit of Purification, so as to illumine the*
> *Upright (the Upright,*' a verbal noun based on the same root as Isaiah
> 40:3's '*straightening the Way*') *with Knowledge of the Most High* (Paul's
> '*Knowledge*' vocabulary that so '*puffs up*' those who '*have*' it in 1 Corin-
> thians 8:1–3 introducing his position in 8:4 – relative to '*things sacrificed*
> *to idols*' – on '*knowing that an idol is nothing in this world*'!) *and the Wisdom*
> *of the Sons of Heaven to teach the Perfect of the Way* (again, language exactly
> paralleling Paul in 1 Corinthians 2:4–8 above and, obviously, an actual
> name for the adherents of this Community), *whom God has chosen as an*
> *Everlasting Covenant* (once more, this language of the '*Everlasting Cove-*
> *nant*' or '*Foundation*' – the idea of '*the Chosen*' or '*the Elect*' in both the
> Damascus Document and the Habakkuk *Pesher* clearly denoting '*the Sons*
> *of Zadok*'), *and all the Glory of Adam will be theirs, without any Unrighteous-*
> *ness.*[49]

Again, not only do we have here a variation on what goes by the name of '*Holy Spirit baptism*' according to New Testament characteriza-tion, but it is not difficult to recognize a version of the '*Essene*'/

'Ebionite'/'Elchasaite'/'Sabaean''Primal Adam'- ideology, also to be found, as we have been showing, at critical junctures of the War Scroll and Damascus Document[50] and so characteristic of all baptizing groups across Jordan up into Northern Syria and down into Southern Iraq – in our view, yet again demonstrating the basic homogeneity and contemporaneous quality of all these documents where Qumran is concerned (palaeographic and/or AMS carbon testing dating-parameters notwithstanding).

As we just saw as well, the text also knows the language of ordinary baptism, prefacing this more 'Holy Spirit'-oriented procedure with an allusion to routine and probably 'Daily' ritual immersion as follows:

> Whoever ploughs the mud of Wickedness returns defiled and he shall not be justified by what his stubborn heart permits (another reference to a genus of a Paul-like nay-sayer or backslider)...nor reckoned among the Perfect Ones (again the 'Perfect' ideology and 'the Perfect Ones' as a name for this Community), nor shall he be cleansed by atonements, nor purified by cleansing waters, nor sanctified by seas and rivers, nor washed clean by any waters of ablution;

for, 'seeking the Ways of Light, he has looked towards Darkness,' 'rejecting the Laws of God' (also called 'the Ordinances of Righteousness').[51] The language of 'rejecting' – in particular, 'rejecting the Laws of God' – will be important throughout the corpus at Qumran and applied quintessentially, in the Habakkuk Pesher in particular, to the opponent of the Righteous Teacher, 'the Man of Lying' or 'Pourer out'/'Spouter of Lying' par excellence.[52]

If we were to look at this from a 'Jewish Christian' or 'Ebionite' perspective (and, in the writer's opinion, that of Qumran as well) – taking an individual like James 'the brother of the Lord' or John the Baptist as the type of 'the Righteous Teacher' – then there can be little doubt that the genus of individual being described so negatively here resembles Paul more perhaps than any other historically-identifiable person.[53] On the other hand, the 'Sins' of a person of the opposite genus, one who 'undertakes the Covenant before God to do all that He commanded' (the 'doing' vocabulary again), not to 'depart from the Laws of His Truth to walk either to the right or to the left' (these very words will be repeated in the last Column of the Damascus Document, not to mention basically by James to Paul in their last confrontation in Acts 21:24), and 'walks perfectly in all the Ways of God,'[54]

> will be atoned for, so he can look on the Living Light and he will be cleansed

of all his sins by the Holy Spirit (there can be no more *'perfect'* picture of 'Holy Spirit' baptism than this) *joining him to His Truth* (our imagery 'joining' again). *And he will be purified of all his sins and his trespasses atoned for by a Spirit of Uprightness* ('straightness' presaging as we just saw the *'making a straight Way in the wilderness'* imagery to come) *and Humility, for only with the humble submission of his soul to all the Laws of God* (clearly not Paul and meaning here the Mosaic Laws, not as Paul in Romans 13 and elsewhere, Roman Laws) will *his flesh be made pure for ablution with cleansing waters and sanctified through the waters of immersion.*[55]

This is also the basic gist of Josephus' picture of the teaching of John the Baptist, according to whose description, as we have just seen (but it is worth repeating in full), John

> *commanded the Jews to exercise Goodness, both as regards Righteousness towards one another and Piety towards God, and so to come to baptism, which cleansing would be acceptable to Him, provided that they made use of it not for remission of sins, but to purify the body, supposing that the soul had been thoroughly purified beforehand by Righteousness*[56] —

of course, the very opposite of the picture of John's baptism in the New Testament, except in so far as there is refraction.

The Community Rule draws to a close with such an outpouring of poetic ecstasy as to to be fairly overwhelming. Amid allusion to *'looking upon the marvelous Mysteries of Eternal Being...concealed from mankind'* (here again, the language of Paul in 1 Corinthians 2:7 — for a perfect match, one has only to substitute *'hidden'* for *'concealed'*), which God gives as *'a Fountain of Justification'* and *'a Well of Glory to His Chosen Ones'* (not only do we have here, again, the *'Glory'* language combined with the definition of *'the Sons of Zadok'* in the Damascus Document or, as the case may be — here in the Community Rule too — *'the Sons of Zedek'/'Righteousness'* or *'the Sons of the Zaddik'/'the Righteous One'*)[57]; it reiterates that God *'caused this Elect'* (*'the Elect of Israel'* in the Damascus Document)

> *to inherit the lot of the Holy Ones and to be in Communion with the Foundation of the Sons of Heaven* (we have already seen this *'joining with the Sons of Heaven'* in the Qumran Hymns previously) *as a Council of the Community* and *the Foundation* ('Sod' again which, it will be recalled, also means *'Secret'*) *of the Holy Building, as an Eternal Plantation with all the Ages of Endless Being'*[58]

Yet again, of course, these are just the words Paul uses – with slightly varying and, in fact, often inverted connotation – when in 1 Corinthians 3:9–11 above he applies *'building,' 'planting,'* and *'laying the Foundation'* imagery to speak about how *'Apollos watered'* (in 1:12 and 3:22, he somehow adds *'Cephas'* to this mix) and describes the Community as *'God's Plantation, God's Building.'* This *'Building,'* whether Community or Temple above (not unlike *'the Council of the Community'* in the Community Rule), he identifies here and elsewhere, as we have seen, as *'Jesus Christ'* or, if one prefers, his *'body.'*[59]

Apollos (another of these *'certain Jew's*) – this time, identified in Acts 18:24 as *'having come to Ephesus'* – according to the often tendentious picture Acts there provides, had been *'instructed in the Way of the Lord,'* but only knew *'the baptism'* of someone it refers to as *'John'* (18:25) – meaning, it would appear, *he only knows 'water baptism.'* Normally this *'John'* is taken to be *'John of Ephesus'* (in the Gospels, seemingly, *'John the son of Zebedee'*) but, according to the picture we are developing here and the one one gets from the literature at Qumran, the baptism being referred to here can only be that of the original *'John the Baptist'* whoever the *'Apollos'* being spoken of here may have been. Moreover, if the *'Cephas'* being referred to here and in 1 Corinthians 15:5, is the same as the individual most – including the Gospel of John, the Pseudoclementines, and Epiphanius – call *'Peter'*; then, according to these latter two testimonies anyhow, as we have shown, *he rose daily at dawn and prayed* (obviously following the *'Essene'* way), *wore only 'threadbare clothes'* (as Josephus tells us *'the Essenes'* did), and was a *'Daily Bather.'*[60]

All this comes to a resounding climax in the Community Rule in the atmosphere of evocation of *'this being the Time of the Preparation of the Way in the wilderness'* and *'zeal for the Law,'* graphically described in terms of *'the Day of Vengeance,'* and *'zeal for the Judgements of Righteousness.'*[61] This may have been a uniquely Palestinian militancy or a 'Jamesian' Palestinian synthesis of some kind not duplicated among *'Daily Bathing'* practitioners outside the Land of Israel or without attachment to it (except, of course, in Islam – though this last, following the new approach of Mani as we have seen, drops many of these extreme purity practices such as *'daily bathing'* or *ritual ablution*). This unique combination of extreme purity-mindedness with militant *'Messianism'* (regardless of the depiction of 'Jesus'' view of *'cleanliness'* or, for that matter, his generally *'pacifistic'* attitude in the Gospels) and xenophobic *'zeal for the Law,'* given voice in these documents, explains the ruthless Roman repression of it at least in Palestine if not elsewhere.

'*The Way in the Wilderness*' and Final Apocalyptic Holy War

To return to the War Scroll which, in the manner of these allusions to '*this being the Time of the preparation of the Way in the wilderness*' and '*zeal for the Day of Vengeance*,' now turns more aggressive – in the blueprint it provides for final apocalyptic Holy War, the reason it gives for '*keeping indecent behavior*' or '*fornication*' away from '*the camps*' is that '*your God goes with you to fight for you against your enemies that he may save you*,' a loose quotation of Deuteronomy 20:2–4.[62] This reference to '*Saving*' or '*Deliverance*' is again based on the same Hebrew root as '*Yeshuᶜa*' or '*Yeshaᶜ*,' that is, the Hebrew root of the name '*Jesus*' as it passes into the Greek, highlighted in a number of Qumran documents and forming the emphasis of climactic key portions of the Damascus Document, as we have seen.[63]

In the Damascus Document, '*Salvation*' and '*Justification*' ('*Yeshaᶜ*' and '*Zedakah*' are promised to '*those who fear His Name.*' Another way of translating this last phraseology is the familiar '*God-Fearers*,' referred to in Acts (for instance, in 10:2 it is applied to *the Roman Centurion Cornelius and all his household!*), as well as in some of the Gospel materials analyzed above, and as previously suggested, seemingly a category of persons attached to synagogues throughout the Mediterranean world in some sort of affiliated (*e.g.*, '*the Nilvim*' or '*the Joiners*') – if not completely orthodox – status. This is a group among whom Paul would seem to have been particularly active.[64] The emphasis, too, in this phraseology on '*Name*' and '*naming*' will be an ongoing one and will, for instance, be echoed in new and, again, often inverted significations normally associated with 'Jesus'' '*name*' – for example, in Acts '*those called by this Name*' instead of the fairly repetitive '*those called by name*' in the Damascus Document.[65]

Such persons, designated under this rubric of '*those who fear His Name*' in the Damascus Document – '*God-fearers*' in other vocabularies – are, in turn, described in terms of '*loving Him*' or '*keeping*' either *His Covenant* or *His Laws* – this last, once again, being both the language of '*Piety*' and '*Righteousness*' we have been encountering in the Community Rule and other venues above. The Damascus Document for instance, even uses in these contexts the language of '*Naziritism,*' *i.e.*, '*keeping away*' or '*apart from*' ('*lehinnazer*' / '*lehazzir*' / '*linzor*') in three or four separate circumstances already alluded to above.[66] In the Book of Acts, for instance too, this language of '*keeping away*' or '*refraining from*' is precisely that of the '*Judgement*' ('*I judge that*') James is pictured as making (in the manner of '*the Mebakker*' or '*the Overseer*' or '*Bishop*' of the wilderness camps in the Damascus Document[67]) at '*the Jerusalem Council*' and the terms of the directives he makes at its conclusion – namely, '*abstain*' or '*keep away from blood, fornication, things sacrificed to idols'* (in one version as we saw, *'the pollutions of the idols'*), *etc.* in Acts 15:19, 29, and 21:25.

In the Damascus Document, all instances of this kind of language are connected in some manner with *'the Well – 'of Living Waters' – which is being dug' in the wilderness,* interpreted to mean, *'the New Covenant in the Land of Damascus,'* and the extreme purity regulations and absolute *'separation of Holy from profane'* associated with this. The exhortative part of the Damascus Document ends some fifteen lines further along, after these references to *'fearing God'* or *'God-Fearers,'* promising – as we have now seen – that those *'who listened to the voice of the Teacher of Righteousness and did not abandon the Laws of Righteousness'* would gain *'Victory over all the sons of Earth.'* Furthermore, that God or possibly His representatives would *'make atonement for them and that they would see His Salvation* (that is, *'see Jesus'* – *'Yeshuʿato'*), *because they took refuge in His Holy Name.'*[68]

The apocalyptic character of this *'promise'* should be clear, as should its relationship to Paul's triumphant language at the end of 1 Corinthians 15 above. Certainly what we have here is an encouragement to martyrdom and a variation of what has gone in Judaism ever since under the denotation of *'Kiddush ha-Shem' / 'Sanctification of the Name'* literally meaning *'martyrdom.'* Certainly, too, those Josephus depracatingly refers to as *'False Prophets,' 'Impostors,'* and *'Deceivers'* whom, he claims, were in intent even *'more dangerous than the cutthroats and Revolutionaries'* – leading the People out into the wilderness, there to show them *'the signs of their impending Freedom'* or *'Deliverance'* – were making claims not unsimilar to these.

The *'wilderness'* regime of *'daily bathing'* and ablution in these *'desert camps'* was part and parcel of this extreme eschatological vision because of the need for absolute purity there. This was necessary because the Final Apocalyptic *'War'* against all Evil on the Earth, as the War Scroll – however fancifully – envisions it, could only be effected, as already explained, by the intervention and participation of the Heavenly Host, who would not or could not *'join' any camps with pollution in them.* Put in another way, their *'Heavenly'* state could not abide human *'pollution'* of any kind. Therefore the stringent purity regulations required in these *'camps'* if *the Heavenly Host* or *'Holy Angels' were going to 'join'* them, setting the stage for that apocalyptic Final *'Judgement,'* which would *come down from Heaven 'on the clouds'* like rain. It is this combination of themes too, as we have seen, that characterizes the presentation of James one gets both in early Church descriptions of him and the Letter the New Testament attributes to his name.

This is the esoteric dimension to these claims about *'rain-making'* as it emerges in the War Scroll, where this kind of imagery is repeated both in the climactic exegesis of the Messianic '*World Ruler Prophecy*' and at its end.[69] It is as dramatic as it is poetic and worth presenting in its entirety, for only then can the reader get the real feeling of this unique combination of uncompromising apocalyptic '*zeal for the Day of Judgement*' and meticulous attention to *bodily purification* and '*Perfect Holiness*' or '*the Perfection of Holiness*' – '*Perfection of the Way*' as the Community Rule refers to it, variations of which being over and over again reiterated in the documents at Qumran.[70] This is the combination exemplified by the militant '*Sicarii*' or '*Zealots*' who, according to Hippolytus' unique picture, were just another group of '*Daily-Bathing*' Sobiai ('*Essenes*') or extreme Nazirites (some people might even consider that the tradition of the combination of these conceptualities carried on in some unique manner to Medieval fighting groups like the 'Christian'Templars, probably via an undetermined transmission of some kind through Jewish groups such as '*the Mourners for Zion*,' who had preceded them by several centuries in their return to Jerusalem and in discovering Dead Sea Scrolls materials, and through them, '*the Karaites*').[71]

We have met many of these concepts before, for instance in Matthew's picture of the Sermon on the Mount. For Hebrews, permeated like Qumran with the imagery of '*Perfection*' – '*Jesus, the Mediator of the New Covenant*' (12:24), who '*was crowned with Glory*' and '*the Leader of their Salvation*,' '*is made Perfect through sufferings*' (2:9–10) '*and, being made Perfect, he became the author of Eternal Salvation to all those who obey him*' (5:9). This last reiterates remonstrances prevalent in definitions of '*the Rechabites*' in Jeremiah 35:6–18 in which they are repeatedly characterized as '*obeying the commands of their father*.'[72] The New Testament Letter ascribed to James, too – whether authentic or simply part of '*the Jamesian School*' – also refers to '*the Perfect Man*' (3:2), '*Perfect and Complete, lacking nothing*' (1:4).

'*Preparation for the Time of the Day of Vengeance*,' as we saw, is the essence of the exegesis in the Community Rule above of Isaiah 40:3's pivotal '*prepare in the wilderness the Way of the Lord – make a straight path in the desert for Our God*.' In the Synoptics, as everyone knows, this is applied to John the Baptist's activities '*in the wilderness*' – in Matthew 3:1, '*of Judea*'; in John 1:28, '*across the Jordan*' – in preparation for *the coming of 'Jesus*.' At Qumran, it is applied to those who '*walk Perfectly, each with his neighbor*' (that is, the second of the two '*all Righteousness*' Commandments – '*Righteousness towards one's fellow man*') and '*do* (with an accent on '*doing*') *all that is found in 'the Torah commanded by the hand of Moses*.'

Here, not only is the emphasis on '*doing*' crucial, especially when

considering parallel '*Jamesian*' insistences and like-minded ones throughout the Qumran corpus – Pauline ones to the contrary notwithstanding;
but the whole, as can be seen, is specifically tied to '*the Torah as commanded
by the hand of Moses*' – something Paul, in turn, never fails to either belittle or pour scorn upon.[73] The one '*walking in (such) Perfection*,' echoing
Paul in 2 Corinthians 6:17 again, shall '*separate from any man who has not
turned his Way* (the '*Way*' terminology as a name for nascent '*Christianity*' – known, for instance, even to someone like Felix in Acts 24:14 and
22[74]) *from all Unrighteousness*' or '*Ungodliness*,' and, as already explained,

> be a man zealous for the Law whose time is the Day of Vengeance, to do His will
> in all his handiwork and His Kingdom, exactly as commanded.

This last, once again then, hints at the '*Rechabite*'-style obedience ('*to the
commandment of their father*'), we have already alluded to above, but also
the closing imprecations of John 20:26–21:24, itself abounding in the
language of '*love*' (now divided between both '*loving Jesus*' and '*the Disciple Jesus loved*'), '*standing*,' and '*Name*' and '*naming*' imagery.

These words in the Community Rule reiterate what was written
earlier, once again containing just the slightest hint, not only of the
'*Rechabite*' lifestyle, but also their '*obedience to the commands of their father*'[75]:

> They shall separate from the midst of the habitation of the Men of Unrighteous-
> ness (or alternatively '*Ungodliness*') to go into the wilderness to prepare there
> the Way of the Lord, as it is written (here the text quotes Isaiah 40:3 as
> already indicated)...and which the Prophets have revealed by His Holy Spirit.[76]

The connection of this citation with parallel allusions in the War Scroll
should be straightforward. The reference to '*volunteering*' one finds in the
War Scroll in connection to such '*going out into the wilderness camps*' is also
important, as it is in the Paean for King Jonathan where, as we saw as
well, a central contingent, designated as '*the Joiners in the War of*,' is also
evoked.[77] Going on to refer to '*the War of God*' and '*mighty works and marvelous wonders*' (here, '*war-like*' ones, not more pacified '*Hellenized*' ones
such as '*raisings*,' '*curings*,' and magical '*transformations*' like those in the
Gospels), as well as Daniel's '*Saints*' or '*Kedoshim*' (applied in the Gospels
to less militaristic Divine activity[78]); the War Scroll turns to its exegesis of
'*the Star Prophecy*' from Numbers 24:17–19, we have been following
above. It does so by introducing it amid reference to '*the likeness*' or '*simil-
itude of Adam*' and imagery bearing on that of '*the Heavenly Host*' – here
'*the Holy Angels*' – as well as its first evocation of the '*clouds*' metaphor.[79]

Of course, this reference to '*the likeness of Adam*' either has to do with '*the Primal Adam*' ideology once again or prefigures the evocation of '*the Son of Man coming on the clouds of Heaven*,' the essence of James' proclamation in the Temple, we have also been following (in the Gospels, it will be recalled, attributed to John the Baptist and Jesus as well) – if the two, '*the Son of Man*' and '*the Primal Adam*,' can in fact be differentiated in any real way.[80] It is at this point that '*the Star Prophecy*' from Numbers is quoted in its entirety, the interpretation of which, as we have re-marked, not only forms its highpoint, but is so fundamental that it is repeated again in the last two Columns of the Scroll (19–20).

The exegesis of it specifically refers to God's '*Messiah*' (singular), '*the Poor*' (*Ebionim*) who have been redeemed by God's '*marvelous Power*' ('*Power*' imagery again), and '*the Poor in Spirit*' (the very words used by 'Jesus' in Matthew 5:3's '*Sermon on the Mount*'). These '*Poor*' will, '*like a flaming torch in the straw, consume Evil and never cease until the Wicked are destroyed*' which is, of course, almost the very imagery John the Baptist is pictured as using in the introduction of him in the Gospels (Matthew 3:11–12 and *pars.*)[81]

The War Scroll, too, at this point twice speaks of '*the hand of the Poor*' who '*will humble the mighty of the Peoples*' – once again, presumably the Romans ('*Peoples*,' as we saw, being an allusion used throughout the Scrolls and in Roman jurisprudence to refer to the assortment of nations under Roman rule in the Eastern part of the Empire including petty, semi-autonomous, tax-collecting '*Kings*' like '*the Herodians*,' labeled in both these milieux, '*Kings of the Peoples*'[82]). This is directly reprised with the words:

> *to whom* (meaning '*to the Ebionim*' or '*to the Poor*'/'*the Ebionites*') *will be delivered the Enemies of all Lands* (of course not in the way the Gospels employ such language which rather apply it to the prototypical '*Enemy*' of all mankind they have fashioned, '*Judas the Iscariot*,'[83] repeatedly pictured in them, as we have seen, as having '*delivered up*' Jesus)...*in order to justify Your true Judgement* (here again the language of apocalyptic '*Judgement*') *on all the Sons of Men and to make for Yourself an Eternal Name* (the '*Name*' and '*naming*' vocabulary once again).[84]

It is at this point, too, that the text quotes Isaiah 31:8 to the effect that this deliverance will be accomplished by '*the sword of no mere man and no mere Adam*' – the implication being that, *together with* '*the Poor*' and '*those bent in the dust*,' someone or *something more than Adam will accomplish this* '*Deliverance*.' Here too the reference to '*the Sons of Men*' is framed in terms of different usages, which do not include this reference to 'Adam,' the implication being that *these are not really the kind of supernatural 'Men' the War Scroll is interested in.*

One should also remark the parallel of these materials with the end of the exhortative section of the Damascus Document, already quoted above but, once again, worth repeating in its entirety:

> *Your Judgements upon us....who have listened to the voice of the Righteous Teacher* (language reiterated, as we shall see, in the Habakkuk *Pesher,* providing yet another linguistic commonality and, therefore, chronological synchronization[85]) *and did not abandon the Laws of Righteousness. They shall rejoice and their hearts shall be strengthened* (a quality we know was applied to James in the Jerusalem of his day[86]), *and they shall be victorious over all the Sons of Earth* (of course, we have already heard this too). *God will make atonement through them and they shall see His Salvation* (again '*Yeshuᶜa*' as we saw – '*Jesus*' in the New Testament), *because they took refuge in His Holy Name* (meaning, 'Jesus" or God's).

This is the kind of '*Name*' and '*naming*' symbolism which recurs generally throughout these and other like-minded documents as, for example, in the Book of Acts – itself, as already signaled, particularly interested in '*the Name*' or '*the Great Name of Jesus*' (3:6 and *pars.*).87

One should also note the parallel between this and Jerome's report of the vow James is reputed to have made in the Gospel of the Hebrews, not to '*eat or drink*' (the Nazirite '*not eating or drinking*' theme again) *until he had 'seen Jesus.*'[88] For the medieval *Zohar* too, in discussing this same '*Star Prophecy*' in Numbers,

> *King David* (meaning, '*the Messiah*') *placed himself among the Poor,...the Pious,...and...those ready to sacrifice themselves...for the Sanctification of God's Name* (not only the '*Name*' and '*naming*' vocabulary once again, but now coupled with the language of '*Martyrdom*' or '*Sanctification of the Name,*' already underscored above).[89]

'Joining the Heavenly Holy Ones' and 'Judgement' upon the Clouds in the War Scroll

That the coming eschatological '*Judgement,*' being pictured at this point in the War Scroll in terms of '*cloud*' and '*rain*' imagery, is something akin to what in normal parlance goes by the designation, '*the Last Judgement,*' is made particularly clear in the Habakkuk *Pesher* in its all-important exposition of the pivotal Habakkuk 2:4, '*the Righteous shall live by his Faith.*' As the Habakkuk *Pesher* pictures it, '*God will save them* ('*the Righteous*' – here the Hebrew is '*yizzilam*' and really does mean, just as in the Gospels, '*save them.*'[90] Moreover, in such an eschatological context, the sense is the same as that of '*Yeshuᶜato*' above or '*Yeshuᶜa*'/'*Salvation*'[91]) *from the House of Judgement,*' a term which it will later apply to that '*House of Judgement* (a better translation would be '*the Decree of Judgement*') *which God would deliver in His Judgement in the midst of many Peoples.*'[92]

At the end of the *Pesher*, as we shall see, it actually makes it clear that this '*Salvation*' or '*Deliverance,*' which will be denied to '*Idolaters*' among the Nations and backsliding Jews, is none other than '*the Day of Judgement,*' a phraseology it repeats twice just so there should be no mistaking it.[93] Not only is this '*Day of Judgement*' terminology widespread in Matthew, 2 Peter, and Jude,[94] it forms the backbone of the Koran which has a particular obsession with just such '*Idolaters*' and '*Backsliders.*'[95] It is no different, of course, from what we just referred to above as '*the Last Judgement.*'

With regard to this '*House of Judgement which God would make in the midst of many Peoples,*' the *Pesher* states even earlier that '*God would not destroy His People by the hand of the Nations,*' but rather '*God would execute Judgement on all the Nations by the hand of His Elect.*'[96] For anyone who takes seriously the widespread idea of '*peaceful Essenes,*' the extreme apocalyptic nationalism of this passage could not be clearer. Nor can there be any mistaking what it is saying.

But in addition, God's '*Chosen*' or '*Elect*' is the definition of '*the Sons of Zadok*' in the key exegesis of Ezekiel 44:15 in the Damascus Document. These, as the Damascus Document puts it in its own inimitable way, '*will stand at the End of Days* (not only is this eschatological but, as we have already underscored, another incidence of the '*standing*' ideology)...*and justify the Righteous and condemn the Wicked.*' This is both '*Justification*' theology with a vengeance, but the opposite of what other '*Liars*' and '*Evil Ones*' do earlier in the Document ('*those that remove the boundary markers which the First* – '*the Ancestors*' or '*Forefathers*' – *have set up*' meaning, as we saw, '*remove the Law*'): *justify the Wicked and condemn the Righteous.*'[97] In the Habakkuk *Pesher* therefore, as in the description of '*the Community Council*' in the Community Rule, it is clear that these same '*Elect of God*' participate in '*the Last Judgement*' and '*will execute Judgement on all the Nations.*'[98]

But this is not very different from many less well-formed ideas circulating about '*the Apostles*' or even Jesus himself in early Christian thought. The same '*execution of Judgement*' – presumably '*at the hand of*

God's Elect' as in the Habakkuk *Pesher* – is, however, expressed in the Letter of Jude 1:14–15 as well. Quoting '*Enoch the Seventh from Adam*' and attributed, as we know, to '*the brother of James*'; this letter has the ideology down just about perfectly:

> *Behold, the Lord is coming among the Myriads of His Holy Ones to execute Judgement against all and to sentence all the Ungodly with regard to all their ungodly works.*[99]

The War Scroll now goes on to describe this eschatological '*Judgement*' in a far more detailed, but completely parallel manner, using imagery and allusions clearly based on Daniel 7:13's '*one like a Son of Man coming on the clouds of Heaven.*' Grouping these '*Holy Ones*' or '*Saints*' ('*Kedoshim*') from Daniel with '*the Angels...mighty in battle*' and, referring seemingly to either *Messianic* or *Divine intervention from Heaven*, it reads in perhaps the most complete exposition of final apocalyptic warfare and eschatological '*Judgement*' ever recorded:

> *You will fight against them from Heaven...and the Elect of your Holy People* (in the Damascus Document, '*the Sons of Zadok*' as we just saw)...*are with You in Your Holy abode...You have recorded for them...Your Covenant of Peace* (accorded Phineas as a result of the '*zeal*' he displayed in killing backsliders in Numbers 25:7–11 above, a '*zeal*' replicated in Judas Maccabee's father's call to arms in 1 Maccabees 2:27), *that You may reign forever throughout all the Eternal Ages. And You commanded* (the same root in Hebrew as the word, '*visit*' or '*Visitation*' which follows – the *real* '*Visitation*' language, if one likes) *the Hosts of Your Elect in their thousands and their Myriads* (the same language as the Letter of Jude above), *together with Your Saints and Your Angelic Army with the authority in war to strike the Rebellious of Earth with Your awe-inspiring Judgements* (again, the meaning here of '*Judgements*' is quite clear)...*And the Assembly of Your Holy Ones is in our midst together with the Elect of Heaven for Eternal help* (here the '*joining*' of the Heavenly Host to the wilderness camps of both the Damascus Document and Community Rule above – more documentary simultaneity). *And we shall despise kings* (including most obviously Herodians but also clearly others – Romans for instance) *and we will mock and scorn the Mighty, because our Lord is Holy* (the word here actually is '*Lord*' and not '*God*' as in some of the more recently-revealed documents from Qumran such as '*The Messiah of Heaven and Earth*' – the interpretation of which is still in dispute[100]) *and the King of Glory together with the Saints* (Daniel 7:21–22) *are with us. The Mighty of the Angelic Host have visited us* (here the use of

the word '*visit*,' just signaled above, in the sense of a '*Divine Visitation*,' as for instance at the beginning of the Damascus Document, and not a '*command*'[101] – perhaps parodied in *the 'visit' the Holy Ghost pays Mary in* 'Christian' ideology) *and the Hero in War is in our Assembly* (in the language of Christianity, '*our Church*') *and the Host of His Spirits* (the Islamic '*Ginn*' mentioned above) *are with our foot soldiers and our cavalry*.[102]

Here we have some of the most triumphant, apocalyptic language in any literary document from this period. Not only are '*the Elect of Your Holy People*' the same as '*the Sons of Zadok*' and the references to both '*commanded*' and '*visited*' the same in Hebrew; but '*the Covenant of Peace*,' as we just saw, is the same as that accorded Phineas in Numbers and, by implication, Noah in Genesis as well. Also the reference here literally is to '*Lord*' not '*God*' and, as with '*the Hero in War*' and in another Qumran text just noted above, specifically evoking the '*Messiah*' as '*commanding both Heaven and Earth*' and making precisely such a '*visit*,'[103] it is unclear if we are speaking about '*God*' or '*His Messiah*.' However, in the parallel represented by '*the Lord coming with the Myriads of His Holy Ones to execute Judgement*' in '*Jude the brother of James*' above, there can be no doubt that we are speaking about *the Messiah*.

At this point in the War Scroll, the imagery shifts to '*cloud*' imagery, because now it is combining the imagery of Daniel's '*one like a Son of Man coming on the clouds*' of Heaven with the exegesis of '*the Star Prophecy*,' both interpreted in terms of an eschatological War against all Evil on the Earth and final Judgement on all mankind. Furthermore, the whole passage, as with the passage from the Kabbalistic *Zohar* representing David as the Messiah already alluded to above, begins with the evocation of '*David Your Servant, who...put his trust in Your Great Name*.' It is at this point the Star Prophecy from Numbers 24:17 is quoted in its entirety and allusion is made to '*Your Messiah*' – the '*hand*' of whom is once again referred to – all the verbs and nouns being in the singular and not the plural.[104]

In this context, the text now adds eschatological '*rain*' imagery, in the sense of implying *Final Apocalyptic Judgement*, not just warfare, and a logical extension of its Messianic '*cloud*' imagery. That the context is, once again, that of Daniel 7:13 is made clear by the words:

They are as clouds, as moisture-laden clouds over the Earth and torrents of rain shedding Judgement on all that grows on it.[105]

This is of course poetic metaphor again '*with a vengeance*' – poetic metaphor often lost on Qumran specialists. Even though it is using figurative language, the meaning could not be clearer. It is followed by what virtually amounts to yet another 'Paean of Praise':

> Arise Mighty One, lead off your captives, Man of Glory. Gather your spoil, Doer of War. Put your hand upon the neck of your Enemies and your foot on the piles of dead (the imagery of 'making your enemies a footstool' from Psalm 110:1. It is alluded to in the Gospels and fairly abounds in Hebrews,[106] a letter also announcing its version of 'the Zadokite Priesthood,' namely 'the Priesthood after the Order of Melchizedek,' the source of which is this very apocalyptic and fairly aggressive – some might even say, bloodthirsty – Psalm 110 as well.[107] Nor is this say anything about the imagery of 'his feet,' so strong in the 'Standing One' ideology and throughout the New Testament and Rabbinic passages, we have been highlighting above). Smite the nations, your Adversaries, and let your sword devour guilty flesh (not only do we have allusion to 'the sword of the no mere Adam' of Isaiah 31:8 above, but even the use of the verb 'consume' or 'devour' here is the same as one finds in that prophet earlier and, as it turns out, pivotal passages in the Habakkuk Pesher – to say nothing of Paul in Galatians 5:15 above[108])...Fill Your land with Glory (could this be more 'filling' imagery – the real kind? It is certainly more of the 'Glory' vocabulary) and may your inheritance be blessed...Zion rejoice greatly! Show yourself with jubilation Jerusalem! Sing for joy all you cities of Judah and may your gates be ever open...Sovereignty is (to the Lord) and Eternal Dominion to Israel (and this is supposed to be 'anti-Nationalist' or 'peace-loving Essene'?).[109]

The sense here is pretty unmistakable. Hyperbole aside, one can't get much more 'Messianic' or 'nationalist' than this. It is followed by six more columns, recapitulating much of this imagery and adding allusions such as: 'Eternal Light,' 'Belial,' 'the appointed times of Salvation' ('Yeshu'a' again), 'the Perfect of the Way,' 'the Day of Vengeance,' 'the Power of God,' 'the burning' (very popular imagery in the Koran as well[110]), 'the Rule of Michael among the gods and Israel in the midst all flesh,' and 'the Gates of Salvation.'

This last, as we have seen, has particularly strong relevance to the question asked of James in the early Church tradition reported by Hegesippus, 'What is the Gate to Jesus?' and James' response:

> Why do you ask me concerning the Son of Man? He is sitting in Heaven on the Right Hand of the Great Power and he is coming on the clouds of Heaven,

which provokes the riot in the Temple on Passover and his stoning. Once again, the intrinsic relationship of James' response in these sources, not only to the materials in Daniel but also to these passages in the War Scroll, should be obvious to all but the most biased observers. Basically a compressed version of these triumphant and climactic passages of the more prolix War Scroll have been put into James' mouth and, by implication, Jesus' and John the Baptist's in the Gospels.

The War Scroll now culminates in a second evocation of eschatological 'rain' and its 'Paean' to the Messianic 'Hero' with which the text ends. These are both, as already noted, word-for-word repetitions of the first. Following another curious reference to 'standing' and 'to You is the Power' ('Power' language again) and in Your hands is the battle' (the omnipresent language of 'hands'), the text again then avers:

> Our sovereign is Holy and the King of Glory (or 'Glorious King' – 'the Messiah' – and an extremely militant and not very pacifistic one) is with us and the Host of His Spirits (the 'Ginn' again) is with our foot soldiers and our cavalry. (They are) as clouds (here the 'clouds' simile begins again), and moisture-laden clouds covering the Earth, and as a torrent of rain (and again, finally the simile of Messianic 'rain') shedding Judgement on all that grows therein.[111]

This could not be more clear or a more clearly poetic metaphor for 'the Last Judgement.' After this commences the praise of the Messianic 'Hero' who will 'devour all flesh with his sword' again.[112] Here is the final crystallization of all the eschatological 'rain,' 'flood,' and 'final Judgement' imagery encountered above. Tied to the exegesis of 'the Star Prophecy,' so intrinsic to events in 66–70 CE Palestine and the cataclysm there – to say nothing of the Gospel portrait of the birth of its 'Messiah' in Matthew 2:2–2:9, and Daniel's imagery of 'one like a Son of Man coming on the clouds'; it also links up with the parallel evocation in the New Testament Letter of James of 'the coming of the Lord' – which, it will be recalled, was connected with 'spring and autumn rain,'[113] 'the prayer of the Just' or 'Righteous One having much Power' (parodied in Josephus' disparaging portraiture of this genre of individual; nor is this to say anything about the more positive one in the Gospels[114]), and Elijah's role as paradigmatic 'rain' and 'Judgement'-making forerunner, setting this final eschatological process into motion.

16

Temple Sacrifice at Qumran and in the New Testament

Spiritualized Sacrifice and Atonement Imagery in Paul and at Qumran

It is curious that this clear hostility to foreigners in Qumran documents like the War Scroll and that evinced in the behavior – real or implied – of those Josephus at times calls '*Zealots*' and sometimes something else, has been for the most part ignored where native Palestinian groups or movements are concerned. This is particularly true in the case of the oft-times too easy acceptance of passages such as the one Epiphanius claims he saw in '*the Gospel in use among the Ebionites*,' that '*Jesus came and announced the abolition of the sacrifices*' – meaning, *Temple sacrifice*.[1] This is also clear from two Qumran texts from the more-recently published documents, the Testament of Kohath and another tantalizing fragment that seem to include allusion to '*binding the wounded*' and other references implying either participation or assistance in a '*war*' of some kind.[2] The reference in the Testament of Kohath, which Professor Wise and myself were the first to call attention to, is particularly striking in this regard. Ascribed in a pseudepigraphic manner to the grandfather of Moses, it reads:

> *And now my sons, be watchful over your inheritance....Do not give your inheritance to foreigners, nor your heritage to Violent Men* (this term in Aramaic can also mean '*Men of Mixed Blood*' or '*Expropriators*' – even '*Tax-Collectors*' which would have particular relevance where Herodians were concerned), *lest you be regarded as humiliated in their eyes and foolish, and they trample upon you* ('*the Holy Things*' or '*pearls*,' '*trampled upon by the feet*' of either '*pigs*' or '*dogs*' in 'Jesus" first precept in Matthew 7:6 above about '*dogs*,' '*casting*,' and '*feet*'?); *for, though only resident aliens, they will become your masters* (and again, too, the '*masters*' language of the second in Matthew 15:27).[3]

Nor is this to say anything of similar language in the all-important Paean to King Jonathan which, as we saw, actually makes reference to '*those*

Joining the War of....'[4]

Though it is not clear how this '*Gospel in use among the Ebionites*' differs, if at all, from the one Jerome or Eusebius call '*The Gospel of the Hebrews*' and another that Jerome, at least, calls '*The Gospel of the Nazoraeans*' (all no longer extant)[5]; the passage in the Gospel of the Ebionites which has to do with '*the abolition of the sacrifices*,' as Epiphanius records it, reads as follows:

> *They do not say that He (Christ) was begotten of God the Father, but that He was created like one of the Archangels and that He rules over the Angels and all things created by the Almighty.*[6]

We have already encountered this idea that '*the Messiah*' is above the Angels in '*The Messiah of Heaven and Earth*' text, also first discovered and published by Professor Wise and myself in 1990 when the monopoly over publishing the Dead Sea Scrolls was broken.[6] It is present as well, as already also remarked, in Muhammad's position in the Koran that '*Adam*' – again echoing '*the Primal Adam*' ideology – was '*above the Angels.*' As he puts it they, rather, '*must bow down*' or '*submit*' to him, '*all save Iblis*' (2.35) – this last, patently, '*the fallen Angel*' notion of books like Enoch and Judeo-Christian tradition generally[8] and, as we have seen, the counterpart in Arabic of the Dead Sea Scrolls '*Belial*' language and Paul's defective '*Beliar*' ('*Diabolos*'/'*the Devil*' as it moves into more familiar Western tongues – two letters, '*B*'-'*L*,' being sufficient in linguistic theory to establish a loan).[9]

Not only does this text, which we named '*The Messiah of Heaven and Earth*,' include tantalizing references to '*healing the wounded*' and '*liberating the captives*'; it also alludes to '*glorifying the Pious on the Throne of the Eternal Kingdom.*' Here, again, the allusion is to '*the Hassidim*,' reflecting the vocabulary of the '*Piety*'/'*Righteousness*' dichotomy and, not surprisingly, it is directly followed by evocation of '*the Righteous*.' One should also pay particular attention, here, to the vocabulary of '*the Throne of the Eternal Kingdom*,' which will be part of two other '*Messianic*' texts, we have already mentioned above and will encounter further below, the *Florilegium* and the Genesis *Pesher* on Jacob's promises to '*the House of Judah*' concerning the Davidic Kingship.[10]

Aside from additional allusions to '*bringing Good News to the Meek*' (both '*the Good News*' and '*the Meek*' being very much a part of New Testament usage[11]), '*calling the Righteous by Name*' (the same '*called by Name*' language that permeates the Damascus Document, in particular, when speaking about one of the clear variations of '*the Righteous*' or '*Zaddikim*' vocabulary, '*the Sons of Zadok*'), and a direct and unambiguous allusion to '*resurrecting the dead*'[12]; that '*the Heavens and the Earth will obey His Messiah*' also incorporates the theme of '*Heaven and Earth*' again (now being used in a slightly new way).[13] Nor should it be overlooked that the reference to '*Messiah*' here is *singular*, meaning the type of the singular '*Davidic*' Messiah familiar to both Judaism and Christianity, not the widely-circulated, though perhaps somewhat tendentious, '*two Messiah*'-theorizing of the early days of Qumran research, if there ever were really '*two Messiahs*' as such referred to at Qumran and not just a single '*Messiah*' from the two genealogical roots of '*Aaron and Israel*'.[14] However this may be, to repeat, in this text we are clearly dealing with is a *single* '*Davidic*'-style Messiah.

Where the relation of the Angels to this '*Messiah*' is concerned – one, the Archangel '*Michael*', is referred to in several passages dealing with the coming eschatological '*Judgement*' (further elaborating those already mentioned above in the War Scroll), as *commanding* '*the Kingdom Above*' or '*the Heavenly Host*'.[15] These passages aver that he *will overthrow* '*the Prince of the Kingdom of Evil*' – certainly an allusion to the Scrolls' '*Mastema*' or '*Belial*' (Muhammad's '*Iblis*') – *and bring* '*Eternal help*' *and* '*Knowledge*' *to the* '*Sons of His Covenant*' *and* '*the Sons of His Truth*' (more of the language of '*Gnosis*', this time coupled with that of Divine '*Sonship*' – the latter as usual, as at Qumran generally, referred to plurally[16]), the destiny of whom is said to be '*of the Redeemed*'.[17]

This same '*Michael*', traditionally the Guardian Angel of Israel, is in other Qumran texts pivotally identified with '*Melchizedek*' or '*the King of Righteousness*', the prototypical High Priestly forerunner in the New Testament Letter to the Hebrews.[18] He is purportedly referred to in '*The Gospel of the Hebrews*' too, which according to St Cyril of Jerusalem (375–444 CE) contained the following passage:

> *When Christ wished to come upon the Earth to men, the Good Father summoned a Great Power in Heaven* (again the '*Great Power*' vocabulary of Simon *Magus*, the Ebionites, the *Elchasaites*, and others), *which was called Michael* (this very definitely equates with the '*Michael*', we are encountering above and in the War Scroll) *and entrusted Christ to the care thereof. And the Power came into the world and it was called* '*Mary*' (or '*Mareim*' – in some later contexts also identified with '*Mary Magdalene*', an identification which is enjoying a particular vogue today).[19]

This '*Mareim*' is also mentioned at Nag Hammadi in both Apocalypses of James as receiving the Hidden Wisdom of James and, in one such presentation, this even occurs by means of a '*kiss*' – a quasi-reversal of the '*kiss*' Judas *Iscariot* is alleged to have given '*Jesus*' in the Synoptics. In Hippolytus, he ('*Mareim*') is even known to those he denotes as '*Naassenes*,' seemingly a very early Gnosticizing amalgam of the two groups we refer to as '*Nazoraeans*' and '*Essenes*.'[20]

To return to the '*Gospel*' Epiphanius claims was in use, seemingly a generation before his own, '*among the Ebionites*:'

> *And that he (Christ) came and declared, as their so-called 'Gospel' reports, 'I have come to do away with the sacrifices and, if you do not cease from sacrificing, the Wrath of God will not cease upon you.'*[21]

Of course, this issue of the inefficacy or cessation of Temple sacrifice is widespread in Paul's letters, though admittedly from a somewhat more '*allegorized*' perspective. For Paul and the Gospels – with, as they have come down to us, their generally pro-Pauline cast – Jesus *is the very sacrifice itself.*

Paul says as much in 1 Corinthians 5:7 in a discussion supposed to be about one important aspect of James' directives to overseas communities, '*fornication*.' Not only does this discussion use the vocabulary both of James' proscriptions and Gospel allusions to 'Jesus'; but, like 2 Corinthians 6:14–7:1 above and unlike what is now directly to follow in 1 Corinthians 6:11–11:29, it actually has more in common with the ethos of both '*the Essenes*' and Qumran, in terms of not keeping '*table fellowship*' with '*fornicators*,' '*idol-worshippers*,' '*Scoffers*,' '*wine-bibbers*,' and such like, and even goes so far as to recommend both '*shunning them*' and/or '*expelling them*' (1 Corinthians 5:9–11).

Nevertheless, it is this same context and continuing its allegorical evocation of such key allusions as '*the Name*,' '*the Power of our Lord Jesus Christ*,' and '*someone being delivered unto Satan*' for '*the destruction of the flesh, so the spirit might be saved on the Day of the Lord Jesus*' (more esoteric juxtaposition of '*flesh*' and '*spirit*,' this time in the context of what we have just been alluding to as '*the Last Judgement*' or '*the Day of Judgement*'); it avers that, '*for also Christ, our Passover, was sacrificed for us*' (1 Corinthians 5:4–7).

Here not only do we have the familiar '*Christ*' as '*the Paschal Lamb*' image, but this is now actually couched in yet another allegorizing discussion of the '*leaven*' the Jews reject on their Festival of Passover. This is presented in the usual disparaging and one-sided manner, recommending – seemingly in all innocence, but actually playing off all the inherent imageries – '*celebrating the Feast*' (meaning '*the Passover*') not with the old '*leaven of malice and Wickedness*' – one is quite staggered here by the derisive and polemical way Paul alludes to the previous tradition to which he, too, supposedly claims to be an heir), but with the new *'unleaven of sincerity and Truth'* (5:8 – this last implying himself, of course, and the Communities he has founded). Not only are we again in the world of pure allegory, in which Paul is always on the side of the *'good,'* but none but the most naive observer could possibly miss the acrimonious thrust of the several imageries he packs into these allusions – imageries which are, of course, to be found in the Gospels, in particular, in the several discourses or *'Parables'* we have already encountered above in which Jesus is either portrayed as speaking about or warning against *'the leaven of the Pharisees'* and alluding to them as *'Blind Guides,'* i.e., *'the Blind leading the Blind'* and *'both falling into the Pit'* (Matthew 15:12-14 and 16:6-12)

Paul continues this metaphor of spiritualized sacrifice in Romans 12:1, though this time his rhetorical barbs, while present, are a little more subdued. Returning to his previous characterization of *'the Body of Christ'* in 1 Corinthians 6:15 and 12:12–12:27 as applying to the whole Community, he once again characterizes *'the bodies'* that compose it as *'a Holy and living sacrifice well pleasing to God,'* only adding the incidental if condescending aside, and a more *'reasonable service.'* This is exactly the sort of imagery we have just pointed up with regard to *'the Community Council'* in the Community Rule, a document including some of the same allusions and also considered opposed to Temple sacrifice, though if it was, this was probably only because of the perception that the then-reigning Priesthood – in our view *'the Herodian'* – was corrupt.[22] What would have been its position, for instance, if the Jerusalem Priesthood were *'a Perfectly Righteous'* One? That would be a whole other question.

We have just seen how the Community Rule in emphasizing this kind of *'Perfection of the Way'* in its evocation of Isaiah 40:3's *'making a straight Way in the wilderness'* citation and prefiguring Paul in 1 Corinthians 3:9, itself seemingly playing on the opening description in the Damascus Document – as we saw as well – about how *'God visited them and caused a Root of Planting to grow from Israel and from Aaron...to prosper on the good things of His Earth,'* characterizes the members of this *'Council'* as *'an Eternal Plantation,'* *'keeping Faith in the Land with a steadfast and humble Spirit,'* and *'atoning for sin by doing Judgement and suffering the sorrows of affliction.'*[23] Of course, the New Testament is fairly awash with similar allusions when discussing the theological significance of its 'Jesus.'[24]

But at this point the Community Rule parts company with Paul. In addition to *'being Witnesses of the Truth for Judgement and the Chosen'* or *'the Elect of His Will'* (a few lines further on, the same idea is expressed in terms of *'being an acceptable free will offering'*[25]) *to make atonement for the Land and pay the Evil Ones their Reward'* (here, as previously, both Paul's '*spiritualized*' atonement imagery but also, as the Habakkuk *Pesher* puts it and as we shall see further below, to both *participate in* '*the House of* or '*Decree of final Judgement*' that '*His*'/*God's* '*Elect would execute on all the Nations*' and '*pay back the Wicked* – like '*the Wicked Priest*' – *their reward*'[26], '*to do Truth, Justification, Judgement, Love of Piety, and Humility each with his neighbor*' (a variation, as we saw above, of James' '*Royal Law according to the Scripture*' – '*to love every man, his neighbor as himself*'); the members of '*the Council*' are admonished – just as Jesus admonishes those he is addressing in the Sermon on the Mount – *to be* '*Perfect in all that has been revealed about the whole Torah,*' only Matthew 5:48 substitutes '*Your Father in Heaven's Perfection*' for the '*Perfection*' of '*the whole of the Torah,*' as it is delineated here in the Community Rule.[27]

The members of this Council are also '*to offer up a pleasing fragrance*' – the very words Paul uses in 2 Corinthians 2:14–15 when he describes what those followers of Jesus (seemingly in Macedonia, but also in Achaia) are supposed to offer up meaning, where he is concerned, for the most part, *monetary contributions* – but secondarily, an allusion as well to *the fruitfulness of his mission*.[28] As usual, here too Paul is at his rhetorical and deprecating best. Evoking once again both his and the Scrolls' language of '*Triumph,*' he implies that others, who also speak both of such '*a sweet fragrance*' and '*being saved,*'[29] are rather bringing '*an odour of death to death*' not '*life to life*' (cf. the putrid '*smell*' which Lazarus' body, dead in the grave '*for four days,*' emits in John 11:39 above).

Furthermore, again employing another usage, '*the Many,*' fundamental to the Community Rule and the same vocabulary, the Habakkuk *Pesher* uses to indict '*the Last Priests of Jerusalem who gathered Riches and profiteered from the spoils of the Peoples*'; these others, his competitors – who like himself also speak of '*the sweet odour of the Knowledge of Him*' – are actually '*profiteering* (language we shall in due course also encounter in the Habakkuk *Pesher*[30]) *by corrupting the Word of God*' (2:14–17).

The Attack on Moses, the Temple, and the Earthly Stones

Paul continues this metaphor of bringing '*death*' rather than '*life*' into the next chapter of 2 Corinthians where he starts his attack on the '*some*' again, now those '*who need letters to recommend*' them – or, as he puts it thereafter in 2 Corinthians 10:12, referring to the same '*some who commend themselves, measuring themselves by themselves and comparing themselves to themselves*' (again, clearly a belittling attack on James and his Leadership who, we know, required those who would be teachers of '*Apostles*' to carry letters of appointment from James[31]) – by introducing a whole new cluster of polemical juxtapositions in the strophe/anti-strophe/epode rhetorical style centering on key words such as '*Service*'/ '*Ministry*,' '*veil*'/'*being veiled*,' and, as always '*written words*' – in this instance, '*in ink*' but also, momentarily, *to ridicule Moses*, '*in stone*' – as opposed to those (as he puts it) '*written of*' or '*by the Spirit of the Living God*' (2 Corinthians 3:1–3).

This he does while numbering himself and his associates as '*competent Servants of the New Covenant*' not like the others, whom he describes as serving '*the Ministry of Condemnation*' (*Diakonia*). He means by this, of course (just as he does in Galatians 4:25 on '*Agar*''s *Sinaitic* '*slavery*'), Mosaic Law! He then goes on to compare this '*Ministry*' which, in his view, '*was being annulled*' – as we have seen – to how '*Moses who put a veil over his face*' in order to deceive '*the Children of Israel*,' so that they '*would not have to look at the end of that which was bound to be annulled*' (*sic* – 2 Corinthians 3:13).

To put this in another way, according to Paul, Moses was a kind of '*Deceiver*' who didn't want the people to know that '*the shining Glory*' of their tradition was coming to an end. Indeed, so enamored is Paul of the metaphors he is creating that he goes on to characterize Moses' Com-mandments, '*cut in stone*' as they were, as *the Service of death* ('*Diakonia*' – the same '*Diakonia*' we have seen above in Acts 6:1–5 on the '*choosing of Stephen*' and his Hellenized companions '*to serve*'/'*wait on tables*' or in Luke and John's parallel and only slightly less defamatory '*Mary*' vs. '*Martha*' '*table-serving*' materials), triumphantly concluding this par-ticular allegorical polemic with: '*for the letter kills, but the Spirit brings life*' (2 Corinthians 3:5–13).[32]

The above '*offering up a sweet perfume*' or '*a pleasing fragrance*' imagery is from Column Eight of the Community Rule, but in Column Nine, as we have to some extent already observed, the whole metaphor is reprieved – this time seemingly applied, as in Paul – though with a more more graceful and high-minded rhetorical elegance – to '*the Men of the Community, the Walkers in Perfection*' (implying the whole Community and not just '*the Council*') now being called '*the Community of Holiness*.'[33] After playing on the combination in the Damascus Document of '*Israel and Aaron*' as the laity and the Priesthood – pictured in these Columns too of the Community Rule, it will be recalled, as '*a Holy House*' or '*the Temple*' itself or, as it expresses this, '*a Temple of the Community for Israel*' and '*a House of Holiness*' or '*Holy of Holies for Aaron*' – it is set forth that either '*the Men of the Community*' or '*the Council*' (it is not clear which)

will establish (in their '*Perfection*') *the Holy Spirit on Truth Everlasting to atone*

*for guilty transgression and rebellious sinning, and forgiveness for the Land
without the flesh of holocausts and the fat of sacrifices; and the offering of the lips
will be for Judgement like the pleasing fragrances of Righteousness; and Perfection
of the Way, an acceptable free-will offering.*[34]

Once again, this is about as '*spiritualized*' as one can get, even as '*spiritualized*' as Paul thinks he is being, the only difference, as usual, is that the
one is *a hundred and eighty degrees the reverse* of the other. To rephrase this,
whereas the group at Qumran is *inseparably attached to the Torah of Moses
both spiritually and figuratively*, Paul never misses an opportunity, as just
demonstrated, to belittle and/or undermine it whether rhetorically or
allegorically.

We have already seen in Philippians 2:25 how Paul refers to his
'*brother, partner, and comrade-in-arms*' Epaphroditus – possibly Josephus'
patron and also Nero's secretary for Greek letters by the same name (executed later under Domitian). Now he actually alludes to the contributions brought to him by this person he refers to as well as '*Apostle and
Minister to my need*' (also 2:25), '*the odour of a sweet fragrance, an acceptable
sacrifice well-pleasing to God*' (Philippians 4:18). Of course this is totally in
line with the Rabbinic tendency, following the destruction of the Temple, to consider charity – thereafter in Judaism known as '*Zedakah*' or
'*Justification*' (picked up and seemingly compressed in Islam as '*Zakat*') –
as an acceptable substitute for sacrifice in the Temple.[35] Even more to the
point, this is exactly the language used in the Community Rule above
when speaking about '*the Community Council.*'

At the same time and with a congeniality he never displays towards
his more '*Jewish*' of colleagues whatever their rank, Paul in turn sends
greetings, seemingly via this same '*Epaphroditus*,' to '*every Saint* – literally,
'*every Holy One*' as in the Community Rule and War Scroll above though
here, admittedly, with a slightly more ethereal connotation – *in Christ
Jesus*' and '*especially those in the household of Caesar*' (4:18–23). Whatever
else one might conclude, it is hard to avoid the impression that 1) Epaphroditus has connections very high up in this '*household*' and 2) when
he uses this language of an '*odour of a sweet fragrance, an acceptable sacrifice
well-pleasing to God*,' Paul is displaying familiarity with the passages, just
quoted, from the Community Rule at Qumran above.

Using exactly the same vocabulary, Paul or the Pauline author of
Ephesians now goes on to characterize '*Christ*' in the same manner,
namely, as '*giving himself for us as an offering and a sacrifice to God for an odour
of a sweet fragrance*' (5:2). 1 Peter 2:5, playing on the '*Precious Cornerstone*'
and *spiritualized Temple and Priesthood*-imagery, that is, the imagery of '*a*

House of Holiness (Temple) for Aaron in union with the Holy of Holies and a House of the Community for Israel,[36] we have just been following above, applies this *'spiritualized sacrifice'* imagery to the members of the Community it is appealing to as well:

> *You, also, as living Stones are being built up into a Spiritual House, a Holy Priesthood to offer spiritual sacrifices acceptable to God by Jesus Christ* (one should note the quasi-parallel here with Paul in 2 Corinthians 5:1, also using *'House'* and *'Building'* imagery: *'We know that if our Earthly House of the Tabernacle is destroyed, we have a Building from God, a House not made with human hands, Eternal in the Heavens'*).

In either case, we could not be closer than this to the passages in the Community Rule above. Even the connection of the *'Spiritual House'* to the *'Holy Priesthood'* is the same. In the latter, this language also evoked the imagery of *'a Precious Cornerstone, the Foundations of which will not shake or sway in its place'* from Isaiah 28:16 – imagery which, it should be appreciated, was used in conjunction with that of *'a Tested Wall'* or *'an Impregnable Bulwark'* (imagery which in early Church literature, as we have seen, was actually applied to James). But this exact imagery of a *'Wall'* or *'Bulwark'* that *'would not sway on its Foundations or move in its place'* is also used in the Qumran Hymns, once again attesting to the general synchronization or contemporaneity of all these documents, at least at Qumran.[37]

Peter as *'Stone'* and the *'Belial'* / *'Balaam'* and *'Balak'* Imagery as Applied to Herodians.

Of course the *'Peter*,' to whom this kind of *'Stone'* imagery is usually applied in early Christian documentation (the *'Cornerstone'* symbolism – incorporating, in particular, the notion of *'the Stone which the builders rejected has become the Cornerstone'* of Psalm 118:22[38] – usually rather being applied to 'Jesus'; *'the Tested Wall'* / *'Fortress'* / *'Tried Bulwark'* imagery, as just remarked, usually to James[39]), can hardly be the *'Zealot'* Simon, who is pictured in Josephus as *wanting to bar Herodians from the Temple as foreigners* and who *visits King Agrippa I's household in Caesarea to see 'what was done there contrary to Law.'*[40] This *'Simon'* rather has a lot in common with the second brother of Jesus whom we consider identical with the individual called *'Simon Zelotes'* / *'Simon the Zealot'* in Luke's Apostle lists above (*'Simon the Cananaean'* / *'Canaanite'* in Mark and Matthew as we have seen[41]) and his parallel in some early Church sources *'Simeon bar*

Cleophas'[42] – '*Cleopas*' in Luke 24:18/'*Clopas*' in John 19:25 – '*a Priest of the Sons of Rechab, a Rechabite*' in Eusebius' version of Hegesippus' picture of James' death.[43]

But whoever the '*Peter*' is to whom 1 Peter (which even evokes the metaphor of '*the living Stone, Elect and Precious to God*' in 2:4) is ascribed, 2 Peter – which in 1:1, not unremarkably, calls Peter '*Simeon,*' just as in James' speech in Acts 15:14, not '*Simon Peter*'[44] – is completely different from it in style and tone. Except for a few Paulinisms at the end, including in 2 Peter 3:15 a seemingly over-effusive reference to Paul as '*our beloved brother*' – which in the context of the rest of the letter has to be considered an interpolation – 2 Peter is replete with Qumranisms. For example, it knows the language of '*the Way of Righteousness*' (2:21) and calls Noah, very presciently, '*the Preacher of Righteousness*' (2:5). Not only does it know about the torment of '*the soul of the Righteous One*' (2:8), essential language in both the Qumran Hymns and the Damascus Document[45]; but it refers to '*the Way of Balaam the son of Besor*' (it means, of course, '*Be^cor*') who loved '*Unrighteousness*' (2:15) and, as usual, the '*Star*' (1:19) – evoking, of course, '*the Star Prophecy*' of Numbers 24:17 already sufficiently discussed above.

One would almost have to say that its author, who shows himself so intimately acquainted with Qumran doctrines, must have spent time there. This is also true of the author of '*Jude the Brother of James*' above which, in addition to '*the coming of the Myriads of His Holy Ones to execute Judgement*' against all the Ungodly, also knows the language of '*fornication,*' '*Balaam,*' '*Everlasting Fire,*' and '*the Scoffers of the Last Days*' (1:7–18).

This allusion to '*Balaam the son of Besor*' is, of course, reprised in Revelation which also fairly overflows with '*Star*' imagery,[46] where it becomes an attack on:

> *those holding the teaching of Balaam, who taught Balak to cast* (*balein*) *a net before the Sons of Israel to eat things sacrificed to idols and commit fornication* (2:14 – this is very definitely not Pauline!).

Not only is it directly followed up by an allusion to '*making war on them with the sword of my mouth*' (*cf.* Isaiah 11:4 – extant and, as we have seen, quite patently interpreted '*Messianically*' in one of the Isaiah *Peshers* at Qumran[47] – and Isaiah 49:2); but the whole is but a variation on the pivotal '*Three Nets of Belial*' passage in Column Four of the Damascus Document, there in exposition of Isaiah 24:17 ('*Panic and Snare and Net are upon you, O inhabitants of the Land*'). This last, as we have already remarked on several occasions, reads:

Its interpretation (Peshero) concerns 'the Three Nets of Belial,' about which Levi the Son of Jacob spoke (Testament of Levi 14:5–8⁴⁸), by means of which he (Belial/Balaam/Balak/the Devil) ensnares Israel, transforming them into three kinds of Righteousness.

The equivalence of language here with both 2 Peter and Revelation above should be obvious. CDIV continues:

The first is fornication, the second is Riches, and the third is pollution of the Temple.[49]

The rest of Column Four and Five is largely devoted to fleshing these accusations out. Not only is it manifestly an attack upon the Herodian Royal Family and the Priesthood it promoted – a proposition which I have already covered extensively elsewhere[50] – but the key chronological allusion, besides congruence of language with all these other documents we have been examining above (and of course their very real similarity to James' directives to overseas communities), is the combination of the *'pollution of the Temple'* and *'fornication'* charges into one complex whole, the crux of which is put very succinctly in what follows.

Not only do such persons *'not separate'* Holy *from profane 'as prescribed by Torah,'*

but they lie with a woman during the blood of her period and each man takes (to wife) the daughter of his brother and the daughter of his sister.... 'All of them are kindlers of Fire and lighters of firebrands' (Isaiah 50:11). Their webs are spiders' webs and the offspring of vipers are their eggs (compare this with the speech attributed to John the Baptist in Matthew 3:7–12 and *pars.* above).

The applicability of this passage to the Herodian Royal Family – *who married their nieces and close agnatic cousins as a matter of direct family policy –* and none other, should be self-evident.[51] This is particularly true of the allusion to *'sleeping with women during their periods,'* which is how the easygoing contact of Herodians with Romans and their inter-marriage with non-Jewish wives would have been perceived by persons in this period with this kind of native Palestinian-Jewish mindset.[52]

But the next phrase, using the *'cleanness'/'corruption'* language, *'whoever approaches them ('unless he was forced') cannot be cleansed,'* extends this to the Priesthood that owed its appointment to such *'Herodians'* (to wit, *'like an accursed thing, his house is guilty'*[53]) and fraternized willingly and regularly with them. In particular, this meant not only accepting their appointment as '*High Priests*' from them, but also accepting their sacrifices in and gifts to the Temple, even if the more purity-minded extremists regarded them as '*polluted*' – therefore the pivotal accusation in '*the Three Nets of Belial*' passage of the Damascus Document above of '*pollution of the Temple*' (*cf.* as well, the tradition communicated to R. Eliezer b. Hyrcanus by '*Jacob of Kfar Sechania*' above on what '*Jesus the Nazoraean*' said should be done with '*gifts to the Temple from prostitutes*,' in our view, a catchphrase for '*Herodians*' – in fact, at one point *even Queen Helen of Adiabene*).[54]

As we have been signaling, the '*Balaam*' and '*Balak*' language of the above allusions is just an extension of the *B-L-ᶜ/ballo* circle-of-language – in Hebrew, meaning '*to eat*,' '*swallow*,' or '*consume*' and used generally at Qumran in the sense of '*to destroy*'[55]; in Greek, '*to cast down*' or '*cast out*,' used in the literature we have been examining to express how 'Jesus'' Apostles '*cast down nets*' or '*cast out Evil Demons*' and how James or his stand-in in Acts, '*Stephen*,' were either '*cast down*' or '*cast out*' (in Josephus, the latter being used to describe what '*the Essenes*' did to backsliders, that is, '*cast them out*').[58] The transformation of this charge in Revelation, above, from the Damascus Document's '*pollution of the Temple*' into the more 'Jamesian' ban on '*things sacrificed to idols*' (a motif present as well, as we have seen, in both *MMT* and the Temple Scroll – the latter with particular reference to '*skins*'[61]) and what Hippolytus' '*Sicarii Essenes*' *refused* '*to consume*' *on pain of death* – that is, not Josephus' '*forbidden things*,' but the more Jamesian '*things sacrificed to idols*' – certainly tightens the circle of all these interrelated allusions or aspersions making the reader's brain, perhaps, spin in dizzying astonishment.[59]

For the Pseudoclementines, too, *the baptismal fountain of Jesus extinguishes the fires of sacrifice*. As the *Recognitions* puts this, not insignificantly, again Peter speaking:

> *When the time drew near that what was lacking in the regime of Moses should be made up..and the Prophet should appear* (here the '*True Prophet*' ideology of Ebionite expectation based on Deuteronomy 18:15, extant as well at Qumran in both the Community Rule and, as we have seen, the list of Messianic proof-texts called *The Testimonia*, where it is immediately followed by '*the oracle of Balaam the son of Beᶜor...who knows the Wisdom of the Most High*' that '*a Star shall come out of Israel, a Sceptre to rule the World*,' that is, '*the Star Prophecy*'[60])...(*to*) *warn them...to cease from sacrificing* (almost the precise words Epiphanius attributes to James in the *Anabathmoi Jacobou*). *However, lest they, therefore, suppose that because of the cessation of sacrifice, there was no remission of sins for them, he instituted water baptism among them*

(this point, clearly now, an '*Elchasaite*' or '*Mandaean*' ideological perspective, not specifically paralleled at Qumran as such) *in which they might be absolved from all their sins...and, following a Perfect life* (the '*Perfection*' ideology again), *they might abide in immortality, being purified not by the blood of beasts, but by the purification of the Wisdom of God*' (here, of course, again a kind of '*Holy Spirit*' Baptism).[61]

Finding ideas of this kind in documents that are supposed to be anti-Pauline, as for instance the Pseudoclementines and the Gospel of the Ebionites are considered to be, certainly is strange. Nevertheless, the documents found at Qumran along with some readings from Josephus can probably provide an answer of sorts to this kind of conundrum.

As we have observed, side-by-side with the '*spiritualized atonement*' imagery of the Community Rule above, there are at Qumran also a number of documents and passages convincingly demonstrating that '*the Community*' had a considerable and even an unwavering attachment to *the Temple Law of sacrifice*. The letter called by most scholars, appropriately or otherwise, '*MMT*' ('*Some Works of the Torah*'), is a perfect example of this as is the Temple Scroll, which lovingly dwells over details of Temple sacrifice even more comprehensively. So does the Damascus Document, the only caveat being that, in it, Temple sacrifice must either *be unpolluted* or *presided over by* '*Righteous*,' '*Zadokite*,' and '*Perfectly-uncorrupted Priests of Higher Purity*.'[62]

The same seems to be true of James personally (not to mention individuals like 'Peter and John' along with other 'Apostles' even in the portrait in Acts[63]) who, if our sources are reliable, seems to have *spent most of his earthly existence in the Temple*.[64] Nor does he hesitate to *send Paul into the Temple* to carry out an obscure '*temporary Nazirite-oath*' procedure of some kind and pay for '*four others*,' described as '*taking a vow upon themselves*' (Acts 21:22–26). Compare this with those persons, two chapters later, *now archly referred to as* '*Jews*' (23:12 – n.b., too, the ever-present '*plotting*' language here[65]), who '*put themselves under a curse* (also expressed in Acts 23:14, thereafter, as, '*with a curse we have cursed ourselves to taste nothing*'), '*vowing not to eat or drink till they had killed Paul*,' repeated again in Acts 23:21 – these clearly being '*Nazirite*' Sicarii Essenes!

How are we to reconcile these conflicting ideologies and motivations? The answer probably lies in the charge of '*unclean pollution*,' in particular, '*pollution of the Temple*,' so important to so many documents at Qumran. The very fact that James is sending out admonitions concerning '*things sacrificed to idols*' or '*the pollutions of the idols*' – the language of Acts 15:20–29, reflected as already called attention to in *MMT* as well –

to overseas Communities, implies that sacrifice was, in fact, still recognized by 'early Christians' as well (if indeed, they should be called this) – certainly in Palestine and in Jerusalem, if not elsewhere. That Paul too discusses *'things'* or *'food sacrificed to idols'* and *'eating in an idol Temple'* or *'Temple sacrifices'* – it is the same to him – and *'weak'* people who make problems over such matters, in particular, *'consuming the body'* and *'drinking the blood of Christ,'* further reinforces this impression.[66]

James' presence in the Temple from the Forties to the Sixties CE – though perhaps with intermittent periods of absence as, for example, the flight to the area of Jericho recorded in the Pseudoclementine *Recognitions* – certainly implies at least a passive approval of sacrifice procedures there, regardless of whether he felt this was the best way of proceeding or not. So does his *sending Paul into the Temple*, as just remarked, *as a penance of some sort to himself sacrifice* (a demonstration, as he is quoted in Acts 21:24, that Paul himself still *'walks in an orderly Way, keeping the Law'* – note, the Qumran language of *'walking'* and *'keeping'* here – an patent misapprehension) and *pay for the sacrifices 'of four others' under 'Nazirite' oath there* – obviously a very costly procedure even as it is portrayed in Acts. We take this episode to be historical and, clearly, there is no real, absolute disapproval of sacrifices being registered. The literature found at Qumran, despite poetic imagery that may sometimes suggest the contrary, appears to follow a similar approach.

The True *'Sons of Zadok'*: *'A High Priest of Greater Purity'* and *'Higher Righteousness'*

So what then lies behind these conflicting notices? The situation appears to have been twofold. What seems to have been happening is that, when the Temple was perceived of *'as polluted'* by *Unrighteous Priests doing service at the altar* (cf. *'the Way of Balaam the son of Beᶜor, who loved the Reward of Unrighteousness'* in 2 Peter 2:15 above or, if one prefers to use the words of the Damascus Document at Qumran, those who *'do not observe proper separation'* in the Temple, *'pure from impure, Holy from profane'*) as, for instance, *the 'Herodian' High Priesthood (though not the Maccabean), accepting gifts and/or sacrifices on behalf of Romans and other foreigners in the Temple*, the issue that triggered the Uprising against Rome[67], or when that service was otherwise interrupted; then another form of intercession or repentance was preferred.

This is exactly what Paul is implying with regard to his references to the *'well-pleasing' odour of contributions* in Philippians 4:18, *even on the part of 'the Holy Ones'* or *'Saints' in Caesar's household* in 4:22 above. When it was not perceived of as 'polluted' or interrupted, that is, when there was a 'Righteous' or, shall we say, 'Zadokite Priesthood' doing service at the altar as per the parameters of Hebrews and the Dead Sea Scrolls, then sacrifice seems to have been approved of. This, too, is exactly what is implied in the Qumran documents with their charge of 'pollution of the Temple,' one of 'the Three Nets of Belial' in the Damascus Document above or one of the sins of the reigning Priestly Establishment, in our view, founded and promoted by 'Herodians' – even by Herod himself. As Hebrews puts this, 'a High Priest, Holy, innocent, unpolluted, separated from Sinners' – here, our 'Nazirite'/Qumran/'Rechabite' language of 'separation' again[68] – who has 'become Higher than the Heavens' (7:26).

We have been documenting the agitation that broke out after the death of Herod, and even before, by 'the Innovators' (as Josephus often calls them) or 'proto-Zealots,' who from 4 BC-7 CE were already demanding 'a High Priest of greater purity' or 'Piety' or, if one prefers, 'a High Priest of Higher Righteousness.'[69] This is, of course, also the demand being made in Hebrews in its understanding of the language embodied in the circumlocution 'a Priest forever after the order of Melchizedek' (in Hebrew, literally meaning, 'King of Righteousness' – Hebrews 5:6/7:17, quoting Psalm 110:4) and 'loving Righteousness' (Hebrews 1:9, quoting Psalm 45:7).

Once again, the extreme 'Zionism' of these and other Psalms quoted in Hebrews should be stressed. Psalm 110:1, for instance, also makes mention of 'sitting on My right hand and making your enemies a footstool for your feet' (here, of course, the 'feet' imagery that so appealed to sectaries and Gospel writers). The same passage is cited a second time in Hebrews 10:13. It is also quoted in Matthew 22:44/Mark 12:36 after 'Jesus' is pictured as being baited by 'Pharisees,' 'Sadducees,' and 'Herodians' – itself directly following one of his several 'vineyard' parables, this time concluding in 21:42/12:10 with the citation of 'the Stone which the builders rejected has become the Cornerstone' from Psalm 118:22 (of course, in its original context, as already remarked, another totally aggressive, war-like, and Zionist Psalm), imagery evoked in the Community Rule above as we just saw as well.[70] This citation of the 'sitting on My right hand so I can make your enemies a footstool for your feet' also follows 'Jesus'' second (or third) evocation of the 'Righteousness'/'Piety' Dichotomy of 'loving the Lord your God with all your heart' and 'loving your neighbor' (Matthew 22:36-40 – Mark 12:30-31 has 'loving one's neighbor as oneself,' the earlier two in Matthew coming, albeit partially, in 5:49 and 19:19. Luke 20:36-44, on the other hand, omits these at this point, having already evoked them in 10:27 as a prelude to 'the Good Samaritan' encounter and, following this, his version of the 'Mary'/'Martha' 'sitting at Jesus' feet' and 'table-serving' episode) .

Nevertheless Luke 20:39 and Matthew 22:36 – though in different contexts – specifically address Jesus as '*Teacher*' and this imagery of '*making your enemies a footstool*' is, in fact, alluded to throughout the Scrolls.[71] It is hinted at in James 2:3 as well. Psalm 110 also alludes to such telltale '*Zionistic*' and '*Jamesian*' motifs as '*Strength out of Zion*,' '*the Day of Your Power*' (110:2 – as in the War Scroll, this is quite literally *armed Power*, in Islam, '*the Night of Power*' when supposedly the first verses of the Koran were revealed to Muhammad[72]), and, most importantly, *being 'Holy from the womb*' (110:3), imagery we have already seen applied both to James and John the Baptist.[73]

But the demand for '*a High Priest of greater purity*' or '*Piety*' did not just begin in these events from 4 BC-7 CE, consonant with the birth of '*Christ Jesus*,' as Paul would put it and as variously portrayed in the Gospels of Matthew and Luke. In fact, just as Josephus portrays the '*Zealot*' or '*Sicarii*' Movement in the *Antiquities* as beginning with '*the Census*' and the arguments of '*Judas and Sadduk*' with Joezer ben Boethus over the '*tax issue*' in 7 CE; for Luke 2:1–3, in another curious overlap that cries out for attention, it is the birth of '*the Messiah*' that takes place at this moment.[74] In other words, whereas for Josephus it is the '*Zealot*'/'*Sicarii Movement*' (moved as it was – as he admits at the end of the *War* – by the Messianic '*Star*' Prophecy) that begins; in the New Testament, in particular Luke, for all intents and purposes it is '*Christianity*' with the birth of its '*Messiah*' that begins at this moment, a peculiar congruence. But this demand for such an incorrupt High Priest was already, either implicitly or overtly, part of the events that produced the Maccabean Uprising, when there was also just such a struggle between '*Righteous*' High Priests and '*Ungodly*,' '*backsliding*' ones and sacrifice in the Temple was, even, for a time interrupted.

'*Onias the Righteous*,' whom we have already mentioned above – '*this Zealot for the Laws*' and '*Protector of his fellow countrymen*,' as 2 Maccabees 4:2 describes him in anticipation to a certain extent of the way early Church literature will depict James – is martyred at Antioch (this is the '*normal*' or '*real Antioch*') by the hand of a Seleucid King there '*in defiance of all Justice*' (2 Maccabees 4:34). This '*Onias*' was the son of the High Priest of the previous line, '*Simeon the Zaddik*,' whose Righteous atonement in the Temple on *Yom Kippur* is pictured in *Ben Sira*'s climactic '*praise of Famous Men*' – in reality '*praise of Men of Piety*'/'*Anshei-Hesed*,' *i.e.*, once again the theme of '*the Hassidaeans*').[75] Therefore, as we have already seen, this theme of a '*Righteous*' and/or '*Zealot Priesthood*' is a century or two older than our encounter of it with regard to '*Herodians*' and the '*Priests*' involved with and/or appointed by them.

Following the High Priest Onias' *murder by foreigners*, a motif so much a part of this struggle, and the '*pollution of the Temple*' that follows; 2 Maccabees 14:6 portrays Judas as the Leader *par excellence* of those, we have already encountered above, called '*Hassidaeans*,' no intervening presentation of '*Mattathias*' his father whatsoever. Ignoring the '*Zealot High-Priestly*' claims in 1 Maccabees 2:26-28 on behalf of his father in favor of Onias''*Perfect High Priesthood*'; 2 Maccabees 5:27 then proceeds to delineate Judas' own '*wilderness*' sojourn '*with some nine others.*'There is in this, as already suggested too, just the slightest suggestion of '*the Ten Righteous Ones*' or '*the Ten Zaddikim*' of the Abraham/Lot episode in Genesis 18:32, '*for whose sake God would withhold destruction from the Earth.*'This is true both as regards the locale, but also the ideology. 2 Peter 2:6–14 alludes to this episode, as well, after its evocation of Noah as the '*Herald of Righteousness*' and '*the Flood.*' Referring to these same '*Righteous Ones*,' it not only calls Lot '*Righteous*' and '*a Righteous One*'; but, in the style of the Qumran Hymns, highlights the suffering of his '*Righteous soul.*'[76]

Not unlike '*the Teacher*,' Josephus calls '*Banus*' in his *Vita* and with whom he spent a seeming two-year novitiate period,[77] Judas subsists on '*wild plants to avoid contracting defilement*' (2 Maccabees 5:22). Not only, therefore, did Judas at this point avoid all unclean foods, but *he ate only vegetables* and, seemingly, *wild ones* at that – that is, like a '*Rechabite*,' he did not cultivate.[78] The reason for this, as already suggested too, seems to have been that the '*Noahic*' permission to consume meat was withdrawn with the interruption of '*Righteous Temple service*' and '*sacrifice.*'This kind of vegetarianism seems to some extent also to prefigure John the Baptist – the '*fiery torch*' of whose words is depicted (in the style of Ben Sira's portrayal of Elijah's '*fiery zeal*') in Matthew 3:12,[79] Josephus' so-called '*Banus*,'[80] and even James. To repeat, this insistence on vegetarianism, which Paul calls '*weak*' in 1 Corinthians 8:7–13 above and Romans 14:1–2 (continued in 14:13–21), was not mere asceticism; but would appear to have been a consequence of *the extreme purity regulations* being observed by these '*wilderness*'-dwelling *Zaddiks*, and associated in some manner with the perception of '*the pollution of the Temple*' and *the inefficacy* or *interruption either of the sacrifices* or '*the Temple service*' being conducted there.

Where atonement on behalf of the whole people was concerned, it is 'reasonable' (or 'intelligent') to suppose – as Paul would have it in Romans 12:1 on '*the members*' of the *Community* (continuing his '*body*'/ '*members*' metaphor) themselves being '*the living Holy sacrifice well pleasing to God*' – that such a '*working prayer of the Just One*,' so pivotally evoked in James 5:16 when speaking about Elijah's '*powerful*' praying, could not be efficacious unless delivered by '*a Zaddik*' or '*a Priest Zaddik*' like James or of the kind delineated in Hebrews.

This would appear to be the position of Qumran as well in the various attempts there to come to grips with what true '*Sons of Zadok*' were. As we have seen, this phrase was also evoked with regard to Simeon the *Zaddik's* heirs in connection with his splendid *Yom Kippur* atonement in the Temple in the Hebrew version of *Ben Sira* found in the Cairo '*Genizah*,' at Masada, and at Qumran.[81] As in the New Testament, these are sometimes denoted in the Scrolls, as we have already explained, as '*the Sons of Zedek*'/'*the Sons of Righteousness*' or '*the Sons of the Zaddik*'/'*the Sons of the Righteous One*.'[82] Often modern scholars mistake these allusions for scribal errors. But these are really probably not scribal errors – simply rather, interchangeable metaphor.[83]

This then is also the true symbolism commemorated in Jewish *Hanukkah* festivities – meaning, '*Purification*' or '*Rededication of the Temple*,' festivities never really favored very much among '*the Rabbis*' as such (the true heirs of Pharisee Judaism) – therefore, the absence of the Maccabee Books explaining this Festival from their version of Scripture and, mystifyingly, only found in '*Catholic*' recensions of these materials.[84] This '*Purification*' or '*Rededication*' is celebrated in the Temple by Judas Maccabee as a powerful, '*High-Priestly*' Vicegerent of sorts.[85] Modern scholars have been quick to question his qualifications as a '*High Priest*,' but his election to this office is twice attested to by Josephus – and here the idea of '*election*' is important[86] – and, that he presides over these '*purification*' activities in the Temple is not really to be gainsaid. This is also the thrust, real or symbolic, of the presentation of 'Jesus' in the New Testament who, like 1 Maccabees 2:27 and 2:54's picture of these Maccabean purveyors of '*the Covenant of Phineas*' and their '*zeal*,' is pictured in all the Gospels, Synoptic or Johannine, as '*purifying the Temple*' as well.[87]

We know what Pauline groups preferred and, for that matter, Rabbinic ones too. The former went so far in their insistence on a more spiritualized atonement or sacrifice as to turn it into a sacramental religious creed, not only tying it to '*Mystery Religion*'-type ceremonies about '*consuming the body and blood of Christ Jesus*' or '*the living and dying god*,' but barring any other approach. Rabbinic Judaism was already purveying the notion – like Paul – that charitable contributions were equivalent to sacrifice referring to it, as already remarked, as '*Zedakah*'/'*Justification*'–'*Zakat*' in Islam[88] – a verbal noun based on the same root as '*Zedek*' or '*Righteousness*.'[89] This conceptuality and the ideology associated with it were particularly useful after the fall of the Temple, when the sacrifice ritual was for all intents and purposes either interrupted or defunct, but it was already well developed before this time, as the Apocryphal Book of Tobit makes clear.[90] But Paul, too, is well aware of this idea of *'Charity'* superseding Temple sacrifice, having studied with the Pharisaic progenitors of Rabbinic Judaism or, as Acts 23:6 has him express this, *'I am a Pharisee the son of a Pharisee'*[91] – in Philippians 3:5, as he famously puts this himself, *'according to Law, a Pharisee.'*[92]

He refers to precisely this kind of fund-raising activity at the end of Romans and in 1 Corinthians 16:3. In Romans 15:26–27 he speaks about *'the Poor of the Saints in Jerusalem,'* where he makes it clear this involved *'ministering to'* (diakonen again) or *'serving them in bodily things'* – the obvious origin of the presentation of *'Stephen'* and the other *'Six'* doing *'table service'* in Acts 6:2–5. As Paul puts it so inimitably, *'since the Peoples (Ethne) are participating in their spiritual things, they ought to minister to them in bodily things'* as well. Indeed, this notion of charity replacing sacrifice may have been how James *'the Bishop'* or *'Overseer'* – who admonished Paul (even according to the latter's own testimony in Galatians 2:10), it will be recalled, *not to forget to 'remember the Poor'* – may have understood these things as well.

The Pseudoclementines appear to have little doubt that Christ's blood *'extinguished the fire of sacrifice for all time'* which has a peculiarly *'Pauline'* ring. Indeed, this may have been the preferred doctrine among the more sophisticated or refined, but James' behavior, even in Acts – not to mention here in the Pseudoclementines – to some extent belies this as *he did send Paul into the Temple with 'four others,'* as we have just underscored, *to participate in the sacrifice cult.*

Whether groups such as those following James the Just in Jerusalem – who, most accounts attest, *went into the Temple every day for the better part of twenty years* – or *'baptizing'* or *'Nazirite'*-style groups generally, following the approach so clearly enunciated in the Community Rule above, preferred *'spiritualized'* sacrifice and atonement to actual sacrifice in the Temple, even when presided over by a *'Righteous High Priest,'* cannot be determined on the basis of the available evidence. They certainly preferred it to sacrifice offered by or atonement made by a corrupt *'Priesthood'* – a *'Priesthood'* compromised in some manner or *'polluted'* by its *contact with foreigners,* a *'Priesthood'* that collaborated with and received its appointment from *foreign Rulers, Pseudo-Jews,* or *Jewish backsliders.*[93] But this is not to say that these purist, more extreme groups were unalterably opposed at all times and under all circumstances to sacrifice in the Temple, even when it was being exercised by *'Righteous'* High Priests in a *'Righteous'* manner. This is a complex matter and the evidence will not support that.

17

James in the *Anabathmoi Jacobou*
and Paul as Herodian

The Anabathmoi Jacobou and the Literature of 'Heavenly Ascents'

It would now be well to look at the evidence in the book Epiphanius entitles *The Anabathmoi Jacobou* or *The Ascents of James* about the issue of '*Temple sacrifice*' or the lack thereof. This book, which he claims actually to have seen and presents in his discussion of '*the Ebionites*' as being a rival '*Acts of the Apostles*,' has James

> complaining against the Temple and the sacrifices, and against the fire on the altar, and much else that is full of nonsense.[1]

It is passing strange to hear Epiphanius accusing others of being '*full of nonsense*' since this is one of his own manifest shortcomings having said this, one should perhaps accept the reliability of at least some of what he presents. The *Anabathmoi Jacobou* is a lost '*Jewish Christian*' or '*Ebionite*' work, of which we only have these excerpts in Epiphanius and which probably took its title from either a real or symbolic understanding of the debates on the Temple steps with the Jerusalem Priesthood recorded in the Pseudoclementine *Recognitions* debates – as already observed – which were also refracted in numerous notices to similar effect in the first chapters of the Book of Acts (albeit with James' presence neatly deleted or overwritten) and even in the picture of James' death emerging out of Hegesippus.[2]

What remains of the *Anabathmoi* is considered to be either parallel to or incorporated in parts of the Pseudoclementines, particularly the picture of Peter, James, and John debating the Pharisaic/Sadducean Leadership on the steps of the Temple, and perhaps two other lost documents related to these – *The Preaching of Peter* and *The Travels of Peter*.[3] But to be a rival Acts, it must have contained much more than this and, as its title implies, focused more on James than any of the aforementioned appear to have done, which, in more Western orthodox fashion, seem already to prefer to call, whomever they are referring to, '*Peter*.'

The Damascus Document also is a kind of '*Opposition Acts*' from the Qumran perspective and, no doubt, the *Anabathmoi* had numerous points of contact with it too, while all the time remaining more overtly '*Jamesian*' and without the conscious concealment of known or real identities so characteristic of the former and, for that matter, just about all the literature at Qumran. The reason for such dissembling, aside from the doctrinal, usually has to do with fear of powerful external forces.[4] This is certainly the case with the Qumran literature as it has come down to us. The *Anabathmoi* does not seem to have concerned itself with such dissimulation – at least not overtly – and this, therefore, is no doubt an important reason why it did not survive.

These '*Ascents*' (since that is what the title actually means in Greek) – aside from possibly alluding to the steps of the Temple and, therefore, the debates that took place on them in all parallel narratives – can also be looked upon as the '*degrees*' of either mystic or '*Gnostic*' instruction or initiation. This is also the case for Kabbalistic Literature and what is known as '*Hechalot*' or '*Ascents*' Literature. This theme also appears to attach itself to James in the Gnostic variety of the tradition conserved in the Two Apocalypses under his name from Nag Hammadi.[5] In the writer's view, these represent a later stage of the tradition when all hope of a Messianic return or '*Victory*,' or a this-worldly Kingdom, such as the one envisioned at Qumran, had actually evaporated, giving way to the now more familiar other-worldly, ideological perspective.

Indeed, this is something of the thrust one gets in the Qumran Habakkuk *Pesher*'s interpretation of Habakkuk 2:3, leading into its *eschatological* interpretation of the Habakkuk 2:4 ('*the Righteous shall live by his Faith*,' so pivotal to both Jamesian and Pauline theological perspectives[6]) as well. Here, not only is the Righteous Teacher described – just as James is, *from the 'mouth' of Jesus* in the Second Apocalypse of James from Nag Hammadi, where *it is an actual full-mouthed kiss*; in the First Apocalypse, as already remarked, this is '*Mareim*'![7] – as receiving instruction '*from the mouth of God*'; but he is also denoted as '*the Priest*,' a term invariably meaning, as we been signaling, '*the High Priest*' in Hebrew[8] – '*in whose heart* (here another, more positive version of Paul's '*heart*' imagery) *God put the intelligence to interpret all the words of His Servants the Prophets*' and '*through whom God foretold all that was coming to His People*,' '*making known to him all the Mysteries of the words of His Servants the Prophets*' (thus!).[9] In other words, '*the Righteous Teacher*,' who seems just as James to double as '*the High Priest*' or perhaps more comprehensibly '*the Opposition High Priest*,' had virtually *a direct connection to God* and *was, like Moses*, for all intents and purposes '*His mouthpiece*.'

The main '*Mystery*' that '*God made known to him*' – notice the emphasis on '*knowing*' here (or what goes in Greek under the expression
'*Gnosis*')[10] – which is specifically said to have been an '*astonishing*' one and
delivered to him (that is, Habakkuk) as it were '*on the run*' (2:2), seems to
have been that '*the Last Era would be extended and exceed all that the Prophets
have foretold, since the Mysteries of God are astonishing.*'[11] This leads up to the
exegesis of Habakkuk 2:3 (itself leading into Habakkuk 2:4 above): '*If it
tarries, wait for it,*' the exposition of which should already be becoming
clear according to the interpretation of the Habakkuk *Pesher*, which we
shall review in more detail below. It is, of course, exactly the kind of
understanding that was developing in the first centuries of Christianity
into what latterly goes under the heading of '*the Delay of the Parousia,*' that
is, *the delay of the Second Coming of Jesus* and *its accompanying effects* – and
what some moderns refer to as '*the Rapture*' – for which believers have
been waiting quite a long time now and are liable, in the nature of things,
to wait a considerable time more (though some, as then, as always consider all such things imminent).

On the Jewish side however, as just alluded to above, there is also the
literature of '*Heavenly Ascents*' described in Jewish Kabbalistic tradition.
This '*Literature of Ascents*' or '*Hechalot Literature,*' as it is called, is the Literature of the Ascents to Heaven and the various degrees thereof.[12] For his
part, Paul actually describes in 2 Corinthians 12:2–4 meeting one such
'*Man in Christ*' who, in his view, *made one such ascent 'fourteen years before.*'
In this reference, one should note the slight play on the '*Man*'/'*Adam*'
circle-of-language, we have been calling attention to, and the '*being in
Christ*'-allusion as part of the whole '*Heavenly Ascents*' ideology – to say
nothing of Paul's juxtaposition in 1 Corinthians 15:47, above, of '*the First
Man*' as '*made of the dust*' and '*the Second Man, the Lord out of Heaven.*'

The number '*fourteen*' is extremely suggestive here, for it is exactly the
number Paul uses in Galatians 2:1 to describe the interval between his
two visits to Jerusalem, both of which times he met James – the first,
when he '*made the acquaintance of Peter*' and, according to him, saw '*no other
Apostles except James the brother of the Lord* (thus – 1:19)[13] and the second,
when he (Paul) returned for fear the course he had '*been running or had
run*' (the '*running*' metaphor again, this time in quite another context to
that in the Habakkuk Commentary's eschatological interpretation of
Habakkuk 2:2's '*reading it on the run,*' where it forms the background to
'*the Righteous Teacher*'s visionary activity[14]) and to put '*the Gospel, as* (he)
proclaimed it among the Peoples,' before '*those of repute*'/'*those reputed to be
something*'/'*those reputed to be Pillars,*' namely, '*James and Cephas and John*'
(Galatians 2:2–2:9).

Not only does Paul basically give them '*the back of his hand*' by indicating that, to him, their repute '*nothing conferred*' or, as it were, '*made no difference...because God does not accept the person of Man*' (*sic* – again, once more the allusion to '*Man*'). We have discussed this allusion to '*accepting the person of Man*' in regard to James' well-documented '*not deferring to men*' above but, in our view, when all these allusions are taken together – despite Paul's typically subdued tone in referring to persons of James' status here – that James is the one, considered to have made such an '*Ascent*' to '*the Third Heaven*' as Paul describes this in 2 Corinthians 12:2, is probably not to be gainsaid. As Paul expresses this in 12:3 amid allusion to his '*not knowing*' but '*God knowing*': '*whether in the body or out of the body,*' this '*one was caught away into the Third Heaven*' and, again in 12:4, '*caught away to the Paradise*' – in Hebrew, of course, '*Pardess,*' meaning '*Orchard*' or '*Garden,*' this being the typically Kabbalistic and, for that matter, Islamic term for precisely this kind of mystical experience. There, whomever he is referring to ('*the Righteous Teacher*' from Qumran? James?) '*heard unutterable sayings, which it is not permitted to Man to speak*' (yet again, another allusion to '*Man*').

This is certainly a very curious notice, particularly as it comes right in the midst of his attacks on the '*Arch*' or '*Super Apostles*' whom, as we saw, at one point he identifies as '*Hebrews*' (2 Corinthians 11:22), who '*commend themselves*' by '*measuring themselves by themselves and comparing themselves to themselves,*' but who also '*preach another Jesus*' (10:12–11:4). It also comes in the midst of his own '*boasting*' about – and this playing on the motif of these '*Higher Apostles*' or '*Apostles of Surpassing Degree*' just mentioned above – '*the surpassingness of (his own) Heavenly Visions* (here the word is '*Apocalypseon*'/'*Visions*' – 11:22–12:12).[15]

At the beginning of 2 Corinthians 2:12, where Paul speaks of '*a Door having been opened to me in the Lord*' ('*Door*' language not so different from that used in the question asked James by '*the Scribes and Pharisees*' in the portrait in Hegesippus of his death, '*What is the Door to Jesus?*' – James' response immediately coming, as we saw, in his proclamation of '*the Son of Man sitting on the right hand of the Great Power about to come on the clouds of Heaven*'[16]) and God '*leading us in Triumph in the Christ*' and, as already remarked as well,

> making manifest through us the perfume of the Knowledge of him in every place. For we are a sweet odour of Christ in those being saved to God...an odour of life to life (2:14–16 – sound familiar?).

As already underscored as well, Paul is at his allegorical best here; but with his remarks about '*these others*' – whom he calls '*those who are to perish*' (sometimes even, it will be recalled, '*Ministers of Death*' or '*Servants of Satan*' – remarks, however covert, clearly aimed at the '*Arch*' or '*Super Apostles*' and *the Jerusalem Church Leadership*) and, most tellingly and bitingly of all, '*an odour of death to death*'! – he reaches a rhetorical pinnacle (though some might call it, a polemical and rhetorical *nadir*).

We have already seen many of the same themes associated with James including, pre-eminently, that of the role of '*the Zaddik*' and the '*Hesed*'/'*Zedek*'-dichotomy related to it, and the doctrines ascribed generally in all contexts to him along with '*the Righteous Teacher*' from Qumran. Both of these notions have gone underground – along with much else – into Jewish Mystical Tradition only to re-emerge, as we have seen as well, in works like the *Zohar*, some thirteen or fourteen centuries later, in traditions associated with '*the Adam Kadmon*' (Hebrew for '*Primal Adam*') ideology of these earlier doctrinal currents. Some of the ideology of this '*Literature of Heavenly Ascents*' seems also to have gone into the stories about Muhammad's '*Heavenly*' voyaging in Islamic mystical tradition, both to Jerusalem and from there – like the individual here in Paul (James presumably) – to Heaven; and, in this regard, one should also note the title of the '*Surah of the Ways of Ascent*' (70.3–4).[17] There is also one particularly resplendent document of this type at Qumran, itself full of poetic and spiritualized imagery, *The Songs of the Sabbath Sacrifices*, envisioning the analogous sacrifice regime of the Angels in Heaven![18]

In the Koran too, one repeatedly encounters the ideology of '*Paradise*'/'*Pardess*' as '*Garden(s)*' – '*Gardens under which waters flow*'[19], but Muhammad also speaks both of '*journeying from Plain to Plain*' (84.19, that is, '*Hechalot Mysticism*' or '*the Mysticism of Heavenly Ascents*' again) and, of himself, as '*an Honored and Powerful Messenger* – here our '*Great Power*' language again – *established and recognized before the Lord of the Throne*' (81.19–20). Of course this last, too, is clearly a conceptuality which in the literature of *Kabbalah* goes by the companion name of '*Merkabah Mysticism*'/'*the Mysticism of the Heavenly Chariot*' or '*Throne*.' This kind of imagery is widespread in the Koran, but it is also known in both *Hadith* Literature and Islamic Mysticism generally.[20]

As just implied, there may also be something of this idea of James as a mystic teacher suggested by the title of the book about his teachings, the '*Anabathmoi Jacobou*' or the '*Heavenly Ascents of James*' which, Epiphanius claims, *was known to the Ebionites*, that mystic '*Knowledge*,' for instance, communicated by '*the Heavenly kiss*' that either James gives Jesus or – depending on the presentation – Jesus gives James or others in Gnostic variations on such ideologies embodied in books such as the two Apocalypses of James from Nag Hammadi.[21] It is impossible to say because the complete text of '*The Ascents of James*' is unavailable to us.

The Ban on Foreigners in the Temple (including Herodians)

One should note that in 1 Corinthians above, Paul also sees himself as having '*Mysteries*' revealed to him and, in turn, revealing them to his congregants. In 4:1 he actually calls himself and his colleagues – seemingly '*Cephas*' and '*Apollos*,' but others as well – '*Attendants of Christ and Keepers of the Mysteries of God*' (note the Qumran language here, to say nothing of that of the Letter of James, of '*Keeping*'/'*Keepers*,' now being applied to '*Mysteries*' as well as the variation on the language of '*Servants*'/'*Diakonoi*' already remarked several times above as well[22]).

In 1 Corinthians 14:2-4, too, following still another allusion to '*running*' in 14:1 (in this case '*after love*'); Paul, once again, claims that '*he is speaking with a Tongue*' and '*in (the) Spirit*,' and thus, both '*building up*,' '*speaking to God not men*,' and '*speaking Mysteries*' (here, of course, not only the '*building up*' language he uses to attack the '*some with weak consciences*,' '*puffed-up*' by their own '*Knowledge*,' i. e., the Leadership of '*the Jerusalem Church*' itself, but also the vocabulary of the '*Tongue*,' which we have already called attention to in the Letter of James and the Scrolls above, both genres of which language we shall encounter further in the Scrolls below[23]). In fact, even earlier after speaking about '*works of Power*' and his own '*surpassing zeal*' for things like '*speaking in Tongues*' (1 Corinthians 12:28–31) – the '*mastery of all the Secrets of Men and all respective Tongues*' being a basic qualification of the Damascus Document's '*Overseer*'/'*Bishop*' or '*Mebakker*'[24]; in 13:2, he actually seems to be parodying the description of '*the Righteous Teacher*' in the Scrolls, when he speaks of '*having prophecy and knowing all Mysteries and all Knowledge*'[25] while at the same time, in the antistrophe, disparaging this with the words, '*but not having love being nothing*.'

But the Scrolls too speak of such '*Mysteries*,' not only in the Community Rule and relative to unique attributes of '*the Righteous Teacher*' in the Habakkuk *Pesher* above, but in other documents as well – as does Muhammad in the Koran.[26] The same can be said for James in the picture in the Pseudoclementines, though in both them and the Scrolls, teachers are cautioned to keep such things secret, revealing them only to the inner core of colleagues practising real '*Perfection of the Way*.'[27] Paul by contrast, as in Romans 16:25-26 and 1 Corinthians 14:25, wants everything '*made manifest*' and '*nothing hidden*' (at least, after such time that '*the Lord has come*') and in 1 Corinthians 2:4–7, where he again speaks of '*the*

Spirit' and *'of Power'* (the *'Power of God'*) and even applies the *'coming to nothing'* language of 13:2 above to *'the Rulers of this Age'* and *'the Wisdom not of this Age,'* implying they are one and the same; he alludes both to *'speaking among the Perfect'* and *'speaking the Wisdom of God in a Mystery which God has hidden and pre-ordained before the Ages for our Glory.'* In 1 Corinthians 4:5 and 2 Corinthians 4:2–4:6, he even applies Qumran *'Light and Dark'* imagery to these sorts of propositions.

Contrary-wise, regarding Epiphanius' contention that James *'spoke against the Temple and the sacrifices,'* there *is* something to say. Though it is impossible to reconcile it with the material about James from earlier sources like Hegesippus and Josephus, who taken together place him in the Temple *on a daily basis* for the better part of twenty years, or the very solid testimony in the *'We Document'* section of Acts where, as we just saw, James sends Paul into the Temple to pay, not only for his own sacrifices, but also *the sacrifices of four others in a Nazirite oath of some kind*; nevertheless, with the slightest shift in phraseology and signification, it is possible to fit the attitude reported by Epiphanius, himself originally an Ebionite, fairly easily into the situation in Jerusalem in this period and what we know about James generally, to say nothing of the so-called *'Teacher of Righteousness'* at Qumran.

For example, we just saw that in Acts that James imposes this *'temporary Nazirite'*-style penance on Paul – a penance some commentators view as *'a set-up'*[28] – to show that *'there is nothing to all'* the rumors people

> have been informed concerning you, but you yourself still walk undeviatingly, keeping the Law (again, note the *'Jamesian'*/Qumran-style emphasis on *'keeping the Law,'* but also the Qumran-style language of *'walking straight'* and *'undeviatingly'*[29]).

The relevant point in all these matters, as we have been emphasizing, is the *hostility to foreigners*, vividly evinced even in Acts' description of the riot that follows by the Jewish crowd. As Acts 21:24–28 portrays this – in contrast to earlier portrayals, in our view, now fairly accurately – *'Jews coming from Asia'* (which would presumably include those from Asia Minor, Galatia, Cilicia, Northern Syria, Edessa, and even Adiabene), *'saw him* (Paul) *in the Temple and stirred up all the crowd,'* a picture retrospectively incorporated into the Gospels about events circulating around Jesus' death but with, as usual, more historical plausibility where Paul is concerned.[30]

Acts 21:29 even even feels obliged to add, by way of explanation to gainsay this:

> *For they had earlier seen Trophimus the Ephesian* (unlike others in Acts, this character at least appears to be historical – *cf.* 2 Timothy 4:20, which locates him in Miletus not far from Ephesus) *with him in the city and supposed Paul had brought him into the Temple.*

So we also now have here in this picture *the ban on introducing foreigners* or *non-Jews* – according to many extremists including even '*Herodians*' – *into the Temple* that so much exercised this period.[31] '*Laying hands on him,*' these now cry out:

> *Men, Israelites, help! This is the man who teaches everyone, everywhere against the People, against the Law, and against this Place,* (again, in our view, this is an absolutely truthful portrait) *and now he has brought Greeks into the Temple and polluted this Holy Place!*

There can be little doubt that here we have, anyway, the '*pollution of the Temple*' from '*the Three Nets of Belial*' charges at Qumran and in this context, at least, we know the reasons why. One could go even further and observe that what Paul is doing here is acting as '*a stalking horse*' for the Herodian family, testing the ban, mentioned in Josephus, on some of its principal members, such as Agrippa II and Bernice, in the Temple.[32]

However this may be, thereupon he is unceremoniously ejected and '*the doors closed*' or '*barred*' *behind him*. The words Acts 21:30 uses at this point to describe what happened, '*they dragged Paul outside the Temple* (shades of the fictionalized stoning of Stephen in the ahistorical part of Acts earlier) and *immediately shut the doors,*' have an odd resonance with and parallel the phraseology used in the Damascus Document concerning those '*who have been brought*' into '*the New Covenant in the Land of Damascus,*' '*who dug the well with staves*' – the '*staves*' here ('*hukkim*' in Hebrew) being a double entendre based on Numbers 21:18 meaning '*the Laws*' (also '*hukkim*'), which '*the Staff*'/'*Mehokkek*' or '*Legislator*' decreed (*hakak*), complexities to which we shall return in due course.[33]

Initiants such as these are, then, advised '*not to enter the Temple to kindle its altar in vain*' – rather '*they are to be* (as in Acts 21:30 just quoted above) *Barrers of the Door,*' that is, to persons like Paul and his companions. At this point, the Damascus Document goes on to quote Malachi 1:10: '*Who among you will not shut its door* (meaning '*of the Temple*') *and not kindle useless fires on My altar?* – the implication being, '*fires*' like the '*useless fires*' of the corrupt Herodian Priesthood. To put this in another way, if you are going to light the fires of sacrifice in the Temple, then you must abjure the consonant '*pollution of the Temple*' referred to in '*the Three Nets* of Belial' charges just preceding this citation.

Not only is this somewhat the reverse of the language being applied to the treatment of Paul here in Acts, it is precisely the teaching ascribed to James in the testimony, Epiphanius excerpted from the no-longer extant, otherwise-lost document he calls '*The Anabathmoi Jacobou*,' delineating how James *complained against lighting the useless 'fires on My altar'* – yet again, further consolidating the '*Jamesian*' character of the Damascus Document as it has been unfolding to us so far.[34]

Moreover, since the document first found in the Cairo *Genizah* at the end of the last century bears no actual name, it may be that the document Epiphanius is trying to describe is simply a variation of it or, even perhaps, *the 'Damascus Document' itself.* It is impossible to say from the available data. As we have been intent on showing, the Damascus Document *does complain against 'pollution in the Temple'* and now, as just elucidated, *against the sacrifices and 'lighting the fires on its altar in vain.'* A '*Jamesian*' authorship this document and, for that matter, related documents such as the '*Letter*' or '*Letters*' known as '*MMT*' is not something that should be ruled out on the basis of the chronology of Qumran as such or as it presently stands.[35]

The Damascus Document then directly moves on to evoke the idea of '*keeping*' or '*being Keepers*' (*of the Torah* or *the Law* – in Paul above, '*of the Mysteries*')' and to recommend, again, the '*Jamesian*'

> doing according to the precise letter of the Torah in the Age of Wickedness (*cf.* Paul in 1 Corinthians 2:6 above on '*the Rulers of this Age that are coming to nothing*' – that is, '*the present Age*') and to separate from the Sons of the Pit (the '*Pit*' language, again, of Matthew 15:13–14's '*Blind Guides*' and '*every Plant uprooted*' discourse) and keep away from polluted Evil Riches (the '*pollution*' theme once more and the exact language James uses in Acts 21:25, itself preceded by allusion in 21:24 to '*keeping the Law*') acquired by vow or ban and (keep away) from the Riches of the Temple.[36]

Here, not only are we speaking of exactly the same kind of contributions connected to the '*vows*' or '*bans*' that Acts 21:23 is speaking about in the matter of Paul's sacrifice expenses and his unceremonious ejection from the Temple; but the actual phrase used to express this, '*keeping away from*' ('*lehinnazer*'/'*to be set aside*,' in Hebrew), is based on the same root, as we have already pointed out, as the term '*Nazirite*' and plays on the real versions of such activity as exemplified by the Community itself. Nor can there be very much doubt as to what is being said here.[37]

This is immediately followed too by allusion to '*robbing the Poor of His*

People,' which echoes the notices found in Josephus about the High Priests '*robbing the tithes of the Poor Priests*' in the picture he gives of the run-up in Book Twenty of the *Antiquities* to *the stoning of James* and *the War against Rome*.[38] The same accusation will form part of the accusations against the Priestly Establishment in the Habakkuk *Pesher*'s lengthy scenario of the destruction of the character it knows as '*the Righteous Teacher*'.[39] As also already alluded to, the verb based on this '*Nazirite*' root actually appears twice more in as many columns of the Damascus Document. This first evocation is immediately followed by reference to '*the New Covenant in the Land of Damascus*' and citation of the '*Jamesian*' Royal Law according to the Scripture, '*to love, each man, his brother as himself*'.[40] This is accompanied by the admonition, already remarked as well, to '*separate between polluted and pure*,' '*Holy and profane*' – the mirror opposite of what Peter learns on the rooftop in Jaffa in Acts 10:14–15 and 10:28, '*not to make distinctions between Holy and profane*' (this also seemingly direct from the mouth of God!).

In the Damascus Document this is, then, typically followed at the beginning of the next Column with a warning '*to keep away from fornication*,' again expressed by the verb '*lehazzir*,' another variation based on the same root as the Hebrew usage '*Nazirite*'.[41] It should be clear that these are the exact words of the prohibition, as it is expressed in James' directives to overseas communities – once in the context of James' final words to Paul in Jerusalem in Acts 21:20–25, ending with the penance James puts upon him involving '*Nazirite*' oath expenses and procedures.

One final use of the expression in the Damascus Document occurs at the beginning of the next Column (CDviii) in the context of further allusion to '*wallowing in the Ways of fornication and Evil Riches*' and '*each man bearing malice against*' and '*hating his brother*' – the opposite, to be sure, of '*each man loving his brother as himself*' earlier and in the Letter of James above.[42] Here the condemnation of '*Riches*' – as in the Letter of James 5:1–6 as well – is extreme; but, in addition, each man is said to have '*approached the flesh of his own flesh for fornication*' (again, the '*niece marriage*' and '*marriage with close cousins*' charges of '*the Three Nets of Belial*' accusations earlier, the latter even perhaps including the '*incest*' one as well), all matters that can be associated in one manner or another with Herodian marital or sexual behavior,[43]

> *using their power for the sake of Riches and profiteering* (inverting the charge made by Paul in 2 Corinthians 2:17 above on how '*the Many* – a term, as already underscored, used in the Community Rule above to denote the rank and file of Community membership – *profiteered from corrupting*

*the word of God'), each doing what was right in his own eyes and each choosing
the stubbornness of his own heart* (favorite imagery both at Qumran and in
Paul – in the former, usually denoting *'those deserting the Torah'* or backsliders of the genus of a Paul), *for they did not* (and here, the *'Nazirite'*
usage) *keep apart from* (*nazru*) *the People* (probably also meant as inclusive
of *'Peoples'*) *and sinned publicly.*[46]

A better description of the Herodian Establishment could not be
imagined.

This now ends with direct evocation of *'the Kings of the Peoples,'* a term
in Roman jurisprudence used to describe *petty kings in the Eastern part of
the Empire,* mostly *'Greek-speaking'* like the Herodians.[47] This is where *'the
Head (Rosh) of the Kings of Greece'* or *'Greek-speaking Kings,'* that is also part
of the exegesis that follows, will – as we shall see – come into play.[48] In
the Western part of the Empire, integration with the Roman polity generally was more widespread. Identified with Deuteronomy 33:32's
'serpents' – another term with parallels that are almost proverbial in the
Gospels[49] – and playing on the double entendre in Hebrew, *'their venom'*
(*'rosh'* as well, which can also mean in Hebrew, as we just saw, *'Head'* as in
'the Head of the Greek-speaking Kings' – *'yayin'/'wine'* and *'Greece'/'Yavan'*
forming another such homonymous couplet) is identified as *'the wine of
their Ways'* – the implication being, to use Acts' nomenclature in a probably slightly different manner, *'Hellenizing.'*[50] In addition, the Lying
visions of *'the Lying Spouter...who walked in the Spirit'* – a third double
entendre based on Micah 2:11, *'wind'* and *'Spirit'* in Hebrew likewise
being homonyms – is then also directly evoked.[51]

James in the *Anabathmoi Jacobou* and *'Pollution of the Temple'*

We have already provided substantial reason for considering the Damascus Document a kind of 'Opposition' Acts, despite its being in some
passages more exhortative than it and full of the same kind of polemical
invective as Paul. Much in it does have to do with themes one can actually associate directly with James – this on the basis of *'the internal data,'*
we have been providing, and despite what Qumran *'Consensus Scholars'*
might make of its dating.[52] We explained in *Preliminaries* how these scholars make chronological evaluations based on their own preconceptions
and *'external'* investigative devices like their palaeographic sequences and
carbon testing, *none of which in cases as uncertain as dating at Qumran can* or
should be considered definitive.[53] All things being equal, as we have been
stressing, it is the *'internal'* data – that is, *what the documents themselves*

actually say — which must take precedence over the '*external*' data, such as it is where Qumran is concerned and, when there is a conflict between them, the '*internal*' evidence should be *the defining criterion.*[54]

The above evocation of '*doing according to the precise letter of the Torah*' preceded as it is by the telltale allusion to '*keeping*,' not only exactly parallels, as we have underscored, James 2:8–10 about '*keeping the whole Law, but stumbling on one point*' but also the allusion in Jesus' James-like '*Sermon on the Mount*' to '*not one jot or tittle passing away from the Law*' (Matthew 5:18 and *pars.*). Just as the sequence found in the Letter of James, this section of the Damascus Document ends in an allusion to '*the Royal Law according to the Scripture*' as we have just seen.'[55]

We have just seen too how, following this third allusion to '*keeping away from the People*' (one should possibly also read '*Peoples*' here) and in connection with *entering both* '*the New Covenant in the Land of Damascus*' and '*the Well of Living Waters,*' '*setting up the Holy Things according to their precise specifications,*' is now alluded to.[56] It should be appreciated that '*Holy Things*' is synonymous with '*Consecrated Things*' not only, for instance, as regards the Temple Priesthood — which was in fact considered '*Holy to God*' or '*consecrated*' — but also where those following the regime of life-long '*Naziritism*' were concerned.[57]

This new Community '*in the wilderness*' also involved a reunion of the wilderness '*Camps*' under the supervision of an individual referred to as '*the Mebakker*' or '*Overseer*' (as already suggested, a more relevant English equivalent would probably be '*the Bishop*'[58]) or '*the High Priest Commanding the Many*' at Pentecost time — both, roles James is accorded in Christian tradition.[59] One should also note here the vocabulary of '*the Many,*' just encountered in a more derogatory vein above in Paul — this, in particular, in fragments of the Damascus Document not found in the Cairo *Genizah* version, themselves first published by the author.[58] At the same time,

> *all those who rejected* (a typical allusion, always applied to '*the Liar*' or '*the Spouter of Lying*' at Qumran[59]) *the Commandments of God* (we know what this means) *and forsook them, turning aside in the stubbornness of their heart* (again the repetition of both the telltale '*heart*' and '*stubbornness*' allusions — probably we should know what this means as well).

This both included '*all the Men who entered the New Covenant in the Land of Damascus,*' but also those who

> *turned back and betrayed* (the '*Treachery*' allusion so prominent in New

Testament reformulation of same) *and turned aside from the Fountain of Living Waters*[60]

'*Pentecost*' is precisely the festival Acts 20:16 pictures Paul as hurrying to Jerusalem to attend with the contributions he has so assiduously gathered overseas (*cf.* too, 2 Corinthians 1:15–19, 8:13–9:15, Philippians 4:15–19, etc. in this regard). In these more-recently published fragments, tow of which clearly comprising – because of the blank lined space on the bottom and to the left[61] – the actual last Column of the Damascus Document[62]; the oaths taken in connection with *this reunion of the Wilderness Camps*' involve *a total rededication to the Law* and not '*deviating to the right or to the left of the Torah,*' which is exactly the sense of James' directive to Paul in Acts 21:24 above on Pentecost about '*still walking undeviatingly keeping the Law.*'

Similar formulations, as we have seen, are to be found in the Community Rule.[63] Of course, the parallel to all this in Acts 2:1–6 is the descent of the Pauline '*Holy Spirit*' like '*a rushing violent wind*' (compare this with the imagery connecting '*the Lying Spouter*' or '*Windbag*' to '*walking in windiness*' in the Damascus Document above as well[64]) and '*God-fearing men from every People*' ('*Ethnous,*' singular here as in the Damascus Document's '*not separating from the People*' just quoted above) – presumably in preparation for the Pauline Gentile Mission too – '*speaking with other Tongues*' (here again, the '*Tongue*'/'*Tongues*' vocabulary and an ability, as we have just seen, accorded '*the Mebakker*' in the Damascus Document as well.[65] It should be appreciated that the kind of '*separation*' both '*in the Temple*' and '*from the People*'/'*Peoples,*' being recommended in these passages in the Damascus Document, is during such time when it (the Temple) was perceived of as '*being polluted*' by '*polluted Evil Riches*' and, for example, by what was being '*robbed from the Poor*' – not an abandonment of '*Torah*' or '*the Law*' altogether.

But this passage based on Malachi 1:10 above about '*not entering the Temple to light its altar in vain,*' which begins this whole string of allusions in the Damascus Document and brings us full circle back to the *Anabathmoi Jacobou,* Acts, and the Letter of James; also gives us something of the idea of what the issues really were here. What is so exercising Malachi in the background to this quotation is '*putting polluted food on My Altar*' (1:7), this in James' directives, *MMT,* and Hippolytus' picture of '*Sicarii Essene*' willingness to martyr themselves,[66] expressed rather in terms of '*things sacrificed to idols*' (in the Temple Scroll, as a;ready alluded to, '*skins sacrificed to idols,*' a sub-category), not the abolition of the Law of Sacrifice *per se* – the position, as it turns out, attributed to James in the *Anabathmoi*

Jacobou. Again, the problem is '*polluted things*' (in the version of James' directives quoted in Acts 15:20, '*the pollution of the idols*,' as we have seen) or '*pollution of the Temple*' as in the Damascus Document above.

Malachi is also the prophet who alludes to '*sending My Messenger*' to '*prepare the Way before Me*' (3:1) and '*sending Elijah the Prophet before the coming of the Great and Terrible Day of the Lord*' (4:5), again our '*Day of Vengeance*' in the Community Rule and War Scroll above – interestingly enough, in Ezekiel 38:22 and even in the Nahum *Pesher*, expressed in terms of '*torrential rain*,' which actually closes the circle with all these '*rain-making*' *Zaddik*s we have detailed previously.[67] Now we *are* in a more recognizably Judeo-Palestinian milieu. Though this is the Prophecy that is exploited in the presentation of John the Baptist in the Synoptic Gospels, it should be appreciated that '*remembering the Law of My Servant Moses, which I commanded him at Horeb for all Israel*,' is the line directly pre-ceding this in Malachi 4:4, a passage which obviously would not have failed to leave its impression on the sectaries at Qumran – but, as should be easy to comprehend in view of all the foregoing, not on Paul nor in the way its follow-up is exploited in the Synoptics.

But we do not need these passages from Malachi and the Damascus Document at Qumran to make sense of the material about James which Epiphanius cites from the document he is calling 'the *Anabathmoi Jacobou*.' No doubt, the issues really did center – as in the famous letter(s) I entitled '*Two Letters on Works Righteousness*' (*MMT*)[68] – on '*the sacrifices and the Temple*,' but what kind of '*sacrifices*' and what was the concern regarding '*the Temple*'? After the destruction of the Temple, a situation seemingly alluded to in the long passage from Peter's speech quoted above in the Pseudoclementine *Recognitions*,[69] it was easy to reframe or transform these issues in the manner we are seeing in the *Anabathmoi* or the *Recognitions*' debates on the Temple stairs that appears to have relied upon it.

Where the Temple is concerned, the issue is pretty straightforward. I think we can safely say that James complained not simply '*about the Temple*,' as Epiphanius somewhat superficially reduces it, but about '*pollution of the Temple*,' as this is framed in the Damascus Document from Qumran, and the manner in which '*Temple service*,' as the Rabbis for their part would have it, was being conducted by the Herodian Establishment and its '*Sadducean High Priests*,' that is, '*Priests*' appointed by corrupt foreign Governors and a Royal Family that the more extreme groups considered to be foreigners of Greco-Arab descent and not even, for the most part, *Jewish at all*.[70]

This is what makes the Talmudic episode in the *Mishnah* so poignant when it depicts the most respected member of this family, King Agrippa I (37–44 CE – *whose grandmother had been a Maccabean Princess*), *weeping in the Temple on the Festival of Tabernacles*, when the Deuteronomic King Law: '*You shall not put a foreigner over you who is not your brother*' (17:15) was read. Here the Pharisees, who redacted this material, '*cry out*' – as is usual in these stories – three times, '*You are our brother! You are our brother! You are our brother!*' when, of course, in actuality (except for one matrilineal grandmother) for the most part he was not.[71] For the '*Zealot*' Simon, *the Head of '*an Assembly*' (*Ecclesia*) of his own in Jerusalem*, depicted in Josephus at exactly the same time as *wanting to bar Herodians from the Temple just because they were foreigners, Agrippa I was a foreigner.*

Not only is this episode clearly related, on the one hand, to this passage in the *Mishnah* above; but, on the other, it is also related to the descent of '*the Heavenly tablecloth*' episode ('*by its four corners*'!) in Acts 10:17–48 depicting, as we have several times had occasion to remark, another '*Simon*' – in this instance, the so-called '*Simon Peter*' on a rooftop in Jaffa – learning that he '*should not call any man profane*' and *to be more accepting of foreigners* just in time to receive the deputies of and visit in Caesarea, as well, the household of the new '*Christian*' convert, the Roman Centurion Cornelius, a man Acts also describes – somewhat comically, as already observed – both as '*a Pious God-Fearer...doing many good works to the People and praying to God continually*' (10:2).[72]

Not only is '*Peter*' portrayed here as making one of the many '*blood libel*' speeches we have already outlined above too (10:39); but, as we have in numerous other venues set forth, the visit Peter makes to the Roman Centurion Cornelius' household here – having just learned, as he puts it, that he is now '*allowed to come near a man of another race*' (10:28 – this inaccurate characterization is certainly written by a non-Jew, being the way such an individual would have perceived Jewish purity regulations) – is the mirror reversal of the one the '*Simon*' portrayed in Josephus makes to the household of Agrippa I, the most '*Pious*' of all Herodian Kings, a man who *really did* try to '*do many good works for the People,*' '*to see what was done there contrary to Law.*'[73] Of course, as to some degree previously explained, what Acts has done here is simply substitute the Roman Centurion from '*the Italica Regiment*' (a town in Spain which was the birthplace of both Trajan and Hadrian – two of the most-hated enemies of the Jews[74]) for Agrippa I. In our view too, the historical '*Simon*' is the one who was *the Head of his own '*Assembly*' or '*Church*' (*Ecclesia*) in Jerusalem at this time* and *someone who really would have been arrested after the untimely and mysterious death of Agrippa I* (*cf.* Acts 12:21–23).[75]

Of course, the Deuteronomic King Law, which was the passage to be read in the Temple on Tabernacles, has now been found enshrined at Qumran in the Temple Scroll.[76] If we had not found it, we would have had to predicate it. It was statutes such as these and their derivative, *the illegality of foreign appointment of 'High Priests'*; that were, for groups like '*the Zealots*,' the '*jots and tittles*' that should not be deleted from the Law – as, one should add, they were for Qumran – these together with other basic requirements like '*circumcision*' in the matter of conversion and *not divorcing* or *marrying nieces*. As the Temple Scroll puts this last with regard to '*the King*,' '*he shall not take a second wife during the lifetime of the first, for she shall be with him all the time of her life*,' nor '*shall he marry a wife from the daughters of the Peoples*' (this last being particularly relevant where '*Herodians*' were concerned). [77]

James also Complained against Gifts and Sacrifices on Behalf of Herodians and Other Foreigners in the Temple

Where the issue of '*Temple pollution*' is concerned, as we have now several times remarked, it was a central fixture of the '*Three Nets of Belial*' charges in the Damascus Document and was always hovering in the background of the prescriptions in *MMT*.[78] No doubt, too, it was part and parcel of what was being signified in James directives to overseas communities under the rubric of '*things sacrificed to idols*' and '*the pollutions of the idols*.' Josephus repeats the charge over and over again – albeit sometimes with inverted signification – in his description of the run-up to the War against Rome.[79] It was also the backbone of the issue behind '*the Temple Wall' Affair* in which, from our perspective, James was involved and which not only centered on *barring 'foreigners' like the Herodians from the Temple*, but even *their view* and *that of their dining guests of the sacrifices in the Temple*.[80]

But it is the particular variation of it, which Josephus describes in these same descriptions in the *Jewish War*, which provides the key to unlocking the meaning of this second allusion from the *Anabathmoi Jacobou*, as recorded by Epiphanius, that James '*complained against the sacrifice*.' What is particularly exercising Josephus in his description of the run-up to the War against Rome is the *rejecting gifts and sacrifices on behalf of Romans and other foreigners* and *the stopping of sacrifices on behalf of the Emperor in the Temple by the Lower Priesthood*, among whom James' influence seems to have been strong.[81] This event is the direct cause of the outbreak of the War against Rome which, in turn, led inexorably to the destruction of the Temple and the fall of Jerusalem – events so telescoped by early Christian sources relating to the death of James.[82]

Like so many other things he disapproves of and blames on those he refers to derogatorily as '*Zealots*' or '*Sicarii*,' Josephus claims, as already remarked, this cessation of sacrifice on behalf of foreigners in the Temple was '*an Innovation which our Forefathers were before unacquainted with.*'[82] This is certainly *not the case* in the passage leading up to Ezekiel's all-important definition of '*the Sons of Zadok*' (44:15) where significantly, as we saw as well, Ezekiel absolutely *bars any foreigner, 'uncircumcised in heart or body*' (an allusion that will actually be played upon in the description of Habakkuk *Pesher's* '*the Wicked Priest*' at Qumran[84]) from the Temple (44:7–9). In fact, Ezekiel even calls this '*pollution of the Temple*,' but of course – aside from Isaiah – Ezekiel is, not surprisingly, perhaps the most highly-regarded prophet at Qumran.[85]

We have seen that this passage forms the centerpiece of the definition in the Damascus Document of the '*Sons of Zadok*' at Qumran which can, therefore, also be seen as inclusive of *the opposition to just such 'gifts and sacrifices*' *on the part of foreigners in the Temple*. This theme is further reinforced in the Temple Scroll and the Habakkuk *Pesher* – more homogeneity and therefore, in our view, simultaneity – as it is in the '*Two Letters on Works Reckoned as Righteousness*' above.[86] '*The pollutions of the idols*' or '*things sacrificed to idols*' in James' directives, as redacted in Acts and so refracted too by Paul in 1 Corinthians 8–11 and in *MMT*, also links up with the '*polluted food on the table in the Temple*' in Malachi 1:7 – itself relating to the two accusations against *the way 'Temple service' was being conducted* and *the sacrifices that were being accepted there* in both the Damascus Document and the *Anabathmoi Jacobou*.

It is not a very great step, therefore, to attribute these injunctions to James' *teaching 'in the Temple*' and part of what was implied as well in his directives to '*abstain from* (in the Damascus Document, '*to keep away from*'/'*lehinnazer*') *blood, things sacrificed to idols, fornication, and strangled things*' or '*carrion*' in Acts 15:29 and 21:25, at least before things of this kind were retrospectively transformed and moved in these sources slightly sideways or laterally after the fall of the Temple.

We can conclude, therefore, that James *did not 'complain against the Temple and the sacrifices*' *per se*, as Epiphanius via the *Anabathmoi Jacobou* would have it. This has to do with somewhat later more '*Christian*' distortion or misinterpretation. What he did complain about, particularly if he had any involvement in '*the Temple Wall*' *Affair* leading up to his demise and anything in common with the Righteous Teacher at Qumran – which the writer thinks he did – were '*gifts and sacrifices on behalf of foreigners*' and '*pollution of the Temple*,' both to some extent relating to the same issue. In other words, a few extra words clarifying these complaints have been deleted. Deletions such as these change the whole texture of the charges. What James did '*complain against*' was '*sacrifices on behalf of foreigners*' and '*the way Temple service was being conducted*' by the collaborating, '*Rich*' and corrupt '*Herodian Priesthood*,' a '*Priesthood*' that owed its appointment to equally '*Rich*' and corrupt Herodian Kings and foreign Governors.

Seen in this light, James' complaints and those of other Scroll documents along with him really do lead directly to the destruction of the Temple and the fall of Jerusalem, as Christian tradition and others rightly understood in their attempts to portray this sequence of events.[87] The only problem is that Eusebius, Clement, and their sources misunderstood the sense of what they had before them or purposefully reversed it, either out of ignorance or just plain malice – just as the citation from the *Anabathmoi Jacobou*, quoted by Epiphanius, that pictures James as speaking against '*kindling the fire on the altar*' has done. Though James did complain about such things, he did not '*complain*' in precisely in this way. It is by shifting the sense of these materials just the slightest bit and harmonizing them with the facts in other more precise, though sometimes equally subjective sources, such as Josephus and the Dead Sea Scrolls, that one can retrieve their true meaning which lies, as it were, just as in Acts, like a pebble in a clear stream just beneath the surface of the narrative.

The fact of James' person and his discourse or protests in the Temple *did lead directly to the war against Rome* as early Christian tradition, following Hegesippus and Origen, suggests. This broke out *almost exactly* '*three and a half years*' *after his death* – the curious timeframe first spoken of in Daniel 7:25 having to do with cessation of sacrifice and itself an element in the Letter ascribed to James' name in the New Testament as the period between the two '*fervent prayer(s) of a Just One which much prevailed*' (James 5:16–17). This War was precipitated, as just indicated, by *the stopping of sacrifices on behalf of the Roman Emperor and other foreigners (including Herodians)* and *the rejection of their gifts in the Temple*, an act even Josephus bitterly labels '*an Innovation*.' This was done by the '*zealous*,' every-day, working priests of '*the Lower Priesthood*' in the Temple – James' probable constituency – many of whom *had just won the right to wear linen*, as Josephus somewhat enigmatically points out – just as James all the time himself had done according to early Church testimony.[88]

The spirit, therefore, of this martyred '*Opposition*' High Priest/*Zaddik* James suffused the whole process, as it did the sequence of events (including '*the Temple Wall*' *Affair*) leading inexorably up to the final War against Rome. This, as both Origen and Eusebius attest – the one via Josephus and the other via Hegesippus[89] – can be seen as directly relating to his death. The same can be said for the spirit of the martyred *'Teacher of Righteousness'* as he is, in particular, portrayed in both the Habakkuk and Psalm 37 *Peshers* of the Dead Sea Scrolls.[90] As we shall see, this will be precisely what is implied by events surrounding another constellation of notices, those of *'a flight to Pella'* by the followers of James after his death and the mysterious oracle, upon which such a flight was supposed to have been based, which we shall treat in the next chapter.

Paul as Herodian in *The Anabathmoi Jacobou*

Before elucidating what is implied by these materials about the flight across Jordan of *'the Jerusalem Community'* of James after his death, one should look at one more notice from the lost work, *The Anabathmoi Jacobou* or *The Ascents of Jacob*, which Epiphanius shares with us, the only other notice from this book he seems to know or can confirm with any certainty. He apprises us of this, directly following his citation regarding James' discourse *'against the Temple and the sacrifices,'* and rails against it even more than he just did against this one, which he only claimed to have been *'full of absurdities'* and *'deceitfulness.'*[91]

In regard to this second notice, he claims it is *'fabricated by the villainy and error of their false Apostles'* (Paul uses the same words *'false Apostles,'* it will be recalled, in 2 Corinthians 11:12 above), this in spite of knowing beforehand that *'the Ebionites'* he is talking about opposed Paul and considered him *'the Antichrist'* or *'Enemy'* and *'a Liar.'*[92] In fact, after providing their charges from this work against Paul, he goes on to attack them in much the same manner as Eusebius, claiming that they got their name (he thinks *'Ebion'* is a person in much the same manner he does *'Elchasai'* – though he is nevertheless correct in imagining *'he got his name out of Prophecy'*) because of their *'Poverty of understanding, expectation, and works'* (*n.b.*, the telltale emphasis on *'works'* again), not to mention *'the Poverty of their Faith,'* since they *'take Christ as a mere man'* (note the parallel, too, of the *'no mere Adam'* passage from Isaiah 31:38 in the War Scroll above and its exposition).[93]

> *Nor do they blush to accuse Paul there (in the Anabathmoi) with certain inventions fabricated by the villainy and error of their false Apostles (meaning who, James?), saying that he was from Tarsus, as he admits himself and does not deny. But they suppose that his parents were Greek, taking as evidence for this the passage where he frankly states, 'I am a man of Tarsus, a citizen of no mean city' (Acts 21:39). Then they say that he was a Greek, the son of a Greek mother and father, that he went up to Jerusalem, stayed there awhile, and desired to marry*

the (High) Priest's daughter (note, this typically Palestinian way of referring to 'the High Priest', just as in the Habakkuk and Psalm 37 Peshers[94]) and therefore became a convert and was circumcised. But then, because he was still unable to obtain her on account of her high station, in his anger he wrote against the Sabbath, circumcision, and the Law (this is about right, even in the extant Pauline corpus). But this dreadful serpent (he means 'Ebion' – the language also echoes the manner in which Jerome vilifies his old friend Rufinus, presumably for publishing the Pseudoclementine Recognitions and other deficiencies[95]) is making a completely false accusation because of his Poverty-stricken understanding.[96]

I think we can attest, regardless either of its veracity or lack of it, this quotation from Epiphanius *is a classic*. The allusion to '*the Priest*' to signify '*High Priest*' adds to the impression of its authenticity, since with regard to the Gospels and the Dead Sea Scrolls, as just signaled, this is how it would have been expressed in Hebrew. One should also remark the ongoing venom of these accusations which is also typical of writers like Eusebius and Jerome. While at first glance, like much else in Epiphanius, the testimony might strike the reader as patently untrue (and it certainly is bizarre), on deeper reflection, there *is* a way of making sense of or understanding it.

We have already alluded to Paul's putative '*Herodian*' background. That he has connections in such circles is undeniable. Not only were 'the Herodians' making inroads into Northern Syria and Southern Asia Minor, even into what the Romans took to referring to as '*Armenia*' ('*Greater*' or '*Lesser*') where two Herodians with Judaizing pretensions became Kings[97]; but actual marriages of various kinds were being arranged further east in Commagene bordering on '*the Land of the Osrhoeans*' and '*Adiabene*' and west in Cappadocia and Cilicia, the area most usually claim for Paul's origins.[98] In fact, a number of these Rulers were specifically '*circumcising themselves*' in the manner this passage claims Paul did, in order to contract marriages with Herodians, particularly the female line descended from Herod's sole Maccabean wife '*Mariamme*' or '*Mary*.'[99]

But Acts 23:16–22 also makes clear that Paul has important family connections in Jerusalem, where it would appear a sister or, at least, a nephew with entree into Roman/Herodian military and/or administrative circles resides. One possible identification of this '*nephew*,' regarding whom Acts appears to exercise even more than its usual reticence, is '*Julius Archelaus*.'[100] He is an individual Josephus himself mentions in his *Vita* introducing the *Antiquities* as having been interested enough in his works to purchase a copy in later years in Rome after the fall of Jerusalem and the collapse of Revolutionary activities in Judea![101] Josephus does so by way of citing important persons such as Agrippa II who could vouch for the veracity of his history. Julius is the son of an individual mentioned fairly frequently in Josephus, one '*Alexas*' or '*Helcias*,' the Temple Treasurer, and he may even be mentioned in the cluster of '*Herodian*' references at the end of Romans, including the individual Paul refers to as his '*kinsman*,' '*the Littlest Herod*,' and '*Junias*' another of his '*kinsmen*' – read '*Julius*' (16:7–11).[102]

'*Alexas*' or '*Helcias*' seems to have been the son of a daughter of Herod named '*Cypros*' after Herod's own mother, and another old crony of Herod, also called '*Alexas*' or '*Helcias*.'[103] Herod used the whole family as a line of Temple Treasurers and the earliest seems to have been married to his (Herod's) own sister '*Salome*' after Herod executed (Saddam Hussein-style) her first husband '*Joseph*,' following the rumor of this husband's adultery with his (Herod's) first Maccabean wife mentioned above, '*Mariamme*' (the first '*Joseph and Mary*' story?).[104] Julius Archelaus originally married the first of Agrippa I's daughters, also called '*Mariamme*,' after her grandmother. But even this marriage does not seem to have been good enough for this Princess, because she divorced him to make what was obviously an even '*Richer*' marriage to one '*Demetrius the Alabarch of Alexandria*,' whom Josephus calls '*the first in birth and wealth among the Jews of Alexandria*.'

Demetrius must either have been the kinsman or brother of the infamous '*Tiberius Alexander*' mentioned, as we have seen – perhaps a little anachronistically – in Acts 4:6.[105] The nephew of the famous Alexandrian philosopher Philo, noted above, he succeeded Fadus (44–46 CE) as Governor. It was under Fadus that '*the Famine*' occurred and Theudas was executed. Not only was Tiberius Alexander (obviously named after the Emperor by the same name) the type of perfect Roman bureaucrat and, as Josephus describes him, someone who '*abandoned the religion of his Forefathers*'; but it was also under his auspices that the two sons of Judas the Galilean, '*James and Simon*' were crucified (46–48 CE).[106] So trusted was Tiberius ('*Alexander*' in Acts) and so much involved in Vespasian's ascent to power that when Vespasian went to Rome to be acclaimed Emperor by his troops in 69 CE, he left Tiberius behind as military Commander to handle the taking of Jerusalem and the destruction of the Temple that followed and, doubtlessly, to keep an eye on his perhaps not-so-talented son Titus.[107]

Julius Archelaus, who seems to have survived everything, may even have been the younger brother of another individual Josephus associates with the '*Saulos*' in his narrative who so much resembles Paul – one '*Antipas*' of the same general family line, whom Josephus also identifies as '*Temple Treasurer*' – *n.b.*, how '*the Herodians*' kept control of these important and powerful banking and monetary functions. In fact, this '*Antipas*' was executed in somewhat desperate circumstances, when 'the Zealots' took control of the Revolution, around the same time as James' executioner Ananus, the '*Rich*' collaborator '*Zachariah ben Bareis*'/'*Bariscaeus*,' and another backsliding, former Revolutionary, '*Niger of Perea*.'[108]

This last individual, as we have already suggested, may have been the model in Acts 13:1 for Paul's erstwhile colleague in '*Antioch*,' 'Simeon Niger' and the details of his execution may also have gone into the picture of '*Jesus*" in the Gospels.[109] Actually this '*Zachariah*' – *who was also executed by 'the Zealots' in the Temple as a collaborator and whose body was also 'cast down' into the valley below* – and not '*the Prophet Zechariah*,' may have been the model too for the '*Zachariah the son of Barachias*' allegedly murdered in Matthew 23:35 and Luke 11:51 '*between Temple and the Altar*' – here another '*blood libel*' accusation which even includes an allusion to '*Abel the Righteous*' from the Second Generation of Mankind, followed of course by the usual refrain, '*O Jerusalem, Jerusalem, who kill all the Prophets and stone those who have been sent to her*,'[110] the implied meaning once again being, to be sure, '*your blood be upon your own heads*.'

As already explained, there certainly were '*Herodians*' in '*the Antioch Community*,' one specifically called '*the foster brother of Herod the Tetrarch*,' namely our '*Herod Antipas*' again (after which, this '*Antipas*' above – '*Antipas*' being a variation of the name of Herod's father '*Antipater*'). Furthermore, the two brothers, '*Costobarus and Saulos*,' whom Josephus depicts as '*collecting a band of Violent ruffians*' and *causing mayhem in Jerusalem in the aftermath of the stoning of James*,[111] and this youngest '*Antipas*,' together with his putative '*brother*' or '*nephew*,' Julius Archelaus, were all the descendants of interrelated septs descending both from Herod's sister '*Salome*' and one of his (Herod's) daughters named '*Cypros*.'[112]

If the reader's mind reels before the complexities of all these various marital and kinship relationships, so doubtlessly did the minds of the sectaries at Qumran, who regarded many of these relationships as little more than '*incestuous*' and definitely categorized them under what they considered to be '*fornication*' – a charge, as we have repeatedly seen, exercising James to no small degree as well. If Julius Archelaus was '*Paul's nephew*,' referred to in Acts 23:16 above, then his mother too (Paul's *putative sister*) was probably the descendant of Herod's sister, the first '*Salome*' in this family. This is because, after executing Salome's first husband '*Joseph*' –

allegedly on a charge of adultery with his own first wife named '*Mari-amme*' (Herod had two, this one being, as we have already emphasized, *the Maccabean one*) – and before finally marrying her to his close friend (and presumable relative), the original '*Alexas*' or '*Helcias*' in this line of Temple Treasurers above; Herod had previously married her to yet another close associate and probable relative (talk about keeping things in the family and multiple wives and husbands), the original '*Costobarus*,' himself definitively identified as an '*Idumaean*' in Josephus, from whom the '*Costobarus*' in Paul's generation evidently descended and derived his name.[113]

The '*Idumaean*' Line of '*Costobarus*' and the '*Plundering Activities of the Last Priests of Jerusalem*'

Let us start again. Herod's father – whether '*Idumaean Arab*,' '*Greek*,' or a mixture of the two – had married a high-born '*Arab*' woman from Petra named Cypros. Herod's sister Salome had two sons (the genealogies are, chronologically speaking, a little unclear here, as these may have been a generation later and might not be '*sons*,' but 'grandsons'), the individual Josephus calls '*Saulos*' and another – like the putative '*Idumaean*' forebear just mentioned – called '*Costobarus*.' It is to these two that Josephus attributes *the riot in Jerusalem*, just alluded to above, *following the death of James*, which very much resembles *the riot led by Paul in Acts after the stoning of Stephen* (note the correspondence here between '*the stoning of Stephen*' and '*the stoning of James*' which overlap, as we have been suggesting, in other respects as well[114]). Nor is this to mention the riot in the Pseudoclementine *Recognitions*, which ends up in Paul '*casting*' James '*head-long*' *down the Temple steps* and *James breaking at least one if not both his legs*.[115]

Josephus describes these two individuals, '*Saulos and Costobarus*' aside from noting their '*kinship*' to Agrippa (I or II, it doesn't matter), as willing to '*use violence with the People and plunder those weaker than themselves*' – this *in the aftermath of the stoning of James* and the very accusations leveled against the Establishment Priesthood and their '*Violent*' associates *in the aftermath of the destruction of '*the Righteous Teacher*' in the Dead Sea Scrolls.[116] The Habakkuk *Pesher* in particular – but also the Damascus Document – uses this language of '*plundering*' and '*Violence*' in relation to the '*amassing*' or '*collecting*' activities of '*the Peoples*' – in our view, '*Herodians*,' but also their non-Jewish hangers-on (or those perceived as being non-Jewish like the so-called '*Idumaeans*' – another probable term for '*Herodians*,' some pro-Revolutionary, others clearly not – by such

'*Zealot*'-minded Extremists as the sectaries at Qumran).[117]

This kind of '*plundering*' or '*amassing*' is connected then, in particular, to the '*profiteering*' activities of the individual, called in the Habakkuk *Pesher*, '*the Wicked Priest*,' as well as '*the Last Priests of Jerusalem*' generally.[118] To come full circle again, this, in turn, can be connected to '*profiteering from the contributions* or *gifts to the Temple* made by individuals involved in just these kinds of '*Violent*' attacks, namely '*Saulos and Costobarus*' and their '*Violent*' associates (at Qumran, in our view, probably referred to as '*the ᶜArizei-Go'im*' – '*the Violent Ones of the Gentiles*' or '*Peoples*').[119] Regarding these kinds of activities, one should also keep in mind Paul's own admissions in 1 Corinthians 15:9 and Galatians 1:13 to '*persecuting the Assembly of God* – an appellation actually found in the Dead Sea Scrolls – *unto death*.'[120]

The two riots we have just referred to, led by someone called '*Saulos*' in both Acts and Josephus, are in themselves interesting. Although the twenty-year discrepancy in their dating will never be reconciled; the sequencing, however, is the same: the stoning of Stephen followed by the mayhem reported in Acts 8:3, where '*Paul*' (still being referred to even at this point in Acts as '*Saulos*') '*ravaged the Assembly*' or '*Ecclesia, entering house-by-house and dragging out men and women, delivering (them) up to prison*' (the '*delivering up*' the Gospels use to describe '*Judas Iscariot*'s' '*betrayal*' of 'Jesus'[121]); and the stoning of James, followed by the brutal rioting led by '*Costobarus and Saul*' – unless '*Saulos*' really did lead two riots, or Josephus and/or Acts have confused things, which would not be at all surprising. Josephus, it will be recalled, is not writing these things in the *Antiquities* (which he neglected to mention in the *War*) until the early Nineties, thirty years after they occurred. He may have his sequencing wrong or he may simply have misunderstood things, deliberately or otherwise.[122]

That having been said, it seems fairly plain that what Acts is really talking about (or, as the case may be, covering up) in its picture of *the attack on Stephen in the Temple* is *the riot in the Temple led by Paul* in the Pseudoclementines that ended up in James only '*breaking his leg*,' not the *stoning of Stephen*. In fact, there may have been another riot directly after the stoning of James, just as Josephus describes, and '*Paul*' or '*Saulos*' – as the case may be – may have been involved in this too. This depends on what happened to Paul after his initial voyage to Rome and his alleged '*appeal to Caesar*' in 60 CE. (Acts 25:11–28:31, as already underscored, the longest continual narrational sequence of any kind in Acts.)

At this point, Acts 28:30–31 just trails off inconsequentially, only declaring in a fairly formulaic manner (as if to illustrate that the Romans were unconcerned about Paul), he *'proclaimed the Kingdom of God and taught the things concerning the Lord Jesus Christ with all freedom without being hindered'* – the last notice of a substantive kind we have about Paul. This is 62 CE, the date of the stoning of James, but Acts does not bother to mention this and, as far as Christian sources are concerned, Paul did not meet his fate (allegedly by crucifixion) for another four years![123] Nor does Acts have anything to say about what Paul might have been doing in the meantime, where he went or whether or not he returned to Palestine thereafter. Are we to imagine Acts is ignorant of these things or is it just embarrassed – and where is the narrative about the death of James, perhaps the most important single event of the year 62 CE where nascent *'Christianity'* is concerned (and, for that matter, *'Jewish Messianism'* in Palestine)? Romans 15:24–28 hints tantalizingly at Paul's contemplation of a trip to Spain, which would not have been surprising in view of the important contacts like Seneca and his brother Gallio (*cf.* Acts 18:12–17), he seems to have enjoyed, who came from there; and some tradition even appears to have picked this up.[124]

However this may be, just as Paul in Acts, Josephus' *'Saulos'* also makes an appeal to Caesar, but this one apparently not until 66 CE although there may have been an earlier one in the previous decade as well when, like Josephus thereafter, he seems to have made the contacts necessary to enter Roman service – though, in his case, he probably would not have needed such contacts and already had them.[125] In any event, what the *'Saulos'* in Josephus does in 66 CE – after having been the intermediary between *'the Peace Party'* made up, as Josephus tells us, of *'Herodians, Sadducees, and the Chief Men of the Pharisees'* in Jerusalem and the Roman army outside of the city[126] – is, as Paul in Acts and as already alluded to, *appeal to Caesar* presumably with his putative *'kinsman'* Agrippa II's help (a decade earlier, in Acts 23:35 Paul stays in this same Agrippa's Palace in Caesarea as *'Saulos'* seemingly does in Jerusalem). It is to Nero that *'Saulos'* then goes, apparently at that time in Corinth as already indicated, to report on the situation in Palestine generally and, along seemingly with *'Philip,'* Agrippa II's military Commander in Caesarea (we shall discuss below), to justify his own conduct in the matter of the destruction of the Roman garrison in Jerusalem – a report that seems to have triggered the bringing in of the Romans' best general, Vespasian, all the way from Britain to quell the unrest in Palestine.[127]

In the course of our previous discussions we have had occasion to point out the motif of *'circumcision'* or the lack thereof in the marriages of these Herodian Princesses in Asia Minor and Syria, a motif figuring prominently in Paul's activities in these same areas as well;[128] but the announced goal of much of his missionary '*work*' in these areas, that is to found a community where Greeks and Jews could live in harmony and equality (1 Corinthians 1:24, Galatians 3:28, etc.), however noble, was also very much in line with what might be termed *Herodian family interests* or *designs in many of these regions*.[129]

In fact, even after the fall of the Temple, Antiochus of Commagene, on the border west of Edessa, ran afoul of the Romans, as Agrippa I seems to have done a quarter of a century earlier, for precisely such '*imperial*' ambitions.[130] Antiochus' son Epiphanes, who actually fought on the Roman side with his aptly-named '*Macedonian Legion*' in the Jewish War and was even decorated for bravery in the siege of Jerusalem, had himself originally been betrothed to Agrippa I's second daughter Drusilla. This was the same Drusilla who later married the brutal Roman Governor Felix and was identified in Acts 24:24, as we saw, somewhat disingenuously, only '*a Jewess*' despite the fact that Josephus specifically says, she '*abandoned the religion of her Forefathers*.'[131] Nor did Acts consider it, then, relevant to apprise us that she – like her sister, Bernice, who subsequently appears – was an Herodian Princess! This Epiphanes' marriage with Drusilla, presumably because her more '*Pious*' father Agrippa I was still alive, foundered on precisely this issue of '*circumcision*' and *Epiphanes*' *refusal to circumcise himself!*[132] One might opine that in view of Drusilla's later history, her father Agrippa I needn't have bothered.

For her part, Drusilla was then promptly married to the King of Emesa (presentday '*Homs*' in Syria), *who had circumcised himself specifically in order to contract this marriage*, only finally to desert with the Roman Governor Felix to Rome – her father Agrippa I by this time having died – doubtlessly laying the groundwork to some extent for Paul's own eventual '*appeal*' and escape to Rome, which might explain why he was received so well there.[133] As already explained above, her relationship with Felix was clearly connived at by '*Simon*' or '*Atomus*,' '*a Magician*,' that is, the notorious '*Simon Magus*,' and the issues signaled here are probably the real ones in the debates between the latter and the Historical Peter refracted in the Pseudoclementines (and to some extent in Acts!).[134]

For his part, this Antiochus of Commagene also had a daughter, Jotape, who was married to another Herodian, '*Alexander*,' the son of Tigranes, King of Armenia. Tigranes was the grandson of the second of Herod's two sons by his Maccabean wife Mariamme, the original '*Alexander*' in this line – a line that was clearly favored because *it was considered of royal blood* or *the most Kingly*.[135] Josephus tells us that after the War, Vespasian made Alexander '*King of Cilicia*,' presumably for services rendered either by him or his father, '*Cilicia*' of course also being Paul's own alleged place of origin.[136] Though all of this is circumstantial, nevertheless it is instructive.

Tigranes' uncle, also named '*Tigranes*,' was a descendant of this same Maccabean royal wife of Herod, *Mariamme*. He had also been appointed '*King of Armenia*' by the Romans, the first so designated – more confirmation of Herodians as '*the Kings of the Peoples*,' we have been emphasizing above in the Eastern areas of the Roman Empire. Josephus pictures this later nephew of the first '*Tigranes*' as spending a long and agreeable period as a hostage in Rome, so much so that it became his virtual home, as it seems to have done for so many of the persons we are labeling as '*Herodians*' above. There, he and many others like him – Agrippa II, for instance, Aristobulus and Salome (involved in the story of John the Baptist's demise), whose faces appear on the reverse of coinage proclaiming them '*Great Lovers of Caesar*,' and Julius Archelaus – clearly formed part of a sophisticated circle of Greek-speaking, pro-Roman intellectuals with a lot of time on their hands. In earlier work, I have singled out this circle as possibly being the source of much of the material that ultimately ended up being incorporated – along with a good deal of Alexandrian Greco-Roman '*anti-Semitism*' – in what we now call '*the Gospels*.'[137] In any event, like Drusilla with Felix and her sister Bernice with her lover Titus, Josephus tells us fairly matter-of-factly that this latter generation of Herodians '*deserted the Jewish religion altogether and went over to that of the Greeks*.'[138]

Be this as it may, aside from the general atmosphere in the Habakkuk *Pesher* signaling a '*conspiracy*' of some kind surrounding the destruction or death of the Righteous Teacher in which '*the Wicked Priest*' (if not '*the Liar*' too), was involved;[139] there is material in Paul's own letters, as we just saw, that would suggest more than just a casual relationship with the Herodian family and its representatives – *in fact, a genealogical one*. This by itself would explain his rather peculiar idea of Judaism and schizophrenic attitude towards it.

'*The Littlest Herod*' and Paul's Roman Citizenship

We have already called attention to the greetings Paul sends to his '*kinsman Herodion*,' '*the Littlest Herod*,' at the end of Romans 16:11 above – '*Herod*,' of course, not being a commonplace name in this period. This was probably the son of the '*Aristobulus*,' just mentioned above (the evocation of whose '*household*' just precedes it in Romans 16:10) and that '*Salome*' who, as just signaled, was somehow involved in the execution of John the Baptist. Actually it was '*Salome*''s *husband*, as we have explained (not her mother's), who was named 'Philip' and whom – as Josephus makes clear – 'died childless.' This means that 'Philip' was not Herodias' husband, as the Synoptics inaccurately portray (that husband's name was simply 'Herod' after his father, that is, 'Herod Herod'), and the issue of 'raising seed up to her brother' was not really applicable to Herodias' situation where her divorce from this first 'Herod' was concerned and, therefore, probably *was not the central issue* in John's objections to it, as we have already explained – at least as far as the Synoptics portray them.[140]

Rather it was more likely the issues raised at Qumran under the general classification of '*fornication*,' that is, *marriage with non-Jews, nieces* or *close family cousins, polygamy*, and *divorce*, were the issues involved in these confrontations – as they probably were also between '*Peter*' and '*Simon Magus*' in Caesarea a decade later (though Josephus, as we saw, dated John the Baptist's death around 36–37 CE). This was particularly true where like Aristobulus were concerned – *Salome's real husband* and *the one by whom she had all her children*, including '*the Littlest Herod*' above – who *was her mother's uncle, Herod of Chalcis' son* and, consequently, *her first cousin!*[146] To repeat, according to our view, it was their '*household*' that is being alluded to in this cluster of notices in which Paul speaks of his '*kinsmen*,' ending with the evocation of '*Herodion*' their son at the end of Romans 16:7–11.

We have also called attention to the greetings Paul sends to '*the Saints*' in '*the household of Caesar*' in Philippians (presumably Nero) where, as we indicated, he mentions his close collaborator ('*your Apostle*,' as he calls him, the '*your*' seemingly referring to those '*in the household of Caesar*') and '*comrade-in-arms*,' Epaphroditus (2:25 and 4:22). Epaphroditus, as we saw, was Nero's secretary for Greek Letters and held a similar office later under Domitian, of whom he ultimately appears to have run afoul.[142] Josephus himself seems to refer to this same Epaphroditus' '*many great adventures*' and he appears to have been involved in some manner in Nero's suicide or murder which made way, as it were, for the rise of Vespasian as '*Ruler of the World*.'[143] Expediently or otherwise, Domitian accused him of having '*raised his hand against an Emperor*,' but these charges against Epaphroditus were most likely trumped up in the general crackdown against alleged '*Christians*' in the later years of Domitian's reign.[144]

The last notice Josephus provides about the '*kinsman of Agrippa*' he calls '*Saulos*' was his trip to Corinth where, as we just saw, Nero was apparently quartered while he was having the canal dug there. The year, of course, is 66 CE and, after '*Saulos*' informs Nero of the situation in Palestine, Vespasian and Titus are sent out as commanders to deal with the situation in Palestine in the manner Josephus subsequently made famous in his *War*.[145] Just as eight years before, '*Paul*' was under house arrest or, as the case may have been, '*protective custody*' in Agrippa II's Palace in Caesarea; at the outbreak of the disturbances leading up to the Uprising against Rome, '*Saulos*' too – along with his '*cousins*,' '*Antipas and Costobarus*,' and '*Philip*' – seems to have been in this same Agrippa II's Palace in Jerusalem. Not only was this '*Philip*' one of Agrippa II's military commanders and another name overlapping those of either '*Apostles*' or '*Disciples*' in the New Testament (the name of Agrippa I's '*Strategos*' or '*Military Commander*' was '*Silas*'[146]); he too, as Saulos had done, '*appealed to Caesar*' when he was blamed in some manner for surrendering either this Palace or the Citadel to the Revolutionaries.[147]

For his part, everyone knows that Acts 26:32 pictures '*Paul*' as going – apparently on his own recognizance – to appeal to Nero as '*a Roman citizen*' at the beginning of the Governorship of Festus in 60 CE. Aside from a two-year further stay in Rome, where he supposedly hired his '*own house*' (Acts 28:30), nothing more can be said with any certainty about Paul – not even the date of his death which, as already suggested, does not appear to have occurred for another four years – about the time of the final visit this '*Saulos*' in Josephus also makes to Nero when he, too, *just drops out of sight*![148]

The name '*Aristobulus*,' mentioned in the line immediately preceding Paul's greetings to his '*kinsman Herodion*' in Rome, makes the several greetings Paul sends to these kinds of individuals at the end of Romans even more interesting. Not only was '*Aristobulus*' originally a name used by Maccabeans, it turns into an '*Herodian*' name after these latter are '*grafted*' on the tree of the former, as Paul would have it in Romans 11:19, and there were at least four important '*Herodians*' with this name mentioned by Josephus at this time.

Where the identity of the '*Aristobulus*' mentioned by Paul in Romans 16:10 is concerned, probably the only Herodian '*Aristobulus*' this could be in the mid to late Fifties in Rome was Aristobulus the son of Herod of Chalcis, to whom Claudius gave the Kingdom of Lesser Armenia in Asia Minor to compensate him when he took the city of Chalcis from his father's dominions in Syria and added it to his first cousin Agrippa II's domains.[149] Lesser Armenia would be contiguous to or carved out of areas belonging to the Osrhoeans around Edessa and Adiabene, which had fallen by this time to Roman control. As we have seen, another Maccabean of Herodian descent, '*Tigranes*,' had already been given Armenia proper or Greater Armenia. Aristobulus' wife, the infamous '*Salome*,' so celebrated in Gospel story and Western hagiography succeeding to it, had, as we have on several occasions also pointed out, previously been the wife of *the real Philip*. Not only was he the half brother of Herod Antipas above and the Tetrarch of the area around the Gaulon and across into Syria called Trachonitus, but it was he who had *'died childless'* which was to say nothing about either *'Herod Antipas'* or *'Herodias.'*

We have already remarked, too, how on extant coins this couple, Aristobulus and Salome, both advertised themselves as *'Great Lovers of Caesar'* which, no doubt, they were. They obviously spent a lot of time in Rome, as did a good many of these Herodians brought up under or with Claudius. But, even more interestingly, they also had this son, named *'Herod'* who, of course, in this period of the Fifties and Sixties CE, would have been *'the Youngest'* or *'Littlest Herod.'* Nor is this to say anything about the question of collusion between Paul (*'Saulos'*) and Herod the Tetrarch (*'Herod Antipas,'* Salome's mother Herodias' second husband) in the matter of his (Paul's) activities *'in Damascus'* that so disturbed *'Aretas' Governor'* in 2 Corinthians 11:32 and, therefore, in some manner too perhaps, the death of John the Baptist. Though greetings such as these to *'Herodion'* or *'the household of Aristobulus'* in Romans 16:10–11 in themselves prove nothing, they constitute very strong collateral evidence for the proposition, we are arguing, *of Paul's connection to the Herodian family.* Another interesting aside to all this was that this *'Herod'*'s *'first cousin,'* *'Antonius Agrippa,'* the only son of Drusilla and Felix above, died in the eruption of Vesuvius at Pompeii in 79 CE (*Divine Retribution?*).[150]

All these relationships provide a very good reason for the fact of Paul's Roman citizenship, of which all our sources make so much, as they also do his very peculiar and rather elastic attitude towards Judaism. As he puts this in 1 Corinthians 9:19–24:

> *being free from all* (he means here again, of course, *Jewish* or *Mosaic Law*), *I myself became a slave to all* (his usual word-play), *the more that I might win* (Paul's usual idea of *'winning'*). *And to the Jews, I became a Jew, that Jews I might win. To those under the Law, (I became) as under the Law, that those under the Law I might win. To those outside the Law, (I became) as outside the Law – though not outside the Law to God, being within the Law of Christ* (this he hastens to add lest he overstep himself – still, it is a good example of Paul's view of *'the Law'*). *To the weak, I became as weak* (here he uses the *'weak'* simile again, which he uses to attack vegetarians like James in Romans 13:2 or those who *make problems over food*, in particular, *'things sacrificed to idols,'* or otherwise *follow the Law* in 1 Corinthians 8:7–12). *To all these, I have become all things, so that by whatever means, some I might save* (here his usual reference to the ubiquitous *'some,'* which throughout

the New Testament, he and the Book of Acts usually apply to those of the mindset of James or '*the Jerusalem Church*').

This is, of course, a famous diatribe of Paul's and we have quoted it either in whole or in part before. Delivered in response to questions about profiteering from his mission and his credentials and amid allusion to '*the other Apostles* (indeterminate) *and the brothers of the Lord and Cephas*'; he again displays his gift for language, metaphor, and word-play, testimony to an obviously extremely fine Hellenistic upbringing that would have done any Greek polemicist or master of sophistical argument proud.

Paul is at his absolute rhetorical best here and he follows this up by comparing himself and his Mission to '*the runners at the stadium*' and '*the boxers competing for the prize*' (9:24–26). Not only was this calculated to send those of a more orthodox Jewish mindset into paroxysms of rage, so was the ethic he propounds in the midst of this of '*winning*,' i.e., *winning at any price* (9:24). For this reason Paul might be considered one of the first modern men, as '*win*' he did. Nor was Herod very far behind him in this. It is no wonder that those he alludes to as '*having Authority*' and '*wishing to examine*' him in 9:1–13, among whom he no doubt would have included '*the other Apostles and the brothers of the Lord and Cephas*,' would have had difficulty dealing with an individual of this kind.

Where Paul's Roman citizenship is at issue, so conspicuously touted in Acts 22:25–23:27 and elsewhere, Herod's father Antipater, who was so instrumental in the Roman takeover of Palestine – instrumental to the extent that his son, even though he was not Jewish by birth, supplanted its *Jewish Dynasty* – not surprisingly, received this citizenship for himself and his descendants in perpetuity for services rendered to the *Imperium Romanum*. Antipater, in fact, was the first Roman Prefect in Palestine and what he did was turn a regional governorship into a family dynasty. Family connections of this kind to the highest circles of power in Palestine easily explain the fact of Paul's influential sister and nephew living in Jerusalem according to Acts 23:16.[151] They also explain how Paul could have received the powers he did at such a tender age '*from the High Priest*' – to exercise them as far as Damascus which was not, seemingly, even under his control at the time[152] – if this picture of his activities in Acts (echoed in the Pseudoclementine *Recognitions*[153]) is even partially correct.

It is interesting that in the well-known passages about his origins in Romans 11:1 and Philippians 3:5 (reprised in Acts 13:21), where he refers to being of '*the Tribe of Benjamin*,' Paul avoids calling himself '*a Jew*,' a term he does not hesitate however to apply to '*Peter*' in Galatians 2:13–14. Rather he seems to prefer to refer to himself as '*an Israelite, of the seed of*

Abraham, of the Tribe of Benjamin' which, as we saw in the War Scroll above, many *Diaspora* Jews or even converts, such as *'the Herodians,'* may have taken to calling themselves. In Philippians 3:5–6, Paul adds:

> *a Hebrew of the Hebrews – according to the Law, a Pharisee. According to zeal persecuting the Church (Ecclesian –* here he parodies and reverses the language of *'zeal'* of *'the Zealots'* once more, as he also does in Galatians 4:16–18. His statement here is, at least, believable, but not according to the *'zeal'* alluded to in Acts 21:20's picture of the majority of James' *'Jerusalem Church'* or *'Assembly'* as *'Zealots for the Law'* – *'myriads'* as James is quoted as referring to them!). *According to Righteousness in Law, becoming blameless* (here he must mean, clearly, Roman Law, though it is hard to imagine a more self-serving self-portrait).

Aside from his references to *'becoming a Jew'* and *'making himself a Jew to win Jews'* above, these considerations – plus an ambiguous reference in Galatians 1:13 to something resembling conversion to *'Judaism'* – might have convinced his interlocutors that *Paul was really not born a Jew, but had rather converted to Judaism,* as the above testimony from the *Anabathmoi Jacobou* insists. In addition to this, his easy-going attitude towards Judaism, as well as his fairly overt contempt for most things Jewish, could not have failed to make its impression on his contemporaries, as it has left its mark across the breadth of the Gospels and like-minded materials – the Koran, for example.

This is also true of his comments in 1 Thessalonians 2:15 – if authentic which most consider this Letter to be – about *'the Jews'* having

> *killed both the Lord Jesus and their own Prophets and drove you out, and are not pleasing to God and are antagonistic (or 'contrary') to all men* (or, as we have elsewhere rephrased this, *'the Enemies of all Mankind),*

the converse of the Ebionite *'Enemy'* terminology. *Par contra,* see James 4:4 on *'the Friend of the world being transformed into an Enemy of God).* Comments of this kind are made so often in Paul that he does not appear to feel himself to be one of the People he is so denigrating, nor, for that matter, *feel any kinship with them at all.*

The *'Saulos'* in Josephus and Paul

Having said all these things, there is still another way of looking at this curious testimony from the Ebionite *'Acts of the Apostles,'* which Epiphanius entitles '*The Anabathmoi Jacobou*' – that is, having knowledge of Paul's Herodian origins, it is possible that when the *Anabathmoi* was describing the person who was '*a pagan*' or '*a Greek*' coming up to Jerusalem and, *conceiving a desire to marry the High Priest's daughter, converted to Judaism*, and *when frustrated in this design, turned against both the Jews and Judaism*; it was not really talking about Paul at all, but rather Paul's putative ancestor, *the original Herod himself.*

This can be explained by the fact that it was Herod and his father who were perhaps the original '*Herodian*' converts to Judaism – if there ever was a *real* conversion on their part and this was all not simply a charade. It was Herod too who, in decorating Greek temples and cities and giving generously to *Greek* causes (well-documented in all sources[154]) really did make himself – to paraphrase Paul in 1 Corinthians 9:19–21 – '*a Jew to the Jews*' and '*a Greek to the Greek.*' But above all else, like Paul, Herod believed in '*winning*' – *winning at any cost.* And he did – *he really won.*

Finally, it was Herod *who really did want to marry the High Priest's daughter* despite the fact that *he wasn't either native-born* or *originally even Jewish himself.* In fact, he married two of them, both named '*Mariamme*' as we have seen – the reason doubtlessly behind the proliferation of all these '*Mariamme*'s or '*Mary*'s in the next generation and ever since. Herod's killing of all the Maccabeans, including his own wife '*Mariamme,*' his children by her, her mother, her grandfather Hyrcanus II, who had given his father Antipater the chance to rise to power in the first place, her younger brother Jonathan – *the last properly 'Maccabean' High Priest* – and, then, the various *incestuous marriages* he arranged, was genetic engineering with a vengeance. Jonathan he had (in the manner that a latterday Stalin or Saddam Hussein might do) strangled in the swimming pool of his (Herod's) winter palace in Jericho. This he did after Jonathan had for the first time donned the High-Priestly vestments (the clear condition for Mariamme's mother having permitted the marriage in the first place) when he saw how this sight *moved 'the People' to weep with emotion.*[155]

Furthermore, none of these '*Herodians,*' as Epiphanius well understood, were really reckoned as '*Jews*' anyhow – except by themselves when they found it convenient or by their sycophantic '*Pharisee*' supporters.[156] Only Agrippa I, for some reason, really seems to have cared about such fine points.[157] For others, like Paul, legal niceties of this kind were really more of a nuisance than anything else. Eusebius, too, well understood this point for, in quoting the passage he conserves from Julius Africanus about how *Herod burned all the genealogical records of the Jews and* '*the Desposyni*' (Jesus' family in *Nazara* and *Cochaba*[158]), he matter-of-factly observes that Herod did this out of envy '*of his base birth, because he was not of Israelite stock.*[159] In describing Paul as they did, the authors of the *Anabathmoi Jacobou* may have thought they were saying something about his '*Herodian*' origins – in particular, his putative ancestor Herod, who really did marry '*the High Priest's daughter*' and whom some might have considered to have *been a 'convert' to Judaism* – though, for their part, extreme '*Zealot*' groups certainly would not have, which was the basis of a century or more of unrest that followed in this period.

There is one additional subject that needs to be treated where Paul's possible identification with the character Josephus is calling '*Saulos*' is concerned. There is the possibility of Paul having made a return to Palestine after being incarcerated in Rome in time to put in the several appearances described in Josephus' *Antiquities* on the part of '*Saulos*' after the death of James around 63 or 64 CE and another in the *War* in 66 CE above. Before this '*Saulos*' in Josephus went to Corinth – where Epaphroditus, no doubt, was in residence as well – to give his report to Nero on the situation in Palestine; he also served, as we have emphasized, as the intermediary between '*the Peace Party*' in Jerusalem – namely, all those Josephus calls '*desirous for peace*' including the New Testament's *Pharisees*, *Sadducees*, and *Herodians* – and the Roman Army outside the city under Cestius, the Roman Governor of Syria, who had come to Jerusalem to suppress the Uprising.[160] This episode would have been contemporaneous with the death in battle of Queen Helen's own two '*kinsmen*' or '*descendants*,' '*Monobazus and Kenedaeus*,' *who fought valiantly against this same Cestius* in a futile attempt to stop his advance at the Pass at Beit Horon, a site hallowed as well due to Judas Maccabee's earlier exploits.[161]

In the same passage in Romans where Paul sends his greetings to '*those in Aristobulus' household*' and his '*kinsman the Youngest Herod*,' Paul also expressed, as we saw, his perhaps authentic intention to visit Spain, a trip which many think he made (Romans 15:24–28). As already remarked, there is no evidence about whether Paul ever got to Spain or not, just as there is no reliable information as to how or when he died, although most would agree it was sometime after 66 CE. If he did visit Spain, one wonders what contacts he used to get there. Seneca, the famous Stoic philosopher, who acted as Nero's Prime Minister before falling afoul of the latter's changeable temper and being forced to commit suicide himself, was from Spain, as was his brother Gallio whom, as we saw, Acts 18:12–17, too, pictures as treating Paul with such self-evident cordiality. In fact, mercurial as he was, Nero may have found something to find fault with in '*Saulos*'' behavior as well and had him executed, as neither he nor '*Paul*' is ever heard from again. Not long afterwards, Nero himself either committed suicide – with, as we saw above, Epaphroditus' involvement – or was assassinated.[162]

There is nothing to gainsay that Paul actually did get to Spain, just as we cannot be sure that he did not return to Palestine at some point thereafter. Our sources just do not tell us and Acts grows uncharacteristically vague after allowing that Paul was, for all intents and purposes, free in Rome and '*in his own lodgings*' after being sent there by Festus following his '*appeal to Caesar.*' In fact, as this is portrayed in Acts 28:21, even Paul is surprised to find out no one has heard of him there or presumably what he had been doing in Palestine and elsewhere. Felix too, the brother of Nero's financial secretary Pallas, with whom Paul is portrayed as conversing so intimately for two years in Acts 23:25–24:27, had also gone to Rome not long before with his '*Herodian*' wife Drusilla (Acts' '*Jewess*') and possibly even their Rasputin-like advisor '*Simon Magus.*' As already suggested, he could easily have been involved (even with the connivance of Agrippa II, particularly if this '*Paul*' were the '*kinsman*' of both Agrippa II and Drusilla) in arranging this trip to Rome for Paul.

However these things may be, Galba, the first successor to Nero, had previously been Governor in Spain; and Seneca, originally Nero's tutor and finally his Prime Minister, came from Spain as well as we saw.[163] So did Trajan, whose father is given special attention in Josephus' *Jewish War* as a brave Roman Legionnaire. He came from '*Italica*' in Spain.[164] In this context, one should never forget that the Roman '*Centurion*' in Acts 10:1–43 – '*a man Righteous and God-fearing*,' '*doing many charitable acts to the People*,' '*borne witness to by the whole Nation (Ethnous) of the Jews*,' '*whose charity ('Zedakah' in Hebrew) was remembered before God*,' the exact language being applied to '*God-Fearers*' in the final exhortation of the Damascus Document above[165] (as already observed, real challenge to one's credulity) – is described in Acts 10:1 as being from '*the Italica Regiment.*' So was Trajan's personal favorite, Hadrian.

It is certainly not impossible that a man of Epaphroditus' wide acquaintance would have had connections in Spain. In fact, there is a lively correspondence in the apocryphal literature between Paul and Seneca whom Epaphroditus must have known; and Gallio, whom Acts presents as Roman Proconsul in Achaia and Governor in Corinth and who treated Paul with such self-evident cordiality there (much like another Roman Governor, Felix – with extremely close connections to Nero – did, not long afterwards in Caesarea), was, as we have just seen, the Stoic Philosopher Seneca's brother.[166] As Acts 18:12–17 portrays these things, Gallio – whom archaeological evidence now confirms functioned in Corinth about the year 55 CE – pays no attention to Jewish complaints against Paul. He even supposedly goes so far as to allow

Greeks to beat '*Sosthenes*' '*before the Judgement seat*' there.

But there is a problem here, since the man Acts is calling '*Sosthenes the Ruler of the Synagogue*' at this point bears, as already indicated as well, the same name as the character referred to as '*Sosthenes*' at the beginning of 1 Corinthians 1:1, whom Paul calls his '*brother*' and *boon companion* (unless there were two such '*Sosthenes*'s in Corinth at one and the same time, a doubtful proposition). We have encountered this kind of problem in Acts before: for example, in the two trips Paul allegedly makes '*down the walls of Damascus in a basket*' – one in Acts 9:25 to escape '*the Jews who wanted to kill him*' (this one clearly tendentious); and the other in 2 Corinthians 11:31–33, to escape the '*Arab*' Ruler Aretas *who wants to have him* '*arrested*' unless of course, once again, *there were two such trips in a basket* – an equally dubious proposition.[167] In this passage in 2 Corinthians, Paul once again avers he '*does not lie*' (one certainly hopes not). But where there are contradictions between a primary account in Paul's letters and Acts' secondary one, we have already observed (calling it '*a rule of thumb*') that Paul's primary testimony, where authentic, is always to be preferred.

However these things may be, no less an authority than Eusebius is sure that *Paul did go free after his first imprisonment in Rome*, which was, as already signaled, hardly an imprisonment at all but more in the nature of a loose house arrest, or what could be described as (in Caesarea anyhow) protective custody.[168] As already remarked as well, Acts just comes to an end at this point about exactly the time James was killed in Jerusalem, but without a word about this. Why? Though the authenticity of Pastorals like Timothy and Titus is disputed, 2 Timothy 4:16–17 does note how '*at my first trial nobody supported me.*' Whoever wrote this, it would not be surprising that '*no one came to his support.*' Moreover, here anyhow, if reliable and however vague, there is an indication of ongoing legal problems of some sort in Paul's life (unless the reference is to his previous legal complications in Jerusalem and Caesarea before his alleged '*appeal to Caesar*').

Again, with such influential contacts as Gallio and possibly even his brother Seneca, to say nothing of Felix, Drusilla, Epaphroditus, Agrippa II, and Titus' future mistress Bernice, doubtlessly Paul could have made his way to Spain, just as he could have returned to Palestine, either before or after this, to take part in the events Josephus describes there prior to ultimately disappearing from the scene or being done away with in the course of the disturbances that broke out from 66–70 CE, about the same time that Josephus' '*Saulos*' did. We shall never know the true answers to any of these questions, but this does not prevent one from making an intelligent inference on the basis of the evidence.

18

The Pella Flight and
'*Agabus*'' Prophecy

The Reputed '*Pella Flight*' of James' '*Jerusalem Community*'

We should now turn to the last subject we need to discuss before moving on to an analysis of climactic sections of the Scrolls themselves, that is, the famed '*Pella flight*' of the James' '*Jerusalem Community*.' This so-called '*flight*,' which so much resembles the '*departure from the Land of Judah to the Land of Damascus*' of the Damascus Document above, is referred to in three of the main sources we have been consulting: Eusebius (again, probably relying on Hegesippus), Epiphanius, and, surprisingly enough, the First Apocalypse of James from Nag Hammadi.[1]

Eusebius refers to it after documenting the succession to Nero (68 CE) by Galba (68 CE) and Otho (69 CE) – Vespasian having been pro-claimed by his army in Palestine '*Imperator*' or '*Emperor*' also in 69 CE (the so-called '*Year of the Three Emperors*') – and how '*the Jews, after the ascension of our Saviour, followed up their crimes against him by devising plot after plot against his Disciples*' (here the usual '*plot*' language of the Gospels and Acts, which Eusebius glories in repeating, to say nothing of an even more intense malevolence even than in these):

> First, they stoned Stephen to death, then James the son of Zebedee the brother of John was beheaded (at this point Eusebius is following the sequencing in Acts precisely), and finally James, the first after the ascension of our Saviour to occupy the Throne of the Bishopric there lost his life in the manner described (this event as we have just noted, of course, untreated in Acts) and the other Apostles were driven from the Land of Judea by thousands of deadly plots (plots, plots, and more plots).

Having said this, Eusebius immediately contradicts himself with a version of the facts, obviously from another source, different from the first. This reads:

> The members of the Church in Jerusalem, by means of an oracle given by

revelation to approved men there before the War (this is an important qualification), *were ordered to leave the city and dwell in a town in Perea called Pella* (this is the area across Jordan a little north of where John the Baptist was executed. For its part the language is, once again, not unsimilar to that of the Damascus Document above). *To it, those who believed in Christ emigrated from Jerusalem* (this is almost word-for-word from the Damascus Document) *and, as if Holy Men* (as is this) *had completely abandoned the Royal Capital of the Jews and the entire Land of Judea, the Judgement of God at last overtook them for their crimes against Christ and his Apostles* (this, of course, is Eusebius at his best) *completely blotting out that Wicked Generation from among men!*[2]

A little love, humility, and Christian *'charity'* might have been in order from this founder of High Church Christianity as we know it (Greek Orthodox or Catholic). Instead we are confronted with an over-the-top outburst of histrionic invective that would be worthy of more recent practitioners of the art (Goebbels for instance?).

The allusions *'the Land of Judea'* and *'dwelling'* are, of course, to be found in the Damascus Document's depiction of how *'the Sons of Zadok'* and the other *'Penitents of Israel'* – *'the Nilvim along with them'*[3] – *'departed from the Land of Judah to dwell in the Land of Damascus.'* The language of *'plot,'* which Eusebius applies here to – as per his usual wont – *'the Jews'* or *'Jewish People'* is, in the Habakkuk *Pesher,* rather applied to *'the Wicked Priest'* and his associates.[4] In that document, it is he who is described as *'plotting to destroy the Poor'* – here very definitely implying *'the Ebionim'* or *'Ebionites'* – and *'steal'* their sustenance.[5]

Where the Habakkuk *Pesher* is concerned, as we shall see, in a finale as splendid and uplifting as could ever be imagined, the *Pesher* also applies the language of the *'Judgement of God'* – which Eusebius, for his part, is also adroitly turning here against the Jewish People as a whole – to *'all Gentiles'* and *'Worshippers of '* or *'Servants of idols'* generally as well as *'Backsliders among the Jews'* (the gist of what the *Pesher* will be meaning by the allusion, found in this passage, to *'Evil Ones'*).[6] For good measure, Eusebius' reference to *'Holy Men'* (in Hebrew, *'Kedoshim'* or *'Hassidim'*) is exactly the *'Nazirite'* language of *'being Holy'* or *'consecrated to God'* one finds predicated of James in all early Church sources, John the Baptist in the Gospels, and those designated *'the Men of Perfect Holiness'* and other parallel usages throughout the Scrolls.[7]

Not satisfied however with the venom inherent in the above diatribe, Eusebius – now drawing in gruesome detail on Josephus – then goes on at even greater length to list *'the calamities which at that time overwhelmed the whole Nation (of the Jews) in every part of the World.*' In particular, he describes, with both seeming gleeful malice and what can only be construed as hatred not '*love*,' the straits to which the Jews were reduced in Jerusalem, even how they *ended up, eating straw* (the same '*straw*,' to be sure, that we have previously encountered not only in the several Talmudic accounts of both '*Nakdimon*''s and '*Ben Kalba Sabuᶜa*''s philanthropy and, for instance, how Vespasian inspected the excrement of the defenders of Jerusalem and found it '*mixed with straw*'; but also of how '*the Biryonim*' mixed '*straw*' in the mortar used for Jerusalem's defence presumably to make sure the people went on fighting[8]). Finally Eusebius seems almost to revel in reproducing Josephus' account of how, in some cases, *the Jews even ate their own children*, laboring over Josephus' picture of such things in seeming loving detail .[9]

He completes this sketch of 'Christian' history in Palestine with the various signs and portents Josephus lists – in a kind of final summation in connection with the fall of the Temple at the end of the *Jewish War* – by way of introducing his own startling contention that:

> the thing that most moved our People to revolt against the Romans was an ambiguous Prophecy that one from their region would be elevated to Rule the World ('*ambiguous*' because, *whereas the Jews thought it applied to one of their own*, Josephus – along with R. Yohanan ben Zacchai above – obsequiously applies it to *the acclamation of Vespasian by his troops in Palestine as* '*Ruler of the World*'[10]).

In evaluating such oracles, one should always bear in mind the equivalence in early Christian allegorical theorizing of '*Jesus*' with '*the Temple*.'

Even as Eusebius redacts them, quoting directly from Josephus, these '*signs and portents*' included a '*cow giving birth to a lamb in the middle of the Temple*' on Passover (this really is a funny one); *a light shining in the Temple at night so that 'it seemed like full day*' on Passover as well (the mirror reversal of the Synoptic '*there was darkness all over the Land from the sixth hour to the ninth*' also on Passover, following the death of Christ – Matthew 27:45 and *pars*.); '*chariots and armies on high over the whole country, racing through the clouds*' (again the imagery of final eschatological '*Judgement on the clouds*' we have been underscoring in the War Scroll and parallel venues above); ending with '*a Star standing over the city like a sword*' and *a loud voice emanating from the Temple at Pentecost (Shavuᶜot) crying, 'Let us go forth.*'[11] The significance of this last, of course, needs no explanation. All this, even in Eusebius' recapitulation, precedes the Prophecy about the destruction of Jerusalem given by the '*Prophet*,' Josephus says was called

'*Jesus ben Ananias*,' which we shall discuss in more detail below.[12]

Epiphanius provides the same information (though with a little more moderation) about '*the Pella flight*' in the following manner:

> *Today this Nazoraean sect exists in Beroea in Coele Syria (Aleppo), in the Decapolis near the region of Pella, and in Bashan* (which is ancient '*Gilead*' or Transjordan beyond the region of Perea) *in the place called* '*Cocaba*' (the word in Hebrew *meaning* '*Star*'), *which in Hebrew is called* '*Kochabe*' (from which '*Bar Kochba*' seems to have derived his name[13]). *That is its place of origin, since all the Disciples were dwelling in Pella after they departed from Jerusalem* (basically the precise language of the Damascus Document once more), *for Christ had told them to leave Jerusalem and withdraw from it because it was about to be besieged. For this reason they settled in Perea and...that was where the Sect of the Nazoraeans began.*[14]

Not only do we have a reflection of the language the Damascus Document uses, as we just saw, to describe the '*departure from Judah to dwell in the Land of Damascus*,' but also the material here more or less agrees with Mandaean tradition about the withdrawal to Northern Syria of their precursors after the death of John.[15] Here too, it is clear that Epiphanius views the '*Nazoraeans*' – like the '*Ebionites*' – as *the true successors to the Community of James*.

The reference to '*Cocaba*'/'*Cochabe*' also seems to reflect the notice Eusebius preserves from Julius Africanus (c. 170–245) about two villages, '*Nazara*' and '*Cochaba*,' both with '*Messianic*'-sounding names ('*Nazara*' meaning either '*Branch*'/'*Keeper*'/or '*Nazirite*'; and '*Cochaba*' meaning '*Star*,' from which the name, '*Bar Kochba*,' as we just saw, would appear to derive). However, on the other hand, rather than across Jordan or in Lebanon, Julius appears to place the location of these '*villages in Judea*' – whatever he might mean by this.[16] For Julius, this is where '*the Desposyni*' (Jesus' family members) retired after the several tragedies recorded above, where they '*preserved the records of their noble family extraction*' and from which *they sent out members of the family with these proper records* or *genealogies* '*to other parts of the World.*'[17] Of course today, '*Kochaba*,' which may really have been the place of origin of '*Bar Kochba*' and not just his title, seems to be the site of the very old and famous Greek Orthodox Monastery of St. George located in a place called '*Wadi Kelt*' just outside Jericho. Moreover, even today there is also a sizeable town called '*Kaukabe*' (Arabic for '*Star*'), but this is in Southern Lebanon – whatever significance one might accord to this.[18]

Eusebius seems to think, following a writer called '*Aristo of Pella*' (c.

100–160 CE), to whom no doubt many of these traditions relating specifically to '*Pella*' and '*the flight*' remount, that at a later point a small community from Pella re-established itself in Jerusalem after the Bar Kochba War *at a time when Jews were forbidden, not only to enter, but even to look upon the city!*[19] This was probably the beginning of a completely non-Jewish, '*Christian*' group in Jerusalem, now being called '*Aelia Capitolina*' after its latest conqueror, Aelius Hadrian.

This Hadrian (d. 139 CE), like his patron Trajan (d. 117 CE) came, as we just saw, from the Roman Colony of Italica near present-day Seville in Southern Spain and the coincidence of this with the seeming place of origin of the Roman Centurion called '*Cornelius*' in Acts 10:1 and the '*Heavenly Tablecloth*' vision Peter receives, as a consequence of which Peter learns that he is permitted to both '*eat with*' and '*visit the houses of Gentiles*' (*even Roman Centurions from Italica*) should not go unremarked.

'*The Cup of the Lord*' and '*the Avenging Sword of the Covenant*'

For the First Apocalypse of James from Nag Hammadi, too, this oracle '*to leave Jerusalem*' comes – much like the Heavenly '*revelations*' Paul claims always to be receiving[20] – directly from '*Jesus*' ('*Christ Jesus*' in Paul). As this is stated in the first lines of the Apocalypse, '*Jesus*' (referred to significantly now as '*Rabbi*') speaking:

> *Fear not James. You too will they seize. But leave Jerusalem, for she it is that always gives the Cup of Bitterness to the Sons of Light* (*n.b.*, the '*Sons of Light*' imagery which permeates the Scrolls, in particular, the Community Rule, the War Scroll, and Hymns, but also to be found in the Gospel of John 12:36 and Paul in 1 Thessalonians 5:5 and Ephesians 5:8).[21]

Here too is also the '*Cup*' which James and John, the two '*sons of Zebedee*,' will supposedly have to drink in Matthew 20:22 and Mark 10:38 in imitation of Jesus, that is, '*the Cup of Martyrdom*' implying even crucifixion.[22] Both Gospels vary '*the Cup of the Lord*' language, which Jesus supposedly gives James to drink after his resurrection according to the picture in the Gospel of the Hebrews, itself refurbished or, if one prefers, rewritten or overwritten in the '*Emmaus Road*' encounter in the Gospel of Luke.[23]

In this episode, as in the Gospel of the Hebrews, Jesus '*reclines*' to eat with '*two of them*,' '*Cleopas*' and another (later apparently one '*Simon*,' but originally, presumably, '*Simeon bar Cleophas*' and his '*brother*' or '*cousin*' James), '*takes the bread, blesses, and breaks it*' (the second part of '*Communion with the blood*' and '*Communion with the body of Christ*' in

1 Corinthians 10:16, expanded in 11:25–29 with additional reference to '*the Cup*'), and '*gives it to them*,' whereupon he '*became known to them in the breaking of the bread*' (thus – Luke 24:13–35).

Aspects of this '*Emmaus Road*' scenario are, in turn, then revised in the Gospel of John 20:24–31's '*doubting Thomas*' encounter, that is, '*Thomas called Didymus*' or '*Twin Twin*' – in the Gospel of Thomas from Nag Hammadi, more accurately even, '*Didymus Judas Thomas*' – and, therefore, *another putative 'family' member*. This one takes place in Jerusalem and, once again, involves non-recognition in that this time '*Jesus comes and stands among them*' (here both the '*standing*' and '*coming*' notations again) and, at least, '*Thomas*' if not the others do not recognize or are unwilling to recognize him. Instead of '*eating*' with him, '*Thomas*' (in other contexts, '*Judas*' with the sobriquet of both '*Didymus*' and/or '*Thomas*' as we just saw) now actually – as is well known – '*puts*' his hand into one of his wounds. In 21:1–14, this is immediately followed up with yet another '*Manifestation*,' this time by '*the Sea of Tiberias*.'[24]

In this encounter, '*Thomas called Didymus*' is together with '*Simon Peter*,' the '*Nathanael*' and seeming James stand-in – now with the sobriquet of '*from Cana of Galilee*' (i.e., '*the Cananaean Galilean*') – with whom John 1:45–51 began, '*the (sons) of Zebedee*,' and '*two others of his Disciples*' (again unnamed) making '*Seven*' in all. However, instead of Jesus like some Dionysus-like, Hellenized apparition '*coming*' magically through already '*shut doors*' and '*standing in their midst*' as earlier in Jerusalem; now they all rather get in a '*boat*' and '*go fishing*.' It is then, when '*morning had come*' – their having '*caught nothing*' (n.b., how now it is '*morning*' that '*comes*') – that '*Jesus stood on the shore*' and again, *nobody recognizes him*. Finally, after a good deal of '*casting*' of '*nets*' ('*balete*'/'*ebelon*'), Peter then '*drags*' his '*net full of*' – '*a hundred fifty-three* – *large fishes*,' '*two hundred cubits to land*'; and John 21:11 rather comically adds: '*and (though) there were so Many, the net was not torn*' (here now too, again the language of '*nets*' and '*being full*,' as well as the ever-recurring number-motifs). It is now that '*Jesus comes*' and finally '*takes the bread* (and some '*of the fish too*'!) *and gives (it) to them*,' saying, '*come and eat*.' So once more the themes involve non-recognition, '*eating*' together, '*coming and standing*,' and the ubiquitous '*two Disciples*' again.

In the writer's view, the original behind all these episodes is the one in the Gospel of the Hebrews as conserved and excerpted by Jerome. Not only does it also involve '*taking the bread, blessing and breaking it*,' but Jesus now '*gives it to James the Just*' rather than all these '*other Disciples*' – James' cognomen, '*the Just One*,' being used very emphatically. Nor can there any longer be any real doubt as to the identity of the second individual either unnamed or missing from the Lukan refurbishment of this scenario. *It is James himself.* Furthermore, to these words (more or less the same as in Luke and John), Jesus is quoted as adding quite specifically,

> *My brother, eat your bread, for the Son of Man is risen from amongst those that sleep.*[25]

Not only has the usage, *'those that sleep,'* already appeared earlier in this passage from the Gospel of the Hebrews about a first resurrection appearance by Jesus to James, as it is quoted by Jerome; but, to add to the impression of its authenticity, we have already encountered exactly the same kind of phraseology in Paul, when he is speaking about similar subjects in 1 Corinthians 15:20 and 15:51 above, to say nothing of Ephesians 5:14 and, of course, Acts 7:60 on *'the stoning of Stephen.'* One will also find it in the aftermath of the crucial first episode in the Pseudoclementine *Recognitions* about Paul's attack on James and James sending out Peter on his first missionary journey (to be sure, *not to Samaria as in Acts*, but *to confront Simon Magus in Caesarea*[26]).

The above passage from the Gospel of the Hebrews, as it is conserved by Jerome, actually begins as follows:

> *After the Lord had given the linen clothes to the Servant of the Priest* (as we have seen, in Hebrew *'the High Priest'* – again adding to the sense of its authenticity – but, also, compare this with Acts 7:58's introduction of Paul which, as it stands, is virtually meaningless, since it is not *'the witnesses'* who have to be naked as they not the ones about to be stoned, but rather the condemned one as here!), *he went to James and appeared to him* (this is, then, a *first post-resurrection appearance*, paralleling the one *'on the Emmaus Road'* above in Luke), *for James had sworn that he would not eat bread from that hour in which he drank the Cup of the Lord until he should see him rise again from among those that sleep* (here the first occurrence of the *'those that sleep'* idiom but, one might add, this has all the appearances of being the authentic tradition, overwritten and bowdlerized out of all recognition elsewhere).[27]

Once again, not only do we have here a variety of the *'temporary Nazirite'* Oath procedure so much associated with James, but the whole report of this first appearance to James also has its counterpart in the various *'Last Supper'* scenarios about *'the Cup of the New Covenant in my blood'* in the Synoptics and Paul in 1 Corinthians 10:16–17 and 11:23–29 above. Both vary the language of *'the Cup of the Lord'* which Jesus is pictured as giving

James to drink here in the Gospel of the Hebrews after his resurrection.

We shall encounter this same '*Cup*' imagery, too, in the Habakkuk *Pesher*. There it is not just '*the Cup of the Lord*' that is being evoked, but also '*the Cup of Trembling*' of Isaiah 51:17–22 ('*the Cup of Bitterness*' in the First Apocalypse of James above[28]), and applied to *the death of the Righteous Teacher* and consequently, *the retribution God will exact because of it.* In the Habakkuk *Pesher*, when speaking about the '*Vengeance*' which would *also be 'visited upon' the Wicked Priest*, this is expressed in terms of '*the Cup of the Wrath of God*' (*that*) *would come around to*' and '*swallow*' or '*consume him*' as well.[29] This is also the sense of Revelation both in the strophe:

> *Babylon is fallen, Babylon is fallen* (another variation of the '*Belial*' vocabulary and, as we shall see, almost a direct evocation of the mournful dirge, reported by Josephus, on the part of '*Jesus ben Ananias*' – the double citation of '*Woe to Jerusalem*' being the key), *because she has given to all the Peoples* (*Ethne*) *to drink of the wine of the Wrath of her fornication* (14:8 – the imagery of '*fornication*' again, another vivid indicator of how these documents so enjoy mixing up these metaphors and sometimes seemingly, as it were, just hurling them around);

and the antistrophe in 14:10:

> *also he* (anyone worshipping '*the Beast*') *shall drink of the wine of the Wrath of God which is poured out full strength* (this imagery, too, is to be found in the Habakkuk *Pesher*, but also n.b., the reiteration of both the language of '*drink*'/'*drinking*' and '*give to drink*' in so many of these traditions[30]) *into the Cup of His Anger, and he shall be tormented in fire and brimstone* (the very words, as we shall see, that will be applied to the '*chastisement*' of the Wicked Priest in the Habakkuk *Pesher* for '*swallowing*' the Righteous Teacher and '*conspiring to destroy the Poor*').[31]

This imagery of '*the Cup of the Wrath of God*,' '*drinking*,' '*being drunk*,' and '*reeling*' and '*staggering*' is originally to be found, as just signaled, in Isaiah 51:17–23 and Jeremiah 25:15–28. Both make it very clear that what was originally meant by these metaphors was '*destruction*.' The latter even evokes '*the sword*' that, it claims, is to be '*sent against all the Nations on Earth*,' as well as the words '*drink*' (as it puts it, '*take this Cup of Wine from My hand*' – here meaning, '*the Cup of the Wine of the Wrath of God*' – and *make all Nations drink of it*'– here the '*hishkitah*'/'*mashkeh*'/'*Damascus*'/ '*Dammashek*' imagery, we shall elucidate below, when it comes to deciphering '*the New Covenant in the Land of Damascus*'[32]) which Jesus is pictured in the Synoptics as uttering to his Apostles at *'the Last Supper'* in his proclamation of Paul's 1 Corinthians 11:25's *Communion with the Blood of Christ'* above; or, as he puts this: *'Drink of it all,' 'this is the Cup of the New Covenant in my blood which is poured out for you'* (in Matthew 26:28 and Mark 14:24, *'poured out for the Many'* – a significant addition).[33]

In Revelation the whole metaphor is repeated once more in 16:19 and the two earlier versions are combined with yet another evocation of *'Babylon'*:

> *And the Great Babylon was remembered before God* (here again, we have the *'being remembered before God,'* which is almost word-for-word from the Damascus Document – to say nothing of the phrase in both Luke and Paul attributed to Jesus at *'the Last Supper.' 'Do this in remembrance of me.'* It also parallels the language of the passage about the burial memorial for the *'two brothers'* outside of Jericho, who had *'fallen asleep'* in the Pseudo-clementine *Recognitions* above, and because of the viewing of which, James and the rest of his Community – *'five thousand'* strong – had escaped the *'Enemy'* Paul, who was *'pursuing them'*[34]) *to give her the Cup of the Wine of the fury of His Wrath* (so will this be, that is, almost word-for-word from the Habakkuk *Pesher*).

The oracle attributed to Jesus in *'The First Apocalypse of James,'* with which we began the discussion, also plainly parallels those in *'the Little Apocalypse's* of the Synoptics (there being no *'Little Apocalypse'* as such in John), in which Jesus is pictured as predicting *the encirclement of Jerusalem by armies* and *its coming fall* (Luke 21:20–24 and *pars.*). As we have already underscored, this is extremely important because it comprises an internal dating parameter clearly implying the composition of materials of this kind *after the fall of Jerusalem* and *not before*.[35]

In Matthew/Mark, this is *'When you see the Abomination of the Desolation, spoken of by Daniel the Prophet* (we shall encounter precisely the same denominative, *'Daniel the Prophet,'* in the *Florilegium* from Qumran below), *standing where it ought not to stand* (again one should have regard for the language of *'standing'* here, now used, of course, not positively to imply *'Jesus'* is *'the Standing One,'* but negatively by way of an attack presumably on *'Belial'* and those whose language this was – *'Simon Magus,'* for instance?). It should also be appreciated that all these *'Apocalypse's* are introduced by the allusion to *'Jesus going forth from the Temple'* and predicting, *'There shall not be left one stone upon stone that shall not be thrown'* or *'cast down'* (Luke 21:5–6 and *pars.*). In Luke 21:20–22, the operative words of Jesus that follow are:

Let them that are in Judea flee into the mountains and let them that are in the midst of her depart out (again, as in *'Jesus departing from the Temple,'* note the parallel with language of the Damascus Document about *'going out'* or *'departing from the Land of Judah'*)...*for these are the Days of Vengeance.*

Compare this with *'the Day of Vengeance,'* over which we have so labored in both the Community Rule and War Scroll above, but as *per* usual, *reversed.* Now as in all *'Pauline Christian'* literature to follow, the *'Vengeance of God'* is not what we would consider to be *'the Last Judgement'* – or, as Muhammad would put it following the tradition in the Habakkuk Pesher, *'the Day of Judgement'*[36] – but now the *'Vengeance'* which the Roman armies will wreak upon all those who opposed them (those for whom in Paul in Romans 13:4, *'the wearing of the sword'* would bring its own *'Wrathful Vengeance'* and, by implication, all those allegedly involved, as in I Corinthians 11:27–29, in *'the death of the Christ'*).

As we have seen, these *'Apocalypse's,* two of which are introduced in Luke 21:1–4 and Mark 12:41–44 by the use of the language *'casting down'* (*ballei/bebleken/ebalon/balonton*) in the story of the *'certain Poor widow casting her two mites into the Temple Treasury'* (in Mark, anyhow, *repeated six times in four lines* – in Luke, *five*), all speak of the *throwing down of all the stones of the Temple* so that *'there should not be left one stone which is 'not cast down.'* Not only is the *'casting down'* imagery now applied to the stones of the Temple and not James' fall; but the *'Poor widow casting her two mites'* is refurbished, as we have already explained as well, into the portrait of Judas *Iscariot* supposedly *'throwing his thirty pieces of silver into the Temple'* – and here the *'throwing down'* of *'the stones of the Temple'* replaces the *'casting'* by *'the Rich,'* *'the Many,'* and the *'certain Poor widow'* of *'their gifts into the Treasury.'*

There is also the language of *'signs and wonders'* (Matthew 24:24/Luke 21:25, etc.), and *'leading Many astray'* (Matthew 24:4–5, 11, 24, and *pars.*) that permeates all the Gospels. This last expression is precisely the language used at the beginning of the Damascus Document (and throughout the Qumran corpus) to describe the activities of *'the Righteous Teacher's'* ideological nemesis, *'the Lying Spouter'* who *'leads Many astray'* with his words of *'Lying'* (also referred to in the Damascus Document, playing off the language of *'spouting'* applied to him, as *'pouring out'* upon them *'the waters of Lying'*[37]). Furthermore it is implied that, because of such teaching, *'they were delivered up to the Avenging Sword of the Covenant,'* words actually duplicated in the *'delivering up'* language in these *'Little Apocalypse's* (Matthew 24:10 and *pars.*) and to some extent, as just remarked, Paul's comments on the vengeance to be expected for *'wearing'* precisely this kind '*of sword*' in Romans 13:4.[38]

Of course, too, not only do these materials testify to the post-70 CE origins of these '*Apocalypse*'s, but the '*flight*' oracle they contain parallels the '*Logion*,' attributed to Jesus in the Gospel of Thomas, stating (in Jesus' words, as we saw) that '*in the place where you are to go*' ('*you*' meaning '*the Apostles*' or '*Disciples*'; the '*place*,' implying Jerusalem), '*go to James the Just, for whose sake Heaven and Earth came into existence.*' Still the general ethos of the oracle as it is presented in the First Apocalypse of James – if in not Eusebius and Epiphanius – also carries with it the sense of '*bitterness*' *over impending* '*death*' – that same kind of death which is to be visited upon James as it is upon '*the Righteous Teacher*' and his followers among '*the Poor*' or '*Ebionim*,' according to the Habakkuk and Psalm 37 *Peshers* at Qumran.[39]

'*The Pella Flight*' and the Flight to '*the Wilderness Camps*'

But what are we to make of these notices about '*a Pella flight*' in response to some mysterious oracle to those left in '*the Jerusalem Community*' after James' death? Certainly, they have their mythological aspects having to do with actually being able to accomplish such a '*flight*' to a location like Pella in the unstable conditions of warfare at the time, an issue raised by a number of scholars.[40] But if we set '*Pella*' aside for the moment and concentrate on the '*flight*' motif, there are a number of traditions, as already indicated, about similar emigrations or flights in this period.

To start with, there is the '*Theudas*' (c. 44–46 CE), we saw in Josephus above – evoked anachronistically by '*Rabbi Gamaliel*' in Acts and seemingly mentioned as '*the father*' or '*brother of the Just One*' in the Second Apocalypse of James[41] – who attempts to lead a large group of his followers out across Jordan in a '*reverse Exodus*' into '*the Land of Damascus*' or beyond (exactly the reverse of the biblical '*Joshua*' leading them in) before he was caught, beheaded and a majority of his followers butchered.[42]

Then there is the tradition in the Pseudoclementine *Recognitions* about a '*flight*' (reckoned, as we have seen, by the telltale '*five thousand*' – the number Acts 4:4 says joined the Community after Peter and John's first arrest, following their identification of 'Jesus' in 3:22–26 as '*the True Prophet*' in debates manifestly paralleling those '*on the Temple steps*' in the Pseudoclementines and *Anabathmoi Jacobou* above – James, of course, deleted from the narrative; to say nothing of the number of people with whom 'Jesus' is alleged '*to have fled*' to the '*desert*' or '*wilderness*' in the Synoptics or Josephus' estimate of the number of '*Essenes*') of James' Community in Jerusalem to the Jericho area after the attack by the '*Enemy*'

Paul on James in the Temple – the one in which, after *'casting'* James *'headlong down the steps'* and leaving him for dead, Paul misses James and his followers because they were outside of Jericho visiting the mysterious tombs of *'two of the brothers'* that curiously *'whitened of themselves every year.'*[43]

There is also the similar flight of those extreme *'Zealots,'* Josephus calls *'Sicarii,'* to Masada after their leader *'Menachem'* – either the son or grandson of the co-founder of the Movement, named *'Judas the Galilean'*[44] – put on the royal purple of the king at the very beginning of the Uprising in 66 CE.[45] This ultimately ends up in the celebrated suicide of these same *'Sicarii'* together with all their dependents in 73 CE.[46] Much like the stoning of James, three and a half years before this *'flight,'* it should be appreciated that Menachem is stoned by *'Establishment'* opponents – which would include *Pharisees, Sadducees, and Herodians* – in internecine stone-throwing and internal strife on the Temple Mount.[47] Finally, we have already mentioned the flight of the Mandaean partisans of John the Baptist to Northern Syria and beyond, after he too was killed in what has to be regarded as partisan internecine strife.

For the sectaries represented by the Qumran materials, *the reunion of 'the Wilderness Camps'* to rededicate themselves to *'the Torah'* or *'Covenant'* – that is, *'the New Covenant in the Land of Damascus'* – under the authority of *'the Overseer'*/*'Mebakker'*/or *'Bishop'* and/or *'the High Priest Commanding the Many'* – or if one prefers, *'Commanding the Camps'* – in the Damascus Document was, as already indicated, *to take place every year at Pentecost*.[48] In Judaism *'Pentecost'* or *'Shavu^cot,'* it should be remarked, comes fifty days (seven times seven weeks plus one day) after Passover and is the time, if one can put it like this, of *'the descent of the Torah'* or *'the Law'* to Moses in Sinai. This is the festival which Acts 20:16 pictures Paul as hurrying to Jerusalem with his contributions to attend before, what Acts portrays as, *his final confrontation with James*. It is clear that *'Pentecost'* was also the time of the annual reunion of *'the Assemblies'* or *'Churches'* portrayed in Acts as well.

'Pentecost' is also the festival when, as we saw in Acts 2:1–45 above, *'the Holy Spirit'* descended upon the whole Community like *'a violent rushing wind'* – here the *'wind'* and *'Spirit'* correlation of the Damascus Document's description in Hebrew of the *'windiness'* of *'the Lying Spouter,'* already alluded to above too and which we shall discuss further below – accompanied by its *'Gentile Mission'* accoutrement of *'speaking with other Tongues'* (2:41 – though, unlike in 4:4 later, here only *'three thousand'* were added). Where this *'speaking with other tongues'* is concerned, at Qumran *'the Mebakker'* is not only the individual who, along with *'the High Priest*

Commanding the Many' has control over 'the Wilderness Camps' but also 'mastery over all the Tongues of men and their secrets.'[49]

Where 'the Holy Spirit' and 'wind' of Acts 2:1–1 is concerned, 'the Spouter' – who is also the key ideological adversary in the Habakkuk Pesher – is in the Damascus Document (more textual homogeneity, arguing for chronological simultaneity between it and the Habakkuk Pesher) described in terms of being 'of confused wind' (Ms. A – Ms. B, the shorter additional piece found in the Cairo Genizah, has 'walking in the Spirit' – more or less the same but probably more accurate[50]) or, to put it more colloquially, 'a Windbag.' He is called this because he 'misled' (again the vocabulary of 'leading astray') both 'the Builders' and 'Daubers upon the wall,' referred to in Ezekiel 13:10. Ms. B, as we shall see further below, in making such a characterization actually paraphrases Micah 2:11 on 'the man walking in windiness and Lying Spirit, spouting wine and drunkenness to them,' which basically both includes and harks back to the 'wine'/'venom' imagery as descriptive of 'the Kings of the Peoples' ('Herodians' and others, as we have seen) and 'their Ways' preceding this allusion.[51]

Not only in Ezekiel 13:3–10 is it the 'Lying,' 'vain,' and 'Empty visions' of the 'disreputable' or 'obscene prophets following their own spirit' (cf. the odd but constant allusions to 'prophets and teachers' of the early 'Pauline' Gentile Church in Acts 11:27, 13:1, 15:32, etc. – in this last even applied to 'Judas and Silas' whatever that might suggest – to say nothing of the link-up here in the mind of the sectarian exegete at Qumran with Micah 2:11) who 'lead (the) People astray.' It should be remarked that in Ezekiel these 'Daubers on the Wall,' who 'lead the People astray,' do so by 'crying Peace when there is not peace' (13:10), an allusion pregnant with meaning, not only for that time, but all time.

As for the Damascus Document, its conclusion is that, because of 'the windiness' of this 'Lying Spouter's spouting' – obviously meant as the prime exemplar of one such 'Deceiver' – 'the Wrath of God would be kindled against his entire Assembly' or 'Congregation' ('Church' in other vocabularies – also note here, the vocabulary of 'the Wrath of God' of both the Habakkuk Pesher and Revelation and by refraction, as just suggested, even Paul in 1 Corinthians 11:29 above).[52] One last point that should be made regarding this connection of 'Pentecost' with 'the Holy Spirit' in Acts – in the description of 'the signs and portents' anticipating the destruction of the Temple in Josephus, quoted by Eusebius above as well, 'Pentecost' is also the time of 'a loud crashing of gates' in the Temple and the Heavenly Spirit crying out, 'Let us go forth (from it).'

We have already seen how many of these successor groups to 'the Jerusalem Community' of James, such as the 'Ebionites,' 'Nazoraeans,' and

'Sampsaeans' (that is 'the Elchasaite Sabaeans' above), developed in these areas *across the Dead Sea* and '*beyond the Jordan*' in Perea, Bashan, Batanea – what at Qumran might be called '*the Land of Damascus*' – and Northern Syria and beyond. There can be little doubt that there was a lively '*Diaspora*'/'*Dispersion*' (at Qumran, both '*Benjamin*' and '*the Diaspora*' or '*the Peoples of the Desert*') dwelling in these areas. The '*Mandaeans*' – the remnants of '*the Sabaeans*' in Southern Iraq and, also, possibly the descendants of the Izates' conversion around this time there (c. 25–35 CE)[53] – still preserve traditions, as we saw, that the followers of John the Baptist (themselves included) fled after he was executed by '*Herod the Tetrarch*' ('*Herod Antipas*' above), emigrating in the period around 37–38 CE to Northern Syria.[54] Therefore, one should pay some attention to the persistent note of this kind of '*flight*' or '*emigrant*' activity to all these regions.

John the Baptist, in particular – especially in the Gospel of John 1:28, 3:26, and 10:40 – is portrayed as carrying on most of his activities '*across the Jordan.*' Certainly his arrest there by Herod Antipas and execution at the Maccabean/Herodian Fortress of Machaeros, directly across the Dead Sea virtually due east from Qumran, would imply that the activities for which he was imprisoned had transpired in that region.[55] The authority of the '*Herod the Tetrarch*' (Acts 13:1), who executed him, only extended from Galilee into Perea, as we have seen, but not *the Judean side of the Jordan* – at this time still under the control of the Roman '*Prefect*' or '*Governor*' in Jerusalem and Caesarea.[56] This is something of what is implied, as just suggested, in the War Scroll at Qumran about a '*Diaspora*' of '*Jews, Levites, and the Tribe of Benjamin*' in '*the Wilderness of the Peoples,*' meaning the area both north and south of '*Damascus*' and beyond into the Great Desert – what some might today call '*the Fertile Crescent.*' How far beyond must be the subject of some conjecture.

So there is much to support such a '*flight*' tradition, despite the fact of its somewhat fantastic packaging. '*Pella*' was a town just across the Jordan River somewhat further north however, as already indicated, of the region of most of John the Baptist's activities as pictured in the Gospels. It can be looked at as the gateway to this area '*on the Way to the wilderness of Damascus,*' as 1 Kings 19:15 *in its description of Elijah's activities* puts it. But it is doubtful if we can really speak of *an actual 'flight' to the town of Pella itself* which at the beginning of the War, as Josephus recounts, was actually the scene of a good deal of partisan fighting between Jews and more Hellenized native populaces.[57] For awhile Jewish partisans held the upper hand, but ultimately the Jewish populations were for the most part wiped out by the pro-Roman, anti-Jewish, Greek-speaking population in these areas across the Jordan, then known as '*the Decapolis.*'[58]

But a reasonable and viable alternative to an actual '*flight to Pella*' would be to consider Pella, the importance of which is undoubtedly magnified in the writings of '*Aristo of Pella*' in the next century as we saw, as a gateway to these other areas '*beyond Jordan*' *and further North in the* '*Damascus*' *region and beyond*, as implied by such terms as '*the Wilderness*' or '*Desert of the Peoples*' in the Qumran War Scroll and/or '*the Land of Damascus*' in the Damascus Document. This is what is implied, too, in the plethora of notices from writers like Hippolytus, Eusebius, and Epiphanius about the presence of derivative groups like '*Naassenes*' or '*Essenes*,' '*Nazoraeans*,' '*Ebionites*,' '*Elchasaites*,' '*Sampsaeans*,' and '*Masbuthaeans*' in regions such as these.

The totality of the claim, compressed into the idea of a single '*flight to Pella*,' can probably be dated to the fact of the return of a small Gentilized Community to Roman-controlled Jerusalem, '*Aelia Capitolina*,' to set up as a more orthodox '*Christian*' Church there – subsequently referred to as '*the See of James*' – following the failure of the Bar Kochba Revolt in 132–36 CE (similar '*See's*, in fact and legend, came to exist even as far west even as '*Santiago de Compostela*' – '*St. James of the Starry Field*' but there, of course, in the name now of '*James the brother of John*'![59]).

But what of the mysterious '*oracle*' that was supposed to have triggered this '*flight*'? About this perhaps one can be more precise. Certainly it relates to the fact of the removal of '*the Protection of the People*' or the '*Oblias*' James ('*the Wall*'/'*Bulwark*'/or '*Shield*,' '*for whose sake Heaven and Earth came into existence*'), without whose presence Jerusalem could no longer remain in existence or was doomed according to '*the Zaddik-the-Pillar-of-the-World*' ideology of Proverbs above.[60] This is strengthened by all the '*early Church*' testimonies from Hegesippus to Clement to Origen, Eusebius, Jerome, and Epiphanius (Josephus' testimony notwithstanding), insisting that *following the death of James* – either by a '*stoning*' or '*fall*,' it makes no difference – *the Roman armies immediately* '*appeared*.'[61]

Both Origen in the Third Century and Eusebius in the Fourth insist, in fact, that they actually saw in the copy of Josephus' *War*, they were using (both probably in the library at Caesarea and in testimonies at its end concerning '*the signs and wonders*' presaging the fall of the Temple), that the '*immediate cause of the siege*' and *fall of Jerusalem was the death of James*.[62] This is a testimony Origen objects to so vociferously – *insisting that Josephus should have said Jerusalem fell* '*on account of Jesus*' *death*' *not James*' – that doubtlessly it had more than a little to do with its disappearance from all extant copies of Josephus' *Jewish War* that have come down to us; and testimony about James in Josephus, now, is only to be found in the *Antiquities*.[63]

Having said this, it is in fact actually possible to identify both the mysterious oracle that gave rise to this alleged *'flight'* – regardless of the fact of whether it really took place as claimed or not – and its historical provenance, in the *'oracle'* Josephus attributes (also in this section about these *'signs and wonders'* at the end of the *Jewish War*) to the mysterious *'Prophet,'* he designates as *'Jesus ben Ananias'* (n.b., even the prefiguration in this appellation of the name the Gospels give 'Jesus').[64]

This *'Prophet'* too – just as the notices from early Church writings conserved in Eusebius that the coming of the Roman Army occurred *directly following the death of James* – seems to have appeared around *Succot,* 62 CE. We can determine this on the basis of Josephus' own testimony. He, not only tells us about the existence of this later *'Jesus,'* but how he continued prophesying ceaselessly for *'seven and a half years' from the time of his first appearance* (as already suggested above, one should keep an eye on the Daniel-like numerology implicit in this calculus as well[65]) *until he was killed by a Roman projectile during the siege of Jerusalem just prior to its fall.* This means that he started *'prophesying'* in the Autumn of 62 CE, that is, *exactly in the aftermath,* according to Josephus, *of James' death as well.*[66]

But this *'prophecy'* of the destruction of Jerusalem, that *'continued for seven and a half years,'* not only related in some manner to James' death, but also to similar oracles or predictions ascribed to 'Jesus' in *'the Little Apocalypse's.* It also relates, as just remarked, to the proclamation in Revelation, *'Babylon is fallen, Babylon is fallen,'* a proclamation echoing Isaiah 21:9 but, as so often occurs, reversed – Jesus ben Ananias' mournful cry, *relating to the coming fall of Jerusalem*; Revelation's, as normally interpreted, *relating to the fall of Rome.* To bring us full circle, the *'fall of Babylon'* as signaled here in Isaiah 21:9, is uttered in the context of another important allusion found at Qumran, *'taking (one's) stand upon (one's) watchtower'* (21:8). The last, in turn, introduces the Damascus Document's crucial delineation of *'the Three Nets'* – namely, *'fornication,'* *'Riches,' and 'pollution of the Temple'* – with which Belial *'ensnares Israel, transforming them into three kinds of Righteousness'* – but it is also basically replicated in Habakkuk 2:1 *'I shall take my stand upon my watchtower,'* which the Habakkuk Pesher, as we saw – leading up to its equally important exposition of Habakkuk 2:4 – applies to God *'making known to the Righteous Teacher all the Mysteries of the words of His Servants the Prophets.'*[67]

'Jesus ben Ananias' and 'Agabus'' Prophecy

It is also possible to identify Josephus' *'Jesus ben Ananias'* and his *'Prophecy'* in two patently fictionalized refurbishments of the life-story of Paul, as presented in Acts, centering about another equally mysterious 'Prophet,' whom Acts calls 'Agabus,' already described above. In the first in Acts 11:27–30, 'Agabus' is the stand-in, as we saw, for Queen Helen's putative consort in Armenian and Syriac sources – her 'brother' if we take Josephus for our guide or, if a title, also the name of her son by this King[68] – 'Agbarus' or 'Abgarus.'[69]

His second materialization occurs in Acts 21:10–14 just prior to Paul's last trip to Jerusalem and final confrontation with James. In it, like the many notices preceding it in Acts' *certainly peculiar narrative* (which is something in the nature of a freeze-frame, stopping, starting, and then repeating) about a person or persons '*coming down from Jerusalem*' – usually to the ambiguous location called '*Antioch*'[70] – the pretense is that another of these curious '*certain one*'s (now definitively denoted as '*a Prophet named Agabus*') '*came down from Judea*,' this time, not '*to Antioch*' but '*to Caesarea*' (21:10 – in 11:27 earlier, it will be recalled, the first materialization of this 'Prophet' was expressed a little more floridly as, '*and in these days prophets came down from Jerusalem to Antioch*,' '*one among whom was named Agabus*').

It is at this point in Acts 21:11–12 that this '*Prophet named Agabus*' is pictured, rather comically, as '*taking hold of Paul's girdle*' and *warning Paul*, '*not to go up to Jerusalem*' – which, in effect, is the reversal of the '*Pella flight*' oracle – not '*not to go up to Jerusalem*' but '*to leave Jerusalem.*' It is a not incurious fact too that, in tying this oracle to '*a Prophet called Agabus*,' as Acts does in its own peculiar way; it closes the triangle of these three '*prophecies*,' tying the '*Pella flight*' oracle even closer to the mournful cry of the '*Prophet*' who, Josephus designates, as '*Jesus ben Ananias*' just *after the death of James*. It is interesting, too, that the reference to '*Judea*' here, not only bears something of the sense of '*going down*' to a more far-away place, such as '*Antioch*,' than it does to '*Caesarea*'; but also incorporates yet another aspect of the oracle '*to leave Judea*' and the various other references to '*Judea*'/'*Judah*' and '*the Land of Judah*' connected to it above.[71]

Acts 11:27–30 actually describes the first appearance of this mysterious '*Agabus*' in the prelude to its introduction of *the real James* (*James the brother of Jesus*) in the next chapter such as it is. It will be recalled that this first appearance of *the real* '*James*' in Acts 12:17 occurred just after Acts 12:2 had neatly removed '*the other James*' from the scene – the pun here on Matthew 28:1's '*the other Mary*' is intentional – that is, *James the son of Zebedee* '*the brother of John*,' a character we have already linked in the matter of the contemporaneous beheadings in this period to the individual referred to in other contexts as '*Theudas.*'[72]

This introduction of *the* '*real James*' comes, then, directly after its description of how '*Herod the King beheaded James the brother of John with the sword.'* The *'King'* in question here is normally taken to be the first Agrippa I (d. 44 CE), but it is even more likely that someone actually named *'Herod,'* that is, his brother, *'Herod of Chalcis'* (44–49 CE), who succeeded him as King after Agrippa's rather suspicious death and the father, too, of that *'Aristobulus'* who married the notorious *'Salome,'* involved – as already previously underscored – in some manner in *the death of John the Baptist.*[73] All of these points are sandwiched in between the two references to the *'famine relief'* mission on behalf of the *'Antioch'* Community undertaken by *'Barnabas and Saul'* in Acts 11:30 and 12:25, completely drawing our attention away from what happened in the meantime.

It would be well to repeat this first notice in Acts 11:27–28 about this *'Agabus'* in its entirety:

> *And in these days* (c. 45–46 CE, the date of *'the Great Famine'* which, in Josephus, triggered both Theudas' reverse exodus in the *Antiquities* and Queen Helen of Adiabene's own *'famine relief'* activities, in the course of which she *'sent her agents to'* Egypt – patently the source of the story in Acts 8:26–40 of the earlier *'conversion on the way...from Jerusalem to Gaza,'* the traditional gateway to Egypt, of *'the Treasury Agent of the Ethiopian Queen')* prophets came down *from Jerusalem to Antioch* (here, as we just saw, the same datum as Acts 21:10's later *'a certain one, a Prophet came down from Judea to Caesarea')* and Agabus, *rising up from among them* (note the same wording used throughout the Damascus Document, in particular, to describe the *'rising up of the Messiah of Aaron and Israel'* – often this is considered to be *two 'Messiahs'* or *a series of 'Messiahs'* but the singular verbal and adjectival usages, always surrounding it, should be sufficient evidence to convince the reader that the intent of the author was singular[74]), *evoked via the Spirit the Great Famine that was about to engulf the whole habitable world, which actually came to pass under Claudius Caesar* (41–54 CE).

In both the first appearance of this *'Prophet,'* Acts uses to introduce *'the Great Famine'* and Paul and Barnabas' *'famine relief'* operations associated with it, and the second – just prior to Paul's own arrest and ultimately James' disappearance from the scene – *'Agabus'* is the stand-in and mirror replacement for or inversion of this other character in Josephus *'Jesus ben Ananias,'* who *really was 'a Prophet' at this time,* not a made-up one.

In a further curious side-light to Acts' odd presentation of data of this kind, it should be recalled that someone called *'Ananias'* also plays a role in Eusebius' story of the conversion of *'Agbarus'* (*'the Great King of the Peoples beyond the Euphrates'*), as he does in Acts 9:10–20's curious story

about how *'a certain Disciple in Damascus named Ananias,'* after first hesi-
tating *'because of the many Evils this man had done'* to the *'Holy Ones in
Jerusalem,'* goes to *'the house of one Judas'* – in our view, *'Judas the brother of
James'* / *'Judas Thomas'* / *'Theudas'* or even *'Thaddaeus'* – *'on a street called the
Straight'* and, *'having laid hands upon him'* in the style of Mandaean *'Priests'*,
'baptized him.'[75]

Not only is *'Jesus ben Ananias'*' prophecy of the imminent destruction
of Jerusalem related to the *'prophecies'* ascribed to Jesus in *'the Little Apocalypse's* and right before in the *'throwing down'* of the Temple's *'stones'* in
the Synoptics (this should be fairly clear since both sets of oracles relate,
in some manner, *to the destruction of the Temple*); but his *'Prophecy'* must be
seen as being both triggered by James' death and evincing *'Jesus'* reaction
to it, namely, that without the *'Protection-of-the-People'* / *'the Zaddik'* / *'the
Bulwark'* / *'the Tried Wall'* (*'the Zaddik'* being, as Proverbs 10:25 puts it, *'the-
Pillar-of-the-World'*), *Jerusalem was doomed and could no longer remain in existence.* The point here is relatively straightforward. According to Josephus – the most reliable testimony regarding James' demise (more, really,
than early Church sources which are usually dependent in one way or
another upon him) – James died sometime in the year 62 CE.

Josephus describes this as being a miscarriage of justice. So do early
Church sources.[76] The Dead Sea Scrolls present the destruction of their
Leader, tantalizingly referred to – as we have been indicating – as *'the
Righteous Teacher'* or *'Teacher of Righteousness,'* as being totally unwarranted
and react to it in the most violent manner calling down in the Habakkuk
and Psalm 37 *Pesher*s, as we have alluded to, the most horrific curses upon
those responsible for it and their enemies among *'the Idolaters'* and *'the
Evil Ones among all the Nations of the Earth.'*[77]

Josephus places his account of the death of James at the end of the
Antiquities written, in contrast to the *War*, in the early 90s when he seems
to have felt more secure and was, therefore, more forthcoming – perhaps
unwisely so.[78] Just as the notice about Jesus ben Ananias' prophecy is
missing from the *Antiquities*, the notice about the death of James is
missing from the *War* – actually if we go according to Origen's and Eusebius' testimonies, it may have originally have appeared in the *War* –
probably, as just suggested, in the context of this prophecy on the part of
'Jesus ben Ananias' and the other *'signs and wonders' foretelling* and *preceding
the destruction of the Temple and Jerusalem.* The other possibility would be
that this notice about *the death of James, leading to the fall of Jerusalem* was
originally present in the description and account in the *War* of the death
of James' nemesis, the High Priest Ananus – really Ananus II or Ananus
ben Ananus, the son of the High Priest, pictured in the Gospels as

involved in the death of Jesus, and the boon companion of Josephus' friend, Jesus ben Gamala above.[79]

For all intents and purposes James' death is the last episode of any significance in the *Antiquities* and, since we must surmise that Josephus either knew James – having studied '*in the wilderness*' with his mysterious double, '*the Rechabite*,' vegetarian '*Bather*' Josephus cryptically denotes as '*Banus*'[80] – or knew enough about him to include him (if we take this '*testimonium*' to his death to be authentic); it almost seems as if James' death is the climax his *Antiquities* has been building towards.[81] After this, Josephus simply recounts the troubles '*the Sicarii*' stir up, *the riot led by* '*Saulos the kinsman of Agrippa*' who '*used violence with the People*,' how '*the Lower Priesthood*' won the right to wear linen in the Temple (the type of clothing James and Josephus' teacher '*Banus*' also wore), and *enumerates all the High Priests from the return from the Exile to the period of the Uprising*, concluding with the observation that the Roman Governors, Albinus (62–64 CE) and Florus (64–66 CE), *by their venality and brutality*, in effect, *goaded* or *provoked the Jews to revolt against Rome* – even, seemingly, perhaps purposefully. For this latter observation, it is quite likely Josephus was indebted to Agrippa II, with whom he was later intimate in Rome.[82]

The sequentiality here, especially when compared with early Church accounts *associating the fall of Jerusalem with the death of James*, is important. In effect, though not as compressed or nearly as stark, Josephus is following the same sequence as reported in Eusebius (dependent presumably on Hegesippus) – of the stoning of James followed by the immediate appearance of the Roman armies. In effect, too, the Habakkuk *Pesher* (and to a lesser extent that on Psalm 37 connected to it) follows basically the same sequence in describing the destruction of the Righteous Teacher followed by imprecations concerning what was going to happen to '*the Last Priests of Jerusalem*' and in due course, in effect, '*all the Nations that serve stone and wood*' (meaning, of course, '*all Idolaters*').

Josephus' Account of the Death of James

It would be well, therefore, to provide Josephus' testimony to the death of James in its entirety. As just implied, the context is always important. We have described what succeeded James' death in Josephus' narrative. It is preceded in it by the introduction of '*the Sicarii*' who *assassinate the High Priest Jonathan* in 55 CE (the brother of that '*Ananus*' subsequently *responsible for the death of James*;)[83] two additional references to '*the Impostors and Deceivers* (both unidentified) *who urged the masses to follow them into the wilderness*' there to show them '*the manifest signs and wonders of their impending Freedom'* or *'Deliverance'*[84]; *the High Priests sending their servants onto the threshing floors to rob the 'Poor' Priests of the tithes by which they lived*, as already underscored, repeated twice, once before the stoning of James and once after[85]; *'the Temple Wall Affair'* under the Roman Governor Festus (60–62 CE, who succeeds Felix and appears in Acts in a more or less sympathetic light, ultimately sending Paul to Rome – in connection with this *'Affair'?*), *having to do with Agrippa II's dining habits while watching the sacrifices from his Palace balcony*; and finally the decision Agrippa II and the High Priest he has just appointed, Ananus ben Ananus, take to destroy James in 62 CE.

In our view there certainly is a sequentiality in all these things, but it was *'the Temple Wall Affair,'* as we have already suggested, which was actually *the direct cause of the death of James*. This has to do with James' role as Leader or, at least, hero of the *'zealous' Lower Priesthood in the Temple* from the Forties to the Sixties CE. As already to some extent described, a high wall was built in the Temple around 60 CE to block Agrippa II's view of the sacrifices while he reclined and ate, presumably with his pro-Roman, collaborating friends (as a kind of *'Bela^c'/'Belial'/* or *'Balaam'* – one should note here the Temple Scroll's strange injunction against *'Bela^c,'* the biblical name both of the ancestor of the Edomites and the Benjaminites[86] – *'seeing'* or *'coming into the Temple che-balla^c'* or *'as Bela^c'*[87]).

We are not even speaking about what kind of *'foods'* this obviously more accommodating *'Agrippa II'* (in whose *'Praetorium'* in Caesarea, as we saw, Paul was presented as staying in Acts 23:35) might have been eating with his *'friends'* while *'reclining'* and watching the spectacle of the sacrificial ceremonies in the Temple; but it was in connection with protests over this situation that quite a few individuals, including *the Temple Treasurer Helcias (formerly married to Costobarus' and 'Saulos'' sister Cypros)* and *some vegetarian Priests of Josephus' acquaintance* who *ate nothing but 'dates and nuts'* while they were incarcerated (presumably, to avoid *'pollution'*), as well as others – probably even Paul and ultimately even Josephus – went to Rome to plead their case before Nero.[88]

In our view, these two, Agrippa and the younger Ananus – the latter already smarting from the slaying of his brother Jonathan by those Josephus derogatorily calls *'Sicarii'* or *'Assassins'* (see the allusion in Acts 21:38 to the *'Sicarii,'* including even a reference to *'four thousand'* of them being led out *'into the wilderness'*), literally *'Knife People'* (also possibly related, as we shall see, to *'the circumciser's knife'*), who *manifestly did not call themselves this* – take advantage of an interregnum in Roman Governors, caused by the death of Festus in 62 CE, to deal with James. In some manner, therefore, this nefarious act must have been connected to their perception of James' involvement in the various disturbances, just alluded to, centered on the Temple Mount.

It should also be observed that the circumstances of James' death almost precisely fit the circumstances of what the Gospels, seemingly retrospectively, record relative to 'Jesus.' These include the all-important charge of '*blasphemy*,' which is to be distinguished from that of '*sedition*' where Roman administrative Law and local custom are concerned.[89] Nor should it be forgotten that it was by this same Festus, after long and sympathetic conversations in Acts 24:10–26:32 with Felix and Drusilla and then with Agrippa II and Bernice (eventually the mistress of Vespasian's son Titus, who destroyed the Temple), that Paul was sent to Rome as well.

Josephus' complete description of James' death reads as follows:

And now (Nero) Caesar, upon hearing of the death of Festus, sent Albinus to Judea as Procurator, whereupon the King (Agrippa II) deprived Joseph of the High Priesthood and bestowed the succession to this Office on the Son of Ananus, likewise called 'Ananus' (Ananus ben Ananus)..., a man rash in temperament and very insolent (Josephus seems to have changed his view of Ananus here, because in the *Jewish War* he has nothing but praise for him, even going so far as to call him a '*Benefactor*' and *blaming the fall of Jerusalem* – not unlike James, in what would appear to be another case of both reversal and transference – *on his removal!*[90])...*Possessed of such a character and thinking he had a favorable opportunity because Festus was dead and Albinus still on the way, Ananus convened a Sanhedrin of the Judges and brought before them the brother of Jesus who was called the Christ* (here certainly, too, one must be aware of the possibility that a degree of interpolation has taken place[91]), *whose name was James, and several others* (the plural addition of these '*others*' here tallies with certain allusions in the picture of '*the Wicked Priest's destruction* of '*the Righteous Teacher*' in the Dead Sea Scrolls. In them, it is declared, '*he would be paid the reward he paid the Poor*' and '*the Simple of Judah doing Torah*, whom he is also depicted as having '*swallowed*'/'*consumed*'/or '*destroyed*'[92]). *Accusing them of being Law-Breakers, he delivered them up to be stoned.*

Nor should one overlook here Josephus' use – perhaps inadvertently, perhaps otherwise – of the '*delivering up*' language, so widespread as well in the Scrolls, particularly in the Damascus Document, and, as a matter of course, in almost all Gospel presentations of '*Judas Iscariot*,' who is always portrayed, as we have seen, as having '*delivered him up*.' That is, Judas Iscariot is not normally accused of '*betraying Jesus*' or '*being a Traitor*' as such, but rather, in almost every case, as, '*delivering him up*.'[93]

The reference to '*Law-breaking*' in this testimony is very important as well, not only because the charge proliferates across the whole of the Scroll corpus – in particular writings like the Damascus Document as we have seen – but it also has an echo in the counter-charge being made amidst parallel allusion to '*being a Doer*' and *a* '*Keeper*' not a '*Breaker*' in James 2:9–10, etc.[94] Completing this particular language circle, even these latter usages from the Letter attributed to James permeate the Dead Sea Scrolls and, not without significance, the Habakkuk *Pesher's* evocation of similar usages and motifs surrounding its account of *the destruction of the Righteous Teacher* and *those of his followers among* '*the Poor*.'[95]

In going on to describe the reaction to Ananus' stoning of James of those in Jerusalem '*most concerned*' with '*Law-keeping*,' it is not completely clear whether their disapproval had to do only with Jewish Law or Roman Law, or both. As we have seen, Paul often mixes the two as well, playing one off against the other, often to disingenuous effect.[96] Still, this was the kind of language being thrown back and forth between the different '*Party*' groups in Jerusalem as the War against Rome approached. As Josephus describes it:

> *but those residents of the city, considered most concerned with Equity* ('*Right-eousness*') *and strict observation of the Law, were offended by what had been done. Therefore, they secretly sent to King Agrippa, urging him to order Ananus to desist from any further such actions, because what had already been done was illegal from the start. Some of them* (the ubiquitous '*some*' again – this time in Josephus) *even went to meet Albinus, who was on his way from Alexandria, and informed him that it was unlawful for Ananus to convene a Sanhedrin without his consent* (meaning, presumably, *one that would deliver the death penalty*, which only the Roman Governor was empowered to impose and which, even the *Talmud* asserts, *was not within the Jews' power to execute in this period*[97]). *Whereupon Albinus, convinced by these words, wrote in anger to Ananus, threatening to punish him for what he had done. At this point, King Agrippa took back the High Priesthood from him, which he had held for three months* (obviously just enough time to dispose of James, the sole purpose seemingly of his appointment by King Agrippa), *and replaced him with Jesus the son of Damnaeus.*[98]

The picture that emerges from the above testimony could not be clearer. Not only is the antagonism of '*those most concerned with Equity*' to both Ananus II and Agrippa II important, but also the portrait of the vacillating Roman Governor in the Gospels would appear to owe a lot to the depiction of Albinus here and not that of the '*Historical*' Pontius Pilate.[99]

Josephus resumes his tale of mounting violence, stone-throwing and mutual vilification, one group of '*Priests*' against the other – the '*Higher*' usually against the '*Lower*'; the '*Riches*' of various of '*the High Priests*'[100] and how, once again, they sent their '*Violent*' associates (Paul and his Herodian confreres/'*the ʿArizei-Goʾim*' or '*the Violent Ones of the Gentiles*' at Qumran?[101]) to steal the tithes of '*the Poor Priests*' from the threshing floors – all now condoned and even connived at by Albinus.[102] The '*stealing from the Poor*' is one of the accusations against the Establishment actually made in the Damascus Document, but it will also be repeated again in the picture of the destruction of '*the Righteous Teacher*' in the Habakkuk *Pesher*.[103] This is the context, too, in which Josephus now refers to the '*Violent*' behavior of his '*Saulos*,' '*a kinsman of Agrippa*,' and *his band of* '*Herodian*' *thugs*.

It should be clear that Agrippa II, who a decade before had solidified his relationship with Ananus in Rome following similar disturbances in the late Forties and early Fifties, hastened to remove Ananus when his continued presence became inconvenient or an embarrassment to him, but this only after he had accomplished what both of them had been intent on achieving – *the successful removal of James.*[104] It bears repeating that this must also be seen as related in some manner to Agrippa II's discomfiture in '*the Temple Wall Affair*' immediately preceding it, in the aftermath of which many were sent to Rome – including even perhaps Paul. This '*Affair*,' clearly precipitated by so-called '*Sicarii*' or '*Zealots*' and, in our view, *the supporters of James among the Lower Priesthood in the Temple*, had to do with, as already emphasized, *barring Agrippa II's view of the sacrifices in the Temple while he reclined on his balcony dining with his guests.*

It should be appreciated that it also relates to the episode about '*Simon*' two decades before, himself able to convene an '*Assembly*' or '*Church*' in Jerusalem – who wished to bar Herodians like Agrippa II's father Agrippa I from the Temple as a foreigner, an episode we have tied via inversion to Acts picture of Peter going to visit the Roman Centurion in Caesarea and learning to call '*no man unclean*' and *to accept foreigners*. We have already expressed the view that this visit the '*Simon*' in Acts makes to '*Cornelius*' *house*' reverses or overwrites the visit of Josephus' more zealot '*Simon*' (who *wished to bar Herodians from the Temple as foreigners, not admit them*) to the household of Agrippa I who, at least, *made a pretense of Piety*, '*to see what was done there contrary to Law*' – meaning *Jewish Law not Roman Law*.[105]

Needless to say, Agrippa dismissed this poor '*Simon*' with a gift, thereby '*returning good for evil*' – or, as Josephus at one point puts it, '*heaping coals upon his head*' – a favorite behavior pattern of Agrippa I akin to Jesus' teaching '*love your enemy*' in the Gospels.[106] In our view, however, this '*Simon*' would ultimately have been arrested, just as Acts 12:4–11 reports its '*Simon*' was, following upon the execution of '*James the brother of John with the sword*' ('*Judas the brother of James*'/'*Theudas*'?) in the round-up conducted by Agrippa I's more politically-ruthless brother, Herod of Chalcis (Herodias' brother and the father-in-law of her daughter, Salome – the latter, as we saw, having married his son Aristobulus after the death of her/Salome's *first husband* '*Philip*'), after Agrippa I's untimely death in 44 CE.[107]

As the build-up towards this Revolt gathered momentum, both Agrippa II and his sister Bernice were, not only barred from Jerusalem altogether but, in time, both their palaces were burned.[108] These two, Agrippa II and Ananus, *together conspired to remove James* – it is here one encounters the motif of '*plotting*' or '*conspiracy*' reprised in Gospel accounts of Jesus' death and, in the Scrolls, how '*the Wicked Priest plotted to destroy the Righteous Teacher*' and '*the Poor*'[109] – whom they viewed as *the center of all this agitation against gifts and sacrifices on behalf of foreigners in the Temple*, the actual issue invoked by the '*Zealot*' or *the* '*Poor*' *Lower Priest class to precipitate the War against Rome some three and a half years later*, a pretense Josephus denigrates as '*an Innovation with which our Forefathers were before unacquainted.*'[114]

Jesus ben Ananias and '*the Signs*' Prefiguring the Fall of the Temple

However these things or their timing might be, James' death is immediately followed by the appearance of the rustic and seemingly deranged '*Prophet*,' whom Josephus identifies as '*Jesus ben Ananias*.' Though Josephus does not specifically connect the death of James with the appearance of this '*Jesus*,' chronologically speaking, we are justified in doing so because, as already explained, he dates the appearance of this '*Jesus*' seven and a half years before the fall of the Temple in 70 CE and specifically notes his arrest and re-arrest (curiously, just as the portrait of the scriptural '*Jesus*' in the Slavonic Josephus[111]) by the Governor of that time, Albinus.

Even though Josephus declines to mention this '*Jesus*' in the *Antiquities* and one has to go to the *Jewish War* to discover him, it is noteworthy how precise Josephus is with regard to his chronology and events surrounding his activities. Thus, he appeared during '*the Feast of Tabernacles*,' that is, at approximately the end of September or the beginning of October of 62 CE which may, in fact, have been the date of James' stoning –

that is, just following *Yom Kippur*, 62 CE, a possible date too of the '*Yom Kippur*' atonement James is pictured as making '*in the Holy of Holies in the Temple*' in most early Church sources. '*Jesus ben Ananias*' died in March, 70 CE, '*seven and a half years later,' just five months prior to the fall of the City and destruction of the Temple.*

Significantly, Josephus tells the full story of his appearance and death within the context of those passages, we have already referred to at the end of the *Jewish War*, where he sets out '*the signs and portents*' *prefiguring the fall of Jerusalem*. These he calls '*the denunciations God made to them,*' which, again, end pointedly in both his evocation of '*the World Rule Prophecy*' *as the moving force behind the War against Rome and his own application of it to Vespasian.*[112] Because these are so illustrative, it is worth repeating them. As we have already seen, they included a '*Star resembling a sword*' and '*a comet, which stood over the city for about a year*'; '*a brilliant light around the altar of the Temple...for a half hour*' *in the middle of the night* – this supposedly on Passover, 66 CE; *a cow brought for sacrifice during the same Feast,* '*which gave birth to a lamb in the middle of the Temple Court*' (Josephus is nothing if not humorous); *the Eastern brass gate,* '*which was very massive,*' '*opening all by itself*'; in early June, '*chariots and armed troops of soldiers hurtling through the clouds and encompassing cities*' (*i.e*, '*the Heavenly Host coming on the clouds of Heaven*'); and at Pentecost in late June, not long before the War began, '*the Priests at night in the Inner Court of the Temple,...feeling a quaking and hearing a Host of Voices crying out, "Let Us depart"*' – that is, *the Divine Presence departing.*[118]

These are all particularly illustrative of Josephus' frame-of-mind, as they are that of his Roman audience, to which they are addressed. The Gospels, which to some extent probably include materials based on these, are hardly less incredible and sometimes just as funny. To these, Josephus appends the following account which, by its length and detail, he obviously considered perhaps even more important:

> But what was even more alarming...four years before the War began, there came to the Feast, at which it is the custom for everyone to erect Tabernacles to God (meaning, '*Succot*'), one Jesus ben Ananias, a rude peasant standing in the Temple (note here both the telltale motifs of '*being a rude peasant*' in several notices associated with James and his colleagues, and that of '*standing*' once again). And suddenly he began to cry out, '*A Voice from the East, a Voice from the West, a Voice from the four winds, a Voice against Jerusalem and the Temple, a Voice against the bridegrooms and the brides, and a Voice against the whole People.*' Day and night he went about all the streets of the city with this cry on his lips.[118]

In this testimony it is easy to see some of the *leitmotifs* of the story of Jesus as it has come down to us in Scripture, not the least being the note about *'the bridegrooms and brides,'* a favorite theme of many of the parables attributed to him in the Gospels.[115]

But the parallel with 'Jesus' does not stop here. It also continues with Josephus discussing the details of *'Jesus ben Ananias"* arrest and interrogation:

> *Some of the Leading Men of the city, incensed at these ominous words, arrested him, and had him severely flogged, yet did he not utter one word in his own defence or in private to those who beat him* (the resemblance of this to the picture of Jesus' arrest and examination is uncanny – or is it?), *only continuing to cry out as before. Thereupon, our Leading Men, supposing him under some Divine possession, as the case indeed proved to be, brought him* (again, just as 'Jesus' in Scripture) *before the Roman Procurator* (only now, instead of *'Pontius Pilate,'* it is *'Albinus'*). *There, scourged till his bones were laid bare, he neither pleaded for mercy or cried out* (again, the resemblance to the Gospel 'Jesus' needs little further explanation), *but rather in the most mournful tone of voice, responded to each stroke with 'Woe! Woe to Jerusalem!'* (nor does this). *When Albinus, the Governor, asked him who he was and from where he came and why he uttered such words, he said nothing, but unceasingly repeated his heart-rending refrain. Taking him for a lunatic, Albinus dismissed him* (here, yet again, the picture of the sympathetic, lenient Roman Governor).[116]

This dismissal also parallels the many other dismissals by Roman Governors of early Christian Leaders already encountered above, not the least of which being the picture of the dismissal of Jesus himself by Pontius Pilate in the Gospels, before the Jewish crowd forces him to reverse himself. In fact, in the version of these events called *'The Slavonic Josephus'* (real or forged), as just observed, *Pilate does at first dismiss Jesus before ultimately having him re-arrested again and flogged later on.*[117]

Josephus continues:

> *During the whole of the period till the outbreak of the War, he (Jesus ben Ananias) neither spoke to anyone, nor was seen to speak, but daily repeated his foreboding dirge, 'Woe! Woe to Jerusalem!'* (note Josephus' detail here). *Nor did he curse those who repeatedly beat him* (this, too, is a familiar motif of the accounts of Jesus' 'Passion' in the Gospels – modern revisitations of this script should take note), *nor thank those who gave him food* (here Josephus departs somewhat from the familiar scenario)...*His cry was loudest at Festivals. So for seven years and five months he continued this wail* (so much for

the counterfeit accusation, made by both Paul in 1 Thessalonians 2:15 and Muhammad, dependent upon him in the Koran, about *the Jews supposedly killing all their own Prophets* – here's one they did not kill and, if ever '*a Prophet*' invited being silenced or killed, '*Jesus ben Ananias*' surely did), *his voice never flagging nor his strength exhausting, until during the siege, seeing his Prophecy fulfilled, he ceased. For, when making his round of the walls, shouting in the most piercing voice, 'Woe once more to the City and to the People and to the Holy House,' and just as he added the last words, 'and woe to me also,' a stone hurled from one of the* (Roman) *siege engines struck and killed him on the spot* (one hopes this is not one of the '*stones*', to which the Synoptic '*Jesus*' is made to refer in the picture of his '*woes*') *and, as he was adding these very prophecies, he passed away* (here we have Josephus, ever the droll comedian).

Hyperbole or poetic licence aside, we have rendered the entire passage to show how true-to-life it is, not to mention its intensity and the meaning it obviously had for the eye-witnesses who survived these horrific events. At the same time however, as just indicated, it is typical of Josephus' sometimes macabre sense-of-humor. Nevertheless, the cynical parallel to this in the picture of 'Jesus' in the Gospels, predicting the destruction of the Temple '*stone upon stone*' and his '*woes*' upon '*the Scribes and Pharisees*,' in which he also evokes the accusation – as does Peter some five or six times in Acts (as noted in *Preliminaries*) – of '*Jerusalem killing the prophets and stoning those sent to her*' (Matthew 23:1–24:1 and pars.), is to any fair-minded or historically-honest person unmistakable. It is also chilling.

Setting aside its '*Messianic*' implications, which we have already dwelled upon sufficiently above, if one views this '*oracle*' in relation to the '*Pella flight*' oracles, we have been discussing, and the strong 'Christian' tradition associating the destruction of Jerusalem generally with the death of James, it is possible to see that this prophecy has perhaps even more importance than that attributed to it by Josephus. In the light of these early Christian traditions about *an oracle immediately following the death of James, warning his followers to flee Jerusalem,* I think that we can state with some assurance that, in this context, this is precisely what is occurring here and that, therefore even if unwittingly (perhaps even not so unwittingly), *Josephus has provided us with this oracle as well.* Put in another way, we have before us, in this pathetic cry of '*Jesus Ben Ananias*,' *the very oracle* – make of it what one will.

In fact, Josephus omits this '*oracle*' from the normal course of both his narratives, only providing it as the last and most-telling of his '*oracles for the fall of the Temple.'* This, aside from the detail he provides, shows how important he thought it to be. He gives these, significantly, at the end of the *Jewish War* in the midst of his descriptions of how *the Romans burned the Temple and all its associated structures and his excuses for this* and, what must have been even more crushing, *the sacrifice the Romans made to their standards in the midst of this carnage on the Temple Mount facing the very same Eastern Gate*, we have just remarked among these '*oracles for the fall of the Temple*' above. *Here they venerated their standards and acclaimed Titus, 'Imperator!'* The description of this same practice in the Habakkuk *Pesher*, as we shall see and which was, in effect, the very religion of these same Legionnaires – also called '*the Yeter ha-ᶜAmim*'/'*the Additional Ones of the Gentiles*' – in our view, amounts to the most accurate way to date this document and others like it.[118]

Another Oracle by '*Agabus*' and the '*Pella Flight*' Tradition

But it is possible to go further than this. Reviewing these kinds of oracles before us in this period, one comes to the second of the two oracles attributed to the '*Prophet*,' designated in Acts by the nonsense name of '*Agabus*.' It will be recalled that this time '*Agabus*' supposedly '*comes down to Caesarea*' (in his earlier appearance, he had '*come down*' with the other '*prophets from Jerusalem to Antioch*') right before Paul's last trip up to Jerusalem for his final confrontation with James – and, not perhaps unrelatedly, James' consonant removal from the scene just a few years after that.

Not only is Paul acting in these materials in Acts as a '*stalking horse*' for '*Herodians*' in the Temple, in that he appears soon afterwards (Acts 21:26–30) to be *testing the ban in the Temple*, seemingly pronounced on them by '*Zealots*' like the '*Simon the Head of an Assembly*' or '*Church of his own*' in Jerusalem above and possibly, too, the issue of '*the Wall*,' as we have seen, *that had been specifically built at this time to block Agrippa II's view of the sacrifices*; but we shall be able to show that, once again, Acts is appropriating precious materials from its opponents' sources, reversing them, and harmonizing them in line with the demands of its own plot-line – and, in the process, reducing them to banality and/or triviality.

Here Acts appropriates (or misappropriates) the '*oracle*' of '*Jesus ben Ananias*' above about *the coming destruction of Jerusalem*, which he started to proclaim *exactly consonant with the death of James*, and the early Christian '*oracle*' (its basic variation or corollary), *warning James' followers to flee Jerusalem*, reverses them, and turns them into an '*oracle*' warning Paul – not '*to flee*' but, rather, '*not to go up to Jerusalem*' because he would be arrested there – which is, of course, precisely what happens.

We have already shown how the first of these oracles by this '*Prophet*' Acts calls '*Agabus*' at the time of '*the Great Famine*' (that '*was going to come over the whole habitable World*'!) in the reign of Claudius in the mid-Forties, in conjunction with which so much else of consequence was transpiring – almost all, in some manner, connected to James' *tutelege* and '*the Movement*' he led) – was a counterfeit. There, it will be recalled, it was an overwrite of and disguised the Syriac/Armenian legend of the conversion of '*King Agbarus*' or '*Abgarus*', '*the Great King of the Peoples beyond the Euphrates*' (here the origin of Acts' language of '*the Great Famine*'), reprised in Eusebius – who claimed to have personally found and translated it from among the Chancellery records of the city of Edessa – but missing from Acts' tendentious story-telling (and, in fact, demonstrating how '*real*' this reporting on Eusebius' part actually was!).

This fractured nonsense material in Acts also covered over much important material associated with the conversion of Queen Helen of Adiabene and her sons – also missing from Acts' narrative but, as we have shown, *not really* – to a more '*militant*' or '*Zealot*' form of Judaism taught by a '*Galilean*' teacher named '*Eleazar*' ('*Lazarus*' again?), who insisted on '*circumcision*' as a fundamental precondition of conversion (the same '*circumcision*' that was parodied in Acts 8:27's presentation of '*the Ethiopian Queen's eunuch*' – '*circumcision*', in the Roman view, being nothing more than a kind of castration[119]) – the key connecting link here being the legendary generosity of Helen and her son Izates (also possibly '*Agbarus*' or '*Abgarus*' – these names tending to get slurred, as we have seen, and their consonants transposed as they were transliterate from languages like Syriac or Arabic into Greek of Latin) in providing '*famine relief*' to the population of Jerusalem, to say nothing of her possible marital relationship with '*King Agbarus*.' Josephus calls this '*King*,' '*Bazeus*,' while at the same time averring, as we saw, that *she was his sister*.[120]

This is all parodied in the description in Acts 11:27 of how Agabus '*came down from Jerusalem to Antioch*' and '*having risen up*' (the '*arising*' voca bulary again), '*signified by the Spirit*' (and the vocabulary of the '*signs*') his '*Prophecy*' about '*the Great Famine*' which, in fact, '*also came to pass*.' Not only does the reason for this obfuscation or dissimulation have to do with Helen's more militant brand of Judaism and the '*Zealotry*' of her two sons (who, as we saw, ultimately *do decide to circumcise themselves* – therefore Acts 8:27's above derogation of her '*Treasury agent*' as a '*eunuch*' though, for Acts, '*Ethiopian*' would doubtlessly have been derogation enough); it also has to do with the insistent motif of '*circumcision*' and/or '*conversion*' in all these Syriac/Armenian traditions relating to either '*King Agbarus*' or his subjects '*the Edessenes*,' as well as that of '*Zelotes*' or the 'zeal' being attached to the name of one or another of the teachers involved in these 'conversions,' *e.g.*, '*Simon Zelotes*,' '*Judas Zelotes*,' or even, if one prefers, '*Judas Iscariot*' and/or '*Simon Iscariot*'/'*Simon the Iscariot*.'[121]

In turn, these are usually linked to the names of one or another of Jesus' brothers, as we have been underscoring, and the motif of *their having been sent down from Jerusalem* either by one of these, usually '*Judas Thomas*' or even '*James*' himself. In Acts 15:22 it will be recalled, '*Judas Barsabas*' is the one who is '*sent down*' among others by James with his directives to overseas communities – themselves not unrelated, as we have been demonstrating, to the '*Letter*' or '*Letters*' known as '*MMT*.'

Providing additional corroboration of these points, if such were needed, and bringing us full circle, the name of one of Queen Helen's kinsmen, '*Kenedaeus*' – who died bravely fighting the Romans at the Pass at Beit Horon while attempting to block their advance on Jerusalem in the first heady days of the Uprising in 66 CE[122] – may also possibly be a part of the parody in Acts 8:26–40 of the conversion of '*an Ethiopian man, a eunuch in power over all of the Ethiopian Queen Kandakes' Treasury*.' The circumstances surrounding the conversion of this '*Ethiopian eunuch*,' supposedly *on his way down from Jerusalem to* '*Gaza*,' this time by someone called '*Philip*,' would appear to be lifted almost bodily, as we have shown, from those of the conversion of Queen Helen's favorite son Izates together with his brother Monobazus, as portrayed in both Josephus and the *Talmud*.[123] Where the name '*Kandakes*' itself is concerned, Acts has almost certainly found it in the name of a Nubian Queen who reigned in Meroe (in today's Sudan), referred to by Strabo of Cappadocia (c. 30 BC), one of Josephus' sources, and Plliny the Elder dependent on him. But, as we have already pointed out, unfortunately for Acts, the last of these '*Ethiopian*' Queens in Nubia appears to have died in about 20 BC.[124]

In the second of these two prophecies attributed to the ubiquitous '*Agabus*' in Acts, some fifteen years later, we have, as just remarked, another of these inversions – this time of the well-known early Christian '*Pella flight*' oracle warning the followers of James to flee Jerusalem and, by extension, of this tragi-comical, but nonetheless heart-rending, oracle of Jesus ben Ananias about the coming destruction of Jerusalem, an oracle that he started uttering directly following the stoning of the '*Zaddik*' James and never stopped his mournful cry (of which Josephus is well aware) *for seven and a half long years*. This '*oracle*' also finds its way into Gospel presentations – according to the Synoptics anyhow – of another '*Jesus*' who, as we saw as well, is pictured as uttering a more extensive version of it or its equivalent *when coming in sight of Jerusalem* – this time thirty or so years earlier.

As we have shown too, there can be little doubt that '*Jesus ben Ananias*' starts prophesying the coming destruction of Jerusalem at exactly the time James is killed or immediately or a little thereafter. Nor does he cease until he is killed shortly before *his 'Prophecy'* too is fulfilled. Nor can there be much doubt that the mysterious conjunction of these two events must be associated in some manner with James' death. This now explains the widespread belief on the part of '*the People,*' attested to in copies of Josephus available to early Church fathers who spent time in Palestine, *i.e.*, Origen, Eusebius, and Jerome, '*that Jerusalem fell because of the death of James*' (they, it will be recalled, are all angry that Josephus did not say '*because of the death of Jesus*'!).

This deepens tremendously the significance of the events under consideration, showing that the association of James' death with *the coming fall of Jerusalem and destruction of the Temple* was already being proclaimed from *Succot,* 62 CE onwards – and this in a pretty insistent manner – even before these tragic events ultimately occurred. Even though Josephus does not specifically tell us this – as he does, for instance, in the *Antiquities* version of what '*the People*' made of the death of John the Baptist a generation before the death of James (also missing from the New Testament and most early Christian texts), that is, *they blamed Herod the Tetrarch's discomfiture by Aretas in battle* (about the time the latter took over Damascus) *on what he ('Herod') had done to John*[125] – actually *by implication,* as we can now see, he does; and this may have been what the early Church fathers, who saw this testimony, were trying to tell us as well.

Not only do we see the idea of *the connection of James' death with the fall of Jerusalem* directly corroborated by actual events in the Jerusalem of these days, we can say that – aside from the absorption of many of these details into '*the biography of Jesus*' as it has come down to us – we are now getting a parallel absorption of important materials relating to the death of James – and Ebionite history in Palestine generally – into the story of Paul as Acts presents it. As usual, not only is the tragic and momentous import of these events being reduced to the level of banality and/or triviality, the events themselves are actually being reversed or presented with inverted ideological effect.

Paul's Last Days and Agabus' Prophecy in Acts

Let us, therefore, briefly peruse Acts' plot-line up to this point. Here Paul is hurrying to get to Jerusalem in time for *the reunion of the early Church at Pentecost* (20:16). Having just escaped '*the plots of the Jews*' (20:3 and 20:20), he is about to '*set sail for Syria,*' presumably with the contributions he has been collecting *'in Macedonia and Achaia for the Poor among the Saints in Jerusalem'* (Romans 15:25). As Acts 20:22–24 puts it, already *'a prisoner in the Spirit,'* he is about to *'finish (his) race'* and *'the Holy Spirit has made it clear to (him) in town after town that imprisonment and persecutions await'* him (*thus!*). According to *'the We Document,'* in which these materials are embedded, he has been *'earnestly testifying both to Jews and Greeks repentance towards God and Faith towards our Lord Jesus Christ'* (20:21).

As in the episode about *'Kandakes, the Ethiopian Queen'* earlier, *'Philip'* plays an integral part. Previously he was on *a circuitous detour in the South via the road to Gaza* (Acts 8:26 – the route, as we saw, Queen Helen's grain-buyers would have taken to Egypt) *to get from Samaria to Caesarea in the North.* Now like *'Philip,'* the Captain of Agrippa II's bodyguard (associated in the Jerusalem events, we have just delineated, with *'Saulos,'* *'Antipas,'* and *'Costobarus,'* all of whom Josephus portrays as *'kinsmen of Agrippa'* and all, therefore, *'Herodians'*); Acts 21:8's *'Philip the Evangelist'* lives in Caesarea too.[126] Warning *'the Elders of the Assembly'* (*Ecclesian*), he has *'called from Miletus to Ephesus,'*[127] to follow his *'preaching the counsel of God'* and *'to shepherd the Assembly of God'* – a term we have already encountered above in documents like the Qumran Community Rule and Damascus Document, which use it to refer to their *'Congregation'* (*''Ez-ah'*) or *'Community'*[128] Paul tells them before departing *'for Syria'* that,

> *ravening wolves will invade you, not sparing the flock,...even from your own ranks, to pervert the Truth and induce the Disciples to follow them* (20:27–29).

A variation of this quotation is to be encountered also in Hegesippus as conserved by Eusebius about how the family and brothers of Jesus *'presided over every Assembly'* into the reign of Trajan. *'Until then the Church had remained a pure and uncorrupted virgin, since those trying to corrupt (it),' 'if such there were, were skulking in obscure Darkness'* –

> *then godless error crept in through the Lying of false teachers* (here the Qumran-type and Ebionite-style of language resumes again[129]) *who, seeing that none of the Apostles still remained, shamelessly contradicted the preaching of the Truth by falsely preaching so-called Knowledge'* (again, the allusion to *'Knowledge'/'Gnosis'* so important to the Scrolls and Paul in 1 Corinthians 8:1–3 – this last in his typical polemical strophe/antistrophe/epode rhetorical style).[130]

It is interesting that in the passage about Paul calling in *'the Elders'* from Ephesus above, Acts 20:31 pictures him as telling them and, presumably, those at Miletus as well that he '*did not cease warning everyone for three years night and day with tears in (his)* eyes' about these things, which mirrors to no small extent the passage from Josephus' *Jewish War* about '*Jesus ben Ananias*" incessant daily cry of warning '*for seven years and five months.*'

Paul now lands '*at Tyre in Syria.*' There '*the Disciples, speaking in the Spirit*' (as '*Agabus*' previously), warn him '*not to go up to Jerusalem*' (here the '*warning*' theme again) – this, as opposed, as we saw, to the Ebionite '*oracle*' warning James' surviving followers '*to leave Jerusalem.*' But Paul brushes aside their warnings, going down the coast to Caesarea *where he now stays with* '*Philip*' (21:3–8 – the '*Strategos*' of Agrippa II above?). Apart from not being designated as one of '*the Apostles*' here, as in most Gospels, but rather '*the Evangelist one of the Seven,*' '*Philip*' is now further described as having '*four virgin daughters who were prophetesses*' (Acts 21:9), a peculiar description to say the least, which has, again, almost nothing whatever to do with '*Jewish*' Palestine but rather Greco-Roman religious affiliation.

This term '*being of the Seven,*' though not delineated to any extent, doubtlessly harks back to those '*Hebrews*' around '*Stephen*' – most, however, with classical-sounding Greek names – who were appointed, according to Acts 6:3's peculiar narrative, *in response to the* '*murmuring of the Hellenists*' (in line with our other arguments, one should probably rather reverse this and read instead '*murmuring of the Zealots*' or '*those of the Circumcision*') '*to serve tables,*' while the Apostles '*steadfastly continued to pray and serve the Word*' (6:4). As already signaled, apart from '*Philip*' and two names seemingly drawn from Plato's dialogues, '*Timon and Parmenas,*' these so-called '*Hebrews*' include one '*Nicolas a convert from Antioch*' (so he could hardly be called a '*Hebrew*' but, rather, actually a '*Hellenist*').[131] In fact, as already suggested as well, he is doubtlessly a thinly-disguised facsimile of one of Josephus' principal sources, Nicolaus of Damascus, a close collaborator of Herod who ended up in Rome as one of his diplomats there.[132]

Where '*Philip's daughters*' are concerned, at the time of the outbreak of the War against Rome, Josephus specifically alludes to how '*the daughters*' of Agrippa II's '*Strategos,*' '*Philip*' (that is, *his Military Commander in Caesarea*), *miraculously escape the Roman massacre of the population of Gamala*, the fortifications for which Josephus himself was personally responsible – '*Philip*' having already made his way to Jerusalem to join his other erstwhile associates, '*Saulos*' and his Herodian '*kinsmen*' *Costobarus and Antipas.*[133] Unlike Josephus and these others, the population at Gamala on the Gaulon Heights ('*Gaulonitus*') – the birthplace according to the *Antiquities* of '*Judas the Galilean,*' the individual responsible in the first place for the genesis of '*the Movement*' either designated as '*Zealot*'/ '*Sicarii*'/or '*Fourth Philosophy*' – resisted to the end and were pitilessly butchered or jumped to their deaths in a Masada-like mass suicide.[134] But the interesting point and what stands out in the description of these things, that Josephus gives us, is *the fact of Philip's 'two daughters'* and the marvel of how they managed to save themselves by hiding in an underground cave of some kind![135] These now appear to end up in Acts' somewhat bizarre narrative as *'four virgin daughters who were prophetesses'*!

However these things may be, for Acts *'a Prophet named Agabus'* now makes his second appearance. This time, as we saw, he does not *'come down to Antioch from Jerusalem,'* as he did some fifteen years before, but rather *'comes down to Caesarea from Judea'* (21:10 – itself a rather awkward phraseology). Paul is about to *go up to Jerusalem to report to James in time for Pentecost* with the contributions he has so assiduously gathered abroad (manifestly so critical to the success of his enterprise in such quarters and without which he was obviously unwilling to go[136]). As already explained, in the Dead Sea Scrolls *'Pentecost'* is also important as the time when, under the supervision of *'the Mebakker'* (*'the Archbishop'*) or *'the High Priest Commanding the Many,'* the annual reunion of *'the Desert Camps'* took place – *'to curse those who would stray either to the right or to the left'* or deviate in any way from the Torah of Moses.[137]

At this point, obviously because he is perceived as having money (that is, from his overseas fund-raising), Paul is sent *'into the Temple to pay for the sacrifices of four others'* and *be purified himself* in order to show *'there is no truth to the rumors'* they have heard about him and that he *'still walks regularly keeping the Law'* (Acts 21:23–26). But patently there is truth to these rumors and, of course, he does not *'still walk regularly keeping the Law'* or, as the Last Column of the Damascus Document describing the *'gathering (of those inhabiting) the camps in the Third Month (Pentecost) to curse'* those *'who reject the Foundations of Righteousness'* and *'all the Laws found in the Torah of Moses,'* would put it: *those who walk undeviatingly following the Law, not 'straying either to the right or to the left.'*[138]

Once in the Temple, it will be recalled, Paul is mobbed by *'Jews from Asia'* (meaning Asia Minor, Syria and, perhaps, *even Adiabene*), who recognize him, crying out to the people assembled for Pentecost (one of the three annual Jewish pilgrimage Festivals in the Temple at that time):

> *Men of Israel, help! This is the man who teaches everyone everywhere against our People, and the Law, and this Place* (in our view, if Acts' picture of Paul's behavior elsewhere in Asia Minor and Achaia can be credited – to say nothing of his own testimony about himself in those of his Letters considered authentic – truer words could not be imagined), *and now he has also brought Greeks into the Temple and polluted this Holy Place'* (Acts 21:28).

Trying to explain this away in an aside, as already alluded to, Acts 21:29 allows that they had previously seen him in the city with some Greeks from Asia, most notably one '*Trophimus from Ephesus*.' But more important even than this, the key charge from the '*Three Nets of Belial*' section of the Damascus Document of '*pollution of the Temple*,' itself a variation of the '*keeping away from things sacrificed to idols*' or '*the pollutions of the idols*' directive of James in Acts 15:20 and 29, is now definitively linked to the charge of *introducing non-Jews* or *Gentiles into the Temple*!

Was Paul doing this? We consider that he was. It is for this reason we termed Paul a '*stalking horse*' for Herodians and their family interests in Jerusalem – in this instance, *to test the ban on* '*Herodians*' *and other classes of* '*banned*' *or* '*polluted*' *persons in the Temple*. Again, it should be appreciated that such '*Herodians*' were really considered *non-Jews* or '*foreigners*' by '*Zealots*' like the '*Simon*' who visited Agrippa I's household '*to see what was done there contrary to Law*,' as they would have been by '*the myriads of Jews, all Zealots for the Law*,' Acts 21:20 depicts as, making up the greater part of James' '*Jerusalem Church*' followers. It is at this point, too, that they '*drag him outside the Temple*' and, as we have seen, '*bar the doors behind him*' (21:30). As also already noted above, one can find this usage (based on Malachi 1:10) word-for-word in a section of the Damascus Document dealing with '*separating Holy from profane*,' '*doing according to the precise of the Law*,' and '*separating from the Sons of the Pit*.'[139] It is in this context too, as will be recalled, that one encounters the all-important allusion to '*keep away from* (the '*lehinnazer*' usage, based on the same root as '*Nazirite*,' so important to all these '*oath*' procedures, temporary or life-long) *polluted Evil Riches* (*acquired either*) *by vow or oath* (the precise situations described in Acts 21:23) *and* (*keep away*) *from the Riches of the Temple* (here, of course too, the '*pollution of the Temple*' charge being made in Acts here and in 24:6) *and robbing the Poor of His People*' (the '*robbing the Poor Priests of their tithes on the threshing floors*' also described, as we have seen, in Book Twenty of Josephus' *Antiquities* in both the events leading up to and following the death of James).[140]

But to return to '*Agabus*.' It is at this point he takes hold of Paul's girdle and, tying up his own hands and feet with it (the account clearly intends *one to take it seriously here*), said, '*Thus says the Holy Spirit* (a mode of expression most improbable for Palestine at this time), "*The man to whom this girdle belongs will be bound like this by the Jews in Jerusalem* (the provocative racism of this aside – which on the face of it must be considered purely '*Hellenist*' – '*Agabus*' is supposed to be a Jewish '*Prophet*'!) *and delivered up into the hands of the Peoples*"' (Acts 21:11 – '*Ethnon*' again, the '*cAmim*' or '*Yeter ha-cAmim*' of the Habakkuk *Pesher*, who '*plunder the*

Riches of the Peoples,' which '*the Wicked Priest gathered*' or '*collected*' from the '*booty*' stolen by '*the Men of Violence*' – that is, in our view, Herodian '*bully boys*' like '*Saulos and Costobarus*' above[141]).

Here, not only do we have the application of this telltale expression '*delivered up*' again, now coupled with allusion to '*the hands of,*' exactly as in the Damascus Document and War Scroll from Qumran (albeit, as usual, with opposite effect)[142]; but the tenor of the reference to '*the Jews of Jerusalem*' immediately identifies the whole passage as *having been written by non-Jews* – excellent creative writers to be sure, *but non-Jews all the same.* The same allusion to '*the hands of*' is to be found in another allusion at this point in the Habakkuk *Pesher* as well, '*the hands of the Army of the Kittim,*' identified with, as we shall explain more fully presently, '*the Yeter ha-ᶜAmim*' or '*the Additional Ones of the Peoples*' of Habakkuk 2:8 – in our view, *clearly pointing this time to the Romans.* As the detailed description proceeds in Columns 8-9 of the *Pesher,* these are depicted '*in the Last Days,*' not only as destroying '*the Last Priests of Jerusalem*' (again clearly meaning '*High*' or, as the New Testament would have it – in the plural as well – '*Chief Priests*') but, as we just saw, '*plundering*' the '*Riches of the Peoples*' which the Wicked Priest '*stole and collected*' by means of '*the Men of Violence*' (to repeat, in our view, the tithes and gifts given to the Temple by '*Violent Herodians*' such as the ones just enumerated above).[143] For this, '*the Wicked Priest*' is now rather characterized as '*heaping upon himself iniquitous Guilt,*' because he walked '*in the Ways of Abominations of all unclean pollution*' and '*profiteered from the spoils of the Peoples*' – meaning both *in the Temple* and '*the Herodians*' again.[144] Despite my having compressed these striking allusions, their meaning *should be crystal clear.*

Following '*Agabus*'' dire if buffoonish warning in Acts, at this point everyone with Paul in Caesarea begs him:

> *Not to go up to Jerusalem. But Paul answered, 'What are you trying to do, break my heart with your tears? For I am not only ready to be bound, but also to die in Jerusalem for the Name of the Lord Jesus'* (the '*Name*' and '*naming*'-type allusions again). *And when he was not persuaded, we fell silent* (plainly here, we are supposed to be in the sometimes more reliable '*We Document*' again), *saying, 'The Lord's will be done'* (21:12–14).

Paul then goes up to Jerusalem, as we have seen, with his Greek traveling companions '*to lodge with a certain Mnason a Cypriot*' (21:16 – behind the code, probably the ubiquitous '*Ananias*' again) and embark upon the final adventures of his career: being sent in by James and mobbed in the Temple, rescue by the Romans, protective custody in Agrippa II's Palace in Caesarea, and final voyage to Rome. This last included the ritual ship-wreck (27:41), also a fixture of the Pseudoclementines,[145] and a snake-bite episode in Malta (28:3–6) – *where there were no poisonous snakes* – that resembles one told about James' double *'Joseph Barsabas Justus'* (*cf.* Acts 1:23) in Papias[146]; and another about the seeming stand-in for James in the *Talmud 'Jacob of Kfar Sechaniah'* and his further adventures (or misad-ventures) with the straying R. Eliezer ben Hyrcanus above.[147] Once in Rome, as Acts 28:21 reports – much to Paul's surprise – no one seems to have heard anything about him and he appears to continue his activities in a more or less uninhibited manner (28:30–31).

But in the recounting of Agabus' *'Prophecy,'* warning Paul *'not to go up to Jerusalem'* above, one not only has a second of these rather curious *'prophecies'* attributed to Agabus but, as already emphasized as well, the mirror reversal of *the real Prophecy of Jesus ben Ananias*, which Josephus records in such meticulous detail. Furthermore, in this instance, Jose-phus' narrative is definitely not being affected by retrospective historical rewriting, myth-making, or creative writing aimed at the credulous or the simply uninformed. Just as *'the light shining in the middle of the night in the Temple'* on Passover, 66 CE (*'for half an hour'*) from Josephus becomes *'the darkness over all the land'* accompanying *'Jesus''* crucifixion, also on Passover, *for three hours at midday* (*'from the sixth to the ninth hour'*) in the Gospels (Matthew 27:45 and *pars.*); so too the Jewish-Christian oracle warning the followers of James after his death *'to flee Jerusalem,'* now becomes the warning Paul receives before his final arrest *'not to go up to Jerusalem.'* These are simply variations on the same theme. Whereas the one, triggered by the destruction of James, *envisions the eventual destruction of Jerusalem*; the other envisions the binding of Paul and, rather than *the Temple or Jerusalem being destroyed* – what was clearly more important to the writers – *Paul's coming destruction* either in Jerusalem or in Rome.

This parallels other inversions from the biography of James which end up in the biography of Paul as, for instance, when Paul claims in Galatians 1:15–16 that *'God separated'* or *'chose (him) from his mother's womb'* to *'reveal His Son in'* him and *'preach the Gospel about him to the Nations.'* Here a prophecy about the deliverance of the followers of James to *'the Land of Damascus'* on the other side of the Jordan and another in Josephus about retribution for the death of James become an oracle about how *'the Jews in Jerusalem'* were going to mistreat Paul, bind him up, and *'deliver him into the hands of the Peoples'* – all fairly contemporaneous with each other. In *'Agabus''* reference to being *'delivered up to the hands of the Peoples'* above, we also have just the slightest hint or play on the climac-tic exegesis of *'the Star Prophecy'* in the War Scroll, where *'the Mighty of the*

Peoples and the Enemies from all the Lands' were envisioned as going to be '*delivered into the hands of the Poor,*' '*the hands of those bent in the dust,*' and '*the hands of Your Messiah*'![148] More telling notices, pregnant with meaning for the period we have before us, would be hard to imagine.

Paul may really have been warned at this point by someone '*not to go to Jerusalem,*' as the '*We Document*' portrays, but this someone was not '*a Prophet called Agabus.*' It is simply inconceivable that we have two, even three, basically contemporaneous, but mutually-independent '*prophecies,*' being spoken about in different milieux all at about the same time. On the contrary: given Acts' track record of inversion, reversal, and overwriting, the conclusion must rather be that we have *three different versions of a single oracle,* at least one of which is dissembling – the one in Acts.

In the Ebionite or Jewish Christian '*oracle,*' since James' followers are for the most part Jews, the implication is that those who created the climate of discord and internecine strife in Jerusalem were going to perish. In Josephus' heart-rending depiction of '*Jesus ben Ananias*' Prophecy – in our view, *the original behind these other two* – the total annihilation of everything the Jews hold dear was being foretold and by implication, as already underscored, *tied to the destruction of James.* This is how early Church sources seem to have understood the oracle as well *in their insistence on connecting Jerusalem's fall to the death of James.* On the other hand, here in Acts Agabus is simply *foreseeing the annihilation of Paul.* This, of course, does not come to pass – at least not for another eighteen years. With Roman help, Paul escapes, despite the fact that *some* – '*Zealots*' or '*Sicarii*' of a '*Nazirite*' bent – *do wish to kill him* and '*with a curse, curse*' themselves' or '*put themselves under a curse*' not '*to eat or drink until they have killed Paul*' (23:12–14). Though Paul's fate is unclear, it is to Rome that he goes.

However this may be, Acts does seem to appropriate some of these precious materials concerning the devastation of Palestine at this time, particularly Jesus ben Ananias' '*Prophecy*' about the coming fall of Jerusalem and the '*Jewish-Christian*' oracle warning James' followers to flee Jerusalem, inverts or reverses them, and assimilates them into the biography of its hero Paul. *Nor is this second prophecy of '*Agabus*' any more historical than the first* – the one Acts claims he made about '*the Great Famine was then going to cover the whole habitable world.*' Though Agabus' first '*prophecy*' varies elements centering about the story of the conversion of '*King Abgarus*' and Queen Helen's '*famine relief*' efforts, his second varies the heart-rending cry of grief of the mournful '*Prophet,*' '*Jesus ben Ananias.*' In both, the cynical manipulation of history and sardonic mockery of what were the originally tragic events in Palestine are complete.

PART V

THE COMING OF THE MESSIAH OF AARON AND ISRAEL

19

Confrontations Between Paul and James

The Scrolls and New Testament Criticism

The points we have made regarding James' position in early Christianity stand on their own regardless of whether there is a relationship to the Qumran materials or not. There are, however, so many allusions and expressions in the New Testament and related documents which, as we have been showing, overlap with the Scroll materials that it is possible to go further. In previous work we avoided systematic conclusions about the Scrolls because of disagreements over chronological problems, which have still not been resolved and probably never will. What follows, therefore, will have to be evaluated on its own terms, but what has already been proven remains proven.

We could not have arrived at the insights we did regarding '*Palestinian Messianism*,' our understanding of what the true nature of early '*Christianity*' in Palestine was, or problematic portions of the Gospels, without the Dead Sea Scrolls. These provided us with the contemporary control to see what an authentic Palestinian document might look like. This is what is so revolutionary about the Scrolls and the insight they provide into the life and mind of Palestine at that time, as if we had been presented with an untampered-with '*time capsule*' that had not gone through the editorial and redaction processes of the Roman Empire but were, rather, put in caves, as it were, after only the initial redaction process.

Previously, in doing criticism of the New Testament, scholars did not have such contemporary and primary documents to use either for chronological control and by which to measure whether a given passage might be inappropriate or not to its time or place – or *even fictional* for that matter. Now we do, which is what is so revolutionary about having the Dead Sea Scrolls as a research tool. It is for this reason, too, that we can and will go further. Much will depend on one's attitude towards '*external*' parameters such as the '*results*' of palaeographic sequencing analysis or conclusions resulting from archaeology or reached on the basis of A.M.S. carbon dating, such as they are, of the kind we explored in *Preliminaries*.

Actually it would be simpler and easier to take the facile and more well-traveled path, the safe approach most specialists prefer to take, thereby avoiding having to make the specific identifications we shall attempt and insulating themselves from criticism, which is the general rule in this field, because it is almost impossible to be criticized if you do not or cannot say anything definite about a specific issue or hazard a particular identification. But there is enough information from this period that *we should be able to make specific identifications* and not to do so is, in the idiom of the Damascus Document at Qumran, '*to choose the fair neck*' – meaning, that is, '*the easier path*.'[1] If you say, '*I don't know*' and refrain from making real or historical identifications, simply referring to '*unknown person*' or '*persons*,' then you really are on safe ground. But the writer feels this is neither the responsible, nor courageous thing to do, nor is it called for on the basis of the now extensive available data.

First let us state, unequivocally, we are confronted in this period, by the documents from Qumran, with *a major Movement in Judaism*. The scope of the literature guarantees that. Plus, we know enough about the period and have enough data from a variety of sources, not least of which being Josephus himself – to demand that scholars '*toe the line*' on these issues and not simply retreat to the safer ground of not committing themselves. Over and over again we have shown the relationship of the vocabulary of the Community in Palestine which was led by James to the Community represented by the literature at Qumran and this is, in my view, the inescapable thrust of the documents we have before us even though it will never, in fact, be proven to everyone's satisfaction.

Nor could we have had such insights before without such documents. For instance, we could not have known the importance of the *B-L-ᶜ/'Belaᶜ'/'Belial'/'Balaam'* language-circle to Palestinian documents and how this became transformed in the Greek presentation of James' death in terms of being '*cast down*' (in Greek as we have seen, '*ballo*,' based on the same homophonous root as in the Hebrew) by '*Evil*' Establishment conspiracies and forces – and how, in turn, all of this language and imagery of '*being cast down*' went into the final, more sanitized and, one might add, pacified presentation in the Gospels of '*Jesus*' and '*his Apostles*' as either *peaceful* '*fishermen*' *on the Sea of Galilee* '*casting down nets*'[2] or '*casting out Evil spirits*' and similar '*miraculous*' activities often involving this very usage '*casting*.'

Then, too, we could never have understood the importance of Eusebius' '*Letter to Agbarus*' – which he found in the Royal Archives of Edessa ('*Antioch-by-Callirhoe*' on the Upper Euphrates) – in determining the possible provenance of the 'Letter' or 'Letters' from Qumran known as 'MMT', nor, even their extremely 'Jamesian' cast. *Vice versa*, we could never have understood that James' instructions to overseas communities, summarized in Acts and reflected by Paul in 1 Corinthians 6–12, the Pseudoclementines, and in this important Letter or Letters (found in some six or seven different exemplars in Qumran documents even as we have them) is really a letter to a '*zealous*' new convert needing such tuition, in particular, someone like the King of Adiabene on the Upper Tigris, whom Josephus calls '*Izates*,' and not to a '*Jewish*' King at all, whether Maccabean or Herodian.

Finally, we could not have understood the tremendous *lacunae* left in the Gospel narratives after pursuing studies of this kind without comparing them with usages, emphases, and imagery found in the Scrolls. Nor could we have understood how these same Gospels – to say nothing of Acts – were depending on and either parodying or using (often even reversing) identifiable stories, ideas, and episodes taken, not only from Josephus, the Old Testament, and the Scrolls, but also from Rabbinic literature – recondite and unassimilable as it may have been too – and selected '*Christian*' Apocrypha to reconstruct their portrait of the being, ideology, and teaching of the person they were representing as 'Jesus.'

The First Confrontations on the Temple Mount: Stephen, '*the Hellenists*,' and James

The points of contact between the narrative of the First Book of the *Recognitions* of Clement – which pictures debates on the Temple steps, mentions '*Gamaliel*' (probably supposed to be Gamaliel I, Paul's alleged '*teacher*,' the father of the Gamaliel II, who in Rabbinic tradition, as we saw, excommunicates R. Eliezer ben Hyrcanus) and ends with a riot led by Paul on the Temple Mount which triggers the flight of the Jerusalem Community, in this case '*to Jericho*' (and not '*Pella*' or even '*Damascus*'). Acts 1:20–26, following the election to the '*Bishopate*' of '*the Twelfth Apostle*' – or, as the case may be, '*James*' – also pictures, in its more mythologized and highly fictionalized early chapters (3:1–5:25), *debates and confrontations on the Temple Mount, mentions '*Gamaliel*'* (5:33 – in the context albeit of an anachronism relating, not insignificantly, as we also saw, to '*Theudas*'' chronological tie-in with '*Judas the Galilean*'), and ends with a not unsimilar riot in Jerusalem in which Paul, too, plays a central role (8:1–3 – this is '*Saulos*'' or '*Paul*''s introduction) – to say nothing of the letters from the High Priests Paul gets to pursue the Jerusalem Community to '*Damascus*' (9:1–2), a flight depicted in the Pseudoclementine

Recognitions as well. These are the clear points of contact which probably indicate a common source.

In the Pseudoclementine *Recognitions*, as we have seen, the whole presentation is one of debates and arguments on the Temple Mount over the burning issues of the day between the Herodian '*High Priests*' and the Messianic Community, with James functioning either in the role of '*Overseer*'/'*Bishop*'/or '*Archbishop*' (the seeming '*High Priest of the Opposition Alliance*'). These debates finally end in the long speech James delivers, which was, no doubt, originally part of the *Anabathmoi Jacobou*, on the '*two natures of Christ*' and '*the Primal Adam*' ideology.³ There can be little doubt, too, that the attack on James on the Temple Mount (where there really is a physical assault on James and a '*clubbing*' which Acts apparently '*overwrites*' in its picture of parallel events vis-a-vis its hero, the archetypical Gentile convert '*Stephen*,' taken from the accounts of James' stoning, to say nothing of the '*beating*' of the Emperor's '*Servant Stephen*' – thus!– not far from Jerusalem on '*the Beit Horon road*' by '*bandits*'/'*lestai*,' conserved in sources like Hegesippus and Josephus) is what *really* happens at this point in early Church history.

One can also probably assert with some confidence that it is probably James who sends the '*Simon*,' Josephus pictures at approximately this time as wishing to *bar Herodians from the Temple as foreigners*, down to Caesarea – just as the Pseudoclementine *Recognitions* describes in its portrait of James sending out '*Simon Peter*' from a location somewhere outside of Jericho (where the whole Community of some '*five thousand*' has fled after the riot on the Temple Mount provoked by the' *Enemy*' – Paul? – in which James was only injured, but not killed), to confront '*Simon Magus*' in Caesarea where, of course, the Herodian, King Agrippa I (37–44 CE) also *had his palace*.

However this may be, the '*Simon*' in Josephus rather visits the household of this same Agrippa I to see what was being done there '*contrary to Law*' not the household of '*Cornelius the Roman Centurion*,' as Acts 10:1–11:18 portrays parallel materials, deftly subverting them into their mirror opposite. For its part, the exclusionary doctrine ascribed to the '*Simon the Head of an Assembly (Ecclesia) of his own in Jerusalem*' by Josephus is the very reverse of the '*Heavenly*' vision the '*Simon Peter*' in Acts is vouchsafed, which rather ends up in his *thoroughgoing acceptance of Gentiles not their rejection* or, as it were, his absolute '*Paulinization*' – more tendentious mythologization though a tenuous tissue of reality occasionally does shine through.

The confrontations that Peter is pictured as having with Simon *Magus* that follow in Acts 8:9–25 in Simon's birthplace '*Samaria*' – more accurately in '*Caesarea*,' as in the Pseudoclementines – are most likely historical too. These, however, probably relate – as Josephus pictures a parallel episode in the *Antiquities* – to Simon '*Magus*' or '*Atomus*' (*i.e.*, '*the Primal Adam*') subsequent advice to Agrippa II's sister Drusilla to divorce her husband the King of Emesa, who *had specifically circumcised himself* at the insistence of her father (the more '*Pious*' Agrippa I[5]) in order to marry her. Her subsequent marriage to Felix most certainly would have been opposed by those at Qumran on various grounds, already indicated above, had the sectaries there *ever entertained such a person as this 'Drusilla' as being 'Jewish' in the first place.*[6]

As in the case of John the Baptist's complaints against Herodias and Herod Antipas ('*Herod the Tetrarch*' in Acts 13:1's description of the make-up of Paul's '*Antioch*' Community), a decade before these objections '*Simon Peter*' might have had to Drusilla's divorce and subsequent remarriage to Felix; these confrontations with Herodian women always involve what at Qumran goes under the rubric of '*fornication*,' most notably defined there, as we have seen, as '*niece marriage*,' '*polygamy*,' and '*divorce*' – but in the Temple Scroll including, at least where '*the King*' or '*Ruler*' was concerned, *marrying non-Jews* and '*taking more than one wife during the lifetime of the first*' as well.[7]

It should also be appreciated that these confrontations with Herodian women also involve another favorite theme at Qumran and the Letter of James – the second of these '*Three Nets of Belial*' in the Damascus Document – the '*Riches*' of these Herodian women. Of these, Herodias and Bernice would appear to have been the '*Richest*' of all, a point Josephus never fails to note in these descriptions of them.[8] On the other hand, these confrontations had, as already explained, *almost nothing to do with* '*levirate marriage*' – the point so tendentiously seized upon in the Synoptics. These things notwithstanding, complaints of this kind occur at this time – at least in the case of Drusilla and Felix (who both appear conversing amiably with Paul in Acts 24:24–27) – amid the general disaffection between '*Syrophoenician*' Legionnaires and the Jewish inhabitants of Caesarea, so graphically depicted also in Josephus.[9]

Another curious point bearing on this interesting tangle of events, as we have seen as well – Josephus in the *Antiquities* places the riot led by '*Saulos*' and two of his other Herodian '*kinsmen*' or colleagues in Jerusalem in direct succession to *the death of James*.[10] The author of Acts places a similar riot led by the personage it, at least at first, is also referring to as '*Saulos*' following what it considers to be '*the stoning of Stephen*' a stand-in, as we have already sufficiently elucidated, for the attack by Paul on James as detailed in the Pseudoclementine *Recognitions*.

A possible explanation for these kinds of discrepancies between Acts and Josephus on some of this chronology is that Josephus specifically tells us in the *Vita* that he was in Rome at the time James was killed.[11] There he visited Nero's wife, the Empress Poppea, whom he characterizes as *sympathetic to 'religious' causes*, in particular it would appear, *'Jewish' ones*.[12] At the time, Josephus was only about twenty-four years old and already on an extremely important *'mission,'* which itself suggests a certain amount of influence in *'Opposition'* or *'High-Priestly'* circles.[12] As depicted in the *Vita*, the reason he was in Rome – where he, no doubt, laid the foundations for his future betrayal of the Jewish People – was the curious mission he was on (probably in the aftermath of *'the Temple Wall'* Affair above) to rescue some Priests who had been arrested, as he puts it, *'on some slight and trifling charge'* and had been sent to Rome, there to render account to Nero.[14]

As a consequence, Josephus only knew secondhand events taking place in Palestine in the year 62 CE at the time of James' death. He even may have learned of it and other matters through the file of letters he claims King Agrippa II later shared with him when both were in exile in Rome sometime in between his writing the *Jewish War* and the *Antiquities*.[15] There can be little doubt that the *'vegetarian'* Priests, on whose account he goes to Rome and whom Paul, therefore, would have described as *'weak'* (cf. Romans 14:2 and in 1 Corinthians 8:4–13 already underscored above), had been sent to Rome *in the wake of the disturbances in the Temple over the Wall erected to block Agrippa II's view of the sacrifices*. As already suggested, this in our view was the immediate antecedent to the death of James concerning which, we suspect, Paul may have played a part, just as he may have done in circumstances surrounding the War against Rome that followed some three and a half years later.[16]

Nor, in Paul's own description of his experiences above in Galatians 1:15–24, is there any *'vision on the Damascus road,'* only a sojourn of unspecified duration in *'Arabia'* – *'Petra'* as many now refer to it or points further east. As already signaled, Paul's relations with such *'Herodians'* – particularly John's executioner *'Herod the Tetrarch'* – might explain what he may have been doing at the time in *'Damascus'* and the reason he ran afoul of the *'Arab'* Authorities there – not as Acts so tendentiously transforms it, the *'Jewish'* Ones. The *'plotting'* language, Acts 9:22–23 uses in relation to the stratagems these last allegedly employ to try *'to kill Paul,'* is the same as that which the Gospels use to portray what *'Judas Iscariot'* and *'the Jews'* generally do to 'Jesus,' to say nothing of the portrait in John's Gospel of their attempts *to 'kill' Lazarus* as well.[17] Actually, Acts pictures Paul as admitting at several points that he *'persecuted this Way unto death, arresting and imprisoning men and women'* (22:4) or he

> *imprisoned the Saints...,voting against them for execution, punishing them, compelling them to blaspheme in all the synagogues and persecuting them in a mad frenzy even unto foreign cities* (26:10–12).

Paul himself reiterates this in Galatians 1:23, admitting that *'the Assemblies in Judea'* (*Ecclesias*) only knew him as some one who *'persecuted'* or *'ravaged'* them in times past, a portrait which appears to turn into the words 'Jesus' is pictured as uttering in Acts 9:4's famous depiction of Paul's vision on *'the Way to Damascus,' 'Paul, Paul, why persecutest thou me?'*

After this vision, according to Acts 9:26, Paul *'joined himself to the Disciples'* three years later in Jerusalem (*n.b.*, the *'joining'* language occurring here, frequently repeated in the Scrolls, in particular, in the Damascus Document's definition of the *'Nilvim'/'Joiners'* and in the Nahum Pesher[18]). There he ran afoul of the same ubiquitous *'Hellenists'* (*Hellenistas*), whose complaints against *'the Hebrews,'* it will be recalled, triggered *the stoning of Stephen* three chapters before. Here, it is now *'the Hellenists,'* just as *'the Jews'* in Damascus earlier (9:23), who want to *'get hold of'* Paul and *'kill him'* (9:29). Of course, none of this makes any sense whatsoever, since it is Paul who must be considered the real or chief *'Hellenizer'* or *'Hellenist'* not *vice versa*. Nor is it reasonable to think any *'Hellenists'* wanted either *to kill* 'Stephen' or *bother with Paul* – the opposite. Later in Acts 11:20, these same ubiquitous *'Hellenists'* are portrayed as *the first to receive the Gospel 'of the Lord Jesus'* in *'Antioch'* – meaning, of course, *Paul's 'Gospel' not James.'*

The reader will appreciate there is clearly a code of sorts going on here. If this *'code'* was aimed at evasion and disinformation, it certainly has achieved its end over the last nineteen hundred years. Just as Luke was finally forced to attach the real cognomen *'Zealot'* to the Apostle Matthew and Mark are misleadingly calling *'Simon the Canaanite'* or *'Cananaean'*; one would probably ultimately have to read, as already explained, *'extreme Zealots'* or *'Sicarii'* for at least this first cluster of so-called *'Hellenistas'* or *'Hellenists' intent on killing Paul*. The meaning of *'Hellenists,'* then, in such a context – as we have also made clear – would probably have to be *'Zealots'* or *'Sicarii,'* in the sense that they were willing to make no compromises where issues of *'Gentiles'* or *'Gentile gifts in the Temple,' 'foreign rule,'* and *'foreign appointment of High Priests'* – including those *appointed by Herodians* – were concerned. In fact, even Acts 23:12 implies as much when it later goes on to describe those *'Nazirite'*-style *'Jews'* who *make a plot* (here, of course, perhaps the real origin of the telltale '*plotting*' language), *putting themselves under an oath not to eat or drink until they had killed Paul* (repeated in Acts 23:14 and 23:21 – in the manner of vegetarians like James abstaining from '*strong drink*' or alcoholic beverages or of later '*Mourners for Zion*,' who take precisely such an oath *in regard to their steadfastness in 'waiting' to 'see the Temple rebuilt'*).

In Galatians 1:18–21, after describing how he first met James and spent fifteen days with Peter, Paul matter-of-factly notes how he '*then came into the regions of Syria and Cilicia*,' all the time insisting he '*does not lie.*' Not a word about *anyone persecuting him at this point* – the opposite. *He is the persecutor* noting how '*the Assemblies in Judea*' (who did not know him by sight) had only heard that '*their former persecutor was now preaching the Faith he had previously tried to destroy*'! As already remarked, Paul also refers to '*Stephen*' in 1 Corinthians 1:16, whose household he baptized '*in Christ*' as opposed, it would appear, to the water '*baptism of John*' mentioned in Acts 18:25. At the end of 1 Corinthians 16:15–16, he again refers to '*Stephen*' – probably his first convert in Corinth, a focus of his activity – as '*Achaia's firstfruit.*'

We have also remarked that in the opening salutation to '*those of the Assembly of God, which is in Corinth*' in 1 Corinthians 1:1, Paul mentions besides himself as '*an Apostle of Jesus Christ*' – called '*by the will of God*' (it is important to appreciate that, as in Galatians 1:1, this does not mean either '*by men*' or *by the Leadership of 'the Jerusalem Church'*) – one '*Sosthenes the brother.*' As we have seen, Acts 18:17 seemingly portrays this same individual – unless there were two people named '*Sosthenes*' with whom Paul interacted in Corinth at this time – as '*the Ruler of the Synagogue*' in Corinth, whom '*the Greeks*' ('*Hellenes*') rather took '*and beat in front of the Judgement seat*' because of *the false accusations made against Paul there*! Apologists would, of course, say, yes there were *two such people* named '*Sosthenes*', just as there were *two descents* '*down the walls of Damascus in a basket*,' one to escape '*the Jews*' and the other '*the Arabs*,' but this really does strain credibility.

Whatever else one might wish to say about these purposeful mix-ups or overlaps between so-called '*Hellenists*' and '*Hebrews*' in Acts, '*Stephen*' certainly does seem to personify the archetypical Gentile believer who (in a kind of continuation or refurbishment of the Gospel 'Jesus' story) is persecuted and ultimately stoned by Jews – the stoning being, as already several times remarked, a throwback to and drawn from the James story. In fact the charges against him ('*Stephen*'):

> *This man does not cease speaking blasphemous words against this Holy Place and the Law, for we have heard him saying that Jesus the Nazoraean will destroy this place* (note the quasi-overlap with what the Talmudic '*Jesus the Nazoraean*' above is supposed to have '*said*' concerning '*a prostitute's hire*' and the '*latrine for the High Priests*' in the Temple) *and will change the customs handed down to us by Moses* (Acts 6:13–14),

are more or less repeated in Acts 21:28 in the more reliable '*We Document*' in the not unsimilar charges against Paul by the Jewish crowd who, *seeing him in the Temple with Greeks*, think, therefore, *he has introduced foreigners into it*, thereby '*defiling*' or '*polluting it.*' The addition of '*blasphemy*' to the charge sheet against '*Stephen*' here is probably yet another holdover from the original one against James.[19] Concomitantly, the charge of '*destroying this place and changing the customs of Moses*' – doubtlessly, too, the general implication of Pauline doctrine on these issues as well – reflects the '*blasphemy*' aspect of the charges against '*Jesus*' before '*the High Priests, the Elders, and the whole Sanhedrin*' as depicted in the Synoptics (Matthew 26:59–65 and *pars.*).

More Gentilization at Corinth – Sequencing in Acts and Josephus

With regard to the '*Gentilization*' of these kinds of persecutions and sufferings, one should pay particular attention to Acts' picture of Paul's activities in Corinth. Here, as usual, Paul goes straight to the Jewish Synagogue, where he

> *won over Jews and Greeks and…earnestly testified to the Jews that Jesus was the Christ* (Acts 18:4–5).

But Paul was not supposed to do this. According to his own testimony in Galatians 2:9, after going up to Jerusalem as a result of a private '*revelation*' (*apocalypseos*) he says he has received – his usual way of asserting he was under no one's authority or, in this case, that he was not recalled – and putting the Gospel as he '*taught it among the Gentiles*' before the Central Trio of '*James, Cephas, and John*' (not that their '*importance meant anything to*' him since '*God did not have favorites*' or '*accept the person of man*'); these '*Pillars,*' as he puts it, shook hands with him to show, seemingly, their agreement that he '*should go to the Gentiles (Ethnesin), while they to the Circumcision*' (Galatians 2:2–2:6).

This was obviously either the condition of or reservation to their agreement that he was not to teach '*the Gospel as he taught it among the*

Gentiles' to Jews. But over and over again, even according to the picture in Acts, Paul does precisely the opposite and the first thing he does in almost every city he visits is to go directly to the synagogue there. In Corinth, for example, when the Jews *'set themselves in opposition and were blaspheming'* (18:6 – here the *'blasphemy'* language is reversed and applied now to *'the Jews'!*[20]), Paul *'shook out his garments.'* In the Gospels generally, 'Jesus' expresses a similar idea when he councils his followers to *'shake the dust from off their feet'* (Matthew 10:14 and *pars.*) or, for instance, when Pilate *'washes his hands'* of any direct or even indirect responsibility for 'Jesus'' execution (Matthew 27:24 and *pars.*).

Now echoing Pilate's equally proverbial words regarding the latter, Paul is actually even pictured as saying (this, just as with the *'blasphemy'* charge, now in the *Diaspora* and not in Jerusalem),

> *Your blood be on your own heads* (and here, too, echoed by Matthew 27:25's next line, but inverted and attributed in the first person plural instead to *'the Jews'*). *I am innocent. From now on I will go to the Gentiles* (*Ethne* – Acts 18:6),

as if slights or rejections of this kind were sufficient cause to permit such a new direction. These are fateful words regardless of who first uttered them, Paul or Pilate (or, as the case may be, *'the Jews'*), and provide a rare insight into the psychology of, as it were, *'the Gentile Mission.'*

Actually, its anti-Semitism is directed as much against Jews within the early *'Christian'* Movement of principal concern to Paul (we should, with more accuracy, probably call it the *'Messianic'* Movement) as those outside it, since they were, in fact, its principal Leaders – perhaps even more. Just as the presentation of Pilate *'washing his hands'* of any responsibility for the condemnation and death of Jesus earlier, one must see this episode as the total validation of Paul's mission and his position where Jews were concerned – at least this would be true in the eyes of the Roman reader or devotees.

But the problem with the episode, as we just saw, is that *'the Ruler of the Synagogue'* (have we encountered this usage, too, before in Talmudic stories about its *'Rich Men'* or John's description of his *'Nicodemus'?*), Acts 18:17 pictures Seneca's brother – the Roman Prefect Gallio – as allowing the citizens of Corinth 'to *beat before the Judgement seat,'* is apparently the same *'Sosthenes'* Paul greets in the first line of 1 Corinthians, designating him there as a *'brother'* and *a close collaborator in all his work.* In fact, in Acts 18:8, nine lines before this obviously defective notice, this same *'Ruler of the Synagogue'* is rather identified – probably more accurately –

as '*Crispus*.' Again here we would appear to be in the midst of another of Acts' manifold reversals of either real historical persons and/or the real historical situation or both.

With all of the above individuals and activity centered in Corinth, where according to Acts 18:7 Paul stays '*for eighteen months*' at the house adjourning the synagogue of someone (not unremarkably, called '*Justus*'), as well as the designation, too, of '*Stephen*' – clearly another of Paul's close collaborators – as '*Achaia's firstfruit*' (all of this, to say nothing of '*Epaphroditus*' presence at various times in Corinth as well); there would appear to be more going on in Corinth at this time than initially meets the eye. It should be appreciated that Corinth was Nero's summer residence and, as already indicated, he apparently spent a good deal of time there directing one of his pet projects – the digging of the Corinth Canal, for which purpose many of the captives from the shores of the Sea of Galilee at the time of the first engagements of the Jewish War *were consigned and worked to death*.[21]

For instance, if this '*Epaphroditus*' was Nero's confidant (here, too, it would be hard to conceive there would be two Epaphrodituses involved in some capacity in the household of Nero at one and the same time), then he was Josephus' publisher as well and the man who commissioned and to whom Josephus dedicated all his works. Even Josephus refers to him, as we saw, as someone of '*the widest worldly experience*.'[25] Acts 19:22 also refers to one '*Erastus*,' who like '*Timothy*' ('*Titus*'?) was one of Paul's fundraisers in Macedonia. 2 Timothy 4:20, regardless of its historical reliability, refers to said '*Erastus*' as remaining in Corinth which, as should by now be clear, seems to have been a center of Paul's activities '*in Achaia*' as well. Romans 16:23 for its part calls Erastus '*the steward of the city*,' again probably meaning Corinth. It is not without the realm of possibility that this '*Erastus*' is a compression of '*Epaphroditus*,' as consolidations of this kind are common – for instance, '*Prisca*' preceding the reference to '*Erastus*' in 2 Timothy 4:19 for '*Priscilla*,' '*Silas*' for '*Silvanus*,' and even probably – despite some possible indications to the contrary[23] – '*Titus*' for '*Timothy*.' However one looks at it, these are obviously not all separate individuals and the circle of Paul's close collaborators grows ever more concentrated.

If the stoning of '*Stephen*' in Acts is still one more refurbishment of the '*beating*,' as just alluded to – reported by Josephus – by Revolutionaries ('*Innovators*') or '*bandits*' ('*lestai*') of the Emperor's '*Servant Stephen*' just outside the walls of Jerusalem (in Acts 7:58, it will be recalled, *Stephen is 'cast out of the city'/'ekbalontes' before being stoned*) in the wake of the stampede in the Temple at Passover in which '*hundreds*' or '*thousands*' died[24] (following yet another of these proverbial Roman 'Centurion's lifting his skirt, exposing his presumably uncircumcised privy parts, and then – turning around to show his disdain, obviously, for the assembled pilgrimage crowd – *letting off a loud 'fart'*[25]); then we are in very great and potentially very tragic difficulties regarding 'Christian' origins in Palestine.

As already stated, in the author's view the 'Stephen' in Acts is precisely just such a refurbishment and, when combined with the picture of James' later stoning '*for blasphemy*' (now retrospectively inserted into the 'Stephen' story); then the flow of Acts' narrative along with much else becomes comprehensible indeed. While fictional in almost all its aspects, the presentation in Acts 6:1–5 of this archetypical Pauline '*convert*' as one of those '*seven men*' to '*wait on tables*' (*diakonein*) nevertheless combines, on the one hand, the bitterness generated by these events from a pro-Roman perspective and, on the other, elements from both the unmentionable attack by Paul on James (itself likewise deleted even from Pseudoclementine *Recognitions*' sister narrative the *Homilies*[26]) as well as the attack by riotous and revolutionary Jews bent on vengeance and carnage on the Emperor's '*Servant*' Stephen who seems to have come bearing treasure and supplies from *precisely this same 'Corinth'* (and note, too, the use of this same designation, '*Servant*'[27]). There is also just the slightest play in Stephen's name – meaning, as we have seen, '*Crown*' in Greek (as Eusebius likes to portray it, '*he was the first to win the martyr's crown*') – on the '*crown*' of James' '*Nazirite*' hair,[28] not to mention the '*Crown*' of James' own prototypical martyrdom.

The sequentiality in all these matters is, of course, a very important key to understanding their connections. In Josephus, the attack and robbing of Stephen was followed by outbreaks of mayhem between Samaritans and Galileans on their way through 'Samaria' to pilgrimages in Jerusalem, paralleled in Acts 8:4–25 by confrontations between Peter and Simon *Magus* in 'Samaria' (according to the Pseudoclementines, confrontations which actually *rather took place in Caesarea*).[29] In Josephus, too, much inter-communal strife and killing break out in Caesarea between Greeks ('*Syrophoenician's* in Matthew) and Jews, the counterpart of which in these early chapters of Acts is this picture – however far-fetched it might at first appear – in this 'Stephen' episode of *the constant squabbling between 'Hellenists' and 'Hebrews'* (6:1.).[30] From then on, as Josephus portrays it, '*the whole of Judea was overrun with brigands or robbers*' (*lestai* – this last being the actual word used in Greek to describe the '*two thieves*' in the Gospels, between whom 'Jesus' is pictured as having been crucified[31]).

The Roman Procurator from 48–52 CE in Judea, Cumanus, who succeeds Philo's nephew – the Jewish turncoat and later Vespasian's Military Commander during the siege of Jerusalem – Tiberius Alexander (46–48 CE) and precedes Felix (52–60 CE), responds by *taking bribes from and siding with the Samaritans*.[32] Because of the protests he receives, Quadratus, the Governor in Syria (just as Petronius in the earlier affair of erecting Caligula's statue in the Temple and Cestius, later, in his ill-fated attempt to put down the Uprising in Jerusalem[33]) responsible for this area – then at Beirut – settles the issue by beheading some eighteen Jews and, as already described, *crucifying four others at Lydda*. Thus far the *War* but, in the *Antiquities*, Josephus claims *only five were executed, including the 'Doetus'* or *'Dorcas'* already mentioned previously. Furthermore, whereas he includes *'Samaritans'* in this number, Tacitus says only *'Jews' were crucified who had been 'daring enough to slay Roman soldiers'*![34]

Lydda, it will be recalled, was the town on the coastal plain on the way from Jerusalem to both Jaffa and Gaza. Not only do some really fantastic occurrences take place there in the narrative of Acts 9:32–43 at this point, we have also encountered this town in Rabbinic tradition as a focus for the activities, for instance, of teachers such as the heretic Rabbi, Eliezer b. Hyrcanus.[35] But the *Talmud* also mentions at this same '*Lydda*,' one should recall, the crucifixion of an important '*Messianic*' Leader called '*the Messiah ben Joseph*' not only, perhaps, another of these '*Joshua redivivus*es' ('*Joshua*' being in the Bible a '*son of Joseph*'), but because of the '*Joseph*' allusion too – as already explained, possibly the Samaritan '*Taheb*' or '*Messiah*' as well. Even more importantly, one of the individuals mentioned at this point in Josephus' narrative in connection with problems between Jews and Samaritans at '*Lydda*' was the '*Doetus*' or '*Dortus*' just mentioned above.[36] Transmogrified into '*Dorcas*,' just as '*the Taheb*' is transmogrified into '*Tabitha*' ('*his*'/'*her*' equivalent[37]); this '*Dortus*' or '*Dorcas*,' as also already remarked, then becomes an important part of Acts' story about the '*signs and wonders*' or '*miracles*' Peter performed at '*Lydda*,' leading up to his '*tablecloth*' vision preparatory to his visit to the Roman Centurion Cornelius' household in Caesarea that immediately follows.

Concerning these '*four*' or '*five*' crucifixions that seem to have taken place at '*Lydda*' at this time, Josephus also refers to the involvement of another '*certain Samaritan*,' an informer to Quadratus, possibly none other than *the ubiquitous Simon Magus again*. He, it will be recalled, was probably also an intimate of Felix (52–60 CE), the next Governor sent out after Cumanus was removed, an event that occurred two years before Claudius was assassinated to make way for Nero in Rome.[38] The '*Doetus*' or '*Dortus*' we have been talking about here is probably the '*Dositheus*,' who was important, as we saw – along with '*Simon Magus*' – as a '*Disci-*

ple of John the Baptist' in all catalogues of the *'Heresies'* in this period, with views *virtually indistinguishable from the Ebionites.* In turn Acts 8:32–38, for its part, mentions *'Lydda'* – so important to the outcome of these disputes between *'Samaritans and Jews'* in Josephus – some three times in just six lines in this episode, so something of consequence seems to have been going on there, although what exactly is unclear.

In Acts the assault on Stephen, this time by the whole *Jewish Polity* including the High Priests, is followed by notices about *confrontations in Samaria between Peter and Simon Magus,* the affinities with Josephus being palpable – however, as always, reversed. But, where *'Hellenist' complaints against* 'the Hebrews' in Acts 6:1–6 and – following these – *against Paul* in Acts 9:29 are concerned, these are also obviously totally invented. As previously already suggested, surely we have to do with more overwriting here and complaints of this kind against Paul and like-minded personages must rather have been on the part of so-called *'Zealots'* or *'Sicarii'* not *'Hellenists.'*[39]

For the Pseudoclementines, in conclusion then, the whole presentation of *'the stoning of Stephen'* is discarded and replaced by *the assault on James in the Temple by Paul, who incites 'the High Priests' against James not 'Stephen.'* In fact, the whole series of disturbances in the Temple from the Forties to the Sixties CE will probably have ultimately to be associated in one way or another with the kind of activities James and his followers were involved in there, the majority of whom, even according to the description of Acts 21:20, have to be seen as *'Zelotai'* or *'Zealots for the Law.'*

Paul's Missionary Adventures and the Run-up to *'the Jerusalem Council'*

The next meeting between Paul and James may have taken place during the time of *'the Great Famine'* (*'then over the whole habitable world'*!) in the late Forties but, where this is concerned, Acts' testimony cannot really be relied upon because from Chapters 10–16 until the introduction of the *'We Document'* in 16:10 after the so-called *'Jerusalem Council,'* we are presented with such a welter of contradictory notices, fantastic events, and overlaps that little, if anything, can be concluded with certainty.

To continue on the question of sequencing – for its part, having finished its account of Peter's activities in Samaria in confronting Simon *Magus,* Acts now moves directly on to the journey Peter takes to Jaffa and Caesarea and his *'Heavenly tablecloth'* vision, in which he learns that God has *'poured out the gift of the Holy Spirit upon the Gentiles too'* (10:45). Then there are a series of repetitive notices, already highlighted above, about '*prophets and teachers*' coming down '*from Jerusalem to Antioch.*' The first of these follows the so-called '*scattering*' that took place, supposedly '*to Phoenicia, Cyprus, and Antioch,*' after the stoning of Stephen in Acts 11:19 – in the Pseudoclementines paralleled simply by the flight by James' Community to the Jericho area and its wondrous escape while '*visiting the tombs of the two brothers that miraculously whitened of themselves every year.*'[40] Again we hear that '*certain ones of them, men from Cyprus and Cyrene,*' came down and '*preached the Gospel*' to the ubiquitous '*Hellenists,*' now supposedly *residing in* '*Antioch*' (11:20) – here, too, one should probably rather read '*Kanna'im.*'

As we have seen as well, '*Cyprus*' is another one of those curious circumlocutions, sometimes probably meaning – because of its connection to the Greco-Hebrew root '*Cuthaeans*'/'*Kitta*' – '*Samaria.*' It was also one of the destinations supposedly of Queen Helen's '*grain-buying*' agents, an episode we have already characterized as reflected in Acts 8:26–40, too, in the conversion by Philip – after his confrontation with Simon *Magus* in '*Samaria*' – of the Ethiopian Queen's '*eunuch*' (described in Acts 8:27 as responsible '*over all her treasure*'). If Paul was also involved in such '*grain-buying*' operations, as Acts 11:27–30 seems to think (the details of which it reticently fails to provide rather preferring, instead, to dispose of '*James the brother of John*' in 12:1 and then introduce '*James the brother of Jesus*' in 12:17, before finally going on to laconically observe in 12:25: '*and Barnabas and Saul returned from Jerusalem having completed their mission*' – again '*diakonian*'!); he does not refer to it at all in Galatians, where the timeframe of some '*fourteen years*' – after sojourning in Arabia and Damascus before '*again going up to Jerusalem*' (2:1) – certainly takes us into the early Fifties. Of course, these '*grain-buying*' activities – in which he may have been involved along with '*Barnabas*' as one of Queen Helen and her son Izates' '*Treasury*' or '*grain-buying*' agents – may not have taken him up to Jerusalem, as Acts 12:25 seems to think, but simply further afield to Cyprus and/or Egypt.[41]

As already explained, what is really at stake in these episodes about so-called '*prophets and teachers*' such as '*Agabus*' – '*coming down from Jerusalem to Antioch*' – are '*the messengers' from* or '*representatives of James*' like '*Judas Barsabas,*' '*Thaddaeus,*' and even '*Judas Thomas*' sent down to '*Antioch-by-Callirhoe*' or '*Edessa Orrhoe*' either to convert or make sure everyone had correctly gotten the message of obedience to the Law, an obedience which *prima facie* included '*circumcision.*' Persons such as these would also include by refraction '*Judas the brother of James*' ('*Addai*' in the First Apocalypse of James and, '*Theuda the brother of the Just One,*' in the Second) going down to carry on these initial conversion activities in '*the*

Land of the Edessenes,' as Eusebius would express it, and, no doubt, further east in '*Adiabene*' – the roots of these two: '*Edessa*' and '*Adiabene*' (to say nothing of that of '*Addai*' himself) being interrelated.

Paul's adventures, recorded from Chapters 13–15 of Acts, largely overlap those in Chapters 16–18. They are often referred to as his '*First*', '*Second*', or '*Third Missionary Journey's*, depending on how much or how little overlap one thinks there is. The present writer, obviously, thinks there was quite a bit. Ingenious efforts to harmonize these have been largely ineffective and, instead of the picture of '*three*' Missionary Journeys, we are probably really only speaking about one extended one and its offshoots or variations – the one finally told about at some length in the '*We Document*.'

A good example of this overlapping is what happens in '*Antioch of Pisidia*' – another of these ever-recurrent '*Antioch*'s – this one in Galatia. As usual, Paul makes a bee-line on the Sabbath to the Synagogue to preach (Acts 13:14). Once again, as later at Corinth, he '*speaks out boldly*' but the Jews, '*filled with envy, opposed the things Paul said, blaspheming*' (13:45 – again, n.b., the '*blaspheming*' accusation, though '*the Jews being filled with envy*' in this case, anyhow, is probably, simply semantological coincidence). The parallels with Acts 18:6's picture of what supposedly happened later at Corinth are patent. Again, as at Corinth too, in this first incident on mainland Asia Minor at '*Antioch of Pisidia*' ('*Pamphylia*'), Paul goes to the Synagogue on a succession of Sabbaths.

Here, as everywhere, '*the Jews stirred up a persecution against Paul among the honourable, worshipping women and chief men of the city*' and, just as later, Paul exploits this as an occasion to announce his intention to '*turn to the Gentiles*' (13:46-50). This time, however, it is not his '*garments*' that, as in 18:6 at Corinth later, he '*shakes out*,' but now he and Barnabas ('*John Mark having left them*' in 13:13, '*returning to Jerusalem*' – basically '*withdrawing from*' or '*deserting their work*' as Paul will subsequently describe it in Acts 15:38 after '*the Jerusalem Council*') '*shake off the dust of their feet against them*' (13:51 – very impressive). One should also note at the end of this episode (as in the stoning of Stephen earlier, employing the language of '*Essene*' practice of '*expelling*' or '*casting out*' backsliders, as well as that used in traditions both to describe the '*Enemy*''s attack upon James and James' death), the use of '*casting out*' language again in 13:50 (this time, '*ezebalou*'), when the people of '*Antioch of Pisidia*' now '*cast out*' Paul and Barnabas '*from their coasts*' or '*borders*.' This occurs, as we just saw, following Acts 13:13's terse note about '*John Mark*''s sudden return from Pamphylia to Jerusalem – reason unspecified.

Not only are the words Acts 15:38–39 uses to characterize this literally, '*separated*' or '*withdrew from them refusing to (cooperate) with them in work*,' almost precisely those employed in the ostracization of those '*overtly or covertly breaking one word of the Torah of Moses*' in the Community Rule at Qumran[42]; in Galatians 2:12, Barnabas is likewise depicted as either '*withdrawing from*' or '*shunning*' Paul. So do '*the rest of the Jews*' – after the '*some from James*' or '*those of the circumcision*' ('*those insisting on circumcision*'? – *cf.* also Acts 11:2-3 using the same phrase to describe those complaining against '*Peter*'s behaviour after his '*Heavenly tablecloth*' vision) *come down to Antioch* – at which point, it will be recalled, in 2:13 Paul uses the term '*hypocrisy*' to refer to *both Peter and Barnabas.*

At this point, too – between the so-called '*Second*' and '*Third*' *Missionary*' Journeys – Acts suddenly dispenses with all the dissimulation or, as some might characterize it, disinformation and gives us *the real circumstances* behind Paul's return to Jerusalem after his first meeting with James *fourteen years before* (of course, in Acts 11:30–12:25, there had also been an intervening journey for its '*famine relief*' episode *that actually served*, as already remarked, *to introduce James and dispose of the other James*). Hitherto this causality had only been implied but never explicitly stated in all these other highly improbable notices in Acts. It would also appear to be the real reason behind the so-called '*Jerusalem Council*' or '*Conference.*'

As Acts 15:1 puts this, as we have already had occasion to point out, '*Some, having come down from Judea, were teaching the brothers that, unless you are circumcised according to the custom of Moses, you could not be saved,*' and we are right back again in the scenario of Galatians 2:3–2:14 (to say nothing of its converse regarding the same '*Peter*' in Acts 11:1-3 above). One can assume, as well, that this is more or less the truth of the matter and what we have here is what would ordinarily be reckoned as a summons on the part of '*those of repute*' or '*those reckoned to be something,*' as Paul calls them in Galatians 2:6, in Jerusalem – meaning '*James, Cephas, and John*' (note Paul's use of the designation '*Cephas*' here and not '*Peter*'), '*the importance of whom*' for him, it will be recalled, '*nothing conferred*' (this, despite his attempt in Galatians 2:1–4 to make it look as if he had *not been summoned but had come*, as he puts it, *as a result of a private '*revelation*'*– '*for fear that somehow in vain*' he '*should be running or had been running*').

Here too, Paul first makes the accusation in Galatians 2:4, we have already alluded to above of

> *false brothers* (paralleling the one about '*false Apostles*' and '*dishonest*' or '*Lying workmen*' in 2 Corinthians 2:11:13 above) *stealing in by stealth to spy out the freedom we enjoy in Christ Jesus, so that they might enslave us,*

deliberately playing off the issue of *'circumcision'* – in his implication of some *'spying on their privy parts'*[43] – that, as we just saw, according to Acts, triggered the so-called *'Jerusalem Council'* in the first place. Paul means here, of course, as already explained, *'freedom from the Law'* as opposed to *'slavery to it'* and not what would be more apt, given the historical situation, *'freedom from Rome'* as opposed to *'slavery to it'* – a juxtaposition of imagery Paul also picks up again, as we have previously pointed out too, in his *'allegory'* about

> *Agar* (that is,*'Hagar'*), *who is Mount Sinai in Arabia* (here Paul uses the *'Arabia'* notation as the equivalent of the *'Sinaitic'* one, *'the Covenant' from which* – in his view – somehow *'brings into slavery'*) *and corresponds to the present Jerusalem, which is in slavery with her children* (once again, as already explained as well, in the context patently meaning, *'slavery to Mosaic Law'* and not *'slavery to Rome'*!) –

and Sarah, whom he characterizes – against all logic (but *'such things,'* as he eventually goes on to put it in Galatians 4:24 *'are allegories'*) – as *'the free woman through the Promise'* or *'the Jerusalem above which is free.'* Therefore, as he puts it in his own inimical way continuing the *'allegory,'* quoting Sarah's speech in Genesis 21:10 and, once again, parodying every other bit of *'casting out'* and *'casting down'* language we have been underscoring:

> *Cast out (ekbale) the slave woman and her son* (Galatians 4:30).

Whether there was an actual *'Council'* as such, as Acts presents it, and not simply a semi-private audience of some kind between Paul and the Jerusalem *'Pillars,'* as Paul recounts in Galatians 2:1-13 above, is highly unlikely. Reliable or otherwise, Acts 15:2–7 magnifies this into a meeting of *the whole Assembly* (*'the Apostles and the Elders'*). According to it, *this insistence on 'circumcision'* – just like Izates' more *'Zealot'* Galilean teacher, Eleazar, in Josephus' story of his conversion only a little further south in *'Carrhae'* or *'Haran'* or further east in *'Adiabene'* – causes *'an uproar' in the Community at 'Antioch,'* wherever this is thought to have been, whereupon *Paul, Barnabas, and 'certain others'* (again, as usual, unnamed) *are chosen* – just as four chapters earlier, after *'Agabus'* and the other *'prophets had come down from Jerusalem to Antioch'* and *'Paul and Barnabas'* were again chosen (11:27–30) – *'to go up to the Apostles and the Elders in Jerusalem regarding this question'* (15:2).

Apostolic Credentials, '*Boasting*,' and '*the Apostles of Surpassing Degree*' in Paul

Despite the many questions about these events and their chronological sequence, what the so-called '*Jerusalem Council*' really was has been labored over long and hard by numerous scholars with varying answers, usually depending on the theological point-of-view of the given observer or the like. The results achieved are not particularly satisfying because: 1) researchers rarely come to grips with Acts' tendencies to dissimulate – or even, for that matter, its creative writing – to say nothing of its oftentimes mischievousness; and 2) the Dead Sea Scrolls had not yet been discovered and, even when they had, have either simply been shunted aside or not been used – not being considered relevant to the real life setting of this famous confrontation, nor even to hone one's understanding of true events in Palestine of the time. This is still true.

Therefore, we consider that it is better to start from scratch, as it were, using primary sources only and tease the information out of them. The notices we have just encountered above, about persons dogging Paul's footsteps with a contrary doctrine, are rife throughout Paul's Letters and he repeatedly and often bitterly complains, as we have seen, about just that sort of thing.[44] Yet specialists are either still unwilling or unable to definitively determine who these ubiquitous '*some*' or '*certain ones*,' he is constantly complaining about, are. For instance, in 1 Corinthians 9:1 he asserts:

> *Have I not seen Jesus Christ our Lord? Are you not my work in the Lord? Even if I were not an Apostle to others, I should still be an Apostle to you, who are the seal of my Apostleship in the Lord. This is my answer to those who would examine me.*

Paul's wounded pride here is self-evident. So is his feeling of inferiority to those above him whom he refers to in 2 Corinthians 11:13–15, as already underscored as well, by phrases such as '*Super Apostles*,' '*Hebrews*,' and finally, as we have several times had occasion to remark, even '*pseudo-Apostles, dishonest workmen transforming themselves into…Servants of Righteousness, whose End shall be according to their works*' (once again, in this last, note the purposeful play on '*Jamesian*' doctrine). Not only is terminology like '*Servants of Righteousness*' clearly reflected in the Dead Sea Scrolls, but the whole phraseology plays off of the unmistakably '*Jamesian*' approach to '*works Righteousness*.'[44]

His use of the word '*Lord*' here, too, recalls its use in the more-recently published 'Messiah of Heaven and Earth' text, as it does references like that to 'James the brother of the Lord' in Galatians 1:19 above and 'the Cup of the Lord' given to James by Jesus to drink after his resurrection in Jerome's redaction of the Gospel of the Hebrews. The latter allusion would appear to be an extremely early one, which will presently be confirmed in the Habakkuk Pesher's description of the figurative 'Cup of Divine Vengeance' which would ultimately 'come around to' and 'be given by God to' the Wicked Priest 'to drink.'[46]

Continuing on the subject of Apostolic Credentials in 2 Corinthians 3:1, Paul asks rhetorically, his wounded pride and feelings of inferiority again painfully evident, 'Do we begin again to commend ourselves to you?' Then, alluding to the ever-recurring issue of not having official 'written' letters of Apostolic appointment from James (much like a rabbi or some churchmen have even today), a theme which actually permeates the run-up in 2 Corinthians 10:9–18 to his evocation in 11:13 above of the 'dishonest workmen transforming themselves into Apostles of Christ' jibe:

> Unlike some (clearly implying the Hebrew 'Super Apostles'), we need no letters of recommendation either to you or from you.

One should compare this to the Pseudoclementine Homilies picture of Peter teaching at Tripoli:

> Our Lord and Prophet, who has sent us (here both the 'Lord' and Ebionite 'True Prophet' ideologies), declared to us that the Evil One, having disputed with him forty days, but failing to prevail against him (the 'temptation in the wilderness' scenario of the Synoptics), promised He would send Apostles from among his subjects to deceive them. Therefore, above all, remember to shun any Apostle, teacher, or prophet ('the prophets and teachers' of the Pauline, Gentile Christian 'Church in Antioch' of Acts 13:1, with which the picture of Paul's 'Missionary Journeys' began) who does not accurately compare his teaching with James...the brother of My Lord (clearly the kind of 'shunning' Paul himself depicts in Galatians 2:12–13, reiterated in the picture of the break with 'John Mark' and 'Barnabas' in Acts 13:13 and 15:39)...and this, even if he comes to you with recommendations.[47]

The contrast here should be patent.

As we have already seen in 2 Corinthians 3:2–1, using the 'teaching things spiritually' ideology of 1 Corinthians 2:13, Paul then employs the imagery of letters of this kind being written on the 'fleshy tablets' of his

supporters' hearts, not on the cold *'tablets of stone,'* in the process denigrating the most precious attachment of his opponents within *'the
Church,'* to *the Mosaic Commandments*. Since it is such a startling inversion
of Palestinian themes, it is worth citing it fully:

> *You are our epistle, having been inscribed in our hearts, being known and being
> read by all men* (here, of course, Philo's *'allegorical'* methodology with a
> vengeance), *it being manifest that you are Christ's letter, served by us, having
> been inscribed, not with ink, but with the Spirit of the Living God* − not on
> *tablets of stone, but on the fleshy tablets of the heart* (2 Corinthians 3:2–3 − a
> more *'spiritual'* approach could hardly be imagined).

In these polemics, too, Paul employs what here and in the Dead Sea
Scrolls amounts to a central imagery, that of the *'heart.'* For the Scrolls,
'the Wicked Priest,' in the manner of Ezekiel 44:9, refuses to *'circumcise the
foreskin of his heart'*[48] and *'the Man of Lying'/'Spouter of Lying'*'s chief characteristic − aside from *'rejecting the Law'* − is *'stubbornness of heart.'*[49] For his
part, Paul uses the imagery of the *'heart'* in Romans 2:5 and 2:29, where
(just as in the Habakkuk *Pesher* and Ezekiel 44:7 above) he even speaks
about *'circumcision of the heart,'* and in 2 Corinthians 5:12: the first to attack
Mosaic Law and the second, even the same Hebrew *'Apostles of the Highest Degree'* whom, as we saw, for him go around disguising themselves as
'Servants of Righteousness' when they are really *'Servants of Satan.'* Nor can
there be the slightest doubt that what he means by these *'False Apostles'/
'Pseudo-Servants'* is the Jewish Leadership of the *'Jerusalem Church'* itself.

Using the imagery of *'building up,'* not *'puffing up,'* of 1 Corinthians
8:1's prologue to his attack on the *'some'* with *'weak consciences'* (Paul's
euphemism, as we have seen, *for following the Law of Moses*), who *'refuse to
eat things sacrificed to idols'* (8:7–13); in 2 Corinthians 10:8ff.,[50] he launches
into one of his most dizzying displays of rhetorical virtuosity which he
commences by referring, once more, to *'boasting'* − this time, *'about the
Authority which the Lord gave to us for building up and not tearing you down.'*
Once again, we know whom he is referring to by these words, though
one might ask which *'Lord,'* when, and which *'us'* − but Paul is manifestly
employing the royal *'we'* here.

Notwithstanding, we have seen the same claim regarding his Apostolic *'Authority'* above in Galatians 1:1's *'not from men nor through man'* (in
Romans 2:11 above, that God is *'no respecter of persons'*[51]). In 2 Corinthians 10:9 − in alluding to the poor physical impression he apparently
makes in person − he, yet again, follows this in the very next line by
evoking the issue of *'letters,'* asserting, *'so that I may not seem as if frighten-*

ing you by means of letters.' To this he immediately answers antiphonically in 10:11, *'let such a person consider'* – meaning the person complaining about his *'Apostolate in the Lord'* – that, *though we are absent in word, through letters we are present in deed'* – here, too, the ever so slight dismissive parody of the James *'works Righteousness'* doctrine.

He then continues, beginning with his usual note of false modesty, but ending in confident dismissiveness:

> *For we dare not rank (ourselves) among or compare ourselves with some* (the contemptuous and ever-present *'some,'* patently equivalent to Galatians 2:12's *'some from James'* or Acts 15:1's *'some who came down from Jerusalem, who were teaching the brothers, unless you were circumcised according to the custom of Moses, you could not be saved'* that, according to it, triggers *'the Jerusalem Council'* above) *who commend themselves* (the same *'commending'* with which he began the whole polemic in 2 Corinthians 3:1, the biting sarcasm of which discourse growing ever more palpable), *but those measuring themselves by themselves and comparing themselves to themselves do not understand* (10:12 – *'understand'* what, Paul's new *'Gentile Christian'* approach to *'Salvation'/'Jesus'?*).

This is followed by some five lines of the most practiced and strophied discourse, carrying the *'boasting'* theme forward and amply demonstrating his training in this sort of rhetorical and sophistical dialectic, pointedly concluding:

> *For not he that commends himself is the one approved, but (rather) he whom the Lord commends* (10:18).

Nor, once again, can there be any doubt who, he is talking about here, and what – as if somehow he has received his Apostolic Credentials (as he put it in Galatians 1:1), *'not from men or through man,'* that is, *not in the form of direct earthly appointment* (which, it should be clear by this point, *Paul did not have*), or *that of a written letter,* *'but through Jesus Christ and the Father God, who raised him from among the dead,'* which can only mean supernaturally or, as he would put it, *'through Christ Jesus in Heaven.'*

Going back to 2 Corinthians 3:3–6 to repeat somewhat (but such passages cannot be repeated too often):

> *not on Tablets of Stone* (the *'custom'* or *'Torah of Moses'* of Acts 15:1 above), *but on the fleshy tablets of the heart...Not that we are qualified by ourselves to judge anything* (again the obsequious note of false modesty here, not

unlike the similar approach in 1 Corinthians 15:8–9 on his being the '*last*' or '*least of all the Apostles*' – to say nothing of the quasi-parody of James '*judging*' in Acts 15:19 above or, for that matter, that of '*the Mebakker*' at Qumran), *for our qualification is from God* (again here, the '*Apostle not from men nor through man*' of Galatians 1:1 above) *who also made us qualified as Servants of the New Covenant* (this of course to be contrasted with '*the Servants of Satan*' who go around '*transforming themselves into Servants of Righteousness*' above and, to be sure, the whole '*Servant*'/'*serving*' ideology generally), *which is not of letters* (always the attack on the '*letters*' meant in the sense both of those which *would constitute* '*written*' *Apostolic appointment from James*, but also the '*letters*' of *the legal requirements inscribed in the Torah of Moses*, which he then goes on to denigrate as '*the Ministry*' or '*Service of Death*'), *but of Spirit. For the letter kills but the Spirit gives life.*

As already observed, not only do we have here the most perfect example perhaps of Paul's use of Philo of Alexandria's method of allegorization and the whole ethos of the Neoplatonic or Hellenistic schools that preceded him (to say nothing of his teaching '*spiritual things spiritually*' contention); but there is just the slightest hint, again too, of the Gospel/1 Thessalonians 2:15's '*blood libel*' accusation in the way in which Paul alludes to '*the letter kills.*' Even if one is not prepared to go this far, there is the reiteration of '*the Law*' and '*letters*' generally as '*bringing death*' (including by extension, no doubt, those from the same '*some*' who, according to 2 Corinthians 10:12, '*evaluating themselves by themselves and comparing themselves to themselves,*' '*commend themselves*'), like '*the Servants of the Satan*' barb, a most terrible accusation even if meant only '*allegorically*' or, what is even more to the point, '*polemically.*'

20

'Cursed be Anyone Hung Upon a Tree' and 'Boasting in the Flesh'

'The New Covenant' in Paul and 'those Boasting in Appearance'

'*The New Covenant*' Paul is referring to in these astonishing passages from 2 Corinthians is, of course, the total reverse of what is evoked in the Dead Sea Scrolls in the Damascus Document which, as we have been pointing out, rather involves just the opposite approach or, as it were, *rededication to these same 'Letters*' or '*Tablets of Stone.*' But, true to form, Paul's mastery of literary device and rhetorical polemic is simply remarkable here – even if, at times, facile and obfuscating or, perhaps more to the point, sophisitical or "*mystificating.*" Nor has it failed '*to cast*' its spell (again, the pun can be taken as purposeful) over the last Nineteen and a half centuries – from the point-of-view of the present writer not always in a salutary manner and sometimes even positively deleteriously.

Following upon another allusion in 2 Corinthians 5:1 to the '*House*' or '*Temple*' – it and the '*Foundations*' of which he has already alluded previously to having constructed in 1 Corinthians 3:9–17 – being '*a building from God,*' not '*Earthly*' or '*made with hands, but Eternal in the Heavens*' (the '*hand*'/'*hands*' language we have already seen to be particularly strong in the follow-up to the War Scroll's citation of '*the Star Prophecy*' and in the Community Rule above[1]); Paul again picks up the themes of '*persuading men,*' '*commending ourselves to you,*' and '*being manifested to God*' and (he '*hopes*') '*in your consciences too*' (5:11–12).

One should note the play here on his use of the word '*conscience*' in 1 Corinthians 8:7–12, earlier, to signify those blindly '*keeping the Law*' or '*being so weak*' as to make issues over '*eating things sacrificed to idols*' or, in Romans 14:2, '*so weak as to eat only vegetables.*' In another derisive parody in this first passage (8:10), not only will the '*conscience*' of such persons (*i.e.,* '*weaklings*') need some '*building up*'; but in Greek the '*being manifest*' in the 2 Corinthians 5:11-12 passage is the same kind of '*manifesting*' or '*Manifestation,*' we have just encountered throughout the Gospel of John – almost always, of course, together with the idea of '*his Glory*' – in particular, in John 2:11, when Jesus '*manifested his Glory*' after '*doing the signs in Cana of Galilee*' and '*his Disciples believed on him*' or when Jesus '*manifested himself*' or '*was manifested to his Disciples after being raised from among the dead*' at '*the Sea of Tiberias*' in John 21:1-14).

For his part, in this passage from 2 Corinthians 5:11-12, Paul rather uses the ubiquitous '*heart*' imagery– which he often uses in conjunction with '*teaching spiritual things spiritually*' or '*allegorically*' and to justify his own credentials, both to attack those who '*glory*' or '*boast in appearance*' (once more he means by this, not only '*boasting in*' the external trappings of the Law but, as usual and in particular, '*boasting in circumcision*' – the '*glorying*' or '*boasting*' language he uses here being so strong that, at Qumran in the Habakkuk *Pesher*, it is apparently being used in a reverse attack to characterize the Community '*being built*' by '*the Liar*' or '*the Spouter of Lying for his own Glory*'[2] – and to '*boast*' about his Communities, which in 2 Corinthians 3:3 earlier, '*were the seal of his Apostleship*' and his '*work in the Lord*.'

The '*boasting*' or '*glorying*' he does here, which will preoccupy him for most of the rest of the Letter and reach a fever pitch, as already to some extent highlighted, in its closing part in 2 Corinthians 11:5– 12:12, is for him just one more way of demonstrating his Apostolic Credentials. To pick go back and up this passage from 5:11-12, this reads in its entirety:

> *to God we have been manifested and, I hope, also been manifested in your con-sciences* (here his use of the strophe-antistrophe rhetorical method again), *for we do not again commend ourselves to you but, rather, give you occasion to glory* (or '*boast*') *on our behalf as opposed to those boasting in appearance and not in the heart* (here, as just noted, the allusion to '*heart*' and '*circumcision*' imagery, the conjunction of which we have already encountered in Romans 2:25-2:29 above).

Not only does the use of the word '*conscience*'/'*consciences*' allude here to his replacement of the '*Jamesian*' Law-oriented approach – characterized by his use of this same expression '*conscience*' as we just saw – with his now more-allegorized antinomian approach to '*Salvation*'; but it is exactly the reverse of the way he uses the expression in these passages from 1 Corinthians 8:7–12 above where the '*weakness*,' he was speaking about, had to do with '*not eating things sacrificed to idols*' and '*forbidden foods*' gen-erally – or, in short, '*keeping*' or '*observing the Law*.'

Paul's allusion to '*boasting in appearance*' here must be perceived, as just underscored too, as relating at least in part to '*circumcision*.' This is also true of Galatians 2:4 above, where he refers to '*the false brothers who steal in by stealth to spy out our freedom we enjoy in Christ Jesus that they may reduce us to slavery,'* the meaning of which is hardly to be doubted – nor is that of the *'freedom'/'slavery'* contraposition he evokes). When combined with the all-important *'heart'* imagery, as it is here, it must be seen as alluding, as already underscored as well, to 'the Zadokite Covenant' of Ezekiel 44:5–15, so important to the Damascus Document's exposition of who *'the Sons of Zadok'* actually were and the whole ethos of Qumran.

This is particularly the case in the disqualification from Temple service in Ezekiel 44:7 above of an obviously not-so-*'zealous'* previously functioning *'High Priesthood'* for having *'brought foreigners, uncircumcised in heart and flesh, into My Sanctuary to pollute it.'* This is precisely the imagery, it should be remembered, that Acts 21:28 uses to describe Paul's unceremonious ejection from the Temple by persons, obviously *'zealous for the Law,'* in the aftermath of his final encounter with James. It is also the imagery employed in the Habakkuk *Pesher*, as already alluded to, to disqualify *'the Wicked Priest'* – responsible for the destruction of the Righteous Teacher – from *'service at the altar'/'Temple service'* on the basis of *'not circumcising the foreskin of his heart.'*[3] The same language of *'breaking the Covenant'* and *'Abominations,'* used in Ezekiel 44:7 alongside this allusion to *'barring those uncircumcised'* in both *'heart and flesh'* from approaching the altar, is pervasive as well in the Habakkuk *Pesher*, the Damascus Document, and many other documents at Qumran.[4]

Esotericisms of this kind, most to completely opposite effect, are also the basis of Paul's allusions throughout 1 and 2 Corinthians, in particular those to *'God's House,' 'a building from God,' 'not made with hands,' 'Eternal in the Heavens,'* composed of his communities or *'fellow workers'* – these last denoted as its *'members'* just as one would speak about *the 'members'* or *'parts'* of the body – all of which being, once again, pure allegorization and carrying, as is usual for him, the meaning of *'Christ's body.'*[5] In 1 Corinthians 3:9–17 above, in calling – as we saw – his communities *'God's Temple,'* he actually uses the language of *'polluting'* or *'defiling the Temple'*[6] to speak about the rank and file of his Community or, as he puts it, the Temple *'which is Holy, which you are'* – here, once again, referring to its *'members.'* Though, once again too, he is reversing or allegorizing the signification of the language found in both Ezekiel and Qumran of an *'Earthly'* or *'fleshly Temple,'* nevertheless it should not be forgotten that this same language of the Community as spiritualized *'Temple of God'* is amply present in the Community Rule as well.

However, it is this language of *'fleshly'/'physical'* things or *'judging by external appearance'* which he applies to his *'Jamesian,'* mostly *'Hebrew,'* opponents within the early *'Church'* – meaning *those insisting on 'circumcision'* and *the formal letter of the Law* – whose *'hearts'* are always too *'impure'* or gross to understand what for him is the overwhelming creativity of his '*spiritualized*' allegories. It is these persons, as well, he so contemptuously refers to in Galatians 1:7 as the '*some who trouble you,*' '*desiring to pervert the Gospel of Christ*' or, thereafter in 2:12, the '*some from James*' who '*came down*' to Antioch, causing those like Peter ('*Cephas*'?), whose habit previously was '*to eat with the Peoples*' ('*Ethnon*') or to keep '*table fellowship*' with them, '*to withdraw and separate himself.*' These last are then unabashedly identified, it will be recalled, as *the Party* '*of the Circumcision*' or '*those insisting upon circumcision,*' which is obviously the truth of the matter. Furthermore, one should always keep in mind the direct testimony here tying these ever-recurring '*some*'/'*certain ones*' to James.

In 2 Corinthians 3:1 above, it will be recalled, these same '*some*' were those unequivocally and straightforwardly identified as '*needing letters of recommendation*' to '*commend themselves.*' In 1 Corinthians 8:7, they were just as clearly identified as those *refusing to eat* '*things sacrificed to an idol*' and, therefore, *whose* '*weak consciences*' *were all-too-easily* '*defiled*' or '*polluted*' and, consequently, *in need of* '*building up.*' Of course it should be recalled as well, '*refusing to eat things sacrificed to an idol*' is not only a fundamental category of James' directives to overseas communities; it is also a key credo of Hippolytus' '*Zealot*' or '*Sicarii Essenes,*' *willing to undergo any sort of torture even unto death* '*rather than eat food sacrificed to idols.*' It is the dominant motif, too, as already made plain, of an extensive, key section of '*MMT*' on the kind of '*gifts*' and '*sacrifices*' – in particular, *foreign ones* – that would result in '*pollution of the Temple,*' the charge in Paul with which we originally began this excursus.[7]

It should be appreciated that Paul returns to these same '*some*'/'*somebodies*'/'*certain ones*' and the matter of '*written*' credentials in 2 Corinthians 10:8–12 – where he used the language of '*building up,*' he had used earlier in 1 Corinthians 3:9–17, 8:1, and 2 Corinthians 5:1, and the '*building*' for which he claims to have been the '*wise architect*' and whose '*Foundations*' he '*laid*' in 1 Corinthians 3:10 – to once more reaffirm his Apostolic '*Authority.*' It cannot be stressed too often that in 1 Corinthians 8:1 this '*building up*' language had been used to introduce his attacks on those '*puffed up*' with '*Knowledge*' (who should, rather have been '*built up by love*'), language, as we have already to some extent seen and will see further below, fundamental to the Habakkuk *Pesher*. Then in 8:2, continuing his strophe, antistrophe, and epode poetic/rhetorical approach – the contempt underlying which is palpable – he concludes: '*but if anyone thinks he knows anything, he has known nothing yet (in the way) it is necessary to know it*' which is of course, unquestionably, just another attack on the '*Jerusalem Church*' *Leadership* made up of persons like James who, in making problems over '*eating things sacrificed to idols*' and '*whose consciences being weak,*' were unable to stand up to such things and, therefore, saw themselves as '*being defiled*' (8:7–12).

It is this language he now combines in 2 Corinthians 10:8 with the language of '*boasting*' to characterize his '*Authority*' as follows: '*Perhaps I should boast somewhat even more abundantly about our Authority, which the Lord gave us for building up and not for overthrowing you.*' This is the same '*building*' or '*building up*' language which, as we have seen, the Habakkuk *Pesher* will use to characterize '*the Spouter of Lying*' as '*building a worthless city upon blood and erect an Assembly upon Lying*' – and, in so doing, '*vilifying the Elect of God*' – again, extremely strong vituperation.[8]

Nor can there be any doubt that Paul is complaining about those same '*Hebrew Apostles of Surpassing Degree*' whom he claims '*to have been in no way behind*' (11:5 and 12:11) – attempts by Church Authorities at all times (and scholars even today) to diffuse or obscure it with talk of '*unknown*' or '*Gnosticizing*' teachers of some kind notwithstanding.[9] As in the case of '*those reputed to be something*' in Galatians 2:6 above, there can be little doubt that expressions of this kind definitely allude to *the Leadership of the Church in Jerusalem itself* – most notably even, James himself.

'*Written*' Letters, the '*Some from James*' and '*Circumcision*'

Proceeding now in this same vein, but even more bitingly and disparagingly, Paul continues in 2 Corinthians 10:15–18, '*now will we not boast about things beyond measure*' (playing off the motif of '*measuring*' just encountered above), '*nor in others' labors*' (here the tone of taunting dismissiveness is unmistakable) and, exactly as earlier, '*for it is not he that commends himself that is approved*' (meaning, clearly, the '*written letters*' of authorization from persons like James[10]), *but he whom the Lord commends.*' Once again, Paul is using '*the Lord*' language to indicate the Supernatural Being, he has now taken to refer to as '*Christ Jesus,*' or even God Himself. It is interesting that the '*some,*' who '*came down from Judea*' in Acts 15:1 (just as '*Agabus*' came down to Caesarea in Acts 21:10 thereafter) and '*teach the brothers that, unless you are circumcised according to the tradition of Moses, you cannot be saved,*' are obviously, this time, not '*prophesying.*'[11] Rather they are simply *complaining* and, just as obviously – as in almost all these contexts – they are *representatives of James*.

At Qumran, the idea of being '*saved*' – encountered here in *the teaching of the '*some (from James), who came down from Judea,*' about '*circumcision*'* – will also appear in the all-important passages from the Habakkuk *Pesher* interpreting Habakkuk 2:4 ('*the Righteous shall live by his Faith*') in terms of 'being saved from the House' or 'on the Day of Judgement' – an exposition we shall definitively identify as 'Jamesian' and, in fact, specifically confined to those being designated there as 'the Doers of the Torah in the House of Judah.' Though purposefully arcane, this last, as we shall see, obviously carries with it the meaning of 'all Torah-doing Jews.' The contrapositive of this, just as obviously, is that it does not apply to 'non-Torah-Doers' either inside or outside 'the House of Judah' – that is, in particular, it does not apply to 'non-Torah-doing Gentiles' (the constituency of Paul's 'Gentile Mission'). As it will also turn out, it is eschatological – that is, it concerns 'the Last Times'/'Last Things.'[12]

We have already demonstrated that the issue here is 'circumcision,' and through it, attachment to the Law of Moses. But this is made even clearer at the end of Galatians 6:11 above. Here too Paul says:

> See in what large letters I have written you in my own hand: 'As many as desire to make a show of (or, in the language of 2 Corinthians 5:12, 'have an appearance in') the flesh, these force you to be circumcised, so that they may not be persecuted for the Cross of Christ' (thus)!

This is so direct and intimate, it is hard to gainsay. Plus it is completely uncharitable and the polemical vindictiveness, it embodies, fairly takes one's breath away. Paul then goes on in 6:12–13 to reiterate the 'blood libel' charge, already encountered in 1 Thessalonians 2:14–15 above. Though we have referred to it before, this material from 1 Thessalonians, rarely if ever remarked by most commentators, is so important for early Christian history and, for that matter, Islam succeeding it (where it has been picked up and repeated ad nauseam – even in the modern world – as an authentic statement of 'the Prophet') that it is worth requoting in its entirety:

> For brothers, you have become the imitators of the Assemblies of God in Judea which are in Christ Jesus (his 'Christ Jesus' vocabulary, obviously typifying, as it were, 'Gentile Christianity' though not 'Jewish'), because you also suffered the same things from your own countrymen (in this context, clearly meaning the 'Jewish' or 'Hebrew' Jerusalem Community of James the Just) even as they from the Jews, who both killed the Lord Jesus and their own Prophets (an accusation being both patently untrue and a terrible distortion of history, yet one hears it, despite its baselessness, mindlessly repeated – particularly in the Koran – by those completely ignorant of the subject around the world even today. Nor will it cease germinating its maleficent consequences until it is either retracted or corrected – moreover, here, too, 'the Lord' notation again, 'the Lord Jesus' perhaps being just the

slightest bit different from that of the '*Christ Jesus*' preceding it here and elsewhere in Paul) *and expelled you* (something, we have seen, Josephus' '*Essenes*' did to malefactors and backsliders[13]) *and do not please God and are the Enemies of all Mankind* (again '*the Enemy*' accusation made against Paul in '*Ebionite*' literature and possibly even in James 4:4 above, about which Paul in Galatians 4:16 is himself not completely ignorant – *now inverted* or *reversed*).

The difference is that in Galatians, Paul applies this deicide accusation not to Jews as a whole as in 1 Thessalonians 2:15–16 above, but pointedly to persons seemingly within the very '*Assembly*' or '*Movement*' itself like James (although, as just indicated, there is a hint of something of this kind, too, in the 1 Thessalonians 2:14 passage just cited).

To pick up again from Galatians 6:12–13 and to repeat, as Paul puts this:

> *They want to force you to be circumcised so that they can escape persecution for the Cross of Christ* (if Paul were not venerated as a '*Saint*' by perhaps over half the world, an objective observer might be forgiven for thinking this man is not only unbalanced, but actually mad. In fact, if one listens to the timbre of the voice, sad as it may be to have to say, the way this accusation comes across – as already previously remarked – in an earlier environment, now hopefully past, he might even be thought of as sounding like nothing so much as an incipient fascistic propagandist). *For even though they are circumcised, they themselves do not keep the Law. They want you to be circumcised, so they can boast in your flesh* (here again, he is repeating the language of 2 Corinthians 5:12 above and sad, again too, as it may be to say, one can unfortunately definitely hear the cadences or see '*the seed*'s, as it were, of such provocative and alarming propaganda here).

Again we can recognize in allusions such as '*keeping the Law*' and '*circumcision*' the parameters of the '*Zadokite*' Movement as delineated in Ezekiel and elaborated in the Damascus Document and Habakkuk *Pesher*, not to mention an echo of the same argument with Peter and others, Paul had the temerity to call '*hypocrites*' – an accusation with which he began the whole unseemly diatribe from Galatians 2:13 onwards.

This is a terrible libel for, along with 1 Thessalonians 2:14–15 above, it both begins the '*Deicide*'/'*Blood libel*'-accusation and strikes at the very motives of the '*Servants of Righteousness*' themselves like James who actually made up *the Leadership of* '*the Jerusalem Assembly*.' Here too is contained the same allusion to '*glorying*' or '*boasting*' in external '*appearance and* not in the heart' ('boasting in your flesh' or 'making a show of appearance,' as Galatians 6:12–13 would put it), we just encountered in 2 Corinthians 5:12 above. That he is speaking in exactly the same vocabulary of Ezekiel 44:5–7's 'uncircumcised in heart and flesh' allusion – so important to the imagery at Qumran above but, as per his (Paul's) wont, now used to opposite effect – is also undeniable.

It is the view of this book that he is also speaking about the same persons who considered him 'the Enemy' in Galatians 4:16 because, as Paul saw it, he was telling his communities 'the Truth' – that is to say, he 'was not Lying' or not 'the Spouter of Lying.' As we saw, he calls such persons in Galatians 4:17–18 – manifestly playing on both the 'Enemy' terminology of the Pseudoclementines and Gospels and their own sobriquet of 'Zealots'[14] – 'zealous to exclude' and 'zealous after' (as it were, Paul's own communities), but not 'zealous in the right (way),' meaning obviously, 'as they should be.' In these allusions in Galatians – which also play on the 'cutting off' language in Column Three of the Damascus Document about the Children of Israel being 'cut off' in the wilderness for 'eating blood'[15] – he concludes, expressing the hope and actually caricaturing, as we saw as well, 'circumcision' in a fairly ribald manner, that they would, 'themselves cut off' (5:11–12).

This exactly parallels the 'Galilean' teacher at the beginning of Josephus' all-important Book Twenty of the Antiquities, who finds Queen Helen's son Izates – the recipient in our view of the Qumran 'Letter' or 'Letters' known as 'MMT' – reading the words of the Torah of Moses, but not understanding their true import; or, to put this another way (as James 2:10 would have it), 'keeping the whole Law but stumbling over one small point' – language also being parodied, including the allusion to 'stumbling block,' in these passages from Galatians 5:6–26 here in Paul above.[16] When Izates hears this criticism, it will be remembered, he and his brother Monobazus immediately circumcise themselves.[77] The person in this episode advocating the opposite position (that is, conversion without 'circumcision') was, it will be remembered as well, someone by the name of 'Ananias,' the name of a known associate of Paul he supposedly first encounters in Acts 9:10–17 – tendentiously or otherwise – on a 'street called the Straight at the house of Judas' in Damascus and of a person, too, who was a central figure in the 'Agbarus' correspondence as discovered and translated by Eusebius. This is to say nothing about the whole tangle of materials, just reviewed above, relating to the 'Prophet' Josephus calls 'Jesus ben Ananias' and the several oracles in this period – two attributed to 'Agabus' – relating both to Paul's (and probably Ananias') purported 'famine relief' activities and the equally curious tradition of the 'Pella flight' of James' '*Jerusalem Church*' followers after his death.

Paul's Attacks on '*the Zealots*' and '*the Children of the Flesh*'

These passages from Paul are so full of evident pain and feelings of self-pity and inferiority – in some instances, as we have seen, even verging on the maniacal – they are almost embarrassing to read. The '*boasting*' or '*glorying*' they incorporate gains further momentum in 2 Corinthians 11:10 where he contends, '*the Truth of Christ is in me*' – another of these '*vainglorious*' statements such as that in Galatians 1:15–16 where he insists (unmistakably, again, in competition with James) that '*God chose me from my mother's womb and called me by His Grace to reveal His Son in me.*' He insists, as well, that he does not intend to cease '*boasting*' about himself '*in all the regions of Achaia*' – clearly a favorite locus of his activities.

It is in this context that he accuses '*those claiming equality with us in what they boast of*' as being '*Pseudo-Apostles*' and '*Lying workmen disguising themselves as Apostles of Christ*' (11:13). Here we get another typical Qumran play on the idea of '*work*'/'*service*'/or '*mission*,' which in Hebrew is expressed by the word '*ʿavodah*,' and '*works*' of a more eschatological kind – at Qumran, '*maʿasim*,' based on the Hebrew root '*to do*' or '*doing*' as, for instance, in '*the Doers of the Torah*' just alluded to in the Habakkuk *Pesher* above and in parallel usages in the Letter of James.[18] Both, therefore, are parodied in the conclusion in 2 Corinthians 11:15 above by his threat, '*whose End shall be according to their works.*' Not only is this distinction between '*work*' in the sense of '*service*' or '*mission*' and '*works*' of a more soteriological kind clearly drawn concerning '*the Liar*''s activities as opposed to those of '*the Righteous Teacher*' in Qumran texts such as the Habakkuk *Pesher* where even '*the Lying Spouter*''s '*vaingloriousness*' is evoked[19] but in these pregnant passages from 2 Corinthians, aside from the harshness of his malediction, Paul shows his awareness, as we can now see, of the doctrinal contrasts and shifts implicit in language of this kind.

Having said this, Paul goes on to continue '*boasting*' about all his sufferings and privations (again evoking, as above, '*the Lord*' designation):

> *What I say, I do not say according to the Lord, but in folly in the conceit in this boasting. Since Many boast according to the flesh, I will boast too* (we have already seen above both whom he means by the '*Many*' as well as '*those who boast according to the flesh*' – 11:16–18).

Here, of course, he is not speaking about the more spiritualized '*Children of God*' or '*Children of the Promise*' reckoned instead of '*the Children of the flesh*' in the more Gentilized allegorical scheme of '*Salvation*,' we have already encountered in Romans 9:8; but more of what Ezekiel 44:5–7 means by '*circumcision of the body*' – this combined with the additional implication of '*nationality*' or '*race*,' what he will also go on to refer to in Philippians 3:5 below as '*genous*.'

Even before this, however, in Philippians 3:3 he is still emphasizing the bodily '*circumcision*'-aspect of the allusion when he characterizes himself as being '*of the circumcision*,' albeit in his case and the case of those following him, qualifying this and retracting it somewhat with the proviso,

> *who serve God in (the) Spirit and boast in Christ Jesus* (again we understand what he is '*boasting*' about here, the spiritualizing thrust of which could not be clearer) *and do not trust in the flesh* (this could not be clearer either and we are back to his favorite reservation – *not trusting* in either *circumcision* or, true cosmopolitan that he is, '*Genous*'/'*Nationality*' or '*Race*').

Showing his sensitivity on this whole subject, in the very next line in Philippians 3:4 he steps back somewhat – in his usual strophe/antistrophe/epode rhetorical approach (the compositional structure, basically, of the Greek lyric ode) – from his contentious competitiveness:

> *For I too trust in the flesh, but if another trusts in the flesh* (here he is, once again, evoking *the Leadership of the-Jerusalem-Church*,' '*Hebrew*' '*Super Apostles*,' '*trusting in the flesh*'), *I more*.

It is at this point in 3:5 that he immediately, as we have seen, follows this up with his famous statement about '*being circumcised on the Eighth Day*,' '*a Hebrew of the Hebrews*,' '*of the Race*' or '*Genous of Israel*,' but not significantly – and this is important – '*a Jew of the Jews*,' that is, '*a Jew*' or '*Jewish*' *per se*.[20] As we have been suggesting, his claim and the one of all probable '*Herodians*' like him[21] is rather that of being of '*the Tribe of Benjamin*' and, although not explicitly so stated, the implication is certainly not of descent from '*the Tribe of Judah*' or being '*of the House of Judah*,' as the Damascus Document and the Habakkuk *Pesher* would so archaically refer to it.[22] In fact, regardless of his reference to himself in 3:3 as being '*of the circumcision*,' '*being circumcised on the Eighth Day*' would have been true for all those descended from either '*Israel*' or '*Judah*' – and, for that matter, probably *all* '*Herodians*' whether making '*Edomite*' or '*Benjaminite*' claims as well. Moreover, because of mutual descent from one '*Bela*' – whether in Esau's genealogy in Genesis or Benjamin's[23] – '*Benjaminite*' and '*Edomite*' claims would have been seen as more or less equivalent.[24]

In talking about these things in Philippians 3:6, Paul also, once again, evokes the denominative '*zeal*' – as always used negatively and this time alluding to himself and expressed as his own '*zeal*' in '*persecuting the Assembly*' *of God* (note the precision of his vocabulary here). He did the same in Galatians 1:14 after, significantly, assuring the '*brothers*' in 1:10–12 that not only was he *not* '*seeking to please men*,' but the Gospel he taught '*was not according to man*.' Nor had he '*received it from (any) man*,' but '*was taught it*' directly '*from a Heavenly Revelation* ('*Apocalypseos*' again) *of Jesus Christ*.'

Here in Galatians 1:13–14, he again studiously avoids calling himself '*Jewish*,' but rather appears to parody others making, no doubt, a similar claim to the '*zeal*,' '*zealousness*,' or '*zealotry*' just noted above (as, for example, those in Acts 21:20's probably accurate characterization of the greater part of James' '*Jerusalem Church*' followers as '*Zealots for the Law*' / '*Zelotai tou Nomen*') in describing how advanced he was

> at one time in the Jewish Religion ('*Judaismo*' as he calls it, one of the first perhaps to do so) *when (he) was beyond measure persecuting and ravaging the Assembly of God* (once again here, the same vocabulary as Philippians 3:6 above and clearly meaning '*the Jerusalem Church*' of James the Just[25]) –

then directly after that in Galatians 1:14, describing how he

> was progressing in Judaism ('*Judaismo*' again) *beyond many contemporaries of (his) own Race* (again '*Genous*' – does he mean once more here, '*Herodians*' who, though not really '*Jewish*' or born '*Jews*,' affected a kind of '*Judaism?*') *being even more abundantly zealous* (the word he uses now actually is '*zelotes*' – the cognomen too, according to Luke, of one of Jesus' '*Apostles*') *for the Traditions of my Fathers*.

Here, one might legitimately ask which '*Fathers*' and the idea of Paul as a convert to '*Judaism*' really does begin to make sense as, once again, however one reads this, there is no specific claim to *being born* '*Jewish*' as such. On the contrary, he studiously seems to avoid it and his sudden use of the expression '*advancing*' or '*progressing in Judaism beyond many of (his) contemporaries*' is curious indeed. Nor does he make any claim to being '*Jewish*' or '*a Jew*' in any other part of the corpus attributed to him. As against this, however, one should have regard to the assertion in 1 Corinthians 9:20: '*and to the Jews, I became as a Jew*' – here he does actually use the denotation '*Jew*,' while at the same time making it clear *he never really was* '*a Jew*' *as such* – that is, all the time he appears to be both *alluding to* and, at the same time, *covering up his* '*Herodian*' origins.

However this may be, *The Traditions of the Fathers* (*The Pirke Abbot*) was, as already remarked, a key juridical basis of Pharisaic *cum* Rabbinic Judaism though not, significantly, of Qumran.[26] After reiterating this same genre of non-genealogical type claim in Philippians 3:5 – that of being '*according to Law, a Pharisee*' – it is at this point, as we just saw, that he again evokes the '*zeal*' usage. Once more, he reverses it and uses it pejoratively, much as he did in the run-up to Galatians 1:14 above, to deride '*Zealotry*'; and in 4:17–18 after that, where he describes with not a little bitterness how his presumable '*Zealot*' colleagues undermined his teaching against the Law so that his communities abandoned him and began to see him as '*their Enemy*.'[27] Referring once again to '*the Assembly*' (*Ecclesian*), he has just referred to in Galatians 1:16, meaning of course '*the Jerusalem Community*' of James the Just (the greater part of whose supporters, as we just saw, '*were all Zealots for the Law*'); in Philippians 3:6, incorporating the same negative sense as Galatians 1:13, he now puts this a little more cryptically, while all the time still parodying his '*Zealot*' opponents: '*according to zeal* ('*zelon*'), *persecuting the Assembly* (*of God*).' Though for a change he is being straightforward and speaking guilelessly, in the very next line (again a kind of antistrophe), the dissimulation or obfuscation resumes with: '*according to Righteousness which* (*is*) *in* (*the*) *Law, having become blameless*.' What can he possibly mean by this? Whatever else, he is – as at Qumran – at least *associating* '*Righteousness*' *with* '*the Law*.'

Despite this admission, his contempt for the '*Circumcision Party*,' with which he commenced this particular series of allusions in Philippians 3:2 is palpable; and for some reason he calls them, probably either derisively or facetiously, '*those of the Concision*' (meaning '*those of the Cutting*' or '*the Cutting off*,' that is, '*beware of*' or '*watch out for the Concision*' or '*the Concision Party*') which is, therefore, patently the same party he is attacking in Galatians 2:12 and 4:7–6:15). Not only does he, yet again, in Philippians 3:2, call them '*Evil workmen*,' making the links with the '*Deceitful*' or '*Lying workmen*' and '*Pseudo-Apostles*' of 2 Corinthians 11:13–15 explicit; whether intentionally or otherwise, he even employs a new allusion, namely that of the '*dogs*' we have so assiduously been following, that is, '*beware of dogs*,' warning against them – meaning both the '*Evil workmen*' and '*the Concision Party*' – and *referring to them as* '*dogs*'! But in Galatians 5:11–15, when talking about '*circumcision*,' '*the flesh*,' presumably *the Circumcisers* '*themselves cutting off*' – and just after evoking James' '*you shall love your neighbor as yourself*' – Paul, speaking of '*biting and devouring one another*' (the '*dogs*' metaphor again), warns – as we have seen – of '*being consumed*.' Once again, it is impossible to know whether the linkage evoked by these allusions is simply accidental or he is aware of the analogues; but an allusion, such as that in Philippians 3:2, especially when looked at in the context of statements about such '*dogs*' as relating to the '*Salvationary*' state of Gentiles in both Matthew and Mark, is simply breathtaking.

More Attacks on '*the Children of the Flesh*'

That being said, in his run-up to his conclusion in Romans 9:8–9, just alluded to above, about '*the Children of the flesh*' not being '*the Children of God*' while, on the other hand, recommending '*the Children of the Promise be reckoned in place of the seed*' ('*seed*' here, as '*flesh,*' meaning genealogical descendants); Paul picks up all these themes again. These include being '*kinsmen according to the flesh*' (Romans 9:3), '*the seed of Abraham,*' and '*the seed of Isaac*' (9:7) – a favorite formulation. In this regard, it should be appreciated that '*Edomites*' or '*Idumaeans,*' too, could with some legitimacy, biblically-speaking, characterize themselves as '*Children of Abraham*' and/or '*of Isaac*'; but not, most notably, '*of the House of Judah,*' '*Jews,*' or even '*Jacob*' or '*Israel*' – '*Esau*' or '*the Edomites*' being of '*the seed of Abraham*' and '*Isaac*' but not, significantly, of '*Jacob*'. '*Jacob*' is a character Paul only mentions twice, both in Romans and both a little pejoratively. The first almost in the very next line and this to gainsay (after having called, '*Isaac our father*' in 9:10) the passage from Malachi 1:2–3: '*Jacob I have loved and Esau I have hated*' (9:13); the second, two chapters later (11:25–28), in a fairly free translation of Isaiah 59:20 on '*the Redeemer*' who '*shall come out of Zion*' to explain how '*all Israel*' could be the '*Enemies*' ('*of God*') – namely, because of their ('*Jacob*''s) *ungodliness*' which '*the Deliverer*'/'*Redeemer*' would '*turn away*' (in Isaiah 59:20–21, which rather speaks of '*Covenant,*' '*Spirit,*' and Jacob's '*seed's seed forever,*' this is '*pardoning sin in Jacob,*' the same words that Column Twenty of the Damascus Document uses to describe how '*the Penitents from sin in Jacob kept the Covenant of God*'!).[29]

Likewise, where '*Jews*' in particular – the descendants of this '*Jacob*' or '*Israel*' – are concerned, throughout the corpus attributed to him, Paul never fails to refer to them in the most negative manner imaginable – a manner he never uses when speaking about the descendants of either '*Abraham*' or '*Isaac.*'[29] In Romans generally, unlike in either Galatians, 1 and 2 Corinthians, or Philippians, it should be kept in mind, he is at his most guarded and conciliatory best (though not always, as just illustrated, successfully) attempting to present his rather contemptuous views of '*Israel the seed,*' '*Jews,*' and '*Judaism*' in as inoffensive and ambiguous a manner as possible. In this Letter, unlike some others, what he is clearly most concerned about is people, such as the '*some from James*' in Galatians and their colleagues – probably '*of the Concision*'/'*Circumcision*' as Philippians would have it – or, as Galatians 2:4 would: '*coming in by stealth and spying on the liberty we enjoy in Christ Jesus, so that they might reduce us to bondage.*'

In Romans 9:8 he actually makes the comments about '*the Children of God*' or '*the Children of the Promise being reckoned instead of the seed*' after alluding to such pivotal terminologies as '*those who love God*' (8:28 – again the second part of the '*Righteousness*'/'*Piety*' dichotomy), alluded to in James 2:5 as well, followed by '*separating*' – here '*separating us from the love of Christ*' – another clever rhetorical reversal (8:35), '*Justification*' (8:30ff. – a variation on the '*Righteousness*' part of the above dichotomy and based, of course, on the crucial Isaiah 53:11 passage, '*My Servant the Righteous One will justify Many*' or '*make Many Righteous*'), and, perhaps most importantly, yet again the assertion, '*I lie not*' (9:1), directly linking up, as we shall see, with the name of the ideological adversary of '*the Righteous Teacher*': '*the Liar*,' '*Spouter*,' or, as Column One of the Damascus Document would put this most graphically perhaps, '*the Scoffer*' who '*poured out upon Israel the waters of Lying.*'[30]

We have, in fact, already encountered Paul's defensiveness on the subject of '*Lying*' twice before – once at a crucial juncture in Galatians 1:20 when describing how, contrary to the tendentious portrayal in Acts 9:27–29, he was '*unknown by sight to the Churches in Christ in Judea*,' '*having of the other Apostles*' met only '*Peter*' and '*James the brother of the Lord*'; and again in 2 Corinthians 11:31 right before his description – also gainsaying Acts 9:23's equally tendentious picture of '*the Jews plotting together to kill him*' – of how he was let down the walls of Damascus '*in a basket*' to escape '*the Ethnarch*' of the '*Arab*' King Aretas who '*was wishing to arrest*' him.

As in the comments he makes in Romans 9:8, which were also made after a whole series of allegorizations, he arrives at the same conclusion in Galatians 4:28. There, he also compared himself and his fellow congregants to '*Isaac*,' viz., '*we, brothers, like Isaac are Children of the Promise*,' thereby confirming the connection of this '*Isaac*' allusion to '*the Children of the Promise*' above in Romans. This in Galatians 4:22–31 came, it will be recalled, at the end of another series of sometimes outrageous allusions. In these, after starting with '*being born according to the Spirit*,' and '*the Children of the free*'/'*free woman*' and claiming simply to be citing '*Scripture*,' he rather cynically and again a little disingenuously (substituting '*son of the freewoman*' for Sarah's '*my son*') quotes Sarah's words in Genesis 21:10: '*cast out* (*ekbale* – as presumably he was himself from either '*the Essenes*' or those at Qumran[31]) *the slavewoman and her son*'! Nevertheless, though ostensibly talking about '*Agar*,' whom he identifies with '*Mount Sinai in Arabia*' which he admits '*corresponds to presentday Jerusalem*'; it is clear that, by '*the Children of the slave woman*,' he means '*the Jews*,' '*born* – as he puts it again so tortuously (such things being '*allegories*') – *of the flesh*' and *attached*, as he sees them to be, to '*the Law*' or '*Torah of Moses*.'[32]

For Romans 9:8, as we just saw, these same '*Children of the flesh* (meaning again, of course, '*Israelites*' or '*Jews*') *are not the ones who are the Children of God*' but, rather, it is '*the Children of the Promise*' – just equated in Galatians 4:29 with '*the Children of Isaac*'; and in Romans 9:8, now with '*the Children of God*' – again, of course, meaning Paul's new '*Gentile Christian*' converts or '*Community*,' that are '*to be reckoned as the Children of the seed*.' The expression '*reckoned*' being used here is, to be sure, the very same '*reckoned*' or '*counted for*' used in connection with the description of Abraham's '*Faith being reckoned to him as Righteousness*' in Genesis 15:6 – employed in such a pivotally-conclusive theological manner by Paul in Galatians 3:6 – or, as Romans 4:2–5 and James 2:21–24 would rephrase it, again folding the terminology of Isaiah 53:11 into it – '*justifying him*.' All of this is the most clever (albeit at times somewhat facile) verbal polemics and, to reiterate, it is not surprising that it has both captivated and dazzled generations of adherents and all-too-easily overawed well-meaning and believing, yet rhetorically-unskilled, partisans ever since.

The '*Many*' who '*boast according to the flesh*,' he is referring to in these telling lines from 2 Corinthians 11:10–18 above, certainly cannot easily be distinguished from '*the Many*' making up the rank and file of Qumran '*Community*' Membership, as we have been trying to explain, the recipients presumably of the '*justifying*' activity of '*the Righteous Teacher*' as per the scheme of Isaiah 53:11 ('*My Servant the Righteous One justifying*' or '*making Many Righteous*') as well. As Paul continues this note of '*boasting*' two lines further along in 2 Corinthians 11:20:

> *For, being intelligent, you gladly bear fools, for you gladly bear anyone reducing you to bondage, devouring you.*

Here again, of course, again we have the same '*devouring*' of the '*biting and devouring*' passage from Galatians 5:15 above. Nor can there be any doubt of either the context or meaning of this gibe as well. Again, Paul means by this '*slavery*' or '*bondage*,' as in both Romans and Galatians above – now he is using it in 2 Corinthians 11:20 as well – '*bondage*' or '*slavery to the Law*' and its most contentious derivative, '*bondage to circumcision*.' Aside from the whole relationship of this kind of imagery to the '*dogs*' allusion of Philippians 3:2 above, it also reverses the kind of '*eating*' the Habakkuk *Pesher* was talking about, to say nothing of the '*Balaam*'/'*Belial*'/'*Bela^c*' language running through the literature of this period in general.[33]

In the Scrolls, as will be recalled, the language of '*eating*' or '*consuming*' actually mean '*destruction*.' It was applied, particularly in the Habakkuk *Pesher* again, to 'the *Kittim*' or, as we have argued, the Romans, who were described as '*eating*' or '*consuming all the Peoples year by year*',[34] as it was to some extent the '*swallowing*,' '*consuming*,' or '*destruction*' of the Righteous Teacher and his followers – denoted as '*the Poor*.'[35] In Rabbinic literature, the same connotation, '*devouring*' or '*consuming*,' arose out of the description there of the analogue of '*Belial*' or '*Belaʿ*' – '*Balaam*,' one of the *Talmud*'s several '*Enemies of God*'[36] – as his name is split into its constituent parts, '*Ballaʿ*'-'*Am*,' specifically defined as '*swallowing*' or '*consuming the People*.' Again, one should note, the inversion or reversal above of what Paul is saying is happening to his communities in 2 Corinthians 11:20, in which he also uses the term '*devouring*' but, as usual, to opposite effect.

At this point Paul utterly *loses control over his 'tongue*' – another important imagery, again both in the Letter of James and at Qumran, generically related to, at least, where the latter is concerned, the '*spouting*'/'*Lying*'/'*Spouter of Lying*' imagery there.[37] At this point in 2 Corinthians 11:21–23, too, Paul is speaking – as in Philippians 3:5 and Romans 9:6 – directly to the '*Israelites of the flesh*' or '*by Race*:'

> But if anyone may be daring (I am speaking in foolishness), then I am daring too. Hebrews are they, so am I. Israelites are they, so am I (again no 'Judeans'/ 'the House of Judah'/or 'Jews' here). The seed of Abraham are they, so am I. The Servants of Christ are they (I am speaking as besides myself), I much more (here his '*vainglory*' as his sense of inferiority creeps in). I have labored more abundantly (again '*work*' in the sense of '*labor*' or '*Mission*' as opposed to '*works*' in the sense of '*doing*' of the Law') and in stripes beyond measure.

Paul really is losing control of his '*tongue*' here. Not only do we again have the allusion, '*measure*,' to some extent reversing the sense of '*those measuring themselves by themselves*' of 10:12; but the passage should be compared, of course, with 11:13–15 earlier where, instead of '*the Servants of Christ*,' he uses the imagery of '*Righteousness*' to compare '*the Servants of Satan*' with '*the Servants of Righteousness, whose end shall be according to their works*'! As we have already several times remarked, the play in this last on the '*works*' highlighted in the Letter of James and, for that matter, the whole vocabulary of '*works Righteousness*' at Qumran should be obvious. Again, there can be little doubt whom he is talking about here even though generations of scholars have attempted to avoid such conclusions and, intentionally or otherwise, temporized in this regard. With the Dead Sea Scrolls now at our disposal, one should perhaps temporize no longer.

In describing his so-called '*labors*' (again, the Qumran language of '*mission*'/'*toil*'/or '*work*' as opposed to '*works*'[38]) and how he '*worked harder,*' Paul also includes '*five times forty (stripes) minus one I received from the Jews*' (11:24). Just as in Philippians 3:5 above, where he seems deliberately to talk in terms of '*the Tribe of Benjamin,*' '*the Race of Israel,*' or '*the Hebrews*' but not '*the Jews,*' Paul does not appear here, as just signaled, even to reckon himself among '*the Jews*' *as a* '*Nation*' or '*People*' at all (concomitantly, the same can be said for the way 'Jesus' is presented in the Gospels or '*Stephen*' in Acts[39]) and, among the dangers he has endured, he also specifically cites '*dangers from false brothers*' (11:26).

Nor can there be any doubt that his interlocutors, as in Galatians and 1 Corinthians above, despite innumerable attempts by scholars to prove otherwise, are none other than the Leading Apostles ('*the Apostles of Surpassing Degree*') of '*the Jerusalem Church*' – in our view, here and at Qumran, those who *really were* '*Servants of Righteousness*'! Paul sums this up very neatly a second time in the next Chapter in 2 Corinthians 12:11 when, more or less bringing this whole immoderate diatribe against '*letters of recommendation*' to an end, he insists that '*in nothing*' was he '*behind the Apostles of the Highest Rank.*' This is approximately the same position he adopted in Galatians 2:2–6, when speaking about '*those* (in '*the Jerusalem Assembly*') *reputed to be Pillars*' or '*those reputed to be something*' (meaning, '*James, Cephas, and John*'), whose '*importance,*' as far as he was concerned, '*nothing conferred.*'

'Cursed be Anyone Hung upon a Tree'

Right from the start of Galatians Paul emphasizes that, like his '*Apostleship,*' the Gospel which he preached was '*not according to man*' (1:11), but rather that he '*was taught it by a (Heavenly) revelation of Jesus Christ*' (*apocalypseos* – 1:12). In saying these things, however, he not only demonstrates what a poor '*foot-soldier*' (as he puts it in Philippians 2:25) he was, but just how unbending he could be, incapable of taking orders or obedience – just the opposite of what was required, for instance, at Qumran. But '*obedience,*' as the Letter the Pseudoclementine *Homilies* attribute to James makes clear, was the essence too of what was expected in order to receive '*Apostolic Certification*' and '*be recommended.*'[40]

As the Community Rule at Qumran puts this, demonstrating an equal rigidity to the way James is portrayed in the prelude to the Pseudoclementine *Homilies* and employing the language of '*House*' or '*Community of God,*' we have already seen Paul employing in 1 Corinthians 3:9–17 and 2 Corinthians 5:1–2:

Every man of the House will know his Standing (or '*rank*') *in the Community of God according to Eternal design. And no man of the House shall move down from his rank or move up from his allotted place. Because all will be in a Community of Truth…the Sons of the Eternal Foundation* (or '*Secret*').[41]

But as far as Paul is concerned in Galatians 1:8, ostensibly in response to the '*some who trouble*' his communities '*desiring to subvert the Gospel of Christ*' (later identified in Galatians 2:12 as the '*some from James*'):

Even if we or an Angel from Heaven should preach a Gospel to you contrary to what we announced to you, let him be accursed (Galatians 1:8 – compare this with 2 Corinthians 11:14 above about how '*even Satan can transform himself into an Angel of Light*').

In fact later in Galatians 3:10–13, Paul builds this whole '*cursing*' concept into the very fabric of his presentation of his new doctrine of how '*Christ redeemed us from the curse of the Law.*' He bases this on the somewhat disingenuous notion – quoting a version of Deuteronomy 27:26 and again evoking the language of '*works Righteousness*' – that '*as Many* (the '*Many*' language of the Scrolls again) *as are of the works of the Law are under a curse*' (and the language of '*the works of the Law*'). As is usually the case with the way he reproduces biblical writ – which, for the purposes of the argument he very often takes out of context and oversimplifies – this is certainly, even where polemical allegorizing is concerned, both an incredible and a fairly tendentious representation of the concepts involved.

Then, alluding to '*the Righteous shall live by Faith*' of Habakkuk 2:4 and the Habakkuk *Pesher* (the original, of course, being '*the Righteous shall live by his Faith*') and incorporating the '*doing*' concept, conspicuous throughout the Scrolls and in the Letter of James, he continues with the actual Deuteronomy 27:26 passage which he now works into his own:

Cursed be everyone who does not continue in all things which have been written in the Book of the Law to do them (Galatians 3:10 – the original in Deuteronomy 27:26 being '*the words*' or '*things of the*' or '*this Torah to do them*');

he then proceeds with his polemic that Christ

became for us a curse for it is written (this time quoting a version of Deuteronomy 21:23, again somewhat tendentiously) *cursed* (*be*) *everyone who hangs upon a tree* (Galatians 3:13).

While this is not the precise language of the Hebrew Deuteronomy it does, as we shall see, almost exactly reproduce the language of the Temple Scroll from Qumran.[42]

In the original version of this imprecation from Deuteronomy 21:22–23, the words 'upon a tree' are missing from the concluding statement that 'the hanged man' or 'the one who has been hung is accursed of God.' Even more to the point – the sense of both lines, when read together, is that someone whose 'body is hung upon a tree' for an entire twenty-four hour period is 'accursed of God' and it is this which results in, as Deuteronomy 21:23 would have it, the 'pollution' or 'defilement of the Land.'[43] In other words, 'hanging up the body' of an executed person – presumably to deter or as a cautionary example – was not in and of itself 'polluting' or 'defiling' and, therefore forbidden, unless (and this is an important 'unless') it extended beyond the duration of a single day. At that point, that is, if it remained a whole day and night, because the executed individual was denoted an 'accursed of God' (otherwise, presumably, he would not have been executed), it 'defiled the land.' To be sure this is a fine point, but an important one. As Deuteronomy 21:23 renders this, you must not allow 'his body to hang upon the tree overnight' – the 'body' being, as we shall emphasize further below, the relevant point – rather 'you must bury him the same day.' So it is clear, if the body was buried on the same day (regardless of whether or not the body was hung), there was no 'defilement' or, as the case may be, 'curse'; and the exemplary nature of the punishment was satisfied.

But Paul, as we just saw – for the purposes of his polemical dialectic and in the usual untrustworthy way he reproduces biblical proof-texts – conflates and collapses this into a single sentence, specifically, 'cursed (is) anyone who hangs upon a tree' which is not precisely what we have above and clearly misses the nuances of what Deuteronomy seems to have been trying to say. The latter is, in fact, clarified to much better effect in the Nahum Pesher from Qumran. That document makes it clear that 'hanging up of a man alive upon a tree' is the problem and here the key new word is 'alive.' In so doing it adds – in addition to the word 'alive' – another qualifying declaration, 'a thing formerly never done in Israel.'[44] The implication of the rest of the Pesher, about the 'vengeance' that would be taken on Israel because of this and 'the defilement of the Land' that would ensue, appears to be that, whatever curse was seen to be involved in this was now more the fault of the person perpetrating the hanging and not necessarily vice versa as Paul, somewhat disingenuously, rather presents it. It is this 'hanging a man up alive' not the 'hanging' per se which, to use words of Deuteronomy 21:23, 'defiled the Land' and brings about a terrible vengeance.

That being the case, two points emerge: 1) 'hanging up a man alive' was something '*not formally done in Israel.*' There is some question about the reconstruction here, but this is the most-widely accepted translation and, in fact, the only one that really makes any sense.[45] We can assume the individual being spoken of at this point in the *Pesher* to be Alexander Jannaeus (c. 103–76 BC) as he was portrayed in Josephus, and again, this is the normative interpretation of the passage.[46] It is interesting to consider that this is basically the time that '*crucifixion*' as a punishment first seems to have come to the attention of the reading public of the day, as it was being widely employed in a wholesale and rampant manner by the Romans against malefactors and insurgents on the mainland of Italy – in particular, during the Spartacus Uprising in 88 BC, a point with which Josephus is even familiar.[47]

2) It is '*because of*' this '*hanging (a man) up alive upon a tree*' that the next line of the biblical Nahum 2:12 is quoted: '*Behold I am against you saith the Lord of Hosts. I will burn up your multitudes etc.*,' again meaning, it is not because the man '*hung upon the tree*' is '*accursed*' but it is, rather, more the fact of his being '*hung up alive, a thing formerly not done in Israel,*' that will produce these devastating results – this and leaving the body in such an egregious condition for *more than a whole day.*

To sum up: the implication of both Deuteronomy 21:22–23 and the Nahum *Pesher* from Qumran is that it was permissible to hang someone up who had already been executed (as a caution, presumably, and a deterrent to others). Both agree on this, but '*the body*' *should not remain overnight*, that is, it was the '*hanging up overnight of the dead body*' that was the '*defiling*' activity and not the '*hanging up*' in and of itself. To this the Nahum *Pesher* then adds the new proposition of '*hanging up alive upon a tree*' because it had – and this is the writer's view – obviously suddenly become such an issue *in the First Century* BC *and the First Century* CE, though not previously. For his part, as per his usual *modus operandi* of taking citations or pieces of citations out of context, just so long as their superficial meaning suited his exegetical and polemical purposes, Paul refines this in Galatians 3:13 above into his new doctrinal and salvationary scheme of how '*Christ redeemed us from the curse of the Law*' – this, despite the fact that even in the Christian tradition as it has come down to us, '*Jesus*' is not presented as remaining '*overnight upon a tree.*'[48]

Furthermore the Temple Scroll, as we have now found it, varies the whole set of citations in Column 64:6–13 to develop an even more striking contemporary meaning. There, '*if a man slanders his People* – a point having particular relevance, as any fair-minded person might realize, where Paul is concerned – *and delivers his people to a foreign*' or '*a Gentile Nation*' (here the '*delivering up*' language occurs, just as in Gospel characterizations of what '*Judas Iscariot*' supposedly did to 'Jesus'; so there, yet again, we can see the same language in use as here in the Temple Scroll[49]) or '*does evil to his People*' in general – that is, if he is '*a Traitor*' (there is no parallel to this in Deuteronomy nor even in the Nahum *Pesher*, though the people Alexander Jannaeus '*hung up alive*' or '*impaled on stakes*' were manifestly considered by him to be '*Traitors*' and the Temple Scroll's startling new formulation unquestionably fits more updated times such as these[50]) – '*you shall hang him on a tree until he dies*'!

It is interesting that the new charge is now made explicit. It is not a negative injunction (that is, '*not to leave his body on the tree all night*') but, so deplorable were contemporary conditions evidently thought in this regard to be, it has now become a positive commandment. In fact the penalty, as it is being revamped in the Deuteronomy-like '*New Torah*' (as the Temple Scroll is generally thought by scholars to be, presumably in the First Century but, barring this, certainly in the Second Temple Period[51]) and given a whole new rider related to '*traitorous*' activities, is expanded even further with the addendum that

> *if a man, found guilty and under a death sentence, flees to the Gentiles* (cf. Acts' portrayal of Peter's similar flight in 12:17 – though I would consider the situation being described there not a little tendentious – or, for that matter, Paul's rescue by Roman troops in Acts 23:12ff.[52], probably a completely authentic portrayal) *and curses his People and the Children of Israel, you shall also hang him upon a tree until he dies* (n.b., again the positive directive and not the negative injunction – in the new light of this Temple Scroll, one can well understand why someone like Paul would have been so concerned about the issue, since he was himself now under direct liability).

But it is here that the usual caveat from Deuteronomy 21:23 above, though missing curiously enough from the Nahum *Pesher*'s presentation of the issue, is incorporated – a matter of which both Josephus and the authors of the Gospels are, it would appear, keenly aware:[53]

> *but his body* (once again, the Temple Scroll also makes it clear that it is '*the body*' which is the '*defiling*' problem) *shall not remain overnight upon the tree. Rather you shall bury him* (or '*it*') *the same day for...you must not pollute the Land which I am giving you as an inheritance.*[54]

So the Temple Scroll has, in fact, added one or several related infractions for which it was actually appropriate to '*hang a man alive upon a tree.*' This was not delineated in the previous '*Five Books of Moses*' or '*Torah*' to any extent – what Paul in Galatians 3:10 above calls '*the Book ('Biblio') of the Law*' – nor any other context of which I am aware.

Nor, if the Nahum *Pesher* is to be credited – and the author considers it should be – do there appear to have been any previous instances of the application of such a punishment (that is, '*hanging a man up alive*'). However this may be, it is a punishment with enormous ramifications for the period before us, when there were an incredible amount of malefactors who could meet this description of the Temple Scroll, both because of the attractiveness of Hellenistic cultural cosmopolitanism generally (a point made painfully clear even in the Maccabee books[55]) and the power of the Roman Empire – namely, '*cursing*' *one's own people*, '*slandering*' *them to foreign nations*, '*betraying*' *them*, and '*doing Evil to them*.'

How incredibly prescient and appropriate to the times we are considering, peopled by teachers such as Paul, turncoats like Josephus (though in the *Vita* he strives manfully to refute this[56]), Tiberius Alexander, Zachariah ben Bariscaeus (executed as a Traitor in the Temple by '*Zealots*' and his body '*cast down*' into the valley below – probably the original behind '*the blood of Zachariah ben Barachias*' allusion in Matthew 23:35 and Luke 11:51, '*murdered between the Temple and the altar*'[57]), Josephus' '*Saulos*,' Saulos' '*kinsmen*' Costobarus and Antipas the Temple Treasurer[58] and, for that matter, almost the whole Herodian family consisting of Agrippa II, Bernice, Drusilla, and Mariamme (who was first married to the son of the Herodian Temple Treasurer Helcias and Josephus' admirer in Rome Julius Archelaus and, later, another of Philo's nephews, one '*Demetrius*' – probably *Tiberius Alexander's brother*) – whether or not one considered them '*Jewish*' or '*Idumaean*' *Greco-Arabs*.

In the Temple Scroll, too, the following words are added at this point:

for accursed (is) everyone hung upon a tree...;[59]

but these, as we just saw, are almost the precise words Paul has reproduced in Galatians 3:13 above – '*cursed (is) everyone who hangs upon a tree*' – not the extant version of Deuteronomy 21:23, nor really that of the Septuagint either. Of course it is possible to argue, Paul is reproducing the words of the Septuagint here but, while conserving the phrase, '*hung upon a tree*,' common to it, the Temple Scroll, and Galatians, the extant Septuagint does not precisely read the way Paul reproduces it, nor does it match the Greek Paul uses.[160] In fact, Paul does not even reproduce the words of the extant Septuagint in the way he phrases Deuteronomy 27:26 above – for him, '*Cursed (is) everyone who does not continue*

in all things which have been written in the Book of the Law to do them,'
paralleling the *'cursed of God (is) anyone who is hung'* of Deuteronomy
21:23 above – and, in the writer's opinion, the words in the Temple Scroll
are a good deal closer to those Paul actually conserves than any of these.[61]

What does this mean? In the present writer's view – which admittedly might be wrong – *Paul knew the version of these matters circulating and
being reproduced at Qumran*, as he is familiar with much else of what we
now know was being written there.[62] Again, this is a conclusion of
immense proportions concerning which, some might disagree; but if
true, it has enormous implications. Of course, his concern here over this
penalty would be entirely appropriate as no one could have been a
greater *'slanderer of his People'* and *'turncoat'* than he – if indeed it was *'his
People'* (a matter about which, as we have been underscoring, he invariably temporizes). Even Josephus is not entirely his equivalent where
these things are concerned – though the two are similar; since Josephus
was clearly not trying to *'slander his People'* – at least not consciously (as
he himself struggles to make clear on several occasions) – the opposite.[63]

'Cursing' in the Documents at Qumran and in Paul

However this may be, a parallel emphasis on *'cursing'* is strong throughout the Qumran corpus only, as always, the signification is reversed – the
'curse,' as per the actual sense of Deuteronomy and not Paul's more antinomian one, being always upon the *'Turners-aside from the Way'* or those, as
we shall see, *'departing from the Laws of His Truth to walk either to the right or
to the left.'*[64] As this is put in the Last Column of the Damascus Document
found at Qumran (first published by Professor Wise and myself) at the
annual *'gathering of the inhabitants of the (wilderness) Camps in the Third
Month'* or *'Pentecost'* (not unlike the picture in Acts 21:21–27 of Paul
being obliged by James – also at *'Pentecost'* – to do a *'Nazirite'* penance of
some kind in the Temple) *to condemn anyone who 'breaks the boundary
markers' or 'to curse those departing to the right or (to the left of) the Torah'*[65]:

> *And in another place it is written, 'return to God with weeping and fasting.'*[66] *As
> for the person who rejects these Commandments* (here of course is another
> instance of the *'rejecting'* language, used throughout the Scrolls to charac-
> terize the position of the nemesis of *'the Righteous Teacher,' 'the Spouter of
> Lying' / 'Scoffer'*[67]) *which are in keeping with all the Laws found in the Torah of
> Moses* (what Paul in Galatians 3:10 above calls *'the Biblio of the Law'*); *he
> will not be reckoned among all the Sons of His Truth, for his soul has rejected the
> Foundations of Righteousness* (of course, what is being described here is a

'*penance*' or '*repentance*' of some kind and there is the use of the verb '*reckoned*' again[68]). *For rebellion, let him be expelled from the presence of the Many* (here the typical '*Essene*' expulsion practice, as we have seen, which we contend was pronounced upon people like Paul, not to mention these telltale allusions to '*the Law of Moses*,' '*the Many*,' and '*rebellion*').

The Priest Commanding the Many (the meaning here is '*the High Priest*' or '*the Opposition High Priest*' again which in the second half of the First Century, in our view, was '*the Mebakker*' or '*Bishop*' James, '*the High Priest of the Opposition Alliance*'[69]) *shall speak against him...and say:* '*You chose our Fathers and, to their seed* (here the same '*seed*' language Paul used in Romans 9:7–8, 11:1, 2 Corinthians 11:22, and Galatians 3:16–29 above), *You gave the Laws of Your Truth and the Ordinances of Your Holiness, which a man shall do and thereby live*' (*cf.* Leviticus 18:5 and Deuteronomy 4:1, 28:14, and 30:16–19 and note again the emphasis on the '*doing*' language, not to mention the allusions to '*live*' which Paul also makes such good use of in Galatians 2:20, 3:12, and 5:3 above).

And boundary markers were laid down for us (the same '*boundary markers*' with which CD began and which '*the Lying Scoffer*' '*removed*'[70]). *Those who cross over them, You curse* (the '*blessing* and *cursing*' of Deuteronomy 11:26–29, 27:13–28:46, and 30:19 above). *We, however, are Your Redeemed* (here Paul's '*redeemed us from the curse of the Law*' of Galatians 3:13 above, now reiterated in an entirely different, but perhaps the original context) *and the sheep of Your pasture* (Psalms 79:13, 95:7, and 100:3). *You curse the Breakers of them* ('*the Laws of Your Truth*' – here the '*Breaker*' allusion which pervades these materials, in particular, James 2:9–11 above) *while we uphold them* (*them* – again meaning '*the Laws of Your Truth*').

At this point comes the actual expulsion practice of '*the Essenes*:'[71]

Then he who was expelled must leave and whosoever eats with him (the '*table fellowship*' issue of the early Church together with the '*banning*' one, already elucidated above) *or asks after the welfare of the man who was excommunicated or keeps company with him* (the split between John Mark and Barnabas and Paul and Silas, according to Acts 13:13 and 15:37–39 above, and the whole scenario of the split delineated in Galatians 2:12–13, resulting in the final '*shunning*' of Paul), *that fact should be recorded by the Mebakker* ('*the Overseer*' or '*Bishop*') *according to established practice and the Judgement on him will be completed.*[72]

597

In the Community Rule, as we have already remarked, this kind of *'cursing'* reaches a crescendo and is fundamental, running through several columns. It takes place against a background of evocation of the *'two Ways' of 'Light'* and *'Darkness,'* expressed in terms of *'holding fast to the Covenant'* as opposed to *'breaking it'* or *'backsliding from it,'* very much resembling Paul in Galatians 5:15–26 and the early Christian work known as *The Didache.*[73] In Paul, this is expressed by the typical allusion to *'works of the flesh'* (sarcastically alluding, as we have seen, to *'circumcision,' ritual purity, dietary legislation,* and the like) as opposed to *'works of the Spirit'* or, as he revels in expressing it, *'living by the Spirit.'*[74] In the Community Rule, this *'cursing'* is directed against *'all the Men of the Lot of Belial'* – the counterpart of that *'Satan'* referred to by Paul in 2 Corinthians 11:14 above – and reads as follows:

> *Cursed be you without mercy because of the Darkness of your works. Be damned in the netherworlds of Everlasting Fire. May God not comfort you when you cry out to Him, nor forgive you by pardoning your sins* (again, in the 'Christianity' in the process of developing, 'Jesus' becomes the one *'to forgive'* or *'pardon your sins'*). *On the contrary, may He raise up His angry countenance to take Vengeance upon you* (here the usual *'vengeful'* attitude of Qumran – no *'peace-loving Essenes'* these) *and may you enjoy no peace!*[75]

Similar words, again embedded in a general *'curse'* directed against *'Belial'* and *'those of his Lot'* (probably to be seen as a term – depending on one's chronology – as inclusive of *'Herodians'* or, as the *Talmud* would put it as we have seen in its exposition of the name of one of its principal archetypical *'Enemies of God,' 'Balaam'*: *'Balla^c ha-^{c}Am'* or *'One who swallows'* or *'devours the People,'* which *'Herodians'* did most characteristically) are to be found in another document also first published by Professor Wise and myself in 1992, which I entitled after an allusion in the actual text, *'The Chariots of Glory,'* and which others now group under the heading 4Q*Berachot/Blessings.*[76] Probably originally part of the Community Rule, it contains a section abounding in the most fulsome and repeated *'cursing of Belial'* (for which reason I included the separate subtitle of: *'The Community Council Curses Belial'* to describe it[77]). So intense is it, it too is worth reproducing in its entirety:

> *The Community Council shall recite in unison, 'Amen, Amen.' Then (they) shall curse Belial and all his guilty Lot. And they shall answer and say, 'Cursed be Belial (in his Satanic scheme) and damned be he in his guilty rule. Cursed be all the Spirits (of his Lot* – here seemingly, again, Paul's *'Spirit'* language –

as always, with a kind of inverted signification, '*cursing*' people like him and not *vice versa*) *in their Evil schemes and may they be damned in the schemes of their unclean pollution* (again too, the anti-'*uncleanness*' and '*pollution*' position, as opposed to the opposite in Paul, Acts, and on the part of the New Testament's 'Jesus'). *Surely (they are of the) Lot of Darkness. Their punishment will be the Eternal Pit*' (the '*Pit*' language we saw above regarding Jesus' '*declaring all foods clean*' and his arguments with those he characterizes as '*Blind Guides*,' who shall themselves '*fall into a Pit*'). '*Amen, Amen.*' *And cursed by the Evil One in all his Dominions and damned be all the Sons of Belial* (the synonym clearly of those of '*the Lot of Darkness*') *in all their times of service until their consummation* (forever. '*Amen, Amen*').

And they are to repeat and say, '*Cursed are you, Angel of the Pit and Spirit of Destruction in all the schemes of your guilty intention (and in all the) abominable purposes and counsel of (your) Wickedness. And damned be you in (your) sinful dominion (and in your Wicked and guilty rule) together with all the Abominations of Sheol and the reproach of the Pit and with the humiliations of destruction with (no remainder or) forgiveness in the Fury of (God's) Wrath forever (and ever)* '*Amen. Amen.*' *And cursed be all who perform their Evil schemes* ('*Herodians*' such as Paul?), *who establish your Evil purposes (in their hearts against) God's Covenant, so as to (reject the words of those who seek) His Truth...* (here, not only do we have the language of '*rejection*' again, meaning of course, as ever, '*rejecting Mosaic Law*,' but also just a touch of the language of Paul in Galatians 4:17 above: '*So by speaking Truth to you, your Enemy have I become?*' It is interesting, too, that this kind of language is picked up in John 8:12–59, where '*Jesus*' is pictured in 8:15 as speaking about '*judging according to the flesh*'; in 8:45 as '*speaking the Truth*' and, famously, '*the Truth shall set you free*' – the '*freedom*'/'*bondage*' issue again – and the people in 8:48, who respond in terms of '*being Abraham's seed*,' think '*Jesus*' is '*a Samaritan*' and '*has a demon*,' i. e., he is either '*Simon Magus*' or '*the Taheb*,' but he escapes by '*hiding himself*' – 8:59).

I think the meaning is quite clear here and can be compared with the '*Light*' and '*Darkness*' imagery, not only of 2 Corinthians 11:14 about how even '*Satan*' goes around '*disguising himself as an Angel of Light*' and *those of his Lot '*transforming themselves into Servants of Righteousness*'; but 2 Corinthians 6:14–7:1 above as well, *comparing* '*Christ with Beliar*,' '*Light with Darkness*,' '*Righteousness with lawlessness*,' and '*the Temple of God with idols*'! Continuing in this vein and specifically evoking those '*entering the Covenant with idols on their hearts*,' itself totally relevant to Paul's positions in 1 Corinthians 8:1–13 and 10:18–21; the Community Rule prefaces the first passage quoted above with:

> *Cursed be you because of all your guilty works of Evil. May God deliver you up
> to torment* (this is the same '*delivering up*' language, we saw was used to
> express the application of such '*Anger*' to the '*Visitation*' by God for
> '*Vengeance*' in the Damascus Document[78] and also applied in the Tem-
> ple Scroll to the one who '*delivered up his People to a foreign*' or '*Gentile
> Nation*' – the same language the Gospels so exploit in portraying the
> '*treachery*' of the character portrayed under the catch-all pseudonym
> '*Judas Iscariot*' or '*the Iscariot*'[79]) *at the hand of* (here again, the '*hand of*'
> imagery of the War Scroll and other like-minded Qumran documents)
> *all the Avenging Avengers. And may you be commanded to destruction by the
> hand of all the Payers-back-of-Rewards* (this last will be the exact language
> used in the Habakkuk and Psalm 37 *Peshers* to describe the '*Vengeance*'
> that would be inflicted upon '*the Wicked Priest*' for what '*he did to the
> Righteous Teacher*' and his followers among '*the Ebionim*' or '*the Poor*').[80]

Where Paul is concerned, he repeats the '*curse*' with which he began
this whole excursus on '*cursing*' in Galatians 1:8 with even more inflexi-
bility in Galatians 1:9, when he answers the critique that was clearly
being directed against him of '*seeking to please men*' – paralleling similar
charges raised in James 3:2–4:4, in the section dealing with the '*violent
winds*' of '*the Tongue*'[81] and the '*mouth out of*' which '*issues forth* (both) *blessing
and cursing.*'[82] But unlike in the Community Rule and 4QBerachot above,
the '*cursing*' no longer has to do with '*backsliding*' or '*breaking the Law,*' but
teaching '*a Gospel*' *different from the one he is teaching* (in fact a '*contrary*' one):
'*If anyone announces to you a Gospel contrary to what you have received, let him
be accursed.*' Intolerance, even anathema then – as at Qumran (but as ever
to opposite effect and reversed) – was built into the fabric of his teaching. Nor was he unaware of this.

As a concomitant of the above discussion, we are in the situation now
of having to decide which version of events is accurate, the one presented by Paul himself or those claiming to write about Paul? The rule
of thumb, we have always followed is that, where there was a contradiction between the first-person witness of Galatians, other authenticated
Letters by Paul, and the overwritten, conglomerate third-person *melange*,
we have come to know as '*Acts*'; Galatians or its counterparts were to be
preferred. With this in mind we should, nevertheless, now turn to Acts'
account of the penultimate confrontation between Paul and James at the
so-called '*Jerusalem Council,*' since this is what most people think happened and this is what has come down to us.

21

'Re-erecting the Fallen Tent of David' and 'the Fountain of Living Waters'

The Qumran Parallels to the Speeches of Peter and James at '*the Jerusalem Council*'

Though for Acts 15:6, the so-called '*Jerusalem Council*' is a grandiose Assembly of the whole Church or, at least, the Council composed of '*Apostles and Elders*' (*Presbyteroi*); for Galatians 2:2 it is, as we have seen, a '*private*' visit Paul says he made – as a result of the ever-recurring '*apocalypsin*' he claims to be having – '*going up to Jerusalem with Barnabas and taking Titus*' with him to see the Central Three, '*James, Cephas, and John, those esteemed* (*as*) *Pillars*' whose importance for him, '*nothing conferred.*' The Dead Sea Scrolls, on this point anyhow (if relevant) back the position of Acts, for they have the man they call '*the Spouter*' or '*Man of Lying*' – if he and Paul can be connected – '*rejecting the Torah in the midst of their entire Congregation*' or '*Assembly*' ("*Edah*' – '*Church,*' the English equivalent for '*Ecclesia*' or '*Assembly*' in Greek).[1]

For Acts 15:3, surreal as it and the Gospels often seem, Paul and Barnabas,

> *pass through Phoenicia and Samaria, telling of the conversion of the Gentiles (Ethnon) and they caused great joy to all the brothers.*

But why Paul and Barnabas should have come this way or announced these things is difficult to imagine, since the more direct route from '*Antioch*' (if, indeed, they were coming from '*Antioch-on-the-Orontes*' in Northern Syria) would have been via Damascus and Jericho.

Where '*Samaria*' is concerned, as already suggested, there was probably a code of some kind at work concerning this locale. But the reference to '*Phoenicia*' probably reflects Paul's next visit to Jerusalem – in Acts, anyhow, his last – the one he makes in 20:15–21:3 laden with contributions he has collected in '*Achaia*' (*cf.* 1 Thessalonians 1:7–8, etc. above) when, having bypassed Ephesus,[2] he was rushing from Chios, Samos, and Miletus to Cos, Rhodes, and past Cyprus in order '*to be in Jerusalem in time for Pentecost.'* There it is specifically noted – and this *is* in *'the We Document'* – that *he landed at Tyre in Phoenicia and made his way down the coast to Caesarea* (21:1–3).

Where the actual portrayal of this *'Council'* in Chapter Fifteen is concerned, preceding the first intrusion of the *'We Document'* in 16:10, there are several correspondences in the two speeches Acts 15:7–33 pictures Peter and James as making, which – in addition to the James' *'rulings'* at the end of *'the Conference'* – further tie these to a number of documents from Qumran albeit, as is the usual case, inverted or reversed – in particular, the Damascus Document; but also a compendium of *'Messianic'* proof-texts relating to promises made to *'the House of David'* called in the jargon of the field, as already signaled above, *'The Florilegium.'* These, in turn, are tied – because of the *'Messianic'* nature of the vocabulary and allusions in them – to three other documents: the *'Son of God'* text; the fragment of the War Scroll identifying *'the Branch of David'* with *'the Nasi ha-ᶜEdah'* / *'the Leader of the Community'* or *'Church'* above; and the exposition of *'the Shiloh Prophecy'* (part of Jacob's final bequests to his children, in particular where this *'Prophecy'* is concerned, *'the House of Judah,'* in Genesis 49:10), which were all published together for the first time in a publicly accessible manner in 1991 in *The Dead Sea Scrolls Uncovered.*[3]

The first such correspondence comes in the speech Acts 15:7–11 pictures Peter as giving to the *'Assembled Apostles and Elders.'* Curiously in the speech by James that follows in 15:13–21, Acts depicts James, for some reason, as referring to Peter as *'Simeon'* not *'Simon.'* In other words, though possibly a copyist's error, this may not be the proverbial *'Simon Peter'* who, according to Acts 12:17, had already fled the country *with a death sentence on his head.* Nor even the so-called *'Cephas,'* whether the same as or different from *'Peter,'* but arguably, possibly, *'Simeon bar Cleophas,'* the second successor to 'Jesus' in Palestine and James' *'cousin germane'* – even, as we have suggested, *his second brother*[4] (in this regard, one should take particular note of the possible homophonic connection in Greco-Hebrew transcription of *'Cleophas'* / *'Cephas'* / and even *'Alphaeus'*).

Be these things as they may, at this point Peter *'having risen up* (words repeated in some of these prophecies[5]), *says'*:

> You know that from early days God chose from among us the Gentiles (again, literally *'Ethne'* / *'Peoples'*) were to hear by my mouth the word of the Gospel and to believe (as we shall see, this will be directly counter-indicated in the Damascus Document below) and the heart-knowing God bore witness to them (this, in fact, sounds suspiciously *'Pauline'*), giving them the Holy Spirit (as does this) as well as to us, and put no difference between us, having purified

their hearts by Faith (and especially this – *n.b.*, in particular, the significant allusion to '*purification*' or '*being purified*').

Here Peter – if it really is the '*Peter*' (we all assume it is) – as just indicated, yet again basically affirms the position of Paul's '*Gentile Mission.*' In doing so, he uses the '*heart*' imagery so important, not only to the '*fleshy tablets of the heart*' metaphor Paul uses in 2 Corinthians 3:2–3 above to describe the '*letter*' he sends from Christ '*with the Spirit of the Living God,*' but also, as we have seen, to Qumran, generally, particularly the Damascus Document.[6]

In the very First Column of the Cairo recension of this document, it is set forth that '*God has a dispute with all flesh* (again the '*flesh*' imagery of Ezekiel 44:5–7 and similar allusions in Romans and Philippians above as well as 2 Corinthians 3:2–3 just underscored) *and will do Judgement* (again note the use of the '*doing*' allusion here) *on all those who despise Him*' – this last, even possibly, '*blaspheme Him,*' is the usual vocabulary applied to '*the Man of Lying*'/'*Spouter of Lying*' at Qumran – and following this, as we have already to some extent seen, that

> *God considered their works, because they had sought Him* (here the Hebrew is '*darshuhu,*' the basis of the all-important '*Doresh ha-Torah*' we shall encounter further below in both the Damascus Document and the Florilegium) *with a whole heart, and He raised up for them a Teacher of Righteousness to guide them in the Way of His heart.*[7]

Not only is this addressed to '*the Knowers of Righteousness who understand the works of God*' while at the same time using '*heart,*' '*works,*' '*Guide,*' and '*Way*' vocabulary; but it comes right after the citation, already quoted several times above too, that God '*visited them and caused a Root of Planting to grow*' to '*inherit His Land and prosper on the good things of the Earth,*' itself giving way to the allusions to '*they knew that they were Sinners*' and their being '*like Blind Men groping for the Way*' – again all in the First Column of the Cairo version of the Damascus Document.

One can also see now that '*seeking Him with a whole heart*' is almost certainly the allusion being played off in the claim in Acts 15:8–9's picture of Peter's speech that '*the heart-knowing God*' (in addition, to '*putting no difference between us and them*' – meaning '*the Peoples*') '*purified their hearts pure by Faith.*' A more Pauline presentation of these various theological currents, as already suggested, is hard to imagine.

In the Damascus Document, the opposite side of the coin to '*those seeking Him with a whole heart*' were those '*walking in stubbornness of their heart*' – corresponding to Ezekiel 44's '*uncircumcised heart*' metaphor – who '*did not keep apart from* ('*nazru*' – again, the same root as '*Nazirite*' in previous variations) *the People(s)*' – a parallel to Acts 15:7 and 12–14's '*People*'/'*Peoples*' imagery.[8] For its part, the Community Rule – in the midst of allusion both to '*Holy Spirit*' baptism and the '*Primal Adam*'-ideology – expressed this in terms of how *the two Spirits*, '*the Spirits of Truth and Unrighteousness, have until now struggled in the hearts of man*.'[9]

So not only do we have in this First Column of the Damascus Document and what follows, therefore, the same kind of imagery Paul uses with regard to the '*heart*,' now combined with that of '*the Way*' (presumably '*the Way in the wilderness*'), that is, it was '*because they sought Him with a whole*' or '*Perfect heart*' (as, for example, that of the '*Perfect work*' that made one '*Perfect and complete*,' James 1:4 applies to '*being a Doer of the word*' and/or '*of the work*') that '*God raised up for them a Teacher of Righteousness*' – this, as opposed to the individual who cannot '*control his Tongue*' thereby '*deceiving his heart*' of James 1:22–27, the '*Religion*' of whom was '*worthless*.'[10]

Thereafter, the Damascus Document moves on to portray '*the Lying Scoffer*' as '*removing the boundary markers, causing them to wander astray in a trackless wilderness*,' followed by allusions to '*justifying the Wicked and condemning the Righteous*,' '*Traitors*,' and '*the Last Generation*.'[11] These end in a succession of references, as we have seen, to '*being called by Name*,' paralleled by notices in the early chapters of Acts about debates on the Temple steps between Community Leaders and Temple Authorities, evoking '*the Name of Jesus*' (3:6–5:41) and '*those calling on this Name*' (9:21).[12]

Then in 15:13, James responds. The picture provided by Acts 15:14–21 also parallels somewhat the second body of material having to do with the apparent last confrontation between Paul and James in Chapter Twenty-One. In that confrontation too, the major speech was attributed to James because, as Acts 21:18 put it (now in the first person plural): '*The next day Paul went in with us to James and all the Assembled Elders*' and, as earlier in Chapter Fifteen, upon hearing '*what (great) things God had worked among the Peoples through*' Paul's '*Ministry (Diakonias* – the same vocabulary used in Acts 7:2 and 7:4 to describe the '*Table Service*' being done by those in the '*Stephen*' episode earlier still), '*they glorified the Lord*' (21:19–20 – here too both the '*glorying*' and '*Lord*' motifs).

As Acts 15:12 expresses this same situation following Peter's speech and preceding James', *Barnabas and Paul* '*related the signs and wonders God did among the Peoples through them*' (as in Acts 21:19 to follow, '*Ethnesin*' again). One should note here, too, how it is Paul now who is doing '*the signs and wonders*' (though what these might have consisted of is difficult to imagine), not 'Jesus.' As already remarked, repetitions of this kind are quite typical of Acts, particularly before the introduction of the 'We Document,' since the author(s) have really no original material to speak of, but are constantly refurbishing or repeating what they have from other sources.

In Acts 21:20, it will be recalled, James interrupts all this 'glorying' with the negative comment, but 'you see brother how many Myriads of Jews there are who have believed and all Zealots for the Law.' This is the 'Jamesian' position par excellence and it is succinctly put in the Letter under his name in the affirmation in it of 'belief and works working together' – a position over and over again reiterated as well, as we have seen, by Muhammad in the Koran as 'believe and do good works' with an accent on 'doing'![13] For Acts 15:5, this becomes: 'But there were certain ones,' now said to be 'of the Sect ('Heresios') of the Pharisees who believed.' As we have shown, while not at first apparent, this is a parallel statement. What has occurred is the phrase, 'Sect of the Pharisees,' has simply been substituted for the phrase, 'Zealots for the Law,' six chapters later in the more reliable 'We Document' in Acts 21:20.

We had already understood this from the way 'Pharisees' is often used in these New Testament materials as either a 'blind' (this is quite a good pun, particularly when one considers how in Matthew it is 'the Blind leading the Blind, both falling into the Pit,' whereas in the Damascus Document those alluded to as 'Blind' and 'groping for the Way' were henceforth to be 'guided by the Righteous Teacher' – nor should one miss here the evocation of 'the Guide' as well) for James' 'Jerusalem Church' followers or 'Zealots for the Law,' or both. Notwithstanding, this earlier passage in Acts 15:5 – in the midst of these 'Jerusalem Council' materials – is usually cited to explain what is called in the field the 'Judaization' of Early Christianity, an astonishing notion. Notwithstanding, such ideas will not stand up to scrutiny. On the contrary – the more likely scenario, particularly after the fall of the Temple, was a thoroughgoing 'Gentilization' of Early Christianity.

But the meanings of these two passages – the earlier one in Chapter Fifteen forming the background to the supposed 'Jerusalem Council' about the alleged 'Pharisees' who were said to 'believe' and the later one about 'the Myriads of Jews who believed, all Zealots for the Law' forming the background in Chapter Twenty-One to the final confrontation between Paul and James – are virtually the same, only the positions in the former have been overwritten and slightly reversed again. This is reinforced by what follows, not only in Peter's speech, but also in James' in Chapter Fifteen. In addition to telling how 'the heart-knowing God purified the hearts of the Peoples by Faith' (clearly meaning 'Gentiles' here, as we just saw –

note here, as well, the important *'spiritualization'* of Jewish *'purification'* ideologies), Peter announces that from the earliest days God chose *'that the Gentiles were to hear the word of the Gospel'* and *'to believe'*; consequently, just as in Acts 10:11–16 earlier, the *'Gentilization'* of Peter or, even more accurately, the *'Paulinization'* of Peter is complete.

The Damascus Document in later columns actually presents a parallel picture when it is talking about those *'who put idols on their heart and walked in the stubbornness of their heart having no share in the House of the Torah.'*[14] Here, *'House of the Torah,'* it will be recalled, is the analogue of *'God's Building'* or the *'House not made of human hands'* Paul pictures himself as erecting in 1 Corinthians 3:10 and 2 Corinthians 5:1 above. For the Damascus Document, these people with their *'stubborn'* and *'idolatrous hearts'* – just as those *'who turned aside with the Men of Scoffing'* (another expression usually applied to *'the Man of Lying'* as, for example, in the First Column where *'the Man of Scoffing'* or *'Jesting,'* listed there alongside *'the Assembly'* or *'Church of Traitors'* and *'the Turners-aside from the Way,'* *'poured out over Israel the waters of Lying'*[15]) – *'shall be judged,'*

> because they spoke falsely against the Laws of Righteousness and rejected the Covenant and the Faith (also *'Compact'*), the New Covenant which they erected in the Land of Damascus (again, here too, the word *'reject'* is the characteristic verb almost always used to describe *'the Liar'* or *'Spouter of Lying'*s activities at Qumran[16]).

One can now better appreciate the importance of the vision of the Heavenly *'tablecloth'* in Acts 10's picture of Peter's original *'Paulinization'*/*'Gentilization'* above. Not only does Peter learn through it that *'table fellowship'* with Gentiles was not an issue – which it most certainly was for his alter ego in these confrontations at *'Antioch'* according to Galatians 2:12–13 – and not to make problems concerning it and the inclusion of *'Gentiles'* generally in God's *'Salvationary'* scheme; at this point Acts indirectly demonstrates, as we have shown, that 'Jesus' never regulated the issue in his Earthly incarnation, otherwise his closest associate, *'Peter,'* would have known of it and not have required a *'Heavenly'* vision to resolve it. From here, Peter hastens to keep *'table fellowship'* with and *even enter* *'the house'* of the Roman Centurion at Caesarea, Cornelius (*'Cornelius,'* as we have already underscored and shall further elaborate, being the actual title of *'the Lex Cornelia de Sicarius et veneficis'* forbidding practices like *'circumcision'* to Roman citizens as a species of bodily mutilation). However absurd these events might seem, historically speaking, there is a certain cunning logic to them from a theological perspective.

As Acts 15:13 pictures it, James now stands up and supports Peter's position (never mind that Peter has fled Palestine, as already remarked, some three chapters before, presumably with a death sentence on his head). Sequencing aside, it is apparent that here too, just as in the first five chapters of Acts, one is in the world of the Pseudoclementine *Recognitions* where each Apostle stands up in turn and gives his speech to debate '*the Chief Priests*' in the Temple – in both narratives, '*Peter*' being the last speaker before James. For Acts 15:14, James begins this speech as follows:

> *Simeon has related how God first visited and took out of the Gentiles a People for His Name.*

Like '*the Righteous Teacher*' from Qumran ('*in whose heart God put the discernment to interpret all the words of His Servants the Prophets*'), James is then depicted as quoting a pivotal scriptural passage from Amos 9:11–12 – found and expounded in at least two milieux at Qumran[17] – following which he then goes on to make his '*Judgement*,' namely, giving his '*rulings*' concerning overseas communities, with which we have become so familiar and which were the upshot of this '*Conference*' as Acts reports it.

The Language of *God's Visitation* in James' Speech and at Qumran

Before proceeding to the substance of these '*rulings*' and inasmuch as we are already somewhat familiar with both them and the last confrontation between Paul and James in Acts 21 (since James is eliminated from the scene not long after it, who knows if even here there might not be some causality?); it would be well to point out in some detail the Qumran parallels to this speech attributed to James as Acts 15:13–21 records it, because now we have yet another common esotericism found both in the New Testament and in the Dead Sea Scrolls – but, even more to the point, one actually put into the mouth of James.

Short as it, there are several very significant ones. In the first place, before actually citing this passage from Amos 9:11–12 on '*rebuilding* (in Amos, '*raising up*') *the Tent* ' or '*Tabernacle* ('*Succot*' in Amos) *of David which is fallen*'; James is pictured as adding to his description of '*Simeon*"s announcement, of '*how God first visited the Gentiles and took out a People for His Name*,' the phrase: '*and the words of the Prophets agree with this, as it has been written*,' after which the quotation from Amos 9:11 is set forth verbatim (15:16–17). Not only does this agree with like-minded statements in the Habakkuk *Pesher* having to do with '*the Righteous Teacher*' just cited above, to say nothing of the picture of James in early Church texts (*about whom*, according to Hegesippus via Eusebius, '*the Prophets*' were said to '*have declared*'); unlike the way '*Peter*' was pictured as expressing these things, Acts 15:14 now has James specifically use the term '*visited*' and, by implication, the language of a '*Visitation*' generally so absolutely fundamental, as we have seen (and shall see further) to several documents at Qumran, particularly the Damascus Document and the War Scroll.[18]

In the way James' speech is depicted, the sense is inverted again to mean that God '*visited*' *the Gentiles* (literally '*the Peoples*'/'*Ethnon*') *in order to take out a 'People'* (now '*Laon*' not '*Ethnon*') *for Himself* or, more specifically, '*His Name*' rather than the '*Visitation*' God is said to have made at several junctures of the Damascus Document either as a kind of '*Judgement*,' *to take Vengeance upon Backsliders*, or the Messianic-style '*Visit*' or '*Visitation*,' *to 'cause a Root of Planting to grow*' and '*inherit His Land*,' with which the narrative begins. This is '*Gentilization*' with a vengeance.[19]

If we reverse this, however – which was surely the case originally – it really does correspond very closely to this opening pronouncement in the Damascus Document, a document we have already seen to contain so many other '*Jamesian*' conceptualities. We have frequently called attention to this reference to how '*God visited*' *the Community, causing a Messianic* '*Shoot*' or '*Root of Planting to grow*' (*yizmach*)' and '*to inherit* (*lirosh*) *the Land*. Not only is this '*lirosh*' the infinitive of '*yarash*,' which we shall have cause to emphasize further below; but '*yizmach*' is a variation of '*Zemach*'/'*Branch*,' as in '*the Branch of David*' so much a part of '*Messianic*' Prophecy as it is expressed and as we shall encounter in other Qumran documents too as we proceed.[20]

It should be observed in passing that like '*the Messiah of Aaron and Israel*' – who returns also on several occasions later in the Damascus Document – the allusion here in the First Column to '*Root*' is singular.[21] So are the adjectives and verbal usages surrounding it.[22] Moreover, in the speech attributed to James at this so-called '*Jerusalem Council*,' before he '*makes his rulings*' and where *he is clearly in command even of Peter*[23]; the scriptural passage from Amos, he is depicted as quoting, makes reference to the parallel formulary of words, '*My Name being called*,' refracting to some extent the '*being called by Name*,' we have encountered as well in these first columns of the Damascus Document.

The citation in James' speech in the Greek version, in which it is quoted in Acts 15:16–17, reads as follows:

> *After these things, I will return and rebuild the Tabernacle of David which is fallen. And I will rebuild the ruins of it and set it up, so that the Remnant of*

Men will seek out the Lord (here, of course, is the verb '*seeking*' we have just alluded to in the First Column of the Damascus Document – and which we shall see later later in the same document in the term along with its associated phraseology, '*the Doresh*' or '*Seeker after the Torah, who came to Damascus*' – though it is not to be found in the Hebrew original), *and all the Gentiles upon whom My Name has been called, says the Lord, who is doing all these things.*

It is interesting that the Hebrew version of this passage, which is somewhat more Zionist or nationalistic than what we are encountering here, rather reads '*Edom*,' meaning the country not '*Adam*,' meaning the '*Man*' or '*Men*' – '*Edom*' and '*Adam*' being homonyms in Hebrew. By the same token, it includes the usage '*called by My Name*' not '*upon whom My Name has been called*,' as we just saw, phraseology connecting up ever so slightly with formulations – as just indicated as well – found in the Damascus Document even more than the way Acts rephrases it.

It would, therefore, be helpful to provide the complete Hebrew version of it as it appears in Amos 9:11–12:

On that day (the day on which '*all the Sinners of My People shall die by the sword*' – not the militancy here, completely in accord with the documents at Qumran), *I will raise up* (nor is there any word '*return*,' either, in it or the Septuagint) *the Tabernacle of David which is fallen and restore its ruined parts* (while not certainly of the utmost importance and somewhat redundant, it is also worth remarking that this last clause is completely missing from Acts and, this time, the Septuagint too) *and I will raise up its ruins* (we will encounter this usage '*raise up*'/'*Akim*' quite often as we proceed) *and build it up as in days of old* (Acts following the Septuagint here renders this '*ancient times*' in Greek) *that they may possess* (or '*inherit*' – here the Septuagint followed by Acts or Acts followed by the Septuagint substitutes '*darash*'/'*seek*' for '*yarash*'/'*inherit*' or '*possess*,' as we just saw and as in '*seeking the Lord with a whole heart*' in the First Column of the Damascus Document above, once again an obviously more cosmopolitan and less nationalistically aggressive signification) *the Remnant of Edom and all the Nations called by My Name, says the Lord* (*YHWH*) *who is doing this* (again, the '*doing*' usage we have been so emphasizing).

Whether there was a version of Amos that originally incorporated the '*darash*'/'*seek*' of Acts and not '*yarash*'/'*possess*' as here in the normative Hebrew text is impossible to say; but whatever the answer, the text Acts presents – which is ostensibly following the Septuagint as we just saw –

is taking significant liberties with the original in line with its exegetical purposes since it is hardly interested in a restoration of either the '*days of yore*' or of '*ancient times*' – whereas the sectaries at Qumran, on the other hand, most certainly were.

However this may be, once again it should be appreciated that what follows in the next three lines from Amos 9:13–15 (the last three) is, once again, *completely* '*Zionistic*' material about '*inheriting*' or '*restoring the Land*' (an allusion, as just underscored, familiar from the '*Root of Planting*' prelude of the Damascus Document above), '*building up the waste cities*' and '*its vineyards*,' and *bringing an end* '*to the captivity of My People Israel*' – material which could not be more irredentist, if one can use the term here, and totally unlike the purposes Acts is imputing to it in the speech it is attributing to James.

But one can go so much further than this all-important allusion. Not only does this prophecy from Amos 9:11–15 include the allusion to '*building up the fallen Tabernacle of David*' which will presently reappear, not just in the Damascus Document but, as we shall see as well, in the '*Messianic*' Compendium ('*The Florilegium*') of the Promises to David's '*Seed*' after him and to '*the Salvation of Israel*' in '*the Last Times*' below; but it ends with allusion to '*planting*' them on their Land, the imagery of '*growing*,' and '*prospering on the Richness of the Earth*' which is closer to the vocabulary and with more nationalist intent even than the imagery being employed in these opening lines of the Damascus Document about God's '*Visitation*' and evoking the '*inheritance of His Land*' by the Messianic '*Root of Planting*' above.

In fact, these last seem too seem clearly based on these closing lines from Amos 9:12; and Amos 9:15 (the very last line) actually concludes by alluding to being '*no more uprooted from the Land*' upon which '*I have planted them*' – that is, even here one has the '*Root*'/'*uprooting*' imagery which is the basis of the Damascus Document/Gospel of Matthew repartee concerning the so-called '*Pharisees*' as '*Blind Guides*,' '*leading the blind*' (both the '*Blind*' and '*guiding*' immediately even following here in the Damascus Document as we have seen) and '*falling into the Pit*.'

Not only is James in this speech in Acts being portrayed as a personage similar to the Righteous Teacher at Qumran – himself also described in the Habakkuk *Pesher*, in addition to the earlier point about '*God having put in his heart the discernment to interpret the words of His Servants the Prophets*,' as the individual '*to whom God made known all the Mysteries of the words of His Servants the Prophets*'[24] – but, even here, it must be observed that we have an almost word-for-word analogue to the phraseology of James' speech as reproduced by Acts. Right after James uses this allusion '*visit*' in recounting how '*Simeon related how God first visited the Gentiles*' (even the word '*First*' here will have a direct correlative in the language the Damascus Document will now go on to use, as we shall see, in these important allusions in Columns Seven and Eight concerning there being both '*First*' and '*Second Visitations*'); he adds, as we saw above, '*and the words of the Prophets agree with this.*' Furthermore, as just remarked as well, this too is a word-for-word correspondence with how the Righteous Teacher will be described in the Habakkuk *Pesher* including, as we just saw, even the phrase '*the words of the Prophets.*'

Again, the parallels with the Scrolls do not end here. Before making his '*rulings*' or '*judging,*' Acts 15:18 has James add in a seemingly innocuous manner, '*All His works are known to God from Eternity,*' words not found in Amos, but clearly meant to be James' own. Words, however, to this effect are almost exactly what we encounter in the passages about '*being called by Name*' in the Second and Fourth Columns of the Damascus Document above (also varying this '*called by My Name*' or '*upon whom My Name has been called*' imagery here in Acts 15:17 and Amos 9:12 as we have seen), before the subject matter changes to condemning '*fornication, Riches and pollution of the Temple.*'

To demonstrate this, it is worth quoting this exhortation from CD II in its entirety:

> *Now listen to me all who enter the Covenant* (meaning, clearly, '*the New Covenant in the Land of Damascus,*' to be evoked later in Column Six) *and I will unstop your ears concerning the Ways of the Wicked* (the '*unstopping*' the ears of deaf mutes Jesus is presented as accomplishing in favorite Gospel episodes above)....*Enduring patience and abundant forgiveness are with Him to make atonement for the Penitents from sin* ('*Penitents from sin*' also appearing later in the Document and a synonym plainly too for '*the Penitents of Israel who went out from the Land of Judah*' or '*the Penitents of the Wilderness*' we shall further encounter both in it and the Psalm 37 *Pesher* below[25]).

> *But Power, Might, and overwhelming Wrath with sheets of Fire in which are all the Angels of Destruction upon those turning aside from the Way* (again, the '*turning aside*' metaphor) *and abominating the Law* (as we saw, this can also be read as '*blaspheming the Law*'). *There shall be no Remnant nor survivor for them* (the '*Remnant*'/'*survivor*' imagery of Amos 9:11-12 and Acts 15:17 above – not only do we have here '*the Way*' imagery and the kind of aggressively militant language the Gospels use to characterize John the Baptist's activities in the wilderness,[26] but the reverse clearly of Acts' cosmopolitanism), *because God did not choose them from the beginning*

of the world and He knew their works before ever they were established.[27]

Here, then, are the exact words attributed to James in Acts 15:18 just highlighted above, '*all His works are known to God from Eternity,*' but reversed, in the sense of '*condemning*' those whose '*works*' God '*knew from the beginning*' would be '*Evil*' or '*backsliding,*' not condoning them. Interesting too, what is added here is that God '*abominated their generations on account of blood,*' meaning either *the consumption of 'blood*' or *coming in contact with* '*blood*' as, for example, in the matter of '*sleeping with women during the blood of their periods,*' a charge soon to follow in CDv's exposition of the '*pollution of the Temple*' and '*fornication*' accusations of the '*Three Nets of Belial,*' but also an integral part of James' injunctions, themselves about to be reprised too in Acts Fifteen at the end of James' speech – to wit, '*keep away from blood*' – certainly an injunction, as already explained, that would never have entertained Paul's '*communion with the blood.*'

They are exactly the reverse, as well, of Peter's words preceding these words of James in Acts 15:7: '*Brothers, you know that from early days, God chose the Gentiles from among us to hear the word of the Gospel and believe*' – this, as opposed to the words just quoted from Column Two of the Damascus Document above, '*God did not choose them.*' Can there be any doubt that we have here, not only the imagery – albeit reversed to support Paul's new initiative to the Gentiles, but also the very vocabulary Peter is pictured as using in alluding to the '*heart-knowing God purifying the hearts of the Peoples*' above?

As the Damascus Document continues directly upon the allusion to '*knowing their works and abominating their generations on account of blood*':

> *And He hid His face from the Land until they were consumed* (here, too, the language of '*eating*' or '*consuming*' to imply '*destruction*' we have encountered above). *He knew the years of their Standing* (again, a touch of '*the Standing One*' ideology) *and the number and precise determination of their Eras for all Eternal Being and what would happen in their Eras for all the years of Eternity.*[28]

Though more prolix, there can be little doubt that we have here just about the exact words James is presented as using in Acts 15:18 about '*all His works being known to God from Eternity.*' Even the allusion to '*Eternity*' is the same only the signification, as always, is completely reversed. Moreover, the writers in Acts are certainly showing pretty precise knowledge of the documents they are bowdlerizing.

The Damascus Document – Columns Two and Four

The Damascus Document, continuing in Column Two but now changing gears, goes on to speak about – as per the passage James is pictured
as citing from Amos in Acts 15:17 above – 'the Residue of Men seeking out
the Lord and all the Peoples (Ethne) upon whom My Name has been called' (as
in the exegesis of Ezekiel 44:15 two columns later, 'and the Nilvim with
them'[29]) or, as the Damascus Document would rephrase both, here in the
very next line in Column Two and in the exegesis of Ezekiel 44:15 as
well, in Column Four, 'Men called by Name so that a Remnant might remain'
or 'survive' (note the additional parallel here, 'Remnant' with 'Residue'):

> And in all of them he raised up for Himself Men (even the word 'Men' here
> has a counterpart above) called by Name (this, of course, the slight
> rephrasing – if it is a rephrasing – of Acts 15:17 and Amos 9:12 above,
> both also connected to a 'Remnant') that a Remnant might remain on the
> Land and fill (more 'filling' vocabulary should one choose to regard it) the
> face of the Earth with their generations (this, too, not only varying the lan-
> guage of Amos 9:13–15 above, but the gist of Column One's description
> of how God 'caused a Root of Planting to grow' and 'inherit His Land and
> prosper on the good things of His Earth'). And He made known His Holy Spirit
> to them by the hand of His Messiah (this, of course too, is very definitely
> singular – though some in the interests of a more tendentious exposi-
> tion, as we have seen, have translated this as 'His anointed ones'![30]). And He
> (or 'it') is Truth (this, too, is singular though, as already remarked, it is
> actually left out of some of the more normative translations!) and, in the
> precise explanation of His Name (so is this – that is, both left out and sin-
> gular) their names (are to be found – again the 'Name' and 'naming'
> symbolism), and those whom He hated He led astray (as in the First Column
> and a fitting end to the homily[31]).

The allusion here to 'the hand of His Messiah' is, of course, the same as that
to 'by the hand of Your Messiah' in the War Scroll's exegesis of 'the Star
Prophecy' above. Again, the sense of both is singular not plural! Also, the sentence, 'He' or 'It is Truth,' and 'in the precise explanation of His Name, their
names (are to be found)' is, as just signaled, usually either inexplicably
deleted or bowdlerized in most translations of this passage – why, is
incomprehensible.[32]

Likewise, there can be no mistaking the vengeful and xenophobic
nature of these passages. Moreover, this passage contains the language of
'the Holy Spirit' which Peter is portrayed as having included in his speech

about '*the heart-knowing God giving (the Gentiles) the Holy Spirit as well as us.*' In Peter's version of all these usages, as we saw, the sense is again reversed and opened up, claiming no special prerogatives for the Jews regarding '*the Holy Spirit,*' while at Qumran it is more inward-looking and, as usual, xenophobic.

This material in Column Two now concludes in an intense first-person exhortative:

> And now my sons, listen to me, and I will uncover your eyes so that you may see and understand the works of God (the equivalent of '*He who has eyes, let him see*' in the Gospels combined, of course, with the '*works*' language of Qumran[33]) *in order to choose what pleases Him and reject what He hates to walk in Perfection in all His Ways.*[34]

These same elements are more or less repeated in the all-important Fourth Column of the Damascus Document where Ezekiel 44:15's '*Zadokite Statement*' or '*Covenant*' is being elucidated. But before this in Column Three, the whole story of Israel – from the '*cutting off of the Sons of Noah*' (that is, after '*the Flood*') to the '*delivering up to the sword*' of all those who '*deserted the Covenant of the First*' – is told in terms, significantly, of '*keeping the Commandments.*'[35] Interestingly, these '*Deserters*' (elsewhere, '*backsliders*') are described as '*choosing their own will*' and '*following after stubbornness of heart*' – a more pointed description of a Pauline-type adversary would be hard to imagine.

In it, the climax is actually expressed in terms of those who, on the contrary, '*remained steadfast*':

> But as for those who remained of them ('*the Remnant*' vocabulary again of both Acts and Amos above), *those who held fast* ('*the Mehazikim*' – this '*holding fast*' or '*strengthening*' language, as we shall see, will be important throughout and permeate the Damascus Document) *to the Commandments of God, God would raise up* (this is the same '*raising up*'/'*hakim*' of the '*raising up fallen Tent of David*' we just encountered above) *His Covenant with Israel forever.*[36]

Furthermore, beginning with Noah and the Flood, the whole presentation actually focuses on Abraham, Isaac, and Jacob as these very same '*Keepers of the Commandments*' and '*Friends of God* (the language, of course, James 2:23 applies to Abraham) *and Heirs to the Covenant Forever.*' Therefore, not only does this '*Keeper*' language comprise the definition of '*the Sons of Zadok*' in the Community Rule and echo the '*Rechabite*' motif we have encountered earlier; it can also be construed as a synonym for the '*Friends*' and '*Heirs*' vocabularies. For its part this same '*Heirs*' language is also strong both in Paul's Letter to the Galatians and that to the Romans.[37] By the same token, it should be appreciated that at no time does this discourse say there will come a time when such '*Mehazikim*' or '*Steadfast Ones*' will not be considered such '*Heirs*' or '*Heirs to the Covenant*.' On the contrary, it ends, leading up to the all-important quotation of the Zadokite Covenant of Ezekiel 44:15 in Column Four, with allusion to how:

> God pardoned their sins and built a House of Faith for them, the likes of which has never stood in Israel from ancient times until now. Those who hold fast to it (again meaning '*the Covenant*' and, again, the '*holding fast*' or '*strengthening*'/'*mehazikim*' language that will reappear throughout the Damascus Document) are destined for Victorious Life (implying '*Eternal Life*' and paralleling the language of the '*Victory over the grave*' that God '*gives us through our Lord Jesus Christ*' in 1 Corinthians 15:51–57) and all the Glory of Adam will be theirs (here, of course, another variation of the Ebionite '*Primal Adam*' ideology once again).[38]

In Peter's speech in Acts, it should be observed that, when he is speaking about '*the heart-knowing God purifying the hearts of the Gentiles by Faith*,' not only is a similar '*House of Faith*' or '*Faithful House*' being evoked; but this '*House*' is presumably both the one being evoked by Paul in 1 Corinthians 3:9 – using the imagery of himself as '*wise architect*,' '*laying the Foundations*,' and '*building*' we shall, once again, encounter throughout the Scrolls[39] – and in 2 Corinthians 5:1's '*a Building given by God, a House not made with human hands but eternal in Heaven*.' We have already seen, too, that at the end of 1 Corinthians 15:45–55 Paul evokes '*the Primal Adam*' ideology, being alluded to here, ending with a play on the Hebrew name '*Adam*.' He does so by not only contrasting '*the First Man Adam*' with '*the Last Adam*' or '*Second Man*' (*Anthropos*) in terms of being '*the Lord out of Heaven*' but, as we have seen, with an exultation – equivalent to that in the Damascus Document here – of '*death being swallowed up in Victory*' as well.

At the end of this Column Three of the Damascus Document, too, in addition to there being a hint of the '*Primal Adam*'-ideology and the '*Standing*' language of '*the Standing One*' notation[40] – which will now continue into the esoteric definition of '*the Sons of Zadok*' that follows in Column Four; there is also, in this paean to how '*God in His marvelous Mysteries atoned for their iniquity and forgave them their sins*' (the equivalent of Mark 1:3/Luke 3:3's picture of John '*preaching – in the wilderness – the baptism of repentance for remission of sins*'; in Luke 1:77–78, together with an allusion to God '*visiting us*,' this is: '*giving Knowledge of Salvation to His People in remission of their sins*' – thus![41]), the first evocation of '*digging a Well rich in waters*' – later in Columns Six and Eight to be expressed in terms of '*digging the Well of Living Waters*'![42]

Here commences the definition of '*the Sons of Zadok*' as '*the Elect of Israel, called by Name, who will stand at the End of Days*' (there is no mistaking the allusion to '*Standing*' here, nor its eschatological import):

> Behold, the precise explanation of their Names, according to their generations and the Era of their Standing (or '*Duration*') and the number of their sufferings and the years of their existence and the precise explanation of their works (again, the '*works Righteousness*' ideology).

Though the text is a little broken at this point, it reads approximately:

> They are the First (Men) of Holiness, through whom (or '*for whom*') God made atonement, and they justified the Righteous and condemned the Wicked (here, of course for Qumran, the proper exposition of the '*Justification*' theology of '*justifying the Righteous and condemning the Wicked*,' not '*justifying the Sinners*').[43]

These '*Men of Holiness*' would – according to '*Nazoraean*' ideology as we have been trying to expound it – be the first '*Nazirites*' or '*Consecrated Ones*.' Not only does the '*Nazoraean*' ideology come into play here; but, as already signaled as well, there would even appear to be a note of participation in what normally goes under the title of '*the Last Judgement*.'[44] One cannot get more '*Christian*' than this.

This, of course, is the proper '*Salvationary*' order as opposed to the earlier one – the one envisioned by '*the Lying Scoffer*' and those '*seeking Smooth Things and choosing illusions*' at the end of Column One. These last, it will be recalled, '*justified the Wicked* (even possibly, as just remarked, '*the Sinners*') *and condemned the Righteous, breaking the Covenant and violating the Law*' – the very reverse of God's soteriological plan. They even

> banded together against the soul of the Just One and the Walkers in Perfection (clearly the followers of '*the Righteous One*'), abominating their soul (or '*life*' – as already suggested, even probably comprising that '*blaspheming*' so constantly alluded to in Acts). And they pursued after them with the sword and rejoiced in dividing the People...and their works were as unclean before Him

(here, too, the opposite of the proper '*works*' ideology).[45]

One should also not be unaware of the possible parallel to this in the attack by Paul on James in the Pseudoclementine *Recognitions* above.

As the Damascus Document continues here in Column Four:

> *And all those coming after them are to do according to the exact letter of the Torah,* *which the First* ('*the Forefathers*' or '*Ancestors*' we have already called attention to above and, of course, the reiteration of the '*doing*' ideology) *transmitted, until the completion of the Era of these years, according to the Covenant which God made with the First* (the '*Mosaic*' one Paul so derides as '*Agar*' / '*Hagar*' in '*Mount Sinai in Arabia*' in Galatians 4:25 above) *to atone for their Sins – so God made atonement through* (or '*for*') *them.*[46]

The meaning could not be clearer. Not only do we have here the 'Jamesian' emphasis on '*doing*.' echoed in the language of '*works*' just preceding it; but also the implication of – in '*doing according to the exact letter of the Torah*' – not '*stumbling in one small point of the Law*' of James 2:10 above or the '*not one jot or tittle shall pass from the Law*' of the Synoptic Gospels – to say nothing of the '*First vs. Last*' language of these last.

This passage closes with the evocation of '*each man standing on his own net*' or '*watchtower*,' noted earlier, and there being '*no more attachment to the House of Judah*.'[47] Though the meaning here is obscure, it can be enhanced by reference to the Habakkuk *Pesher*, as we saw, where the same '*watchtower*' allusion is used to evoke Habakkuk's own visions; and it does look as if we are moving in the next '*Era*' into the situation devoid of any unique national affiliation – a position being radically exploited by Paul.[48] From here till the end of Four, the Damascus Document moves into its James-like exposition of the '*Three Nets of Belial*.' Nor can there be much doubt of the relationship of the gist of much of this material to the speech attributed to James at '*the Jerusalem Council*' above before he makes his '*rulings*' regarding Gentiles according to Acts.

The use of the term '*Visit*' as Divine Judgement in Columns v–viii of the Damascus Document

Three columns later in the Damascus Document, the very passage from Amos 9:11 on '*rebuilding*' or '*raising up the Tabernacle of David which is fallen*' – which, as already remarked, Acts 15:16 presents as an integral part of James' speech – is actually quoted verbatim. (Nor is this completely aside from the evocation of '*the House of Faith*' God '*built for them*' wherein '*all the Glory of Adam would be theirs*' at the end of Column Three leading directly into the exegesis of Ezekiel's '*Zadokite Covenant*' at the beginning of Column Four.) The exposition of this citation about '*re-erecting the fallen Tent of David*' actually occurs in the middle of Column Seven of Manuscript A (the first and longer version – it will be recalled – of the Damascus Document found in the *Genizah* in Cairo, a citation not paralleled in Ms. B – the shorter and to some degree overlapping version – where the quotations are rather from Ezekiel and Zechariah again[49]) at the climax of this very important section where '*the Star Prophecy*' from Numbers 24:17 (already cited in the War Scroll above and about to be cited in the *Florilegium* below), so much a part of '*Messianic*' agitation in the First Century literally ending in the germination of '*Christianity*,' is also quoted in full and combined with a series of other '*Messianic*' prophecies. These, in fact, begin in Column VI earlier with rarely cited and somewhat esoteric passages from Numbers 21 and Isaiah 54-56's '*Song of the Well*' (passages which follow in Isaiah '*the Song of the Suffering Servant*' in 53 – at least the exposition is esoteric) and extending in Ms. A to the end of Column VII.

In turn, the series of the expositions of these somewhat obscure '*Messianic*' proof-texts in the Cairo Damascus Document culminate – in the first instance – at the end of Column VI of Ms. A. with the initial delineation of what will be meant by '*the New Covenant in the Land of Damascus*,' then leading into the evocation of '*the Well of Living Waters*' (a formulation to be found uniquely at the end of Column XIX of Ms. B not in Ms. A) – clearly baptismal waters – to be '*dug*' there in association with the erection of '*the New Covenant in the Land of Damascus*.'[50] It is at this point – basically at the end of both Columns VIII of Ms. A and XIX of Ms. B – that Ms. B introduces the completely new material, as the overlapping between them begins to come to an end, designated by all commentators as Column XX (though it actually continues directly on from Column VIII of Ms. A too).

Not only this, but it was at the point where the overlap between the two began at the end of Column VI and the beginning of Column VII of Ms. A during the first enunciation of '*the New Covenant in the Land of Damascus*' in the latter (the overlap between them actually beginning at approximately the end of line 5 of Column Seven of Ms. A more or less equivalent to the first line of Column Nineteen of Ms. B) that both manuscripts the words (line VII.9 of Ms. A – line XIX.6 of Ms. B) with which the First Column of CD started off about '*God visiting the Land*' – in this instance, the '*Visit*' which God makes alludes to '*the reward which would be paid to Evil Ones*' or '*paying back the reward on Evil Ones to them* (meaning presumably, '*to all those turning back from,*' '*rejecting,*' or '*betraying*' both '*the Laws of God*' and '*the New Covenant in the Land of Damascus*'[51]) *when God visits the Earth'* – itself a neat bit of ideological reversal from the way the language of '*God visiting the Earth*' is first alluded to in Column One.[52]

The expression '*paying back the reward*' or '*the reward which would be paid to Evil Ones*' appears to be based on Isaiah 3:10–11, a key exegetical component of proof-texts applied in early Church literature to the death of James and at Qumran to '*the Righteous Teacher.*'[53] As such, it completes this '*paying the reward*' circle of like-minded phraseologies in this complex at Qumran since it is also to be found in both the Habakkuk and Psalm 37 *Peshers* (not to mention in a more generalized manner in the Community Rule as applied to '*all the Men of the Lot of Belial*'[54]) where, as already underscored, it refers to how '*the Wicked Priest would be paid the reward with which he rewarded the Poor*' or '*the reward*' which would '*be paid*' the Wicked Priest when he was going *to be* '*delivered into the hands of the Violent Ones of the Gentiles*' who were, then, going to '*execute the Judgement of Evil*' upon him.[55]

The evocation of '*God visiting the Earth*' in Columns VII and XIX is the third use in CD of this allusion to '*visit*' or '*Visitation,*' which Acts 15:14 pictures James himself as using in his speech at '*the Jerusalem Council*' about how God '*visited the Gentiles to take out a People for His Name.*' We have already to some extent seen how in Column Twenty of Ms. B these same '*Gentiles*' ('*Nilvim*' or '*God-Fearers*' as the case may be – for whom, as in the case of the proclamation of '*Communion*' in the Synoptic Gospels and Paul in I Corinthians 11:24, '*a Book of Remembrance was*' also '*be written out*' – for the latter this becomes '*Do this in Remembrance of Me*'[56]) are also referred to either as '*reckoning His Name,*' '*fearing His Name*' (here we are not saying whose '*Name,*' only that '*God*' will soon '*reveal Salvation*' / '*Yesha*[c]' to them) and, as we saw as well, that '*they will see His Salvation (Yeshu*[c]*ato) because they took refuge in His Holy Name.*'[57]

Not only is the first occurrence of this usage '*visit*' associated in Column One with the foundation of the Community – more or less paralleling what in Christianity is reformulated as *God* or *the Holy Spirit* '*visiting*' *Mary to produce a child* – it is not without note that the Gospel of Luke 1:68 and 1:78 actually uses the same expression, '*God visited His People,*' and even adds, '*and wrought Redemption for them,*' in exactly this manner. It does this together – not unremarkably too in addition to this note of '*Redemption*' – with both allusion to '*giving Knowledge of Salvation to His People in remission of their sins*' and '*God raising up a Horn of Salvation for us in the House of His Servant David*' (1:69 – the note of '*Salvation,*' of course, paralleling the two references to 'Salvation' – Yesha^c/'Yeshu^{c}a – at the end of Column Twenty of the Damascus Document above). Once again, this is an incredibly strong correlation.

The second incidence of the use of this verb 'visit' in the Damascus Document comes in Column Five right after the exposition of the 'Three Nets of Belial' – in particular, 'each man' approaching his 'near kin' for 'fornication' (meaning, of course, 'close cousins and nieces' – the key charge implying that we have to do here with the 'Herodian' and not the 'Maccabean' Establishment), where it is opined that 'in ancient times God visited their works' (clearly meaning, 'for destruction') – 'and His Wrath was kindled by their actions.'[58] This charge is repeated or, perhaps more accurately, recapitulated at the start of Column Eight/Nineteen where it is also opined:

> And this also will be the Judgement (this clearly meaning something like we would call 'the Last Judgement') on all those who entered His Covenant (again clearly, 'the New Covenant in the Land of Damascus') who did not hold fast to (yahziku – the 'strengthening' imagery again) these (Laws and Statutes). Their Visitation (also possibly, 'Command' – the two are the same in Hebrew) will be for destruction by the hand of Belial (here the recapitulation of the 'Belial' reference earlier in Column Four and 'hand of'). This is the Day which God commands (or 'in which God visits' – again, the two words are the same in Hebrew, but there can be no mistaking their meaning, 'the Last Judgement,' a connotation also directly picked up in the Koran).[59]

Two more incidences occur at the end of Column Seven and the beginning of Column Eight directly following citation of a passage also from Amos (5:26–27) about 'exiling the Tabernacle of your King' from 'My Tent in Damascus,' 'rebuilding the Tabernacle of David which is fallen' from Amos 9:11, and 'the Star Prophecy.' These not only refer back, literally, to 'the First Visitation' – clearly meaning the 'destruction' at the time of the end of the First Temple Period – but also use both the words the Gospels apply pejoratively to the conduct of 'Judas Iscariot' towards Jesus, that is, 'delivering up' – in this case, as we saw, 'delivered up to the sword.'

In Ms. A, this last is associated with the time 'when the two Houses of Israel separated' and 'Ephraim departed from Judah' – therefore clearly associating it with the Assyrian destruction of the Northern Kingdom. But in Ms. B, where actually five such references to 'visit' or 'command' occur in some nine lines, this is rather represented in terms of a Heavenly or Angel-like 'scribe dressed in linen' who, to quote Ezekiel 9:3–4, goes through the city, beginning first with the Temple, marking out all those destined for survival while – expressing this even more vehemently than

Ms. A – '*the Rest were to be delivered up to the avenging sword of the Covenant*,' reprised in Ms. A above by the words '*while the Backsliders were delivered up to the sword*'[60] (note here, the slight variation in the second of these from Ms. B, '*given over to*,' for '*delivered up to*' in the one expressed in conjunction with '*the Coming of the Messiah of Aaron and Israel*' – to say nothing of '*the Rest*' as opposed to '*the Backsliders*').

Not only is the context here (as against the Assyrian milieu of Ms. A) the Babylonian destruction of Judah; but in both contexts this serves to introduce a Third '*Visitation*' (the Fourth, if one counts the Assyrian one), the present one on all those who '*rebelled against*' and '*betrayed*' the '*Covenant of Repentance*' (as Ms. B expresses it[61]), which is either about to occur or is in the process of occurring – the one in which, as we just saw above, '*their Visitation will be for destruction by the hand of Belial.*' Nor can it be emphasized too strongly that this '*Visitation*' (in our view, *the Roman one*), which is now envisioned in terms of a prophecy from Zechariah 13:7 about the '*escape*' of '*the Meek of the flock*' or '*the Little Ones*,' is now about to take place or in the process of happening.[62]

These references to God '*visiting the Land*' and the two or three '*Visitations for destruction*' – both those previous and the coming one – follow upon the material in Column Six having to do with a quotation from Numbers 21:18, already alluded to above, about '*digging the Well*,' '*which the Princes*' and '*the Nobles of the People dug with the Staff*' ('*the Mehokkek*,' playing off the underlying root, '*hakak*' or '*hok*,' also carrying the additional meaning of '*law*' or '*legislate*' – in this case meaning '*the Legislator*,' which we shall further analyze in Chapter Twenty-two below), '*the Well*' being that of '*the Many*' or '*Living Waters*' just referred to above.[63] But the important thing about this passage is that '*the Princes*' and '*Nobles*,' who comprise these '*Diggers*,' are now interpreted (replicating those Priestly '*Penitents of Israel*' who '*went out from the Land of Judah*' in exposition of Ezekiel 44:15 in Column Four earlier) in terms of '*sojourning*' or '*dwelling in the Land of Damascus*' and '*the New Covenant*' that was to '*set up the Holy Things according to their precise specifications*' there – '*to separate between polluted and profane*,' '*to distinguish between Holy and impure*' (the very opposite, as we have seen, of what Peter learned in Acts 10:15 and 10:28 above, and – perhaps the most important of all – '*to love each man his brother as himself*' (a direct quotation of James 2:8's '*Royal Law according to the Scripture*,' as we have seen as well – to say nothing of its quasi-inversion by Paul in Romans 13:9 into '*loving*' the Governing Authorities in order to pay them the taxes they '*require*,' again quite the opposite of the import of its citation here at Qumran!).[64]

Not only is this tied to '*strengthening the hand of the Meek* (ᶜ*Ani*), *the*

Poor (Ebion), and the Convert (Ger),' the allusion to '*Ebion*' of course again connecting it to the Letter of James and that to '*Ger*' making it indisputably clear that we have to do with the association with the Community of a category of Gentile converts (implied by such words, as we have been showing, as '*Nilvim*'/'Joiners,' 'God-Fearers' and, in the exegesis of Numbers 21:18, as we shall see, '*the Nobles of the People*' – probably playing off, as already remarked, '*Peoples*'); but also to the directive '*to keep away* – again, based on the root '*lehazzir*' or '*Nazirite*' in Hebrew – *from fornication according to the Statute*' (quite literally here, '*Judgement*,' agreeing with James' reputed words in Acts 15:19, '*wherefore I judge*,' and, literally too, the precise words of the second component of James' instructions to overseas communities in Acts 15:20 and 29 following his speech evoking '*rebuilding the Tent of David which is fallen and setting it up*'), '*to separate from all pollutions according to their requirements.*' Here again the word '*Judgement*' is used, this last being a variation on the first element in James' directives as quoted in Acts 15:20, '*to keep away from the pollutions of the idols*' – in Acts 15:29 and 21:25 rephrased, as we have seen, as '*to keep away from things sacrificed to idols.*'[65]

This word '*Judgement*' also appears several times in the next Column (VIII of Ms. A and XIX of Ms. B) – first in the sense of an extremely positive one '*upon the Penitents of Israel*' again, now specifically identified as *those who did not follow* and '*turned aside from the Way of the People*' (again here meaning, as already explained, '*People*' or '*Peoples*' – in our view, '*Herodians*' and their hangers-on[66]); but then a decidedly negative one on '*those who rejected the Commandments of God and forsook them, turning away in the stubbornness of their heart*' (the typical allusion to a Pauline-type adversary) – in particular, as the exhortation mounts to its impassioned conclusion in XX about even '*the God-Fearers seeing His Salvation/Yeshuʿa,*

> *all the Men who entered the New Covenant in the Land of Damascus, but turned back and betrayed and turned aside from the Well of Living Waters....*[67]

And again:

> *This is the Judgement on any member of the Assembly* (or '*Church*') *of the Men of the Perfection of Holiness* (again a '*Nazirite*'-style allusion familiar to Paul in 2 Corinthians 6:17–7:1) *who hesitates to do* (again note the typically '*Jamesian*' emphasis on '*doing*' to be encountered in '*the Doers of the Torah*' allusion relative to Habakkuk 2:4 in the Habakkuk Commentary below) *the Commands of the Upright* (that is, '*the Straight*' as in '*make a Straight Way in the wilderness*'). *He is the man who is melted in the Furnace* (Ezekiel

22:20–22[68]). *According to the appearance of his works, he shall be expelled from the Assembly* ('*Church*' – again, of course, the '*works*' language expressed, a few lines further along, in terms of doing '*according to the interpretation of the Torah/Midrash ha-Torah in which the Men of the Perfection of Holiness walk*'[69] – here too the '*expulsion*' or '*shunning*' practices of '*the Essenes*') *like someone whose lot had never fallen among the Disciples of God* (another name for the Community)....*Nor shall anyone cooperate with him in Purse* (literally '*Riches*') *and work* (this is '*cavodah*' in the sense of '*service*' or '*mission*' – not '*macasim*'/'*works*.' Compare this with how '*Barnabas*' and '*John Mark*' part from Paul in Acts 15:38–39 above), *for all the Holy Ones of the Most High have cursed him* (the '*cursing*' language, again, of the first three columns of the Community Rule and Paul in Galatians 1:8–9).

And this is the Judgement too, which will be upon those among the First and the Last (here '*the First*' and '*the Last*' language of the Gospels again), *who have put idols on their heart and walked in the stubbornness of their heart* (the '*walking*' language here and elsewhere as, for example, James' admonition to Paul in Acts 21:24 before the reiteration in 21:25 of his '*Judgement*' to '*abstain from things sacrificed to idols*,' '*blood*,' '*fornication*,' and '*carrion*' – to '*pay the expenses*' of four men under a temporary '*Nazirite*' oath of some kind and '*be purified with them*' to show that he still '*himself also walks regularly keeping the Law*.' Not only do we also have here the '*idolatry*,' '*heart*,' and '*stubbornness*' language again, but one should compare this with how Paul expresses himself generally in 1 Corinthians 8:3–7 in attacking James' ban on '*things sacrificed to idols*' by those who allegedly '*have Knowledge*').

They shall have no share in the House of the Torah (yet a third self designation in this section, repeated three lines further along and part and parcel of the '*House*' language we have been following). *They shall be judged according to the Judgement* (about the fifth use of this expression too in this section) *upon their confederates who turned aside with the Men of Scoffing* (a variation on '*the Man of Scoffing*'/'*Jesting*'/'*Lying*' language with which CD began and at Qumran generally[70]), *because they spoke wrongly about the Laws of Righteousness and rejected the Covenant and the Compact which they raised in the Land of Damascus – and this is the New Covenant.*[71]

'*The Coming of the Messiah of Aaron and Israel*' and '*the Avenging Sword of the Covenant*

In fact, as this '*New Covenant in the Land of Damascus*' was first defined at the end of Column Six of Ms. A just before the beginning of the material from Column Seven overlapping that in Column Nineteen of Ms. B; it concluded with this same genre of imperative that '*all should walk in these things in the Perfection of Holiness*,' vocabulary varying the '*walking in Perfection*'/'*Perfection of the Way*' language throughout the Community Rule[72] and paralleling James' admonition to Paul about demonstrating that he still '*walks regularly keeping the Law*' in Acts 21:24 above. Furthermore, this sort of allusion, as we just saw, again ties things indisputably with Paul in 2 Corinthians 7:1 – the only difference being that in Paul the words, '*on the basis of the Covenant of God in which they were instructed*' that follow (meaning, apparently, both '*the First*' and '*the New*') and with which this definition of '*the New Covenant*' in Column Seven close, are discarded.[73]

Ms. B of CD then makes its appearance directly after these same words: '*on the basis of the Covenant of God in which they were instructed*,' picking up the idea of (recapitulated – and referred back to – in CDxx[74]):

> *faithfully promising them that they would live for a Thousand Generations, as it is written* (in Deuteronomy 7:9), *keeping the Covenant and the Piety* (here '*Hesed*' – but doubtlessly meaning something more akin either to '*Favor*' or '*Grace*') *promised to those who love* (*Him* – as we have seen, this is quite literally the definition of '*Piety*' in Josephus' descriptions of both '*the Essenes*' and John the Baptist, paralleled in James 2:5 above as '*the Kingdom promised*' both '*to those that love Him*' and '*the Poor*' – '*the Ebionim*' at Qumran as well as in '*Ebionite Christianity*') *and keep His Commandments for a thousand Generations*.[75]

It makes it clear that this coming '*Visitation*' – which is to occur consonant '*with the coming of the Messiah of Aaron and Israel*' (here the usage is to '*coming*' but in later, more legislative portions from CDix-xviii of Ms. A, where it occurs some two or three times as well, it is rather expressed in terms of '*rising*'/'*shall arise*'/or '*stand up*'[76]) – like the several references paralleling it at this point in Ms. A, is to be a violent one.

In Ms. B's exposition of Zechariah 13:7, which prefaces its evocation of Ezekiel 9:3–4 above and basically intrudes about five lines prior to this, it is only these '*Little Ones*' (cf. Paul in Galatians 4:19)– who in the exegesis turn into '*the Meek*' – who are '*to escape*,' '*the remainder to be delivered up to the avenging sword of the Covenant*' (repeated twice, the first only in terms of '*given over*' as we saw – the second in terms of '*delivered up*'[77]).

For Ms. A, it will be recalled, it was only '*the Backsliders*' who were to be '*delivered up to the sword*' while '*the Steadfast* ('*Ha-Mehazikim*' – meaning '*those who held fast to the Covenant*') escaped to the Land of the North.'[78]

Therefore, to some extent, one can assume that '*the Meek of the flock*' in Ms. B's exegesis of Zechariah 13:7 are equivalent to '*the Steadfast*' in Ms. A's parallel exegesis of Isaiah 7:17 about '*the two Houses of Israel separating*' and '*Ephraim turning aside from Judah*.'[79] In Ms. A, too, Ms. B's allusion to '*the coming of the Messiah of Aaron and Israel*' (obviously singular) is paralleled by its exegesis of '*the Sceptre*' of Numbers 24:17, which it is quoting instead, i.e., '*with whose arising* (or '*standing up*') *all the Sons of Seth*' would be '*destroyed utterly*,' clearly implying – just as in the parallel exegesis of the same prophecy in the War Scroll, where they are called both '*the Hordes of Belial*' and '*the Seven Nations of Vanity*' – a whole host of Gentile Nations.

We have already connected '*Messianic*' allusions of this kind to '*standing up*' to something of what is meant in Hebrew by the idea of '*being resurrected*' and '*the Standing One*' ideology among '*Ebionite*'-type '*Daily Bathing*' groups in the East, at least as far as Ms. A is concerned regarding its exegesis of '*the Sceptre*' in '*the Star Prophecy*' from Numbers 24:17 and its several allusions to '*the Messiah of Aaron and Israel*.'[80] It can also include the idea of a return following a preliminary appearance, that is, a '*resurrection*,' though some might wish to dispute this. Nevertheless, what cannot be disputed is that in both cases, whether the verb used is '*coming*' or '*arising*,' the references *are* singular, though many commentators on Qumran texts have – as we have been at pains to point out – circulated a contrary impression thereby confusing the general public about this.[81]

However, even in translation, the non-specialist will be able to see that in every case – as just underscored – *the verbs and pronouns surrounding allusions of this kind are singular*[82] and that what we have to do with here (regardless of any references in any other context) is *a Davidic-style singular 'Messiah'* not a dual one (whatever might be understood by an ideology of this kind[83]) of the kind one encounters in the text we named '*The Messiah of Heaven and Earth*'[84] or, for instance, in the reference to the Davidic '*Shiloh*' of the Tribe of Judah, equated in the text we also denoted '*A Genesis Florilegium*' (the Genesis *Pesher*) with '*the Messiah of Righteousness*.'[85] Again, it should be stressed that, though a '*Teacher*' ('*Moreh*'), '*Legislator*' ('*Mehokkek*'), '*Guide*' ('*Maschil*' or '*Yoreh*'), '*Seeker after the Torah*' ('*Doresh ha-Torah*'), '*Mebakker*' ('*Bishop*'), or even a '*High Priest Commanding the Many*' may exist at Qumran[86]; all usages regarding '*the Messiah*' per se – whether referred to as '*the Root of Planting*,' '*the Sceptre*,' '*the Branch of David*,' '*the Nasi ha-ʿEdah*' (namely, '*the Leader*'/'*Prince*'/or '*Head of the Community*'), or even '*the Son of God*'[87] – are always singular.

Here too, with regard to '*being given over to the sword*' or '*delivered up to the avenging sword of the Covenant*,' while in Columns VI-VII of Ms. A, it is Isaiah 7:17, Amos 5:26–27, 9:11–12, and Numbers 21:18 and 24:17 that are being quoted; in Ms. B these citations are replaced, as we just saw, by material from Zechariah 13:1–9 and Ezekiel 9:2–11, the latter having to do with *'putting a mark'* or *'cross on the foreheads of those who weep and cry'* because of *'all the Abominations done in Jerusalem'* at the time of the destruction of the First Temple. In passing, one should perhaps again remark that this reference to *'weeping and crying'* in Ezekiel 9:4 might just be the scriptural warrant for *'the Movement,'* we have already called attention to, designated *'the Mourners for Zion,'* so important in the Jewish Middle Ages as a forerunner of the group that succeeded it called *'the Karaites'* – both, not only harking back to many of these Scroll materials but also possibly all the allusions to *'vowing not to eat or drink'* (that is *'not to eat meat or drink strong drink'*) we have encountered circulating about the person of James and those connected with him.[88]

Not only is this *'scribe'* – who is referred to in Ms. B as *'putting a mark on the foreheads of those who cry and weep'* – depicted in Ezekiel 9:3 as having a writer's inkwell at his side and four times described as *'clothed in linen'*; but both Ms. B and Ms. A come together at this point by applying the phraseology of *'the Era of the First Visitation'* to refer to the devastation of the land by foreign armies at this *'Time'* (meaning of course, at least in Ms. B, *the destruction of the First Temple*).[89] Though the sense is the same, there to some extent the resemblance ceases because Ms. B is using these references from Zechariah and Ezekiel comparatively – to compare with and as anticipating the present; whereas the *'Messianic'* references at this point in Ms. A, intentionally or otherwise, are more declarative. Still, by the time of VIII.1–2 and XIX.18–19 and the allusion in both to *'destruction by the hand of Belial,'* the discrepancy is made good.

Actually this reference in Zechariah 13:7 to God *'scattering the flock and stretching (His) hand over the Little Ones'* in Ms. B is not completely unrelated to Ezekiel 5:2–17 and 9:3–11, to which it is prefixed, further elaborating these things. These both describe how *'the Glory of the Lord God of Israel'* departed from the Temple and how the prophet divided his hair into three parts to depict the destruction thereafter of Jerusalem's people by famine, fire, sword, and exile, while at the same time *'binding a few in the folds of (his) cloak'* equivalent to those whom, later, the Angelic *'scribe'* marked *'on the foreheads'* so that they would not be destroyed.

Here Zechariah 13:17 too summons *'the sword,'* but it also has clear connections with subsequent material in Ezekiel 13:2–16 on *'the Daubers on the wall'* and the *'Lying Prophets'* with their *'empty visions,' 'misleading (the) People'* by *'crying Peace when there is no peace,'* already evoked in Column IV on *'the Three Nets of Belial'* earlier in conjunction with Micah 2:6–11 about *'the Lying Spouter who would surely spout'* – this also about *'two of* these,' 'fornication' and 'pollution of the Temple,'[90] and to be expounded again in both Columns VIII and XIX to follow.[91] In Zechariah 13:2–9, not only is the subject to some extent these same 'Lying prophets' with their 'unclean spirit's speaking 'Lies in the Name of the Lord,' but also how the country's 'idols would be cut off' and the inhabitants of Jerusalem 'purified' once more (again, this last being favorite imagery of both the Scrolls at this point and Paul – but, even more to the point, James' ban on the 'pollutions of the idols' directly following his evocation in this pregnant passage from Acts 15:19 of 'the Tabernacle of David which is fallen').

Interestingly enough, in this context Zechariah 13:4 even refers to 'the cloaks of hair' of prophets, which may or may not be the origin of the Synoptic picture of John the Baptist as wearing a cloak of 'camel's hair' (it is not in either Josephus or the Gospel of John[92]). Moreover there is also an allusion to how those that are left 'will call on My Name' (13:9). Not only does this language permeate the Damascus Document, but it also seems to preview to some extent the manner in which Acts 15:16–17 – after depicting James evoking how 'the ruins' of Amos 9:11's 'fallen Tabernacle of David' were to be 'set up' once again – turns this (and the phraseology of Amos 9:12 following it) around into its pro-Gentile Mission portrait of how 'all the Gentiles upon whom My Name has been called' were to be considered part of this 'Remnant of Men seeking out the Lord.'[93]

Interestingly too, the very first line of Zechariah 13:1 actually refers to how:

> a Fountain will be opened to the House of David and to the inhabitants of Jerusalem to (wash away their) sin and uncleanness (or 'impurity'),

the relation of which 'Fountain' to 'the Well' from Numbers 21:18 'which the Princes' and 'Nobles of the People dug with the Stave' in Column VI, the 're-erection of the Tabernacle of David which is fallen' in Column VII, and 'the Fountain of Living Waters' epitomizing 'the New Covenant in the Land of Damascus' in Column VIII is unmistakable. In fact, as this section of Zechariah draws to a close – after the allusions to 'smite the Shepherd and the flock will scatter' and 'I will stretch My hand over the Little Ones' in 13:7 – the phrases from Ezekiel 9:4 that follow citation of it here in Ms. B and earlier ones from Ezekiel 5:3 about the division of the People into 'thirds' (including an allusion to the 'being scattered' in 13:7 above) – are actually being further elaborated, as we saw, in 13:8–9 in terms of the first 'two parts to be cut off and die,' but 'the third part left' as the 'Remnant,' 'tested and refined through fire,' as gold and silver are 'tested and refined.'

Furthermore, as Ms. B now expounds these several imageries, it refers back to '*those who keep the Covenant and love and keep My Commandments*' of Deuteronomy 7:9 with which Column XIX began, harking all the way back to '*those who held fast* (the commencement of the '*Steadfast*' language) *to the Commandments of God, those who remained of them*' (and '*the Remnant*' language) and '*those who entered the New Covenant in the Land of Damascus*,' '*walking in these things in Perfect Holiness according to the Covenant of God in which they were instructed*,' in the connecting passage from Columns VI–VII of Ms. A by which the additional material from Ms. B was introduced. To these Ms. B now attaches a deliberate evocation of '*the Keepers of it*' – that is, '*the Keepers of the Covenant.*'[94] But, of course, this is precisely the definition of '*the Sons of Zadok*' as implied by the exposition of Ezekiel 44:15 three columns earlier in Ms. A as well.[95] These '*Keepers*' – the actual definition, too, of '*the Sons of Zadok*' at two junctures in the Community Rule above – were, it will be recalled, in the column before that in Ms. A (CDIII) clearly being referred to, as in the Letter of James, as '*the Friends of God*' as well. Moreover, in Ms. B's description of this '*Second Visitation*' which, together '*with the coming*' or '*arising of the Messiah of Aaron and Israel*,' was imminently about to occur; they are now – combining the allusions to these '*Little Ones*' over whom God '*stretched (His) hand*' and '*the flock*' He '*scattered*' from Zechariah 13:7 above – definitively identified with '*the Meek of the flock.*'

This purposeful shift from '*the Little Ones*' in Zechariah 13 (the same '*Little Ones*,' presumably, we have seen 'Jesus' portrayed as referring to so sympathetically in Matthew 18:2–14 above and now Paul in Galatians 4:19 as well) to '*the Meek*' ('*ʿAnayyim*') in the exposition of Zechariah 13:7 is important because, not only are '*the Meek*' – already alluded to earlier in Ms. A in connection with '*each man loving his brother as himself*' in the first elaboration of '*the New Covenant in the Land of Damascus*' in Column VI preceding this – always a synonym at Qumran for the all-important '*Poor*' ('*the Ebionim*' or '*Ebionites*' – alluded to in this earlier elaboration in Ms. A above of this '*New Covenant in the Land of Damascus*' as well[96]); but these '*Meek*' are clearly the ones who are '*going to escape at the Time of the Visitation*' (that is, '*the Second Visitation*' or the one which was coming), just as they did '*at the Time of the First Visitation*' when Ezekiel '*put a mark on the foreheads of those who cry and weep.*'

This, in turn, connects up with the two references in Ms. A, as we have just seen, to '*the escape*' of '*those who held fast*' or '*the Steadfast*' (*Ha-Mehazikim*) *to the Land of the North*,' which bracket the exegeses of Amos 9:11 and the extremely obscure earlier passage from Amos 5:26–27 preceding it. As we shall interpret these things here and at the end of the book, these arcane and extremely recondite allusions actually refer to *the re-establishment* (or the hope for its '*re-establishment*') *of 'the fallen Tent of David*' in a Land '*north*' of Damascus – in other words, '*the Land of the Edessenes*' or '*the Royal Kingdom of Adiabene*' in Northern Syria and Northern Iraq, contiguous to and probably a part of it.

'The Star of your God' and *'the Saccut of your King'*

We have already to some extent discussed the exegesis of Amos 9:11–12, so graphically evoked as well in the speech Acts 15:13–21 pictures James as making in support of '*Simeon*' ('*Simeon bar Cleophas*'?) describing how '*Firstly God visited the Gentiles* (here, of course, the link-up with the several evocations of '*the First Visitation*' in both manuscripts of the Cairo Damascus Document above) *to take out a People for His Name*' – again, a speech specifically put into James' mouth. Here in these equally '*Messianic*' (though even more recondite and complex) materials from Ms. A – which are obviously supposed to represent a parallel to those in Ms. B citing Zechariah and Ezekiel and evoking '*the coming of the Messiah of Aaron and Israel*' – the exegesis of Amos 9:11 is expressed in terms of a highly '*spiritualized*' conception of '*the Community*' ('*the Jerusalem Community*' of James the Just?) and '*the Books of the Torah,*' which would have done even a Paul proud (*cf.* his 1 Corinthians 2:13 program of '*expounding spiritual things spiritually*'). It is also linked inextricably both with the interpretation of Amos 5:26–27, the citation of which precedes it, and '*the Star Prophecy*' from Numbers 24:17 which follows it.

This passage from Amos 5:26–27 is preceded in extant Amos by allusion in 5:20 to '*the Day of Yahweh*' and an expectation that '*Judgement should rain down and Righteousness* (or '*Justification*'), *a mighty stream*' in 5:24 (the source probably too of James' proclamation in the Temple of '*the Angelic Host coming on the clouds of Heaven*' and the climactic imagery of a similar genre in the War Scroll of '*Judgement*' *falling down* '*like rain on all that grows on Earth*'). It is followed in 6:1 by '*woes*' upon '*those making themselves at ease in Zion*' and a vivid description of the coming '*Exile.*' But, once again, the citation of it here in CDvii – though paralleled in more recently-released Cave 4 Damascus Document fragments – does not read exactly like the received version of Amos 5:26.

Curiously enough, the biblical Amos 5:26 actually does contain an allusion to '*the Star of your God*' which, though missing from the citation of the passage here in the Damascus Document, does pivotally in fact reappear in its exposition. Moreover, it appears to be the connecting link to '*the Star Prophecy*' from Numbers 24:17 about to be quoted, as we have already signaled, here in Column vii of Ms. A as well. This passage in Amos 5:26–27 follows directly upon an allusion in 5:25 to the unnecessariness of having to '*bring sacrifices and offerings to Me in the Wilderness for forty years*,' which may or may not bear upon the Community's attitudes towards Temple sacrifice during the time of its exodus to '*the Land of Damascus*' and dwelling in Wilderness '*Camps*' there. In addition, it may be the origin of the curious reference to '*forty years*' for '*the Period of Wrath*' which was to follow the '*gathering in*' or '*death of the Righteous Teacher*' (called at this point '*the Unique Guide*') '*until the end of all the Men of War, who turned aside* (clearly, '*from the Fountain*' or '*Well of Living Waters*' mentioned previously) *with the Man of Lying*.'[97] It reads as follows:

> *Rather you carried the Tabernacle of your* '*Moloch*' (this actually reads '*Siccut of your Moloch*' or, even possibly '*Siccut of your King*' – '*Moloch*' and '*Melech*'/ '*King*' being based on the same root and, in effect, homonyms in Hebrew, as are '*Siccut*' or '*Saccut*' – which seems to be a designation for an Assyrian Deity – and '*Succah*'/'*Tabernacle*,' which will now be how these terms will be read and exploited in the exegesis to follow) *and* '*Kiyyun*' (or '*Kaiwan*' – also apparently an Assyrian Deity) *of your images,* '*the Star of your God*,' *which you made by yourselves* (this will go on to connect in the text of Column VII with '*the Star that shall go forth from Jacob*' from Numbers 24:17, as just explained). *Therefore I will exile you far beyond Damascus* ('*mehalah le-Dammashek*' – crucially, this will be changed in Ms. A to '*me-Ohali Dammashek*'/'*from My Tent of Damascus*' – a pivotal transformation, albeit retaining the geographical sense of the original). *Thus says the Lord, whose Name is the God of Hosts* (here both the references to God's '*Name*' as, for example, in '*God first visiting the Gentiles to take out a People for His Name*' in James' speech in Acts 15:14 and in Acts 15:17 loosely quoting Amos 9:12 – James still speaking – '*all the Nations upon whom My Name has been called*').[98]

As just indicated, this is subtly transformed in the citation of it in Ms. A, we shall now provide below (as it is to some extent in Acts). Nevertheless traces of the underlying original are still present, so it is obviously a very important proof-text for the sectaries at Qumran and, as just remarked, it is paralleled in the fragments of the Damascus Document that were finally released following the request by Professor Davies and myself in 1989 which triggered the more recent struggle '*to free*' the Scrolls – this being the kind of thing we were seeking to ascertain[99] – though the reworked or compressed variant represented by Ms B, however inspiring and brimming with significance, has not yet been paralleled in these extant Cave 4 fragments.[100]

This is an extremely important point because, not only does it mean that *the Damascus Document was probably still not circulating in a final fixed form* at the time of the deposit in Cave 4 (that is, there was more than one if not several versions of it in circulation outside of Cave 4) and that therefore, probably, *it was a comparatively late document in the life of the 'Community'* of those responsible for having written it; but that *both versions of it had been seen by those who copied the document ending up in the Cairo Genizah* or, at least, they or those from whom they received it, *thought they were dealing with two versions of the same document* and were already trying to harmonize them or put the two versions together in the same document.[101]

It also probably means that those who were apparently using it to write their version of the history in the Book of Acts, only knew, or seemed to only know the first version, the one presenting '*the Star*' as '*the Doresh*' or '*Interpreter of the Torah that came to Damascus*' who, for them, was obviously Paul – though *what he was doing was, rather, 'interpreting the Law' out of existence*. One might even say (if we could pry the dating of these documents from the previously rigid casing in which they have been ensconced – as if they are fixed in stone – over the last fifty-five years since their discovery) that what we have here is not simply the literature of a '*Movement*' we all call '*Essenes*,' as we have explained in the early chapters of this book; but rather, also, a cache of what might be called '*Ebionite*' Documents, of which the fulsome term of self-reference they so often applied to themselves, '*the Ebionim*,' provides vivid evidence – a type of militant or apocalyptic '*Ebionite Movement*' of course – of which we were before unaware.[102]

Be these things as they may, just as with these other parallel '*Movements*,' whether precursors or successors – not least of which one must include the '*Christianity*' of a *Paul*; the signification of this passage from Amos 5:26–27 is now reversed or, at least, altered through creative rewriting and compression – in the exegesis especially the reversal of the original sense is made plain – and it reads as we have been signaling:

> *But the Steadfast* (the '*Ha-Mehazikim*,' we have been accentuating, that is, '*those who held fast to the Torah*' or '*Covenant*' and '*its Ordinances*' – this takes it out of the '*Pauline*' sphere right from the start and even makes it look as if those writing this and other documents – just as '*the Ebionites*' they so much resemble – were aware of a Pauline-type '*Adversary*' who was emphasizing just the reverse) *escaped to the Land of the North* (here the '*beyond Damascus*' of the underlying original from Amos 5:26, the pull of which, while not specifically quoted in the citation as it is being com-

pressed, still makes itself felt). *As He said, 'And I will exile* (or *'cause to go into Exile'* – in the original biblical Amos 5:26, this is: '*and you have carried,*' the '*causing to go into Exile*' of the citation being taken from the next line, Amos 5:27 – another important compression which at the same time demonstrates awareness of the original) *the Siccut of your King* (this can also be read '*Saccut*' and in the exegesis, as we have already indicated, is transformed into the pregnant '*the Succat of the King*' – n.b., the transposition of the two '*waw*'s representing the vowels '*o*' and '*u*' really does take place in the text. This new expression – '*the*' substituted for '*your*' – will then be used to evoke '*the fallen Tabernacle*'/'*Succat of David*' from Amos 9:11 that immediately follows in this all-important exegesis in Column VII. This is how subtle and complex these expositions really are) *and the Kiyyun* (or '*Kaiwan*') *of your images* (this, too, through a subtle shift in spelling ,will be re-interpreted in the exegesis as '*the bases*'/'*kiyyunei of the statues*' – if it has not already been understood as such in the citation – in order to develop the sense of the foundational nature of '*the Books of the Prophets*' about to be esoterically evoked in the exegesis as well) *from My Tent in Damascus.*'[103]

Needless to say, again this exposition is extremely recondite, '*the King*' ('*Melech*' – revised from '*Moloch*' in the original), as per Pauline exposition in 1 Corinthians 12:12–27 about Jesus being '*the Community*' and John 2:21 about his body being '*the Temple*' (for 1 Corinthians, there being little difference between '*the body*' and '*the Temple*' anyhow), is definitely stated to be '*the Community.*'

Interestingly enough, the citation of Amos 5:25–27 (like Amos 9:11–12) is actually paralleled too in Acts 7:42–43 – this time in the speech attributed to '*Stephen*,' whom we have already identified as a stand-in for James. Not only is this curious, but whatever the truth-value of '*Stephen*''s speech, the citation – which, as always as the speech progresses, is turned against the Jewish People as a whole with the accusation of being '*stiff-necked and uncircumcised in heart and ears*' (thus!), '*always resisting the Holy Spirit,*' persecuting '*the Prophets,*' and '*killing the ones who prophesied the coming of the Just One, whose Betrayers and Murderers you now have become* (this certainly does go, as it were, a little '*over the top*') and, just as the one later in Acts 15:16–18, is reflected in the Septuagint – makes it clear that the original of Amos was being read as referring to '*Moloch.*'

Even perhaps more importantly, the speech put into Stephen's mouth in Acts 7:43 also includes the introductory line from Amos 5:25, we noted above as so relevant to Qumran ideology: '*Did you offer up to Me victims and sacrifices forty years in the wilderness, O House of Israel?*'; and, for some reason, re-interprets – as in the Septuagint as well – '*Kiyyun your god*' as '*the god Rephan*,' whatever this means. Moreover, it includes the fairly unique phraseology, '*written in the Book of the Prophets*,'[104] paralleled by the phrase in James' speech in Acts 15:15 introducing the citation of Amos 9:11: '*the words of the Prophets…as it has been written*,' also about to be evoked in this exegesis of Amos 9:11 here in Ms. A that follows in the Damascus Document as well. Just as relevantly, these are also basically the words the Habakkuk *Pesher* uses in Columns II and VII when describing, as we have seen, '*the Righteous Teacher*' as a scriptural exegete.[105]

'The Doresh ha-Torah who Came to Damascus' and 'the Escape of the Steadfast to the Land of the North'

The allusion to '*Books*' is about to appear as well (as will the evocation of '*Israel*') in the several pivotal exegeses that now follow in Column VII of Ms. A – in the first place, in the exegesis of '*the Tabernacle of the King*,' now reformulated in the place of '*the Siccut*' or '*Siccat of your Moloch*' of original Amos 5:26. This new phraseology is then used, as just underscored, not only to link up with the explicit evocation of Amos 9:11's '*fallen Tabernacle*' or '*Tent of David*' but, from thence, on to the Messianic '*Star Prophecy*' of Numbers 24:17:

> *The Books of the Torah* (here the first '*Books*'), *they are* '*the Tabernacle of the King*' (the '*the*' now replacing the '*your*' of '*your Moloch*,' as we just saw, in original Amos above), *as He (God) said* (at this point the link to the more '*Davidic*' Amos 9:11 develops), '*I will raise up* ('*establish*' or '*re-erect*') *the Tabernacle of David which is fallen*' –

itself, of course, word-for-word the words of James' speech in Acts 15:16.

The second evocation of the allusion to '*Books*' then follows on immediately in the totally esoteric exegesis of the combined and reformulated two original passages from Amos that now ensues:

> '*The King*' *is the Community and* '*the Bases (Kiyyunei) of the Statues*' (once again here, the '*the*' replaces the '*your*' and the suffix, '*ei*,' transforming it into a plural and confirmed by the Cave 4 fragment-parallel of CD, is added) – '*the Kiyyun of the images*' (not only is this *a quasi-redundancy which does not include the plural suffix*, it probably reflects the Medieval redactor or copyist's own confusion over the citation, as it does not seem to appear in the extant Cave 4 parallel – itself a little fragmentary at this point[106]) – *they are* '*the Books of the Prophets*' (here the '*Books*'/'*words*'

allusion *which does appear in James' speech* in Acts 15:15, *as it does in Stephen's* in Acts 7:25 and *the two evocations of the Righteous Teacher's exegetical powers* in the Habakkuk *Pesher*), *whose words Israel despised* (and here, the allusion to '*Israel*,' we just highlighted, from Amos 5:25 above).[107]

In the first place, this is an allegorical exposition of the utmost import since it makes clear that the bedrock foundation of the Community, esoteric or otherwise, really is *both 'the Books of the Torah'* and '*the Prophets.*' Moreover, it leads right into both the evocation of '*the Star*' – the '*Star*' that was present in Amos 5:25-26's original '*the Star of your God*,' in apposition to the '*Kiyyun of your images*' but which dropped away from the quotation of it in Ms. A (as should now be clear – only superficially) – and from thence into citation of the all-important '*Star Prophecy.*' All are now – in, one might add, typical Pauline and/or New Testament style – completely reversed. The '*Siccut of your Moloch*' is now '*the Tabernacle of the King*,' interpreted esoterically as '*the Books of the Torah*' as well as the resultant restored '*fallen Tabernacle of David*;' and '*the Kiyyun of your images, the Star of your God*' are no longer negatives and idols '*which you made for yourselves*' but, now, complete positives – namely '*the Doresh ha-Torah*' (picking up on all the allusions to '*seeking*' that preceded it and, as we shall see, playing off the homophone, '*yarash*' – '*inherit*' / '*possess*' – below, probably equivalent to '*the Righteous Teacher*' himself) – and, by implication, '*the Messiah*' of '*the Star*' / '*Sceptre*' language of Numbers 24:17 (paralleled in Ms. B by '*the Messiah of Aaron and Israel*'). Also the '*Kiyyun of your images*' is reversed into '*the Bases of the Statues*' and what was originally a negative is now turned into an esoteric positive, namely '*the Books of the Prophets.*'

The whole now reads as we have to some extent already seen:

And the Star is the Interpreter of the Torah (Doresh ha-Torah – here the verbal noun of Acts 15:17's and the Septuagint's '*darash*' in place of the Hebrew '*yarash*' / '*possessed*' of Amos 9:12 and CD 1.7's '*Root of Planting*,' as evoked in Acts' presentation of James' '*the Remainder of Men seeking the Lord*'), *who came to Damascus, as it is written, 'A Star shall go forth from Jacob and a Sceptre shall arise* (or '*stand up*') *out of Israel.' The 'Sceptre' is the Prince* ('*Nasi*' – the actual name applied to Bar Kochba on the coins in his name in the 132–36 CE Period during the Second Jewish Revolt[108]) *of the whole Assembly* ('*Congregation*' / '*Church*') *and with his standing up* (or '*arising*' – again, as we have seen, which can also mean '*be resurrected*'), *he will utterly eradicate all the Sons of Seth* (in the War Scroll, '*the Seven Nations of Vanity*,' as already remarked as well).

All of this is recapitulated, it will be recalled, with the assertion that: '*These escaped at the Time of the First Visitation while the Backsliders were delivered up to the sword*,' a reference which clearly goes back to '*the Steadfast who would escape to the Land of the North*' with which the whole passage in Column VII began. Also, though the two manuscripts now come together here again, the words turning these arcane allusions into a comparison, '*as it was at the Time of the First Visitation*,' which occur at this point in Ms. B, have either somehow dropped away or are considered to have been implied in Ms. A.

In Ms. B, it will be recalled as well, these '*Escapees*' or '*Emigrants*' – in Ms. A '*to the Land of the North*' – were '*the Keepers*' ('*of the Covenant*' par excellence – '*the Sons of Zadok*' in the Community Rule and earlier in Column IV), '*the Meek of the Flock who would escape* (as '*at the Time of the First Visitation*' when, in Ezekiel 9:4, the Angel-like '*scribe*' marks '*the foreheads of those who weep and cry*')...*the avenging sword of the Covenant*'; so, even here in Ms. A, there would appear to be an '*as it was*' of comparison left out, meaning that in this '*Time of the Second Visitation*,' '*the Steadfast*,' too, *would* '*escape to the Land of the North*' as they had '*at the Time of the First Visitation*.' Though this clearly relates to the earlier Assyrian Exile, the way these several quotations from Amos are being parsed in Ms. A – all the words being deconstructed and taken separately – the whole (as in Ms. B, as we already underscored) is being interpreted '*Messianically*' as the evocation of '*the Star Prophecy*' of Numbers 24:17 – also evoked in the climactic section of the War Scroll above – will and does irrefutably proves.

Other than a completely esoteric meaning, the only sense that can really be made out of it is that something – either '*the Tabernacle*,' '*Tent*,' or the Davidic-style '*Kingship*' – is being exiled to '*a Land north of*' or '*beyond Damascus*' – for our purposes, as already indicated, Northern Syria or further East in Adiabene and Northern Mesopotamia. However one interprets these passages, we are in a '*Damascus*' or '*Land of Damascus*' milieu and surrounding allusions to '*the Tabernacle of the King*' or '*Tabernacle of David*' being '*exiled from My Tent in Damascus*' seem to point to a '*Land*' even further '*North*' than this. In my view, this points to Jewish '*Messianic*' hopes being focused upon a Royal family '*North*' of Damascus which, in turn, bears on the contemporary conversions of King Agbar in Edessa/Antiochia Orrhoe and Queen Helen and her son Izates further East in Adiabene. Since the events are for the most part contemporary, they are hard to separate and minor differences in detail may be due largely to the vantage points of the individual sources involved.

In the way we propose to re-interpret these things, imagery of this kind will have to do with attempts to re-establish this *'fallen Tabernacle'* or *'Tent of the King'* among such Gentile *'Convert'* Kings in this region, just as our various *'conversion'* stories imply – Kings (or Queens) who were willing to take their relationship to *'David'* and the Mosaic Covenant and *'Torah'* or *'Law'* seriously – a little more seriously, for example, than do those we can with some certitude refer to as *'Herodians.'*

It is clear that to more nationalist Jewish *'Zealots'* like Izates *'Galilean'* teacher *'Eleazar'* (thus) including, probably, Qumran-style *'Nazirites'* of whom Helen seems to have been inordinately fond, the Royal Family of Adiabene would have been seen as a more salutary replacement for the hated *'Herodians.'* Its members were prominently involved in the earliest engagements of the War against Rome – two in particular, as we have emphasized, Monobazus and Kenedaeus, martyring themselves to stop the Roman Army coming up the Pass at Beit Horon in the first heady days of the First Jewish Revolt.[109] Its members also appear to have been involved, as we have been observing as well, in the Bar Kochba or Second Jewish Uprising and R. Akiba's marriage to a scion of this family connected to it (in such a context, Bar Kochba would then be *'the Nasi ha-ᶜEdah'* and R. Akiba, *'the Doresh ha-Torah who came to Damascus,'* though this is probably a little far-fetched, depending upon the vagaries of dating).

However this may be, combined as this second reference to God's coming *'Visitation'* is to *'going out from the Land of Judah and dwelling in the Land of Damascus'* and *'the New Covenant'* God would *'raise up' there* (starting in Column IV but continued and more fully delineated in Column VI); this begins to look like nothing so much as either a companion to or variety of *'the Pella Flight'* tradition recorded, as we have seen above, in all early Church tradition and tied to the death of James.

We have already encountered this *'holding fast'* or *'Steadfast'* imagery with regard to the *'Victorious Life,'* those *'holding fast'* to *'the House of Faith'* would enjoy, at the end of Column III (in Column XX of Ms. B also seemingly referred to, as we have seen, as *'the House of the Torah'*). It is connected to the very important *'strengthening'* imagery found throughout the Damascus Document and, as we shall see below, the *Florilegium*[110]. At the end of Column XX of Ms. B, too, which both parallels and in the end adds on much material to Column Eight of Ms. A, we have already seen, how these same *'Penitents of sin (in) Jacob'* – who *'held fast to these Ordinances'* or *'Judgements,'* who *'listened to the voice of the Righteous Teacher and did not abandon the Laws of Righteousness,'* *'confessing their Sins'* (this, of course, further strengthens the oblique allusion to the same *'Deliverer'* Paul evokes in Romans 11:20 above who – as he says – *'will turn away Sin in Jacob*') would, as several times underscored as well, '*see His Salvation, because they put their trust in His Holy Name*'![III]

All this, then, is the Qumran parallel to Acts' presentation of James' speech at the climax of '*the Jerusalem Council*' – following Peter's pro-Pauline oration about the '*heart-knowing God purifying the Gentiles' hearts through Faith*' – about how '*God first visited to take out of the Gentiles a People for His Name*' (again note the analogue to the allusion to a '*First Visitation*' here). Not only does the correlating passage in the Damascus Document come after allusion – amid strong '*Messianic*' imagery – to '*the New Covenant in the Land of Damascus*' but, as we just saw, the biblical passages evoked are obscure and the surrounding text difficult to decipher. That the texts from Amos and Numbers are only present in Ms. A deepens the puzzle, but even Ms. B is '*Messianic*' at this point, unflinchingly referring to '*the coming* (and not the '*arising*') *of the Messiah of Aaron and Israel.*'

In Ms. A the allusion to and exegesis of '*establishing*' or '*re-erecting the Tabernacle of David which is fallen*' are directly followed, as we have seen as well, by the famous exposition of Numbers 24:17 of '*the Star*' as '*the Interpreter of the Law* ('*the Doresh ha-Torah*') *who came to Damascus*' (here, Acts' and the Septuagint's '*darash*' of '*the Gentiles seeking the Lord*' above instead of Hebrew Amos' '*yarash*' of '*possessing the Remnant of Edom and the Gentiles called by*' God's '*Name*'), material seemingly paralleled in Acts' presentation of Paul's equally famous *conversion* '*on the road to Damascus.*'

Of course the '*Jacob*' here – just as several columns later in the obscure allusion to '*the Penitents of Sin (in) in Jacob,*' harking back to the famous '*Redeemer*' or '*Deliverer*' of Isaiah 59:20 and Paul in Romans 11:20 above, who '*will come out of Jacob,*' which seems to parallel both '*the Priests*' who were '*the Penitents of Israel*' in Column IV and, as we shall see, '*the Diggers*' of '*the Well of living waters*' in '*the Land of Damascus,*' who *will be* '*the Penitents of Israel*' in Column VI – may literally refer to James, the basis of his name in Hebrew. Whereas for Acts '*the Interpreter of the Torah who came to Damascus*' is certainly presented as being a Paul (and in this regard, one should not forget *the reversals involved in all these designations*), though, as we already saw, *his* '*interpretation*' *was to interpret it out of existence.*

These matters are certainly as complex as they are recondite, a fact working to the advantage of the authority of those during the last Nineteen Centuries who would attempt to simplify them. But they are not impossible and, with a little diligence, the reader should be able to see through to the relationships underlying them. Plus now we have the Dead Sea Scrolls – themselves quasi-contemporary '*Messianic*' documents.

22

'The Star who Came to Damascus' and 'the Song of the Well'

The Florilegium: A Compendium of Messianic Promises to David and *'his Seed'*

To properly understand this cluster of esotericisms and '*Messianic*' allusions, one should probably go back a few columns to the citations from both Numbers and Isaiah in Column Six of Ms. A; but, before doing so, we should perhaps have a closer look at the peculiar document John Allegro called the *Florilegium* (so named, because it seemed to him a '*Bouquet*' of texts – more specifically, in fact, '*A Bouquet of the Promises to David and his Seed in the Last Days*'[1]). Strikingly, the Amos 9:11 proof-text found in James' speech in Acts 15:16–17 above and Column Seven of Ms. A – '*I shall raise up* ('*hakimoti*' in CDVII.16; in received Amos, just '*akim*') *the Succat of David which is fallen*' – also appears in it.[2] Though its thrust is slightly different – in this instance seemingly applied along with the promises to David in 2 Samuel 7:5–17 – to which it is appended – and those in Psalm 89:7–24, to both '*the Doresh ha-Torah*' and '*the Branch of David*' (as we have seen, identified in '*The Messianic Leader*' fragment – probably of the War Scroll – found by Professor Wise and myself in 1990, with '*the Nasi ha-ʿEdah*' or '*the Head*' or '*Prince of the Congregation*' or '*Church*'[3]). Still it is completely '*Messianic*' – even perhaps more than CDVI-VII and xix-xx.

Actually this is probably more or less the interpretation of Ms. A as well where, as will be recalled, the string of '*Messianic*' proof-texts in Column VII was held together by an underlying allusion to '*the Star*' from Amos 5:26 (never quoted as such in the actual text, but implied), used to trip-wire the quotation of Amos 9:11 and evocation of '*the Star Prophecy*' that directly followed. The exposition of this last (just as in the case of '*the Branch*') in the *Florilegium*, then focused on – in addition to '*the Doresh ha-Torah*' – '*the Sceptre*' who '*would arise out of Israel*.' He, in turn – once more emphasizing his '*arising*' or '*standing up*' – was identified with '*the Nasi Chol ha-ʿEdah*' ('*the Head*' or '*Prince of the Entire Community*'), who would – in a paraphrase of the second part of Numbers 24:17 and laying the stress on his militancy as well – '*utterly destroy all the Sons of Seth.*'⁴

As the *Florilegium* puts a parallel idea in its exposition of 2 Samuel 7:12–14 together with Amos 9:11, either one or both of these – that is, '*the Zemach*' or '*Branch of David*' (identified in 4Q285, as just underscored, with '*the Nasi ha-ᶜEdah*') '*together with the Doresh ha-Torah*' – would also '*arise*' or '*stand up in Zion at the End of Days.*' Here the verb '*arise*'/'*stand up,*' redundant or otherwise, is repeated twice and perhaps even more.⁵ Perhaps more tellingly yet, still another portentous expository phrase is added: '*to save Israel*' (the actual Hebrew here is '*lehoshiᶜa*' as in '*Salvation*'/ '*Yeshuᶜa*'/'*Joshua*'/'*Saviour*' – not '*lehazzil,*' the alternate way of express-ing a similar idea as, for instance, in the Habakkuk *Pesher's* exposition of Habakkuk 2:4 – '*the Righteous shall live by his Faith*' – '*saved from the House of*' or '*Last Judgement*').⁶ Nothing could be more '*Messianic*' than this.

In addition, it is well to remember that this verb, '*stand up,*' will be attached in later columns of Ms. A – just as at this point in Column VII it is to '*the Sceptre*' – to '*the standing up of the Messiah of Aaron and Israel,*' identifying this last as an obvious synonym of this '*Sceptre,*' to say nothing of '*the Nasi*' or '*the Branch*' – as it is in Column XIX of Ms. B anyhow.⁷ As already remarked, these things are as recondite as they are complex. Nor is it without relevance that this '*Zemach-David*' or '*Branch of David,*' as the *Florilegium* and 4Q285 would express it, is exactly the same '*Root*' (no pun intended) as CD Ms. A uses in its prelude to characterize how God '*caused a Root of Planting to grow (yizmach) out of Aaron and Israel*' to '*possess*' or '*inherit His Land*' ('*lirosh*'). Here '*yizmach*'/'*to cause to grow*' is a variant of the designation '*Zemach*'/'*Branch.*'

Here, too, the root of this infinitive '*lirosh*'/'*Y-R-Sh,*' as will be recalled, is the same as that found in Amos 9:12 concerning '*possessing the Remnant of Edom and all the Nations upon whom My Name has been called*' – changed in the Septuagint and James' speech, for some reason, into '*darash*'/'*seek*' as in '*seeking the Lord*' or '*the Doresh ha-Torah*'/'*the Seeker after*' or '*Interpreter of the Torah*' In applying this same '*seeking*'/ '*darash*' in the Greek of Acts 15:17 – in line, seemingly, with the new, more cosmopolitan thrust of the exegesis being attributed to James – to '*the Remnant who seek the Lord and all the Gentiles upon whom My Name has been called*' '*the Doresh*' or '*Seeker after the Torah*' in CDvii.16–18's exe-gesis of Amos 9:11 and in the *Florilegium* above – to say nothing of the original sense of Amos 9:12 in Hebrew of '*possessing*' or '*inheriting the Land*' (clearly being played off, as we can now see, in Column One's pres-entation of the Messianic '*Root,*' God '*had planted,*' '*to possess His Land,*' *never to be* '*uprooted*') – has gone by the boards.⁸

This is not the only usage in the *Florilegium* with parallels to the

Damascus Document, thereby identifying it as one of a cluster of documents – along with *MMT*, the War Scroll, the Temple Scroll, the Habakkuk and Psalm 37 *Peshers, etc.* – all probably written at about the same time. This is what is meant by having regard for the internal data, as we have emphasized it, especially where the external data is as fragile as it is where Qumran is concerned.

Having said this, the sequence of texts which the *Florilegium* represents is truly extraordinary where '*Messianic*' and '*Davidic*' Prophecy is concerned. Not only does it begin with a quotation from Psalm 89:23, the interpretation of which is eschatological, meaning, having to do with '*the Last Days*,' and involving '*the House*' or '*Temple*,' '*the Temple*' in which '*the Lord will reign forever and ever*,' as the quotation then included from Exodus 15:17–18 expresses it; this is followed by the above prophecy, which in Samuel 7:5–13 is attributed to Nathan, *conferring on David* and '*his seed*' the '*Throne of his Kingdom forever*' and *instructing him* '*to build*' this same '*House*' or '*Temple*' *in which* God '*would dwell.*' Furthermore, it even avers, perhaps even more significantly, that God '*will be for him a Father and he will be (for God) a son*'!

Not only is this one of the most completely pro-David texts in the whole Old Testament and, if one were going to choose a text relating *the* '*Messianic*' *promises to David and* '*his seed*' *forevermore*, one could not find a better one; but also a more pro-'*Zionist*' passage also is hard to imagine.[9] Moreover, the above points from 2 Samuel 7:10–16 are preserved in the extant passages of the *Florilegium* even though some of it is fragmentary. Not only is the above passage from 2 Samuel 7:12 – alluding to the '*seed*' of David – actually referred to but, perhaps even more significantly, it does so in conjunction with the all-important verb '*hakimoti*' ('*I will set up*') again, used in Amos 9:11 to express how the '*fallen Tabernacle of David*' *will be* '*rebuilt*' or '*restored.*' This is a telltale combination.

Likewise, '*the Establishment of the Throne of his Kingdom forever*' is twice promised in 7:13 and 16 and, as just alluded to, this vision 2 Samuel attributes to Nathan goes even further, averring '*I shall be his Father and he shall be My son*,' a promise of the most inestimable significance for '*Christianity*' to follow, which has not failed to leave its mark on the Scrolls as well, both in the document most refer to as '*the Qumran Hymns*' and '*the Son of God*' text we shall treat in more detail below. Just as strikingly, the '*planting*' language, the basis probably of '*the Root of Planting*' allusion in the First Column of the Damascus Document above, is part of this oracle as well in the affirmation, attributed to Nathan, that God

would appoint a place for (His) People Israel and plant them so that they might dwell in it and never be disturbed again (7:10).

In fact, this promise should probably be considered the source of the whole passage, as it presently stands in CDi.7-8 and paralleled, too, in extant Qumran fragments from Cave 4.

Psalm 89:23–36 with which this first and best-preserved part of the *Florilegium* commences is also, it should be appreciated, one of the most completely *pro-David, Sinaitic Covenant-oriented*, and '*Messianic*' Psalms in the Old Testament as well. In it, '*his seed will be forever*,' paralleling 2 Samuel above and meaning David's, is repeated not once but twice (89:29 and 36 – *cf.*, too, Paul's '*seed*' language including '*the seed of David*' in Romans 1:3, 4:13–18, 9:7–8, 2 Corinthians 11:22, Galatians 3:16–29, etc., already remarked above). Moreover, it also includes the phrase in 89:30, paralleling 2 Samuel 7:13 and 16 above, '*his Throne will be as the Days of Heaven.*' Also – in line with its overtly pro-David orientation and '*the Kingship*' promised him and '*his seed forever*' – it is completely xenophobic, that is, it is not sympathetic or friendly to the admission of '*Gentiles*' or '*foreigners*' into either this '*Community of the Last Days*' or '*the Temple*' or both (as Acts 15:7–21 portrays Peter and James to be). The opposite.

Not only is this '*House*' – which in the interpretation is equivalent to '*the Place*' God was going to '*appoint*' for them '*in the Last Days*' (itself probably based on 2 Samuel 7:10 above on '*appointing a Place for My People Israel*' and presaged as well, probably, by the line from Psalm 89:22 preceding the first quoted line 89:23, '*with the oil of My Holiness, I have anointed him*'/'*meshahtaiv*,' one of the fundamental bases for all actual '*Messianism*' derived from such idioms subsequently) – the same, for example, as CDiii.19's '*House of Faith in Israel, the likes of which has not stood from ancient times till now*' (also called, '*the House of the Torah*')[10]; it is, also,equivalent to the '*House of Holiness for Israel*' in the Community Rule (based on the esoteric meaning of the '*Twelve*' Israelite members of the Community Council and meaning, as in the above exposition in the *Florilegium*, '*the Temple*'[11]) or the '*House*,' Paul characterizes in 2 Corinthians 5:1 as:

> *a Building from God, a House not made with (human) hands, (but)*
> *Eternal in the Heavens.*

Furthermore, clearly paralleling the latter but probably in a more corporeal way, the *Florilegium* – interspersing at this point, and as per its methodology, a quotation from Exodus 15:17–18 – describes this '*House*' (that is, '*the Temple*' of the Community Rule above) as the one '*the Lord* (the source of Acts 15:17's '*seeking the Lord*' above?) *will* '*establish with His own hands*' and *in which He* '*shall reign for ever and ever.*'[12] Here the parallel with Paul in 2 Corinthians 5:1 is just about exact – though '*a House,*' as just alluded to, clearly *not* '*in the Heavens,*' but in line rather with more revanchist and restorative Jewish '*Messianic*' ideals, *the Earthly Jerusalem.*

Here too a xenophobic or nationalist streak clearly shines through, as the *Florilegium* specifically asserts that this is going to be '*a House*' in which no '*Ammonite or Moabite*' or '*foreigner or alien*' shall ever be allowed '*to enter until Eternity, because His Holiness* (or '*Holy Ones*') *is there.*' As already suggested, this is almost the exact opposite of the exegesis of Acts 15:7–17 above, but totally in accord with passages from both '*MMT*' and the Temple Scroll[13] and the sort of '*internal*' data that argues, in our view, for a more or less contemporaneous authorship of all these kinds of documents.[14]

Moreover, if the allusion is to '*Holy Ones,*' then of course here we have the typical Qumran view that '*the Holy Angels*' dwell with either '*the Community*' or the People, whether in the '*the Camps*' where the '*Nazir-ite*'-style extreme purity regulations were in effect *because* '*the Holy Angels were with*' their inhabitants[15], or in '*the Chief of the Camps of Israel*' – as '*MMT*' would put it[16]– meaning '*Jerusalem*' and, in particular, '*the Jerusalem Temple.*' In fact, if the allusion to '*alien*' or '*resident alien,*' which the present writer prefers (the underlying Hebrew usage being simply '*ger*'), were also to be read as '*proselyte,*' as some translators suggest,[17] then this is even more xenophobic than just about any document in the entire Qumran corpus.

However this may be, though all this is seemingly in exposition of Exodus 15:17–18 introducing the '*Messianic*' promises to David and '*his seed*' in 2 Samuel 7:12–14 above, to some extent, as the *Florilegium* continues this exposition; it echoes the words of 2 Samuel 7:10 about Israel '*being planted*' and '*dwelling*' in its own *Land* and not '*being afflicted by the Children of Evil anymore*' ('*Belial,*' as the usage ultimately becomes below) in asserting,

> (*For the Glory of the Lord*) *shall appear over it always* (meaning '*the Temple*' again) *and no foreigners will lay it waste again as they formerly did.*

It is at this point it adds the pregnant allusion about '*the Temple of Israel because of their Sin*' (note here that, if Jesus in the New Testament is equated with '*the Temple*' as some characterizations insist, then this pretty much harmonizes with the outlook of a number of New Testament documents as well), which seems almost to imply the Temple has at this point already been destroyed.[18]

Just as strikingly, in then going on to characterize the offerings that were going to be made in this 'House – clearly the one 'to be raised up for (God) at the End of Days' of the second line of the preserved text – as 'works of the Torah' ('ma'asei-Torah' – again note the emphasis on 'doing' and its correlating vocabulary of 'works Righteousness'); the Florilegium actually employs another mystifying allusion in describing the 'command' God gave 'to build for Himself a Temple of Man' or 'Mikdash Adam'![19] The word being employed here really is 'Adam' which can in a sense, of course, also be construed as an evocation of 'the Primal Adam' ideology again. But we have already seen how, in Acts 15:16's version of James' evocation of 'building up the ruins' of 'the fallen Tabernacle of David,' instead of the allusion, 'possessing the Remnant of Edom' that actually follows in Biblical Amos 9:12 and evoked after a fashion in CDI.7-8 as well; Acts 15:17 rather goes on – somewhat tendentiously in view of the above – to describe how this 'Tabernacle' is going to be 'set up'

> so that the Remnant of Men may seek out the Lord and all the Peoples (Ethne) upon whom My Name has been called.

Here we again have the 'seeking' language – in our view, to some extent derived, as we already saw, from 'the Doresh ha-Torah' in these exegeses at Qumran; but also the 'Edom' of Amos 9:12's original, which is generically not really distinguishable – as we also saw – from either 'Adam' or 'Man' in Hebrew. Though not immediately apparent, this devolves into 'Men' in the Greek. It is an intricate conundrum the writer is unable to penetrate further unless the same language complex is underlying all three of these documents: Acts, the Florilegium, and the Damascus Document, which would also mean that the authors of Acts are already changing their version of the language of Hebrew Amos 9:12 by incorporating usages derived from these exegeses at Qumran.

However this may be, the text now goes on to expound yet another part of the phraseology of 2 Samuel 7:11 about how the Lord would obtain for David 'rest from all (his) enemies,' now interpreted – as earlier regarding how 'foreigners would no longer lay waste' the Temple – in terms, again presumably, of the 'My People Israel' of Psalm 89:23 in the second line of the preserved text. This now becomes, as already suggested as well, how the Lord 'would obtain for them (that is, those presumably, too, who 'hold fast to the Commandments at the End of Days') rest from all the Sons of Belial' – the 'Sons of Belial' usage now taking the place of 'the Sons of Evil' of 2 Samuel 7:10 above (again, not specifically quoted in the text, but implied).[19] This 'Sons of Belial' idiom is, of course, more characteristic of and an important one at Qumran, which is also found elsewhere in the Scrolls.[20]

It usually refers, in the writer's view – because of the 'Balaam'/ 'Bela^c'/'swallowing' symbolism underlying it – to a complex of persons in and around the Herodian Establishment.[21] Not only does this 'Sons of Belial' usage and two other references to 'Belial' – generally coupled with another to their antithesis 'the Sons of Light' – precede these all-important citations from 2 Samuel 7:12–14 about 'raising up (David's) seed after (him)' and 'establishing the Throne of his Kingdom forever'; they introduce the pivotal 'I will be a Father to him and he shall be a son to Me,' which is then interpreted, as just highlighted, in terms of 'the Branch of David who will stand up in Zion together with the Doresh ha-Torah,' itself both introducing and tied to the pivotal evocation of 'raising up (the same 'hakimoti' too, as we saw, in 'raising up the seed of David after him' in 2 Samuel 7:12) the fallen Tabernacle of David' from Amos 9:11. This, in turn, is then yet again specifically and somewhat redundantly interpreted to mean:

> It (that is, 'the Tabernacle of David which is fallen' just mentioned above) is the Tabernacle of David which will stand up to save Israel.[22]

Though by this time the reader's head will, no doubt, be reeling – particularly if not directly consulting a text – nevertheless one can say that this whole complex of citations tied to the exegesis of Amos 9:11–12 both here and in the Damascus Document – and to be fair, the speech attributed to James in Acts 15:13–20 – presents us with the entire scriptural underpinning of 'Messianism' in this period, including 'the Throne,' 'the Branch,' 'the Sceptre,' 'the Root of Planting,' and 'the seed,' which also becomes so much a part of early 'Christian' ideology to follow. In fact, even in its somewhat fragmentary or incomplete state of preservation, the 'Pesher' – and 'the Florilegium' is a Pesher on a 'Bouquet' or 'Selection' of Messianic and Davidic eschatological proof-texts, the only question being its original length and what other passages might have been included in it, if any – basically represents a kind of proto-Gospel of the kind of a Matthew, it being understood that it is not from a 'Paulinized' point-of-view sympathetic to 'the Gentile Mission' of a Paul, but rather the opposite – the nationalist, Hebrew, xenophobic, or Mosaic Covenantal.

It cannot be stressed too much that this reference to Amos 9:11, quoted here in the Florilegium exactly as it is in Column Seven of the Damascus Document, comes precisely following the citation by it of

644

2 Samuel 7:14 (itself reprised in the Qumran Hymns below[23]): *I shall be a Father to him and he shall be a son to Me.'* What is more, the *Florilegium* then connects this quotation with *'the Branch of David,'* it insists this 2 Samuel 7:14 passage refers to, who *'in the Last Days will stand'* (again, together with *'the Doresh ha-Torah'* – more intertextuality) or *'rise up in Zion to save Israel'* (*lehoshiʿa*), introducing an eschatological dimension to the whole complex of interrelated citations. In so doing, it equates at least *'the Branch of David,'* if not *'the Doresh,'* with the *'erection of the fallen Tabernacle of David'* just as Ms. A of CD does, in combining and interpreting this passage with and in terms of *'the Star Prophecy,'* again, tying all these terminologies together. By the same token, not only is it basically repeating the thrust of CDvii on these subjects but Column xix of Ms. B as well – which, it will be recalled, was also *making reference to 'the coming of the Messiah of Aaron and Israel'*!

'Adoptionist Sonship,' 'the Sons of Zadok,' 'Casting Down,' and *'the Branch of David'* Once Again

Nor does its eschatological *'Messianism'* stop there. These pericopes give way, as the *Florilegium* moves towards its finale, to two passages from Psalms 1 and 2 (one wonders how many more passages from Psalms were invoked in the complete text) – the second actually alluding to how *'the Kings and Rulers of the Nations plot together against the Lord and His Messiah'* (2:1 – here, as usual, *'Messiah'* once again singular!). Moreover, it is also well to remark that this is a Psalm containing the all-important prooftext for Early Christian history in Palestine, *'You are My son. On this day have I begotten you.'* Not only is this passage from Psalm 2:7 pictured in Acts 13:33 as part of a speech Paul gives *'on the Sabbath'* at the Synagogue in Antioch at Pisidia together with several allusions to God *'raising up David'* and even one to David's *'seed'* (13:23)[23]; it is also twice referred to in Hebrews 1:5 and 5:5 – the first one together with the passage from 2 Samuel 7:14, *'I shall be a Father to him and he shall be a son to Me,'* just quoted in the *Florilegium* above – and, perhaps most importantly, in the Gospel of the Hebrews as reported by Jerome as what *'the Voice out of Heaven'* calls out to Jesus when he emerges from his baptism by John in place of the obviously defective, *'You are My beloved son. In you I am well pleased,'* as it is refurbished in the Synoptics.

One says *'refurbished,'* because the doctrine as it is reported in Hebrews, Acts, and the Gospel of the Hebrews reflects the way it was being viewed in Palestine in documents such as the Dead Sea Scrolls and, in succession to these, by groups like *'the Ebionites'* – that is, as one became

'*Perfectly Righteous*' (or as '*Jesus*' in Matthew 5:20 and 48's '*Sermon on the Mount*' would put it, '*Unless your Righteousness exceeds that of the Scribes and the Pharisees, you shall in no way enter into the Kingdom of Heaven.... Therefore be Perfect even as your Father who is in Heaven is Perfect*'[24]), one became *like unto* '*a Son of God,*' a signification to a large extent arrived at in the '*Resurrection*' and '*Sons of Zadok*' passages from Daniel and Ezekiel by the end of the *Florilegium*.[25] In the jargon of the field, this is known as '*adoptionist sonship*' and the fear of this more native, Palestinian doctrine – as '*Christianity,*' as it were, went 'overseas' and became evermore Hellenized – is at least part of the reason for the shift in this regard to a more absolute '*Divine Sonship*' as the more '*Paulinized,*' '*Gentile Christian*' Gospels emerged and took on their final form.[26]

It should be appreciated, too, that where Wisdom 2:16 is concerned, '*the Righteous One*' or '*the Zaddik is the Son of God*' – the same really too for *Ben Sira* 4:11 – an idea to some extent reflected as well in Matthew 5:9 in connection with '*the Peace-Makers*' (hardly a very '*Palestinian*' notion) and Luke 20:36, which speaks about '*the Sons of the Resurrection*' in terms of being '*equal to the Angels and the Sons of God.*' This last, of course, is exactly the doctrine one finds reflected at the end of the *Florilegium* in its references to '*the Book of Daniel the Prophet*' (n.b., for it, there is no doubt that Daniel *is* a '*Prophet*') and, as it puts it based on Daniel 11:35 and 12:10, '*the Righteous Ones shall be whitened and refined.*' Note too, though the text becomes fragmentary and is poorly preserved here, the usage '*become strengthened,*' paralleling the many similar ones in the Damascus Document, also occurs – to say nothing of this notion of '*being made white and refined*' as one finds it in the Pseudoclementine *Recognitions*.[27]

We also have an echo of this ideology in an oracle, largely either a rewrite of or based on Daniel, in another text from Qumran which more latterly appeared and is designated by most, '*The Son of God.*' Again, this is another text describing the Messianic promises, derived from Daniel 7:14–27, of an '*all powerful,*' '*Eternal Kingship.*' This could even be appended in a kind of amplification to this Messianic *Florilegium*, though without its scriptural proof-texts and without the specific mention of David or his '*seed*' as such.[28] The '*King,*' who is mentioned in it and called '*Great,*' whose '*Kingdom* (as in Daniel 7:27) *will be an Eternal Kingdom*' and '*the Dominion of whom will be an Eternal Dominion,*' is both designated as '*the Son of the Most High*' and '*the Son of God*' and described, as in Daniel, as '*judging the Earth in Truth.*'

On the other hand, more recently, controversy has arisen concerning whether '*the Son of God*' and his several attributes, described in the text, really is a 'Messianic' individual at all and not rather an opponent of some kind of those alluded to in the text as 'the People of God' – in fact, someone akin to what is normally thought of as being 'the Antichrist'![29] While the text is, like Daniel, in Aramaic and only partially preserved, this disagreement largely resembles that between those who wish to press all the data in the Scrolls as far back as possible and away from Christian origins in Palestine, desiring to date the greater part of Qumran documents in the Second Century BC, and those who are pre-pared to entertain a more First-Century chronological ambiance.

Where this particular text is concerned, since it is heavily recon-structed, much depends on the translation of several possessive adjectives found therein, namely 'their' or 'his' and whether, for instance, we are talking about 'their Kingdom' or 'his Kingdom,' whether 'his Dominion will be Eternal' or 'theirs will' and whether it is 'he will judge the earth with Truth' or 'they.'[30] The conclusion will depend on whether the text is interpreted either positively or negatively. If negative and a past event or 'Kingship' of a negative kind, which is the present trend among many scholars, then it must be seen as relating to a 'King' like Alexander the Great (as it very often does – according to modern scholarship – in Daniel[31]) who, like the Pharaohs in Egypt and to some extent the Persian Kings he was dis-placing, and Roman Emperors later on, actually styled himself in this manner. If positive, as in the manner we have translated these key phrases above, then he can be taken as being something of the kind of Ruler alluded to in Daniel 2:44–45, 7:13–14, and 7:27 above.

However this may be, the words from this text in fact do actually appear in Luke 1:32–33, where they are put into the mouth of 'an Angel' reacting to Mary's 'betrothal to a man' of 'the House of David': 'He shall be Great and be called the Son of the Most High' and 'His Kingdom will be Eternal' (literally, 'without End'). Not only must it almost certainly be con-cluded that the author of the Gospel of Luke knew this Aramaic Apocalypse relating to Daniel conserved in the Dead Sea Scrolls and was interpreting it more or less as we are doing; but at this point, too, the text in Luke actually adds the 'Davidic' aspect to the promise: 'And the Lord God shall give him the Throne of David his father' which is almost word-for-word the sense of the Florilegium as we have just expounded it. Of course, the conflict here of having both 'David' and 'God' as his 'father' has never been resolved. In the Florilegium, of course, it needs no resolution, since the whole sense is – as it is in 2 Samuel above – symbolic or that of the 'adop-tionist sonship' ideology of 'Jewish Christianity' and its offshoots.

That being said, though many have attempted to use this negative interpretation of the text as relating to one or another of these overly pretentious '*Enemy*' Kings or even the so-called '*Antichrist*' himself – whatever might be meant by this in the Second Century BC, to say nothing of the First Century CE – as already suggested, this ideology of '*the Son of God*,' when taken figuratively or according to its esoteric sense, is simply another of these synonymous variations of the '*Perfection*' ideal, as for example '*the Friend of God*,' '*the Son*' or '*Sons of Righteousness*,' '*the Sons of the Resurrection*' as we just saw it above too in Luke, and even the variation actually present – as we shall see – in the *Florilegium* as well, '*the Sons of Zadok*'![32] That being said, even here in the *Florilegium*, the '*sonship*' ideal is in play, as we have been remarking, regarding David and his progeny – as it is, however symbolic and '*adoptionist*,' in a more generalized manner in other documents at Qumran, such as Hymns where in Column XVII, as already noted as well, it is talking about '*knowing*' the author '*from his father and the womb (of his) mother*' and '*succouring (him) with Deliverance for all Eternity*.'[33] Here the conclusion is rendered in no uncertain terms that

> *my father knew me not and my mother abandoned me to You, for You are a Father to all the Sons of Your Truth* (another of these interchangeable ideological characterizations as, for example, earlier in the same document, '*the Ebionei-Hesed*' or '*the Poor Ones of Piety*,' combining two of the favorite appellations of these '*Opposition*' alliances).[34]

Where the pericope cited from Psalm 1:1, '*Blessed is the man who walks not in the counsel of the Evil Ones*,' is concerned (*Reshaᶜim* – an allusion usually applied to the Adversary of '*the Righteous Teacher*' known as '*the Wicked Priest*' and the Establishment associated with him), it is immediately and specifically expounded – in what the *Florilegium* itself refers to as a '*Midrash*', that is, the verbal noun of and how someone like '*the Doresh ha-Torah*' would expound a given text[35] – fairly straightforwardly as '*turning aside from the Way of the* (Evil Ones – paralleling '*Your Enemies*' and '*the Sons of Evil*' in 2 Samuel 7:9–11, themselves equated in the exegesis of the *Florilegium* above to '*the Sons of Belial*'), phraseology of the sort we have already encountered in important contexts in the Damascus Document as well.[36]

Furthermore, in the labyrinth of the way all these interrelated citations are put together, this is itself, then, in turn directly interpreted in terms of what was '*written in the Book of the Prophet Isaiah*'; and here the phrase, '*about the Last Days*,' is specifically added[37] – meaning, that by this time, not only has '*the Prophet Isaiah*' already become a '*Book*' (not necessarily '*a Scroll*') but that passages such as this one were going to be taken in an 'eschatological' manner. In particular, for 4QFlor the addition of the phraseology, 'about the Last Days,' means that 'Isaiah the Prophet' – together, as we shall see, with both 'Ezekiel the Prophet' and 'Daniel the Prophet' (again, just as in the Damascus Document) – were now going to be taken as eschatological 'Last Times'/'Last Days' Prophets.

The passage, which turns out to be Isaiah 8:11, basically repeats the gist of Psalm 1:1 and 'the Midrash' or 'Interpretation' just provided it, but with the addition of the important allusion to God's 'Strength' – as in the Lord's 'strong hand' – which will have additional significance, as we proceed, where James is concerned[38] and a slight twist: instead of 'the Way of the Evil Ones,' 'the Way' is now expressed in terms of 'the Way of this People' or, if one prefers, 'the People.' Otherwise, this passage in the Florilegium now reads in a largely parallel fashion:

> And behold, with a strong hand (the 'hand' imagery also found in the War Scroll and elsewhere above[39]), He (the Lord) turned me aside from walking in the Way of (the) People.

As just suggested, both the allusions to 'turning aside' and 'the Way of the People' have strong parallels in the Damascus Document, primarily in the follow-up material in Column VIII to the exegeses in Column VII of 'erecting the fallen Tabernacle of David' from Amos 9:11 and that of 'the Star' from Numbers 24:17 as 'the Doresh ha-Torah who came to Damascus.' In this material in Column VIII, here overlapping that of Column XIX, both 'not walking in the Way of the Evil Ones' (whose 'wine is the Venom of Vipers and the cruel poison of asps' of Deuteronomy 32:33[40]) and not following 'the Way of the People' and 'not keeping apart from ('nazru' – here the parallel 'Nazirite' language of 'separating oneself from' again) the Way of the People' are stressed – a 'Way' also condemned as 'the Way of Traitors.'[41] As this is expressed, as we have seen, in both Ms. A and Ms. B:

> All the men who entered the New Covenant in the Land of Damascus, but turned back and betrayed and turned aside from the Well of Living Waters...shall be expelled from the Assembly ('the Church') like someone whose lot had never fallen among the Disciples of God (here yet another new name for the Community, 'the Disciples of God,' pregnant with significance, but also a clear allusion to expulsion practices similar to those Josephus is calling 'Essenes'[42]).

So, once again, we are in a nexus of common vocabulary and, probably, a common chronological provenance.

Interestingly enough, this Chapter Eight from Isaiah which climaxes the recitation of these parallels – carrying over into the beginning of Chapter Nine – actually ends, once more, with yet another proverbial passage, famously evoked in Matthew 4:15–16 to describe Jesus' '*withdrawal*' *into Galilee* after '*having heard that John had been delivered up*' in 4:12 (again, the '*delivering up*' language we have been following throughout the Damascus Document above and elsewhere in the Gospels[43]):

> *Land of Zebulon and Land of Naphtali, Way of the Sea beyond the Jordan, Galilee of the Peoples* ('*Ethnon*'), *the People who were sitting in Darkness have seen a great Light* (Isaiah 8:23–9:1).[44]

Here again '*the Way*,' '*the Peoples*,' and '*the Light*' vs. '*Darkness*' allusions so fundamental to the imagery at Qumran.

In the *Florilegium*, furthermore, '*the Midrash*' of Psalm 1:1's '*not walking in the counsel of the Evil Ones*,' the interpretation of which was '*turning aside from the Way of the Evil Ones*' – in turn, also interpreted by evocation of Isaiah 8:11's '*not walking in the Way of (the) People*' – is itself then expounded, as we approach the end of the readable portion of 4QFlor, as just underscored, by evocation of '*Book*'s in the names of two further '*Prophet*'s, Ezekiel and Daniel. The first (aside from Isaiah) is, as we have seen, perhaps the most important eschatological prophet in the Qumran corpus[45]; and the second, '*Daniel the Prophet*,' already evoked in '*The Son of God*' text above and, interestingly enough as already remarked as well, not really even considered '*a Prophet*' in Rabbinical tradition to follow, though at Qumran – just as in subsequent '*Christian*' tradition – he quite definitely *is* clearly considered '*a Prophet*.'

The allusion, which combines two passages from '*the Book of Daniel*' (11:32 and 12:10 as we saw), is absolutely fundamental and at the root of what is perhaps one of the first complete statements of the doctrine of '*the Resurrection of the Dead*' in any known Biblical document.[46] Following specific reference to Daniel 12:2 – '*And Many (Rabim) that sleep in the dust of the earth shall awake, some to Everlasting life*' – the passage as it is reconstructed here in the *Florilegium* has to do both with the state of '*the Righteous Ones*' after the Resurrection and '*condemning the Wicked*' – a usage already evoked in the all-important exegesis of Ezekiel 44:15 in CDiv.7 when elucidating the role '*the Sons of Zadok*' in '*the Last Days*' (presumably at '*the Last Judgement*'[47]) and '*the Time of the End*.'

Though the text is poorly preserved here, it does allude to '*doing the Torah of Moses*,' that is, we are in the '*Jamesian*' milieu of '*doing*' and a '*works Righteousness*' environment. Furthermore, it harks back to the pivotal words of Daniel 12:10, 'Many (the 'Rabim' – as already encountered at Qumran, the designation applied to the rank and file of members particularly in documents like the Community Rule[48]) will be purified, refined and made white'[49]; but it turns these words around, prefacing them with what in the normative Daniel in fact directly follows this allusion to 'being made white': 'But the Evil Ones will behave wickedly (or 'condemn the Wicked') and will not understand.'

The reason for this, even in the fragmentary state of the text as it has survived at Qumran, should be plain. What the exegetes are doing is playing on the constant contrast of 'the Righteous' with 'the Wicked' – 'Justification' with 'condemnation,' based on the same 'Z-D-K' and 'R-Sh-ᶜ' roots, one finds continually throughout the most important Qumran texts – in particular, the Damascus Document's presentation of 'the Sons of Zadok' about to be mentioned in the Florilegium, but also in the Pesharim generally where 'the Righteous Teacher' and 'the Wicked Priest' are also continually contrasted.[50]

As opposed to its reference to Psalm 1:1's 'Evil Ones' earlier and 'those subject to the control of Belial' (alluded to in the previous 'pesher' on the first part of 2 Samuel 7:11 as well[51]) – to complete and emphasize the ongoing contrast between 'Righteousness' and 'Evil,' 4QFlor,ii.4 now substitutes the pregnant allusion to 'Righteous Ones' ('Zaddikim') for Daniel's underlying 'Rabim' – that is, not only will 'the Evil Ones behave wickedly' or 'be condemned'; but it is now 'the Righteous Ones' who 'shall be made white, purified, and refined,' adding the phraseology from Daniel 11:32, 'but the People knowing God will be strengthened' – words repeatedly averred in one form or another throughout the Damascus Document, as we have been illustrating,[52] thus completing the sweeping parallel with the Damascus Document above.

Not only is this idea of 'strengthening' – picking up the allusion to 'a strong hand' in the passage from Isaiah 8:11 just quoted above – part and parcel of imagery used throughout the Damascus Document when evoking the Righteous Teacher's role among the People, it is also continually used in early Church literature to describe James' role as both 'Zaddik' and 'Oblias' (according to Hegesippus, 'the Protection of the People,' probably based on the Old Testament phraseology, 'ᶜOz-le-ᶜAm'/'Strength of the People'[53]) and 'Bulwark.'[54] Even perhaps more interesting, the allusion to 'being made white' from Daniel 12:10, which precedes it, also both explains and, to some extent as just alluded to, evokes the usage in the Pseudoclementine Recognitions above, where the followers of James flee with his unconscious body from Jerusalem (detail of this kind not lightly dismissible) and subsequently miss the 'Enemy' (Paul) who is pursuing them with letters from the High Priests because they have gone to a location somewhere outside of Jericho *'to visit the tombs of two of the brothers that miraculously whitened of themselves every year.'*[55]

We can now understand just some of what was implied by a statement of this kind in this sort of literature. These are just some of the parallels found in these very striking passages from the *Florilegium* – fragmented as they may be – surrounding its allusion to *'raising the Tabernacle of David which is fallen,'* but there is more. To return to the mention of *'the Book'* preceding the mention of *'the Book of Daniel the Prophet,'* namely *'the Book of Ezekiel the Prophet'* – in particular, Ezekiel 44:10 and, as in Column Four of the Damascus Document, *'the Zadokite Covenant'* again: in 4QFlor,I.17 going back to evocation of the passage from *'the Book of Isaiah the Prophet'* (Isaiah 8:11) and *'the Midrash'* therein provided on those *'who do not walk in the counsel* – or *'turned aside from the Way'* – of the Evil Ones'* (also called *'the Way of the People[s]'* or *'the Way of the Traitors'*[56]); it is at this point, not surprisingly, that *'the Sons of Zadok and the Men of their Council'* are evoked. Though the sense is disputed because the passage is so fragmentary, it seems natural to assume that these are the ones now being described as *'those who pursue Righteousness enthusiastically'* – once again, directly linking *'the Sons of Zadok'* ideology with the one of absolute *'Righteousness,'* to say nothing of the implication of their *'zeal.'*[57]

Not only does this passage then move directly into the Psalm 2:1 pericope: *'Why do the Nations rage and the Peoples imagine a vain thing? The Kings of the Nations set themselves against the Lord and their minions take counsel against His Messiah,'* interpreted in terms of *'raging against the Elect of Israel in the Last Days'* – again the interpretation is eschatological (*'the Elect of Israel,'* it should be observed, also occurring as part and parcel of the definition of *'the Sons of Zadok'* in the Damascus Document and in the Habakkuk *Pesher* as *'the Elect by whose hand God will execute Judgement on all the Nations'*[58]); but there is once again also this allusion to *'Peoples.'*

This time the evocation of the word *'Peoples'* is tied to the idea of *'Emptiness'* or *'Vanity'* – allusions not only important in the Letter of James 2:20 responding to *'the Man of Emptiness'* who does not *'know that Faith without works is dead,'* but which will also be crucial in the Habakkuk *Pesher's* characterization of the character it calls *'the Spouter of Lying'* as *'leading Many astray'* (the *'Many'* language again), *'building a worthless city upon blood and erecting an Assembly upon Lying for the sake of his own Glory'* or *'Vanity,' 'tiring out Many with a worthless service (or 'Mission') and instructing them in works of Lying, so that their '*camal (the *'suffering works'* vocabulary of Isaiah 53:11 too) *will be of Emptiness.'*[59]

As 4QFlor,I.16-17 now puts this in the words of *'Ezekiel the Prophet,'* these '*Sons of Zadok*' – reversing Ezekiel 44:10's original description of those Levites '*who abandoned Me when Israel turned aside from Me to follow idols*' (here of course the original prototype of the '*turning aside*' language in both the Damascus Document and the *Florilegium*, linking up as well with the injunction of James and of those Hippolytus calls '*Sicarii Essenes*' to '*abstain from things sacrificed to idols*' – or, to use the words Acts 15:20 also attributes to James – '*the pollutions of the idols*'[60]) – are now described as those who '*shall not defile themselves anymore with all their idols.*' The reader should not forget that what these '*Renegades*' or '*Rebels in the House of Israel*' (that is, '*the Priests and Levites*' serving in an '*unclean*' or '*polluted*' state at the altar) had done – in the words of Ezekiel 44:7 – was to have

> brought foreigners (once again, the general xenophobic attitude of this compendium of Messianic proof-texts, as opposed to the speeches we have already seen reported in Acts 15:7–17 above) *uncircumcised in heart* (this is even more extreme than the '*some of the sect of the Pharisees*' insisting on '*circumcision,*' who are pictured as triggering '*the Jerusalem Council*' in Acts 15:5 above) *and uncircumcised in flesh to be in My Temple to pollute it;*

when, in fact, in the words of Ezekiel 44:9,

> no foreigner uncircumcised in heart and uncircumcised in flesh shall (be allowed to) enter My Temple, nor any foreigner (meaning, as we have seen, seemingly, '*resident alien*') that is among the House of Israel.

Again, therefore, we would seem to be in an almost totally opposite milieu than Acts 15's portrayal of '*the Jerusalem Council*' or, for that matter, the situation Josephus so fulminates against in his picture of the run-up to the War against Rome in 66 CE, when he contends that *opposition to sacrifices on behalf of such foreigners* was an '*innovation,*' of which '*our people were unaware.*'[61] Also the true import of what this '*raising up the fallen Tabernacle of David*' in '*the Land of Damascus,*' as well as this kind of evocation of '*the Sons of Zadok*' (both as regards its basis in '*Righteousness*' ideology underlying the meaning of the root in Hebrew and in the context of allusion to '*the Last Days*' and Messianic imagery generally), is now emerging as forcefully in the *Florilegium* as in the parallel represented by the Damascus Document.

It should be appreciated that in addition to these allusions to '*the Last Days*' and the '*standing up of the Branch of David*' (a verb also used, as we have seen, in the Damascus Document to depict the '*standing up of the Messiah of Aaron and Israel*' and/or the one who '*will pour down Righteous-*

ness at the End of Days'[62] – here, as elsewhere, '*pouring down*' too is a verb in the singular case, paralleling that applied to '*the Branch of David*' in the *Florilegium*, '*the Sceptre*' in the Damascus Document, and '*the Messiah of Righteousness*' in the Genesis *Pesher*), '*to save Israel*' and '*in Zion in the Last Days*'; there is also in this pregnant collection of '*Messianic*' proof-texts relating to '*the promises to David and his seed*' the usage, repeated twice and tied to what '*Belial*' and not God *intended to do* to '*the Sons of Light*' above, that is to say, '*cause them to stumble*' or '*fall*' (*hamachshilim/lehachshil*) – or, in the language of other vocabularies we have been following above, '*cast them down*' – here specifically defined as meaning '*destroy them.*'[63]

'*Lehachshil*' also forms a key aspect of a passage in the Habakkuk *Pesher* describing what the Wicked Priest did to the Righteous Teacher and those of his persuasion on *Yom Kippur*, that is, '*caused them to stumble*' or '*cast them down*' – the synonymous allusion, '*to destroy them,*' appearing also in a follow-up passage about what '*the Wicked Priest did to the Poor*' (*Ebionim*), manifestly denoting the followers of '*the Righteous Teacher.*'[64] I should not have to add, but I will – this expression, '*casting down,*' in Greek forms the central thrust of all descriptions of the death of James in all early Church accounts (the followers of whom, too, were known as '*the Poor*'!), as it does the attack by the '*Hostile Man*' or '*Enemy*' (Paul) on him in the Pseudoclementine *Recognitions*.

Let us, therefore, just sum up these points-of-contact between the *Florilegium*, the Damascus Document, and the New Testament once more. In the *Florilegium*, '*Re-erecting the Fallen Tent of David*' is now directly expounded in terms of the '*arising*' or '*standing up of the Branch of David with the Doresh ha-Torah in Zion in the Last Days,*' which is the same language one encounters in the Damascus Document regarding the '*standing up*' (the secondary meaning of which is '*to be resurrected*') of both '*the Sons of Zadok*' and '*the Messiah of Aaron and Israel,*' to say nothing of '*the Pourer Down of Righteousness* ('*the Yoreh ha-Zedek*' as opposed to '*the Moreh ha-Zedek*'[65]) *at the End of Days.*' In the latter, strictly speaking, it is '*the Sceptre*' from '*the Star Prophecy,*' now equated with '*the Nasi Chol ha-*ᶜ*Edah,*' who '*will stand up and utterly destroy all the Sons of Seth,*' but otherwise the language is about the same.[66]

In the *Florilegium*, too, the whole sequence which, as in the Damascus Document not to mention Acts, is arcane in the extreme, is introduced by:

> *And the Lord declares to you that He will build you a House. I will raise up your seed after you* (meaning, as we saw, David's) *and establish the Throne of his Kingdom* (again, David's – one of the unique references to a '*Kingdom*'

of this kind in the Dead Sea Scrolls, unless one considers '*The Son of God*' Apocalypse[67] – to say nothing of the '*Throne,*' though this is more common[68]). *I will be a Father to him and He will be a son to Me,*

from 2 Samuel 7:12–14. Paul paraphrases at least the last part of this in 2 Corinthians 6:18 above where – after speaking about: '*Christ with Beliar,*' '*Righteousness with Lawlessness,*' '*Light with Darkness,*' and '*coming out from among them and being separated and touching no unclean thing*' (that is, being '*a Nazirite*'), but before concluding: '*cleansing oneself from every pollution of the flesh and the spirit, Perfecting Holiness in the fear of God*' (this last, the '*God-Fearer*' language, again of Column Twenty of Ms. B of the Damascus Document, as we have seen, combined with the '*pollution*' language of those of '*uncircumcised heart and body*' in Ezekiel's '*Zadokite Covenant*' above) – he avers:

> *And I will be a Father to you and you shall be sons and daughters to Me, says the Lord Almighty.*

This overt evocation of the '*sonship*' language (present in the Qumran Hymns as well) – the application in the *Florilegium* of which seems to be to '*the Branch of David who will stand up in Zion together with the Doresh ha-Torah who will (arise) in the Last Days to save Israel*' – would also seem to apply, at least figuratively, to '*re-erecting the fallen Tabernacle of David*' in the Damascus Document as well. In the last-named anyhow, as we have seen, one encounters a kind of esoteric '*Messiah*' as '*Temple*' imagery not unlike what Paul uses in 1 Corinthians 12:14–27. This might point the way to a similar sense as the allusion occurs in James' speech in Acts as well. It is certainly present in Column Seven of Ms. A of the Damascus Document.

Though the sense in all these documents is arcane, just the fact of its presence here in 4QFlor and CD, not to mention in Acts in a speech – however tendentious – attributed to James, is significant. But it is the use of this and related allusions in Columns IV-VII of the Damascus Document that will, as already suggested, enable us to get some indication of how all these conceptualities are connected.

'*The Song of the Well*,' '*the Kings of the Peoples*,' '*Gehazi*,' and Pauline-style '*Grace*' in the Damascus Document

It is now possible to return to the Damascus Document and show how these Columns VII–VIII and XIX–XX, introduced by IV–VI, in fact, do in some sense also involve '*Gentiles.*' This will allow us to firm up the link between the presentation of '*re-erecting the Tabernacle of David which is fallen*' in the Damascus Document and *Florilegium* and in Acts. Acts 15:22–23 claims that the '*rulings*' James made at the conclusion of its grandiose picture of the so-called '*Jerusalem Council*,' just before the commencement of '*the We Document*,' were incorporated in a '*letter*' he sent down via '*Chosen Men*' (n.b., the parallel here both with '*the Elect*' and '*those called by name*' in Column IV of the Damascus Document above), *Paul and Barnabas and Judas surnamed Barsabas and Silas*,[69] addressed to '*the brothers who are of the Gentiles in Antioch* (in our view, *Edessa and beyond*) *and Syria and Cilicia.*'

This idea of '*brothers who are of the Gentiles in Syria*' to a certain degree harmonizes with the picture of parallel passages in the Damascus Document and the '*Letter*'(s) at Qumran known as '*MMT*' as well. Setting aside what Acts considers to be the upshot of James' '*rulings*' at this '*Council*' – '*rulings*' very much in the character of those that would have been made by a character such as '*the Mebakker*' or '*the High Priest commanding the Many*' at Qumran; it is now possible to turn to allusions in CDVI, fleshed out further in VIII and XIX-XX, to get some indication of how the various conceptualities highlighted above are connected and apply to these events.

Paralleling the earlier exposition in Column IV of Ezekiel's '*Zadokite Covenant*' (this time Ezekiel 44:15 not Ezekiel 44:10, though the two passages are part of the same basic whole); an archaic '*Song*' – said in Numbers 21:14 to be from an old lost text called '*The Book of the Wars of the Lord*' and transcribed in 21:16–18 – is expounded in Column VI of Ms. A, then leading into the exegeses of Amos 5:26–27, 9:11–12, and Numbers 24:17 in Column VII (Ezekiel 9:4 and Zechariah 13:7 in Ms. B; 2 Samuel 7–12–14 and Amos 9:11 again in 4QFlor).

This '*Song*,' embedded in a very arcane section of Numbers leading up to '*the Star Prophecy*,' celebrates how – when Moses '*gathered the People together*' and the Lord '*gave them water*' to drink in the wilderness – the People sang a welcoming song, '*singing out to the Well*,' '*the Well* (repeated three times in the passage) *which the Princes*' or '*Leaders dug, which the Nobles of the People trenched* (or '*dug*') *out with the Staff* (here the transcription has been slightly changed from that of the normative Numbers 21:18 in the interests probably, as so frequently in the Gospels, of the exegesis – but note once again, too, the emphasis on '*People*' or '*Peoples*').[70] The meaning of this last, '*the Staff*' or '*the Mehokkek*,' upon which the exegesis will play and turn, can also be understood in Hebrew as '*the Law-Giver*,' playing off the underlying sense of the root, '*Hok*' or '*Hukkim*'/'*Laws*.' This, in turn, will add to the prosody and alliteration of the new meaning being developed, '*hakak ha-Mehokkek be-Mehokkekot*' – '*the Law-Giver decreed Laws.*'[71]

Before proceeding to analyze the much-underestimated and all-important esoteric exposition of this passage from Numbers 21, which will lead into another from Isaiah 54:16 about '*creating an instrument for His works*' and be crucial for the Community's sense of self-definition and historiography; it should be appreciated that, as already to some extent pointed out, it largely repeats that of Ezekiel's '*Zadokite Covenant*' two columns earlier. This, it will be remembered, explained how '*the Priests*' – now defined, somewhat curiously, as '*the Penitents of Israel*' – '*went out from the Land of Judah* (no doubt, an archaic allusion to '*Judea*' but, at this juncture anyhow, no '*dwelling in the Land of Damascus*' sub-joined – this will be added in Column VI's exposition of Numbers 21:18 we are presently in the process of examining) *and the Joiners* ('*ha-Nilvim*') *with them*' – this in exposition of Ezekiel's '*Levites*' ('*Ha-Leviyyim*'), not '*the Priests*' – '*the Sons of Zadok*' being defined as '*the Elect of Israel called by Name* (and, paralleling allusions made in the *Florilegium* above), *who would stand in the Last Days.*'

Furthermore, it is important to note that this expression, '*the Penitents of Israel*' – which is, first of all, not a normative definition of '*Priests*' at all but an esoteric and highly unorthodox one[72] and, second of all, just as obviously, carries with it something of the familiar ideology of '*seeking*' either '*forgiveness for sin*' or '*remission of sins*' – is also referred to twice more later in CD. The second of these, '*the Penitents from sin in Jacob,*' which occurs in the midst of the highly emotive climax in Column XX and, as we have seen, plays off the promise in Isaiah 59:20 of a '*Deliverer coming to Zion for the sake of the Penitents from sin in Jacob,*' referred to so sophisticatedly by Paul in Romans 11:24–35 – as always – in the context of '*the fullness of the Gentiles* (*Ethnon*) *coming in*'! Before proceeding, one should also note how in Isaiah this leads into the passage in 60:21 about '*your People all becoming Righteous*' or '*Righteous Ones*'/'*Zaddikim*' and, therefore,

> *inheriting* (*lirosh* again) *the Land forever, the Branch of My Planting* (this time, this is '*Netzer,*' a synonym of both '*the Zemach*' in the *Florilegium* and '*the Shoresh*'/'*Root*' or '*Shoot*' in Column I of the Damascus Document above and an obvious additional source of the allusion there to the '*Root of Planting*' with which it begins), *the work of My hands, Glorifying* (*Me*).

Not only does this allusion to '*Penitents*' in Column XX evoke the twin ideas of '*forgiveness of sin*' and '*keeping the Covenant of God*' (that is, they were '*Keepers*' again not '*Breakers*'[73]) but it precedes, as we have been underscoring, the incredibly passionate evocations of '*the Love Commandment,*' '*the Book of Remembrance being written out for God-Fearers,*' the '*Hesed*' or '*Grace*' reserved for '*the thousands of them that love Him*' (Exodus 20:6), and '*God making atonement for*' or '*through them,*' so that '*they might be Victorious*' and '*see His Yeshuᶜa' / 'Salvation, because they took refuge in His Holy Name*'!

The earlier allusion in overlapping Columns VIII of Ms. A and XIX of Ms. B, which actually was to these same '*the Penitents of Israel,*' had to do with '*the Judgement upon*' them, this time meaning an extremely positive one, because '*they turned aside from the Way of the People and God so loved the First*' ('*the Forefathers,*' as we have seen) that, as we shall also see further below, '*He loved those coming after them because theirs is the Covenant of the Fathers*' – again, a more '*Palestinian*' form of '*Grace*' is hard to imagine.[74]

It comes at the conclusion of the tremendous attack – in the context, as previously remarked, of the '*Visitation*' or '*Judgement*' that was to be '*visited upon them*' and this time an extremely negative one – both on '*the Kings of the Peoples*' or '*the Greek-speaking Kings*' and '*the Daubers with Plaster*' of Ezekiel 13:10 or '*the Builders of the Wall,*' already fulsomely condemned earlier in Column IV in '*the Three Nets of Belial*' accusations in the matter of '*fornication*' – in particular, where '*taking two wives in their lifetimes*' (meaning '*divorce*') and '*the Ruler*' ('*the Nasi*' or '*Prince*') '*multiplying wives unto himself*' were concerned.[75] If this does not involve '*Herodians*' it is hard to imagine what does.

The allusion to '*the Kings of the Peoples,*' as already signaled as well, develops out of a citation from Deuteronomy 32:33: '*Their wine is the venom of vipers and the cruel poison of asps,*' the exegesis of which while extremely opaque is nonetheless fierce. One should note too, here again the parallel in the Gospels with '*Generation of Vipers,*' a parallel played upon in Column Five earlier where the words of Isaiah 59:5 (our key '*Deliverer out of Zion*' Chapter again),

Their webs are spiders' webs and their eggs are the eggs of vipers,[76]

are cited. Its exegesis, too, which is a classic – while previously provided in part – is worth quoting in detail:

The '*Vipers*' *are the Kings of the Peoples* (again, in our view, '*Herodians*' who, in the eyes of the Romans, were just this – '*Kings*' chosen from among '*the Peoples*'[77]) *and* '*their wine*' *is their ways, and* '*the poison of asps*' *(rosh) is the*

Head (Rosh) of the Kings of Greece who comes to execute Vengeance upon them.[78]

Not only is the allusion here to '*coming to execute Vengeance upon them*' both a familiar and indicative one; but, as previously explained to some extent too, that to '*the Head (Rosh) of the Kings of Greece*' (*Yavan*) is pivotal and plays off the word '*wine*'/'*yayin*' in the underlying text from Deuteronomy 32:33 – to say nothing of '*Rosh*,' playing off of its homonym '*rosh*'/'*poison*.' In turn, the evocation of these telling expressions follows upon the allusion we have already underscored as well to:

> *not keeping apart* (here, again, the root is '*Na-Za-Ra*' or '*Nazirite*') *from the People and knowingly sinned, walking in the Way of the Evil Ones*' (all this, too, we have just heard in the *Florilegium* above),[79]

itself provoked by an earlier attack in the same column on '*the Rulers of Judah*' as the '*Removers of the Bound*' – we heard so condemned in the description of '*the Lying Spouter*''s activities with which CD commences in Column One – and '*diseased without a cure*.' This, in turn, picks up from the assertion that '*their Visitation will be for destruction by the hand of Belial*' (this, the '*Second*' or '*Third Visitation*' – depending on the reckoning – and the one presently transpiring) at the beginning of Column VIII/the middle of the overlapping Column XIX, we have already referred to above.

Not only does '*yayin*'/'*wine*' in the citation: '*Their wine is the venom (rosh) of vipers*' give way to '*Yavan*' ('*Ion*' as in '*Ionic*')/'*Greece*,' the two being based on the same root-word in Hebrew); but so too, as we just saw, does '*rosh*'/'*poison*' – in the underlying Deuteronomy – give way to its homonym '*Rosh*'/'*Head*' in the exegesis. Of course, all such transformations are purposeful and examples of the penchant for word-play these Qumran exegetes display so abundantly. The key identification is that of the '*Vipers*' with '*the Kings of the Peoples*' – introduced, of course, by the earlier allusion to '*the Rulers of Judah are those who are Removers of the Bound*' (having '*become diseased without cure*') preceding it – terminology, as already signaled as well, known to Roman jurisprudence at the time and designating those semi-independent, '*Greek-speaking*,' satrap '*Kings*' in the Eastern parts of the Empire where – different from the West – Roman Administration had not yet been directly imposed, nor citizenship extended.[80]

Furthermore, it must be understood that this allusion to '*Rosh*'/'*Head*,' cleverly playing off the underlying allusion to '*rosh*'/'*venom*' or '*poison*,' implies a situation where one over-arching Ruler – *in this case the*

Roman one – is '*Head*' over an assortment of *petty 'Kings'* – such as, for example, Antiochus of Commagene, Azizus of Emesa, Archelaus of Cappadocia, Tigranes of Armenia, and even the Herodians themselves, all '*Greek-speaking*' or, as it were, '*Grecian*' and, therefore, the exploitation of the underlying allusion to '*yayin*'/'*wine*' in Deuteronomy 32:33 above (upon which the designation '*Yavan*' in Hebrew might originally have been based or *vice versa*) – not to mention that such persons were undoubtedly perceived as '*drinking*' a lot just as Alexander himself originally was.[81]

It is for this reason we take the meaning of '*the Head of the Kings of Greece*' to mean '*the Head of Greek-speaking Kings*,' which is to say nothing of the fact that this '*Head*' of an Alliance of such petty '*Greek-speaking Kings*' actually did '*come and execute Vengeance upon them.*' Again, this individual cannot be either Pompey, Antiochus Epiphanes, or even Alexander the Great earlier. It can only be Nero or his successor, Vespasian or Titus (we will leave Trajan and Hadrian aside for the moment in this process). Moreover, it is just this allusion which then proceeds immediately in Column Eight/Nineteen into the evocation of Ezekiel 13:10's '*Daubers with Plaster*' and '*the Builders of the Wall*' (and here, both mss. agree), already alluded to above and referenced earlier in the context of the '*Three Nets of Belial*' transgressions attributed to the Establishment – in particular, '*niece marriage*' and '*polygamy*' are the ones cited which can only entail '*Herodians*' and, as we have seen, certainly not Maccabeans.

Once again, this exegesis of this '*Dauber*' passage, combined as it is with Micah 2:11 on '*walking in the Spirit and spouting Lying*,' is another of these arcane expositions, but also one of incredible ingenuity. As Ms. A would have it, as already to some degree elucidated, such persons ('*the Daubers*' and '*Builders of the Wall*' of Ezekiel 13:10 above) '*have not understood because one of confused Spirit*' or '*windiness*' ('*wind*' and '*Spirit*' – as in '*Holy Spirit*' – being homonyms in Hebrew; here, probably implying in English, what we would call, among other things, as previously underscored, '*a Windbag*'), *a Spouter of Lying, spouted to them.*' Ms. B, which is probably more accurate, rather has here – directly evoking the citation from Micah 2:11 upon which the whole esotericism is based, which also includes '*spouting Lies about wine and strong drink*,' thereby connecting it to the evocation of Deuteronomy 32:33 directly preceding it in CDVIII.10/XIX.23 – '*walking in the Spirit.*' Both end up – from the allusion at the end of Column Four to '*those following Zaw ha-Zaw* (Hebrew for '*So-and-So*'), *the Spouter about whom it was said* (in Micah 2:11), *and he will surely spout*' – with,

and the Spouter of Lying spouted to them, which kindled God's Wrath upon his entire Congregation (or '*Church*').[82]

It is this, in turn, again without even a break, which then leads directly into not only the second evocation of '*the Penitents of Israel who turned aside from the way of the People*' ('*Peoples*'), but also what we have already suggested might be called – based on a combination of passages from Deuteronomy 9:5 and 7:8 – a kind of Palestinian version of '*Grace*':

> *Not for your Righteousness* (again '*Zedek*' or '*Zedakah*') *or the Uprightness of your heart* (based on the '*straightening the Way*' vocabulary of Isaiah 40:3 found, for instance, in the Community Rule – to say nothing of the the the language of the '*heart*') *are you going to possess these Nations* (Deuteronomy 9:5 – the same '*lirosh*' we have heard in the interchanges with '*darash*' in the various quotations of Amos 9:11–12 and the '*Root of Planting*' exposition in Column One above[83]), *but because of His love for your Fathers and keeping the oath* (what was called in CDXIX.1 above, also quoting Deuteronomy 7:8–9, '*keeping the Covenant*').[84]

It is at this point that it is declared in no uncertain terms that this would be '*the Judgement*' (the consequence of that same '*Visitation*' just alluded to, but in this case clearly meaning something akin to what should be called '*the Last Judgement*') upon '*the Penitents of Israel* (that is, those who were identified with '*the Priests*' in the previous exegesis – two columns before – of Ezekiel's '*Zadokite Covenant*'). Now these same '*Penitents*' are defined – as we already saw and picking up the sense of vocabulary present in the *Florilegium* – as those '*who turned aside from the Way of the People(s)*.' This imagery of '*turning aside from*' is again to be found in Ezekiel 44:10 above and in the ideology of life-long '*Naziritism*' generally, alluded to even by Paul – amid reference to '*being sons and Daughters to Me*' and '*touching no unclean thing*' in 2 Corinthians 6:17–18 above – as '*being separated*' (cf. too, the exposition in Columns VIII-IX of the Community Rule of Isaiah 40:3's '*Prepare in the wilderness a Way for the Lord. Make straight in the desert a Pathway for our God*' and '*making a Way in the wilderness*' as '*separating (themselves) from the midst of the habitation of the Men of Unrighteousness*' and '*from any man who has not turned his Way away from all Unrighteousness*').[85]

Again it is intoned, as we just saw above:

> *Because God loved the First* ('*the Forefathers*' in CD One's picture of how '*the Comedian poured over Israel the waters of Lying* – meaning he was also '*the Man*' or '*Spouter of Lying*' – *causing them to wander astray in a trackless*

waste without a Way' – another play on the '*Way in the wilderness'* imagery – '*abolishing the Pathways of Righteousness and removing the boundary
markers'* – meaning, of course, '*the Torah.'* We have just seen this allusion
to '*removing the boundary markers'* – regarding Column VIII/XIX's condemnation of '*the Rulers of Judah'* upon whom, not just Column One's
'*the waters of Lying,'* but the '*Wrath'* of Hosea 5:10 would now '*be poured
out'* and – *which 'the First'/'the Ancestors had marked out as their inheritance.'*
Compare this, too, with John 3:16 and *pars.* on '*God so loving the World that
he gave His only-begotten son,*[86] *so everyone who believes on him will not die but
have life Eternal.'* The resemblance is uncanny but of course the sense, as
always, inverted) *who testified on His behalf* (Ms. B has: '*testified on behalf of
the People of God'*), *He loved those coming after them, because theirs is the Covenant of the Fathers* ('*Avot'* as in '*The Fathers according to Rabbi Nathan'* or
'*The Traditions of the Elders'* or '*Fathers'* in Matthew 15:2/Mark 7:5 above).

Likewise, '*the Judgement* (continuing this theme of the '*Judgement upon
the Penitents of Israel'* and that of this '*Second'* or '*Third Visitation'* generally)
upon all those who reject the Commandments of God (a typical allusion at
Qumran to '*the Lying Spouter'* or '*Scoffer'*[87]) *and forsake them, turning away
in the stubbornness of their heart'* (this '*stubbornness of heart,'* too, being characteristic of the way '*the Spouter of Lying'* is described at Qumran[88]) is now
compared to the way Jeremiah rebuked Baruch and Elisha, '*his Servant
Gehazi.'*[89] The suddenness of this analogy is not only striking but very
telling as well because, setting aside the Jeremiah and Baruch side of it,
as we have already underscored, '*Gehazi'* in Talmudic literature – along
with Moses' '*Enemies,'* Do'eg, Jannes, and Jambres (these last two, as we
shall see below, also alluded to as '*Removers of the Bound,'* '*speaking Rebellion against the Commandments of God as given by the hand of Moses,'* and
'*raised up by Belial at the time of the First Salvation of Israel'* – again here, the
'*yakim'* of the '*Raising up of the Tabernacle of David'* and the '*Hoshea'* allusion of the '*saving Israel'* exegesis in the *Florilegium*) – is one of the three
or four individuals designated as '*Enemies of God.'*[90]

Furthermore, in this literature – as censored and, therefore, bowdlerized as it has often become[91] and as also previously alluded to – this
'*Gehazi'* is a known blind or *nom-a- clef* for Paul. This was because of the
way the former was perceived in 2 Kings 5:20–27 as *having disobeyed the
command of his master Elisha*, in particular, in the matter of *selling his teaching to Royal Personages for money*. But this may also have to do with the
fact of Gehazi's having been condemned by Elisha to suffer '*leprosy'* the
remainder of his life (5:27), Paul too being considered to suffer from an
illness of some kind which he himself referred to in 2 Corinthians 12:7

as '*a thorn in the flesh*' but which also seems to have made him unpleasant to encounter in person.[92] This then leads directly into the theme, begun a few lines earlier with the assertion that '*this is the kind of Judgement which will be upon all those who reject the Commandments of God and forsake them turning away in the stubbornness of their heart*' and, as we have several times had occasion to remark, *condemning*

> *all the men who entered the New Covenant in the Land of Damascus* (with this Column Eight of Ms. A definitively ends and Column XIX of Ms. B, as we have seen, picks up the narrative), *but turned back, betrayed, and turned aside from the Well of Living Waters*' (not only the evocation of '*the Well*' of Column VI again – now termed '*the Well of Living Waters*,' and an allusion known even to the Spanish/Jewish Philosopher/Mystic, Ibn Gabirol and his '*Fons Vitae*' in the Middle Ages[93] – but, as we have seen above, the '*turning back*'/'*turning aside from*' vocabulary once more)[94]

to that same '*Angry Wrath of God*' with which the allusion to '*the Lying Spouter's spouting*' was already said to have condemned them to earlier in Column VIII/XIX. Notwithstanding, the qualification is then conjoined at this point: '*until the standing up of the Messiah of Aaron and Israel*' or '*until the Messiah of Aaron and Israel will arise*' and this last – which is paralleled in Cave 4 fragments as '*ᶜad ᶜamod Mashiah Aharon ve-Israel*' – is definitively singular and not plural as the singular form of the verb confirms, all the rest being wishful thinking![95]

Here of course there can be little doubt that what we have characterized in both allusions, and especially the one '*on all his Congregation*' or '*Church*,' is a Paul-like cadre of previous believers and internal adversaries – at this point being grouped with external enemies like those called '*the Sons of the Pit*' or '*the Princes of Judah*'/'*the Kings of the Peoples*'/'*the Builders of the Wall*' – who '*turned aside*' from the New Covenant and its '*Well of Living Waters*' and followed '*the Way of the People*,' '*forsaking the Commandments of God*' in '*the stubbornness of their hearts*.' Nor can there be any doubt that the issue here, both where '*the New Covenant*' is concerned and the Paul-style '*Grace*' to be bestowed on '*the Penitents of Israel, who turned aside from the Way of the People(s)*' in '*the wilderness*, hinged upon their willingness to recommit themselves to and follow '*the boundary markers which the First*' or '*the Ancestors had marked out for their inheritance*' – meaning, '*the Law*.'

Where Paul is concerned, perhaps the best discussion of this '*Grace*' – always replete with a wide range of Qumranisms – is to be found in Romans 5:1–21 which, not only includes the idea of '*Justification by Faith*' (5:1), but also that of '*the love of God being poured out into our hearts*' (5:5), '*being saved*' despite having previously '*been Enemies*' (5:9) and, finally, '*through the obedience of the one* (meaning '*Jesus Christ*' or '*Christ Jesus*'), *the Many will be constituted Righteous Ones*' (5:20 – in this line alone, he twice refers to '*the Many*.' Again one can't get much more Qumran-like than this).

Numbers 21:18's '*Song about the Well*,' Jannes and Jambres, and a Cadre of Gentile '*Nilvim*' or '*Believing God-Fearers*' at Qumran

To go back now to the key exegesis of the archaic '*Song*' from Numbers 21:18 about Israel '*singing out to the Well*,' a '*Well*' defined as

> the Well which the Princes dug, which the Nobles of the People trenched (or '*dug*') out with the Staff (Mehokkek) –

another phrase, '*with their staves*' ('*be-mish^canotam*' – also '*their supports*') is not included in the citation in CDvi.3-4, but a variation of it, '*be-Mehokkekot*'/'*with Laws*' – as in '*hakak ha-Mehokkek be-Mehokkekot*'/ '*the Law-Giver legislated Laws*,' the intense prosody of which we have already remarked above – is picked up in the exegesis.[96]

Before launching into this very telling exegesis, however, there is another reference to '*Belial*' at the end of Column Five preceding and describing how '*Belial in his guilefulness raised up Jannes and his brother*' – '*Jannes and Jambres*' – at the time of the First Salvation of Israel' (once more, as just alluded to, here is another analogue to the '*Akim*' of the subsequent antithesis of this in Column Seven of Ms. A, the '*raising up of the Fallen Tabernacle of David*') – '*the First Salvation*' (Hoshe^ca), as we have already seen, being a prior parallel to the '*First Visitation*' but in the context alluding, not to *the escape at the time of the Babylonian destruction of the Temple*, but *the Exodus from Egypt*.[97]

For CDv.18-19, as we saw, not only are Moses and his brother watched over by '*the Prince of Lights*' while '*Jannes and his brother*' (Jambres – unnamed here, but he is named in apocryphal literature generally[98]) are '*raised up*' by '*Belial*' (an interesting analogy); but the connections of this with the New Testament are clear, since these two individuals – who are, in fact, normally thought of as, like Simon *Magus*, '*magicians*' of some kind – are actually mentioned in 2 Timothy 3:8 as '*withstanding Moses*.' Nor is this the only analogy with the Damascus Document in 2 Timothy, as this allusion is itself preceded by a host of other Qumran-like allusions in it, such as '*empty babblings*' (2:16), '*naming the Name*' (2:19), '*pursuing Righteousness*' (2:22), '*being granted repentance*' (2:25 – as '*the Pen-*

itents from sin in Jacob' in 'the Land of Damascus' were likely 'to have been granted'), 'the Snare of the Devil' (2:26 – that is, 'the Net of Belial'), 'the Last Days' (3:1), 'Traitors,' 'puffed up' (3:4), and 'turning away from' (3:5).[99] Moreover, as already signaled, in Rabbinic literature Jannes and Jambres are – along with 'Do'eg' and 'Gehazi' among others (and, one might add, Paul in the Pseudoclementine *Recognitions*) conceived of as the quintessential 'Enemies of God.'[100]

At this point at the beginning of CDvi – like the condemnation of 'the Man of Scoffing' / 'Comedian' in CD1.14-18, who 'poured out over Israel the waters of Lying' (that is, he is equivalent to 'the Pourer out of' or 'Spouter of Lying'[101]), as 'removing the Boundary Markers which the First had marked out as their inheritance' above (again too, the language of 'inheriting') – all of these are grouped together under the heading of 'the Removers of the Bound,' the accoutrements of which are, yet again, the proverbial 'leading Israel astray' and 'speaking Rebellion against the Commandments of God (as given) by the Hand of Moses.'[102] Not only have we heard all of this before, all are descriptive of the kind of ideological adversary (and this *within* the Movement not *outside* it) who taught 'straying' from 'the Law' and 'betrayed (just as their prototypes did 'the Covenant of the First' – in particular, as 'Gehazi' had done Elisha) the New Covenant in the Land of Damascus.'[103]

It is just at this point too, as we move into the exegesis of Numbers 21:18 on 'the Song of the Diggers of the Well,' that the striking phrase, 'and also against His Mashiah Ha-Kadosh,' is conjoined – that is, they also spoke 'Rebellion' or 'blasphemies against His Holy Messiah,' a phraseology familiar in 'Christianity' as well. Once again, not only is this startling allusion a foretaste of things to come, it is *very definitely singular*. Though it specifically refers to 'His Holy Messiah,' whatever the meaning of this might have been in the context, it is often rendered in most popular English translations – tendentiously one might add – 'His holy anointed ones' – as usual, *plural and uncapitalized* (though how one could get a plural out of this is beyond comprehension)![104]

As opposed to all this, prefacing this decisive exposition of Numbers 21:18 with yet another implied allusion to 'Grace' – but 'Grace,' Torah and Covenant-of-Moses-oriented *not* 'New Testament'-style; the text now avers that 'God remembered the Covenant of the First (again 'the Forefathers') and took from Aaron Men of Discernment and from Israel (Men) of Wisdom and made them listen.' Once again, this echoes the earlier material in CD1-11 and the various 'he who has ears' metaphors in the Gospels.[105] At this point at the beginning of Column vi, in describing how 'they dug the Well' and quoting Numbers 21:18 (just as in the identification in the Community Rule of Isaiah 40:3's 'the Way in the wilderness' as 'the Study of

Torah'/'Midrash ha-Torah' – again note the telltale *'darash'/'Doresh'* root-cluster of the key *Florilegium* exegesis above and an expression which actually reappears in the last words of the Damascus Document according to the Cave 4 fragments[104]); *'the Well'* is actually and specifically identified as *'the Torah.'*

But now it is the two categories of *'Diggers,'* namely, the *'Princes'* and *'the Nobles of the People,'* that take the place of *'the Priests'* and *'the Nilvim'/'Joiners'* of the previous exegesis of *'the Zadokite Covenant'* two columns earlier (in the process showing both to be equally esoteric); and, instead of Ezekiel's *'Priests,'* it is *'the Diggers'* who are now defined, as already explained, as *'the Penitents of Israel who went out from the Land of Judah'* – and it is at this point that the additional portentous phraseology is actually attached, *'to sojourn'* or *'dwell in the Land of Damascus.'*[107] Taken in its overt sense, this constitutes the first concrete reference to the Syrian heartland *per se*, the earlier exegesis having only spoken of, as will be recalled, *'to depart'* or *'go out from the Land of Judah'* – nothing more.

It is interesting too that, since the term *'Mehokkek'/'Staff'* includes a play on the underlying idea of *'Hok'* or *'Hukkim'* (*'Laws'/'Ordinances'/*or *'decrees'* – in the actual underlying text from Numbers 21:18, this is *'mish-ᶜanotam'/'their supports,'* words which, as we saw, do not appear in the portion of the citation quoted in CDVI.3-4 but, as one should be plain, are nevertheless implied); this *'Staff'/'Mehokkek'* (playing off its secondary meaning of *'Law-Giver'* or *'Legislator'*) is also, as just underscored too, identified in the exegesis that follows as *'the Interpreter'* or *'Doresh ha-Torah.'* It will be recalled that we have already encountered this individual in the *Florilegium* above, connected to both *'the Fallen Tent of David'* and *'the Branch'* who *'will stand up in Zion in the Last Days to deliver'* or *'save Israel'*; and he will reappear as well in the exposition of Numbers 24:17 in the next column of Ms. A (VII.18-19) as *'the Star'* who *'came to Damascus,'* an allusion we shall try to flesh out more fully below.

Here in Column Six, however, he is now further delineated in terms of another passage – this one from Isaiah 54:16 about *'the Smith creating a weapon'* or *'instrument for His works,'* in this instance, clearly meaning God's Divine *'works'* and His *'Holy'* plan. Whereas the overt meaning of the passage as it exists in Isaiah is that of *a 'weapon' created by God that can destroy any weapon used against it* (note the atmosphere of impending military threat and national catastrophe even in Isaiah 54 and note as well that this passage following directly on from the all-important Isaiah 53 and *'the Song of the Suffering Servant,'* perhaps the fundamental proof-text in all 'Christian' theology); the subjects of this particular additional *'Song'* in Isaiah, as it continues, are significantly called *the Servants 'established in*

Righteousness' (54:14), who 'do Righteousness' and 'keep Judgement' (56:1) and 'love the Name of the Lord' (56:6). Again here, we have the 'Righteousness'/'Piety' dichotomy predicated, as we have been stressing, of all 'Opposition' groups from 'the Essenes,' to John the Baptist, to Jesus, and James – words having particular significance, of course too, for Qumran.

As just observed, this passage follows directly on from and, in fact, really is another 'Song' continuing – for continue it surely does – the famous 'Song' of 'the Suffering Servant' in the previous chapter (Isaiah 53). Furthermore, this whole succession of allusions closes in Isaiah 56:3–6 with actual ecstatic evocation of those same 'Nilvim'/'Joiners' so much a part of the exegesis of Ezekiel 44:15 two columns earlier in CD, just highlighted above. But here in both Isaiah 56:3 and 56:6, it is explicitly stated – just as in Esther 9:27 later (where, as already remarked, such persons are described as 'joining with them' – meaning, 'the Jews' – in their celebrations) – that the 'Nilvim'/'Joiners' are 'foreigners who have joined themselves to the Lord' – repeated twice.

Of course, the 'joining' imagery is significant here and it is found too, as already signaled as well, in the Nahum Pesher.[108] There it is applied to 'the Simple of Ephraim,' extremely pregnant language which should be ranged alongside 'the Simple of Judah doing Torah' at the end of the Habak-kuk Pesher and may, as previously suggested, even imply – if not simply referring to 'Ger-Nilvim' or 'Resident Aliens' generally – 'Samaritans.' Again it should be emphasized and Isaiah makes this unequivocally clear (as does Esther) that we are speaking about 'Gentiles' or 'foreigners' here.[109] We are also coming extremely close to what Acts is picturing Peter as saying in 15:7–9 and James, in 15:16–17, in alluding to 'building up again the fallen Tabernacle of David' and 'the Gentiles upon whom My Name has been called.'

For over two decades now, I have been stressing the fact that these 'Nilvim' mentioned in CDiv.3's exposition of Ezekiel's 'Zadokite Covenant' – that is, 'and the Nilvim with them,' the 'them,' as we can now see, being 'the Penitents of Israel who went out from the Land of Judah to dwell in the Land of Damascus' – were, in fact, Gentile converts attaching themselves to the Lord.[110] Now in these pregnant passages being cited from Isaiah 54–56 here in CDvi.7-9, one finds further confirmation of this proposi-tion.

At least where James' speech in Acts was concerned, to say nothing of these other contexts – in particular, MMT, the Nahum Pesher, and here in the Damascus Document – the addressees are at least partially to be considered 'Gentile' converts or exactly such 'Nilvim' or 'Joiners,' whether in Edessa in Northern Syria or Adiabene further East where we know conversions of the kind we are talking about were going on.[111] In fact, one can say the same thing about Paul's counter-positions in Romans 3:18–5:10, 8:12–11:32, and Galatians 3:2–5:16 (the quantity of Qumranisms in in which passages are also quite numerous), all evoking Genesis 15:6 on Abraham's salvationary state (as opposed for instance to how James 2:7–26 would express this) and clearly meant to be the allegorical and sophistical antithesis of these positions, not only in James but also on *'being Steadfast'* and *'keeping the Covenant'/'doing the Torah'* in this *'New Covenant in the Land of Damascus'* in the Damascus Document as well.

Be these things as they may – according to Isaiah 56:4-6 as long as such *'Gentiles'* or *'Nilvim'* *'keep the Sabbath, choosing what pleases (Him) and holding fast to the Covenant'* (*'Mehazikim'* again, which both anticipates the imagery of *'strengthening'* in the Damascus Document above and extends it to specifically apply to *'any foreigner joined to the Lord'* – including even *'eunuchs'*[112]); they will also be found acceptable in the Temple and added to those *'already gathered'* there.

This *'holding fast'* or the language of *'being steadfast,'* which itself encompasses that of *'strengthening'* is, as we have seen, a persistent usage throughout the Damascus Document and other texts from Qumran. In particular, it is to be found in the closing language of the exhortation in Column XX of Ms. B as it is in Columns VII–VIII of Ms. A, as we have on several occasions remarked (but it is so important it is worth repeating again),[113] about how *'all those that hold fast to the Statutes –* '*Mehazikim,'* as in Isaiah 56:6 above *– coming and going according to the Torah and listening to the voice of the Teacher'* (*'Moreh'* – almost certainly meant to imply the proverbial *'Moreh ha-Zedek'* or *'Teacher of Righteousness'* already mentioned in CDi.11 and pervasive at Qumran[114]), who *'do not desert'* or *'turn aside from the Laws of Righteousness'* (*'Hukkei ha-Zedek,'* just as implied with regard to *'the Mehokkekot'* of *'the Mehokkek'* earlier),

> *their hearts will be strengthened* (here the verb is *'ya^ciz'* as in the cognomen applied to James according to all early Church reports, that is, the *'^cOz-le-^cAm'* or *'Strength'* or *'Protection-of-the-People'*[115]) *and they shall prevail against* (or *'be Victorious against'*) *all the Sons of Earth...and see His Salvation* (*Yeshu^cato*), *because they took refuge in His Holy Name* (that is, as even Paul implies in the passages from Romans 3:18 and 8:15 above, they were *'God-Fearers'*).[116]

In conclusion, therefore, this *'Mehokkek'* or *'Staff'* of Numbers 21:18 – whom God, in the words of Isaiah 54:16, *'created as an instrument for His works'* –is defined in this dramatic follow-up exposition in Column Six as *'the Doresh'* or *'Seeker after the Torah.'* In an esoteric exercise of some alliterative inventiveness, it is he '*who decreed (hakak) the Mehokkekot*' ('*Ordinances*' or '*Staves*' – as we have already explained, this double entendre is not only an obvious plural parallel of '*the Mehokkek*' / '*Law-Giver*' but also plays on and replaces the '*Mish͑anotam*' / '*their Supports*' in the underlying original from Isaiah 54:18) with which '*the Princes and the Nobles of the People dug the well*' and '*in which they should walk until the Standing up* (or '*Arising*') *in the Last Days of the One who Pours down Righteousness*' ('*ha-Yoreh ha-Zedek*,' that is, '*Yoreh*' or '*Pourer*' instead of its homophone, '*the Moreh ha-Zedek*' / '*Righteous Teacher*' – but also possibly a scribal error). Not only does this '͑*Amod*' evoke the *Florilegium*'s '*Branch of David who would arise together with the Doresh ha-Torah in Zion in the Last Days to save Israel*' again; but the allusion to the same '*Last Days*' in both in large measure demonstrates their circularity and that not only are the authors part of the same general mindset or '*Movement*,' but that the two documents were written at approximately the same time.[117]

This is Ms. A, but the idea of '*being given over*' or '*given up to the sword*' in both Mss. makes it unmistakably clear that we are speaking about the parallel allusion in Ms. B to '*the coming of the Messiah of Aaron and Israel*' as well.[118] Though the imagery, admittedly, is complex and obscure, the thrust is clear. Not only does it appear that '*the Doresh ha-Torah*' and '*the Righteous Teacher*' are, for all intents and purposes, the same person; but '*the Penitents of Israel*' are in this second exegesis in CDVI.5, now, both '*the Diggers*' and also clearly identical with '*the Priests*' in the first exegesis of Ezekiel 44:15 in CDIV.2. They are also clearly identical to '*the Princes*' of the underlying Numbers 21:18, who just as these same '*Priests*' must, in turn, be seen as '*the Emigres*' par excellence '*who went out from the Land of Judah to dwell in the Land of Damascus*' and who, like the '*Doresh ha-Torah*,' are plainly described as '*seeking*' (*darshuhu* – God) '*and whose honour was questioned by no man.*'[119]

In addition, these '*Princes*' are slightly different from '*the Nobles of the People*' from the same text and with whom – just as with '*the Levites*' in CDIV.3 earlier – they are in apposition in the original citation from Numbers 21:18. Though both are described as '*Diggers*' (in the second case, though, they are characterized rather as '*Rooter-Uppers*'[120]); it should be appreciated that – just as in '*the Sons of Zadok*' exposition earlier, where one had three groups – here one has at least two groups: '*the Princes*' and '*the Nobles of the People.*' These will be interpreted slightly differently in the exegesis and one should always be cognizant of these differences however minuscule or seemingly redundant.

As with Ezekiel's original '*the Priests who were Sons-of-Zadok Levites*,' the phraseology of the original underlying passage from Numbers is being deliberately broken open and the appositives treated separately. It would also appear that '*the Doresh ha-Torah*' or '*Seeker*'/'*Interpreter of the Torah*' is included among the first group – that of '*the Princes*' (*Sarim*) – because, like him, they too are being described in terms of '*seeking*' – in his case, '*seeking the Torah*'; in theirs '*seeking God*,' the operative word, as we can plainly now see, continuing to be '*seeking*.' In fact, he is also probably the prototypical '*Prince*' and, as such to be identified with the third group of the earlier exegesis of Ezekiel 44:15, '*the Sons of Zadok*' as well.

However this may be, since he has already been specifically identified as '*the Staff*' or '*Mehokkek*' as well, it is he – as we have seen – who '*decrees (hakak) the Laws*' or '*Staves*' with which these '*Nobles of the People dig the Well*.' Here, then, the seeming redundancy represented by the phrase '*the Nobles of the People*' with whom '*the Princes*' are in apposition – just as '*the Levites*,' '*the Priests*' in the Ezekiel 44:15 before – can fairly easily be accounted for by identifying them with '*the Nilvim*' or '*Joiners*' of both this earlier exegesis and now Isaiah 56:6, the connecting piece being the allusion to '*People*' or '*Peoples*' meaning (as in Paul) '*Gentiles*.' These are the ones who apply '*the Ordinances*'/'*Staves*'/'*Mish^canot*'/'*Mehokkekot*' ('*the Laws of the Covenant*' or '*the Laws of His Holiness*' or '*the Laws of Right-eousness*' at the end of CD[121]) and so the imagery of '*the Well of Living Waters*,' which will be picked up later in Columns VIII and XIX when '*the New Covenant in the Land of Damascus*' is being elucidated, is complete.[122]

The reason all of these are attached to the all-important phraseology emerging out of Isaiah 54–56 (even from Isaiah 53) is that this whole section is being presented as a '*Song*' or '*singing*' – in the minds of the exegetes, the same '*Song*' or '*singing*' of the classical song of Numbers 21:18 above. As Isaiah 54:1 puts this: '*Sing, O barren, who did not bear. Break forth into singing*' but, even in 52:7–10 earlier, it is intoned that the Lord '*is making Salvation* ('*Yeshu^cah*' again) *heard to Zion*,' '*with one voice shall they sing, for the Lord has comforted His People*' and '*all the ends of the Earth shall see the Salvation of Our God*' (here again the last line of CDxx.34 of Ms. B above). It is from here, too (Isaiah 52:11), that Paul extracts the unchar-acteristic passage, we just alluded to in 2 Corinthians 6:17 above, '*Be Separated and come out from among them. Touch no unclean thing*.'

As already remarked as well, the whole tenor of these passages from Isaiah 52–56, even earlier, is one of national catastrophe followed by hope directed towards '*the barren that did not bear*,' '*the sons of the forsaken one being no less than (those of) the married*,' '*the ashamed*,' '*the confounded*,' '*the cast-off wife of youth*,' '*for a moment forsaken*' but promising and *looking for-ward to* – just as the Habakkuk *Pesher* does[123] – ultimate '*Salvation*' or '*Redemption*.' Here, too, the thrust then in both documents, the Damascus Document and the Habakkuk *Pesher*, of remaining hopeful even in the face of overwhelming national disaster is the same – once more pointing towards a common chronological origin. Just as significantly – now that the basis for the language of the closing promise of '*seeing Yeshuʿa*' of the Damascus Document can be seen to be Isaiah 52:10 and the citation of Isaiah 54:16 and 56:1 earlier; it is hard to imagine that the person or persons responsible for writing this document were not also reading Isaiah 53:2–12, perhaps the fundamental proof-text of 'Christianity,' as we have seen, with equal diligence.

Again the '*Nazirite*' Language of '*Separation*' and that of Divine '*Visitation*'

Immediately following the exegesis of this arcane '*Song*' from Numbers 21:18 and Isaiah 54:16, the Damascus Document proceeds into its description of '*the New Covenant in the Land of Damascus*,' referred to at the end of Column VI.19, and '*the Fallen Tabernacle of David*' to be, presumably, '*re-erected*' or '*established*' there – referred to in Column VII.16, the *Florilegium* above, and in Acts 15's picture of James' speech to '*the Assembly*' *of the Jerusalem Church* (the parallel to which in the Damascus Document would probably be to '*the Assembly*' or '*Church of Perfect Holiness*'[124]). It does so by progressing through allusions to '*doing according to the precise letter of the Torah*' and the use of '*Nazirite*' language ('*lehinnazer*' / '*lehazzir*' / '*linzor*') to describe how one '*separates from the Sons of the Pit*' and '*keeps away from polluted evil Riches*,' including those of the Temple (presumably polluted by Herodian and Roman contributions)[125] to announce its final theme: '*distinguishing between Holy and profane*' and '*separating polluted from clean*' (though a parallel to Paul in 2 Corinthians 6:18–7:1 – the exact opposite, as we have seen, of what Acts 10:15–28 pictures Peter as learning in its '*Heavenly tablecloth*' scenario).[126]

Even the use of '*Nazirite*' language of this kind should be seen as paralleling the '*Judgement*' James makes in Acts 15:19 (clearly in his role of '*Bishop of the Jerusalem Church*' – '*the Mebakker*' at Qumran[127]) and the directives he gives to overseas communities also expressed, as we have seen, in terms of '*keeping away from*' ('*things sacrificed to idols*' / '*pollutions of the idols*,' '*blood*,' '*fornication*,' and '*strangled things*' / '*carrion*') directly following his speech evoking '*the fallen Tabernacle of David*' above. The sequencing here is important and it is '*internal data*' of this kind that has to be seen, as we have been emphasizing, as calling into question the supposedly secure results of '*external*' evidence such as palaeography or radiocarbon dating opposed to this '*internal*.'

A third evocation of this kind comes in Columns VIII and XIX. This is
'*nazru*' or '*linzor*' and has to do with '*not separating from the People*' (again,
possibly also '*Peoples*' and the '*People*'/'*Peoples*' vocabulary) and, not
insignificantly, directly following an injunction against '*fornication*.'[128] This
last is defined here as elsewhere in CD as '*approaching close family relatives
for fornication*' – in particular including '*nieces*.'[129] In the earlier exegeses of
'*the Zadokite Covenant*' and '*the Three Nets of Belial*,' it will be recalled that
it was said that one of the reasons the Temple was '*polluted*' was because
those in control (referred to in both Columns IV and VIII/XIX in terms
of the two other images from Ezekiel 13:3–16, '*the Builders of the Wall*' and
'*the Daubers upon it with Plaster*,' themselves delineated in terms of the
'*Empty visions*' of '*Lying prophets*' who '*cry Peace when there is no Peace*'[130])
'*did not separate according to the Torah*,' meaning '*clean from unclean*' and '*Holy
from profane*.'[131] Rather, the accusation was that '*they slept with women
during the blood of their periods*' – another aspect of the '*fornication*' charge
combined with that of '*abstention from blood*,' both now directly evoked in
Acts 15:20–29's picture of James' injunctions to overseas communities –
and '*each man married the daughter of his brother or the daughter of his sister*'
(the original expression of the '*niece*' marriage charge).[132]

The sense of what follows at the end of Column Five of CD was that
the Temple Establishment, the seeming object of this castigation, did not
itself necessarily do all these things but, by having contact with persons
who *did* – in our view, clearly indicating Herodians, Romans, and/or
other foreigners and, in implying a context of foreign domination of
Palestine, another firm dating parameter – they acquired their '*pollution*'
and '*could not be cleansed*' unless they '*had been forced*' (the meaning of this
last should also be clear).[133] However this may be, these descriptions, all
of which turn on the issue of '*not separating according to the Torah*' (that is,
'*in the Temple*' and again meaning, '*not separating Holy from profane*'), are
clearly expository of both the Second and Third '*Nets of Belial*' and
combine the '*pollution of the Temple*' charge with the '*fornication*,' one as just
indicated and two of the areas of concern in the correspondence known
as '*MMT*' as well.[134]

Following this admonition '*to separate between clean and unclean and distinguish between Holy and profane*' and, of course, the directive '*to keep the
the Sabbath Day according to its precise letter and the Festivals*' (which Paul
refers to in Galatians 4:9–10 – playing off his contempt for and the
'*Ebionite*' sense of the whole complex – as '*beggarly*') *and the Day of Fasting*' (*Yom Kippur*[135]) at the end of CD Six – points already encountered
and specifically applied to Gentiles in Isaiah 56:2 and 56:6 above; '*the New
Covenant in the Land of Damascus*' is for the first time specifically evoked,

as we have seen, and set forth in the context of the associated Command, 'to set up the Holy Things according to their precise specifications,' again also the basic thrust of large sections of the admonitions in *MMT*.[136]

Following this and the first in importance obviously in this catalogue of Commandments associated with this '*New Covenant in the Land of Damascus*' is the Commandment '*to love each man his brother as himself*.'[137] Not only is this patently a principal foundation piece of '*the New Covenant in the Land of Damascus*' and immediately recognizable as '*the Royal Law according to the Scripture*' of James 2:8; it is also the basis, as we have been underscoring, of '*the Righteousness Commandment*' of Josephus' '*Essenes*' and his picture of John the Baptist's teaching (in the *Antiquities*, '*Righteousness towards one's fellow man*'[138]), as it is the Gospel picture of 'Jesus' and Paul's recommendation in Romans 13:4–10, *to pay taxes to Rome* – that is, paying taxes to Rome, was '*Righteousness towards one's fellow man*'! It is also, as also stressed, the first part of the '*Righteousness*'/ '*Piety*' dichotomy and the first of the two '*Love*' Commandments – the second being '*loving God*' or, as the Damascus Document would put a similar idea, '*setting up the Holy Things according to their precise specifications*.'

Following the evocation and seemingly in exposition of this '*all-Righteousness*' Commandment and continuing the '*strengthening*'/'*steadfastness*' imagery, as applied by Isaiah 56:6–7 above to '*Gentiles*' or '*Nilvim*,' the admonition '*to strengthen the hand of the Meek, the Poor (Ebion), and* – equally as notable in terms of the implications for a cadre of Gentiles or God-fearing '*Nilvim*' at Qumran – '*the Ger*' or '*the Convert*,' referred to esoterically in the previous exegesis as '*the Nobles of the People*,' is subjoined.[139] Following this too, in this list of ordinances associated with '*the New Covenant in the Land of Damascus*,' is the directive (at the beginning of Column Seven) '*not to uncover the nakedness of near kin*,' expressed in the more normative Qumran manner in terms of the injunction '*to keep away from fornication according to the Statute*' (here the '*Nazirite*' vocabulary affixed now to the first of '*the Three Nets of Belial*').[140]

All these things are then summed up by the next phrase, to '*walk in these things in Perfect Holiness*,' which is both the point of their '*Nazirite*' focus and the reason for these extreme purity regulations in effect in '*the Wilderness Camps*' in the first place – that is, we have to do with what should almost be referred to as *a Community of 'life-long Nazirites*' or, if one prefers – to use an earlier vocabulary – '*Rechabites*' (but '*Revolutionary Rechabites*'[141]). They are also summed up, as we have just seen, by Paul in 2 Corinthians 6:17–7:2 above (also a '*Florilegium*' of sorts on 2 Samuel 7:14, Isaiah 52:11, etc.), which includes, not only almost exactly the same phraseology (this time, for a change, not reversed), '*Perfecting Holiness in fear of God'* (*n.b.*, the '*God-fearing*' vocabulary), but also the allusions to '*separate from all pollutions*' and '*touch no unclean thing*' (including, '*I shall be a father to you and you shall be My sons and daughters*,' based on 2 Samuel 7:14 above), by implication, again applied as in Isaiah 56:3–6 *to Gentile converts as well.*

It is at this point, too, that both narratives more or less converge. Less complex than Ms. A at this juncture, Ms. B does not, as will be recalled, refer to '*those who were Steadfast escaping to the Land of the North*' (again *n.b.*, the '*strengthening*' imagery here, based on the Hebrew root '*H-Z-K*' of CD Six earlier and CD Twenty later, not to mention Isaiah 56:6 above)[142]; but rather it is '*the Little Ones*' or '*the Meek of the Flock*' who '*escape*' while, with the '*coming of the Messiah of Aaron and Israel* (equivalent to the '*arising of the Sceptre*' in Ms. A; '*the Branch*' and/or '*the Tabernacle of David*' in the *Florilegium*), *those that remained would be given over to the sword.*' This is repeated again with specific reference to Ezekiel 9:4 about '*putting a mark on the foreheads of those who cry and weep*' (this last obviously implying '*those seeking repentance*' and, thereby, '*Salvation*' – that is, '*the Penitents from sin in Jacob*'), '*but the rest shall be delivered up to the avenging sword of the Covenant*' or Ms. A's '*the Backsliders would be delivered up to the sword.*'[143] There can be little doubt that this is the vengeful war-like '*Messiah*' of the War Scroll. Nor can there by any doubt of the background atmosphere of impending national disaster or of suffering.

In the parallel material in Ms. A, as we have seen, this is paralleled by the '*standing up of the Sceptre*' from '*the Star Prophecy*' of Numbers 24:17 above, equated with '*the Nasi Chol ha-cEdah*' and described, '*upon his arising*' (singular), as going to '*utterly destroy all the Sons of Seth.*'[144] This, in turn, parallels the sense of the *Florilegium*'s '*Tabernacle*' or '*Branch of David*,' just noted above, '*who would arise in Zion in the Last Days*' to '*deliver*' or '*save Israel*' as well as the War Scroll's '*sword of No Mere Man*' from Isaiah 31:8 – as in Ms. A, again in continuing its exposition of Numbers 24:17 – that was going to '*devour*' Assyria (it is important the verb here is '*eat him*,' that is, '*eat Assyria*' or what '*Assyria*' *was supposed to represent*[148]), interpreted in terms of the destruction of '*the Kittim.*'[146] It is at this point at the end of Column Seven of Ms. A, too, that all this is compared to the '*escape at the time of the First Visitation*' – clearly meaning '*the Steadfast*,' pictured only a few lines before as '*those who escaped to the Land of the North*' – '*while the Backsliders were delivered up to the sword.*'[147] Here, as just remarked and previously explained, the two manuscripts briefly come together again.

In all four documents, therefore, the *Florilegium*, the War Scroll, and the two versions of the Damascus Document, it should be clear that this

'*Messiah*' primarily *comes to destroy Gentiles and not Jews*, at least not '*Penitent*' or '*Righteous* Jews' – a '*Messiah*,' in fact, of the cut of Shimon Bar Kochba/'*the Son of the Star*.'[148] As we have seen too, this '*Messiah*' in Ms. A is also referred to as '*the Nasi Chol ha-ᶜEdah*'/'*the Head*' or '*Prince of the Whole Assembly*' or '*Church*.' Notwithstanding, in the very next Column VIII of Ms. A and to some extent Ms. B as well, this same '*Judgement*' or '*Visitation*,' as earlier underscored too, was also to be upon '*those who entered the Covenant* (clearly, '*the New Covenant in the Land of Damascus*') *who did not hold fast to these Statutes*' and '*turned aside*,' '*back*' or '*away in stubbornness of heart*.'[149] To put this in another way – not only was this '*Judgement*' or '*Visitation*' to be upon *hated foreigners* and *conquering* '*Gentiles*' but *upon backsliding Jews* as well, possibly even including those '*Nilvim*' or '*Joiners*' in associated status '*with them*,' particularly if they were '*Paulinists*' (not only '*possibly*' but '*probably*').[150] '*Their Visitation would be for destruction by the hand of Belial*' – presumably Herodians and/or Romans.

> *This is the Day on which God commands* (or '*in which God visits*' – here '*commands*' and '*visits*,' as already explained, are basically the same word in Hebrew[151]).

Again, there can be little doubt of the meaning of this, nor of the tragic nature of the times.

'*The Nasi ha-ᶜEdah*' also appears, as we have seen, in the curious fragment 4Q285, discovered by Professor Wise and myself and which, because of it, we called '*The Messianic Leader*' – afterwards, not surprisingly, identified as part of the War Scroll. Not only does this fragment, like the *Florilegium*, refer to '*the Prophet Isaiah*,' it is steeped in Messianic terminology, mostly taken from Isaiah 11:1–5, about which there is another, largely parallel *Pesher* extant at Qumran.[152] Taken together, both include such terms as '*the Shoot*' or '*Root of Jesse*,' '*the rod*,' '*the Staff*,' '*the Netzer*,' '*a Throne of Glory*' (somewhat like 2 Samuel 7:16 above), and '*woundings*.'[153] Even more strikingly, '*the Nasi ha-ᶜEdah*' is actually placed in it in apposition to or identified with '*the Branch of David*' (*Zemach*), itself in apposition to '*the Shoot of Jesse*.'[154]

In conclusion, just as with '*the Princes*' and '*the Nobles of the People*' earlier, '*the Star*' and '*the Sceptre*' seem to be different characters. In the Damascus Document, the more war-like '*Sceptre*' – identified in the *Florilegium* with 4Q285's '*the Branch of David*,' itself identified in the Genesis *Pesher* (in which '*the Mehokkek is the Covenant of the Kingdom*'[155]) with '*the Shiloh*' or '*the Messiah of Righteousness*' – is now rather '*the Nasi*' (a term actually used by Bar Kochba on his coinage[156]) who is identified with '*the*

Sceptre' – so one has to assume all three are identical.[160] On the other hand '*the Star*,' who along with '*the Sceptre*' is part of the terminology of Numbers 24:17 above, is actually identified in the Damascus Document with '*the Interpreter of* or '*Doresh ha-Torah who came to Damascus*.' There is no way of penetrating the mind of the exegete here.

Not only would this seem to have not just a parallel but a parody in the present Book of Acts; but in CDvii.18-21, '*the Interpreter*' or '*Doresh*' seems to be achieving a sort of equality with '*the Sceptre*' or '*Nasi ha-'Edah*' because of what he appears to be accomplishing at Damascus – or in the wilderness thereof and in '*the Land of the North*' as a part of the process of '*erecting the Fallen Tabernacle of David*' there.

In CDviii.2/xix.14 this exposition is immediately followed by allusion, already underscored above, to a coming '*Second Visitation*' involving that Judgement '*for destruction at the hand of Belial*' on '*Backsliders*' from '*the New Covenant*' ('*in the Land of Damascus*'), '*who did not hold fast to its Laws and Statutes*' and '*betrayed*' its '*Well of Living Waters*.' This very definitely has overtones of James' evocation of a '*Visitation*' upon new Gentile converts in Acts 15:14, where '*the Men who remain*' (seemingly replacing '*the Remnant of Edom*' of Amos 9:12 in Hebrew) were described in 15:17 in terms of '*seeking out the Lord*' (note again the emphasis on and use of the word '*seeking*' even though this, too, seems to derive from a reworking of Amos 9:12's '*possessing*' – as in '*possessing the Remnant of Edom and the Nations upon whom My Name has been called*'[158]) preceding his rulings with regard to '*those from the Peoples*' (*Ethnon*) who in 15:19, '*turn to God*' (here even the '*turning to*,' '*back*,' or '*aside from the Way of idolatry*' or '*of the People(s)*' of the Damascus Document's various formulations above).

'*Raising the Fallen Tabernacle of David*' in James' Speech and at Qumran

This allusion to God's coming '*visit*' to the land and the '*escape to the North*' in these First and Second Visitations – in both versions clearly involving '*the avenging sword of the Covenant*' (no '*peaceful*' Essenes these, although there is '*humility*' or '*meekness*,' in the sense of '*obedience*') – is directly followed in Ms. A, as we have seen, by the two quotations from Amos: the first from 5:26–27 about '*exiling the Tabernacle*' or '*the Saccut of your King*' (also readable as '*your Moloch*' as already explained) *and the Kiyyun of your images*' (transformed as well in the rendering of CDvii into '*the bases of your statues*') '*beyond Damascus*.'[159]

What seems deliberately left out in Ms. A (one should not forget that the passage is replaced by the citations from Ezekiel and Zechariah in Ms. B) is the rest of the passage from Hebrew Amos: '*the Star of your God you made'* and *'being exiled beyond Damascus'* just alluded to. However, these are picked up, by implication as we have seen – the first in the next proof-text, evoked from Numbers 24:17, which actually then speaks of *'the Way of the Star from Jacob,'* the second having already been deliberately reworked into *'from My Tent(s) of Damascus'* and transferred in the interests of the exegesis as a complement to the first part of the passage about *'exiling the Tabernacle of your King and the bases of your statues'* (that is, *'from My tents of Damascus'*).[160]

The reason behind this should be clear. This passage from Amos 5:26–27, which on the surface is ostensibly about *'idols'* and *'idolatry,'* appears to have been purposefully altered to refer to the *'Tents of Damascus'* (once again, most translations read singular *'My Tent of'* here, but the usage can also be plural). In any event, the allusion to *'My Tent'/'Tents of'* (*'Ohali'* or *'Ohalei'*) does not appear anyhow in the original Amos but rather, as we just saw, the homonym *'me-hal'ah le-Dammashek'/'beyond Damascus.'*[161] Changing a word like *'me-hal'ah'/'beyond'* in received Amos 5:27 to *'me-Ohali'* (meaning *'God's Tent'*) or *'me-Ohalei'* (meaning *'the Tents of'* – in this case, *'Damascus'*) is typical of Qumran exegesis as it is Paul's and even the Gospels. Furthermore, it is reversed in the exegesis to refer to matters dear to the Community and the idolatry charge is completely ignored – in the event, *'the Flight'* or *'Exile to the North'* (in any case, *'north of'* or *'beyond Damascus'*) and/or *'the Tents'* in *'the Land of Damascus.'*

As the exposition continues, *'the Tabernacle of the King,'* paralleling *'the House of Faith whose like never existed in Israel previously'* earlier, is interpreted esoterically as *'the Books of the Torah'* (in the Genesis *Pesher*, it was *'the Mehokkek'* or *'Staff'* from Genesis 49:10 that was interpreted – here clearly seeming to mean *'the Legislator'* – as *'the Covenant of the Kingdom'* which, two lines later, was *'given'* to *'the Branch'* or just *'David'* and *'his seed'* forever[162]). In CDVII.17 in support of this, Amos 9:11, as we have seen, is quoted: *'as God said, I will raise up the Tabernacle of David which is fallen.'* Again, this is the precise text James is pictured as quoting in the passage above about Gentiles being accepted in the new Community, which brings us full circle. This is direct and incontrovertible evidence of *interdependence* between Acts and the Damascus Document, the *'Opposition Acts'* from Qumran, too flagrant to be denied or to be mere coincidence.

Now it is interpreted and the parallels go further. In the exegesis which follows directly preceding the citation of *'the Star Prophecy,'* as already indicated, *'the King'* is said to be *'the Community.'* In the Genesis *Pesher*, too, it was *'the feet of the Sceptre,'* from the same line of Genesis 49:10, that were interpreted esoterically and, not unsimilarly to this *'Community'* metaphor, as *'the Thousands of Israel.'*[163] But this is exactly the sense of Pauline exegesis in 1 Corinthians 12:27 above, where the *'members of the Community'* are identified with *'the body of Christ,'* a letter answering, as we have been elucidating, some of the materials in Acts relative to James' directives to overseas communities, which themselves now directly follow his evocation of Amos 9:11–12. In CDVII.15, *'the Kiyyun of your images'* from Amos 5:27 above is also now read as *'the bases of your statues'* and completely reversed, as just underscored too, from an allusion appertaining to paganism and idolatry to *'the Books of the Prophets whose words Israel despised.'*[164] This is esoteric exegesis at its best and one could well imagine an alternate interpretation of these same passages of the kind one seems to be getting in these speeches in Acts attributed to both Peter and James and supporting *'the Gentile Mission'* of Paul!

In conclusion, the actual allusion in this exegesis to *'raising up the Tabernacle of David which is fallen,'* a scriptural allusion attributed to James in Acts' version of the *'Jerusalem Council,'* would appear to be definitive – this not to mention James' reverse use of the language of God's *'Visitation'* in his own exegesis of this passage. Furthermore, if anything is illustrative of the First-Century authorship of the Damascus Document – aside from the many other allusions we have already shown to have a First-Century provenance and in spite of scholarly attempts to assert otherwise on the basis of palaeography or some other such *'external'* indicator – this is.

In Acts' presentation, James' speech – introduction of whom, despite the disappearance of the *'other'* James, seemingly being considered unnecessary – is preceded by a short description of how *'Simeon* (as already remarked, this could with more logic be presumably James' *'cousin'* – or *'brother'* – the second Successor to 'Jesus' in *'the Jerusalem Church,'* 'Simeon bar Cleophas,' since Peter had supposedly already fled abroad with a price on his head) *has related how God first visited the Gentiles to take out of them a People for His Name.'* Here four expressions jump immediately from the page, *'the words of the Prophets,' 'visited,' 'People,'* and *'Name.'* Though CD at this point uses the possibly defective *'the Books of the Prophets,'* 'MMT' for instance repeatedly uses this same allusion, *'the words of the Prophets.'*[165] *'The words of the Prophets'* also permeates documents like the Habakkuk *Pesher* above where it is used to highlight the extraordinary exegetical powers of the Righteous Teacher.[166]

Though it is not necessarily an uncommon expression, the allusion to *'visited'* is. Once again, as we have been showing, it is found almost exclusively in the Damascus Document where it occurs repeatedly – beginning with the description of how God *'visited them and caused a Root of Planting out of Aaron and Israel to grow'* in Column One to *'visiting their works,*' used in terms of '*Judgement*' in Column Five,[167] and from '*the Era of the First Visitation*' of Column Seven to the '*Visitation*' of '*Judgement on all those who entered His Covenant but did not remain steadfast in the Torah*' in Column Eight (literally, '*the Judgement Day*' or '*the Day on which God visits*' or '*commands*' – Muhammad knows the same expression: '*The Day on which God commands is Allah's*'[168]). As James is presented, applying it to Gentiles being saved in Acts 15:14-17, *i.e.*, '*how God First visited and took out of the Gentiles a People for His Name*'; it is a '*Visitation*' *for reward or goodness.* This is also a sense known to the Damascus Document and, if one looks closely, one will also find it emanating from *MMT*'s promise to its Royal addressee of '*works of the Torah*' for his '*own good and that of (his) People.*'[169] The operative term in all these formulations, as we have been emphasizing throughout, is '*People*' or '*Peoples*' – the same word, of course, Paul is applying to his '*Gentile Mission.*'

Again, this term '*Peoples*' is generally being used at Qumran as a term for Gentiles, as it is, for instance, in Eusebius' rendering of Agbarus as '*the Great King of the Peoples beyond the Euphrates*' – meaning both '*the Land of the Edessenes*' and countries such as '*Adiabene*' further East – areas to which Josephus appears, as he himself attests, to have first addressed his Aramaic and original version of the *Jewish War.*[170] This use of this allusion '*Peoples*' is the same in Greek as it is in Hebrew (and as it is, in fact, in Latin) and the next column of the Damascus Document will actually employ just such a term, '*the Kings of the Peoples,*' well known to Roman jurisprudence and, in our view, *inter alia* applying to Herodians.[171]

'The Star who Came to Damascus'

At this point, Ms. A now folds the allusion to '*the Star of your God*' from Amos 5:26, which it omitted from its original citation and regardless of its original import into a quotation of '*the Star Prophecy*' from Numbers 24:17, a central fixture of both Messianic allusion in the War Scroll and, according to Josephus, the general Messianic unrest in Palestine in the First Century leading up to the final War against the Romans.

Though most of what follows in the next two sections of this chapter we have already analyzed in one way or another previously, it is perhaps worth just summarizing it all for the benefit of the reader one more time. '*The Star*' is now identified with '*the Interpreter*' or '*Doresh ha-Torah who came to Damascus*' – the opposite, clearly, of *Paul's coming to Damascus* in Acts. '*The Sceptre,*' who shall '*arise out of Israel*' with '*the Star from Jacob*' in Numbers 24:17 and the *Florilegium*, is identified as '*the Leader of the whole Assembly*' – '*Assembly*' as in James' *Jerusalem Assembly.*'

These two terms, '*the Leader of the Assembly*' and '*the Sceptre*,' are now to be found in two other Qumran documents I first named and published fifteen years ago, '*the Messianic Leader*' (4Q285) and '*the Genesis Florilegium*' (4Q252). In the former, '*the Leader of the Assembly*' is identified as '*the Branch*' and in the latter, interpreting '*the Shiloh* Prophecy' from Genesis 49:10, '*the Branch*' is defined as '*the Messiah of Righteousness*' (singular).[172] In Ms.A these matters are connected to the '*escape*,' seemingly for comparative purposes, '*in the Era of the First Visitation when the Backsliders were delivered up to the sword.*'

In Ms. B, which at times seems superior to Ms. A — certainly it is just as '*Messianic*' — and adds much completely new material at the end of Column Eight (called, therefore, by its original editor '*Columns Nineteen*' and '*Twenty*'), this is now connected, as with those having Ezekiel 9:4's '*mark*' or '*cross*' on their foreheads at the time of '*the First Visitation*' (that represented by the coming of and destruction by the Babylonians), *to the escape of* '*the Meek*' (a synonym for '*the Poor*') *at the time of the coming* and, seemingly, *Second* or *final* and/or *present* '*Visitation*,' *when* '*the rest would be given over to the sword with the coming of the Messiah of Aaron and Israel.*'[173]

At this point in Columns Eight and Nineteen, both manuscripts (now more or less identical) launch into an all-out assault on '*the Princes of Judah*' — also labeled '*the Kings of the Peoples*,' whom we have previously identified as Herodian or other Greco-Roman (or '*Greek-speaking*'), petty '*Kings*' from Asia. Drawing on Deuteronomy 33:32 about '*their wine being the hot Venom of Vipers*' and echoing John the Baptist's and Jesus' attacks on the Establishment in the Gospels, these '*Kings of the Peoples*' are now specifically identified with the '*Vipers*'; and '*the Venom*' in this citation, '*the wine of their ways.*'[174]

In Hebrew, '*Venom*,' playing on the idea of '*Hotness*' or a '*burning stinging*' inherent in the underlying root, '*Hamah*,' is also a homonym for '*Wrath*' or '*Fury*.' The allusion to this '*Hemah*' or '*Wrath*' or '*Hot Anger*' will also reappear below in the description of the Wicked Priest's '*pursuit*' of or attack on the Righteous Teacher.[175] Also '*wine*' here plays on the idea of being '*Greek*' — '*wine*' and '*Greek*' being homonyms in Hebrew. All provide an unmistakable further and, in our view, *absolute dating provenance for the Damascus Document in the Herodian Period.* This is the context, too, in which '*the Lying Spouter*' is again now referred to. If he is Paul, then this is just what one would have expected, since it hints at *his links with both petty Herodian Kings and the Establishment High Priest.* Acts does the same. As already underscored, this '*Spouter of Lying*' is now described as being either of '*confused windiness*' or '*a Windbag*' or, as it were, '*walking in the wind*' or '*the Spirit*' — '*wind*' and '*Spirit*' being homonyms in Hebrew as well – and '*surely spouting to them*'![176]

The reference here is to Micah 2:6–11 and picks up earlier references to such '*spouting*' or '*pouring*' ('*spouting*' and '*pouring*' also being homonyms in Hebrew) and Ezekiel's 13:9–15's '*Daubers*' or '*Plasterers upon the wall*' in CD One and Four. The original context of both of these citations involved '*Lying prophets*' and their '*Empty visions*,' in particular – significantly in the context of both Paul's claims to '*Revelation*' and Josephus' Saulos' role as the intermediary between the Romans and '*all those desirous of Peace*' in Jerusalem – '*crying Peace when there was no Peace*' (Ezekiel 13:16). For Paul's claims to '*Revelation*'/'*Apocalypseos*,' one should see Galatians 1:12, 2:2, 1 Corinthians 14:6 and 26 (together with the always telltale allusions to '*Tongue(s)*,' '*Gnosis*,' '*building up*,' and '*prophecy*'), 2 Corinthians 12:1 (even evoking '*visions*' too), 12:7, and Romans 16:25 (itself overflowing, like 1 and 2 Corinthians, with Qumran usage and imagery).

Here too Ezekiel 13:14 speaks of the torrential rain or hailstones that God unleashes in his '*Fury*' (again '*Hemah*'), a torrential rain of the kind already encountered in the follow-up to the events surrounding the stoning of James' putative forebear Honi and which we shall see to have been included in the newer Cave 4 fragments of the opening First Column of the Nahum *Pesher*[177]; so, once again, all our imageries involving '*Lying prophecies*' and '*torrential flood*' are joined.

In CD One this '*Lying Spouter*,' as we have now on several occasions had cause to remark, was also referred to as '*the Scoffer*' or '*Comedian who poured down on*' (a possible play on baptism as well) or '*spouted to Israel the waters of Lying*.' As will also be recalled, it was he who is blamed for '*removing the boundaries which the First had set down as their inheritance*,' '*abolishing the Pathways of Righteousness*' and '*causing them to wander astray in a trackless waste without a Way*.'[178] But in addition, it was also he that '*banded together against the soul of the Just One*' and the other '*Walkers in Perfection*,' '*kindling God's Wrath against*' them. These are just the words, too, which CDviii.13/xix.26 uses to close its characterization of '*the Lying Spouter's spouting*,' '*so that God's Wrath was kindled against his entire Assembly*' or '*Church*' (the only question is here, whose '*Church*' are we referring to?)[179]

Importantly, it is here as well, as both Mss. of CD continue their exposition of the genus of '*the Lying Spouter*' by immediately evoking *Elisha's relations with Gehazi* – someone who went to Damascus and betrayed his master there (2 Kings 5:20–27) and a *nom a clef* for one of '*the Enemies of God*' in Talmudic literature which some consider was used to denote Paul.[180] Here too '*the Man of Lying*' and his colleagues, '*the Violent Ones*' and '*the Traitors*,' are described as having '*turned aside from and betrayed* –

the language of '*Treachery*' here is always something to keep an eye on – *the New Covenant in the Land of Damascus*.'[180]

Once more it set forth that an individual of this kind '*who entered the New Covenant in the Land of Damascus*' or '*the Assembly of the Men of Perfect Holiness but hesitates to do the commands of the Upright*,' '*turning aside from the Well*' or '*Fountain of Living Waters*' (Ibn Gabirol's *Fons Vitae?*);

> when his works are revealed, he shall be expelled from the Assembly (or '*Church*') like one whose lot had never fallen among the Disciples of God.[182]

Here, again, we have the '*Jamesian*' emphases on '*doing*' and '*works*.' The usage '*Disciples*,' too, is important, the Community being variously referred to, as we have seen, as '*the Community of God*,' '*the Assembly of His Holiness*,' or '*the House of the Torah*.' Not only will a person of this genus not '*be reckoned in the Foundation of the People*' – here the language of '*reckoned*,' as in '*Abraham's Faith being reckoned to him as Righteousness*' of Genesis 15:6 above and elsewhere, is also important[183] – but when

> his works reveal themselves, according to the exact letter of the interpretation of the Torah in which the Men of Perfect Holiness walk, no man shall cooperate with him in purse and work (*ᶜavodah* – meaning, '*service*' or '*Mission*' as we have seen, not *maᶜasim/'works*' and *cf.* Acts 15:38 above), for all the Holy Ones of the Most High have cursed him.

This is a total anathema of the kind we have already signaled in the Community Rule above and Paul seems to be complaining about in Galatians 2:12–14. It is interesting, too, that the imagery Paul uses in this passage in Galatians 2:14 of '*not walking Uprightly*' is precisely that used here in these portions from the Damascus Document.[184] CD now specifically applies this to the kind of individual '*among the First and the Last*' (like Gehazi or Paul) who '*rejected the Law*' and '*put idols on their heart*,' adding: '*they shall have no share in the House of the Law*.'[185]

Contrariwise in Galatians, Paul's attacks on those '*keeping the Law*' and '*slavery to it*' occupy most of the rest of the Letter, including, '*no one can be Justified by keeping the Law*' (2:17) and '*if Righteousness were through the Law, then Christ died for nothing*' (2:21). These lead directly into his doctrine of *the saving death of Jesus Christ*, who '*redeemed us from the curse of the Law*' (3:13), in the end concluding: *you are* '*set aside from Christ*' if you '*are justified by the Law, fallen from Grace*' (5:3). Again, here too, one should note the play on the '*setting aside*' language of Naziritism.

We have already encountered this language of '*cursing*' and excommunication in the Community Rule. There too, it will be recalled, the individual '*with idols in his heart*' will be

> *consumed without forgiveness. God's Anger and Zeal for His Judgements will burn him in Everlasting destruction. All the curses of the Covenant will cleave to him and God will separate him for Evil, and he shall be cut off from among all the Sons of Light, because he has turned aside from God. Because of his idols and the stumbling block of his sin* (it should be recalled that for Paul, in Galatians 5:11 above, *the crucified Christ* is a '*stumbling block*' to the Jews), *his lot shall be among those who are cursed forever.*[186]

Here, of course, we again have both the '*setting aside*' and '*cutting off*' language, which Paul in Galatians 5:3–12 above also applies to his opponents' insistence on '*circumcision.*'

This kind of excommunication and '*cursing*' is also the sense of what follows in these passages from CDxx.8–13 of Ms. B turning '*the First*' vs. '*the Last*' language, attributed to Jesus in the Gospels, against those who '*reject the Law*' and '*put idols on their hearts*' (the same ban on '*idolatry*' one finds implied in James' directives to overseas communities, itself overtly stated in '*MMT*' as well[187]) *and walked in stubbornness their heart.*' This reads:

> *They shall be judged according to the Judgement upon their confederates who turned aside with the Men of Scoffing* (the plural of '*the Man of Scoffing*' clearly implying '*the Liar*' and his kind), *because they spoke mistakenly about the Laws of Righteousness and rejected the Covenant and the Compact* (or '*Faith*' – '*the Compact*' of Deuteronomy 7:9, we have already seen referred to in Column VII.4-6/XIX.1-4 earlier, '*faithfully promising them to live for a thousand years*'), *which they erected in the Land of Damascus – and this is the New Covenant* (here, again, making it clear that '*the New Covenant*' is just a rededication to the '*Old*'). *Neither they nor their families* (meaning, of course, *those who 'break' or 'reject' this 'New Covenant*' as '*the Liar*' and his followers were seen to do) *will have a share in the House of the Torah.*[188]

As we have seen, this '*judging*' will now reappear both in the '*rulings*' James is said to make at the Jerusalem Council in Acts, but also in later columns of Ms. A of CD, where the role of '*the Mebakker*' or '*Bishop*' is delineated.

Not only does the allusion to '*House of Torah*' repeat what came three lines before, but the emphasis on this '*Covenant*' being '*the New Covenant*' makes it seem as if someone else, as just suggested, might have been talking about a different '*New Covenant.*' However this may be, this leads into the affirmation, as we have seen, that:

the Penitents from Sin in Jacob, who kept the Covenant of God, shall speak then, each man to his neighbor, each strengthening (again here, probably both the language of '*strengthening*' and '*the all-Righteousness Commandment*') *his brother to support their step in the Way of God...until God* (as we saw) *shall reveal Salvation* (*Yesha^c*) *and Righteousness* (literally '*Justification*') *to those fearing His Name*' (namely, '*the God-Fearers*' again, a term which, in our view, includes '*Gentiles*' – but '*Torah*' and '*Righteousness*'-oriented ones).[189]

Here again, most translations reproduce '*the sin of Jacob*' but, as we have seen, in Isaiah 59:20 above, the name '*Jacob*' would appear to go with '*the Penitents*' and not their so-called '*sin*' (*pace* all those whose mindset is dominated by this aspect of 'Christian' theology).

Here it is averred that '*each man shall be judged according to his Spirit in His Holy Council*' and, once again, the imagery of CD1.16 about '*removing the boundary which the First had marked out*' is recapitulated and the '*cutting off*' language applied:

> *And with the appearance of the Glory of the God to Israel, all among the members of the Covenant who transgressed the boundary of the Torah, shall be cut off in the midst of the camp, and with them, all who condemned Judah during the days of its tribulations* (clearly no so-called '*anti-Semitism*' here).[190]

In many of these allusions in this section of CDXX, there are clear parallels to the language of the Letter of James which counsels, as we have seen, '*patience until the coming of the Lord*' (5:7). While the text of Ms. B is somewhat defective in alluding at this point above to '*each man to his neighbor*' or '*brother*', as just intimated, it appears to be repeating a second time '*the Royal Law according to the Scripture*' of the Letter of James or a variation of it. James 5:8 even adds at this point – it is talking about '*Final eschatological Judgement*' and *the prayer of the '*Just One*' for rain* – '*make your hearts strong because the coming of the Lord has drawn near.*' Not only does this recapitulate the earlier '*heart*' imagery but, as already indicated, almost the very words will now reappear as CDXX.33–34 draws to a close: '*they shall exult and rejoice, and their heart will be strengthened* (here the '*strengthening*' language really does occur), *and they shall be victorious over all the Sons of the Earth.*'

That the Letter attributed to James is using imagery and materials also found in the Damascus Document, to the extent that the former has almost the appearance of a shorter condensation of the latter and that, both it and the Damascus Document – not to mention other materials about James – home in on differences with a '*Lying*' adversary who denies the Law and cannot control his '*Tongue*,' would seem to move these materials very close to a final identity.

Where these allusions to '*the midst of the camp*' and these '*First*' and succeeding '*Visitation*'s are concerned, this language is reprised at the end of the judicial sections that make up most of the rest of CD in its *Genizah* format. These give the rules for life in the '*camps*' presumably in '*the Land of Damascus.*' These '*camps*' are under the control of '*the Mebakker*' or '*Overseer*' who, as we have seen, resembles nothing so much as '*the Bishop*' or '*Archbishop*' of early Christian usage, and his role too is set forth. '*In the camps,*' the *Mebakker* is to make Judgements '*according to the exact letter of the Torah*' and '*instruct the Assembly about the works of God,*' '*His mighty wonders,*' and the '*essence of His Eternal Being.*'[191] One should compare this with what Peter and James say about God in the picture of the Jerusalem Council in Acts 15:7–18, before James gives his final rulings, the '*miracles and wonders of God*' even reappearing in the intervening remark attributed to Barnabas and Paul in 15:12. '*The Mebakker*' is also to be '*merciful to them as a father his children*' and again, as in James above, '*strengthen the hand of the Meek and the Poor*' (Ebion).[192]

As we have seen, not only does '*speaking in Tongues,*' associated with the Gentile Mission in Acts, and the '*Tongue*' imagery applied to the Adversary in the Letter of James, find an echo in the mastery attributed to him over '*all the secrets of men and the Tongues according to their enumeration*'; but Paul speaks about the very same things from 1 Corinthians 13:1–14:39 on making known '*the secrets of the heart*' and '*speaking in the Tongues of men.*' Yet again, this exact parallel in 1 Corinthians confirms, as little else can, Paul's intimate knowledge of the parameters and ideology of Qumran. To be contrary here, Paul limits speaking with '*a foreign Tongue to two or the most three*' (14:27), but he even parodies Qumran vocabulary and attitudes again by speaking about being '*zealous of Spirits*' in 14:12 and '*zealous to prophesy*' in 14:39 ('*zelotai*' and '*zeloute*' – as in '*Simon*' and '*Judas Zelotes*' again).

The *Mebakker* is also to examine entrants (Paul protests about just this kind of thing in 1 Corinthians 9:3–27), as well as those who have erred and repented, and make all judicial rulings, including who is to be admitted and who is not.[193] As in the War Scroll:

> No madman, lunatic, simpleton, fool, blind man, maimed, lame, deaf, and no adolescent is to enter the Community, because the Holy Angels are with them.[194]

There is to be no association with '*the Sons of the Pit,*' except by his express permission, and on three different occasions it is stated that

These are the Laws...and the order of the Colony of the Camps, in which they are to walk during the Era of Evil, until the standing up of the Messiah of Aaron and Israel...(and) of the habitation of the Camps for the whole (Era of Wickedness and he who does not hold fast to these) will not be saved to inhabit the Land when the Messiah of Aaron and Israel shall stand at the End of Days...until God will visit the earth...And this is the exact interpretation of the Ordinances (in which they are to walk until the Messiah) of Aaron and Israel stands up and forgives their Sins. [195]

The word '*saved*' here, envisioning seemingly a '*Messianic*' return to Palestine as part of it, is exactly the same as that we shall encounter in the Habakkuk *Pesher* where it will mean '*saved from the House*' or '*Day of Judgement*.' [196] Not only do we have here again the idea of the '*Visitation by God of the Earth*,' connected either to '*the coming*' or '*the return of the Messiah*' – *all usages surrounding which are singular* – but, also, the explosive idea, so prominent in early Christian thought, that at that time *the Messiah will also have the power to forgive Sin*. That this is a Rule for a Messianic existence in a Colony of '*Camps*' beyond the Jordan '*in the Land of Damascus*,' preparatory to some kind of '*Messianic*' return and a '*New Covenant*' under the rule of an all-powerful '*High Priest*' or Bishop '*commanding the Camps*,' is hardly to be denied. [197]

As we have seen, the 'Jesus' of Scripture is portrayed as interested only in the other-worldly spiritualized '*signs and wonders*,' both Paul and Barnabas evoke in 15:12, in Acts' picture of '*the Jerusalem Conference*' and Paul, too, in these incisive passages from 1 Corinthians 12:1–14:40. Nor is he interested in going out in the wilderness, in Josephus' words, '*to show them the signs and wonders of their impending freedom*' or '*Redemption*,' as these charismatic, camp-dwelling '*Revolutionaries*' seem to have been. This basically demonstrates the Gospels to be on the whole works of pure fiction, largely reflecting an imaginary reality retrospectively conceived of and imposed by persons enthralled/possessed by a Hellenized worldview.

James' Rulings to '*Abstain from Pollutions*' and Jannes and Jambres

To return to Acts' presentation of its Jerusalem Council: after Peter's speech against '*the Pharisees*' insisting on circumcision (read here '*Zealots*') to '*the Apostles and the Elders assembled to see about this matter*' (15:2–6), '*Barnabas and Paul relate what signs and wonders God worked for them among the Gentiles*' (15:12), the '*signs and wonders*' – as we just saw – delineated in the description of '*the Mebakker*'s duties in the Damascus Document above.

Not only does Peter's speech contain the '*heart*' imagery we have been emphasizing above and a version of Paul's '*Gentile Mission*' doctrines – including allusion even to his '*Grace*' doctrines; it also alludes to '*being saved*' – this in Peter's belief that he '*will be saved*' in precisely the same manner as the Gentiles (note his use of the term '*Disciples*' in 15:10 instead of '*Gentiles*' in exactly the manner of the Damascus Document) without the '*yoke*' of the Law, '*which neither our Fathers or we were able to bear*' (15:10–11). In the Damascus Document's description of the duties of '*the Mebakker*' or '*Bishop*' above, this was '*being saved by walking stead-fastly in the Law during the whole Era of Wickedness*' in order to be ultimately able to return to the Land.[198]

At this point, James is depicted as '*judging*' or '*making the judgement,*' precisely in the manner laid down for '*the Mebakker*' or '*Bishop*' in the Damascus Document above, that '*We are not to trouble the Gentiles turning to God*' (15:19 – this also employing the '*turning aside,*' '*to,*' or '*back from*' language of CD above). There is no vote, no general consensus. It is only James ruling in his role as absolute Overseer and unquestioned Ruler. He judges, as we have seen, '*to write to them to keep away from the pollutions of the idols and fornication, and strangled things, and blood,*' rephrased in the words of the epistle he writes that follows – which '*the Apostles and the Elders*' send '*down to Antioch*' via '*Chosen Men*' ('*Judas Barsabas,*' '*Silas,*' '*Barnabas,*' and '*Paul*') – as, '*to keep away from things sacrificed to idols, and from blood, and from strangled things, and from fornication*' (15:19–29).

Later in James' final confrontation with Paul, where he lays on him the penance to '*be purified with*' those who '*have taken on themselves a vow, so that all might know...that you still walk regularly keeping the Law,*' James reminds him of these points:

> We wrote, judging that they ('*the Gentiles*' or '*the Peoples*')...keep themselves from things offered to idols, and blood, and strangled things, and fornication (21:23–25).

Here again we have the '*judging*' and '*N-Z-R*' language of '*keeping away from*' both, as we have seen, permeating the Damascus Document above. These are the parameters of James' rulings concerning overseas communities as they have come down to us in Acts. Since this last is now from the '*We Document,*' we probably have a more authentic version of them than those read back into Acts' more fictionalized presentation of '*the Jerusalem Council*' in Chapter Fifteen before the introduction of the '*We Document*' in Chapter Sixteen. They also form the subject matter, as we have been underscoring, of some of Paul's hand-wringing responses in 1 Corinthians 8–11, basically dealing with *'eating things sacrificed to idols'* and even *'reclining and eating in an idol Temple.'*

It is interesting that in his discussion of *'fornication'* – so prominent in materials associated with James and in the Damascus Document where it becomes part and parcel of the *'pollution of the Temple'* charges against the Establishment – preceding this in 1 Corinthians 5–8 that, though ostensibly talking about Corinth and not Palestine, Paul still begins his discussion with the curious allusion to *someone taking his father's wife* (1 Corinthians 5:1). This is the proposition basically generalized in the *'Three Nets of Belial'* section of the Damascus Document into the key attack on this Establishment for *'marrying nieces,'* where it is considered just a further extension of *'the law of incest'* Paul is referring to as well.¹⁹⁹

It is interesting, too, that now it is Paul doing the *'judging'* and he literally recommends – in language almost paralleling such expulsions or excommunications at Qumran – *'expelling the Evil person from among yourselves'* (1 Corinthians 5:13). The phraseology could not be more similar to that we have just encountered in CDviii and xix above, to say nothing of the Community Rule.²⁰⁰ Within the same context of what Qumran would refer to as *'separating Holy from profane'* (for Paul, *'not keeping company with'*), Paul recommends that *'you should not even eat* (meaning, *'keep table fellowship'*) *with such a person'* (5:10–11). Like *'the Mebakker'* at Qumran too, he makes it clear that he is *'judging'* persons within the Community not outside it (5:12) and follows this up with the injunction *'not to go to law before the Unrighteous'* (6:1), by which he obviously means persons outside the Community. Again this precisely parallels the second part of the Damascus Document concerning these *'judgements'* of *'the Mebakker'* or *'Bishop'* in the wilderness *'Camps,'* where it is specifically laid down, as previously underscored, that: *'Anyone having another condemned according to the laws of the Gentiles shall himself be put to death'* – basically substituting *'Gentiles'* for Paul's usage, *'the Unrighteous.'*²⁰¹

It is an incontrovertible fact that the Letter of James and Acts contain Qumran-like materials. So do James' rulings about overseas communities. In addition to confirming James' preeminent role in the Leadership of the early Church not simply as *'Bishop'* of Jerusalem – whatever might have been meant by this usage – but actually *'Bishop of Bishops'* or *'Archbishop'* – the two last episodes in the confrontations between James and Paul demonstrate James to have clearly been on the side of the strict constructionists. Certainly this is the thrust in the portrait of him throughout Galatians – now watered down or glossed over to a certain extent in these presentations in Acts.

We have already shown that the prophecy Acts pictures Agabus as making to Paul in Caesarea is basically a rewrite of '*the Pella Flight*' Oracle in Early Christian tradition and an inversion of the '*prophecy*' about the coming destruction of Jerusalem that Josephus pictures '*Jesus Ben Ananias*' as making *in the direct aftermath of the death of James approximately two years later*. But in the speech Acts 22:6–14 pictures Paul as making – with the help of the Roman '*Chief Captain*' and his soldiers, who allow him to '*stand on the steps*' of the Temple (just as James and the other Apostles in the Pseudoclementine *Recognitions*) after having been unceremoniously expelled from the Temple and force the crowd to listen to him – Paul tells the whole story of his conversion '*drawing near Damascus about midday.*' In doing so, however, this time he recounts that '*a certain Ananias, a Pious Man according to the Law*,' told him him that God had appointed him '*to see the Righteous One and hear a voice out of his mouth*,' a way of expressing these things we had not heard before.

After this, instead of telling how he returned to Jerusalem and met James – '*speaking boldly in the Name of the Lord Jesus*' as Acts 9:28 earlier would describe this – Paul rather tells how, after *returning to Jerusalem* and '*praying in the Temple*,' he fell into a trance and received his vision, either from Jesus ('*the Lord*') or from God (22:17). But now this vision is *to leave Jerusalem*, '*because they will not receive your testimony about me*' (22:18). The overtones, too, of this with James praying daily in the Temple and receiving his vision of '*the Son of Man coming on the clouds of Heaven*' in early Church tradition, to say nothing of '*Stephen*'s, should not be overlooked. Nor is this to mention the individual Paul describes in 2 Corinthians 12:2–4, directly after referring to '*Damascus*' and again insisting that he '*does not lie*.' As in Galatians 2:1 and as already remarked, this was also '*fourteen years before*,' the individual in question '*being caught away into*' the Third Heaven of Paradise, there having '*heard unutterable words it is not permitted a man to speak.*'

But in Paul's speech '*on the steps of the Temple*' here in Acts 22, the Pella-Flight Oracle '*to leave Jerusalem*' has been revamped and combined with his other '*visions and revelations of the Lord*' (*cf.* 1 Corinthians 12:1 above). Now the '*flight*' is not because Jerusalem could no longer remain in existence – as it was in the aftermath of the death of James, the '*Bulwark*' of '*the Righteous One*' having been removed[202] – but rather *to teach the Gentiles his new Gospel* (Acts 22:21). Paul is even pictured as referring in this speech to '*the blood of Stephen*' and it is now Stephen's '*blood*' that is '*poured out*' – should one add '*for the Many*'?[203] Furthermore, not only does Paul note how – for some reason – he '*kept the clothes of those who killed him*' (though, as already alluded to, why he should have done this, when it was the man about to be stoned whose clothes were removed is hard to comprehend); but also that he was '*standing by* (just as '*Simeon Bar Cleophas*' or '*one of the Priests of Rechab*' in early Church literature, but not as what follows) *and consenting to putting him to death*' (22:20). One is tempted to ask, which '*him*' Paul is actually referring to here, James or Stephen?

There is one other parallel in New Testament contexts with these materials in the Damascus Document that should be remarked. This comes in 2 Timothy, a letter of questioned authorship but nevertheless steeped, as we have seen, in Qumranisms, including '*the Last Days*' (3:1), '*being made Perfect by good works*' (3:17), and '*the Crown of Righteousness*' (4:8). Directly after mentioning *being saved in Christ* '*with Everlasting Glory*' (2:10), those '*naming the name of Christ, departing from Unrighteousness*' (2:19), and '*the snare of the Diabolou*' (2:26 – in the Damascus Document, as already underscored, '*of Belial*'); 2 Timothy 3:8, evokes the example – already discussed to a certain extent above – of how '*Jannes and Jambres withstood Moses*' and '*resisted the Truth, being men completely polluted in mind and worthless as regards Faith*.' The use of this last word '*worthless*' is important as well because, not only does it reflect James 2:10's characterization of '*the Empty*' or '*Worthless Man's Faith*' but also the description we shall encounter in the Habakkuk *Pesher* below of the '*worthlessness*' of both '*the Lying Spouter*''s '*building*' activities and '*service*' and the '*Lying*' nature of his '*works*.'[204]

In the reference to this incident at the end of the '*Three Nets of Belial*' section of the Damascus Document, '*Belial*' is, once again, referred to and described as '*in his cunning, raising up Jannes and his brother*.'[205] Not only are '*Jannes and Jambres*' like '*Balaam*,' '*Gehazi*,' and others in Talmudic literature archetypical '*Enemies of God*' but, just as Gehazi betrayed Elisha on the way to '*Damascus*' in 2 Kings 8:4–14, so '*Jannes and Jambres*' were considered to have led the rebellion against Moses *in the wilderness* – both '*wilderness*' and '*Damascus*' being motifs of the utmost importance to those '*dwelling*' in the wilderness '*camps*.' Furthermore, equally as important no matter how improbable, '*Jannes and Jambres*' are both considered in Rabbinic literature to be '*Sons of Balaam*.'[206]

In the previous Column Four, where the reference to Belial's '*nets*' followed upon the exposition of Ezekiel's '*Zadokite Covenant*,' the charges against the Establishment – as will be recalled – were '*sleeping with women in their periods*,' '*marrying nieces*,' and '*not observing proper separation*' in the Temple '*between clean and unclean*,' thereby '*polluting it*.' Moreover, the reference to '*Belial*' in Column Five, as just underscored, comes amid reference to '*the Removers of the Bound who led Israel astray*,' language applied in the First Column to '*the Lying Spouter*''s removal of '*the bound which the

Forefathers had set down,' and it is also more or less the manner in which Revelation 2:14 describes those *'holding to the teaching'* of *'Belial'*'s double

> *Balaam who taught Balak to cast a net (balein) before the Sons of Israel to eat things sacrificed to idols and commit fornication.*

Not only could one hardly get closer to Damascus Document ideology than this, it is precisely at this point in the reference to these *'Net's*, *'the builders of the wall,'* and *'the Lying Spouter's Spouting'* at the end of Column Four and preceding those to *'the Removers of the Bound,' 'Belial,'* and *'Jannes and his brother'* in Column Five that, as we have seen, the *'incest'* commandment of Leviticus 18:13 is cited concerning not approaching *'near kin'* for *'fornication.'* Now, however, it is generalized to include, in addition to *'your mother's near kin,'* also a *'father's* – even *'the daughter of a brother uncovering the nakedness of the brother of her father,'* in a word, *'niece marriage'* – in its tortuous complexity, this very definitely, yet again, aimed at *'Herodians.'*[207]

Furthermore, the extension of this law to *'the male'* (in a manner greatly resembling the modern jurisprudential technique of analogy) is to some extent perhaps also reflected – however imperfectly – in Paul's I Corinthians 5:1 condemnation as *'fornication'* of someone marrying his father's wife, from which he launches in 5:5–12 into a veritable barrage of additional *'judgements'* against *'Satan,' 'fornicators,' 'worshippers of idols,'* *'idolaters,'* etc. In CD 5, this conclusion is then neatly reversed – just as Paul in I Corinthians 5:11–13 above – into its contrapositive, *'whoever approaches them could not be cleansed and his House would be accursed.'*[208] This kind of *'cursing'* is also exactly replicated in Paul's imprecations to his communities in Galatians 1:8–9 that anyone teaching a Gospel different than the one he has announced (*'even an Angel from Heaven'*) is to *'be accursed,'* to say nothing of just the slightest hint – accidental or real – of play on this kind of *'House'* language in I Corinthians 3:9–17 and 2 Corinthians 5:1–11 above.

Here in Column Five of CD, playing off the anti-*'Herodian'* theme as it is developed later in Columns Eight and Nineteen, these references to *'incest'* and *'fornication'* are directly followed up by the note based on Isaiah 59:5: *'their eggs are vipers' eggs,'* already highlighted above and so reminiscent of Gospel portraits of John the Baptist's (and Jesus') attack upon the Establishment – this again clearly *'the Herodians.'*[209] This, in turn, leads into yet another citation from Isaiah 50:11, *'they are all kindlers of the Fire and lighters of firebrands,'* again, demonstrating the absolute reliance of CD on these last chapters from Isaiah and clearly reflecting an allusion to

'*Hell-Fire*' not unreflective, as well, of the imprecations attributed to John by Matthew 3:7–12 and *pars.* about '*fleeing from the Wrath to come*,' '*being cast into a furnace*,' and '*burned with an unquenchable fire*.'

Here, the Damascus Document combines this imagery with another seemingly anti-Pauline and possibly anti-Herodian attack – if the two can, in fact, be separated – on those who:

> *pollute their Holy Spirit and open their mouths with a Tongue full of insults* (also possibly '*blasphemies*' – here again, too, the '*Tongue*' imagery of 3:5–15 of the Letter of James, to say nothing of the '*spouting*' imagery generally) *against the Laws* (the same '*Hukkim*' we have just encountered above in Column Six – where '*the Mehokkek*' is concerned – and Column Twenty, to say nothing of the '*zeal for*' them evoked in the Community Rule's exegesis of Isaiah 40:3's '*make a straight Way in the wilderness*' citation[210]) *of the Covenant of God.*[211]

For it, such individuals behave like Jannes and Jambres, '*preaching apostasy from the Commandments of God (given) by the hand of Moses*.' For this reason, the Column basically concludes, '*in ancient times God visited their works* (the language of '*Visitation*' again) *and His Wrath was kindled*,' as well as the '*Kindlers of firebrands*' imagery of the John the Baptist-like passages above.[212]

But this is exactly the kind of thing, as we have seen, being said in 2 Timothy 3:8 above as well. Furthermore the phraseology about '*apostasy from the Commandments of God*' exactly reflects James' words in the climactic last confrontation scene with Paul, as pictured in Acts – and this in the '*We Document*' – that he (James) was informed that Paul,

> *teaches all the Jews among the Nations (Ethne) apostasy from Moses telling them not to circumcise their children* (the '*circumcision*' theme again – what could be more accurate than this?) *nor to walk in the Ways* (or '*Customs*') –

this in words *actually* attributed to James by Acts 21:21. The fit here could not be tighter including even the Qumran 'walking' language.[213]

For its part 2 Timothy 3:9, as we have also seen, uses the language of '*folly*' and '*foolishness*' in referring to such persons. But these words also crop up in the Damascus Document at this point in the Biblical citations preceding this allusion to '*Belial in his guilefulness raising up Jannes and his brother*.' Here Isaiah 27:11 and Deuteronomy 32:28 are quoted, to the effect that, it is '*a People without understanding*' and '*a Nation devoid of counsel*.' But this is exactly the sort of thing we see cropping up as well in

James 3:14–4:4 above on he '*who makes himself a Friend of the world trans-forming himself into an Enemy of God.*' One need not comment further on the commonality of vocabulary here.

For the Pauline writer of 2 Timothy, the foolishness of such persons '*will be fully manifest to all as was theirs,*' meaning '*Jannes and Jambres*' (3:8–9). He also counsels both '*turning away from*' and '*keeping away from*' such persons (here our '*Nazirite*'-based language again), who as at Qumran he calls '*Traitors.*' Playing off the Qumran/Essene '*Piety*' Commandment of loving God, he also calls such persons '*lovers of money*' and, as above in the Damascus Document, '*blasphemers*' and '*not lovers of God*' (3:2–5). For its part, the Damascus Document, having already evoked the '*removing the bound*' imagery applied to '*the Pourer out of Lying*' in Column One, now goes on in Column Six to '*barring the doors*' of the Temple to such persons, the language – as we have seen – that Acts 21:30 uses to describe Paul's unceremonious ejection from the Temple after being accused of introducing foreigners into it and his last meeting with James.

This allusion, based on Malachi 1:10, now develops into the one about '*separating from the Sons of the Pit and keeping away from polluted Evil Riches (acquired by) vow or ban* (our Nazirite oath-gifts again) *and the Riches of the Temple,*' we have also already highlighted above, all expressed in terms of the Hebrew root '*N-Z-R*' and ending in allusion to '*robbing the Poor of His People*' (which we shall again encounter further in the Habakkuk *Pesher* below), to say nothing of evoking '*the New Covenant in the Land of Damascus.*'[214]

Again, the fit could not be closer and the relevance of all these allusions to the events we have been highlighting in the First Century should be clear. Where the matter of '*whoever approaches them*' incurring their pollution ('*unless he was forced*'[215]) is concerned, this, of course, would be just how those, coming into direct or indirect contact with Herodians and Romans and their unclean gifts or sacrifices in the Temple, would have been seen by '*Opposition*' groups in this period – such as the one expressing itself in the Letter or Letters known as '*MMT.*'

PART VI

JAMES AND QUMRAN

23

The Destruction of the Righteous
Teacher by the Wicked Priest

*Cursing those 'Straying to the Right or the Left of the Torah' at Pentecost in
the Cave 4 Damascus Document*

We have repeatedly been pointing out the relevant allusions in principal
Qumran documents (many known for fifty years – in some cases more),
not only as they connected to the position of James the Just/'*the brother
of the Lord*'/'*the brother of Jesus*' in early Christianity, but also to the
written ideas and vocabulary of the Letters of Paul and usages and allusions – albeit radically disguised and transformed – in the Gospels and
the Book of Acts. Principally, these have included the Damascus Document, first found in the Cairo *Genizah* in 1896 and paralleled now in
fragments from Cave 4, and the Habakkuk *Pesher*, the Community Rule,
and the War Scroll, all found in the first Qumran Cave discovered in
1947. One might wish to add to these the Qumran Hymns, also found
in Cave 1, the Psalm 37 and Nahum *Peshers*, the compendium of Messianic proof-texts bearing on the promises made to '*the House*' or '*seed of
David*' known as '*the Florilegium,*' and *MMT*.

In *The Dead Sea Scrolls Uncovered*, I pointed out the relevance of some
of the newer fragments that came to light as a result of the struggle we
led to achieve complete and unimpeded access to the entire corpus of
Qumran materials, which ultimately proved successful and created the
situation in which we presently operate today.[1] These contained many
specific usages that link up with ideas and vocabulary already discussed
above. These included the constant use of the terminology '*the Meek*'
('*Anayyim*) and '*the Poor*' (*Ebionim*),[2] additional materials about a Messianic '*Leader,*' '*Branch,*' '*Sceptre,*' or '*Messiah of Righteousness*' – which give
more substance to the expectation of a singular, Davidic-style Messiah at
Qumran, paralleling what was already known in Ms. A and B of the
Damascus Document as '*the Messiah of Aaron and Israel,*' not a dual one as
some basing themselves on earlier texts had originally claimed[3] – and an
insistence that Abraham's '*works*' were to be '*counted for him as Righteousness*' as opposed to the more Pauline doctrine of '*Justification by Faith.*'[4]

Also found in these newer documents is the condemnation of ideo-logical adversaries in terms of '*the stumbling block of the Tongue*,' central to parallel formulations in the Letter of James and reflected in the language Paul uses as the antithesis to James, as for instance in Galatians 5:1, where he even uses the vocabulary of '*holding fast*' or '*standing firm in the freedom with which Christ made us free*' (more strophe/antistrophe poetic-rhetorical technique) as opposed to '*being held again in the yoke of slavery*' (by which he means, of course, '*freedom from the Law*') and '*being separated from Christ*' (typical language at Qumran and, as we have seen above, the basis in the Community Rule of the exposition of the '*making a Straight Way in the wilderness*' passage[5]) by '*doing the whole Law*' (*cf.* James 2:10 on '*keeping the whole Law but stumbling on one point*') or thinking to '*be justified by the Law*' in the attack in 5:3–5:12 on '*circumcision*' which he frames in terms of '*the stumbling block of the cross*.'

Or the arguments in 1 Corinthians 8:1–13 attacking those '*who have Knowledge*' (the '*Jerusalem Church Leadership*') as '*puffed up*.'[6] Not only does he identify these with the omnipresent '*some*,' this time the '*some with con-science*' (again, his euphemism for '*observing the Law*'), whose '*weak conscience will be wounded*' should they see someone, with '*strength*' (playing off the '*strength*' allusions we have been highlighting) and who '*has Knowledge*' (that is, '*the Knowledge that an idol is nothing in the world*' – 8:3), '*reclining*' or '*eating in an idol temple*' – meaning '*eating things sacrificed to idols*'; this he, then, says '*will become a cause of stumbling*' or '*a stumbling block to those who are weak*,' that is, those whose '*consciences are so weak*' that they see themselves as '*defiled*' or '*polluted*' (8:7-12). He then concludes, as we have seen:

> So if meat causes my brother to stumble (or '*scandalizes my brother*'), I shall never eat flesh (again) forever that my brother shall not be scandalized (or '*caused to stumble*' – the verb carries this dual meaning in Greek).

Notwithstanding, two chapters later in 1 Corinthians 10:23 he goes on to aver for the second time that '*for me all things are lawful*,' followed by the affirmation in 10:25: '*Eat everything sold in the marketplace, in no way inquiring on account of conscience*' – cynically and self-servingly quoting the first line of Psalm 24: '*For the Earth is the Lord's and the fullness thereof*,' which he knew full well was hardly its intended application. So here, too, he makes it crystal clear that what he means by '*conscience*' is '*inquiring because of the Law*.'

Not only are these perhaps some of the most cynical and manipula-tive rhetorical displays in the disappointing history of theological dialectic; but even here Paul makes it absolutely clear that, even if Acts' presentation of James' minimal directives for overseas participants is genuine, he is really only willing to observe one of them, the ban on '*fornication*.' The ban on the other three, '*blood*,' '*carrion*,' and '*things sacrificed to idols*' have clearly already gone by the boards – the ban on '*blood*,' in particular (again so definitive in the Damascus Document[7]), playing off additional allusions to '*zeal*,' '*building up*,' and '*strength*,' having been cast aside, as already signaled, in his evocation of '*Communion with the blood of Christ*' that preceded this in 10:11–22 and the recommendation to '*drink the Cup of the New Covenant in my blood*' following it in 11:23–29.

But he has already attacked these same vegetarians (like James) in Romans 14:2 in the equally equivocal:

> One believes he may eat all things; another, being weak, eats (only) vegetables (here the governing usage is the term '*weak*').

Of course, this would not be the position most '*pure foods*' advocates today would endorse, nor that of its reflection in the Synoptic picture, discussed previously, of 'Jesus' declaring '*nothing entering from outside defiles the man*,' both condoning '*eating with unwashed hands*' and '*making all foods clean*' (Mark 7:1–23 and pars.) – nor would most people consider the pursuit of a 'Jamesian'-style vegetarianism '*weak*.'

But these kinds of statements in Chapter Fourteen of Romans come within the framework of yet another sophistical and equivocating (in the sense of equivocal) argument alluding to the same '*stumbling*,' '*being scandalized*,' and '*weakness*.' In it, he adjures: '*Do not destroy the work of God for the sake of food*' (literally '*meat*'), '*let him who eats not, not judge* (the '*judging*' terminology again of Acts 15:19 and of '*the Mebakker*' at Qumran) *the one who eats*' and again, actually following another somewhat tendentious allusion – this time to Isaiah 45:23 evoking the '*Tongue*' ('*every Tongue shall praise God*'):

> No longer, therefore, should we judge one another. Rather (speaking euphemistically and somewhat facetiously) judge this: '*Do not put a stumbling block or cause of offence* (literally '*cause of scandal*' again) *to the brother . . . for whom Christ died...All things are indeed pure, but Evil to the man who, through stumbling, eats* (the '*some with weak conscience*'s – and, again equivocally – therefore, it is) *not right to eat flesh or drink wine* (all positions connected to James), *nor anything in which your brother stumbles or is scandalized or is weak* (Romans 14:13-21).

A more cynical presentation of one's opponents' views is hardly to be imagined.

Finally – actually even employing the language of '*adoptionist Sonship*'[8] and again applying the language of '*judging*' to condemn '*the one who judges*' – Paul really does use the language of the key section of the Damascus Document (albeit again reversed or, shall we say, used somewhat self-servingly) to insist that such a one, or the one '*God has adopted for Himself*,' '*stands or falls to his own master*' (see both the language of '*standing on his own net*' or '*watch-tower*' following the exposition of '*the Zadokite Covenant*' in terms of '*justifying the Righteous and condemning the Wicked*' and '*the Covenant God made with the First to atone for their Sins*' in CDIV.7–12 and that of '*the Poor man to his master*,' following the second citation of '*the Preparation of the Way in the wilderness*' passage in the Community Rule above) – and even more pointedly:

> And he shall be made to stand, for God is able to establish him (or '*set him up*' or '*make him stand*'; and here, too, the language of '*establishing*' or '*setting up*' of both CDVII and the *Florilegium* – Romans 14:1-4).[9]

Compare this with CDIV.3–4's description of '*the Sons of Zadok*' above as '*the Elect of Israel called by Name who still stand in the Last Days*' as well.

But in these newer documents too as, for instance, the Last Column of the Damascus Document (the actual subject of the letter Professor Davies of Sheffield University and myself wrote in March, 1989 requesting access to the previously unpublished fragments of the Damascus Document – a letter which actually set in motion the whole process of '*freeing the Scrolls*,' this with a slightly different sense than Paul might use the term! – so we could compare them with the Cairo *Genizah* versions of the mss.); not only is there the reiteration of '*the New Covenant in the Land of Damascus*' as a rededication to the '*Old*,' but also the constant reiteration of this '*judging*' or '*Judgement*' ('*according to all the Laws found in the Torah of Moses*' – this then clearly a pro-Mosaic document as opposed to Paul's anti-Sinaitic Covenantal attitude of Galatians 4:22–30 as '*bringing forth slavery which is Agar*' wherefore '*cast out the slave woman*'), presumably by either '*the Priest Commanding the Many*' – an individual unreferred to in the corpus previously known to that time – or '*the Mebakker*' (both meaningful titles in it as we have seen), as legitimate and quite proper.

Not only does this Last Column (clear from the blank space to the left of the written material – Hebrew being a language written from right to left – and extant in two exemplars from the previously unpublished corpus[10]) sum up and recapitulate motifs and themes first evoked in opening Columns of the Cairo *Genizah* redaction,[11] such as '*rejecting the Foundations of Righteousness*,'[12] '*expulsion from the presence of the Many*,'[13] '*the Sons of His Truth*,' allusion to '*the Peoples*' as '*wandering astray in a trackless waste without a Way*' (word-for-word from CD1.15 – a good summation), and the actual words delivered by '*the Priest* (clearly implying '*the High Priest*') *Commanding the Many*' concerning the expulsion of, as we have seen, the one '*rebelling*' against '*the Laws* (here, of course, '*Hukkim*' again) *Your Truth*' – this, a very different definition of '*Truth*' than one might encounter in the Pauline corpus – in terms of '*boundary markers being laid down*';

> *Those who cross over them You curse. We, however, are the flock of Your pasture* (paralleling the reference to being '*the Meek of the flock*' in the exposition of Zechariah 13:7 in CDXIX.8–9 of Ms. B above[14]). *You curse the Breakers of them* (meaning '*the Laws*' or the '*boundary markers*') *while we set it up* (again the term '*set up*' or '*establish*,' obviously meaning '*the New Covenant*' which was '*set up in the Land of Damascus*' previously, *etc.*)

The '*cursing*' language at this point – as we have discussed in detail in Chapter 20 but it is worth repeating – obviously derived from the '*blessing and cursing*' of the Book of Deuteronomy and so much a part too of the subject matter of the first three columns of the Community Rule[15] – is fundamental, as well, for Paul. This is true, not only in the opening passages of Galatians '*cursing anyone who would teach a Gospel different than we have preached*' (1:8–9), but also in his whole development of how '*Christ redeemed us from the curse of the Law*' having, in his view, '*become a curse for us*' or, if one prefers, taking our '*curse*' (including clearly and presumably Paul's own) upon himself, '*as it has been written, cursed be everyone hung upon a tree*' (3:13). We have already discussed the somewhat tendentious presentation of this citation – in line with the scriptural exegesis desired – for this is not precisely the emphasis of Deuteronomy 21:22–23, which rather focuses on the point that '*the one who has been hung*' has already been executed and '*cursed*' beforehand, having been guilty of a capital offence; and it is rather the fact of his being '*hung*' which is the '*accursed*' thing – that and, in particular, '*allowing the body to remain on the tree overnight*.'[16]

But this is beside the point where Qumran is concerned in any event since, as we have already pointed out as well, in the Nahum *Pesher* it is clear that the Qumran sectaries not only oppose crucifixion as such, considering it '*a thing previously not done in Israel*' – and in fact, as the Damascus Document itself would express it, anyone who aids in the process of '*vowing another to death by the laws of the Gentiles shall himself be put to death*'[17] – but the focus is on '*hanging a man alive upon a tree*;' and it is for this that the Prophet is made to proclaim, '*Behold I am against you, saith the Lord of Hosts*' (Nahum 2:13).[18]

Again the Language of '*Cursing*' both at Qumran and in Paul

However this may be, the whole discussion in this section of Galatians gives the impression that Paul considers that in some sense he and those of '*Gentiles*' ('*the Ethne*'/'*Peoples*' again) like him have in some manner been '*cursed*,' which brings us right back to these passages in the Last Column of the Damascus Document where the actual speech of excommunication delivered by '*the High Priest Commanding the Many*' is transcribed. Not only does this have to do with '*choosing our Fathers and to their seed giving the Laws of Your Truth*' (the Mosaic *Torah*, as we have seen), and '*cursing the one expelled*'; but, also, '*establishing the Peoples according to their families and national Tongues*' – something we shall also hear about below in the way Acts 2:1-11 will portray '*the pouring out of the Holy Spirit*' (this is the way Acts 10:45 describes it) at Pentecost upon '*God-Fearers from every nation of those under the Heaven*,' '*each one hearing spoken words in (their) own Languages*' (2:1–11 – '*Tongues*,' as in these passages above at Qumran[19]).

In '*the High Priest Commanding the Many*''s expulsion order, only must '*the individual who was expelled leave*,' but the rank and file – presumably '*the Many*' in the Camps being instructed to '*return to God with weeping and fasting*' (Joel 2:12 – also this is to be found in CDxix.11-12's citation of Ezekiel 9:4 about '*those who weep and cry*' and in all likelihood, as we have seen as well, probably the basis of '*the Mourners for Zion*'' Movement' so important in the centuries to follow in producing a '*return to Zion*' and for the development of '*Karaite Judaism*'[20]) – are instructed not '*to eat with him* (that is, not to '*keep table-fellowship with him*') *or ask after the welfare of the individual who was excommunicated or keep company with him*' (or, as the Community Rule would have it, '*not to cooperate with him in purse or Mission*'). Importantly, the individual who does not observe this ban '*will be recorded by the Mebakker according to established practice and his Judgement* (that is, again the positive reference to '*Judgement*' or '*judging*' by either '*the Mebakker*' or '*Priest Commanding the Many*,' or both – as we have seen) *will be completed*.'

We have already referred as well to similar '*shunning*' procedures being described by Paul regarding his break with both Peter and Barnabas in Galatians 2:12–13 which Paul contemptuously characterizes as '*playing the hypocrite;'* but also in both Acts 13:1 and 15:37–39 where Paul breaks with both Barnabas and John Mark. However preceding this *'Judgement'* of excommunication, following the reference by *'the Priest Commanding the Many'* to *'choosing our Fathers and giving the Laws of Your Truth to their seed,'* an even more important allusion is made based on Leviticus 18:5 (echoed in Deuteronomy 4:1 and 8:1) – since it actually parallels the same allusion Paul makes in his comments about *'being cursed'* in Galatians 3:12 – *'and the Ordinances (or 'Judgements') of Your Holiness which a man must do* (again, note the continuation of the emphasis, of course, on both *'judging'* and *'doing'* here) *and thereby live.'* But these are exactly the words cited by Paul in Galatians 3:12 above.

Furthermore these passages from Paul in Galatians 3:2–29 on *'Christ redeeming us from the curse of the Law,'* not only actually refer to two of the three key scriptural proof-texts for Gentile Christianity (the third being, as we have seen above, Isaiah 53:11) from Genesis 15:6 about how *'Abraham believed God and it was reckoned to him as Righteousness'* (3:6) and Habakkuk 2:4: *'the Righteous shall live by Faith'* (3:11); but also these passages from Deuteronomy *'cursing anyone who does not continue in all things written in the Book of the Law* (in Deuteronomy 27:26, *'the words of the Torah')* *to do them'* (3:10) and actually even the words just highlighted above in the Last Column of the Damascus Document from Leviticus 18:5, *'but the man who has done these things shall live through them,'* now seemingly applying it, not a little tendentiously – as Acts 8:32–33 does Isaiah 53:7–8 to Philip's baptism of *'the Ethiopian Queen's eunuch'* – to *'those of Faith being blessed with the blessing of Abraham'* or *'the Righteous who shall live by Faith'* (3:9–12).

It is from this Paul – using the language of the Damascus Document above of *'the Many'* – derives his conclusion: *'for as Many as are of the works of the Law are under a curse,'* the same *'curse'* from which he seems to have considered himself to have *'been redeemed by Christ.'* In our view, it is just these passages here in the Damascus Document that actually delineate not only the kind of *'curse'* with which he had *'been cursed,'* but also the reason for it, that is, the *'curse'* which was pronounced both by *'Essenes'* and now here at Qumran on backsliders – meaning those from among *'the Sons of His Truth'* who *'rebelled against'* or *'rejected the Judgements in accordance with all the Laws found in the Torah of Moses.'*

But even more importantly than any of these things is the reference in the Last Column of the Damascus Document, with which the Damascus Document seems to conclude, to a *'reunion of the inhabitants'* of the wilderness *'camps in the Third Month'* seemingly every year – that is, at Pentecost. It is important to note here too, as already indicated, that this would appear to be the same '*reunion*' to which Paul is hurrying in Acts 20:16, laden with funds he has collected, particularly in Thessalonia but also probably '*Achaia*,' though not wishing at this point '*to lose time in Asia*,' '*so as to be in Jerusalem*' in time for '*the Day of Pentecost*.'

Moreover, we have already referred above to the picture in Acts 2:1–6 of the '*gathering together in one place*' (language having a quasi-parallel again here in this Last Column of the Damascus Document) and '*the Descent of the Holy Spirit*' during '*the accomplishment of the Day of Pentecost*' on '*Jews dwelling in Jerusalem and God-fearing men from every Nation under Heaven*.' Not only do we have here another quasi-parallel to the language of CD, should one choose to regard it, such as '*dwelling*' and, of course, the multiple references to '*God-Fearers*' or '*Fearing God*'; but unlike these episodes in Acts, as several times now underscored, what is to be accomplished in this '*gathering together of the inhabitants*' of these desert '*Camps*' at Pentecost is the '*cursing*' of all '*those departing to the right or to the left of the Torah*' (and the word being employed in this last usage is '*Torah*' despite the tendency of many translators to render it by the more nondescript or general term, '*Law*').[21] This is followed by the conclusion that:

> *This is the exact sense of the Judgements which they are to observe* (literally '*to do*' again) *for the entire Era of the Visitation with which they will be visited* (again, probably the '*Visitation*' language) *in all the Periods of Wrath...for all those dwelling in their Camps and those dwelling in their cities* (here the parallel with Acts' '*dwelling in Jerusalem*' above). *Behold, this is the whole of what is written concerning the Last Interpretation of the Torah* (the '*Midrash ha-Torah ha-Aharon*' based, as already underscored, on the same '*Doresh*' or '*Seeker after the Torah*' as earlier in CDvii.18).[22]

Immediately it should be observed that this allusion to '*cursing all those departing to the right or to the left of the Torah*' – the point here of the Pentecost reunion of the '*Camps*' and the very opposite of '*the pouring out of the Holy Spirit*,' which Acts 2:4 and 18 takes to be its point, and the point in 'Christianity' ever after – actually has a parallel as well in what James appears to understand is the the point of this festival in Acts 21:21 when, as we have several times remarked – even alluding to '*walking*' – he tells Paul in the '*We Document*' that '*They have been told that you teach apostasy from Moses, telling all the Jews among the Peoples (Ethne) not to circumcise their children, nor to walk in the Customs*.' It is at this point he directs Paul to take '*four men we have with us who are under a vow upon themselves*' (clearly a temporary '*Nazirite*' oath of some kind, the procedures for which are specifically outlined in both Numbers and the *Talmud*, and the probable origin of all the '*Nazoraean*'/'*Nazrene*' terminology regarding early Christianity of the '*Jamesian*' persuasion[23]) and '*be purified with them and pay their expenses*' (since Paul was obviously seen, at this point, as being flush with money from his collections abroad) *so that they may shave their heads*' – a thing which he himself had already been pictured as doing in Acts 18:18 previously[24] and, clearly, part of the temporary '*Nazirite*' oath procedures (as it is to this day in Islam during the *Hajj* in Mecca at the Ka^cabah).[25]

But more important still is the manner in which James (the one clearly speaking at the time) expresses this: '*and all may know there is nothing to all that they have been informed concerning you and that you yourself also still walk regularly keeping the Law*' (21:23–24). Directly following this, James adds, '*But concerning those who have believed among the Peoples* (here, plainly the '*Peoples*' vocabulary of the Cave Four material above), *we wrote, judging to observe nothing other than to keep from themselves things sacrificed to idols, etc., etc.*' But, of course, we know that Paul is doing no such thing regardless of the fact that he then does precisely as James has directed him to do – a course of action in line with his *modus operandi* in 1 Corinthians 9:19–27 of '*being free from all myself, becoming a slave to all*' (by which he again is euphemistically speaking of '*the Torah of Moses*'): '*I became a Jew to the Jews, that Jews I might gain*'; '*to those under the Law, I became as under the Law to gain those under the Law*'; '*to those outside the Law, as outside the Law*'; '*to the weak I became as weak*' (we know by now what he is referring to by '*being weak*' here); '*so that by all means I might save some*' (and we know too who these '*some*' are).

But James' allusion to demonstrating '*that you yourself still walk regularly keeping the Law*' is exactly what is being required here at Pentecost to avoid the '*cursing*' prescribed for those '*not keeping*' or '*departing to the right or to the left of Torah*' in these last lines of the Damascus Document, and allusions like '*walking in these things in Perfect Holiness*' actually permeate both the Damascus Document and the related Community Rule.[26] In fact, the latter actually begins in its First Column with exactly the same words the Damascus Document is using here:

> *Nor shall they depart from the Laws of His Truth to walk either to the right or the left...undertaking the Covenant before God to do all that He commanded* (here, of course, both the emphasis on '*doing*' again and the addition of the allusion to '*walking*' found not in 4QD266 and 271 above, but actually in James' speech as recorded in Acts 21:21 here).[27]

In 1QS,ii.1-2, those who are '*blessed*' – just as Paul speaks of those '*blessed with the blessing of Abraham'* in Galatians 3:12 above – are *'those who walk Perfectly in all His Ways,'* a column that also speaks repeatedly about *'cursing'* the one *'who enters the Covenant'* with *'the stumbling block'* of *'idols upon his heart.'* Here, again, we have not only the *'heart,' 'stumbling block,'* and *'idols'* imagery so much in evidence in Paul, but Column Three adds that such a one *'will not be justified by what his stubborn heart permits because he looks upon Darkness instead of the Ways of Light,'* repeating (again using both the *'Perfection'* and *'Walking'* vocabulary),

> *Let him then order his steps so as to walk Perfectly in all the Ways of God, as He commanded concerning His Festivals, neither straying to the right or to the left, nor infringing on one of His words.*[28]

Not only should one compare this with James 2:11 on *'whoever shall keep the whole of the Law but stumble on one point, shall become guilty of (breaking it) all'* or even the Synoptic portrait of 'Jesus'' words: *'not one jot or tittle shall disappear from the Law till all these things are accomplished'*[29]; but also James' admonition to Paul here at *'the Festival'* of Pentecost in Jerusalem, *'that you yourself also walk regularly keeping the Law.'* But Paul, too, in Galatians also uses this language, at first in his accusations of *'hypocrisy'* against Peter and Barnabas in 2:13, but slightly shifted in 2:14 with *'the Gospel'* as he *'taught it among the Peoples'* when he says he saw that they *'did not walk uprightly according to the Truth of the Gospel.'*

Here, of course, we have the expression, *'the Truth of the Gospel,'* in the place of *'the Laws of Your Truth'* of the Last Column of the Damascus Document or *'the Laws of His Truth'* (to say nothing of *'the Community of Truth'* or *'the Community for His Truth'*[30]) in the Community Rule. But the way Paul transforms this kind of allusion to *'regularly walking'* reaches a climax at the end of Galatians 5:1-15 in his arguments about *'neither circumcision or uncircumcision being worth anything in Christ Jesus'* or those *'justified in (the) Law falling from Grace.'* Here he ends with those originally *'running well'* not *'obeying the Truth'* and, finally, *'biting,' 'devouring,'* and *'destroying one another,' 'for the whole Law is fulfilled in one word, you shall love your neighbor as yourself,'* not only a central focal point of *'the New Covenant in the Land of Damascus,'* as we have been underscoring, but – again – a more cynical manipulation of *'the Love Commandment'* is hardly to be imagined. Moreover, it is at this point he speaks about *'walking in the Spirit'* (5:16), by which he means here and elsewhere, *'not walking in the flesh'* and, of course, *'the Commandments of the Covenant'* (that is for *'the flesh'*), concluding, using the language of Leviticus and Habakkuk earlier:

If we live by the Spirit, we should (then) also walk by the Spirit (5:25).

Once again, as he proceeds along his Hellenizing and Neoplatonic trans-mutation, this is '*allegorization*' or '*spiritualization*' with a vengeance.

Esotericisms in Qumran Documents Continued: '*the Wicked Priest*' and '*the Liar*'

However these things may be, it is sufficient to prove such link-ups between usages and ideology at Qumran and their transformation and reflection in various New Testament cognates and correlatives by relying on the older, more widely-known, documents by themselves, augment-ing these by occasional reference to less familiar ones for additional verification only. We have already signaled widespread parallels in the Damascus Document to many of the subjects we have been considering above. Among such references one should, no doubt, include '*the Man of Lying*' or '*Scoffing*'/'*Spouting Windbag*' together with a group variously referred to as '*the Violent Ones*'/'*the Men-of-War*'/'*the Men of Violence*' (the word for this last is '*Hamas*,' the same as the one presently appearing in more recent Middle Eastern struggles) and/or '*Traitors*' (an-other usage dear to Gospel artificers) as '*removing the boundary markers which the First had set down as their inheritance, bringing low the Everlasting Heights*' – a clear reference to what becomes in the Habakkuk *Pesher*, '*denying the Torah in the midst of their whole Assembly*' or '*Church*.'[31]

Most such allusions are to be found in documents known as '*the Pesharim*' or '*Commentaries*.' These are idiosyncratic commentaries on prized Biblical texts or combinations of texts, specifically chosen for the interesting exegetical possibilities they provide. Often, however, they bear little or no relationship to the meaning or interpretation being ascribed to them except a linguistic one. We have already shown the same process to be at work in the Gospels, Acts, and Paul's Letters which, as opposed to Qumran, often *ignore* and even *reverse* the ambiance or sur-rounding ethos of the original Biblical texts. Then, too, the Gospels and Acts are arranged in a more-or-less Greek narrative form, whereas the Qumran documents are more eclectic and uneven, only providing the semblance at times of a narrative – at other times, small episodic bits. There are even some *pesharim* or compendiums that combine various texts, as the Gospels and the Book of Acts often do – most of which are '*Messianic*' or, as we have seen, of otherwise obvious importance, resem-bling nothing so much as modern collections of '*proof-texts*.'[32]

This is what is meant by saying the documents at Qumran are

homogeneous. The same allusions, attitudes, and *dramatis personae* move from document to document across the entire spectrum of the corpus. This allows us to date many of what can be said to be specifically '*sectarian*' documents in the non-Biblical part of the corpus ('*sectarian*' often meaning simply documents never seen before, of which there are some 650, many in multiple copies) as largely contemporaneous and referring to the same set of events – events seen by the Community as cataclysmic often having to do with '*the Last Days*' or '*the Final Era*' and imbued with the most pregnant and portentous significance. This is also the reason why the literature at Qumran must be seen as that of a '*Movement*' and not simply a random or eclectic collection of documents reflecting the general flow of the literature of the period, as some have suggested – though documents of this latter kind do exist, as they would in any library or manuscript collection.[33]

These specifically '*sectarian*' documents mainly focus, as we have observed, on an individual called '*the Righteous Teacher*' or '*Teacher of Righteousness*' and not so much on the '*Messiah*' or '*Messiah of Righteousness*' (in the Genesis *Pesher*, '*the Shiloh*') *per se*, though background references do allude to an individual of this kind as well. There are also references in the Damascus Document to other parallel individuals such as '*the Maschil*,' '*the Yoreh ha-Zedek*,' '*the Doresh ha-Torah*,' '*the Mehokkek*,' and the like, who may or may not be the same as '*the Righteous Teacher*'[34] – though at least the last three probably are. In the *Pesharim*, this latter individual seems to double as '*the Priest*' as well, clearly meaning, as already explained, as per normative Hebrew usage of this period – as opposed simply to '*a Priest*' as such – '*the High Priest*.'

There are also references, as we just too, to '*the Mebakker*' – '*the Overseer*' or '*Bishop*' – and a '*High Priest Commanding the Many*,' again expressed simply in terms of being '*the Priest*.'[35] This '*Mebakker*,' who very much resembles James, is described at length in the Damascus Document, though there are references to him as well in the Community Rule. What he does is to '*command*' both '*the Many*' and '*the Camp*' or '*Camps*,' '*instructing them*' – including even Priests – '*in the exact interpretation of the Torah*.'[36] He also examines new entrants, '*records*' infractions and makes '*Judgements*,' and, as also just underscored, is '*the master of all the Secrets of Men and every Language* ('*Tongue*') *according to their families*.'[37]

For their part, the references to '*the Righteous Teacher*' focus on his two opponents as well – one a more ideological adversary, we have often mentioned above, known variously as '*the Man of Lying*'/'*Liar*,' '*Spouter of Lying*'/'*Pourer out of Lying*'/ '*Comedian*'/'*Scoffer*' (described in the Damascus Document as having '*poured out over Israel the waters of Lying*'), and

56 Left: Augustus under whom Judea was pacified and given over to the Herodians as tax-farmers and the first Imperial deifications occurred.

57 Above: Presumed bust of the Jewish historian Josephus.

58 Above: A coin issued by Nero in honor of Poppea, whom he kicked to death in 65 CE and who was visited by Josephus not long before.

59 Left: Columns IX–X of the Habakkuk *Pesher* mentioning '*the Riches of the Last Priests of Jerusalem*' '*given over to the Army of the Kittim*' and '*the Worthless City*' the Liar '*built upon Blood*.'

60 LEFT: The entrance to Petra, Herod's mother's place-of-origin and the capital of the '*Arab*' King Aretas, her possible kinsman (and also, therefore, the possible '*kinsman*' of Paul).

61 BELOW: Column XVI of 4QD271 describing how Abraham was threatened by '*the Angel Mastemah*' ('*Satan*') for not circumcising all members of his household, whereupon he promptly did so.

62 ABOVE: The amphitheatre at Hellenistic Petra, a city Paul may have visited when he speaks in Galatians 1:17 of '*going into Arabia.*'

63 ABOVE: The ruins of Pella across the Jordan in Perea, to which the Community of James was reputed to have fled after his death.

64 RIGHT: The ruins of Palmyra, a key city on the trade route going North to Syria, Adiabene, and beyond.

65 BELOW: The Cave 4 parallel to CDVI where the all-important '*going out to dwell in the Land of Damascus*,' '*digging of the Well*,' and '*the New Covenant*' to be erected there are mentioned.

66 BELOW RIGHT: The ruins of Hellenistic Jerash, like Pella, another city of '*the Decapolis*' but further inland.

67 LEFT: A scene from old Damascus, down the walls of which Paul allegedly escaped *'in a basket'* from the *'Arab'* King Aretas and the venue of many important allusions at Qumran.

68 BELOW: The City of Edessa (*'Antioch Orrhoe'*) with the Pool of Abraham in the foreground and the Plain of Haran – Abraham's childhood home – in the background.

69 BELOW: The end of the Second Part (*'the Second Letter'*) of *MMT* speaking of *'the works of the Torah which would be reckoned for your Good'* as *per* Abraham in Genesis 15:6, James, and Paul.

70 RIGHT: The *MMT* passage banning *'things sacrificed to idols'* so important to James' directives to overseas communities and *'Sicarii Essene'* martyrdom/resistance practices.

71 Left: Baptism scene of the Mandaeans/'*the Subba^c of the Marshes*'/'*Masbuthaeans*'/'*Elchasaites*' of Southern Iraq.

72 Above: Mandaean Elders and Priests.

73 Above: The First Column of CD mentioning '*the Root of Planting,*' '*the Teacher of Righteousness,*' and '*the Pourer out*'/'*Spouter of Lying.*'

74 Above right: 4Q268, paralleling the First Column of the Cairo *Genizah* version, showing the link with earlier material instructing '*the Sons of Light to keep away from the Paths*'/'*the Ways (of pollution).*'

75 **Left:** Voluptuous Hellenistic sculpture found around Italica in Spain, the birthplace of both Trajan (98-117 CE) and Hadrian (117-138 CE).

76 **Above:** Bust of Hadrian who ruthlessly suppressed the Bar Kochba Revolt and rebuilt Jerusalem under his own name as '*Aelia Capitolina.*'

77 **Above:** Amphitheatre at Italica, birthplace of Trajan and Hadrian and perhaps home of '*the Regiment*' mentioned in Acts 10:2.

78 ABOVE: Sumptuous reconstructed floor mosaic found in ruins in the area of Italica.

79 BELOW: Silver Sestertius with portrait of Trajan, under whom Egyptian Jewish Community was wiped out in disturbances around the years 105-115 CE.

80 BELOW RIGHT: Silver dinar with portrait bust of Hadrian.

81 LEFT: The Pinnacle of the Temple with the Kedron Valley tombs – in particular, the Monument of Absalom just visible below.

82 BELOW LEFT: Rock-cut '*Tomb of Zadok*' in the Kedron Valley below the Pinnacle of the Temple next to James' – a hiding place mentioned in the Copper Scroll.

83 ABOVE: The Tomb attributed by pilgrims to James, but an inscription identified it as that of the '*Bnei-Hezir*' Priest Clan ('*the Boethusians*') and probably at the root of the burial legends about Jesus.

84 LEFT: Burial chambers inside '*the Tomb of St. James.*'

85 ABOVE: The excavated entry to the family Tomb of Queen Helen of Adiabene built for her and her son Izates by her second son Monobazus.

86 RIGHT: Absalom's Monument next to James' Tomb. It or pyramids like it probably stood above Queen Helen's Family Tomb on the other side of Jerusalem.

87 ABOVE: Column IV of the Psalm 37 *Pesher* describing how '*the Violent Ones of the Gentiles took Vengeance*' on the Wicked Priest for what he did to the Righteous Teacher and referring to '*the Church of the Poor seeing Judgement.*'

88 RIGHT: Burial niche inside the Family Tomb of Queen Helen of Adiabene.

89 Above: Ruins surrounding the steps of the Temple in Jerusalem with the Pinnacle and Mount of Olives Cemetery in the background.

90 Below: Tomb directly alongside James,' attributed to Zechariah the Prophet, but the designation probably has more to do with '*Zachariah ben Bariscaeus*,' the '*Rich*' collaborator '*cast down*' by Revolutionaries from the Temple wall into the Kedron Valley below.

91 Above: The Temple steps upon which James lectured the People when he was supposedly '*cast down*' by '*the Enemy*' Paul.

92 Below: The Third Column of the Nahum *Pesher* referring to '*messengers*' / '*Apostles*' to '*the Gentiles*' and '*deceiving*' converts with '*a Lying Tongue.*'

93 ABOVE: '*The Golden Gate*,' towards which the Romans made their final adoration of their standards after storming and burning the Temple in 70 CE.

94 ABOVE RIGHT: What is left of '*Herod's Palace*' in Jerusalem where Saulos and his Herodian colleagues took refuge at the beginning of the Uprising.

95 BELOW LEFT: Greek/Hebrew warning block in the Temple forbidding non-Jews to enter its sacred precincts on pain of death.

96 ABOVE: Fragment from the Genesis *Pesher* (49:14) identifying '*the Sceptre*' as '*the Messiah of Righteousness*' (singular) and '*the Branch of David*.'

97 LEFT: 4QBerachot/'*The Chariots of Glory*' '*cursing*' Belial as '*the Angel of the Pit*.'

98 LEFT: The ruins of strategic Emmaus where Jesus appeared to '*Cleopas*' and Jewish defenders were sealed in their caves and starved to death by the Romans.

99 BELOW: A passage verifying the presence of CDVII at Qumran evoking '*the Star who came to Damascus*,' '*the Doresh*,' '*the Sceptre*,' '*the Nasi*,' and '*destruction by the hand of Belial*.'

100 BELOW: Columns IV–V of the Nahum *Pesher* referring to '*the Nilvim*' rejoining '*the Glory of Judah*,' '*the Cup*,' '*perishing by the sword*,' and '*going into captivity*'

101 ABOVE: The ruins of the seaport at Caesarea, where Paul visited '*Philip*' and was incarcerated for two years by Felix in the Palace of Agrippa II, his putative '*kinsman*.'

102 ABOVE: The Synagogue at Gamala just above the Sea of Galilee in the Gaulon, the birthplace of '*Judas the Galilean*' (the progenitor of '*the Zealot Movement*').

103 RIGHT: The two '*Camel*'-like humps from which Gamala received its name and from which the first Jewish mass suicide occurred in 67 CE as the Romans made their bloody way down from Galilee.

104 ABOVE: Ruins near Mt. Gerizim in Samaria where the Samaritan Redeemer figure, '*The Taheb*,' crucified by Pontius Pilate, performed his '*Signs*.'

105 **Above:** The Western or '*Wailing Wall*,' the only part of Temple left standing after its destruction in 70 CE.

106 **Above:** Columns XI-XII of the Habakkuk *Pesher* referring to how the Wicked Priest both '*swallowed*' the Righteous Teacher and '*destroyed the Poor*' and how '*the Cup of the Right Hand of the Lord*' would then '*come around*' and '*swallow him*.'

107 **Above:** The last Column XIII of the Habakkuk *Pesher* evoking '*the Day of Judgement*' on '*Idolaters*' and '*Evil Ones*' and announcing that '*God is in His Holy Temple, let all the world be still*.'

108 **Right:** Coin from '*Year 2*' of the Uprising against Rome depicting a ceremonial amphora on the obverse and a grape leaf with the logo '*the Freedom of Zion*' on the reverse.

109 ABOVE: The Colosseum, built by Vespasian from the proceeds of the Temple Treasure and the numerous slaves he took, the survivors among whom (martyrs all) probably died in it.

110 BELOW: The underground walkways of the Priests in the Jerusalem Temple which survived its destruction by Vespasian, Titus, Titus' mistress Bernice, and Philo's nephew Tiberius Alexander.

111 BELOW RIGHT: The Arch of Titus, celebrating his victory over the Jews, still standing in the Roman Forum today – his father Vespasian's Colosseum visible just behind it.

112 ABOVE: Vespasian's '*Judea Capta*' coin, displaying his image on its obverse and the Roman dominion over a weeping Judean woman on its reverse – the palm tree signifying the Jewish State.

113 ABOVE: The image on the Arch of Titus showing his great Triumph, the Jewish captives carrying their sacred objects, particularly the seven-branched, gold candelabra given by Queen Helen to the Temple – presumably melted down to help to pay for the Colosseum.

114 ABOVE RIGHT: Jewish Revolutionary coin from the rare Year 4 depicting the real '*Cup of the Lord*' ('*the Cup*' of Divine Vengeance?) and bearing the logo '*the Redemption of Zion.*'

even a '*Windbag*.'[38] The '*pouring*' aspect of this notation ('*hittif* /'*Mattif*)is also part of '*the Spouter*' terminology – literally, therefore, '*the Pourer*' – which can also be seen as incorporating a play on the language of '*baptism*' – particularly '*Holy Spirit baptism*' – and should be contrasted with '*the standing up of the Yoreh ha-Zedek*' or '*He who pours down Right-eousness at the End of Days*.'[39]

As we have seen as well, in the Damascus Document there is also a plural reference to these '*Men of Scoffing*' that comes in the context of '*putting idols on their hearts*' (compare this allusion to '*idols*' here and else-where in CD and 1QS with James in Acts 15:19 banning '*the pollutions of the idols*'),

> *speaking mistakenly about the Laws of Righteousness, and rejecting the Covenant and the Compact* (literally, '*the Promise*' or '*the Faith*'), *that is, the New Covenant which they raised in the Land of Damascus*,[40]

followed by the evocation of '*the end of all the Men of War who walked with the Man of Lying*' (*n.b.* the '*walking*' allusion again with an entirely new or reverse signification[41] – this coupled with an allusion to '*the gathering in of the Yoreh*,' the implication being that, whoever he was, he has already in some manner died[42]).

Combinations such as '*the Comedians*' or '*Scoffers of Lying*,' together with allusion to '*Belial*' and '*his nets*,' also appear in documents like the Qumran Hymns.[43] These further demonstrate the proposition that all these kinds of usages are more or less circular denoting the same indi-vidual and his associates. In fact, '*Scoffing*' imagery of this kind seems actually to have gone into Islamic eschatology as denoting '*the Dajjal*' or '*Joker*.' This character is portrayed as being in conflict with '*the Mahdi*' or '*Expected One*' (the '*Messiah*'-like individual in Islam) who is finally to be destroyed *with the coming of Jesus Christ*! How this ideology developed is impossible to say.[44]

This '*Spouter of Lying*' (*Mattif ha-Chazav*) who '*spouts*' or '*pours out to them*' (*hittif*) is even referred to, as we have seen, in CDviii.13 of Ms. A as '*spilling out wind*' or '*being of confused Spirit*' ('*wind*' and '*spirit*' being, as already explained as well, synonymous in Hebrew) – in xix.25-26 of Ms. B, even as '*walking in the wind*' or '*walking in the Spirit*,' phraseology we have just seen Paul actually employ at the end of Galatians (5:11–26) where he is heaping scorn on those who '*teach circumcision*' as being either '*in the flesh*' or '*of the flesh*' (cf. Romans 8:1–9:8 and *pars.*) – here in Gala-tians 6:12–13 '*in your flesh*.' As he explains, he means by this, '*they want you to be circumcised so they may Glory*' or '*boast in your flesh*,' certainly an ungenerous exposition going even so far as to, once again, allude – as we have seen too – to the '*blood libel*' accusation, this time in an entirely new format, that is, the omnipresent '*these force you to be circumcised only that they should escape persecution for the cross of Christ.*'

This too is really an ungenerous accusation and, as already suggested, is reminiscent of the one in 1 Corinthians 11:27, relating to his previous announcement of '*Communion with the blood of Christ,*' that '*whoever shall drink the Cup of the Lord* (an expression we shall presently encounter in the Habakkuk *Pesher* but with an entirely different signification) *shall be guilty of the body and the blood of the Lord*' – itself coming on the heels of the '*do this in remembrance of me*' allusion in 11:25.[45] Whatever he means by these things, the fearful virtuosity of the rhetorical displays, especially in the first, which again follows the strophe/antistrophe/epode format of Greek lyrical poetry, are portentous. If authentic, the version of these things in Ms. B, describing '*the Spouter*' as '*walking in the Spirit*' would, as previously alluded to as well, have particular import where Paul's design in 1 Corinthians 2:13 to '*teach the spiritual things taught by the Holy Spirit spiritually*' is concerned.

In fact, most of these passages from the two versions of CD have since been confirmed in the previously unpublished Cave 4 fragments of the Damascus Document.[46] There is even a reference in one of these 4QD fragments – exactly as in the Pseudoclementine literature – to '*not revealing the secret of His People to Gentiles or cursing or (preaching) Rebellion against His Messiah of the Holy Spirit, turning aside from (or 'disobeying) the word of God.*'[47] Here the allusion can also be read '*the Anointed Ones of the Holy Spirit,*' since there are no verbs or adjectives associated with it that can help determine whether it should be read as a singular or plural; but if it parallels reference to '*the Messiah of Aaron and Israel*' elsewhere, where there are, then we can take it as singular.

However this may be, it is an extremely important allusion and the tenor of the allusion to '*Rebelling*' which accompanies it – also permeating CDVIII, XIX, and XX – is, it should be appreciated, exactly the same as that used at the end of Column V and the beginning of Column VI above to describe how '*Belial raised up Jannes and his brother*' (*Jambres*) and the other '*Removers of the Bound*' to '*lead Israel astray*' as a prelude to its description of how '*the Diggers*' (equivalent to '*the Penitents of Israel*') '*went out from the Land of Judah to dwell in the Land of Damascus,*' there '*to dig the Well*' (of '*Living Waters*') and explain why '*the Land was decimated*':

because they preached rebellion against the Commandments of God (as given) by the hand of Moses and also against His Holy Messiah (once again, as there is a singular adjective, '*Holy*' or '*Kadosh*,' that goes along with the usage here; it is singular, though the most widely used English translation renders it '*His holy anointed ones*' – plural[48]). *They prophesied Lying to turn Israel aside from God.*[49]

This really is a pregnant passage and, as should be clear, it too will be picked up later in Columns VIII and XIX in '*the wall-daubing*' and '*prophesying Lying*' materials from Ezekiel 13:6–12 and Micah 2:6–12. In such a context, the references to either '*rebelling against His Holy Messiah*' or '*the Messiah(s) of the Holy Spirit*' are nothing less than astonishing and, whatever else one might wish to say about them, especially the latter combines the conceptuality of '*the Holy Spirit*' with either '*His Messiah*' or '*the Messiahs*' in an unforgettably striking manner.

What unites all references to this '*Lying Spouter*' or CD's '*Zaw Zaw*' allusion, tied to the one who '*will surely spout*' (Micah 2:6) in IV.19-20, is that not only does he '*pour out on Israel the waters of Lying and lead them astray in a trackless waste*,' '*removing the boundary markers which the First* ('*the Forefathers*') *had laid out as their inheritance*' – imagery, as we have seen, picked up again and recapitulated in the 4QD fragment containing the Last Column of the Damascus Document[50]; but this sort of behaviour takes place in '*the Last Days*' when – as if all these things were not enough – in the Habakkuk *Pesher* he will be distinctly described as '*rejecting the Torah in the midst of their whole Assembly*' (or '*Church*') and '*not believing in*' the Scriptural interpretations of '*the Righteous Teacher*' which the latter '*had received from the mouth of God*'!

He would even appear to have been involved along with these other '*Covenant-Breakers*' in CDi.20 in physical violence – some of which might even be described as '*mortal*' – '*against the person* (or '*soul*') *of the Righteous One* (again singular, though some specialists prefer to render it as plural[51]) *and all those walking in Perfection*' – here again the '*walking in Perfection of the Way*' or '*in Perfect Holiness*,' meaning '*not deviating to the right or the left of the Torah*' – imagery, we have been following, as opposed to Paul's more generalized '*walking in the Spirit*' imagery.[52] In other descriptions, these confrontations between '*the Liar*' or '*Spouter of Lying*' and '*the Righteous Teacher*,' however, are usually verbal and not so violent or physical and this '*Lying Spouter*' or '*Man of Jesting*'/'*Scoffing*' is clearly depicted as an *ideological* adversary of '*the Teacher of Righteousness*' within '*the Movement*,' not outside it, since he attends the scriptural exegesis sessions of '*the Priest*'/'*Righteous Teacher*'/'*Zaddik*.'[53]

'The Wicked Priest' and the *'the Simple of Judah doing Torah'*

On the other hand, the other opponent of the Righteous Teacher is easier to delineate. Though called *'the Wicked Priest,'* in the early days of Qumran research no distinction was ever made between him and *'the Man'* or *'Spouter of Lying,'* that is, before I made this clear in *Maccabees, Zadokites, Christians and Qumran: A New Hypothesis of Qumran Origins* (Leiden, 1984).[54] On the contrary, all opponents of *'the Righteous Teacher'* were lumped indiscriminately together and referred to as a single individual. One scholar in the Introductions to both his widely-circulated *The Dead Sea Scrolls in English* (4th Edition) and *The Complete Dead Sea Scrolls in English* was particularly particularly aggressive in attributing this view to me, thereby unwittingly demonstrating that he had never really seriously read my theories.[55] Nevertheless, by so doing and setting up this particular *'straw man'* – as already made clear in my *'Preliminaries'* – he made it especially easy for himself and others to depreciate my ideas.[56]

But despite this erroneous and misinformed representation of my position and points I have been arguing for thirty years now[57] – it is quite clear, according to the position I am arguing, that *'the Righteous Teacher'* has *two* separate opponents and these are two *separate* individuals – one *inside the Movement,* 'the Man of Lying' / 'Spouter' / 'Comedian'; and the other *outside it,* 'the Wicked Priest.' That the latter is also a *'High Priest'* as we just saw – in this case the Establishment *'High Priest'* – is made clear as well from the appellation *'the Priest'* attached to him in both Habakkuk and Psalm 37 *Peshers*; but *he is not is not the same as 'the Lying Spouter.'*[58] He is also referred to as *'the Priest'* (meaning the Establishment *'High Priest'* again) who *'did not circumcise the foreskin of his heart'* and *'rebelled against and broke the Laws (of God'* – here again, both the language of *'breaking'* and *'Rebelling').*[59]

The use, too, here of the allusion *'the Priest'* is exactly the opposite of how it is used with regard to *'the Righteous Teacher.'* The one is more or less the mirror reversal of the other – *'the Righteous Teacher,'* therefore, being *'the Opposition High Priest'* of his time, which links up strongly with allusions associated with James and *his role in the Jerusalem of his day*, a position first delineated regarding him in the 1920s and 30s by Robert Eisler even before the discovery of the Dead Sea Scrolls (though he did have the Cairo *Genizah* Damascus Document to work with).[60]

The allusion to the Wicked Priest's being *'uncircumcised in heart'* is also, ideologically speaking, of importance for our purposes and this, not only in relation to Paul's use above of *'heart'* imagery in his letters. It also means that, though he may have been *'circumcised in the flesh'* – Paul's main concern relating to those ideological adversaries he is always denigrating[61] and important, as much for the Community of James and those following '*the Righteous Teacher*,' as it was for those '*Revolutionaries*' demanding a High Priest of '*greater purity*' and '*higher Righteousness*' from 4 BC onwards[62] ('*the High Priest after the order of Melchizedek*,' '*Perfectly Holy, unpolluted, separated from Sinners, and higher than the Heavens*' of Hebrews 7:26, *etc.*[63]) – his '*heart*' was '*impure*' or '*polluted*.' Furthermore, he was obviously not a '*Righteous Priest*'[64] as '*the Righteous Teacher*,' to say nothing of the '*the Priest after the Order of Melchizedek*,' certainly appears to have been. As the Habakkuk *Pesher* puts this: '*he* ('*the Wicked Priest*') *acted*' or '*worked in the Ways of Abominations in all unclean pollution*.'[65]

It is also important vis-à-vis the esoteric allusions in Ezekiel that are the basis for the definition of who *the true* '*Sons of Zadok*' were. These are the passages from Ezekiel 44:5–9 that also put the lie, as we have stressed, to Josephus' claims that the rejection of gifts and sacrifices on behalf of Gentiles in the Temple in the run-up to the War against Rome in the Sixties CE (the decade in which James died) was '*an Innovation with which our people were before unacquainted*.' It is clear that this idea of banning foreigners and gifts and sacrifices from them or on their behalf from the Temple goes all the way back to these passages from Ezekiel 44:5-9. In fact, they make '*rejecting such gifts and sacrifices*' a requirement for proper '*Temple service*' and accuse those behaving in the opposite manner of '*breaking the Covenant*,' the very words the Habakkuk *Pesher* uses to describe the activities of '*the Wicked Priest*' and those opposing '*the Righteous Teacher*' in general.[66] With this in mind, there can be little doubt that this kind of allusion is meant to disqualify persons of the type of '*the Wicked Priest*' from doing '*Temple service*,' despite any genealogical claims to the contrary they may have been making.

Earlier in the Habakkuk *Pesher*, these '*Covenant Breakers*,' '*Violent Ones*,' and '*Traitors to the New Covenant*' were presented as '*walking with*' or being allied to '*the Man of Lying*.'[67] This '*breaking*' language too, as we saw, was also part and parcel of Letter of James – in particular, the recommendation at its beginning to be a '*Doer*' (1:22–26, 2:13, and even later in 4:11–17) or a '*Keeper*' not a '*Breaker*' (1:27 and 2:8–2:11) and condemning thereafter the one '*not bridling his Tongue*' (1:26) or '*stumbling over one small point of the Law*' (2:10) Such persons are '*Breakers*' or '*Law-Breakers*' as opposed to '*Doers*' and '*Keepers*' – familiar terms in James and used throughout the Damascus Document and the Habakkuk *Pesher*.[68]

As will be recalled, it is in these passages that Ezekiel 44:7 explains what is meant by the '*pollution of the Temple*' charge made in the '*Three Nets of Belial*' section of CDIV.14–VI.2 directly following its exposition of

Ezekiel 44:15:

> *Because you have brought foreigners uncircumcised in heart and uncircumcised in flesh into my Temple to pollute My House..., you have broken My Covenant because of all your Abominations'*

Even this word *'Abominations'* will be directly applied to *'the Wicked Priest'* below and it will be these kinds of esotericisms from crucial Biblical passages that will show what the problem concerning him was. It will be for us to interpret such esotericisms as we proceed as we have already to a large extent been doing – but disqualifying *'the Wicked Priest'* from *'service'* at the Temple altar must certainly be seen as part of their thrust.

In the *Pesharim* too, we also find esoteric, yet meaningful, expressions such as *'the Simple of Judah doing Torah.'* These are basically identical with *'the Ebionim'* or *'the Poor'* – both, for all intents and purposes, describing the rank and file of the Community (in other contexts, *'the Rabim'* or *'the Many'*).[69] Parallel to these are *'the Simple of Ephraim,'* urged in the Nahum *Pesher 'to turn aside from the one who deceives'* or *'lies to'* them,[70] who have a parallel in the New Testament usage, *'these Little Ones'* – a usage as we have seen also possibly reflected in the quotation from Zechariah 13:7 encountered in Ms. B's version in CDxix.7–9 of *'Messianic'* events centering around the coming (*'Second'* or *'Third'*) *Visitation'* above. In the New Testament, as we saw, Jesus is pictured as using the expression in Matthew 18:5 and *pars.* in such a way that it is obviously meant to be a stand-in for those among *'the Gentiles'* to whom Paul's *'Gentile Mission'* is addressed – in the sense of being unsophisticated in Scriptural matters and, to a certain extent, not even aware of *'the Torah'* (*cf.*, for instance, how Paul uses the expression in Galatians 4:19 above).

When evaluating its use in the Nahum *Pesher* at Qumran one should bear in mind, as previously underscored, its relationship to another favorite New Testament allusion, *'Samaritans,'* who – *bona fide* or not – claimed descent (as they still do today) from those in the Northern Kingdom, most generally known as *'Ephraim.'*[71] In the *Pesher*, which makes use of the first three Chapters of Nahum, the usage *'the Simple of Ephraim'* was tied to another, *'Resident Aliens'* (*Ger-Nilveh*), which for its part relates to the Hebrew *'joining'* or *'Joiners'* (*'nilvu'* or *'Nilvim'*). Not only have we already encountered this expression in the exegesis of *'the Zadokite Covenant'* above, but it conveys the sense of *'joining'* or *'attaching oneself' to the Community in an associated* or *adjunct status* of some kind as the *'God-Fearers'* were seen to be doing to the Synagogues throughout the Mediterranean at this time.

For its part, we have seen how this expression, '*fearing God*,' crops up in critical passages among the promises made towards the end of the exhortative section in of Ms. B, Column XX.19–20, which include the allusion to '*a Book of Remembrance being written out before Him for God-Fearers and those reckoning His Name*' (meaning '*God's Name*') and which so much resemble Paul's and the Synoptics' '*Do*' or '*Drink this in Remembrance of me.*'[72] It too occurs throughout the New Testament corpus as, for instance, in Acts 10:2 and 10:22, as previously underscored too, where someone like the Roman Centurion '*Cornelius*' is even described as '*a God-Fearer*'! Not incuriously, in these passages and in Acts 10:7, he is also described as '*Righteous*,' '*Pious*,' '*praying to God continually*' – the kind of language normally associated with either '*the Essenes*' or someone like James – and even as '*continually waiting for him*'!

But even more importantly, there are actually two further references in regard to his '*charitable works going up*' (the very subject of the beginning of the Last Column of the Damascus Document and the references there to Leviticus 26:31 and Joel 2:13) and '*being remembered before God*' (10:4 and 10:31), almost the very words just encountered in CDxx.19 of Ms.A as well. Moreover, this allusion to '*remembered before God*' is almost word-for-word that of the description in the Pseudoclementine *Recognitions* of '*the two brothers*' who were, also, '*remembered before God*'; and, because of having visited the burial monument of whom ('*which miraculously whitened of itself every year*'), James and the rest of his Community of '*five thousand*' were missed by '*the Enemy*' Paul, who was pursuing them on his way to Damascus *with letters from the High Priest*![73] In scientific investigation, it is generally considered that the ability of a given theory to arrive at insights as precise as these constitutes very good confirmation of its validity. It is furthermore worth observing, once again, that it is to '*God-Fearers*' such as these that Paul generally directs his message.

The '*doing Torah*' language – as in '*the Simple of Judah doing Torah*' and '*the Doers of the Torah*' – will not only be absolutely fundamental to the Habakkuk *Pesher*'s exposition of Habakkuk 2:4: '*the Righteous shall live by his Faith*' and, as we shall see, of the one, related to and preceding it, Habakkuk 2:3 (which will turn out to be the basis of what normally goes in Christian theory under the heading: '*The Delay of the Parousia*'[74]); but it also underlies the general usage in Hebrew that translates into English as '*works*.' These allusions to '*Doer*' and '*doing*' are pregnant with meaning for the approach of James and actually appear several times, as we just saw, in the New Testament Letter associated with his name (1:2, 1:25, 2:8, 2:13, 4:13, and 4:17) – the second, '*the Doer*' shall '*be blessed in his doing*,' and, the third, in conjunction with '*doing the Royal Law according to the*

Scripture.' In James, as at Qumran, this emphasis on *'being a Doer'* and *'doing,'* as just indicated as well, is ranged against the allusion to being a *'Breaker'* or *'breaking the Law'* (2:9–11), an ideology which also permeates the two Letters) we have highlighted above known as *'MMT.'* Some have even gone so far as to see this allusion to *'Doers'/'Osei ha-Torah* as the basis for the denotation in the Greek of Josephus and Philo's *'Essenoi'* or *'Essenes.'*[75] For his part, Epiphanius relates the appellative *'Essenes'* to either the name *'Jesus'* itself – namely *'Jessaeans'* – or that of the father of David and, therefore, the New Testament's *'Jesus'*'putative ancestor, *'Jesse.'*[76] However one looks at the problem, both kinds of derivations relate to either Early Christianity or Qumran.

Other esotericisms found in the *Pesharim*, important for solving the puzzle of the Scrolls, are phrases like *'the City of Blood'* in the Nahum *Pesher* or *'a worthless City built upon blood and an Assembly'* or *'Church erected* (or, as in Amos 9:11 above, *'raised'*) *upon Lying'* in the Habakkuk *Pesher.*[77] As already suggested, not only can these be looked upon in terms of both Paul's *'architectural'* and *'building'* imagery in 1 Corinthians – particularly 1 Corinthians 3:6-17, where he actually does use the imagery of CD (and of Isaiah 60:21-61:4) of *'planting'* and *'God causing to grow'* and really does call himself *'the architect'* or *'builder'* – but, as we shall see, also his understanding of *'Communion'* both with the *'body'* and *'blood of Christ,'* found later in 1 Corinthians 10:14-17.

At least where it is found in the Nahum *Pesher*, this expression *'City of Blood'* (Nahum 3:1) – as it is interpreted in the *Pesher*, *'the City of Ephraim, the Seekers after Smooth Things at the End of Days, who walk in Deceitfulness and Lying'* – will have real meaning where the related phrase *'the Simple of Ephraim'* tied to the idea of *'joining'* is concerned.[78] It is possible to interpret it, anyhow, in terms of *'Pauline Christians'* (*'Gentiles'* of course) or Resident Alien *'Joiners'* in an associated status with the new *'Community of God,'* the attitudes of whom with regard to *'Torah'* have not yet been clarified or sufficiently consolidated. This is of course, as just emphasized, the other side of the coin of the expression *'the Simple of Judah doing Torah'* – identified in the Habakkuk *Pesher* with *'the Ebionim'* or *'the Poor.'* These are the kind of esotericisms which abound in Qumran literature and have so much puzzled scholars for so long. Yet they are consistent and homogeneous and provide clues for finally unraveling the meaning of the documents in which they are found.

The Language of Psalm 37

It is in the Habakkuk *Pesher* that one really has the most extensive picture of things of this kind and it is to the Habakkuk *Pesher* we must turn in order to find the exposition of the destruction or death of the Righteous Teacher. The atmosphere surrounding this event will so link up with circumstances surrounding the death of James that, when properly expounded, one virtually arrives at convergence or almost absolute proof. This will be augmented by several notices in the Psalm 37 *Pesher*, a document also found – like all the other *Pesharim* so far found at Qumran – in single exemplar only, meaning it comes probably from the last stages of the Community's literature.

Like the Habakkuk *Pesher*, the Psalm 37 *Pesher* is in a very good state of preservation and was published early on by the controversial Qumran scholar, John Allegro – whose publishing efforts, one might add, were then overwritten by the equally-controversial John Strugnell.[79] The Psalm itself is replete with imagery beloved at Qumran and, like the Nahum *Pesher* and passages from Habakkuk 1:4 and 2:4 above, it is yet another '*Zaddik*'-Psalm, contrasting '*the Wicked*' with '*the Righteous*' (37:12), imagery intrinsic to the literature at Qumran.

This was probably the reason for choosing these texts and others in the first place and the contrast of this '*Wicked devouring*' or '*encompassing the Righteous*' is exploited to produce the several exegeses relating to the destruction of '*the Righteous Teacher*' and the vengeance taken on '*the Wicked Priest*,' apparently responsible for this, at Qumran. This is exactly paralleled in the presentation of the Habakkuk *Pesher* as well as in the passage from Isaiah 3:10 applied to the death of James in early Church literature. In addition, Psalm 37 is permeated by the vocabulary so beloved at Qumran like '*the Poor*' (*Ebion*) and '*the Meek*' (*ʿAni* – 37:14).

But its imagery can also be found to underlie the Letter of James, particularly in the recommendation: '*to wait for the Lord and keep His Way*' (37:34), phraseology specifically evoked in James 5:7, as we have seen. This imagery also has its counterpart in the recommendation in Habakkuk *Pesher* 2:3: '*If it tarries, wait for it*,' itself specifically interpreted in the Habakkuk *Pesher*, as we shall see, in terms of what goes by the name of '*the Delay of the Parousia*' in Christianity – '*the Delay of the Last Times*' and '*Second Coming*' leading up to the all-important interpretation of Habakkuk 2:4, '*the Righteous shall live by his faith*,' a passage as important for Pauline theological thought as it is Jamesian.

In addition, Psalm 37 contains the kind of rebuke – found in the First Chapter of the Letter of James – cautioning,

Cease from anger and turn aside from wrath. Do not upset yourself to bring yourself to Evil (37:8).

As the Letter of James puts this in its opening lines, after cautioning: '*have patience, so you may be Perfect and Complete*' (1:4 – language also present in Psalm 37:37: '*mark the Perfect and see the Upright*'), condemning '*Riches*' or '*the Rich*' (1:10–11), and emphasizing the language of '*being Doers of the word*' (1:22 – in 1:25, as we have seen, being a '*Doer of the work*'):

> *So my beloved brothers, let every man be swift to hear, slow to speak, slow to anger, for man's wrath does not (carry out) the Righteousness of God's works* (1:19–20).

In Chapter Three in its attack on '*the Tongue*,' recapitulating its earlier allusion to '*bridling one's Tongue*' and '*deceiving one's heart*' in 1:26, James 3:14–16 cautions not to

> *have bitter jealousy and contention in your heart, nor boast and lie against the Truth…For where jealousy and contention are, there is commotion and every Evil thing.*

In Chapter Five, in the context of repeatedly counseling '*patience*,' James once again reiterates,

> *You should also be patient. Make your hearts strong, because the Coming of the Lord is drawing near* (his proclamation in the Temple, as we encountered it in early Church literature, but also note the parallel with '*the coming of the Messiah of Aaron and Israel*' in Ms. B of CDXIX.10–11 above). *Do not grumble against one another, lest you be condemned, because the Judge is standing before the door* (5:8–9).

We have already noted this language of '*making your hearts strong*' throughout CD, particularly at the end of its exhortative section above. One should also remark CD's language of '*judging*' and '*standing*' again too. There is even just the slightest hint here of that '*door to Jesus*' encountered in early Church accounts of the death of James.[109] '*Grumbling*,' for instance, is banned outright in both the Damascus Document and Community Rule and the penance for it, '*thirty days*,' is one of the '*Judgements*' made by '*the Mebakker*' or '*Bishop over the Many*' in '*the Camps*.' In fact, CD and 1QS overlap at just this point, making it seem as if they were both part of a single whole that was originally joined and there is a fragment in the Cave 4 parallels to CD that actually does combine them at this juncture in just this way.[81]

This idea of '*being Strong*' is also part and parcel of the '*Protection*' imagery applied to James in early Church accounts including '*Fortress,*' '*Bulwark,*' and the mysterious '*Oblias*'-language – possibly '*Strength of the People.*' It too is found in Psalm 37, which reads:'*the Salvation of the Righteous is from the Lord, who is their Strength in time of distress*' (37:39 – the Hebrew here being '*Ma^coz*' or '*Shield*'). In addition, there is the reference to '*His Way,*' noted in 37:4 above in conjunction with the idea of '*waiting patiently for the Lord*' – not only an alternative name for Christianity in Acts 16:17, 18:25-26, and 24:14-25, but imagery conspicuous across the whole Qumran corpus. So are the ideas of '*Perfection,*' '*Salvation,*' and '*being saved*' (37:40), prominent at Qumran and prominent in James. The same for the idea of being '*cursed and cut off*' found in Lines 37:9, 22, 28, and 38.

We have already seen how this language of '*cursing*' and '*cutting off*' is conspicuous at Qumran – in CDIII.6–7, the Children of Israel '*were cut off*' in the wilderness because '*they consumed blood*' – and conspicuous in the Letter of James. But in these instances, they are also strong in Paul's formulation in Galatians 3:10-26 above of how Jesus took his (Paul's) '*curse upon himself*' and, in so doing, freed Paul and others like him from the Law while, at the same time, providing an exemplar of redemptive death – as they are in 5:12 in his imprecation that the circumcisers should '*themselves* (meaning their own sexual members) *cut off.*'

It is interesting too, that in the interpretation of these things in the Psalm 37 *Pesher,* the allusions to '*Perfect*' and '*Way*' in the underlying text are applied in the exposition to the same '*Penitents in the wilderness,*' encountered in the Damascus Document above, continuing the circularity of these documents.[82] For the *Pesher* these '*shall live for a thousand generations*'! In the Damascus Document, it will be recalled, we found this same phrase, '*they shall live for a thousand generations,*' in interpretation of Deuteronomy 7:9 on the effects of '*keeping the Covenant*' and the '*Hesed*' ('*Grace*' in Paul) due to those that '*love God*' (the '*Piety*' Commandment) '*and on the Keepers of the Commandments for a thousand generations.*'[83]

Preceding this, the Damascus Document reiterated that these same '*Penitents of Israel...went out from the land of Judah to dwell in the Land of Damascus.*' Again, one should not forget the '*Rechabite*' aspects of both such '*dwelling*' and '*keeping the Commandments.*' To review the sequencing here: later it is explained that they were to '*turn aside from the Way of the People(s)*' – in our view the Herodians but not unrelated, as well, to the usage '*Galilee of the Gentiles*' in Matthew 4:15.[84] Earlier still, in the exegesis of '*the Zadokite Covenant,*' these same '*Penitents of Israel who went out from the Land of Judah,*' were identified with the '*Priests*' of Ezekiel 44:15's '*Priests, Levites, and Sons of Zadok.*' Furthermore, it will be recalled, '*the Levites*' were interpreted esoterically to mean our '*Nilvim*' above:'*and the*

Joiners (Nilvim) with them,' that is, *they went out 'with them.'*[85]

This allusion to *'living for a thousand generations'* in CDvii.6 and xix.1, reiterated – as we can now see – as well in the Psalm 37 *Pesher*, immediately follows the reference there to Paul's *'Perfection of Holiness'* and a string of allusions to *'separating from all pollutions,'* *'loving each man his brother as himself,'* *'strengthening the hand of the Meek (ᶜAni) and the Poor (Ebion)'* and *'not uncovering the nakedness of near kin,'* so as *'to keep away from (lehinnazer) fornication according to Law.'*[86]

But in addition to all these, there are two other usages in Psalm 37 that are fundamental to our discussion. The first is to *'plotting'* or *'conspiring'* – in this instance, *'the Wicked plotted against the Righteous'* (37:12). This is expressed in terms of *'zamam,'* the Hebrew verb which will be literally picked up in the exegesis of the Habakkuk *Pesher* in its discussion of how the Wicked Priest destroyed the Righteous Teacher and, after this, *'destroyed the Poor.'* Inversely, it is also a term which fairly permeates Acts' presentation of either Jewish or (so-called) *'Hellenist'* plots against Paul.

The second is to being *'cast down'* and *'falling'* (37:14). Here again the reference is to *'casting down the Meek (ᶜAni) and the Poor (Ebion).'* Furthermore allusion to *'the Righteous'* (*Zaddik*) abounds in the background to the Psalm (37:12–21). Basically the point is made that, *'though he falls, he shall not be cast down, because the Lord upholds him with His Hand'* (37:24). As should be clear, all of these usages are pregnant with import where the death of James, as pictured in early Church accounts, is concerned. This wording will, in turn, be transposed via the Hebrew into the death of the Righteous Teacher in the Habakkuk *Pesher* and how *'the Wicked encompassed* – usually expressed in terms of either *'he swallowed'* or *'he consumed'* – *the Righteous,'* interpreted to mean *'the Righteous Teacher'* and/or his followers among the *'the Poor'* (*Ebionim*)

What will become clear in our analysis of the Habakkuk *Pesher* is that we shall be able to elicit additional meaning from this text by comparing it with accounts of the death of James from early Church sources which we would not have expected before starting – points that would not otherwise have been appreciated without considering data relating to the death of James. This in itself, as it mounts up, will constitute very powerful proof that James and the Righteous Teacher are one and the same and the kind of proof that will verge on certainty and cannot be counter-indicated or repeated with regard to any other *known* character from this period – and we should work with *known characters* not unknowns, as our historical data is substantial enough to do so.

The Destruction of 'the Righteous Teacher' by 'the Wicked Priest' in the
Habakkuk Pesher from Qumran

The Habakkuk Pesher is – along with the Damascus Document, the
Community Rule, and the War Scroll – one of the most important
documents at Qumran. It is certainly one of the best preserved. A few of
the first columns are fragmented – normal where Scroll preservation is
concerned – as these would have been on the outside of the roll and,
therefore, suffered the most wear and tear. It is also somewhat frayed
along the edge, so one or two lines at the bottom of each column are
sometimes difficult to read. The rest is more or less intact.

Where handwriting is concerned, even those relying on palaeography have dated this document to the First Century CE, though those
employing an over-zealous use of 'first' and 'second sigma's in carbon
dating have tried to push this back into the First Century BC.[87] Notwithstanding such efforts, its First-Century dating, like that of the Psalm 37
Pesher it so much resembles (both had probably to be written at more
or less the same time), is reinforced by a wealth of internal allusions
within the document itself which make it impossible that the document
could have come from any century earlier than the First, whatever external dating tool might be applied. In particular, carbon testing should not
gainsay this, because, whatever the claims, as already emphasized, these
results involve outside interpretation or analysis and are in no way secure
or powerful enough to counter-indicate the kind of 'internal evidence' we
have been citing above and will cite further below.[88]

The most obvious and important of these internal allusions is the reference to 'the Kittim,' the foreign, invading armies, 'who come to lay waste
the earth' (obviously from the West, since they 'come from afar, from the
Islands of the Sea, to consume all the Peoples like an insatiable eagle' – the
'eating' and 'Gentiles'/'Peoples' allusions again), and are characterized as
'sacrificing to their standards and worshipping their weapons of war.'[89]

As we shall see, this allusion – which is general, indicating habitual
and not specific action – can apply to no time during the entire period
we have been considering other than that of Rome – and this Imperial
Rome, after the deification of the Emperors had taken hold and the
Emperor's medallion busts were affixed to the standards. Josephus specifically describes one such sacrifice the Romans made facing the Eastern
Gate after they had stormed the Temple in 70 CE.[90] But there were others
they obviously would have made – a whole series of them as they made
their bloody way down from Galilee, reducing fortress city after fortress
city, all vividly described in Josephus.[91]

Josephus also describes the incident of Pilate trying to smuggle such Roman military standards – in this case probably bearing the image of Tiberius Caesar (14–37 CE) – into Jerusalem just before the '*Jesus*' as '*the Christ*' *testimonium* and the '*Mundis and Paulina*' and '*Fulvia*' seduction episodes in the *Antiquities*. These last – one about a man impersonating the Egyptian god Anubis in the Temple of Isis to seduce one '*Paulina*' and the other about Tiberius' expulsion of an itinerant renegade Jewish teacher (who had been expelled for some infraction also from Jerusalem) and his associates from Rome, because they had swindled a high-born '*convert*' to Judaism (one '*Fulvia*'), and with them '*all the Jews of Rome*' – are certainly very peculiar and seem to have replaced something a little more worrisome and serious.[92] For his part, Pilate introduced the Roman military standards into Jerusalem and the Temple *by night* causing a frantic reaction the next day. The 'Jesus' episode, as it would have appeared (if it really did appear) or was over-written in the original Josephus, was probably somehow connected to these events and the revolutionary reaction they elicited from the crowd. This incident is also clearly connected with the attempt by Gaius Caligula to have his own portrait bust set up in the Temple five or six years later in 40–41 CE. In turn, Caligula was assassinated before this could be effected, thus paving the way for Claudius' rise – an altogether more sympathetic Ruler.[93]

Aside from the references to '*the Ebionim*' or '*the Poor*,' the *Pesher* also alludes to '*the Riches and booty*' of '*the Last Priests of Jerusalem*,' Jerusalem's fall, and how these '*Priests*' (plural not singular – *ergo*, the '*Herodian*' High-Priestly clans not the singular hereditary High Priest of the Maccabean Period) enriched themselves and literally '*profiteered from*' the elicit '*plunder of the Peoples*.'[94] Again, in our view, these last are '*Violent Gentiles*' or, more specifically, '*Herodians*' viewed as Gentiles by groups as '*Pious*' as the Qumran sectaries. The ambiance for this, as we have shown, is amply developed in the all-important, final Book Twenty of Josephus' *Antiquities*, where he twice notes how the '*Rich*' High Priests sent their servants and other thugs to the threshing floors to raid the tithes, so that '*the Poor*' among the lower priests died of want.[95] He also delineates in the *War* how these '*Herodian*' High Priests accepted gifts and sacrifices in the Temple on behalf of Romans and other foreigners, including both the Emperor and Herodians, which led directly to the War against Rome and was considered '*pollution of the Temple*' by their opponents.[96]

But the most obvious dating tool, based on '*internal data*' in the Habakkuk *Pesher* and not the '*external*,' is the citation and exegesis of Habakkuk 2:4, the climax of the *Pesher* – '*the Righteous shall live by his faith*' – the scriptural passage, as we have seen, forming the basis of a good deal of Paul's scriptural exegesis, to say nothing of James.' In addition to this, there is also, as in James 5:7-11, the counseling of '*patience*' tied to the exegesis of Habakkuk 2:3: '*if it tarries, wait for it*,' which directly precedes this. As we have seen, both of these passages are interpreted eschatologically, that is in terms of '*the Last Days*' or '*End Time*.' In fact, the interpretation of Habakkuk 2:3 is specifically related to the delay of this '*End*' and resembles nothing so much, as we just saw as well, as the scriptural warrant for what goes in Christianity even today under the heading of '*the Delay of the Parousia*' – the delay of the second coming of Christ and the final eschatological events associated with this.

As the *Pesher* puts this:

> The Last Era (or '*Last End*') *will be extended and exceed all that the Prophets (primarily Daniel) have foretold, since the Mysteries of God are astounding.*

The exposition – just as with that of Habakkuk 2:4 which follows – then goes on to apply this, like James 1:22-24 above, to '*the Doers of the Torah*.'[97] Presumably this exegesis repudiates a more '*Lying*' one on the same materials being circulated by '*the Man of Lying*' or '*Lying Spouter*.' These are the kinds of characteristics that make anything other than a First-Century ambiance for these arguments hard to imagine.

Again, this document too is found, as is normal with the *Pesharim* at Qumran, in a single exemplar only. As such, it would appear to be a record of the scriptural exegesis sessions of the Righteous Teacher who, as already emphasized, is specifically referred to as being able to give authorative scriptural exegeses and to whom '*God made known all the Mysteries of the words of His Servants the Prophets*.'[98] Elsewhere, he is said to be able '*to interpret*' these words. In this case, if '*the Righteous Teacher*' is not James – since he is clearly referred to in the exegesis as being destroyed along with several members of his Council – then we have to do with someone like James' successor according to all early Church tradition, Simeon bar Cleophas who, not unlike the individual designated as '*Elchasai*,' certainly functioned somewhere in the Judean wilderness or across Jordan in the Pella or Damascus region following the death of James (there being no real Jerusalem left at this point to function in).

As the *Pesher* puts it in interpretation of Habakkuk 2:2: '*write down the vision and make it plain on tablets*':

> *And God told Habakkuk to write down what was coming in the Last Generation, but He did not reveal to him (the Time of) the Completion of the Era (or 'when the Age would end').*

One should compare this with words attributed to 'Jesus' in Matthew 5:18 and 24:34: '*until all these things shall be accomplished*' or '*completed*.' Earlier, the same *Pesher* had identified '*the Traitors together with the Man of Lying*' as '*not believing what the Righteous Teacher expounded from the mouth of God*' (n.b., the emphasis here and in the rest of the column on '*believing*').[99]

Identifying these '*Traitors*' as not only betraying '*the New Covenant*' and '*the Last Days*' but also as '*Violent Ones and Covenant-Breakers*' (note the parallel here with James 2:9's '*Law-Breakers*'); these together with *the Liar*

> *did not believe all that they heard was going to happen in the Last Generation from the mouth of the Priest* (i. e., the *High Priest* – here, as we have seen, identified with '*the Righteous Teacher*') *in whose heart God put the intelligence to expound all the words of His Servants the Prophets, through whom* (literally '*through whose hands*') *God foretold all that was going to happen to His People.*[100]

These passages are only a little inverted from the kind of thing one encounters in Early Christian sources about James, namely that '*the Prophets declare concerning him*' – meaning not necessarily that he would do the expounding but that his name was to be found by searching Scripture where the events of his life were prefigured, particularly in these ever-present '*Prophets*.' Again, not only do these kinds of allusions link the *Pesher* very closely to the scriptural ambiance and eschatological expectation of Early Christianity, but we even have in it something akin to Paul's '*fleshy tablets of the heart*' allusion in 2 Corinthians 3:3 above, should one choose to regard it.

The *Pesher* focuses on several important events. These transpire against a backdrop of *the coming of foreign armies into the country* called, as we have seen, '*the Kittim*.'[101] While these are extremely violent – '*swift and terrible in war causing many to perish*' and '*plunder the cities of the Earth*,' '*parceling out their yoke and their taxes* (that is, '*tax-farming*'), *eating all the Peoples year by year, giving many countries over to the sword*' – they are not the *Pesher*'s principal concern, though the exegete is very distressed by the ferocity and pitilessness of their efficiency. Not only this, but it would even seem that we have here a direct allusion to the Romans appointing '*Kings of the Peoples*' such as '*the Herodians*' to rule in the East and '*profiteer*' from their tax-collecting and it is difficult to conceive of this description applying to any ancient people other than the Romans.

Aside from '*not believing in the Laws of God*,' it is specifically noted that '*they come from afar*,' '*from the islands of the sea*,' '*trampling the Earth with their horses and pack animals,*' '*consuming all the Peoples like an eagle that is never satisfied.*'[102] The last is normally taken to be an allusion to the Roman Eagle. Furthermore, '*they overthrow the Fortresses of the Peoples, laughing at them in derision,*' an allusion that would confirm our earlier identification of '*the Peoples*' as '*the Herodians*' and, more than likely, refers to '*the Fortresses*' which they either built or enlarged such as Masada, Machaeros, Hyrcania, and Cypros, named by Herod in honor of his mother.[103]

As the *Pesher* continues, they '*encircle*' cities, and '*destroy them because of the iniquity of their inhabitants.*' One should not overlook that the genre of this accusation is one familiar to the New Testament and in early Church literature. Plus, '*they gather their Riches together with all their booty like the fish of the sea*' – this, not insignificantly, in exposition of an allusion to '*fishermen*' and their '*nets*' again in the underlying language of Habakkuk 1:14–15 and tied to the '*tax-collecting*' motifs above. Nor do they pity '*youths,*' '*old men, women, children,*' not even '*the fruit of the womb.*'[104] It should be clear that, aside from the accompanying allusion to '*sacrificing to their standards and worshipping their weapons of war,*' these passages can hardly be describing a Dynasty or a war machine as ineffectual as the Seleucids and *can only relate to the Romans* – any and all external dating parameters to the contrary notwithstanding.

But despite the horror of this heart-wrenching picture, it only forms the backdrop and is secondary to the *Pesher's* two other really main concerns, between which it swings its attention back and forth despite this background picture of mayhem and slaughter – maybe even because of it. The first is the ideological conflict between '*the Man of*' or '*Spouter of Lying*' – in CD1.14-15, as we saw above, the '*Scoffer who pours out Lying*' – and '*the Righteous Teacher.*' Ultimately the focus on these two overwhelms all other concerns including the coming of the rapacious and all-powerful '*Kittim,*' to whom the *Pesher* also refers as '*the Additional ones of the Peoples.*' Since, in our opinion, '*the Herodians*' are '*the Peoples,*' the Romans are '*the Additional Ones of the Peoples.*'[105]

The second concern is the conflict between the Righteous Teacher, clearly identified as '*the Opposition High Priest*' by the literature at Qumran, and the Wicked Priest, clearly meant to signify the reigning '*Establishment*' High Priest of the day. Moreover, the Wicked Priest plainly ends up destroying the Righteous Teacher and, it would appear, being in turn '*destroyed*' himself. These are the exact words of the *Pesher* and under what appear to be very gruesome circumstances indeed at the hands of a group called '*the Violent Ones*' or, as the Psalm 37 *Pesher* would put this, '*the Violent Ones of the Gentiles.*'[106] In the background to these two conflicts and the warp and woof, as it were, of the *Pesher* is the constant antagonism to foreigners, 'robbing the Poor' (in the Damascus Document, 'robbing the Meek of His People'), and the predatory, 'profiteering,' and conspiratorial activities of the Wicked Priest and his colleagues (called, as already remarked, 'the Last Priests of Jerusalem') with what appear to be 'Herodians.' This last is true if 'Peoples' (Paul's 'Ethne' or 'Gentiles') can be identified with 'Herodians.' We think they can.

In the Pesher, the 'Wicked Priest' is clearly responsible for removing or, as it appears, 'destroying' his adversary and opposite number 'the Righteous Teacher,' referred to as we have seen as 'the Priest,' i.e., 'the Opposition High Priest' or 'the High Priest of the Opposition Alliance.' For the Pesher, the Wicked Priest 'swallows' or 'consumes' the Righteous Teacher (the 'Ba-La-ᶜa' language again – this in the sense of 'consumes' or 'destroys,' a variation on the 'eating' theme already encountered above). The latter, in turn, is always identified with a reference to 'Zaddik' or 'Righteous'/'Righteous One' in the underlying Biblical text. In the penultimate column, as already underscored, it is specifically stated that, just 'as he plotted to destroy the Poor' (Ebionim – identified with 'the Simple of Judah doing Torah'), so would 'he be paid the reward he paid the Poor' and 'God would condemn him to destruction.' The verb at this point, notwithstanding the tantalizing allusion to 'swallow'/'consume' preceding it, is quite literally 'destroying the Poor.' Moreover, because of this, he is 'condemned to destruction' himself.[107]

'The Wicked Priest' in the Psalm 37 Pesher

This presentation is reinforced in the Pesher on Psalm 37 which is also – in the jargon of the field – considered 'a late document.' Not only is the Psalm 37 Pesher clearly from the last days of the Community; in many of its concerns it overlaps the vocabulary and subject matter of the Habakkuk Pesher. As already noted, both appear to be written in approximately the same script from the same palaeographic Period (called 'the Herodian') which, in itself, counter-indicates what some consider to be the earlier radiocarbon date of the latter.[108] A 'Zaddik' text like the Habakkuk Pesher, as just remarked as well, the allusion to 'Zaddik' and 'Zaddikim' permeates the underlying Biblical material, forming the underpinning of 4QpPs 37's exposition – in particular, the struggle of 'the Righteous' with 'the Wicked' and the latter's invariable destruction of the former. This is exploited in the exposition to produce 'a Pesher' about the Wicked Priest 'overwhelming' or 'destroying' the Righteous Teacher.

The first incidence of this is the variation we noted above using 'the Meek' and 'the Poor' – interchangeable with 'the Righteous' throughout the Pesher – which reads: 'The Wicked have drawn the sword...to cast down the

Meek and the Poor' (37:14). This, it will be recalled, was preceded by: '*The Wicked plots against the Righteous and gnashes upon him with his teeth*' (37:12). The first of these and then what is more or less yet a third variation in the Psalm – '*the Wicked watches out for the Righteous and seeks to put him to death*' (37:32) – are both subjected to exegesis. The *Pesher*, which is repeated twice with slight variations, basically describes how the Wicked Priest '*laid hands upon*' the Righteous Teacher/'*the Priest and the Men of his Council...to put him to death*,' but would himself ultimately '*be delivered over to the hand of the Violent of the Gentiles for Judgement.*'[109] This is the same kind of '*Judgement*' we shall encounter in the Habakkuk Commentary – again emphasizing the basic circularity of these documents where *dramatis personae* and subject matter is concerned.[110]

Not only do we have here the language of '*being delivered up*' or '*over*,' applied in the New Testament to what '*Judas Iscariot*' supposedly did to Jesus and, as we have seen, permeating the Damascus Document (here the language is not strictly speaking, '*delivered up*,' but rather the '*paying him his Reward*'/'*Gemulo*,' we shall encounter in the penultimate Column of the Habakkuk *Pesher* below and in the passage from Isaiah 3:10-11 applied by all early Church testimony to the death of James[111]); but, for its part, the *Pesher* does not particularly follow '*the Meek*' part of the '*ʿAni*'/'*Ebion*' dichotomy. Rather it twice refers to '*the Assembly*' or '*Church of the Poor*' (*Ebionim*), whom it calls '*the Leaders and Pride of the flock.*' Here too, we have usages already encountered in the Damascus Document above.[112] These it opines '*will possess the High Mountain of Israel and His Holy Place*,' while '*the Violent Ones of the Peoples and the Wicked of Israel will be cut off and blotted out forever.*' Again one should note how the '*cutting off*' language, variously remarked above too, is used here.[113]

The same thing happens at the end of the Habakkuk *Pesher*, particularly where the destruction of the Righteous Teacher and his followers, '*the Poor*' and '*the Council of the Community*,' are being described. Though the expression '*ʿAni*' does occur in Habakkuk 3:14 as '*consuming the Meek*,' it is not used in the *Pesher* which, in any event, breaks off at 2:20. Rather the terminology, '*the Poor*' or '*Ebionim*,' is purposefully introduced into the exegesis of Habakkuk 2:17 in the penultimate column (1QpHab,xii.3–5) about '*Lebanon*,' '*the dumb beasts*,' and '*the violence done to the Land*,' though it nowhere occurs in the underlying text. In the writer's view, this is deliberate, because the commentator knows that he is, in fact, dealing with a Community already known as '*the Poor*' or '*the Ebionites*' and, as it were, the followers *par excellence* of James.[114]

In the Psalm 37 *Pesher*, too, the commentary on the extremely interesting allusion to '*the Wicked plotting against the Righteous*' (37:12), noted above, is missing – presumably because of the fragmentary state of the text – but its main lines can be detected. In any event, this *lacuna* is made good in the Habakkuk *Pesher*, where Psalm 37's allusion to '*conspiring*' or '*plotting*' (*zamam*) is now, once again, seemingly deliberately introduced into the commentary on Habakkuk 2:16–17's '*the Cup of the Lord's right hand coming around to you*,' '*the violence of Lebanon*,' and '*the destruction of the dumb beasts*.' Here it is worthwhile to note in passing the allusion to '*the Cup of the Lord*,' words already encountered in Paul's presentation of '*the Lord Jesus*" words at '*the Last Supper*' in 1 Corinthians 11:27-29 (themselves, as already underscored, not without a tinge of vengefulness) and imbedded in the scenario of the first post-resurrection appearance of Jesus to James in Jerome's '*Gospel of the Hebrews*.'[115]

The words used here are that '*he (the Wicked Priest) plotted to destroy the Poor*.' This basically reprises the language of Psalm 37:12–14, though neither '*conspiring*' or '*the Poor*' appear at this point in the underlying Biblical text of Habakkuk 2:17 exploited to produce the *Pesher*. Nevertheless, '*destruction*' does, since '*the dumb beasts*' – interpreted to mean '*the Simple of Judah doing Torah*' – are the ones '*he is conspiring to destroy*.'

This exposition precedes the last several allusions to '*the Day of Judgement*' (*Yom ha-Mishpat* – in the Koran, as we have seen, '*Yom ad-Din*' or what is more popularly referred to as '*the Last Judgement*') being called down upon '*idol-worshipping*' '*Gentiles, serving stone and wood*,' and what would appear to be the same Jewish backsliders – in the Psalm 37 *Pesher* above, expressed as '*the Evil Ones among His own People*.'[116] Again, this is what we meant by saying the documents are homogeneous and the same terms move from document to document, *Pesher* to *Pesher* – the same allusions – in fact, overlapping and complementing one another, thus betokening '*a Movement*' and not a random collection of documents or '*Jerusalem libraries*' as some have posited.

In this *Pesher* on Habakkuk 2:16–17, '*Jerusalem*' is denoted as '*the City*,' '*where the Wicked Priest committed works of Abominations, polluting the Temple of God*,' more excellent examples of our constantly recurring vocabulary and immediately recognizable as the same accusation in the Damascus Document aimed at the Jerusalem Establishment and the third of the '*Three Nets of Belial*' which they set up as '*three kinds of Righteousness*.' Nor is this to say anything about the allusion to '*Abominations*' in Ezekiel 4:6–7, the basis of these, about '*breaking (the) Covenant*' by '*bringing foreigners, uncircumcised in heart and uncircumcised in flesh into (the) Temple to pollute it*.' In these accusations, it was not observing proper '*separation but sleeping with women in their periods*' or, as we have explained, approaching or associating with people who did – namely, *Herodians and other foreigners.* One good example of this association was accepting appointment to the High Priesthood from them, to say nothing of the ever-recurring theme of accepting their polluted gifts and sacrifices in the Temple.

In this exposition of the Habakkuk *Pesher* too, '*the Cities of Judah*' are identified as the locale '*where (the Wicked Priest) robbed the Riches* – or '*the sustenance*' – *of the Poor.*' We have already shown the connection of this notice and its complements in the Damascus Document to the two notices in Josephus' *Antiquities*, one just preceding and the other just following the death of James – and reflected in the *Talmud* too – about how the High Priests sent their violent associates to the threshing floors to rob the '*Poorer*' priests of their sustenance so they died of want.[117]

The word used here to describe what the Wicked Priest did, harking back to '*the destruction of the dumb beasts*' (that is, '*the Simple of Judah doing Torah*') and, '*the violence done to Lebanon*' ('*Lebanon*' interpreted in the commentary, because of the root-meaning of the underlying syllable '*lavan*' or '*whiteness*,' to mean '*the Council of the Community*' – this harking back to the '*white linen*' its members presumably wore and also possibly the symbolism in 1QS,VIII.5-11 and IX.3-6 of '*the Community Council*' as '*Temple*') is not simply '*swallowed*' or '*consumed*,' but it *actually is* '*destroyed.*' It is for this God would '*pay him the reward he paid the Poor*' of the Psalm 37 *Pesher* and Isaiah 3:10-11 above and '*the Cup of the Wrath of God would swallow him*,' meaning '*God would condemn him to destruction*' as well.

This, in fact, parallels the usage, noted above, of how the Wicked Priest, '*who did not circumcise the foreskin of his heart*,' '*swallowed*' the Righteous Teacher '*with*' or '*at his House of Exile*,' which we will interpret in terms of the Sanhedrin Trial of James.[118] Here '*swallowing*' really does mean '*destroy.*' We referred to this '*swallowing*,' too, in our discussion of the constant reiteration of James '*falling*' or '*being cast down*' in all early Church accounts in Greek of James' destruction. Moreover, we also showed how the Hebrew of this usage was connected with '*Devilishness*'/'*Belial*'/or '*Balaam*'; and the same regarding its homophone in Greek, '*ballo*' or '*cast down*' with '*Diabolos.*'

Ananus ben Ananus

Josephus specifically tells us that the High Priest, Ananus ben Ananus, was appointed by Agrippa II and convened the Sanhedrin that destroyed James. Ananus' brother Jonathan had been assassinated in the mid-Fifties by those whom Josephus had just started to call '*Sicarii*' – and this probably because of this assassination – an event we identified as one of the main incidents setting in motion the succession of occurrences that ended up in James' death and the Uprising against Rome. Ananus seems to have been sent to Rome at the end of the previous decade in the Roman Governor Cumanus' time (48–52 CE), along with Helcias the Temple Treasurer and possibly Jonathan his brother, after the beating of the Emperor's Servant '*Stephen*,' we have already referred to above, and the Messianic disturbances between Samaritans and Jews in 49 CE which resulted in the crucifixions outside Lydda.[119]

In Rome, Ananus was kept as a hostage because Nero and his wife Poppea seemed to be looking for bribes, that is, until Agrippa II intervened to free him – an altogether more convincing story than the one Acts 24:27 presents regarding the relations of Felix and Paul. Here, the close relationship developed between Ananus and Agrippa II that seems ultimately to have resulted in '*the conspiracy*' to remove James – this, as already suggested, probably had its roots in '*the Temple Wall Affair*' which was erected to block Agrippa II's view of the sacrifices in the Temple.

Josephus gives further details that explain, in the words of the Habakkuk *Pesher*, how he could have been

> *called by the name of Truth at the beginning of his Office, but when he ruled in Israel, his heart became puffed up and he forsook God and betrayed the Laws for the sake of Riches.*[120]

Not only is this fairly vivid, but it is directly followed by the description of how

> *he stole Riches and collected the Riches of the Men of Violence, who rebelled against God. And he took the Riches of the Peoples, thereby further heaping upon himself guilty sinfulness.*[121]

'*Riches*,' of course, was the second of the Damascus Document's '*Three Nets of Belial*' and widely condemned both in the Letter of James and elsewhere at Qumran, so once again we have consistency here. As we also saw, Paul in fact refers to just this expression '*puffed up*' in 1 Corinthians 8:1-13 when attacking those with '*Knowledge*' like James and facilely laboring over the issue of James' – and, as we have also now explained, *MMT's – condemnation of 'things sacrificed to idols*'.

Consensus Qumran scholarship attempts to see in this description one or another of the Maccabean High Priests (mostly Alexander Jannaeus); and '*the Righteous Teacher*,' therefore, some unknown individual in the First Century BC opposed to Alexander. But there is no indication that any Maccabean ever took anyone else's '*Riches*' and '*polluted the Temple*' with them, nor '*profiteered*' in any manner from the predatory activities of '*Violent*' persons such as the Herodians and their accomplices; nor were they ever pictured as being particularly '*Rich*,' though this accusation can be used against any Ruling Class at any time or place. On the other hand, in these passages having to do with Paul and James, we have a clear ambiance of one side opposing '*Gentile*' *gifts in the Temple* (including those by '*Herodians*') and the other side accepting them.

For his part, Ananus '*ruled Israel*' on two separate occasions: the first when he destroyed James in 62 CE; and the second, during the early stages of the Uprising between 66–68 CE before the final siege of Jerusalem began. Before he and his associates were exterminated by *the '*Violent*' Idumaeans* – '*the ᶜArizim*' / '*Anshei-Hamas*' / '*Men of Violence*' of the Habakkuk *Pesher*; '*the ᶜArizei-Go'im*' or '*Violent Ones of the Gentiles*' of the Psalm 37 *Pesher*; '*the Anshei ha-Milhamah*' / '*Men-of-War*' of CDxx.14? – whom '*the Zealots*' called in when the Revolt moved into what could be referred to as its more '*Jacobin*' phase, he did '*rule*' in Israel in virtually an absolute manner. Having said this, *all* High Priests can be said to have '*ruled Israel*' and this is the actual thrust of Paul's allusion, quoted in Acts 23:5, to '*Ananus*'' alter ego, '*Ananias*.'

As we have been attempting to point out, despite this ambiguous reference to '*ruling in Israel*,' almost all the internal allusions in these very important *Pesharim* and related documents such as CD gainsay this identification, on the part of '*Consensus*' Scholars of '*the Wicked Priest*' with one or another of the Maccabeans. This is particularly true when one takes into consideration the militant and uncompromising character of the data accompanying allusions to his antagonist, '*the Righteous Teacher*' which rather accord with the ethos of the Maccabeans, particularly Judas Maccabee – '*Judas the Hammerer*' as he was surnamed – and Alexander Jannaeus, his grand nephew, not to mention his great grand nephew, Aristobulus II, whose conflict with his more accommodating brother Hyrcanus II we have already delineated to some extent above.

The latter, it will be recalled, was supported by the newly-emerging Pharisee Party, the accommodators *par excellence*, whose willingness to bow to Roman hegemony finally brought the Romans into the Country. Ananus' own father had held the High Priesthood from 10–18 CE, a murky period not covered to any extent in Josephus. This is the period in which, according to the allegedly '*spurious Acts*' being circulated in Pontius Pilate's name – therefore called '*The Acti Pilati*' – and mentioned by Eusebius, the *real* 'Jesus' may have died, that is, if we can speak in any really historical way about this death and the events surrounding it.[122]

Ananus the Elder is pictured in John's version of events as participating in the interim examination of Jesus, before he was turned over to Pilate for more secular examination. This episode mainly focuses on how Peter denied he was Jesus' 'Disciple' three times (John 18:13–24). This is paralleled in the Synoptics by an improbable midnight meeting, called on Passover evening by Caiaphas at 'the High Priest's House' (Luke 22:54 and pars.) and consisting of High Priests, Elders, and Sanhedrin – an improbable scenario to say the least. Caiaphas was Ananus' son-in-law and, therefore, the brother-in-law of James' judicial executioner Ananus ben Ananus.

The Psalm 37 Pesher's exegesis of the passage, mentioned above, about 'the Wicked casting down the Meek and the Poor' makes it clear that somehow 'the Wicked of Ephraim and Manasseh' were involved in the destruction of 'the Priest and the Men of his Council.'[123] As almost all commentators agree that this is an esoteric allusion of some kind to what most now call 'Pharisees and Sadducees,' it would be absurd in such a context to put this back into either the First or even Second Century BC. At that time the Sadducees would mainly have been a pro-Maccabean Party. Nor would it be a simple matter to identify any 'Violent Gentiles' at that time to take vengeance on 'the Wicked Priest' for what he did to 'the Righteous Teacher' which is the gist, in fact, of the Pesher. These are the problems that are rarely, if ever, addressed when evaluating Establishment theories of Qumran origins, the majority of which holding one or another of the Maccabees to have been the Wicked Priest.

'The Violent Ones of the Gentiles'

This matter of the vengeance taken by 'the Violent Ones of the Gentiles' for what had been done to the Righteous Teacher is treated in two separate expositions in the Psalm 37 Pesher. The second of these at the end of the Pesher uses, as we just saw, almost the exact language of the Habakkuk Pesher – to say nothing of Isaiah 3:10-11 above, namely 'God will pay him ('the Wicked Priest') his reward by delivering him into the hand of the Violent Ones of the Gentiles.' These 'execute Judgement upon him,' a Judgement which is then described as 'the Judgement on Evil.'[124] In the parallel material in the Habakkuk Pesher about the admonishment of the Wicked Priest, these 'Judgements' reappear as 'the Judgements on Evil,' which they (identity unspecified) inflicted upon 'the flesh of his corpse.'[125]

The Psalm 37 Pesher is replete with the kind of language we have been following and links up perfectly with allusions in the Habakkuk Pesher and the Damascus Document again confirming the interrelatedness of these documents. Its subject is God's 'Righteousness which will be *revealed like Light and (His) Judgement like midday'* (37:6). The interpretation of this and analogous phrases is applied to *'the Assembly'* or *'Church of the Poor' (Ebionim)*. It, like the Messianic *'Root of Planting out of Aaron and Israel'* in the Damascus Document, *'will inherit the Land'* and *'prosper on its good things,'* this last in direct interpretation of an underlying reference to *'ᶜAnayyim'/'Meek'* in 37:11, again deliberately transmuted in the *Pesher* (as in the Habakkuk *Pesher*) into *'the Assembly of the Poor' (Ebionim)*.

Also called *'the Assembly of His Elect,'* as in the Damascus Document, they are again characterized, as we saw, as *'the Penitents of the wilderness who will live for a thousand generations.'*[126] Here not only does the usage *'of the wilderness'* take the place of the *'of Israel'* in CDIV.2, VI.5, and VIII.16/XIX.29, but the phrase *'be-Yeshuᶜa'* – seemingly *'in Salvation' ('Jesus')* – is added and it is stated – in what appears to be yet another variation of the *'Primal Adam'* ideology – that *'all the inheritance of* (instead of *'all the Glory of') Adam will be theirs.'* As in the Habakkuk *Pesher* too, *'God will save them* – the *'saving'* here really being eschatological *'saving'* in the sense of *'Salvation'* – *and deliver them from the hand of the Evil Ones'* (this both quoting and interpreting Psalm 37:40). Because they *'waited on'* Him and *'kept His Way'* (here, of course, both the *'waiting on'* and *'keeping'* language again), they would both *'be exalted'* and – using the words of both Psalm 37:34 and CDI.7–8 above – *'inherit the Land'* and *'see the destruction of '* the same *'Evil Ones.'*[127] Here the *Pesher*, once again, applies this to *'the Assembly'* or *'Church of the Poor'* who will not only *'see the Judgement on Evil'* but, *'with His Chosen Ones'* or *'Elect, rejoice in the True Inheritance'* – a more eschatological promise is hard to imagine.

As in the Habakkuk *Pesher*, *'the Priest'* (meaning *'the Opposition High Priest'*) is specifically identified with *'the Teacher of Righteousness'* and, paralleling usages in the Damascus Document and *Florilegium* again, too, about *'the Star who came to Damascus'* and *'the Interpreter of the Torah'*; it is he whom *'God chose to stand before Him'* (the *'Standing One'* ideology again or, if one prefers, the *'Imam'* who *'stands in front of'* in Shiᶜite Islam). Contrary to *'the Spouter of Lying'* or Paul himself in 1 Corinthians 3:9–17, he has been *'prepared'* or *'established'* by God *'to build* (the *'building'* imagery, the Habakkuk *Pesher* will apply to *'the Assembly on Lying'* and *'worthless service'* the Liar will *'erect'* and which Paul in 1 Corinthians 8:1 uses to describe himself and attack those opposed to him as *'puffed up'*) *the Assembly of His Chosen Ones for Him'* – in CDIV.3–4, the same *'Chosen Ones'* or *'Elect'* who are *'the Sons of Zadok'*; here in the Psalm 37 *Pesher*, they are *'the Assembly'* or *'Church of the Poor.'* These will *'be saved* (again, the usage is the same as in the Habakkuk *Pesher*) *from all the Nets of Belial.'*[128]

Here, not only do we hear – again replicating the language of both the Habakkuk *Pesher* and Damascus Document – about how '*the Wicked plotted against the Righteous gnashing his teeth at him*' (Psalm 37:12); but a new category of individual is now evoked, '*the Violent Ones of the Covenant in the House of Judah*' – referred to also, as the text proceeds – as '*the Evil Men of Israel*.' These, too, are '*cursed by Him and will be cut off*' (37:23) – again our '*cutting off*' language used throughout the *Pesher* and CD and by Paul in Galatians 5:12 above.[129]

This allusion to '*gnashing of teeth*' is a familiar one in the parables attributed to 'Jesus' in the Gospels. Acts 7:54, in particular, however, uses it to describe how *the Jewish mob behaved towards Stephen* – they '*gnashed their teeth at him*' – after Stephen accused them of '*being uncircumcised in heart and ears*' (sic), '*always resisting the Holy Spirit*,' '*persecuting the Prophets*' and *being* '*the Traitors and murderers of the Just One*' (very congenial allegations) right before his vision of '*the Son of Man standing at the right hand of God*' (7:50-56). When one realizes that Stephen (whose name in Greek, as we saw, means '*Crown*' – '*the Crown of Righteousness*' in 2 Timothy 4:8 above and '*the Crown*' of James' unshorn '*Nazirite*' hair – in Acts is a stand-in for James), one appreciates the significance of finding this important allusion about '*gnashing his teeth*' at this point in the Psalm 37 *Pesher* where '*plots against the Righteous One*' are being described.

Again, just as in the Nahum *Pesher* previously, '*the Man of Lying*,' right from the beginning of the Psalm 37 *Pesher*, is described as:

> *leading Many astray with deceitful words, for they have chosen Emptiness and did not listen to the Interpreter of Knowledge* (is this the same '*Emptiness*' as in the '*Empty Man*' allusion in James 2:10? It is certainly the same '*worthlessness*' as evoked with regard to '*the Lying Spouter*''s '*service*' in the Habakkuk *Pesher* where, as in the Damascus Document, the fact of his '*leading Many astray*' is also referred to).[130]

Moreover, the *Pesher* also refers to the period of '*forty years*' – alluded to in the Damascus Document as the '*approximate time*' that would pass from '*the gathering of the Unique Guide*' ('*Yoreh ha-Yahid*,' as opposed to '*Moreh ha-Yahad*') to the Completion of the Time of the Men-of-War (*Anshei ha-Milhamah*), *who walked with the Man of Lying*' – '*to the Completion of (the Time of) all Evil*.' In fact, the very same word '*completed*' is used regarding this eventuality in both documents.[131] Again, just as in CDxx.13-17, during this period '*the Wrath of God would be kindled against Israel*' and '*there will be no King, no Prince, no Judge, no one to rebuke with Righteousness*' (Hosea 3:4); here in the Psalm 37 *Pesher*, at the end of this Time, '*there would not be found on Earth a single Evil Man*' – to be sure, a slight exaggeration –

and '*the Man of Lying*' and his confederates – in the Habakkuk *Pesher*, '*the Traitors*' who in CDxx.11–12 '*reject the Covenant and the Faith they erected in the Land of Damascus which is the New Covenant*') would be '*cursed*' (just as he presumably would '*curse*' others), '*cut off*,' and '*exterminated*' (37:34).

This allusion to '*approximately forty years*' is clearly imprecise, '*forty*' being the usual number in the Bible used to indicate a fairly long, if indeterminate period of time, and, in this instance, '*not a single Evil Man to be found on Earth*' clearly being a little over-optimistic as well. Furthermore, '*the Man of Lying*' has either not yet died or the author(s) have no idea of his exact fate, nor of those '*Rebels who did not turn aside from the Way of Traitors*'[132] ('*Traitors to the New Covenant*'/'*Covenant-Breakers*'/ and '*Violent Ones*' in CD and 1QpHab), who are his confederates. If these have anything in common with either the New Testament's Paul or Josephus' '*Saulos*' and their other colleagues' this completely accords with what one would expect; since after one or the other of these went off to Rome to appeal to Caesar or the like, the writers of documents of this kind would have had little or no idea of the actual fate of these sorts of individuals, only that immediately after the death of James ('*the gathering of the Unique Teacher*'?), they were still alive.

For the *Pesher*, '*the Violent Ones of the Covenant who are in the House of Judah*' (meaning again, '*Jews*' not *non-Jews*) '*plotted to destroy* (here the usage really is '*destroy*' and not simply '*swallow*' or '*consume*') *the Doers of the Torah who were in the Council of the Community* (these are the same '*House of Judah*' and '*Doers of the Torah*' found in the Habakkuk *Pesher*'s decisive interpretation of Habakkuk 2:4); *but God will not deliver them into their hand.*'[133] Moreover it is also the same '*plotting*' as that of '*the Wicked Priest*' in the Habakkuk *Pesher* who '*plotted to destroy the Poor.*' Here in the Psalm 37 *Pesher*, it is almost immediately followed by the description of how '*the Evil Ones of Ephraim and Manasseh* – also referred to in the Nahum *Pesher* and normally thought of in this context as analogues of '*the Scribes and Pharisees*' or '*the Pharisees and Sadducees*' of the Gospels – *who sought to lay hands on the Priest and the Men of his Council in the time of trial that came upon them*' (this is the same '*period of testing*' that was referred to earlier in the same column regarding '*the Congregation*' or '*Church of the Poor*' who were ultimately going to be '*saved from all the snares of Belial*').[134]

'*Afterwards* – that is, after his destruction of the Righteous Teacher and the Men of his Council – they (meaning '*the Wicked of Ephraim and Manasseh*,' including '*the Wicked Priest*' who would '*be paid his reward*' as well – this is a different kind of '*Reward*' than that '*paid to Judas iscariot*' in the orthodox Gospels) *will be delivered into the hand of the Violent Ones of the Gentiles for Judgement* ('*the* ^c*Arizei-Go'im*').' Despite an earlier reference to

'*God redeeming them from their hand*' and the later one in exposition of Psalm 37:33-34 – after '*the Wicked Priest laid hands on the Righteous Teacher*,' *attempting to* or actually '*putting him to death*' (the text is fragmentary here and the meaning imprecise) – about *God* '*not abandoning him, nor permitting him to be condemned at His Judgement*' ('*the Last Judgement*'?) and '*being exalted*' and '*rejoicing in inheriting Truth*' and '*being saved*'; one should appreciate that '*the Righteous Teacher*' and '*the Men of his Council*' were for the most part destroyed and this, like the previous '*God will not deliver them into their hands*,' and there '*not remaining upon the Earth a single Wicked Man*,' simply represents a pious hope or – what is probably more to the point – an expression of certitude in *their ultimate* '*Salvation*.'[135]

Regarding '*the Men of his Council*' (in the Habakkuk *Pesher*, equivalent to '*the Simple of Judah doing Torah*' and '*the Poor*'), it should be appreciated as well that in Josephus, James is executed with several others.[136] We should also keep a firm hold on these allusions to '*the Violent Ones*' (*ʿArizim*), a usage appearing in several Gospel allusions to the coming of John the Baptist – '*from whose days until now, the Kingdom of Heaven is taken by Violence and Violent Ones seize it by force*' (Matthew 11:12/Luke 16:16). The problem, however, is that the elapsed time between the time when Jesus supposedly says these things and John's coming is, at least superficially, quite negligible.[137] Still, the allusion is illustrative.

It is also paralleled in the Habakkuk *Pesher*. There, '*the Violent Ones*' are simply '*the ʿArizim*' – no '*Goʿim*' or '*Gentiles*' attached – nor, for that matter, any '*House of Judah*' or '*the Evil Ones of Israel*.' Rather, these '*Violent Ones*' together with '*the Man of Lying*' are identified with '*the Covenant-Breakers*' and '*the Traitors to the Laws of God and the New Covenant*' (this last, a reconstruction) and '*to the Last Days*.'[138] As already suggested, all seemingly participate in the Scriptural exegesis sessions of '*the Priest*'/'*the Righteous Teacher*,' as they are specifically described as '*not believing what they heard*' from his '*mouth*' concerning '*all that was going to happen to the Last Generation*.'[139] Clearly, therefore, some of these, like '*the Violent Ones of the Covenant in the House of Judah*' or '*the Evil Ones of Israel*' are not simply external adversaries, but also have to be seen as internal ones too.

Later in the commentary, these same '*ʿArizim*' seem to be referred to as '*the Men of Violence*' (*Hamas*), but the context would appear to be the same – that of the Wicked Priest, '*whose heart became puffed up*' and *who* '*stole and collected the Riches of the Men of Violence, who rebelled against God, and took the Riches of the Peoples*' ('*Peoples*,' in our view, once again denoting '*Herodians*' – what '*the Wicked Priest*' was doing here, as we shall also see below, was illegally '*gathering*' and '*collecting the Riches*' which they '*stole*' and depositing them in the Temple, thereby '*polluting it*').[140]

As we just saw above, these would also appear to be described in another particularly critical juncture of the Damascus Document, as '*the Men-of-War who walked with the Man of Lying*' *after the seeming death of the* '*Unique*' or '*Righteous Teacher.*' Here '*Men-of-War*' seems to better encapsulate the sense of the term than '*Anshei-Hamas,*' but both will do. In the Habakkuk *Pesher,* as we just saw, in the context of the exposition of 2:5-6, following the exposition of how '*the Torah-doing Jews*' were to '*be saved from the House of Judgement*' and picking up Habakkuk 2:4's '*puffed up,*' these '*Men of Violence*' (*Anshei-Hamas*) are described as '*rebelling against God*' and the'*puffed-up*' '*Wicked Priest,*' as '*deserting God and betraying the Laws* ('*Hukkim*' again) *for the sake of Riches.*' At the same time, '*the Last Priests of Jerusalem*' – identical in our view with '*Chief Priests*' in the New Testament – are described as '*gathering Riches and profiteering from the spoils of the Peoples*' ('*the Peoples*' again, in our view, signifying '*Herodians*').[141]

Herodian '*Men-of-War,*' Costobarus, and the '*Idumaean*' Connection

Though these are extremely complex allusions, if one is careful about them and their translation, their sense does emerge. It is our position that we must see these allusions to either '*Violent Ones,*' '*Men of Violence,*' or '*Men-of-War*' on both sides of the political and religious spectrum as either pro- or anti-Revolutionary Herodians or other people with military training. Individuals of this kind certainly existed in the context of the events we are speaking about in the First Century – people like Niger of Perea, Philip the son of Jacimus, and Silas – preceding him as the Head of Agrippa I's Army – all described in Josephus. Nor is this to mention warriors like those in Queen Helen of Adiabene's family, namely, Izates, Monobazus, Kenedaeus and others – for the purist, ostensibly foreigners, but still part and parcel of the Revolutionary Struggle.

Even Paul would originally seem to have been an individual of this kind. As we have seen, his Herodian namesake '*Saulos,*' a relative of King Agrippa, is portrayed in just such a '*Violent*' manner, *creating mayhem after the stoning of James* (or '*Stephen*' as the case may be). So are the '*Violent*' henchmen of '*the High Priests,*' who are depicted in several notices in this context here in the *Antiquities* – but also in the *Talmud* – as '*stealing the sustenance of the Poor.*' They too are not really differentiable from this sort of person. As for '*Saulos,*' Josephus describes him, together with his two violent, '*Herodian*' relatives, '*Antipas and Costobarus,*' as already highlighted, as '*getting together a multitude of wicked wretches...finding favor because of their kinship to Agrippa, but using Violence with the People and very ready to plunder those weaker than themselves.*' One should note here the vocabulary parallels with Qumran above, in particular the allusion to '*using Violence with the People*,' but also '*plundering*,' '*Wickedness*' and, even possibly, '*the Many*' denoting the rank and file of the Community. It is at this point Josephus laconically notes, '*and from that moment, it principally came to pass that our city suffered greatly – all things growing from bad to worse*.'[142]

We have already shown that Paul, Agrippa II, and Bernice, his fornicating sister – with whom Agrippa II also possibly had an illicit connection – were acquainted, and all had connections going high up in Nero's household. So did Josephus' '*Saulos*.' In Josephus' last notice about him, Josephus describes him as going to Corinth to personally brief Nero about the disastrous situation in Palestine. Interestingly enough, as previously remarked, both Josephus' '*Saulos*' and Paul disappear from the scene at approximately the same time or, at most, within a year or two of each other, and both seemingly after appeals to Nero.

We have already noted the stoning of Stephen in the Forties as a stand-in for the stoning of James in the Sixties and how both the former in Acts and the latter in Josephus are followed by the account of the violent and predatory activities of someone named '*Saulos*' – in both instances undertaken because of high-level influence. These are the kinds of connections that move beyond coincidence. As we have observed as well, the mention of '*Antipas*' and '*Costobarus*' always in connection with Saulos may have something to do with either his or their genealogical origins, Costobarus being the real '*Idumaean*' in Herodian genealogies.

This Costobarus had originally been married to the first Herod's sister – the first (or second) '*Salome*' – and seems to have been descended from an upper-class '*Idumaean*'/'*Edomite*' background. These last are the People in Southern Transjordan and Judea, claiming an ancient relationship to Jews, especially through Esau but also possibly Ishmael, and virtually indistinguishable from what in Roman Times came to be known as '*Arabs*.' During the Maccabean Era, groups of these seem to have been forcibly converted to Judaism. When Herod executed his own uncle Joseph after the rumor of unfaithfulness between him and his own Maccabean first wife '*Mariamme*' ('*Mary*' – the first '*Joseph and Mary*' story), he appointed Costobarus to replace him as Governor of Idumaea and Gaza, the two areas from which Herod's family came, as we have seen.[143]

Costobarus, then, promptly entered into intrigue with Anthony's consort Cleopatra (and Herod's mortal enemy) to get what he considered to be his proper patrimony. Discovering this, Herod waited for his opportunity to deal with Costobarus and found it when Salome divorced him.[144] This is the first, clear instance of that '*divorce*' among Herodians so roundly condemned at Qumran. So totally contrary to Jewish

Law was it seen to be – at least, divorce on the part of a woman – that even Josephus stops his narrative at this point to launch into his first excursus on why it should be condemned. The last time he mentions it is in regard to Drusilla's and Bernice's excesses in this regard a century later.[145] One cannot emphasize too strongly that these are things condemned at Qumran as '*fornication*,' particularly in the '*Three Nets of Belial*' section of CDiv.15-v.15.

There is a direct line from these behavior patterns to those of Herodias, over whose infractions in this regard too – not to mention '*niece marriage*' – John the Baptist was executed. Herodias' niece Drusilla behaved in exactly the same manner – to say nothing of Herodias' own behaviour and that of her daughter Salome (as we can now see, probably named after Herod's sister – if not the first Maccabean, Alexander Jannaeus' wife '*Salome Alexandra*') – when she divorced Azizus the King of Emesa (present day Homs in Syria, who had specifically circumcised himself at her father Agrippa I's insistence in order to marry her) to contract a more advantageous marriage – with the connivance, as we have seen, of the omnipresent '*Simon Magus*' – with the brutal Roman Governor Felix. So did her sister Bernice (whom Josephus describes as the '*the Richest Woman*' in Palestine) when, after having been accused of '*incest*' with her brother Agrippa II, she married Polemo, King of Cilicia, who had also circumcised himself to marry her (Josephus says, '*because she was so Rich*'), but whom she too ultimately divorced in order to take up her illicit relationship with Titus, the destroyer of Jerusalem. She had also originally been married to her '*uncle*' – her father's brother, Herod of Chalcis – another example of the '*niece marriage*,' so frowned upon at Qumran. The catalogue of all these '*incestuous*'-style marriages and divorces on the part of '*Herodian*' women is so extensive as to be definitive.

Not only does the original Herod end up executing this Costobarus but, having also executed his own wife, Mariamme, her grandfather Hyrcanus II, and her mother Alexandra – all of whom, as Josephus himself makes plain, abetted his rise to power – he takes the opportunity too to dispose of all other pro-Maccabeans, whom this first '*Costobarus*' seems to have been sheltering in Idumaea. The connection of this '*Costobarus*' with pro-Maccabeans is certainly an interesting one. So effective was Herod in extirpating Maccabeans, when he was not marrying them – and even when he was, that even Josephus himself was forced to remark:

There were none left of the kindred of Hyrcanus (i.e., Mariamme's grandfather, the most pliant and accommodating of all Maccabeans) *and no one left with sufficient dignity to put a stop to what he did against the Jewish Laws.*

Josephus continues, using the *exact* phrase, '*rebelled against the Laws*' that the Habakkuk *Pesher* used above regarding those it described as '*the Men of Violence*' (*Anshei-Hamas*):

> *Herod rebelled against the Laws...polluting the ancient constitution by introducing foreign practices...by which means we became guilty of great Wickedness thereafter, while those religious observances that used to lead the multitude to Piety were now neglected.*[146]

This is a very strong indictment and here, again, are the two points about '*Piety*' and antagonism to foreign practices we have been following.

Later, in discussing how Herod thought higher of the two Pharisees, Pollio and Sameas (Hillel and Shammai?) '*than their mortal nature deserved*' and describing his vindictiveness, Josephus tells how Herod brought endless numbers of malcontents to fortresses like Hyrcania and Machaeros on either side of the Dead Sea – this last being the '*Fortress*' a half century later in Perea where his son Herod Antipas, himself a probable '*kinsman*' of riotous '*Herodians*,' such as Saulos and Costobarus above, put John the Baptist to death.[147] In doing so, Josephus baldly tells us that it was Herod who was the first to introduce '*Innovations into the religious practices of the Jews to the detriment of their Ancestral Customs*' – meaning that it was he, Herod, who was the first '*Innovator*' not '*the Revolutionaries*,' as Josephus later claims when discussing the latter's decision to reject gifts and sacrifices in the Temple on behalf of foreigners, which triggered the War against Rome. These later '*Innovators*' were only attempting to restore the *status quo ante*. This, of course, is exactly the sense of the manner in which CDiv.15-17 describes the '*nets*' Belial set up as '*three kinds of Righteousness to ensnare Israel.*' It is on the basis of allusions and notices of this kind that we can link up the '*Belial*' usage with '*Herodians.*'

There is more however. Since, as we saw, '*Bela^c*,' a name based on the same Hebrew root as '*Belial*,' was the first Edomite King according to Biblical genealogies (Genesis 36:32 and *pars.*); this relationship has an even more concrete foundation and relates not only to the perception of the '*Herodian*' dynasty as '*Idumaean*,' but also to the language circle centering about the name '*Balaam*,' another linguistic variant of both '*Belial*' and '*Bela^c*' in Hebrew. In fact, the only really pure '*Idumaean*' in Herodian genealogies is '*Costobarus*' himself. For its part, '*Balaam*' pops up in the New Testament as a linguistic variant of '*Belial*' in the Damascus Document. For Revelation 2:14, as we saw,

> *Balaam taught Balak to cast down (balein) a net before the Sons of Israel to eat*

things sacrificed to idols and commit fornication.

Here, of course, we have the telltale '*casting down*' language in Greek, linking up with the '*swallowing*' language in Hebrew which reappears in the Habakkuk *Pesher's* description of the destruction or deaths of the Righteous Teacher and '*the Poor*' of his Council – and what God, in turn, did to the Wicked Priest, that is, '*swallowed him.*' The relationship of this '*casting down*' language in Greek and this '*swallowing*' language in Hebrew to Herodian behavior and both, in turn, to each other, should not be too difficult to recognize.

This section of Revelation is also steeped in the language of '*works Righteousness*' ('*I will give to each of you according to your works*' – 2:23) and antagonism to '*fornication*' and '*Riches.*' It combines both the language of '*Satan*' (2:9–13, mentioned three times) with that of how '*the Devil (Diabolos) is about to cast*' (*balein*) some of those being addressed '*into prison*' (2:10). Not only does it transform the language of the Damascus Document's third of Belial's '*nets*' into the language of James' instructions to overseas communities in Acts, it takes on a distinctly '*Jamesian*' cast. Now that this very allusion to '*things sacrificed to idols*' has appeared in '*MMT*' in the context of *opposing Gentile gifts of grain in the Temple*, '*skins sacrificed to idols*' (a principal concern of the Temple Scroll too), and *Gentile sacrifices generally*, we can see how all these things are connected.[148]

2 Peter 2:15, another letter which, as we have seen, is drenched in the imagery of Qumran, also speaks of those '*led astray from the Straight Way, following the Way of Balaam the son of Beᶜor,*' and replicates almost precisely the description of '*the Liar's*' activities in CD1.14–18 as well. It also speaks of the '*soul of the Righteous*' (2:8), duplicating the language the Damascus Document uses at the end of the First Column to describe the attack on '*the Righteous One*' by those '*rejoicing in strife among the People*' as well as like-minded phraseology used throughout the Qumran Hymns.[149] The same is true of the Letter of Jude, James' '*brother,*' referring to '*the error of Balaam*' (1:11).

Both Belaᶜ and Balaam, as previously remarked as well, however improbably, were also in some sense considered '*Sons of Beᶜor,*' thus completing this whole circle and tying these esotericisms even closer together. It is not incurious that in the Temple Scroll where '*ballaᶜ*' / '*Belaᶜ*' – either reading is possible – is evoked amid reference to the classes of persons to be debarred from the Temple and where '*skins sacrificed to idols*' are alluded to as an aspect of '*polluting the Temple*' and banned from the Temple for the same reason as '*things sacrificed to idols*' were in James' directives to overseas communities ('*skins,*' of course only being the special case); the language again appears to incorporate an esoteric play of some kind on the name '*Be^cor*,' that is, '*be-^corot*'/'*with skins*,' just as it does the term '*balla^c*'/'*swallowed*' or '*Bela^c*.'

Where the '*Idumaeans*,' in particular, are concerned – these are the same '*Idumaeans*,' according to Josephus, that a century later take the side of '*the Zealots*' and come into Jerusalem at their request and annihilate all the collaborating classes among the Jews including the High Priests – most notably James' judicial executioner Ananus and a few others, whose deaths, as we have already indicated, Josephus describes in gory detail.[150] It is these '*Idumaeans*,' no doubt including an assortment of pro-Revolutionary Herodian '*Men-of-War*' and other '*Violent*' persons that we identify with these '*Violent Ones of the Gentiles*' – mentioned in these critical passages from the Psalm 37 *Pesher* as taking vengeance for what was done to '*the Righteous Teacher*' (whatever this was) – which dovetail so impressively with similar notices in the Habakkuk *Pesher*, we have already described and will describe further below.

They are probably to be identified as well with '*the Violent Ones*' who, at the beginning of the Habakkuk *Pesher*, take part in the scriptural exegesis sessions of '*the Righteous Teacher*' and at this point would appear to be allied with '*the Liar*' and other '*Traitors to the New Covenant*' against him. It is interesting that in the materials in CDxx.13–17 where '*the Men-of-War*' are said to '*walk with the Liar*' after the '*gathering in*' or *death of 'the Unique*' or '*Righteous Teacher*,' such '*Men of Scoffing*' are said, it will be recalled, to have '*spoken mistakenly about the Laws of Righteousness and rejected the Covenant and the Compact, the New Covenant, which they erected in the Land of Damascus*' – the Hebrew word '*reject*' (*ma'as*) always being tied to '*the Spouter of Lying*'s activities in the Scrolls.

As we saw, Josephus specifically designates the Leader of these Idumaeans as '*Niger of Perea*' – Perea being the area across Jordan where John the Baptist was active and met his death at the hands of Herod Antipas around 34-36 CE (Josephus' dating).[151] This would be around the same time that Aretas, *the 'Arab' King of Petra* – no doubt connected in some manner to such '*Idumaeans*' – took control of Damascus, coeval with the mission of some kind, '*Saul*' or '*Paul*' undertakes to '*Damascus*,' when clearly still a young man, from which he has to escape from Aretas' soldiers by having himself '*let down in a basket*' from its walls – the same episode that Acts 9:3-25 exploits to describe Paul's conversion on the way to Damascus and his subsequent attacks on the Jews there. All this is very murky, but clearly the situation is somewhat different than Acts describes it.

Niger of Perea and other '*Violent*' Herodian '*Men-of-War*'

It is a not incurious coincidence that individuals with names paralleling these '*Herodian*' Men-of-War, like Niger, Silas, and Philip, again turn up in the career of Paul. For Acts 13:1, it will be recalled, one '*Simeon called Niger*' appears among the '*prophets and teachers in the Assembly ('Church')* *at Antioch*,' along with Barnabas, Luke (most likely, '*Lucius of Cyrene*') and someone, as we saw, called '*Manaen the foster-brother of Herod the Tetrarch.*' This name, as already noted, is obviously an obfuscation of some kind, probably for the '*Ananias*' whom Acts portrays as greeting Paul in '*Damascus*.' We have already remarked how an individual by the same name converts Queen Helen of Adiabene in a chronologically parallel manner, taking a patently Pauline line on the circumcision of her two sons Izates and Monobazus.

'*Herod the Tetrarch*,' of course, is the same '*Herod Antipas*,' who married his half-brother's wife, Herodias, on which account John the Baptist was executed. If we consider the '*Saul*' in Josephus and the '*Saul*' in the New Testament to be identical, then, as already suggested, it would make more sense to think the ascription '*foster-brother*,' more properly, applied to Paul than to the garbled '*Manaen*' and that, on the contrary, *Paul was the one* '*brought up with Herod the Tetrarch*' – therefore his various connections with him, including his mission to Damascus where he fell afoul of Aretas' soldiers and had to run for his life, not from '*the Jews*' but from '*the Arabs*,' as depicted in another typical New Testament reversal.

Both Niger and Silas (whom Josephus describes as '*a deserter to the Jews from the Army of King Agrippa*' – meaning, he was another Herodian '*Man-of-War*') also take part in the heroic assault on the Roman troops coming up the Pass at Beit Horon to put down the Revolt in Jerusalem, in which Helen of Adiabene's two descendants, Monobazus and Kenedaeus, were killed.[152] Though Josephus calls this Silas '*a Babylonian*,' like Queen Helen's descendants, he was probably from Northern Syria or Iraq too and, together with another individual – not inconsequentially named '*John the Essene*' – was one of the early Commanders of the Uprising. These three, Niger, Silas, and John the Essene, thereafter, launch one of the initial attacks along the sea coast at Ashkelon, formerly the birthplace of Herod's father. While John and Silas are killed in this engagement, Josephus never stops recounting Niger's '*numerous feats of valor*' – in other words, he clearly very much admired him.

In the aftermath of this assault, Josephus tells another story with strong connections to the Gospel picture of 'Jesus' about how Niger, after leaping from a burning tower and being left for dead by his friends, rather '*found refuge in a subterranean cave*':

> *Three days later his lamenting friends, while searching for his corpse to bury it,*
> *overheard his voice beneath them. His reappearance filled all Jewish hearts with*
> *unlooked-for joy, thinking that God's Providence had preserved him to be their*
> *Commander in future conflicts.*[153]

To be sure, the resemblance of this story to the New Testament presentation of 'Jesus' spending three days in the tomb before being resurrected should be plain, but this is not the only overlap between the Gospel 'Jesus' and '*Niger.*' Josephus recounts the story of Niger's death by execution at the hands of '*the Zealots*' after they had taken control of the Uprising and one can imagine the bitterness this would have caused among Niger's erstwhile '*Idumaean*' supporters, which would be extremely fertile ground for similar stories about 'Jesus' in the Bible. In fact, it almost seems as if some of the Gospel picture of 'Jesus'' death is created out of deference to these supporters.

In Josephus' account of Niger's death as a '*Traitor*' – like the picture of 'Jesus'' death in the Gospels – Niger is '*dragged through the midst of the city,* *vehemently protesting and pointing to his wounds*' for execution outside Jerusalem's gates.

> *In his dying moments, Niger called upon their heads the vengeance of the*
> *Romans ('the Kittim' in the Habakkuk Pesher), famine and pestilence on top*
> *of the horrors of War and, to crown it all, internecine strife. All of these curses upon*
> *these miserable people were executed by God, including the most Righteous*
> *Judgements, which they were now fore-ordained to suffer because of their outra*
> *geous behaviour.*[154]

Not only does this almost completely recapitulate and, yet, reverse the language of the Habakkuk and Psalm 37 *Peshers*, it is incorporated almost precisely into the '*Little Apocalypses*' the Gospels attributed to their 'Jesus' on the eve of *his* not unsimilar execution. One sees in the Qumran documents the opposite side of the coin of the point-of-view of Josephus and these New Testament stories.

It is individuals such as '*Niger*' and Josephus' '*Silas*' that we would group under the designation found in the Psalm 37 *Pesher* of '*the Violent* *Ones of the Gentiles*' ('*Arizei-Go'im*). Niger would have been seen, no doubt, as an only-superficially '*Judaized*' Gentile by groups as extreme as those '*Zealots*' who executed him for fraternization with the enemy. By contrast, Helen's two sons – not to mention her two kinsmen who martyred themselves at Beit Horon – because of their '*zeal*,' would seem to have enjoyed greater acceptance. '*Philip the son of Jacimus*,' another of these Herodian '*Men-of-War*' of questionable loyalty and, also, possibly of mixed blood, cannot be separated too far from the mythologized '*Philip*,' encountered from time to time in the Gospels and Acts and at the same time characterized as one of '*the Apostles*' and one of '*the Seventy*,' depending on which reckoning one chooses to follow.[155]

'*The Seventy*' is, of course, the number of Jewish judges in the Sanhedrin with the authority to pass death sentences, such as the one above. One particularly graphic description of such an execution, after the Uprising had begun, is presented by Josephus in relation to one '*Zachariah*' right after the '*Zealot*' execution of Ananus and before that of Niger. This '*Zachariah*,' whom Josephus calls '*very Rich*' – thereby fulfilling another Qumran and '*Jamesian*' bugaboo – was actually put on trial before a '*Council of the Seventy*' which '*the Zealots*' called for the purpose of dealing with '*Traitors*' of this kind. Josephus repeatedly refers to this '*Council*' as '*the Seventy*' though he claims in this case they had actually voted for acquittal. Nevertheless, '*the Zealots slew him in the midst of the Temple*' and '*forthwith cast his body*' – like Stephen in Acts – *without burial* from '*the Pinnacle*' or '*ramparts of the Temple*' *into the valley below.*

This is the more likely origin of the portrayal of 'Jesus'' reference to the murder of '*Zachariah son of Barachias whom you slew between the Temple and the altar*.' Of course, though ostensibly directed against '*the Blind Guides*' and '*the Scribes and Pharisees*' in Matthew's '*Little Apocalypse*' once again; it ends up, as we have seen, in the horrendous and famous '*blood libel*': *Jerusalem, Jerusalem which kills all the Prophets and stones those who have been sent to her*' (23:16–37 and pars.). Moreover, it is at this point that Jesus is also portrayed as using John the Baptist's words earlier: '*Serpents, Offspring of Vipers, how shall you escape the Judgement of Hell*' – this, rather than any other '*Zechariah*' whether in Chronicles or the Prophets.[156]

It would also appear more likely that this episode in Josephus (written when the latter was in a particularly vicious frame of mind because of the matching murder of his friend '*Jesus ben Gamala*') formed the basis for naming the '*Tomb of Zechariah*' in the Kedron Valley beneath the Pinnacle of the Temple – this perhaps, too, part of the origin of the legend of James being '*cast down*' *from the Pinnacle of the Temple* –next to the tomb Christian tradition attributes to James and the reason probably for this ascription as well. To complicate this situation still further, recently an inscription was found on the needle-like tomb on the other side of this 'Tomb of Zechariah,' usually called '*The Tomb of Absalom*' after David's son by that name. But the inscription, which was translated by Emile

Puech and Joseph Zias and dated by them to the Fourth Century CE, instead attempts to tie that tomb to the individual Luke 1:5-79 refers to to as '*Zachariah the father of John the Baptist*,' calling him '*a Martyr*' and '*a very Pious Priest*,' at least the second of which is interesting. Notwithstanding, in what way John the Baptist's father could be seen as '*a Martyr*' (implying, therefore, that he was '*a Christian*') stretches credulity to the breaking and both the designation and the inscription should probably to be ascribed to a Fourth-Century pilgrim – himself '*a very Pious' one!*[157]

Where '*Philip*' is concerned – '*one of the Seven*' in Acts and '*one of the Seventy*' in early Church literature – we have already seen that he was the Commander of Agrippa II's bodyguard. He would also appear to have been a close associate of Josephus' '*Saulos*' and went with him and Costobarus on a mission on behalf of the '*Peace*'-Coalition inside the City, composed of '*the Men of Power*' (the Herodians), '*the Chief Priests*,' and '*the principal Pharisees*,' to the Roman Army outside Jerusalem to get them to come into the City and put down the Uprising.[158] These kinds of parallels in the lives of the two '*Saulos*''s, to say nothing of the two '*Philip*''s, just increase the suspicion of some kind of correlation between them.

Philip even went on a parallel mission to Nero to explain his behavior in surrendering Agrippa II's Palace and/or the Citadel at the start of the War. In fact, he and Saulos were either in Agrippa's Palace or the Citadel when its garrison surrendered and all were butchered except the Chief Captain (the predecessor of whom rescued Paul from the Jewish mob in Acts 21:31-38). He, it will be recalled, had agreed to circumcise himself at the intervention of one '*Gurion the son of Nicomedes*' (probably a reversal of '*Nakdimon ben Gurion*') and someone again called '*Ananias the son of Zadok*.' In Acts 21:8–14, as we saw, Paul stays with Philip in Caesarea and receives the second of '*Agabus*''*prophecies*.' It was here, too, that Acts 21:9 exaggerated the number of his daughters from two to '*four virgin daughters who prophesied*,' never really heard from again and all now part and parcel of its evasive obscurantism. Josephus, too, remarks one '*Philip the son of Jacimus*'' two daughters, but for him, as we saw as well, they miraculously escaped the wholesale butchery that occurred following the fall of Gamala on the cuff between Galilee and Gaulonitus.[159]

Even if people like Saulos, Philip, and Costobarus were not originally part of this Movement and reckoned among '*the Men of Violence*' or those called '*the Violent Ones*' who, in both in the Habakkuk *Pesher* and the Damascus Document, were probably to be reckoned as '*Covenant-Breakers*' and '*Traitors to the New Covenant in the Land of Damascus*,' there can be little doubt that '*Men-of-War*' like Niger carried on the revolutionary tradition across the Jordan in Perea and Idumaea before he was eventually executed. Furthermore, men like Silas, John *the Essene*, and Queen Helen's *'kinsmen Kenedaeus and Monobazus'* certainly were part of this tradition and the overlap of three of these with the names of persons associated with Paul in the New Testament, such as *'Philip,' 'Silas'* (a name which, like another of Paul's traveling companions *'Titus'* or *'Timothy,'* probably corresponds to his more Latinized *alter ego 'Silvanus'*), and *'Niger'* – while admittedly speculative – certainly is curious. If the *'Paul'/'Saulos'* identity holds, so do a number of these others.

The matter of *'Philip,'* living with his *'four virgin daughters who prophesied'* in Caesarea, is especially vexing, since we can definitely link *'Philip the son of Jacimus'* and Josephus' *'Saulos'* very closely together in their activities. In fact, Acts 23:35 definitively places Paul in Agrippa II's Palace in Caesarea after his rescue by Roman troops from Jerusalem. There, as we saw, he spent two years or more in extended conversations with persons like Felix and Drusilla and Agrippa II and Bernice before going to Rome to see Nero. In conclusion: Philip, Saulos, Costobarus, and Antipas all appear to have been in Agrippa II's Palace or the Citadel in Jerusalem – presumably representing his interests since he had been barred from Jerusalem together with his sister – when it was besieged by *'the Zealots'* some four years afterwards when the War broke out.

Later this *'Antipas'* who, like his father *'Helcias,'* Josephus says was *'Treasurer of the Temple,'* was pulled from prison and butchered by an assassin sent by such *'Zealots'* or *'Brigands,'* Josephus claims was actually called either *'John'* or *'Dorcas.'*[160] Who are we to imagine this person was supposed be (does this have anything to do with the weird *'Dorcas'* referred to in Acts 8:39)? Though no final conclusions can be drawn from all of this data, the implications are truly worrisome. If Paul came back to Palestine after going to Rome in 60 CE – the note upon which Acts ends coincident with James' death in 62 CE – before or after going to Spain and as something resembling Nero's agent or *in his service*, as his close colleague Epaphroditus seems to have been; then of course the missing link would be filled, as would the reason for Saulos' return four years later to see Nero in Corinth and report on the situation in Palestine.

However these things may be, it is these *'Violent Ones of the Gentiles'* who, according to the Psalm 37 *Pesher*, *'take Vengeance'* or *'execute the Judgement (on Evil) on the Wicked Priest,'* the same *'Judgements on Evil,'* we shall see, they execute *'upon his corpse'* in the Habakkuk *Pesher* below. Having said this, these *'Violent Gentiles'* are not necessarily looked upon in a friendly manner, any more than *'the Idumaeans'* are in Josephus by *'the Zealots,'* one of whose leaders, Niger of Perea, they finally executed presumably for being, despite his heroics, what they saw as a lukewarm partisan.

Concerning Herodian Kingship, the Psalm 37 *Pesher* – in exegesis of an allusion in the underlying text, '*they shall vanish like smoke*' (37:20) – appears to have this to say:

> This concerns the Princes of Evil, who have oppressed the People of His Holiness and who shall disappear like the smoke of fire in the wind.[161]

Not only do we have here the '*Nazirite*' language of '*Holiness*' again, but these are doubtlessly the same '*Princes of Judah*' who, in the Damascus Document, '*remove the bound*' (Hosea 5:10), and '*are diseased without cure*,' '*wallowing in the Ways of fornication and Evil Riches*,' and upon whom '*Wrath shall be poured out*' (n.b., once again, the New Testament '*pouring out*' imagery here). They are also characterized there, as already underscored, as '*Rebellious*' (clearly, against '*the Laws*') '*being vengeful*,' and '*bearing malice, each man hating his brother*,' instead of '*loving his brother*,'

> each man sinning against the flesh of his own flesh, approaching them for fornication (again, niece marriage). And they have used their power for the sake of Riches and profiteering, each doing what was right in his own eyes and each choosing the stubbornness of his own heart.[162]

These '*Princes of Evil*,' as the Psalm 37 *Pesher* characterizes them, as will be recalled, at this juncture of CDviii.3–12/xix.15–26 are described as '*walking in the Way of the Evil Ones*' and identified there with '*the Kings of the Peoples*,' whose '*wine is the venom of vipers and the cruel poison of asps*' (Deuteronomy 32:33) and characterized – playing off the identity in Hebrew between '*wine*' and '*Hellenized*' – as '*their ways*.' By contrast in the Psalm 37 *Pesher*, '*the Assembly of the Poor*' (*Ebionim*), continuing its exegesis of '*those whom He curses shall be cut off*' (37:22),

> shall possess the High Mountain of Israel and enjoy the blessing of His Holiness forever, while 'those who are cut off' are the Violent Ones of the Peoples (the text is defective here, reading either 'the Violent Ones of the Peoples' or 'the Violent Ones of the Covenant' as earlier) and the Evil Ones of Israel, they are the ones that shall be cut off and blotted out forever.[163]

Again one should note, not only the remorseless intensity here, but also the imagery of '*cutting off*,' reversed in the Pauline approach in Romans 11:22–24 and 2 Corinthians 11:12 above and used even scatologically in Galatians 5:12 to counter just such claims as these.

'*The Spoils of the Peoples,*' '*the Last Priests of Jerusalem,*' and the '*Pollution*' of the Temple Treasury

We can now pass over to the Habakkuk *Pesher* in which many of these same allusions or usages occur. In the very First Column, which is somewhat fragmentary, there is the idea of '*the Wicked encompassing the Righteous*' (Habakkuk 1:4) where, paralleling the Psalm 37 *Pesher* above, '*the Wicked*' is specifically identified as '*the Wicked Priest*'; '*the Righteous,*' as '*the Righteous Teacher.*' [164] Immediately, too, one sees the idea that '*they executed upon him* (the Wicked Priest) *the Judgements on Evil,*' which we just encountered in the 4QpPs 37,I.11-12 and with which it draws to a close. This is sometimes not appreciated because of faulty translations of the sense. The allusion occurs at the beginning of Column IX (1–2) of the Habakkuk *Pesher*, directly after the material in VIII.11–12 about how *the Wicked Priest* '*stole and collected the Riches of the Men of Violence (Anshei-Hamas), who rebelled against God and took the Riches of the Peoples*' (ʿ*Amim*).

It speaks about how '*they tortured*' or '*inflicted upon him the Judgements on Evil,*' '*taking vengeance upon the flesh of his corpse*' which we shall discuss further below. This comes just preceding the interpretation of a passage in the underlying text of Habakkuk: '*because of the blood of Man* ('*Adam*') *and the Violence done of the Land, the City, and all its inhabitants*' (2:8, repeated in 2:17). It should be appreciated that, in light of the '*the Primal Adam*' ideology, it would be possible for someone to read the reference to '*Adam*' in the underlying text of Habakkuk at this point as another reference to '*Christ*' and all further passages should be considered with that in mind. The *Pesher* reads:

> *This concerns the Wicked Priest whom, as a consequence of the Evil he committed against the Righteous Teacher and the Men of his Council, God delivered into the hand of his enemies to afflict him with torture in order to destroy him in agony, because he condemned His Elect.* [165]

Not only then, do we have this '*torturing*' allusion running through a good part of Column Nine, but this idea of '*His Elect*' also occurs in 4QpPs 37,III.6 in the run-up to the material about '*the Princes of Evil vanishing like smoke.*' To recall the Damascus Document's exposition of Ezekiel 44:15's '*Sons of Zadok,*' these are '*the Elect of Israel, called by Name, who will stand in the Last Days*' and '*justify the Righteous and condemn the Wicked*' – again the '*condemned*' usage just encountered in 1QpHab,IX.11. Preceding this in 1QpHab,V.3–4, too, it is stated in exegesis of Habakkuk 1:12–13 *that God would not destroy His People by the hand of the Nations but rather, by the hand of His Elect, God will execute Judgement on the Nations. And with their chastisement, all the Evil Ones of His (own) People, who kept His Commandments only when convenient, would be punished.*

This is an extremely pregnant exposition. Not only do we have in it the repeated allusion to '*hand of*,' previously encountered in '*Messianic*' passages of the War Scroll above about '*the hand of the Messiah*,' '*the sword of no mere Adam*,' and '*the hand of the Poor*' – '*the Downcast of Spirit consuming Ungodliness*'; but the implications of this for native Palestinian conceptualities of '*the Day of Judgement*' and the fact that '*the Backsliders among His own People*' were to be judged along with all others are considerable.[166]

The pronouncement is as well delivered in exegesis of Habakkuk 1:12, which refers to God as '*my Rock*' who has '*ordained them for Judgement*' and '*punishment*,' the implications of which for the designation of Peter as '*Rock*' and his role in early Christian eschatology – like '*the Elect*' in this passage at Qumran – are noteworthy. In 4QpPs 37,III.1-13 above, '*the Elect*' are '*the Assembly of His Elect*' – in Christian terms equivalent to '*the Jerusalem Assembly*' or '*Church*' of James the Just. In turn, these are equivalent, as just underscored, to those who in the next passage are called '*the Assembly of the Poor* (in other vocabularies, '*the Ebionites*') who will possess the High Mountain of Israel forever.*'

In the view of the Psalm 37 Pesher, '*the Assembly of His Elect*' are to be the '*Leaders and Princes, the choice of the flock among their herds*,' this in exegesis of an underlying reference in 37:20 to '*the most valuable of the lambs*.' It is interesting that, to produce this very positive exegesis, the underlying Hebrew of the original has been reversed from the received version of Psalm 37:20, which rather alludes to '*the Enemies of the Lord*.' This is now transformed in the text as it is quoted into the homophonic phrase in Hebrew, '*whoever loves the Lord*'[167]; and it is these who are identified – just as '*the Meek of the flock*' in CDXIX.9 of Ms. B who '*will escape at the Time of the Visitation*' and '*the coming of the Messiah of Aaron and Israel*' – with '*the choicelings of the flock*,' '*the Assembly of His Elect*,' and '*the Assembly of the Poor*.' This is typical of Qumran textual redaction and interpretation and the liberties taken there, as it is the New Testament.

In this transformation, one immediately recognizes the '*Piety*' part of the '*Righteousness*'/'*Piety*' dichotomy that has become so familiar to us as the fundamental basis of Josephus' descriptions of John the Baptist's teaching in the wilderness and the doctrines of '*the Essenes*,' not to mention of Jesus and James in early Christian texts. Here at Qumran, these '*Lovers of the Lord*' – along with several allusions in the underlying text of Psalm 37 (12, 21, 30, and 32) to '*the Righteous One'/'Righteous Ones'* as well – are obviously to be identified with '*the Penitents of the Wilderness,*' (in the Damascus Document, both '*the Penitents of Israel*' and '*from sin in Jacob*') *who will live in Salvation* ('*Jesus*') *for a thousand generations*' and to whom, '*all the Glory of Adam will be theirs*' mentioned above.

The evocation of these '*Penitents of the Wilderness*' comes amid exegesis of '*the days of the Perfect, whose portion shall be forever*' of 37:18. Following this, preceding evocation of '*the Assembly of His Elect*' and '*the Assembly of the Poor*'/'*the Righteous,*' allusion is made to '*the days of the famine and the Wicked perishing*' (37:19). In the *Pesher,* this is interpreted in terms of '*the Penitents of the Wilderness*'/'*the Assembly of the Poor*' being '*kept alive*' or redeemed – the whole ambiance being a juridical one – while '*the Wicked,*' described as '*all those who did not depart (from the Land of Judah),*' '*will perish from famine and plague.*'[168] Once again, even here, it would appear that we have yet another possible oblique parallel to what in Christian tradition goes under the appellation of '*the Pella Flight of the Jerusalem Community.*' This whole section, of course, immediately follows the first reference to how '*the Evil Ones of Ephraim and Manasseh*' – later simply '*the Wicked Priest*' – would be '*delivered into the hand of the Violent Ones of the Gentiles for Judgement.*'

In the Habakkuk *Pesher,* just prior to the references in Column Nine to how '*the Wicked Priest was delivered over to the hand of his enemies*' as a '*consequence of the Evil he did to the Righteous Teacher and the Men of his Council*' and just after reference to '*torturing him with the Judgements on Evil*' (both paralleled in these passages from the Psalm 37 *Pesher* above); another delineation of the sins of '*the Wicked Priest*' and '*the Last Priests of Jerusalem*' in general is presented. Of course, it should be appreciated that an allusion such as '*the Last Priests of Jerusalem*' – which certainly does mean '*High Priests*' or '*Chief Priests*' and, as a plural, parallels the references to these same '*High Priests*' or '*Chief Priests*' in the New Testament – makes no sense anytime before the destruction of the Temple in 70 CE and their decimation by '*the Zealots*' and their '*Violent*' Idumaean allies when the Revolt moved into its more extreme '*Jacobin*' phase, as it were, and *all collaborators were dealt with.* Along with James' destroyer Ananus, among these, as just indicated, was Jesus ben Gamala, whose father managed to get word to Josephus in Galilee about a plot in Jerusalem to remove him when he (Josephus) was commanding there in the early days of the Uprising.[169] These are the passages in which Josephus describes how '*the Idumaeans,*' whom he calls '*turbulent and unruly, ever on the alert to create mayhem and delighting in Innovation,*' butchered all the High Priests and, in particular, '*cast out*' the bodies of Ananus and Jesus ben Gamala, his friend, *without burial,* '*naked as food for dogs and beasts of prey.*'

As Josephus recounts all these matters, these '*Idumaeans,*' introduced by stealth at night into the city by those he has started now to call '*Zealots,*' were '*of the most murderous and savage disposition,*' '*pests,*' '*the sum total of the offal of the whole country.*'[170] In an extremely vivid description, he describes how, *together with* '*the Zealots,*'

> *they stealthily streamed into the Holy City, Brigands of such incomparable Impiety* (note the reversal going on here too) *as to pollute even that hallowed Sanctuary...recklessly intoxicating themselves in the Temple and imbibing the spoils of their slaughtered victims in their insatiable bellies.*

Once again, in good collaborationist style, Josephus is reversing not just the '*Piety*' ideology (as just alluded to) but also the '*pollution of the Temple*' accusation that so characterizes the ethos of Qumran and applying it, like his ideological look-alike Paul, to '*the Zealots*' and those allied to them; not as Qumran or James would do – *to the* '*Establishment*' *High Priests.*

In addition to using the language of the Scrolls about '*pollution of the Temple,*' '*Piety,*' '*Riches*' and, in particular, '*the spoils,*' '*the Last Priests of Jerusalem gathered*' in the Temple – the very language the Habakkuk *Pesher* actually is using at this point, though, as in Paul, always reversed; Josephus has already told us that James' destroyer Ananus – who basically had total control of the government for the two years since the outbreak of the War – was the whole time trying to make the necessary inroads that would make it possible for the Romans to once more enter the city; and was just on the point of succeeding when '*the Zealots,*' aided by '*the Idumaeans,*' overwhelmed him and his fellow collaborating '*Chief Priests.*'[171]

The allusion to '*the Last Priests of Jerusalem,*' which the *Pesher* now makes as a concomitant to this general allusion to '*plundering*' and '*profiteering*' (in effect, '*tax-farming*' – the language is very precise here[172]), is entirely appropriate because, at this point, the *Pesher* actually knows it is speaking about *the total destruction of these* '*Last*' *collaborating* '*High Priest*' *clans.* Nothing like this *ever* happened before and the *Pesher* is quite cognizant of its significance. There is no possibility such wholesale destruction of High Priestly clans can be read into any events prior to 68–70 CE. Even at the time of Pompey in 63 BC or Herod's later assault on the Temple with the help of Roman troops in 37 BC, Josephus makes it very clear that *neither allowed any plundering or booty-taking to go on!* This is the definitive point and Josephus explicitly says as much both as regards Pompey's behavior in the Temple and Herod's directives to his troops – unless we are speaking about Antiochus Epiphanes here, a dubious proposition.[173] That leaves only Titus and his father Vespasian and we know they took 'booty' – a good deal of it, because, *inter alia*, they used the proceeds of it and the labor force they acquired to build the Colosseum in Rome.

Exploiting references to the Babylonians '*plundering many Nations*' (*Go'im*) and '*Additional Ones of the Peoples*' (*Chol Yeter-ᶜAmim*), in turn, '*plundering*' in the underlying text from Habakkuk 2:7–8 and the Babylonians '*gathering the Nations*' and '*collecting the Peoples*' preceding these in Habakkuk 2:5; the *Pesher* produces the picture of '*tax-farming*' begun three columns earlier. There, it will be recalled, '*the Kittim*' (here clearly, '*the Romans*') were described as '*collecting their Riches together with all their booty like the fish of the sea*' (Habakkuk 1:14) and '*parceling out their yoke and taxes*' – this in interpretation of Habakkuk 1:16, '*his portion is fat and his eating plenteous*.' Now the text asserts:

> Its interpretation (meaning the '*spoiling many Nations*' and '*the Additional Ones of the Peoples spoiling you*' of Habakkuk 2:8 above), *concerns the Last Priests of Jerusalem, who gathered Riches and profiteered from the spoils of the Peoples*.[174]

Here the text has, once again, been deliberately altered to produce the desired exegesis. Not only have '*the Last Priests of Jerusalem*' now been substituted for the '*collecting*' and '*gathering*' activities of the Babylonians in the underlying text from Habakkuk 2:5-8, but a new allusion, '*profiteering*,' is introduced which is not in the underlying text – at least not yet, that is, not until Habakkuk 2:9 and '*the profiteer's profiteering – Evil unto his house*.'

This word used here, '*bozeᶜ*'/'*bezaᶜ*,' is also used in the Damascus Document where the '*pollution*,' '*Riches*,' and '*fornicating incest*' of the Establishment classes – '*each man sinning against the flesh of his own flesh, approaching them for fornication, they used their power for the sake of Riches and profiteering*' – are being described.[175] The Hebrew here definitely carries the sense that '*the Last Priests are profiteering from the spoils of the Peoples*' (in our view, as by now should be clear, '*Herodians*'), not the sense one finds in most translations, that '*the Last Priests*' are '*plundering the Peoples*.'[176]

This is the kind of imprecision one gets in 'Consensus' interpretation of texts in the interests of promoting a theory of the Maccabeans as '*the Wicked Priests*' and, in some sense therefore, conquering foreign peoples. But this is not the sense of the *Pesher*. Rather, it is '*the Peoples*' and '*the Men of Violence who rebelled against God*' who are the ones doing the '*plundering*' – namely, '*the Herodians*' and '*other Violent Gentiles*' – and '*the Last*

High Priests' (plural), in the sense both of multiple High-Priestly clans an something of the imagery of '*the First vs. the Last*,' '*profiteering*' from this kind of predation – as we have already made amply clear, *by accepting gifts and sacrifices from persons of this type in the Temple*, not only the theme of the Damascus Document, but also of '*MMT*.' Furthermore, it is for this reason, as we have seen, that '*the Wicked Priest*' is specifically described as '*acting in the Ways of Abominations (and) of all unclean pollution*.'[177]

The text now adds – laconically in view of its consequence:

> *But, in the Last Days* (or '*Last Times*' – note the eschatological character here of such '*Last*' *Things*), *their Riches together with their booty will be given over to the hand of the Army of the Kittim, because they are the Additional Ones of the Peoples*.[178]

As the *Pesher* would have it, this last is now '*Yeter ha-ᶜAmim*,' and not '*Yeter-ᶜAmim*' as in Biblical Habakkuk 2:8 underlying it. The reason for this would seem to be to further emphasize the contrast between '*ha-ᶜAmim*'/'*Herodians*' and '*the Yeter ha-ᶜAmim*'/'*Romans*,' both basically two parts of a single exegetical complex.

There can be little doubt what is transpiring here. The reference to '*the Army of the Kittim*' would appear to be definitive. Again, allusion to '*the Kittim*' has been deliberately introduced into the *Pesher*, even though it does not appear as such in the underlying text because the exegete knows very well that these are going to *appropriate all the wealth and plunder that the* '*Herodian*' *High Priests have* '*collected*,' and take it to Rome. This cannot apply to any previous period, except the long-ago Babylonian one on which the *Pesher* is based, because at no time, as we have explained, did we have any foreign armies plundering the country in such a massive manner – probably not even during the Maccabean Uprising and certainly not after 167 BC until 70 CE. But it also means that the text is being written by eye-witnesses to this either shortly before 70 CE or sometime not long afterwards.

The Method of the Qumran Commentators

This is an extremely important *Pesher*, as the reader may well appreciate, for not only does it provide definitive historical proof of the backdrop to the events in question, but it shows the method of the Qumran Scriptural exegetes – if '*method*' it can be said to be. The exegetes are for the most part interested in the useful vocabulary from the underlying Biblical passage, as they have been in other instances above, not always the actual sense of the passage. This is also true of the Gospels, even though the scriptural exegesis developed there, as we have seen, is often the reverse of the one here at Qumran.

For instance the term, '*ha-ʿAmim*'/'*the Peoples*,' we have been following both here and in the Damascus Document, does not really appear, as we just saw, in the underlying passage from Habakkuk 2:8, though '*Goʾim*'/'*Nations*' and '*Yeter-ʿAmim*'/'*Additional Ones of the Peoples*' do. Rather the exegetes purposefully introduce it into their interpretation because it means something to them, that is, '*Herodians*.' Also it contributes to the balance they are looking for between '*ha-ʿAmim*'/'*Peoples*' and *Yeter ha-ʿAmim*'/'*Additional Ones of the Peoples*.'

The underlying Biblical text from Habakkuk 2:6–7 has the foreign armies – in this instance, the Babylonians – doing the plundering and oppressing and '*the Remnant of the Peoples*,' meaning all the others, *being oppressed and being plundered*. Nothing loathe, the exposition now has the '*Additional Ones*' or '*Remnant of the Peoples*,' identified with brutalizing foreign armies from the West (*i.e.*, '*they come from the Islands of the Sea*') – in this instance undoubtedly the Romans – and it is they who finally '*plunder the Riches*' that '*the Last High Priests of Jerusalem*' have already '*amassed and profiteered from*' the '*Violent*' predation activities of the Herodians and their '*Violent*' henchmen or thugs like Saulos and Costobarus.

One need only add to all of this that, according to Josephus, Bernice (the mistress at this point of Titus) was *the 'Richest' woman in Palestine* – as was, doubtlessly, *her aunt Herodias before her*. This was in part, no doubt, as already suggested, the source of her attractiveness to people like her uncle, Herod of Chalcis, and Polemo, a foreign King from Cilicia (Paul's alleged birthplace), who was – as we have already seen as well – even willing to circumcise himself to marry her. This is not to mention her third sister Mariamme's marriage to: first, the son of the Temple Treasurer (and Paul's possible '*kinsman*') Julius Alexander who read Josephus' works in Rome, and after divorcing him ('*contrary to the Laws of her Country*'[179]), next to Demetrius, the son of the Alabarch of Alexandria (and probably, therefore, Tiberius Alexander's brother and Philo's nephew), the Richest man in Egypt.

The sense of this commentary is crystal clear, once one dispenses with the cloud of unknowing of much Qumran 'consensus' or what is seen as 'normative' scholarship – which for the most part avoids literary or historical criticism in favor of handwriting or related philological analyses – and once one penetrates the charming, if sometimes rather obscure, code the Qumran exegetes are using. Normative Qumran translations by scholars with little sense of literary analysis or metaphor make it look as if, as just detailed, '*the Last Priests of Jerusalem*' were '*gathering the booty*' and '*doing the plundering*' and not '*the Peoples*' and '*the Men of Violence.*' They were, but indirectly, through these '*ᶜArizim*' and '*ᶜAmim*' – '*Violent Ones*' and '*Peoples.*'

This is the sense of the passage preceding this one (based as it is on Habakkuk 2:7-8) as well, interpreting Habakkuk 2:5 about an arrogant man who never gets enough wealth into his mouth, collecting the Nations and Peoples unto himself – in the Biblical Habakkuk, *meaning the Babylonian King.* This is expanded in the interpretation in the text, as we have seen, *into the Wicked Priest 'collecting the Riches of the Men of Violence*' and '*taking the Riches of the Peoples,*' meaning '*the Riches*' of the violent Herodian tax-farmers by which means he '*heaped upon himself guilty Sinfulness.*' In the process, it is allusions of this kind that make a mockery of the famous and beloved New Testament passages about 'Jesus' keeping '*table fellowship*' with '*tax-collectors*' and '*harlots*' – *i.e.*, persons like Bernice, her sisters Drusilla and Mariamme, and her aunt Herodias above.

This passage about how *the Wicked Priest 'deserted God and betrayed the Laws,*' ends with an allusion, as just highlighted, to how '*he acted in the Ways of the Abominations (and) of all unclean pollution.*' Here '*the Way*' terminology, usually applied to '*the Way of the Perfection of Holiness*' or '*the Way in the Wilderness,*' is inverted to encompass the behaviour patterns of the Evil Establishment and, at this point, the *Pesher* is fairly running away with itself with derogatives and can hardly restrain its disgust and outrage at all these '*Abominations*' or '*blasphemies.*' It does not interest itself in the subject of '*the Riches of the Men of Violence*' or '*Peoples*' *per se*, though like the Letter of James, it does condemn '*Riches*' in a general sense – therefore its self-designations, '*the Poor*' or '*the Simple of Judah doing Torah.*'

What it and its counterpart '*MMT,*' however, cannot abide, as we have been emphasizing, is *the receipt of such 'polluted Riches' into the Temple* and, therefore, their condemnation of this – along with '*fornication*' and '*Riches*' of '*pollution of the Temple*' – is self-explanatory in these circumstances. The '*fornication,*' being repeatedly alluded to here, has to be that of the '*Herodians*' because of the charge '*each man marries the daughter of his father or the daughter of his brother,*' and because there is no indication in our sources of widespread '*niece marriage,*' '*divorce,*' '*polygamy,*' and indiscriminate coupling with near kin, to say nothing of unrestrained and rampant enrichment, among Maccabeans. This is how to read texts – with one's eyes open – but in order to do this, *one has to have a proper sense of history and literary genre and not just ignore them or set them aside on the basis of a set of some other somewhat 'artificial' parameters one might be following.* This is what we have been attempting to do in this book.

24

He '*Swallowed*' the Righteous Teacher with '*his Guilty Trial*'

'Profiteering from the Spoils of the Peoples'

But how were these '*Last Priests of Jerusalem*,' – the so-called '*Chief Priests*' in New Testament terminology (all equally *illegitimate* in the eyes of Qumran) – '*profiteering*'? The answer is – *by accepting gifts and sacrifices in the Temple from foreigners.* This specifically meant sacrifices on behalf of the Roman Emperor who had been paying from his own revenues for a daily sacrifice in the Temple.[1] But it also extended, as we have been showing, *to gifts and sacrifices from and on behalf of* '*Herodians*' regarded for these purposes, too, as '*foreigners*' – and, therefore, '*polluted*' – by these various groups of '*Zealot*'-type extremists including the authors of the documents at Qumran. This was the issue and the thing which so infuriated the '*Zealot*'*-inspired* Lower Priesthood when it stopped sacrifice in August, 66 CE on behalf of any and all such individuals, thus triggering the War against Rome.

This too is why these texts at Qumran fulminate about '*pollution*,' '*uncleanness*,' and '*Abominations*' to such a degree. Properly appreciated, it is also the thrust, as we have been underscoring, of the '*Three Nets of Belial*' accusations in the midst of like-minded remonstrations about *not observing proper* '*separation*' *in the Temple between* '*clean and unclean*' connected to the peculiar charge that '*they sleep with women in their periods*.' Of course, almost the whole of Columns Five to Eight of the Damascus Document inveigh against such things, including the use – as already remarked – of the imagery of John the Baptist's attacks on the Sadducees and Pharisees in the Gospels, as '*Offspring of Vipers*,' adding even '*their nets are Spiders' nets*.'

As we have seen, these complaints also include the charges of '*polluting the Temple Treasury*' and '*each man among them uncovers his brother's flesh and approaches them for fornication*.' As the text itself explains, this last includes *close family cousins* as well as *nieces*.[2] This it does by extending the Biblical ban on consanguinity in an egalitarian way or, as CDv.9-10 itself puts it, '*the Laws of incest for men as well apply to women*.' This then even applies to uncovering one's sister's flesh which, as Josephus reports was supposed to have occurred between Agrippa II and his sister Bernice.

Here the text even gives the mechanism of such *'pollution'* as we have seen: *'every man who approaches them shares their uncleanness, unless he is forced.'* The Damascus Document does not actually think that all Jerusalem High Priests were *'sleeping with women in their periods,'* conduct forbidden in the *Torah* of Moses. Even the compromised and corrupt *'Herodian'* Jerusalem High-Priestly Clans would probably not have gone that far. As the several texts make abundantly clear, they were only guilty of *'profiteering'* and *'gathering Riches'* and consorting with and taking their appointment from people who probably did *'sleep with women during their periods'* or were perceived of as so doing.

What the Damascus Document and *'MMT'* are trying to say – after one gets their chronology straight – is that by *'accepting gifts and sacrifices in the Temple'* from the Roman Emperor, Roman Governors, *'Herodians,'* and their hangers-on – including *'Violent Gentiles'* and *'Men-of-War'* – the High Priests were *contracting their pollution* and, in the process and as a consequence, *'polluting the Temple.'* In particular, this would include accepting appointment from such classes of persons to the very High Priesthood itself which, to be sure, *they did.*

This is the thrust of all the various usages of the *'Belial'*-terminology, refracted along with *'Balaam'*-imagery in Paul, 2 Peter, Jude, and Revelation above and the *'idolatry'* charge associated with both – that is, as we have been at pains to point out, this imagery relates to both the *'Herodian'* family itself and the Establishment they sponsored, not to mention to a certain extent, *'the Liar.'* If the latter is Paul, he probably also carries *'Herodian'* blood even if Paul is not identical with the *'Saulos'* in Josephus – which we think he is.

The kind of *'swallowing'* and *'casting down'*/*'casting out'* imagery, one finds implicit in these charges, has nothing whatsoever to do with the Maccabean Priesthood, which on the whole was considered legitimate and highly respected even by Josephus – who makes it plain that he is quite proud of his own Maccabean blood[3] – and even Herodians themselves. Concerning these, one should study the genealogies of Herodians to note how assiduous they were in arranging marriages to preserve every bit of Maccabean blood possible.[4] This was parceled out among the descendants of Herod's own line and that of his sister, Salome – originally married to Costobarus before she divorced him to marry the first *'Helcias'* – and that of the line of his brother *'Pheisal'* (*i.e.,* *'Feisal,'* a good Arabic name even today). All this, the Dead Sea Scrolls help clarify. This is also how to date these documents as well, as we have been insisting, by properly understanding the internal allusions and imagery, however obscure, not by simply relying on some of the external parameters more recent scholarship has found acceptable.

An Historical Synopsis

Josephus himself becomes so upset at what those of a '*Zealot*' frame-of-mind are doing in the Temple that, as we have seen, he rails against them as '*Innovators*' and their rejection of gifts and sacrifices on behalf of foreigners in the Temple as an '*Innovation.*' We have already shown as well how the latter accusation was more appropriate to Herod's own changes '*to the disuse of the Jews' own ancestral traditions*' than to anything the '*Zealots*' were doing. For his part, Josephus does not decline to accept appointment as commander or commissar in Galilee – he perhaps exaggerates his role here – from the cabal in charge in Jerusalem, though these were hardly '*the Innovators.*'[5]

Before the Revolution moved into its '*Zealot*' or '*Idumaean*' phase (in something like its '*Phony War*'), those directing it were biding their time while they tried to negotiate for themselves a separate deal with the Romans. This is the clarity Josephus does provide. That the more extremist groups, which took over the Uprising with the wholesale destruction of these more accommodating High Priests, looked askance on Herodians is clear from their earlier treatment of Agrippa II and his sister (or '*consort*') Bernice, *barring them from the Temple* (and, in time, *all Jerusalem as well*). This, some of them wished to do to their father before them – who Josephus already told us was of such refinement as to surpass all others of his generation in '*Chrestos*'/'*Kindliness.*'[6]

It is he that the '*Zealot*' Simon – the Head of an '*Assembly*' or '*Church*' in Jerusalem in the early Forties – wanted to have barred from the Temple as a foreigner.[7] We have already identified this '*Simon*' with the demythologized '*Simon Peter*' in Scripture, himself possibly identical with one or another of the New Testament's '*Simon the Zealot*' or even '*Simeon bar Cleophas.*' Whereas Josephus' '*Simon*' wants to *bar Herodians from the Temple as foreigners*, the '*Simon*' in Acts actually '*learns*' to *accept foreigners into the Community of Christ* and that, as we have seen, *it was permissible to keep 'table fellowship' with them* even though they themselves were not observing the Law (Acts 10:9–11:18).

As the Pauline author of Ephesians 2:19–22 puts this, using the familiar '*building*' imagery again and reversing the sense of the Mecca-like warning-markers barring foreigners from the Inner Courtyard of the Temple on pain of death: *in Christ Jesus 'you are no longer foreigners or*

resident aliens, but fellow-citizens of the Holy Ones and of God's Household.'
We have already encountered this language of being *'joined to the Holy
Ones'* and of *God's 'House'* at Qumran.[8]

The scriptural Peter even goes so far as to visit the household of the
Caesarean Centurion of the contingent from *'Italica,'* the birthplace of
Trajan whose father had campaigned with Vespasian and Titus in Pales-
tine – the Caesarean legionnaires being, it will be recalled, the very ones
whose brutality Josephus blamed for goading the Jews to revolt against
Rome. Moreover, we have already shown Peter's visit here to be but a
stand-in for this visit by the *'Zealot'* Simon – probably at James' request
(this would be the picture of the Pseudoclementine *Recognitions*) – to
Agrippa I's household in Caesarea to see *'what was done there contrary to
Law.'*[9] Though this *'Simon'* is pictured in Josephus as being dismissed by
Agrippa I with some gifts, no doubt he would ultimately have been
arrested either by Agrippa himself (before he died under very suspicious
circumstances) or his brother Herod of Chalcis (his daughter Bernice's
husband) who succeeded him and indulged in just such wholesale arrests
during the five more years he ruled. This last, most likely, is what Acts
12:1–9 is trying to depict (in its own outlandish way) in its curious picture of Peter's arrest and escape, leading up to the introduction of James.

It will be recalled that Peter's miraculous escape from prison, for
which *'Herod the King'* executed the jailers, and the general denigration
of the more *'Jewish'* Peter, one encounters in the Gospels, contrasts markedly with Acts 16:25–40's picture of Paul's more Socratic/Platonic and
properly *'Christian'* behaviour of declining to escape when he might
have, after which *he 'eats with' and converts all the jailers* (sic)!

For Pharisaic Judaism and Rabbinic Judaism succeeding it, this question of whether the Herodians were foreigners or not is also a burning
one – as illustrated by the episode in *Mishnah Sota*, where Agrippa (I or
II, it is of no import) is portrayed reading the *Torah* in the Temple at
Tabernacles.[10] It will be recalled that this is the third great Jewish pilgrimage Festival after Passover and Pentecost and the Festival at which
the curious *'Prophet,' 'Jesus Ben Ananias,'* appears directly following the
death of James (probably around *Yom Kippur*) to proclaim the coming
destruction of Jerusalem. Here Agrippa (to judge by his sensitive behaviour, probably Agrippa I) comes to the Deuteronomic King Law, *'You
shall not put a foreigner over you who is not your brother'* (17:15), a passage also
found – as if foreordained – in the Temple Scroll at Qumran where,
among other things, it is set down that *the King should marry only one wife
and this a Jewess and for her whole life* – therefore, *no divorce.*[11]

When King Agrippa comes to this passage, he begins to weep. *A*

Jewish King was supposed to read the Law in the Temple on Tabernacles, the cel-ebration of the wilderness experience of the Jews. For his part, Agrippa I had been appointed '*King*' by his friends, the Emperors Gaius Caligula and Claudius, after being freed by them from prison. He was also always being abetted by Tiberius Alexander's family in Alexandria, which managed Claudius' estates in Egypt and into which, as we just saw, one of his daughters Mariamme married. The Temple Scroll, which is considered by some to be a Sixth Book of the Law, also includes the general ban on '*niece marriage*' and, as pointed out previously, '*Bela^c' in the Temple* – at least when read esoterically – *along with other classes of polluted persons*, and the additional curious ban on '*skins sacrificed to idols*,' what-ever was supposed to have been meant by this.[12]

By contrast to what Simon '*the Head of an Assembly of his own in Jerusalem*,' '*the Zealots*,' and presumably the Temple Scroll might have thought – the *Talmud* pictures the assembled Pharisees as crying out, sycophantic to a fault, '*You are our brother, you are our brother, you are our brother*,' three times, exactly in the manner of the '*Voice*' *out of Heaven* to Peter in Acts 10:13–16 that also cries out '*three times*': '*Get up, Peter, kill and eat*' in anticipation of his visit to the house of the Roman Centurion Cornelius in Caesarea – an utterly charming '*Heavenly*' message! Nor is it an inconsequential point that in all four Gospels, Peter is pictured as '*denying*' the Messiah '*three times*' before the cock crowed the morning of his crucifixion (Matthew 14:30 and *pars*. – again part of the general den-igration of '*Peter*' throughout all these materials).

The gist, basically, of all these episodes is that Peter misunderstood the 'Paulinized' message of the Messiah 'Jesus.' This is also the gist of the Heavenly '*tablecloth*' episode where, as we have seen, the words following '*kill and eat*': '*What God has made clean, do not make profane*,' have become decisive for Western civilization ever since; and Peter learns he can *eat forbidden foods* and keep '*table fellowship*' with Gentiles. Peter misunderstood the Master's message or, at least, this is what we are supposed to con-clude. What is more to the point, and the converse of this, is that Peter was *never* taught these positions in the first place. Otherwise, why would he need a '*Paul*'-style vision to understand them when the Gospels portray '*Jesus*' as preaching just such a message? But we have already covered this point previously.

As for '*the* Zealots' or '*Sicarii*' and those causing the Uprising against Rome generally, they stopped sacrifice and refused to any longer accept gifts from or on behalf of foreigners in the Temple just as, prior to James' death in what we have called '*the Temple Wall Affair*,' they had previously built an obstacle to stop '*Bela^c*' (*i.e.*, the first Edomite King) or the Herodian King from *even seeing the sacrifices*. But, as already explained, this too is the gist of the *'balla^c'/Bela^c'* episode in the Temple Scroll, where such classes of persons were forbidden even from *'seeing the Temple.'*[13]

It is a doleful twist-of-irony that the Romans, after two Uprisings and endless troubles over these issues, in effect turned the tables on the Jewish extremists, forbidding them even *to come within eyesight of the Temple* and Jerusalem after its final transformation by Hadrian (another Roman legionnaire from Italica in Spain) into Aelia Capitolina in the wake of the Bar Kochba Uprising. It is interesting, too, that during this time the Rabbis are alleged to have put a ban upon upon those taking Nazirite-style oaths not to *'eat or drink'* until they had *seen the Temple rebuilt* – language clearly reflected in Acts 23:12–14's picture of those wishing *'to kill Paul.'* The symbolism here, where Paul's doctrine of *'Jesus'* as the *'Heavenly Temple'* is concerned, is also so intrinsic as to be impossible to ignore.

Not only were foreign gifts and foreign sacrifices – seen as both *'polluting the Temple'* and *corrupting the High Priesthood* – banned by these religious *'Innovators'* and *'Zealot'*-style extremists; *foreign appointment of High Priests* was also abjured, including either by Herodians or Roman Governors in succession to them. This is the thrust of James' *opposition to the High Priests in the Temple* and his *'Opposition'* High Priesthood, as pictured in early Church sources. It is also finally the basic thrust of a *'Jamesian'* Letter(s) like *MMT*, not to mention Epiphanius' *Anabathmoi Jacobou's 'he complained against the Temple and the sacrifices.'* In this last text, too, *Paul is specifically pictured as a foreigner*.

As we have explained, James did complain about certain things, but not quite in the retrospective manner these early Church documents, through the prism of their ideology, suppose but, rather, in one meaningful to the above context. As already suggested, he *'complained'* about the way *'Temple service'* was being carried out by these Herodian and Roman-appointed Establishment High Priests – as the Qumran documents do in their way – and he *'complained against'* gifts and sacrifices from or on behalf of foreigners in the Temple – just as the *'Zealot'* Lower Priesthood and *'MMT'* do – when Acts 21:20 itself admits the majority of James' *'Jerusalem Church'* followers were *'Zealots for the Law.'* Even earlier, Acts 6:7 also admitted that *'a great multitude of the Priests had become obedient to the Faith'* (n.b., this same word, *'Faith'* or *'Compact,'* used to describe *'the New Covenant which they erected in the Land of Damascus'* above).

This is the essence of the controversy over the first of James' directives to overseas communities, *'things sacrificed to idols.'* All of these things were seen as *'pollution of the idols'* or *'idolatry,'* as both *'MMT'* and the Habakkuk *Pesher* so vividly illustrate. This is also the thrust of the election to fill the '*Office*'/'*Episcopate*' of the Twelfth Apostle in Acts 2:20 – as we have argued, really the election of '*the Mebakker*' (as Qumran would have it) or '*the Bishop*' James ('*the Righteous One whom* – as Eusebius and Hegesippus put it – *everyone must obey*') as '*High Priest of the Opposition Alliance*.' It is to him all groups – '*Zealots*,' '*Sicarii*,' '*Nazrenes*,' '*Essenes*,' or '*Messianic Sadducees*' (if there was any real difference between these except of degree) – paid homage.

Judas Maccabee had been elected High Priest two centuries previously after defeating the Greco-Syrian Seleucids and '*purifying the Temple*,' a notice repeated twice in Josephus but which all modern scholars manage to ignore in developing their portrayal of one or another of the Maccabeans as '*the Wicked Priest*' or '*usurpers*.'[14] They are mistaken here. Election by lot was simply the ancient, more egalitarian way of choosing the High Priest (the '*Perfect*' High Priest of '*Higher*' Righteousness, as Hebrews 7:26 and 9:11 would have it – its '*Priesthood after the Order of Melchizedek*' being but a variation, playing on the '*Z-D-K*' or '*Righteousness*'-ideology, of this and the '*Zadokite*' one at Qumran).

The Revolutionaries or so-called '*Zealots*' first made this demand at the beginning of the '*Seventy-Year*' Period of '*Wrath*,' pictured in the Prophet Daniel – so highly valued both at Qumran and in Early Christianity[15] – when the '*Messianic*' disturbances broke out in earnest after the death of Herod in 4 BC. As Josephus pictures this, they demanded '*to elect a High Priest of Greater Purity*' and, by implication, '*Higher*' Righteousness.'[16] This was not, as previously signaled, primarily a genealogical demand but, as at Qumran, a qualitative one. Nor would they accept one or another of the '*polluted*' appointments made by the same Roman or Herodian Authorities they were subjected to, a process which began after Herod achieved supremacy and carried out his various '*Innovations*' – in particular, to use Paul's words, his '*grafting*' his family on the '*Maccabean*' tree. For Paul in Romans 11:9–24 – using '*net*' (11:9), '*Riches*' (11:12), '*zeal*,' '*some*' (11:14), '*casting*' (11:15), '*Root*' (11:16–18), '*Branch*' (11:19), '*standing*,' '*fearing*' God (11:20), and '*cutting off*' (11:22–24) allusions – the new Christians ('*Ethnon*'/'*Ethnesin*') were all '*grafts*' upon the tree (11:13–19).

The '*election*' of James (the majority of whose supporters were '*all Zealots for the Law*') as '*Bishop*' of the '*early Church*' – so unceremoniously jettisoned in favor of Paulinizing fantasy and the traces of which can still be made out by the discerning reader beneath the surface of Acts 2:20ff. even in its present version – was another of these elections. After the elimination of the collaborating High Priests, gruesomely delineated by Josephus in his description of the demise of James' nemesis Ananus, '*the Zealots*' or '*Sicarii*' proceeded to elect their own High Priest, a simple

'*Stone-Cutter*' named '*Phannius*' or '*Phineas*,' the name, of course, of the archetypical purveyor of the '*Zealot*' ideal and against whom, snob and collaborator that he is, Josephus rails because of the purported baseness or meanness of his origins.

But those of the more xenophobic and probably Jamesian '*Zealot*' mindset had already barred Agrippa II from the Temple and, together with his sister and allegedly '*incestuous*' consort Bernice, all Jerusalem as well. This was some twenty years after the earlier '*Simon*''s attempt to bar their father Agrippa I from the Temple too and a decade after they had built a wall to block Agrippa II's view of the sacrifices. It is no wonder that individuals such as these spared no pains to convince the Romans to destroy the Temple when it was put in their power in the aftermath of the Uprising finally to do so – thereafter going to Rome to live.[17]

For example, at the beginning of the Uprising in 66 CE, Josephus describes how those he calls '*Sicarii*,' together with members of the '*Poorer*' classes, not only burned the palaces of '*Rich*' High Priests like the '*Ananias*' presented to us in Acts 24:1, but also '*the Palaces of Agrippa II and Bernice.*' As Josephus goes on to describe this in his usual laconic manner, they then burned the public registrars to '*destroy the money-lenders' bonds... in order to cause the Poor to rise against the Rich.*'[18] I think we can safely say that we have, in the description of these events, a true depiction of the state of affairs in Jerusalem in these portentous times.

This is also the thrust – in our view – of the '*swallowing*' or '*Ba-La-ᶜa*' language applied to the destruction of '*the Righteous Teacher*' by '*the Wicked Priest*' and then to '*the Wicked Priest*''s own destruction in the Habakkuk *Pesher*. Usages of this kind parallel the '*casting out*'/'*casting down*' language (*ekballo*/*kataballo*), applied to the deaths of James and Stephen in early Church texts and, as we have just seen, parodied by Paul in Romans 11:15 above. As we discussed above too, both of these Hebrew and Greek language circles are related to the '*Belial*'/'*Diabolos*' synergy and, of course, the '*Belaᶜ*'/'*Balaam*' usages spinning off, in turn, from these.

Not only is '*Belaᶜ*' the name of the first Edomite or Idumaean King as we have seen, his father '*Beᶜor*' is also the name of Balaam's father in Numbers, Deuteronomy, and elsewhere. This usage, '*be-ᶜorot*'/'*with skins*' – in this instance, '*skins sacrificed to idols*' – is also possibly played upon to produce another example of '*pollution of the Temple*,' in this case a variation on James' proscription on '*things sacrificed to idols*' in Acts 15 and 21, in both '*MMT*' and the Temple Scroll.[19] The quotation of this in Acts 15:20, generally echoed in '*MMT*,' is even wider still, '*the pollutions of the idols*' or a ban on '*idolatry*' generally. This is also the gist, as we have seen, of the language Paul uses in 1 Corinthians 8–10 countermanding it.

But, as we have explained as well, '*Bela^c*' is also the firstborn son of Benjamin (Genesis 46:21, etc.), producing yet another overlap in these New Testament and Scroll esotericisms – this one having to do with Paul's alleged affiliation with '*the Tribe of Benjamin*' (Romans 11:1, Philippians 3:5, Acts 13:21, etc.). For Judges 19–20 the Tribe of Benjamin are called '*Sons of Belial*,' the usage often being applied to those in association with '*Saul*.'[20] This may well have been the derivation of Paul's claims to be of '*the Tribe of Benjamin*' – this and his association with '*Edomites*' – there being really no discernible '*Benjaminites*' left among Jews, as we have explained, in the First Century.

As also already described above, for the *Talmud*, '*Balaam*' together with '*Gehazi*' and CDv.18-19's '*Jannes and his brother*' were among the commoners who would have '*no share in the world to come*.' In the same breath, Talmudic tradition interprets '*Be^{c}or*' as '*be^{c}ir*'/'*animal*' ('*i*' and '*o*' being interchangeable in First-Century epigraphy as at Qumran), imagery, as we have seen, that also recurs in Jude 1:9–11, where both '*Balaam*' and '*the Diabolos*' are referred to as well. This same section of *Talmud Sanhedrin* then plays on the meaning of the name '*Balaam*,' to produce the construct, '*balla^c-^{c}Am*' or '*he who swallows the People*,' which is, of course, exactly how the Herodians were seen by their opponents.[21]

'The Peoples' and 'The Additional Ones of the Peoples'

This way of looking at Herodians is also the thrust of the '^{c}*Amim*'/'*Yeter ha-^{c}Amim*' vocabulary, as we have seen, found in the Habakkuk Commentary when describing what would happen '*in the Last Days*' to the '*Riches*' and '*booty*' of '*the Last Priests of Jerusalem*.' All these juxtapositions are nothing if not purposeful, one balancing and playing off the other. Since '*the ^{c}Amim*' or '*the Peoples*' are – according to our explanation – the '*Herodian*' puppet Kings, '*the Yeter ha-^{c}Amim*' or '*the Additional Ones of the Peoples*,' whose army would eventually gather all the spoils, are their Roman puppet-masters.

That '*the Kittim*' in the Habakkuk *Pesher* have to be seen as the Romans would appear to be self evident. The *Pesher* spends long lines delineating their behaviour, which forms the background against which its entire presentation plays out. We have already delineated these things above. They include:

> *the fear and dread of (the Kittim) is upon all the Nations, and...they deal with all Peoples with cunning and deceitfulness...They trample the earth with their horses and pack animals, and they come from afar, from the Islands of the Sea*

(hardly the Seleucids in Syria) *to consume all Peoples like an eagle* (nor this)...*They deride the Great and have contempt for honorable men. They ridicule Kings and Princes and scorn large populations* (hyperbole notwithstanding, once again, this can hardly relate to the Seleucid Syrians)...*They cause many to perish by the sword, youths, grown men, old people, women and children, and take no pity even on babes in the womb* (this last, of course, is particularly important since this is just what Josephus tells us the Romans did around the Sea of Galilee at Tarichaeae[22]).

In addition, we hear that '*their Commanders, one after another come to despoil the Earth*' and, of course, that '*they sacrifice to their standards and worship their weapons of war.*'[23]

We have already alluded to the significance of this reference to '*sacrificing to their standards and worshipping their weapons of war*' in deciphering the meaning of all these allusions as relating to Roman military practice. But, in addition, it has already been recognized that this has to be '*Imperial*' Rome, when the Emperor's bust was on the standards and the Emperor had already been '*deified,*' *not* Republican Rome, *i.e.*, basically First Century CE.[24] Moreover, as we have seen, this is a general reference and not – as some have assumed – a specific one, such as, for example, the adoration of their standards, described by Josephus, which the Romans performed on the Temple Mount after taking the Temple. Moreover, the Romans must have made many such sacrifices as they made their bloody way down through Galilee in 67 CE. But even if this were not the case, as previously noted, these descriptions can hardly be thought of as applying to the Greco-Syrian Seleucids operating out of Antioch, themselves in the process of collapsing before the military might of Rome.

Again one must point out that flights of fancy of this kind have been the problem with previous scholarly consensuses and elites, to a certain extent ongoing and now reforming. They just *do not read the texts.* To be sure, *they translate them*, sometimes imperfectly and often poorly, but *they do not read them* or *take their content seriously*. Furthermore, because the public rarely reads the texts in question for itself, nor feels any confidence when it does so, these kinds of misconceptions and sometimes obvious fallacies have gone unchallenged until more recently. Even though, for instance, in the Nahum *Pesher*, '*the Rulers of the Kittim*' are specifically said to have come '*after the coming of the Kings of the Greeks,*' whose rulers themselves are definitely said to have begun with '*Antiochus*'(obviously, Antiochus Epiphanes, the villain of the Maccabee Books), meaning the Seleucids[25]; these kinds of preconceptions and misconceptions are allowed to stand. Indeed they persist and are renewed.

We have just noted, too, the allusion in 1QpHab,IV.5-8 above to how: '*The Commanders of the Kittim have contempt for the Fortresses of the Peoples and laugh at them derisively.*' To take them, '*they encircle them with a mighty host and through fear and dread, they are delivered into their hands* (the same species of 'delivering' one encounters in New Testament lore) *and they destroy them because of the Sins of their inhabitants.*'[26] This is exactly how Josephus describes things (not to mention the echo of this last in the '*blood libel*'-type accusations found in all four Gospels), how the Romans encircled city after city, reducing each in turn, as they made their way down from Galilee to Jerusalem. We have also seen how this usage, '*Fortresses of the Peoples,*' provides a key identification tool, because '*the Herodians*' built a series of semi-impregnable '*Fortresses,*' the most famous of which being Masada, the very name of which means '*Fortress*'/ '*Metzad.*'[27] Though this was actually originally built by the Maccabeans, others of this kind, as already remarked, were Hyrcania, Cypros, Herodion, and Machaeros in Perea across Jordan.

Since many of these documents overlap, one such usage in the Damascus Document seals the identification of '*the Peoples*' with the Herodians. Though we have looked at these passages in the Damascus Document before, it is worth looking at them again because of their importance. Of course, the very usage, '*the Peoples,*' preserves the sense that the Herodians, as we have been suggesting, were not real Jews. In the *Talmud*, for instance, one encounters a parallel usage, '*'Am ha-Aretz*' – a '*Person*' or '*the People of the Land,*' used contemptuously to refer to backsliders and persons the *Talmud* does not really consider to be Jews as such but who are nevertheless living in the country.[28] This, of course, might well be a later usage applying to a chronologically-succeeding period.

In Columns Five to Eight of the Damascus Document, in the endless harangue against the Establishment that includes the several '*Messianic*' Prophecies from Numbers and Deuteronomy and the allusions to '*Offspring of Vipers and Spiders' Nets*' one comes upon what for our purposes is the definitive allusion with regard to '*the Peoples*' and the Establishment, '*the Kings of the Peoples.*'[29] This occurs, as we have already pointed out, in exegesis of the second quotation from Deuteronomy 32:33, this time mentioning both the '*Venom of Vipers*' and '*Poison of Asps,*' and having to do with the Sins of the Establishment.

Among these Sins, it will be recalled, was '*wallowing in the Ways of fornication and Evil Riches*' (one can't get more '*Jamesian*' than this), '*every man hating his neighbor*' – in contrast to two columns earlier in CDvi.19-20, '*every man loving his neighbor*' ('*the Royal Law according to Scripture*' in the Letter of James) – and '*every man sinning against the flesh of near kin,*' *approaching them for fornication, and using their power for the sake of Riches and profiteering' (bezaᶜ).*[30]

We have already noted this '*profiteering*' usage above in the Habakkuk *Pesher* and this just furthers all these terminological overlaps. The earlier allusion to '*Vipers*' and '*Spiders*,' it will be recalled, was from Isaiah 59:5 and 50:11 and included the allusion, '*they are all Kindlers of Fire and Lighters of Firebrands.*' In Matthew 3:11–12, John the Baptist's words against '*Many of the Sadducees and Pharisees*' (is this more code?) read, as we saw as well.

> *He shall baptize with the Holy Spirit and with fire, the fan of which is in his hand, and he will thoroughly purge his threshing-floor...the chaff will He burn up with an unquenchable fire.*

Preceding these allusions in the Damascus Document was the material about how '*they also pollute their Holy Spirit and open their mouth with a Tongue full of blasphemies against the Laws of the Covenant of God, saying, "they are not sure," but they speak blasphemously concerning them.*'[31] This, in turn, grew out of the explanation of the '*Three Nets of Belial*' about '*polluting the Temple, because they do not (observe proper) separation according to the Torah.*' Rather it is observed, as we also saw, how '*they sleep with women in their periods, and all marry the daughter of their brother or the daughter of their sister.*' Here '*Moses*' was quoted to explain why one '*should not approach the sister of your mother, she being your mother's near kin*' (Leviticus 18:13). If this does not directly relate to the marital practices of the Herodians, it is difficult to imagine what would.

After some three columns of material of this kind, as we saw as well, Hosea 5:10 is quoted in Column Eight about '*the Princes of Judah being like Removers of the Bound.*' There can be no doubt that this is a reference to their '*Law-Breaking*' activities, and here it is not the Holy Spirit that will be '*poured out upon them*' but rather '*God's Wrath.*'[32] Later in this column it is stated that '*the Penitents of Israel departed from the Way of the People(s)*' and '*just as God loved the First ('the Forefathers'), so too would He love those coming after them because the Covenant of the Fathers was theirs.*' This is clearly a recapitulation of the language of Columns I–VI earlier, where it is '*the Scoffer*' or '*Liar*,' who '*poured out the waters of Lying on Israel*' and '*removed the bound that the First have marked out for their inheritance.*' There, '*the Penitents of Israel*' were, it will be recalled, defined as '*departing from the Land of Judah to dwell in the Land of Damascus.*'

This process is opposed to one centering about '*the Princes of Judah*' who '*removed the bound,*' soon to become '*the Kings of the Peoples*' or

'*Vipers*' and including '*the Windbag*,' described either as '*walking in the Spirit*' or '*of confused Spirit*,' '*who poured down Lying on them*' or '*who spouted to them, against whose whole Assembly* (or '*Church*'), *God's Anger would be kindled.*'[33] These things, as we have seen, are associated with a prophecy from Ezekiel 13:10, railing against '*worthless and Lying visions*,' '*prophets prophesying their own hearts and Lying to the People*' and, in particular, '*crying Peace when there is no Peace.*'

Earlier the same language was used in the context of the exposition of '*the Three Nets of Belial*' to characterize those following the Lying Spouter's '*spouting*' (Micah 2:6), and these were the ones said to be caught in '*fornication*,' itself defined in terms of divorce, polygamy, marrying their nieces, and, in the process, '*polluting the Temple, because they do not separate according to Torah.*' Now they are defined as '*rejecting the Commandments of God...and turning aside in stubbornness of heart*,' language typical of that always used to describe the character and behaviour of '*the Spouter of Lying*,' just referred to as '*spilling out wind*' as well as '*pouring out Lying*' and, thus, '*kindling the Wrath of God.*'[34]

These epithets are now associated with Elisha's rebuke of Gehazi, another of the individuals in Rabbinic literature like '*Balaam*,' who would have '*no share in the world to come*' and who is often, in fact, a stand-in in it for Paul. As we saw, this '*Gehazi*' confrontation (something like the one in Acts 8:18–20 with Simon *Magus*) – also tied to a '*Damascus*' ambiance – relates to 2 Kings 5:20–27 and the point there was *taking money for his master's miraculous curing*. The text then goes on to speak about '*cursing*' an individual of this kind and '*not cooperating with him in purse and work.*' Because it is speaking about '*the Men of Scoffing*,' '*who put idols on their heart and walk in stubbornness of their heart*' and '*speaking slanderously against the Laws of Righteousness and rejecting the Covenant and the Faith, the New Covenant, which was erected in the Land of Damascus*,' '*the Man of Lies*' is once more evoked together with the '*Men-of-War*' who walked with him.

It was at this point that the passage from Deuteronomy 32:33 was applied to these malicious and vengeful renegades, '*who did not depart from the Way of Traitors*' and '*walked in the Ways of the Evil Ones*,' about '*their wine being the Venom of Vipers*' and '*the cruel Poison of Asps*,' interpreted in terms of '*the Kings of the Peoples*' and '*their Ways.*' Here '*the Head of the Asps*' is said to be '*the Ruler of the Grecian Kings who comes to take vengeance upon them.*' This incorporates another interesting play, since, as in English, not only can '*Head*' be used to denote '*Ruler*' or '*Leader*' but, it will be recalled, it is substituted for the allusion to '*Poison*' in the underlying text – '*Head*' and '*Poison*' being homonyms in Hebrew.

This is an extremely important *pesher* embedded, as it is – like other important Biblical *Pesharim* – at this critical juncture of the Damascus Document. This is also, it should be noted, something of the method of Acts and Gospel narratives, which is the reason I have called the Damascus Document – to say nothing of the Pseudoclementine *Recognitions* – a kind of '*Opposition Acts*.' This *Pesher*, as we saw, is delivered following the points about '*the Princes of Judah removing the bound*' – in Hebrew, one should appreciate, '*Princes*' and '*Ruling Officials*' are equivalent usages – and '*Wrath being poured out upon them*.' Moreover, it fits right in with the scheme of 1QpHab,ix.7 about the Romans being '*the Additional Ones of the Peoples*.' Here, too, we have an analogue to the language of *Divine* '*Wrath*' put into the mouth of John the Baptist in his attacks on the Establishment above who, in turn, was a also killed by *Herodian Governing Officials*.

But the *pesher* in the Damascus Document is permeated as well with the kind of word-play which would be hard for the unschooled reader to appreciate, word-play which also permeates the Habakkuk *Pesher*. In the first place, there is the play, just noted, between '*Head*' and '*Poison*,' which is built into the very fabric of the *Pesher* itself. But then there is the related reference to '*Hemah*' in the underlying text, another synonym which, as we have seen, can either mean '*Venom*' or, based on its underlying sense of '*hotness*' or '*stinging*,' *Hot Angry* '*Wrath*.' The same connotation also exists in English as in '*to be hot under the collar*.' This will be the meaning that will reappear in the all-important exposition in the Habakkuk *Pesher* describing how the Wicked Priest pursued the Righteous Teacher to swallow him either '*with*' or '*in his hot anger*.'

The same language will also reappear in another important Qumran Document, which we also published and named the *Hymns of the Poor* (*Ebionim*).[35] This document, which parallels the language of the Habakkuk *Pesher* almost word-for-word at this point – showing the two to be basically contemporary – speaks about how God did not judge '*the Poor*,' nor '*kindle His Wrath against them*,' that is, '*His Hot Anger*' or '*fiery zeal*.' Rather '*He circumcised the foreskin of their hearts*' (here the '*circumcised heart*' language again) and '*saved them*' (as well as the '*saving*'), '*delivering them out of the hand of the Violent Ones*' and '*from among the Gentiles*,' '*hiding them in the shadow of His wings*' (this same language is used to opposite effect in Luke 13:34 and elsewhere in Paul).[36]

But in these passages in the Habakkuk *Pesher* about how the Wicked Priest '*swallowed*' the Righteous Teacher and how '*the Cup of the Wrath of God*' would, in turn, '*swallow him*,' there are at least three other plays-on-words: one, between '*Hera⁽c⁾el*/'*Trembling*' – as in '*Cup of Trembling*' from

Isaiah 51:22 – and '*he-ʿarel*,' the same '*foreskin*' just mentioned above; and another, related to it, between '*moʿadeihem*'/'*their festivals*' and '*meʿorei-hem*'/'*their privy parts*.' A third, which is less well-grounded, but nonetheless probably also present, is between '*Hamat*'/'*Wrath*' or '*Venom*' above and '*Hanut*,' a name used to designate, as we shall see, the location where the Sanhedrin sat in the period in which James was stoned and for which '*Hamat*' is a quasi-anagram or homophone – these, not to mention the additional implied play on '*Hemah*' in the Hebrew word *Raʿal*, also meaning '*Poison*.'

There is also the play, as we saw, on the word '*yayin*' for '*wine*' (the English comes from the same root) in '*their wine is their ways*,' which in Hebrew can also be read – as previously indicated – as '*Yavan*' or '*Greece*.' Once again, the two words are homophones in Hebrew. This also helps explain the troublesome usage '*the Head*' or '*Leader of the Kings of Greece*.' First it is based, as we have seen as well, on two plays on the wording of the underlying biblical text itself (Deuteronomy 32:33), that is, on both '*wine*' and '*poison*.' Secondly there is the implied play in the former on the *Hellenization* exemplified by '*their ways*'!

But this is not all. As we have been at pains to point out, it should be appreciated that the Roman Administration in the East was different from Italy proper or even Greece in places like Corinth. Further east in 'Asia,' particularly in areas of what we now call Asia Minor, Northern Syria, and, in fact, extending down as far as Palestine and Transjordan, the Romans left petty *Greek-speaking 'Kings'* in control (therefore the allusion '*Kings of Greece*' or '*Grecian Kings*'), most of whom, as we have seen, were really only *Hellenized Arabs*. Therefore the references we have been following to these various '*Kingdoms*,' such as Commagene, Cilicia, Chalcis, Emesa, Little Armenia, Edessa, Adiabene, Arabia, and the like – though sometimes, as in Palestine or Damascus, these were replaced by Governors, depending on the circumstances involved or the availability of a suitable '*Rulers*.' In these cases, '*the Herodians*' made themselves particularly useful. But this is not the end of the proof involved.

The actual word used to refer to such '*Kings*' in Roman legal jargon, as we have now several times explained, was, '*the Kings of the Peoples*,' basically the '*Ethnon*' or '*Ethnesin*,' we have already singled out above and the words Paul uses over and over again to characterize his '*Mission*' – in Latin, '*Gentium*,' the root of the English usage '*Gentiles*.'[36] It is for this reason that the Roman Emperor can be denoted as '*the Head*' or '*Ruler of the Grecian Kings*,' these '*Kings*' or '*Kings of the Peoples*' actually being the '*Hellenized*' or '*Greek-speaking*' Roman puppet Kings that were the basic building blocks of Roman administrative practice in the East.

So what the Damascus Document on the surface seems to be referring to as '*Greek Kings*' are not really that at all but, first of all, rather a play on the '*wine*' or '*Hellenization*' of '*their ways*' and second of all that, though they were under Roman control, ostensibly they spoke Greek. This term, used in Roman administrative practice to refer to such '*Kings*,' is actually the one found here in these passages in the Damascus Document referring to '*the Rulers of the Jews*' who '*robbed the Poor*,' '*did not separate clean from unclean*' in the Temple, '*slept with women in their periods*,' '*wallowed in the Ways of fornication and Evil Riches*,' '*polluted the Temple Treasury*,' and '*approached near kin for fornication*,' '*each man marrying the daughter of their brother or his sister*.'

This is what we are calling a *valid* internal proof, based on the clear sense of the '*internal data*' of the text itself – not the usual approach of Qumran research. And this same word '*Ethne*' (Romans 11:12–13 above, etc.), '*the Nations*'/'*Peoples*'/or '*Gentiles*' – in English we derive the word '*ethnic*' from it also – is, of course, how Paul and his later propagandists or apologists chose to formulate his '*Apostleship*' or '*Mission*,' calling him '*the Apostle to the Peoples*' or '*Gentiles*,' (Romans 11:13), however offensive this might have been to those '*of importance*' or '*those reckoned to be something*' in Jerusalem, given the reality of the political and religious turmoil there and the hatreds so amply documented in these passages in the Damascus Document. In our view, at this point, we are virtually in a '*QED*' situation.

This, too, is how the word '*Peoples*' is used in the Habakkuk *Pesher* when describing how the Wicked Priest '*betrayed the Laws for the sake of Riches*' and '*collected the Riches of the Men of Violence who rebelled against God and took the Riches of the Peoples* (meaning '*the spoils*' the Herodians '*collected*' as we have explained), *heaping upon himself guilty Sinfulness and acting in the Ways of Abominations in all unclean pollution*' – or '*how the Last Priests*' (one should not miss the eschatological note here, complementing the allusion to '*Last Times*'/'*Last Days*' that follows) '*gathered Riches and profiteered from the spoils of the Peoples, but in the Last Days their Riches together with their booty* (this now the '*Riches*' and '*booty*' of '*the High Priests*') *would be delivered into the hand of the Army of the Kittim, because they are the Additional Ones of the Peoples*.'

It should also be clear that this relates to the stopping of sacrifices in the Temple on behalf of these same '*Peoples*' and/or '*the Kittim*' by those resisting them of the opposite persuasion – in our view, the viewpoint of James, of Qumran, and of those wishing to make it more difficult, not easier, for '*Gentiles*' *to come into* '*the Covenant*' (and not '*be born in Sin*') – this perhaps equivalent to the real '*New Covenant in the Land of Damascus*' not the one reworked, as we shall see below, in the light of overseas realities or expediencies. Such persons, in fact, opposed the so-called '*Gentile Mission*' – at least on the terms Paul unilaterally proclaimed in Romans 11:13 and Galatians 2:2 (as he avers in Galatians 1:17, 2:2, *etc.* – '*without consulting anyone*'), retrospectively confirmed in the Scripture as it has come down to us and put into the mouth of '*the Risen Christ*' (Matthew 28:19 and *pars.*).

Over and over again from the Forties to the Sixties we have shown James to be at the center of this kind of agitation in the Temple and involved in debates on the Temple stairs concerning issues such as these. But he did not protest simply against '*the Temple and the sacrifices*,'as the *Anabathmoi Jacobou* would have it, but – as we have been delineating – against the way '*Temple service*' was being carried out by the '*polluted Herodian Priesthood*' and *against accepting gifts and sacrifices in the Temple on behalf of* '*Gentiles*' and '*Rich*' *Herodians* generally. It was gifts and sacrifices made on behalf of these last that were seen as '*spoils*' or '*booty*' and, as a consequence, according to the terms of Qumran documents like CD and '*MMT*,'they were '*polluting the Temple*.'

This too is how Habakkuk 1:14–15, about '*fishing*,' '*dealing with Man* ('*Adam*') *like the fish of the sea*,' and '*collecting them in a dragnet*,' is interpreted in 1QpHab,v.12–vi.11 above. This passage, which is so important for identifying '*the Kittim*' who '*sacrifice to their standards and worship their weapons of war*' as the Romans did – and apparently parodied, in our view, in the Gospel portrait of peaceful '*Apostles*' casting their nets and fishing like '*Fishers for men*,' on the Sea of Galilee – rather interprets such '*fishing*' and '*casting of nets*' as '*parceling out their taxes*' and '*eating all the Peoples year by year*' (and here the verb literally is '*eating*' or '*devouring*'), '*collecting their Riches with all their booty*'!

This is why the removal of James was seen as so imperative by the Herodian Establishment and this is what was accomplished in 62 CE. at the first opportune moment by Ananus, as a follow-up both to the assassination of his brother, the High Priest Jonathan, by Zealot '*Sicarii*' in 55 CE and all the turmoil centering around '*the Temple Wall Affair*' in 61–62 CE directed against his patron, the *Herodian* '*King*' Agrippa II. These, in turn, have not failed to make their impression in the various documents that have come down to us, particularly Acts – if, albeit, in a rather distorted and often unrecognizable fashion. The same controversies were also at the root of the earlier disturbances involving '*Simon*,' around 44 CE – the *real* '*Simon Peter*' (and probably '*Simon the Zealot*') – '*the Head of an Assembly of his own in Jerusalem*' who wished to bar *Agrippa I from the Temple as a foreigner.* This is how complex these kinds of allusions *really* are.'

'They Took Vengeance upon the Flesh of his Corpse'

These same Columns Eight to Nine of the Habakkuk *Pesher* contain the parallel allusion to the one in the Psalm 37 *Pesher* about how the Wicked Priest would be '*delivered into the hand of the Violent Ones of the Gentiles for Judgement*' and how these '*executed (the Judgements on Evil) upon him.*' The passage in the Habakkuk *Pesher*, which contains the phrase '*they inflicted upon him the Judgements on Evil*' and '*took vengeance upon the flesh of his corpse,*' has created not a little misunderstanding among commentators because of the arcane quality of its vocabulary and the difficulty in translation.

It occurs directly following the material about how the Wicked Priest '*collected the Riches of the Men of Violence who rebelled against God*' and preceding that about how in the Last Days the Riches and the booty of the Last Priests of Jerusalem '*would be delivered into the hand of the Army of the Kittim.*' Interpreting an underlying reference from Habakkuk 2:7 to being '*bitten by torturers,*' the *Pesher*, as usual, totally ignores the sense of the underlying text, which relates to the King of the Babylonians, only paying attention to the vocabulary it is interested in to develop an exposition condemning '*the Priest* (meaning, that is – this time the Wicked Priest) *who rebelled against and broke the Laws of God.*'

These last two usages are based on the exact same roots as those of the '*Rebels*' and '*Covenant-Breakers*' in Columns One, Eight, and Nineteen of the Damascus Document, to say nothing of the allusion to '*the Men of Violence rebelling against God*' directly preceding this passage in the Habakkuk *Pesher*.[37] It comes at the bottom of Column Eight of the Habakkuk *Pesher*, which is frayed at this point, so after a slight break in the text it continues, as we have just seen, at the top of Column Nine which is complete:

> They inflicted the Judgements on Evil and committed the outrages of Evil pollutions upon him in taking vengeance upon the flesh of his corpse.

This passage had caused a good deal of confusion in Dead Sea Scrolls Studies, because the word we are translating here as '*pollutions*'/'*mahalim*' in Hebrew has a primary meaning of '*diseases.*' But this cannot mean simply '*diseases,*' since it is *twice* explicitly stated that a person or persons '*inflicted these* ('*pollutions*' or '*diseases*' – we prefer '*defilements*')*upon him.*' Also the phrase '*flesh of his corpse*' has been translated by some as '*his body of flesh,*' despite the fact that this is a redundancy and virtually meaningless in English.[38] Not only is it clear that we have direct action and the same plural '*they*' who are '*committing the outrages of Evil pollutions*' are also '*inflicting the Judgements on Evil on him*'; it is equally clear that these '*Judgements on Evil*' or this '*Vengeance*' is being inflicted in the sense of direct action by unspecified third-person plural parties on the '*flesh of his corpse*' (*geviyah*).

But what is most interesting about this obscure allusion is that it can be made sensible by looking at the biography of James – in fact, more sense than we knew before. This is very powerful testimony that our analysis and the way we are proceeding is correct. When a theory or paradigm can not only make sense out of given materials, but also elicit more from the text than one might have known previously, then this is very persuasive evidence that the theory we are propounding here about the identity of James and '*the Righteous Teacher*' actually *works*. Indeed, this is the very essence of what it means for a proof to be valid in scientific theory.

In the history of Qumran Studies, '*Establishment*' or '*Consensus*' Scholars, because of the obscurity of translations of this kind and a real paucity of historical insight, began speaking in terms of '*diseases of the flesh*,' from which some Maccabean High Priest might have been suffering in this period and identifications spinning off from this became legion.[39] The problem with '*diseases*' however, as we just saw, is that these are not normally thought of as being '*inflicted*' by third parties – unless we are talking about Angels! – which is very definitely the sense of the passage here. Furthermore, we are very definitely talking about the word '*corpse*' here. Once this is understood, looking at the biography of James helps elucidate this. Though on the surface, it is true, the Hebrew word '*mahalim*' does look something like '*diseases*,' it is impossible to speak of a person or persons inflicting diseases – plural – on another individual. On the other hand, '*geviyah*' here really does have a primary meaning of '*corpse*,' i.e., '*dead flesh*" not simply '*body*' – '*his flesh*'/'*besaro*' also being alluded to in the *Pesher* and attached to this usage. This means we probably have an idiomatic or esoteric usage of some kind here.

Taking the parallel with the Psalm 37 *Pesher* again about '*the Violent Ones of the Gentiles*' '*inflicting the Judgement on Evil*' upon '*the Wicked Priest*' and observing that the word '*outrages*' or '*violations*' really is associated with this process in the text of the Habakkuk *Pesher* above; one then can look at the word '*mahalim*' here as rather having more to do with '*defilements*' or '*pollutions*.' In fact, this would be the primary meaning, had we taken the usage to relate to the Hebrew root '*halal*,' with two *lamed*s or *l*'s, meaning '*pollute*,' '*defile*' or, even, '*sustain a wound*.'[40] '*Pollutions*' of this kind, in the sense of '*defiling a corpse*,' can be inflicted by others on a third party; diseases cannot (except perhaps more recently through modern germ warfare or AIDs). The '*Vengeance*' theme, of course, precisely parallels the sense of the Psalm 37 materials above, once again implying that they took '*Vengeance*' upon him and something had been '*done to him.*'

If we now look at the combination of these usages with reference to the biography of James and his opposite number, Ananus ben Ananus, the man along with Agrippa II who was responsible for his death, these things are clarified. Since the second problematic word in the above translation, '*geviyah*,' means '*dead body*,' '*carcass*,' or '*corpse*' in Hebrew, the redundancy implicit in most English translations of this passage disappears. Now we really can identify a situation with regard to James' destroyer Ananus where '*they took vengeance upon the flesh of his corpse*' just as we have translated it and we can now see this is exactly what the *Pesher* is talking about with regard to the fate of '*the Wicked Priest.*' Here material from the biography of James can elicit further meaning from the text than we would previously have been aware of had we not known it.

The High Priest Ananus ben Ananus' death, per usual, is recorded in Josephus, who in fact does make a good deal of it. As Josephus describes Ananus ben Ananus' death, '*the Idumaeans*' had been allowed surreptitiously into the city by those he has only just started to call '*Zealots.*' As already underscored, previously he had not been using this terminology to any extent, if at all, but was calling such individuals '*Innovators*,' '*Revolutionaries*,' '*Brigands*,' or '*Sicarii*,' but not '*Zealots*' per se – cryptically referring to '*the Movement*' they represented as '*the Fourth Philosophy*,' nothing more. Josephus' first real use of this pivotal terminology, then, comes in relation to those '*who take vengeance*' on Ananus (reason unspecified), who are his mortal enemies. Therefore, James and the Zealots are distinguished by their common opposition to or abhorrence of this Ananus.[41]

As Josephus describes it in detail, these '*Zealots*,' '*taking some of the Temple saws, sawed open the bars of the gates nearest the Idumaeans, who were shivering outside the city in a violent thunderstorm*'! These so-called '*Idumaeans*,' thereupon, rushed through the city '*sparing no one*' – notice the precise detail in Josephus here, including even '*saws*' and '*a violent storm*'! '*Considering it pointless to waste their energies on the common people, they went in search of the High Priests, focusing their greatest zeal against them.*'[42] Josephus now concentrates specifically on the fate of Ananus, saying,

> As soon as they caught them (meaning Ananus and Josephus' friend Jesus ben Gamala), *they slew them. Then standing upon their dead bodies* (here is the note of abusing or, as it were, '*desecrating their corpses*'), *they mockingly upbraided Ananus for his caring attitude towards the People.*

This last is a little far-fetched and, once again, it is hard to suppress a guffaw, since in his later *Vita*, Josephus accuses this Ananus of having been involved in an olive oil scam and other illicit activities.[43] Nothing loath, in the *War*, he now goes on to see all this as 'sacrilege,' explaining,

> So far did they go in their Impiety (i.e., that of Ananus' torturers) that they threw their bodies outside (the city) without burial, although Jews were so scrupulous in the burial of men that they even took down malefactors who had been condemned and crucified and buried them before the setting of the sun.[44]

This last, of course, has not been lost on the Gospels, particularly the note in the Gospel of John (19:31–33) about 'bodies not remaining on the cross on the Sabbath' – which John identifies as 'the Sabbath' of their Passover commemoration (by which he appears to mean 'a day of rest') – and that of the Roman soldiers coming to 'break the legs'/'break his ('Jesus'') legs,' repeated three times.[45] In Josephus, of course, the notice has nothing to do with 'the Sabbath' or, for that matter, 'the Passover.' However Josephus does reiterate the point about 'violating dead corpses' when, in continuing this description about what happened to Ananus and his friend 'Jesus ben Gamala,' he describes even more graphically how 'they were cast out naked and seen to be the food of dogs and beasts of prey.' It is hard to imagine he could have described Ananus' death in terms of any greater outrage or 'defilement' than this.

So here we actually do have the gist of the meaning of the above passage in the Habakkuk *Pesher* about 'inflicting the outrages of Evil pollutions'/'diseases and taking vengeance on the flesh of his corpse.' Without consulting the events of James' life and those involved in his demise we could never have suspected it. On the other hand, with such data, otherwise obscure usages are immediately clarified. So terrible does Josephus consider this 'Impiety' to be that – as we have just seen – he compares it to the Jews being so careful in the burial of men that they even 'took down malefactors who had been condemned and crucified and buried them before the setting sun,' though he never mentions the additional points in John's 'Gentilizing' portrait of 'Jesus'' death about 'breaking their legs' or 'breaking his legs' or the 'Sabbath.' What Josephus is rather interested in – as we were above – is 'nightfall' and Deuteronomy 21:22–23's injunction that the 'hanged man is not to remain upon the tree all night.'

Rather the first point now reappears with slightly differing sense in the Pseudoclementine *Recognitions* account of the attack by the 'Hostile Man'/Paul on James in the Temple and its refraction in Jerome's later account of how James 'was cast down, his legs broken' – the second such '*casting down*' report about James in early Church reporting, this one '*from the Pinnacle of the Temple*'; the first, as we just saw in the Pseudoclementine *Recognitions*, '*down the Temple steps.*'

Where Josephus is concerned, his account of the '*Impiety*' involved in the treatment of '*the corpse*' of James' murderer Ananus actually seems to have been transferred to Gospel accounts of Jesus' crucifixion, at least that is the indirect effect of his having compared the '*Impiety*' involved in the treatment of Ananus' corpse by '*Zealots*' and '*Idumaeans*' to the care Jews *even accorded the corpses of malefactors in crucifixion*.

But he doesn't stop here. In the long panegyric to Ananus, which he now interrupts his narrative to deliver, curiously he says the very same things about Ananus that early Church sources say about James – including calling him '*a man revered on every ground and of the Highest Righteousness.*' The obsequiousness of these words rather takes one's breath away, especially when one is aware – as we just saw – of what Josephus said about this Ananus in the *Vita*. But he even goes on to attribute the eventual fall of Jerusalem and the ruin of its affairs to '*the death of Ananus*':

> *I should not be mistaken in saying that the death of Ananus was the beginning of the destruction of the city, and that the very overthrow of her wall(s) and the downfall of their State began on the day on which the Jews saw their High Priest, the Procurer of their Salvation, slain in the midst of the City* (one should compare this title '*Procurer of their Salvation*'/'*Soterias,*' meaning '*the Saviour of his Fellow Countrymen,*' with the title applied to James in early Church sources, '*Oblias*' or '*Protection of the People*'!).[46]

It is difficult to consider all these parallels and overlaps accidental and there seems to be more going on beneath the surface of these events than originally is apparent. This is especially true when early Church accounts are saying almost the very same things about James as Josephus here is saying about Ananus; and when Origen, Eusebius, and Jerome all say that in the copy of Josephus' works they saw (presumably in Caesarea – *and this in the War not the Antiquities*), Josephus *attributed the fall of Jerusalem to the removal and death of James!*

Nor can there be much doubt that what one has in these graphic scenes in Josephus is vengeance for the death of James, whose memory seems to have been held in particular regard by these so-called '*Idumaeans*' – including, obviously, some pro-Revolutionary '*Herodians*' like Niger of Perea – which also seems to have been the case among other '*Arabs*' like Queen Helen's family and kinsmen from either Edessa or Adiabene.[47] In fact, these passages extolling Ananus to such a degree that

Josephus has the temerity even to call him '*a lover of Liberty and enthusiast for Democracy*' may even have overwritten something else Josephus originally said at this point in the version of the *War* in the East – prepared, as he told us in his Preface, for his own countrymen in these areas in their native language – *about the death of James.*[48]

Little else can explain the '*Violence*' these so-called '*Zealots*' and '*Idumaeans*' exhibited and their single-minded and extreme animus towards Ananus. What else could have infuriated them to such a degree as to commit such '*Impieties*' and to violate Ananus' body in this manner? One can even imagine that, in standing over Ananus' dead body here, instead of '*berating*' it, as Josephus more politely recounts, they rather went so far as to defile it by urinating upon it or even cutting off its sexual parts – not unusual in these circumstances, since Josephus makes a specific point of *the bodies being naked when they 'cast them out of the city as food for dogs and jackals,*' and not perhaps, as Josephus more modestly puts it, that '*they upbraided Ananus' corpse because of his benevolence*'![49] These are the kinds of '*defilements,*' aside from *not burying the body at all*, that would cause Josephus to compare what had transpired to '*crucifixion*' or '*beheading.*'

They are also the kinds of things the extreme description in the Habakkuk *Pesher* seems to have in mind by '*their inflicting upon his corpse the outrages*'/'*horrors*'/or '*Abominations of Evil pollutions.*' Furthermore, as always, the Qumran document refers to acts such as these with approval while the pro-Roman collaborator Josephus is outraged – at least he makes out that he is for the purposes of public consumption. He even goes on, in the same breath that he does about Ananus' '*love of Liberty and enthusiasm for Democracy,*' to extol *the dignity of his rank* and *the nobility of his lineage* but notes that, despite these, '*he treated even the humblest of men with equality*' and '*ever preferred the public welfare to his own advantage*' – unctuousness that would make anyone but a Josephus blush.[50]

Once again, however, this is exactly the point made in all early Church sources about *James*, that as '*Zaddik,*' he '*did not defer to*' or '*consider persons,*' the very charge Paul is so anxious to parry in Galatians 1:10 of '*attempting to please persons*' – expressed in James 4:4 as '*making himself a Friend to the World.*' Again, an overlap of this kind, when speaking of the death of the man responsible for James' death, can hardly be considered accidental. One might even conclude that we have here the very place in the text where Origen and Eusebius saw their Josephus' testimony that '*Jerusalem fell because of the death of James.*' In addition, it is hard to gainsay the parallels in this account with New Testament materials about 'Jesus' who, of course, is '*the Soter*' or '*Saviour*' par excellence, not to mention those about James as '*the Righteous One*' and '*Protection-of-the-People.*'

In perhaps the cruelest cut of all, in emphasizing how much Ananus *'preferred Peace above all things'* and *'was sensible that Roman Power was irresistible'*; Josephus concludes, *'I cannot but think that, because of its pollutions* (meaning the desecration of Jesus ben Gamala's and Ananus' *corpses*, language absolutely echoing the Habakkuk *Pesher* above – only reversed), *God had condemned this City to destruction.'* In the Habakkuk *Pesher*, God *'condemned the Wicked Priest to destruction.'* In fact, these are the very words it uses in 1QpHab,XII.5–10 where, it will be recalled, it is the Wicked Priest who *'polluted the Temple of God'* because of *'the works of Abomination he committed'* there. So, actually Josephus turns the thrust of the implied accusation in the Gospels about Jesus around here and, in the process, gives vivid testimony as to why persons in the Third, Fourth, and Fifth Centuries thought he said *'Jerusalem fell because of James.'* There is certainly something very peculiar going on in these various like-minded testimonies, so perhaps he did.

Josephus closes with the aside, *'and (He – God) was resolved to purge the Temple by fire, that He cut off these its greatest defenders and benefactors.'* Not only is this last basically the charge being made in early Church texts with regard to James' death but, taken as a whole, it is generally the charge that Eusebius or other early Church writers are making against *'the Jews'* for killing 'Jesus.' (*'the Saviour'*).[51] It also employs the *'cutting off'* language, we have been following and just seen used in the Psalm 37 *Pesher* applied to similar events. Paul does not make this charge as such, though he does use the *'cutting off'* language, as we have seen, probably because the events had not yet transpired at the time of his writing. Nevertheless, to reiterate, in Josephus we get the interesting anomaly that *the charge is being made against 'the Zealots' and their confederates, 'the Idumaeans' for killing Ananus and Jesus ben Gamala* (another *'Jesus'*) and *'casting' their corpses out of the city without burial.* For Josephus, as we just saw, these actions are comparable to the *'profanation'* or *'sacrilege'* of leaving the bodies of those crucified on the crosses without taking them down to bury them before nightfall, a singular and most unexpected comparison.

But for Qumran, the group resembling these unruly *'Idumaeans,' 'the Violent Ones of the Gentiles,'* is praised for *'inflicting the Judgements on Evil upon the Wicked Priest'* and their behavior is considered justified and applauded *'because of what he did to the Righteous Teacher.'*[52] We can only assume that in the early Church in Palestine the same attitude would have prevailed regarding what was done to James. Nor can there be any doubt that what is being described at this point in the Habakkuk *Pesher* are *these monstrous 'defilements' inflicted on 'the body' of 'the Wicked Priest.'* That Josephus also then goes on to compare the *'Impiety'* and sacrilege involved in *violating the corpses of the dead in this manner* to the revulsion Jews felt about leaving bodies up on crosses without taking them down and burying them before nightfall brings the whole complex to a kind of conclusion. If this connection is, in fact, real and not just a coincidence; then, once again, we have an echo of themes circulating about James' life – in this case relating to his death or demise (to say nothing of Ananus' and Jesus b. Gamala's) reappearing in material relating to that of 'Jesus' in Scripture.

The reason for all these pollutions, *e.g.*, severing the head from the body as in John's case, the '*curse*' of crucifixion, or '*inflicting the disgusting abuses of Evil pollutions*' on Ananus' naked body, was probably because they were seen as impediments to resurrection, the ultimate reason for their perpetration. It is a '*curse*' of this kind, namely the '*curse*' of being '*hung upon a tree*,' whether applied to the object as in Deuteronomy or the action as at Qumran that, as already explained, Paul in Galatians 3:10-13 develops into the basic '*Saving*' ideology of Christianity as we know it, that Jesus, in taking this '*curse*' upon himself freed him (Paul) from '*the curse of the Law*' (here an additional bit of reversal) and, thereby, all '*Christians*' following him – a most astonishing piece of exegetical acrobatics.

The Death of the Righteous Teacher in the Habakkuk *Pesher*

The Habakkuk *Pesher* now goes on in Columns Eleven and Twelve to discuss the destruction of the Righteous Teacher and some members of his Council or '*the Poor.*' It is here it uses Josephus' words about the Temple above, '*God condemned him* (the Wicked Priest) *to destruction.*' It is in this context as well that it goes on to delineate how he '*plotted to destroy the Poor*' ('*the Ebionites*' again), *robbing them of their sustenance in the Cities of Judah, committing '*his Abominable works*' in Jerusalem*, and '*polluting the Temple of God.*'[53] The sequence here is very close to the one in early Church texts where the death of James is immediately followed by the appearance of Roman Armies outside Jerusalem. The coming of these Armies in 1QpHab,IX.6-7, an event actually referred to in the *Pesher* under the designation, '*the Armies of the Kittim*,' follows the description of the predatory actions of the Wicked Priest, '*profiteering from the spoils of the Peoples*' and/or '*Violent Ones*' and '*the Judgements on Evil being inflicted upon the flesh of his corpse.*'

Because the underlying text of Habakkuk 2:8 is, once again, speaking of '*the blood of Men and the Violence done to the Land*,' this is followed by a repeat of the description of '*the Evil the Wicked Priest committed against the Righteous Teacher and the Men of his Council*' (also referred to, as earlier, as

God's 'Elect') and 'the Vengeance,' in turn, which would be visited upon him. In these passages about 'the handing over in the Last Days of the Riches and booty of the Last Priests to the Army of the Kittim,' the destruction of Jerusalem and, with it, the Temple is certainly implied.[54] This is also true for the additional descriptions in Columns Eleven and Twelve, culminating in that of 'the Day of Judgement' – also referred to in Column Ten after the description of the Vengeance 'they meted out' to the corpse of the Wicked Priest as 'the House of Judgement (Beit ha-Mishpat) which God would deliver in His Judgement in the midst of many Peoples.'[55]

In this second set of descriptions about the destruction of the Wicked Priest in Column Twelve, it is simply stated that since the Wicked Priest 'robbed the sustenance of the Poor' and 'plotted to destroy the Poor,' 'so too would God condemn him to destruction.' The same idea is stated again in slightly differing fashion in the previous sentence, 'the Wicked Priest would be paid the reward which he paid the Poor.' Of course, as we have already pointed out, the introduction of 'the Poor'/'Ebionim' terminology is purposeful here, as the usage nowhere occurs in the underlying text of Habakkuk at this point. But what is really interesting about all this is that this usage, 'the reward of his hands (that is, 'the hands of the Wicked') would be paid back to him,' actually occurs in the passage following that of Isaiah 3:10: 'Let us take away the Righteous One, because he is offensive to us' (this in Septuagint reformulation), applied to James' death in all early Church literature.[56]

The idea is very clear. Since this phrase about 'the Wicked being paid the reward he paid the Poor,' too, nowhere appears in the text of Habakkuk at this point; the implication is that it is being deliberately imported from Isaiah 3:10–11 (another 'Wicked vs. the Righteous text – just as in Habakkuk 1:4–2:20), so once again in our view we have 'QED' Again, too, the note of 'Vengeance' in all of this is unmistakable. Nor can there be any doubt that we are speaking about 'destruction' here, that is, the 'destruction' of 'the Righteous Teacher' and 'the Wicked Priest' – in effect, one succeeding the other.

There is no way that any of these descriptions can apply to any earlier assault on the Temple and a destruction of Jerusalem prior to that of 70 CE – and certainly not the two of 63 and 37 BC. In these earlier attacks, as already underscored, there was not the slightest implication of any 'booty given over to' foreign Armies of the kind being alluded to here in the Pesher and in Titus' triumphal parade following his 70 CE conquest, the evidence of which still stands in the ruins of the Roman forum today – to say nothing of the Colosseum reputed to have been built by Titus and his father (Vespasian) out of the proceeds of this 'Victory' (and, of course, with the help of the tens of thousands of prisoners they took). These notices probably cannot even be said to relate to the incursions in the time of Antiochus Epiphanes and the Maccabean War, because this was hardly on the scale of the Roman one and nothing else in the text can be thought of as relating to it.

Before continuing the analysis of this crucial material in Column Twelve, it would be well to return to that in Columns 9–10 just cited above, following the descriptions of the Vengeance *they took upon the corpse* of the Wicked Priest and the coming of the Army of the *Kittim*. The actual words of the second description of this *'Vengeance'* or *'chastisement'* at the end of Column Nine are that *'as a consequence of the Evil he did to the Righteous Teacher and the Men of his Council, God delivered him into the hand of his enemies to torture him.'* *'His enemies'* are unspecified here, but they are clearly not the Righteous Teacher and his confederates, but individuals additional to these, or, as we have been attempting to explain employing the parallel material in the Psalm 37 *Pesher, 'the Violent Ones of the Gentiles'* ('*Idumaeans*' in Josephus).

These *'torture him'* or *'bring him low, with punishment unto destruction'* or *'to consume him with (mortal) soul-embittering (torments), because he condemned His Elect.'* The *'consuming'* or *'destroying'* vocabulary here anticipates and plays off the *'consuming,' 'destroying,'* and even *'swallowing'* imagery we shall encounter in Columns Eleven and Twelve when it comes to describing both what he (*'the Wicked Priest'*) *'did to the Righteous Teacher and the Men of his Council'* – clearly identified with *'the Poor,'* that is, *'he consumed'* or *'destroyed them'* – and what would be done in return to him. Furthermore, the note about *'condemnation'* again carries something of a judicial-meaning here, should one choose to regard it.

Not only is it clear that what is being done to the Wicked Priest is to *'pay him back'* for something he did and a *'Vengeance'* of some kind, but again it is *being done by others to him*, in particular, *'Violent'* third parties such as *'the Idumaeans'* above who, for some reason, treat him *'abominably.'* Nor can this be a disease of some kind, as we have already made clear, but rather something resembling the kind of *'polluted'* and *'abominable'* treatment meted out to Ananus because he had *'condemned'* God's *'Elect.'* We shall presently be able to connect this up with *'the Sanhedrin proceedings'* this same Ananus *'pursued'* against James the Just and several of his companions as Josephus records it.

The play of *'causing Evil to'* or *'condemning God's Elect'* on the idea of *'condemning the Righteous'* is clear. Not only is *'condemning the Righteous'* the characteristic activity of *'those who sought Smooth Things,' 'breaking the Covenant and transgressing the Law'* (*Hok*), who in the end would be *'delivered up to the Avenging Sword of the Covenant'* and who actually made a mortal attack on '*the Righteous One*' (James?) *together with all Walkers in Perfection,*' '*pursuing them with the sword*' at the end of the First Column of the Damascus Document[57]; it is the opposite of the kind of '*justifying*' activity ('*justifying the Righteous*' / '*yaziku Zaddik*') predicated of '*the Righteous Teacher*' and those '*of his Council*' in documents like the Damascus Document and Community Rule. This is implicit in the way Hebrew works, Hebrew having a causative verb – in this case, '*justifying*' connected to the underlying root-meaning of '*Righteous*' / '*Righteousness,*' namely, '*making Righteous*' (as in '*making Many Righteous*' in Isaiah 53:11) or '*justifying*' as opposed to the '*making Evil*' or '*condemning*' here in the Habakkuk *Pesher* and the Damascus Document – that is, *whereas the Wicked Priest* '*condemns*' *people, the Righteous Teacher* '*justifies*' *them.*

This is the kind of exposition one encounters as well, as we saw, in the interpretation of the designation '*the Sons of Zadok*' in CDiv.3–10, who are referred to there – just as the Righteous Teacher and his Council are here in the Habakkuk *Pesher* – as '*the Elect of Israel.*' '*Righteousness*' is the actual root of the designation '*Zadok.*' In the Damascus Document '*the Sons of Zadok,*' as will be recalled, are '*the Elect of Israel called by Name*' ('*called by this Name*' in Acts 4:17, 9:21, etc. above), *who will stand in the Last Days,*' the characteristic activity of whom is '*justifying the Righteous and condemning the Wicked*' – that is, as in early Christianity and fragments of other materials at Qumran,[58] they participate in *the Final* or '*Last Judgement,*' a '*Judgement*' about to be evoked in the Habakkuk *Pesher* as well.

This connection of the name '*Zadok*' ('*Justus*' in Latin) with the person of the Righteous Teacher (who can be looked upon as '*the Son of Zadok*' or '*the Zaddik*' *par excellence)* is exactly what one gets in early Church literature with the constant attachment of the name or title '*Justus*' to James' person. The best example of this comes in the narrative of James' death in Eusebius via Hegesippus, where the designation is sometimes used in place of James' very name itself – for example, when the Scribes and the Pharisees place James on the Pinnacle of the Temple and cry out to him '*O Just One, whom we all ought to obey, since the People are led astray after Jesus the Crucified One, tell us what is the Gate to Jesus?*'[59]

The use of the language of '*consumed*' / '*destroyed*' here in the description of the Vengeance inflicted on the '*soul*' of the Wicked Priest because of '*the Evil he had done to the Righteous Teacher and the Men of his Council,*' will have a variation in the '*swallowing*' language, which the Habakkuk *Pesher* will now use to describe the destruction of the Righteous Teacher by the Wicked Priest at the beginning of Column Eleven (Column Ten having been devoted to a description of '*the House of Judgement God would pronounce in the midst of many Nations'* and the Spouter of Lying's *'building' a worthless 'Assembly upon Lying for the sake of his (own) Glory.'*[60]

The presentation of this death plays off this *'Ba-La-ᶜa'* vocabulary of *'swallowing'* or *'consuming'* – a circle-of-language, as we saw, related to the *'Balaam'*/*'Balak'*/and *'Belial'* language above, not to mention parallel notions circulating about the allusion in Greek, *'ballo,'* that is, *'casting'* or *'throwing down,'* usually in a violent manner. When the Greek preposition, *'kata'*/*'down,'* is added, the signification then becomes that used to describe James being *'thrown down from the Pinnacle of the Temple'* in almost all early Church sources – although this event probably never happened. In the Pseudoclementines *Recognitions,* as we saw, this becomes his being *'thrown down the Temple steps,'* which probably really did happen.[61]

As just indicated too, in the aftermath of the attack by *'the Zealots'* and *'Idumaeans'* on the High Priests in Jerusalem, something resembling this *'casting down'* (*kataballo*) from the Pinnacle of the Temple probably really *did* happen in this case. This was the death of *'Zachariah ben Bariscaeus'* (probably, *'Zachariah ben Barachias'* in Matthew 23:35), whom Josephus describes rather improbably as being both *'very Rich'* and a *'lover of liberty.'* He uses the same allusion, *'lover of liberty,'* to describe Ananus, as just signaled as well, whose murder both preceded and was, no doubt, in some manner connected to this *'Zachariah'*'s. Paul also uses a variety of this language to characterize *'the liberty'* he enjoys *'in Christ Jesus'* and the contrasts he draws between it and *'slavery to the Law'* throughout his Letters (Galatians 2:4, etc.).

The execution of *'Zachariah'* by *'the Zealots'* in the Temple after a mock Sanhedrin trial by *'the Seventy'* which preceded the trial of Niger of Perea, not only parodies James' trial and execution, but was probably connected to it – perhaps even part of the retribution for it. Tradition always locates *'the Tomb of Zechariah,'* as remarked above, right beside James' in the Kedron Valley directly beneath the Pinnacle of the Temple.[62] When *'ballo'* is coupled with a different preposition, *'dia,'* for instance, or *'against,'* the expression then turns into the Greek *'Diabolos,'* meaning *'to throw against'* or *'complain against,'* the basis of our modern word *'the Devil.'* To be sure, many of the usages connected to these crucial allusions to *'swallow'* (*levalᶜo*/*levalᶜam*/*tevalᶜeno*) in the Habakkuk *Pesher,* on how *the Wicked Priest 'swallowed' the Righteous Teacher and his followers among 'the Poor,'* are obscure even in the Hebrew but by elucidating them, as we have shown, we shall be able to tie this description very closely to the death of James as described in early Church sources.

Aside from this *'ballo'*/*'ballaᶜ'* language complex, the exegesis, as we have it, also plays on another word *'Hemah'*/*'Venom'* or *'Wrath,'* which we have already encountered in CDviii.9–11/xix.21–24's description of '*the Princes of Judah*' and '*the Kings of the Peoples*' above. This is evoked relating to an underlying text from Habakkuk 2:15 about '*making his neighbor drink and pouring out His Fury*' ('*Venom*'). All these denotations will be used in the *Pesher*. It also contains another phrase, '*looking on their festivals*,' which will be applied, thereafter, to problems relating to '*their*' Yom Kippur observances. '*Hemah*' / '*Hamato*' can mean '*Venom*' (as in '*the Venom of Vipers*' in the Deuteronomy 32:33 text above) or it can mean, as we saw, '*Anger*' or '*Wrath*,' as in the Wicked Priest's '*Hot Anger*' or '*Wrath*,' which will be the sense the 1QpHab,xi.2–15 will utilize. But, as we shall see, it can also mean, '*dregs*,' which is the sense of the Received Version of 2:15, which actually reads, '*your dregs*' in the sense of the '*dregs of the Cup*' not '*His Venom*' – nor is this to say anything about the '*Divine Wrath*, which is also the sense of the passage. The *Pesher* on it reads as follows:

> *Its meaning concerns* (that is, the meaning of '*pouring out Anger*' – the '*giving one's neighbor to drink and making drunk*' to follow after that) *the Wicked Priest who pursued after the Righteous Teacher to* ('*in*' or '*with*') *his House of Exile to swallow* ('*consume*') *him in his Hot Anger* (*Cha*^*as Hamato*' – the Hebrew of '*to*,' '*in*,' or '*with his House of Exile*' being defective, but it *is* a preposition).

The allusion to '*his Hot Anger*' or '*Furious Wrath*' will be extremely important for understanding the delineation of the Vengeance upon '*the Wicked Priest*' that inevitably follows. So is the allusion to '*swallow*' or '*consume*,' the sense of which, as we have been underscoring and which the rest of the *Pesher* plainly demonstrates, is clearly '*destroy*' (regardless of the fact that some translators give the patently absurd reading, '*confuse him*' here which is simply wrong). '*The Wicked Priest*' did not wish to '*confuse the Righteous Teacher*,' he wished '*to destroy*' him.

'*His House of Exile*'

The above *Pesher* is a most incredible one. In the first place, it contains a defective usage in Hebrew, '*a-Beit-Galuto*' – something about '*in*' or '*at*' '*the House of his Exile*' or '*his Exiled House*,' the meaning of which is obscure but which we shall ultimately be able to decipher. In addition, the *Pesher* introduces an additional word '*Cha*^*as*' not found in the underlying text from Habakkuk 2:15.

The reason for this will also become clearer as we proceed. For a start, this word '*Cha*^*as*' will play on another usage which presently appears in the *Pesher*, '*Chos*'/'*Cup*,' which will further refine the '*giving drink*,' '*drunkenness*,' or '*drinking to the dregs*' metaphor, which appears in the underlying text. Though these usages are admittedly obscure, it will not take much Hebrew to begin to grasp the wordplay that is going on. Even without Hebrew, the reader can attempt to grasp this.

This interpretation of Habakkuk 2:15, of course, does contain the usage we have just highlighted above, '*Hamato*,' which when linked with '*Chaᶜas*' produces the meaning '*his Hot Anger*' or '*Furious Wrath*.' Above, it will be recalled, '*the Venom of Vipers*' from Deuteronomy 32:33 in the Damascus Document was interpreted to relate to '*the Kings of the Peoples and their ways*' or, as we have explained, '*Herodians*.' The usage also occurs in the '*Hymns of the Poor*,' where the meaning parallels the sense we are seeing here, but reversed. There, as we saw, '*the Poor*' are said to be '*saved*' from '*the Fiery Wrath of God's Hot Anger*' because they '*circumcised the fore-skin of their hearts*.' This is surrounded by allusions to '*walking in the Way*,' '*judging the Wicked*,' '*kindling His Wrath*,' and '*being saved*,' all paralleling usages we have been considering above. In the Damascus Document and here, of course, they relate to an illicit Establishment and its High Priests.

But, in addition, what has further confused scholars in the passage from 1QpHab,XI.4-6 before us is the multiplication of '*him*'s or '*his*'es. These occur in three successive variations: '*to swallow him*,' '*the House of his Exile*,' and '*his Hot Anger*' or '*Venomous Fury*.' In Hebrew, pronouns of this kind are always expressed by the same pronominal suffix '*o*'/'*him*' or '*his*.' But the problem is, when one has a series of these, it is often impossible to know to whom they refer – the subject of the action or its object. The same is true in Semitic languages like Arabic and the problem often occurs even in English writing where it is considered poor style not to specify this. In Hebrew and Arabic it is quite normal and you have to figure out the sense of the attribution by what is being said and the drift of the material. This is often a dangerous activity for academics.

In the interpretation of this passage one sees everywhere, the sense of the '*swallow him*' and '*in his Hot Anger*' are quite clear. They refer to '*the Righteous Teacher*' and '*the Wicked Priest*' respectively, that is, '*the Righteous Teacher is being swallowed by the Wicked Priest in his Hot Anger*' or '*Venomous Fury*' – the '*Chaᶜas*' in '*Chaᶜas Hamato*,' as we have seen, meaning even more specifically, '*Anger*' or '*Wrath*.' This will give way to another usage in Hebrew also having to do with the imagery of '*Anger*' and '*Wrath*,' particularly in apocalyptic literature, '*Chos*' or '*Cup*.'

This is the kind of language interplay and imagery that so appealed to the authors of the Dead Sea Scrolls. It is certainly to be found in passage(s) before us from the Habakkuk *Pesher*. It is also to be found, as we have shown, in the Book of Revelation in the New Testament almost word-for-word as we have it here (Revelation 14:10) – another good dating tool for the Habakkuk *Pesher*. We will also find it in the '*Cup*' which Jesus '*must drink*' and that the two brothers, John and James, the so-called '*Sons of Zebedee*,' '*will have to drink*' after him in order to follow him (Matthew 20:22–23/Mark 10:38–39).[62]

It is, however, the third '*him*' or '*his*' that produces all the problems in this text, not only the '*his*' but the expression it is attached to, the defective *a-Beit-Galuto*/ '*to*' or '*in*'/ '*with his House of Exile*' – '*Galut*' meaning, as already indicated, '*Exile*' in Hebrew. In the normal interpretation of this phrase by scholars over the last forty years (what has come to be called in popular literature '*the Consensus*'[64]), the '*him*' or '*his*' here is also taken as referring to the Righteous Teacher, that is, *the Wicked Priest pursued the Righteous Teacher* '*to swallow him in his Hot Anger*' at *the Righteous Teacher's* '*House of Exile*.' In their mind of these scholars or of this '*Consensus*,' this last meant Qumran or what they theorize to have been the '*Essene*' Settlement situated there.

This then gave rise to certain other interpretations having to do with what they considered to be the Wicked Priest's supposed '*drunkenness*' (how silly can one be?) and confrontations at this so-called '*Essene Monastery at Qumran*' between the Righteous Teacher and the Wicked Priest over a different calendrical reckoning for *Yom Kippur*.[65] Therefore the defective '*to*,' '*at*,' or '*with the House of his Exile*' was Qumran – '*the Righteous Teacher*'s purported '*House of Exile*' even though this was only some twenty miles from Jerusalem.

But comparison with the life of James – as in the case of the desecration of the Wicked Priest's '*corpse*' and, as will become plain, this same '*Wicked Priest*'s purported '*drunkenness*' as well – produces an even more rational and plausible explanation. When data relating to James' life and death are introduced into references of this kind in the Dead Sea Scrolls, they help clarify and extract more meaning – meaning one could not otherwise have expected – whereas previously there was only obscurity. This is the kind of powerful corroboration that '*builds up*' (once more, no pun intended), when one considers the internal evidence of these texts, and that begins to approach certainty.

First of all, reference to the biography of James makes one think that this third '*his*,' the one attached to the defective '*his House of Exile*,' does not apply to the object being '*pursued*' with such '*Hot Anger*' and then '*swallowed*' – namely '*the Righteous Teacher*' – but rather the subject doing the '*pursuing*' and/or '*swallowing*,' meaning '*the Wicked Priest*.' This makes the sequence of the three '*him*'s/'*his*'es more plausible: that is, the first '*to swallow*' or '*consume him*' applies to the Righteous Teacher; the second, '*in his Venomous Anger,*' applies to the Wicked Priest; and the third, '*with*'/'*in his House of Exile,*' once again, applies to the Wicked Priest too. This then makes our sequence of '*him's*/'*his*'es expressible in terms of *a-b-b* ('*a*' being the Righteous Teacher and '*b*' being the Wicked Priest) instead of *a-b-a* as most take it to be. This is far more rational than thinking the '*swallow*' or '*consume him*' applies to the Righteous Teacher; the '*in his hot anger,*' to the Wicked Priest; and the '*with*'/'*to his Exiled House,*' back to the Righteous Teacher again which is, at best, confusing – at worst nonsensical.

Then what would the sense of this '*his House of Exile*' or '*Exiled House,*' seen in this manner, be? The Hebrew for this expression, as just noted, is the defective '*a-Beit-Galuto.*' The introductory preposition here is an '*a*' or '*alef*' which is meaningless in Hebrew. '*Be*' – or '*Bet*' in Hebrew here – would give the meaning '*with*' or '*in.*' Anything else would probably not be a single Hebrew letter nor readily be confused with '*alef,*' nor make any sense. Furthermore in Hebrew, terms like '*Beit-Din*' or '*Beit ha-Mishpat*' normally have to do with judicial proceedings of some kind. In fact, as already intimated, the latter was even used in the *Pesher* in the previous Column X.3-5, when it came to describing '*the Judgement that God would make in the midst of many Peoples,*' where He would '*judge*' the Wicked Priest '*with fire and brimstone.*'[66]

Moreover this imagery of this '*Judgement*" permeates the last Columns of the Habakkuk *Pesher*, giving them a completely eschatological cast, i.e., '*the Judgement*' that in common parlance is normally referred to as '*the Last Judgement.*' This is referred to in Columns XII.12–XIII.4 of the *Pesher*, following the passages we are analyzing here, as the '*Yom ha-Mishpat*'/'*the Day of Judgement*' (an expression paralleled in the Koran 82:17–18 by the expression '*Yom ad-Din*'[67]). This would make Column X.3's '*House of Judgement*' (which we have already encountered at the beginning of Column VIII.2 in the eschatological interpretation of Habakkuk 2:4) an idiomatic expression of some kind having to do with *the actual decision of* '*Judgement*' God '*delivers*' on '*the Day of Judgement.*'[68]

In fact, this '*Judgement*' is already being referred to in the *Pesher* as early as Column V.1-5, where '*His Elect,*' meaning, '*the Righteous Teacher and the Men of His Council*' – '*the Poor*' in the Psalm 37 *Pesher* whom we have already shown to be the object of the Wicked Priest's condemnation in the Habakkuk *Pesher* both in Column IX.9–10 and Column XII.2–6 – are those who will '*execute God's Judgement on the Nations.*' We have also already seen this expression '*His Elect*' to be equivalent to '*the Sons of Zadok*' in CDIV.3-4 which would make '*the Sons of Zadok*' almost supernatural, participating along with God *in the process of final eschatological Judgement.*

This scenario fits in very well with that of the War Scroll too, in which the Heavenly Host, together with His Messiah (the *'no mere Adam'* and presumably the *'Returning'* One, though this is not clear), will come *'on the clouds of Heaven'* – as per Gospel presentations – and participate along with *'the Penitents in the Wilderness'* Camps *'in the Land of Damascus'* *in the process of final eschatological Judgement,* once again tying the circle of all these allusions in our texts very closely together. This, in any event, as we have seen, is the proclamation James is pictured as making in the Temple prior to his death in all early Church texts. This proclamation of *'the Son of Man standing on the right hand of God'* or *'coming with Power on the clouds of Heaven,'* is also repeatedly ascribed to Jesus (to say nothing of John the Baptist) in a variety of contexts throughout the New Testament as already pointed up as well.[69]

For Column v.3 of the Habakkuk *Pesher,* as we have also seen, *'God would not destroy His People by the hand of the Gentiles.'*[70] This last is the same term the Psalm 37 *Pesher* attaches to *'the Violent Ones'* who visit God's *'Judgement on Evil'* upon the Wicked Priest. The term *'destroy,'* being used here, is also the same one ultimately applied to the condemnation of the Wicked Priest by God towards the end of the *Pesher* in Column XII.5-6.[71] Rather, in the most hopeful expression of nationalism, this Column Five *Pesher* on Habakkuk 1:12–13 concludes:

> By the hand of His Elect, God will execute Judgement on all the Nations (Go'im again) and with their Punishment, all the Evil Ones of His (own) People, who kept His Commandments only when convenient (the meaning here clearly being 'Jewish Backsliders').

These *'Ebionim'/'Sons of Zadok'/'God's Elect'* are then said *'not to have fornicated after their eyes during the Era of Evil.'*[72] The use of the verb, *'fornicate,'* in this context is particularly meaningful once again as well. As will be recalled, *'being a Keeper not a Breaker'* is the language one encounters in James 2:8–9 (in exposition of *'loving your neighbor as yourself'*), which can now be seen to be permeating 1QpHab as well, *'the Covenant-Breakers'* in Columns II.3–7 and v.4–12 being identified with *'the Traitors (to the New Covenant)'* and *'the Violent Ones.'* It is also the definition of *'the Sons of Zadok,'* which one encounters on two occasions in the Community Rule, again completing the circle of the identification of *'the Sons of Zadok'* with *'the Elect of Israel'* who are, therefore, *'the Keepers of the Covenant'* or *'the Shomrei ha-Brit'* par excellence.

Where '*the Evil Ones among (God's) People who kept His Command-ments only when convenient*' are concerned: for a start these should probably include '*the Wicked Priest*,' Ananus himself, responsible for the death of James; Philo's nephew, Tiberius Alexander, responsible with Ves-pasian and Titus (and probably Paul's listeners in Acts 25:13–26:32 – one of Acts' longest continuous episodes – Agrippa II and Bernice) for the destruction of the Temple; and people of this ilk, among whom (where the parameters of Qumran are concerned), one would probably have to include R. Yohanan ben Zacchai, Paul himself, Josephus, and *many others*.

The usage '*House of Judgement*'/'*Beit ha-Mishpat*,' as just signaled, will also appear in the eschatological exposition in Column VIII.1–3 of how those with '*Faith in the Righteous Teacher*' and '*suffering works*' will be '*saved* ('*in the Last Times*') *from the House of Judgement*.' All these exegeses set up a purposeful tension between the death of '*the Wicked Priest*' and the worldly or profane trial he '*pursued*' against the person, we consider to be James, and the Heavenly or eschatological '*Beit ha-Mishpat*' or '*Judgement*' God pronounces by the hand of '*the Sons of Zadok*' or '*His Elect*' against him in Column V.4 and at the beginning of Column X, '*of fire and brim-stone*' which God delivers '*in the midst of many Peoples*' (to say nothing of X.12–13 and XII.6–XIII.4 above).[73]

Seen in this manner and with the actual historical scenario of James' Sanhedrin trial in mind, one can think of the reference to his '*pursuing him with his House of Exile*' as being an esotericism or an expletive of some kind for the Sanhedrin trial that '*the Wicked Priest*' Ananus actually '*pursued*' against James. This would also seem to be something of the import of the interpretation of the words, '*the Wicked spies on the Right-eous, seeking to kill him*,' but God did not allow him '*to be condemned when he is tried*' in the *Pesher* on Psalm 37:32–33 (and, for that matter, the early Church *Pesher* on Isaiah 3:10–11) above, which is deliberately turned around in the exposition to signal, once again, as here in the Habakkuk *Pesher*, the '*reward God would pay*' the Wicked Priest, '*delivering him into the hand of the Violent Ones of the Gentiles to execute Judgement upon him*.'[74]

Put more explicitly – so abhorrent, therefore, were the proceedings '*pursued*' by Ananus against James in the Pharisee/Sadducee-dominated Sanhedrin – here denoted by the '*Beit-Galuto*'/'*his House of Exile*' – to '*the Assembly*' or '*Church of the Poor*,' they would not deign to acknowl-edge these either as a proper '*Beit-Din*' or a '*Beit ha-Mishpat*' ('*Court*' or '*Trial*'). Therefore the words, '*his Galut*' or '*Exile*' here are not a location or an actual '*Exile*' *per se*, which is the normative understanding of the expression in Qumran Studies, but an expression of their loathing or disgust for just this place and these proceedings.

This is another and altogether more sensible way of looking at the expression '*His Exiled House*,' taking the pronominal suffix tied to it to mean not *the Righteous Teacher's* '*House*,' the usual understanding of Dead Sea Scrolls' scholars, but *the Wicked Priest's*. In fact, one encounters this exact sense in the allusion, '*the House of the High Priest*,' mystifyingly evoked in the Gospels to denote precisely *the Sanhedrin Trial by* '*all the High Priests, Scribes*, and *Elders*,' and '*the whole Sanhedrin seeking testimony against Jesus in order to kill him*' in the middle of the night at '*the House*' or '*Hall of the High Priest*' (Mark 14:53–55 and *pars*.).

One need be mystified no longer. Not only are the exact words '*seeking to kill him*' of the Psalm 37:32 *Pesher* above employed here; but it is directly following this that Jesus is pictured as evoking the proclamation we have already seen attributed to James, '*You will see the Son of Man sitting at the right hand of Power and coming on the clouds of Heaven*,' and the High Priest, for some reason – again mystifyingly – then rending his clothes and saying, '*He has spoken blasphemy*.' (Matthew 26:65). One says '*mystifyingly*,' for it was not '*blasphemous*' to say the sorts of things 'Jesus' is pictured as saying at this point in the narrative.[75] Nor could anything better recapitulate the events converging on James' death than this. Moreover, as already underscored, we would not have thought to look at these parallels without looking into the materials surrounding James' Sanhedrin Trial and death.

'*The Exile*' of the Sanhedrin in Talmudic Sources

This exposition of '*His House of Exile*' would suffice as an alternative suggestion as to how to translate this curious phrase, but it is possible to carry this further and develop a more convincing exposition even than this which really must be seen as final and a *definitive* proof – a proof based on '*the internal data*' much stronger, in fact, than any of the presently-reigning orthodox scholarly consensuses regarding palaeography or the rather imprecise measure of AMS C–14 dating. In most Biblical contexts, the words, '*pursued after*,' are usually accompanied by the phrase '*with the sword*.' This is true of Pharaoh's '*pursuit*' of the Israelites in Exodus 14:8 and Saul's '*pursuit*' after David in 1 Samuel 23:25. This is also true of the depiction of the attack on '*the soul of the Righteous One*' and '*all the Walkers in Perfection*' by '*the Pourer out of Lying*'s confederates, '*the Seekers after Smooth Things*' and '*those who broke the Covenant*' and '*transgressed the Law*' at the end of the First Column of the Damascus Document.[76]

Often such a '*pursuit*' involves the name '*Jacob*,' as in Jacob's pursuit by his father-in-law Laban (Genesis 31:23 and 36), which no doubt would have appealed to the Qumran exegetes if James was the subject of their exegesis – James' original name in Hebrew being '*Jacob*.' This theme is recapitulated in Amos 1:11's accusation, this time '*against Edom*,' that '*he pursued his brother with the sword*.' Again the '*Edomite*' connection here would have been particularly attractive to Qumran exegetes; but what is certain is that in all these contexts, the pursuit signaled by the word '*pursue*' was mortal and carried with it the intent '*to kill*' or '*destroy*.'

This is also true in the mirror reversal of this, '*the Law of the Pursuer*' of Deuteronomy 19:6, which actually includes the idea of the '*heart*' of the Pursuer in '*blood Vengeance*' being uncontrollably '*Hot*' just as we have here in the Habakkuk *Pesher*. It is also true in recent variations of this theme among groups of more nationalist Jews, with a mindset today similar to what we are seeing here, permitting mortal '*pursuit*' of someone having caused fellow Jews to be killed by Gentiles.[77] There even seems to be a hint of the inversion of these matters in the present exposition of the Habakkuk *Pesher* we have before us. Of course, if one does admit the identification of Ananus with '*the Wicked Priest*' and, along with this, the connection possibly in his mind of James with the assassination some six years earlier of his brother, the High Priest Jonathan, by those Josephus at this point had started denoting as '*Sicarii*' (as tenuous as this may be), then the fact of a species of '*blood Vengeance*' being involved in, according to his view, *the judicial proceedings he 'pursued' against James* has to be entertained.[78]

Looking at the words '*he pursued the Righteous Teacher*' in or with '*his Beit ha-Mishpat*' in the Greek can also be somewhat illustrative. We have already found this helpful in terms of looking at other allusions in Hebrew, but it is especially true when looking at perhaps the most interesting parallel between how 'Jesus' was portrayed in the Gospels (apart from '*the Voice of Heaven*' that convinces Sophocles' '*Philoctetes*' to go back and fight for the Greeks at Troy and the way Dionysus is treated by the local townspeople in Euripedes' *Bacchae*) to the archetypical destruction of '*the Righteous Teacher*' in the Hellenistic literature, *the Courtroom Trial of Socrates*. In Plato's *Euthyphro*, for instance, Socrates comes to the court and outside meets one Euthyphro who is later to be among those who accuse him (Socrates) of '*Impiety*' which leads to his death. An Oracle of sorts, Euthyphro is '*pursuing*' courtroom proceedings against, as it turns out, his own father! The word used here to express this in the Greek is '*pursued*' in the sense of *pursuing judicial proceedings against someone*.[79] As far afield as this might originally seem, it is nevertheless useful in bringing home the mindset of the individuals responsible for documents of the kind before us, and we suggest that this is the sense of the word as it is being used at this critical juncture of the Habakkuk *Pesher*.

If we now look at Talmudic sources relating to Sanhedrin proceedings carrying the death sentence and the legitimacy or illegitimacy of these, one finds materials that *directly relate to this usage in the Habakkuk Pesher*. Once again, the reader should realize that we would not have thought even to consult these, where the fate of '*the Righteous Teacher*' at Qumran is concerned, were we not looking at *the paradigmatic fate of James*. There, it turns out, that on at least *six* different occasions, when the issue of capital punishment is being discussed – particularly that *relating to passing a death sentence for* '*blasphemy*' – it is specifically claimed that, in the Period under consideration (from the 30's–60's CE), the Sanhedrin '*was exiled*' – these are the words Talmudic tradition actually uses – from its normal place-of-sitting in '*the Chamber*' on the Temple Mount to a place-of-sitting outside these precincts cryptically referred to as '*Hanut*.'[80]

As these sources generally recount this tradition, this is expressed as '*before the destruction of the Temple* (here, also expressed as '*ha-Bayit*' or '*the House*'), *the Sanhedrin* was *exiled (galtah) and took up its sitting in Hanut*' – or more simply even, '*the Sanhedrin was exiled...from the Chamber of Hewn Stone to Hanut*.'[81] In the Tractate *Rosh Ha-Shanah*, where this notice or its counterparts are recorded *three times*, it is specifically linked to two passages from Isaiah 26:5 and 29:4, about '*the fall of the Lofty Ones*' or '*the Lofty Ones being brought low*.' The same words are specifically evoked, particularly as regards '*the fall of the Cedars of Lebanon*' – as, for instance as already explained above, in the *Pesharim* on Isaiah 10:33–34 introducing the famous '*Rod*' and '*Branch*' material '*from the Roots of Jesse*' in 11:1–5 ('*white*' in the sense of underlying '*Lebanon*,' '*levan*' meaning '*white*' in Hebrew, almost always signifying '*the Temple*' and '*the Cedars*,' its '*wood*') – both at Qumran and in Talmudic literature to refer to the fall of the Temple and, in the *Talmud* anyhow (if not at Qumran), the fall in 70 CE; never an earlier fall.[82]

Some of these Talmudic references to this peculiar fact of the Sanhedrin changing its residence to a place outside the Temple called '*Hanut*,' specifically emphasize that the Sanhedrin's '*Exile*' (*Galut*) during this period from its original home in the Chamber of Hewn Stone on the Temple Mount was widely known. But the reference in Tractate *Rosh ha-Shanah* is to six such '*Exiles*' or '*Banishments*' – and here the actual word used is that '*Galut*' being used in Column XI.4–6 of the Habakkuk *Pesher* above to describe how the Wicked Priest '*swallowed the Righteous Teacher*.'[83] This kind of '*Exile*' was '*the Exile*' or '*Banishment of the Sanhedrin from the Temple*' during the period in question, namely, from approximately 30–70 CE. The point being made in the enumeration of these is that these kinds of *'Exiles'* also presaged *the departure of the Divine Presence from the Temple*, echoing a similar causality *between the death of James and the fall of Jerusalem* which we have already encountered in early Church sources above.

The same language is repeated in Tractate *Sanhedrin*, where the subject under discussion is the number of witnesses required for conviction in capital cases and procedures for acquittal in close votes. We have already had occasion to refer to this Tractate both as regards *'the Enemies of God,'* who would have no share in the *'world to come,'* and as it threw light on the stoning of James, particularly as recorded at Nag Hammadi.[84] Again the tradition of the Sanhedrin's *'Exile'* to its place-of-sitting in *'Hanut'* in the years just prior to the destruction of the Temple in 70 CE is repeated. But the focus of the discussion concerns the permission or non-permission to try capital cases in such a setting – the polemical conclusion being that *outside the Chamber of Hewn Stone such permission was withdrawn* and *sentences of this kind in such an exterior-setting were illegal.*[85] This is a conclusion fraught with significance where the Sanhedrin proceedings *'pursued'* against James (to say nothing of others) are concerned.

Therefore, we now have extremely telling testimony that in the Period in which we would place the documents before us, the middle of the First Century CE, the word *'Exile'* is being *specifically applied to Sanhedrin proceedings having to do with the death penalty involving blasphemy.* In our view, it is not possible to find stronger proof relating to the exposition of this obscure expression, *'a-Beit-Galuto,'* than this; but, in addition, the actual formulation one finds in more of these testimonies, aside from *'Galut'/'Exile,'* is *'galtah min ha-Bayit,'* meaning *'exiled from the House'* – *'House,'* in this instance, being the manner in which *'the Temple'* is often referred to in Hebrew. This is the phraseology used in these notices about *'the Exile'* of the Sanhedrin from its former place-of-sitting in the Chamber of Hewn Stone on the Temple Mount to a location outside these precincts in the *Talmud* and the way this is formulated – only slightly reversed from the expression *'Beit-Galuto'/'His House of Exile'* in the Habakkuk *Pesher* – makes it look as if those writing the *Pesher* were familiar with the fact that the Sanhedrin was, in fact, *'exiled' from the Temple Mount to a place called Hanut* in the period just prior to the War against Rome and Jerusalem's fall. Furthermore, in our view – and connected to this – *they were aware of the judicial proceedings being 'pursued' against James.*

Once more our case is demonstrated, at least on this point, and we have come full circle. The phrase *'Sanhedrin Trial,'* as well as its reflection in *the Sanhedrin Trial of Jesus* at '*the Palace*' or '*House of the High Priest*' in the Gospels, now fits this otherwise totally obscure usage, '*a-Beit-Galuto*,' in 1QpHab,xi.6. In the latter, as now forcefully emphasized, this comes at a key juncture focusing on *the destruction of the Righteous Teacher by the Wicked Priest* – itself preceding *both his own destruction and the fall of the Temple*, also alluded to in Columns Nine, Eleven, and Twelve of the *Pesher* above.[86]

It is reference to the few known facts of James' life and his death, such as they are, that allow us to approach these shadowy allusions. This meets two criteria: 1) it expounds material we would not otherwise be able to understand; and 2) it leads to new, hitherto unsuspected, insights not explainable by any other theory. Once again, the point is that by consulting the biography of James we are able to elicit additional meaning out of otherwise obscure usages in the Dead Sea Scrolls that have been a continual puzzle to scholars. For what most have made out of these without benefit of the James hypothesis, one has only to consult their works – that of any of my colleagues will do. This is powerful verification of the applicability of the positions we are adopting indeed.

'*Seeing their Privy Parts*' and '*Seeing their Festivals*'

But it is possible to reach even further still and, using the James hypothesis, elicit more from the text. *This cannot be done with any other hypothesis.* As it turns out, there are *transmutations of words* in this text, not only in this interpretation but in the two that follow. As already previously remarked, there is a second part of the *Pesher* on Habakkuk 2:15 which turns on the allusion in the underlying text to '*looking upon their festivals*.'[87] Not only is this interpreted in terms of confrontations at the so-called '*Essene Monastery at Qumran*' between the Righteous Teacher and the Wicked Priest but, once again the imagery of '*swallowing*' is introduced into the *Pesher* and the exposition expressed in terms of this imagery.

The problem is that in the normative reading of the underlying text in both the *Masoretic* (Hebrew) and *Septuagint* (Greek) versions, the phrase '*looking upon their festivals*' (here *moᶜadeihem*) does not exist, but rather '*looking on their privy parts*' (*meᶜoreihem*) and a '*dalet*' has been substituted for a '*resh*.' Since the *Pesher*, when speaking about '*the Cup of the Wrath of God shall swallow (the Wicked Priest)*' at the end of Column xi.15, in xi.13 will also speak about the Wicked Priest's '*foreskin*,' as we have seen, *i. e.*, '*he did not circumcise the foreskin of his heart*'; we can only assume that the transmutation in the underlying text from Habakkuk 2:15 was purposeful and those at Qumran knew the original of this passage.

But this also triggers a transmutation in the underlying text of Habakkuk 2:16, where the received *Masoretic* and *Vulgate* read, '*Uncover your foreskin*' (*he-ᶜarel*), but which here in 1QpHab,XI.9 and in the Greek *Septuagint* read '*make tremble*' (*heraᶜel*). But the sense of the Masoretic original and of the preceding '*privy parts*' from 2:15 is again, then, recovered in the *Pesher* which interprets this, as we have also seen, in terms of the Wicked Priest '*not circumcising the foreskin* (*ᶜorlah*) *of his heart.*'[88] Besides the play on the word '*Raᶜal*' ('*Poison*') in CDviii/xix, etc. above, one should remark the curious parallel that exists regarding this in Galatians 2:4, where Paul basically uses this '*looking on their privy parts*' charge to accuse some in the Jerusalem Church Leadership of '*coming in by stealth to spy on*' *the freedom* he and his colleagues '*enjoy in Christ Jesus*,' meaning *their circumcision* or *lack of it*, and adding, '*so that they might enslave us.*'What an incredible turnabout.The point is, is it intentional?

In our view, the *Pesher* is also involved in at least two other transmutations or word-plays in this section: '*Chos*' ('Cup') from '*Chaᶜas*' ('*Wrath*') in the underlying text – also related to Isaiah 51:21's '*Chos ha-Tarᶜelah*/'*the Cup of Trembling*' above, now expressed as '*Chos Hamato*'/'*the Cup of the Wrath of God*' and '*Hemah*'/'*Hotness*' or '*Anger*' and '*Hanut*,' the putative venue in the early 60's of James' illegal trial for blasphemy. The first three or four of these transmutations or plays are indisputable – the last, '*Hamat*' for '*Hanut*,' will remain a matter of opinion. In view of the transmutations in the rest of the *Pesher* it is not far-fetched.

The *Pesher*'s transformed version of this all-important text from Habakkuk 2:15 then reads as follows:

> *Woe unto the one who causes his neighbor to drink, pouring out his Fury* ('*Hamato*,' which can also mean '*dregs*') *to make them drunk, that he may look upon their Festivals* ('*moᶜadeihem*' in place of '*meᶜoreihem*' – '*their privy parts*' in the received Biblical text, as we just saw).

To some extent, the first part of the exposition of this passage, which we have treated in the foregoing, plays and will play further on the allusions in the underlying text to '*giving one's neighbor drink*,' '*pouring out the dregs*' (this, the '*hamato*' in the underlying text), and '*drunkenness*.'

The second part will now be interpreted in terms of additional confrontations connected to *Yom Kippur*, called in the *Pesher* '*the Festival of Repose of the Day of Atonements*,' '*the Day of Fasting*,' and '*the Sabbath of their Repose*.'[89] This last, as already noted, would appear to be reflected in or to incorporate something of the thrust of John 19:31 above about not leaving the condemned on crosses '*into the Sabbath*,' '*for that Sabbath was a*

Great Day' – here again, the double use of '*Sabbath*,' since '*the Festival of Repose*' can be translated in Greek as '*the Sabbath*.' Moreover, '*Great Day*' is clearly a reference to '*Festival*' – only in John, the '*Festival*' is the Passover whereas, in the Habakkuk *Pesher*, it is '*the Day of Atonements*' (thus!).

The phraseology '*in his Hot Anger*' is redundant and also introduces a new usage, '*Cha^cas'/'Wrath*' or '*Anger*.' This is not mentioned in the underlying Biblical text from Habakkuk 2:15, but it will be played upon momentarily to produce the homophonic '*Chos'/'Cup*,' which will then produce '*the Cup of the Wrath of God*' in the *Pesher*. Nor is this to say anything about '*the Cup of the right hand of the Lord*' in the underlying text from Habakkuk 2:16. This, in turn, plays off the allusion to '*make tremble*' (*hera^cel*) in the underlying text from 2:15 as redacted in the *Pesher*, not to mention '*the Cup of Trembling*' (*Tar^celah*) from Isaiah 51:21, which then moves in the *Pesher* into the Wicked Priest '*not circumcising the foreskin* (*^corlah* or *^carlah*) *his heart*.' As previously remarked, this is how complex these texts really are.

It is our view that, like the transmutation of '*privy parts*' into '*Festivals*,' at the beginning of the *Pesher*, all this word-play is purposeful. The same can be said for the illegality concerning the proceedings '*pursued*' against '*the Righteous Teacher*' or James by the Wicked Priest '*in his Exiled House at Hanut*.' The fortuitous conjunction of '*Hanut*' and '*hamat*' would have been just the kind of word-play or transmutation of words that appealed to the sectaries in their exegetical exposition of these matters. The term '*Hanut*' for the actual location of the Sanhedrin during the Period of its '*Exile*' (coinciding almost precisely with the time of the Sanhedrin proceedings '*pursued*' against James) would have been seen by them as significant as it is in the *Talmud*. If this is true, then we have a direct reference, however veiled, to events in James' life even in the *Pesher* as it stands.

Once again, nothing could be more powerful proof of the relationship of these passages to James' death than this – not to mention the evocation of a *Sanhedrin Trial* at '*the House*' or '*Court of the High Priest*' in the Gospels above. We shall now be able, in '*pursuing*' the next few notices in this Scriptural exposition (again no pun intended), to follow some of this word-play to its inevitable conclusion, in the process elucidating some of the grossest errors and intellectual miscues that have plagued Qumran Studies from their inception.

More '*Swallowing*' Related to the Day of Atonement and '*the Reward he Paid the Poor*'

Proceeding with this kind of word-play, the text now moves on to the second part of its exposition of Habakkuk 2:15 – the '*he looked on their Festivals*'/'*looked on their privy parts*' phraseology – and again uses the vocabulary of '*swallowing*,' as we saw, to represent what the Wicked Priest did to the Righteous Teacher and his confederates. This time the pronominal suffix attached to the action is the plural '*them*,' '*he swallowed them*' not '*him*,' as in '*he swallowed him*,' and the action is connected to a reference to '*Yom Kippur*' above – this being the *Pesher*'s clear elucidation of the revamped usage, '*their Festivals*,' in the underlying text.[90] Though this is often interpreted in normative Qumran studies as '*to confuse them*,' as already intimated, there is no real '*confusing*' going on here, only a reference to '*swallowing*'/'*consuming*' in the sense of '*he destroyed them*.'

This language of '*swallowing*' will now be applied a third time, in the context of some of the most overpowering imagery in the Qumran corpus – or, for that matter, any other post-Biblical context – to describe how '*the Cup of the Wrath of God would swallow*' the Wicked Priest and, here, it cannot mean anything but '*destroy*.' We have already seen how in the next *Pesher* in the next Column XII on Habakkuk 2:17 about '*the Violence of Lebanon*' and '*the destruction of the dumb beasts*,' these ideas are reiterated, namely, that the Wicked Priest '*would be paid the reward he paid the Poor*,' and '*as he plotted to destroy the Poor*' (Ebionim), so too '*God would condemn him to destruction*.'[91] '*The Poor*' here are clearly meant to be identified with either '*the Ebionites*' or '*the Essenes*' (if the two groups can, in fact, really be separated) and incorporate both '*Lebanon*' – this presumably because like Priests in the Temple, as already remarked, they too only *wore white linen* – and '*the dumb beasts*' in the underlying Hebrew of Habakkuk 2:17. Not only does the *Pesher*, as the Psalm 37 *Pesher*, really identify '*the Poor*' ('*Lebanon*') with '*the Council of the Community*' but '*the dumb beasts*' too, as previously signaled as well, are identified with '*the Simple of Judah doing Torah*' which harks back to the archaic '*Torah-Doers in the House of Judah*' (*i.e.*, all '*Torah-Doing Jews*') to circumscribe the exegesis of both Habakkuk 2:3 on '*the Delay of the Parousia*' in Column VII.5–14 and Habakkuk 2:4 in Column VIII.1–3. Again, to repeat, the Hebrew here really does mean '*destroy*' (*lechalah*/*lechalot*) and not something else like '*confuse*.'

One should note the telltale emphasis on '*doing*' again, the same emphasis one finds throughout the Letter of James and the Damascus Document – also the basis of the Qumran usage '*works*'/'*maᶜasim*' as we saw. This allusion to '*Torah-Doers*' will, as already remarked as well, reappear in the restriction in Columns VII and VIII earlier of the scope of the application of both Habakkuk 2:3 and Habakkuk 2:4 on '*the Righteous shall live by his Faith*.' Earlier still, in Column V.3, we saw the verb '*destroy*' (*yechaleh*) used to express how God '*would not destroy His People by the hand of the Nations, but rather by the hand of His Elect ('the Poor') execute Judgement on all the Nations'* and *'the Evil Ones of His People who kept His Commandments only when convenient,'* presumably meant to include *'the Wicked Priest'* and all Backsliding or Renegade Jews as we saw as well.

The reason for this *'Judgement'* and *'destruction,'* where *'Gentiles'* were concerned was simple – they are all perceived of as *'Idolaters.'* In the words of the very last lines of the *Pesher* (Column Thirteen):

> *Its interpretation* (Habakkuk 2:19–20 warning *'Idolaters'*) *concerns all the Nations* (here the usage is *'Go'im'* again as in *'the Violent Ones of the Go'im'*) *who serve stone and wood. But on the Day of Judgement, God will destroy (lechalah) all the Servants of Idols* (the opposite of *'the Servants of Righteousness'* we already encountered in 2 Corinthians 11:15 above) *and Evil Ones from off the Earth.*[92]

The parallels too here with Koranic imagery, when both *'the Idolaters'* and *'the Day of Judgement'* are pivotal, should be patent.[93]

As the Habakkuk *Pesher* now details this confrontation relating to *Yom Kippur* in Column XI.6–8, as already underscored:

> *And at the completion of the Festival of Repose of the Day of Atonements, he (the Wicked Priest) appeared to them to swallow them, causing them to stumble* (or, more significantly perhaps, *'casting them down'*) *on the Fast Day, the Sabbath of their Repose.*

One encounters this same sense in James 2:10 about *'keeping the whole Law, but stumbling on one small point'* and throughout the Pauline corpus reversing this. Here, however, because of the imagery of *'swallowing'* or *'destruction'* surrounding it, the sense would appear to be more that of *'casting them down'* than of *'causing them to stumble,'* though what one has here may be a double entendre implying or incorporating both senses.

Much speculation has arisen concerning how the Qumran sectaries were using a different calendar than the Jerusalem Establishment.[94] This was no doubt true but, once again, all of this has assumed that the defective and clearly esoteric *'a-Beit-Galuto'* meant that the Righteous Teacher's *'House of Exile'* – and, *ergo*, that the Community was celebrating a different *Yom Kippur 'Fast Day' in the wilderness* or at Qumran itself, when the Wicked Priest appeared to them to, supposedly, *'confuse them.'*[95]

But this is to miss the intense sense of *'destruction'* surrounding the passage. As just emphasized, this is not some innocent *'confrontation'* simply involving *'confusing'* people or *'causing them to stumble'* in their observations, though this may have been part of it as even an Establish-ment Trial for *'blasphemy'* would imply. To be sure, there is *'confrontation'* going on here but, once again, the sense would appear to be mortal, not simply verbal. As we have emphasized, as well, this is what the telltale usage *'leval*ᶜ*am'/'swallow them'* and what follows in the *Pesher* in the next Column XII.2–6 – about how *God would 'pay'* the Wicked Priest *'the reward he paid the Poor'* and *'condemn him to destruction,'* because *'he plotted to destroy the Poor'* – clearly implies.

This is also the sense of the underlying allusions to *'the Violence done to Lebanon'* and *'the Land'* and *'the predation on the dumb beasts,'* upon which these *Peshers* are based. If so, then the allusion to *'causing them to fall'* or *'casting them down'* would have import, in particular, *vis-à-vis* all Greek versions of the death of James where, as we have seen, the *Ba-La-ᶜa/'swal-lowing'* language moves into the *'ballo'/'casting down'* language. Though the allusion here may mean something as innocuous as *'causing them to stumble'* over differences about legal observance concerning *'the Day of Atonements,'* the totality of the phraseology seems more portentous than that. This is especially true in view of what immediately follows XI.9–15, as the *Pesher* proceeds, evoking the imagery of *'drinking the Cup'* and *Divine Retribution* and *'destruction,'* one encounters in the fanatically apoc-alyptic and emotionally-charged atmosphere of Revelation too. Before moving on to consider this, it is important to look quickly at the usage *'Day of Atonements, the Fast Day the Sabbath of their Repose'* and its signif-icance, not only for Jews but also in the life of James.

For Jews today, of course, *'Yom Kippur'/'the Day of Atonement'* (singu-lar) is still the Holiest and most solemn day of the year associated, as it is, with forgiveness of Sin – inadvertent or collective. Classically, it was the one day of the year when the High Priest, dressed in his full regalia including mitre and breastplate, went into the Holy of Holies alone – there, kneeling before the Judgement Seat, to ask for forgiveness on behalf of the whole People before God,. This is precisely the picture, for example, one gets in the presentation of *'Simeon the Righteous'* in *Ben Sira* 50:5–23 (because it has a colophon, almost certainly a Second-Century BC book).[96] It was, also, the day on which the High Priest was permitted (in the manner of Moses addressing God face-to-face in the Tent of Meeting) to pronounce the forbidden Name of God, *'YHWH'* (so tor-tuously transliterated into modern approximations because everyone has forgotten how to pronounce it).

But this is precisely the picture of James in early Church accounts – particularly in Epiphanius and Jerome – going into the Holy of Holies, there to *render atonement before God 'until the flesh on his knees turned as cal-*

loused as a camel's for all the supplicating before God he did,' meaning, *before the Judgement Seat.* One way of construing this is to see it as nothing other than an early Church attempt to provide a picture of James making at least one such *Yom Kippur* atonement – if not many – in his role as '*Opposition High Priest*' or the incarnation of all '*Perfection,*' '*the Righteous One*' or '*Zaddik*' of his Generation, acknowledged across the board by all groups, as early Church documents so vividly testify.[97] But who was James that he had the right to go into the Holy of Holies in this manner, whether once or often, to make such an atonement? Why, as we have been trying to suggest, he was '*the People's Priest*' or '*the High Priest of the Opposition Alliance*' *par excellence*; and it is the '*Zadokite*' ideology at Qumran – which, *inter alia,* was applied to '*the Righteous Teacher*' there, that provides us the wherewithal to understand this.

Before the Qumran documents appeared, we could not have predicted this which is what is so startling about them, though the approach was hinted at in Hebrews with its emphasis on a '*High Priesthood after the Order of Melchizedek*' (a variation on the '*Zadokite*' one at Qumran) and its insistence on a '*Perfect High Priest of greater purity*' or '*higher Righteousness*' – Hebrews 7:26–8:1). This was much of what the '*Zealots,*' too, were demanding from the first stirring of their '*Movement*' in the 4 BC–7 CE events, following Herod's death, to the fall of the Temple in 70 CE and beyond.[98] It was also being fairly clearly enunciated in the Damascus Document – then called the '*Zadokite Document*' – first discovered among the materials in the Cairo *Genizah* in 1896.

With these materials, blurred by arcane scholarly discussions about the differences between Qumran and Pharisee/Rabbinic calendrical reckonings and misunderstandings over the true thrust of references like the one here to '*his Exiled House*' – '*Exiled*' because it was *no longer sitting in the Chamber of Hewn Stone on the Temple Mount* – we do, now, have the instrumentality for approaching this notice about James in the Temple performing something resembling '*a Yom Kippur atonement,*' to say nothing of the one in the Habakkuk *Pesher* above, about difficulties between '*the Wicked Priest*' and '*the Community*' of '*the Righteous Teacher*'/'*Zaddik*' relating to events circulating around '*Yom Kippur*' or its aftermath. Even from the paucity of materials that have survived about James, we also have something of the same kind regarding him.

Regardless of what may or may not have happened between '*the Righteous Teacher*' and '*the Wicked Priest*' on '*the Day of Atonements*' ('*the Fast Day*' or '*Sabbath of their Repose*') or between '*the Wicked Priest*' and '*the Poor*'/'*the Simple of Judah doing the Torah,*' who made up '*the Council of the Community*' and who were, seemingly, led by '*the Righteous Teacher*'; one can, as already suggested, perhaps surmise that it was because of *James'* *atonement in 'the Inner Sanctum' of the Temple on behalf of the whole People on* *Yom Kippur* – attested to in sources stemming from the Second-Century early Church writers, Hegesippus and Clement of Alexandria – that his arrest took place, probably in 62 CE, the year of his '*Sanhedrin Trial*' on charges of '*blasphemy*'; and here too, of course, the substance of the '*blasphemy*' charge – *pronouncing the forbidden name of God* which the High Priest did on *Yom Kippur* and *in the Inner Sanctum of the Temple*.[99] Put in another way, we also have materials in these sources, as sketchy as these are, which specifically imply activities connecting James to the Temple and centering about a *Yom Kippur*-atonement of some kind. Again, that we should have such notices and such a link-up, even in the scanty materials before us, is of the most noteworthy significance.

Since, as we know from the above, Jesus ben Ananias appeared during the Feast of Tabernacles, 62 CE, which occurs immediately following *Yom Kippur* in the same month and as a culmination of the Festivities initiated by this atonement. He, in turn, seems to have reiterated, as already described, *one thing and one thing only for seven and a half straight years*:'*Woe to Jerusalem...Woe to the City, and the People, and the Temple,*' until he was killed by a stray Roman projectile shortly before the fall of the Temple in 70 CE, In some manner, as already suggested, this was connected to the removal and recent death of James, '*the Oblias'* / '*Bulwark*' / '*Protection of the People*' or '*Perfectly Righteous' High Priest.*

Therefore, one can say with some certainty that Jesus ben Ananias, the '*Prophet*' bowdlerized in Agabus' oracle of warning to Paul before his last visit to Jerusalem according to Acts 21:7, began his mournful prophesying immediately following *Yom Kippur* 62 CE and the events culminating in the death of James. We have also described how this '*oracle*' seems to have been the basis of the Early Christian '*Pella Flight*' Tradition connected to the death of James. It is even possible to conceive that in some manner the three and a half years in Daniel 12:7 – '*a time, two times, and a half,*' the period of the interruption of sacrifice in the Temple during which '*the Abomination of the Desolation*' held sway in Jerusalem – may have been, as already suggested as well, interpreted to relate to the period between James' death and the suspension of sacrifice on behalf of Romans in the Temple leading to the outbreak of the War.

This is also something of the implication of additional obscure numerology in Daniel 12:11–12 of '*1290–1335 days.*' This is connected to another section of Daniel with slightly-differing numerology *relating to the daily sacrifice and the cleansing of the Temple*, which uses the language of '*casting down*' – namely, '*casting down the Truth*' / '*casting down the Temple*' and a variation of both of these, '*casting the Heavenly Host and the stars to the ground and stamping upon them*' (Daniel 8:10–14). The '*causing them to stumble*' or '*casting down*' verb, used along with '*swallowing them*' in this obscure passage from 1QpHab,XI.2–XII.12 about tragic events connected to *Yom Kippur*, is somewhat parallel to these. Neither of these – the allusion to '*swallowing them*' and the allusion to '*causing them to stumble*' or '*casting them down*' – is to be found in the underlying text from Habakkuk 2:15. At this point this only contains the allusions to '*pouring out His Venom*' or '*pouring out His Wrath*,' '*causing his neighbors to drink*' (this is the same '*mashkeh*' or '*give to drink*' we shall encounter in the esoteric analysis we shall do at the end of this book on '*Damascus*' or '*Dammashek*' in Hebrew as '*Dam-mashkeh* – '*give Blood to drink*'), and '*to the dregs*' or '*unto drunkenness in order to gaze on their Festivals*'/'*privy parts*,' as we have seen. Both of these phrases are deliberately added in the *Pesher*. But it should be appreciated that this '*casting down*' or '*being thrown down*' language is the basis of all early Church accounts relating to '*the Enemy*' Paul's attack on or the death of the look-alike of '*the Righteous Teacher*,' James.

The Isaiah 3:10–11 '*Pesher*' in Early Church Literature

This is also the thrust of the material preceding Isaiah 3:10–11, the Scriptural passage, as we just saw, applied to James' death in Eusebius' long extract from Hegesippus' now-lost Second-Century account in the manner that '*Zaddik*'-texts were applied to the death of the Righteous Teacher at Qumran. Hegesippus also attests, as previously signaled, that James' name was to be found by searching Scripture, clearly meaning either his name '*Jacob*' or '*the Zaddik*' (probably the latter), just as in these texts at Qumran, like Psalm 37:32 and Habakkuk 1:4, to say nothing of Isaiah 53:11. But this text from Isaiah 3:10–11 actually fulfills both of these qualifications being, first of all, a '*Zaddik*'-text about '*the Wicked overwhelming the Righteous*' and those involved in such activity '*being paid the reward of their doings*' and, second of all, no less significantly, it was addressed to the '*House of Jacob*' (Isaiah 2:5).

Furthermore, not only is it surrounded by references to '*robbing the Poor*,' '*swallowing the Way*,' '*standing up to Judge the Peoples*,' and '*the reward of the Wicked*'; but it is also a '*cedars of Lebanon*'-text referring to '*the fall of the Lofty Ones*' and that '*the Lord of Hosts is taking away from Jerusalem and Judah the Stay and the Staff*' (2:5–3:15). Whether there was actually a *Pesher* concerning it in the manner of the Habakkuk and Psalm 37 *Peshers* at Qumran is a matter of opinion but what the exegetes at Qumran would have made of these passages is crystal clear.[100]

It is worth remarking, in the Greek version of this passage from Isaiah 3:10-11, the note of *'conspiring'* or *'plotting'* that one finds as well in the Habakkuk *Pesher*, in which the Wicked Priest *'plotted to destroy the Poor.'* Here it is expressed in terms of *'conspiring an Evil counsel against themselves,'* translated in the Greek by the words *'bebouleuntai boulen.'* Again one recognizes the bare outlines of our *'bale'/'ballo'* symbolism permeating all these parallel Greek texts relating to the death of James. As we shall presently see, the allusion here will not be unrelated to the *'Babulon'/'Babylon'* usage one finds in Revelation 14:8 and 16:19 as well.

But these words nowhere appear in the Hebrew version of Isaiah 3:10-11 nor, for instance, in the version of Isaiah found at Qumran, nor the Vulgate. Here the words are, *'Woe to the Wicked'* (basically the sense of Jesus ben Ananias' forlorn *'prophecy'* above) *'for they have rewarded ('paid')* *themselves Evil.'* Therefore these surprisingly different words in Greek seem to have at some point found their way into the *Septuagint.* Accordingly, it then goes on to read:

> *Let us bind the Just One, for he is an annoyance to us. Therefore shall they eat the fruit of their works.*

This is the version of the text that is reproduced in the early Church testimony as applied to James with the repercussions we have been explaining above.[101] For their part, however, the Hebrew and other received versions of this text preserve almost the opposite sense and give the passage a more positive cast that does not fit the exegesis developed in Hegesippus and his dependents:

> *Say to the Righteous (Zaddik) that it will be well, for they shall eat the fruit of their actions. Woe the Wicked (Rasha^c), (to him) Evil (Ra^{c}ah), for the reward (gemul) of his hands shall be done to him (Isaiah 3:10–11).*[102]

In both of these versions we have the usual references to *'eating'* carrying the implied meaning of *'destroyed'* or *'being paid a reward.'* One should also note here just the slightest play on the usage *'doing'* or the *'works'* ideology. The same sense is reiterated in the Hebrew version of Isaiah 3:9 above: *'for they have paid' (gamlu)* or *'rewarded' themselves Evil (Ra^{c}ah).* The Isaiah 3:11 part of this all-important passage is more or less the same in all versions. This having been said, as already remarked, the words being used in this proof-text will immediately be recognized as the basis of the *Pesher* we have just reviewed above from Column XII.2–3 of the Habakkuk *Pesher* which actually uses the same Hebrew words '*gemul*' and '*gamal*' ('*reward* and '*rewarded*'/'*paid*') twice, '*gemul asher gamal*' ('*the reward which he rewarded*' or '*the reward which he paid*'), just as one finds them here in the Hebrew of Isaiah 3:9–11. In both the Hebrew and the Greek of Isaiah 3:11, this is expressed as '*the reward of his hands will be done to him*' or '*he shall be paid according to the works of his hands.*'

1Q,XII.2-3 uses parallel words to express the same idea, '*he (the Wicked Priest) will be paid the reward which he paid* ('*rewarded*') *the Poor*'(Ebionim), even though none of this exists in the underlying text of Habakkuk 2:17 being expounded. As in the case of the '*swallowing*' or '*casting down*' in the interpretation of Habakkuk 2:15 in XI.2-15 just preceding this, the allusion to '*the Poor,*' which will not have a parallel until, as already remarked, the eschatological (and '*Messianic*') reference to '*the Meek*' ('*Ani*) in Habakkuk 3:14 to follow, has been deliberately introduced. But so has the language of dual allusion to '*reward*' (*gemul*) and '*rewarding*' (*gamal*) which does not exist as such in the underlying Hebrew of Habakkuk 2:17 and which only refers to '*the Violence done to Lebanon,*' '*the Violence to the Land,*' '*the dumb beasts,*' and '*the Blood of Man* ('*Adam,*' repeated twice). We have already signaled the possibilities presented by this reference to '*Man*'/ '*Adam.*' This, too, has been deliberately introduced. Nor is this to say anything about the incredibly '*Messianic*' language of Habakkuk 3:3–19 which the *Pesher* has not yet even bothered to expound.

In our view, what the exegete has done here (either because the Community has another *Pesher* relating to the language in Isaiah 3:9–11, or remembers it) is taken this language – in particular that of Isaiah 3:11 which did involve the phraseology of '*Woe to the Wicked*' (in the vocabulary of Qumran exegesis, always '*the Wicked Priest*') – namely, '*the reward of his hands shall be done to him,*' and introduced it here into his *Pesher* about '*the reward which would be paid to*' the Wicked Priest for what he did to '*the Poor*' – i.e., in our view, the followers of James.

But, of course, where Isaiah 3:10–11 is concerned, this is the exact passage, as we now know, that was applied to the death of James in early Church literature. But the parallels do not end there. Not only does the Habakkuk *Pesher*, at this point, refer to the '*conspiracy*' by the Wicked Priest '*to destroy the Poor,*' it ends with the reference that he '*robbed the Riches of the Poor*' (*gazal Hon-Ebionim*). Once again, the phrase does not appear at this point in the underlying text Habakkuk 2:17, only '*Violence,*' '*Lebanon,*' '*beasts,*' and '*Blood,*' as we have seen, but nothing about '*robbing the Poor*' (*gazal*). Rather this allusion is to be found two lines further along in Isaiah 3:14, directly following the materials from Isaiah 3:10–11 being applied to James' death by Hegesippus and his dependents. Here '*robbing the Poor*' (*gezelat he-'Ani*) is specifically referred to, as is '*burning the vineyard*' and '*grinding the face of the Poor*' (3:15). The only difference between the sense of the two texts is that '*ʿAni*'/'*Meek*' is used instead of '*Ebion*'/'*Poor*.'[103]

We just saw how this usage of '*Ebionim*,' the name for James' Community in Early Christianity, was deliberately introduced into the reference to the '*robbing*' and '*destroying*,' the Wicked Priest does in this Column to '*the Poor*,' even though – just as in Isaiah 3:15 above – an allusion to '*ʿAni*'/'*Meek*' did not appear until Habakkuk 3:14's '*eating*' or '*devouring*' *the Meek in secret*.' The same is true of the Psalm 37 *Pesher*, which also refers to *God paying the Wicked Priest* '*his reward*' (*gemulo*) in exegesis of '*the Wicked watching out for the Righteous and seeking to kill him*,' the underlying text for which generally, too, refers to '*the Meek*' (Psalm 37:11 and 14). There, it will be recalled, these allusions were tied both to evocation of '*the Doers of the Torah*' and '*the Assembly of the Poor*' – phrases, as should by now be appreciated, of absolute significance to the identification our two Communities.[104]

But this '*eating*' or '*devouring*' is exactly the sense of '*eating the fruit of their actions*' ('*works*' in the *Septuagint* translation) of Isaiah 3:10 above. In addition, this allusion to the '*robbing the Poor*' in the Isaiah passage, applied to James in early Church exegesis, also directly follows an allusion in 3:12 to '*leading the People astray*' and '*swallowing (billeʿu) the Way of Your Paths*' – again the imagery of '*swallowing*' we have been following – not to mention '*the Lord standing up to judge the Peoples*' in 3:13 (our '*standing*,' '*judging*,' and '*Peoples*' vocabularies once more). Once again, we have the clearest kind of proof – if such were needed – that the sectaries are mixing the imagery found in Isaiah 3 with those of Habakkuk 1–2 to produce the exegesis they are seeking. Having said this, the passage from Isaiah 3:10–11 is the one being applied to James' death and what Ananus ('*the Wicked Priest*'?) did to him in the earliest Church testimony. Nor can we find a clearer illustration of the connections between the two passages than to see that the language from the one is deliberately being introduced into the interpretation of the other.

One should also note both the allusions to '*standing up*' (the '*standing*'/'*Standing One*' ideology again) and the parallels represented by the language of '*eating*'/'*devouring*' and '*swallowing*'/'*consuming*,' which are particularly strong in the *Pesharim* at Qumran. One cannot ask for clearer textual proof of the identity of '*the Righteous Teacher*' from Qumran with the '*James*' ('*Jacob*') of early Church sources than the convergence of these Scriptural materials being used to apply to the deaths of them both.

25

'The Cup of the Wrath of God Will Swallow Him'

Daniel's Chronology and James' Stoning

We shall now be able to elucidate these allusions to '*making one's neigh-bor drink, pouring out His Fury* ('*pouring out Your Venom*' or '*dregs*' in received Habakkuk – here the shift from '*Your*' to '*His*,' to say nothing of that from '*privy parts*' to '*Festivals*,' already underscored above, is portentous) *unto satiety*' or '*drunkenness*' – possibly, also, '*make them drink*' or '*drunk*' – in the underlying passage from Habakkuk 2:15 being expounded here in 1QpHab,XI.2–10. Before doing so, it should be noted that this passage from the end of Daniel which alludes to '*a time, two times and a half*' and the odd numerology of '*a thousand three hundred and thirty-five days*' (about '*three years and eight months*') also closes with an allusion to '*standing up to your Fate* (also '*Lot*') *at the End of Days*' (12:13). Not only is this language of '*the Last Days*' or '*the End of Days*' a part of the ethos of most of these *Pesharim* on Biblical texts at Qumran, we have already encountered it in terms of the '*standing up*' or '*return of the Messiah*' in the Damascus Document – alluded to there (as we saw) in at least three different places.

That is to say that, according to the ideology of the Damascus Document, as already suggested, it is possible to consider allusions such as this as meaning that '*the Messiah*' had already come and that, not only is his return anxiously awaited but the events, we have been describing, are taking place in the aftermath of this. While these things are obscure and not, strictly speaking, admissible of proof; this is the problem of depending on the chronology of 'Consensus' Qumran Scholarship as it has (until recently) been purveyed. As we have said, this scholarship does not attempt to make ambiguous readings of this kind intelligible to the general public or come to grips in any significant way with the internal data of the texts themselves – rather the opposite.

Where the '*three and a half years*' from Daniel 12:7 are concerned, reiterated in Josephus' description of the interruption of sacrifices at the time of Antiochus Epiphanes' incursions in the *War*[1]; this is, as just remarked, also the numerology of the eschatological ending of the Letter of James. Not only are the coming of apocalyptic '*Judgement*,' '*standing*,' '*the Last Days*,' '*the coming of the Lord of Hosts*,' and '*the End*' – most of which found in Daniel – alluded to in the last Chapter of James (5:4–5:11); but, as will be recalled, the reference there to '*three and a half years*' comes amid evocation of '*the Prayer of Faith*' for forgiveness of Sins, that is to say, *an atonement*.

Here the assurance is given that '*the Lord will rise him up*' and the efficacy of '*the fervent working prayer of the Righteous One*' evoked (5:15–16). This then is followed by evocation of '*the prayer for rain*,' delivered by a previous '*Righteous One*' Elijah, which we have already shown to be not unconnected with the evocation of final apocalyptic '*Judgement*' and '*the coming of the Messiah*' (also deriving from Daniel) together with '*the Heavenly Host on the clouds of Heaven*.' In the War Scroll, the coming of this eschatological Judgement is twice compared to the coming of rain – apocalyptic rain – which, as Matthew 5:45 would phrase it, is '*sent on the Just and Unjust*' alike.[2] In Rabbinic literature, as already noted too, the coming of rain in its season is associated with proper '*Temple service*,' the very thing delineated in James' reported critique of the Temple Establishment in the *Anabathmoi Jacobou*.[3]

Here in James 5:7–8, '*the coming of the Lord*' is also expressed in terms of '*early and late rain*.' In *Talmud Ta'anith*, this '*early rain*' (*yoreh*) is also referred to with regard to final eschatological Judgement[4]; and, in the Damascus Document, it is a name for the stand-in for '*the Righteous Teacher*,' '*the Yoreh ha-Zedek*'/'*Guide of Righteousness*,' mentioned above, not '*the Moreh ha-Zedek*.'[5] In the Letter of James, too, '*three and a half years*' is the period in between which Elijah – John the Baptist's prototype and the forerunner of the Messiah in the Gospels – both '*prayed for it not to rain and then to rain*,' i.e., the period *during which* '*rain*' *was withheld*.

It is possible to view this period, as just signaled, as a complicated numerology of some sort relating to the period in between the stoning of '*the Zaddik*' James for '*blasphemy*' and the final rejection of gifts and stopping of sacrifice '*on behalf of foreigners*' in the Temple by the '*Zealot*' Lower Priesthood some *three and a half years later*. Though admittedly speculative, in such a scenario James, then – as '*the High Priest of the Opposition Alliance*' and the individual whose '*fervent prayer*' and '*atonement*' on behalf of the whole People on his knees in the Holy of Holies before the Judgement Seat at Yom Kippur – provoked the events the Habakkuk *Pesher* seems to be referring to, that from its vantage point resulted in *the swallowing of the Righteous Teacher* or, from Josephus' point-of-view, *the Trial for '*blasphemy*' of James*.

We have already discussed this Trial of James and several of his associates – in the Habakkuk *Pesher* referred to as '*the Poor*' and '*the Simple of Judah doing Torah*' – on a charge of '*blasphemy*' by Ananus to which, as Josephus avers, those in Jerusalem '*most concerned with Equity and scrupulous observation of the Law objected.*' This is followed in all early Church sources by the immediate coming of the Roman Armies and the destruction of Jerusalem – which is also the overall sense here of the Habakkuk *Pesher* though, for it, all of these events may not yet have been accomplished but in the process, perhaps, of only being accomplished. Such a scenario would allow us to place what is being described in these incredible materials in the Habakkuk *Pesher* in the very midst of these events having both to do with the fall of Jerusalem and the destruction of the Temple, so fraught with significance for the history of Western Civilization thereafter, just as a greater part of Daniel appears to have been written in the midst of the Maccabean Uprising.

This complex of events and allusions is a very important dating tool for the Habakkuk *Pesher* because otherwise, as we have seen, we would have to put the events it is describing back into the days of the storming of the Temple with Roman help by Herod in 37 BC or Pompey in 63 BC when there was absolutely no indication of any subsequent seizure of spoil. This would be patently absurd, not only because there is nothing remotely resembling the events we have been describing here, but because, on the contrary, Josephus is very specific in asserting that, aside from going in and viewing the forbidden Holy of Holies with some of his officers, Pompey *touched nothing* – *no spoil*. Nor did Herod thereafter, for the reasons we have already delineated above, that is, wishing to avoid the animosity of his subjects-to-be, he promised to pay his soldiers out of his own pocket.[6]

We have already seen how these '*blasphemy*' charges – which more properly appertain to the Sanhedrin Trial of James – are absorbed into all accounts of the trial and death of Jesus,[7] unless Jesus did what James did, that is, *render atonement on behalf of the whole people in the Holy of Holies on at least one Yom Kippur*. He may have, as he is pictured in Mark 11:16 as stopping commerce in the Temple, but we have no way of knowing if he did. In any event this is the way Paul, in his spiritualization of these affairs, interprets his death though now Jesus becomes the very atonement itself and the sacrifice. However this may be, the most important basis for the charge of '*blasphemy*,' according to Talmudic tradition is pronouncing the forbidden Name of God ('*YHWH*') or encouraging others to do so[8] – except, that is, by the functioning High Priest who on *Yom Kippur* was permitted to pronounce this Name as part of his general supplication in the Holy of Holies.

But, as already explained, this is exactly what James is pictured as doing in the very *Yom Kippur* atonement scenario, portrayed in early Church tradition regarding him, that is, we have an actual basis for the '*blasphemy*' charge against James in the reported events of his very life itself whereas for Jesus, ostensibly anyhow, we do not – claims to the contrary in the Gospels notwithstanding. Furthermore, even in the picture of the Gospels, Jesus does not undergo the prescribed punishment for '*blasphemy*' – stoning – but one for subversive activities or Revolutionary actions according to Roman parameters – therefore his appearance before Pilate, according to Gospel portraiture, who would probably not normally review a punishment for '*blasphemy*' according to Jewish ones.[9] A Jewish Sanhedrin would not and could not impose a crucifixion penalty since, as we have been showing, it was forbidden under Jewish Law, even in Paul's convoluted transformation of it in Galatians 3:13. Only a Roman Governor could do this, a fact the Gospels and the Book of Acts are anxious to obscure in their many accusations about '*Jewish plots*' – themselves doubtlessly based on the Qumran picture of Establishment '*plots*' against '*the Righteous Teacher*' – and their picture of the rushed Sanhedrin proceedings for '*blasphemy*' at the Jewish '*High Priest's House*' – itself probably based on the biography of James.

Here the usage '*Court*,' '*House*,' or '*Palace*' in the portrait in the Gospels is very important, as we have seen, and probably the true explanation for the allusion to '*a-Beit-Galuto*'/'*(at/with/* or *in) His House of Exile*' in the Habakkuk *Pesher*, not to mention the plethora of Talmudic notices about just such an '*exile of the Sanhedrin*' from its normal place of sitting in *the Chamber of Hewn Stone on the Temple Mount* during this period. However these things may be, James *was stoned for blasphemy* and we have in the events, we are considering, the probable basis for such a charge – warranted or otherwise. A '*Rechabite Priest*,' to wit, a '*Priest*' obeying the purity strictures of extreme Naziritism or what some might call an '*Essene Priest*,' James as a '*Covenant-Keeper*' was certainly a '*Priest*' according to the definition at Qumran – a '*Son of Zadok*' or one of '*the Elect of Israel, who would stand at the Last Days and justify the Righteous and condemn the Wicked*.'

It was most likely in this period, symbolized by the erection of the wall in the Temple to bar an '*Herodian*' King from even seeing it or sacrifice-performance activities in it (as per the parameters of the '*che-balla*ʿ'-section of the Temple Scroll[10] – that James and his partisans developed the power to effect such an atonement by a '*Perfectly Righteous*' or People's '*Priest*' in the Temple on '*their Yom ha-Kippurim*'/'*Day of Atonements*' if not the Establishment one. After James' death in 62 CE on the heels of Agrippa II's discomfiture in this same '*Temple Wall Affair*,' some might have seen the stopping of sacrifices and accepting gifts on behalf of Romans and other foreigners – including Herodians and their associates – in 66 CE by persons of a '*Jamesian*' mindset and revering his memory as fulfilling some kind of Scriptural warrant.

Such '*Zealots*' are, in fact, referred to as the partisans of James in Acts 21:21 and earlier, as we have remarked, Acts 6:7 speaks of '*a large number of the Priests*' coming over to the nascent '*Movement*' or, as it puts it, '*the Faith*' (*cf*. CDVII.4-6/XIX.1 and XX.12 above) – not that it is able to make any sense of this notice. It is these '*Priests*,' called by some '*the Lower Priesthood*,' who win the right to wear the High-Priestly linen following James' death at the end of the *Antiquities*[11] and who are at the core of the events leading up to stopping sacrifice on behalf of Romans and other foreigners in the Temple, the signal for the start of the final War against Rome.

Since Daniel seems to have been so instrumental in so many of the prognostications relating to this War, calculations in Daniel may have been part of the process of deciding the time and date such steps were called for. For instance, the year 66 CE also has the virtue of completing the 70–year '*Period of Wrath*,' referred to in Daniel 9:24, reverberating in references at Qumran in documents like the War Scroll and the Damascus Document.[12] This was perhaps thought of as coming into play with the outbreak of '*the Zealot*'/'*Sicarii Movement*' in the 4 BC disturbances following Herod's death until the final purification of Temple sacrifices in these events surrounding the beginning of the War in 66 CE. These are only possibilities – they are not realities, but they are sensible within the framework of the Scriptural mindset being evinced here.

'The Cup of the Wrath of God' and *'the Blood of Man'* in the Habakkuk Pesher

This now brings us to the destruction of the Wicked Priest, as vividly delineated in the *Pesher* in interpretation of the passage that follows the allusion to '*giving his neighbor to drink*' and '*pouring his Fury*'/'*Hamato*' in the underlying text. The underlying Biblical text that follows this from Habakkuk 2:16 is quoted as follows:

> Drink also and stagger (hera^{c}el – in the received text, this is, '*uncover your foreskin*'/he-^{c}arel, as we have seen). *The Cup of the right hand of the Lord shall come around to you and shame shall cover your Glory*.[13]

We have already noted the discrepancy between the word for *'stagger'* or *'tremble'* in this text and *'foreskin'* in the normative Hebrew Bible. In the past, this was interpreted – rather laughably – by *'Consensus Scholars'* from Harvard to Oxford to the French Ecole Biblique in Jerusalem to Notre Dame as implying that the Wicked Priest had been *'drunk'* in some manner or a *'drunkard'* and the conspicuous eschatological sense of the passage was missed! This sent most of such individuals and their acolytes scurrying around looking for one or another of the Maccabeans who might have been *'drinking'* or *'drunken'* at some point.[14]

Nothing could be further from the truth. They, then, came up with the textual warrant in the Maccabee books – since they thought one or another of the Maccabeans was *'the Wicked Priest'* delineated in the Dead Sea Scrolls – that either Jonathan Maccabee or Simon Maccabee had been destroyed by treachery at a banquet of some kind! But the *Pesher* that follows in 1QpHab,XI.4–XX.12, as just intimated, has nothing whatever to do with *'drunkenness'* on the part of *'the Wicked Priest,'* that is, except figuratively – but rather, *'drinking his fill* (or *'drinking to the dregs'*) *from the Cup of the Wrath of God.'* So much for the Scriptural perspicuity and understanding of Hebrew metaphor on the part of philological experts. A grammar school child or novice could have done better, but failure to relate to literary metaphor, as already alluded to, has been a distinct failure on the part of Qumran researchers.

The key allusion here, of course, is *'Cup'* (*Chos*). This is an extremely important usage at Qumran, as it is in Christianity paralleling and succeeding it. We have even seen this usage relating to James in Jewish Christian sources, that James would *'not eat or drink from the time he drank the Cup of the Lord, until he should see Jesus'* – this is in the so-called *'Gospel of the Hebrews'* reported by Jerome. At Qumran the allusion is almost always to *'Wrath'* (*Cha^cas*), as it is here in the *Pesher* – *'Chos'* and *'Cha^cas'* being *homophonic*. Here, in the *Pesher*, quite rightly, *'the Wicked Priest'* is going to *'drink to the dregs'* or *'drink to satiety,'* but this, of course, has nothing whatever to do with actual *'drunkenness,'* nor means, as our commentators would have it, that he was a drunkard! He would be *'drunk,'* it is true, but his *'drunkenness'* would be from *'the Cup of the Wrath of God, of which 'he would drink his fill.'* Here again, of course, we see the sort of word-play and metaphor that so fascinated our militant exegetes. Nor is this to say anything about the *'giving to drink'* and the various plays we shall encounter in Gospel portraits and the one in Paul of Jesus' words at *'the Last Supper,' 'taking the Cup and giving them to drink'* (in 1 Corinthians 11:26–27, connected to *'Blood'* and called *'the Cup of the Lord'*) at the end of this book in our analysis of *'the New Covenant in the Land of*

Damascus.'

The phrase, as it is given at the end of Column XI.13-15, is: '*but the Cup of the Wrath of God shall swallow him*' (*teval^ceno*). Once again we have our play on the language of '*swallowing*' that so permeates these Scriptural exegeses. Our Oxford translator in English, G.Vermes – at one time a seminarian but latterly a returnee to synagogue-membership – again translates this as '*might confuse him.*' More likely, the translation itself is insufficiently nuanced or, as it were, somewhat '*confused*' and as a result has '*confused*' a whole generation of devotees entirely dependent on its thin thread in English. The meaning here is clear, as we have just underscored: just as '*he swallowed the Righteous Teacher*' and his associates (possibly connected to observances they were conducting on their *Yom Kippur*) so, too, would he himself be '*swallowed,*' *i.e.*, '*consumed*' – not '*confused.*'[15]

That this, in fact, involved '*the destruction*' of '*the Righteous Teacher and the Men of his Council,*' called in what follows '*Ebionim*' or '*the Poor,*' is made clear in the next two columns ending in the climactic finale about '*the Last Judgement*' in XII.13–XIII.4. Because the word being used there is now '*destroy*' (*lechalot*) not '*swallow,*' this reads quite straightforwardly as we saw: '*He will be paid the reward he paid the Ebionim*'/'*the Poor.*' Just so there should be no mistaking the import here, this is repeated using the language of '*conspiracy,*' just highlighted above as well: '*as he plotted to destroy the Poor, so too would God condemn him to destruction.*'[16]

There can be no mistaking the sense of this. As noted, the language of '*the Poor*'/'*Ebionim*' is introduced into the *Pesher*, though it nowhere occurs in the underlying Biblical passage, just as the language of '*swallowing,*' '*being cast down,*' and '*paying the reward*' was previously. The sectarians *want* this language in the exegesis; *therefore they put it there.* They do the same with the language of '*Chos-Hamato*'/ '*the Cup of His Wrath,*' the variation of which has already preceded its use here in the description of the Wicked Priest's '*angry wrath*'/'*cha^cas hamato.*' (transformed from '*Your Fury*' in normative Habakkuk 2:15 above).[17] The word-play here should be obvious *even to the amateur.*

There is no '*Cha^cas*'/'*Wrath*' as such in the underlying text from Habakkuk 2:15 (though there is '*Hamatchah*' – '*Your Fury*' as we just saw). This is purposefully introduced into the *Pesher* by the exegetes, in the same manner that they introduce important words like '*Festivals,*' '*staggering,*' '*swallowing,*' and '*the Poor.*' An additional variation on this '*Hemah*' ('*Venom*' or '*Poison*') and itself connected to '*wine,*' as we have also seen, is the way the '*Vipers*' or '*Kings of the Peoples*' are portrayed in the exegesis of Deuteronomy 32:33 in CDVIII.9–11/XIX.21-25 above. Where '*the*

Wicked Priest' is concerned, it is his '*hot wrath*'/'*cha^cas hamato*' or '*venomous fury*' that – in the manner of '*the Pursuer*' in Deuteronomy 19:6 above generally – drives him to '*pursue the Righteous Teacher to swallow him.*'

In the case of God's '*Vengeance*' and '*Punishment on the Wicked Priest*' that follows, it is '*the Cup of the Wrath of God*' that '*will swallow him*' (the Wicked Priest), meaning, just as the latter '*swallowed*' the Righteous Teacher and his followers '*with*' or '*in his House of Exile*' so, too, would he be '*swallowed*'/'*consumed by God's Wrath,*' of which – as just made clear – '*he would drink his fill*' or '*drink to satiety*'/'*to the dregs.*'

But the imagery here of '*the Cup of Divine Wrath*' is familiar to anyone who has sung the Civil War inspirational, *The Battle Hymn of the Republic*, because it is based on the same Biblical passages. The whole imagery is present, as already pointed up, in almost the same detail in Isaiah 51:17–23, including a related metaphor, '*the Cup of Trembling,*' which links up with the transmutation of the underlying text of Habakkuk 2:16 from '*he-^carel*'/'*foreskin*' to '*hera^cel*'/'*trembling*' above. This has nothing to do with any '*drunkenness*' on the part of the Wicked Priest except tangentially. In other words, the Wicked Priest '*will stagger*' or '*be trembling*' not from actual '*drunkenness,*' but rather from '*drinking the Cup of the Wrath of the Lord*' (who wouldn't?)!

'*The Cup of the Wine of the Wrath of God*' and '*the Scarlet Beast*' in Revelation

The best exposition of this vivid metaphor is to be found in of all places (though this not surprisingly), the Apocalypse of the New Testament, *The Book of Revelation*, itself drenched in language and imagery of this kind and revelling in it. We have already highlighted these parallels to some degree but it is worth looking at them again. In the context of repeated allusion to '*blaspheming the Name of God*' (13:1–6) and '*One like a Son of Man sitting upon the cloud*' (14:14 – here '*a white cloud*'), it reads:

> *He shall also drink of the wine of the Wrath of God, which is poured out full strength into the Cup of his Anger. And he shall be tormented in fire and brimstone before the Holy Angels and before the Lamb* (14:10).

These allusions should all be by now familiar and, in this context, there can be no doubt that we are speaking about '*the Wrath of God*' and '*Divine Vengeance.*' It will be immediately appreciated that the allusion here even incorporates the underlying language of Habakkuk 2:15, just used in CDxi.3–8 to develop the exegesis concerning how the Wicked Priest '*swallowed the Righteous Teacher,*' '*causing his neighbor to drink, pouring out His Venom*' or '*Wrath to make them drunk.*'

This was even preceded in CDx.3–5 and 13 by allusion to executing '*Judgement upon him with fire and brimstone*' in '*the House of Judgement which God would deliver.*'[18] Revelation, of course, fairly overflows with this language of '*pouring*' and '*Judgement,*' just as it does that of '*blasphemy.*' In what to some might appear as '*an orgy of obfuscation,*'[19] Revelation endlessly repeats:

> And the third Angel poured out his bowl onto the rivers and onto the Fountain of waters (language present in CDVIII.22/XIX.34 as we have seen[20]), and they become blood...For they poured out the blood of the Holy Ones and the Prophets, and You gave them blood to drink, for they deserve it (16:4–6).

Not only was this '*Fountain*' or '*Well of Living Waters*' referred to in the Damascus Document in the context of the allusion to '*the Yoreh*'/'*Guide,*' Gehazi's admonishment, '*betraying the New Covenant in the Land of Damascus,*' '*the Assembly of the Men of Perfect Holiness,*' and the '*standing up of the Messiah of Aaron and Israel*'[21]; these are the same accusations about the Jews '*killing all the Prophets*' one encounters first in Paul but also probably retrospectively attributed to 'Jesus' in the Gospels, and picked up, as we have seen, by Muhammad in the Koran.[22] There is also the variation on James' directive in his instructions to overseas communities, '*abstain from blood*' (which in the Hebrew of the Damascus Document would have been expressed as the '*Nazirite*'-style verb, '*lehinnazer*'). Nor is this to say anything about what we shall see at the end of the book as the Hebrew esoteric exposition of '*Damascus*' as '*to give blood to drink*' and what we have further seen as the additional play on and reversal of these matters by Paul in 1 Corinthians 10:21 and 11:27–29.

> And the Fourth Angel poured out his bowl upon the sun (this, very obscure)...and men were scorched with great Heat, so that they blasphemed the Name of God (Revelation 16:7–9).

This last is, of course, the accusation against James in the Temple, reversed in various ways in the accusations against '*the Wicked Priest*' in the Habakkuk *Pesher*. In addition, we also have here the '*great Heat*' of '*his* (in 1QpHab,XI.5–6, '*the Wicked Priest*'s) *Hot Anger*' as well as the reference underlying it in Habakkuk 2:15 to '*pouring out His Anger (Hamato) unto drinking his fill*' or '*drunkenness.*' All this is delivered under the heading in Hebrews 16:1 of '*Go and pour out the bowls of God's Anger unto the Earth.*'

In 1QpHab,XI.10–15 above this would read '*Cup*,' but the Greeks drank wine out of '*bowls*.' In Revelation too, we even have allusion to '*the Beast*,' '*with a mouth speaking great things and blasphemy*,' again tied to a timeframe of *three and a half years*, that is, '*forty-two months*' (13:5). In the interpretation of Habakkuk 2:17 following these allusions to '*the Cup of the Wrath of God swallowing him*,' '*the dumb beasts*' were '*the Simple of Judah doing Torah*' and there was also the pregnant allusion to '*Blood*' – there, as just underscored, '*the Blood of Man*' (*Adam*), interpreted to mean '*the destruction of the Poor*' and '*robbing them of their substance*.'

In Revelation, this is reversed, as per usual in early Church texts of a Pauline mindset and even later by 'Christian' theologians such as Eusebius – himself partially responsible for the Christian takeover of the Roman Empire.[23] Instead of '*the Simple of Judah doing the Torah*' and '*the Community Council*' of '*the Poor*' as in the *Pesher*, this '*Blood*,' as just underscored too, now becomes the Jews '*pouring out the Blood of the Holy Ones and the Prophets*' which is, again, not to mention Paul's whole ideology of '*Communion with the Blood of Christ*' succeeding these kinds of allusions in the documents at Qumran.

This is re-affirmed with the words, '*You gave them Blood to drink*' – also a play, as just noted, on both the 'Jamesian'/Jewish '*abstinence from blood*' and what we shall now try to show is the esoteric exposition of '*the New Covenant in the Land of Damascus*' – '*for they deserve it*.' This is neatly summed up by Paul above in 1 Corinthians 11:27–29: whoever shall '*drink the Cup of the Lord unworthily shall be guilty of the Body and Blood of the Lord*,' for *he, who drinks unworthily, drinks Judgement to himself*. How terrifyingly accusative these passages read in the light of Qumran texts as we now know them to be and subsequent Western History as it has unfolded. Their gist has even been picked up in the shrill and, one might add, almost always unfounded accusations of a similar kind also just underscored in the Koran above.

The '*blasphemy*' accusations that accompany all this are not really separable from the Gospel presentations of the Trial of Jesus at '*the High Priest's House*' where he is pictured as both claiming to be either '*the Christ*' or '*the Son of God*' and delivering the proclamation about the latter attributed to James in early Church literature (Matthew 26:57–68 and *pars.*). At this point in Revelation, these accusations are tied to the imagery from Daniel of '*the beast with ten horns*.' As Revelation 13:1 puts this: '*On its heads was the Name of blasphemy*' and '*it opened its mouth for blasphemy against God, to blaspheme His Name and His Temple and those in the Temple of Heaven*' (13:6). Not only does this play on the imagery in Daniel 7:8 of the '*little horn*' (the one coming after the Tenth '*with a mouth full of boasts*'), but also the '*blasphemy*' charge against James in the episode in Hegesippus about his proclamation of '*the coming of the Son of Man*'; instead of '*pronouncing the forbidden Name of God in the Temple*,' as we have decided James did in his *Yom Kippur* atonement, '*the beast*' is '*blaspheming the Name of God and the Temple*.' The ethos, however, is basically that of the charges made against Paul by '*the Jews from Asia*' in the Temple in Acts 21:27–28 (how fortuitous this location, as it is essentially the same as in Revelation), in '*Jewish*' or '*Ebionite Christianity*' generally, and against '*the Liar*' at Qumran – '*blaspheming the Temple*' or '*insulting the Law*.'

Notice, too, how this charge of '*blasphemy*' is also used earlier in the section, in which '*Balaam taught Balak to cast a net before Israel*,' amidst negative allusion to '*works*,' '*Riches*' and '*fornication*' (Revelation 2:9). Even '*Poverty*' and '*suffering*' are mentioned. As usual, the '*blasphemy*' is now on the part of '*those claiming themselves to be Jews*' but who are really '*the Synagogue of Satan*' paralleling material in 2 Corinthians 10:12–11:15 about the *Hebrew* '*False Apostles*' who '*recommend themselves, comparing themselves to themselves*,' claiming to be '*Servants of Righteousness*.' These are really '*the Servants of Satan, whose End shall be according to their works*' (11:15). In Revelation 2:23, this is: '*giving you each according to your works*.'

In addition to the virtual reproduction of Paul's words, this chapter of Revelation mixes the language of '*the Diabolos*'/'*the Devil*' with that of '*Satan*,' as do the Gospels and as at Qumran. In Revelation 2:10, the reference is to how '*the Devil casts (balein) some of you into prison*.' This moves on to an allusion to '*ten days of suffering*' and final death, ending in evocation of '*the Crown of Life*.' In James 1:12, this was '*promised by the Lord to those that love Him*'; and in 2 Timothy 4:8, '*the Crown of Righteousness*' – all expressed in terms of the Greek '*Stephanos*.' Not only does the reference to '*the Diabolos*' here parallel the one to '*Belial*' and '*the nets he set up to ensnare Israel*' in CDiv.15–18 but it, too, begins by evoking, '*He knew your works*' (Revelation 2:9). Again, this is word-for-word from CDii.7–8: '*God knew their works before ever they were established*,' preceded by reference to '*God's Anger being kindled against them*,' because '*their works were unclean before Him*.'[24]

Furthermore, we have also already seen that this '*Belial*'/'*Devil*' evocation of the '*Three Nets of Belial*'-section of the Damascus Document is present in the evocations of '*Balaam*' and '*Balak*' which follow in Revelation 2:14. So are the parameters of James' prohibitions to overseas communities in Acts: '*eating things sacrificed to idols and committing fornication*,' which so parallel the basic thrust of '*Three Nets*' in the Damascus Document, in which Belial '*caught Israel*,' '*transforming them into three kinds of Righteousness*' (note the additional parallel here to Paul in 2 Corinthians

11:14 above, in the sense of the verb *'transforming'* as in *'Satan transforming himself into an Angel of Light'* or *'his servants'* into *'Servants of Righteousness'*). These parameters are repeated again in Revelation 2:20 in slightly variant form in terms of *'leading My Servants astray'* – here also the *'Servants'* language of 2 Corinthians 11:15, not to mention *'leading astray'* in Qumran vocabulary generally – *to commit fornication and eat things sacrificed to idols,'* only now it is *'Jezebel'* who is being attacked as the Deceiver. One should appreciate that even in her name one has another clear variant of the *'balla^c'/'ballo'* terminology here.

This reference to *'Jezebel'* is of the utmost interest, as are the references to *'the great whore'* and *'the whore of Babylon'* that appear later in Revelation 17:1–18 and 19:2 amid the language of another of these categories of James' prohibitions, *'Blood.'* Surrounding the *'Jezebel'* references, *'knowing your works'* from Revelation 2:9 is repeated in 2:19 and, varying this, *'keeping My works'* in 2:26 – note the Qumran *'keeping'* vocabulary in this last again. In fact *'he that keeps My works until the End'* – *'keeping the Law'* in James; *'keeping the Covenant'* at Qumran – *will be given Authority over the Peoples'* (*Ethnon* – the Qumran *'Peoples'* vocabulary again, not to mention that of the Pauline *'Gentile Mission'* to these same *'Peoples'*). This is basically the eschatology of the Habakkuk *Pesher* (v.3–5) where *God's 'Elect* (*'the Assembly of the Poor'* in the Psalm 37 *Pesher)* execute Judgement on all the Nations'*!

The references to Jezebel's *'fornication'* in Revelation 2:21–22, seemingly with multiple partners, makes it more likely than ever that the author has one or another of the Herodian Princesses in mind, most likely Bernice – ultimately the mistress of the destroyer of Jerusalem and the Temple Titus. Once again, the *'bel'/'ballo'* language – denoting in our view *'Herodians'* and their confrères – which is omnipresent throughout, must be considered determinant. Of course, what we have in these allusions in Revelation *are Qumran materials* – and, by extension, *those of the Community of James* – being tossed around indiscriminately and overwritten in obfuscating fashion. Sometimes these usages are trivialized or even reversed, but sometimes they are presented as per normative Palestinian usage. Knowing this, the imagery can be at times quite amusing.

'Babylon the Great' and *'Jezebel'*

For good measure, in these later passages, Revelation 16:19 now goes on to apply *'the Cup of Wrath'*-metaphor to *'Babylon the Great,'* rejoicing over how God would remember to give her – in Greek, *'Babulon'* – *'the Cup of the Wine of the Fury of His Wrath.'* Once again, these are precisely the words used at Qumran to describe what happened to the Wicked Priest as a result of what he did to the Righteous Teacher and yet another variation of the *'Jezebel'*/*'ballo'*/*'Bela^c'* language cluster. Once again, too, we are getting transmutation of Hebrew usages into Greek.

Here the allusion includes even the redundancy, *'Cha^{c}as Hamato,'* (*'the Fury of His Wrath'* in Hebrew), the Habakkuk *Pesher* uses to describe the Wicked Priest's action in *'swallowing'* (again *'balla^c'*) the Righteous Teacher and Revelation even employs the same reversal as the Habakkuk *Pesher* does, that she would be paid with the same *'drink'* or *'Cup'* – in the Habakkuk *Pesher,* *'Chos'* (*Cup*), also playing on this same Hebrew *'Cha^{c}as'* (*Wrath*) – she paid to others. Earlier in Revelation 14:8, repeating the multiple *'drinking'* allusions of the Habakkuk *Pesher,* this was expressed as: *'Babulon, which gave all Peoples the wine of the Fury of her fornication to drink,'* adding the *'fornication'* imagery which was associated with *'Jezebel'* in Chapter Two and which we just associated with the Herodian miscreant Bernice above as well.

Not only does Revelation 14:8–12, following an allusion to *'the Fountains of Water'* – right out of another Qumran text, *'The Chariots of Glory,'* we first named in 1992[25] – apply this imagery, as we saw, to *'Babylon,'* but also to *'anyone worshipping the Beast.'* As this was expressed in Revelation 14:10, it will be recalled – *'he would be made to drink the wine of the Wrath of God, which is poured out undiluted in the Cup of His Anger,'* this is precisely – in fact, almost word-for-word – the imagery applied to *'the Wicked Priest'* in the Habakkuk *Pesher* above, even including that of *'the Cup of the Wrath of God,'* varied slightly, and in the allusion *'undiluted,'* Habakkuk 2:15's *'drinking to the dregs.'* This is immediately followed up with the words, also in Revelation 14:10, *'he shall be tortured by fire and brimstone before the Holy Angels.'* But this, as we just saw, is precisely the scenario followed in the admonishment of the Wicked Priest in Column Ten of the Habakkuk *Pesher* above, in exposition of Habakkuk 2:10 about *'the profiteer's profiteering'* and *'cutting off many Peoples.'*[26] This last, too, is again interpreted in terms of *'the House of Judgement'* which God would pronounce *'in the midst of many Peoples.'* There, to repeat, *'He (God) would lead him* (here the *'him'* is the Wicked Priest) *for Punishment'* or *'Admonishment* – this in interpretation Habakkuk 2:10's *'the Sins of your soul'* obviously now being taken eschatologically – *and condemn him among them, judging him with fire and brimstone'* – the same *'fire and brimstone'* just referred to in Revelation 2:10 above.

But these repeated allusions to *'being made to drink the wine of the Wrath of God'* in Revelation even recapitulate the words of CDviii.6–10/ xix.23–24, following allusions to *'wallowing in the ways of fornication and*

Evil Riches,' 'incest,' 'profiteering,' and *'not keeping apart (nazru) from the People(s)'* we have cited above. In that context, *'their wine is the Venom of Vipers'* of Deuteronomy 32:33 – *'Venom,' 'Anger,' 'dregs,'* and *'Fury'* being, it will be recalled, homonyms in Hebrew – was not applied, as here in Revelation to *'Babulon the Great,'* but to *'the Kings of the Peoples'* – in our view, as several times elucidated, *'Herodians.'* In this material, as will be recalled too, not only was *'the Head'* of the petty Greco-Roman Kings (in Deuteronomy, *'the cruel Poison of Asps'*), the Roman Emperor, who was going to *'come to execute Vengeance upon them'* (basically the eschatological point-of-view of the Gospels and early Church literature as well though with, of course, slightly differing signification); but in the material directly following this, *'the Spouter of Lying'* was characterized as *'pouring out wind'* or *'pouring out'/'walking in the Spirit'* or *'Lying,'* thus *'kindling the Wrath of God on all his Assembly'* (or *'Church'*)[27]

In Revelation, these allusions to *'drinking the Cup of the Lord's Fury'* – themselves based on imagery, as previously underscored, found in Isaiah 51:17 associating *'the Cup of His Fury'* (*Chos Hamato*) with *'drinking the dregs of the Cup of Trembling'* (*Chos Ha-Tarʿelah*) and in Jeremiah 25:15–30 on drinking *'the Cup of the wine of the Fury'* of God – are often accompanied by a quotation from Psalm 2:8–9 about *'ruling the Nations with a Sceptre of iron and shattering them like pots of clay.'* This is repeated at several key junctures in Revelation 2:27, 12:5, and 19:15, the last time in conjunction with *'treading the press of the wine of the Fury and Wrath of God'* and *'striking the Nations with the sharp sword of his mouth'* from Isaiah 11:4 and 49:2.

This allusion from Isaiah 11:4, as well as the phrases leading up to it from 11:1–3, about *'a Shoot from the stem of Jesse and a Branch that would grow from his roots'* who would *'judge the Downcast (Dallim) with Righteousness'* and *'treat the Meek of the Earth (ʿAnayyim) with equity,'* are also to be found in the *Pesher* at Qumran on Isaiah 10:20–11:5, already mentioned above, about *'the Branch of David standing at the End of Days.'* Not only does it seem to be connected with 4Q285 – called by some *'The Pierced Messiah'*-text, but which we have called *'The Messianic Leader'*[28] – which also quotes Isaiah 10:33–11:3, but it also employs the *'Sceptre'* imagery from above and refers both to his *'Throne of Gory'* and *'Holy Crown'* (*Nezer*)/*'Crown of Holiness,'* all apparently interpreted in terms of *'the Branch of David who shall stand'/'arise at the End of Days.'*[29]

Regardless of translation, it is the use of common imagery of this kind and these emphases that make it absolutely certain that Qumran Documents of this genre, which are homogeneous in this regard, were written in the First Century CE. It is interesting that in the *Pesher* on Isaiah 11:1, the '*Netzer*' or '*Branch*' in the underlying text becomes the '*Nezer*' ('*Crown*' or '*Diadem*') of the High Priest – or, in more colloquial Hebrew, as we have seen, even possibly, '*the Holy Crown*' of the *Nazirite's* hair (in 4Q285, it will be recalled, this '*Branch (of David)*' was '*the Nasi ha-ᶜEdah*' – '*chol ha-ᶜEdah*' in CDᵥᵢᵢ.20's exegesis of Numbers 24:17).[30] Again we have the shift from '*Netzer*' to '*Nezer*,' we have been discussing with regard to the terminology, *Nazoraean*/'*Keeper*' and *Nazirite*/'*Consecrated One*' or that between '*Nazareth*' and '*Nazrene*' in Christianity generally – but this time in an actual text from Qumran further adding to the impression of the interchangeability of these language clusters.[31]

Following the allusion to '*pouring out the bowls of God's Wrath onto the Earth*' in Revelation 16:1, which becomes '*pouring out the Blood of the Holy Ones and Prophets*' and, in return, God '*giving them Blood to drink because they deserve it*' in 16:6; Revelation 16:20–21 continues its ongoing mystification and conflation of all these imageries:

> *And every island fled and no mountains were found, and great hail, like the weight of a talent came down out of the Heaven upon men. And men blasphemed God, because of the plague of the hail, for its plague was exceedingly great.*

Though all this is, of course, total nonsense, it does evoke both the imagery of James' final proclamation in the Temple of '*the Son of Man coming on the clouds of Heaven*' and the War Scroll's *Heavenly Host* '*like clouds, clouds covering the Land,*' raining final eschatological '*Judgement*' on all the Sons of Men. This is to say nothing of the imagery of the whirlwind in both Jeremiah 25:32, probably evoked in the previously unpublished First Column of the Nahum *Pesher*,[32] and Ezekiel 13:11–13 on the Damascus Document's '*Daubers upon the wall,*' evoking God's '*Anger*' (*Hemah*) and '*hailstones*' as well and recapitulated in 38:22, including reference to '*fire and brimstone.*'

This excursus in Revelation ends in the next chapter with allusion to being '*carried away in Spirit into (the) wilderness*' – again playing on similar allusions in the Gospels and, possibly, the Scrolls – and '*seeing a woman sitting upon a scarlet beast (kokkinon) full of Names of blasphemy*' (17:3) – the same '*seven headed, ten-horned beast,*' based upon Daniel 7–8, we saw earlier in 13:1. The woman, too, '*was dressed in purple and scarlet*' (*kokkino*) and on her head was written '*MYSTERY: Babylon the Great, the mother of whores and of the Abominations of the Earth*' (17:4–5). In her hand is '*a golden Cup full of Abominations and the uncleanness of her fornication*' and she is '*drunk with the Blood of the Saints and with the Blood of the Witnesses of Jesus*' (17:6 – a new kind of nomenclature). Here, of course, is the imagery of 'Abominations' connected to the person of 'the Wicked Priest' in both Columns Eight and Twelve of the Habakkuk Pesher, but the imagery of this last (Column XII.1-10), which – as we have seen – above, does include these various allusions to 'beast(s)' and 'Blood,' is much simpler.[33]

The reason for the startling introduction of the allusion in Greek, 'scarlet' or 'kokkinon,' i.e., 'the scarlet beast' on which she rode or her 'scarlet clothing,' is also perhaps explained by inspection of the underlying text from Habakkuk 2:16 relating to both 'drinking' and 'staggering'/'trembling' and 'the Cup of the Lord's right hand and shame (kikalon) upon your Glory.' The Pesher now applies this allusion to 'kikalon'/'shameful spewing,' adding another allusion related to it, 'kalono' (also 'shame'), as part of Column Eleven's accusation that the Wicked Priest's 'shame was greater than his Glory because he did not circumcise the foreskin of his heart,' which precedes the fact that he would, therefore, 'walk in the Way of satiety.'[34]

Not only is this the passage which is interpreted in terms of 'the Cup of the Wrath of God swallowing him,' but also it is said that it is of this he would 'drink his fill' or 'drink to the dregs.' This is the same language applied to 'the whore of Babulon' or 'Great Babulon' in Revelation 14:8 and 16:19, as well as the Worshippers 'of the Beast' in 14:10. Once again, we possibly have one of these startling overlaps and esoteric transmutations – like 'balla[c]' into 'ballo' above – moving from Hebrew into Greek, in this case, now 'kalon and kikalon'/'shame and disgrace' into 'kokkinon' – the esoteric and completely unnecessary allusion to 'scarlet.'

'The Cup of Trembling' and 'not Circumcising the Foreskin of his Heart'

Not only, therefore, is this 'Bowl' or 'Cup' imagery, as applied to Vengeance and martyrdom, to be found in Revelation and the Habakkuk Pesher, it is also to be found, as we have seen, in the Gospels relating to John and James 'the sons of Zebedee,' the latter generally an overwrite of the real James. The 'pouring' imagery one finds in these chapters of Revelation also plays on the general imagery at Qumran with regard to 'the Man of Lying' who, in a variation of the 'Belial' terminology itself, 'pours out the waters of Lying over Israel,' and is just as often referred to as 'the Spouter' – specifically, that is, one who 'pours out,' seemingly, in addition to 'Lying,' 'water,' and/or 'wind,' even 'the Spirit.'[35]

Not only is this 'Cup' imagery systematically transformed by Paul in his treatment of 'the Lord's Cup' or 'the Cup of the New Covenant in my blood' in 1 Corinthians 10:16–21 and 11:25–29, it also culminates in the drinking of 'the Cup of the New Testament in my blood which was poured out for you' in Gospel 'Last Supper' scenarios. Here, too, the 'pouring' imagery is now attached to Paul's new and more *'spiritualized'* (or *'allegorical'*) theology of *'the Cup of the Lord.'*

At this point, as we saw, the text of the Qumran Habakkuk *Pesher* even picks up the imagery of Isaiah 51:17–22, adding its additional *'the Cup of Trembling'* (*Chos ha-Tar'elah*) to its quotation of the underlying text from Habakkuk 2:16: *'You drink also and tremble'* (*hera'el*). The *Pesher* to this reads as follows – the reader should again note the shift from *'hera'el'* to *'he-'arel'/'foreskin'*:

> *Its interpretation concerns the Wicked Priest, whose shame was greater than his honour because he did not circumcise the foreskin of his heart* (*kalono/kikalon* – this, as just suggested, possibly transmuted into the Greek *'scarlet'* or *'kokkinon'* of *'the whore of Babylon'* riding a *'scarlet beast'* in Revelation 17:3 above).

Not only is there recourse to the same *'heart'* imagery Paul so often exploits in his Letters –though here (as usual at Qumran) with completely inverse signification – but, as even the amateur will see, the *Pesher* has simply reversed the letters in its version of the underlying reading, *'to tremble,'* to produce the allusion to *'foreskin'* instead. This is typical again of Qumran word-play and the freedom with which underlying texts were both cited and utilized. As should be plain, this same word-play is present in the Greek of the New Testament's Revelation, but with a more obscurantist and transparently anti-Semitic point-of-view.

Though, as we saw, received versions of Habakkuk 2:16 seem to have conserved this switch from *'hera'el'/'tremble'* to *'he-'arel'/'foreskin,'* the Greek Septuagint version still retains the Qumran *'tremble'/'shake'/*or *'stagger'* here. But the Qumran *Pesher* seems to understand this kind of word-play and, though conserving *'tremble'* in the underlying Habakkuk 2:16, interprets it – utilizing Isaiah 51:17–22's *'Cup of Wrath'/'Cup of Trembling'* duality to produce its *'foreskin'* metaphor – in terms of the Wicked Priest's *'uncircumcised heart,'*. It is these things our exegetes in modern Qumran Studies prefer to translate in terms of the Wicked Priest *'staggering'* from *'drunkenness.'* But there is no *'drunkenness'* here, as we have been at pains to point out, only – as Revelation would have it – *'the wine of the Wrath of God, which is poured full strength into the Cup of His Anger.'*

In fact, this *'Cup of Wrath'/'the Lord's Cup'/'Cup of the Lord'* metaphor is picked up again in the next passage of the *Pesher* (XI.15) which sets forth how *'the Cup of the Wrath of God would swallow him.'* This, again, many translate as *'confuse'* but, as we saw, God did not want *'to confuse'* the Wicked Priest any more than the Wicked Priest wanted *'to confuse'* the

Righteous Teacher and his associates 'with his Beit-Galuto' on Yom Kippur. In the case of the latter, anyhow (if not the former), *he wanted to destroy him.*

This allusion to *'not circumcising the foreskin of his heart,'* whether in the original Habakkuk or transmuted from an allusion to *'hera^cel'* there, should also be seen as not unconnected with Ezekiel 44:9's *barring 'foreigners uncircumcised in heart and uncircumcised in flesh' from the Temple* – itself part and parcel to the run-up to the enunciation of *'the Zadokite Covenant'* in 44:15 so dear to Qumran exegetes in the Damascus Document. Not only does it form there, as will be recalled, the basis of the eschatological definition of *'the Sons of Zadok'* and *'Priests'* as *'Penitents in the Wilderness'*[36]; in Ezekiel 44:17–31 it also leads up to the admonitions *'not to drink wine,' 'not to shave their heads but to poll them,' 'not to wear wool but only linen,'* and *'not to eat carrion,'* all matters central to the descriptions of James as they have come down to us. All of these reinforce the idea of his connection to a *'Nazirite'*-style, *'Consecrated'* Priesthood.

The issue of *'linen garments'* or *'clothes'* has particular relevance to James *'being cast down'* from the Pinnacle of the Temple and his brains being bashed in by a *'laundryman' wielding a club* in early Church texts – itself connected to *'stoning'* scenarios in Rabbinic ones.[37] Interestingly enough, the Hebrew word we saw possibly connected to such allusions in the exegesis of Habakkuk 2:15 about the Wicked Priest *'appearing to them to swallow them, causing them to fall'* or *'be cast down'* on Yom Kippur, also appears in Ezekiel 44:13 about the Priests in the Temple *'ministering to them before idols and causing the House of Israel to fall'* or *'be cast down.'*

In this context, one should also remark the allusions to the new *'Priests,' 'the Sons of Zadok,' 'standing up to judge according to My Judgements and keeping My Torah and My Laws in all My Assemblies'* in Ezekiel 44:24 and *'teaching My People the difference between Holy and profane, polluted and clean'* in Ezekiel 44:23, both also dear to the Qumran mindset. The first is actually evoked in the description of *'the Mebakker'* in the *'Camps'* in the Damascus Document.[38] The second too, as will be recalled as well, is also cited there in the *'Nazirite'*-like description of *'the New Covenant in the Land of Damascus,'* which actually mentions *'keeping the Day of Fasting according to the precise letter of the Commandment.'*[39]

Not only do we have in these passages from Ezekiel 44:6–31, as reflected in the Damascus Document, the very reverse of what Peter is pictured as learning in Acts 10:15 and 10:28, *in anticipation of his visit to the Roman Centurion's household in Caesarea* – an episode, as we saw, ending with *'the Holy Spirit being poured out on the Peoples'* (10:44–45); but the main lines of what could have been exploited to produce a very interesting Qumran-style *Pesher* on aspects of James' life and practices. The point, preceding these in Ezekiel 44:7–9 about '*foreigners uncircumcised in heart and flesh not entering My Temple*,' of course, certainly could have been and probably was interpreted to relate to *Herodians being barred from entering the Temple* and in the wake of the death of James it would seem, *all Jerusalem as well*. It also, as we have been emphasizing, relates to *the rejection of gifts and sacrifices from foreigners in the Temple*, the issue which sparked the outbreak of the War against Rome. We have identified this issue as the basis for the Third '*Net of Belial*' reflected in James' directives to overseas communities, as reported in Acts 15/21, 1 Corinthians 8:10, and *MMT* – namely, abstention from '*the pollutions of the idols*' or '*things sacrificed to idols*.' In fact, the ban in the last line of this chapter from Ezekiel on things '*dying of themselves or torn, whether fowl or beast*' (44:31) is clearly the basis, as we saw, of the last category of James' directives to these same overseas communities, the Islamic ban on '*carrion*,' garbled in Greek translation/transliteration into '*strangled things*.'

Here too, whether by coincidence or design, one has the omnipresent allusion to '*Beast*' again. Therefore, not only do we have in all three of these documents, Ezekiel, Habakkuk, and Revelation, the constant reiteration of this theme of '*Beast(s)*,' but in the first, the makings of what could have been developed into a more complete Qumran-style *Pesher* relating to James' person and experiences as well. In the second two of these, this allusion to '*Beast*' is accompanied by the common imagery of '*Blood*,' '*pouring out the Blood of the Saints*' and '*giving them Blood to drink*' – reversed, of course, in the ban on '*Blood*' in James' prohibitions to overseas communities (in the Habakkuk *Pesher* '*the Blood*,' it will be recalled, has to do with the '*destruction of the Poor*'/'*the Ebionim*') – and the retribution for this, either '*drinking the wine of the Wrath of God*' or '*the Cup of the Wrath of God*.'

Where 1QpHab,XI.13 specifically is concerned, it now applies this allusion to '*being uncircumcised in heart*' from Ezekiel 44:7–9 to a Jewish High Priest, one of those Jewish backsliders or '*Wicked Ones of His People*,' it condemned – along with Gentile idolaters '*serving stone and wood*' – in its description of the '*Judgement God would execute by the hand of His Elect*' earlier and the final '*Day of Judgement*' with which the *Pesher* closes.[40] By introducing this peculiar charge against '*the Wicked Priest*' at this point and under these circumstances, the *Pesher* leaves little doubt that the issue it had in mind was *accepting Gentile gifts and sacrifices in the Temple* or, as the Damascus Document, *MMT*, or even Ezekiel 44:23 would put it, *not observing proper separation* '*between clean and unclean, Holy and profane*' in the Temple or bringing '*polluted things into the Temple*' and, as a consequence, '*incurring their pollution*' – the same issues exercising

'*Zealots for the Law*' and extreme Purists generally in the run-up to the War against Rome.

Persons doing such things are called in Ezekiel 44:7 '*Covenant-Break-ers*,' the term used in the Habakkuk *Pesher* – in conjunction with '*the Man of Lying*,' '*Violent Ones*,' and '*Traitors to the New Covenant*' generally – to describe the Alliance opposing '*the Righteous Teacher*'/'*the (High) Priest*.' The allusion in these contexts to, '*Breakers of the Covenant*,' as in James 2:9, is obviously meant to signal the very opposite of what a true '*Son of Zadok*' was supposed to have been, namely a '*Keeper of the Covenant*' and a '*Doer of the Torah*' *par excellence*, the reference to which then permeates these lines from Ezekiel 44:8–15, Qumran generally, and, of course, James. That a variation of this ban on foreign gifts and sacrifices in the Temple is found here in Ezekiel 44:7–15, puts the lie, as we have been indicating, to Josephus' attempt to portray objections of this kind on the part of '*Sicarii*'/'*Zealot*' extremists after the death of James in the run-up to the War as '*Innovations which out Forefathers were unacquainted with*' – as it does the attempt by Josephus (like Paul in the New Testament) to turn their complaints against themselves by accusing these same extremist '*Zealots*' of '*polluting the Temple*' by their acts of '*bloodshed*,' an accusation par-alleled with only slightly differing signification in these passages here – as it is in the Gospels[41] – in Revelation as well.

The phrase '*because he did not circumcise the foreskin of his heart*,' there-fore, is based on these passages from Ezekiel on '*the Zadokite Priesthood*.' The sense of purposefully introducing it in the Habakkuk *Pesher*'s exe-gesis of '*looking upon their Festivals*' (in original Habakkuk 2:15, '*their privy parts*') and '*drink and tremble*' to characterize '*the Wicked Priest*' was to specifically apply the general parameters in Ezekiel to him despite his '*Jewishness*' and even though he was not a foreigner. The point it is making is that he should be treated just like a foreigner because, not only was he *enriching himself by accepting such foreign gifts and sacrifices* – another aspect of the sense of the next charge at the end of Column XI.13-14, '*walking in his way of greediness for the sake of slaking his thirst*' or, as the *Pesher* put it earlier in IX.5, '*profiteering from the spoils of the Peoples*' – but *his very appointment to the High Priesthood itself came from them*. For this, the *Pesher* makes it clear, by deliberately altering the underlying text and introducing the changes it does, *he was disqualified from service as High Priest on the basis of the parameters of Ezekiel's 'Zadokite Statement'* and, in fact, worthy of death.

As Ezekiel 44:13 puts it in these passages about these backsliding Priests who '*went astray from Me after their idols*' and '*brought foreigners into*' the Temple '*uncircumcised in heart and body to pollute it*,' '*breaking My Covenant with all their Abominations:'*

> *They shall not come near to Me to serve as Priests* (basically, the second of the two complaints attributed to James in the *Anabathmoi Jacobou*), *nor approach any of My Holy Things or the Holy of Holies, but they shall carry their shame (kelimmah) and the Abominations they committed.*

Even the word '*Abominations*' (*To*ᶜ*evot*) now appears in the *Pesher's* description that follows of '*the Abominations the Wicked Priest committed*' in '*polluting the Temple of God.*'[42]

Moving on to its definition of the true '*Sons of Zadok,*' who are henceforth to approach the altar of God and render this '*service,*' these are now described in the passage expounded in the key exposition of the CDiii.21–iv.12 as '*those who kept charge* (literally '*the keeping*') *of My Temple when the Sons of Israel went astray from Me*' (44:15). They are also described as '*keeping My Laws (Hukkim),*' '*Festivals,*' and '*Sabbaths,*' not only alluded to elsewhere at Qumran as '*the monthly flags.*'[43] They are also all things, by contrast, Paul heaps abuse on in developing his theology of the saving death of '*Christ Jesus,*' describing them in Galatians 4:9–10 as '*Beggarly*' or '*Poverty-stricken elements*' (note the play here on '*the Poor*' terminology associated with James) only good for '*weaklings*' and those '*preferring bondage*' – as he makes clear in the 'allegory' that follows in Galatians 4:21–31 contrasting '*the slave woman*' Hagar, who '*is Mount Sinai in Arabia,*' with '*the free woman*' Sarah – meaning '*to the Law.*'

Furthermore, he makes this allusion, as will be recalled, in the aftermath of discussing how '*as Many are of the works of the Law are under a curse*' and '*the Righteous shall live by Faith*' in 3:10–11. We showed in discussing the last Column of the Damascus Document earlier that Paul turns the '*cursing*' of those '*straying to the right or left of the Torah,*' one finds there, in upon those who had most probably anathematized him. Making it clear in Galatians 3:13 that he considered himself to be in some manner under '*the curse of the Law,*' he argues that Jesus too was '*cursed*' by being '*hung upon a tree*' according to the very Law those would execrate him held so dear. Therefore, by implication, by taking this '*curse*' upon himself or, in some of the most dazzling theological footwork ever evinced, Paul argues that, '*having become for us a curse,*' 'Jesus' redeemed all Mankind too.

We also showed how in the next chapter of Galatians (4:16–18), Paul is primarily teaching against those '*zealous*' for such things – meaning '*Zealots*'– when he asks, '*Have I now become your Enemy by telling the Truth to you?*' In so doing, he shows his awareness that epithets of this kind, namely *both* the '*Lying*' and '*the Enemy*' ones, were being applied to him

by his detractors – epithets that have not failed to leave their mark in
'*Jewish Christian*' or '*Ebionite*' tradition. In this last, the Paul–like attacker
of James is specifically referred to, as we saw, as the '*Hostile Man*' or
'*Enemy*' in the account of the physical assault he makes on James in the
Temple in the Pseudoclementine *Recognitions*. Not only is the basis for
this epithet to be found in James 4:4, but reflections of it are to be found
in Matthew's '*Parable of the Tares*,' which recounts how an '*Enemy*' came
and sowed the tares among the good seed, but at the End of Time ('*the
Completion of this Age*') – as the Gospel raconteur avers – the tares will be
uprooted and '*cast* (*balousin* – more '*casting*' usage) *into the furnace of fire*'
(Matthew 13:39–42). This will be exactly the same approach as the
Habakkuk *Pesher* and the note of extreme hopefulness it manifests
regarding such matters in its climactic conclusion.

'The Cup of the Wrath of God will Swallow him'

As already highlighted, it is in this context that the Habakkuk *Pesher*
describes the destruction of the Wicked Priest in terms of '*drinking his
fill*' from '*the Cup of the Wrath of God*.' This would also be '*the Cup of Trembling*' from Isaiah 51:17 implied, as we saw, by the purposeful substitution
of '*tremble*' for '*foreskin*' in the underlying text from Habakkuk 2:16. This
is also clearly '*the Cup*' of Divine Vengeance – *ergo*, now '*the Cup of the Wrath
of God (Hamat-El) would swallow him*' (*tevalceno*).

We have already seen this kind of '*Venomous Anger*' imagery used in
the Damascus Document to apply to the '*Establishment*' and '*the wine*' of
'*their ways*.' Here it is being applied to the '*Reward*' (*Gemulo*) of the
Wicked Priest. In the Psalm 37 *Pesher* above, this was '*the Reward* (again,
gemulo) *God paid him by delivering him into the hand of the Violent Ones of
the Gentiles*.' These we have identified as the Idumaean allies of the
'*Zealots*,' all thirsting for vengeance for James. Not only did they '*execute
the Judgements upon Evil on him*,' in this *Pesher* this involved '*taking
Vengeance on the flesh of his corpse*.' As we have seen too, the text also plays
on the expression '*shame*' (*kalon/kikalon*), repeated twice, to express the
Wicked Priest's behavior and final defilement. A variation of this '*shame*'
(*kelimmah*) is also found, combined with reference to '*Abominations*'
(*To'evot*) as here in the Habakkuk *Pesher*, in these key passages of Ezekiel's
'*Zadokite Statement*' about *the disqualification of Priests like* '*the Wicked Priest*'
from service at the Temple altar (44:13).

As we have seen, his destruction is described in 1QpHab,XI.12–15 in
the following manner:

His shame was greater than his Glory, because…he walked in his Way of satiety (also possibly, '*greediness*') *by way of drinking his fill* (this, the '*filled with shame*' and '*drinking*' in the underlying text of Habakkuk 2:16), *but the Cup of the Wrath of God shall swallow him, adding to* (*his shame and dis*)*grace* ('*his kalon/kikalon*)…

The column breaks off here. This was the passage that was translated in the early days of Qumran research in terms of the Wicked Priest's '*walking in the Ways of drunkenness that he might quench his thirst*' and '*the Cup of the Wrath of God confusing him*'; but, as already several times now reiterated, *God did not wish* '*to confuse*' *the Wicked Priest. He wished to* '*destroy him*.'

The whole exposition, we are presenting here, is born out by what follows in the next column of the *Pesher*, Column XII – the penultimate one. Pursuing an underlying reference to the '*Violence done to Lebanon*,' '*the destruction of the dumb Beasts*,' '*the Blood of Man* (*Adam*) *and the Violence* (*done*) *to the Land, the City, and all its inhabitants*' (as we have seen, all allusions with counterparts in the Book of Revelation), the *Pesher* now focuses on the '*conspiracy to destroy the Poor*' and '*to rob*' *them of their sustenance* ('*Riches*').[44] As will be recalled, this '*plot*' or '*conspiracy*' was, in our view, the one between Ananus ben Ananus and the Herodian Agrippa II '*to destroy*' the Righteous Teacher James. It is this which is '*the Blood of Man*' (which may have additional overtones both as regards the '*Christ Jesus*' of received Scripture, but also the related theology of '*drinking his Blood*,' to say nothing of the noisome '*Blood libel*') and '*the Violence done to the Land*' and '*its inhabitants*.' '*The City*' is specifically identified in XII.7–9 as Jerusalem. The text makes no bones about this, averring that this was '*Jerusalem, where the Wicked Priest committed his works of Abominations and polluted the Temple of God*.' On the other hand, '*the Violence* (*done to*) *the Land*' is said to be '*the Cities of Judah*' where '*he stole the Riches of the Poor*' (*Ebionim*).[45]

This is the same '*stealing from the Meek of His People*' and '*grinding the face of the Poor*,' referred to above in those passages surrounding Isaiah 3:10–11 and applied in early Church literature to the death of James. The reference to the Wicked Priest's '*works of Abominations*' harks back, as already remarked, to the parameters of Ezekiel's '*Zadokite Covenant*' above and, first and foremost, consisted of his '*destruction of the Poor*' – meaning, in our view, the destruction of James and several of his colleagues. They are also a play on the proper '*works*' associated with and recommended by James and, for that matter, the Qumran Letter(s) ('*MMT*') on '*the Works that would be Reckoned to you as Righteousness*' or

'*Justifying you*.'[46]

This '*stealing from the Meek of His People*' also comprises part of the passages in CDvi.11-14 above having to do with '*barring the door of the Temple, so as not to light its altar-fire in vain*' (Malachi 1:10) and '*separating from the Sons of the Pit*' during '*the whole Age of Evil*' (the '*seventy*' years of Daniel 9:3 and Jeremiah 25:11 – the latter also so strikingly going on to refer to '*drinking*,' '*drunkenness*,' and '*drinking the Cup*' of the Lord unto '*Judgement*' and what is most clearly '*destruction*'?) – all part of what was meant there by '*separating between clean and unclean*,' '*Holy and profane*' and '*keeping away from (lehinnazer) polluted Evil Riches*' and '*the Riches of the Temple*.'[47] There can be little doubt too that this is the same '*stealing the tithes of the Poorer Priests*' in the areas around Jerusalem ('*the Cities of Judah where he stole the Riches of the Poor*') by the thugs and servants of the High Priests, to which Josephus twice refers directly before and directly after the stoning of James, in his description of the run-up to the Revolt.

As we have seen too, the accusation of filling Jerusalem with '*pollution*,' '*Abominations*,' and '*Blood*,' is exactly what – again reversing this accusation – Josephus says '*the Zealots*' and their '*Violent*' Idumaean colleagues did in destroying James' murderer Ananus, Saulos' kinsman Antipas, and Zachariah (the '*Rich*,' pro-Roman merchant, whose body the Zealots '*cast down*' from the Temple Wall – just as James' murder is portrayed in early Church sources – and whose name would still appear to be attached along with James' – despite variant traditions to the contrary – to the two tombs directly beneath '*the Pinnacle of the Temple*' in the Kedron Valley), that is to say, they '*polluted the Temple of God*' thereby bringing upon the Jews His (God's) just '*Retribution*.' As previously explained, this accusation should be a familiar one by now and it is only slightly transformed in the version of it one gets in New Testament contexts and in the theology of the early Church.

Furthermore, the allusion here to '*works*' also inverts the proper '*works*' attributed to '*the Righteous Teacher*' throughout the Scrolls and, as just signaled, the traditions of Western Civilization associated with the name of 'James' – the allusion to his '*Abominations*' (*To'evot*) being exactly the same as in Ezekiel 44:13 above. In this last, these even were specifically connected with the verb '*do*,' the root in Hebrew – as should by now be fully appreciated – of the word '*works*' – and '*the shame and the Abominations which they did*' (here, again significantly, the use of the word '*shame*' and the opposite of what the new Priesthood, '*the Sons of Zadok*,' were to '*do*' in Ezekiel 44:14 there) and the Wicked Priest is being disqualified from such '*service at the altar*,' not only for allowing Gentiles into the Temple (in particular, Herodians) and accepting their gifts (including Caesar's), but also for '*the Blood*' of the Righteous Teacher (James) and his colleagues, '*the Poor*' (*Ebionites*).

'*Lebanon*,' because of the '*whitening*'-imagery implicit in the original Hebrew (elsewhere, we saw it had to do with the garb the Priests wore in the Temple), is specifically interpreted as '*the Community Council*,' imagery also encountered both as regards '*the tombs of the two brothers that miraculously whitened every year*' in the *Recognitions* and Jesus' clothing at his '*Transfiguration*' and that of the Angel in his tomb, '*white as snow, such that no fuller on earth could whiten*,' in the Gospels.[48] These wore white linen, as per Ezekiel's directives in 44:17 – just as '*the Essenes*' seem to have done – as if they were '*Zadokite Priests*' permanently serving in the Temple before God. '*The Beasts*,' as we saw too, are '*the Simple Jews*' who actually '*do the Torah*'; and here we have the '*doing*' usage again, just encountered in the various contexts above and actually referred to several times throughout the Letter of James in terms of being '*a Doer of the word*'/'*the work*'/or '*the Law*,' which was used four columns earlier in VIII.1–3 to restrict the applicability of '*the Righteous shall live by his Faith*' to '*Torah-Doers in the House of Judah*,' that is, only '*Torah-doing Jews*.'

Just so that there would be no mistaking any of these things, the *Pesher* at this point, as earlier underscored, avers that the Wicked Priest '*would be paid the Reward he rewarded the Poor*' (*Gemulo asher gamal*), '*the Poor*' also being identified with '*the Community Council*' – which wore white – and with '*Lebanon*'; and '*just as he plotted to destroy the Poor, so too would God condemn him to destruction*.' The verb here, as already remarked as well, is '*lechalah*'/'*lechalot*' and literally means '*destroy*'; so there cannot be any doubt that the language of '*swallowing*' or '*eating*,' used throughout these passages to evoke the fate of '*the Righteous Teacher*' and '*the Poor*' ('*the Dumb Beasts*' or '*members of his Council*'), ultimately '*comes around to*' the Wicked Priest and means '*to destroy him*' – nothing else.

Here we should recapitulate the significance of the usage '*swallowing*' as it relates to the '*destruction*' of the Righteous Teacher and some of his colleagues on '*the Community Council*' in 1QpHab,XI.13–XII.10. In such a context, these last would be equivalent to the so-called '*Twelve Apostles*' of Gospel portraiture. In the Community Rule, '*the Community Council*' – which is reckoned as '*an Eternal Planting*,' '*a Precious Cornerstone*,' and a kind of spiritualized '*Holy of Holies for Aaron*' and '*Perfect Temple of God for Israel*' – is, as may be recalled, presented as composed of '*Twelve Israelites and Three Priests*.[49] This, of course, can immediately be recognized as the '*Twelve-man*' Apostle-scheme of the Gospels and Acts and that of '*the Inner Triad*' or '*the Central Three*' – '*those reputed to be Pillars*' (not that '*their importance*' to him '*anything conferred*') as Paul in Galatians 2:6–9 refers to them using the language of 'building' and 'architecture' so typical of him. In the Scrolls, it is not clear whether these 'Three' are part of or in addition to the 'Twelve,' though the latter is more probable.[50] This same confusion is reflected in the Gospels and compounded in Acts and early Church tradition, where it is not clear exactly who is an 'Apostle,' nor how these relate to 'the Inner Three,' nor who, in fact, really comprise the latter.[51]

This 'swallowing' imagery, as already stressed, is being deliberately applied throughout 1QpHab,XI.5-15 to the destruction of the Righteous Teacher and some members of this Council, referred to collectively as 'the Simple of Judah doing Torah' or 'the Poor.' It, along with 'the Poor,' are being purposefully applied to this 'destruction,' as neither appear in the underlying passages of Habakkuk 2:15–18. We have made it clear that this 'swallowing' means 'consume' or 'destroy' here and that, in a kind of poetic justice, it is finally turned around and applied to 'the destruction of the Wicked Priest' – presumably by 'the Violent Ones of the Gentiles' or those Josephus is calling 'Idumaeans' – that is, just as the Wicked Priest 'swallowed' the Righteous Teacher and some of his followers among 'the Poor,' so too would he himself be 'swallowed' or 'consumed.'

We have shown too that this imagery of 'swallowing' and the circle-of-language related to it were based on the Hebrew root B-L-ᶜA. It forms a parallel and opposing one to the Z-D-K or 'Righteousness' language-circle and also relates to allusions like 'the wine' or 'the Venom of the Kings of the Peoples' and 'their ways' (meaning 'the Herodians') in other Qumran documents such as the Damascus Document. This is the thrust, too, of the various adumbrations of this imagery we encounter – including allusions to 'the Three Nets of Belial,' 'Balaam,' 'Balak' and even 'Jezebel' and 'Babylon' in Revelation, not to mention 'Beliar' and 'the Diabolos' – even 'Beelzebub' – elsewhere in the New Testament.

In fact, the first of these individuals and the original instigator of all these 'Innovations into the Customs of the People' was Herod himself; and the Rabbinic decipherment of the nomenclature 'Balaam' in terms of its root-meaning, i.e., 'he who swallowed the People,' was absolutely characteristic of 'the Herodians,' particularly as they disposed of Revolutionary 'Opposition' Leaders such as John the Baptist, James, and many others.[52] They 'ballaᶜ' or 'Belaᶜ (the first 'Edomite' King-name) them,' meaning, 'they swallowed' or 'destroyed them.' This is the reason, too, this imagery is being used at this point in the Habakkuk Pesher because it describes what the Herodian-sponsored High Priestly 'Establishment' did to the Righteous Teacher/James. They destroyed him. Furthermore, the 'conspiracy' hinted at is the one between Ananus and Agrippa II to remove 'Opposition' Leaders, particularly 'Opposition High Priests' such as James, who opposed

Herodian gifts and sacrifices in the Temple and *supported the building of a wall in the Temple to block their view of the sacrifices.* These took advantage of the chance provided by an interregnum in Roman Governors to remove the key individual they considered responsible for the agitation against them in the Temple – 'the Opposition High Priest of his time,' James.

'Stumbling,' 'Casting Down,' 'Leading Astray,' and 'Slaying with the Rod of his Mouth'

To draw all these imageries even more closely together, early Church texts are saying the same things about James and his entry into the Holy of Holies on at least one *Yom Kippur* (if not many) – there to make atonement on behalf of the whole People (the atonement of a 'Righteous Priest' / 'Zaddik') – that Ezekiel is saying about the true 'Sons of Zadok' in the 'Zadokite Covenant' in 44:6–31 above.

Even without the reference to it in CDIII.21–IV.2, we could have connected James to the 'Zadokite'-ideology by the constant reiteration of the 'Righteousness'-ideology regarding his person and the title in Latin tied to his name, 'Justus,' which is 'Zadok' in Hebrew – this, to say nothing of the constant reiteration of the word 'keeping' in all sources (including 'Rechabite' ones) connected to his being, which (aside from the word-play centering around the 'Z-D-K' ideology) is the actual definition of the true 'Sons of Zadok' in the Community Rule at Qumran.[53] But early Church texts are indeed applying, as we just saw, many of the parameters listed in Ezekiel's 'Zadokite' materials in consequence of this, including, 'wearing only linen,' 'a razor never touching his head,' 'abstaining from wine,' 'barring carrion,' etc.; so it is possible to discern the traces of a conscious effort to present him as a true 'Son of Zadok' even in these texts and according to the parameters recognized at Qumran, not to mention those of the 'Nazirite' / 'Rechabite' ideology in general.[54]

But early Church texts are also at pains, as we have been accentuating, to portray his death in terms of the verb in Greek that basically contains the same root letters as that of 'swallowing' in Hebrew – namely, 'casting down': 'ballo' / 'kataballo' / 'ekballo' / or the like. We have also seen above how the equivalent of this verb 'casting' or 'throwing down' – also 'causing to stumble' in Hebrew – was linked, together with 'swallowing' in the Habakkuk *Pesher,* to how the Wicked Priest destroyed the Righteous Teacher and some colleagues, and this related to *Yom Kippur,* even though the word nowhere appeared in the underlying Biblical passage from Habakkuk 2:15 on which the exegesis supposedly was based.

Interestingly enough, as also already remarked, it does appear in

Ezekiel 44:12 regarding *'causing the House of Israel to stumble into sinning,'* not to mention a variation of it in the Letter of James, also following quotation of *'the Royal Law according to the Scripture'* and in conjunction with allusion to *'keeping'* (2:10). On the other hand, together with this imagery of *'swallowing'* and additional allusion to *'the Poor,'* as just pointed up, it seems purposefully to have been introduced into the vocabulary of the Habakkuk *Pesher* at this point.

We have also shown above how this imagery related to that of *'Belial'* (in Revelation, *'Balaam'*) *'casting down his net'* generally to *'deceive Israel'* or *'lead Israel astray,'* imagery picked up in the picture of the Apostles *'casting down'* their nets in the Gospels (Matthew 4:18–19 and *pars.*) who, in a kind of parody of this imagery, are then said to have become *'Fishers of Men'* (Matthew 4:20–21 and *pars.*). Interestingly enough, as we have called attention to as well, this same imagery is present in the Habakkuk *Pesher* in exposition of Habakkuk 1:15–16 on *'fishing,' 'nets,'* and *'plenteous eating'*; but there the *'nets'* and *'fishing'* were those *cast by 'the Kittim'* or, as it were, *the Romans, 'parceling out their yoke and their taxes'* and the *'eating,' destroying 'all Peoples, year by year,' 'with the sword.'*[55]

As we have elsewhere explained, in the Gospels this imagery even went further afield to encompass the authority received by the Apostles, *'to cast out demons'* or *'Evil spirits'* (*ekballo* – Mark 3:15 and *pars.*) – a parody, as also suggested, of *the expulsion by groups like the Essenes* or *those at Qumran of Backsliders and Law-Breakers* (like Paul?).[56] It was also edifying to note the further use of this language in the *'casting out'* from Jerusalem of Ananus' body without burial as food for jackals or that of the *'Rich'* collaborator *'Zachariah'* and of *'Stephen'* in Acts 7:51–53 by allegedly blood-thirsty Jews, who *'gnashed their teeth at him'* after being accused by him themselves of *'not keeping'* the Law and being *'uncircumcised in heart and ears'*![57]

It was interesting, too, how this idea of being *'cast down from the Pinnacle of the Temple'* in the manner of James occurs in the famous stories about Jesus' *'Temptation in the Wilderness'* in Matthew 4:1–11 and Luke 4:1–13. The picture of this in these two Gospels (unlike Mark 1:12–13) is on the whole equivalent with only slight variations. Both use the language of the *'Diabolos'* and *'kataballo'* to signify being *'cast down'* (4:5 and 4:9). Also, in the typical style of Qumran, Revelation, and Paul in 2 Corinthians, both insert the usage, *'Satan,'* into the fabric of their narrative, even though they seem initially to be referring to the *'Diabolos'* or *'Belial'* (4:10 and 4:8). Both episodes are given a Pauline or pro-Roman cast in that Jesus is offered Authority over *'all the Kingdoms of the World and their Glory'* (4:8–9 and 4:6). He declines with the now proverbial words,

'*Get thee behind me Satan,*' quoting Deuteronomy 6:13, to the effect that, it is God alone whom he serves (4:10 and 4:8). The only difference is that in Luke this offer follows the Devil's suggestion '*to cast himself down from the Pinnacle of the Temple*' while in Matthew it precedes it.

This implied rejection of this-worldly '*Messianism*' makes no sense at all, since in the Palestinian version of '*Messianism*' – for instance, in the War Scroll and other texts from Qumran not to mention Revelation – *the Messiah was to come and crush all the Nations with '*a rod of iron*' and make them his '*footstool.*'*[58] In support of this, Revelation repeatedly cites the passage from Psalm 2:8–9 about being given '*the ends of the Earth for a possession*' and '*breaking the Gentiles with a rod of iron,*' not to mention Isaiah 11:4's '*smiting the earth with the rod of his mouth*' – '*the sharp sword of his mouth*' in Isaiah 49:2 – a passage extant in Qumran *Pesharim* as we have seen. As it turns out, the mentality typical of these '*footstool*' passages in Revelation are completely typical of Qumran as well.[59]

Nor should it be forgotten that the ambiance of Isaiah 11:4 is the citation about '*the Rod of the Shoot of Jesse and the Branch (Netzer) from his Roots,*' subjected to exegesis at Qumran, as we have seen above, in two separate contexts; and the context of Psalm 2:8–9 is the all-important reference to '*You are My son. On this day I have begotten you*' (2:7). It should be appreciated, as we have laid stress on, that this last appears in one of the so-called '*Jewish Christian*' Gospels, attributed by Epiphanius to '*the Ebionites,*' in place of the extant text in the Synoptics which, in depicting John's baptism of Jesus rather inserts the phrase, '*This is my only-begotten Son. In him I am well pleased*' (Matthew 3:17 and *pars.*).[60] *Par contra,* Epiphanius' Ebionite Gospel conserves Psalm 2:7 and, consequently, the impression of an '*adoptionist baptism,*' similar to that at Qumran,[61] rather than a supernatural birth or '*Immaculate Conception*' as it is now called. As this is the approach reiterated in Hebrews 1:5 and 5:5, a letter replete with the imagery of the Messiah '*sitting on the right hand of God and making his enemies his footstool*' (Psalm 110:1, the Psalm which in 110:4 also contains the imagery of '*a Priest forever after the order of Melchizedek*'). It seems very likely that this was the original tradition. However this may be, so much does Revelation expand on quotations of this kind that it appears like something of an extended, Qumran-style *Pesher* as well.

But in Matthew and Luke's descriptions of *the Temptation '*in the Wilderness*' by the Devil,* which not only almost directly follow this baptism scenario but, in the same breath, seem directly to be targeting these '*wilderness-dwelling*' sectarian groups; '*Jesus*' is basically also being presented within the '*Jamesian*' scenario of '*being cast down from the Pinnacle of the Temple*' by the Devil ('*Diabolos*'/'*Belial*'). The words are almost exactly those of early Church accounts of James' death except, instead of *'being cast down*,' 'Jesus' is asked to *'cast himself down'* (Matthew 4:6 and Luke 4:9). Declining, he says in words now proverbial and continuing to quote Deuteronomy 6:16, *'you shalt not tempt the Lord your God.'* The implication is the James tradition is that James willfully cast himself down from the Pinnacle of the Temple and, in so doing, somehow tested the Lord his God, but, as just intimated, none of this makes any sense whatsoever and it is simply a further example of a tradition related to James' death and the *'ballo'*/*'balla^c'*/*'Belial'*-terminology being retrospectively incorporated into the life of 'Jesus.' There is also the derivative implication, should one choose to regard it, that *'temptation in the wilderness'* materials of this kind could not have assumed this form until after the traditions about James' *'fall'* or *'having been cast down'* were concretized. These traditions have their further adumbrations in the materials about the Apostles *'casting down their nets'* into the Sea of Galilee before recognizing and joining Jesus on the shore, folkloric inventions taking this imagery even further afield.

The traditions relating to the *'casting down'* of James occur in early Church testimony, as will be recalled, in two separate variations – one having to do with the attack by *'the Enemy'* Paul in the Forties CE which does not result in his death, but only a fall from the Temple stairs in which he *'breaks his leg.'*[62] This is the more likely scenario. The second attack, which occurs in the Sixties CE, supposedly results in his *'being cast down'* or a fall *'from the Temple Pinnacle.'* On top of this last, *there is the stoning* and *the coup de grace delivered to him by a laundryman's club.*[63] As we showed in *James the Brother of Jesus*, the second is really a conflation of both the earlier one – apparently by Paul – in the Forties (which Acts is so anxious to disguise masking it with *'the Jews'* allegedly stoning a paper-mache character like *'Stephen'*) and the later one, James' stoning in 62 CE as described by Josephus.[64] This last is the one that most fits the Dead Sea Scrolls' account of how *'the Wicked Priest pursued the Righteous Teacher with'* or *'in his Beit-Galuto* (*'his House of Exile'* or *'his Exiled House'*) *to swallow him,'* that is, *pursued judicial proceedings against him that resulted in his stoning.*

Where Paul's 'Herodian' affiliations and, therefore, part and parcel of the *'Belial'*/*'balla^c'* terminology are concerned; in Acts 23:35, as we saw, he stays in Agrippa II's Palace in Caesarea and converses with him and his sisters in a kind of quasi-protective custody – not to mention the Roman Procurator Felix – with easygoing congeniality for, apparently, *more than two years while they protect him from Temple 'Zealots'* and *'Nazirite oath'-taking would-be Assassins* (*'Sicarii'*?). Finally they pack him off to Rome where he again appears to flourish under another kind of loose house arrest (Acts 28:30–31). In addition, there is the reference he makes in Romans 16:11 to his '*kinsman Herodion*'/'*his kinsman, the Littlest Herod.*' We take this to be the son of that Aristobulus, the son of Herod of Chalcis Agrippa I's brother, who was married to the Salome involved in John the Baptist's death – probably mentioned under the heading '*all those of the household of Aristobulus*' in Romans 16:10 as well.

This nicely explains Paul's easy access to Temple Authorities (according to Acts) as a comparatively young man, since the aunt of the '*Saulos*' he so much resembles was married to the Temple Treasurer Helcias[65]; as well as why the High Priest would give him letters to arrest so-called '*Christians*' (by Acts 11:26's own testimony, the name wasn't even in use at this time until a decade or so later in Northern Syria!), *i.e.*, extreme '*Zealots*' or '*Sicarii*,' and what he was doing in Damascus around 36–37 CE. There he was probably in the service of Herod Antipas, the individual responsible, along with Agrippa I's and Herod of Chalcis' sister Herodias, for the death of John the Baptist and, by his own testimony, in 2 Corinthians 11:33, he was '*let down its walls in a basket*' and had to flee the soldiers of the Arab King '*Aretas*' with whom the said '*Antipas*' was at war.

All of this would, of course, be most understandable if Paul ('*Saulos*'?) gave the Authorities the information they needed to identify James as the center of agitation against them, Gentile gifts and sacrifices in the Temple generally, and related issues (for these, see the two Letters, I called, '*On Works reckoned as Righteousness*') and to remove him at the first opportunity. Therefore the '*balla^c*'/'*swallowing*' imagery one comes upon at this point in the Habakkuk *Pesher* – in our view, relating to '*Herodians*' – which would be even more comprehensible if James were seen as the center of agitation against them in the Temple, in particular, *wishing to bar said '*Herodians*' from the Temple as foreigners.*

Therefore too, the penance put upon Paul by James in Acts 21:23–24, Paul's mobbing in the Temple on precisely such grounds and his unceremonious ejection from the Temple that follows can simply be seen as part and parcel of these struggles against *the admission of foreigners and their gifts and sacrifices* – seen as '*polluted*' or '*polluting*' – into *the Temple.* Therefore, too, the dire warnings of a conspiracy against Paul in Jerusalem presented through the mouthpiece of the non-existent '*Prophet called Agabus*' in Caesarea in Acts 21:10–11. Looked at in this way, Paul can simply be seen as a '*stalking horse*' for Herodian family interests in the Temple, as he so often seems to be in areas further afield such as Northern Syria, Asia Minor, and Iraq ('*Ethiopia*' or '*Meroe*' in Acts – '*Arabia*' or '*Agar*' in Galatians).

Even if these things are only partly true, it would not be surprising at all if Paul held his rough treatment in the Temple in Jerusalem against

James during his more than two years of what have the appearance of debriefing sessions in Caesarea, first with Felix and his wife Drusilla and then with Agrippa II and his sister Bernice. The '*Saulos*' in Josephus is, in fact, involved in just such debriefing sessions with Nero in Corinth six years later in 66 CE after the Roman Governor Cestius' defeat in the first heady days of the Uprising.[66] Nor would it be surprising if Nero sent this '*Saul*' or '*Paul*' back to Palestine in his service following this first appeal.

The '*Saulos*' in Josephus – '*a kinsman of Agrippa*' – at this point in the two converging narratives becomes the intermediary between the '*Peace Party*' in Jerusalem (consisting High Priests, principal Pharisees, and Herodians) and Roman and Herodian troops outside the City.[67] Before finally going to see Nero in Corinth, this '*Saulos*' goes to Agrippa II's camp also, presumably, to give him a first-hand report on the situation in Jerusalem, where (it will be recalled) he had been in the latter's palace before it surrendered along with several other Herodian '*Men-of-War*,' including Philip, Costobarus, and Antipas the Temple Treasurer, his cousin.

The same language circle – in Greek having to do with '*casting down*' and connected to '*the Diabolos*' or '*the Devil*' (rather than the '*swallowing*,' connected in the Hebrew to '*Belial*') – is being applied to the death of James in early Church texts even though James probably did not die in precisely this way, that is to say, on this point anyhow the texts are somewhat farfetched. This proves, as little else can, that the application of such language to James' death *was purposeful*, just as it was in its application to the destruction (or death) of '*the Righteous Teacher*' at Qumran. Though James was probably not '*cast down*' *from the Pinnacle of the Temple*, as these texts imagine, he probably was '*cast down*' from the top ('*headlong*') of the Temple steps where he had been positioned to speak to the crowds – whether twenty years before, as reported in the *Recognitions*, or as a prelude to his final stoning. Whatever the case, instead of calming them, he proclaimed the imminent coming (or return) of the Messiah '*standing on the right hand of Power*' and '*about to come on the clouds of Heaven*,' as per the parameters of the War Scroll from Qumran and as so widely refurbished in the Gospels and Acts. This doubtlessly happened in some manner.

'*The Wicked Encompasses the Righteous*' and '*Swallows One more Righteous than He*'

The application of these two parallel homophonic imageries, *ba-la-ʿa* and *ballo* in both the Hebrew and the Greek, the former to the destruction of the Righteous Teacher at Qumran and the latter to the death of James in early Church texts, from our perspective proves as little else can the final identity of these two individuals. Texts such as '*the Wicked swallows one more Righteous than he*' (Habakkuk 1.13), are almost always exploited to produce expositions like those encountered above. This is particularly the case if they are accompanied by words like '*Traitors*' (of parallel import in Gospel presentations), '*Violence*,' '*Riches*,' '*Lebanon*,' and the like.

This is also true of the First Column of the Habakkuk *Pesher* where, though poorly preserved because of the way the Scroll was rolled, one can still make out a *Pesher*. This seemingly has to do with '*the Last Generation*,' tied in the underlying text to references from Habakkuk 1:2 to '*Violence*,' '*destruction*,' and '*You save*' – the word '*Salvation*' or '*Yeshuᶜa*'/ '*Jesus*' is based upon in Hebrew. Though the text is fragmentary, there would also appear to be a reference to '*rebelling against God*' tied to a reference to 'ᶜ*amal*' or '*suffering works*' in the underlying text from Habakkuk 1:3. This usage, 'ᶜ*amal*,' will be important later in the *Pesher* when it comes to discussing the '*suffering toil*' of '*the Righteous Teacher*' – that is, how '*the Righteous shall live by his Faith*' – in Column VIII.2 as opposed to the '*Lying service*' of '*the Spouter of Lying*' that follows in Column X.11-12.

As later in the *Pesher*, this reference to 'ᶜ*amal*' from Habakkuk 1:3 is followed by another allusion to '*robbing Riches*.' There is also a reference to '*division*' or '*quarrelsomeness*' in the underlying text from 1:3 which follows this as well, a usage that appears in the First Column of CD1.21 describing the attack by '*the Liar*' and other '*Covenant-Breakers*' on the '*Soul of the Righteous One*' and the other '*Walkers in Perfection*.'[68] In 1QpHab, 1.8–9, this is followed by an underlying citation from Habakkuk 1:4 having to do with '*the Torah being weakened and Judgement never going forth*,' interpreted in terms of '*those who rejected the Torah of God*' (plural). This usage '*ma'as*' for '*reject*' or '*deny*' is an important one and, when singular, is repeatedly used at Qumran to characterize the actions of '*the Spouter of Lying*' – so much so that this, '*rejecting the Torah*,' would appear to be his defining activity.

This introduces the key reference in the underlying text, '*the Wicked encompasses* (based in Hebrew on the same root as, for instance, '*Crown*' or '*Diadem*'[69]) *the Righteous. Therefore perverted Judgement goes forth*' (Habakkuk 1:4). This is very similar to the text and exposition of Psalm 37:32, '*the Wicked looks out for the Righteous and seeks to kill him*,' we looked at earlier and, once again, the possible parallel here to the illegal trial of James should not be ignored. In any event here in 1QpHab,1.10 it sets the tone for the whole *Pesher* that follows.

Though the exposition of the second half of this is missing, it should be immediately recognizable that the first part parallels and is simply a variation on Habakkuk 1:13 later in Column v.8-9, '*the Wicked swallows one more Righteous than he*' – the imagery of '*surrounding*' or '*encompassing*' having the same negative signification as '*swallowing*.' Though the exegesis is fragmentary at this point too, it is nonetheless made clear that '*the Wicked*' in the text applies to *the Wicked Priest* in the *Pesher*, as it does everywhere else at Qumran, and '*the Righteous*' (*Zaddik*) is likewise explicitly tied – as always – to '*the Righteous Teacher*.' In fact, it is this allusion to '*the Righteous One*' or '*Zaddik*' that introduces '*the Righteous Teacher*,' concretizing the basic consistency of these textual correspondences.[70]

This is also the approach of all early Church accounts of the death of James at the hands of '*the Wicked Priest*' of his generation '*Ananus ben Ananus*.' This too, in our view, is '*the Last Generation*' as in the 1.11 *Pesher* on Habakkuk 1:2 above as well as when '*the Last Priests of Jerusalem gathered Riches and profiteered from the spoils of the Peoples*' in IX.4-7. There can be little doubt of the relationship of these kinds of allusions to text applied in these sources to the death of James (an individual actually surnamed '*the Righteous One*,' namely Isaiah 3:10–11, another *Zaddik*-text – in its Greek Septuagint version, to repeat: '*Let us bind the Just One for he is an annoyance to us. Therefore shall they eat the fruit of their works*.'

Once again, the '*eating*' in this allusion, as in the received Hebrew and Latin versions, basically parallels the sense of '*swallowing*' or '*being swallowed*' as it is expressed here in the Habakkuk *Pesher*. As in the characterization of '*the Kittim*' or the Romans in 1QpHab,VI.7-8 as '*eating all the Peoples...with the sword*' too, the sense of all these allusions in Isaiah is of '*violent destruction*.' One should also keep the double entendre implicit in usages such as this in mind when evaluating related allusions such as '*glutton*' in the Gospels (in Matthew 11:19 and Luke 7:34, not insignificantly, tied to being '*a wine-bibber*' and '*a Friend of tax collectors*' – thus!) which, in Hebrew, literally translates out as '*bela*[c]' – but also Paul's related almost total fixation upon '*eating*,' by which he means (as do the Gospels) *being free of Jewish dietary regulations and Mosaic Law*.

As we have seen to some extent as well, this section of Isaiah 2–3 also includes references to '*Jerusalem being fallen*,' '*Judea in collapse*,' '*Lebanon*,' '*robbing the Meek*,' '*grinding the face of the Poor*,' and '*Judgement*.' This is not to mention allusion to '*abolishing the idols*' and '*casting down his idols of silver and his idols of gold, which they made for each other to worship, to the moles and the bats*' (2:20). This, too, will be directly reprised from XII.12–XIII.4, the end of the Habakkuk *Pesher*, with the phraseology:

This interpretation of this passage concerns all the idols of the Gentiles, which they create in order to serve them and bow down before them. These will not save them (the same word '*save*'/'*yizzilu*' used in Column VIII.1–2 in the eschatological interpretation of Habakkuk 2:4, '*the Righteous shall live by his Faith*' and '*the House of Judgement*') *on the Day of Judgement*.

It repeats this in the next column in the following manner:

> *This concerns all the Gentiles, who serve stone and wood. But on the Day of Judgement, God will destroy all idolaters* (literally, '*the Servants of Idols*') *and Wicked Ones* (Resha'im – e.g., Jewish '*Backsliders*' and '*Traitors*' like '*the Wicked Priest*') *from the Earth*.

In the *Pesher*, this is given in interpretation of Habakkuk 2:19–20: '*Behold, it is covered with gold and silver and there is no spirit at all within it. But the Lord is in His Holy Temple. Be silent before Him, all the world*.'[71] The pathos and hopeful constancy of this Faith, even in the face of the disastrous circumstances overwhelming everyone at this moment in the *Pesher*, is poignant.

This point-of-view is also evident at the end of the Letter of James in the condemnations one finds there and the note of coming eschatological '*Judgement*' (4:11–5:12). In Isaiah 2:21 above, this is expressed in terms of '*the Lord arising to terribly shake the Earth*.' James 5:3, like Isaiah 2:20 and Habakkuk 2:19 above, at this point is also using the imagery of '*gold and silver*' to condemn the '*Rich*.' These it blames for '*condemning* (what '*the Wicked do to the Righteous*' in the Damascus Document[72]) *and putting the Righteous One to death*,' contrary to Paul in 1 Thessalonians 2:14–15 who, as already laid stress on, typically blames '*the Jews*.' For James 5:1–3, this reads as follows:

> *As for you Rich, weep, howl over the miseries that are coming upon you. Your Riches have rotted and your clothes have become moth-eaten. Your gold and silver has been eaten away, and their decomposition shall be a witness against you and shall eat* (again the word '*eat*'/'*consume*' – this time in the Greek) *your flesh like fire*.

This is all described in terms of '*the Judge standing before the Door*' (5:9), '*the coming of the Lord*' (5:8), and *the cries of the Downtrodden reaching* '*the Lord God of Hosts*' (5:4).

Curiously, the Greek of this term '*annoyance*' or '*burdensome*,' as applied to '*binding the Just One*' in the Septuagint version of Isaiah 3:10 above, is expressed in terms of '*duschrestos*,' a term some might have been able to interpret as a hidden reference to '*the Antichrist*.' Be this as it may, it could not have failed to appeal to our exegetes holding the events of James' life in such reverence as to think they could find them by searching Scripture whether the Hebrew or the Greek.[73] However this may be, in contrasting 'the Wicked' (Rasha[c]) with 'the Righteous' (Zaddik), the Greek version of this passage reverses the underlying sense of the Hebrew – and, as it would seem, the Latin – making it appear as if the negative things are being done to 'the Righteous One' not 'the Wicked', though the succeeding reference to 'he shall be paid the reward of his hands' is the same. Moreover, we have already seen how these kinds of recasting or inversions of Scripture in favor of a preferred exegesis were fairly common, not only at Qumran, but also in early Church usage.

In the Septuagint version given by Hegesippus *via* Eusebius, this was actually seen to reflect the death of James. Its contrast of 'the Wicked' and 'the Righteous' parallels that at the beginning of the Habakkuk *Pesher* of 'the Wicked encompasses the Righteous' (1.10–11) which was specifically interpreted to apply to 'the Righteous Teacher' and 'the Wicked Priest.' It, too, is immediately followed in Habakkuk 1:4 by a reference to 'Judgement' though, in this case, delivering 'perverted Judgement.'

In Isaiah 3:11, as well, all versions immediately follow with some rendition of 'the reward of his hands will be done to him' meaning, as this seems to have been interpreted, 'the Wicked Priest' as well. This is echoed almost precisely, as already remarked, in 1QpHab,XII.2–3's 'he ('the Wicked Priest') would be paid the reward he rewarded the Poor.' In the Septuagint Greek, following the allusion to 'they shall eat the fruits of their works' in 3:10, 3:11 is translated as, 'Evils shall happen to him according to the works of his hands.' In all versions too, this is immediately succeeded in the next line – as already to some extent related – by allusion to 'leading the People astray' and 'swallowing the Way of Your Pathways' in 3:12. This, in turn, was followed by allusion to 'the Lord standing up to Judge the Peoples' and 'the Lord entering into Judgement with the Elders and Rulers of the People' in 3:13–3:14.

The Introduction of 'the Liar' in the Habakkuk *Pesher* from Qumran

In the Habakkuk *Pesher* too, the next reference to what 'the Wicked' does to 'the Righteous' occurs in Column v.8–9 and actually refers to 'the Wicked swallowing one more Righteous than he' (Habakkuk 1:13), following a reference to 'Judgement' in the underlying text of Habakkuk 1:12 which is interpreted in terms of a vivid picture of 'the Judgement on the Gentiles by the hand of His Elect' – 'the Sons of Zadok' in CDIII.21–IV.9 above.

This is the single instance in any Qumran *Pesher* of an allusion to 'the Wicked' and 'the Righteous' not being applied to 'the Wicked Priest' per se.

The same is true of the word '*swallowing*' in this passage. Rather it appears to be applied to an inner session of '*the Assembly*' or Community where, exploiting a reference to '*Traitors*' (*Bogdim*) in the underlying text from Habakkuk 1:13, one group within the Community is admonished for '*keeping silent at the time when the Righteous Teacher was reproved.*' This admonishment seems to have been by the tongue of '*the Man of Lying*,' though this is not clear. What is clear is that he is described revealingly as '*rejecting (ma'as* again) *the Torah in the midst of their whole Assembly.*'[74]

The evocation of '*the Judgement*' participated in by '*the Elect*' at the beginning of Column Five (IV.14–V.5) comes after a long excursus on the might and ferocity of '*the Kittim*'/Romans – including '*their Council Chamber*' (presumably their Senate) as '*their Guilty Council House*' – in Columns III-IV.[75] follows a stubborn, if nationalistic insistence, as we saw, '*that God would not destroy* (as in the last Column of the *Pesher* on '*the Day of Judgement*') *His People by the hand of the Gentiles, but rather God would render Judgement on the Gentiles by the hand of His Elect.*' This would also be in line with the eschatology of Revelation – such as it is – as we have signaled it above. This '*Elect*' is described as '*not lusting after* (literally, '*fornicating*' – once again playing off the language of '*fornication*' so characterizing the Herodian Establishment) *their eyes during the Era of Evil.*'[76]

Again, this '*rejection of the Torah in the midst of their whole Assembly*' must be seen as characteristic of '*the Lying Spouter*'s behavior and his rebuke of the Righteous Teacher. The confrontation between them, which this time would appear to be internal and verbal not mortal – this is the import of the verb, '*ma'as*' or '*reject*' as opposed to '*eating*' or '*destroy*' – in that sense, resembles nothing so much as '*the Jerusalem Council*' or, at least a '*Council*' of some sort. The word '*balla°*'/'*swallowing*' in the underlying text from Habakkuk 1:13, however, is not applied in any real sense in the exegesis as it stands. Rather it is put on intellectual hold, as it were, and employed later in the *Pesher* to describe what the Wicked Priest did to '*the Righteous Teacher*' and his followers among '*the Poor*,' as we have seen, and what in turn the Lord would do to him, *i.e.*, '*swallow him.*'[77]

That this was seen in some manner also to refer to '*the Man of Lying*''s activities – if it was – can, as well, only be understood if in some way the latter was seen either to represent or be part and parcel of '*the Herodian Establishment.*' As we have seen, this is the case where Paul is concerned above and adds to the conclusion that Paul was, indeed, '*an Herodian.*' If we take the '*Saulos*' in Josephus to be another, alternate presentation of this Paul –a we have been doing – then this is certainly the case. That '*Saul*' or '*Paul*' in all versions of the data was able to get letters from the Chief Priest in Jerusalem to arrest '*any he found of the Way*' and '*confound the Jews dwelling in Damascus'* (Acts 9:2 and 22), further reinforces this perception or, at least, that he would have been perceived of as a member of this Establishment. The *Pesher* then moves on at the end of v.12–vi.5 to present the picture of *'the Kittim'* or Romans, *'sacrificing to their standards and worshipping their weapons of war,'* also delivered in exegesis of an underlying text having to do with *'casting down nets'* and *'fishing'* from Habakkuk 1:16, which we have already discussed above.[78]

In fact this *'Liar'* is introduced at the end of Column I.12–II.3 and the exegesis of a passage in the underlying text of Habakkuk 1:5 referring to *'not believing even though it was explained'* and specifically addressing *'the Gentiles.'*[79] Once again, this is explained in relation to *'the Traitors'* (*Bogdim*), now *'Traitors to the New Covenant,'* the significance of which language, as it relates to parallel stories in the Gospels about the alleged *'Traitor,'* Judas *Iscariot*, should not be difficult to appreciate. Though the term *'Traitors'* is repeated three times in the exposition that follows, which is indeed exceedingly long and descriptive, once again it nowhere appears in the actual text of Habakkuk 1:5 being expounded but rather later, as we just saw, in conjunction with *'the Traitors who kept silent when the Righteous One was swallowed by one more Wicked than he'* of Habakkuk 1:13.

These *'Traitors'* at the beginning of Column II.1 – later *'the Traitors to the New Covenant'* and *'the Traitors to the Last Days'* in II.3–6 (both reconstructed and not necessarily present as such, though the words *'New'* and *'Traitors'* are) – *'together with the Man of Lying'* are described, as already highlighted, as *'not believing what the Righteous Teacher expounded from the mouth of God.'* Later in the *Pesher*, it will be recalled, we hear in Column VII.4–10's exposition of Habakkuk 2:2 that *'God made known to the Righteous Teacher all the Mysteries of the words of His Servants the Prophets.'*[80]

This *Pesher* in Column II.1-10 on Habakkuk 1:5, which actually has to do with *'wonders'* and *'wonder-working,' 'believing,'* and *'the Last Generation'* again, is astonishing because it is a *Pesher* within a *Pesher*, the verb *'liphshor'/'to interpret'* literally being used to express the exegetical powers of *'the Righteous Teacher.'* Because it is completely in the past tense, by implication, it would appear to imply that *'the Righteous Teacher'* is already past, gone, or dead as well. It also implies that *'the Righteous Teacher'* – or, as it calls him, *'the Priest'* had *direct* communication with God – *i.e.,* just as in these early Church texts which insist that *'the Prophets declare concerning him'* (James), *he declared concerning the Prophets!*

These are also the kind of *'revelations'* (*'apocalypses'*) Paul, too, claims competitively and repeatedly to be having in 2 Corinthians 12:1 and 12:7, not to mention the *'Mysteries'* he also claims to be expounding in 1 Corinthians 4:1 and 15:51. Nor should one miss the point about *'belief'* or '*believing*' here (in this case, '*not believing*'), the key element in the Pauline theological approach, not to mention Paul's other claims to be in direct communication – via '*apocalypsin*' as it were – not only with '*the Holy Spirit*' but '*Christ Jesus*' in Heaven as well (Galatians 1:12, 2:2, etc.).

Just as Paul terms his new understanding, '*the New Covenant in the Blood of Christ*,' so the language of '*the New Covenant*' now permeates the rest of this *Pesher* about '*not believing what was explained*.' As in the Damascus Document, '*the New Covenant*' in the Habakkuk *Pesher* is, once again, nothing more than a reaffirmation of '*the Old*.' But now the *Traitors* are '*the Traitors (to the Laws of God and) the New Covenant, who did not believe in the Covenant of God (and profaned His) Holy Name*.' Identified a third time as '*the Traitors to the Last Days*' and now designated as coextensive with '*the Violent Ones and the Covenant-Breakers*'; a third time, too, these are described (as also several times already pointed out) as:

> *not believing all that they heard was (going to happen in) the Last Generation from the mouth of the Priest (i.e., 'the Righteous Teacher'/'Opposition High Priest,'* the role played by James in all early Church accounts), *in whose heart* (Paul's '*fleshy heart*'-language of 2 Corinthians 3:3 again), *God put the intelligence to interpret (liphshor) all the words of His Servants the Prophets, by whose hand God foretold all that was going to happen to His People* (this probably the '*working a wonder in your days*' with which the *Pesher* began)[81]–

all this in exposition of the two words in the underlying text from Habakkuk 2:5 '*not believing even though it was explained*.'

This is, of course, a very complicated exegesis but, on top of this, it should be recognized that *there is absolutely no anti-Semitism in it*, no self-hatred – not even a jot of any – that is, *it doesn't hate its own people*. On the contrary, it is very nationalistic. Rather it hates '*Traitors*,' '*Covenant-Breakers*,' '*the Violent Ones*,' and '*the Man of Lies*' but not its *own* '*People*'– '*the People of God*,' '*the Prophets*,' or '*the Covenant*,' '*Old*' or '*New*.' Nor does it *love its enemies*; *it hates them*. *These are the hallmarks of a native Palestinian text*. One cannot emphasize this too strongly.

There is sectarian and internecine strife to be sure and one's enemies are hated, unlike the approach of the New Testament, which is so '*New*' that it is no longer even either Palestinian or Jewish. Anything deviating from this norm *is simply not* a native Palestinian document. This does not mean it is bad, just that it is *not* '*native Palestinian*' and probably rather '*Hellenistic*.' Moreover, one can lump a whole group of texts under this rubric, as we have been doing.

Whether these '*Violent Ones*' are the same as '*the Violent Ones of the*

Gentiles,' who took Vengeance for the death of the Righteous Teacher on the Wicked Priest in the Psalm 37 *Pesher*, is impossible to say; but one assumes that they are, the Habakkuk *Pesher* perhaps being expounded from a slightly different perspective. That these '*Violent Ones*' participate in the Scriptural exegesis sessions of '*the (High) Priest*'/'*Righteous Teacher,*' who is the authorative Scriptural exegete, should also be clear. So do '*the Man of Lies*' and other '*Traitors to the New Covenant*' and '*the Last Days,*' with whom all or perhaps some seem to have been allied – at least originally. This would certainly accord with Paul's more violent early days, which may well have been resumed in the mid-Sixties in Jerusalem, if Josephus' '*Saulos*' has anything to do with the New Testament character by that name. That there are pro- and anti-Revolutionary Herodian '*Men-of-War,*' we have already explained above, and that some of the latter are also allied with the '*Saulos*' in Josephus should also be clear. This is also the situation in the Damascus Document, where '*the Men-of-War*' are portrayed as '*walking with the Man of Lying.*'[82]

But, be this as it may, all are considered '*Covenant-Breakers*' and '*Traitors to the New Covenant and the Laws of God,*' which the final treatment meted out by '*Zealots*' to Niger of Perea, *a Leader of 'the Violent Idumaeans*' and, seemingly, one of these same pro-Revolutionary Herodian '*Men-of-War,*' helps illustrate. In Acts 13:1, it will be recalled, someone called '*Niger*' was also a colleague of Paul in '*the Assembly of the Prophets and Teachers*' where '*the Disciples were first called Christians in Antioch.*'

The language of '*Covenant-Breakers*' here comes right out of that surrounding '*the Zadokite Statement*' of Ezekiel 44:7 of '*those uncircumcised in heart and flesh*' who also '*pollute the Sanctuary.*' It is also evoked in the Letter of James, where '*the Covenant-Breakers*' are distinctly ranged against '*the Doers*' and '*Keepers,*' meaning '*the Covenant-Keepers*' (the '*Sons of Zadok*' in the Community Rule) in the introduction to the famous material about '*keeping the whole of the Law, yet stumbling on one small point*' in James 2:9–2:11.

Finally, that '*the Righteous Teacher*' has, '*in his heart,*' '*the intelligence to expound all the words of His Servants, the Prophets*' is, of course, what makes him a *truly 'Righteous'* High Priest, fulfilling the proper role of '*the Mebakker*' or '*High Priest Commanding the Camps*' in the Damascus Document, '*in whose heart*' God has put all '*the mastery of all the secrets of men and (their) Languages*' ('*Tongues*') and Scripture as well. It is the opposite side of the coin to '*the Wicked Priest,*' the real Establishment High Priest, whose '*heart is uncircumcised*' – as the *Pesher* goes on later to declare – and who is, therefore, *disqualified on that basis from service in the Temple.*

26

'He Rejected the Law in the Midst of Their Whole Assembly'

The First Confrontations between the Righteous Teacher and the Liar

We now come to what for our purposes are the climactic sections of the Habakkuk *Pesher*. These concern the confrontations of '*the Righteous Teacher*' with '*the Liar*' which – together with the confrontations with '*the Wicked Priest*' – really preoccupy the attention of the *Pesher*. All occur against the backdrop of foreign Armies invading the country.

We have just delineated an initial confrontation between '*the Man of Lying*' and '*the Righteous Teacher*,' expressed in terms of the characteristic verb '*rejecting*' or '*denying*,' to wit, '*he rejected the Torah in the midst of their whole Assembly*' (or '*Church*'). That this confrontation was *internal* and *verbal* we deduced from the fact that the individuals involved were clearly attending the Scriptural exegesis sessions of '*the Righteous Teacher*' and the sense of the allusion there to '*ma'as*' or '*rejected*,' which is not '*Violent*' (in fact, this could have involved an additional play on the characteristic emphasis of both '*the Righteous Teacher*' and James on '*works*' or '*ma^casim*' which, though based on a completely different root in Hebrew, is nonetheless homophonic).

The version of this confrontation between '*the Righteous Teacher*' and '*the Man of Lies*' here in 1QpHab, V.8–12 is certainly being presented from a perspective hostile to persons like '*the Liar*,' '*the Traitors to the New Covenant*,' or a Paul. In Acts, we have the diametrically-opposite point-of-view. This non-violent, verbal confrontation is alluded to in exegesis of a passage, as we just saw, about '*Traitors*' (*Bogdim*) in the underlying text from Habakkuk 1:12 –13. These were said to have '*watched*' or '*stared*,' '*remaining silent at the time of the Reproof* or '*Chastisement*' (this, in ongoing exegesis of '*O Lord, You have ordained them for Judgement; O Rock, for Chastisement You have established them*' from 1:12) of the Righteous Teacher.' Furthermore, as just noted, it was at this point the usage '*swallowed*' was first introduced into the text, which becomes so important for Columns XI –XII later in the follow-up of 1:13, i.e., '*O Traitors,...(why do you) remain silent when the Wicked swallowed (balla^c) one more Righteous than he?*'

As already underscored as well, these 'Traitors' were not referred to in the earlier passage from Habakkuk 1:4, underlying an exegesis in which they, too, were referred to in 1QpHab,II.1–5 *three times in just five lines.* There, the complaint, it will be recalled, was that '*they ('the Violent Ones,' 'the Covenant-Breakers,' and 'the Man of Lies')...did not believe what they heard was going to happen to the Last Generation from the mouth of the (Righteous Teacher/High) Priest'*; so, once again, we have a usage referred to in the middle of the *Pesher* which seems to over-arch the whole presentation and, as in the Gospels, not just refer to one single happenstance. In the exegesis of Habakkuk 1:13, three columns later in v.9, these '*Traitors to the New Covenant,' 'Violent Ones,'* and '*Covenant Breakers*' are evidently being subsumed under yet another curious esotericism, '*the House of Absalom and the Men of their Council,'* in which the notion of '*betraying*' is paramount – '*Absalom*' theoretically having betrayed his father David.[1]

These, interpreting the underlying passage about '*Traitors staring and remaining silent*' just highlighted above, are described as '*being silent at the time when the Righteous Teacher was reproved*' (presumably by '*the Liar*') and '*not coming to his aid against the Man of Lying.*'[2] This may relate to what goes by the name of '*the Jerusalem Council*' in Acts 15:6–29, where Paul must have done something of the same or, at least, been perceived by his opponents as so doing. Later columns of the *Pesher*, most notably VII.17–VIII.3 and X.6–XI.1, will again focus either on disputes or issues between '*the Righteous Teacher*' and '*the Man of Lying*' – in the second such context being called '*the Spouter of Lying*' – as they shift back and forth from the subject of '*the Liar*' to the oncoming '*Kittim*' and finally, as we have seen, the various descriptions of how the Wicked Priest destroyed the Righteous Teacher in Columns VIII–IX and X–XII as well.

Not only was this '*destruction*' ultimately expressed in terms of the language of '*swallowing*' from Habakkuk 1:13 above; but '*the Judgement*' that would overtake him this '*Wicked Priest*' was expressed in terms of '*the Cup of the Wrath of God swallowing him*' giving way, as we saw, to the Final eschatological '*Judgement*' that would be pronounced on those who had plundered and destroyed the Holy Land in general, expressed in XIII.2–4 in terms of the pious hope that '*on the Day of Judgement God would destroy*' all Gentile '*Idolaters*' ('*the Servants of wood and stone*') and Jewish '*Backsliders*' (*ha-Reshaᶜim*) '*from off the Earth.*' As explained, these last were clearly seen as being no better than '*Idolaters*' and, no doubt, would have included persons like Philo's nephew, the Alexandrian turncoat Tiberius Alexander – who, by Josephus' own testimony, had apostated himself from Judaism and went over to the Romans – together with Herodians generally, who would have been perceived by the mindset exhibited at

Qumran – and one would imagine that by John the Baptist – as never having abandoned '*idolatry*' in the first place.

All of these matters follow the terrifying and graphic descriptions of the merciless behavior of '*the Kittim*'/Romans who, as we have seen as well, are pictured in Columns v.12–vi.11 in exposition of Habakkuk 1:14 (using the '*Net*' imagery associated with '*Belial*' and '*Balaam*' in CD and Revelation above) as '*collecting their Riches with all their booty like the fish of the sea*'. Included in this all-important '*gathering*' simile and '*fish*' analogy, so familiar in New Testament usage, was the allusion to how '*they parcel out their yoke and their taxes*,' another burning issue for both the Gospels and '*the Zealot*'/'*Sicarii*' Movement (begun by '*Judas and Sadduk*' at the time of '*the Census of Cyrenius*' in 6–7 CE[3]).

As already explained, this is a clear allusion to '*tax-farming*,' so descriptive of the actual role played by Herodians and important where New Testament allusions to '*publicans*' or '*tax collectors*' are concerned. As we have suggested this '*Net*'-imagery relates to the one Jesus applies to the Apostles as '*Fishers of Men*' in the Gospels – an endearing variation of the same metaphor albeit, however, both inverted and reversed. This imagery relative to the issue of '*tribute*' or '*taxation*' is actually applied in a '*Paulinizing*' episode in Matthew 17:24–27 (which, not only uses the language of '*stumbling*' or '*scandalization*,'[4] but concludes '*therefore the Sons are free*'[5]) to the matter of an Apostle – in this case, Peter – '*casting down*' (*bale*) a hook into the Sea of Galilee to catch a fish with a coin in its mouth which is to be given *to those collecting these taxes* – another beguilingly tendentious variation on the '*tribute*' theme which the Habakkuk *Pesher* rather connects to the *omnivorous appetite and might of Rome*. Which version of the metaphor more accurately expresses the mindset of Palestine and which that of the overseas rewrite should be clear.

In the all-important teaching about Habakkuk 2:3–4 in Column vii.1–8.3 and the nature of '*the Liar*'s approach to these and similar matters in Column x.6–12, as just signaled, '*the Man of Lying*' turns into '*the Spouter*' or '*Pourer out of Lying*.' Similarly, in the Damascus Document, he is also called, as several times remarked, either '*the Windbag*,' '*Comedian*' or '*Scoffer*' who '*poured over*' – '*spouting*' being based on the Hebrew root, meaning '*to pour*' – *Israel the waters of Lying*.' The plays here on another, probably characteristic, activity of '*the Man of Lies*,' '*pouring out*' – aside from '*Lying*,' even perhaps '*the Holy Spirit*' or '*baptism*' (*cf.* CDxix.25–26) – are also probably purposeful.

As we have seen, this imagery is present not only in the Gospels, where it relates to '*the Cup of the New Covenant in my Blood which was poured out for you*' (slightly condensed in 1 Corinthians 11:25); but also in

Acts where it is expressed in terms of 'pouring out' the Holy Spirit upon all flesh (2:17–18) and 'the gift of the Holy Spirit being poured out upon the Gentiles too' (10:45) – typical 'Pauline' activity. It is also present in Revelation where, as we have seen as well, like the imagery in the Habakkuk Pesher, it rather relates to 'the wine of the Wrath of God which is poured out full strength into the Cup of His Anger' (14:10) – but then, inverting and reversing this again, the accusations against the Jews of 'pouring out of the Blood of Holy Ones and the Prophets' (16:6).

In the allusions in the Damascus Document, the Lying Scoffer's 'pouring out the waters of Lying upon Israel,' in fact, had to do – as will be recalled – with 'removing the bound which the Forefathers had marked out as their inheritance,' 'Justifying the Wicked and condemning the Righteous,' and 'exulting in dividing the People.' All of these are formulations that have to do with both 'the Man of Lying''s characteristic activity – and Paul's – of 'rejecting the Torah in the midst of their whole Assembly' ('Church'), which again reinforces the impression of exceedingly bitter, internal ideological differences, themselves finding clear expression in the Pauline corpus.

Matters of this kind are again implicit in the description of the 'Jerusalem Council' in Acts. This is portrayed in Acts as a kind of pro-Pauline love fest where the only discordant note are the parvenu 'Pharisees,' who want to make 'the Peoples' circumcise themselves and 'keep the Law of Moses' (15:5 – in the Habakkuk Pesher here, 'the Torah'). As Paul puts a similar proposition in his Galatians 2:4 version of these events, they are 'the false brothers who crept in furtively to spy on the freedom we enjoy in Christ Jesus that they might enslave us.' Aside from the 'spying' and 'freedom' allusions which have real significance vis-a-vis some of the materials, we have already expounded above, this is exactly what Acts 15:1's 'certain ones who came down from Judea' are insisting on in the first place, which sets in motion the series of events pictured in the next lines as 'the Jerusalem Council.' In Galatians 2:12, where even 'the Ethnon' in the allusion to Peter 'previously eating with the Gentiles' is the same as in Acts; the 'certain ones,' it will be recalled, were from James.

In the version here in 1QpHab,v.8-12, we have both allusion to 'Council' and 'their Assembly.' In the picture in Acts 15:1, as just reiterated, these 'some from Judea' are teaching the brothers – for Paul in Galatians 2:4 above, 'false brothers' – 'unless you are circumcised according to the custom of Moses, you cannot be saved.' But this will be recognized as basically the key precondition of the coming eschatological exegeses of both Habakkuk 2:3 and 2:4 in Columns VII–VIII of the Habakkuk Pesher, where both the precondition of being a 'Torah-Doer' and this usage, 'saved,' will form the essence of the interpretation that finally emerges.

Before moving on to consider this and the description of '*the Spouter of Lying*'s '*worthless service*' and '*Lying works*' connected to it, one should also recall how Galatians 2:13 uses the phraseology '*separating himself*' to describe Peter and Barnabas' '*hypocrisy*' in drawing back and no longer being willing '*to eat with Gentiles*.' In the Community Rule, it will be recalled too, this was '*separating from the habitation of the Unrighteous and going out in the wilderness to prepare the Way of the Lord*'; in the Damascus Document, '*separating from the Sons of the Pit*.'[6] It is a demand, as should be clear, that is evinced across a whole range of documents at Qumran, most interestingly perhaps in '*MMT*' – '*The Letter(s) on Works that would be Reckoned to you as Righteousness*' – which end by applying the 'Jamesian' position on Abraham '*being justified by works*' to a '*Kingly*' respondent not unsimilar to Izates or his brother Monobazus in Adiabene.

The Letters to James in the Pseudoclementine *Homilies* and the Dead Sea Scrolls

These crucial exegeses, which now follow in Columns VII–VIII of the Habakkuk *Pesher* and relate to these quotations from Habakkuk 2:3–4, end – one should not forget – with the all-important citation '*the Righteous shall live by his Faith*.' This should be recognized (along with Genesis 15:6 on how '*Abraham's Faith was reckoned to him as Righteousness*' and Isaiah 53:11, '*My Servant, the Righteous One (Zaddik) will Justify Many*') as, perhaps, the fundamental building block of 'Christian' theology as we know it even today. This is particularly true of the manner in which they have been interpreted, as we have seen, by Paul and what would appear to be, at least in part, the response to him in the Letter – authentic or otherwise – ascribed to James' name.

There are *two* letters from James on record. One is in the Introduction to the Pseudoclementine *Homilies* and the other, the famous one (whether written by James or by someone in his '*school*') under his name in the New Testament. The one that introduces the version of the Pseudoclementine romances called the *Homilies* comes following a short note from Peter to James dealing with the issue of '*secrecy*' and not revealing '*anything to Gentiles*' – or, for that matter, even other Jews – before the acolyte has gone through a proper initiation period.[7]

In this Letter, attributed to Peter and prefacing the *Homilies*, James is addressed as '*the Lord and Bishop of the Holy Church*' – in Clement's Letter to James, which follows, he is addressed as '*the Bishop of Bishops (i.e., 'the Archbishop' or 'Mebakker') who rules Jerusalem, the Holy Church of the Hebrews, and the Churches everywhere*.'[8] It cautions that one should not teach, '*unless *he has first learned how the Scriptures must be used.'* Not only is this seemingly a riposte to Paul, it is comparable to the kinds of interpretations in the Habakkuk *Pesher* we have just been discussing above. In conclusion, Peter cautions that his *'teachings'* or *'preachings'* should themselves not be communicated *'to anyone, whether one of our own People or of another People before a qualifying period'* – here Peter's clear attachment to Judaism or rather to the Jews as a *'People'* is manifest. The language used, including consigning the one *'opposing the Law of God which was spoken by Moses'* to the *'Pit of Destruction,'* have repeated parallels at Qumran, where similar issues are treated and *'the Pit'* several times actually referred to.[9]

One should perhaps not forget that it is in the *Homilies* that Peter is not only presented – like, one presumes, John the Baptist – as a *'Daily Bather'* who bathed every day before praying at sunrise to greet the sun or, as Epiphanius would have it (probably dependent on the *Homilies*), *'before eating even bread'*[10]; but he is also the prototypical 'Jamesian' who preaches a version of James' directives to overseas communities fuller and more perfect than anything even encountered in Acts, instructing the followers in Tripoli *'to shun any Apostle, teacher, or prophet* (n.b., the 'Pauline' language here), *who does not accurately compare his teaching with that of) James'* – *'the brother of My Lord'* – and *'this, even if he comes to you with recommendations.'*[11]

Most interesting, however, is Peter's attack in this Letter on an individual, clearly of the Pauline genus, which is expressed in terms of *'some from among the Gentiles have rejected my Legal Teaching, attaching themselves to a certain Lawless and trifling teaching of the Man who is my Enemy.'*[12] Here, of course, not only do we have the *'Enemy'* terminology again and the parallel to the *'Scoffer'/'Jesting'/'Comedian'* language at Qumran, but the word *'rejected'* is the same as the one we have been following vis-a-vis *'the Man of Lies'* in the Habakkuk *Pesher* above.[13] This is the same *'Enemy'* terminology we have been tracing with regard to this *'Man of Lying who rejects the Law,'* which Paul shows himself to be completely aware of when discussing *'telling the Truth'* and *'slavery to the Law'* in Galatians 4:16.

James' response to Peter at the end of this Letter is also most interesting. In it, James sets down a novitiate period for teachers of six years. At Qumran the initiate period for the rank and file of the Community – as with Josephus' *'Essenes'* – is two or three years; in particular, for *'approaching the pure food or drink,'* it is two years.[14] Still at Qumran, there are different requirements for higher Offices – some, for instance, having a minimum age of *'twenty-five'* or *'thirty years'* as, for example, that of *'the Mebakker'* or *'High Priest Commanding the Many.'*[15] There is an interesting law regarding those who preach apostasy *'under the dominion of the spirits of Belial' too*, language also reflected in the Gospels particularly as regards 'Beelzebul.' These are to be put to death as per the Law of possession by Evil spirits (Leviticus 20:27). Also *'those who go astray profaning the Sabbath or the Festivals'* are to be observed or tested for seven years, after which they shall again be allowed *'to approach the Congregation.'*[16] This period of *'seven years'* not only has implications *vis-a-vis* the periodicity here of Clement's reports to James (the implied basis for how these Pseudoclementines are constructed), but also when considering Queen Helen of Adiabene's series of seven-year *'Nazirite'* penances allegedly imposed on her by the Rabbis. Certainly the *'novitiate'* period would have approached the first of these – and that required for *'teaching,'* much of the rest.

In both the Qumran Damascus Document and the response of James to Peter, the initiate is made *'to swear to secrecy.'* The response James makes to Peter actually gives the oaths the probationary is obliged to take against communicating any of the Community's secrets to any unworthy person. In every way these resemble the series of oaths set forth in detail in the first columns of the Community Rule already quoted above.[17] Interestingly enough, in the Damascus Document these abjure swearing by *'the Name'* (that is, *'of God'*) or by *'the Torah of Moses,'* lest an entrant breaking such an oath be guilty of *'profaning the Name.'*[18] These *'oaths'* in the Community Rule end with a series of bringing curses or eternal Divine Vengeance on oneself, again abjuring mention of the Divine Name. They resemble nothing so much as the curse the assassins in Acts 23:12–14 and 21 *'put themselves under not to eat or drink until (they) have killed Paul.'* The actual wording of these, as already remarked, is: *'with a curse we have cursed ourselves to taste nothing until we have killed Paul.'*

Once again, these kinds of things are paralleled in the response of James to Peter at the beginning of the *Homilies*, but with the additional telltale allusion to the *'Lying'*-notation so widespread in the Qumran documents and, by refraction, in Paul's own repeated, self-conscious assertions that he *'does not lie.'*[19] This reads:

> *Should I lie in these things, I shall be cursed living and dying and punished with Everlasting punishment,*

adding for good measure, *'anyone who acts otherwise* (meaning, breaking this oath) *shall with good cause incur Eternal punishment.'*[20] One should compare these to the words, quoted in the Community Rule, which again use the verb *'destroy'* (*lechalah*) applied to *'the Wicked Priest'* in 1QpHab,XII.6 (not to mention the language of *'zeal'*): *'God's Wrath and zeal for His Judgements shall burn him in Eternal destruction'* or

May God visit you with terror by the hand of all the Avengers of Vengeance and command destruction (challah) upon you by all the Payers-of-Rewards (Gemulim)....All the curses of this Covenant shall cleave to him and God will separate him for Evil.[21]

Again here we have the language of God's '*Wrath*,' and '*paying Rewards*' (*Gemul/Gemulim*) we saw in the Habakkuk *Pesher* above, co-opting that of Isaiah 3:11 where the fate of '*the Wicked Priest*' was concerned. Surely it cannot be coincidental that James' speech at this point to '*the Elders*' in the *Homilies* regarding just such '*oaths*' and '*Eternal punishment*,' employs the words: '*For why should he who is the cause of the destruction of others not be destroyed himself?*' Not only do we have here the two allusions to '*destruction*,' but this is also almost word-for-word the language of the beginning of Column XII of the Habakkuk *Pesher* about '*the reward which the Wicked Priest paid the Poor being paid to him.*' This read, as will be recalled: '*He will be paid the Reward he paid the Poor*,' even using the words '*gamlu*' and '*Gemul*' of 1QS,II.6 above, or '*as he plotted to destroy the Poor so too would God condemn him to destruction.*' Here again are the two allusions to '*destroy*' and '*destruction*' just attributed to James in the *Homilies* above. These are the kinds of improbable overlaps one finds when one inspects the language in these parallel documents closely.

Even Josephus' description of '*the Essenes*' uses similar language. In the section outlining the same novitiate period of two years '*before approaching their society and touching the pure food*' – '*bathing*' already began one year prior to this – it is stated that the initiate is obliged to take terrible oaths '*not to reveal any of their doctrines to others even if compelled to do so on pain of death*,' a point with particular import for Paul's claims in 2 Corinthians 4:2 to have '*forsaken the hidden things*,' not '*walking in craftiness, nor falsifying the word of God*' – terrifying accusations when one appreciates their target (there would also appear to be an echo of this '*being compelled to do so*' in CDvi.15 as we have seen).[22]

Moreover the initiate swears not to communicate their doctrines to anyone other than in the way he received them himself, also of import for Paul's claims in 1 Corinthians 11:25 on '*drinking the Cup of the New Covenant*' ('*in the Blood*') and 15:5 on the order of post-resurrection sightings. As in James' response to Peter in the *Homilies*, this injunction is accompanied by the telltale allusion to '*hating Lying and loving Truth*,' following that to '*exercising Piety towards God and Righteousness towards one's fellow man*' which, of course, is exactly what Josephus says John the Baptist taught dividing the practices of '*the Essenes*' into the same two categories[23] and which are, then, reprised in James' speech in response.[24]

For this speech of James which, as we just saw, provoked 'an agony of terror among the Elders'; the communication of doctrine, as at Qumran and among Josephus' 'Essenes,' occurs in stages, the last being what James refers to as 'the initiation of Moses' (no Galatians-like antagonism to the Mosaic Covenant here). In it, teachers are brought to 'a river or a fountain, wherein there is living water and the regeneration of the Righteous takes place.' There the initiate is made to adjure – though not 'swear,' that is, 'not by the Divine Name' or 'by the Torah of Moses,' just as in the case of the oaths in the Community Rule – not to sin, not to communicate the Books of the Preachings to anyone except 'those who wish to live Piously and to save others.'[25] We have already encountered precisely such a 'Fountain of Living Waters' in CDVIII.22/XIX.34 in the follow-up to Elisha's rebuke of Gehazi and the condemnation of those who 'betrayed and turned aside' from 'the New Covenant in the Land of Damascus' and 'the Assembly of the Men of the Perfection of Holiness.'

In the Community Rule, following the curses which we have already set out previously and which so parallel the curses in this speech of James as well as those here in CDxx.8 on 'all the Holy Ones of the Most High cursing him,' we hear – as will be recalled – in Column Three following the above that 'He who rejects ('ma'as' again) the Ordinances of God shall receive no instruction,'

> nor shall he be justified by what the stubbornness of his heart permits, because instead of the Ways of Light, he looks towards Darkness. He shall not be reckoned among the Perfect, nor purified by atonements, nor cleansed by purifying waters, nor sanctified by seas and rivers, nor purified by any waters of ablution.[26]

It is easy to recognize the practices of those we have been calling 'Nazirite Essenes' or 'Elchasaite Sabaeans' in these descriptions.

Furthermore, in what follows in the Community Rule, we also hear that:

> He shall not come to the water to partake of the Pure Food of the Men of Holiness (i.e., 'the Saints'), for (such individuals) will not be cleansed unless they repent from their Evil, (here, of course, is an echo of the New Testament's presentation of John: 'preaching the Baptism of Repentance unto remission of sins' in the wilderness, as Luke and Mark refer to it), because all the Breakers-of-His-Word are polluted.[27]

We also have here both the echo of the Nazirite 'Holy from his mother's womb' and 'Holy to God' vocabulary, applied to James in all early Church sources, to say nothing of John the Baptist and Jesus in Luke 1:35 and 2:23, as well as 'Herod''s alleged words according to Mark 6:20 and the 'pollution'/'breaking' usages again. This 'Breaker-of-the-Word' vocabulary actually parallels that in James 1:22–23 on being 'a Doer' or 'Hearer of the Word' but, because the point is negative, the sense is being reversed once again:

> For they are not to be reckoned in His Covenant, because they neither inquired after or studied His Laws to know the Hidden Things, in which they have gone astray unto sin. And did the Revealed Things with contempt, kindling the Wrath for Judgement and the Avenging Vengeance of the curses of the Covenant, which shall be executed upon them in Great Judgements for eternal destruction without a remnant (lechalah again).[28]

It is easy see here why the Elders, hearing James' imprecations against 'Lying' and the threat of 'being accursed living and dying' at the beginning of the Homilies, would be in such 'an agony of terror.' Here, too, we have just the slightest hint of the kind of 'studying His Laws,' the Galilean teacher Eleazar demanded on seeing Prince Izates reading the Torah of Moses, but not understanding it.

Throughout these curses in the Community Rule – both the ones here and the ones we enumerated earlier – there is the evocation of the 'reckoning' so much a part of Genesis 15:6's language of 'Abraham's Faith being reckoned to him as Righteousness' and, in turn, so important to Paul. As we have now seen as well, it is intrinsic to the opposite point-of-view in 'MMT' of 'the works we reckon' or which would 'be reckoned to you as Righteousness' or, to use Paul's language again, 'justify you.' As we have also suggested, this Letter(s) was possibly even addressed to someone like this Izates or his brother for whom, coming from the Land from which he was supposed to have come, Abraham would have been a figure of immense importance.

Furthermore, in these passages from the Community Rule too, one has actual reference to 'the Hidden Things' (as opposed to 'the Revealed' ones), Paul so rancorously and contemptuously refers to in 2 Corinthians 4:2 above, literally accusing those harboring such notions as 'walking in craftiness and falsifying the Word of God.' For the Community Rule too (as to some extent we have already seen as well):

> God, in the Mysteries of His Understanding and his Glorious Wisdom, has decreed an End of to the existence of Unrighteousness, and at the time of the Visitation, will destroy it forever. Then Truth...will emerge Victorious in the world

(Paul's language of 'Victory' again), and God will refine with His Truth all the works of Man and purify him from among the Sons of Man, Perfecting all the Spirit of Unrighteousness within his flesh and purify him with the Holy Spirit of all Evil Sinfulness and pour upon him the Spirit of Truth like baptismal waters (washing him) of all the Abominations of Lying, immersing him in the Spirit of Purification, that He may cause the Upright to understand and instruct the Perfect of the Way with the Knowledge of the Most High and the Wisdom of the Sons of Heaven, for God has chosen them for an Eternal Covenant, and to them will be all the Glory of Adam and no Unrighteousness.[29]

As in the Damascus Document, not only do we again have here the essence of the '*Primal Adam*' ideology, combined with both the '*Visitation*' language and that of God's '*Elect*' elsewhere at Qumran; but of course, nothing less than the '*Holy Spirit*' Baptism which the Gospels, too, delineate – however, in the light now of these passages from Qumran, not a little tendentiously.

In the *Homilies* – just as after these oaths and repeated references to the '*Pure Food*' (literally '*Purity*') in the Community Rule – after repeating the oaths '*not to communicate the preachings or secrets to anyone unworthy*' and after re-affirming the commitment to absolute obedience, the initiate is allowed to '*participate in the bread and the salt*' – in 1QS, v.13 above, '*the Purity* (apparently, '*the pure Food*') *of the Men of Holiness.*'

But in these imprecations by James about those who will be teachers, the language of '*keeping this Covenant*' – used throughout the Community Rule as the definition of '*the Sons of Zadok*' – is important, as it is, for instance, in '*the Rechabite Covenant*' generally (found in Jeremiah 35: 2–19).[30] For James herein the *Homilies*, such '*Keepers*' will have '*a share with the Holy Ones.*'[31] Once again this is precisely the language of the Community Rule which also abounds with references of this kind to '*the Holy Ones*'; and, for the War Scroll and the Damascus Document, these purity regulations, as we have seen, are necessary '*because the Holy Angels are with them*' or '*with their Hosts.*'[32]

It would be difficult to doubt, after seeing all these overlaps, that all these '*Baptizing*' or '*Daily Bathing*' Groups, such as the Community of James here in the Pseudoclementine *Homilies* or Josephus' '*Essenes*' or, for that matter, Qumran are equivalent. The only difference is that for Paul and in Josephus' picture of '*the Essenes*,' these oaths included '*keeping faith with all men and especially those in Authority*' – '*Authority*' here implying secular – in fact, Roman – '*Authority.*'[33] That this is not the position of Qumran should be abundantly clear. Plus Qumran and, no doubt, John the Baptist's and James' Communities as well, added the more militantly apocalyptic note of the Messiah 'about to come upon the clouds of Heaven,' which was certainly nothing if not an uncompromising one.

Statements such as the preceding one from Josephus have confused the issue of the relationship of his 'Essenes' to Qumran immeasurably. Whereas in Romans 13:1–9, in perhaps the most facile manner conceivable, Paul interprets this so-called 'keeping faith' as owing obedience to the Governing Authorities – the implication again plainly being Rome – at Qumran, it is clear that absolute obedience was owed only to the Community Leadership and to God – no others. This was no doubt true of James' 'Jerusalem Community' as well – if there was any difference – certainly as reflected in James' imprecations here in the Pseudoclementine Homilies where absolute obedience to those conveying the traditions is twice enjoined. Moreover, when the ambiguity of translating Greek characterizations is dispensed with, this was doubtlessly true of Josephus' 'Essenes' as well.

For the Homilies' portrait of James, these rules are delivered for those who are 'Righteous and Pious' – the 'Righteousness'/'Piety'-dichotomy Josephus applies to the oath the Essenes take 'not to lie' or 'reveal any of their doctrines to others' – and teachers should be both 'circumcised and believing.' Where Paul's contrary 'Mission' is concerned, this is unbelievably important. Moreover, this is ultimately expressed in terms of 'those wishing to live Piously and save others' as we have seen. For James in this portrait, too, these teachings were not to be given out 'indiscriminately and corrupted, thereby, by insolent men or perverted by interpretations' causing others, as it were, 'to wander astray.' But, of course, this last will be immediately recognizable as the language CD1.15, etc. applies to the activities of the insolent 'Man of Scoffing, who poured over Israel the waters of Lying and caused them to wander astray in a trackless waste.'

Qumran Language and Abraham 'Made Righteous by Works' in James

Where the Letter of James in the New Testament is concerned, we also encounter parallel language and exactly the same kinds of allusions, this time to the insolent 'Tongue,' symbolizing someone who is 'the Enemy' of the position being enunciated, particularly as regards the issue of 'Faith vs. works.' This sort of 'Tongue' imagery also abounds in the Dead Sea Scrolls where it is related, as we have to some extent already remarked, to that of 'spouting,' 'insolence,' 'blasphemy,' and 'scoffing.' In both the Community Rule and the Damascus Document, for instance, 'the Spirit of Unrighteousness,' is defined in terms of 'a Tongue full of insults' or 'blasphemies.'[34]

In the Damascus Document, this allusion comes against a background tapestry of reference to 'fornication,' 'Vipers' eggs,' and 'Kindlers of the Fire'/'Lighters of Firebrands.' These are described, it will be recalled, as 'polluting their Holy Spirit, opening their mouth with a Tongue full of insults against the Laws of the Covenant of God.'[35] In the Community Rule, the same 'Spirit of Unrighteousness,' the second of the 'Two Spirits' God put into man in equal parts, is described as 'slackness in the Service of Righteousness' (the 'Servants of Righteousness' language Paul uses above in 2 Corinthians 11:15), 'brazen insolence,' 'impatience,' 'zeal for lustfulness and works of Abomination in a Spirit of fornication, the Ways of uncleanness in the service of pollution, and a Tongue full of insults' ('blasphemies' – here the turning around of all the favorite usages: 'zeal,' 'works,' 'Holy Spirit,' 'service,' 'fornication,' 'uncleanness,' etc.).[36]

In the recently-published document from Qumran, I named after one of its more striking allusions 'The Demons of Death' and others call 'Beatitudes,' it is connected – paralleling imagery at this point in James 3:1–15, a chapter which starts off with allusion to both 'stumbling' (repeated twice) and that kind of 'windiness' associated with 'the Lying Spouter's spouting' in CDviii and xix above – with 'the Stumbling Block of the Tongue.'[37] For Paul such 'stumbling block' imagery is again turned around and applied to the fact that the new theological position he is enunciating either is a 'stumbling block' to or 'scandalizes' (he uses these two vocabularies interchangeably) those with 'weak consciences' and those who cannot get over their previous attachment to the Law. In 1 Corinthians 1:23, he applies it even to his proclamation of 'the Crucified Christ' and, in 1 Corinthians 8:9, to those who make problems over the 'things sacrificed to idols' of James' directives to overseas communities and 'MMT.'

The same is the general approach in Romans 14:13–21 where, it will perhaps be recalled, 'eating only vegetables' and 'food' in general are what cause the 'weak' brother 'to stumble' or 'be scandalized.' Earlier, in Romans 9:31–33 and 11:6–11, Paul referred to the 'Stone of Stumbling' (an allusion from Isaiah 8:14 and 28:16) which he characterized, amid a plethora of allegorizing, as a 'Righteousness achieved through Faith' not by Israel's 'works of the Law' (this last being the same 'Righteousness,' of course, demanded in the Scrolls generally and here in the Letter of James), and 'a Grace no longer of works.' He even refers to this using a barrage of 'Messianic' proof-texts (i.e., Isaiah 29:16, 10:22–23, 1:9, 8:4, 28:16, Hosea 2:1, 2:25, etc.) culminating in quoting 'David' (that is, Psalm 69 – a Psalm used in the Synoptic Gospels to show how 'Jesus' was 'given vinegar to drink'; the Gospel of John in picturing 'the Disciples' crying out on witnessing 'Jesus'' 'Temple-cleansing,' 'zeal for Your House consumes me'; and Acts 2:20, after Judas Iscariot's 'headlong,' 'bloody' fall in anticipation of the election to succeed him, 'Let his camp be desolate and let there be no one dwelling in it' –

only substituting a '*him*' for '*their*' and an '*it*' for '*their tents*' – how convenient) to exploit this '*net*,' '*snare*,' and '*stumbling block*' language, to the effect that '*their own table* – the multifaceted edge of this barb ought to be clear – *should prove a net, snare, stumbling block* (or '*scandalon*'/'*cause of offence*') *and a reward* – in the sense of '*punishment*' or '*payback*,' as in the Habakkuk *Pesher* – *to them*' (Psalm 69:23 – Romans 11:9). Here he gets the pronominals right but adds the '*stumbling block*,' '*scandalize*' and '*punishment*' or '*reproof*'/'*reward to them*'! Moreover, he then goes on to claim (leading into his use of '*Root*,' '*Branch*,' '*Standing*,' and '*cutting off*' imagery from 11:14–24 and, in the process, that of '*zealotry*' and '*saving some from among them*' against them and from 11: 25–28 – '*mysteriously*' – in the follow-up of Isaiah 27:9's '*Deliverer that shall come out of Zion to turn away Ungodliness from Jacob*' to qualify the '*Enemies of God*' accusation in 1 Thessalonians 2:15 above to '*only Enemies on your account as regards the Gospel*' – whatever he means by this), like Peter and James in Acts 15:7–18's picture of '*the Jerusalem Council*' and James' exposition of Amos 9:11, that because of '*their* ('*the Jews*") *stumbling*' or '*falling away*'; '*Salvation was granted*) *to the Nations*' / '*Peoples*' (*Ethnesin*). He makes this claim, as we have seen, despite the fact that Psalm 69:36–37 rather specifically ends with the promise that '*God would save Zion*' ('*yoshi^ca*,' relating to '*yeshu^ca*') and, like CDVII-VIII and XIX-XX, '*build up the Cities of Judah*' and '*those who love His Name*' would '*inherit it*' or '*have it for a possession*' and '*dwell therein*.'

For James 2:10, less metaphorically but nonetheless striking, the '*stumbling*' was rather '*keeping the whole of the Law, but stumbling over one small point*.' Not only does it reinforce this in 3:2 with the two allusions to teachers '*stumbling*'; right from the beginning in 1:4, it will be recalled, it uses the language of Qumran of '*being Perfect and Complete*' from the description of Noah in Genesis 6:9 as '*being Righteous and Perfect in his Generation*' and in 1:10–25 antagonism to '*Riches*.' Counseling '*patience*' both here and later, it recommends '*listening*' and cautions against '*anger*' (1:19–20) – all matters it groups in 1:12 under the rubric (just as in Josephus' picture of '*the Essenes*') of '*loving God*' – '*Piety*' in Josephus' descriptions both of '*the Essenes*' and of John the Baptist's '*Way in the wilderness*.' Promising a '*Crown of Life*' (as does Revelation 2:10 and as it later promises '*the Poor*' in 2:5 '*the Kingdom*') '*to those who love Him*' and putting this in terms of '*man's anger never serving God's Righteousness*'; as we have seen, it uses the '*Doer*' language from 1:16–25 three times in four lines to express the idea of not '*being led astray*' but following, rather, '*the Word of Truth*.' It is at this point that James 1:26 makes its first allusion to the '*Tongue*.' This it combines, as per usual, with '*heart*' imagery to conclude that he who *does not keep control over his Tongue, in the process deceiving his heart, such a one's Religion is worthless.*

We shall momentarily encounter similar language in 1QpHab,x.5-12, which uses the language of '*worthlessness*' to describe '*the Spouter of Lying*''s '*Mission*' or '*Service*,' '*works of Lying*,' and the general '*Emptiness*' of his doctrines (as we have already done in James 2:20's characterization of its antagonist, the '*Empty Man*').

For its part James 2:2–2:8, stressing its concern for '*the Poor*' and its antagonism to '*the Rich*' (this time four times in five lines), moves on to its citation of the second of the two '*Love Commandments*,' '*the Righteousness Commandment*'– '*love your neighbor as yourself.*' In doing so, it shows that it is this '*Commandment*' that produces the economic concern that results in the self-designation of so many of these groups, '*the Poor*' – because for it, obviously, if there are economic distinctions between you and your fellow man, *you cannot be* '*loving him as yourself.*' This is the '*Righteousness*'/'*Piety*' dichotomy we have been accentuating throughout this work as the hallmark of all '*Opposition*' groups in this period whether '*Essenes*,' '*Christians*,' or, like those at Qumran or the Community of James, actually designating themselves as '*the Poor.*'

It is at this point that James 2:8 speaks in terms of '*doing*,' that is, '*if you truly keep the Royal Law*,' '*you do well*' – language, once again, combining that of the '*keeping*' with the '*doing*', which we have been underscoring as so fundamental to the approach of Qumran (in particular too, in the evocation of '*works*' in 1QpHab,x.12 above). Moreover, 2:9 connects it to the issue of being a '*respecter of persons*' (a point labored over so disingenuously, as we have been emphasizing, by Paul in his arguments with James[38]) which it characterizes as '*breaking the Law*' (here again, the '*breaking*' language). It is this and the citation of '*the all Righteousness Commandment*' preceding it that produces the assertion in James 2:10 that '*whosoever keeps the whole of the Law, yet stumbles on one small point, becomes guilty of (breaking) it all*' which is echoed in the constant reiteration in documents such as the Damascus Document at Qumran of '*doing according to the precise letter of the Torah.*'

In this vein, the Community Rule specifically enjoins, where those who '*enter the Council of Holiness to walk in Perfection of the Way as they were commanded*' are concerned, that any man:

who breaks one word of the Torah of Moses, whether overtly or covertly, shall be expelled from the Council of the Community never to return and no one of the Men of Holiness shall have anything to do with him in purse or doctrine in any matter whatsoever.[39]

This, as we have seen, is the kind of *'excommunication'* or *'shunning'* Jews like Peter and Barnabas exhibit towards Paul in 'Antioch' in Galatians 2:12–13, after the *'some from James'* came down from Jerusalem – nor could it be an closer to the sense of James. The same point accompanies the *'cursing'* and excommunication of *'those who depart to the right or left of the Torah,' 'going astray in the wilderness without a Way'* in the Last Column of the Damascus Document. There, this injunction is actually accompanied by the ban on *'eating with them'* or even *'asking after their welfare.'*[40]

The condemnation on *'Law-Breakers,'* repeated twice in James 2:9–11 – and echoed in this language at the end of the Damascus Document – and James 2:12–13's evocation of *'keeping the whole Law'* and *'Judgement without Mercy to him who does not,'* lead directly into the discussion in 2:14 of *'Faith vs. works.'* Specifically this reads: *'if anyone says he has Faith but does not have works, can Faith save him?'* Not only is this phraseology fundamental to all disputes centering around Paul and James, it is also implicit in the Habakkuk *Pesher's* interpretation of Habakkuk 2:4: *'the Righteous shall live by his Faith,'* as we have seen, cited as well by Paul in Galatians 3:11 just following his evocation in 3:6 of how *'Abraham believed God and it was reckoned to him as Righteousness'* from Genesis 15:6.

In James 2:20, this rebuke of the individual characterized by *'saying he has Faith,'* is directed against an opponent scathingly referred to as the *'Empty Man'* or *'Man of Emptiness'* and the well-known point that will ultimately be made here and five lines further on is that *'Faith without works is dead.'* But this *'Empty'* or *'Emptiness'* vocabulary also appears, whether by accident or design, in the aspersions in 1QpHab,x.12 – two columns after its exposition of Habakkuk 2:4 – on the *'worthlessness'* of the Lying Spouter's *'Service'* and the *'Emptiness'* of his *'Lying works.'*

It is in directly following this rebuke to *'the Empty Man'* who thinks his *'Faith can save him'* that the Letter of James cites the example of Abraham, quoting as well – as in Paul above – Genesis 15:6 that *'Abraham believed God and it was reckoned to him as Righteousness'* (2:23). It is in this context, too, that James 2:21–23 first remarks that Abraham *'was called the Friend'* or *'Beloved of God,'* asserting that he *'was justified by works.'* This assertion of the *'saving'* nature of Abraham's *'works'* is pivotal since it is through the figure of Abraham that Paul, as we have seen, develops his theology of *'Salvation by Faith'* based on Genesis 15:6 on how *'Abraham believed God and it was reckoned to him as Righteousness'* (thus) in Galatians 3:6–29 (quoting, as we just saw, Habakkuk 2:4 on *'the Righteous shall live by Faith'* in 3:12) and Romans 4:3–22 – Abraham becoming for him both the prototype and the embodiment of this 'Faith.'

Similar phraseology is also pointedly utilized, as we have seen as well, in the recommendation at the end of 'MMT' where it is, rather, rephrased in terms of 'the works that would be reckoned to you as Righteousness,' clearly meaning 'the works of the Torah,' it is urging the 'King' it is addressing 'to perform.' Notwithstanding, the implication regarding the archetypical figure of Abraham is unchanging. Such an evocation of Abraham's 'Salvationary' state, as previously emphasized, would have been particularly meaningful for people like Queen Helen of Adiabene's two sons, Izates and Monobazus – Abraham being a figure of no mean import in the Northern Syrian culture sphere in places like Edessa, Haran, and Adiabene, where much of the action we have been alluding to transpires.

For Paul, *since Abraham came before Moses, his 'Faith' came before the Law of Moses.* This is also the approach of Muhammad in the Koran, another 'Prophet' focusing on the persona of Abraham and claiming to be an 'Apostle to the Gentiles' (in his case, one 'Gentile People,' 'the Arabs') and the heir, as we have been suggesting, to some of the cultural traditions of this area. The only difference between his approach and Paul's is that in Muhammad's presentation in the Koran, the word 'Religion' – *actually used* in James 1:26 above – is substituted for what in Paul's dialectic is called Abraham's 'Faith' though 'Faith,' too, is important in Muhammad's designation of 'Islam' as 'the Faith of Abraham.'[41]

As James 2:20 puts this in one of the most famous formulations of Western Religion, '*O Empty Man, don't you know that Faith apart from works is dead?*' It is worth repeating that here again is the allusion to 'Empty' or 'Emptiness,' we shall meet in the Habakkuk *Pesher's* characterization of the '*worthless Assembly*' the Spouter is '*building on Lying*' and '*upon Blood.*' James 2:21 then goes on to use the very same formulations as Paul in Romans 4:9 and Galatians 3:6 above and the '*Abraham*' example he cites to such good effect to ask, as we just saw as well, '*was not Abraham, our Father, justified by works?*' This is basically the same formulation too, as we have been arguing, translated just slightly laterally, in '*MMT*' above. It is important because it harks back to Paul's discussions of Abraham, the only difference being that (as we have seen, just as in '*MMT*') the sense is one hundred-and-eighty degrees the reverse of Paul.

James 2:21 then goes on to give an example of just such a paradigmatic example of '*works*' as we have seen as well, Abraham's readiness to sacrifice his own son Isaac. Not only is this also reflected in Muhammad's Koran – reinterpreted in Islam, however, as Abraham's '*firstborn*' son '*Ishmael*'[42] – but probably, too, it had significance to an individual like the

'*Izates*' of Adiabene, a name of course probably based on '*Isaac*,' the details of whose conversion we have already largely covered above.[43]

As Paul puts it for his part (this somewhat disingenuously in the interests of his all-consuming '*allegorizing*'), *Isaac is the 'freeborn' son, 'the Son of the Promise*.' This is also how Izates is presented in Josephus who calls him, just as Hebrews 11:17 does '*Isaac*' and the Synoptics do '*Jesus*,' '*only begotten*.'[44] Playing on his favorite theme of '*bondage to the Torah*' of Moses and, once again, the language of '*casting out*' (*ekbale*) – this time, not '*Stephen*' or '*Evil Spirits*,' but stringing together passages from Isaiah 54:1 and Genesis 21:10 in, as already remarked, perhaps the most tendentious manner possible and in the interests, once again, of developing the most antinomian exegesis conceivable; he allegorizes the latter, '*casting out the slave woman*' which is '*Agar*' (by whom he means '*Hagar*'), into '*Mount Sinai in Arabia*'; and '*the Children of Israel*' (because of their '*bondage to the Torah of Moses*'), into '*the Children*' of this '*slavewoman*' (Galatians 4:25–31, reflected, too, in Romans 8:16–9:14).

For its part James, as also already underscored, concludes its discussion by evoking Genesis 15:6 about Abraham's Faith '*being reckoned as Righteousness*,' the passage along with Habakkuk 2:4 upon which Paul bases his entire '*Salvationary*' scheme of '*Justification by Faith*.' One should pay very close attention to the Hebrew vocabulary of '*counted for*' or '*reckoned*' here, widespread too at Qumran where it moves over into the characterization of '*the works being reckoned to you as Righteousness*,' as just pointed up, evoked on behalf of the addressee of '*MMT*,' whoever he was. For its part James 2:23 concludes:

> And he (Abraham) was called Friend of God. You see, therefore, that a man is justified ('made Righteous') by works and not by Faith only.

For good measure it adds, '*You see that Faith was working with his works and by works was Faith Perfected*' (2:22). In fact, it was probably not a particularly good example, inasmuch as *Abraham's willingness to sacrifice Isaac cannot really be considered a 'work.*' As already remarked, Hebrews 11:17 cites it as an act of '*Faith*.' on top of this, since Abraham never actually completes the sacrifice as such it is, in any event, only an intent. This in itself illustrates Paul's perhaps greater mastery of dialectic and/or rhetorical argument, not to mention the allegorical technique he employs of Philo of Alexandria Philo of Alexandria, his older contemporary and possible acquaintance – since, as we have seen, several '*Herodians*' married into Philo's family.[45]

By the same token, where Abraham was concerned James could have cited a host of other examples (including '*circumcision*'), this illustrates its straightforward, guileless approach but the reason it did not must also have been purposeful. In fact, Hebrews 11:1–31 – which cites the same two examples, James 2:25 cites here in describing '*Rahab the harlot*' as being '*justified by works*' (another allusion, which could be seen as aimed at Queen Helen of Adiabene and which, in our view, it was) and evoking Abraham's sacrifice of Isaac (also possibly directed at Helen's son) – does list a whole series of these, but – in the nature of its polemics – rather supporting the '*Pauline*' position and declaring them all '*justified by Faith.*'

Where the parallel citation of '*Rahab the harlot*' as possibly directed at the activities of Queen Helen of Adiabene is concerned, it should be recalled that Helen was supposed to have undergone *three consecutive, seven-year* '*Nazirite*'-style penances for infractions of some kind committed outside of Palestine.[46] As suggested, her possibly anomalous marital situation with King '*Agbar*' or '*Bazeus*', as the case may be, or being a member – married or not – of the harem of '*an Edessene King*' might have been at the root of some of these allegations or perceived infractions (this is to say nothing of a possible '*affair*' with Simon *Magus*); but however things may be, we know that it was she who paid for the plaque containing '*the suspected adulterers*' passage from Numbers 5:11–31 to be displayed in the Temple *in gold letters*!

The potency of citing Abraham's willingness to sacrifice his '*only begotten son*' Isaac (Hebrews 11:17 – again the very word Josephus uses to characterize Queen Helen of Adiabene's favorite son, Izates as we have seen – here now the conjunction of vocabularies concerning these two personages begins to converge), should not be underestimated in this locale in this period. Not only does it evoke the example of Abraham's '*Faith*', so important to individuals of this kind in this region of Northern Syria and Mesopotamia, but it also prefigured just the kind of death the '*Sicarii*' Revolutionaries chose for themselves and their families three years after the collapse of the Uprising only a decade after James' own.

In fact, *these* '*Sicarii*' ('*Christian*'?) *partisans finally did actually sacrifice their own children* before killing each other and committing suicide themselves on Masada in 73 CE. No doubt they, too, saw themselves as operating within this same '*Abrahamic*' paradigm – or should we say the '*Jamesian*' paradigm (now this *is* '*works Righteousness*' with a vengeance) – and one can well imagine someone making just the kind of exposition James 2:21 makes regarding Abraham's willingness to sacrifice his own son Isaac as an inspiration to do so. These people, in fact, *actually did sacrifice their children and themselves* going even further than Abraham went in this regard for the '*Sanctification of His Holy Name*.'

Abraham as 'Friend of God' in Jubilees, James, and Paul

We have already seen how Abraham is called 'the Friend' or 'Beloved of God' both in James 2:22 at this point and in the Damascus Document – as the latter puts it in III.2, because 'he kept the Commandments of God and did not choose the will of his own Spirit.' Not only is this latter assertion absolutely relevant to the position of Paul, but that this 'keeping' should be seen as the basis for the 'Friend' or 'Beloved of God' denotation in CDIII.2–4 is a statement of the most inestimable importance. In James 2:23 it was, as we saw, because 'Abraham believed God and it was reckoned to him as Righteousness.'

The Damascus Document also adds:

> And he transmitted (the Commandments) to Isaac and to Jacob, and they kept (them) and were inscribed as Friends of God, Heirs of the Covenant forever.

The parallel represented by this last to Paul's vocabulary of 'the Children of the Promise' in Romans 9:8 and Galatians 4:28 above should not be underestimated. Nor did 'they go astray,' as the Damascus Document would put it, nor were 'they cut off' like those after them, who 'walked in the stubbornness of their hearts' (here Paul's 'cutting off' imagery used positively).[47] Here again too, we have Paul's 'heart' imagery and a typical aspersion, used at Qumran to describe the genus of the 'Lying' Adversary of 'the Righteous Teacher' – 'complaining against the Commandments of God, each man doing what seemed right in his own eyes.' Rather, as already alluded to, it was because 'they ate blood' that 'their males were cut off in the wilderness.'[48] Again, the importance of these characterizations, not only for James' prohibitions for overseas communities but, as we shall see, for Paul's new conceptuality of 'drinking the Cup of the New Covenant' in 'the Blood' of Christ Jesus, should not be underestimated.

It is allusions such as these which now go on to play a part in the condemnation of the Pauline-type adversary at Qumran. They are also reflected in the non-canonical, Apocryphal book known as Jubilees, found in multiple copies at Qumran, where Abraham is again called 'the Friend of God' and described as commanding Isaac 'to eat no blood.'[49] As this document puts it in passages actually extant at Qumran, 'for the blood which is poured out defiles the Earth and the Earth cannot be purified from blood except with blood' (Jubilees 19:9–21:20). As reflected in the Letter of James, it is precisely because Abraham 'was tested and found Faithful' that he 'was called' or 'recorded the Friend of God' – 'recorded' here being almost precisely the kind of language in the Damascus Document.[50]

Not only is this 'Friend' ascription identified in Jubilees with 'the Righteous One' and 'being found Faithful,' it is also identified with 'fulfilling the Law' or 'Covenant,' and not 'breaking' or 'transgressing' it, again language absolutely reflected here in these passages from James. Furthermore these 'Covenant-Breakers,' who 'work uncleanness in every way,' are 'recorded on the Heavenly Tablets as Enemies to be destroyed out of the Book of Life' and 'uprooted out of the Earth' (Jubilees 30:20–22). Here, of course, we have both the language Paul uses in 2 Corinthians 3:3 about the 'tablets of the heart' and the 'uprooting' metaphor – should one choose to regard or consider it relevant – already encountered in CD1.7–8, reversed in 'Jesus'' dismissal of 'the Pharisees' as 'Blind Guides' in the prelude to his 'casting out the Toilet Bowl' Parable, now re-reversed to its original 'Palestinian' sense.

Nor is this to say anything about the definition *par excellence* of the 'Enemy' epithet both he and James are alluding to in these various exchanges. Whereas for Paul in 1 Thessalonians 2:15 above, it is 'the Jews' as a People who are 'the Enemies of the World' (circumscribed in Romans 11:28, in the context of 'the Redeemer' Prophecy from Isaiah 29:10, as just indicated, to the 'Enemies of the Gospel for your sakes,' whatever Paul means by this); for James 4:4, it is the man attempting to become 'a Friend to the world' (here the reversal of the status of Abraham and his 'heirs' as 'Friends of God' in both CDiii.2–4 above and James 2:23 earlier) 'transforms himself into' or 'is constituted an Enemy of God.'

We have also noted how James' 'Royal Law according to the Scripture,' the second of the two parts of the 'Righteousness'/'Piety'-dichotomy making up the sum total of all man's obligations in this world, is several times evoked either in whole or in part in the Damascus Document.[51] In this regard one should note the conjunction of 'keeping and doing according to the precise letter of the Torah during the Era of Evil to separate from the Sons of the Pit and keep apart from polluted Evil Riches' (expressed in terms of the Hebrew verb 'lehinnazer') that leads into a full citation of it in CD vi.19–21 It is in this context, in conjunction with evocation of 'the New Covenant in the Land of Damascus and setting up the Holy Things according to their exact interpretation,' that the Damascus Document instructs 'each man to love his brother as himself, to strengthen the hand of the Meek (ᶜAni), the Poor (Ebion), and the Convert' (Ger). As will be recalled, this is followed up immediately in Column Seven by the command 'not to sin against the flesh of near kin' and 'abjure fornication according to the Law' – again expressed in terms of the Hebrew verb 'lehazzir' (N-Z-R)/'to keep apart from.'[52]

This ends with the admonition 'to separate from all pollutions' and 'not defile one's Holy Spirit, which God separated for them, but to walk in these things in Perfect Holiness on the basis of the Covenant of God.' This last, of course, not only reflecting the ethos of James instructions to Paul in Acts 21:24 above but, as we have seen, the very term, '*separate*,' Paul uses in 2 Corinthians 6:15–7:1 when addressing the '*Beloved Ones*' and evoking '*Beliar*' while, at the same time, the command '*be separated*' and '*cleansed from all pollution of flesh and Spirit.*' It is impossible to escape the conclusion that the person writing these reproofs from 2 Corinthians knew and was actually using these materials from CDvii.3–5, not to mention 1QS,viii.13–14 and ix.20–21. But unlike elsewhere, as already pointed out, for a change Paul preserves their original sense, as per Damascus Document and Community Rule parameters, and does not reverse them, though, as always, his thrust is more cosmopolitan and he directs them to his new communities of overseas Gentiles.

Paul, too, twice cites James' '*Royal Law according to the Scripture*' verbatim, '*you shall love your neighbor as yourself*,' once, as we have seen, in Romans 13:8, in the context of recommending paying taxes to Rome and, by implication, '*loving the Authorities*'; and once, towards the end of his long excursus against taking on Mosaic Law and these same '*Holy Things*' from Galatians 3:19–6:15 (the '*keeping*' of which he over and over again refers to in terms of either '*weakness*' or '*slavery*'). Just as in Romans 14:2–21, where the citation of this passage from Leviticus 19:18 in 13:8 gave way to his critique of '*throwing down the work of God*' and '*setting up stumbling blocks over food*'; in CDvi.19–20 above, it was '*setting up the Holy Things according to their precise interpretation.*' In particular, Paul cites '*eating flesh or drinking wine*' here as the things he feels a '*weak*' brother either '*stumbles in*' or is '*scandalized by.*'

In Galatians 5:11–15, the citation of the '*Righteousness*' Commandment '*to love your neighbor*' is also accompanied by allusion to '*the stumbling block*' or '*scandal of the Cross.*' In addition, it is pointedly accompanied by evocation of '*biting and devouring*' or '*swallowing*,' clearly seemingly parodying, as we have already suggested, these same usages at Qumran. As at Qumran, these end up in the characterization of such persons as being either '*consumed*' or '*destroyed*' and all are seemingly variations on the language of '*eating*' and a play on the same language one finds there. To repeat this section from Galatians 5:14 in Paul:

> For the whole of the Law is fulfilled in one word: '*You should love your neighbor as yourself.*' But if you bite and swallow one another, take heed you be not consumed by one another.

In any event, that this is the analogue to the language of the '*whole of the Law*,' James 2:10 uses, should be patent but, as we have already pointed out as well, there is also a certain threatening aspect to the language here should one choose to regard it.

As we have shown, this allusion to 'the stumbling block' or 'scandal of the Cross' in 5:11 – accompanied as it is by an allusion to how he 'still preaches (the doctrine of) circumcision' (though it is hard to see how) and followed by these allusions to 'fulfilling the whole Law' and 'loving your neighbor' in 5:14 – also evokes the language of these passages from CDII–III and VIII/XIX–XX about the Jews 'being cut off,' now turned around and used against Jewish traveling teachers – clearly a 'Jamesian' mindset – proclaiming this doctrine. In CDiii.1-12, it will be recalled, it was applied to both the Children of Noah 'not keeping the Commandments' and, therefore, 'being cut off after the Flood and the Children of Israel 'murmuring in their tents' and 'complaining against the Commandments of God, each man doing what seemed was right in his own eyes' and this, specifically, 'eating blood' in the wilderness (it would be hard to miss an implied allusion to Paul here).[53]

In Galatians 5:12, however, the 'cutting off' language is expressly applied to the issue of 'circumcision,' the biggest 'scandal' or 'stumbling block' of them all. As we have shown, Paul phrases this: 'I even wish that those throwing you into confusion would themselves cut off,' a not-a-little-shocking bit of profanity which recalls Acts 9:22's picture of his throwing the Jews 'dwelling in Damascus' into confusion by the way he 'proved Jesus was the Christ.' Paul continues on this theme of 'circumcision' until the end of the Letter, making it clear that this is what they – the Jews and his interlocutors within the Church – are doing to the Galatians and that he means that, instead of circumcising you, he wishes they would 'cut' their 'own privy parts' off. However improbable it may seem, first of all, it is clear that this is what he meant at the beginning of the Letter when he spoke of it in 2:4, to wit, 'the false brothers who stole in by stealth to spy out the freedom we have in Christ Jesus in order to reduce us to bondage' (we know, of course, by now what he means by 'bondage' here); but secondly, also possibly more plays on the 'looking on their privy parts' language shifts we have already seen in the Habakkuk Pesher, XI.13 above.

This is what, he contends, his Jewish opponents within 'the Church' are doing to newcomers like the Galatians, forcing them 'to be circumcised so that they can – reversing his 'boasting' claims – boast in your flesh'; and, even negatively, 'so that they may not be persecuted for the Cross of Christ' (Galatians 6:12–13)! Not only does he raise in conjunction with this charge that even though 'they being circumcised do not themselves keep the Law' – the basis of the 'Sons of Zadok' esotericism in the Community Rule above – still, this is one of the most incredible slurs yet encountered in Paul, for he is clearly aiming it at the Jamesian party and the very Leadership of the Jerusalem Church itself. Combining this with the 'scandal of the Cross' accusation and complaints about his own persecution within the Church in 5:11, leading into his citation of the second of the two 'Love Commandments' in 5:14, what he rather has done here is make and flesh out the original 'blood libel' accusation. This, he develops further, as we saw, in 1 Thessalonians 2:15 in terms of the very 'Enemy'-terminology, James 4:4 directed against its Paul-style adversary and which he himself has just alluded to regarding himself in Galatians 4:16. No wonder some of his interlocutors might have considered him 'Diabolical.'

To once again reiterate: the Damascus Document's evocation of how the Israelite males were 'cut off' in the wilderness because they 'walked in stubbornness of heart,' 'complained against the Commandments of God,' and 'consumed blood,' is now employed in Paul to express his wish that those throwing his communities 'into confusion' over the issue of circumcision would, rather, 'themselves cut off.' We have already seen how this theme of 'Blood' and its consumption resurfaces, not only in the Habakkuk Pesher but, also – as we shall see further – in the Pauline and Qumran versions of 'the New Covenant in the Land of Damascus' or 'in the Blood of Christ.'

Paul's Interpretation of Abraham's Salvation by Faith

Paul really develops his doctrines about 'the Faith of Abraham' in Romans and Galatians, where he is also very interested in 'Abraham's seed' and Abraham as the father 'of us all,' particularly, 'the father of all those who believe among the uncircumcised' (Romans 4:1–11) – again, all matters that would have been important for those in the Haran area, Abraham's original place of origin or homeland. Whether he means this literally or figuratively is difficult to say. We have already seen how, in Romans 11:1 and Philippians 3:5, he asserts how he himself was 'of the seed of Abraham through the Tribe of Benjamin'; and that, if he was an 'Idumaean' Herodian, such a claim might have made sense to him, 'Bela'' in Genesis genealogies being both the first 'Edomite' King and also one of the principal 'Sons of Benjamin' (46:21), to say nothing of 'the Sons of Belial.'

We have already seen too how in leading up to this point in Galatians 5:3–12 that 'every man, being circumcised, is required to do the whole Law' – again the language of James 2:8–12 even including the emphasis on 'doing' – Paul contends, somewhat maddeningly, that 'Agar' the bondwoman both corresponds to 'Mount Sinai in Arabia' and is the equivalent to 'the present Jerusalem,' 'such things being allegorized' (Galatians 4:24f.). Having already asserted two chapters earlier, that 'if you are Christ's, then you are Abraham's seed and heirs according to the Promise' (3:29), by implication it is clear that this '*Jerusalem*' is the Jerusalem of slavery, while '*the Jerusalem above ('the Heavenly Jerusalem') is free and the mother of us all*' (4:26).

Here he adds another convoluted allegory from Genesis about how '*he who was born according to the flesh persecuted him who was born according to the Spirit*' (4:29). What he means here is how '*Ishmael persecuted Isaac*' and, even possibly, how '*Esau persecuted Jacob*' – it is not completely clear (we have already seen the '*pursuing them with the sword*' allusion in CD1.20–21 concerning how '*the Covenant-Breakers banded together against the soul of the Righteous One and all the Walkers in Perfection*' and '*the Wicked Priest pursued the Righteous Teacher*' in 1QpHab,XI.4–5 – both presumably based on the idea of how '*Esau pursued Jacob*'). What is clear is that, once again, the other Israel, '*the Israel according to the flesh*,' are those whom Paul claims here are persecuting him, primarily over '*circumcision*' – but also other things. Because of their '*enslavement to the Law*' (of course, he is either not interested in or forgets about their '*enslavement to the Romans*'), these are really the '*Arab*' bondchildren of Hagar, while he and his communities are '*the Children of Isaac*' (called in Hebrews 11:17–18 above, the '*only-begotten*' and '*in whom your seed will be called*').

Paul actually says this in so many words, asserting, '*but we, brothers, are like Isaac, Children of the Promise*,' which brings him to the conclusion, already noted several times above but worth repeating: '*Therefore cast out (ekbale) the bondwoman, for the Son of the Bondwoman shall in no wise inherit with the Son of the Free Woman*' (4:30). Not only is this another reversal of the '*balla^c'/'ballo'/'Belial*' language-complex, but it is the actual wording of the Greek *Septuagint* version of Genesis 21:10, the text of which Paul is freely quoting here. He adds: '*Therefore, brothers, we are not Children of the Bondwoman, but of the Free*' (4:31), meaning of course Sarah. How this would appeal to real '*Arab*' converts to '*Judaism*' or '*Christianity*,' like King Agbar, Queen Helen, or her sons, Izates and Monobazus, in the geographical area of Haran (Abraham's original homeland), is difficult to say.

Paul launches into his discussion of how Abraham '*was justified by Faith*' – which would, of course, have held such significance for such persons – more fully in Romans 4–5 by again referring to the same '*Righteous shall live by Faith*' passage from Habakkuk 2:4, we have already encountered so frequently above, and '*changing the Truth of God into Lying*' in Romans 1:17–25. Referring throughout these passages to the problem of who should teach and who should not, '*hating idols*,' '*circumcision*,' '*Law-breaking*,' and '*Lying*,' he even evokes again the key '*circumcision of the heart*' in Romans 2:29 and how '*the Doers of the Law shall be justified*' (2:13) – the same '*Doers of the Law*' appearing several times in the Letter of James and forming the backbone of the Habakkuk *Pesher*'s exposition of

Habakkuk 2:3–4 too.

Noting that there is 'no respecting of persons with God,' an issue James 2:9 gives as the prototypical example of 'working Sin' and being 'convicted by the Law as Breakers,' Paul concludes (somewhat evasively), 'for as Many as sinned in the Law shall be judged by the Law' (Romans 2:11–12). Not only do we have here again the 'Many' usage, but the whole varies the language James 4:11 uses in referring to slandering one's brother or speaking against the Law – 'but if you judge the Law, you are not a Doer of the Law.' Here, too, is both 'the Days of Wrath' of 'God's Righteous Judgement' (2:5) of the Habakkuk Pesher and his own 2 Corinthians 3:3–6 imagery of 'the New Covenant' letters 'written not with ink,' 'but on the fleshy tablets of the heart' here, 'the work of the Law written in their hearts' (Romans 2:15).

Moreover, Paul asks in Romans 3:7–8 (ever so unctuously and playing with the 'Lying' and 'Truth' duality again), 'If in my Lie the Truth of God abounded to His Glory, why am I yet judged' and follows this up with the complaint which again exploits another rhetorical duality about being 'wrongly accused' of 'practicing Evil things so Good things may come.' Though the logic is convoluted, the reference to Qumran parameters should be clear. Furthermore his conclusion is also clear. Asserting 'a Law of Faith' not 'of works' (3:27) and having already stated that 'God's Righteousness has now been revealed apart from the Law' (3:21); he concludes, clearly using the language of Genesis 15:6 and absolutely counter-indicating 'MMT,' though operating in the same linguistic framework: 'So we reckon that a man is justified by Faith without works of (the) Law' (3:28).

Having already raised the issue of 'circumcision' in Romans 2:25 and 3:30, this conclusion, once again, leads him into a discussion of Abraham, who he refers to as 'our Father according to the flesh' (4:1). It is difficult to know if he means by this only himself or Jews generally, 'Herodians,' or even the People of 'the Land of the Edessenes,' however ambiguity of just this kind was probably precisely his point. Now he cites the very passage from Genesis 15:6 he has been leading up to all along and which we have already seen James 2:23 cite in conjunction with its designation of Abraham as the 'Friend' or 'Beloved of God,' viz., 'and Abraham believed God and it was reckoned to him as Righteousness' (Romans 4:3).

Not only has he just used this pivotal allusion to 'reckoned' in 4:3 to apply to how Abraham was a man 'justified by Faith,' he also uses it in 4:4 to pointedly express the 'reward of him who works' (once again, the pregnant vocabulary of 'gemul'/'gemulo') which he asserts was 'not reckoned according to Grace but according to debt.' Puzzling or mystifying as this may be, he now proceeds in 4:9–12 to bring up this language of 'being reckoned' again in relation to the issue of 'circumcision' (the very issue that so preoccupied Izates and his brother Monobazus in Josephus' and *Talmud's* picture of their conversion), specifically Abraham's '*circumcision*' and the time at which this occurred, asking, '*How then was this reckoned, being in circumcision or uncircumcision?*' (Romans 4:10).

The question is for rhetorical purposes only but one cannot get much cleverer, rhetorically-speaking, than this. Clearly, having had a high degree of training in the skills of Greek sophistical and dialectical argument, he is using this knowledge to punch holes in the 'Jewish' scheme of '*Salvation*' of some of his '*teaching*' opponents. This is the question, as we just saw as well, that so exercised Helen in the matter of Izates' conversion (not to mention its parody in Acts 8:27's picture of the '*eunuch*' Treasurer of '*the Ethiopian Queen*' – i.e., her son *Izates*). It is an important question, for Paul is actually asking whether this '*reckoning*' or '*Salvation*' occurred before Abraham was circumcised or afterwards. As these materials percolate down in the next six centuries from Northern Syria into the '*Arabian*' cultural sphere further south they will be, as we have seen, only slightly, laterally transformed in Muhammad's Koran into the question of which came first, '*Abraham's Religion*' (meaning Islam) or Judaism and Christianity – both lumped together under the rubric '*Lying*.'[54]

Paul immediately – and triumphantly – provides the answer: '*not in circumcision but in uncircumcision*,' the point being, as anyone familiar with chronological sequencing in the Hebrew Bible will realize, that this promise concerning Abraham's '*Faith being reckoned as Righteousness*' in Genesis 15:6 came before the Commandment telling him to circumcise himself and those of his household in Genesis 17:10–14.

This is all Paul needs. He then concludes that the '*the Promise that was made to Abraham or his seed* (persons presumably like King Agbar, Paul Helen, Izates, and others too) *to be heir of the World was not by Law but the Righteousness of Faith*' and, further to this, that Abraham was the '*Father of all those who Believe in the Uncircumcision*' (Romans 4:11–13) – the whole presentation being rather figurative like that of Isaac's relationship to '*the Children of the Promise*' in Galatians 4:28 above. One cannot get more skillful in Hellenizing semantics or show much more agility in dialectical argument than this – the only problem was that persons like Izates who, basically, were really only warriors were, no doubt, a little too unsophisticated to catch his drift or understand his allegorizing polemic.

In 4:17–18, Paul even applies the various promises God made to Abraham in Genesis 15:5 and 17:5 about being '*the Father of many Nations*' (*Ethnon*) and his '*descendants being as many as the stars.*' His use of the '*Peoples*' (*Ethnon*) vocabulary here, playing on and inverting a parallel usage found, like that of being '*heir to the World*,' at Qumran – in the

Damascus Document, this is 'heirs to the Covenant' – is purposeful. More-over, here and later in the Letter too, as in both 1 Corinthians and Galatians, he hurls at his opponents the 'weakness' allegation (usually asso-ciated with their 'consciences') – a usage he had already evoked in 2:15 – now turning it around in 4:19 to assert that Abraham's 'Faith was not weak' (even though he was already a hundred years old!); the implication be-ing – as in the instance of the Biblical 'Peter' who sank into the Sea of Galilee in Matthew 14:30–31 because of the inadequacy of his 'Faith' – that theirs was. It was 'for this reason, too, that it (Abraham's 'Faith') was reck-oned to him as Righteousness' (4:22), not like the 'some' in 1 Corinthians 8:3–13 (in exposition of the first 'Love' or the 'Piety' Commandment'[55]) who 'stumbled over food' and whose 'weak consciences' required dietary reg-ulations in general, as well as abstention from 'things sacrificed to idols' in particular, and who like James 'would eat only vegetables' (Romans 14:2).

'The Seed of Abraham'

Paul returns to this 'seed of Abraham' and the language of 'reckoning' in Romans 9:7–8 where, again, referring to Genesis 21:12: 'in Isaac shall seed be called to you,' he asserts:

> The Children of the flesh are not the Children of God; rather it is the Children of the Promise who are to be reckoned as the seed.

This dovetails perfectly with the arguments in this regard we have just reviewed in Galatians above. Also he punctuates these kinds of construc-tions with regular cries of 'Amen' (Romans 9:4 and Galatians 6:18 – just the kind of 'Amen, Amen's we have encountered in the excommunica-tion-style texts at Qumran from exactly the opposite point-of-view![35]). Paul's development of these materials in Galatians 3:2–5:26, ending in the allusions to 'Agar' and the 'Righteousness' Commandment, we have reviewed above, are equally hard-hitting. These, too, were triggered in 2:8–12 by the issue of 'circumcision' which from Acts' perspective (together with the 'table fellowship'-one related to it) prompted Paul's return to Jerusalem and James' directives to overseas communities following it. Not only did these emanate out of Paul's visit to Jerusalem and the so-called 'Jerusalem Council' assembled there, but they end up in Galatians 5:3 in Paul's insistence that 'circumcision' requires one to 'do the whole Law.'

As Paul puts this in his attack on Peter and 'the rest of the Jews,' includ-ing Barnabas and the 'some from James' in 2:12–14 earlier: 'a man is not justified by works of the Law but through Faith in Jesus Christ' and, again, 'for *by works of the Law* shall *no flesh be justified*' (or '*made Righteous*' – 2:16). Pushing this point even further and employing the '*building*' imagery, we have encountered and will presently encounter again where the '*works*' and '*City of Blood*' built by '*the Liar*' are concerned in the Habakkuk *Pesher*[57]; he asserts, '*for if Righteousness were through the Law, then Christ died for nothing*' (2:21). Nor could he possibly be more emphatic than this.

Chastising his respondents, he then goes on to ask – marshalling his '*Spirit*'/'*Faith*' duality as opposed, presumably, to that of his opponents of '*works*' and '*the Law*' – '*was it by works of the Law or report of Faith that you received the Spirit* and, '*having begun in the Spirit, are you to be Perfected in the flesh*' (3:2–3). He clearly means this last to be a euphemism for '*circumcision*' again and, it is at this point, he cites Genesis 15:6 about how Abraham's Faith '*was reckoned to him as Righteousness*' now arguing that '*they that are of Faith, these are Sons of Abraham*' (Galatians 3:6–7).

Here Paul cites an additional scriptural passage from Genesis 12:3 relating to the blessings Abraham received *before he was circumcised* and how God promised Abraham that '*all the Peoples (Ethne) would be blessed in*' him (Galatians 3:8), language picked up too in the speeches Peter and James are pictured as making in Acts 15:7–17's version of '*the Jerusalem Council.*' As Paul now concludes in Galatians 3:9, '*those of the Faith are being blessed along with the believing Abraham.*' We have already called attention to the impression a polemic and promise such as this might have made on persons in areas like Edessa (Antioch-by-Callirhoe) adjacent to Abraham's Haran (Carrhae) in Northern Syria.

It is at this point in 3:10–14 that Paul launches into the development of his new theology of the '*Redeeming*' death of '*Christ Jesus.*' He does this, as we saw, by reversing the '*cursing*' language found in Qumran documents like the Damascus Document and the Community Rule. In the Last Column of the former, as already underscored as well, such '*cursing*' was reserved for those '*breaking*' the '*Laws of Your Truth and the Judgements of Your Holiness,*' '*departing to the right or left of the Torah,*' and '*anyone rejecting (ma'as)...all the Laws found in the Torah of Moses*' – again the language of '*rejecting,*' so important for describing the behaviour of '*the Man of Lying*' in other documents at Qumran.[58] These, it pregnantly characterized, as will be recalled, as '*abhorring the Foundations of Righteousness*'; but, even more tellingly (in view of our above discussion and Paul's parallel contention that, '*by telling you the Truth, your Enemy have I become*'), '*these will not be reckoned among any of the Sons of His Truth.*'[59] Here this kind of '*rejection*' is also described, just as earlier in CD, as '*Rebellion.*'[60]

Interestingly, as we have remarked too, the '*cursing*' of such persons at the assemblage '*of the inhabitants of the Camps*' takes place at, of all times,

'*Pentecost,*' the very Festival that Acts 20:16 has Paul hurrying to attend in Jerusalem. It was during the course of this Festival after Jesus' '*Ascension*' in Acts 2:1–41 that '*the Holy Spirit*' was pictured as being '*poured out*' upon the Community and that those '*assembled*' were pictured as learning '*to speak in Tongues*' and begin the process of learning to accept non-Jews. The language of these '*Tongues*' is recapitulated both in these passages at the end of the 4QD, and several columns earlier, in the skills required of '*the Mebakker.*'[61] But here all resemblance ceases, because in this the Last Column of the Damascus Document, such an individual, who '*departs to the right or left of*' and '*rejects the Laws of the Torah of Moses,*' is to '*be expelled from the presence of the Many*' (Paul's vocabulary of the '*Many as are in the Law*' just encountered in Romans 2:12 above) and excommunicated.

This outlook is also reflected in the Community Rule, where the language of '*separating from all the Men of Unrighteousness who walk in the Way of Evil*' and '*are not to be reckoned in His Covenant,*' as we saw, again occurs. This is accompanied by the strictures about '*not entering the water*' or '*touching the Pure Food of the Men of Holiness*' where the language of '*the Many*' abounds.[62] This point is reiterated three columns later in 1QS,viii.16–17 following its all-important citation of Isaiah 40:3's '*Prepare in the wilderness the Way of the Lord.*' In interpreting this, once again, in terms of '*separating from the midst of the habitation of the Men of Unrighteousness*'; the point was added about '*going into the Wilderness to prepare the Way of the Lord,*' which itself was, then, interpreted with reference to '*the Study of the Torah*' ('*the Midrash ha-Torah*' – the identical phrase with which this Last Column of 4QD ended[63] and the same root as the appellative, '*the Doresh ha-Torah*' above) and in terms of *being obliged to* '*do all*' that was '*commanded by the hand of Moses,*' '*which the Prophets have revealed through His Holy Spirit*' from '*age to age.*'[64]

For its part, the expulsion and '*cursing*' in the Last Column of 4QD refers to '*the Peoples*' just as in Paul; but now, in a play on this same language of *the preparation of this* '*Way in the wilderness,*' with which the original condemnation of '*the Lying Scoffer*' began in CD1.9–15, these '*Peoples*' are described as being made '*to wander astray in the wilderness without a Way.*' As against this, as far as the Damascus Document is concerned, as we saw, God

> chose our Fathers and to their seed gave the Laws of (His) Truth and the Ordinances of (His) Holiness, which a man shall do and thereby live.[65]

Again here, not only do we have yet again the '*Jamesian*' emphasis on '*doing,*' but the language Paul just used about '*the seed of Abraham.*' Nor is this the tendentious interpretation of Genesis 21:12's '*in Isaac shall seed be called to you*' of both Romans 9:7and Hebrews 11:18.

Not only is this seemingly restricted to the '*People*' Israel, but '*living*' now is through '*the Torah of Moses*' not through the '*Redeeming*' death of '*Christ Jesus,*' as Paul now presents it '*Mystery-Religion*' style. This is the same '*living*' we just saw Jubilees 30:30 record above on the part of '*the Righteous*' or '*Friends of God, who did not transgress the Judgements or break the Covenant.*' In Jubilees, this was to be for '*a thousand generations,*' the same period referred to in CDvii.6/xix.1 and xx.22 as the legacy of those '*walking these things in Perfect Holiness on the basis of the Covenant of God,*' promised in Exodus 20:6 and Deuteronomy 7:9 to those '*loving*' God and '*keeping (His) Commandments for a thousand generations.*'[66]

It is this '*living,*' too, that Paul now advances, not only as he freely paraphrases Hosea 2:25 in terms of '*being called Sons of the Living God*' in Romans 9:26, but in his interpretation of both Habakkuk 2:4 ('*the Righteous shall live by Faith*') and Leviticus 18:5's '*doing*' and '*living in them*' (that is, '*the Laws and Ordinances*') in Galatians 3:10–13, ending up in another absolutely dizzying display of rhetorical and sophistical virtuosity also affirming in 3:26 '*all*' to '*be Sons of God through Faith*' – but in 3:21, to exactly opposite effect, *denying* '*a Righteousness by the Law*'.

As opposed to this, this closing section of 4QD now reiterates its position using the very same language. we just saw used at the beginning to condemn the Scoffer '*who poured over Israel the waters of Lying,*' not to mention its condemnation of him and the others along with him Columns viii.21–23/xix.33–35, who '*betrayed the New Covenant in the Land of Damascus,*' by '*turning aside from the Fountain of Living Waters*' and would, therefore, no longer '*be reckoned among the Foundation of the People.*' Now it rather avers, as previously already stressed: '*Boundary markers were laid down for us. Those who cross over them*' and '*break them You curse, while we uphold them.*'[67] Not only do we have here again the '*breaking*' language of the Habakkuk *Pesher* and James, it is this language that Paul then goes on to play upon and reverse, turning it into its mirror opposite in, as just underscored, his canny mastery of mystifying polemic.

Again returning to his allegorizing dialectic based, as it is, on revered Biblical passages and alluding to the terminology of the '*Many,*' he states (as partially quoted to some degree earlier):

> *For as Many as are of the works of the Law are under a curse, for it is written, 'Cursed is anyone who does not fulfill all the things which have been written in the Book of the Law to do them.'*

Not only is this the same language, we have before us here in this Last Column of 4QD, but the play on Qumran doctrine should be patent. The quotation is from Deuteronomy 27:26, the language of which runs right through the Damascus Document, particularly the Last Column.

In fact, even Abraham's 'circumcision' is specifically evoked in CDxvi.4– 6 as part and parcel of 'the fulfillment' or 'completion of the Torah of Moses.' This, it is said, Abraham performed 'on the day he (came to) know it' as illogical, chronologically-speaking, as this may seem in the light of Paul's analysis above. But there was no contradiction in these matters at Qumran.[68] Nor is it conceivable that an argument of this kind was not being made against someone making precisely the arguments of Paul.

Paul's Citation of Habakkuk 2:4's 'the Righteous shall Live by Faith'

To clinch these arguments, Paul now quotes the very same passage from Habakkuk 2:4, 'the Righteous shall live by his Faith,' the Habakkuk *Pesher* also now goes on to expound but, in his version, he drops the adjective 'his' and, in doing so, adopts exactly the opposite position, to the one we have seen embraced in 1QpHab,viii.1-3 (and, in effect, embraced in the Letter of James), to argue his proposition 'that no one is justified with God by virtue of the Law.' For Paul these things are obvious and again in Galatians 3:11–12, he puts it in another way – freely quoting, as we just saw, a variation of Leviticus 18:5 and stressing the common thread of 'living' to arrive at 'the Law is not of Faith, but the man who has done these things shall live in them – the emphasis on 'doing' now being shifted over to 'of Faith.'

Paul makes exactly the same point in Romans 1:17 above, again quoting Habakkuk 2:4, this time in the context of reference to 'Greeks,' 'Romans,' and 'Barbarians' amid thinly-veiled threats about 'God's Wrath from Heaven being revealed ('apocalypsed'!) upon all (the) Ungodliness and Unrighteousnes of (the) men who hold the Truth in Unrighteousness' (1:18). Also evoked are 'the Jews' and 'other Gentiles' (Ethnesin – 1:13). So does Hebrews 10:38 in the beginning of its long Paulinizing discourse (or harangue?) on 'Salvation by Faith' (11:1–26) which cited among other examples, as we have seen, the two evoked in the Letter of James. By contrast, as James 2:25 put it, Abraham 'was justified by works when he offered his son Isaac on the altar' and Rahab the Harlot too 'was justified by works when she took in the messengers and sent them out another way.'

For Hebrews 11:17 and 11:31, however, it was rather 'by Faith' that Abraham when he was tested, it will be recalled, offered up his 'only begotten' Isaac in whom his 'seed would be called' and Rahab the Harlot 'did not *die with the ones who did not believe.'* Not only have we seen the relevance of these two examples to historical events in Palestine in this period – in particular, the situation of the Queen of Adiabene, both as regards her son Izates and possibly her own questionable past; but this emphasis will be shifted back to '*doing*' and '*the Doers of Torah*' in the Column VIII *Pesher* of 1QpHab on Habakkuk 2:4 we shall analyze further below.

One should again remark the emphasis on '*living*' in these passages expounding Habakkuk 2:4 in Paul, which end by denying that *the Law 'can give life*' and a '*Righteousness*' by '*the Law*' (Galatians 3:21), as we just saw above. Rather they affirm – in yet another canny if '*biting*' metaphor for '*circumcision*' and '*works*' – that '*sowing*' in '*the flesh*' shall '*reap corruption*,' but '*sowing to the Spirit shall reap everlasting life from the Spirit*' (Galatians 6:8). This is the same '*living*' encountered in the '*cursing*' of the '*Law - Breakers*' in the Last Column of 4QD above relating to what '*a man must do and thereby live*' – precisely the words Paul has just used, but with the *entirely opposite* signification.

Paul moves from these two points about '*life*,' by which he means Eternal life, into his interpretation of the passage about '*cursing*' from Deuteronomy 21:23. Though this Biblical injunction can be taken to mean that it is a '*curse*' to *hang a man upon a tree at all* – this is what we saw to basically be the position of the Nahum *Pesher*[69] – the sense is ambiguous even in Paul's reading of the phrase. The operative part, as already discussed too – though Paul does not quote it – has to do, however, with *not leaving a 'body all night upon the tree*' which neverthe-less, then, made such a deep impression on New Testament chroniclers.

But Paul's twist on this, as we saw, is quite different. He has already cited the passage from Deuteronomy 27:26 about, as he sees it, those '*of the works of the Law being under a curse*' (Galatians 3:10). This is the second '*cursing*' passage connected to '*Abraham's Faith being reckoned to him as Righteousness*' and *the Peoples 'being blessed with the believing Abraham*' (the warrant for Paul's '*Gentile Mission*') in almost as many lines. Since, as Paul sees it, those '*doing the Law*' – again terminology which we shall see as integral to Columns VII.11, VIII.1, and XII.4 of the Habakkuk *Pesher* – are under what is, in fact, the threat of a '*curse*'; for him, '*Christ redeemed us from the curse of the Law by having become a curse* – that is, by '*being hung up-on a tree*,' i.e., '*crucified*,' and, therefore, '*accursed*' – *for us*' (Galatians 3:13).

It is from this '*that Abraham's blessing might come to the Peoples (Ethne) in Christ Jesus that (they) might receive the Promise of the Spirit through Faith*' (Galatians 3:14), and it is on this basis that he now goes on to develop his whole understanding of the redeeming death of Christ Jesus, not only for himself, but for all mankind as well. Though, obviously masterfully

dialectical, as already emphasized, one can plainly see this to be based upon the same kind of '*cursing*' language just encountered in the Qumran
documents above, only '*reversed.*' Furthermore, Paul clearly realizes that
individuals of the *genus* of '*the Man of Lying*' like himself, who '*reject the
Law*,' are for a whole series of Qumran documents '*accursed*,' as per the
injunction from Deuteronomy 27:26 he has just quoted so perversely
above – a passage also plainly in wide use at Qumran. This is particularly
clear in the Community Rule and Damascus Document above, but also
4Q *Berachot* (which, reflecting its subject matter, I entitled '*The Chariots
of Glory*') in the section '*The Community Council Curses Belial*' – itself
plainly a part of the Community Rule.[70]

It is this denunciation that can be viewed as the moving force behind
the '*plots*' against Paul's life, so repeatedly signaled in Acts, particularly on
the part of '*Nazirite*'-vowing extremists who take an oath in Acts 23:12
'*not to eat or drink until they have killed Paul.*' This is not the same for Jesus
and James, though Scripture would have us think it is. In Paul's case, it is
plots on the part of '*Zealot*'-style sectarians; for Jesus and James, it is
clearly the very opposite kind of Establishment '*plots*,' because all reports
confirm that they were very *popular among the People*. So, however interpreted, it is clearly not '*Jewish*' *plots*. The same is true for John the Baptist.

Ultimately Scripture as it has come down to us and early Church
theology have taken advantage of the general lack of historical sophistication concerning this period to make these two, diametrically opposed
types of '*plots*' appear equivalent, but now the Dead Sea Scrolls have
come to light to restore the balance and give us a unique contemporary
witness into the intellectual heart of this period. Without them, previously one might have suspected this, but it could not be proved. Now it
can. This is the point one must appreciate when considering historical
matters in this period. James is able to function in Jerusalem for twenty
years or more from the Forties to the Sixties with no discernible problems among the mass of the People – the opposite – until he is removed
by what has to be considered Establishment '*plotting*,' whereas Paul can
hardly set foot in Jerusalem without being mobbed by the People or
protected by Roman troops and has to spend years abroad while the
memory of his previous behaviour recedes. Even this is insufficient.
However this may be, knowing that he '*is*' or '*has been cursed*' by those certainly of a '*Nazirite*' or Qumran frame-of-mind; in the best Greco-
Hellenistic rhetorical style, he reversed the language of '*cursing*,' his opponents are throwing against him, to hurl back upon them instead.

Not only does he use here the language of '*excommunication*' or
'*banning*,' just encountered in 4QD above, there can be little doubt – just

as in the positions he adopts in Romans 13:1–10 – that his adversaries were not '*Jews*' from the '*Herodianizing*' Jewish Establishment. One can well imagine how the kind of verbal invective he is indulging in here would have infuriated his opponents who were themselves the partisans of just such a '*crucified Messiah*.' That someone was claiming that '*the crucified Messiah*,' whom they loved, '*was cursed*' because *foreigners* '*had hung him on a tree*' – '*cursed*' in the exact manner they considered persons such as '*Lying Spouter*'s like Paul to be – would have enraged them.

Just this kind of outrage is to be encountered in the Habakkuk *Pesher* when, after speaking about the Liar's '*misleading Many*' and '*erecting an Assembly*' or '*Church upon Lying*' or '*Self-Glorification*' and '*upon Blood*,' it will call down upon him and those like him the same '*Judgements of Hellfire*' with which they '*blasphemed and vilified the Elect of God*.'[71] Furthermore, 1QpHab, VII.17–VIII.3 also uses the very same formulation, '*Doer of*' or '*doing of the Torah*,' Paul uses in Galatians 3:10 (quoting Deuteronomy 27:26 above) and in Galatians 5:3, to restrict the effect of just this Habakkuk 2:4, '*the Righteous shall live by his Faith*,' Paul so tendentiously interprets in Galatians 3:11. This is about as powerful a demonstration of the convergence of these documents as one could devise – not to mention the use of this same expression, '*Doer of the Law*,' in James 4:11 above.

For Paul now in Galatians 3:13, '*Christ redeemed us from the curse of the Law*' by having become a '*curse*' according to the Law himself. As we have implied, this is one of the most astonishing ideological reversals in the whole complex of Western intellectual history and has had the most profound effects even until today, but it is the Qumran documents that allow us to see it in perspective. Without them, we probably would be able to do so, but with them, a completely new perspective is afforded.

Paul now uses this proposition to assert that Abraham's blessing will now come to the '*Peoples*' (*Ethne*) as well, again the complete ideological reversal of Qumran's perspective on these same '*Peoples*.' Taking the opportunity to counter-indicate 4QD's position on '*the Covenant*' and '*the Law*' or '*Torah*' being able to give '*life*,' he states – as we just saw – '*for if a Law had been given that was able to give life then, indeed, Righteousness would have been by the Law*'; but, of course, this was not the case. Therefore '*Righteousness*' was '*the Promise by Faith of Jesus Christ*' (3:22). He can now go on to evoke the '*Sonship*'-ideal on behalf of Gentiles since, strictly speaking according to Jewish writ, *all the Righteous Ones were Sons of God*, all were now '*Sons of God through Faith in Christ Jesus*' (3:26).[72]

This leads into his concept of '*the Children of the Promise*' being *the true Sons of Abraham's seed*. As we saw, in Galatians 3:29, he puts this as follows: '*But if you are Christ's, then you are Abraham's seed and Heirs to the Promise*.'

Moreover, it echoes Romans 9:7 above where he was rather interpreting Genesis 21:12, 'in Isaac shall your seed be called,' and using the language
of 'reckoning' from Genesis 15:6 to assert that this meant 'the Children were
to be reckoned as the seed.' Muhammad's presentation of this, as we have
explained, involved only a slight refurbishment so as to apply to all his
followers, now called 'Muslims' (in James 2:23 and 4:4 this would be
'Friends of God'; in Paul, as we just saw, 'the Children of the Promise'). But
Paul, too, uses it to move into a slightly more universalist program. As he
had expressed this earlier in Romans 1:16–17, in interpretation of 'the
Righteous shall live by Faith' as well: 'the Power of God saving (or 'giving Salvation to') everyone who believes, both the Jew first and the Greek.' It is this
language of 'saving' we shall presently encounter in the Habakkuk Pesher's
crucial interpretation of this same Habakkuk 2:4.

The same is true in Romans 10:1–14, where, playing on the issue of
the 'uncircumcised heart' again, Paul now rather expresses 'the desire of (his)
own heart' for the 'Salvation' of Israel (10:1– sic). In doing so, he acknowledges that the fundamental issue was 'being saved,' at the same time
deliberately invoking the counter-position of those in Israel whom he
acknowledges 'have zeal for God but,' as he expresses this – taking back
what he has just accorded them – 'not according to Knowledge' (Gnosis –
10:2). Continuing this critique, he then goes on to criticize these as 'being
ignorant of God's Righteousness' – the very words with which the Cairo
version of the Damascus Document begins ('Now listen, all Knowers of
Righteousness, and comprehend the works of God'[73]) – and in 'trying to set up
their own Righteousness, did not submit to the Righteousness of God' (10:3)!

It is now a quick step to: 'Christ is the end of the Law for Righteousness
to anyone that believes' in Romans 10:4 – but another a-little-too-ingen-
ious-perhaps exegetical leap. Here he again alludes to Leviticus 18:5
about 'doing these things and living' and Moses writing 'a Righteousness of
the Law' (10:5). This he now counters by again using the language of the
'heart' (so familiar both at Qumran and his 2 Corinthians 3:3 metaphor
to similar effect): if 'you believe in your heart..., you shall be saved, for with the
heart is belief (leading) to Righteousness...and Salvation' (10:9–10), concluding with the completely cosmopolitan proclamation:

> For there is no difference between Jew and Greek, for the same Lord of all is Rich
> towards all who call on Him. For everyone, whoever calls on the Name of God,
> shall be saved (Romans 10:11–12).

Not only does this mix both Hellenistic and Hebraic allusion, but here
we again see the play on the 'Riches' and 'being called by Name'-imagery

in both Qumran documents and in James (the latter in 2:7, criticizing *'the Rich'* who despise and oppress *'the Poor,' 'dragging you before tribunals,'* and *'blaspheming the good Name by which you were called'*). Furthermore, this language of *'being saved'* reappears in both James and the *Pesher* on Habakkuk 2:4 at Qumran as well.

Colossians 3:9–11, a letter considered to be in the *'Pauline school,'* also reverses the language of James 3:5–10's attack on *'the Tongue'* – complaining about *'blasphemy'* and *'the filthy language'* generally that comes out of the mouth, not to mention the *'fornication,' 'uncleanness,' 'idolatry,'* and *'the Wrath of God'* allusions, usually associated with the *genus* of *'the Lying Spouter'* at Qumran. Instructing its respondents – as at Qumran and in the Pseudoclementine *Homilies* (and by refraction also in Paul[74]) – *'not to Lie to one another'* as well; it too concludes: *'there is neither Greek nor Jew, circumcision or uncircumcision, Barbarian, Scythian, bondman or free,' 'only Christ.'* For Paul in 1 Corinthians 1:24, this is: *'To those who are called, both Jews and Greeks, Christ is God's Power and God's Wisdom.'*[75] He also puts the same proposition in Galatians 3:28: *'There is not Jew or Greek, bondman or free, male or female. All are one in Christ Jesus.'* As usual, this leads directly into his attack on those *'who wish again to be in bondage,'* scrupulously *'keeping days and months and times and years,'* the very elements, as we have previously remarked, that in the Damascus Document are so much a part of *'separating'* in the wilderness, *'setting up the Holy Things according to their precise letter,' 'to love each man his brother as himself,'* and *'not defiling one's Holy Spirit,'* but *'walking in these things in Perfect Holiness.'*[76]

In 4QBerachot (*'The Chariots of Glory'* text above), which punctuates its *'excommunications'* and *'cursing' with 'amen, amen's,* these are *'the weeks of Holiness,' 'the Festivals of Glory,'* and *'the embroidered Splendor (n.b.,* the *'Kabbalist'* language here) *of the Spirits of the Holy of Holies'* (and that of *'Naziritism'* or esotericized *'Holiness'* here). For Paul, as already highlighted, they are the *'weak and beggarly elements'* that reduce his constituents to *'the bondage (they so) desire'* (Galatians 4:9). Is it possible to conceive of anyone being more insulting than this? Also the allusion to *'weak'* here, not only meshes with the allusions to *'weakness'* we have seen him use throughout the totality of his polemical assaults, but now it includes the point about how he *'labored in vain'* regarding these matters for his Communities (4:11). This will, again, be absolutely reproduced in the language the Habakkuk *Pesher* uses to condemn the *'vain labor'* of *'the Spouter of Lying,'* which he has expended to *'build (his) Worthless City upon Blood* – language also paralleled in Hebrews 11:16 above – *and erect (his) Assembly* (possibly even *'Church'*) *upon Lying'* – this paralleled too in its antithesis in CDvii and its analogues: *'erecting the fallen Tabernacle of David'*!

James and the Liar

Before proceeding to the interpretation of '*the Righteous shall live by his Faith*' in Columns VII–VIII of the Habakkuk *Pesher*, we should look at the figurative evocation of '*the Tongue*' in James 3:5–8, a chapter replete with the imagery of Qumran. Not only does it contain an allusion to the '*blessing and cursing*' from Deuteronomy, which Paul also makes use of in Galatians 3:10 above, upon which most of the language of '*cursing*' in these documents is based; it even alludes to the problem of '*mixed liquids*,' a subject which also occupies not a little attention in '*MMT*.'[77] As James 3:11–12 puts this, '*out of the same fountain orifice pours forth sweet and bitter*' (note here the metaphor of '*pouring*' again), which it compares to '*the death-bringing poison*' of the Tongue (another Qumran simile), out of whose '*mouth goes forth the blessing and cursing*' at the same time. It also uses the '*heart*' imagery, we have just seen Paul use above and used at Qumran with inverted effect. In James 3:13–14 this is tied, not insignificantly, to '*showing one's works in the Meekness of Wisdom*,' followed by the words: '*If you have bitter jealousy and contentiousness in your heart, do not boast or Lie against the Truth*.'

We have just seen how important this language of '*Truth*' is at Qumran, not to mention how Paul uses it in Galatians 3:1 and 4:16 to assert, in particular – just as in Colossians 3:9 – he '*does not Lie*.' Moreover it was, according to him, that by telling his communities '*the Truth*,' namely, that the Righteousness of the Law has been superseded by the death of Christ above, he has become their '*Enemy*.' In James 4:8–10, this kind of language is always followed by further requests to '*purify your hearts*,' '*humble yourselves*,' and '*do not slander one another*' which, just as the above, all have their direct counterparts in the literature of Qumran. As 4:11 puts this:

> He who speaks against (his) brother and judges his brother, speaks against the Law and judges the Law. But if you judge the Law, you are not a Doer of the Law, but a Judge.

These kinds of allusions are also tied in James to references to '*the Diabolos*' again (4:7) or '*animal*' or '*beastliness*' (3:15). But this is exactly the kind of phraseology we have already encountered in Rabbinic literature regarding the name '*Be'or*' (or *be'ir*/animal, '*o*' and '*i*' being largely interchangeable in Qumran epigraphy as we have seen) – in the Bible reckoned as the father at once of both '*Bela'*' and '*Balaam*.' We have also seen this imagery of '*biting*' and '*swallowing*' reflected in Paul in Galatians 5:15

and one can find it reflected in 2 Peter 2:15–16 and Jude 1:10 and 1:19 above, also evoking *'the error of Balaam'* – referred to in 2 Peter as *'the Son of Be'or who loved the Reward of Unrighteousness'* (here, of course, the *'Gemul'* / *'Gemulo'* language again). But it is the attack on *'Lying against the Truth'* in James 3:14 which is most pregnant in this regard and related, not only to Paul's claims of *'speaking Truth'* in Galatians 4:16 but the imagery of *'the Tongue,'* by which it is introduced in James 3:5–12. Nor can there be any doubt that this genre of imagery is generically related to or parallels that of the *'pouring out'* or *'spouting'* imagery applied to the depiction of *'the Lying Spouter'* at Qumran. In turn, it is related to *'mouth'* and *'lips'* imagery both here and throughout the literature at Qumran.

For instance, in James 3:15–16, the language that follows this allusion to *'the Tongue'* and *'Lying against the Truth'* is:

> *This is not the wisdom which comes down from above, but rather it is fleshly, animal-like, Demonic, for where jealousy and contentiousness are, there is confusion and every Evil Thing.*

We have already seen the same kind of imagery in Jude and 2 Peter above. In the Colossians passage recommending *'not Lying to one another,'* one has the same imagery of *'disobedience,'* *'anger,'* *'malice,'* and *'filthy language out of the mouth.'*

We can also see the same kind of recitations in the Community Rule in its enumeration of *'the Ways of the Spirit of Falsehood,'* as opposed to *'the Crown of Glory with the Garment of Majesty in Unending Light'* which *'the Sons of Truth and the Sons of Righteousness'* will enjoy. These are the two Spirits of Light and Darkness, Truth and Lying, exactly equivalent to the *'Two Ways'* in the early Church teaching document known as *The Didache.*[78] As this is put in the Nahum *Pesher*, *'those who lead Ephraim astray'* – whatever this esotericism *'Ephraim'* might mean (*'Nilvim,'* a cadre of new *'Gentile'* believers in the sense of being *'God-Fearers'*?[79]) – are specifically said *'to teach Lying and, with a Tongue full of Lies and deceitful lips, lead Many astray.'* This, of course, is the very opposite of the proper *'justifying'* activity of both the Damascus Document and Isaiah 53:11 of *'making Many Righteous,'* applied in the former to *'the Sons of Zadok'* and, in Pauline theology, to 'Jesus.'[80]

For James 3:1–8, delineating its view of this *'Tongue'* in the context of both who should or should not teach but also, as we have seen, with reference to *'stumbling'* and *'being driven by violent winds'*:

> *The Tongue is only a little member and boasts great things. But see how a little*

fire can kindle a large forest and the Tongue is a fire, a world of Unrighteousness. So the Tongue is set among our members, yet the polluter of the whole body, both setting on fire in the course of nature and being set on fire in Hell. For every species, both of beasts and birds, creeping things and sea creatures, is tamable and has been tamed by mankind, but none among men is able to tame the Tongue, (which is) an uncontrollable Evil, full of deadly venom.

Here, not only do we have the *'kindling,' 'fire,'* and *'Wrath of God'* imagery, used in CDv–vi to condemn those who *'polluted their Holy Spirit and opened their mouth with a Tongue of blasphemies against the Laws of the Covenant of God, saying they were not sure'*; but also the *'venom'*-language it uses in Columns VIII and XIX thereafter.

This intense concern over *'the Tongue'* in the Letter of James parallels a similar hatred of *'the Enemy'* in Pseudoclementine *Recognitions* and *'the Parable of the Tares'* in Matthew 13:24–44 – where, as we saw, the plants that he has planted would *'be gathered up'* (or *'uprooted'*)and *'cast into a Furnace of Fire'* – to say nothing of *'the Spouter of Lying'* in the Qumran tradition. In fact, in CDvIII.13/XIX.25-26, as we saw as well, the very same imagery of *'violent wind'* is applied to *'the Spouter of Lying'* as is applied to him here in James 3:4. There, too, we also heard about *'walking in wind'* or *'Spirit'* or *'pouring out wind'* or *'being of confused Spirit,'* and it is this which *'kindled God's Wrath on all his Assembly'* or *'Church.'*[81] It will be recalled, the imagery was based on Micah 2:6: *'they shall surely spout,'* which in 2:8 also refers to the *'Enemy,'* and Ezekiel 13:6–16 about *'the Builders of /'Daubers upon the wall,'*which also included allusion to Lying prophets *'deceiving the People,'* and the *'vanity'* or *'worthlessness of their Lying vision,'* not to mention *'making the heart of the Righteous sad'* over Lying, and *'strengthening the hand of the Wicked by promising him life'* (13:22).[82]

As we have also seen, these are *'the Daubers on the wall,'* referred to in both CDIV.19-20 and VIII.12-13/XIX.11-13, who followed *'Zaw Zaw ('So-and-So'), the Spouter,'* as it is said, *'He shall surely spout,' 'whose works God would visit'* and *'upon whom Wrath would be poured'* (in the unwillingness to utter the name of this inimical opponent there is clearly expressed the fear of powerful outside, secular forces).[83] We have already explained, too, that the *'Lying visions,'* referred to in Micah 2:6–8 and Ezekiel 13:10–16, involved *'crying Peace when there is no peace,'* which is just the point Josephus emphasizes regarding *'Saulos'*' role among *'all those desiring peace'* and accommodation with Rome in Jerusalem and harmonizes perfectly with Paul's approach, enunciated in Romans 13:1–8 on the Commandment *'to love your neighbor as yourself'* (thus!).

Not only do these allusions in CDvIII and XIX to *'the Lying Spouter'*'s '*pouring out wind*' and '*spouting to them*' begin with the allusion to '*the deadly Venom of Vipers and the cruel Poison of Asps*,' they end with allusion to '*rejecting the Commandments of God, forsaking them and turning aside in the stubbornness of their heart*,' all prototypical of the behavior of '*the Lying Spouter*' at Qumran. After comparison of this to Elisha's rebuke of Geha-zi, they move directly into evocation of '*the New Covenant in the Land of Damascus*" reference to '*betraying*' it and '*departing from (its) Fountain of Living Waters*' and '*not being reckoned in the Foundation of the People*.'[84] Not only do we have here the possible play on Paul's insistence in Galatians 3:21, above, about the Law '*being incapable of giving life*' but, again, also the language of '*being reckoned*,' applied by both Paul and James to Abraham and in '*MMT*' to its '*Royal*' addressee.

Here too there follows the typical expulsion from '*the Assembly of the Men of Perfect Holiness*' (again see Paul in 2 Corinthians 7:1 on '*Perfecting Holiness in the Fear of God*') because '*the manifestation of his works*' were not in conformance with '*the precise letter of the teaching of the Torah*.'[85] Once again, '*all the Holy Ones of the Most High have cursed him*,' nor is anyone '*to cooperate with him in purse* ('*Riches*') *or Mission*' ('*labor*'/ '*cAvodah*').[86] Here too, the Letter of James, in raising the issue of '*blessing and cursing*,' notes the contradiction of the same '*Tongue*,' '*blessing God the Father*,' '*curses men made according to the likeness of God*' (3:9–10).

As we just saw, in introducing the description of the Tongue's '*boast-ing*,' '*uncontrollable Evil*,' '*pollution*,' and '*death-giving Poison*' or '*Venom*,' we also hear about '*violent winds*' driven by a helmsman's '*rudder*' which is, in turn, also compared to '*the Tongue*' (3:4). In James too is the parallel imagery of '*kindling fire*.' While somewhat obscure at this point, perhaps purposefully, it also contains the variation on this Qumran allusion to '*the Fountain*' or '*Well*,' mentioned above, as well as these curious allusions to '*the Tongue*' both '*cursing*' and, in turn, '*being cursed*.'

It is at this point, too, ending its recitation on '*the Tongue*,' that it makes the charge that '*whoever makes himself a Friend of the World turns himself into an Enemy of God*' (4:4). That Paul already knows he is being termed '*a Friend of the World*' is made clear, as previously underscored, by his own statements about '*seeking to please men*' and his rhetorical assertion about his Gospel '*not being according to men*' in Galatians 1:10–11. He is such '*a Friend*' – or should we say '*Enemy*' – that, according to his detractors, he makes things too easy for such '*men*'; and it is precisely at this point, as should be recalled, that Paul twice resorts to using the '*cursing*' language of his opponents: '*If anyone teaches a gospel contrary to what you received* ('*even if an Angel from Heaven*'), *he is to be accursed*' (Galatians 1:8–9).

27

The Cup of the New Covenant
in His Blood

The First Description of '*the Man of Lies*' in the Damascus Document

Before going on to see the further treatment in the Habakkuk *Pesher* of this *genus* of '*Liar*' and his differences with '*the Righteous Teacher*,' we should look at the additional notices regarding this subject at the beginning of the Damascus Document which start towards the end of the Column One and run on into the first line of the Column Two where, once again, they end with the notice that '*the Anger of God was kindled against their Assembly*' and '*their works were unclean*' or '*polluted before Him.*'[1]

Not only is this point about '*their works being unclean before Him*' significant, but the Cairo Recension opens with the address to '*all the Knowers of Righteousness, who seek to understand the works of God*,' so paralleling Paul in Romans 10:3 above about those whose '*zeal for God*,' he admits, but which was '*not according to Knowledge.*' '*Being ignorant of God's Righteousness*,' these – as he puts it – '*sought to establish their*' own (again, note here the possible play on allusions in the '*Messianic*' vocabulary at Qumran to '*setting up*' or '*establishing*' – as in CDvii.16's '*setting up the Tabernacle of David which is fallen*' or in the quotation of 2 Samuel 7:12's the '*setting up of [his] seed after [him]*' in 4QFlorilegium,i.10 above – not '*submitting to God's Righteousness.*' By this, among other things, he obviously means (as in Romans 13:1–7) submitting to the power and Rule of the Roman Empire. His double entendres and innuendo here are always strong and worth remarking.

In CD1.3–4, these references to '*knowing Righteousness and understanding the works of God*' also end up in allusion to God hiding his face '*from His Temple and delivering them up to the sword.*' This, of course, was at the time of '*the First Visitation*' and '*the Era of the desolation of the Land*' when they '*spoke Rebellion against the Commandments of God as (given by) the hand of Moses*' as described in CDv.20–21 and vii.21–viii.3/xix.10–16 Nevertheless, because God '*remembered the Covenant of the First*' ('*the Forefathers*') and '*they understood their sinfulness and knew they were guilty men*' (that is, John the Baptist-like, they '*repented*'), '*He left a Remnant to Israel and did not deliver them up to be destroyed* ('*lechalah*' again).[2] As previously explained, the notice about '*the Forefathers*' here should be seen in terms of '*the First*' vs. '*the Last*' language Jesus is portrayed in the Gospels as employing in the Parables. But here '*the First*' are the Forefathers, Abraham, Isaac, Jacob, and Moses, and '*the Last*,' which Paul also applies to himself in 1 Corinthians 15:8–9, is '*the Last Generation*' and '*the Last Days*,' presumably the time of writing or the present.

It is at this point that the Righteous Teacher is introduced in the Damascus Document. It should be appreciated that this occurs after the description of the second, probably even the third (an even earlier one seemingly being at *the time Pharaoh 'pursued' Moses into the wilderness*), '*Visitation*' by God and how He '*caused to grow*' the Messianic '*Root of Planting from Israel and from Aaron.*' In the context of the coming of this '*Teacher of Righteousness*,' we hear that '*God raised him up*' (again, the language of '*setting up*' is important and the same as we just highlighted and as Paul is using in Romans 10:3 above, seemingly parodying this process) out of consideration for '*their works*' and because they '*sought Him with a whole heart.*'[3] Here not only do we have an evocation of the all-important '*Salvationary*' element of '*works*' again and the '*darash*'/'*seeking*' of '*the Doresh* ('*Seeker*') *ha-Torah*' above, but also the '*heart*' imagery that we have been encountering throughout our consideration of Paul and James.

In fact, as will be recalled, the Righteous Teacher was '*to guide them in the Way of His (God's) heart.*' Here too the '*heart*' imagery is combined with that of '*the Way*,' language employed repeatedly – as already pointed out – throughout Acts as an alternate way of referring to early Christianity in Palestine.[4] Not only is this '*preparation of the Way in the wilderness*' part and parcel of the vocabulary applied to John the Baptist's missionary activities in the Synoptics in exegesis of Isaiah 40:3 as well as parallel expositions of this in the Community Rule at Qumran; it explains the use of '*the Way*' terminology generally throughout the documents there and, for instance, in Acts. In fact, both here in CD1.15 and in the Last Column of 4QD, as we just saw, the opposite language is applied to '*the Pourer-out of Lying*'/'*Scoffer*' and '*the Peoples*,' namely, '*causing them to wander astray in a wilderness without a Way*' – one simply reversing the other.

Here, too, as in the Habakkuk *Pesher*, '*the Assembly of the Traitors*' are also introduced and described as '*Rebels against the Way*' and with them, of course, '*the Lying Scoffer.*' Just as in the Habakkuk *Pesher*, where '*the Traitors*' (there '*the Traitors to the New Covenant*' and/or '*the Last Days*,' also called '*the Covenant-Breakers and Violent Ones*') and '*the Man of Lies*' attend the Scriptural exegesis sessions of the Righteous Teacher/(High) Priest and '*did not believe*' what he told them was going to happen to His (God's)

People '*in the Last Generation*'; so here in the Damascus Document, again demonstrating the basic circularity of these documents, '*he made known to the Last Generations what God would do to in the Last Generation to the Congregation (Assembly) of Traitors*' (here *n.b.*, again the '*doing*' language).[5]

Just as with the quotations from Micah and Ezekiel in Columns IV and VIII/XIX about the Spouter's '*spouting*' and '*Lying visions*,' this is described in terms of a passage from Hosea 4:6 comparing Israel's '*straying*' or '*Rebelliousness*' to the '*straying*' of '*a Rebellious heifer*.'[6] It is this passage CDI.13-14 uses to introduce '*the Scoffer*' or '*Man of Jesting*' / '*Comedian, who poured over Israel the waters of Lying*.' Since the same vocabulary is used to describe what '*the Man of Scoffing*' or '*Comedian*' does here, as is used in 4QD later and in the Habakkuk *Pesher* to describe '*the Pourer out*' or '*Spouter of Lying*,' we can – as already explained – take these two to be identical. What he does is '*pour out Lying*,' here expressed in terms of '*causing them to wander astray in a trackless waste without a Way*.'

We have already seen that the '*leading astray*' or '*deceiving*' language is important where the activities of '*the Man of Lying*' are concerned and the opposite of the '*justifying*' or '*making Many Righteous*' activities, predicative of the Righteous Teacher – as well as how these were recapitulated in the Last Column of 4QD where '*the High Priest Commanding the Many*' condemns anyone '*rejecting the Laws found in the Torah of Moses*' and characterizes God as having '*caused the Peoples*' (Paul's '*Gentiles*') '*to wander astray in a trackless waste*' or '*a wilderness without a Way*.' But where Israel was concerned, as we have also seen, '*the Priest*' avers: '*You chose our Fathers and to their seed* (again, Paul's '*seed*' language above) *gave the Laws of Your Truth and the Ordinances off Your Holiness, which a man shall do and thereby live. And boundary markers were laid down for us. Those who cross over them You curse* (here, clearly, the very passages from Deuteronomy 27:26 and 30:6 that Paul is so disingenuously interpreting in Galatians 3:10 and 3:21 above, following which he then goes on to cite Habakkuk 2:4: '*the Righteous shall live by Faith*,' the Habakkuk *Pesher* will now go on to expound counter-indicating it).[44]

Moreover, Deuteronomy 30:6 *actually* refers to God '*circumcising your heart and that of your seed to love the Lord your God with all your heart*' to express the promise concerning '*thereby living*.' It is clear, too, that what is meant by the '*boundary marker*'-imagery here *is* the Law. So too for the description of '*the Pourer out of the Waters of Lying*' at the beginning of the Damascus Document: '*He brought low the Everlasting Heights, rebelling against the Pathways of Righteousness* (Paul's Righteousness '*by the Law*' in Galatians 3:21 and '*trying to establish their own Righteousness*' in Romans 10:3) *and removing the boundary markers which the First had marked out as their inheritance*.' There can be no doubt that what is being talked about so exaltedly is, once again, '*the Law*'; and '*the First*' are none other than the Patriarchs and Moses, the *Forefathers*, conceived of as having laid it down.

The text now turns to the effect of '*removing these Pathways of Right-eousness*' and '*boundary markers,*' once more resorting to the '*cursing*' and '*Covenant*' language of Deuteronomy 27–31 above, continuing:

> *for which reason He (God) called down on them the curses of His Covenant and delivered them up to the avenging sword of Vengeance of the Covenant.*

We have already remarked the importance of these notices about '*delivering up*' to those characterizing '*Judas Iscariot*' in the New Testament, who is also always described as '*delivering him up*.' The double reference to '*Vengeance*' reiterates similar such references in the '*cursing*' in the Community Rule, emphasizing just how terrible this '*Vengeance*' was going to be – in our view, as in the New Testament and the theology of the early Church, '*the avenging sword of the Romans* who, in the words of the Habakkuk *Pesher*, '*consume*' or '*eat all the Peoples year-by-year, delivering many Countries up to the sword.*'[7]

Curiously enough, '*Law-breaking*' activities of '*the Lying Spouter*' are tied, in the view of these extreme visionaries – who, just like the early Christians say they did, seem to have removed themselves from the struggle – to the coming '*Vengeance*' of the Romans. In their view, this '*Vengeance*' is going to be '*visited*' upon almost everyone, but they – much like the partisans of the '*Pella Flight*' Tradition after the death of James – seem to have removed themselves, as we have seen, to the Land across Jordan in the neighborhood of Damascus and beyond. This too is the thrust of the statement in CD1.21–II.1above, with which this section ends, that '*God's Wrath was kindled against their Congregation, devastating all their multitude, for their works were unclean before Him.*'

Interestingly enough, this is now tied to two quotations from Isaiah 30:10-30:13, also having to do with visionaries '*preferring illusions*' and '*looking for breaks*' in the Wall – presumably '*the Wall*' in Ezekiel 13:10 referred to in Columns IV and VIII/XIX, '*daubed upon by Lying Prophets,*' who '*cried Peace when there was no Peace.*' These passages from Isaiah 30:10–13 actually relate to the same subject as, not only Ezekiel 13:10, but also Micah 2:11 about the '*spouting*' of '*Lying Spouter*'s or visionaries and even use the same word, we have been following here, '*ma'as*'/'*reject,*' in this case '*rejecting this Word and trusting in oppression and guile*' (Isaiah 30:12). Here, too, is the language of '*Smooth Things,*' viz., '*prophesying Smooth Things and seeing delusions*' or '*jests*' ('*mahatalot,*' also a play here on the Hebrew word '*Halakot*'/'*Smooth Things*' – Isaiah 30:10).

Elsewhere, as in Columns II–IV of the Nahum *Pesher* at Qumran, '*prophesying Smooth Things*' from Isaiah 30:10 is expressed in terms of '*the Seekers after Smooth Things*,' usually tied, as we have seen, in some manner by almost all commentators to Pharisees and considered to be a play on their characteristic activity of '*seeking Halachot*' or '*seeking legal Traditions*.' I have extended this usage in the light of the claims by Paul of '*being by Law, a Pharisee*' and the consonant behaviour pattern of '*seeking accommodation with foreigners*' (the most perfect formulation of which is to be found in Romans 13:1–7 above, a completely anti-nationalist and non-'*Zealot*' text) to '*Pauline Christians*' as well.[8] In the Nahum *Pesher*, it will be recalled, this euphemism, '*Seekers after Smooth Things*,' is related – amid the imagery of '*walking in Lying and Deceitfulness in the Last Days*' and a '*Lying Tongue and Deceitful lips leading Many astray*' – to an underlying allusion in Nahum 3:1 to '*the City of Blood*.'[9]

Not only is this esotericism associated in Column II of 4QpNahum with the historical action by the Pharisees of *inviting foreign armies into Jerusalem in Alexander Jannaeus' time* (103–76 BC) – the paradigmatic act, as we would define it, of '*seeking accommodation with foreigners*' – but in the Third and Fourth Columns with '*the City of Ephraim*,' defined as '*the Seekers after Smooth Things at the End of Days*,' and reference to '*joining*' or '*Joiners*' ('*Nilvim*' in CDiv.3 above), clearly interpreted to include '*resident aliens*' or '*the stranger*' (*ger-nilveh*) – in this case, clearly meaning '*Gentiles*.'[10] This '*City of Blood*' imagery will have important ramifications as well when it comes to analyzing the activities of '*the Lying Spouter*' in the Habakkuk *Pesher* below.

There is, in fact, an extant commentary on these materials from Isaiah 30 at Qumran, but it is very fragmentary. Still, it does refer to this same '*Assembly*' or '*Congregation of the Seekers after Smooth Things who are in Jerusalem*,' '*the Last Days*,' and '*rejecting the Law*.'[11] There are also two just as fragmentary commentaries on Hosea and Micah, the first referring to adopting '*the Festivals of the Gentiles*'; and the second, '*the Spouter of Lying who leads the Simple astray*' though '*the Spouter*' and '*the Simple*' are nowhere mentioned in the underlying text from Micah 1:5–6. By contrast, it should be noted that '*Samaria*' is. While this allusion to '*the Spouter*' *clearly* links up with the allusions to '*he will surely spout*' in Micah 2:6 and '*walking in wind ('the Spirit') and Lying, spouting Lies*' in Micah 2:11, '*Samaria*' links up with '*the Simple of Ephraim*' in the Nahum *Pesher* above – '*Samaria*' and '*Ephraim*,' as already noted, being coextensive. This *Pesher* also contains a reference to '*the Righteous Teacher*' and '*those volunteering to join the Elect of God*.'[12] Not only do we have in this last allusion another variation on the language of '*joining*' but, seemingly, another reference to those 'Doers of Torah' ('the Elect') so disparaged by Paul but so important to the interpretation of Habakkuk 2:4 in the Habakkuk *Pesher*. For the Micah *Pesher*, anyhow, 'these will be saved on the Day of (Judgement).'[13] Again we can see this allusion to 'being saved' is eschatological, but we shall now find precisely this language, 'being saved on the Day of Judgement'– as already remarked – in the Habakkuk *Pesher* as well.

In the Damascus Document too, as we have seen, we now hear of another attack against 'the Righteous One,' probably to be identified with the Righteous Teacher and possibly James. The description of what these 'Seekers after Smooth Things' – who 'chose illusions (mahatalot from Isaiah 30:10 above) and watched for breaks, choosing the easiest way' (literally, as previously remarked, 'the choicest of the flock') – do, is very germane to our subject. What they did, as the text goes on to tell us and as we have seen, was 'justified the Wicked and condemned the Righteous,' 'transgressing the Covenant and breaking the Law' (the language of 'Covenant-breaking' again).[14]

This is an incredible description because, as already emphasized, it completely reverses what the proper 'justifying' activity in Column Four of the true 'Sons of Zadok' was considered to be, namely, 'justifying the Righteous and condemning the Wicked.' If one considers the word 'Wicked' ('Evil Ones') here in the Hebrew to include what Paul is calling in Galatians 2:15, 'Gentile Sinners,' then this phraseology, 'justifying the Wicked,' can be seen as exactly how Paul's 'justifying' activities – and, for that matter, those the Gospels predicate of 'Jesus' – might have been seen by his opponents, that is, as 'justifying the Sinners.' As Paul actually puts this in Galatians 2:15–16, 'Though by nature Jews and not Gentile Sinners, we know that a man is not justified by works of the Law but through Faith in Jesus Christ.'

What immediately follows at the end of Column One in the Damascus Document, as just alluded to, is what can only be considered to be a description of another attack on 'the Righteous Teacher,' led in our view by 'the Lying Scoffer.' As already suggested too, this in turn can be seen as the attack by 'the Enemy' Paul on 'the Righteous Teacher' James in the Temple – certainly in coordination with 'the High Priests' and presumably 'the Pharisees' – in the Forties, as recorded in the graphic description of the Pseudoclementine *Recognitions*.

Interestingly enough, as we just saw as well, in this passage the terminology 'Righteous Teacher' is abjured in favor of James' actual sobriquet, 'the Righteous' or 'Just One.' As this is described:

> they banded together against the soul of the Righteous One and against all the Walkers in Perfection, execrating their soul. And they pursued them with the sword, attempting to divide (or 'rejoicing in the division of') the People.

Nothing could be a better description of the attack on James and his followers in the Temple by Paul and his '*Violent*' colleagues, converted by Acts into '*the stoning of Stephen*', than this.

The Vision of the End and '*the Delay of the Parousia*'

Following the description of how the Liar '*rejected the Torah in the midst of their whole Assembly*' or '*Church*' and '*the Traitors*' did not come to the aid of '*the Righteous Teacher*' against him in Column V.8–12 and the '*tax-farming*' rapaciousnes and merciless brutality of '*the Kittim*' or '*the Romans*' in V.12–VI.11, the Habakkuk *Pesher* moves on in Columns VII–VIII to its interpretation of Habakkuk 2:3: '*If it tarries, wait for it*,' and Habakkuk 2:4: '*The Righteous shall live by his Faith*' and what, for our purposes, constitute the key passages of its whole exposition. These would also appear to have been crucial to and the climax of the author's entire presentation as well. It is surprising, therefore, that they have been so little considered by '*Consensus Scholars*' and the question naturally arises of '*why*'?

These interpretations actually begin at the end of Column VI with the exposition of Habakkuk 2:1–2. Though the text is, as usual, broken because it is the bottom of the column, it is clear that the underlying passage is from Habakkuk 2:1–2 speaking about '*standing up*' (our '*standing*' imagery again) and being a '*watchman*' of sorts. It reads:

> But I will stand up upon my Watchtower (Mishmartî) and take my stand upon my Fortress (Metzuri) and look (or '*spy*') out to see what He will say to me and wh(at I will ans)wer when I am reproved (or '*rebuked*' – Habakkuk 2:1).[33]

Habakkuk 2:2 continues: '*And the Lord answered and said, "Write down the vision and make it plain on tablets, so that he may read it on the run."*' Once again, we are in the realm of the '*visions*,' already encountered in Isaiah 30:10, Ezekiel 13:10, and Micah 2:6 above, now the '*true visions*' of the Prophet '*Habakkuk*' and '*the Righteous Teacher*,' not the '*Lying*' ones of '*the Lying Spouter*.' Here, too, is the allusion to '*being reproved*' or '*admonished*' and the reason, probably, it was applied to the exposition of Habakkuk 1:13 in the previous Column V.10–12 about '*the admonishment of the Righteous Teacher*' and '*the Traitors remaining silent*' and '*not coming to his aid*,' when '*the Man of Lying rejected the Torah in the midst of their whole Assembly*.' In this regard, it is worth remarking that this underlying Biblical passage from Habakkuk 1:13 contains the first reference to '*Wicked*' – in this case, '*the Wicked swallowing (balla^c) one more Righteous than he*,' as we saw, which will basically dominate the historical action of the rest of the *Pesher* (usually applied to 'the Wicked Priest' and 'the Righteous Teacher,' though here the meaning is a little more obscure).[16]

This passage from Habakkuk 2:1 is a very important one to the Qumran exegete because, as we saw, it is actually used at the end of the climactic exposition of 'the Zadokite Covenant' of Ezekiel 44:15 in the CDIV.10-12. To understand how, one must recall precisely what was said there. This exegesis of how 'the Sons of Zadok' (also referred to as 'the First Men of Holiness') 'justified the Righteous and condemned the Wicked' also was eschatological, meaning, it was connected to or evoked 'the Last Days.'[17]

This was followed by the James-style 'all those coming after them were to do according to the precise letter of the Torah, which the First (i.e., 'the Ancestors') had transmitted, until the Completion of the Era of these years'; and then, the assertion: 'According to the Covenant which God made with the First to remit their sins, so too would God make atonement through them' – meaning seemingly through or by 'the Sons of Zadok' or in succession to them. This, in turn, was immediately followed by, 'And with the Completion of the Era of the number of these years, there would be no more association with' or 'joining to the House of Judah' – apparently meaning, at least on the surface, that there would be no more specifically being Jews per se.

To this was added the note, as already alluded to, 'rather each man would stand on his own net' (metzudo) or 'Watchtower' (Metzuro). Here, not only will this archaic phraseology, 'House of Judah'– clearly an archaism for 'Jews' – also be important for the exposition of both Habakkuk 2:3 and 2:4 about to follow in 1QpHab,VII.5–VIII.3; but so is this passage from 2:1, 'taking one's stand upon one's watchtower and looking out' – now also about to be expounded as a prelude to these in VI.12-VII.5.

The problem is that in this phrase, as we saw, in Column IV.12 of the Cairo Damascus Document; the scribe redacted 'each man would stand on his own net'/'metzudo,' not 'watchtower' or 'fortress'/'Metzuro,' which really does make things obscure – seemingly miscopying dalet (D) for resh (R), virtually identical in written Hebrew.[18] But such a scribal error would be very understandable in view of the context of what follows in the Column IV.12–V.11, the 'Three Nets' (Metzudot) in which Belial 'catches Israel, transforming these things before them into three kind of Righteousness.'

Even were the substitution purposeful – meaning possibly, 'each man standing on his own record' or 'Righteousness' – still the language would clearly appear to be that of Habakkuk 2:1, now being subjected to exegesis here in the Habakkuk Pesher (VI.12–VII.8). Once again we have dramatic proof, if such were needed, of the basic homogeneity of all these documents – but what is even more startling, that the writer of the Damascus Document seems to be using the very same passage as the writer here in the Habakkuk *Pesher* – if so, intending us to understand that this, too, was the new state of affairs Habakkuk was envisioning.

Be this as it may, for the Habakkuk *Pesher* at this point at the end of Column VI.12–13, the '*standing upon one's Watchtower*' and '*looking*' or '*spying out to see what (God) would say*' is interpreted to refer to *both* the Prophet Habakkuk and '*the Righteous Teacher*' (God's exegete *par excellence*) and their mutual '*visions*' of '*the End Time*' – obviously an extremely important subject. Judging by the amount of space the Habakkuk *Pesher* devotes to it, almost the whole of Column VII, its writer thought so as well. The *Pesher*, in fact, is particularly graphic about this, connecting the '*reading and running*' in the underlying text from Habakkuk 2:2 to the exegetical mastery of the Righteous Teacher, '*to whom God made known all the Mysteries of the words of His Servants the Prophets.*' With regard to these, one should also recall the kind of '*revelations*' or '*apocalypseon*' Paul always claims to be having, in particular in Romans 16:25 and his proclamation of '*the Gospel of Jesus Christ, according to the revelation of the Mystery, kept secret of the times of the Ages and by the Prophetic Scripture, but now made plain.*' The parallel of this with the language being encountered here in the *Pesher* should be plain.

By contrast, here in the *Pesher* the reference is directly to the Righteous Teacher, who is being described in precisely the manner he was in the earlier scriptural exegesis sessions of '*the Priest*' ('*the High Priest*'/'*Righteous Teacher*') in Column II.8–9, '*in whose heart God has put the insight to interpret all the words of His Servants the Prophets*' – that is to say, *his heart was truly circumcised* as opposed to the Wicked Priest's or, even more germane to the material before us, those '*fleshy tablets of the heart*' upon which Paul claims to be writing '*Christ's Letter*' in 2 Corinthians 3:3 '*with the Spirit of the Living God.*' In fact, in the rest of the text from Habakkuk 2:2 being cited here: '*write down the vision and make it plain on tablets, so that he may read it on the run,*' we have allusion to the *very* '*tablets*' Paul is referring to. But now these '*tablets,*' upon which God told Habakkuk to write down his vision, are interpreted, as just indicated, in terms of '*the Righteous Teacher, to whom God make known all the Mysteries of the words of His Servants the Prophets.*'[19] If such were not clear in Column II earlier, it is now unmistakably so that, as in early Church texts about James, '*the Priest*'/'*High Priest*' here and '*the Righteous Teacher*' are *one and the same*.

Since the underlying passage from Habakkuk 2:3 that follows this speaks enigmatically about '*there shall yet be another vision of the Appointed Time, and it will speak of the End and it will not lie,*' the whole interpretation is then framed eschatologically, '*the End*' now being both '*the Last Generation*' and '*the Last End,*' just encountered in the Damascus

Document's exposition of '*the Sons of Zadok*' as '*the Elect of Israel, called by Name, who will stand up in the Last Days*' – '*the First Men of Holiness,*' '*who would justify the Righteous and condemn the Wicked*' as it were. So, once again, we are in the same exegetical milieu.

This language of '*the First*' vs. '*the Last*' is very important at Qumran, as we have seen, as it is in the New Testament. At Qumran, however, as should be evident, it is eschatological – this, despite the kinds of trivializations one encounters in prized allusions attributed to 'Jesus' in the Gospels, such as '*the First shall be Last and the Last shall be First*,' a '*code*' basically disqualifying Jews and enfranchising the new Gentile believers of Paul not difficult to decipher. At Qumran, it absolutely had to do with '*the Last Generation*' or '*Last End*' in which, the group writing these documents, clearly felt itself to be. In this regard, one should a final time remark Paul in 1 Corinthians 15:8, enumerating the post-Resurrection appearances of Jesus: '*and Last of all, as if to an abortion, he appeared to me.*'

The Habakkuk *Pesher*'s interpretation of Habakkuk's '*writing down his vision so he could read it on the run,*' reads, '*And God told Habakkuk to write down what was coming in the Last Generation, but he did not make known to him when the Age ('End') would be completed.*' Again one should immediately remark parallel New Testament phraseologies in sayings attributed to 'Jesus' in the Gospels, like '*not one jot or tittle shall pass away from the Law until all is completed*' or, even more germane, '*this Generation shall not pass away until all these things are completed.*'[20]

Attached to the next passage from Habakkuk 2:3 about '*there yet being another vision of the Appointed Time*' is an allusion in the underlying text, as we just saw, to '*it shall tell of the End and shall not lie,*' presumably harking back to citations from Isaiah 30:10 and Micah 2:6 relative to '*Lying visions*' and the '*spouting*' of '*the Lying Spouter*' in the Damascus Document above. Again, the appeal of such a Biblical text to Qumran exegetes or, for that matter, those in the early Church should be plain. One should, also, appreciate the kind of connections that could have been drawn to Paul with his repeated protestations to '*not Lying*' in the corpus attributed to him. The thrust given it in the *Pesher*, of course, is that the Righteous Teacher's interpretation is '*the Truth,*' as opposed to '*Lying*' ones like those of '*the Man of Lying*' or '*Lying Spouter.*' Nor, in this regard should one forget Paul's own protestations in Galatians 4:16: '*So, by speaking Truth to you, your Enemy have I become?*'

Here the interpretation of '*the Righteous Teacher*' is actually given, namely that '*the Last Age*' or '*the Final End will be extended and exceed all that the Prophets have foretold, because the Mysteries of God are astonishing.*'[21] As already suggested, anyone familiar with early Christian history will immediately recognize this interpretation as equivalent to what goes in modern parlance as *'the Delay of the Parousia'* or *'the Delay of the Second Coming'* or *'Return of Christ'* – and as anyone with this understanding will appreciate, too, this *'Delay'* is still going on. But here in the Habakkuk *Pesher*, we actually have the scriptural warrant for it – at least from the Qumran perspective – Habakkuk 2:3. Not only this, it leads up to and actually introduces the Qumran exposition of Habakkuk 2:4, *'the Righteous shall live by his Faith.'* Even perhaps more significantly, it was in the Scriptural exegesis of the Righteous Teacher of *'the Appointed Time'* and *'the End'* of Habakkuk 2:3 that this interpretation first appears to have been made, at least this would appear to be the purport of the text before us – a startling and even eye-opening conclusion.

'If it Tarries, Wait for it'

The sense of this interpretation is reinforced and further expounded in the exposition of the second half of Habakkuk 2:3: *'If it tarries, wait for it, for it will surely come and not be late.'* Of course, as the Habakkuk *Pesher* turns this around, it will *'be late'* or *'delayed'* in view of the events transpiring in Palestine before the eyes of the exegete – *very late*. In any event we have seen that this is typical of Qumran usage, just as it is New Testament usage, which sometimes even changes the phraseology of an underlying text in favor of a given exegesis, not to mention reversing it.

One sees a variation of this in John 21:22–23's portrait of Jesus telling one of his *'Disciples,'* in his post-Resurrection appearance along the shores of the Sea of Galilee to them, *'to remain'* (another significant usage at Qumran) or *'wait for (him) until (he) comes.'* In this case, it is *'the Disciple Jesus loved'* who is told to *'abide'* his coming. It should be noted, too, that this notion of *'waiting on the Lord'* or patiently for *'the God of Judgement'* is part and parcel of the eschatology of Isaiah 30:18, which we just highlighted, directly following the material about visionaries *'foretelling Smooth Things,'* so integral to the presentation of *'the Liar'* and his *'Covenant-Breaking'* associates in the Damascus Document above. It is also part and parcel of the ideology of James 5:7 on being patient, because *'the coming of the Lord is drawing near.'*

At this point the Habakkuk *Pesher*, VII.10–11, introduces the terminology, *'the Doers of the Torah'* in apposition, significantly, to *'the Men of Truth'* and the analogue to which has already been encountered several times in James applied to those *'speaking against the Law and judging it'* and to opposite effect by Paul in Galatians 3:10, quoting Deuteronomy 27:26 above, or Galatians 5:3 cautioning that *'circumcision'* requires one to *'do the*

Law.' Evoking this terminology here, so much a part of the Letter attributed to James and so disparaged by Paul, is of the profoundest importance. This is particularly true since, as if by way of emphasis, it is then immediately introduced into the exegesis of Habakkuk 2:4 that follows, a fundamental proof-text we have already seen Paul expound on behalf of '*Gentile*' non-'*Torah-Doers*' and bringing '*Salvation*' to *Gentiles* generally.

Here in the *Pesher*, it is connected – as just remarked – to another concept important to the ideology of Paul and James, '*the Men of Truth doing the Torah*' or '*Torah-Doers*.' We have already seen how intent Paul is that by telling his communities '*the Truth*' he should not be viewed as their '*Enemy*' (Galatians 4:16) and telling '*the Truth*' about the prophecies so dear to God, at least as he sees this to be. This is particularly the case regarding Abraham's '*Faith*' in Genesis 15:6 but also, as we have seen, the '*Salvation by Faith*' he sees in Habakkuk 2:4.

This would relate to '*the Truth of the Gospel*' (Galatians 2:5 and 2:14) or '*the Truth of Christ*' and '*of the Cross*' (2 Corinthians 11:10) as well. In Romans 1:18–25, for instance (actually evoking Habakkuk 2:4), he calls down '*the Wrath of God in Heaven*' upon those who '*disguise the Truth in Unrighteousness*' or '*change God's Truth into a Lie*' and, later, again speaking about the '*Truth in Christ*,' he reiterates his assurance elsewhere that he '*does not lie*' (Romans 9:1). However, here in the Habakkuk *Pesher*, the phraseology '*the Men of Truth who do the Torah*' counter-indicates those having the opposite or '*Lying*' interpretation of these pivotal passages as, for instance, someone of the *genus* of '*the Lying Spouter*' it so reviles.

It is for this reason that this allusion to '*it will not Lie*' in the underlying text of Habakkuk 2:3 is so important to the exegetes, meaning that the eschatological exegesis that is to follow will not be a '*Lying*' one (like some others – as, for example, those of '*the Spouter of Lying*'). Furthermore, because it seems to restrict the exegesis to '*the Men of Truth who do the Torah*,' the implication is that *it does not apply to those who do not*. One cannot stress the emphasis on '*Torah-doing*' here too much. It will reappear four columns later in 1QpHab, XII.4–5 in the description of the '*conspiracy to destroy the Poor*,' described there too as '*the Simple of Judah who do the Torah*' (note again, not only the usual emphasis on '*Torah-doing*' but also the archaizing allusion to '*Judah*' to mean, simply, '*Jews*').

We have already delineated many of the allusions to '*Doers*' and '*doing*' (in Hebrew, based on the same root as '*works*') throughout the Qumran corpus. The same is true in James, where we also heard about '*the Doers of the word*' and '*the Doers of the word of Truth*' (1:18–22), not to mention – when condemning '*rancor and bitter jealousy in (one's) heart*' – '*boasting and Lying against the Truth*' (3:14) and the typically-Qumran '*straying from the*

Truth' (5:19). For its part, the *Pesher* in its exposition of Habakkuk 2:3 goes one better, repeating this word *'Truth'* as if for emphasis:

> This concerns the Men of Truth, the Doers of Torah, whose hands shall not slacken from the Service of Truth, though the Last Age be extended.[22]

This is the same construct, *'Last Age'* or *'End Time,'* used in the previous *Pesher* in VII.5–8 first evoking this *'Delay of the Last Era.'* It now continues somewhat formulaically:

> For all the Ages of God come to their appointed End as He determined (them) in the Mysteries of His insight.

Again, it would not be without profit to compare this to Paul in Romans 16:25 on *'the revelation of the Mystery kept secret in the Times of the Ages.'*

But there is another usage, we have been following, which is introduced here: *'labor'* or *'work'* – not 'Jamesian' works, which in Hebrew is based on a different root – but *'works'* in the sense of *'Service'* or *'Mission.'* We have been observing this usage, both in Paul's Letters and at Qumran, in documents like the Community Rule and Damascus Document.[23] It is not to be confused with *'Salvationary'* works, but rather simply with *'work'* as *'work'* or, if one prefers, *'Service,'* or *'Mission.'*

Not only is this used in excommunication texts at Qumran, banning having anything to do with such a person either *'in service or purse'*; but two columns later in 1QpHab,x.9–12, it will have important ramifications in the evaluation of *'the Lying Spouter'*'s *'labor'* or *'Service'* and the *'worthlessness'* of the *'Service'* with which he *'tired out Many'* (by *'instructing them in works of Lying'* – these now proper eschatological *'works'*) and *'the Assembly he erected upon Lying'* for his own *'Glorification.'* This, too, is something of the thrust of Paul's contemptuous reference in 2 Corinthians 11:15 to *'the Servants of Righteousness'* – only reversed – whom he really thinks are *'Servants of Satan'* and *'whose End (in another satirical play and reversal) shall be according to their works'*!

In the *Pesher* in VII.10–14 about *'not slackening in the Service of Truth though the Last Age be prolonged before them,'* the sense is, once again, reversed to that of *'Truthful Service'* not, as three columns later, the *'worthless Service'* of *'the Lying Spouter.'* But 1QpHab,x.10–12 restricts the application of Habakkuk 2:3 only to *'the Servants of Righteousness'* or *'the Men of Truth who do the Torah.'* That is to say, it is only to such persons that *'the Righteous Teacher'*'s exegesis about the *'Delay of the Last Age'* or *'End Time'* (*'the Parousia'*) applies. This will have particular relevance now for the exegesis of Habakkuk 2:4 that follows and its clear anti-Pauline thrust.

Since we are at the end of Column Seven, the text is again fragmentary, but the *Pesher* is quite clear. It has to do with the first phrase from Habakkuk 2:4: '*Behold, his soul is puffed up and not Straight* (or '*Upright*') *within him*,' the language of '*straightening*' being evocative of that of '*straightening the Way in the wilderness*' both in the Community Rule and as it is applied to John the Baptist in New Testament Scripture. As already underscored, Paul is also playing on this imagery of being '*puffed up*' and uses it to introduce his observations about the '*weak*' brothers whose '*conscience are defiled*' and '*stumble*' over the issue of '*meat*' and dietary regulations in general in 1 Corinthians 8:1–13.

As we have seen, specifically concentrating on '*eating things sacrificed to idols*' (8:1), his attacks here are clearly directed against the Jerusalem Leadership, parodying two of their favorite pretenses: superior '*Knowledge*' and '*loving God*' (or their '*Piety*' – also a favorite pretense of those Josephus is calling '*Essenes*'). As Paul expresses this in his own inimitable way, '*Knowledge puffs up*' whereas '*loving God*' – which they ought to espouse (again more contemptuous reversal, while at the same time complimenting his own '*architectural*' activities) – '*builds up*.' Put in another way, if they followed his prescriptions, then their '*weak consciences*' would '*be built up enough to eat things sacrificed to idols*' (8:10) not *vice versa*. The *Pesher* (1QpHab,x.10), too, will presently use this '*building*' imagery when it comes to describing the activities of '*the Liar*.'

The exposition of this in the *Pesher*, as it stands in VII.14–16, also plays on the allusion to '*puffed up*' (a homophone in Hebrew of the word '*doubled*'). Pregnantly, this is now expressed in terms of how '*their Sins will be doubled upon them and they will not be pleased with their Judgement*.'[24] That it has to do with '*Judgement*' – in this instance, most certainly, '*the Last Judgement*,' which Paul too is evoking in his aspersion about '*the End*' of the '*Servants of Righteousness*' in 2 Corinthians 11:15 above – is undeniable and will have decisive meaning for the *Pesher* that now follows on the second part of Habakkuk 2:4, the most important one of the whole Commentary and perhaps all the literature at Qumran.

That the *Pesher* on Habakkuk 2:4 is eschatological, too, is clear from everything that has gone before and the repeated references to '*the Final Age*'/'*Last End*' in the exposition of Habakkuk 2:3 preceding it. It is also clear from several additional usages within the *Pesher* itself. This idea of '*Judgement*,' having to do with the kind of '*tarrying*' and '*extension*'/'*delay of the End Time*'/'*Final Age*' and the counseling of '*patience until the coming of the Lord*' and '*seeing the End of the Lord*' is also part and parcel of the last Chapter of the Letter of James, as we have seen (James 5:7–11). There it is accompanied by allusion to '*the Judge*,' who '*is able to save and destroy*' (4:12) '*standing before the door*' (5:9) – also the imagery of the Islamic '*Imam*.'

The Exposition of Habakkuk 2:4, '*the Righteous shall Live by His Faith*,' in the Habakkuk *Pesher*

We are now at the most crucial *Pesher* of all, the interpretation of Habakkuk 2:4, '*the Righteous shall live by his Faith*,' at Qumran. Unlike Paul's citation in Galatians 3:11 and Romans 1:17, the possessive pronoun has not been dropped from '*live by his Faith*' and the phraseology is correct. It reads: '*Its interpretation relates to*' or '*concerns all the Doers of the Torah in the House of Judah*.' The phraseology '*Osei ha-Torah*,' from the previous *Pesher* on Habakkuk 2:3, is actually picked up and repeated again. Nor is there any doubting the meaning of the usage '*House of Judah*' here.

We have just encountered it in the allusion to '*each man standing on his own net*' or '*Watchtower*' and '*with the Completion of the Era of the number of these years, there shall be no more joining to the House of Judah*' in the conclusion of the eschatological interpretation of Ezekiel's '*Zadokite Covenant*' in CDiv.10–11 above. It is simply an archaizing or grandiloquent way of saying '*Jews*.' Once again, we have the linking of these two key expositions at Qumran. It is also paralleled by another expression, also involving '*doing the Torah*,' that follows four columns later in the *Pesher* in exposition of '*the dumb beasts*,' as we just saw in xii.3–5, '*the Simple of Judah doing the Torah*,' identified with the '*Ebionim*' or '*the Poor*,' whom – along with '*the Righteous Teacher*' – '*the Wicked Priest*' also '*destroys*.'

Now we can take the thrust of this expression, '*House of Judah*,' to be double-edged or doubly attributive. Just as the James-like recommendation of '*patience*' – in the eschatological exegesis preceding it relating to '*the Delay of the Parousia*' in viii.9–12 – is circumscribed to '*the 'Osei ha-Torah*' or '*Torah-Doers, whose hand would not slacken in the Service of Truth though the Final Age would be extended beyond anything the Prophets foretold*'; here the efficacy of Habakkuk 2:4 is, not only circumscribed to '*the Doers of the Torah*,' but now there is an additional qualification: *these must be native-born Jews as well*.

That the thrust of this is explosive should be obvious. To state the contrapositive: Habakkuk 2:4 *does not apply to non-Torah-doing non-Jews*, that is, *non-Torah-doing Gentiles*. It does not even apply to *non-Torah-doing Jews*. Put in another way, this *Pesher* is stating that Habakkuk 2:4 *should not be applied to Gentiles at all*, as Paul does. This qualification in its applicability would appear to be purposefully inserted in the exegesis and *directed against someone*. There can be little doubt *whom*. In addition, it clears up a lot of misunderstandings about the way Scripture is used in the rather free and eclectic manner of Paul or, for that matter, by the New Testament generally. Nor can this limitation in the scope of the applicability of the *Pesher* on Habakkuk 2:4 be thought of as being accidental. It would appear to be framed precisely with foreknowledge of the position of '*the Man of Lies*' or the Pauline position on these passages and issues in mind and, *a priori*, to *disqualify them* – the only disqualification possible given the manner and style of Pauline argumentation as we have reviewed it. It is a very powerful argument indeed and just what one would have expected from a *native-born Jewish Community* interested in the apocalyptic and eschatological interpretation of Scripture as well.

What it does is preclude the Pauline interpretation of this passage out of which, as we have seen, much of the theology about the '*Redeeming*' nature of 'Jesus'' death in Galatians 3:13 and the extension of '*the Power of God unto Salvation to everyone that believes, both to Jew first and to Greek*' in Romans 1:16, emerges. It is also an extremely telling dating tool for the *Pesher* as a whole, since it shows that the text could not have been written – external parameters such as A.M.S Radiocarbon Dating notwithstanding – before this theological position was enunciated. This is what *dating according to the internal data really means*.

The text now moves on to the rest of its interpretation of Habakkuk 2:4: '*The Righteous shall live by his Faith*,' which, given the presentation we have already encountered in James, must be seen as '*Jamesian*.' It reads:

> Its interpretation concerns all the Torah-Doers in the House of Judah whom God will save from the House of Judgement, because of their works (or '*suffering works*' – '*camal*' as in Isaiah 53:11) and their Faith in the Righteous Teacher.[25]

This is nothing less than '*Faith working with works*' or '*Faith made Perfect*' or '*complete by works*,' given in riposte to the '*Empty Man*''s interpretation of how '*Abraham was justified*' and/or '*saved*' in James 2:20–24.

It is also expressed, as we saw, in James 2:14 in the following manner: '*If someone says he has Faith, but does not have works, can Faith save him*'? The individual making such claims, also interpreting Habakkuk 2:4 and presumably identified with '*the Tongue*' in James 3:5–8, must be seen as the same person who – as opposed to this believing Abraham, '*the Friend of God*' – by making himself '*a Friend to the world transformed himself into the Enemy of God*.' In fact, the allusion to '*save*' here (Hebrew: '*yizzil*') is very important. Its import has usually been missed by most scholars who, because of generally poor translations, see what we have before us here as simply a mundane '*courtroom*' confrontation of some kind.[26] But we have already encountered this usage 'save' in James, not only as regarding 'the Doers of the Word' and 'the Doer of the work' above, but also in the prelude to its discussion of 'Faith vs. works' where, after quoting 'the Royal Law according to the Scripture' and 'keeping the whole Law, while stumbling on one small point,' it alludes to how Abraham was 'saved.'

Paul, as we saw, also uses the term following his discussion of how Abraham was saved in Romans 4:1–5:5. This occurs in conjunction with allusion to 'being justified by his blood' and how, 'having previously been Enemies, we are reconciled to God by the death of His son' and 'saved by his life' in 5:9–10. He, also, alludes to it in 1 Corinthians 15:1–2, evoking the Gospel 'in which you stand, by which you are also being saved' in conjunction with the clear Qumran language of 'holding fast' to his preaching and 'not believing in vain.' In 1 Corinthians 15:14, this becomes: 'If Christ has not been resurrected, then our preaching is worthless and your Faith too is worthless.' These kinds of allusions to 'believing in vain' and 'being worthless' will now recur, as we just saw, in the later Pesher in x.10–12 on Habakkuk 2:12–13, evaluating 'the Spouter of Lying''s 'vain Service' and 'worthless works.'

That we are dealing, where this passage from Habakkuk 2:4 is concerned, as just signaled, with 'Judgement' or 'the Last Judgement' is clear from just about every text quoting it from Paul to James and to these documents from Qumran. We have shown how this term 'House of Judgement,' used here in conjunction with the allusion to 'being saved' in 1QpHab,VIII.2, is again used two columns further along in x.3–5 to specifically describe the 'decision of Judgement that God would decree in making His Judgement in the midst of many Peoples,' in particular, upon 'the Wicked Priest.' 'There (God) would arraign him and condemn him in their midst and judge him with fire and brimstone,' an obvious picture of Hell-Fire or what, in ordinary parlance, usually goes by the title of 'the Last Judgement.'

In such a context, there can be no doubt of the eschatological nature of the usage, 'House of Judgement' (not 'condemned house' as in some translations[27]) from which 'God would save them' (yizzilam); and that it means something like the actual 'Decree of Judgement, God would make in the midst of Many Peoples,' which we also just saw pictured in Columns IV.14–V.5 leading up to the first (seemingly verbal, though it may have been physical) confrontation between 'the Man of Lying' and 'the Righteous Teacher.'

The basically eschatological nature of the Pesher is absolutely confirmed, further along in Columns XII.10–XIII.4, at the end with two clear references to 'the Day of Judgement,' at the time of which 'God would destroy all the Servants of Idols – here again, as we saw, the reference to 'Servants' and/or 'Service' or 'labor' – and Evil Ones from off the Earth.'[28] This is introduced by allusion to, in interpretation of Habakkuk 2:18 above, *all the idols of the Nations, which they create in order to serve and worship them. These will not save them on the Day of Judgement (thus!).*

Here, not only do we again have the usages *'serve'* and *'the Day of Judgement'*; but the use of the word *'saved'* (*'yizzilum,'* exactly the same phrase that was used – except it is plural for *'idols'* – in the eschatological exegesis of Habakkuk 2:14 earlier) to express the ideological thought of *'being saved from the Last Judgement'* is definitive. As just noted too, this is precisely the way the term is being used in the small fragment of the *Pesher* on Micah 1:5, which seems to refer to *'the Doers of the Torah in the Community Council'* as *'those who will be saved on the Day of Judgement'* as well.

Where the exegesis of Habakkuk 2:4 in VII.17–VIII.3 specifically is concerned, both the allusion to *'saved'* and the one to *'works'*– *'suffering works'* or *'spiritual toil'* (as we saw, *'˓amal'* in the text) – are important. In the general interpretation of Qumran materials that one reads, the whole eschatological nature of the *'Salvation'*-situation before us here in the *Pesher* is for the most part either completely ignored or missed. As we have seen, the *'saving'* (*'yizzilam'* in the text), that is occurring, is simply taken as relating to some real *'trial'* or *'courtroom'* scenario, from which either *'the Righteous'* or *'all the Torah-Doers in the House of Judah'* (i.e., *'all Torah-doing Jews'*) *'were to be saved from the House of Judgement.'* This is as silly as thinking that being made to *'drink the Cup of the Wrath of God,'* in the exegesis about *'the Wicked Priest'* that follows in XI.2–XII.6, has to do with the Wicked Priest *'getting drunk'* or *'being a drunkard'*! Unfortunately, this is the analytical level on which a good deal of studies in the field of Qumran has taken place – even at some of our greatest universities – and still does. An interpretation of this kind, so lacking in literary-critical insight, is as senseless as it is absurd; but this is the reason the struggle in this field took place, witnessed, as it turned out, (fortunately) by a good part of the public at large – enabling it to draw its own conclusions.

Not only is the eschatological effect of this passage restricted only to *'Torah-Doing Jews'* and not *'non-Torah-Doing non-Jews'* as, for example, the kind towards which the *'Salvationary'* activities of the Paul's so-called *'Gentile Mission'* were directed. As if with the competing Pauline exegesis in the New Testament in mind, the *'saving'* being referred to in this *Pesher* is actually *'saving'* in the sense of *'Salvation'* and – as it is at the end of the *Pesher* – the sense of the *'saving'* in this sequence about being *'saved from the House of Judgement'* is very definitely eschatological. This is how the Hebrew verb *'saved'* (*'yizzil'*) is being used here, as it is in Paul.[29]

Aside from the other examples cited above, another good example of the use of this term by Paul comes in 1 Thessalonians 2:15, the passage in which – operating within the parameters of the '*Friend of God*,' '*seeking to please men*,' and '*Enemy*' allusions – he makes the baldest of his '*blood libel*' charges against '*the Jews who both killed the Lord Jesus and their own Prophets*' too. As we have explained, these have even been picked up and mindlessly repeated in documents like the Koran, so that now they have come to be seen as truisms and to dominate the thinking of Western Mankind. His conclusion, as several times underscored, is that '*they*' ('*the Jews*' now, not himself) were, therefore, '*not pleasing to God* (the language the Community Rule applies in reverse to '*the Community Council*'[30]) *and the Enemies of all Men.*' Can there by any doubt that he is operating within the framework of the '*attempting to please men*'/'*Enemy*' accusations?

Directly after this, he makes another interesting charge: that '*the Jews*'

> *are forbidding us to speak to the Peoples (Ethnesin) so that they may be saved, so that their Sins may be filled up always* (this second '*so*' clearly meaning, as he would put it, '*the Jews*'). *But the Wrath (of God) will come upon them to the fullest* (1 Thessalonians 2:16).

Here, not only do we have the double use of the phraseology '*filling*' which we have been following in many of the overlapping Talmudic and Gospels episodes above – to say nothing of the '*Wrath of God*' we have been following in the several characterizations of the Damascus Document as well; but he actually seems to be using the same double entendres of the Habakkuk *Pesher's* interpretation of the first part of Habakkuk 2:4, '*his soul is puffed up and not upright within him*,' which played on and transmuted the Hebrew, '*puffed up*' (*ʿuphlah*), to produce '*their doubling*' or '*filling up their Sins upon themselves*' (*yichaphlu*).[31]

This is quite an amazing turn-about and confluence of both vocabulary and themes. Of course, Paul does not really mean that all Jews '*are forbidding (him) to speak to the Peoples, so that they may be saved*' but, quite obviously, the *Jewish* Leadership of '*the Jerusalem Church*' and James and his associates, that is, '*those of the Circumcision*' or, as he also calls it '*the Concision*,' to whom such a circumstance more appropriately pertained. Nor can there be any doubt what his allusion to '*saving*' means here. Moreover, as we just signaled, he is even using the eschatological language of '*the Wrath of God*,' but he is doing so even more specifically in the manner encountered in the Habakkuk *Pesher's* presentation in these columns of '*the Cup of the Wrath of God*' which would '*have to be drunken to its fill.*'[32]

Furthermore here, too, he is bearing out precisely what is being said, as well, in the Habakkuk *Pesher* in Column x.5–12 in discussing the '*Emptiness*' of the '*ʿamal*' ('*suffering works*') taught by '*the Spouter of Lying*' and how he 'instructed them in works of Lying' – this, it should be appreciated, in interpretation of passages from Habakkuk 2:12–13 about 'building a City upon Blood' and 'the Peoples laboring for the sake of Fire' and 'tiring themselves out for the sake of Nothingness' or 'Emptiness,' preceding 2:14: 'the Earth being filled with the Knowledge of the Glory of God like waters covering the sea' (here, the 'filling' language from the opposite perspective).[33]

Not only would these 'works' (that is, 'the works of Lying' taught by 'the Lying Spouter') be 'in vain' or 'for Nothingness' – literally, 'for Emptiness'; but 'the Many,' being 'instructed' in them by him, 'would come to the (same) Judgements of Fire, with which they blasphemed and vilified the Elect of God' – these last, it will be recalled, identified in the Psalm 37 Pesher with 'the Assembly of the Poor'; in the Damascus Document, 'the Sons of Zadok'; and in the Micah Pesher, seemingly, 'the Doers of the Torah in the Community Council' who would 'be saved on the Day of Judgement.'[34]

The second usage found here, 'ʿamal'/'works' or 'suffering works,' is interesting as well. As we have to some extent already observed, it differs slightly from the 'works' language we have been following at Qumran and in the Letter of James – based on the Hebrew root 'to do' (therefore, the interesting 'Doers of the Torah' and the general stress on 'doing' throughout the Letter of James and the Dead Sea Scrolls in general – in the Psalm 37 Pesher even, 'the Assembly or 'Church of His Elect, the Doers of His will'[35]).

'ʿAmal' seems to have been slightly more eschatological and it occurs in several interesting places, most notably in the language of the famous 'Suffering Servant' Messianic proof-text from Isaiah 53:11f., so much a part of Scriptural expectation in Christianity and – because of the use of this term 'ʿamal' and other usages, such as 'making Righteous' and 'the Many,' here in the Pesher on Habakkuk 2:4 and elsewhere in the corpus – probably at Qumran as well. In Isaiah 53, this read: 'by his Knowledge (in Greek, 'Gnosis'), the Righteous One, My Servant (again 'Zaddik' and consequently another 'Zaddik' text), will justify' or 'make Many Righteous and their Sins will he bear' and was attached to an allusion to: 'and he will see by the ʿamal of his soul,' seemingly meaning, 'the spiritual travail' or 'suffering of his soul.'

Again, this 'ʿamal' is probably best translated by the term 'works' in the sense of 'suffering works,' but perhaps even more accurately, 'works with soteriological' or 'eschatological effect.' It would appear to be purposefully introduced both at this point in VIII.2 and earlier in the Pesher as descriptive of how – along with 'their Faith' – the Righteous were to 'be saved.' This is the way it is also used in The Children of Salvation (Yeshaʿ) and the Mystery of Existence text, which others call 'A Sapiential Work' (whatever this might mean), but which I and my colleague, Professor Wise, published too and named accordingly.[36] Following allusion to 'the Salvation of

His works' and, in the context of one to *'justifying by His Judgement'*; the evocation of this *'ʿamal'* – used as a verb – leads directly into reference to *'the Children of Salvation'* (here *'Yeshaʿ'* as in the concluding material in CDxx.20) *'inheriting Glory'* and, again, the *'Poor One'* (*Ebion*).[37]

A similar idea of making atonement *'by doing Judgement and suffering travail'* occurs in the Community Rule's description of the Community Council.[38] In undergoing this, its members are not only said to *'keep Faith in the Land with steadfastness and a humble Spirit'* but *'to atone for the Land and pay the Wicked their reward'* (again *'gemulam'*) – the language of Isaiah 3:10–11 we saw introduced into the Habakkuk *Pesher's* description of how *'the Cup of the Wrath of God would swallow'* the Wicked Priest, *'paying him the reward with which he rewarded the Poor'* (*n.b.*, all the similar language circles again).[39] Thus they become *'a Precious Cornerstone'* and *'sweet fragrance of Righteousness,' 'well-pleasing to God'* (the language we just saw Paul use in 1 Thessalonians 2:15 above to disqualify Jews *'Christ-Killers'*), *'establishing'* both *'the Council of the Community upon Truth as an Eternal Plantation'* and *'the Holy Spirit according to Everlasting Truth'* – more interesting language circles and all concepts that should by now be familiar.[40]

The allusion to this *'ʿamal'* also reoccurs, as just underscored – in our view purposefully – two columns later in 1QpHab,x.12 where the *'worthless Service'* and *'Empty'* teaching of *'the Spouter of Lying'* are subjected to *fulsome* rebuke (this time our play *is* purposeful). That, in addition, this *'ʿamal'* is also part and parcel of the language of Isaiah 53:11–12:

> *for he shall bear their Sins...because he poured out his soul unto death...and the sins of the Many he bore and made intercession for their iniquities,*

could not have failed to make its impression on the sectaries at Qumran, given their ideological outlook. Moreover, we have already seen the evocation of key passages from Isaiah 52-56 in the exegeses of CDvi above.

This is certainly the case, too, where the language of *'My Servant the Zaddik justifying Many'* is concerned introducing this. In fact, at Qumran the terminology, *'the Many,'* as already several times explained, was the designation for the rank and file of the Community, the presumable recipients, as per *'Christian'* re-presentation, of the *'justifying'* activity of *'the Righteous Teacher'* or *'the Zaddik.'* That this same *'ʿamal'* will now reappear as an extremely important element in the *Pesher's* final scathing evaluation of the Spouter of Lying's *'building'* activities clinches the case for the centrality of this concept as well as the parameters of Isaiah 53:11–12 – so important to early Christian exegesis – at Qumran.

Therefore, what we have here in this exegesis of Habakkuk 2:4 at

Qumran is nothing less than astonishing. What it appears to be is the 'Jamesian' position on this passage, '*the Righteous shall live by his Faith*,' before it was reversed in the '*Gentilizing*' Pauline exegesis, with which we are all now so familiar. With this new understanding we can now see that, as opposed to Pauline exegesis, not only does the *Pesher* in VIII.1–3 restrict the efficacy of Habakkuk 2:4 solely to '*Torah-doing members of the House of Judah*' – that is, '*Torah-Doing Jews*' – or, at the very least, those who have made formal *conversion via circumcision to this* '*House*,' '*joining such Torah-Doers*' (contrary to the demands of a Paul); but, perhaps even more importantly, a man '*will be saved*' from '*the decree of Judgement*' God *would pronounce* '*in the midst of many Nations*' (or '*the Last Judgement*') '*by his Faith in the Righteous Teacher and by his works*' – the curious allusion to '*being saved from the House of Judgement*' in the *Pesher* meaning just this.

Not only is this 'Jamesian,' that is, '*Faith and works working together*' or '*Faith being completed by works*'; but, once again, elements from the presentation of '*the Righteous Teacher*' – or, as the case may be, of James – are being absorbed into the presentation of 'Jesus' in Scripture, in the sense that, according to the received understanding, it is '*Faith in Jesus Christ that saves*.' It is this term '*ᶜamal*,' which the *Pesher* will now employ in describing the '*Worthless Community which Liar builds on Blood*' as well as '*the Assembly*' or '*Church which he erects upon Lying*' (the same '*erect*' of CD VII.16 and 4QFlorilegium, 1.10 –12 above) *for the sake of his (own) Glory*.'[41]

Here the '*ᶜamal*' or '*Salvationary works*,' which '*the Liar*' teaches, are said to be '*Empty*,' i.e., *empty of soteriological* or *saving effect*. But bringing us full circle and showing we are, once more, in the same ideological and spiritual ambiance of James, this last will be the very word James 2:20 uses to characterize its ideological opponent, when the '*worthlessness*' of his spiritual program concerning how '*Abraham was justified*' is being analyzed: '*O Empty Man*' or '*Man of Emptiness*' (often translated more imprecisely as '*Foolish Man*'), *don't you know that Faith apart from works is dead?*'

'*He built a Worthless City upon Blood and Erected a Congregation on Lying*'

The last discussion of '*the Man of Lies*' in the Habakkuk *Pesher* – now called, following the presentation of CD1.14–17, '*the Spouter of Lies*' – occurs two columns later as we have seen (though we have been calling him '*the Spouter*,' the pseudonym is not actually used in any document until x.9–13), directly following the first description of the '*Judgement*' inflicted on the '*corpse*' of the Wicked Priest and the '*profiteering*' and '*booty-gathering*' activities of '*the Last Priests of Jerusalem*' in IX.1–7 and the vivid portrayal of the eschatological '*House of Judgement*' God delivers '*in the midst of many Peoples*,' where '*He would arraign him for Judgement*' (seemingly '*the Wicked Priest*' but, because the commentary at the bottom of IX.16 is so fragmentary, this cannot be verified with complete certainty) and '*condemn him with fire and brimstone*.'

This final discussion of the Liar's activities and '*Justification*' doctrine, as just signaled, is presented in terms of an underlying allusion from Habakkuk 2:12, decrying the person who '*builds a City on Blood and establishes a township on Unrighteousness*.' Importantly, this is followed by a quotation from the underlying text Habakkuk 2:13, we just alluded to, about '*the Peoples laboring for the sake of Fire and the Peoples tiring themselves out for the sake of vanity*.' This could not be more convenient, because we have the very word '*Peoples*' (*ʿAmim*) – repeated twice in the underlying text – upon which the word '*Gentiles*' in the Latin ('*Ethne*' in the Greek, as in Paul's conception of a '*Mission to the Gentiles*') is based. We have already seen how Paul uses this phrase '*vanity*' or '*in vain*' in Galatians 2:21 – e.g., that '*if Righteousness is through the Law, then Christ died in vain*' or Galatians 3:3–4 (leading up to his citations of Genesis 15:6 and Habakkuk 2:4) actually applying the word '*foolish*' to those abandoning the Spirit for '*works of the Law*' or '*Perfection in the flesh*' (meaning, of course, as usual '*circumcision*'), whose '*suffering*' (again the allusion to '*suffering toil*') was, therefore, '*in vain*.' In Galatians 4:11, following his attack on '*keeping the weak and beggarly elements*' of '*days and months and times and years*,' this becomes how he '*labored in vain*,' meaning, *with his communities*.

In the crucial 1 Corinthians 15:2–58 passages about the Gospel Paul '*received*' and '*in which you* (his recipients) *also stand*' and the order of the post-resurrection appearances of '*Christ*,' Paul also repeatedly alludes to this '*Worthlessness*' and '*being in vain*' beginning in 15:3. There he speaks about his communities – '*being saved and holding fast to the word* (he) *preached*' (here the language of '*steadfastness*' together with that of '*the Word*' constantly reiterated in the Damascus Document and Community Rule above and in the Letter of James) – '*not believing in vain*'; and three times insists that, if Christ did not rise from the dead, both their '*Faith*' and his '*preaching*' were '*Worthless*' (15:12–14). Here, too, he ends by encouraging, again as in CD, 1QS, and James, '*steadfastness*' in '*the work of the Lord*,' '*knowing that your toil* – the '*ʿamal*' in Isaiah 53:11 and the Habakkuk *Pesher* – *is not in vain*' (15:58).

In the underlying passage from Habakkuk 2:13, the actual word used is not exactly '*vain*' – though effectively it is the same – but, as we saw, '*Emptiness*' or '*Nothingness*.' This text is exploited to swing back from the subject of the '*profiteering*' activities of '*the Last Priests of Jerusalem*' to develop, once again, a *Pesher* about '*the Liar*' – now referred to as '*the*

Spouter of Lying.' This *Pesher* ends, as just signaled, by calling down in x.12–13 the same *'Judgements of Fire'* on him that it called down at the beginning of Column x.3–5, seemingly, on *'the Wicked Priest'* when he was being *'arraigned in the midst of many Peoples'* and *'judged with fire and brimstone.'*[42] For this *Pesher*, these are a response to the same kind of insults and curses with which the Man of Lying *'insulted and vilified the Elect of God.'*[43] It should be noted that, contrary to *'the Wicked Priest,'* his offence against *'the Righteous Teacher'* and *'the Elect of God' – 'the Sons of Zadok'* or *'the Assembly of the Poor'* or *'of Holiness'*– is intellectual, not physical. This is in keeping with the *'Lying'* epithet applied to him, the analogue of *'the Tongue,'* figuratively-speaking, in the Letter of James.

In describing the teaching or doctrine of *'the Lying Spouter,'* it is the imagery of *'Blood'* which is all-important, the same imagery so integral to Paul's conception of *'the Cup of the New Covenant in (his) Blood,'* not to mention its variation in the other Gospel *'Blood'* scenarios including even one attributed to Pilate when he is portrayed in Matthew 27:24 as characterizing himself as *'being guiltless in the Blood of this Righteous One.'* In the first place, the *Pesher* applies the *'building a City on Blood'* in the underlying text from Habakkuk 2:12 to *'the Spouter of Lying who leads Many astray in order to build a Worthless City on Blood.'*[44]

'Leading astray' is, as we have seen, always the contrary language to the proper *'Justifying'* activity of the Righteous Teacher of *'making Many Righteous.'* It is the language used in the Damascus Document's introductory description of the activities of *'the Lying Scoffer'/'Comedian,'* who poured out *'the waters of Lying and caused them to wander astray in a trackless waste without a Way.'* That it is the contrary to the Righteous Teacher's *'Justifying'* activity is made clear by the inclusion of the terminology *'Many'* and, seemingly thereby, employing Isaiah 53:11's language of *'the Righteous One justifying Many'* in this *Pesher* on *'the Peoples laboring for the sake of fire'* and *'tiring themselves out for the sake of Emptiness'/'Nothingness.'*

But the parallels do not end here because the *'ʿamal,'* too, from this same Isaiah 53:11 will also momentarily be invoked. For the Habakkuk *Pesher*, x.9–10, the way the Spouter of Lies *'leads Many astray'* was, as we just saw, by *'building a Worthless City upon Blood and erecting an Assembly'* or *'Church upon Lying.'* The *'building a City upon Blood and establishing a township on Unrighteousness'* in the underlying text from Habakkuk 2:12 are being transformed in the *Pesher* by the addition of the allusion *'Worthless'* to qualify the *'City'* and the phrase, *'erecting an Assembly on Lying,'* instead of the *'Unrighteous township.'* We have already encountered this usage *'established'* in the several descriptions of the Community Council and Holy Spirit being *'established on Truth'* in 1QS, VIII.5, etc., above. Here in the *Pesher* it is seemingly being deliberately replaced by the slightly different terminology, 'erecting' or 'setting up', which is the same usage as the 'raising up of the fallen Tabernacle of David' in the Damascus Document or of both it and David's 'seed' in the *Florilegium* above (the 'established' being reserved in that document for 'the Throne of His Kingdom'[45]).

This 'Congregation'/'Assembly'/or 'Church', which has also been deliberately substituted for the word 'township' in the underlying text of Habakkuk, is, of course, the same one we earlier heard about in v.12 regarding the Liar's 'rejection of the Torah'. The replacement of 'Unrighteousness' in underlying Habakkuk 2:12 with 'Lying' is, of course, significant as is the addition of 'setting up' or 'erecting of an Assembly' to the extant language of 'building' (in the sense of 'building it up'). In fact, it is this allusion to 'building a Worthless City upon Blood' that is pivotal for the *Pesher*.

We have already noted Paul's repeated use of the word 'Worthless' in 1 Corinthians 15:14–17 to characterize the value of his communities' 'Faith' when not 'holding fast to' his teaching things such as 'the Crucified Christ – to the Jews, indeed, a stumbling block' (1 Corinthians 1:23). We have also seen Paul's criticisms of James' prohibitions to overseas communities from 1 Corinthians 5:1–9:27 (note, too, the inversion of the language of 'rejection,' 'laboring over Holy Things,' and 'freedom' from 9:13–27). These lead directly into his presentation of 'the Cup of the Lord' not being 'the Cup of Demons' (by which he seems to mean *both* 'idols' and 'the Temple') and 'Communion with the Blood of Christ' in 10:16–22 and 11:25–29.

Not only does he appear to be discussing the former in some ongoing exposition of James' prohibition on 'eating things sacrificed to idols,' but the latter has been retrospectively assimilated into 'Last Supper' scenarios in the Synoptic Gospels as 'the Cup of the New Covenant in (his) Blood which is poured for you' or 'poured out for the Many for remission of Sins' (Luke 22:20 and Matthew 26:28 – again, note the Qumran language in this last). In providing his version of this in 'this is the Cup of the New Covenant in my Blood,' Paul adds – as we have seen – his own proviso to it: 'For as often as you eat this bread and drink this Cup, you are announcing the death of the Lord until he comes' (1 Corinthians 11:26). In enunciating this, Paul – interestingly enough – is using the 'Cup' language which follows the material we have before us in the Habakkuk *Pesher* XI.10 but with entirely different signification. It should not be forgotten, too, that this allusion, 'the Cup of the Lord,' is also integral to the scenario of the first post-resurrection appearance to James in the Gospel according to the Hebrews. There is is the 'Cup' 'Jesus' gives his 'brother' James to 'drink.'

Where the Habakkuk *Pesher* is concerned, reiterated in the language used by Revelation, this language of 'the Cup of the Lord' symbolizes *the*

Anger of God and *His Divine Retribution on His Enemies*. This is the meaning of both the overt sense of the metaphor in Columns xi–xii of how '*the Cup of the Wrath of God would swallow*' or be '*repaid to the Wicked Priest*' because of how '*he swallowed*' the Righteous Teacher and of '*the reward he paid the Poor*'; but also how it is being played on in the signification '*Anger*' or '*Wrath*' – '*Chaᶜas*' in Hebrew, a homophone, as we saw and shall analyze further, for '*Cup*'/'*Chos*' in Hebrew.

Preceding this, too, at the end of the 1QpHab,x.10–11, this '*Divine Vengeance*' that will be exacted will be the outcome of what is going to happen to '*the Spouter of Lies*' and those who are the recipients of his '*Worthless Service*' and '*Empty ᶜamal*' as a result of their '*blaspheming and vilifying the Elect of God*'.[46] But as Paul closes his discussion of this '*Cup of the New Covenant*,' again archly hinting – as already suggested – at '*Blood*'-libel accusations, he too moves over into this kind of language of implied threat – this time directed against those seemingly within the Church with the opposite point-of-view to his own, *to wit*, persons like James:

> *Therefore, whoever shall eat this bread or drink this Cup of the Lord in an unworthy way shall be guilty of the body and the Blood of the Lord* (1 Corinthians 11:27).

Not only is the underlying thrust of this quite aggressive, but just so that there should be no mistaking it, Paul repeats it:

> *For whoever eats and drinks unworthily – not seeing through to the Blood of the Lord – eats and drinks Judgement to himself.*

Again, not only is its accusatory and menacing aura obvious; but this, of course, is exactly the gist of the language centering around these various '*drinking the Cup of the Wrath of God*' allusions, we have been highlighting in the Habakkuk *Pesher* and Revelation, including even the '*eating*' and '*drinking*' metaphors as meaning Divine '*Judgement*' or '*being consumed*' or '*destroyed*' Therefore, it should be quite clear that in all such contexts this language of '*the Cup of the Lord*' is present, albeit with widely varying, if not simply completely unrelated, significations.

'*The City of Blood*' in the Nahum *Pesher*, James' '*Abstain from Blood*,' '*Crucifixion*' again, and '*Communion with the Blood of Christ*'

Directly following the use of this language of '*the Cup of the Lord's right hand*' (Habakkuk 2:16) and '*the Cup of the Wrath of God*' to apply to how the Wicked Priest would himself '*be swallowed*' or '*consumed*' in the Habakkuk *Pesher*, Column XI.10–15, another allusion to '*Blood*' occurs in the underlying text of Habakkuk 2:17 in Column XII.1,'*the Blood of Man*' (*Adam*). As earlier suggested, some might have taken this anomalous reference to '*Adam*' more figuratively as an esotericism bearing on the ideology of '*the Primal Adam*' they were espousing and, further to this, as involving *his* '*Blood*' and/or even his death.

However this may be, in the *Pesher*, as we saw, this language is clearly being applied to how the Wicked Priest '*plotted to destroy the Poor*,' '*the Violence*' he did to the Righteous Teacher and his followers (called '*the Simple Jews doing the Torah*'), and his '*works of Abominations polluting the Temple of God*.' It should be appreciated, however, that this is not the same kind of '*Blood*' one finds, two columns earlier in Column X.6 and 10 as we saw). There it was more ideological and/or allegorical, dealing with the underpinning or outlook of a given Community (namely, that of '*the Liar*'s or one like Paul's). In this climactic end of the Habakkuk *Pesher* it is, rather, more like the '*Blood*'-accusations one gets in the Gospels – here related clearly to the spilling of '*the Blood of the Poor*' and '*the works of Abominations*,' seemingly of the '*Herodian*' Establishment, connected to it.

As opposed to this, however, Column Ten – as we have been demonstrating – is rather describing the ideas and activities of the Liar in an unusually prescient manner. As already implied, in our view this allusion to '*building a Worthless City upon Blood and erecting an Assembly*' or '*Church upon Lying*' is not something '*Violent*' but rather relates to the perception of what Paul is doing in his '*Missionary*' activities generally, particularly abroad – but, further to this and even more specifically, his enunciation of his controversial doctrines of both '*the Cup of the Lord*' or '*the Cup of the New Covenant in (his) Blood*,' and '*Communion with the Blood of Christ*' in 1 Corinthians 10:16–11:29.

This occurs, as we have already seen, right after and as a continuation, seemingly, of his responses to James' directives to overseas communities '*to abstain from fornication, blood, things sacrificed to idols*' and dietary matters generally from 1 Corinthians 5:1–10:33. In our view, as just intimated, this is made clear by the purposeful shift in emphasis in the *Pesher*, signaled by the addition to the underlying text from Habakkuk 2:12–13 of the new words, '*Worthless*' and '*erecting a Congregation upon Lying*.'

We have already encountered a variation of this '*City of Blood*' allusion in the Nahum *Pesher* where, it will be recalled, it was related to '*the City of Ephraim*' and '*Gentile*'-style converts referred to as '*resident aliens*' or '*Ger-Nilveh*'/'*Nilvim*,' that is, evoking the '*Joiners*' language we encountered in the Damascus Document's exegesis of Ezekiel's '*Zadokite*

Covenant.'⁴⁷ 'The City of Blood' ('Blood' for some reason being expressed here in the Nahum *Pesher* in the plural) was not even a real '*City*' in the *Pesher* but actually directly connected to '*the Congregation of the Seekers after Smooth Things*.'⁴⁸ This *Pesher*, as previously underscored (aside from its *real* historical references) was primarily directed against those it called '*Seekers after Smooth Things*' seemingly holding sway at the time of writing or presently in Jerusalem, whose '*counsel*' – specifically described in terms of '*inviting*' *foreign Kings and foreign Armies into Jerusalem* (at an earlier time before '*the coming of the Rulers of the Kittim*' or '*the Romans*,' i.e., the time of '*Demetrius, King of the Greece*'⁴⁹ – from Josephus, we know these to have been '*the Pharisees*') – is identified as being directly responsible for the disasters overtaking the People, both in the past and at present.⁵⁰

Not only does its scheme more or less parallel that of the Habakkuk *Pesher* of '*the Riches collected by the Last Priests of Jerusalem*' ultimately '*being given over*' to this same '*Army of the Kittim*,'⁵¹ but in its Second Column – the First evoking *the final* '*fiery*' *Judgemental Hurricane of* '*God's Wrath*,' particularly upon '*the Kittim*' – it refers to '*Messengers* (Hebrew for '*Apostles*') *among the Gentiles*.'⁵² Moreover, as already explained too, it also actually evokes the very passage that Paul uses to develop his '*Salvationary*' theology of how '*Jesus Christ redeemed us from the curse of the Law*' and, in the process, '*justified*' in Galatians 3:6–14 all Mankind along '*with the believing Abraham*' by himself being '*hung upon a tree*.'

However, interestingly enough, 4QpNah,2.6–8 on Nahum 2:12–13, citing '*victims*,' adds the important qualification '*hanging up living men*' to the passage, Paul is evoking from Deuteronomy 21:23, which originally seems only to have banned, as previously underscored, '*the hanging up of dead corpses overnight*.' In the process, the *Pesher* turns this into a passage rather condemning what has since come to be understood as '*crucifixion*' (obviously, this has to be understood, most particularly, in terms of *Roman crucifixion*!) as '*a thing not done formerly in Israel*' and, just as obviously, not '*glorifying*' it as the pivotal '*building*' block of a future theology – on the contrary. To explain this more unequivocally – while Paul, following the letter of Deuteronomy 21:23, but also applying it specifically to '*crucifixion*' *per se*, sees '*the hanged man*' as the '*thing accursed*'; the *Pesher*, by applying – as we saw – a later passage from Nahum 2:12: '*Behold I am against you says the Lord of Hosts*,' rather turns this, seemingly purposefully, into a condemnation of '*crucifixion*' itself – a matter obviously of intense emotional interest, as just observed, *probably only in the Roman Period*!

From here the whole *Pesher* turns completely eschatological – *i. e.*, relating to '*the Last Days*'/'*End Time*' (just as in the Habakkuk *Pesher*) –

defining 'the City of Blood' curiously, as earlier alluded to, as 'the City of Ephraim, the Seekers after Smooth Things at the End of Days, who walk in Deceit and Lying.'[53] These last make it pretty clear we are in the same milieu as 'the Spouter of Lying' of the Habakkuk Pesher again – and that 'Ephraim' must (or should) in some way relate to him. This is further clarified in terms of 'those who lead Ephraim astray' – here our paradigmatic usage 'leading astray' again. This also includes, once more, the use of the term – just as in Paul above too – 'Many,' to wit: 'those who, through teaching Lying, their Lying Tongue and Deceitful lips, lead Many astray.'[54]

Column Three is also about 'the Last Days,' a time that clearly has to be seen in terms of the 'coming of the Rulers of the Kittim' (the plural here would imply Republican Rome), but after the departure of the Greeks, when 'the sword of the Gentiles' was never far from their midst.[55] It expresses the hope that 'the Simple of Ephraim' – paralleling 'the Simple of Judah' in the Habakkuk Pesher, but without the qualification of 'doing the Torah' – 'shall flee their Congregation, abandoning those who lead them astray and joining Israel.' In my view, that this is an attack on Paul, which at the same time begins to clarify the nature of this pseudonym (as with the term 'Samaritan' in the New Testament to which it is related) 'Ephraim' as having something to do with new 'Gentile' converts, is indisputable.

We have already identified this language of 'joining' – expressed in the Pauline corpus as 'joining the body of Christ,' rather than 'being joined to the body of a prostitute' (I Corinthians 6:16–17) – as being expressive of Gentiles 'joining themselves' to the Community in an associated status of some kind much as 'God-Fearers' were associated in this Period with synagogues around the Eastern Mediterranean, meaning, people who had not yet entered the Community as full-status converts, but were 'Joiners'/ 'Nilvim.' In fact, this kind of language relative to 'God-Fearers' – 'for whom a Book of Remembrance would be written out'[56] – comes through very strongly in the last Columns of the Cairo Damascus Document

As already underscored, one finds this expression, 'Nilvim,' which is used in Esther 10:27 to denote precisely such a status, in the interpretation of 'the Zadokite Covenant' in the Damascus Document at Qumran and this is, in fact, the kind of imagery being used throughout the Nahum Pesher with regard to 'resident aliens' (Ger-Nilvim) above, meaning, those 'joining themselves to the Community.' In this sense 'the Simple Ones of Ephraim' is the counterpart to 'the Simple Ones of Judah doing the Torah' in the Habakkuk Pesher, the former being Gentiles associated with the Community in some adjunct status but without the qualifier 'doing the Torah' yet added.

It is, of course, to just such persons that Acts presents James as addressing his directives to overseas communities, including the prohibition on *'Blood'* – which in the context before us is *primary* – as well as the *'things sacrificed to idols'* or *'the pollutions of the idols'* (also important in *MMT* as we have seen), *strangled things ('carrion'), and fornication.'* But, as just signaled too, it is in discussing in 1 Corinthians 8:10 and 10:7–28 exactly these injunctions, particularly that concerning *'things sacrificed to idols'* but also *'Idolatry'* generally (also alluded to in the conclusion of the Habakkuk *Pesher* above), that Paul first raises, as we just saw too, the issue of *'Communion with the Blood of Christ'* including, most astonishingly of all, these several evocations of the imagery of *'the Cup'* – present with widely differing signification in these passages of the Habakkuk *Pesher* as well.

In fact, Paul is playing on this imagery of *'the Cup'* in 1 Corinthians 10:16, even evoking *'the Cup of the Lord'* language of Habakkuk 2:16 above in 1 Corinthians 11:27 as we just saw as well. These are very complex matters, but the reader should pay careful attention to them. We have treated them to some extent above, but now it is important to see them in relation to Paul's reversal and spiritualization of the Qumran language of *'the New Covenant in the Land of Damascus'* generally. In fact, it is at this point in 1 Corinthians 10:18, as also already underscored, that Paul heaps total abuse on the Temple and the Temple cult – including *'the other Israel,'* the one he terms *'according to the flesh'* (this, too, a double entendre) – ending up with his final directives to *'eat anything sold in the market place'* (1 Corinthians 10:25) and *'all things for me are lawful'* (10:23). This is his final riposte to the prohibitions from James – and presumably those in *'MMT'* – on *'things sacrificed to idols, blood, and carrion.'*

As just remarked, Paul even goes so far as to compare the things which the other Israel eats in the Temple to *eating at 'the Table of Demons'* (earlier in 1 Corinthians 8:9–10, *'reclining in an idol Temple'* and *'a cause of stumbling to those who are weak'*), and his *'Cup'* is *'the Cup of the Lord'* or *'the Cup of Communion with the Blood of Christ'* as opposed to their *'Cup'* – *'the Cup of Demons'* as it were in 1 Corinthians 10:18–21). Once again, he has *'turned the tables,'* as it were (to coin a pun), on his interlocutors with his dizzying dialectical acrobatics and allegorization.

But the *'Blood'* he is talking about here – symbolic or real – as we just saw, has already been *specifically forbidden in James' prohibitions to overseas communities,* even according to the picture in Acts 15:19–29. It is also forbidden in the Damascus Document. There, it will be recalled, in the same breath as asserting that Abraham *'was made a Friend of God, because he kept the Commandments of God and did not choose the will of his own spirit'* (n.b., the possible play on Paul's *'Holy Spirit'* doctrine here) – that is, by Qumran definition, because he was a *'Keeper'* he was a *'Son of Zadok'* (as, according to CDiii.2-4, were Isaac and Jacob after him too) – it is asserted that the Sons of Israel '*were cut off in the wilderness*' because '*they ate blood*' (this, as opposed, it will also be recalled, to Paul in Galatians 5:12 above, wishing the circumcisers '*would themselves cut off*' – more inverse word-play, CDiii.1 beginning with '*the Sons of Noah...going astray*' and '*being cut off*'!).

Moreover the Children of Israel are described here in CDiii.5–6 as '*walking in the stubbornness of their heart*,' '*complaining against the Commandments of God, and each man doing what seemed right in his own eyes*,' language particularly appropriate to the genus of the Pauline-style '*Liar*.' Not only does Paul show in this all-important 1 Corinthians 10 that he knows the terms of James' instructions to overseas communities (including '*fornication*' – 1 Corinthians 10:8), he actually uses the same example one finds here in CDiii.7 and words paralleling the Hebrew meaning of '*being cut off*' to describe how the Children of Israel '*were overturned*' or '*cut off in the wilderness*' (1 Corinthians 10:5).

But the proof that he is following the text of the Damascus Document, albeit inverting its sense, doesn't end here. In the latter, this allusion to '*cutting off*' is immediately followed by the allusion: '*and they (the Children of Israel) murmured in their tents*.'[57] But this same allusion occurs in 1 Corinthians, following this evocation of how they '*were overturned in the wilderness*.' As Paul puts this in 1 Corinthians 10:10, '*nor should you murmur as some of them murmured*.' But this is almost word-for-word the language of these important passages about Abraham as '*Friend of God*' in CDiii.2–4 proving, as almost nothing else can, that Paul, not only knows the Damascus Document, but is even following its sequencing. This – even though he now proceeds to reverse the position of the Damascus Document on the issue of '*Blood*' – and with it, not insignificantly, that of his presumed Leader, James the Just – using it, rather, to '*build*' or '*erect*' *his whole Congregation based upon, not banning Blood, but consuming it* – in this case, '*the body and Blood of Christ Jesus*.' In doing so, he claims to be advocating to his '*Beloved Ones*' – his '*Friends*' – *to flee from Idolatry*' (1 Corinthians 10:14) – again the very reverse of the language about such '*Beloved Ones*' or '*Friends*' we have been following here in Column Three of the Damascus Document.

'*The Cup of the New Covenant in (His) Blood*' and '*the New Covenant in the Land of Damascus*'

This is what Paul is doing with James' directive to *abstain from blood* (in the Damascus Document, this would have been referred to in terms of the language of '*Naziritism*') in I Corinthians, a letter in which he earlier refers to his community, as we saw, as '*God's building*' in the context of speaking about the familiar '*each receiving his reward according to his own labor*' and where he actually compares himself to '*the architect*' (3:6–14)! In this passage, he is also even using the '*laying the Foundation*' imagery of both the Community Rule and Hymns at Qumran, not only stressing the necessity of '*building*' on '*the Foundation of Jesus Christ*,' but several times referring to the fact of his '*building*' as opposed to '*Apollos' watering*.'

This, in our view, is what is meant by the allusion to the Lying Spouter's '*leading Many astray*' and '*building a Worthless City upon Blood*,' with the additional aside of '*raising a Congregation upon Lying*' in 1QpHab,x.9–10, which will now go on to characterize his '*Service*,' too, as '*Worthless*,' his '*works*' as '*Lying*,' and his '*ʿamal*' as '*Empty*.' But it should also be clear that Paul's treatment of '*Blood*' in I Corinthians 10:16–11:29 is also the import of how he treats the Qumran '*New Covenant in the Land of Damascus*.' Not only does he treat it esoterically, turning the written word '*Damascos*' in Greek – '*Damascus*' in Latin and English, but '*Dammashek*' in Hebrew – into '*the Cup of Blood*,' as per the meaning of its *homophonic* root in Hebrew, *dam/Blood* and *chos/Cup*; he is *reversing* it once again! In fact, as we shall see, the parallel will go even further than this, both in I Corinthians 11:24–29 and the Synoptics related to it, in the phrase always connected to this formula, '*Drink this in Remembrance of me*' – in Hebrew, '*mashkeh*' or '*dam-mashkeh*,' '*give blood to drink*' – to say nothing of the phrase in CDxx.18–21 just highlighted above, '*the Book of Remembrance that was written out before Him for God-Fearers*.'[58]

In I Corinthians 11:20–30, he claims to have received his view of what he calls '*the Lord's Supper*' directly '*from the Lord*' (11:23), though how and by what mechanism he does not explain. Rather he moves directly into connecting this with the language of '*the New Covenant*,' also the language used in climactic sections of the Damascus Document, where, as we have been underscoring, it becomes associated with an even more extreme rededication to '*the First*' or '*Old*.'[59] It is Paul's approach to this '*New Covenant*,' too, that becomes the manner in which it is attributed to Jesus in Gospel portrayals of '*the Last Supper*,' at least in the Synoptics. Luke 22:20 perhaps puts this most graphically, reflecting the language Paul uses here in I Corinthians 11:26 almost exactly and incorporating the '*Cup*' (or '*Chos*') imagery from Qumran, itself developed – as we just pointed out – in terms of a play on the word, '*Wrath*' or '*Chaʿas*' there.

In the process, of course, Paul in I Corinthians 11:25 reverses this as well: '*This Cup is the New Covenant in my Blood. As often as you drink it, do this in Remembrance of me*' (n.b., the Damascus Document's '*Remembrance*' language above – to say nothing of its 'doing'). All three Synoptics also add the language of 'being poured out for the Many' – Matthew 26:28 adding 'for remission of Sins.' Even this language is reflected in the Damascus Document's presentation of 'the Covenant which God made with the First (i.e., 'the Ancestors' again) to atone for their sins' or 'for remission of their Sins' directly following its exegesis of the Zadokite Covenant.[60]

Not only does the language of 'the Cup of the New Covenant in (his) Blood' in the Gospels recapitulate that at Qumran of 'pouring out of Lying' (the root of 'the Spouter of Lying' appellation) and 'the Many,' the Letter to the Hebrews too – not surprisingly – discusses both 'the New Covenant' and that of 'the Old' extensively. It does so in the context of quoting Jeremiah 31:31–34, perhaps the original provenance of this language of the 'New Covenant with the House of Judah' and probably, also, the origin of these several archaizing allusions to 'the House of Judah' in both the Habakkuk Pesher and the Damascus Document (Hebrews 8:8). Hebrews 9:20 also evokes Exodus 24:8's 'this is the Blood of the Covenant, which God has enjoined upon you' and makes repeated reference to the Damascus Document's 'Covenant of the First' (8:13 and 9:15).[61] In extensive, if esoteric, discussion of these two 'Covenant's, not only does Hebrews express this 'New Covenant in the Blood of Christ' in terms of 'Perfecting the one who serves' (9:9,), 'a Perfect Tabernacle' (9:11), and 'making Perfect the Spirits of the Righteous' or 'Just' (12:23); but in evoking Habakkuk 2:4's 'the Righteous shall live by Faith,' it even uses the Habakkuk Pesher's language of the 'City,' combining it with that of 'building' and 'erecting' (10:38–11:16)!

Here the parallel with both Paul in 1 Corinthians and the Habakkuk Pesher is patent: 'For he was waiting for a City, the Foundations of which were built and erected by God.' This reference comes in the section about how Abraham 'became the Heir of Righteousness according to Faith' and about the other 'Heirs to the Promise,' such as Jacob, Joseph, and Moses, we have already discussed with regard to how 'Abraham's was justified by works when he offered up his son Isaac on the altar' and Rahab the harlot, 'when she received the messengers' in James 2:21–25 above (cf. Hebrews 11:17–31).

Paul expresses this idea, as we just saw, in 1 Corinthians 11:25 – precisely prefiguring Luke 22:20 above – as 'This Cup is the New Covenant in my Blood.' He not only follows this up by reference to 'the Cup of the Lord,' but here all resemblances end because he then rather speaks, as we have several times pointed out, about 'drinking the Cup of the Lord unworthily' and, thereby, 'drinking Judgement to oneself, not seeing through to the body of the Lord' (1 Corinthians 11:27–29).

In doing so, he mixes the two separate 'Cup' imageries we have been following, by implication demonstrating that he, anyhow, appears to realize the two are interrelated – the one having to do with Divine *'Vengeance'*; the other a *'spiritualized'* or *'allegorical'* reinterpretation of a *'Mystery Religion'*-type *'Covenant'* of some kind. Therefore we can conclude that what is referred to on three separate occasions in the Damascus Document at Qumran as *'the New Covenant in the Land of Damascus'* becomes for Paul, in a figurative and esoteric transformation revealed only probably to a few adepts, *'the New Covenant in the Blood of Christ.'*

It should be recalled that in the first description of the Scriptural exegesis sessions of *'the Righteous Teacher'*/*'(High) Priest'* in Column Two of the Habakkuk *Pesher*, this *'New Covenant'* was expressed in terms of a two or threefold allusion to *'Traitors,'* that is, it appears, *'the Traitors to the New Covenant'* and *'the Traitors to the Last Days,'* who *'did not believe in the Covenant of God and defiled His Holy Name,'* nor *'what they heard was going to happen to the Last Generation from the mouth of the Priest* (himself, as we saw, seemingly identical to *'the Righteous Teacher'*), *in whose heart God put the insight to interpret all the words of His Servants the Prophets.'*[62] Nor is this to mention those *'Covenant-Breakers,'* also alluded to in the key original citation above in Jeremiah 31:31–34 about the coming *'New Covenant'* – the *'Torah within them'* that, as Paul would put, was going to be *'written upon their hearts'* as well! – who, along with those designated as *'Violent Ones'* and these two or three species of *'Traitors,'* would appear – as we have seen – to attend the Scriptural exegesis sessions of *'the Righteous Teacher.'*[62] At *'the Last Supper'* in the Gospels too – coincidentally or otherwise – it is just prior to Jesus *'taking the Cup'* and announcing *'the New Covenant in (his) Blood'* (that in Matthew and Mark *'is poured out for the Many'*) that, as we saw, he raises the issue of his coming *'betrayal'* (Matthew 26:21 and *pars.*) or that in John 13:29, anyhow, *'the Traitor'* Judas (once again designated in 13:27 as *'of Simon Iscariot'*) leaves to betray him.

But the relationship between *'the New Covenant in the Land of Damascus'* at Qumran and *'the New Covenant in the Blood of Christ'* in Paul does not end there. There is the additional connection, just signaled above, which also may or may not be coincidental. In our view, it is purposeful. As already explained, the word for *'Blood'* in Hebrew is *'Dam'* – in the Nahum *Pesher*, for whatever reason, the plural *'Damim.'* But this is the first syllable in the place name *'Damascus,'* whether in Hebrew (*Dammashek*) or any other language. In the Greek of the New Testament, as already explained, it is *'Damascos,'* just as it is in Latin and English.

The word in Hebrew for *'Cup,'* as we saw in our analysis of the word-play surrounding the two words, *'Chos'* and *'Cha*ᶜ*as'* – *'Cup'* and *'Anger'* – in the Habakkuk *Pesher* above, is *'Chos'* (in fact, the Wicked Priest really did give, in a manner of speaking, the Righteous Teacher *'the Cup of*

Blood to drink'). Therefore the place name 'Damascos', in Greek and other derivative languages really does mean, taken according to its precise homophonic or literal transliteration in Hebrew, 'Blood' and 'Cup' ('Dam' and 'Chos') or 'Cup of Blood'. Just as in the case of the overlaps between 'swallowing' in Hebrew (balla᷅) and 'casting down' in Greek (ballo) in the usages surrounding the deaths of both the Righteous Teacher at Qumran and James, it is hard to conceive of additional overlaps such as these as mere coincidence.

This makes 'the New Covenant in the Land of Damascus' at Qumran the very same thing as 'the Cup of the New Covenant in (his) Blood' in Paul (and the Gospels) – only the one estericizes and, in due course, absolutely reverses the sense of the other. The parallel between 'Drink' and 'Give to drink' in Greek and 'Mashkeh' in Hebrew just increases the correspondence further, making it seem as if the relationship – esoteric as it may have been – had to have been a conscious one. This is a perfectly astonishing conclusion, one that – to coin a euphemism – turns the history of Christianity 'on its ear' – this, too, from a document, which on the basis of an analysis of the hand-writing of one or two fragments, scholars insist on placing in the Second Century BC.[64] On the basis of an analysis of the internal data and its vocabulary, such an early date is patently absurd.

If Paul was conscious of this relationship – and it is hard to conceive that he was not, since even the Book of Acts avers he spent time in 'Damascus' – then we must conclude he was very much aware of the language of 'the New Covenant' at Qumran and the way it was being expressed there in terms of the word 'Damascus.' Moreover, he was simply transforming this in the light of his own more allegorical and even more esoteric approach – what he himself calls in 1 Corinthians 2:13, 'communicating in words taught by the Holy Spirit spiritual things spiritually.' In the process, enjoying all these plays on words, he was, no doubt, having a good laugh as well – which is, of course, precisely the implication at Qumran in 'the Scoffer' or 'Comedian' epithet applied to 'the Man of Lying' there.

The only question which remains is whether in some sense 'the New Covenant in the Land of Damascus' at Qumran actually did have a secret or esoteric meaning of the kind Paul is exploiting or whether this new, more esoteric approach was entirely his own creation. Based on the documents at our disposal, we shall probably never know definitively as this is what it means for something to be 'esoteric.' Given the thrust of the surrounding allusions in these documents, it is difficult to detect what this might have been and probably it did not, except for the esoteric evocation in the Damascus Document of: 'with the Completion of the Era of these years,' 'each man will stand on his own net' (or 'Watchtower') and 'all the Glory *of Adam will be theirs,*' there being no more specific attachment to '*the House of Judah*' *per se* – this being something of the manner in which Paul is reconstructing it or construing these things too.

'*Building a Worthless City upon Blood*' and '*Communion with the Blood of Christ*'

We can now return to the allusion to '*building a Worthless City upon Blood and erecting a Congregation on Lying,*' where the Lying Spouter's '*Service*' or '*labor*' is concerned, the second part of which, as we saw, purposefully replaces the phraseology '*establishing a township upon Unrighteousness*' in the underlying text of Habakkuk 2:12.[65] '*Building a Worthless City upon blood*' is just what was in the underlying text, except for the *significant addition* of the deprecative term '*Worthless.*'

We have already seen how Paul uses this word '*Worthless*' or the allusion to '*in vain*' above. In the *Pesher* that follows, this word, '*Worthless*' or '*vain,*' will also be used to characterize the kind of '*Worthless Service*' or '*Lying works,*' the Liar causes '*the Many*' to perform – expressed contemptuously as '*tiring out Many*' – '*for the sake of (his) Glory.*' This is expressed, as we saw, as follows:

> *The interpretation of the passage* (Habakkuk 2:12–13) *concerns the Spouter of Lying, who leads Many astray, building a Worthless City upon blood and erecting an Assembly upon Lying, for the sake of (his) Glory, tiring out Many with a Worthless Service and instructing them in works of Lying, so that their ʿamal* ('*suffering works*' or '*suffering toil*') *would be for Emptiness.*[66]

These are the exact words of the *Pesher*. One can only assume that the addition of the word '*Worthless*' here – repeated twice (as already indicated) – was purposeful and it, in fact, characterized the *Soteriological* value or efficacy of the '*Service*' taught by the Lying Spouter, by which he '*leads Many astray,*' or that of '*the City*' he was '*building.*' The play on the usage '*the Many*' from Isaiah 53:11 here – also repeated twice – would appear to be purposeful as well, as would, therefore, the play on the idea of '*the Righteous Teacher*''s James-like '*works of Righteousness*' – these as opposed to the Lying Spouter's '*works of Lying*' – the usage '*works*' now being the one based on the verb '*to do,*' as in '*doing the Torah,*' not 'ʿ*avodah.*'

We have already discussed the allusion to '*City of Blood*' above, including its relevance to the Qumran usage '*Dammashek*' and the Greek '*Damascos.*' In some sense, in the Nahum *Pesher*, as we saw as well, this usage is connected to '*the Simple of Ephraim*' (as we have interpreted it,

924

the 'Pauline Christian' contingent among 'the Seekers after Smooth Things,' 'seeking accommodation with foreigners' – in this instance, meaning Rome and including 'the Violent Ones of the Gentiles' and 'the Traitors to the New Covenant' above). The 'City' metaphor as opposed to the 'township' – which is transformed in the Pesher into the allusion to 'erecting' or 'raising a Congregation'/'Assembly'/or 'Church upon Lying' – stays in the Pesher.

Paul very much enjoyed using the imagery of 'citizenship.' In this regard, one should look at Ephesians 2:19, where Paul or its Pauline-minded author attacks 'Jewish' exclusivity – particularly the kind, we have already reviewed, directed against Herodians in the Temple. This reference in Ephesians is preceded by allusion in 2:11–13 to 'the Peoples' ('Ethne' again), those it claims the Jews were calling the 'Uncircumcision in the flesh' and whom, for its part, it is referring to as 'Strangers from the Covenants (sic) of the Promise' (note here, the variation on the 'Ger-nilveh' language in 4QpNah,III.9), originally being 'thought of as aliens from the Commonweal Israel' and 'apart from Christ' (also, as we have seen, 'the body of Christ'), but now 'an offering and sacrifice to God, a sweet fragrance' (5:2 – of course, one recognizes this 'sacrifice,' 'offering,' and 'sweet fragrance' language as the kind of metaphor applied to the description of 'the Community Council,' 'atoning for the Land' by 'suffering works' and 'without the flesh of burnt offerings and the fat of sacrifices' in the Community Rule above[67]).

In this context, Ephesians also cautions – yet again, seemingly, reversing the 'Emptiness'/'Empty Man' language against these very same persons it seems just to have called the 'Circumcision in the flesh made by hand' – 'not to be deceived by Empty words, for the Wrath of God comes upon the Sons of Rebellion' (here, of course, again the inversion of 'the Wrath of God' phraseology, to say nothing of that of 'the Sons of Rebellion' – also language with not unsimilar parallels in the Damascus Document above[68]) and 'not cooperating' with such persons, 'for once in Darkness, but now in the Light of the Lord, you walk as Children of Light' (5:6–5:8). But, of course, this too is exactly paralleled in the Qumran Community Rule, III.5–IV.8. Even the Sermon on the Mount in Matthew 5:14 uses such 'Light' imagery – combined with an allusion to 'a City situated upon a hill that cannot be hidden' – to characterize 'the Disciples of Jesus.'

Moreover, in bolstering Paul's 'in the flesh' or 'glorying in your flesh' arguments elsewhere (as, for example, the allusion to this last in Galatians 6:13 above) and completing this particular circle of artful rhetorical footwork, it actually uses the language of 'Ethne in the flesh' (once 'far off, but now become near by the Blood of Christ'!) to appeal – even perhaps a little archly – to such 'Gentiles' (2:11-13). For good measure, as just indicated, it calls such new converts the 'Uncircumcision' (cf. Galatians 2:7–12), while the Jews – or those it has just denoted, '*the Commonweal Israel*' (sic) and seemingly again, perhaps even, somewhat contemptuously – it calls the '*Circumcision in the flesh made by hand*' (here *n.b.*, the incredibly able polemic exemplified in this allusion to '*made by hand*').

We have already seen in Hebrews 11:10 and 11:16 above, discussing how '*Abraham was saved by Faith*,' how this '*City*' imagery here in the Habakkuk *Pesher* was combined with '*building*' and '*erecting*' imagery – to say nothing of the '*Foundation*' – to allude to '*a City, the builder and erector of whose Foundations is God.*' The imagery of such '*Foundations*' is present in these lines from Ephesians 2:19–20 about '*being fellow-citizens in the Household of God*' and is extremely widespread at Qumran as well.[69] Which brings us to the second element in this '*City of Blood*' construction, the '*building*' imagery again – imagery which, as should by now be clear, fairly permeates the Pauline corpus. Whether one considers Ephesians authentic or, like Hebrews, of '*the Pauline School*,' it is part and parcel of its '*citizenship*' metaphor too. As Ephesians 2:19 puts this, '*you are no longer strangers* (again, '*ger-nilvim*' at Qumran) *and foreigners, but fellow citizens of the Holy Ones and of the Household of God.*' Not only should one note here '*the Holy Ones*' usage, so widespread in the Dead Sea Scrolls and prominent in all descriptions of James, but also the language, just alluded to above, of the '*ger-nilveh*'/'*resident alien*' in the Nahum *Pesher*.[70] Ephesians 2:20–22 continues:

For you have been built on the Foundation of the Apostles and the Prophets, Jesus Christ himself being the Cornerstone, in whom all the building is joined together, growing into a Holy Temple in the Lord – in whom you, too, are being built together as a dwelling place for God in the Spirit.'

Here we have all our imageries and this is also about as close to the language of Qumran as one can get. Nor can one get very much more '*spiritualized*' than this. Not only do we have here the Community Rule's further imagery regarding '*the Community Council*' above being a spiritualized '*Temple*' and '*Holy of Holies*' and '*the Cornerstone*,'[71] but also the '*joining*' and '*building*' vocabulary again. The imagery here is, of course, also that of Paul in 1 Corinthians 12:12–27 above – following his proclamation of '*the Cup of the New Covenant in* (his) *Blood*' and '*Communion with the Blood of Christ*' in 10–11 – of the Community and its '*members*' being '*the body of Christ.*' The double entendre involved in this '*member*' metaphor is being played upon, too, by the counter-imagery in James 3:5 of '*the Tongue being one small member of the body*' but '*boasting great things.*' It is also part and parcel of the '*Temple*' and '*body*' imagery in the Gospels where 'Jesus,' questioned as to what he meant by saying he would '*destroy the Temple of God and raise it up again in three days,*' is pictured as saying, he '*meant his (own) body,*' i.e., his own resurrection (John 2:19–21).

For Mark 14:58, this '*Temple,*' which 'Jesus' will destroy (the symbolism is nothing, if not '*devastating*'), is '*made with hands*'; while he will go on, using the Habakkuk *Pesher's* and Paul's '*building*'-imagery again – '*in three days to build another not made with hands,*' language absolutely reflected in Ephesians 2:11's condescending characterization above of '*those called Circumcision in the flesh made by hand*' as opposed to '*the Peoples in the flesh who are called* – by these same '*Circumcision*' – *Uncircumcision.*' Again we have extremely well-crafted and consistent – if biting – metaphor here. Moreover, the allegorizing polemic, whether embedded in Gospel or Letter, is '*devastating.*' For Ephesians 2:20–22 too, as just noted, '*Jesus Christ himself is the Cornerstone, in whom the whole building, joined together, grows into a Holy Temple in the Lord.*' Here again in this '*building,*' '*joined,*' '*growing,*' and '*Holy Temple*' imagery we have all the allegorizing metaphor of not only Community Rule but a whole range of other Qumran documents as well.

We have seen how Paul refers to himself as '*Builder*' or '*Chief Architect*' in 1 Corinthians 3:9–11. Here Paul, using the metaphor of the Community as '*God's building and the Temple of God*' and himself as the Builder '*laying the Foundations well,*' also employs the language of '*being saved from the Fire,*' evoked here in 1QpHab,x.5 and x.13 as well, cautioning '*each should be careful how he builds*' and concluding, '*for no one can lay any other Foundation, except...Jesus Christ*' (1 Corinthians 3:11–15). In Romans 15:20, operating within the same metaphor, he expresses his concern '*to preach the Gospel where Christ had not been Named*' – meaning, it would seem, mainland Greece, Rome, and Spain – so as '*not to build on someone else's Foundations.*'[72]

Not only should the implications of this last symbolism relating to the Community led by the Archbishop James be obvious, the whole, in fact, relates, as we have been demonstrating and as just underscored, to the '*Stone*'/'*Cornerstone*' and '*Foundations*' imagery so very widespread at Qumran. This is particularly true of the Qumran Hymns, where amid allusion to the James-like '*Bulwark of Strength*' and '*a Strong and Tested Wall,*' as well, significantly, as '*the Gates of Protection through which no foreigner can pass*'[73]; we are told about erecting '*My building upon Rock*' (in the previous column this was '*setting the Foundation on Rock and tested Stones for a Building of Strength*'), '*the Foundations of which are Eternal Principles that will not shake*'[74] – obviously meaning here '*the Torah*' and/or '*the Law*' again. This is immediately followed in the Qumran Hymns by two allusions to the '*Tongue*,' '*Lying lips*,' '*condemning in Judgement*,' and finally, the protagonist applying both the language of '*separation*' (just applied in Ephesians above to '*Gentiles in the flesh*,' but here in Hymns, obviously, in the sense of '*Naziritism*') and the language of '*the Righteous vs. the Wicked*' to himself, *i.e.*, '*separating between Zaddik and Rasha° through me*.'[75]

The above imagery of '*shaking*' is also connected two columns earlier in these Hymns to that of Final Eschatological Judgement – again basically evoking the imagery of '*Heaven*' (or '*the Heavens*') and '*coming on the clouds of Glory*.' Here, using imagery, familiar in both the writings of Paul and Muhammad's Koran, '*the mountains like flames*' and '*running like molten pitch*,' we hear how:

> the Heavenly Hosts cry out and the Eternal Foundations quake and shake. Then the War of the Heavenly Mighty Ones scourges the Earth, not ending before the decreed-upon destruction which shall be Forever.[76]

Again the same language of '*decreed-upon destruction*' is used in the Habakkuk *Pesher* above.

This spiritualized '*Temple*' imagery, as just signaled, is also to be found in the Community Rule, VIII.5–10 and IX.6. There, as we saw, amid the imagery of spiritualized '*sacrifice*' and '*atonement*,' it is applied to the Community Council as a spiritualized '*Plantation*' and '*House for Israel*' (in 1 Corinthians 3:9 above, '*God's Field, God's Building*,' introducing Paul '*laying the Foundation as a wise architect*') and, as already also highlighted, a spiritualized '*Foundation of the Holy of Holies for Aaron*.'

> It will be a Tested Rampart, a Precious Cornerstone, whose Foundations shall not rock or sway in their place (here the '*Foundation*' imagery of 1 Corinthians 3:10, Ephesians 2:20, and Hebrews 11:10), a Dwelling Place of the Holy of Holies for Aaron with Everlasting Knowledge of the Covenant of Judgement,...a House of Perfection and Truth in Israel, erected as a Covenant of Eternal Laws.

This is the imagery of the '*Perfect Tabernacle*' in Hebrews 9:11 above, followed immediately in Hebrews 9:12 by evocation of '*the Holy of Holies*' and '*Eternal Redemption*,' presaging the laborious discussion of '*the New Covenant, the First Covenant*,' and '*the Blood of Christ*' that follows. One cannot get a much closer convergence of language than this.

Not only do the Qumran Hymns, when speaking of '*establishing My Building on Rock*,' also allude to '*the Council of Holiness*' of the Community; but this language of '*erecting*' or '*raising*' in the Habakkuk *Pesher*, also present in these allusions in the Hymns, is clearly applied in the Community Rule above to '*the Covenant of Eternal Laws.*' This, in turn, can be nothing other than the Damascus Document's '*House of the Torah*' or '*the Covenant and the Faith they erected in the Land of Damascus, the New Covenant*' – reflected, too, in the Habakkuk *Pesher*, labored over so profusely in these passages from Hebrews, and varied so disingenuously in Paul and the Gospels.

All of the foregoing should be clear proof that Paul knew and was using the '*building*' imagery – alluded to in this final description of '*the Spouter of Lying*' with which the Habakkuk *Pesher* draws to a close – and applying it to himself. One cannot imagine marshalling anything stronger. In conclusion, one can only assume that those writing these *Pesharim* at Qumran understood this too, just as they seem to have understood '*the Lying Spouter*''s more cosmopolitan analysis of '*Salvation*' – as in Paul, probably also based on this passage from Habakkuk 2:4.

'*Erecting an Assembly on Lying*' and '*Tiring out Many with a Worthless Service*'

We now come to the last part of this all-important *Pesher*. It reads, as we saw, that the person '*building*' this '*Worthless City upon Blood and raising a Church*' or '*Assembly on Lying*' caused '*Many*' to perform '*a Worthless Service for the sake of his vainglory*' or '*self-glorification.*' The term '*Service*' here in Hebrew is the other kind of '*Service*' or '*work*' – the kind presumably that '*Martha*' and others indulged in above or what Paul several times refers to as '*toil*' or '*labor*' and what we have also been translating as '*Mission.*' That it differs from '*works*' based in Hebrew on the verb '*doing*' – meaning, therefore, '*doing the Torah*' – should by now also be clear.

The term '*Worthless,*' deliberately applied in the *Pesher* to the '*Service*' with which the Spouter of Lying '*tires out Many*' or, for that matter, '*leads Many astray,*' of course, recapitulates the '*Worthless*' applied to the value of the Spouter's '*building a City upon Blood*' above, as well as the '*erecting an Assembly*'/'*Church upon Lying*' coupled with it. Here it should be clear that the '*Worthless Service*' is synonymous with the '*Worthless City,*' so our arguments with regard to this last are sustained. That this is a characterization of the Pauline '*Gentile Mission,*' the accoutrements of which like '*speaking in Tongues,*' we have described above; we feel is more than clear, especially when it is grouped with all the other usages (we have been delineating so extensively) in the context in which it is presented here.

To recapitulate: Paul uses this word '*Worthless*' or '*void*' twice in I Corinthians 15:14 after speaking not only about '*holding fast,*' '*Standing,*' and *'being saved'* in 15:2, but also in 15:5–8 about 'Jesus'' post-resurrection appearances *'to Cephas,' 'to James,'* and *'last of all to (him)'* – *'the least of the Apostles'* – expressing the hope that his communities did not *'believe in vain'* (also in 15:2). He even contends in 1 Corinthians 15.10 that he *'labored more abundantly than them all,'* twice concluding, as we just saw, that *'if Christ was not raised from the dead, then'* both his *'preaching'* and their *'Faith'* were *'worthless.'* In 1 Corinthians 15:58, again using the language of *'being strong'* and *'not wavering'* of the Community Rule, Damascus Document, and Hymns, he summarizes this position, encouraging his followers to *'be firm and immovable.'*[77] Here he repeats the words the Habakkuk *Pesher* is employing in this passage about the Spouter of Lying *'leading Many astray'* almost verbatim: *'knowing that your labor is not Worthless in the Lord.'*

In 2 Corinthians 6:1, again alluding to *'working together,'* he speaks of *'not receiving the Grace of God in vain'* and in 2 Corinthians 9:3, his hope that his *'boasting (about his communities and his labors) should not have been in vain.'* Significantly, he is referring at this point to *'the funds'* he is collecting from his communities. In Galatians 2:2 he speaks of *'running in vain,'* this *a propos* of the Gospel as he teaches it *'among the Peoples'* (*Ethnesin*) – even possibly recapitulating the language Habakkuk 2:2 applies to the Prophet *'running'* with his vision which the Habakkuk *Pesher* interprets in terms of *'God making known to the Righteous Teacher all the Mysteries of the words of His Servants the Prophets'* (n.b., too here the use of the word *'Servants'*)[78] – and in Galatians 4:11, of *'having labored in vain'* regarding his communities (this, it will be recalled, concerning *'keeping'* feasts, fast *'days,'* and other *'beggarly'* calendrical reckonings).

In Galatians 5:15 and 5:26, he even evokes the term *'Glory'* or *'vainglory'* again, in cautioning his communities *'not to seek vainglory'* or *'self-glorification'* by *'envying,'* and, as we have seen, *'biting and swallowing one another'* – strange words coming from his perspective. This would appear to be the same *'vainglory'* or *'self-glorification'* the Habakkuk *Pesher* is referring to at this point here. There is so much *'vainglory'* of this kind in the corpus ascribed to Paul that to enumerate it all would be endless.

Where the Letter of James is concerned, we have already seen how in the First Chapter, following the characteristic caution to its recipients not to be *'led astray'* (1:16), nor to be *'only hearers, Deceiving yourselves, but Doers of the word'* (1:22 – in 1:25, it may be recalled, this was *'be a Doer of the work'*). James 1:26 then concludes, *'If anyone among you seems Religious, not bridling his Tongue, but rather Deceiving his heart* – here both the *'heart'* and *'Tongue'* imagery in one phrase – *such a one's Religion is Worthless.'* As previously suggested, *'Religion'* here basically approximates or takes the place of the references to *'Service'* and *''amal'* in the Habakkuk *Pesher*.[79]

The *'heart'* imagery here, too, is presaged by Jeremiah 31:31–33's *'making a New Covenant'* with *'the House of Judah'* described, as we saw above, in terms of *'putting My Torah inside them and writing it upon their heart.'* But, it should be clear that, when combined with Habakkuk 2:2's *'writing and running'* above, this produces Paul's play on the appointment *'Letters'* written by James – and, for that matter, *'written letters'* generally – in 2 Corinthians 3:3, referring to *'Christ's Letter, served by us, not written in ink,'* but *'on the fleshy tablets of (the) heart.'*

This too ends with his evocation of his and, doubtlessly, his companions' being *'able Servants of the New Covenant'* in 2 Corinthians 3:6 (here, note again, the Habakkuk *Pesher's 'Servants'* language just signaled above). Paul immediately then adds, as already emphasized and obviously alluding to the *Torah,* *'not of letters but of the Spirit, for the letter kills, but the Spirit gives life'* (here both his *'letters'* and *'the Spirit'* vocabularies). Aside from the clear derogation here, he then concludes speaking fairly plainly this time:

> But if the Ministry of death, having been cut in letters in stones (the Ten Commandments), was produced with Glory...how much rather shall the Ministry of the Spirit be with Glory? For if the Ministry of Condemnation was Glory, how much rather does the Ministry of Righteousness exceed it in Glory (2 Corinthians 3:6–9).

Not only do we have here his strophe/antistrophe/epode lyrical poetry, rhetorical style, but how much more hostile to *'Palestinian'* parameters can one show oneself to be and, of a completely philo-*'Hellenistic'* mindset, can one display?

Not only does one have here the *'condemnation'* and *'Justification,'* descriptive of the eschatological role of the true *'Sons of Zadok'* in the Damascus Document above, to say nothing of the total usurpation of the *'Righteousness'* doctrine itself; but the constant play in the Habakkuk *Pesher* on both the *'Worthless Ministry'* of the Liar and his *'Vainglory.'* The Letter of James, directly following its allusion to *'making yourself a Friend of the World'* and *'turning yourself into an Enemy of God,'* also reverses the thrust of Paul's repeated evocation of this term *'Worthless'* or *'in vain'* by asking, *'Does Scripture speak in vain'*? (James 4:5). For more of Paul's *'Vainglory'* and his *'Tongue,'* one has only to consult 2 Corinthians, which is full of what even Paul himself admits is *'boasting.'* Nor could not find more appropriate examples to illustrate the identity of outlooks between the Habakkuk *Pesher* and the Letter attributed to James.

For its part, the *Pesher* seems to refer to just this kind of activity by adding the phrase to its *'Vainglory'* allusions, *'and instructing them in works of Lying.*'This is how '*the Lying Spouter*' is building his '*Worthless Assembly*' or '*Church upon Blood*' and '*Lying*,' i.e., just as the '*works*' of '*the Righteous Teacher*' are '*Righteous*' and '*full of Righteousness and Justification*'; so, too, the '*works*' of '*the Man of Lies*' are '*of Lying*' and '*Empty.*'We have all of the allusions necessary to connect this material to the kind of person seen as '*the Enemy*' or '*Liar*' – in Islam '*the Dajjal*' or '*Joker*'[80] – in '*Jewish Christian*' or '*Ebionite*' texts such as the *Recognitions* or the *Anabathmoi Jacobou*. There can be little doubt that the '*Worthless City*' referred to at this point in the *Pesher* is an intellectual or spiritual one – the reference to '*Blood*' in this instance, as in Pauline Christianity generally, also being figurative. Nor in this regard should one forget the allusion being attributed to 'Jesus' in Matthew 5:14's '*Sermon on the Mount*' – following ones to '*Strength*,' '*being thrown out*,' '*trampled upon*,' and '*Light*' – of his Community being '*a City on a hill*' that '*could not be hidden*' (*n.b.*, again the '*hidden*' ideology).

Moreover, the *Pesher* does not stop here. It now adds the third kind of works – those we have identified as '*suffering works*' or '*works with eschatological effect*,' the same kind of works the *Pesher* evoked two columns earlier in VIII.2 in its eschatological interpretation of Habakkuk 2:4. This kind of '*works*,' as will be recalled, described how those following the teaching of '*the Righteous Teacher*' would '*be saved from the House of Judgement, because of their works (ᶜamal) and their Faith in the Righteous Teacher.*'

We identified this with the '*works working with Faith*' of James 2:18–26, only now it was '*works*' working with '*Faith in the Righteous Teacher*,' another excellent example of materials relating either to James or '*the Righteous Teacher*' (or both) being retrospectively absorbed into the presentations of 'Jesus' such as Paul is now using in Galatians and, to a lesser extent, in Romans to construct his ideology of the '*Salvation by Faith.*' In the Habakkuk *Pesher*, the same term 'ᶜamal' is now applied to how the Liar '*tired out Many with a Worthless Service, instructing them in works of Lying, so that their ᶜamal (or 'works') would be Empty*' or '*for Emptiness*' – '*Empty*' here, clearly meaning '*Empty of saving*' or '*eschatological effect.*'

In regard to this, it is instructive to look, for instance, at Paul's encouragement at the end of 1 Corinthians 15:58 above to his '*Beloved brothers*' to '*be super-abundant in the work(s) of the Lord always, knowing that your toil is not Empty.*' But this is obviously almost word-for-word the description in the Habakkuk *Pesher* above about the 'ᶜamal' of the Spouter of Lying '*being Empty.*'[81] The counterpoint between this and the Habakkuk *Pesher*, not to mention Paul's reference to '*Super Apostles*' elsewhere, cannot be accidental and even the '*James*'-like '*works*,' now called '*the work(s) of the Lord*,' is here evoked. This word '*Empty*' – and the word in the Habakkuk *Pesher* in Hebrew at this point *is* '*Empty*' – is also the basis of the epithet

James 2:20 uses to describe the '*Wicked*' Ideological Opponent, who doesn't know that '*Faith without works is dead*' nor that, '*just as the body apart from the Spirit is dead, so Faith apart from works is also dead*' (2:26).

James calls this individual the '*Empty Man*' or '*Man of Emptiness*,' obviously alluding to that individual's position on how '*Abraham was justified*' and the eschatological value of the '*suffering works*' or '*toil*' with which '*he instructed* (or '*misled*'?) *the Many*' – that is, that '*they counted for Nothing*' or were '*Empty*' of soteriological effect where the matter of eschatological '*Salvation*' or '*being saved*' was concerned. In thinking that '*Abraham was justified by Faith*' and not '*works*,' this individual – who in his very being gainsaid the idea of Abraham as '*the Friend of God*,' he being '*the Enemy of God*' – did not know that '*Abraham was justified by works when he offered up his son Isaac on the altar*' (2:21).

There can be no doubting the implication of these words and the purposeful introduction of a notation like that of '*camal*' into the Qumran exposition of both Habakkuk 2:4 – which we have already identified as '*Jamesian*' – and 2:13 about '*the Peoples laboring for the sake of Fire and the Peoples tiring themselves out for the sake of Emptiness*' in terms of the value of the teaching of the Ideological Adversary of '*the Righteous Teacher*.' With this last, we approach – where matters of this kind are concerned – about as close to absolute convergence as one could imagine.

The exegesis of these passages from Habakkuk 2:12–13 now closes by calling down '*Hell-fire*' on precisely the kind of individual who has been '*building (this) Worthless City upon Blood and raising a Church* ('*Congregation*'/'*Assembly*') *upon Lying*,' '*blaspheming and vilifying the Elect of God*.' There can be little doubt that throughout the corpus of Letters attributed to him in the New Testament, particularly Galatians and 1 and 2 Corinthians, Paul did precisely this – '*insulted and vilified*' the Leadership of '*the Jerusalem Assembly*' or '*the Church*' led by James.

It will be recalled, Paul even went so far as to characterize the '*Hebrew*' Apostles as '*those reckoned to be something*' or '*those who wrote their own letters of recommendation*,' '*not that their importance*,' as far as he was concerned, '*anything conferred*' (Galatians 2:6). For him, these '*Super Apostles*' were really Servants of Satan '*transforming themselves into Servants of Righteousness*' and, parodying the actual doctrines of these last, as already noted, their '*End would be according to their works*' (2 Corinthians 11:15). In addition to their doctrine of '*works*,' he is also parodying the language of '*the Last End*' and '*Service*' in the Habakkuk *Pesher* above.

To repeat once again, as the *Pesher* now responds to this: those who '*blasphemed and vilified the Elect of God*,' instructing others '*in works of Lying*' and '*tiring*' them out '*with a Worthless Service*,' would themselves be brought, as just indicated, to '*the (same) Judgements of Fire with which they had insulted and vilified the Elect of God.*'[82] Paul calls down similar '*Judgement*' against the Jerusalem Leadership in 2 Corinthians 11:15 above whereas James 2:13, in its discussion of '*the Tongue*' being '*a Fiery World of Unrighteousness,*' also speaks about '*Judgement without Mercy for him who does no Mercy.*' For him, this same Tongue, '*set among our members,*' '*setting on Fire in the course of nature,*' will itself '*be set on Fire by Hell*' (3:5–3:6).

Final Things: '*On the Day of Judgement God will Destroy all the Servants of Idols from the Earth*'

Before moving on to its treatment of the fate of the Righteous Teacher and Wicked Priest in Columns XI–XII, the Habakkuk *Pesher* pauses to interpret a passage from Habakkuk 2:14, as we saw, about '*the Earth filling with the Knowledge of the Glory of the Lord like waters covering the sea.*' Though coming at the end of Column X.14–16 and, therefore, fragmentary again – aside from the fact that it was from this citation (to say nothing of the ones about '*the City of Blood*' in 2:12 and '*laboring for the sake of Fire*' in 2:13) that the extraordinary exegesis about how '*the Spouter of Lying led Many astray*' was constructed – the reference to '*waters*' in the underlying text seems to be interpreted in terms of '*repenting*' or '*a repentance*' of some kind and it is after this that it is asserted that '*Knowledge, like the waters of the sea, should be revealed to them abundantly.*'

Here, not only can something of a parallel to the '*abundant works of the Law*' alluded to in 1 Corinthians 15:58 above possibly be discerned, but also possibly one to what is portrayed as '*the descent of the Holy Spirit*' in Acts or '*Holy Spirit-baptism*' generally. Whatever this '*Knowledge of the Glory of God*' from 2:14 is interpreted to be, it is clearly the opposite of the '*puffed up Knowledge*' of those forbidding the consumption of '*things sacrificed to idols,*' to whom Paul so contemptuously refers in 1 Corinthians 8:1ff. But it is the opposite as well of '*the waters of Lying,*' '*the Comedian*' or '*Lying Scoffer*' is said to '*pour over Israel*' in the First Column of CD.

After turning again to the subject of what '*the Wicked Priest*' did to '*the Righteous Teacher*' and '*the Poor*' and how '*the Cup of the Wrath of God,*' in turn, would come around and '*swallow him*' in Columns XI.4–XII.9, the *Pesher*, as already signaled, concludes on the note of '*Idolatry*' and '*serving Idols.*' This was also the theme, seemingly reversed in Paul and applied to '*the Table of the Demons*' and that of '*reclining in an idol Temple*' generally and '*eating things sacrificed to idols*' in 1 Corinthians 8:1–13 and 10:14–33.

Here at the conclusion of the Habakkuk *Pesher*, it is connected to the evocation of '*the Day of Judgment*' and '*Salvation*' or '*being saved*' at the time of this Last Judgement, language and themes – as we have also stressed – part of the all-important eschatological exposition of Habakkuk 2:4 four columns earlier in VIII.1–3 as well. Not only is the theme of *'Idolatry'* important in the *'Three Nets of Belial'* accusations against the Establishment and, as we have now seen, the Letter(s) known as *'MMT'*; it is also part and parcel of James' directives to overseas communities in the sense of what Acts either calls *'the pollutions of the idols'* or *'things sacrificed to idols.'*

This is the context in which Paul is responding to it in 1 Corinthians too, the letter in which he ultimately sets forth his ideas of *'Communion with'* and *'the New Covenant in the Blood of Christ'* – the very same *'Blood,'* as already underscored as well, ostensibly forbidden in James' prohibitions to overseas communities. Paul refers to this *'idol-worship'* in the run-up to his presentation of *'Communion with the blood of Christ'* in the conclusion of his discussion of James' *'eating things sacrificed to an idol'* – also in conjunction with *'Cup'* imagery – in 1 Corinthians 10:16–21 as we have seen.

As this same imagery emerges, but with opposite signification, in these final columns of the Habakkuk *Pesher*, it is of such poignancy and immediacy as to be heart-rending. Moreover, it is an example of that long-suffering *'patience'* and *'steadfast'* Faith, we have seen encouraged in the Letters of both Paul and James above despite their differing points-of-view. In the Habakkuk *Pesher*, this is perhaps best evidenced by the exegesis of Habakkuk 2:3: *'If it tarries, wait for it'* – an exegesis seemingly attributed to *'the Righteous Teacher'* and clearly paralleled in the last Chapter of James by the admonition, *'Be patient brothers until the coming of the Lord,'* *'strengthen your hearts because the coming of the Lord approaches.'* In the Damascus Document this last is referred to – together with the same *'Strengthening'* imagery – as *'the Visitation of the Land.'*[83] This is the same kind of *'Strengthening'* also signaled by Paul in 1 Corinthians 15:58 above.

The sequence that is followed here at the end of the Habakkuk *Pesher* also almost precisely follows that of early Church accounts delineating the death of James. In these accounts, James' death, it will be recalled, is pictured as immediately being followed by the appearance of foreign Armies outside Jerusalem and the final destruction of both City and Temple presumably because, as we have explained, *'the Protection'*/*'Pillar'*/or *'Bulwark,'* provided by *'the Righteous One'* James, had been removed. In Columns VIII–XI of the Habakkuk *Pesher*, the sequence is: the destruction of *'the Righteous Teacher,'* the destruction of *'the Wicked Priest'* and *'the Last Priests of Jerusalem'* – this last, paralleling what the Gospels call *'the Chief Priests'* – and their *'Riches'* and *'spoils'* (collected, seemingly, by the agency of *'the Peoples'* or *'Herodians'* and other *'Violent Ones'*) given over to 'the Army of the Kittim' or 'the Additional Ones of the Peoples.'[84]

But in the immediacy and poignancy of this commentary, it is the 'Pious Faithfulness' that stands out. These people have undergone every reversal and tragedy. Their Community has been decimated. 'The Righteous Teacher' – just as in the Gospels – has been destroyed. Jerusalem is either in the process of being destroyed or already destroyed. 'The Kittim' are overrunning the Land, 'taking no pity on' anyone, 'youths, men, old people, women and children, even babes in the wombs' (of course, a more accurate description of the Romans could not be imagined[85]). In the words of the Nahum Pesher, supported by Josephus' descriptions: 'the corpses are stacked up everywhere' and 'there is no end to the sum of the slain.'[86]

In particular, the group responsible for these writings has lost everything and 'the Last End will be extended beyond anything the Prophets have foretold' – an exegesis of Habakkuk 2:3 seemingly ascribed, as we have seen, to 'the Righteous Teacher' ('to whom God made known all the Mysteries of His Servants the Prophets') in his role as God's exegete on Earth.

In short, we have an eye-witness account of these events – as the Gospels are supposed to be but are not – written as they are actually going on. Nothing could be more immediate or compelling. Nor as 'Men of Truth' and 'Doers of the Torah' are they 'to slacken from the Service of Truth – as opposed presumably to 'the Service of Lying' – though the Final Age is to be extended beyond anything the Prophets have foretold.' Therefore, the author(s) of this document call down on the kinds of 'Enemies' they are facing the only 'curses' they have left, those of 'the Day of Judgement,' wherein will be their ultimate 'Salvation' – that is, they do not give up.

This is delivered from Columns XII.10–XIII.4, as already alluded to, in exposition of an underlying reference to 'Lying' and 'dumb idols' from Habakkuk 2:18: 'Of what use are graven images, whose makers formed a casting and images of Lying' and directed against both 'those who serve idols' (that is, 'the Servants of Idols') and 'the Wicked Ones' ('Reshaᶜim' – plural). The former are, in fact, overtly identified in the Pesher as 'Gentiles' (Go'im). The latter, as already suggested, have to be identified as 'backsliding Jews'– people like 'the Wicked Priest,' responsible for the destruction of 'the Righteous Teacher,' who 'did not circumcise the foreskin of his heart'; or persons like the Alexandrian Jewish turncoat, Philo's nephew and Titus' Commander-in-Chief at the siege of Jerusalem and the destruction of the Temple, Tiberius Alexander, whom Josephus specifically identifies as just such a 'Backslider.'[87] In fact, where the Pesher is concerned, they would probably also include the whole Pharisee/Sadducean Establishment or collaborators such as R. Yohanan ben Zacchai above or Josephus himself and, of course, Paul. There are many – enough to go around – and all are to be subjected to the same '*Hell-Fire.*'

It is the allusion to '*serve*' here which is so pivotal in the evocation of '*serving the idols of the Nations,*' the same '*Service*' or '*labor*' we have already seen referred to in the description of the Liar's efforts as '*Worthless*' or '*vain*' and the same language Paul over and over again applies to his own activities – what the world often describes as '*Mission.*' This is roundly condemned. As we saw earlier, this is put in the following manner:

> *This concerns all the sculptures of the Gentiles, which they create in order to serve and bow down to them. These will not save them on the Day of Judgement.*[88]

Here, of course, are the same words, '*save them,*' we have just seen used in the eschatological interpretation of Habakkuk 2:4 in the *Pesher* in viii.2. The phrase '*Day of Judgement*' is, of course, related to the previous formulation in that *Pesher*, '*House of Judgement*' (not '*condemned house*' as in some translations) which, in turn, will be used two columns later in x.3 to describe '*the Judgement God would deliver in the midst of Many Peoples.*'

The same sentiment is encountered over and over in the Koran where, as already underscored, the same phrase in Arabic, '*Day of Judgement,*' is also used. In fact, the author of the Koran – a latterday '*Apostle to the Peoples*' (much like Paul) – designates his enemies by the same terms, '*Idolaters*' and '*Backsliders*' as here in the Habakkuk *Pesher*, repeatedly calling down upon them the same imprecations.[89] So parallel are these imprecations that it is possible to suspect a more than casual connection.

1QpHab,xii.16–xiii now closes by repeating this fulsome condemnation, extending it to all '*Evil Ones*' generally, presumably including all Jewish Backsliders, as we have explained. It does so in exegesis of a passage from Habakkuk 2:19–20: '*Can this guide? Behold it is covered with gold and silver and there is no spirit at all within it.*' Not only does this delineate the problem with '*idols,*' it specifically alludes to the telltale words, '*gold and silver,*' that we also encountered in the eschatological Judgement section of the last Chapter of the Letter of James condemning '*the Rich*' (5:3). We have also encountered the same phraseology in the passage about coming eschatological Judgement in Isaiah 2:20–21, preceding the Isaiah 3:10–11 passages – applied to James' death in early Church sources and incorporated, as we illustrated, into exegeses about '*the destruction of the Poor*' in the Habakkuk *Pesher*.

There is also the pious hope, expressed in the second part of the underlying text from Habakkuk 2:20 here in the Habakkuk *Pesher* too, seeming sadly forlorn in these disastrous and devastating times of complete and general collapse: '*But the Lord is in his Holy Temple, let all the*

Earth be still before Him.' One cannot avoid the conclusion that whoever is subjecting words of such sublime hopefulness to such interpretation is doing so in the midst of total disaster and that we have in this document an eye-witness account – as just remarked but also worth reiterating – of the most awe-inspiring devotion and Piety of the events leading up to and surrounding the the fall of Jerusalem in 70 CE. One has to assume that whoever the exegete was, the passages were chosen purposefully.

As the *Pesher* closes, it interprets the passage, as we have already seen as well, as follows:

> *Its interpretation concerns all the Gentiles, who serve but stone and wood (i.e., idols). But on the Day of Judgement God will destroy all the Servants of Idols and (all) Evil Ones from off the Earth.*[90]

The display of such '*Faithfulness*' and undying commitment is stunning in such circumstances.

The use of the word '*destroy*' here is the same one we saw used earlier in the description of what would happen to '*the Wicked Priest*' for what he had done to '*the Righteous Teacher*' and his '*plots to destroy the Poor.*' We have also seen it used in precisely this manner in eschatological '*Judgement*' sections of the Qumran Hymns and the Community Rule above.[91] It means *utter* '*destruction.*' There probably never was a more forlorn and pathetic document ever penned, now come back – in a state of almost perfect preservation – some Twenty Centuries later to haunt and unsettle us all.

Not only have we proven our case, it is clear that these allusions in the Scrolls, if not identical with the situation in early Christianity, at least are almost the exact parallel to it – so much so that the two sets of allusions approach what only can be considered identity. But, in addition, we have shown through the Dead Sea Scrolls and a close analysis of early Church texts and literature, the *lacuna*, overwrites, and ofttimes even outright falsification in the early Church presentation of its own history.

The keynote here is reversal – always reversal. Everything is being reversed and turned around from the way it was in Palestine in this Period as attested by eye-witness accounts like the Dead Sea Scrolls (which are completely homogeneous in this regard) and other documents. Palestinian Messianism is being, as it were, '*turned on its ear*' and reversed and turned into Hellenistic and allegorical mythologizing, some of which redacted in the form of exquisite Gospel narratives which have not failed to catch the imagination of Mankind ever since – though, as always, not without an often rather-unpleasant barb of anti-Semitism.

28

From Adiabene to Cyrene: The Cup of the Lord, the Blood of Christ, and the *Sicaricon*

Northern Syrian Conversion Stories: '*ᶜAd and Thamud*' and '*Hud and Salih*'

Despite a certain amount of repetition – which in circumstances as recondite and complex as these is probably unavoidable – it would be worth
recapitulating some of the key issues addressed in this book. Before
doing so, however, it one should look more closely at the stories in the
Koran about '*ᶜAd and Thamud*' and '*Hud and Salih*,' touched on previously
but not delineated in any detail. These have always been thought of as
showing Muhammad's acquaintance with unknown cities and '*Prophets*'
in the '*Arabian*' cultural sphere. The normal understanding is that these
stories have to do with little remembered '*Arab*' Holy Men, functioning
in some quasi-identifiable locale in the Arabian Peninsula at some time
in the primordial past before the coming of Islam. The usual explanations
are replete with forced connections and nonsensical rationalizations. All
is hazy or unknown and nothing of any certainty emerges.

A typical commentary or explanation runs something like this:

> *ᶜAd was the name of a tribe who lived in the remote past in Arabia. At one time
> they ruled over most of the fertile parts of greater Arabia, particularly Yemen,
> Syria, and Mesopotamia (i.e.,* just about everywhere). *They were the first
> people to exercise dominion over practically the whole of Arabia* (this is from an
> '*Ahmadiyya*' commentary, but almost all present the same or similar
> insights).[1]

Another runs:

> *The Thamud People were the successors to the culture and civilization of the ᶜAd
> People.*[2]

Almost all connect these persons or peoples in some manner with
Abraham because, in the Koran, all such references are almost always

followed up by evocation of '*Abraham.*' In the context of our previous points about the importance of Abraham, this connection is probably true but in a different manner than most might think. Nor, probably, have they anything to do with a genealogical connection with either '*Abraham*' or '*Noah,*' another individual mentioned prominently in these traditions.

Here is a third:

> The Thamud Tribe lived in the western parts of Arabia, having spread from Aden northward to Syria. They lived shortly before the time of Ishmael. Their territory was adjacent to that of ᶜAd, but they lived mostly in the hills...The Prophet Salih lived after Hud and was probably a contemporary of Abraham[3];

and a fourth:

> The Thamud People were the successors to the culture and civilization of the ᶜAd People...They were cousins to the ᶜAd, apparently a younger branch of the same race. Their story also belongs to Arabian tradition, according to which their eponymous ancestor, Thamud, was a son of ᶜAbir (brother of Aram) the son of Sam (Shem), the son of Noah (thus!).

Most of these comments are drawn from real or imagined references in the Koran and on the whole represent a total garbling of only dimly recalled and little understood oral tradition. What we would now like to show is that they come from traditions which Muhammad or his voices (Angelic or real) derived from either Northern Syria or Southern Iraq – probably the latter.

We have already remarked the general connection of many of Muhammad's ideas with sectarian movements in Southern Iraq such as the Mandaeans and Manichaeans and, if the additional relationships we shall now illustrate are true, then they considerably reinforce the connections of traditions of this sort with the kind of visits Muhammad was reputed to have made to Southern Iraq and even, perhaps, Northern Syria – and to the caravan trade, which could have easily carried him, or those he came in contact with, to such locales. However, of perhaps even more significance, what we shall attempt to demonstrate is that these notices, in fact, have to do with cities, '*Peoples,*' or '*Prophets*'/'*Warners*' (as the Koran would put it[4])/or '*Messengers*' within the '*Arabian*' culture sphere. Furthermore, what is not generally appreciated and, as we have been showing, the allusion '*Arab*' had a much wider connotation in the Greco-Roman Period than is normally considered nowadays to apply. As

a result, these stories had, geographically-speaking, a much wider transmission framework and actually reflect Northern Syrian conversion
stories of the kind we have been highlighting in this work – themselves
very important to both '*Jewish*' and '*Christian*' history in this region and,
as we have been suggesting throughout this work, the Dead Sea Scrolls
and, along with them, the person of James.

Having said this, the key connections are '*^cAd*' with '*Addai*'/
'*Edessa*'/and '*Adiabene*'; '*Thamud*' with '*Thomas*'; '*Hud*' with the characters
we have otherwise been calling '*Judas Thomas*' (as we have seen, the other
or real name of '*Thomas*'), also equivalent to '*Thaddaeus*', '*Judas Barsabas*',
'*Judas the Zealot*', and, in this sense, '*Judas Iscariot*' – in fact, just about all
the '*Judas*'es) in this Period; and '*Salih*' (the Arabic for '*Righteousness*' or
'*Righteous One*'), of course, with '*James the Just*', the '*brother*' either of
'Jesus' or this '*Hud*'. Even Muslim sources and commentators have gar-
nered this conclusion, no doubt based on his name, appreciating that
'*Salih*' was '*a Just and Righteous Man*.'[5]

The reason these stories are so important, too, is because they unify
the several conversion stories we have been following in both Early
Christian and Jewish sources (and now probably also those at Qumran)
relating to this region. As already made clear, in our view these stories
have to do with the conversion of '*the King of Edessa*', known in early
Christian and Greco-Latin sources as '*Abgarus*' or '*Agbarus*', called in
Christian sources '*the Great King of the Peoples beyond the Euphrates*.' Furthermore, they have to do with the Kings and Queen of the Royal
House of Adiabene – according to Syriac and Armenian sources, the
consort of this '*Agbarus*'[6] – contiguous to this '*Edessa*' and a little further
East '*beyond the Euphrates*.' They also have a direct link to the development of the tradition that '*James the Righteous One*' sent down one '*Judas
Barsabas*' (among others – supposedly '*Silas, Barnabas, and Paul*') in Acts
15:22–32 to regulate matters having to do with this evangelization in a
place it knows as '*Antioch*' but, as we have been trying to demonstrate,
probably also '*Edessa*' and, in any event, a '*Northern Syrian*' locale.

These '*Northern Syrian*' conversion stories are also important, because
they throw light on the puzzling terminology '*Sabaean*' in the Koran (and
elsewhere), which in Islamic sources – as well as it turns out (as we have
been pointing out too), as '*Christian*'[7] – is often confused with '*Saba*'' or
'*Sheba*' in Southern Arabia or Ethiopia

Let us take these matters one at a time. In the first place it is rarely, if
ever, realized that the word '*Arab*' or '*Arabia*' was being used, as just indicated, in Roman times to encompass a much wider expanse both of
territory and personalities. Roman historians, such as Tacitus, routinely

use the term 'Arab' to refer to Northern Syrian personages and Kings –
as, in fact, persons still do today.[8] For Tacitus, 'King Acbar' or 'Abgar' (we
have already commented on this kind of confusion concerning Semitic
names above[9]) is 'King of the Arabs.'[10] Other sources, in fact, also refer to
him as 'the Black,' a sobriquet, as we have already signaled as well, which
will have more than the normal significance.[11]

Furthermore, we have treated the matter of this greater expanse of
land going by the designation 'Arabia' in the map section of this book,
illustrating it to have extended up into Mesopotamia as far as Edessa and
Adiabene in Northern Syria and modern Iraq. Petra, across the Jordan
River and on the other side of the ʿAravah, is a locale whose Kings were
definitely being referred to as 'Arab.' We have already made it clear that
this would make Herod – whose mother was from an aristocratic family
in Petra, not improbably, related to its King – what would loosely be
called an 'Arab.' Modern scholars, following one or two leads in Josephus,
are fond of referring to this culture as 'Nabataean' after 'Nabaioth,' one of
Ishmael's sons in Genesis 25:13[12]; but it is doubtful if these Peoples really
ever referred to themselves in such a manner or, for that matter, anything
other than 'Arab' which, as we have been showing, had wide currency in
the Roman First–Second Centuries. It is this state of affairs that
Muhammad seems unwittingly to be echoing in his general references
to these legendary Peoples of 'ʿAd and Thamud.'

Such a broader definition also imparts an entirely new dimension to
Paul's notice in Galatians 1:16 about how, after receiving his 'version of the
Good News as he taught it among the Gentiles' (here 'Peoples'/'Ethnesin'
again), he did not return to Jerusalem or 'discuss it with any living being' (his
usual allusion to 'flesh and blood' – of course, he did 'discuss it' with more
'Spiritual' or 'Supernatural' Beings such as his 'Christ Jesus' in Heaven, the
source of many of his supernatural 'visions'/'apocalypseis') or, for that
matter, 'those who were Apostles before (him'). On the contrary, he 'went
straightway into Arabia' and, only thereafter, 'again returned to Damascus'
(1:17). The question is, precisely what did he mean by this reference here
to 'Arabia'?

Normally it is only thought of as having to do with Arabian 'Petra' or
some such locale – even a Qumran or an 'Essene'-style novitiate of some
kind in the Judean or Transjordanian Desert ('the Land of Damascus'?).
But this broader definition allows us to consider that it meant (as we have
been suggesting) as far north as 'Edessa' or 'the Land of the Edessenes' or
'Osrhoeans' ('Assyrians' – this, it will be recalled, is how Eusebius refers to
it); or even, as just suggested too, 'Adiabene' neighboring 'Edessa' some
hundred miles or so further East; or as far South as 'Messene' (Mani's

birthplace) or '*Antiochia Charax*' (presentday Basrah), the area where Josephus first traces Izates' contact with the merchant he is calling '*Ananias*' who, as we saw – together with another teacher unnamed in Josephus' account – teaches a sort of conversion to what is supposed to be Judaism which does not require '*circumcision*'[13]!

This would mean that what Paul is alluding to by '*into Arabia*' could be much further afield than is generally appreciated, even as far North and East as '*Antioch-by-Callirhoe*' or '*Antioch Orrhoe*' and/or '*Adiabene*' – today's Kurdistan – in Northern Mesopotamia. This is before his return to '*Damascus*,' from where he later – or perhaps earlier, depending on how one evaluates his own account in 2 Corinthians 11:32 – seems to have escaped from representatives of the '*Arab*' King Aretas of Petra. As already remarked, one must appreciate that Acts 9:25's tendentious account of these same events is secondary. As already underscored as well, all these episodes also involve the contact with the mysterious and unidentified personage named '*Ananias*' – as we saw, the same '*Ananias*' who (as Eusebius reports it) will reappear in the Syriac accounts of '*King Agbar*' or '*Abgar*''s conversion.

'*The Land of Noah*,' the Location of Mt. Ararat, '*the Elchasaites*,' and Other '*Daily Bathers*' there

There is another oddity that comes to light in the context of the notices about these '*Lands*' and the conversions that took place there and that is the location of the fabled Mount Ararat where Noah's ark came to rest, which the perspicacious reader of the Koran will realize is associated in most of these allusions with '*Hud*' and '*ᶜAd*,' '*Salih*' and '*Thamud*.' Modern hagiography has, of course, placed the ark in Northern Anatolia on the Russian border next to a mountain now called '*Mt. Ararat*.' This is partly due to the wandering of '*Armenia*' northwards ('*Armenia*' presumably being the area where Aramaic was originally spoken), so that the only real Armenia left – particularly after the Turkish devastations – is in Southern Russia. The point is that this ark was always associated in some manner with '*Armenia*' and, as we shall see, this is basically the implication of these notices in the Koran as well.

But for early historians, such as Josephus or Hippolytus (the manuscript '*On Sects*' attributed to him was found at Mount Athos in Greece at the end of the last Century), the ark came to rest in '*the Land of the Adiabeni*' – that is, the '*Adiabene*' we have so assiduously been following above[14] – which turns out to be modern Kurdistan or the area of Northern Iraq, moving up into the mountains of Southern Turkey and *not*

Northern Turkey. In fact, one of the best witnesses to this is the Twelfth-Century Jewish traveler Benjamin of Tudela. He actually visited the mosque on an island in the Tigris dedicated to the place where the ark was supposed to have come to rest and, unless he was dreaming (which I very much doubt that he was), this is just North of presentday Mosul – in fact, he locates it between Nisibis and Mosul.[15] As he puts it, leaving Haran (the *'Carrhae'* or *'Carron'* of Josephus' narrative) and passing through Nisibis, he comes to:

> an island in the Tigris at the foot of Mount Ararat, four miles distant from the spot where the ark of Noah rested. Omar ibn al Katab removed the ark from the summit of the two mountains and made a mosque of it.

However mythological this may appear to be or sound, it perfectly accords with what Hippolytus in the Third Century and Josephus in the First are telling us almost a millennium previously. It also accords with Talmudic data connecting the ark to the Land from which Queen Helen came – that is, *'Adiabene'* or *'Kurdistan.'*[16] Whether Benjamin of Tudela is accurate in this tradition or not (who can be accurate in any tradition concerning *'Noah's ark'*?) is unimportant. The point is that this is where *he thinks* the ark came to rest, as did a number of his predecessors – some already cited. Because of the notices, already alluded to above, connecting *'cAd and Thamud'* with *'the Folk of Noah'* – not to mention to *'the People of Abraham'* – and the place where the ark came to rest, it would appear that the Koran seems to think so as well.[17] Mosul, of course, is connected to ancient Nineveh and both are but a little distant from Arbela, considered by most to have been the capital of Adiabene on the Northern reaches of the Tigris.

But more to the point *'cAd,'* even if looked at only superficially, is, in fact, linguistically related not only to *'Edessa,'* but also to the place name *'Adiabene.'* One can go further than this. In all these stories about conversions in Northern Syria to some form of *'Christianity,'* retrospectively it is always *orthodox 'Christianity'*; but, as we have been suggesting, it was most probably heterodox or one of the manifold varieties of what is now sometimes referred to as *'Jewish Christianity'* – and this is also the case with regard to Helen's or her son Izates' conversion to what is supposed to be a form of *'Judaism'* further East connected to these.

'Jewish Christianity' is poor nomenclature. Even the Arabic *'Sabaean,'* as we have been implying, would be more appropriate. The terms *'Ebion-ites,' 'Elchasaites,' 'Masbuthaeans'* (as we saw, *'Daily Bathers,'* from the root in Syriac and/or Aramaic, *'S-B-c'/'to immerse'* – therefore its Arabic

variation, 'Sabaeans' or 'Subba^c'), 'Mandaeans' and, in Palestine, even 'Essenes,' all have a common focus on 'bathing' or 'ritual immersion.'These are the more technical terms – many arising out of the works of early Christian heresiologists of the Second to Fifth Centuries or Josephus – unfortunately, not widely comprehended by the population at large. Where the *Talmud* is concerned, it applies the appellatives 'Minim' or 'Saddukim' to groups of this kind.[18] For example, as already remarked, Epiphanius at the end of the Fourth/the beginning of the Fifth Century refers to an unknown bathing group in Transjordan and beyond, descended from 'the *Essenes*' and '*Ebionites*' and interchangeable with these '*Elchasaites*,' that he calls '*Sampsaeans*.'[19] Writing in Greek, he has no idea of the derivation of the term but, as we have already suggested, this last is almost certainly what goes by the name of '*Sabaean*' in Islamic tradition.

It should be appreciated that even Benjamin of Tudela, in his seemingly very-late Twelfth-Century account, identifies one of two synagogues, he claims actually to have visited in Mosul, as that of '*Nahum the Elchasaite*,' i. e., '*Nahum the Daily Bather*'[20] or, in Islamic terms, '*al-Mughtasilah*' or '*al-Hasih*,' as the Encyclopaedist of that period, known as '*The Fihrist*,' calls the Leader of such '*Mughtasilah*' (not to be confused with the later philosophical group, known to Maimonides and others as '*al-Mu^ctazilah*').[21] In fact, it is possible that this term in Arabic may even be a variation of what goes in Hebrew under the designation '*Karaite*' (though this is probably a stretch), which would make the links between these two groups of Jewish sectarians interesting indeed.

However this may be, this means that even in Benjamin of Tudela's time in the Twelfth Century – unless his manuscript is completely corrupt – there were '*Jewish*' sectarian '*Daily Bathers*' living in Mosul or Arbela, that is, the area that was formerly '*Adiabene*.' Many of these groups move on in the Third and Fourth Centuries – again in Southern Iraq – as we saw, into what come to be known as '*Manichaeans*' – the only real difference being that, whereas '*the Elchasaite*'/'*Ebionite*'/'*Mughtasilite*'/and '*Sabaean*' groups stressed '*Daily Bathing*,' '*the Manichaeans*' abjured it – and from there on into Islam. In fact, Mani, it has become clear from more recently uncovered texts, as already remarked as well, was actually from an '*Elchasaite*' family in this same Messene area of Southern Iraq.

The point that all these groups actually have in common, including the latterday Muslims (who like the Manichaeans discarded the '*bathing*' ideology of the earlier though still-extant '*Subba^c of the Marshes*' – The *Fihrist* calls them '*the Mughtasilah of the Marshes*') is '*the True Prophet*' ideology. As already underscored, this ideology is very definitely strong at

Qumran where the passage underlying it from Deuteronomy 18:18–19 is actually one of the '*Messianic*' proof-texts cited in 4QTestimonia.[21] It is also definitely alluded to in the Community Rule.[22] Furthermore, as we have been stressing as well, it is also strong among '*the Ebionites*,' important to '*the Elchasaites*' – allegedly following a '*Prophet*' the heresiologists are calling '*Elchasai*' which they claim means '*Hidden Power*' – and strong among followers of Mani. From there it too proceeds into Islam.

This is not the only Dead Sea Scroll/'*Jamesian*'/Ebionite idea that proceeds into Islam. Two others, as we have been signaling, are the formulation '*believe and do good works*,' which fairly permeates the capsule descriptions of Islam in the Koran[23] – no different than the James 2:22 formulation '*Faith working with works*' and similar phraseologies at Qumran such as the Habakkuk *Pesher* exegesis of '*the Righteous shall live by his Faith*' above – all emphasizing '*doing*.' The second is Islamic dietary regulations, quoted some five times in the Koran and consisting of, among other things, both the '*Jamesian*' '*things sacrificed to idols*' ('*that immolated to an idol*' in the Koran) and '*carrion*.'[24] The reader will, of course, by this time readily recognize these as based on James' directives to overseas communities, repeated three times in Acts 15 and 21 and labored over so disingenuously by Paul in 1 Corinthians 6–12 to produce his own formulations that '*all things are lawful to me*' and '*Communion with the Blood of Christ*'!

The Koranic versions as we have them here, as already several times perhaps explained, are probably based on the Pseudoclementine *Homilies* – originally probably a Syriac work and also the source of much deliberation both about the '*True Prophet*' ideology and '*bathing*.' Its translator, Rufinus, took it into Greek at the end of the Fourth Century and its companion volume, the *Recognitions*, went into Latin at approximately the same time. The formulation, '*carrion*,' reproduced in these pronouncements in the Koran, is clearly delineated the *Homilies* in place of the rather abstruse '*strangled things*' in the Greek New Testament – though even the idea of '*carrion*' can be deduced from this last.[26]

The Conversion of '*Agbar Uchama*,' the Activities of '*Hud*,' '*Salih*,' '*Addai*,' and '*Thaddaeus*' in '*cAd and Thamud*,' and '*MMT*'

We are now ready to approach these notices about a conversion that took place in Northern Syria in a place our sources are calling '*Edessa*' – as we have seen, a late Greco-Syriac/Aramaic name for that city – presumably in the First Century and having to do with a King there known as '*Agbar*' or '*Acbar*' (the Latin pronunciation) or '*Abgar*' (the Semitic). The document Eusebius claims to be translating, as already noted, calls him '*Abgar Uchama*' or '*Agbar the Black*' and he is, most probably, to be identified with Abgar V, c. 4 BC–50 CE.[26] The Fifth-Century Armenian historian, Moses of Chorene (some consider this a pseudonym for a later Ninth-Century Armenian historian), is already testifying to the difficulty Westerners are having with names based on Semitic originals[27] and such a reversal of letters, as we have seen, is a common phenomenon for those familiar with the vagaries of translating Middle Eastern nomenclature.

We have been using the Latin derivative, '*Agbar*,' because of its clear connections with the garbled name '*Agabus*' in Acts 11:28, the '*Prophet*' who was supposed to have '*come down from Judea to Antioch*' and predicted the Famine. This idea of a '*Famine*' will also bear some connection with these Koranic notices about the problems in either '*ᶜAd*' or '*Thamud*.'[28] The names '*Edessa*' and even '*Adiabene*' also have, as just pointed out, a clear relationship with the terminology '*ᶜAd*' and the '*Prophet*' called in some sources – in particular, the Syriac – '*Addai*.'[29]

When the name '*Edessa*' gained currency is not clear at all but, before it was called '*Edessa*,' it was apparently called '*Antiochia Orrhoe*' or '*Antioch-by-Callirhoe*' – there being not one, but at least four '*Antioch*'s in the Seleucid Empire previously, as we have seen: the one at the bottom of the Tigris Delta – '*Antiochia Charax*' (in Greek sometimes, '*Charax Spasini*'), '*Antioch-on-the-Orontes*,' '*Antioch-in-Pisidia*' mentioned in Acts, and this one. The fact that Antioch Orrhoe or by-Callirhoe was on the upper reaches of the Euphrates, not far from Carrhae or the ancient city of Haran, that is, Abraham's place of origin, as already explained at length, had a not inconsiderable bearing on not only Early Christian and Jewish sources but also quite clearly the Koran itself. We have already made it clear as well that, in our view, the '*Antioch*' intended in these several notices in Acts about individuals, such as this '*Agabus*,' '*some insisting on circumcision*' (the '*some from James*' in Galatians 2:12), and '*Judas Barsabas*' who brought down '*the Letter*' James wrote in Acts 15:23–30, was not Antioch-on-the-Orontes near the Mediterranean Coast; but rather the one in Northern Syria, connected to this name '*ᶜAd*,' where these legendary conversions took place (and neither coincidentally nor insignificantly, from where the celebrated '*Holy Shroud*' was ultimately alleged to have come[30]).

These notices, also reflecting Galatians and Paul's confrontations at '*Antioch*' with the '*some from James*' of '*the Party of the Circumcision*,' are about individuals like '*Agabus*,' '*Judas Barsabas*,' and the '*some insisting that, unless you are circumcised you cannot be saved*' who trigger, as we have seen, the equally-celebrated '*Jerusalem Council*.' Furthermore, they contain the note that it was '*in Antioch that the Disciples were first called Christians*' (11:26 – *thus!*). As already made clear, in our view there was nothing of note really happening at this time in '*Antioch-on-the-Orontes*' and the only reason we think there was – as the authors of Acts have made us do – is because of our and their respective ignorance (or purposeful dissimulation). What was happening was happening here in Northern Syria with these legendary conversions in '*the Land of the Edessenes*' or '*Osrhoeans*'/ '*Assyrians*' – '*the Lands*' of '*the Great King of the Peoples beyond the Euphrates*.' In our sources these '*Lands*,' as already underscored too, are also being called '*Arab*.' It turns out that the intermediary in this correspondence between this '*Great King*' and Jerusalem in the Syriac source, that Eusebius claims to have found and translated, was, yet again, this same '*Ananias*' – a not unnoteworthy coincidence.

The story, as we have already reviewed it and as Eusebius presents it, concerns two characters he calls '*Judas Thomas*' and '*Thaddaeus*,' neither of whom are really properly identified in any other '*Christian*' source. In the Gospel of John, for instance, '*Thomas*' is called '*Didymus Thomas*,' i.e., as already underscored, '*Twin*' in Greek' and '*Twin*' in Aramaic or, quite literally '*Twin Twin*.' In the newly-recovered Gospel of Thomas found at Nag Hammadi, he is '*Didymus Judas Thomas*,' combining the two sorts of appellations but, once more, manifestly unaware of the inherent redundancy of referring to both '*Didymus*' and '*Thomas*.'[31] All Gospel presentations, too, of '*a Disciple*' or '*Apostle*' called '*Thomas*' must be seen as either suspect, uninformed, or dissimulating as well. Even in John 20:24, when he appears as the '*missing*' Apostle, *he sometimes overlaps* '*Judas Iscariot*' *in the Synoptics*. Nor does '*Thomas*' seem to be mentioned in the newly-released '*Gospel of Judas*' which doesn't seem to make it clear if its '*Judas*' is surnamed '*the Iscariot*' or distinguish him from the '*brothers*' or '*Thomas*.'

It is, however, only in the Syriac sources – and we would include in these the source Eusebius is working from to produce his narrative about the correspondence with King Agbarus – that this appellative '*Judas*' is always and probably accurately joined to his other title.[32] That in some sense this '*twin*' theme has to do with the '*brother*' theme in sources about James and the other '*brothers*' is also, probably, not to be gainsaid. Moreover, that all have in some sense to do with one '*Judas*,' in some manner related either to Jesus or James, should also be clear. The attaching of '*Judas*' to '*Thomas*'' name in Eusebius' source but not Eusebius' own actual narrative, also bears out its authenticity, though not necessarily its accuracy in terms of *dramatis personae* – that is, the source is not necessarily reliable in terms of characters and subject matter, only that something of this kind appears to have happened and it does, at least, have some idea of the true names.[33]

Where '*Thaddaeus*' is concerned, once again, in the Apostle lists in Matthew and Mark, he parallels the '*Apostle*' Luke 6:16 is calling '*Judas of James*' ('*Judas the brother of James*' in the Letter of Jude). For some recensions of Matthew and in Syriac documents such as the Apostolic Constitutions, he bears the additional surname of '*Lebbaeus*,' perhaps – as we have already suggested – a distortion of '*Alphaeus*,' as in '*James the son of Alphaeus*' in the Synoptics (Matthew 10:3 and *pars.*); or of '*Cleophas*,' the name of Mary's other husband ('*Clopas*' in John 19:25) and the seeming father of these '*brothers*'[34]; or a garbling of James' mysterious cognomen in Hegisippus also *via* Eusebius above – '*Oblias*,' meaning in this pivotal source, '*Protection of the People*.'[35] Eusebius, for example, doesn't even know if '*Thaddaeus*' is an '*Apostle*' or a '*Disciple*' (if there is any difference) and what finally emerges in all these sources is that these two individuals '*Thaddaeus*' and '*Thomas*' are for the most part all but indistinguishable.[36]

For the two Apocalypses of James from Nag Hammadi, '*Addai*' and someone actually referred to as '*Theudas*' (probably '*Thaddaeus*') are also parallel figures.[37] Finally, in Syriac texts '*Thaddaeus*' is none other than '*Addai*' himself – as should have been suspected all along – the eponymous figure associated with all these stories and traditions centering around '*Edessa*' and the conversion of '*the Great King of the Peoples beyond the Euphrates*' to what is pictured, at this point anyhow, as '*Christianity*').[38] As opposed to this, however, it should be appreciated that there is another Divine figure called '*ᶜAd*' or '*Addai*' associated with this region from remotest antiquity.[39]

As we saw, Eusebius claims to have personally found the report of this conversion in the Chancellery Office of Edessa and, much as Rufinus did in the next generation the Pseudoclementine *Homilies* (probably also stemming from Syriac records), translated it himself into Greek. The reader should recall that, in this story, first there is a correspondence between this individual, '*Agbar*,' described as '*the Great King of the Peoples beyond the Euphrates*' – phraseology which certainly has interesting overtones with Paul's '*Mission*' to these same '*Peoples*' or '*Ethnon*' ('*Gentiles*' in Latin) – and '*Jesus*,' the courier in this correspondence being '*Ananias*.' Furthermore, a '*portrait*' of sorts is exchanged (the origin of the legend of '*the Holy Shroud*' just mentioned above?).

Then after Jesus' death, '*Judas known as Thomas*' sends '*Thaddaeus*' down from Jerusalem to continue the evangelization of the Edessenes and, in due course, follows up this mission with one of his own. In the two accounts Eusebius provides – his own and the Chancellery Office one from the '*official*' records of Edessa – it is not clear whether '*Thomas*' sends out '*Thaddaeus*' *before the death of Jesus* or *afterwards*. However this may be, one can dismiss any report of a correspondence (including the report of an exchange of portraits!) between '*Jesus*' and '*the Great King of the Peoples beyond the Euphrates*' with the omnipresent '*Ananias*' as courier as retrospective. Rather – if it is to be entertained at all and the writer thinks to a certain degree it can (at least where James is concerned) – it should be put under the stewardship of James, who also sent Letter(s) and messengers '*down to Antioch*' (*i.e.*, Edessa) and who, even Acts concedes, was pre-eminent from around the time of the Famine (45–48 CE) until 62 CE. For Eusebius, following Hegesippus (2nd c. Palestinian) and Clement (3rd c. Alexandrian), James was '*Leader*' or '*Ruler*' of the early Church in Palestine even earlier than this – after '*the Assumption*' when he '*was elected*.'[40]

The reason, therefore, why this exchange of communications should rather be attributed to James is quite simple: even in Acts' evasive, achronological, and somewhat refurbished account, an actual correspondence of James to '*Antioch*' carried by one '*Judas*' (in this instance, with the cognomen of '*Barsabas*') is definitively described – and this in the more reliable '*We Document*' of the latter part of Acts. Acts even knows the subject matter of this correspondence, as we have been accentuating: '*things sacrificed to idols*,' '*carrion*,' '*fornication*,' and '*blood*' – and which, as we just saw, any perspicacious observer will immediately recognize as the basis of Islamic dietary law to this day.

I have already traced the relationship of these notices to a '*Letter*' or '*Letters*' called '*MMT*' from the '*Daily-Bathing*' Community at Qumran (which some call '*Essene*,' some '*Ebionite*,' some '*Zadokite*,' etc.) – the only '*Letter*'(s) found among the manifold remains of that corpus – addressed to a '*Pious*' King of some kind, somewhere (location unspecified, though obviously not in Jerusalem[41]); and also dealing with matters such as '*things sacrificed to idols*,' '*the ban on Gentile gifts to the Temple*,' '*fornication*,' and even, somewhat esoterically, '*carrion*' – though in far more detail such that the one recorded in Acts above appears a simplified epitome of the other.

We have already discussed the geographic relationship of the two place-names '*Antioch*' and '*Edessa*.' At Qumran, as well, there are further references – as we have also elucidated in detail above – to a '*New Covenant in the Land of Damascus*,' a '*Diaspora*' Community of '*Camps*' in the '*Wilderness of the Peoples*,' and a '*King*' in '*the Land of the North*,' '*beyond Damascus*,' where '*the Tabernacle of David which was fallen*' was to be '*re-erected*,' as well as a paradigmatic '*circumcision*' of Abraham (Genesis 17:9–14) as a *sine qua non* for conversion.[42]

In putting all these notices together, it is possible to come out with the following conclusions: 1) '*Addai'/'Thaddaeus'/'Theudas'/*and '*Thomas*' are really the same person – one '*Judas*.' In some Syriac texts he is actually also called '*Judas the Zealot*' (just as in Luke's Apostle lists, '*Simon the Cananaean*' is less covertly revealed to be '*Simon the Zealot*') – terminology little different from '*Judas Iscariot*,' it being appreciated, as we have already to some extent signaled and shall explain further below, that '*Sicarios*' carries with it the secondary meaning of '*Circumciser*.'

2) It is James who sends *his 'brother' Judas 'down to Edessa'* with the '*Epistle*' containing his directives – as we have stressed, it is important to keep one's eye on the '*brother*' theme in all these overlapping accounts – or possibly, as already suggested as well, even further East to Adiabene, itself probably one of the provinces owing allegiance to this '*Great King of the Peoples beyond the Euphrates*.' It is this '*Epistle*' which in other parlance goes by the designation '*MMT*' or the '*Letter*' from Qumran on '*Works Reckoned as Righteousness*' or '*Things we Reckon as Justifying you*.'

3) Finally, the '*Antioch*' in the interconnected notices in Acts and Paul's Galatians is really '*Edessa*' or these provinces further East, all having to do with the underlying notation '*ᶜAd*' – and, in some sense, '*Addai*' as well – so important to these regions. This '*Judas*' too has to do with '*Thomas*' or, as the Koran would so typically deform it, '*Thamud*.'

4) It is important to repeat that the '*Prophet called Agabus*,' who predicts the '*Famine*' in Acts, really has to do with this '*King Agbarus*' story and the related one of the conversion of Queen Helen – probably one of his many wives and his half-sister, as Aramo-Syriac texts aver[43] – further East and her legendary '*famine-relief*' activities, as well as those of her son Izates. Furthermore, in this earlier context anyhow, he is probably none other than that '*Ananias*' who constantly reappears in the stories of Paul's conversion '*in Damascus*,' Josephus' story of King Izates' conversion, and, of course, Eusebius' curious account of the conversion of '*King Agbarus*.' The '*Letter*' in question is, as several times now remarked, the one comprising James' directives to overseas communities – themselves ultimately re-emerging in Koranic dietary regulations.

5) All these episodes, including the associated references in the Scrolls and the Koran, not to mention Paul's allusions to '*the Faith of Abraham*' and James, to Abraham as the '*Friend of God*' (turns-of-phrase found in both the Koran and at Qumran as well) and how he was '*tested*' by his willingness to sacrifice Isaac, have to do with *the importance of Abraham for these Northern Syrian locales* – where holy sites are still dedicated to his name – in particular Haran, Abraham's place-of-origin in Northern Syria near Edessa and, apparently, the Kingdom bestowed upon Izates by

his father (*'Bazeus'/'Monobazus'/*or *'Agbarus'*), a *'Kingdom'* Josephus calls *'Carron,'* i. e., probably *'Carrhae'* or ancient *'Haran.'*

The conversion story of Izates and his mother Queen Helen, as just underscored, also involves the participation of the same *'Ananias'* of Acts and Eusebius' story of *'Agbarus'* conversion and takes place both in Southern and Northern Iraq. It is found in both Josephus and Talmudic sources.[44] Three of its principal fixtures are the location of the landing place of Noah's ark *'in their realm'* (here *'the People of Noah'* reference to these same events in the Koran), the three-year Famine and their munificence in relieving it in Jerusalem, and a focus on Abraham, whose paradigmatic act of circumcising both himself and all those traveling with him is evoked in the story of Izates' conversion both in Josephus and the *Talmud*. We have sufficiently explained how this *'circumcision'* and conversion is parodied by another episode in Acts – chronologically commensurate with that of *'Agabus'* first *'Prophecy'* (though not the obviously equally-spurious story of his second) and Paul's activities in *'Damascus'* and, after that, *'in Arabia'* – having to do with the conversion of the Treasurer of the Ethiopian Queen on his way home *'from Jerusalem to Gaza'* and characterized in Acts 8:27 as *'a eunuch'*!

There are several parodies here – none of which without malice. One, as already explained, is of Izates' circumcision. It is important to note that the Roman *'Lex Cornelia de Sicarius et veneficis'* (c. 95–136 CE, which we shall discuss further below) viewed *'circumcision'* as a form of bodily mutilation – in this, too, the connection of the terminology *'Sicarios'* (*'Iscariot'*) with the act or idea of *'circumcision'* is a fundamental one – it is also a good *terminus a quo* for Acts as a whole. Another is the perceived *'Racial identity'* of these new *'Arab'* converts, that is, in Greco-Roman eyes they were *'black,'* a matter *'Agbar Uchama'*'s cognomen, *'the Black,'* further concretizes. The last is of the mix-up, we have highlighted, known as well in the Koran, between *'Saba'* (with an *'alif'*)/Southern Arabia/Ethiopia (*'Sheba'* in the Bible) and *'Saba^c'* (with an *'^cayin'*)/*'Bather'* – again implying that the conversion of this *'Ethiopian'* Queen did involve *'bathing'* and/or *'Bathers,'* namely, Eusebius' *'Masbuthaeans'* or those Islam knows as *'Mughtasilah'* or *'Sabaeans.'*

Furthermore, it should be appreciated that there was no *'Ethiopian Queen'* at this time, who sent her *'eunuch's* to Jerusalem with all her *'treasure.'* What there was, was Queen Helen of Adiabene – the *'^cAd'*-part of all our stories – who sent *'her Treasury agents'* (possibly including even *'Saul and Barnabas'*) to Egypt and Cyprus to buy grain for Palestine – therefore, the *'Gaza'* allusion, *'Gaza'* being the gateway to Egypt from Palestine. Finally, as we have stressed, the whole episode parodies the presentation in Josephus and the *Talmud*, where Izates is studying Genesis 17:10–14 about Abraham's '*circumcision*' (also evoked – as we have underscored and will see further below – in CDxvi.5–7) when he is asked by the unknown '*Zealot*' teacher '*Eleazar from Galilee*' if he understands the meaning of what he is reading. Whereupon Izates and his brother both immediately circumcise themselves. In Acts 8:32–33, the Queen's '*eunuch*' is reading Isaiah 53:7–8, when he is asked the same question by '*Philip*' whereupon he too, it will be recalled, immediately descends from his chariot and is '*babtized*.'

The Koran Takes over

If we now look at the Koranic reflections in the allusions to '*Hud and Salih*'/'*ᶜAd and Thamud*' of these really pivotal conversions in Northern Syria and Iraq, these occur primarily in *Surahs* 7:65–84, 11:50–68, 14:9–17, 26:123–144, 29:38, 46:21–35 (mentioning '*the brother of ᶜAd*') and 54:18–32. In almost every instance, they are immediately preceded by reference to '*the Folk of Noah*' and the story of Noah (7:69, 11:32ff., 14:9, 25:37, 51:46, 54:9, *etc.*), with particular reference to the matter of the ark, which we have already shown to be related to this area of Adiabene between the Euphrates and the Tigris – the area too of Eusebius' '*the Peoples beyond the Euphrates*' ('*Peoples*,' as we have seen, having particular relevance to the Paul '*Gentile Mission*' and important to the technical vocabulary at Qumran) – where almost all these so-called '*Peoples*' considered the ark to have come to rest.

They are also often accompanied by allusion to '*the People of Abraham*' and Abraham's trial and suffering, in particular, the '*testing*' exemplified in the proposed sacrifice of his son. In the Letter of James and that to the Hebrews, this '*testing*' relates to the sacrifice of Isaac which, as already several times pointed out, would have had particular importance to someone like King Izates – in our view, the putative respondent for the Letter or Letter(s) known as '*MMT*'– who had already demonstrated his interest in '*Abraham*''s soteriological state by recognizing '*circumcision*' as a *sine qua non* for conversion.

Though Muslims generally tie this reference to the sacrifice of Ishmael rather than Isaac, it should be appreciated that Ishmael is not mentioned in these contexts even in the Koran, only Isaac (11:50–84 and 37:101–14). It is important to note as well that Agbar VII (c. 109–117) was also known as '*Abgar bar Ezad*' ('*Abgar the son of Ezad*') – nominally '*Izates*,' whom Josephus at one point too even calls '*Izas*.' The point is that one of '*Izates*'' sons does nominally seem to have been called '*Agbar*' or

'*Abgar*,'[45] thus tying these two families as close as Syro-Armenian tradition seems to think they are and, in effect, merging them, making the conversion episodes involving all these persons more or less part of a single complex.

Several other themes also tie these notices in the Koran to the themes of the conversion stories from Eusebius, Josephus, and the *Talmud* and traditions swirling about the persons of James and '*Judas Barsabas*' ('*Judas Thomas*'/'*Judas the brother of James*'/'*Judas the Sabaean*'/'*Judas the Zealot*'/ '*Thaddaeus*'/'*Theudas*,' etc.). In the first place, there is the matter of the '*drought*,' always associated with allusions to ''*Ad*' and '*Hud*' and the suggestion, connected with the '*warning*,' Hud delivers, that he too was a '*Rain-maker*' – a drought that, for some reason, Muslim tradition considers to have lasted *for three years*.[46] This is the same timeframe of '*the Great Famine*' in Josephus and Acts' '*Agabus-as-Prophet*' notices (45–48 CE) and a collateral aspect of the stories of the conversions of King Agbarus and his putative sister or half-sister, the legendary Queen Helen. Connected to this is the subtheme of '*whirlwind*' or '*rain-making*' (*Surahs* 11:52, 46:24, etc.) – a theme extremely strong in the newly-reconstructed First Column of the Nahum *Pesher*, as we have seen, and strong too in traditions about James and his reputed '*rain-making*,' as well as that of another of James' putative ancestors and that of these '*Rain-makers*' in general, Onias *the Just* or Honi *the Circle-Drawer*.

There is also the theme of '*fornication*' attached to both Noah's and Salih's teaching, as well as the one of '*Righteousness*' and '*Justice*.'[47] One of these traditions in the Koran even uses a familiar Qumranism '*turning aside from the right Way*' to describe the warning Hud gives his '*People*' (11:56–7, etc.). Then, there is the '*brother*' theme that runs through all these Koranic traditions – not only that '*Hud*' is the brother of ''*Ad*' ('*Thaddaeus*'/'*Addai*'), but that '*Salih*' is the brother of '*Thamud*' ('*Thomas*'/'*Judas Thomas*'). At one point, the allusion to '*brother*' occurs in regard to '*Thamud*' (just as with ''*Ad*' above) without even referring to '*Salih*''s proper name[48]; but, however it is seen, the term '*brother*' is an important element of all these stories as they are presented in the Koran. In our view, '*Hud*' *is* the '*brother*' of '*Salih*' just as '*Judas*' is the brother '*of James*.'

Finally, the countryside in question in these Koranic traditions, though admittedly rather obscure, sometimes '*sandhills*,' sometimes '*whirlwind*,' is at one point said to abound in '*hills, springs, plains, and date palms*' (7:75 and 26:148–9), but always broad plains, richly fertile, with olive trees and the like, which is a very good description of the cattle-grazing country around Edessa and Haran and the area between the Euphrates and Tigris Rivers towards Mosul or Adiabene generally. In our view the connections are clear: '*ʿAd*' is to be equated with '*Edessa*'/'*Adiabene*'/'*Addai*'/and, by extension, '*Thaddaeus*' (even '*Theudas*'); '*Hud*' with '*Judas of James*,' '*Judas the brother of James*,' '*Judas Barsabas*,' '*Judas the Zealot*,' '*Judas Thomas*' – and even possibly '*Judas Iscariot*.' This is perhaps one of the first – if not *the* first – time that the relationship of the name '*Hud*' with that of the Hebrew '*Yehudah*' has ever been pointed out; but of course it makes absolute sense, even though those who conserved the tradition had – not surprisingly – long ago forgotten its linguistic basis. Still, the information concerning it is based on a certain reality.

Even the '*Barsabas*' allusion, also mentioned at the beginning of Acts in relation to one '*Joseph*' who '*was surnamed Justus*' (no doubt a stand-in for James or the family of '*Joseph*' in general) – the defeated candidate in the '*election*' to succeed '*Judas Iscariot*' – may be another of these allusions to '*bathing*' or '*Bathers*' as we have seen, *i.e.*, '*Sabaeans*.' In fact, Syriac and Muslim sources make it clear that this term means '*Daily Bather*' – in Greco-Syriac, as already remarked, '*Masbuthaean*' ('*Sampsaean*'?), the remnants of which group are still known as '*the Subbaᶜ of the Marshes*' today (in so far as they have survived Saddam Hussein's recent attempts to annihilate them) as they were to both al-Biruni and *The Fihrist* in their day. '*Thamud*' is to be associated with '*Thomas*' in these various stories; and '*Salih*,' with '*James the Just*' or '*the Righteous One*' – the individual who set all these various traditions in motion.

Not only is the '*Arab*' ancestry of all these stories important – ancestry which the '*Paulinizing*' narrative of the Book of Acts is quick to relegate to '*Ethiopia*'; so is the connecting theme of the ban on '*things sacrificed to idols*' – the basis, as we have now several times accentuated, not only of Koranic dietary regulations but also that of '*MMT*'s polemicizing directives aimed at a '*Pious*' King, it seems to imply, was wishing to emulate Abraham. It is also the focus of Acts' picture of James' directives to overseas communities and Paul's diminution of these in 1 Corinthians 8 above – where because of which, he disingenuously concludes he '*will never eat meat again forever*' and that, for him, '*all things are lawful*' (repeated twice).

The conclusion is that somehow Muhammad came in touch with these Northern Syrian conversion stories and other quasi-Syriac materials from the Pseudoclementines about James – either through caravan trips to Southern Iraq, where the '*Subbaᶜ of the Marshes*' only just still survive or further North, to the remnants of these lost cultures in Northern Syria. These too are not completely lost but still survive in groups like the presentday '*ʿAlawwis*' or, as they also refer to themselves, '*the Nusayris*' (*i.e.*, '*the Nazoraeans*' once more – another group obviously recognizing multiple '^{c}Ali's or 'Imam's/'Standing One's). In all these contexts, the constant emphasis on 'Abraham,' whose homeland this was, is decisive (of course, for Muhammad, 'Abraham's House' turns into 'the Ka^{c}bah' at Mecca instead!).

Not only is 'Abraham' a focus for the genesis of Koranic doctrine about Islam, but also for the antecedents to this – the debates between Paul and James regarding Abraham's 'Salvationary' State that permeate the history of Early Christianity and now, seemingly, Qumran as well. By focusing on 'Abraham,' the Qumran Damascus Document (III.2–4 and XVI.6–8) throws light on these seemingly arcane and certainly very obscure Koranic references to 'Arabian' Holy Men or 'Warners' as well. Moreover, by insisting that because he and Isaac, and Jacob 'kept the Commandments' and 'remained Faithful' (not 'straying from them in stubbornness of heart' as some others may have done), they were 'to be reckoned Beloved of God' or 'Friends,' an expression paralleled in Surah 2:124–141 of the Koran by the new terminology – focusing like James 2:21–24 on Abraham's obedience to God – 'Muslim' or 'He that surrenders to God.' This is the context, too, which in our view can throw light on these seemingly impenetrable and otherwise certainly very recondite Koranic references.

Sicarii Essenes and Zealot Essenes

Another subject, having to do with the relationship of early 'Christian' origins in Palestine to the 'Jerusalem Church' of James the Just and to Qumran that we should consider in more depth before closing is the related one of those Hippolytus and perhaps Josephus, in turn, are calling 'Sicarii Essenes' and/or 'Zealot Essenes' – those Paul and the Book of Acts seem to be alluding to as 'the Circumcision' or 'those insisting on' or 'the Party of the Circumcision.' In a much overlooked description of 'the Essenes' – usually attributed to the Third-Century early-Church theologian/heresiologist in Rome named 'Hippolytus' (an attribution that is by no means certain – the sole exemplar was found in the late Nineteenth Century at Mount Athos as we saw) – there exists the completely original and different presentation of just who and what 'the Essenes' were, probably going back to a variant version of the received Josephus, perhaps even based on the earlier version of the Jewish War he claims he did in Aramaic for the benefit of his Eastern brethren (meaning those in Northern Syria, Adiabene, Mesopotamia, and Persia) most likely to impress upon them the power and might of Rome and discourage them from any attempt to overturn the outcome of the Jewish War.[49]

In this version of the two famous descriptions in the normative

Josephus (the originality of which probably identifies it as being based on an earlier source and not a creative effort of Hippolytus himself – if, indeed, he can be definitively identified as the author in question), '*Four*' Groups of '*Essenes*' are identified and not '*four grades*' as in the *Jewish War* or '*four philosophical schools*' or '*sects*' generally as in the *Antiquities*.[50]

To be sure, the version in Hippolytus has all the main points of the received *Jewish War*, though at times it is somewhat clearer – for example, in its description of the progress of the novitiate relative to the tasting of '*the pure food*' of the initiates, the resurrection of the body along with the immortality of the soul, and the clear evocation of a '*Last Judgement*'.[51] It also includes (aside from '*the Four Parties*' of '*Essenes*') the additional point about there being *two other* '*Groups*' – marrying and non-marrying ones.[52] Regarding aspects such as these, both the texts in the *War* and the alternate version in Hippolytus are virtually the same. On the other hand, whereas Josephus speaks of '*four grades*' in basically descending order of '*Holiness*,' Hippolytus rather speaks of a '*division into Four Parties* (perhaps also in some sense relating to stricter or less-strict '*Holiness*' or '*Naziritism*') that,'*as time went on*,'*did not preserve their system of training in exactly the same manner*,' that is, his version contains *an element of chronological development and perhaps even devolution or changes that occurred over time*.[53] This is a new point nowhere mentioned in the normative Josephus and, in this, he is much clearer than the received Josephus.

It is at this point, too, having raised the issue of '*the passage of time*,' that Hippolytus adds the new details connecting both '*the Sicarii*' and '*the Zealots*' to '*the Essenes*,' that, in the writer's view, have particular relevance to the materials at Qumran and the problem many commentators have encountered during the course of Dead Sea Scrolls research in trying to sort the '*Essene*' character of the Scrolls at Qumran from the '*Zealot*' one,[54] a delineation which will have particular relevance to the picture of both '*Early Christian*' History and Palestinian '*Messianism*' as well.

The first '*Party*' of Essenes, Hippolytus *cum* Josephus identifies, is the familiar one, we know from descriptions in the received Josephus – which also seems to have found its way into depictions of the New Testament's 'Jesus' – that is, that '*they will not handle a current coin of the country*' because '*they ought not to carry, look upon, or fashion a graven image*.' Here we have the actual Scriptural warrant for the ban – only hinted at in Gospel portraiture.[55] The implication, too, is of '*land*' or '*countries*' in general, not a particular '*Nation*' or '*Country*,' since it is immediately followed up by another familiar attribute: that they will not enter into a city '*under a gate containing statues as this too they regard as a violation of Law to pass beneath (such) images*' – yet again, a variation on the '*Mosaic*' ban on '*graven images,'* but this one having particular relevance regarding the unrest we have already chronicled where First-Century Palestinian history is concerned.[56]

So much for Hippolytus' first Group of '*Essenes*' – the earliest one, if one takes his note about chronological sequentiality seriously. The second Group is even more striking and gives us the distinct impression that those Josephus pejoratively refers to (again in the First Century) as '*Sicarii*' – and not until 68 CE onwards as '*Zealots*' – grew out of '*the Essene Movement*' and not as some might have thought from a too-credulous reading of normative Josephus,'*the Pharisees*' – a point the present writer has always taken as self-evident.[57] As Hippolytus puts this:

> *But the adherents of another Party* (the second '*Party*' seemingly chronolog-ically-speaking or in the '*course of time*'), *if they happen to hear anyone maintaining a discussion concerning God and His Laws and, supposing such a one to be uncircumcised, they will closely watch him* (something Paul seems particularly concerned about in his description in Galatians 2:4–8 of '*false brothers stealing in by stealth and spying on the freedom*' he enjoys '*in Christ Jesus*') *and when they meet a person of this description in any place alone, they will threaten to slay him if he refuses to undergo the rite of circumcision* (not only does the detail of this have the ring of truth, but so much for the normative picture most people have of '*Peace-loving Essenes*'– one might say, these are *more intolerant*, of the stripe, should we say, of Qumran). *Now if the latter kind of person does not wish to comply with this request* (a member of this Party of '*Essenes*') *will not spare* (him), *but proceeds to kill* (the *offender* – this is something of the nature of what we are familiar with in Islam to this very day). *And it is from this behaviour that they have received their appellation being called* (by some) '*Zealots*' but, *by others, 'Sicarii.'*[52]

Not only does this resemble something of what happens to Paul in Acts 21:38 where '*Sicarii*' are for the only time specifically alluded to and others take a '*Nazirite*'-style oath '*not to eat or drink until* (they) *have killed Paul*' (23:12–21); but it is nowhere to be found in the extant Greek version of Josephus' *Jewish War*. Nor, as already observed, is it something 'Hippolytus' (whoever he was) was likely to have made up on his own, but it is so striking in its originality as to fairly take the reader's breath away. Whoever was writing it, even if it was not Josephus (the writer thinks that it was Josephus – a Josephus who, for some reason, was willing to be more forthcoming), certainly knew something about this period beyond the usual superficialities. In particular, it also helps explain certain puzzling aspects of the notations '*Zealot*' and/or '*Sicarii.*'

Nor could these individuals be considered '*Peace-loving*' Essenes as just underscored. On the contrary, they are quite violent or at least extremely '*steadfast*' in their '*dedication to the Torah*,' exhibiting something of the ethos the writer contends one encounters in the documents at Qumran, which is why in the early days of Qumran research, scholars such as G. R. Driver and Cecil Roth were inclined to identify the Qumran Group as '*Zealots*.'[49] Nor can anyone who reads the literature at Qumran fail to be impressed by the extreme '*Zealotry*,' as we have been highlighting, of the larger part of its attitudes, particularly where '*the Last Days*,' '*the Torah of Moses*,' '*Backsliders*,' and '*the New Covenant*' were concerned.[59]

Actually, we have already suggested in *James the Brother of Jesus* that the term '*Sicarios*' might be an anagram for '*Christian*' or the latter, at least, a homophonic play on the former. This is certainly the case where '*Judas the Iscariot*' (the '*son*' or '*brother of Simon* [*the*] *Iscariot*' – most likely the last) is concerned, as all that has occurred is that a '*theta*' has been substituted for a '*sigma*' and the first two letters – as is often the case, as we just said, in Semitic philology (take the case in Arabic of '*Aphlaton*' for Greek '*Plato*,' not to mention '*Agbarus*'/'*Acbarus*'/ or even '*Albarus*' for '*Abgarus*' above), have been reversed.[60] But if we abandon the term '*Christian*' for '*Messianist*' – as we would most certainly have to do in the '*Palestine*' of this Period – then '*Judas*' becomes the archetypical '*Violent*' or '*aggressive Essene*' and/or '*Messianist*,' just the kind of person the New Testament is trying to distance itself from or distance the person of the 'Jesus' it is portraying from.

This is perhaps the most subtle reversal of all and, at the same time, one of the most insidious ironies, to have turned the person who was perhaps the epitome of '*the Messianic Movement*' in Palestine (now we have further confirmation of this in the newly-revealed esotericizing '*Gospel*' supposedly in his name) – and probably the third '*brother*' of James if not of 'Jesus' (*i.e.*, in Lukan '*Apostle*' lists, '*Judas of James*'; in Syriac texts, as already remarked, '*Judas the Zealot*'[61] – just as the putative second brother of James, '*Simon*' or '*Simeon*,' is designated in these same lists as '*Simon the Zealot*') – into the actual '*Betrayer*' or, what in the Scrolls would be termed, a '*Traitor*' to the kind of '*Movement*' its 'Jesus' is supposed to represent (of course, this view of '*Judas*' as '*Traitor*' will now have to be reconsidered in the light of the newly-discovered '*Gospel of Judas*').

What adds to the impression of the truth of this proposition is the fact that Josephus vividly documents how '*the Sicarii*' did not all die on Masada; but some – for whom he himself is either mistaken (much as Paul is for '*the Egyptian*' in Acts 21:38 above) or identified with – fled to Egypt, causing the Romans to likewise destroy the Temple that had also been constructed there,[62] and even carried on the agitation in Cyrenaica (modernday Libya) in North Africa, which was eventually severely repressed in Josephus' own lifetime even there.[63] So to escape such stigmatization, 'Christian' might have been a very useful reformulation or even a term in Greek that might have been used to deride or ridicule – or, *vice versa*, 'Christians' demanding '*circumcision*,' as we shall see, might have been called '*Sicarii*' (just as Hippolytus' '*Essenes*' are here), again meant to caricaturize or to mimic but always – as in Acts – disparagingly.

'*The Gospel of Judas*,' which was found, and this, not insignificantly, together with a slightly different version of the First Apocalypse of James and was – as already indicated in our Introduction – known because of denunciations of it by its detractors such as Irenaeus to have existed since the Second Century,[64] actually portrays '*Judas*' as 'Jesus'' favorite '*Disciple*' or '*Apostle*' which would certainly have been the case, as we can now see, if either of them can be said to have existed in any real '*Historical*' sense and if we are not just dealing in these things with '*literature*' (which in fact, of course, we actually are). Still, here anything resembling *a truly* '*Historical*' situation ends.

Though called '*The Gospel of Judas*' and definitely appears to intend this to be '*Judas Iscariot*' (though it does not appear to use this terminology or for that matter, as just intimated, distinguish him in any way from the person among Jesus' '*brothers*' by that name or even '*Judas Thomas*'), it naturally abjures the reference to '*Judas*'' suicide – as alleged in Matthew 27:5 – in favor (as we have explained) of a more Neoplatonic or Hellenizing mysticism, with which one is familiar in other Nag Hammadi or so-called '*Gnostic*' texts in general. Moreover, not only is it completely antinomian portraying Jesus '*laughing*' (a typical feature of such texts) at his Apostles' worrying over dietary regulations and other legal trivialities; but, in fact, there are even doctrines in it resembling the outlines of '*the Primal Adam*' ideology, we have been so assiduously accentuating above, including reference to denying the body in favor of releasing the Eternal, more spiritual, '*Self*' or '*Inner Man*' or '*Being*' – '*the Adam Kadmon*' of Kabbalistic and '*Jewish Christian*'/'*Ebionite*'/ '*Gnostic*' tradition generally. In setting out this doctrine, it actually refers to '*Jesus*' wishing to shed his body as '*a cloak*,' just as one finds in the Pseudoclementines and other Gnosticizing '*Primal Adam*'/'*Incarnationist*' literature, and it is, in this regard that he designates '*Judas*' as a '*Deliverer*' of sorts with regard to him (very esoteric!) or '*Star*' – another interesting allusion.[65]

But, comparing '*the Gospel of Judas*' with the literature at Qumran, one can immediately see that (just as the other '*Gospels*') it contains little or nothing that is actually '*Palestinian*' at all; on the contrary, it is clearly a product of Egyptian Neoplatonic Enlightenment mysticism. Nevertheless and despite the fact of its '*Platonizing*,' what it does do – and this quite properly – is reverse the deleterious and gratuitously defamatory picture of '*Judas Iscariot*'/'*the Iscariot*,' to which we have all been '*Heirs*' these Twenty some Centuries. In the process it demonstrates, as we have also emphasized in our Introduction – in a way that almost nothing else could – what a lively, complex, and layered literature was actually circulating about these '*Hellenizing*' God-tales of an Osiris/Dionysus-like or Ovid-like/Senecan cast, one level building upon another, incorporating the most up-to-date version of transcendental or mystical thinking – that of '*seeking Union with the Divine*' – to produce a novelizing literature of Hellenizing Enlightenment almost none of which is '*Historical*' at all. On the contrary, for the most part it is dialectical or allegorical.

The Gospels we have, of course, are just some of the more easily-accessible and exoteric versions of this literary activity; '*the Gospel of Judas*' and its companion literature, the more esoteric. Having said this, *the problem of mistaking literature for history remains*. These documents (as already emphasized in our Introduction too) are the literature, some of which quite dazzling but literature nonetheless. Where the Dead Sea Scrolls and Josephus – and now these testimonies from Hippolytus – are concerned however, after parting the curtain of unknowing, *one does actually begin to approach real history*.

To summarize: three things immediately emerge from this new material attributed to '*Hippolytus*' (none of which, to be sure, to be found in the Gospel of Judas or its analogues which – as just underscored – are thoroughly antinomian and, as such, just the opposite of whatever can be called '*Essene*' at Qumran), which the writer cannot imagine as invented by this '*Hippolytus*' if he was indeed the author, but rather drawn from suppressed information previously extant in the various versions of these matters in Josephus: 1) that '*the Zealots*' or '*Sicarii*' were known for *their insistence on circumcision* – a new point we never heard before but which might have been surmised; 2) that according to their view, one first had to come in under '*the Law*' as delineated by '*the Torah of Moses*' before one could either even discuss God or the subject of the Law (something Paul would have found extremely prohibitive, given his *modus operandi* and intellectual point-of-view); 3) it was permissible to forcibly circumcise individuals on pain of death or to offer persons interested in such subjects – much as in Islam – *the choice of circumcision or death* (one is not recommending any of this, just pointing out the situation as it then obtained).

Put in another way, like Paul (we shall reserve judgement about

James), 'Essenes' of this kind were also interested in non-Jewish converts, but for them 'circumcision' was a *sine qua non* not only for conversion, but *even to discuss questions appertaining to Mosaic Law* – meaning, *you first had to come in under the Law before you could discuss it.* No wonder certain 'Zealots'/'Sicarii'/or 'Nazirites' (in particular those designated as the greater part of James' 'Jerusalem Church' adherents in Acts 21:20) wished to 'kill Paul' (Acts 23:12). Anyone carefully reading Galatians would have to acknowledge that 'circumcision' was a subject utterly obsessing Paul.[66] In addition, however, if one has carefully read it together with Acts 15:1–5's prelude to 'the Jerusalem Council' – tendentious or otherwise – asserting that it was triggered by 'some who came down from Judea' who 'were teaching the brothers that, unless you were circumcised, you could not be saved'; then one will realize that what one has before us in Hippolytus' version of Josephus' description of 'the Essenes' is a 'Party of the Circumcision' par excellence – in fact, those Paul is calling in Galatians 2:12 either the 'some from James' or 'of the circumcision.'

Hippolytus' 'Sicarii Essenes'

Hippolytus rounds out his description of the 'Four Groups of Essenes,' corresponding to the 'four grades of Essenes' in Greek Josephus, with a Third 'Party.' These, he claims, would 'call no man Lord except God even though one should torture or even kill them,' which not only overlaps Josephus' testimony about the Essene refusal 'to eat forbidden foods' or 'blaspheme the Law-Giver' (meaning Moses) in the *Jewish War*,[67] but also, even more closely, 'the Fourth Sect of Jewish Philosophy' founded by 'Judas the Galilean,' Josephus describes in the *Antiquities*.[68] In other words, there is a slight shift even in received Josephus in the two accounts in the *War* and the *Antiquities* from 'Essenes' to 'Fourth Philosophy.' Actually what Josephus, in effect, seems to have done is cut a piece from his description of 'the Essenes' in the former and added it to his description of 'Judas the Galilean"s 'Fourth Philosophy' in the latter.[69]

As he continues in both, normative Josephus identifies this 'Fourth Philosophy' – which at first he had declined to name – as 'the Sicarii' but, as already noted, he never actually employs the term 'Zealot' until midway through the *War* around 68 CE at the point when, along with those he is calling 'Idumaeans,' they slaughter James' nemesis and judicial murderer, Ananus ben Ananus, along with Josephus' own close friend, 'Jesus ben Gamala,' and throw their naked bodies outside the city without burial as food for jackals.[70] As also described, Josephus follows this up in the *War* with a picture of 'the Zealots' that is so hysterical (including dressing themselves up as women and wearing lipstick) as to verge on the absurd, but by this time he, too, is beside himself with animosity.[71]

For his part, Hippolytus rather follows up his picture of his '*Third Group*' – '*those who will call no man Lord*' (presumably, not even 'Jesus') – with a '*Fourth Group*,' who are basically schismatics and who have '*declined so far from the (Ancient) Discipline*' that those '*continuing in the observance of the customs of the Ancestors* ('*the First*' in documents such as CD1.16 and IV.6 above[72] – '*Law-Keepers*' in James) *would not even touch them.*'[73] This '*Group*' resembles, of course, nothing so much as Pauline '*Christians*' or perhaps some later, even more '*Gentilizing*' or '*Gnosticizing*' group. Furthermore,

> *should they* (the Habakkuk *Pesher's* '*Torah-Doers*'?) *happen to come into contact with them, they would immediately resort to water purification as if they had come into contact with someone belonging to a foreign People.*[74]

One should note the resemblance of this last to Acts 10:28's picture of Peter's words, accurate or not, to '*Cornelius*' (described – as previously underscored – not a little dissimulatingly in Acts 10:7 and 10:22 as '*a Pious*' Roman '*Centurion*' – the name of whom will also have relevance to the complex of materials we are developing) that it was '*unlawful for a Jewish person to keep company with or come in contact with one of a foreign race.*'

Not only do these appear in the context of Peter's '*tablecloth*' vision, the effect of which is the declaration of '*all foods being lawful*' enabling him – because he then learns '*not to make distinctions between Holy and profane*' (10:14 – meaning, of course, 'Jesus' never taught any such doctrine or why would 'Peter' require a Paulinizing vision to learn it) – to make his subsequent visit, however fantastic, to the '*Righteous and God-fearing*' Roman Centurion '*Cornelius*'; but we have already observed and shall further explain the significance in this encounter with '*Cornelius*' in Caesarea with regard to the Roman '*Lex Cornelia de Sicarius et Veneficis.*' This Law, in effect, banned '*circumcision*' – at least for those not originally born Jewish – and other similar '*bodily mutilations*,' '*circumcision*' being considered in Roman jurisprudence, as previously observed as well, '*a bodily mutilation*' equivalent to '*castration*' (therefore, the allusion to '*eunuch*' in Acts' '*Ethiopian eunuch*' episode), the application of which became particularly stringent after the fall of the Temple and the War against Rome from 66–73 CE – itself, not significantly, ending in the suicide of '*the Sicarii*' at Masada.[75]

Though a fourth '*grade*,' not unsimilar to Hippolytus' '*Fourth Group*,' does appear in Josephus' extant *Jewish War*, there it is the more innocuous matter of being in an inferior state of apprenticeship or novitiate as compared with those already far-advanced where '*Holiness*' or bodily and spiritual '*purity*' were concerned but not as having slipped, as it were, out of the '*Jewish fold*' altogether, as in Hippolytus, to be looked upon as virtual '*foreigners*' and/or '*untouchables*.'[76] This is a significant discrepancy between the two accounts and, on the face of it, Hippolytus' makes more sense, since it is hard to imagine such a horror of contact or '*touching*' directed simply against junior members in a less-advanced state of '*ritual purity*.' In this context too, one should recollect all the various '*touching*' episodes with regard to 'Jesus' in the Gospels we have several times pointed up.[77] In fact, Hippolytus' '*Fourth Group*' resembles nothing so much as the new more '*Paulinized*' Christians we have been highlighting (of the kind '*Peter*' has just learned in Acts 10:28 to accept) following, in the writer's view, a less stringent, more extra-legal form of '*Essenism*' totally alien to those preceding it. It is for this reason that it becomes impossible either to '*associate with*' or even '*to touch them*' as Hippolytus would have it.

This being said, Hippolytus now returns to his earlier description of the Three Groups of Essenes – or, at least, the two earlier ones, that is, those he calls '*Zealot Essenes*' and '*Sicarii Essenes*,' if in fact they can be distinguished in any real way from the Third (those willing to undergo any form of torture rather than '*call any man Lord*') – because he now picks up the points paralleled in normative Josephus about the longevity of Essenes, their temperateness, and the incapacity, they display, of becoming angry.[78] But he also now returns a second time to his previous description of how '*they despised death*' and the willingness they showed to undergo torture of any kind amalgamating, as just indicated, parts from both Josephus' descriptions of '*Essenes*' in the *Jewish War* and '*the Fourth Philosophical Sect*' (later either '*Sicarii*' or '*Zealots*') in the *Antiquities*.[79]

In any event, in this passage from Hippolytus' presentation, the reader will immediately recognize the description in the *War* of the bravery shown by the Essenes in '*our recent War with the Romans*' (that is, unlike so-called '*Pharisees*,' '*Herodians*,' '*Establishment Sadducees*,' and '*Christians*' – meaning '*Pauline*' ones and not '*Sicarii*' – the Essenes did participate in the *War against Rome* and *they were on the side of the insurgents, whatever the orientation*[80]) that no matter how much they were '*racked and twisted* (of course, here we have the first *real '*Martyrs*'*) *burned and broken*,' they could not be made to '*blaspheme the Law-giver* (meaning Moses – here the '*blaspheming*' charge again) or '*eat forbidden things*.'[81]

It is this last which is the pivotal point, for Hippolytus now refines it as well – in the process, bringing it in even closer agreement with and, as a consequence, the actual reverse once again of what Paul is so concerned about from 1Corinthians 8–11 above where he is in the process, not only of attacking persons like James, but all persons *'with weak consciences'* such as these same *'Essenes'* in Hippolytus – persons whose *'conscience was so weak'* (8:4) that they would not even *'eat things sacrificed to idols,'* considering such fare *'polluting'* or *'defiled'* (8:7). This point is not only pivotal, it is decisive. Considering the commitment, personal sacrifice, and dedication of such persons, as Hippolytus (in this, supported by normative Josephus) will now go on to describe them; this position expressed by Paul in 1 Corinthians is, not only disrespectful, deceitful, and unnecessarily abusive, it is contemptible. As Hippolytus now expresses this:

> *If, however, anyone would attempt even to torture such persons in order to induce them either to blaspheme the Law* (n.b., the parallel to Josephus' *'blaspheme the Law-giver'* in the *War* above, not to mention *'blaspheming the Name of God'* or *'the God of Heaven'* in Revelation, now recurring in this passage, in what has to be regarded as confirming the identity of the two groups) *or eat things sacrificed to an idol, he will not achieve his end for* (an Essene of this kind) *submits to death and endures any torment rather than violate his conscience* (here, of course, Paul's very *'conscience'* language from 1 Corinthians 8:7–10, just quoted above. Nor is this to mention again the combined picture of both *'Essenes'* and *'Zealots'* who are willing to undergo any torture and martyrdom in both the *War* and the *Antiquities* – in the latter, as will be recalled, *'rather than call any man Lord'*).[82]

The reader now has the option of deciding which version of Josephus is more accurate – or are all three accurate? – the *Jewish War's* less specific and vaguer *'rather than eat forbidden things'* (its *'not blaspheming the Law-giver'* and the *Antiquities'* *'Fourth Philosophical Sect's'* unwillingness to *'call any man Lord'* aside) or the more precise and, as we can now see, *'MMT'*-oriented *'refusal to eat things sacrificed to idols'* reflecting James' directives to overseas communities. Nor is this to say anything about Paul's attack on those refusing to eat these same *'things sacrificed to idols'* in 1 Corinthians 8:3–10:23 climaxing – as we have been signaling – with his proclamation of *'Communion with the Blood of Christ'* in 10:16 above.

'Sicarii Essenes,' *'the Lex Cornelia de Sicarius,'* and *'the Sicaricon'*

Therefore we now approach a conundrum: the sort of *'Essenes'* described by Hippolytus – in particular, those he is calling either *'Zealot Essenes'* or *'Sicarii Essenes'* or both, who apparently will not tolerate anyone discussing the Law or *Torah* who is not circumcised and are prepared to kill anyone doing so who refuses or declines to be circumcised (if not a direct, certainly a tangential attack on Paul and his '*Gentile Mission*') – are, also, prepared to undergo any sort of torture rather than '*eat things sacrificed to an idol.*' This certainly does represent a refinement of Josephus with particular relevance both to '*the Party of the Circumcision*' and those Paul refers to with such evident antipathy in Galatians 2:12 as the '*some from James*' and '*those of the circumcision.*'

We have already called attention to the section of '*MMT*' having to do with this complete and total ban on consuming '*things sacrificed to idols.*' Furthermore, we have also called attention to Columns XLVI–XLVII of the Temple Scroll dealing with '*pollution of the Temple*' as well and barring various classes of '*unclean*' persons and things from the Temple – in particular, enigmatically evoking someone or something called '*Bela^c*' and including '*skins sacrificed to idols.*'[83] Moreover, looked at from another perspective and through another vocabulary, these kinds of bans represent just another variation of the theme of '*pollution of the Temple*' – which the version of James' directives in Acts 15:19 refers to as '*the pollutions of the idols*' and which Paul was accused of doing by the crowd in the Temple in Acts 21:28 by '*bringing Greeks into the Temple*' – the third and perhaps most decisive of '*the Three Nets of Belial*' charges in the Damascus Document above, the '*Nets*' with which he *both deceives and subverts Israel.*[84]

Before pulling all these strands of inquiry together, we should perhaps turn to one final source relevant to discussing such '*Sicarii Essenes*' and bearing on the possible circumcision they indulged in – possibly with the '*sica*'-like knife, from which Josephus claimed they originally derived their name[85] – and the view in Roman jurisprudence of '*circumcision,*' just noted above, as a kind of castration-like bodily mutilation (*cf.* the same sense in Acts' characterization of the Ethiopian Queen's '*Treasury agent*' as a '*eunuch.*' an episode we have already identified several times above as a parody of the crucial circumcision of Queen Helen of Adiabene's two sons, Izates, and Monobazus, at the chronologically-concurrent moment in both the *Talmud* and the *Antiquities*).

Before doing so, however, it is important to remark that even in the *Jewish War*, as we have it, forcible circumcision was to some extent part of the program of those Revolutionaries, Josephus sometimes is calling '*Zealots*' and at other times '*Sicarii.*' This is particularly the case in the episode at the start of the War against Rome, when the Jewish insurgent forces have been successful (with the help, it should be appreciated, of two other descendants of Queen Helen, the Monobazus and Kenedaeus, we have identified above, who martyred themselves at the Pass at Beit Horon) and where the Commander of the Roman garrison in Jerusalem is offered and, in fact, accepts just such a choice, while the rest of those under his command are butchered by those Josephus likes to call '*the Innovators*' (he means, those '*Innovations*' into customary legal practice of which he claims – not a little facilely – '*our Ancestors were before previously unaware*').[86] There are also further examples of this in the *Jewish War*.[87]

Curiously, the first clue one comes upon relating to the '*circumcision*' aspect of the terminology is the denotation by Origen of '*Sicarii*' as those who have either circumcised themselves or forcibly circumcised others in violation of the Roman '*Lex Cornelia de Sicarius et Veneficis*' – the Roman Law, as just signaled above, banning such '*circumcision*' (except, it would appear, where Jews *per se* were concerned – meaning it obviously applied to converts who were Gentiles) and mutilation of the sexual parts generally as a kind of castration.[88]

In *Contra Celsus*, Origen specifically describes '*the Sicarii*' as being called this '*on account of the practice of circumcision*,' which in their case he defines as '*mutilating themselves contrary to the established laws and customs*' and as being inevitably, therefore, '*put to death*' on this account.[89] Of course, this is in Origen's time in the Third Century CE. It does not necessarily mean that such a total ban would have been in effect prior to the First Jewish Revolt against Rome when the problem would probably not yet have been deemed sufficiently serious to merit it – not probably until the aftermath of the Second Jewish Revolt, when it is clear things became more and more repressive in this regard. Nor, as he continues, does one ever hear – that is, in his own time – of a '*Sicarius*' reprieved from such a

> punishment (*even*) *if he recants, the evidence of circumcision being sufficient to ensure the death of him who has undergone it.*

Not only should one not ignore the harshness of this, but the text is doubly ironic for we know that Origen himself was just such a person, that is, '*a Sicarius*,' and reportedly had castrated himself – not, presumably, because of his '*zeal for the Law*' or '*circumcision*' but rather for celibacy.[90] Nevertheless, where non-Jews, anyhow, were concerned – and this, no doubt, included Pauline-style '*converts*' – '*castration*' of this kind was clearly being seen as the equivalent of '*circumcision*' – or, rather, *vice versa*, the Romans viewed '*circumcision*' as just such a bodily mutilation of the flesh and a variety of '*castration*.'

Jerome confirms this in claiming that Origen '*castrated himself with a knife*' (thereby clarifying the '*sica*' part of the '*Sicarius*' vocabulary) and ridiculing him by quoting, significantly, Paul's own critique of 'zealotry' and 'Zealots' from Romans 10:2 above, saying he did this out of 'zeal for God but not according to Knowledge.'[91] In this regard, not only should one bear in mind Jesus' statement in Matthew 19:12 above about 'those making themselves eunuchs for the Kingdom of Heaven's sake,' which is obviously what Origen had done; but also that Jerome is using here the very language Paul uses in 1 Corinthians 8:1–2, in his usual strophe/antistrophe/epode lyric-poetical/rhetorical style having to do, as we have seen, with 'things sacrificed to idols' and 'Knowledge puffing up,' not 'building up' (as it should):

> but if anyone thinks he has known anything, he has not known anything as he ought to know it.

In this manner, both he and the passage from Paul he is quoting from Romans 10:2 show their awareness of 'Zealots' (as Paul does elsewhere as we have shown[92]) and that the whole matter had something to do with such 'zeal' (Paul displays the same 'Knowledge' in Galatians 4:16–5:13 where he is speaking about 'becoming your Enemy,' 'zeal,' and, of course, such 'cutting off') – in particular, that such an act would have been typical of just such 'Sicarii Essenes' or 'Zealot Essenes,' as the case may have been – to say nothing of 'the Circumcision Party' of James.

In fact, Paul goes on in Romans 10:3–4, much like he does in 1 Corinthians 8:1–4 about 'things sacrificed to idols,' to ridicule the reputed 'Righteousness' of such persons (as already underscored, a basic concept at Qumran), a concept he even evokes in Galatians 5:14 above after expressing his desire (in speaking about 'the flesh') that he 'wished' such persons who were 'troubling' his communities would 'themselves cut off' and, facetiously parodying James, 'for all the Law is fulfilled in one word, "you shall love your neighbor as yourself"'(thus). He also does so as follows:

> For being ignorant of God's Righteousness (in 1 Corinthians 8:1–3, just highlighted above, it was their reputed 'Knowledge' and 'loving God' – their 'Piety' he was parodying) and seeking to establish their own Righteousness (here too, a possible play on the 'seeking of the Torah' of 'the Mehokkek' and/or 'the Teacher of Righteousness' above, to say nothing of the language both of 'establishing' or 'setting up the fallen Tent of David' and 'the New Covenant in the Land of Damascus'), they do not submit to God's Righteousness, for Christ is the End of the Law for Righteousness (once again, a perfect example of his strophe-antistrophe-epode poetic rhetorical approach).

One could not have a better example of the sophistic manner in which Paul is transforming the *'Righteousness'*-oriented interpretation of '*the Zadokite Covenant*' and those like '*the Doresh ha-Torah*,' who '*sought (God) with a whole heart*' and, presumably for that reason, '*went out from the Land of Judah to dwell in the Land of Damascus*' and erect '*the New Covenant*' there. Nor is this to say anything further about Acts 21:20's final designation of the greater part of James' '*Jerusalem Church*' followers in Paul's seeming final encounter with James as '*all Zealots (Zelotai) for the Law*'!

The Roman '*Lex Cornelia de Sicarius*' which, as we saw, seems actually to have been attributed to Publius Cornelia Scipio (therefore the '*Cornelia*' part of the statute's designation) and which, Origen attests, the judges in his time were so zealously enforcing; according to Dio Cassius, as we saw, seems to have first come into real effect in Nerva's time (96–98 CE),[93] that is, in the aftermath of the First Jewish Revolt against Rome. But the sudden interest in it and its connection, in particular, to '*circumcision*,' in fact, appears to be linked both to the '*Sicarii*' and the whole issue of the First Revolt and, even finally, the Second.

Certainly by Hadrian's time (117–138 CE) and his actual prohibition of '*circumcision*' in the period of the Second Revolt, this linkage is reflected in a law, '*the Ius Sicaricon*,' which related to the confiscation of enemy property – primarily, it would seem, in Palestine. It was also, it appears, in some manner connected to those defying his decree banning '*circumcision*' who at the same time appear to have *participated – as in the First Jewish Revolt – in the War against Rome*.[94] The repression of '*circumcision*' particularly in relation to those Jews being called '*Sicarii*' – now, seemingly, *because of their insistence on circumcision* and not so much, as Josephus had previously (perhaps somewhat disingenuously) presented it, *their pro-pensity for assassination* – by Hadrian's time had become extraordinarily severe and this had to mean, once again, *where non-Jews were concerned*.

In Tanaitic literature the term '*Sicaricon*' actually describes the property, including land and slaves, which was expropriated from Jews by the Roman Authorities in the aftermath of the Second Jewish Revolt because of the perception of their participation in this War.[95] Against this background, it seems clear that the term '*Sicarii*,' at this point, was not only being used both to characterize the most extreme partisans of Revolt against Rome, but also those '*insisting on circumcision*' as a *sine qua non for conversion* – in particular, '*the Party*' or '*those of the Circumcision*,' as we have been encountering it or them above – now, in the wake of all the unrest, being expressly prohibited in an official manner by Rome. In this regard one, should pay particular attention to the designation of '*Judas*

Iscariot' or *'the Iscariot'* in the Gospels as having some relationship to or, in some manner, parodying or holding practices of this kind up to contempt, ridicule, or loathing, that is – if one likes – he is *'Judas the Circumciser,'* a matter rarely if ever addressed in New Testament or Scrolls research.

'The Party of the Circumcision'

There is no doubt that those represented by the literature at Qumran were extremely *'zealous for circumcision'* too. This position is perhaps made most forcibly, as already emphasized, in CDxvi (according to the Cairo recension, renumbered more recently as CDx) at the beginning of the more statutory part of the Damascus Document where

> *the oath of the Covenant which Moses made with Israel...to return to the Torah of Moses with a whole heart and soul* (again note the *'whole heart'* allusion)

is the paramount proposition.[96] One should also compare this with Romans 10:5 where Paul, quoting Leviticus 18:5, speaks as well of how *'Moses writes of the Righteousness which is of the Law that the man who has done these things shall live by them'* (again here, note the allusion to *'doing'* and, of course, as usual the whole Qumran position on *'living'*[97]) before going on to trump it in Romans 10:6 with what he calls *'the Righteousness of Faith speaks.'*

Par contra, however, CDxvi emphasizes *the binding nature of oaths taken 'to return to'* and *'keep the Commandments of the Torah at the price even of death'*[98] – again a particularly important emphasis for those prepared, as *per* Hippolytus' and Josephus' descriptions of both *'Sicarii Essenes'* and *'Zealot Essenes'* above, *'to undergo any torture rather than disavow the Law.'*[99] This is repeated with the admonition, evoking both Deuteronomy 23:24 and 27:26 and the *'curses'* of the Covenant attached thereto, that:

> *even at the price of death, a man shall not fulfill any vow he might have sworn to turn aside from the Torah* (n.b., once more this very important allusion to the phraseology of *'turning aside from the Torah'*).[100]

It is in this same Column, and in this context, that Abraham's *'circumcision'* is evoked and, as already intimated, *the most fearsome oaths of retribution attached to the performance of it.* In other words, once again, we are not really in an environment of *'Peaceful Essenes,'* however such are defined, and certainly not of Paulinism, but rather one of absolute and violent vengeance and a life-and-death attachment to *'the Torah of Moses'* however it might have been acquired – whether undertaken at birth or by conversion. As this is put at this point in the Damascus Document:

> *And on the day upon which the man swears upon his soul* (or *'on pain of death'*) *to return to the Torah of Moses* (here, of course, the *'turning back'* language again meaning, however, as earlier in the Document, *'returning to the Torah'*), *the Angel of Divine Vengeance* (here expressed as *'the Angel of the Mastema'* – this is the way the Scrolls, as we saw, express what in other vocabularies goes by the designation of *'Satan'*[101]) *will turn aside* (here the *'turning aside'* notation, now expressed in the new context of *'Satan'* being checked from his usual behaviour – the play is certainly purposeful) *from pursuing him* (and here, again, the *'pursuit'* vocabulary already examined above too), *provided that he* (the oath-taker) *fulfills his word. It is for this reason Abraham circumcised himself on the very day of his being informed (of these things).*[102]

The reference is to Genesis 17:9–27, in particular, Abraham's obligation to *'circumcise the flesh of his foreskin'* and *that of all those of his household* – the addition of this last being an important addendum – as *'a sign of the Covenant'* which, the text observes, he accomplished (just as in CDxvi.6 above) *'on that very day'* – though he was *ninety-nine years old*!

But, of course, as we have been tirelessly pointing out, this is the very same passage, the *Talmud* says, Queen Helen of Adiabene's two sons, Izates and Monobazus, were reading when the more *'Zealot'* teacher *'from Galilee,'* identified by Josephus as one *'Eleazer,'* gainsaid Ananias' and his associate's (Paul's?) previous tuition, asking them rather (just as *'Philip,' 'the eunuch of the Ethiopian Queen'* in Acts 8:30 above) *whether they 'understood the meaning of what'* they were reading? It is at this point, having understood the true nature of the *'conversion' they had undertaken 'to fulfill'* that, in both Josephus and the *Talmud* – *'on that very day'* they, too, immediately *went out* and *circumcised themselves.*[103]

As already pointed out, the very words attributed to *'Eleazar'* here are being parodied in Acts' version of the *'Philip'*'s encounter with *'the Ethiopian Queen's eunuch'* who asks the very same question. The caricature of *'circumcision'* as *'castration'* here is certainly purposeful, as is that of the *'Queen'* as a *'Black'* or an *'African'* – much like *'Agbar Uchama'* (her putative *'husband'* or descendant). Only now the *'eunuch,'* as we saw, is reading Isaiah 53:7–8 (central lines in the fundamental *'Christian'* proof-text Isaiah 53:1–12) not Genesis 17:10–14 and, in Acts 8:38, he likewise *'orders the chariot to stop'* and immediately *proceeds to be baptized.* In fact, the creation of this canny caricature can undoubtedly be dated within the complex of notices we are discussing regarding this subject.

To go back to CDxvi.1–8 above, there can be little doubt of the aggressive and uncompromising ferocity of this passage and others like it in the Scrolls where even *'the Avenging Fury of the Angel of Mastema'*[104] and *'a person vowing another to death by the laws of the Gentiles being put to death himself'*[105] are also evoked. The ferocity in question is more in keeping with Hippolytus' description, tendentious or accurate (we consider it accurate), of *'the Sicarii Essenes'* who would either *'threaten to kill a man'* or *'forcibly circumcise him'* if they heard him discussing *'God and His Laws'* but who, by the same token, would *'submit to any death or endure any torture rather than violate (their) conscience'* (i.e., *'blaspheme the Law'* in Josephus and Paul's *'conscience'* language again) or *'eat that which was sacrificed to an idol.'*

We have continually stressed how this issue of *'abstaining from things sacrificed to idols'* is the backbone of James' directives to overseas communities at the conclusion of *'the Jerusalem Council'* in Acts 15:20 and 15:29. It is reiterated in Acts 21:26 when Paul is sent into the Temple by James for a *'Nazirite'*-style penance because the majority of James' supporters are *'Zealots for the Law.'* Not only does the subject preoccupy Paul from 1 Corinthians 8–11, where he uses it as a springboard to introduce his idea of *'Communion with the Blood of Christ'*; but also to affirm that *'an idol is nothing in the world'* (8:4 – nor is *'that which is sacrificed to an idol anything'*) and to insist that one should *'not inquire on account of conscience'* (10:25–29).

As already described, the subject forms the background to the whole section in *'MMT'* on bringing *gifts and sacrifices on behalf of Gentiles into the Temple* (a ban, according to Josephus, of which *'our Forefathers were previously unaware'* and the issue which, according to him, triggered the War against Rome in 66 CE[106]) – *'sacrifices by Gentiles'* in the Temple, in particular, being treated under the expression that *'we consider they sacrifice to an idol'* or *'they are sacrifices to an idol'* generally.[107] Though the exemplars are a little fragmentary here, the meaning is clear and the words *'sacrifice to an idol'* shine clearly through.

The conclusion should probably be that the picture of *'the Sicarii'* in Josephus, as descending from the teaching of *'Judas and Sadduk'* during the unrest of 4 BC–7 CE (coincident with what the Gospels picture as *'the birth of Christ'*) and at the forefront of the unrest in the Fifties–Sixties CE in the Temple, when Josephus is finally willing to explain – however tendentiously – the meaning of their several denotations, is only partly accurate. As these events transpire, these same *'Sicarii'* are also the ones who commit mass suicide at Masada while others flee down to Egypt, resulting in the additional destruction of the Temple at Leontopolis there[108] – and finally into Cyrenaica in North Africa where unrest continues well into the Nineties and beyond, as Josephus also reports.[109]

But Josephus is perhaps only being partially forthcoming when he tells us that '*the Sicarii*' derived their name from the beduin or Yemeni-style dagger (which resembled the Roman '*sica*') they carried beneath their garments to dispatch their enemies, thus giving the impression that they were simply cutthroats or assassins and nothing more. As just underscored, this picture is picked up in Acts – probably also somewhat tendentiously – where Paul, after disturbances provoked by the perception of his having brought Gentiles and, presumably, their gifts into the Temple (*cf.* the outcry in Acts 21:28 that '*he has brought Greeks into the Temple and polluted this Holy Place*'), is queried by the Roman Chief Captain, who rescues him from the Jewish mob '*seeking to kill him*,'

> '*Are you not the Egyptian who recently caused a disturbance and led four thousand Sicarii* (the usual number of either '*four*' or '*five thousand*' Essenes, partisans of James, or even those 'Jesus' feeds in his various exoduses '*beyond Gennesareth*' and '*into the wilderness*'[110]) *out into the desert*'?

This is only true as far as it goes. In the light of the materials from Hippolytus, Origen, Dio Cassius, and Jerome, highlighted above, designating those who circumcise or forcibly circumcise others as being '*Sicarii*' too, we can perhaps go further. As we have seen, this designation was based on the eponymous body of Roman traditional law, attributed to Publius Cornelius Scipio (hence the name), forbidding castration and other similar bodily mutilations particularly of the *genitalia*, the '*Lex Cornelia de Sicarius et Veneficis*,' which grew evermore onerous from the time of Nerva to Hadrian and beyond so that, by Origen's time, Third-Century Roman magistrates were applying it as a matter of course.

This law evidently bounced back on the Revolutionaries of the Bar Kochba Period – who were, obviously, also seen as '*Sicarii*' – to the extent that a Regulation, known in the *Talmud* as '*the Sicaricon*,' was applied to them which allowed the Government to confiscate their property in the aftermath of the Uprising. The conclusion would appear to be that '*the Sicarii*,' everyone always talks so confidently about, were also known for '*forcible circumcision*' – or rather (as just suggested, something like the '*Islam*' of a later incarnation), they offered those having the temerity to discuss the validity of Mosaic Law without first entering '*the Covenant*' (*whether converts or foreigners*) *the choice of circumcision or death*.

Judging by the severity of the efforts expended against them in this period, this conduct does not seem to have been very well received by their Roman Overlords, who abrogated all the privileges the Jews had previously enjoyed regarding this practice, at least where those perceived of as being '*Sicarii*' *Revolutionaries* ('*Sicarii*' or '*Zealot Essenes*,' as Hippolytus would call them – with a distinctly '*Jamesian*' cast) were concerned. Since the Romans looked upon '*circumcision*' as little more than a variety of bodily mutilation or castration, this is something of the private joke shining through Acts' tendentious picture of the convert characterized as '*the Ethiopian Queen's eunuch*.' Based on the somewhat incomplete and perhaps even dissembling picture in Josephus – he certainly seems to have known more, as his furious remonstrances and self-justifications in both the *War* and the *Vita* on the subject of '*Sicarii*' unrest in Cyrenaica at the end of the First Century indicate[111] – readers have concluded that the '*knife*' from which the Greek version of their name was derived (this could hardly have been what they called themselves in Hebrew or Aramaic) was simply that of '*the Assassin*.' In the light, however, of the picture arising out of the new material, we have assembled above, there is no justification whatever for this conclusion.

So great was the attachment of '*the Sicarii*' to and their insistence on '*circumcision*' that they probably were far better known as '*the Party of the Circumcision*' *par excellence,* as Paul seems to so contemptuously dismiss them. Not only is this the name Paul seems to give in Galatians 2:12 to the '*Party*' led by James, but it is an issue with which he wrestles, as we have seen, with extremely high emotion throughout Galatians, including his final contemptuous jibe at those he claims in 5:12 '*are disturbing*' his communities (presumably with '*circumcision*'): '*would they would themselves cut off.*' Even the expression '*cut off*' in this context is but a thinly disguised play on '*Essene*' and Qumran '*excommunication*' practices and a euphemism, as we have seen, in wide use in the Damascus Document, particularly where '*Backsliders from the Law*' were concerned.[112]

Therefore this '*knife*,' which some saw as the assassin's, probably doubled as that of the circumciser's. In fact, the emphasis should probably be the other way round. The '*knife*,' '*Sicarii Essenes*' were using *to circumcise* or *forcibly circumcise those they heard discussing the Law in an illegitimate manner*, probably doubled as *the one they used to assassinate*; and, just as Origen who had himself mutilated his own sexual parts reports, this is how such '*Mutilators*' or '*Circumcisers*' were known in the Greco-Roman world. In our view this is a more insightful way of understanding the literature found at Qumran which, as we have been demonstrating, did contain a contingent of Gentile believers in associated status, referred to CDiv, vi, and xx, for instance, as '*the Nilvim*'/'*God-Fearers*'/or '*Joiners*.'[113]

As stated in Column xx.19f. and 34 of the Damascus Document, it was for such persons – to whom *'God would reveal Salvation ('Yesha^c')* and who would *'see His Salvation'* (*Yeshu^{c}ato*) because *'they reckoned'* and *'took refuge in His Holy Name'* – that *'a Book of Remembrance would be written out.'* It is this which, we contend, is parodied in the words, *'Do this in remembrance of me,'* attributed to 'Jesus' by Paul in 1 Corinthians 11:25 and echoed in *'Last Supper'* scenarios in the Synoptics (Luke 22:19 and *pars.*).

Early commentators had difficulty reconciling the self-evident militancy, intolerance, and aggressiveness that run through almost all the Qumran documents with their self-evident *'Essene'*-like characteristics. This conundrum is resolved if we take Hippolytus' additions to Josephus at face value – additions which, as already argued, Hippolytus would have been incapable of inventing or fabricating himself in the Third Century but which were either suppressed or diffused in alternate versions of Josephus' *Jewish War*, either by himself in Rome or others, as the true apocalyptic *'Messianism'* of the *'Essenes,'* represented by the literature that has now been found at Qumran, came to be more fully realized.

Therefore, it should be clear that what we have before us in this literature are the documents of the *'Sicarii Essene'* or *'Zealot Essene Movement'* (for Hippolytus, they are the same), a *'Movement'* which (as the First Century progressed) became indistinguishable from those Paul is identifying as *'the representatives'* or *'some from James,'* those who were insisting – to use the language of Acts 15:1's prelude to *'the Jerusalem Council'* – that, *'unless you were circumcised according to the Custom of Moses, you could not be saved'* (here, of course, too the *'yesha^c'* / *'yeshu^{c}a'* language of these extraordinary passages from CDxx above – to say nothing of similar language in the Habakkuk *Pesher*) or, as Paul characterizes them too, *'the Party of the Circumcision.'*

When one takes Dio Cassius, Origen, and Jerome at face value – understanding *'the Sicarii'* in the light of *'the Lex Cornelia de Sicarius'* – not as *'Assassins'* or *'Cutthroats,'* as their enemies would have us see them, but as *'Circumcisers'* utilizing *'the Circumciser's knife'* (even sometimes, when they heard someone improperly discussing the Law, *'forcible Circumcisers'*) and even sometimes – as at Qumran and Masada – as *'Messianists'* (*'Christians'* according to some vocabularies or, as we have also described them, *'Messianic Sadducees'*) – then, I submit, most of the difficulties hitherto surrounding these issues in considering the Dead Sea Scrolls evaporate.

'The Cup of the Lord' and *'the Blood of Christ'*

Let us close by recapitulating the arguments for the relationship of Paul's and the Synoptics' *'Cup of the New Covenant in (the) Blood'* of Christ and the Damascus Document's '*New Covenant in the Land of Damascus.*' At first glance there is no relationship between the two at all except the reference to '*the New Covenant.*' On further analysis, however, there is – a lingustic and/or an esoteric one. This will depend, as we have been demonstrating, on letters that have a certain signification in the Hebrew moving over into the Greek to produce a slightly different one.

Earlier, we pointed out that letters with unusual significance in Hebrew – for example, *B-L-ᶜ/'swallowing*' and the root of '*Belial*,' '*Belaᶜ*,' and '*Balaam*' – moved over into the Greek with entirely different signification as if the letters themselves ('*ballaᶜ*' in the Hebrew/'*ballo*' in Greek) carried some special importance whatever their meaning. In particular, this usage – which had to do in both languages with a sort of '*Devilishness*' – was important. To illustrate this, we just showed that the '*swallowing*'/'*levalᶜo*'/'*tevalᶜeno*' language, applied in Hebrew in the Habakkuk *Pesher* to the destruction or death of '*the Righteous Teacher*' and his followers among '*the Poor*' (as well as to '*the Wicked Priest*'), had a certain linguistic relationship to the '*casting out*'/'*casting down*' language in New Testament, Josephus, and early Church accounts of the deaths of Stephen, Ananus, James, and Zachariah ben Bariscaeus respectively.

This '*casting out*' language was also to be found in '*Nets*' and exorcism symbolism generally in the New Testament, not to mention the '*expulsion*' language Josephus employs in his description of '*Essene*' banishment practices. In addition, it was easy to see how '*Belial*' and his '*Nets,*' in the language of Qumran allusion, moved into '*Balaam*,' '*Balak*,' their '*Nets*,' '*Babylon*,' and even '*Beelzebul*' in Revelation and the Gospels. As an aside to this, '*Belial*' itself (to say nothing of Paul's '*Beliar*' bowdlerization in 2 Corinthians 6:15) connects in the Greek with '*Diabolos*' – in English, '*the Devil*' – and, in Arabic, with '*Iblis*' in the Koran.[114]

When considering '*Damascus*,' as in '*the New Covenant in the Land of Damascus*' in CDvi.19 and viii.21/xix.33–34, the Hebrew for '*Blood*,' as previously explained, is '*Dam*' and, for '*Cup*,' it is '*Chos*,' both forming the two parts of the transliteration into Greek of the Hebrew place name '*Damascus.*' Though in Hebrew, this particular homophone appears only to work for the first syllable, '*Dam*' or '*Blood*'; if the second part of the Hebrew expression for '*Damascus*' – '*Dammashek*,' namely '*mashek*'/'*mashkeh*,' a fourth form verbal noun, meaning, '*to give to drink*' – is taken into consideration, it also works out for the second syllable even in Hebrew.

Not only will this ultimately link up with the same phraseology, '*giving to drink*' or the command to '*drink this*,' a staple of New Testament accounts of these solemn pronouncements, attributed by all – except the Gospel of John – to 'Jesus' himself; but it is also an allusion Paul seems to take particular (if malicious) pleasure in enunciating when – after picturing in 1 Corinthians 11:24–25 '*the Lord Jesus,*' '*having dined*' and '*saying,*'

> '*This Cup is the New Covenant in my Blood. Do this as often as you drink it* (here one has the first allusion to '*drinking*' in combination with the imagery of the '*Cup,*' '*Blood,*' and '*the New Covenant.*' Furthermore, one should again note the evocation of '*doing*' playing off this usage, as one finds it throughout the Dead Sea Scrolls and '*Jamesian Christianity*') *in Remembrance of me*' (and here CDxx.19's '*Book of Remembrance written out for God-Fearers*' as the material in Ms. B reaches a climax);

and proceeding in the typical strophe-antistrophe-epode style to affirm (often it is difficult to know who is speaking, Paul or '*the Lord Jesus*'):

> *For as often as you eat this bread and drink this Cup, you proclaim the death of the Lord until he comes* (whatever he means by this, now clearly it is Paul speaking – but note here, the variation on the evocation of '*the coming of the Messiah of Aaron and Israel*' in CDxix.10–11 of Ms. B and, for that matter, in James 5:7–8 as well);

he then, seemingly, parodies these '*drinking*' connotations in his twofold epode (or, should one say, in his thesis-antithesis-synthesis rhetorical style, his '*synthesis*'?) with the belligerent and intolerant passages, we have already remarked:

> *So that whosoever...shall drink the Cup of the Lord unworthily shall be guilty of the body and Blood of the Lord* (11:27) –

and, once again, reaffirming this:

> *For he who eats and drinks unworthily, eats and drinks Judgement to himself, not seeing through to the body of the Lord* (11:29).

Whatever one may think of the theological and personal attitudes he displays here, these denotations in Hebrew at the root of the Greek transliteration '*Damascus*' become the essence of the New Testament theological approach of '*the New Covenant*' – now not '*in the Land of Damascus*' – but '*in the Cup of (the) Blood*' of Christ. Though the arguments in support of this insight are linguistic and textual, given the importance of the material under consideration, one would be unwise to ignore or pass over the correspondence between these two formulations, treating it as if it did not exist or was simply a fortuitous accident. Even if only the 'Blood' part of the equivalence were to be entertained – which in itself would be sufficient corroboration – what is the mathematical probability of such a surprising correspondence being accidental?

To put this in another way: is it logical to think that a focus such as this on the twin concepts of 'Cup' and 'Blood' – the homophonic equivalents in Hebrew of the syllables 'Dam' and 'Chos' composing the Greek transliteration 'Damascus' – is simply accidental? Investigators in the field of criminology are fond of insisting that 'coincidences' in their field are rare. One should perhaps say the same thing about 'coincidences' in the area of linguistic transfer or, for that matter, in Dead Sea Scrolls and/or Early Christian Studies generally. This is especially the case in a document like Hebrews where from Chapters 8–13, as we have shown, the focus on 'Blood' verges almost on an obsession.

But the second part of the designation 'Damascus,' involving the Hebrew root 'Sh-K-H' – in its verbal fourth-form morphology, 'mashkeh,' meaning, as just indicated, 'give to drink' – works out as well; and, in addition to the self-evident 'Dam'/'Blood' and 'Chos'/'Cup' equivalences in the Greek, this additional 'mashkeh'/'give to drink' equivalence in Hebrew would appear to be definitive.

Even if it should be granted that New Testament writers such as Paul, to say nothing of those producing the Synoptic Gospels – understood an esoteric or allegorical equivalence such as this (the fusion of 'Damascus'/ 'Dammashek' providing an especially bountiful harvest for those interested in esoteric exegesis of this kind); the question remains whether those who composed the documents found at Qumran understood the allusion 'Damascus'/'Dammashek' in this manner as well. From the perspective of the interpretation of texts (if not philology itself), the only plausible way to answer a question such as this is to look at the texts themselves and see how the expression 'the New Covenant' is used in them.

Allusion to 'the New Covenant' is first found in the prophecies of Jeremiah 31:31–34 which are, as it turns out – so important were they then evidently thought to be – quoted in full in the sections of Hebrews 8:8–12, already alluded to above. These are followed up by 'new heart and new Spirit' imagery in Ezekiel 11:19 and 36:26 which Paul variously adopts to his own purposes throughout the corpus attributed to him, as we have seen, while conveniently discarding the phrase 'keep My Laws' associated with the phrase in almost all original contexts.[115]

The usage is then picked up again in 'Last Supper' scenarios in the Synoptics (though not in John) and 1 Corinthians 11:25, as already remarked as well. Thereafter it is fleshed out definitively in Hebrews 8:13, 9:14–15, 10–20, and 12:24 (here not 'New' but 'fresh' Covenant), though in these last with an emphasis on the 'Blood' aspect of the phraseology rather than the 'Cup.' In the Dead Sea Scrolls, aside from the one negative evocation of 'the New Covenant' in the context, seemingly, of an allusion to 'Traitors' attached to it in 1QpHab,II.3 already called attention to above, it is found almost exclusively in the Damascus Document and, there, almost never unaccompanied by allusion to 'the Land of Damascus.'

In the Damascus Document, the first allusion to 'Damascus' occurs in Column VI.19 in the extension or recapitulation of the earlier exegesis of 'the Zadokite Covenant' in III.21–IV.4. Though in the latter exposition – 'waw' constructs seemingly having been deliberately added to break up the original appositive of 'the Priests, the Sons of Zadok Levites' in Ezekiel 44:15 – 'the Priests' were defined (obviously somewhat esoterically) as 'the Penitents of Israel who went out from the Land of Judah and the Nilvim with them' (seemingly in exposition of or esoterically-equivalent to the term 'Levites' in Ezekiel). The third group, of course, were 'the Sons of Zadok' who were defined both more eschatologically and, as we have seen, in terms of 'standing.'

For its part 'the Land of Damascus,' which did not actually appear at this point in Column Four, was rather picked up in the next exposition, this time of Numbers 21:1 in Column Six, which contained a similar apposition, namely, the two parallel categories of 'the Princes' and 'the Nobles of the People.' Not insignificantly, the phrase, 'to dwell' or 'live in the Land of Damascus' added here, enjoys a direct parallel in Acts 9:22 which in detailing Paul's activities in the area, it will be recalled, actually makes reference to 'the Jews who dwelt in Damascus' and in Acts 26:20, now picturing Paul himself describing this as 'Damascus first and Jerusalem and in all the region of Judea and to the Gentiles,' the whole passage containing several inversions of known Qumran usage or ideology.[116]

Furthermore, we have already pointed out that a certain amount of the exposition of Columns IV-VIII and XIX-XX of CD seems to be addressed to or signal a cadre of Gentiles associated with the Community, that is, in an associated 'God-Fearer' status.[117] This is particularly true of the manner in which Column IV.3, as just alluded to, expounded the term 'Levites' from Ezekiel 44:15 in terms of 'Nilvim'/'Joiners' – a typical expression in Hebrew documents for 'Gentiles attaching themselves to the Torah' – and the way Column VI.3–11 applies the language of Isaiah 54:16 to its evocation of 'the Staff' or 'the Mehokkek,' an individual which it defines (in another esoteric exegesis) as 'the Doresh' or 'Seeker after the Torah.' In fact, that Isaiah 54–56, from which this latter expression is taken, is being directly applied to such 'Nilvim,' to wit,

> the foreigners who have joined themselves to the Lord..., keep My Sabbaths...and hold fast to the Covenant (here note, in particular, the 'keeping' and 'holding fast' allusions again, language permeating these last sections of the Damascus Document as we have seen),

is made explicit in Isaiah 56:3–6.

In the second appositive cluster in CDvi.3–9, 'the Nobles' or 'Leaders of the People,' subsequently defined as 'those who came to dig the Well with the staves' – meaning the 'hukkim' or 'Laws' legislated by 'the Mehokkek' / 'Doresh'/'Interpreter'/'Seeker' (all these, as we saw, are play-on-words) – are now combined with 'the Princes' to develop a third overall category 'the Diggers.' This, in turn, produces the exposition:

> the Diggers are the Penitents of Israel who went out from the Land of Judah to dwell in the Land of Damascus.

'The Diggers' here are, self-evidently, synonymous with 'the Priests' in the earlier exposition in Column iv.2–3 of Ezekiel 44:15, 'the Land of Damascus' now being expressly and specifically added, probably because of the coming evocation of 'the New Covenant' which is going to be described in Columns viii.21 and xix.33 as being 'erected' there in connection with the 'digging of the Well.' For their part, 'the Nobles' or 'Leaders of the People' – 'People'/'Peoples' probably being a deliberate play on 'Gentiles' (Ethnon in Greek), as we have been explaining – are presumably those already in 'the Land of Damascus' who 'came to dig the Well' with 'the Seeker's or 'Doresh's 'staves,' that is, his 'Laws' or 'Statutes.'

As already remarked, much of this is rather obscure or arcane – in fact about as arcane as Pauline/Hebrews' exposition of 'the Cup of the New Covenant in (his) Blood' though from a completely opposite ideological perspective – but some sense can be made of it. 'The Leaders of the People' ('Peoples' carrying on the 'Gentiles' theme) are now to be identified with 'the Nilvim' of the earlier exegesis – 'People'/'Peoples,' as repeatedly indicated, being a typical Qumran/Damascus Document/Habakkuk Pesher allusion to 'Gentiles.' According to Acts 26:17 above, even Paul evokes similar usages when he speaks of

> being taken out from among the People and the Peoples to whom I now send you.

In fact, throughout the rest of CD, as we have emphasized, there is continual allusion to '*fearing God's Name*' and '*God-Fearers*,' accompanied by pointed allusions to '*being steadfast*' or '*holding fast*' – meaning '*to the Covenant*' or '*the Torah*'/'*the Law*.'

This is typically put, as will be recalled, in Column XX.17–20 of Ms. B as follows:

> *But the Penitents from Sin in Jacob kept the Covenant of God. Then each man shall speak to his neighbor, each strengthening his brother, to support their step in the Way of God* (this passage relates to one from Jeremiah 31:34: '*each one to teach his neighbor and each one to teach his brother*,' also cited in Hebrews 8:11)...*and a Book of Remembrance was written out before Him for God-Fearers* (here, the '*Book of Remembrance*' allusion, we have so often called attention to, linking up with '*Last Supper*' scenarios of '*do this in Remembrance of me*' in both 1 Corinthians 11:24–25 and the Synoptics – which, in effect, is the same idea but from a different perspective) *and for those reckoning His Name until God shall reveal Salvation* (Yesha^c – '*Jesus*' again) *and Justification to those fearing His Name.*

It should also be noted that these are exactly the parameters of Isaiah 56:1 above, '*Zedakah*' ('*Justification*') and '*Yeshu^{c}ati*' ('*My Salvation*'/'*My Jesus*'), introducing the material that follows in 56:4–5 about '*foreigners attaching themselves to the Lord to serve Him and to love His Name and be His Servants*' (cf. Paul in Acts 25:16 on being appointed '*a Servant*' and 2 Corinthians 3:6 on being '*competent Servants of the New Covenant*' as well). The same idea is repeated again at the end of Column XX, as we have also been repeatedly remarking:

> *For He does Mercy to (the thousands) of them that Love Him and...all those who hold fast to these Statutes, coming and going in accordance with the Torah* (cf. James 2:5 above on '*the Kingdom He Promised to those that love Him*') *and...listening to the voice of the Righteousness Teacher...Their hearts will be strengthened and they shall prevail against all the Sons of the Earth, and God will make atonement for* (or '*through*') *them, and they will see His Salvation* ('*Yeshu^{c}a*,' another variation, as we have seen, of '*Yesha^c*'/'*Jesus*'), *because they took refuge in His Holy Name.*[118]

The first allusion to '*the New Covenant*' associated with these promises comes in CDVI.14–16 amid allusion to '*separating from the Sons of the Pit*' and the '*Nazirite*'-rooted language of

> *keeping away from (lehinnazer) polluted Evil Riches...and from the Riches of*

the Temple...and (from) robbing the Poor (Ebionim).

In the newer fragments of the Damascus Document from Cave 4 (4Q266), this language is also found in the First Column in the instructions *'to the Sons of Light'* *'to keep way from the Paths'* (again *'lehinnazer'*) probably *'of Evil'* or *'of Wicked pollution,' 'until the completion of the Time of Visitation.'*[119] It is because of allusions such as this that we have been referring to this language as *'Nazirite'* and this Community as a *'Consecrated One'* or *'a House of the Torah'* dedicated to God – or, to use more familiar language, *'Nazirites'/'Nazoraeans'/'Nazrenes'* as the case may be.

'The New Covenant in the Land of Damascus' and *'Drink this in Remembrance of Me'*

The actual reference to *'the New Covenant in the Land of Damascus,'* as we have seen, comes in Column VI.20 where *'the Staff's 'decrees,'* in which they are commanded *'to walk during all the Era of Evil,'* are defined in terms of

> *separating between polluted and pure ('separation' here, a synonym for 'lehinnazer' above)...Holy from Profane and to keep the Sabbath Day* (the language again, one actually finds in Isaiah 56:4 and 56:6 above regarding *'Nilvim'* or *'Gentile'* and n.b., the *'keeping'* language too)...*the Festivals and the Day of Fasting (Yom Kippur) according to the precise letter of the Commandment of those entering the New Covenant in the Land of Damascus.*[120]

This of course is the direct opposite of what Peter is presented as learning in the Acts 10:15 and 10:28 version of what it considers ultimately to be *'the New Covenant,'* namely, as we saw (but it is worth repeating), *'not to make distinctions between Holy and impure'* and *'to call no man impure'!*

In Column VI.20–VII.3, on the other hand, this *'Covenant'* is then specifically defined, as we have been accentuating, as:

> *to set up the Holy Things according to their precise specifications, to love every man his brother* (again, James' *'Royal Law according to the Scripture'*), *to strengthen the hand of the Meek (ʿAni), the Poor (Ebion), and the Convert (Ger* – here *'Converts'* are distinctly referred to and combined with the *'steadfast'/'strengthening'* language we have been emphasizing as so important to this orientation and, of course, James' role among *'the People'* as defined by his cognomen, *'Oblias'/'Protection-of-the-People'*[121])...*and not to uncover the nakedness of near kin (i.e., 'niece marriage' or 'incest'), but to keep*

away from fornication according to the Statute (here *'lehazzir'* based on the same *'N-Z-R'* or *'Nazirite'* root as *'lehinnazer'* above, the second category of James' directives to overseas communities in Acts 15:20, *et. al.*)...*to bear no rancor...but to separate from all pollutions according to Statute* (*cf.* James in Acts 15:20, too, on *'keeping away from the pollutions of the idols'* and *n.b.*, the Nazirite *'separation'* ideology again).

Now that we know the terms of *'the New Covenant in the Land of Damascus,'* the presentation turns *'Messianic'* and Column VII.13–21 proceeds to evoke the imagery from Amos 9:11 – common to James' speech in Acts 15:16 – about *'raising the Tabernacle of David which is fallen,'* combining it with the imagery from Amos 5:26–27 earlier, including – as we have seen – *'the Star of your King,'* which it expresses rather in terms of *'exiling the Tabernacle of your King and the bases of Your statues from My Tent* (or *'from the tents'*) *of Damascus.'* For its part, the speech accorded James in Acts 15:13–21 puts an esoteric spin on *'rebuilding'* this *'Tabernacle'* compressing a good deal of what follows in CDVII-VIII and XIX-XX.

In both Acts and at Qumran, the exposition – as will be recalled – is esoteric. In the latter *'the Tabernacle of the King'* (thereafter, seemingly, to be refined in terms of Amos 9:11's *'the Tabernacle of David which is fallen'*) is identified with *'the Books of the Torah'* – this, of course, the very opposite of how *'the Gentile Mission'* would see these things. Notwithstanding, *'the King'* – as in Paul in 1 Corinthians 12:12–27 – *'is the Community and the Bases of the Statues are the Books of the Prophets whose words Israel despised.'* By contrast, in Acts 15:16–21 the esoteric exegesis of this passage from Amos is rather presented, it should be recalled, as having something to do with James' support of Paul's *'Gentile Mission'* or, as this is put, *'all the Gentiles (Ethne) upon whom My Name has been called,'* which then triggers the various versions of James' directives to overseas communities.

That the whole complex, as it is presented in the Damascus Document, is to be taken in a *'Messianic'* way is clear from the evocation of *'the Star Prophecy'* which follows in Ms. A and *'the coming of the Messiah of Aaron and Israel'* in Ms. B. Bringing the whole series of usages full circle: as this prophecy is expounded it is now connected in some manner both with *'the Diggers'* materials (that is, *'those who dug the Well in the Land of Damascus'*) and *'the New Covenant in the Land of Damascus'* preceding it from Columns VI.3–VII.6. In turn, both are connected to Numbers 21:18's *'Well'* which *'the Princes'* and *'Nobles of the People dug,'* *'the Penitents who went out to the Land of Damascus'* materials, and Isaiah 54–56's *'Staff'*/ *'Mehokkek,'* described as *'an instrument for His works.'* The last link between all of these is then, of course, *'the Doresh'* or *'the Seeker after the Torah'* (the '*seeking*' theme being fundamental here), that is, '*the Interpreter of the Torah*' who is both '*the Staff who decrees the Laws*' ('*Hukkim*,' a play on '*the Mehokkek*' as well as '*His staves*' as we just saw), who is then identified in the next exegesis as '*the Star who came to Damascus.*'

This is quite a complex structure. Nevertheless, we are now in the realm of Acts' presentation of early 'Christian' history on two counts: 1) in the matter of '*the Seeker after the Torah*' ('*the Star*') '*who came to Damascus*'; and 2) in the use of these Amos materials, particularly those relating to '*re-erecting the Tabernacle of David which is fallen*' constituting the jumping-off point, as it were, to Acts' presentation of James' directives to these same '*Nilvim*' or '*Joiners*' to the Community in its picture of the outcome of '*the Jerusalem Council.*' The '*rebuilding*' or '*re-erecting*' of this '*fallen Tabernacle*' is then used in Acts to present James as definitively supporting Paul's '*Gentile Mission*' (a presentation I dispute – he might have supported the '*Mission*' but, clearly, not its '*Pauline*' parameters), as well as to introduce the specific ban in these instructions on '*Blood.*'

The two, of course, are incompatible – that is, one cannot support both the '*Mission*' as Paul (followed by Acts) frames it and the ban on '*Blood*' – my reason for denying the historicity of this genre of application of Amos 9:11's Prophecy about '*raising the Tabernacle of David which is fallen*' in the picture of James' discourse in Acts 15:16–17 to Paul's '*Gentile Mission.*' A prohibition of this kind on James' part, concerning which Paul feigns ignorance throughout 1 Corinthians – if taken seriously – would preclude what Paul claims in 1 Corinthians 11:24 he '*received*' directly '*from the Lord.*' A claim of the latter kind, if entertained, can only mean via direct visionary experience or '*apocalypsis*,' the kind of experience he also claims as both the basis of his '*Apostleship*' – '*not from men nor through man*' – in Galatians 1:1, as well as his view of the entire '*Gentile Mission*' in Galatians 2:2. Furthermore, even if one were to insist that the claim should only be taken allegorically or symbolically, this would inevitably make 'Jesus' a quasi-'*Disciple*' of Philo of Alexandria just as Paul.

As Paul now pictures '*the Lord Jesus*' describing this '*New Covenant in (his) Blood*' in 1 Corinthians 11:25–27, as we just saw (possibly adding the '*Cup*' from an esoteric understanding of '*Damascus*'):

> '*This Cup is the New Covenant in my Blood*'...*As often as you drink...this Cup you drink the death of the Lord...whoever shall...drink the Cup of the Lord unworthily shall be guilty of...the Blood of the Lord.*

A more esoteric or allegorical understanding of '*the New Covenant*' is hard to envision. In Matthew 26:27–28, this becomes:

> *Taking the Cup...he gave it to them, saying,'This is my Blood, that of the New Covenant which is poured out for the Many for remission of Sins'* (Mark 14:23–24 is the same, but omitting the *'remission of Sins'* part)

Luke follows Paul, even including in 22:21–22 the two references to *'delivering up'* of the kind found in 1 Corinthians 11:22 above and only adding the further variation, *'which is poured out for you.'*

According to Acts 15:14, as we have seen, James' evocation of *'rebuilding the fallen Tabernacle of David'* even includes the allusion to how God *'visited the Gentiles to take out a People for His Name.'* We have also seen how *'Visitation'* language of this kind permeates the Damascus Document, beginning with the assertion – also preceded by two references to *'delivering up'* – in the First Column of CD that God *'visited them and caused a Root of Planting to grow from Israel and from Aaron'* and continuing to this very juncture of the Document and the exegesis of *'the Star Prophecy'* in CDvii.18–viii.3. Though in Ms. B, *'the Star Prophecy'* is replaced by Zechariah 13:7, Ezekiel 9:4, and evocation of *'the coming of the Messiah of Aaron and Israel'* (continuing this *'Israel and Aaron'* allusion from Column 1.7 earlier – singular), both versions conserve the *'Visitation'* usages.

As already underscored as well, even the word *'First,'* as in the *'First Visitation,'* is included in both Ms. A and B versions of the text, *e.g.,'these escaped in the Era of the First Visitation,'* and the language of *'Visitation'* or *'God visiting them'* is repeated some three or four times. In James' speech in Acts (no mention of who this *'James'* was – the other *'James'* having already disappeared from the scene), this becomes, *'Simeon has told you how God First visited the Gentiles to take out a People for His Name'* (n.b., not only the *'Visitation'* language but also the allusion to *'for His Name'* replacing more familiar allusions *'called by this Name'* earlier in Acts and *'called by Name'* in the Dead Sea Scrolls[122]). Just as in Column vii.18's *'the Prophets whose words Israel despised,'* Acts 15:15 also evokes *'the words of the Prophets,'* but adds Amos 9:11's *'and I will build the ruins of it again and I will set it up'* to CDvii.16's more circumscribed version of Amos 9:11.

It will be recalled that in CDvi.8, quoting Isaiah 54:16, *'the Mehokkek'* was defined as *'the Seeker after the Torah'* and characterized as *'an instrument for His works.'* Stitching the whole together, CDvii.18–19 then defined *'the Star'/'Stave'/'Mehokkek,'* as we saw, as *'the Interpreter of'* or *'Seeker after the Torah who came to Damascus.'* But in James' speech in Acts 15:18, not only is *'the Tabernacle of David which is fallen'* invoked (*'its ruins to be rebuilt'*), but this becomes an explanation of why *'the Remnant of Men'* or '*the Men who are left may seek out the Lord*' – '*those who are left*' or '*the Remnant*' also being language familiar to these sections of CDVII/XIX.[123] Once again, the '*seeking*' language is pivotal as it is in CDVII.18–19's exposition of both Amos 9:11 and Numbers 24:17 in terms of '*the Doresh ha-Torah.*' It is also the explanation earlier for why God called '*the Diggers*' of Numbers 21:18 (that is, '*the Penitents who went out from the Land of Judah to dwell in the Land of Damascus*') '*Princes, because they sought Him and their honour was questioned by no man*' (CDVI.4–7)!

At this point in Acts 15:18, as if by way of explanation, James is pictured as adding: '*all his works are known to God from Eternity.*' Here, of course, we have the '*works*' language of Isaiah 54:16 and CDVI.8 and '*the Staff*'/'*Seeker*' being '*an instrument for His works*' – not to mention the earlier material from CDI.10 (following on from how '*God visited them and caused a root of Planting to grow from Israel and from Aaron*'): '*And God considered their works because they sought him with a whole heart*' (here the '*seeking*' language connected to the '*whole heart*' allusions, we have been following in this work). Nor is this to say anything about the allusion to '*God visiting their works*' later in CDV.17. Even more germane, almost the exact words are to be found in CDII.5–8, where '*the Penitents from Sin*' among those '*who enter the Covenant*' (i.e., '*the New Covenant in the Land of Damascus*') are characterized in terms of being blessed, but:

> *Power, Might, and overwhelming Wrath with sheets of Fire...upon those who turn aside the Way and abominate the Law...because, before the World ever was, God chose them not and, before they were established, He knew their works.*

Here CDII.8 adds, as if for emphasis and a *coup de grace* of sorts: '*and abominated their Generations on account of Blood.*' Once again, one should compare this allusion to God '*knowing their works*' with James quoted in in Acts 15:18 as concluding: '*All his works are known to God from Eternity.*'

Directly, Acts 15:19 has James proceed with his '*judgements*' or '*rulings*': '*Therefore I judge those from the Peoples who turn to God*' (n.b., this same '*turning*'/'*returning*' we have been underscoring above and familiar to Columns VI–VIII and XIX–XX of CD as well), a speech which then gives way to the overt use of the '*Nazirite*' language '*abstain from*'/'*keep away from,*' we have also seen as permeating these Columns of the Damascus Document. In this regard, we just highlighted the key importance of the '*keep away from*' language ('*lehazzir*'/'*lehinnazer*'/and '*linzor*') specifically as regards '*fornication*' in VII.1 and its parallel '*to separate from all pollutions*' in VII.3, which certainly would have included '*the pollutions of the idols*' in Acts 15:20; but also, in the Column preceding the First Column of CD from 4Q266, where '*the Sons of Light*' were instructed to '*keep away (lehin-nazer) from the ways*' – probably '*of Evil*' or '*Evil pollutions*,' the last-mentioned being expressed in CDVI.15 (in a seeming attack on the Herodian Establishment) as '*polluted Evil Riches*.'

Aside from the almost hysterical attack on '*Blood*,' just highlighted in CDII.8 above, there are at least two other specific references to '*Blood*' in the Damascus Document – both negative: one that immediately follows this in Column in III.2-7, after explaining why Abraham

> *was made a Friend of God* (also of interest to James 2:23–24) *because* (and this significantly) *he kept the Commandments of God and did not choose the will of his own Spirit* (as '*some*' might consider Paul to be doing)...*But the Sons of Jacob turned aside in them* (the '*turning aside*'/'*backsliding*'/'*going astray*' vocabulary we have been calling attention to) *and* ...*walked in stubbornness of their heart...*, *complaining against the Commandments of God* (which, of course, Paul does interminably), *each man doing what was right in his own eyes. So they ate blood and their males were cut off in the wilderness.*

The second in Column Five:

> *They also pollute the Temple, because they do not separate according to the Torah* (that is, '*Holy*' from '*profane*' – the opposite of 'Peter''s vision in Acts 10:13–15 above), *but rather they lie with a woman during the blood of her period and each man takes (to wife) the daughter of his brother and the daughter of his sister* (a construct of the '*fornication*' and '*pollution of the Temple*' charges, the First and Third of '*the Three Nets of Belial*' of CDIV.16–18 earlier).

While not relating to the ingestion of food or drink *per se* (as CDII.8 and III.7 do) and, as a consequence, '*Communion with the Body and Blood of Christ Jesus*'; this last passage, nonetheless, vividly illustrates the attitude of the authors towards contact with '*Blood*' of any kind.

To sum up the approach of the Damascus Document, we should look at its closing section containing, as we have seen, its most vivid exhortative passages (Columns VIII and XIX-XX). Here while '*the Spouter of Lying*' and '*his whole Congregation*' or '*Church*' are condemned, the implication is that '*the Penitents of Israel, who turned aside from the Way of the People(s)*' (that is, '*the Way*' preached by '*the Spouter of Lying*' and those like him) are not, '*because God so loved the First* ('*the Forefathers*')...*He also loved those coming after them*' (VIII.13–17/XIX.26–30) – a form, as already remarked, of Pauline '*Grace*' should one choose to regard it but within specifically Qumranic parameters. It was at this point, it will be recalled too, that

'*Elisha's rebuke of Gehazi his servant*' – a favorite Rabbinic allusion for rebuking Pauline-type teachers – is invoked to emphasize God's:

> *Judgement on all those who reject the Commandments of God and forsake them, turning away in stubbornness of their heart* (VIII.20/XIX.33)

It is in conjunction with this that '*the New Covenant in the Land of Damascus*' is for the second time directly invoked – this in order to condemn:

> *All those who entered the New Covenant in the Land of Damascus, but turned back and betrayed and turned aside from the Well of Living Waters*' (VIII.21–22 and XIX.33–35 – here the most complete presentation of the '*turning aside*'/'*turning back*'/'*betraying*' circle-of-language).

Similar expressions are reiterated in the third evocation of '*the New Covenant*' in CDxx.10–13, where it is also designated as '*the Compact which they raised in the Land of Damascus*' and equated with '*the House of the Torah.*' Sentiments of this kind continue to be expressed in the surrounding materials having to do with the fate of all such '*Traitors,*' '*Backsliders,*' and '*Scoffers*' from CD Columns XIX.34–XX.17 of Ms. B. At this point, it will be recalled, the text turns both positive and passionately inspirational, again returning to '*the Penitents from Sin in Jacob who kept the Covenant of God*' (the same '*Penitents*' we heard about in Column II.5 – to say nothing of IV.2, VI.5, and VIII.16/XIX.29 following that – before the condemnation of the '*Turners-Aside from the Way*' or '*Backsliders*' and '*the Abominators of the Torah*' on account of their '*consumption of Blood*' in II.8–9), in particular –as just reiterated – '*God-Fearers*' and '*those reckoning His Name,*' to whom '*God would reveal Salvation (Yesha^c) and Justification*' (*Zedakah* – XX.19–20), the exact vocabulary found in Isaiah 56:1 introducing its position on foreign '*Nilvim*'/'*Joiners*' in 56:3–6 above, for whom '*a Book of Remembrance would be written out*'!

To understand these passages one should again refer back to Acts 15:14–17 and James' alleged connection of God '*taking out of the Gentiles a People for his Name*' in 15:14 with '*rebuilding the fallen Tabernacle of David*' and '*setting it up*' again, reiterating its applicability to '*those left of Men*' or '*the Remnant*' (designated as '*Seekers*') and '*all the Gentiles upon whom My name has been called*' in 15:16–17. In CDxx.27–32, as we have seen, these were particularly to include:

> *all those who hold fast to the Statutes, coming and going in accordance with the Torah...(who have) not lifted up their hand against the Holiness of His Laws and*

the Righteousness of His Judgements and the Testimonies of His Truth. Rather (we) have been instructed in the First Ordinances (or 'the Statutes of the First'), in which the Men of the Community were judged.

Once again, as in James' speech and as previously pointed out too, the word '*First*' appears ('*the First Ordinances*' or '*Statutes*' in XX.31), but here rather relating to '*the First*' or '*the Forefathers*' of the First Covenant, as earlier in CD1.4's description of how God '*remembered the Covenant of the First*' or '*the Forefathers*' – '*the First Covenant*' – and, therefore, '*left a* (tell-tale) *Remnant*' and '*did not deliver them up*' ('*to the sword*') but rather '*visited them and caused a (Messianic) Root of Planting to grow.*'

Furthermore, when they '*listen to the voice of the Righteous Teacher*' ('*Teacher*' repeated twice at this juncture in CDxx.28 and 32), they '*hear*'

the Laws of Righteousness and do not desert them...Their hearts will be strengthened and they shall prevail against all the Sons of Earth. And God will make atonement for (or 'through') them and they will see his Salvation (as we have seen, here as in Isaiah 56:1 above, '*Yeshuʿato*' and, to repeat), *because they took refuge in His Holy Name* (XX.33–34).

This '*Covenant*' is, of course, exactly the opposite of the Pauline one as it has come down to us. How can two such chronologically almost contemporaneous versions of '*the New Covenant*' be so completely and diametrically opposed? As we have been intimating, it is almost as if one is framed in direct reference to or with direct knowledge of the other.

We have already examined a similar kind of diametrically-opposed ideological reversal in the the Habakkuk *Pesher*'s exposition of Habakkuk 2:4, which must be seen – along with Genesis 15:5 on Abraham's '*Faith being reckoned to him as Righteousness*' (*i.e.*, '*Justification*') – as fundamental '*building blocks*' of Pauline theology. In 1QpHab,VII.17– VIII.3, it will be recalled, the applicability of this key Biblical proof-text was circumscribed to '*the Doers of the Torah in the House of Judah*' – in other words, '*Torah-Doers who were Jewish.*' It, therefore, followed that it did not apply to '*Non-Torah-doing Gentiles*' – nor even, for that matter, '*Non-Torah-Doing Jews*'!

It is the position of this book, the partial aim of which has been to collate and highlight these contrasts and reversals, that this kind of stark contrast where '*the New Covenant in the Land of Damascus*' is concerned is invaluable in helping to further highlight the Qumran perspective which, in so far as it was addressed to Gentile converts – *and it was* – was addressed to those '*keeping the whole of the Torah,*' including the Sabbath and the other observances like '*circumcision*' as *per* the parameters of Isaiah 54–56, as expounded in CDVI-VII above – this as opposed to the more allegorized and spiritualized '*New Covenant*' being delineated at such length and with such self-evident rhetorical flourish in his Letters by Paul (and, by extension, a good many passages in the Gospels as they finally crystallized out in the West), who is finally (if carefully) emphasizing to his followers that *it was not necessary to do so* – in particular and *inter alia*, that not only was *it unnecessary to circumcise oneself but one should not do so.*[124]

Building the '*House of Faith in Israel*'

For these last (that is, Paul's positions on these issues), the rhetorical and polemical constructions of the concluding Five Chapters of Hebrews – already remarked to some extent above – are fundamental as well: '*If the First Covenant had not been found wanting, then there would be no need to seek for the Second*' (Hebrews 8:7 – here the telltale '*seeking*' allusion again), quoting in its entirety the passage from Jeremiah 31:33–34 on '*making a New Covenant with the House of Israel and the House of Judah*' – n.b., '*the House of Judah*' language, just called attention to in the Habakkuk *Pesher* exposition of Habakkuk 2:3–4 above. In these passages in Jeremiah, this included a stress on '*keeping the Covenant*' – so conspicuous in the concluding exhortation in the Damascus Document (but so conspicuously missing from Paul's more allegorical exposition of similar proof-texts) – and the reference to '*teaching each one his neighbor and each one his brother*' also found word-for-word in CDXX.17–18:

> Then each man shall speak to his neigh(bor and each on)e his brother to support their steps in the Way of God.

At this point, Hebrews calls the First Covenant '*Old*,' again in stark contrast to that of the '*New*,' as embodied in '*the New Covenant*,' opining '*that which decays and grows old is ready to disappear*' (8:13).

Continuing this theme into Chapter Nine and evoking, too, '*the veil*' between the Outer Sanctum and the Inner – '*the Tabernacle which is called the Holy of Holies*' (9:2–3 – note here, the additional possible play on '*the Tabernacle*' vocabulary in CDVII.14–17 above) – as we have already to some extent described, Hebrews 9:12 now alludes to how Christ '*by his own Blood*' (repeatedly reiterating the redemptive power of '*Blood*') '*entered the Holy of Holiest once for all.*'

In a total allegorical description, Hebrews 9:12–14 now asserts '*how much more the Blood of Christ can purge...the dead works'* of its hearers' *'consciences to serve the Living God.'* Again here, one should note, not only the completely allegorized, Pauline use of language of the kind already encountered throughout 1 Corinthians 8–11 and Galatians 3–4 previously; but, in addition, the allusion to *'conscience(s),'* which Paul evokes so contemptuously in 1Corinthians 8:10–12 too, but which we have also just seen Hippolytus use regarding those *'Sicarii Essenes'* who preferred martyrdom to *'eating things sacrificed to idols'* – the very *'things sacrificed to idols'* we have, also, just encountered in 1Corinthians 8:1–10 above.

This is the point at which Hebrews 9:15 designates *'Christ'* – much as the *'Instrument'/'Seeker'/'Stave'* /and *'Star'* above – *'the Mediator of the New Covenant.'* Picking up the *'Perfection of Holiness'* language, one encounters in CDxx.2–7 and 1QS,VIII.10–20, it concludes in 10:14, *'For by one offering he has Perfected forever those who are sanctified'* (or, in more properly Hebrew terms, *'made Holy'*). Again, quoting Jeremiah 31:33 on *'putting My Torah in their midst and writing it on their hearts'*(for Hebrews 8:12 and 10:16, it was: *'I will put My Laws in their hearts and write them on their minds'*), but completely ignoring Jeremiah's further absolute and repeated insistence on *'keeping the Covenant,'* Hebrews 10:16–17 now states:

> *This is the Covenant I will make with them after those days, saith the Lord. Their Sins and lawlessness will I remember no more* (now a presumable negative variation on the *'Remembrance'* language we have been calling attention to).

This is the *'Covenant,'* Paul also develops in 2 Corinthians 3:6 above when he calls himself and his colleagues *'Servants of the New Covenant'* which he claims – using the language of Jeremiah, just highlighted above, augmented by that of Ezekiel [125] – *'to have written on the fleshy tablets of the heart'* – while, once again, simultaneously managing to ignore both Ezekiel's insistences on *'keeping the Laws'* or *'the Covenant'*!

Picking up the *'moving through the second veil'* allusion of 9:3–15 and, by implication, the allusion to *'the Mediator'* there, the author of Hebrews 10:19–20 now goes on finally and climactically to claim *'to have the boldness to enter into the Holiest (that is, 'the Holy of Holiest')...by a New and living way.'* One should compare this with CDviii.21–22 and xix.33–34's use of the term *'living'* in its description of *'those who turned back, betrayed, and turned aside from the Fountain'* or *'Well of Living Waters,'* directly following its evocation of *'the New Covenant in the Land of Damascus'* above, which it goes on to imply has something to do with *'the words'* with which *'Elisha rebuked Gehazi.'* The author of Hebrews means by this and defines this as – moving now into almost total allegory (so much so as to verge on almost complete mystification) – '*by the Blood of Jesus*' which has been '*consecrated through the veil*' (one often wonders what is actually being said here or is it '*mystery-fication*' simply for '*mystification*' sake?)

Finally, in Hebrews 12:23–24, alluding to the dual efficacy again of '*Jesus*' as '*the Mediator of the New Covenant*' (here, literally expressed as the '*Fresh*' Covenant) and '*the Perfect Holiness of the Spirits of the Righteous*' (literally, '*Perfecting the Spirits of the Righteous*' – again, '*Perfection of the Way*' and '*Perfect Holiness*' being central ideological approaches of both the Damascus Document and the Community Rule) and evoking *MMT*'s '*Camp*' language; Hebrews 13:10–12 and 13:20–21 now states:

> *Just as the bodies of those animals, whose blood was brought into the Holy of Holiest by the High Priest as a sacrifice for Sin,*[126] *were burned outside the Camp; so too Jesus suffered outside the Camp, so he might sanctify the People by his own Blood* (here the Philo-like allegorization is patent)...*It is this Blood of the Eternal Covenant of our Lord Jesus that will make you Perfect in every good work* (the very opposite, of course, of a '*works-Righteousness*' and '*Covenant-keeping*' orientation of a James or Qumran).

Though the allegorized analogy here clearly moves into Hellenizing '*Mystery Religion*' rituality and even displays, in depicting 'Jesus' as having '*suffered outside the Camp*' – this, hardly deducible from the way the Gospels portray their view of how things happened but the '*outside the Camp*' allusion does reverberate across a wide range of Qumran documents as we have seen[127] – what today might be characterized as the inferiority complex of those feeling in some way rejected or '*cast aside*'; still it is mesmerizing in its esoterics and the total Philo-esque allegorization implicit in its mastery of rhetorical display is spell-binding.

The only question remaining is the one we asked at the beginning of this section: did the sectaries at Qumran know the Pauline or New Testament position (if we can refer to it in such a manner) on '*the New Covenant*' to which they were responding? Or was there some secret, hidden, or inner meaning imparted only to central members of the sect, as is sometimes implied in Column Four of CD and elsewhere:

> *And with the Completion of the Era of the number of these years, there will be no more joining to the House of Judah* (here, again, both the Habakkuk *Pesher*'s and Jeremiah's '*House of Judah*' language), *but rather each man will stand upon his own net* (to say nothing of both the '*joining*' and '*Standing*' vocabulary – '*his net*'/'*metzudo*,' as we have seen, probably being a

defective redaction of *'his Watchtower'*/*'Metzuro'* also used in the Habakkuk *Pesher* quoting Habakkuk 2:1)[128]?

Or, as this is put earlier,

> *And he built for them a House of Faith in Israel, the likes of which has never stood from Ancient Times until now. And for them that hold fast to it* (here again, the *'holding fast'* or *'steadfast'* language), *there will be Victorious Life and all the Glory of Adam will be theirs* (a variation probably, as we have seen, of the Ebionite/Elchasaite *'Primal Adam'* ideology).

It is possible, but I consider both options relatively doubtful.

The other possibility is: did someone like Paul – a person whom, I consider, because of the breadth of Qumran language infusing his letters, spent time in the Community before he was, most likely, ejected as *per* the parameters of CDxx.25–27, 4QD266, and 1QS,VII.22–25 above and who, speaking both Hebrew and/or Aramaic and Greek (as he undoubtedly must have done), understood at least to a certain extent the esoteric possibilities inherent in the Greek transliteration of the Hebrew geographical designation *'Dammashek'* or *'Damascus,'* in particular as these bore on the Hebrew terms for *'Cup'* and *'Blood,'* to say nothing of *'drink this'* or *'give to drink'* – understand *'the New Covenant in the Land of Damascus'* in such a manner?

In asking this question, I leave aside the allusions to *'the Cup of the right hand of the Lord'* and *'the Cup of the Wrath of God'* in Column XI.10 and XI.15 of the Habakkuk *Pesher,* which – in my view – carry the true sense of all of these *'Cup of the Lord'* allusions one is encountering in these documents. Curiously enough, as we saw, Revelation also knows this sense, when it states in passages replete with Qumran imagery such as 14:8 (which we have already cited to some extent previously), mimicking and inverting the language of the mournful Prophet, Jesus ben Ananias, whom Josephus pictures as having first made his appearance in Tabernacles, 62 CE directly following the death of James:

> *Babylon is fallen* (another variation, as already pointed out, of the *'Belial'*/ *'Balaam'*/*'Beelzebub'* imagery) *because she has given to all Peoples* (*Ethne* again) *to drink* (here, of course, the precise *'giving to drink'* of the *'mashkeh'*/*'Dammashek'* imagery above) *of the wine of the Fury of her fornication* (and to add to this, the *'fornication'* allusion – to say nothing of those to *'wine'* and *'Fury'*/*'Wrath'*);

and again with regard to the '*Worshipper of the Beast*' (in Hebrew '*Be^cir*' or '*Be^cor*' the father of both '*Balaam*' and '*Bela^c*' and the eponymous ancestor, as we have stressed, of all Herodians [129]):

> *He also shall drink* (again the imagery of '*drinking,*' once more coupled with that of '*the wine,*' '*the Cup,*' and '*the Wrath*'/'*Fury*'/or '*Anger*') *of the wine of the Wrath of God which is poured out full strength into the Cup of His Anger* (Revelation 14:10).

This is repeated again, as we have seen as well, two chapters later amid the imagery of '*blasphemy,*' namely '*blaspheming the Name of God*' and '*blaspheming the God of Heaven*' (16:9–11 – *cf.* the parallel with the official charge against James of '*blasphemy*'), and '*pouring out the Blood*' (here, '*the Blood of the Saints and of the Prophets*' – compare this with '*the Blood of Man,*' '*the Dumb Beasts,*' '*the Simple of Judah doing Torah,*' '*the Ebionim,*' and '*the Violence done to the Land*' of the exposition in 1QpHab,XI.16–XII.10 of Habakkuk 2:17 above), literally expressed in Revelation 16:6 in terms of '*giving them Blood to drink*' – perhaps the very correlative in Hebrew of '*Dammashek*' when taken according to its esoteric decoding:

> *And the Great City Babylon was remembered before God, to give her the Cup of the wine of the Fury of His Wrath* (16:19).

In addition to the '*being tormented in fire and brimstone before the Holy Angels*' (Revelation 14:10) of the picture of God's '*Judgement in the midst of many Peoples*' in 1QpHab,X.4 above, the '*mark on the forehead*' of '*those who cry and weep*' of Ezekiel 9:4 in CDXIX.12 (Revelation 14:9), '*or on the hand*' – perhaps '*the right hand of the Lord*' of '*the Cup of the right hand of the Lord*' of the '*drink and stagger*'-imagery of 1QpHab,XI.9–11; in this passage from Revelation 16:19, one actually has the '*remembered before God*' phraseology – now, of course, reversed – of '*the Book of Remembrance*' that '*would be written out before Him (God) for all God-Fearers and those reckoning His Name*' of CDXX.19–20, to say nothing of the episode in the Pseudoclementine *Recognitions* describing the '*two brothers*' (whose tomb outside Jericho '*miraculously whitened of itself every year*' after the flight of the James Community following the attack on it by the '*Enemy*' Paul), who were also characterized there – as will be recalled – as '*being remembered before God,*' as well as the use of this same phraseology in the various New Testament '*Last Supper*' scenarios already alluded to above.

Not only are these various imageries presaged in the Habakkuk *Pesher*'s pictures of how '*the Cup of the Wrath of God*' would '*come around* to' and '*swallow him*' ('*the Wicked Priest*'), because he '*swallowed them*' ('*the Dumb Beasts*'/'*the Poor*'/the followers of '*the Righteous Teacher*' – a.k.a., '*the Simple of Judah doing Torah*') and '*swallowed him in his hot anger*' (that is, '*swallowed the Righteous Teacher*' – of course here too, as already pointed out, we have the '*swallowing*' imagery implicit in Hebrew in allusions like '*Babylon*' in Revelation above); but it would seem that Paul has some understanding of this variation of the '*Damascus*' or the '*drinking the Cup*' allusion as well when he states in 1 Corinthians 11:26, as we have also now several times remarked (directly following his evocation of '*Communion with the Blood of Christ*'):

> For as often as you drink this Cup, you solemnly proclaim the death of the Lord until He comes (again here, the '*coming of the Messiah of Aaron and Israel*' of CDxix.10–11 as also just remarked above),

following this up in 11:29 with (to repeat one of the passages with which we began),

> for he who eats and drinks unworthily, eats and drinks Judgement to himself, not seeing through to the Body of the Lord ('*the Lord of Hosts*'?).

Allegorization such as this is, in fact, really quite expert.

My conclusion is – yes, in some symbolic or allegorical manner, teachers like Paul and authors even of Books such as Acts – which in my view did know the Damascus Document and who were diametrically opposed to much of what it was saying – did see through to this esoteric understanding of '*Damascus*' and did reinterpret it in this utterly spiritualized and Hellenistic '*Mystery Religion*'-oriented fashion. However, I do not believe, given the intensity of the attachment to '*the Law*' or '*Torah*'– repeatedly avowed in the Damascus Document, unless this is to be considered a species of dissimulation which from my vantage point appears very doubtful – that the sectaries at Qumran entertained any such covert or hidden sense of '*the New Covenant in the Land of Damascus*'; though, given their several intemperate denunciations of contact with or the consumption of '*Blood*' of any kind, it may be that they knew the Pauline one.

We have already pointed out that the esoteric understanding of the formulation '*Damascus*,' outlined above, actually works in the Hebrew as well as it does in the Greek – not only in one but in both syllables of the formulation. In fact, it works even better than the simple homophonic relationship of the Hebrew to '*Cup*' (*Chos*) and '*Blood*' (*Dam*) in the

Greek transliteration. The fact of this unexpected further verification of what was initially just a suggestion provides extremely convincing added corroboration of both its relevance and applicability.

To review this additional verification one last time: in Hebrew the word for the Greek/English '*Damascus*' is '*Dammashek*' but the word for '*drink*' or '*give to drink,*' as already pointed out, is '*mashkeh.*' Therefore the place name '*Damascus*' in Hebrew breaks down in putative esoteric or allegorical delineation to '*Dam*'-'*Mashkeh*' or, as we saw, in Revelation 16:6 above, '*give Blood to drink.*' This, of course, is the phraseology repeatedly evoked in the quotation of this formula involving '*the Cup of the New Covenant in (the) Blood*' attributed to – in Paul's parlance – '*the Lord Jesus*' whether in 1 Corinthians 11–12 or in the Synoptics and even in the face of the ban on the consumption of '*blood*' in the various formulations of James' directives to overseas communities already sufficiently delineated above.

To once again condense the various formulations one encounters:

> ...*he took the Cup saying,* '*This Cup is the New Covenant in my Blood. As often as you drink it, this do in Remembrance of me*' (1 Corinthians 11:25) –

in the Synoptics varied slightly into, '*This is the Cup of the New Covenant in my Blood which is poured out for you*' (Luke 22:20 and *pars.* – here the '*pouring out*' imagery of Revelation above, but also as related to '*the waters of Lying*' as '*poured out*' by '*the Lying Scoffer*' or '*Spouter*' in both the Damascus Document and the Habakkuk *Pesher* and in the latter, anyhow, the putative opposing (but fractured) *Pesher* on Habakkuk 2:14's '*Earth being filled with the Knowledge of the Glory of the Lord like waters covering the sea*') followed – at least in Matthew 26:29 and Mark 14:25 – by:

> I *will not drink of the fruit of the vine again until I drink it again in the Kingdom of God* ('*drink,*' as if for emphasis, repeated twice – in Luke 22:18, this statement comes before the pronouncement about '*this Cup being the New Testament in my Blood which is poured out for you*' in 22:20 and the second allusion to '*drink*' is missing).

If this were not sufficient, it is preceded in Matthew 26:27 by the commandment, '*this drink*' (in Mark 14:23, this is stated rather as: '*they drank of it*').

The combination of the usages '*drink*'/'*drank*'/or '*drinking*' with '*the Cup of the New Covenant*' and '*my Blood*'/'*Blood of me*' in one manner or another in all the contexts outlined above is hardly either to be gainsaid or be considered accidental. The present writer considers that contextual allusions such as these are too insistent and too comprehensive in the sources before us to be simply fortuitous or coincidental. They are indicative of some more persistent esoteric or allegorical wordplay – in fact, some kind of amusingly-clever or aesthetically-pleasing wordplay. What the allegorical sense or meaning, underlying these formulations, might be and whether those at Qumran might also have been aware of or a party to it, as already observed, the author is unable to determine in any definitive manner.

Nor is it possible to determine which came first, the version and sense of '*the New Covenant*' found in Pauline/Synoptic formulation and attributed to the 'Jesus' which they are presenting or the version of it found in the Qumran variation. The writer, as should by now be clear, suspects that the latter – '*the Law*' or '*Torah*'-oriented exposition of it one finds developed in the later Columns of the Damascus Document – is the original and the esoteric play and even quasi-derogatory parody or exposition of it, one finds in both Paul and the Synoptic Gospels, is neither meant positively nor innocently, but rather to invalidate, belittle, or undercut, transforming it into its exact or mirror opposite.

Note on Translations and Endnotes

This book tries to provide everything the reader will need in the text itself without going to secondary sources. Therefore, all important testimonies and sources should be at the reader's fingertips. Standard translations of Old or New Testament texts often sacrifice accuracy for readability or elegance. For instance, important words are not translated in a consistent manner and beauty or inspiration are frequently sought rather than precision. Therefore, in all cases in both Old and New Testaments we have followed the original Hebrew or Greek as accurately and consistently as possible.

The same can be said for the Dead Sea Scrolls. The available translations in English are often insufficient and even, at times, misleading. Consistency and precision are frequently sacrificed in favor of readability, fine points missed and, on occasion, whole and important phrases deleted altogether. The premier translation in English, for instance, often avoids – whether for ideological reasons or otherwise – using words like 'Holy Spirit,' 'Justification,' 'works,' 'the Law,' 'House of Judgement,' 'Belial,' 'the Messiah,' etc., curiously submitting words like 'spirit of holiness,' 'deeds'/'acts,' 'ordinances'/'precepts,' 'condemned house,' 'Satan,' and 'anointed one'/'anointed ones' instead. In one instance, surrounding singular usages are change to plural and an important phrase dropped (seemingly because it either was expressed in the singular or could not otherwise be translated).

The same, for instance, is done in translations of the Letter of James in the New Testament, when it is stated, 'You (meaning 'the Rich') killed the Righteous One. He offered you no resistance' (5:6). For various reasons, this is transformed into the plural, 'You killed the Righteous Ones [plural]. They offered you no resistance.' In this way, startling and important usages are marginalized or minimized.

More recent translations of the Dead Sea Scrolls are not much better and often even worse. One even goes through re-translation in several languages before getting to English and others are actually even less accurate and readable than the more well known one just alluded to above. Therefore we have preferred to make our own translations. The reader should be cautioned in this regard. There is no substitute for the original Greek or Hebrew as the case may be. As one translator cautions against another, so that translator will, in turn, caution against the first. The reader, dependent on translations, will simply have to compare and judge. Where our own translations are concerned, we have preferred to err on the side of precision and accuracy rather than poetry or creative imagination (though we hope a modicum of splendor to be not altogether lacking). The same is true when it comes for translations of both Old and New Testament passages. For my translations of the Damascus Document, Community Rule, and Habakkuk *Pesher* – which it is recommended the reader have at his or her side – the reader should consult *The Dead Sea Scrolls and the First Christians* (Harper Collins/Sterling, 2004).

Where the Early Church Fathers are concerned, we have followed the *Ante-Nicene Christian Library* (1867–71 edition) as the basis for translations. For Eusebius, we have generally preferred for greater precision to follow the original Greek. The same for Josephus, though in both cases we have consulted and sometimes had recourse to the Loeb Library and other translations. Where Eusebius is concerned, we also consulted G. A. Williamson (1966), and the 1890–92 *Nicene and Post-Nicene Christian Library*. The same for Jerome. For Epiphanius, we consulted Philip R. Amidon's version (Oxford, 1990), Frank Williams (1987), Glenn Alan Koch (1976), and A. F. J. Klijn and G. J. Reinink (1973). The several passages from the Gospel of the Hebrews and the Protevangelium of James are based on Jerome, the editions of E. Hennecke and W. Schneemelcher (1959), and M. R. James (1926). All other passages from the Pseudoclementines were based on the *Ante-Nicene Christian Library*.

The point is to make a consistent translation of given terms such as 'Righteousness,' 'Piety,' 'the Poor,' 'the Holy Spirit,' 'Truth,' 'Lying,' 'works,' 'House of Judgement'/'Day of Judgement,' 'Belial' (not 'Satan' – when a text wants to say 'Satan' or 'Mastema' it does so; when it wants to say 'Belial,' it does so too), and 'swallow'/'cast down.' Some translators take extreme liberties in these matters. A book of this kind depends on precise vocabulary and absolute consistency across all texts, so that the reader will be able to recognize the same word, phrase, or term as is appears repeatedly in different contexts. To help in this regard and to emphasize them as pivotal, I have put all quotations in italics. By the same token, all italics throughout the book are my own to emphasize important ideas, words, or repetitions of same.

Where the footnotes are concerned, because of their extensiveness and complexity, the author and publisher have agreed to put these on-line rather than at the back of the book. They can be accessed directly at www.watkinspublishing.com/New Testament Code Footnotes or the writer's own website at www.CSULB.edu/centers/sjco/ where the more dedicated or interested reader can download them or print them out.

The reason behind this and the compromise reached between practicality and scholarship – which might even prove innovative – was that, since both writer and publisher wished the book to be accessible to the more general public and the dedicated specialist at one and the same time – the needs of whom were *prima facie* different – the only way to do this and not sacrifice sophistication was to leave the indications of the numbers in their entirety in the text. The index, which was complete and extensive (even more than most books of this kind) – itself running on to some thirty-six pages – would perhaps be sufficient to meet the needs of the more popular reader. Since most of the key Biblical and Dead Sea Scrolls references (even the Talmudic) were actually given in the book itself, to have also included an additional eighty-ninety double-columned pages to which the footnotes actually extend would perhaps have been too daunting for the first-time or general reader.

Therefore it was decided to try this unique solution that might actually even appeal to a newer computer-literate generation – leave the full complex of footnote numbers in the text, but put these on-line where the specialist, professional, or individual New Testament or Dead Sea Scrolls afficionado, who wanted a more in-depth approach (or even the critic), could easily access them. This, it was thought, might actually prove a challenge and even be enjoyable to the more internet-oriented reader providing the opportunity to stretch his or her inquiry further and deeper while at the same time not frightening away the more general reader, who was just looking for '*a good read*' and might otherwise consider the subject '*too academic*' or '*beyond*' him or her – which it decidedly is not and must not be.

List of Abbreviations

Acts Th.	Acts of Thomas
Ad Cor.	Clement of Alexandria, Letter to the Corinthians
Ad Haer.	Irenaeus, *Against Heresies*
Ad Rom.	Ignatius, Letter to the Romans
ADAJ	*Annual of the Department of Antiquities, Jordan*
Adv. Hel.	Jerome, *Against Helvidius*
Adv. Marcion	Tertullian, *Against Marcion*
ANCL	*Anti-Nicene Christian Library* (1867–71 Edition)
Ant.	Josephus, *The Antiquities of the Jews*
Apion	Josephus, *Against Apion (Contra Apion)*
1 Apoc Jas.	First Apocalypse of James
2 Apoc Jas.	Second Apocalypse of James
Apoc. Pet.	Apocalypse of Peter
Apost. Const.	Apostolic Constitutions
APOT	*Apocrypha and Pseudepigrapha of the Old Testament* (ed. R. H. Charles)
ARN	*Abbot de Rabbi Nathan*
As. Moses	Assumption of Moses
b. A. Z.	Babylonian *Talmud*, Tractate ᶜ*Avodah Zarah*
b. B.B.	Babylonian *Talmud*, Tractate *Baba Bathra*
b. Ber	Babylonian *Talmud*, Tractate *Berachot*
b. Bik	Babylonian *Talmud*, Tractate *Bikkurim*
b. Git	Babylonian *Talmud*, Tractate *Gittin*
b. Hul	Babylonian *Talmud*, Tractate *Hullin*
b. Kid	Babylonian *Talmud*, Tractate *Kiddushim*
b. Ket	Babylonian *Talmud*, Tractate *Kethuboth*
b. Ned	Babylonian *Talmud*, Tractate *Nedarim*
b. Pes	Babylonian *Talmud*, Tractate *Pesahim*
b. R.H.	Babylonian *Talmud*, Tractate *Rosh Ha-Shanah*
b. Shab.	Babylonian *Talmud*, Tractate *Shabbath*
b. Sot	Babylonian *Talmud*, Tractate *Sotah*
b. Suk	Babylonian *Talmud*, Tractate *Sukkah*
b. Taᶜan	Babylonian *Talmud*, Tractate *Taᶜanith*

b. San.	Babylonian *Talmud*, Tractate *Sanhedrin*
b. Yeb	Babylonian *Talmud*, Tractate *Yebamoth*
b. Yom	Babylonian *Talmud*, Tractate *Yoma*
BAR	*Biblical Archaeology Review*
Baroccian.	*Codice Barocciano*
BASOR	*Bulletin of the American Scholls of Oriental Research*
CD	Cairo Damascus Document (Ms. A and Ms. B)
Comm. on Gal.	Jerome, *Commentary on Galatians*
Comm. on John	Origen, *Commentary of John*
Comm. on Matt.	Origen, *Commentary on Matthew*
de Carne	Tertullian, *On the Body of Christ*
de Mens. et Pond.	Epiphanius, *De Mensuris et Ponderibus*
de Monog.	Tertullian, *On Monogamy*
de Verig. vel.	Tertullian, *On the Veiling of Virgins*
Dial.	Justin Martyr, *Dialogue with Trypho*
Deut. *R.*	Deuteronomy *Rabbah*
DSD	*Dead Sea Discoveries*
DSSNT	*The Dead Sea Scrolls: A New Translation* (ed. M. Wise, M. Abegg, & E. Cook)
DSSFC	*The Dead Sea Scrolls and the First Christians* (R. Eisenman)
DSSU	*The Dead Sea Scrolls Uncovered* (ed. R. Eisenman and M. Wise)
Eccles. *R.*	Ecclesiastes *Rabbah*
EH	Eusebius, *Ecclesiastical History*
Enarr. in Ps. 34:3	Augustine, *Discourses on the Psalms*
Eph.	Ignatius, Letter to the Ephesians
Epist. Apost.	Epistle of the Apostles
Epist. B.	Epistle of Barnabas
FEDSS	*A Facsimile Edition of the Dead Sea Scrolls* (ed. R. Eisenman and J. Robinson)
Gen. *R.*	Genesis *Rabbah*
Gos Th.	The Gospel of Thomas
Haeres.	Epiphanius, *Against Heresies* (*Panarion* in Latin)
H.N.	Pliny, *Natural History*
Haer.	Tertullian, *Against Heretics*
Hennecke	*The New Testament Apocrypha* (ed. E. Hennecke and W. Schneemelcher)
Hippolytus	Hippolytus, *Refutation of all Heresies*
Hom. in Luc.	Origen, *Homilies on Luke*

HUCA	*Hebrew Union College Annual*
JJHP	*James the Just in the Habakkuk Pesher* (R. Eisenman)
IEJ	*Israel Exploration Journal*
j. Ta^can	Jerusalem *Talmud*, Tractate *Ta^canith*
Lam *R.*	Lamentations *Rabbah*
M. San.	*Mishnah Sanhedrin*
Mur.	Wadi Murraba'at, Cave 1
MZCQ	*Maccabees, Zadokite, Christians and Qumran* (R. Eisenman)
Opus imperf. C. Iul	Augustine, *Opus Imperfectum contra Secundum Juliani*
pars.	parallels
Protevang.	Protevangelium of James
Ps *Hom.*	Pseudoclementine *Homilies*
Ps Philo	Pseudo Philo
Ps *Rec.*	Pseuclementine *Recognitions*
Quod Omnis	Philo, *On the Contemplative Life*
4QD	The Qumran Damascus Document (Cave 4)
4Q*Ber*	The Qumran Blessings (The Chariots of Glory)
4Q*Flor*	The Qumran *Florilegium* (on Promises to David's 'Seed')
1QH	The Qumran Hymns
1QM	The Qumran War Scroll
4Q*MMT*	The Qumran Letter(s) on Works Righteousness
4QpGen	The Qumran Genesis *Pesher* (Genesis *Florilegium*)
1QpHab	The Qumran Habakkuk *Pesher*
4QpIs	The Qumran Isaiah *Pesher*
4QpNah	The Qumran Nahum *Pesher*
4QpPs 37	The Qumran Psalm 37 *Pesher*
1QS	The Qumran Community Rule
11QT	The Qumran Temple Scroll
4QTest	The Qumran Testimonia
Song of Songs *R.*	Song of Songs *Rabbah*
Suet.	Seutonius, *The Twelve Caesars*
Tos. Kellim	*Tosefta Kellim*
Trall.	Ignatius, *Letter to the Trallians*
Vir. ill.	Jerome, *Lives of Illustrious Men*
Vita	Josephus, *Autiobiography of Flavius Josephus*
War	*The Jewish War*

CHRONOLOGICAL CHARTS

MACCABEAN PRIEST KINGS

Mattathias, 167–166 BC
Judas Maccabee, 166–160
Jonathan, 160–142
Simon, 142–134
John Hyrcanus, 134–104
Alexander Jannaeus, 103–76
Salome Alexandra, 76–67
Aristobulus II, 67–63
Hyrcanus II, 76–67 and 63–40
Antigonus, 40–37

HERODIAN KINGS, ETHNARCHS, OR TETRARCHS

Herod, Roman–supported King, 37–4 BC
Archelaus, Ethnarch of Judea, 4 BC – 7 CE
Herod Antipas, Tetrarch of Galilee and Perea, 4 BC – 39 CE
Philip, Tetrarch of Trachonitis, 4 BC – 34 CE
Agrippa I, Tetrarch and King, 37–44
Herod of Chalcis, 44–49
Agrippa II, 49–93

ROMAN GOVERNORS

Antipater (Herod's father). Procurator, 55–43 BC
Coponius, 6–9 CE
Ambivulus, 9–12
Rufus, 12–15
Valerius Gratus, 15–26 (perhaps 15–18)
Pontius Pilate, 26–37 (perhaps 18–37)
Fadus, 44–46
Tiberius Alexander, 46–48
Cumanus, 48–52
Felix, 51–60
Festus, 60–62
Albinus, 62–64
Florus, 64–66

ROMAN EMPERORS
FROM 60 BC TO 138 CE

Caesar, 60–44 BC
Mark Anthony and Octavius, 43–31 BC
Octavius (Augustus), 27 BC – 14 CE
Tiberius, 14–37
Caligula, 37–41
Claudius, 41–54
Nero, 54–68
Galba, 68–69
Otho, 69
Vitellius, 69
Vespasian, 69–79
Titus, 79–81
Domitian, 81–96
Nerva, 96–98
Trajan, 98–117
Hadrian, 117–138

EARLY CHURCH AND OTHER SOURCES

Philo of Alexandria, *c.* 30 BC – 45 CE
Clement of Rome, *c.* 30–97 CE
Josephus, 37–96
Ignatius, *c.* 50–115
Papias, *c.* 60–135
Pliny, 61–113
Polycarp, 69–156
Justin Martyr, *c.* 100–165
Hegesippus, *c.* 90–180
Tatian, *c.* 115–185
Lucian of Samosata, *c.* 125–180
Irenaeus, *c.* 130–200
Clement of Alexandria, *c.* 150–215
Tertullian, *c.* 160–221
Hippolytus, *c.* 160–235
Julius Africanus, *c.* 170—245
Origen, *c.* 185–254
Eusebius of Caesarea, *c.* 260–340
Epiphanius, 367–404
Jerome, 348–420
Rufinus of Aquileia, *c.* 350–410
Augustine, 354–430
St Cyril of Jerusalem, 375–444

The Maccabeans

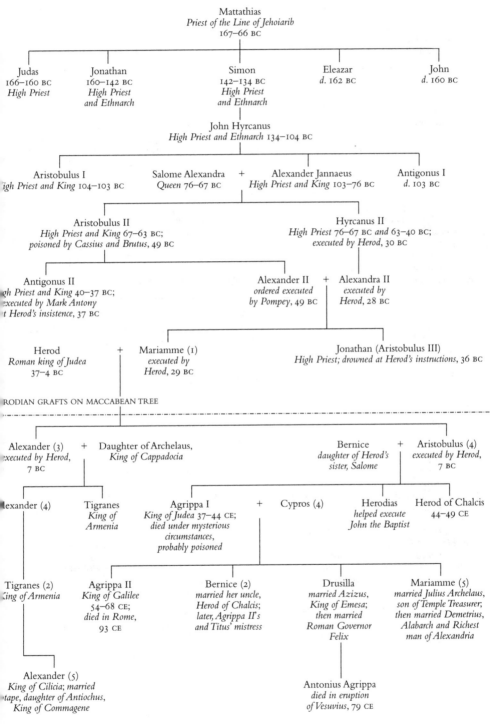

Mattathias
Priest of the Line of Jehoiarib
167–66 BC

Judas
166–160 BC
High Priest

Jonathan
160–142 BC
*High Priest
and Ethnarch*

Simon
142–134 BC
*High Priest
and Ethnarch*

Eleazar
d. 162 BC

John
d. 160 BC

John Hyrcanus
High Priest and Ethnarch 134–104 BC

Aristobulus I
igh Priest and King 104–103 BC

Salome Alexandra
Queen 76–67 BC

+

Alexander Jannaeus
High Priest and King 103–76 BC

Antigonus I
d. 103 BC

Aristobulus II
*High Priest and King 67–63 BC;
poisoned by Cassius and Brutus, 49 BC*

Hyrcanus II
*High Priest 76–67 BC and 63–40 BC;
executed by Herod, 30 BC*

Antigonus II
*gh Priest and King 40–37 BC;
executed by Mark Antony
t Herod's insistence, 37 BC*

Alexander II
*ordered executed
by Pompey, 49 BC*

+

Alexandra II
*executed by
Herod, 28 BC*

Herod
Roman king of Judea
37–4 BC

+

Mariamme (1)
*executed by
Herod, 29 BC*

Jonathan (Aristobulus III)
High Priest; drowned at Herod's instructions, 36 BC

ERODIAN GRAFTS ON MACCABEAN TREE

Alexander (3)
*executed by Herod,
7 BC*

+

Daughter of Archelaus,
King of Cappadocia

Bernice
*daughter of Herod's
sister, Salome*

+

Aristobulus (4)
*executed by Herod,
7 BC*

lexander (4)

Tigranes
*King of
Armenia*

Agrippa I
*King of Judea 37–44 CE;
died under mysterious
circumstances,
probably poisoned*

+

Cypros (4)

Herodias
*helped execute
John the Baptist*

Herod of Chalcis
44–49 CE

Tigranes (2)
ing of Armenia

Agrippa II
*King of Galilee
54–68 CE;
died in Rome,
93 CE*

Bernice (2)
*married her uncle,
Herod of Chalcis;
later, Agrippa II's
and Titus' mistress*

Drusilla
*married Azizus,
King of Emesa;
then married
Roman Governor
Felix*

Mariamme (5)
*married Julius Archelaus,
son of Temple Treasurer;
then married Demetrius,
Alabarch and Richest
man of Alexandria*

Alexander (5)
*King of Cilicia; married
tape, daughter of Antiochus,
King of Commagene*

Antonius Agrippa
*died in eruption
of Vesuvius, 79 CE*

The Herodians

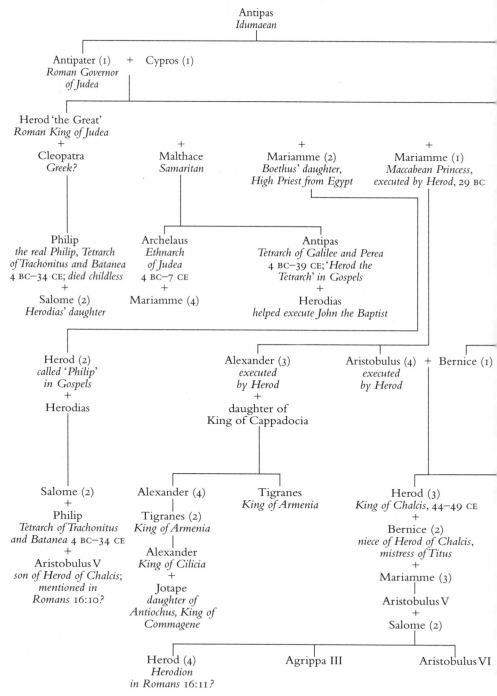

Antipas
Idumaean

Antipater (1) + Cypros (1)
*Roman Governor
of Judea*

Herod 'the Great'
Roman King of Judea
+

Cleopatra
Greek?

Malthace
Samaritan

Mariamme (2)
*Boethus' daughter,
High Priest from Egypt*

Mariamme (1)
*Maccabean Princess,
executed by Herod, 29 BC*

Philip
*the real Philip, Tetrarch
of Trachonitus and Batanea
4 BC–34 CE; died childless*
+
Salome (2)
Herodias' daughter

Archelaus
*Ethnarch
of Judea
4 BC–7 CE*
+
Mariamme (4)

Antipas
*Tetrarch of Galilee and Perea
4 BC–39 CE; 'Herod the
Tetrarch' in Gospels*
+
Herodias
helped execute John the Baptist

Herod (2)
*called 'Philip'
in Gospels*
+
Herodias

Alexander (3)
*executed
by Herod*
+
daughter of
King of Cappadocia

Aristobulus (4) + Bernice (1)
*executed
by Herod*

Salome (2)
+
Philip
*Tetrarch of Trachonitus
and Batanea 4 BC–34 CE*
+
Aristobulus V
*son of Herod of Chalcis;
mentioned in
Romans 16:10?*

Alexander (4)
|
Tigranes (2)
King of Armenia
|
Alexander
King of Cilicia
+
Jotape
*daughter of
Antiochus, King of
Commagene*

Tigranes
King of Armenia

Herod (3)
King of Chalcis, 44–49 CE
+
Bernice (2)
*niece of Herod of Chalcis,
mistress of Titus*
+
Mariamme (3)
|
Aristobulus V
+
Salome (2)

Herod (4)
*Herodion
in Romans 16:11?*

Agrippa III

Aristobulus VI

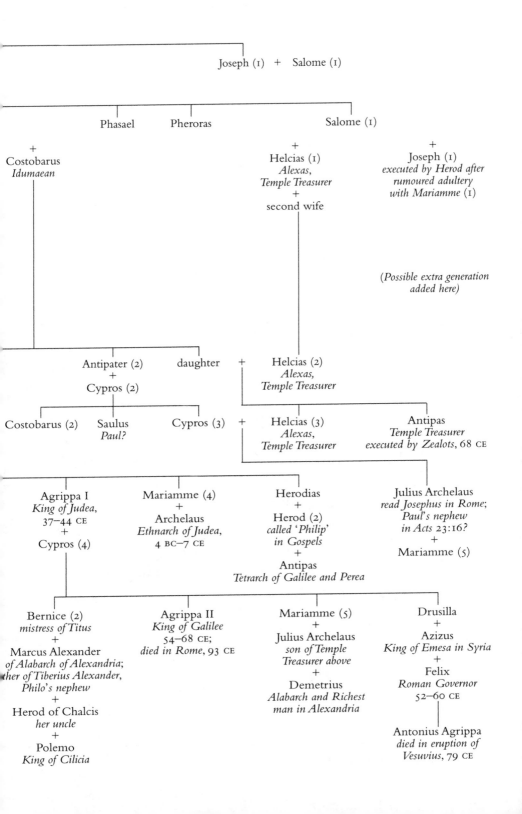

Joseph (1) + Salome (1)

Phasael   Pheroras   Salome (1)

+   +   +
Costobarus   Helcias (1)   Joseph (1)
Idumaean   *Alexas,*   *executed by Herod after*
                                  Temple Treasurer   *rumoured adultery*
                                        +   *with Mariamme (1)*
                                   second wife

                                                          *(Possible extra generation
                                                             added here)*

          Antipater (2)   daughter   +   Helcias (2)
                +   *Alexas,*
            Cypros (2)   *Temple Treasurer*

Costobarus (2)   Saulus   Cypros (3) + Helcias (3)   Antipas
                 Paul?   *Alexas,*   *Temple Treasurer*
                                          Temple Treasurer   *executed by Zealots, 68 CE*

   Agrippa I   Mariamme (4)   Herodias   Julius Archelaus
King of Judea,   +   +   *read Josephus in Rome;*
   37–44 CE   Archelaus   Herod (2)   *Paul's nephew*
        +   *Ethnarch of Judea,*   *called 'Philip'*   *in Acts 23:16?*
   Cypros (4)   4 BC–7 CE   *in Gospels*   +
                                                                           Mariamme (5)
                                                   Antipas
                                        Tetrarch of Galilee and Perea

   Bernice (2)   Agrippa II   Mariamme (5)   Drusilla
mistress of Titus   *King of Galilee*   +   +
                           54–68 CE;   Julius Archelaus   Azizus
Marcus Alexander   *died in Rome, 93 CE*   *son of Temple*   *King of Emesa in Syria*
of Alabarch of Alexandria;   *Treasurer above*   +
ther of Tiberius Alexander,   +   Felix
Philo's nephew   Demetrius   *Roman Governor*
        +   *Alabarch and Richest*   52–60 CE
Herod of Chalcis   *man in Alexandria*
  her uncle   Antonius Agrippa
        +   *died in eruption of*
   Polemo   *Vesuvius, 79 CE*
King of Cilicia

THE MEDITERRANEAN 1012

Caspian Sea

CAUCASUS MOUNTAINS

Sea

PARTHIA

UPPER ARMENIA
MT ARARAT ▲
(Modern location)

YNIA

GALATIA

LOWER ARMENIA

MT ARARAT (Classical location)

PERSIA

MED

Ecbatana

CAPPADOCIA

Samosata

LAND OF THE EDESSENES

Nisibis

Arbela

ADIABENE

Edessa(Antiochia)

Haran(Carrhae)

Tigris

ch of Pisidia

COMMAGENE

CILICIA

Hierapolis

Lystra Tarsus

Beroea (Aleppo)

Euphrates

BABYLONIA

Seleucia

Susa

Antioch

Orontes

Palmyra

Babylon

Charax Spasini
(Antiochia or Basrah

CYPRUS

Tripolis

COELE SYRIA

Sidon

Damascus

Tyre

Jordan

Caesarea

Jerusalem

Ashkelon

Qumran

Gaza

IDUMAEA

Petra

N

exandria

Heliopolis

mphis

EGYPT

ynchus

A R A B I A

Red Sea

500 miles

Bernice

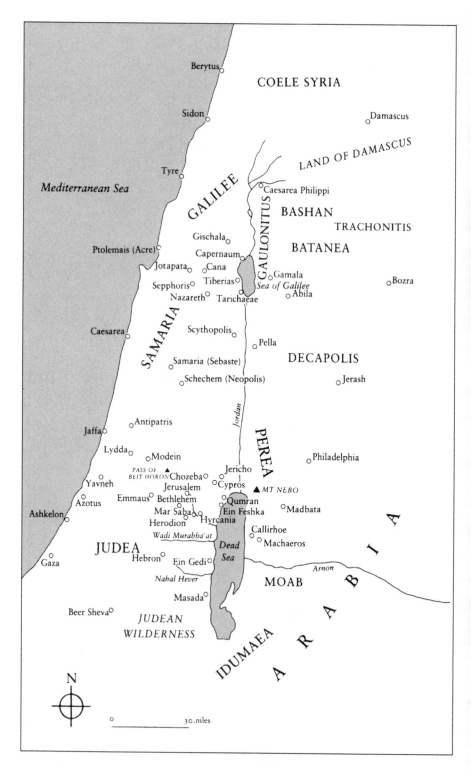

COELE SYRIA

Berytus

Sidon

Damascus

LAND OF DAMASCUS

Tyre

Mediterranean Sea

GALILEE

Caesarea Philippi

GAULONITUS

BASHAN

TRACHONITIS

Gischala

BATANEA

Ptolemais (Acre)

Capernaum

Jotapata

Cana

Gamala

Bozra

Sepphoris

Tiberias

Sea of Galilee

Nazareth

Tarichaeae

Abila

Caesarea

Scythopolis

Pella

SAMARIA

Samaria (Sebaste)

DECAPOLIS

Schechem (Neopolis)

Jerash

Jordan

Antipatris

PEREA

Jaffa

Lydda

Modein

Jericho

Philadelphia

PASS OF BEIT HORON

Chozeba

Cypros

MT NEBO

Yavneh

Jerusalem

Emmaus

Bethlehem

Qumran

Ein Feshka

Madbata

Azotus

Mar Saba

Hyrcania

Ashkelon

Herodion

Callirhoe

Wadi Murabba'at

Dead Sea

Machaeros

JUDEA

Hebron

Ein Gedi

Arnon

Gaza

Nahal Hever

MOAB

Masada

Beer Sheva

JUDEAN WILDERNESS

IDUMAEA

A R A B I A

N

30 .niles

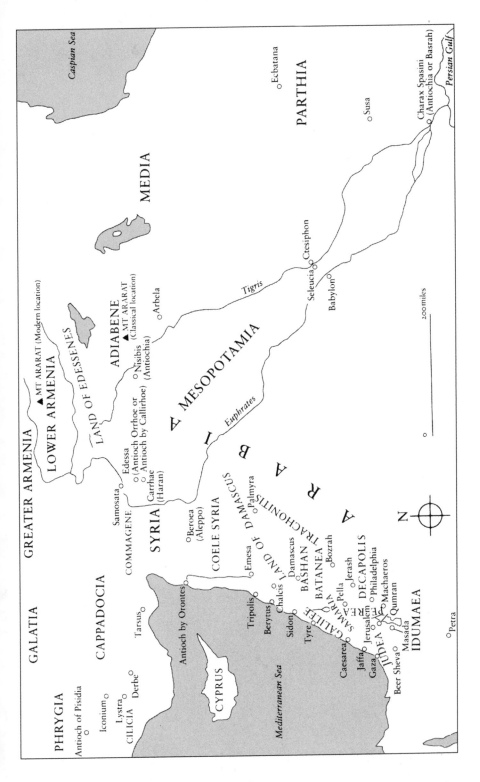

Index

364; Riches/silver couch of, 215, 235-6, 264, 315, 334, 344-5

Bene Hezir, 62; *see* James' tomb

Benjamin/Benjaminites, 530, 583, 765, 871; the *Diaspora* of the Desert, 378, 410-16, 504-5, 523; *see* the War Scroll; *Diaspora*, Paul

Benjamin of Tudela, 69, 97, 113, 944-5

Beᶜor, 464, 741-2, 764-5; *see* Belaᶜ, Balaam

Bernice, 234, 341-2, 352, 481, 509, 530, 533, 555, 595, 738-39, 747, 755-760, 764, 791, 819-20, 839; mistress of Titus 206, 342, 352, 419, 530

Berytus (Beirut), 122

Biblical Archaeology Review, 42-3, 56-7

al-Biruni, 36, 97-8, 112, 955

Biryonim, 334-6, 345-7, 350, 512; *see* Zealots

Bishopric, *see* Episcopate

blasphemy, 150, 155, 394, 560, 566, 559, 616, 665, 692-3, 792; execution/stoning for 180, 794-5, 809-10; in Revelation 815, 818, 822; and James, 150, 395, 530, 796, 801, 809-11; Jesus 204, 530, 559, 810-11

blind/Blind Guides, 220, 265, 267, 276, 288-89, 293, 298-9, 318, 321, 354, 377-80, 459, 610, 745; *see* guide, Pharisees, *Maschil*

blood, 25, 99, 137-8, 162, 169-70, 172, 176, 180, 189, 226, 309-10, 319, 362, 419-21, 467, 473, 560, 595, 672, 689, 719, 758, 781, 793, 812-7, 822, 826, 830-2, 867, 870-1, 905, 914-5, 918, 924, 932, 942, 950, 987-8, 990-4; ban on/horror of, 309, 375, 581, 612, 719, 867, 870-1, 986-8, 992, 995; City of, 716, 876, 893, 914-7, 924, 926, 934; Cup of, 516, 813, 850, 920-23, 977, 995; Communion with, 68, 98, 138, 294, 375, 383, 429, 432, 468, 472, 514, 612, 699, 710, 716, 817, 913, 915, 918, 924, 926, 935, 946, 965, 972, 987, 995; and Damascus, 168, 170, 310, 804, 915, 920-3, 976, 978, 993-4; James' ban on, 98-9, 138, 178, 375-6, 407, 445, 490, 612, 623, 671, 699, 816-9, 826, 914-5, 918-9, 950, 984; in Hebrews, 407, 826, 855, 913-4, 925, 928, 978-9, 992; of Man, 407, 749, 781, 813, 817, 826, 830, 823, 832, 915, 994; New Covenant in, 98, 167-8, 223, 226, 310, 516, 518, 699, 823, 846, 850, 855, 871, 912-4, 919-26 935, 975, 977, 980, 984-5, 992, 996; Paul and, 69, 433, 395, 560, 710, 817, 855, 905, 914, 918-9, 942, 977; Worthless Community/built upon, 294, 436, 578, 652, 716, 733, 864, 882, 884, 901, 908-910-920, 924-5, 929-33; Field of (Akaldema), 9, 33, 163-4, 168; menstrual, 161, 170, 228, 234, 309, 376, 465, 612, 672, 987; price of, 163-4, 169, 171, 234, 249, 319, 342, 860; woman with flow/fountain of 270, 307-10, 328, 421

blood libel, 9-10, 22-5, 30, 35, 95, 319, 488, 495, 573, 579-80, 710, 745, 767, 826, 830, 871, 907, 914

Boethus/Boethusians, 62, 147, 157-8, 200, 236, 243; *see* Martha, daughter of

Boni, 205, 390, 395; *see* Honi

Book of Giants 110, 116

Book, People of the, 91, 110, 113, 145, 152

Books of the Prophets, 631-4, 687, 983

Books of the *Tòrah*, 629-30, 634, 677, 983

Branch/Branch of Planting (*Netzer*), 352, 639, 644, 657, 666, 677, 680, 697, 763, 794, 861; of David, 297, 323, 349, 353-4, 396, 602,

608, 625, 638-9, 644-5, 653-6, 669, 674-5, 821-2, 836; *see* Root of Planting

Braunheim, S., 47

Brill, E. J., 42-3

Broshi, M., 36

Buddha/Buddhism, 153, 173, 395, 669

builder/building imagery, 431, 658, 699, 788, 834, 887, 927-9, 985; of the wall, 663, 672, 691, 716; in Paul 293, 294, 295, 436-8, 443, 463, 576-7, 606, 615, 681, 716, 733, 759, 833, 902-3, 920, 928-9, 968; at Qumran, 733, 785, 864, 876, 902, 908-15, 919, 924, 932-3, 983-990; *see* blood, Worthless City

Bulwark, 181, 427, 431, 463, 542; James as 463, 651, 689, 719, 803

Caesar, 19, 497-8, 722, 735, 835

Caesarea, 11-12, 110, 524, 538, 555, 562, 602, 746-7, 778, 837-8; Cornelius at, 168, 387, 488, 533, 563, 606, 760, 761, 825, 963; Paul in, 502, 508, 525, 542, 546, 689, 839; Peter/Simon *Magus* confrontation in, 35, 37, 102-4, 312, 501, 515, 554, 562, 760; Philip in, 541-2; Simon Jerusalem Assembly Head in, 29, 463

Caiaphas, 247, 732

Caldararo, N., 49

Caligula, 420, 562, 722, 761

camel/camel's, 232, 240, 242; burden, 229, 242-3, 252, 331-4; John the Baptist's cloak of, 626; James' knees hard as, 123, 408-9, 802; Rich Man and Kingdom of Heaven, 229, 243, 250-4, 326, 332

Camps, 32, 172, 390, 416, 423, 444-7, 521, 544-47, 642, 685, 688, 708, 718, 825, 847; banning dogs in, 375-82; *see* Wilderness Camps, *MMT*, War Scroll

Cana, 258-9, 260, 273, 275, 407, 422, 515

Canaanite/Greek Syrophoenician woman, 199, 229, 238, 251, 257, 263, 266, 273, 276, 299-303, 307-8, 367, 380, 384-5; daughter's demons cast out, 211-13, 247, 261, 271-2, 286, 299-301, 317, 390; retort to Jesus, 245, 256-8, 302, 382, 389

Cappodocia, 493

carbon dating, 40-57, 424, 426-7, 441, 484, 551, 671, 721, 726, 904

Carrae/Carrhae, 86, 378, 568, 876, 944, 947, 952, 968; *see* Haran, Edessa

carrion, ban on, by James 98-9, 138, 178, 377, 379, 381, 490, 623, 671, 699, 825-6, 834, 918, 946-7, 950; Sabaeans/in Islam, 97-9, 189, 379, 825, 946; in Ezekiel, 127, 825, 834; in *MMT*, 377-81; *see* James' directives

cast/casting down/out, 33, 164, 166, 191, 266, 321 326, 341, 419, 466, 518-19, 566, 595, 654, 691-2, 700, 720, 726, 732, 744, 751, 758, 763, 785, 789, 800-6, 814, 818, 825, 829, 831, 834-39, 841, 850, 865, 872, 923, 976, 992; and *B-L-ᶜ* language circle, 466, 552, 729, 740-1; demons/spirits, 211, 247, 261, 272, 280, 298, 299-301-7, 382, 390, 466, 552, 835, 865; to dogs, 199, 212-3, 247, 256, 262, 265, 268, 272, 301, 373, 777, 779; James, 38, 180, 191, 212, 236, 466, 496, 729, 744, 764, 777-8, 804, 825, 831, 835, 837, 839; nets/snares, 187, 191, 254, 420, 466, 552, 773, 780, 818, 845, 847, 887; pearls, 212, 256, 316-17, 373, 389; the Poor, 33,

womb'/Naziritism/Justness of, 70, 153-5, 325, 470; not *'eating and drinking,'* 68; objections to Herodias' marriage, 237-8, 343, 555, 739; as True Prophet, 325; vegetarianism, 70, 324; in wilderness, 52, 425, 446, 611, 615, 861, 750; Zealot/*Zaddik*, 177, 401; as *as-Sabi*' ibn Yusufus, 90, 97, 101, 104

Joiarib, 138

Joiners/joining, 28, 427, 429, 442, 447, 618, 664, 666, 668, 673, 716, 896, 903, 910, 984, 988, 992; in Damascus Document, 367, 414-5, 424, 444, 455-6, 557, 613, 619, 622, 657, 667, 670, 675, 714, 720, 915, 917, 974, 979, 982; in Nahum *Pesher*, 367, 415, 667, 714, 886, 915, 917, 926; *see nilveh/Nilvim*,

Jonadab, son of Rechab, 159-60, 167-9, 261, 426

Jonathan brother of Ananus, 399, 529-30, 729-30, 773, 793

Jonathan, brother of Mariamme, 506

Jonathan, Maccabean Priest King, 423-4, 447, 455, 813

Jonathan, Paean to King, 423-4, 447, 455-6

Jordan /Jordan River, 73, 93, 97, 117, 202, 277, 378, 405-6, 410-2, 416, 418, 420, 422, 446, 520, 523, 547, 650, 686, 723, 742, 746, 767, 942

Joseph, 10, 101, 105, 254, 340, 563, 921

Joseph, brother in law of Herod, 62, 494-6, 738

Joseph, father of Jesus, 15, 60, 63, 101, 105-6, 157, 738

Joseph Barsabas Justus, 14, 113-14, 117, 164, 547, 955;

Joseph of Arimathaea, 62, 172, 257, 392, 398, 401-2

Josephus, 4, 7, 9, 12, 17, 35, 38, 52, 54, 62, 67, 72, 74-5, 90, 105, 163, 174-5, 243, 262, 266, 274, 286, 298, 316, 335-6, 341, 343, 352, 354, 397-401, 420, 454, 472, 480, 482, 493-502, 511-2, 532, 542, 555-6, 593-6, 679, 681, 721-2, 729, 730-1, 735, 737-46, 751-2, 758, 763, 766-7, 776-8, 780-1, 784, 791, 793, 808-10, 827, 831, 837, 839, 844, 847, 849, 865, 887, 916, 921, 936, 942-3, 952-3, 961, 965, 972, 974, 976; Acts parallels, 7-12, 77, 119, 175, 488, 554-6, 561-4; and *Banus*, 67, 93-4, 124-5, 167-8, 408, 471, 529; and Domitian, 8, 120, 316; Dositheus/Dortus/Doetus in, 102-6, 116, 563, 747; and Epaphroditus, 8, 120, 462, 501, 561; Essenes/Jewish sects in, 24, 91, 96, 124-7, 198, 212, 239, 251-4, 276, 318, 344, 345, 351, 368, 374, 383, 387, 399, 415-16, 428, 434, 436-9, 455, 466, 469, 470, 520, 580, 624, 673, 686, 716, 853-61, 902, 943-5, 956-66, 969-75; the Famine/famine in, 77, 118, 128, 201-2, 276-7, 298, 335, 391, 406, 527, 954; Gurion son of Nicodemus in, 172, 197-8, 335, 397; Honi/Onias in, 118, 142-51, 198, 205, 394-5; Idumaeans in, 13, 239, 344, 368, 415-6, 496, 742, 747, 751-2, 759, 776, 778, 780, 783, 829, 831, 833, 847, 962; Impostors/Deceivers, 117-18, 174, 178, 259, 276, 325, 407, 422, 445, 529; James' death in, 18-9, 58, 75, 118, 134, 150, 158, 320, 496, 507, 524, 527-34, 545, 597, 689, 729, 736, 738, 763, 778-9, 809-10, 837, 976, 993; Jesus ben Ananias' Prophecy in, 158-9, 320-1, 512, 516-7, 524-8, 534-7, 540-3, 547-8, 581, 689; Jesus son of Sapphias in, 418-21; John the

Baptist in, 18-20, 109, 151, 153, 313, 434, 437, 438, 442, 500-1, 624, 750, 855-6, 890; Queen Helen and family in, 5, 18, 75-8, 80, 86-8, 96-7, 118, 201, 208-9, 255, 276-7, 318, 323, 385, 387-8, 391-2, 398, 406, 527, 539-40, 568, 581, 865-6, 873-4, 943-4, 951-2, 971; Romans in, 936, 967; Simon Head of an Assembly of his own in Jerusalem in, 29, 343-4, 463, 488, 554, 759-60; Simon the Magician/Atomus in, 102, 111, 555; the Star Prophecy in, 56, 208, 408, 470, 679; Stephen in, 7-11, 561; stopping of sacrifice on behalf of foreigners in the Temple in, 141, 163, 381-2, 189-91, 534, 653, 713, 759, 808, 827; Theudas in, 113, 117-9, 128, 174, 202, 277, 405-6, 520, 527; *see Antiquities, Jewish War, Vita, Against Apion*

Joses, 13, 15, 261, 307

Joshua, 10, 105, 198, 278, 520; *Redivivus*, 105-6, 117, 198, 202, 405, 563

Joshua, R. (student of Yohanan), 162, 348, 350-1, 354-6, 362-3, 401; woes, 350, 355

Joshua ben Gamala, *see* Jesus ben Gamala

Josiah, 180; Reform of, 159-60, 173

Jotape, daughter of Antiochus, 499

Jubilees, 46, 867-8, 878

Judah, 164, 277, 378, 418, 453, 526, 624, 684, 729, 781, 831, 900; destruction of, 620-2, 830; Glory of, 367-8; House of, 28, 363, 456, 579, 583, 586, 589, 602, 617, 734-6, 799, 832, 896, 903-6, 910, 921, 924, 931, 989-90, 992; Land of, 78, 81, 101, 117, 140, 277, 353, 369, 378, 411, 415, 420, 657, 666, 669, 710, 719, 734-6, 751, 768, 969, 979-80, 986, 988-92; Princes of, 74, 663, 680, 748, 768, 770, 786; Simple of, 33, 102, 531, 667, 712, 714-6, 726-9, 736, 756, 799, 802, 810, 817, 833, 900, 903, 917, 994-5; Sons of, 411, 413, 415; Tribe of, 583, 625

Judaism, 182, 190, 246, 371, 373, 552, 702, 722, 738, 872, 944; charity (*Zedekah*) in, 462, 472; Helen/Izates conversion to, 80, 88, 113, 209, 280, 539; Herod's conversion to, 506; martyrdom in, 445; Paul and, 83, 500, 503, 505, 583-6, 590; Rabbinic/Pharisaic, 182, 220, 472, 585, 760; Seven Sects of, 92; Pentecost in, 521; *also see* Karaism

Judas/Jude, Jesus' third brother, 5-6, 121, 384

Judas Barsabas, 119, 941; takes James' letter to Antioch, 12, 85, 109, 113, 373, 397, 416-7, 540, 565, 687, 941, 947; overlaps Judas of James, 76, 84, 107, 113, 389, 954

Judas *Iscariot*, 15, 26, 116, 169-70, 227, 361, 343, 389, 539, 735, 845, 922, 948, 959-61, 970; death/suicide of, 33, 163, 165, 169, 249, 341, 860; allegedly *'delivers up'/'betrays'* Jesus, 167, 218, 225-6, 230, 233-4, 238, 249, 329, 338, 368, 448, 531, 556, 594, 600, 620, 727; election to replace, 113, 117, 164; expensive perfume/Poor complaints by, 172, 224, 225, 226, 229-34, 238, 249-51, 265, 271, 314, 319, 333, 361; and *'Field of Blood,'* 9, 33, 163, 164; Jesus' kisses, 458; Judas Barsabas/Thaddaeus/Theudas/Judas of James tangle, 108, 113, 116, 389, 405, 941, 949, 954-5; overlaps Judas the Galilean/Judas Maccabee, 250, 313; 'Price of Blood'/ 'casting into the Temple', 163-4, 234, 319, 342, 346, 347, 518; and *Sicarius/Sicarii*, 238, 250-2, 402;